A Practitioner's Guide to Class Actions

MARCY HOGAN GREER

TORT TRIAL & INSURANCE PRACTICE SECTION

AMERICAN BAR ASSOCIATION
Defending Liberty
Pursuing Justice

14 13 12 11   5 4 3 2

Library of Congress Cataloging-in-Publication Data
A practitioner's guide to class actions / Marcy Hogan Greer, national editor. — 1st ed.
   p. cm.
 Includes index.
 ISBN-13: 978-1-60442-955-8
 ISBN-10: 1-60442-955-0
 1. Class actions (Civil procedure)—United States. I. Greer, Marcy Hogan. II. American Bar Association. Tort Trial and Insurance Practice Section.
 KF8896.P73 2010
 347.73'053—dc22
                     2010030499

Contents

Foreword

MARCY HOGAN GREER, NATIONAL EDITOR

The genesis of this book was a premier class action CLE program known as "The Future of Class Action Litigation in America," which was held in Boston, Massachusetts, and Washington, D.C., in 2003, 2005, and 2007, sponsored by the Business Litigation Committee of the American Bar Association's Tort Trial and Insurance Practice Section. Tom Thagard and Mike Drumke co-chaired the program, and Dave Rief, John McMeekin, and Michele Powers were instrumental in its success. Their fine work in putting together these conferences led the BLC to consider turning the widely acclaimed speeches and papers into a practice guide on class actions. Bob Caldwell's enthusiastic support as chair of the BLC helped us launch the book project. In addition to having the excellent speakers and materials from the Institute, I had a vision of a class action book I wanted as a desk reference containing the materials most useful to lawyers, clients, and others involved in class action cases. Telling myself that it would not be *that* much work, I signed on to be the National Editor.

Our editorial team of Assistant Editor Mike Truesdale and the Editorial Board, Van Cates, Madeleine ("Nikko") Fischer, Bo Phillips, Joanne Swanson, and Tom Thagard, has worked tirelessly over the last 18 months to finalize the concept, identify the most cutting-edge topics, recruit the top legal minds in the country, and review, edit—and, in many cases, write—the chapters of this practice guide. We reached out to judges, law professors, and practitioners nationwide to identify both the best authors and key issues in the class action practice. The TIPS leadership was instrumental in helping us find authors in geographic and topical areas that we needed to round out the project. Our many thanks go to Chair Wyndall Ivey and Chair-Elect Jim Myrick. We were most fortunate that so many first-rate class action experts answered our call, and we ended up with a wonderfully diverse and talented group. These authors did a terrific job on their respective parts, and the collective work surpassed even our ambitious expectations. We believe this book will become the leading class action go-to guide in the country.

The practice guide is organized into three parts. The first, entitled "The Anatomy of a Class Action," is a soup-to-nuts analysis of the various parts of a class action from pretrial to settlement, based on Federal Rule of Civil Procedure 23, which also provides the pattern for class action law in most states. The second part, "Special Issues in Class Actions," contains a variety of current themes, challenges, and practices in class actions from the viewpoint of those who face them regularly. The third section is a comprehensive compilation of class action materials from each of the 50 states and the District of Columbia, focusing on where the local practice differs from federal class action laws and procedures.

I dedicate my work on this book to my mother, whom I lost shortly after I finished the last chapter. She loved the fact that I was producing a book—even if it was not one that she would have read. Through the long process of writing and editing the many chapters, she would ask about my progress and encourage me to "get it done." She wanted to know the minute I was "really finished." My mother was the one who taught me how to turn an idea into a completed project. I also dedicate this book to my late father, whose footsteps I am attempting to follow in the legal profession. Both of my parents taught me the importance of service and excellence. I have tried to live up to those ideals with this book. Fortunately, the other authors did such fine work on their part that I can say without reservation that it is an incomparable compendium of class action resources. I hope you will find it relevant and useful in your work.

About the Editors

NATIONAL EDITOR

MARCY HOGAN GREER is a partner in the appellate section of Fulbright & Jaworski L.L.P. in Austin, Texas. Her practice is focused on complex civil trial and appellate litigation in both federal and state courts throughout the country, and she is a member of Fulbright's Global Class Action practice group. Ms. Greer has been board certified in Civil Appellate Law by the Texas Board of Legal Specialization since 1997. She is admitted to practice before the U.S. Supreme Court, the U.S. Courts of Appeals for the First, Fifth, Seventh, Eighth, Ninth, Eleventh, and Federal Circuits, as well as the federal and state courts of Texas. From 1993 to 1994, Ms. Greer clerked for the Hon. Carolyn Dineen King, the former Chief Judge of the U.S. Court of Appeals for the Fifth Circuit. Ms. Greer is listed in *Best Lawyers in America* in the areas of Appellate, Bet-the-Company Litigation, and Commercial Litigation, and Texas *Super Lawyers*. She is also a Founder of the Center for Women in the Law at the University of Texas School of Law.

ASSISTANT EDITOR

MICHAEL S. TRUESDALE is a solo practitioner in Austin, Texas. His practice focuses on civil appellate litigation in both state and federal courts. He is board certified in Civil Appellate Law by the Texas Board of Legal Specialization. He is admitted to practice before the U.S. Supreme Court, the U.S. Courts of Appeals for the Fifth, Seventh, Ninth, and Eleventh Circuits, and the federal and state courts of Texas. Mr. Truesdale clerked for the Hon. Craig Enoch on the Supreme Court of Texas. He is a member of the American Bar Association, the State Bar of Texas Appellate Section, and other appellate-related bar organizations. He is AV-rated by Martindale-Hubbell and is listed as a Texas *Super Lawyer* in the area of appellate law.

EDITORIAL BOARD

VAN A. CATES is Assistant General Counsel for Veolia Water North America Operating Services, L.L.C. (http://www.veoliawaterna.com), in Tampa, Florida. He has practiced law in the environmental consulting, engineering, construction, operations, and management industries, both in private practice and as in-house counsel, for the past 25 years. His experience includes managing litigation, bankruptcy, and large water and wastewater outsourcing agreements with industrial and governmental entities in North America and the Caribbean. He is licensed to practice law in state and federal courts in Texas and New Jersey and is admitted to practice before the U.S. Courts of Appeals for the Fifth Circuit.

MADELEINE ("NIKKO") FISCHER is a partner in the New Orleans office of Jones, Walker, Waechter, Poitevent, Carrère & Denègre, L.L.P. Admitted to practice in both Louisiana and Texas, Ms. Fischer has represented clients in litigation for more than 30 years and has extensive bench trial, jury trial, and appellate experience in state and federal courts. She is board certified in Civil Trial Advocacy by the National Board of Trial Advocacy (NBTA). Her practice includes class actions, toxic torts, products liability, appellate practice, and insurance coverage and bad faith litigation. She has appeared as counsel of record for clients in a number of state and federal class actions and in several multidistrict litigations. Ms. Fischer has been listed as a Louisiana *Super Lawyer* every year since 2007.

ROBERT D. ("BO") PHILLIPS, JR. is a partner in the Los Angeles and San Francisco offices of Reed Smith L.L.P. His practice consists primarily of defending consumer class actions, and he serves as national counsel in class actions throughout the country. He is a 1978 graduate of Duke University School of Law and returns to Duke often as a guest lecturer on topics including class action issues and ethical considerations faced by litigators in complex litigation.

JOANNE GEHA SWANSON is a member of Kerr, Russell and Weber, P.L.C. in Detroit, Michigan. Ms. Swanson specializes in the areas of civil litigation and appeals. Her litigation practice primarily involves complex commercial disputes, antitrust, class actions, and other related matters. Ms. Swanson also devotes a significant percentage of her professional time to state and federal appellate practice, involving groundbreaking constitutional issues and questions of statutory interpretation, medical liability, tort reform, insurance, business, and other related areas. Ms. Swanson is a former chairperson of the Antitrust, Trade and Franchising Section of the State Bar of Michigan. She is listed in Michigan's *Super Lawyers*, *Super Lawyers Corporate Counsel Edition*, and *DBusiness Top Lawyer*.

THOMAS WERTH THAGARD III practices law at Maynard, Cooper & Gale, P.C., in Birmingham, Alabama. Mr. Thagard focuses his practice on complex business litigation matters, including commercial business litigation, class actions, pharmaceutical defense, insurance fraud, products liability, and antitrust. He has represented clients in Alabama, Florida, Georgia, Louisiana, Mississippi, Pennsylvania, Texas, and Utah. Mr. Thagard has tried cases in various circuit courts in Alabama and arbitrations in various venues. He has handled appeals in the Eleventh Circuit, Fifth Circuit, and the Alabama Supreme Court. He has served as Liaison Counsel for a defendant group in the FEMA Formaldehyde MDL pending in Louisiana. He has been named to *Best Lawyers in America* for both Commercial Litigation and Products Liability Litigation.

About the Authors

PAUL ALSTON is a founder of Alston Hunt Floyd & Ing in Honolulu, Hawai`i. His practice focuses on complex commercial disputes. He has brought or defended over 40 class actions in both state and federal court. He is both a certified civil trial specialist and the only Hawai`i member of the American Academy of Appellate Lawyers. He is listed in *Best Lawyers in America* in six categories, including Bet-the-Company Litigation, Appellate Law, and Commercial Litigation. He is also listed in *Chambers USA, Leading Lawyers for Business* in Commercial Litigation. He was president of the Hawai`i State Bar Association from 1990–1991.

PETER A. ANTONUCCI is a shareholder in the New York office of Greenberg Traurig, L.L.P. Mr. Antonucci concentrates his practice in class actions, products liability, crisis management, and toxic torts. Mr. Antonucci has been an active member of the TIPS Section of the ABA for 20 years and presently serves on its Governing Council.

RICHARD J. ARSENAULT is the senior partner with the Alexandria, Louisiana, law firm of Neblett, Beard and Arsenault. He is listed in the Bar Register of Pre-eminent Lawyers as well as the *Best Lawyers in America*. He has an AV Martindale-Hubbell rating and serves on the LSU Law School's Trial Advocacy faculty. Mr. Arsenault has served as President of the Alexandria Bar Association, President of the Alexandria American Inns of Court, and Chairman of the Louisiana Bar Association's Section on Insurance, Negligence, Worker's Compensation, and Admiralty Law. He has chaired the Louisiana Bar Association's Annual Class Action/Mass Tort Symposium since its inception. He currently serves as a court appointed member of a variety of plaintiff steering committees nationwide, including those involving the Vioxx, Guidant, Medtronic Sprint, Bextra, Zicam, and Toyota multidistrict litigations. He also now serves as a co-chair of the AAJ Gulf Coast Oil Spill Litigation Group. Mr. Arsenault is licensed in Louisiana, Texas, Colorado, and Washington, D.C.

SCOTT J. ATLAS took a leave of absence from law practice to serve as the Finance Chair for Bill White's campaign for Governor of Texas. Before that, he was a senior partner specializing in complex commercial litigation in the Houston office of Weil, Gotshal & Manges. He has substantial experience in matters involving antitrust, arbitrations, business torts, construction, contract disputes, legal malpractice, lender liability, municipal law, securities, trade secrets, trademark infringement, and general commercial litigation. He has been listed repeatedly in *Best Lawyers in America* in Commercial Litigation. Mr. Atlas chaired the 70,000-plus member ABA Section of Litigation in 2002–2003. He received a B.A. from Yale University in 1971 and a J.D. from the University of Texas in 1975.

RUTH A. BAHE-JACHNA is a shareholder in the Chicago office of Greenberg Traurig, L.L.P. Ms. Bahe-Jachna concentrates her practice in class actions, products liability, and product safety counseling.

JASON M. BEACH is an associate in Hunton & Williams L.L.P.'s Atlanta office. His practice focuses on complex commercial litigation in federal and state courts at the trial and appellate levels, including class action defense, commercial contract disputes, data breach forensic investigation, and financial services litigation. He also has experience with internal investigations and with financial services matters including violations of statutes regulating lenders and related common law claims for major national banking associations and mortgage lenders.

ANDREW F. BEHREND is of counsel in the litigation group of Stoel Rives L.L.P. in Anchorage, Alaska. His litigation practice includes employment and large contract litigation, ERISA and employee benefits, business torts, misappropriation of trade secrets, insurance coverage, antitrust violations, and violations of environmental laws. He also counsels employers on a wide range of nonlitigation labor and employment issues. Mr. Behrend was selected as one of the *Chambers USA, Leading Lawyers for Business* (Alaska) in Labor & Employment from 2006 through 2010.

MEGAN M. BELCHER is the Vice President and Chief Employment Counsel for ConAgra Foods, Inc., a *Fortune 500* Consumer Package Goods company based in Omaha, Nebraska. In her position she manages the team of lawyers and professionals who handle the labor, employment, and benefits legal matters for the company, which includes managing employment litigation nationally and internationally. Prior to joining ConAgra, Ms. Belcher practiced in the labor and employment department of Husch Blackwell Sanders L.L.P., defending corporate clients in their labor and employment litigation matters and providing counseling on human resources matters. Ms. Belcher is admitted to practice in the state and federal courts of Missouri, Kansas, and Nebraska.

CAMILLE E. BENNETT is counsel in the Chicago office of Sonnenschein Nath & Rosenthal and specializes in securities and class action litigation. Ms. Bennett graduated from the University of Chicago Law School, where she was a member of the *Law Review*.

AMY BERGQUIST, currently clerking for Justice Ruth Bader Ginsburg of the U.S. Supreme Court, was previously an associate at Faegre & Benson L.L.P. She graduated summa cum laude from the University of Minnesota Law School in 2007, and served as Editor-in-Chief of the *Minnesota Law Review*. At Faegre & Benson, she concentrated her practice on litigation of consumer fraud claims and contract disputes, as well as appellate advocacy.

JAMES L. BERNARD is a partner in the litigation department of Stroock & Stroock & Lavan L.L.P. in New York City. His practice focuses mostly on complex federal litigation, including securities fraud and accounting malpractice actions. He has been representing Grant Thornton International in various litigations arising out of the collapse of Parmalat, as well as other security class actions. He clerked for Loretta A. Preska and Alvin K. Hellerstein, both of the U.S. District Court for the Southern District of New York.

DAVID W. BERTONI is a partner in the law firm of Brann & Isaacson in Lewiston, Maine. He advises clients and serves as litigation counsel in the areas of consumer protection, unfair trade practice, privacy, and e-commerce and telemarketing laws. He is a graduate of the George Washington University Law School and the national winner of the American Intellectual Property Law Association moot court competition. He received his undergraduate degree from the University of Rochester. Mr. Bertoni represented L.L. Bean, Inc.—and prevailed—in a landmark class action case before the Maine Supreme Judicial Court arising out of claims that the company had improperly collected sales taxes on credit card reward coupons (*Flippo v. L.L. Bean*, 898 A.2d 942, 2006 Me. 62).

DAVID M. BIZAR is a partner in the Business & Financial Services Litigation and Bankruptcy & Restructuring groups of McCarter & English, L.L.P., in its Boston, Massachusetts, office, and practices consumer financial services and commercial litigation. Mr. Bizar has defended lenders, finance and debt collection lawyers, and other business clients in putative class action lawsuits challenging their products and services, corporate practices, and regulatory adherence. Mr. Bizar has served as lead or class counsel in more than 20 consumer class actions, including representing one of the largest federal savings banks in a putative nationwide class action challenging the lawfulness of its option adjustable rate subprime mortgage product, and a manufacturer automotive finance company in a putative nationwide class action challenging the legal adequacy of its lease disclosures. Mr. Bizar served as the Chair of the Consumer Law Section of the Connecticut Bar Association from 2005 to 2009 and has served on the Executive Committee of the Litigation Section from 2008 to the present. Mr. Bizar is also a former Army JAG and is a current member of the Standing Committee on Legal Assistance for Military Personnel of the American Bar Association.

C. PATRICK BODDEN is an attorney at Maynard, Cooper & Gale in Birmingham, Alabama. Mr. Bodden received his J.D. from the University of Texas and his B.A. cum laude from Emory University.

JILL D. BOWMAN is a partner at Stoel Rives L.L.P., practicing in the litigation department in Seattle, Washington. She regularly handles federal and state court cases and appeals involving a broad range of corporate and commercial matters, including claims brought under federal and state securities laws, state unfair practices laws, business torts, and labor and employment issues.

JEFFREY A. BRAUER is a litigation partner at Hahn Loeser & Parks, L.L.P. in Cleveland, Ohio. Mr. Brauer graduated from Vanderbilt University School of Law in 1994 and has worked extensively in complex commercial, construction dispute, and class action litigation. He is a frequent speaker and author on a variety of litigation-related topics.

ERNESSA M. BRAWLEY joined the Atlanta, Georgia, firm of Swift, Currie, McGhee, & Hiers, L.L.P. in 2008 upon receiving her law degree from Georgia State University College of Law. Ms. Brawley practices in the firm's civil litigation section, focusing primarily on products liability, automobile litigation, and premises liability. She is also a registered neutral with the Georgia Office of Alternative Dispute Resolution. Ms. Brawley has a B.S. in Biology and a minor in Gerontology. Prior to attending law school, Ms. Brawley marketed several multi-million-dollar products on behalf of Merck pharmaceuticals.

ANN BROWN-GRAFF is a lawyer at Brady & O'Shea, P.C., in Cedar Rapids, Iowa, practicing primarily in the area of civil litigation. She attended Cornell College, where she graduated cum laude with a degree in Political Science, and the University of Iowa College of Law, where she graduated with distinction. Ms. Brown-Graff is admitted to practice in all Iowa state courts, as well as the Northern and Southern Districts of Iowa's federal courts. She is a member of the American Bar Association, Iowa Bar Association, Iowa Association for Justice, and American Association for Justice (Lead Paint Litigation Section and Toxic, Environmental, and Pharmaceutical Torts Section).

JENNIFER CADENA received her J.D. from American University Washington College of Law in 2008 and is a lawyer at Fulbright & Jaworski L.L.P. Ms. Cadena is admitted to practice in the state of New York and is a member of Fulbright's Global Class Action practice group.

ROBERT B. CAREY is a partner at the law firm of Hagens Berman Sobol Shapiro, L.L.P. He concentrates his practice on consumer class actions. Mr. Carey specializes in class action lawsuits from his office in Phoenix, Arizona, handling recent cases such as the NCAA student athlete likeness litigation, the Toyota unintended acceleration MDL litigation, and a claim against the United States for failing to refund unearned passport expedite fees. He has tried numerous cases to verdict with as much as $75 million at stake, and acted as trial counsel on claims for counties and states for damages stemming from tobacco-related illnesses. From 1990 to 1996, Mr. Carey was Arizona's Chief Deputy Attorney General, where he supervised 300+ lawyers, and later served as a superior court judge pro tempore. He currently serves as the Chair of the Arizona State Bar Class Action and Derivative Suits Committee, and has taught graduate law and policy courses at, most recently, the University of Colorado. Mr. Carey earned his bachelor's degree at Arizona State University, and his MBA and law degree from the University of Denver.

CHRISTOPHER CHORBA is a partner in the Los Angeles office of Gibson, Dunn & Crutcher L.L.P. and a member of the firm's Class Action and Appellate & Constitutional Law practice groups.

MARK D. CHRISTIANSEN is an energy litigation lawyer with the Oklahoma City office of Crowe & Dunlevy, P.C. He spends a substantial portion of his litigation practice representing defendants in statewide, multistate, and nationwide class action lawsuits in the energy industry. Since 1985, he has served as lead editor and co-author of national updates on energy litigation in the United States for the *Year in Review* publication of the American Bar Association's Section of Environment, Energy, and Resources. Mr. Christiansen is listed as a first-tier energy lawyer in *Chambers USA, Leading Lawyers for Business*, and in *Best Lawyers in America* and Oklahoma *Super Lawyers*.

EZRA D. CHURCH is an associate in Morgan Lewis's Litigation Practice in Philadelphia, Pennsylvania. Mr. Church's practice focuses on a broad range of litigation matters, with a particular emphasis on complex commercial and class actions. A member of the firm's Class Action Working Group, Mr. Church has a specific background in the area of class action certification. Mr. Church earned his J.D., cum laude, from the University of Texas School of Law in 2005 and his B.A. in History, with a minor in Philosophy, from Northwestern University in 2002. Mr. Church is admitted to practice in Pennsylvania, New Jersey, and Louisiana.

JAMES C. DALE is a partner with Stoel Rives L.L.P. in Boise, Idaho. Mr. Dale is a member of the litigation practice group, where he concentrates on labor and employment matters in federal and state courts and a variety of administrative agencies. He is admitted to practice law in Idaho and Utah and the Circuit Court of Appeals for the Ninth Circuit. Over the past several years, Mr. Dale has been recognized in *Chambers USA, Leading Lawyers for Business* as a first-tier employment lawyer in Idaho. He is also listed in *Best Lawyers in America* and Mountain States *Super Lawyers*. Mr. Dale is a founding member of the Management Labor and Employment Roundtable.

LAURIE WEBB DANIEL is a partner in the Atlanta office of Holland & Knight L.L.P. She is chairman of her firm's Appellate Team and a member of its Class Action Team. Her active motions and appeals practice focuses on complex litigation, including class actions and multidistrict litigation.

CARI K. DAWSON is a partner with the law firm of Alston & Bird L.L.P. in Atlanta, Georgia, and chairs the Class Action Practice Team for the Litigation and Trial practice group. Ms. Dawson handles a variety of complex litigation matters in both state and federal courts nationwide, with a particular focus on class action defense.

NICOLE J. DULUDE is an associate in the litigation department at Adler Pollock & Sheehan P.C. in Providence, Rhode Island. She formerly served as lead law clerk to the Hon. Frank J. Williams, Chief Justice of the Rhode Island Supreme Court (retired).

BARBARA B. EDELMAN is a partner in the Lexington, Kentucky, office of Dinsmore & Shohl, L.L.P. She has extensive complex commercial litigation experience. She served for seven years as an assistant U.S. Attorney, where she prosecuted cases involving money laundering, complex fraud prosecutions, RICO matters, conspiracy, aiding and abetting, bank fraud, and numerous white collar cases. She also served on the Department of Justice's Economic Fraud Commission. For over 20 years, she has litigated, prosecuted, and defended civil cases specializing in business litigation, including breach of fiduciary duty claims, business torts, fraud, and negligent misrepresentation, as well as a number of class actions. She has tried over 50 jury cases and numerous bench trials. She is listed in *Best Lawyers in America* in Appellate Law, Bet-the-Company, and Commercial Litigation. She has also been selected by Chambers & Partners - *Chambers USA* in Commercial Litigation, Kentucky's *Super Lawyers* for 2009, Kentucky's *Super Lawyers* for 2009 Top 25 Women, *Benchmark Litigation* as a "Local Litigation Star," and *The Lane Report*'s "Top Women in Business." She is the chair of the firm's Commercial Litigation practice group.

SARAH BRITE EVANS is a lawyer at Schwartz Semerdjian Haile Ballard & Cauley L.L.P. in San Diego, California, where her practice primarily involves individual and class action employment claims. She is a graduate of the University of Southern California and Notre Dame Law School and has been named to the *San Diego Daily Transcript*'s Top Young Attorneys and *San Diego Metropolitan Magazine*'s Top 40 Under 40.

BLAINE H. EVANSON is an associate in the Los Angeles office of Gibson, Dunn & Crutcher L.L.P., practicing in the firm's Class Action and Appellate & Constitutional Law practice groups. He has defended numerous class actions at both the appellate and trial court levels, principally in cases involving claims under the wage and hour and consumer protection laws. He graduated from Columbia Law School in 2006, where he was a James Kent Scholar and an editor for the *Columbia Law Review*. Before joining Gibson Dunn, he clerked for Judge A. Raymond Randolph of the U.S. Court of Appeals for the D.C. Circuit.

JOSEPH B. G. FAY is a partner in Morgan Lewis's Litigation Practice in Philadelphia, Pennsylvania. Mr. Fay has experience with a wide range of class action cases, including numerous nationwide class actions involving building materials, consumer products, ERISA, and antitrust-related class actions. He is a member of the firm's Class Action Working Group, and in 30 years of practice in class actions he has defended more than 100 such actions, spoken at continuing legal education presentations on the topic, and written book chapters and articles on class action issues. Mr. Fay earned his J.D. from the Georgetown University Law Center in 1980 and his A.B. from Harvard University in 1976. He is admitted to practice in Pennsylvania.

ALEXANDER B. FEINBERG is currently a law student at the Cumberland School of Law in Birmingham, Alabama. He will be joining Maynard Cooper & Gale in Birmingham after passing the bar in 2010.

BRUCE W. FELMLY is a partner in the Manchester, New Hampshire, office of McLane, Graf, Raulerson & Middleton, P.A., and is the co-chairman of the firm's litigation department. He has tried many cases in state and federal court to both juries and judges. His practice involves representing companies and individuals in trial in a wide range of commercial disputes, including employment matters, antitrust, class actions, trade secret and patent litigation, construction, environmental, insurance recovery, real estate, and other business disputes. Mr. Felmly is a former President of the New Hampshire Bar Association, a Fellow in the American College of Trial Lawyers, and is currently serving on the Board of Regents of the College. He has been recognized by *Chambers USA* in Litigation and *Best Lawyers in America* in Appellate Law, Commercial Litigation, Personal Injury Litigation, and Bet-the-Company Litigation.

RICHARD L. FENTON is a litigation partner in the Chicago office of Sonnenschein Nath & Rosenthal, which, on September 30, 2010, will become SNR Denton US L.L.P. Mr. Fenton serves as co-chair of the firm's appellate practice group, and specializes in complex commercial litigation and class action defense at both the trial and appellate levels. Mr. Fenton is a member of the bar of Illinois, of the U.S. Supreme Court, of the U.S. Courts of Appeal for the Second, Fifth, Sixth, Seventh, Ninth, and Eleventh Circuits, and of the U.S. District Courts for the Northern District of Illinois and the Eastern District of Wisconsin. He has been recognized repeatedly in *Best Lawyers in America* and in Illinois *Super Lawyers*.

DONALD R. FREDERICO is a shareholder in the Boston office of Greenberg Traurig, L.L.P. Co-chair of the firm's National Class Action practice group, Mr. Frederico focuses his practice on representing defendants in class actions and mass tort litigation. He is currently President-Elect of the Boston Bar Association.

THOMAS C. GALLIGAN, JR. is the president of Colby-Sawyer College, where he is also a professor of humanities. He has written extensively about tort law and maritime law. Professor Galligan was the Dean of the University of Tennessee College of Law from 1998 to 2006, where he was also an Elvin E. Overton Professor of Law. From 1986 to 1998, he was a professor at Louisiana State University's Paul M. Hebert Law Center, where was also the Dale E. Bennett Professor of Law. He has published and spoken extensively on tort law and maritime law, and his scholarship has been cited by the U.S. Supreme Court, the U.S. Fifth Circuit Court of Appeals, the Louisiana Supreme Court, other courts, and commentators. His co-authored scholarship with Professor Frank L. Maraist has been honored by the *Tulane Law Review* and the *Louisiana Bar Journal*. Professor Galligan has testified before Senate and House committees on liability issues surrounding the *Deepwater Horizon* disaster.

MAUREEN GORMAN is a Senior Media Analyst with Kinsella Media, L.L.C., based out of Chicago, Illinois. She has more than 30 years experience in media buying and planning. Ms. Gorman has held high management positions in the media departments at BBDO Worldwide and Bayer Bess Vanderwarker, as well as positions in media research sales and marketing at The Nielsen Company. She personally directed national spot broadcast buying for accounts such as Wrigley, Dodge, Quaker, Ameritech, and US West. In addition to her work at Kinsella Media, Ms. Gorman conducts professional training seminars in media planning and buying throughout the country as a senior instructor for the Media Buying Academy.

JEFFREY M. GRANTHAM is a shareholder at Maynard, Cooper & Gale in Birmingham, Alabama, where he chairs the firm's Insurance and Financial Services practice group. He has a national practice focusing on the defense of class actions and other complex claims against the insurance and financial services industries. Mr. Grantham also frequently represents companies in the defense of personal injury and other tort claims. Mr. Grantham received his J.D. from Vanderbilt University and his B.S. magna cum laude from the University of Alabama. He has been recognized by his peers in both *Best Lawyers in America* and Alabama *Super Lawyers*.

STEVEN F. GRIFFITH, JR. is a shareholder in the New Orleans office of Baker Donelson Bearman Caldwell & Berkowitz, P.C. He practices in the area of business litigation with a focus on clients in the construction and oil field services industries. He specializes on the unique wage and hour issues in these industries and defends nationwide collective actions brought under the Fair Labor Standards Act, as well as related class actions across the country. He is admitted to practice before the U.S. Supreme Court, the U.S. Court of Appeals for the Fifth Circuit, and the federal and state courts of Louisiana. He has also been admitted on a pro hac vice basis to various courts throughout the country. From 2000 to 2001, Mr. Griffith clerked for the Hon. Pascal F. Calogero, Jr., Chief Justice of the Louisiana Supreme Court.

J. ALAN HARRELL is a partner in the Baton Rouge, Louisiana, office of Phelps Dunbar L.L.P. His practice includes toxic tort and environmental litigation, class actions, and commercial litigation. He also advises clients on environmental regulatory compliance. Mr. Harrell regularly defends clients in class action and mass joinder litigation involving environmental and other theories of recovery. He is the co-author of "Toxic Tort Litigation," in *Environmental Litigation: Law and Strategy,* published by the American Bar Association's Section of Environment, Energy and Resources (May 2009).

KENDRA HARTMAN is General Counsel for Gehl Foods and also works pro bono prosecuting a class action on behalf of adults with developmental disabilities. Ms. Hartman was formerly a partner at Sonnenschein, Nath & Rosenthal L.L.P. in Chicago, where she practiced in the field of complex commercial litigation, concentrating in the defense of class actions. Ms. Hartman graduated from Yale Law School.

JOHN C. HAWK IV is an associate with Buist Moore Smythe McGee P.A. in Charleston, South Carolina, practicing primarily in the areas of products liability and business litigation.

G. CALVIN HAYES is a partner at Fowler White Boggs in Tampa, Florida. His practice focuses on complex commercial, healthcare, and class action litigation in state and federal court. He is admitted to practice before the U.S. Supreme Court, the U.S. Courts of Appeal for the Eleventh and Ninth Circuits, as well as the federal and state courts of Florida. Mr. Hayes is Co-Chair of the ABA Class Action and Derivative Suits Subcommittee on Mass Torts.

ERIC A. HERZOG is a senior associate in the Los Angeles, California, office of Fulbright & Jaworski L.L.P. His practice involves a wide range of complex litigation, including class actions, unfair business practices, insurance, securities fraud, and intellectual property litigation, and he is a member of Fulbright's Global Class Action practice group. In 2009, Mr. Herzog was selected for inclusion in *Super Lawyers—Rising Stars* for Southern California.

HAROLD C. HIRSHMAN is a partner in Sonnenschein Nath & Rosenthal L.L.P.'s Chicago office. He has been litigating securities cases since the early 1970s and has taught securities law. Mr. Hirshman graduated from the University of Chicago Law School, where he was a member of the *Law Review*.

ROBERT L. HODGES is of counsel in the Complex Commercial Litigation group of McGuireWoods L.L.P. in Richmond, Virginia, where he focuses on complex litigation and class action defense, particularly in the areas of vendor-purchaser disputes (including real estate, sale of goods and warranty matters) and lender-borrower disputes (including lender liability and consumer credit matters). He also has a substantial practice representing clients in appellate litigation. He is admitted to practice before the U.S. Supreme Court, the U.S. Courts of Appeals for the Third, Fourth, and Fifth Circuits, the U.S. District Courts for the Eastern and Western Districts of Virginia and Northern District of Illinois, and the Supreme Court of Virginia. Mr. Hodges has taught Sales and Leases (U.C.C. Articles 2 and 2A) as an adjunct professor at the T.C. Williams School of Law at the University of Richmond since 1993.

DAVID HOLLAND is the Executive Vice President of Rust Consulting, Inc.'s Minneapolis, Minnesota, office and has 15 years of experience consulting with clients on class action settlement administration.

TIMOTHY C. HOLM has been a shareholder with Modrall, Sperling, Roehl, Harris & Sisk in Albuquerque, New Mexico, since 1993. His practice focuses on civil defense litigation, including class action, products liability, and consumer protection actions. He is listed in *Best Lawyers in America* (Products Liability, Mass Torts, and Railroad Law). He is also a member of the Local Rules Advisory Committee for the U.S. District Court for the District of New Mexico. He graduated from the University of North Carolina School of Law in 1987 with high honors and still considers himself a Tar Heel.

S. AULT HOOTSELL III is a partner in the New Orleans, Louisiana, office of Phelps Dunbar L.L.P. For more than 23 years, Mr. Hootsell has counseled corporate and individual clients in complex commercial and tort litigation matters. His practice includes the defense of class action and mass joinder litigation in both federal and state court, including products liability disputes and mass tort litigation. He is among a select group of lawyers listed in a nationwide client survey published in *Chambers USA, Leading Lawyers for Business*. He is recognized as a leading practitioner in the areas of Bankruptcy/Creditor-Debtor Rights Law and Business Litigation in *Best Lawyers in America* and *Super Lawyers*, respectively. And he is also a Business Bankruptcy Specialist and is board certified by the Louisiana Board of Legal Specialization and the American Board of Certification.

LOUISE K.Y. ING is a founder of Alston, Hunt, Floyd & Ing in Honolulu, Hawai`i. Her practice focuses on complex commercial, employment, and real estate litigation and dispute resolution, and has included class action litigation. She is listed in *Best Lawyers in America* in the Bet-the-Company Litigation and Commercial Litigation categories and in *Chambers USA, Leading Lawyers for Business* in Commercial Litigation. She is president-elect of the Hawai`i State Bar Association.

WYNDALL A. IVEY is the Managing Member of The Ivey Law Group in Birmingham, Alabama. Mr. Ivey is a labor and employment litigator with an emphasis on representing parties in all types of employment disputes and collective actions brought under the Fair Labor Standards Act. Additionally, Mr. Ivey has tried cases in federal and state courts and before state administrative bodies. He was an inaugural member of the Tort Trial and Insurance Practice Section's Leadership Academy, an inaugural member of Leadership UAB, a member of the Alabama State Bar 2006 Leadership Forum Class, a TIPS Now Fellow, and served on the Board of Directors for the Alabama Defense Lawyers' Association. Currently, Mr. Ivey serves as Chair of the Tort Trial Insurance Practice Section's Business Litigation Committee. He received his B.S. from the University of Alabama at Birmingham in 1996, and obtained his J.D. from Washington & Lee University School of Law in 1999. In

2004, Mr. Ivey was selected by the *Montgomery Advertiser* as one of Montgomery's Leading 20 Under 40, and in 2008, he was selected by the *Birmingham Business Journal* as one of Birmingham's Top 40 Under 40.

THEANE EVANGELIS KAPUR is an associate in the Los Angeles office of Gibson, Dunn & Crutcher L.L.P. She has defended numerous class actions at both the appellate and trial court levels and is a member of the firm's Class Action and Appellate & Constitutional Law practice groups. She graduated from New York University School of Law in 2003, where she was managing editor of the *New York University Law Review*. Before joining Gibson Dunn, she clerked for Justice Sandra Day O'Connor of the U.S. Supreme Court and Chief Judge Alex Kozinski of the U.S. Court of Appeals for the Ninth Circuit.

KERMIT L. KENDRICK is a partner with Burr & Forman L.L.P. in Birmingham, Alabama, practicing in the litigation section and focusing on consumer finance, transportation, and commercial litigation. Mr. Kendrick is also a TIPS member and is a vice chair of the Business Law, Public Relations, and Professional Officers Directors and Liability Committees.

JASON H. KIM is of counsel at Alston Hunt Floyd & Ing in Honolulu, Hawai`i. His practice focuses on commercial litigation, class actions, and health care litigation.

J. BENJAMIN KING is a partner in the Dallas, Texas, office of Diamond McCarthy L.L.P. His practice focuses on civil litigation in both state and federal courts. He has prosecuted and defended class actions in courts across the United States.

MOLLY PRODGERS KING is an associate at Swift, Currie, McGhee & Hiers, L.L.P., in Atlanta, Georgia. She practices in the firm's liability section and focuses primarily on commercial litigation, products liability, and insurance coverage. Ms. King represents corporate clients, individuals, and insurers from pre-suit matters through appeal and settlement. Ms. King received her J.D. from the University of Georgia School of Law in 2005 and her A.B.J., magna cum laude, in Journalism from the Henry W. Grady College of Journalism at the University of Georgia in 2001.

KATHERINE KINSELLA is president of Kinsella Media, L.L.C. in Washington, D.C. She is a leading, nationally recognized expert in the design and dissemination of legal notice in class actions and bankruptcies. Ms. Kinsella has developed and directed some of the largest and most complex national notification programs in cases involving asbestos, home siding products, infant formula, polybutylene plumbing, pharmaceuticals, securities, and tobacco. She brings to her firm and to the courts more than 30 years of experience in high-level communications strategy in the fields of advertising, marketing, and public relations. Her firm has placed over $230 million in paid media and has worked on over 600 cases.

PETER S. KNAPMAN is an attorney with Alston, Hunt, Floyd & Ing in Honolulu, Hawai`i. He joined the firm in 1999 after completing a clerkship with the Hon. Justice Paula Nakayama of the Hawai`i Supreme Court. His practice focuses on complex commercial litigation, consumer class actions, and professional malpractice disputes.

KENNETH E. KRAUS is a partner at Kenneth E. Kraus LLC in Chicago, Illinois, where he represents businesses and individuals in complex litigation including breach of contract, fraud, consumer fraud, trade secrets, covenants not to compete, and disputes over corporate transactions.

JILL A. KRAUSS is an associate practicing commercial litigation at Stroock & Stroock & Lavan L.L.P. in New York City.

LAYNE KRUSE, a litigation partner in the Houston office of Fulbright & Jaworski L.L.P., co-chairs the firm's Antitrust and Competition practice group and heads the litigation department. His practice is focused on antitrust and securities litigation, class actions in particular, and he is a member of Fulbright's Global Class Action practice group. Mr. Kruse has chaired the Antitrust and Business Litigation Section of the State Bar of Texas and the Texas Association of Certified Civil Trial and Appellate Specialists. He is certified in Civil Trial Law by the Texas Board of Legal Specialization. Before joining the firm, Mr. Kruse clerked for Chief Judge John R. Brown, U.S. Court of Appeals for the Fifth Circuit. Mr. Kruse is listed in *Best Lawyers in America* in the areas of Commercial Litigation and Antitrust and was named one of America's Leading Business Lawyers by *Chambers USA*. He graduated from Yale Law School.

JOSHUA D. LICHTMAN is a partner in the Los Angeles, California, office of Fulbright & Jaworski L.L.P. His practice primarily focuses on complex commercial litigation matters, including insurance, banking, antitrust, unfair business practices, and business torts, in both individual and class actions, and he is a member of Fulbright's Global Class Action practice group. Before joining the firm, he served from 1994 to 1995 as a law clerk for the Hon. Irving S. Hill of the U.S. District Court for the Central District of California.

F. A. LITTLE, JR., U.S. District Judge (retired) of the Western District of Louisiana, is of counsel to Stanley, Reuter, Ross, Thornton & Alford, L.L.C. of New Orleans and Alexandria, Louisiana.

SCOTT H. MARDER is a partner in the Baltimore office of Duane Morris, L.L.P. He is a member of the firm's trial department, with a national practice focusing on complex commercial and construction litigation. Mr. Marder received his J.D., magna cum laude, from the University of Miami School of Law in 1991 and is admitted to practice before the federal and state courts of Maryland and Florida.

RICHARD W. MARK is a partner in the New York City office of Orrick, Herrington & Sutcliffe L.L.P., and is a graduate of Dartmouth College and Columbia University Law School. He clerked for the Hon. Thomas P. Griesa of the U.S. District Court for the Southern District of New York, and served as an assistant U.S. Attorney in that district from 1984 to 1996. Mr. Mark's practice includes the litigation of mass civil actions, at trial and on appeal. He has defended manufacturers in product liability cases involving diverse products such as lead pigment and vaccines. From 1988 through 2006, Mr. Mark was an adjunct professor at Fordham University Law School.

PETER H. MASON is partner-in-charge of the Los Angeles, California, office of Fulbright & Jaworski L.L.P. His practice encompasses complex commercial litigation matters, including antitrust, unfair competition, insurance coverage, marketing practices and bad faith, products liability, and energy litigation, and he is a member of Fulbright's Global Class Action practice group. In addition to trial work, he has successfully argued appeals in the California Supreme Court and in the U.S. Courts of Appeals. Mr. Mason is listed in *Best Lawyers in America* in the area of Commercial Litigation.

ROBERT GREGG MAYER practices commercial litigation with Phelps Dunbar L.L.P. in Jackson, Mississippi.

DANIEL M. McCLURE is a partner in the litigation section of Fulbright & Jaworski L.L.P. in Houston, Texas, and is co-chair of Fulbright's Global Class Action practice group. His practice is focused on civil trials and appeals in both state and federal courts, with a concentration in complex commercial litigation and class actions. Mr. McClure is a 1978 graduate of Harvard Law School. He is certified in Civil Trial Law by the Texas Board of Legal Specialization. Mr. McClure is listed in *Best Lawyers in America, Chambers USA, Leading Lawyers,* and the *BTI Client Service All-Star Team.*

J. ETHAN McDANIEL practices law at Maynard, Cooper & Gale, P.C. in Birmingham, Alabama. Mr. McDaniel focuses his practice on complex business litigation matters, including class actions, class arbitrations, commercial business litigation, financial services litigation, insurance sales practices litigation, trademark litigation, and trade secrets litigation. He has represented the firm's clients in Alabama, Florida, Tennessee, New York, New Jersey, North Carolina, Texas, Idaho, and Nebraska.

ALLAN McGARVEY is a partner in the firm McGarvey, Heberling, Sullivan and McGarvey, P.C. in Kalispell, Montana. He has served as class counsel in large-scale litigation including a $97 million profit-sharing settlement (CFAC), class and group claims over the W.R. Grace asbestos contamination in Libby, Montana, and nationwide (ZAI), the Montana Power Company shareholder litigation ($113 million settlement), and numerous class actions challenging insurance company conduct.

MATTHEW P. McGUIRE is a partner in the Litigation & Trial practice group at Alston & Bird L.L.P. in Raleigh, North Carolina, where his practice focuses on complex commercial, financial services, and class action litigation.

DAVID J. MICHALSKI is a litigation partner at Hahn Loeser & Parks, L.L.P. in Cleveland, Ohio. Mr. Michalski graduated magna cum laude in 1994 from Case Western Reserve University Law School and has worked extensively on complex commercial, construction, and class action litigation. He frequently litigates complex matters involving foreign law, cases involving foreign governments, and cases involving cross-border discovery.

ADAM E. MILLER is a partner at Husch Blackwell Sanders L.L.P. in St. Louis, Missouri. Mr. Miller has been extensively involved in complex, mass tort, and class action product liability litigation involving consumer and commercial products containing benzene, solvents, iodine-uptake inhibiting compounds, dioxins, PCBs, caustics, tobacco products, creosotes, and environmental contaminants such as mercury and perchlorate.

CLYDE A. MUCHMORE is a director for Crowe & Dunlevy in the corporation's Oklahoma City offices. A practitioner for more than 40 years, he specializes in civil litigation, appellate law, communications and media law, and constitutional law. Mr. Muchmore has considerable experience in high-profile litigation involving federal and state constitutional issues, 1st Amendment issues, complex business disputes, and appeals in federal and state appellate courts.

MICHAEL J. MUELLER is a partner in Hunton & Williams L.L.P.'s Washington office and is co-head of the firm's nationwide complex commercial litigation group. He has been lead counsel in over 50 class or collective actions in various industries. Mr. Mueller has appeared in all levels of the U.S. courts and the state courts of Connecticut, Delaware, the District of Columbia, Florida, Maryland,

North Carolina, and Tennessee. In 2006 he was lead trial counsel for a national food processing company in an overtime wages case involving over 500 plaintiffs; the defense verdict was listed first in the *National Law Journal*'s 2006 Defense Hot List. Mr. Mueller has been listed as a Washington *Super Lawyer*.

LINDA S. MULLENIX is the Morris and Rita Atlas Chair in Advocacy at the University of Texas School of Law. Professor Mullenix holds M.Phil. and Ph.D. degrees from Columbia University and her law degree from Georgetown Law Center. She has been a scholar-in-residence at the Rockefeller Bellagio Research Center in Bellagio, Italy, and held the Fulbright Distinguished Senior Chair in Law at the University of Trento, Italy. She is an elected member of the American Law Institute and the International Association of Procedural Law. She was the Associate Reporter on ALI Restatement of the Law Governing Lawyers, and a consultant to the ALI Complex Litigation Project and the Transnational Rules of Civil Procedure. She is the author of *Mass Tort Litigation* (Thomson West, 2d ed. 2009) and numerous other books and publications relating to federal practice and procedure, class action, and complex litigation. She has been a regular columnist for 20 years for the *National Law Journal*, writing on topics relating to complex litigation and class actions.

LUTHER T. MUNFORD is with Phelps Dunbar L.L.P. in Jackson, Mississippi. He defends lawyers, represents news media clients, litigates constitutional issues, and handles federal and state civil appeals. He is listed in the Mississippi news media and appellate litigation sections of both *Chambers USA, Leading Lawyers for Business* and *Best Lawyers in America*.

JAMES D. MYRICK is a principal with Buist Moore Smythe McGee P.A. in Charleston, South Carolina, and head of the litigation department. His practice includes business and environmental litigation. Mr. Myrick is listed among the *Best Lawyers in America* and South Carolina *Super Lawyers*.

RAND P. NOLEN is a lawyer with Fleming & Associates, L.L.P., in Houston, Texas. He practices in the areas of products liability, consumer protection, personal injury, mass tort, class action, and appellate law. He is admitted to practice law by the State Bar of Texas, as well as the U.S. District Courts for the Southern, Western, Northern, and Eastern Districts of Texas; U.S. Court of Appeals for the Third, Fifth, and Seventh Circuits; U.S. Court of Federal Claims; and U.S. Supreme Court. He has been selected by the American Trial Lawyers Association as one of their Top 100 Trial Lawyers for 2007, 2008, 2009, and 2010. He has also been selected by *H Texas Magazine* as one of Houston's Top Lawyers for 2006 through 2010 and Houston's Top Lawyers for the People for 2007 through 2010. Mr. Nolen is an associate in the American Board of Trial Advocates and a fellow in the Litigation Counsel of America.

DANIEL C. OCCHIPINTI is an associate in the litigation group of Stoel Rives LLP in Portland, Oregon. Mr. Occhipinti represents and advises individuals, businesses, and corporate clients in a variety of matters, including complex business disputes, shareholder actions, and debtor-creditor litigation.

DANIEL W. OLIVAS is an associate at Lewis, King, Krieg & Waldrop in Nashville, Tennessee. His practice focuses on coverage opinions, appellate work, products liability, ERISA defense, and professional malpractice defense.

LINDA B. OLIVER is a partner with Reed Smith in San Francisco, California, practicing in the area of financial services. She represents insurance companies, mortgage lenders, and other business entities in litigation involving ERISA, bad faith, unfair competition, sales practices, and agency termination, including class action defense.

JAMES A. O'NEAL is a partner in the Minneapolis, Minnesota, office of the law firm of Faegre & Benson L.L.P., where he heads the product liability practice. He graduated in 1978 from Yale Law School, where he was the student chair of the trial practice organization. He concentrates his practice on the litigation of complex product liability and consumer fraud claims, class actions, and mass torts. He is a Fellow of the American College of Trial Lawyers and a member of the Product Liability Advisory Council, the International Association of Defense Counsel, and the American Board of Trial Advocates. He is listed in *Best Lawyers in America* in the areas of Mass Tort and Product Liability Litigation, and by *Chambers USA, Leading Lawyers for Business* in the area of Litigation.

JOSEPH H. PARK is a partner in the litigation department of Fulbright & Jaworski L.L.P. in Los Angeles, California. His practice focuses on the representation of domestic and foreign companies in a variety of industries in complex civil litigation, class actions, commercial disputes, and international litigation. Mr. Park's experience includes the trial of two class actions to verdict. A graduate of Stanford University (B.A.) and UCLA School of Law (J.D.), Mr. Park is admitted to practice before the U.S. Courts of Appeals for the Ninth and Eleventh Circuits, the U.S. Tax Court, the District Courts for the Central, Eastern, and Northern Districts of California, and California state courts. He is a member of Fulbright's Global Class Action practice group.

ROBERT TED PARKER practices law at the Parker Law Firm in Orinda, California, and was formerly a partner in K&L Gates L.L.P.'s San Francisco office. His practice is focused on complex and international civil litigation, including matters in securities and financial fraud, banking and commercial law, construction, products liability, agriculture, film production, and business torts. He is admitted to practice before the U.S. Supreme Court and the U.S. Courts of Appeals for the Second, Ninth, and Federal Circuits, as well as the federal and state courts of California. He was an editor of the *Cornell Law Review*. He has served as Adjunct Professor of Law at Golden Gate University School of Law since 2002, where he teaches E-Commerce Law. During 2001, he served as Visiting Professor of Law at Appalachian School of Law, teaching Commercial Law and Conflicts of Law.

NANCY L. PELL is a partner in the litigation section of Fulbright & Jaworski L.L.P. in Washington, D.C. She represents clients primarily in the energy sector in administrative, judicial, and appellate proceedings, and she is a member of Fulbright's Global Class Action practice group. Ms. Pell is admitted to practice in West Virginia, Virginia, and the District of Columbia.

JACOB B. PERKINSON is a partner with Johnson & Perkinson in South Burlington, Vermont, and since graduating from Vermont Law School in 1995 has practiced primarily in the field of securities and consumer class action litigation in courts throughout the United States, serving as lead and co-lead counsel in numerous cases.

PAUL L. PEYRONNIN is a lawyer in the New Orleans office of Baker, Donelson, Bearman, Caldwell, & Berkowitz, P.C., who concentrates his practice in the areas of construction law and commercial litigation, including real property and landlord/tenant disputes, breach of contract and business torts, commercial recovery, and defense of class action claims. Following his graduation from Tulane Law School, Mr. Peyronnin clerked for the Hon. Henry A. Mentz, Jr. of the U.S. District Court for the Eastern District of Louisiana. Prior publications include co-authorship of *Louisiana Courtroom Evidence* (1993, supplemented in 1996), a treatise interpreting the Louisiana Code of Evidence.

DAN PIROLO is a senior associate in the litigation section of Fulbright & Jaworski L.L.P. in Houston, Texas. His practice is focused on antitrust and securities litigation in federal and state courts, and he is a member of Fulbright's Global Class Action practice group. From 2005 to 2006, Mr. Pirolo clerked for the Hon. W. Eugene Davis, Judge on the U.S. Court of Appeals for the Fifth Circuit. He received his J.D. from the University of Notre Dame.

JULIAN W. POON is a partner in the Los Angeles office of Gibson, Dunn & Crutcher L.L.P. He has successfully defended numerous wage and hour, labor, and other class actions at both the appellate and trial court levels, recently defeating some on the pleadings and without discovery, and is a member of the firm's Class Action and Appellate & Constitutional Law practice groups. Before joining Gibson Dunn, he clerked for Justice Antonin Scalia of the U.S. Supreme Court, and Judge Luttig, formerly of the U.S. Court of Appeals for the Fourth Circuit, and also graduated first in his class and summa cum laude from Harvard Law School.

ERIC L. PROBST is principal of Porzio, Bromberg & Newman in its Morristown, New Jersey, office. He is a member of the firm's Commercial Litigation team. He practices in the areas of complex commercial law, consumer fraud, class action, construction defect and delay claims, mass tort, and product liability. A significant part of his practice over the last several years at Porzio was dedicated to defending pharmaceutical companies in personal injury mass tort actions. He is AV-rated by Martindale-Hubbell and was recognized by *New Jersey Monthly Magazine* as a Rising Star in the State of New Jersey, 2009.

LYN P. PRUITT is a litigation partner with Mitchell, Williams, Selig, Gates & Woodyard in Little Rock, Arkansas. A significant part of her 25-year practice has focused on multiparty litigation, mass tort litigation, and class actions. Ms. Pruitt is a Fellow in the American College of Trial Lawyers. She has been recognized in consecutive years as a Mid-South *Super Lawyer* and has been listed in the *International Who's Who of Business Lawyers*; *Chambers USA, Leading Lawyers for Business*; and *Best Lawyers in America*.

JEFFREY M. PYPCZNSKI is counsel to Porzio Bromberg & Newman in its Morristown, New Jersey, office. He is a member of the firm's Complex Tort Practice group, where he concentrates his practice in the areas of product liability, toxic tort environmental litigation, class actions, and professional liability. Mr. Pypcznski is active in the ABA TIPS Products, General Liability & Consumer Law Committee and has represented a number of *Fortune 500* companies in both state and federal courts.

PATRICIA K. ROCHA is chair of the litigation group at Adler Pollock & Sheehan P.C. in Providence, Rhode Island. Ms. Rocha has successfully tried and defended cases ranging from commercial litigation, product liability and toxic tort, employment discrimination, and redistricting litigation to bribery, wire fraud, honest services, and conspiracy. She has been recognized in *Chambers USA, Leading Lawyers* as one of the "Leaders in Rhode Island," as well as in *Best Lawyers in America* in the fields of Administrative Law, Commercial Litigation, Healthcare Law, White Collar Criminal Defense, and Labor and Employment Law. Ms. Rocha has also been selected as a Rhode Island *Super Lawyer*.

LOIS O. ROSENBAUM is a 1974 Stanford Law School graduate and is a partner with the litigation group of Stoel Rives LLP in Portland, Oregon. She has represented numerous public and private companies and their officers and directors in defending class actions and governmental investigations, has represented both plaintiffs and defendants in fiduciary duty litigation, and has served as special counsel to special litigation and audit committees. Ms. Rosenbaum is listed as one of America's Leading Lawyers for Business in *Chambers USA,* in *Best Lawyers in America,* and in Oregon's *Super Lawyers.*

JASON M. ROSENTHAL is the Managing Partner of Schopf & Weiss L.L.P., a national business litigation firm based in Chicago, Illinois. Mr. Rosenthal's practice is dedicated to representing businesses and individuals in complex litigation. In addition to successfully defending corporations in class action litigation, he has recovered millions of dollars in insurance coverage for class action defendants. For the past three years, he has been recognized as an Illinois Rising Star by *Super Lawyers.*

ANITRA GOODMAN ROYSTER is an associate in the Litigation & Trial practice group at Alston & Bird L.L.P. in Raleigh, North Carolina, where her practice focuses on complex commercial and financial services litigation and the defense of class actions.

DEBORAH M. RUSSELL is a partner in the Richmond, Virginia, office of McGuireWoods L.L.P. and a co-leader of the firm's Life Sciences Industry Team. Her practice primarily focuses on products liability and complex commercial litigation, including individual cases, multidistrict or coordinated litigation, cases consolidated for trial, and class actions. She is admitted to practice in state and federal courts in Virginia and Maryland. Ms. Russell has received a number of honors, including selection by *Best Lawyers in America* in the specialties of Mass Tort Litigation and Personal Injury Litigation.

CHARLES F. RYSAVY is a partner in the Newark, New Jersey, office of K&L Gates L.L.P. His practice is focused on complex class action and other multiparty toxic tort, product liability, and commercial litigation. He has tried numerous jury cases, and filed numerous appeals and amicus briefs, in state and federal courts around the country. He is admitted to practice before the state and federal courts of New Jersey, the U.S. Court of Appeals for the Tenth Circuit, and the Southern and Eastern Districts of New York.

MARK G. SCHROEDER is a shareholder with Briggs and Morgan, P.A., in Minneapolis, Minnesota. In his business/commercial litigation practice, he specializes in class action defense, especially consumer finance litigation. He has defended financial institutions and mortgage lenders as lead trial and appellate counsel in dozens of class action lawsuits in state and federal courts. Mr. Schroeder's other class action experience includes wage and hour claims, securities/shareholder disputes, and mass torts. He received his B.A. from the University of Minnesota and his J.D. from UCLA, where he was a member of the *UCLA Law Review*. After law school, Mr. Schroeder clerked for U.S. District Court Judge Donald D. Alsop in St. Paul, Minnesota. He is admitted to practice in Minnesota and California.

DICK SEMERDJIAN is a partner at Schwartz Semerdjian Haile Ballard & Cauley, L.L.P. in San Diego, California, where he practices in the area of employment and business litigation. He received his B.A. in Cell Biology and Biochemistry at the University of California, San Diego in 1981. He received his J.D. at the University of San Diego in 1985. He was named in *Best Lawyers in America* in 2010 and as a Top Lawyer in San Diego County by the *San Diego Daily Transcript* and *San Diego Magazine*. Mr. Semerdjian has been named a California *Super Lawyer* since 2007. He is admitted to the U.S. Supreme Court and the Southern, Central, Eastern, and Northern Districts of the U.S. District Courts. He is licensed to practice in California.

LISA M. SHARP is an associate in the Environmental Litigation and Toxic Torts department of McGuireWoods L.L.P. in Richmond, Virginia. Her practice is focused on complex civil litigation, including suits brought under Virginia's Multi-Claimant Litigation Act. She is admitted to practice in Virginia and New York.

EDWARD F. SHERMAN is the W.R. Irby Chair and Moise S. Steeg, Jr. Professor of Law at Tulane University Law School. He is a co-author of casebooks on civil procedure, complex litigation, and alternative dispute resolution that are used in law schools around the country and of many articles on these subjects. He has been a counsel or expert witness in a large number of class actions and cases relating to his expertise in complex litigation and he has been an active arbitrator and mediator. He has served as Chair or Reporter of the ABA Task Forces on Preemption (2010), Disaster Insurance Coverage (2007), Asbestos Reform (2005), Class Action Legislation (2003), and Offer of Judgment Rule (1995).

DANIEL M. SILVER is an associate in the Business Litigation group of McCarter & English in Wilmington, Delaware. Mr. Silver's practice spans all areas of civil litigation, including intellectual property, products liability, and employment discrimination. In addition, Mr. Silver regularly litigates disputes on behalf of creditors in Chapter 11 reorganization cases, and counsels clients on various aspects of Delaware law in conjunction with corporate litigation and transactional matters.

JOHN M. SIMPSON has practiced law in the Washington, D.C., office of Fulbright & Jaworski L.L.P. for more than 30 years and has been a Fulbright partner since 1986. Mr. Simpson is currently the partner in charge of Fulbright's Washington litigation practice and serves on the Litigation Committee of the firm. He is also a member of Fulbright's Global Class Action practice group. He has handled jury and bench trials in both federal and state court and before federal administrative agencies and has argued several cases in the U.S. Court of Appeals for the District of Columbia, Fourth, Fifth, and Eleventh Circuits, the Supreme Courts of North Carolina and West Virginia, and the North Carolina Court of Appeals. He is a member of the District of Columbia and North Carolina Bars, the Bar of the Supreme Court of the United States, and multiple lower federal appellate and trial court bars.

LANCE SORENSON is an associate at the firm of Winder & Counsel in Salt Lake City, Utah, focusing primarily on commercial litigation. He is admitted to practice in the state and federal courts of Utah and California. He has worked for the Hon. Michael W. McConnell, former circuit judge for the Tenth Circuit, and is a past chair of the Medicine and Law Committee of the Tort Trial and Insurance Practice Section of the American Bar Association.

GEORLEN SPANGLER is a partner at Kolesar & Leatham, Chtd. in Las Vegas, Nevada. Ms. Spangler's practice is primarily litigation oriented. She regularly handles commercial litigation and construction-related matters, including representation of multiple subcontractors in litigation against major hotel casinos and construction lenders. She has negotiated and customized multiple AIA form construction contracts and sophisticated nonstandard construction contracts. Ms. Spangler received her J.D. from the University of Wisconsin-Madison in 1989, where she was a member of the Jessup International Moot Court team, and her B.A., magna cum laude, from the University of Wisconsin-Milwaukee. She is a member of Phi Beta Kappa and served as a law clerk for the U.S. District Court for the Eastern District of Wisconsin. Ms. Spangler is an arbitrator with the American Arbitration Association for commercial and construction matters and an active member of the American Bar Association's Litigation Section and the American Bar Association Forum on the Construction Industry. She routinely lectures on Nevada construction law issues and is the co-author of *Nevada Construction Law,* published by HLK Global Communications as part of its state construction law book series. She is a member of the State Bar of Nevada and is admitted to practice before all state courts in Nevada, the U.S. District Court for the District of Nevada, and the Ninth Circuit Court of Appeals. Ms. Spangler is a vice-chair of the Construction Law Section of the Nevada State Bar. She has been recognized in the 2006 and 2007 editions of *Chambers USA, Directory of Leading Lawyers* as a top construction lawyer and as a 2007 Mountain States *Super Lawyer* in Litigation. Ms. Spangler is AV-rated by Martindale-Hubbell.

RUSSELL O. STEWART is a litigation partner with Faegre & Benson L.L.P. in Denver, Colorado. He focuses on the defense of prescription drug and toxic torts, and has most recently served as national and trial counsel in Seroquel, pain-pump, and thimerosal litigation. He has extensive experience defending manufacturers of bupivacaine, ropivacaine, second-generation antipsychotics, flu vaccines, DTP vaccines, breast implants, and PPA. Mr. Stewart is an active member of the International Association of Defense Counsel, where he currently chairs the Toxic and Hazardous Substances Litigation Committee.

STACY O. STITHAM, a graduate of Harvard University and Harvard Law School, is an associate at the law firm of Brann & Isaacson. Her practice includes litigation in state and federal courts and proceedings before administrative agencies on behalf of national corporations as well as local businesses and individuals, with a particular emphasis on intellectual property litigation.

LAURIE STRAUCH WEISS is a litigation partner in the New York City office of Orrick, Herrington & Sutcliffe L.L.P. She is a graduate of Cornell University and Boston College Law School, where she was an editor of the *Boston College Law Review*. Ms. Strauch Weiss represents clients in large, complex, and multiparty class action litigation and has handled significant actions involving the chemical and medical device industries. Her practice also includes advising companies on overall strategies, from prelitigation to the final resolution of matters, often involving novel scientific issues. Ms. Strauch Weiss has written several articles and lectured frequently on topics concerning expert witnesses, bankruptcy/mass tort, and claim preclusion issues.

THOMAS J. SULLIVAN is a partner in Morgan Lewis's Litigation Practice in Philadelphia, Pennsylvania. Mr. Sullivan's practice encompasses a variety of product liability and commercial civil litigation in state and federal courts, with a focus on the defense of putative class actions, mass torts, and other complex, serial, and multijurisdictional product-related litigation. He is a member of the firm's Class Action Working Group and has experience with class action litigation involving consumer products, RICO, and ERISA violations. Mr. Sullivan earned his Ph.D. in Philosophy from the University of Pennsylvania in 2003, his J.D., cum laude, from the University of Pennsylvania Law School in 2001, his M.A., with highest distinction, in Moral, Political, and Legal Philosophy from the University of Reading, England, in 1996, and his B.A., cum laude, in Philosophy from the College of the Holy Cross in 1995. He is admitted to practice in Pennsylvania.

ALLAN A. THOEN is an associate in the Philadelphia office of Pepper Hamilton L.L.P. and a member of the Health Effects Litigation and White Collar & Corporate Investigations practice groups. He has a litigation practice with a primary emphasis on representation of clients in the health care sector.

ANDREW S. TULUMELLO is a litigation partner and vice-chair of the class action practice group in the Washington, D.C., office of Gibson, Dunn & Crutcher L.L.P.

JAMES A. WALKER is a partner at Triplett, Woolf & Garretson in Wichita, Kansas. Mr. Walker has had a general, civil, and business litigation practice for over 33 years in the various state and federal courts in Kansas. Virtually his entire career has been in representations where litigation was either threatened or, more usually, filed. His broad litigation practice has included matters involving securities law, antitrust, noncompete agreements, oil and gas, real estate, legal and accounting malpractice, derivative claims, estate and probate disputes, commercial fire loss, and higher asset divorce cases.

JUSTICE JOSEPH T. WALSH was appointed as a judge of the Delaware Superior Court in 1972, a Vice Chancellor of the Court of Chancery in 1984, and a Justice of the Delaware Supreme Court in 1985. He was reappointed as a justice to a 12-year term in 1997. Justice Walsh retired from the Delaware Supreme Court in April 2003. He joined McCarter & English as Of Counsel June 1, 2003, and his practice focuses on mediation, arbitration, and counseling in connection with Delaware corporate and business law matters.

CLIFFORD H. WALSTON is a partner in the Houston, Texas, law firm of Farrar & Ball, L.L.P. He is a trial lawyer who handles all types of complex commercial litigation with a special emphasis on financial disputes, class actions, lender liability cases, and product liability litigation.

KIMBERLY R. WARD is an associate at Ashe, Rafuse & Hill L.L.P. in Atlanta, Georgia. Her experience includes class action motions and appeals, and clerkships for Judge Joel F. Dubina of the U.S. Court of Appeals for the Eleventh Circuit and Justice Champ Lyons, Jr. of the Alabama Supreme Court.

GEOFFREY C. WEIEN is a litigation associate in the Washington, D.C., office of Gibson, Dunn & Crutcher L.L.P.

PAUL D. WELLER is head of litigation at Coventry Health Care, Inc., a *Fortune 500* company. In that capacity, he is responsible for all litigation involving the company. Previously, he was a partner in the litigation section at Morgan, Lewis & Bockius L.L.P., where his practice focused on a wide range of commercial litigation, including class actions. He is admitted to practice before the U.S. Courts of Appeals for the Second and Third Circuits, as well as the federal and state courts of New York and Pennsylvania.

MARK WHITBURN is a litigation associate in the Dallas, Texas, office of Gibson, Dunn & Crutcher L.L.P.

AMY M. WILKINS is an associate at Hagens Berman Sobol Shapiro L.L.P., in Phoenix, Arizona, with an emphasis on consumer class action lawsuits. Her recent cases include several actions against vehicle manufacturers, including involvement in the Toyota Sudden Unintended Acceleration class action, and against a major trucking company. Ms. Wilkins serves as Vice-Chair of the Arizona State Bar Class Action and Derivative Suits Committee. She received her law degree from the University of Arizona, where she served as Editor-in-Chief of the *Arizona Law Review*.

BRADLEY S. WOLFF is a partner with Swift, Currie, McGhee & Hiers, L.L.C. in Atlanta, Georgia. Mr. Wolff practices in the areas of products and personal liability defense, with an emphasis in medical and pharmaceutical products. Mr. Wolff represents domestic and international manufacturers of biological and pharmaceutical products and various other medical products in cases filed in several jurisdictions across the United States. Mr. Wolff graduated from Vanderbilt University with honors in Philosophy in 1983. He received his law degree, cum laude, in 1986 from the University of Georgia School of Law. Mr. Wolff practices throughout the United States, and is admitted to practice before the U.S. Supreme Court. He is a member of the State Bar of Georgia, the Defense Research Institute, and the International Association of Defense Counsel.

LARRY R. ("BUZZ") WOOD, JR. is a partner in the Philadelphia, Pennsylvania, and Wilmington, Delaware, offices of Pepper Hamilton L.L.P. Mr. Wood's practice focuses primarily on complex commercial litigation, including business tort litigation, intellectual property litigation, employee noncompete litigation, employment litigation (including discrimination and ERISA/benefits), and financial services litigation. He has particular experience in all aspects of class action litigation.

Preface

RICHARD A. NAGAREDA[1]

A Practitioners' Guide to Class Actions continues the American Bar Association's tradition of providing up-to-date guidance to practicing lawyers concerning areas of significant real-world concern. The ABA *Guide* gathers timely work on the part of leading class action lawyers and academics, all facilitated by the able editorial and organizational skills of Marcy Greer (Fulbright & Jaworski L.L.P. in Austin, National Editor), Mike Truesdale (Law Office of Michael S. Truesdale in Austin), Van Cates (Veolia Water North America Operating Services in Tampa), Nikko Fischer (Jones, Walker, in New Orleans), Bo Phillips (Reed Smith in San Francisco and Los Angeles), Joanne Swanson (Kerr, Russell & Weber in Detroit), and Thomas Thagard (Maynard, Cooper & Gale in Birmingham).

The present time is an especially auspicious one for lawyers and scholars to step back and assess both the path and the future trajectory of the class action device. In parallel with the ABA's work on the *Guide*, the American Law Institute has developed its *Principles of the Law of Aggregate Litigation*. Professor Samuel Issacharoff (New York University School of Law) served as the Reporter for the project; and I, along with Dean Robert Klonoff (Lewis & Clark Law School) and Professor Charles Silver (University of Texas School of Law), served as Associate Reporters.

The publication of the ALI *Principles* in 2010 represents the culmination of a multiyear project that involved as advisors a broad cross-section of leading plaintiff- and defense-side practitioners, prominent judges, and distinguished academics. In the collaborative tradition of the ALI, the *Principles* also benefited from multiple presentations before the Institute membership as a whole at its Annual Meetings, during which my co-reporters and I received countless comments, suggestions, and constructive criticism that, together, made for major improvements in the final

---

1. Richard A. Nagareda is the Professor of Law and Director, Cecil D. Branstetter Litigation & Dispute Resolution Program, Vanderbilt University Law School.

product. In keeping with the growing globalization of law practice, moreover, the ALI *Principles* also were the subject of conferences in Florence, Italy, and Beijing, China, as well as a conference of U.S. class action scholars at George Washington University Law School in Washington, D.C.

The chapters of the ABA *Guide* speak to the richness of class action law today and need no introduction here. The enterprise of this Preface, instead, is to provide a brief and necessarily selective overview of the main features of the ALI *Principles* with respect to class actions. Six such features bear attention, from a bird's-eye perspective.

1. The ALI *Principles* situate the class action device within the larger landscape of "aggregate litigation." This move is apparent from the title of the project itself, consciously chosen so as not to be limited to the class action. The same move also is in keeping with the recognition by the Supreme Court that "class actions constitute but one of several methods for bringing about aggregation of claims, *i.e.*, they are but one of several methods by which multiple similarly situated parties get similar claims resolved at one time and in one federal forum."[2] Indeed, it is only now—upon 40-plus years of experience with the class action in its modern form— that both its uses and its limitations have come more sharply into focus.[3]

The move to urge the consideration of class actions as part of the larger category of aggregate litigation is in keeping with the nature of a "Principles" project in ALI parlance, as distinct from the Institute's famous "Restatements." Unlike Restatements that—as their title suggests—aspire to restate existing law, Principles projects are explicitly normative. They seek to set forth the view of the Institute on what the law *should* be—albeit, of course, with due regard for its existing content. Indeed, quite apart from their treatment of class actions, the ALI *Principles* arguably bear attention first and foremost for their proposal for reform of the "aggregate settlement rule" in the law of legal ethics[4]—a major source of guidance today for the resolution of related civil claims in a nonclass, aggregate posture.

2. The ALI *Principles* offer a synthesis of the longstanding debate concerning the relationship between the "predominance" requirement of Rule 23(b)(3) and the additional specification in Rule 23(c)(4) of judicial authority—"when appropriate"—to certify class actions confined to particular issues, as among all those

---

2. *Sprint Comm's. Co. v. APCC Servs., Inc.*, 128 S. Ct. 2531, 2545 (2008).

3. Scholarly literature offers a window on nonclass aggregation. *See, e.g.*, Howard M. Erichson, *A Typology of Aggregate Settlements*, 80 NOTRE DAME L. REV. 1769 (2005); Samuel Issacharoff, *Private Claims, Aggregate Rights*, 2008 S. CT. REV. 183; Richard A. Nagareda, *Embedded Aggregation in Civil Litigation*, 95 CORNELL L. REV. (forthcoming Sept. 2010), *available at* http://papers.ssrn.com/sol3/papers.cfm?abstract_ id=1506460; Charles Silver & Lynn Baker, *I Cut, You Choose: The Role of Plaintiffs' Counsel in Allocating Settlement Proceeds*, 84 VA. L. REV. 1465 (1998); Charles Silver & Geoffrey P. Miller, *The Quasi-Class Action Method of Managing Multidistrict Litigations: Problems and a Proposal*, 63 VAND. L. REV. 107 (2010).

4. American Law Institute, Principles of the Law of Aggregate Litigation §§ 3.17–.18 (2010) [hereinafter ALI *Principles*].

presented by a given litigation. These two Rule subsections have perplexed practitioners, courts, and scholars for some time. Rather than adopt a view that effectively would read either subsection out of the Rule, the ALI *Principles* seek to capture the core insight conveyed by the two subsections as a synthetic whole. In this enterprise, once again, the ALI *Principles* draw on the now-40-plus years of experience with the class action device. Section 2.02(a)(1) does so by recognizing that a court "should exercise its discretion to authorize aggregate treatment of a common issue by way of a class action if the court determines that resolution of the common issue would"—among other things—"materially advance the resolution of multiple civil claims by addressing the core of the dispute in a manner superior to other realistic procedural alternatives, so as to generate significant judicial efficiencies."

This language is far from a license for courts to pluck out common issues for certification wherever they might be found. Rather, the remaining sections of Chapter 2 within the ALI *Principles* elaborate the limiting nature of the language in section 2.02(a)(1) by situating substantive law, preclusion principles, and considerations of judicial management as significant constraints on class certification. Comment *c* to section 2.01 conveys the "broad generalization in light of accumulated, real-world experience with class actions" that

> common issues will tend to arise more frequently with respect to "upstream" matters focused on a generally applicable course of conduct on the part of those opposing the claimants in the litigation rather than on "downstream" matters centered upon the individual situations of those claimants themselves. Similarly—again, as a matter of broad generalization from experience—common issues will tend to arise more frequently with respect to economic injuries from a generally applicable course of conduct than with regard to personal injuries, as to which the "upstream" inquiry likely would not materially advance the disposition of claims.[5]

In addition, section 2.09 underscores that issue class certification should come only along with the possibility of interlocutory appellate review as to both "the class-certification determination" (in the manner of Rule 23(f) in current law) and "any class-wide determination of a common issue on the merits."

3. The ALI *Principles* endorse the emergence in lower-court decisions of a distinctive law of class certification in recent years.[6] Those decisions offer considerable clarification of the posture from which courts should approach the class certification determination—a matter famously clouded by language in the Supreme

---

5. *See also id.* at § 2.02 cmt. *a*. The contrast between "upstream" and "downstream" matters stems from Samuel Issacharoff, *Class Action Conflicts*, 30 U.C. Davis L. Rev. 805, 831–32 (1997).

6. *See, e.g., In re Hydrogen Peroxide Antitrust Litig.*, 552 F.3d 305 (3d Cir. 2008); *In re Initial Pub. Offerings Sec. Litig.*, 471 F.3d 24 (2d Cir. 2006); *Szabo v. Bridgeport Machines, Inc.*, 249 F.3d 672 (7th Cir. 2001).

Court's 1974 opinion in *Eisen v. Carlisle & Jacquelin.*[7] Section 2.06(a) of the ALI *Principles* specifies that "[i]f the suitability of multiple civil claims for class-action treatment depends upon the resolution of an underlying question concerning the content of applicable substantive law or the factual situation presented, then the court must decide that question as part of its determination whether to certify the class."

4. The ALI *Principles* recast the legal vocabulary on the dividing line between mandatory classes and opt-out classes. Rather than cast that dividing line in terms of a formalistic, law-versus-equity distinction in the manner of the language used in Rule 23(b)(2), section 2.04 of the ALI *Principles* looks functionally to the divisibility of the remedy involved. "Indivisible remedies"—such as the classic sorts of injunctions or declaratory judgments vis-à-vis a general course of alleged misconduct—"are those such that the distribution of relief to any claimant as a practical matter determines the application or availability of the same remedy to other claimants."[8] An indivisible remedy already situates the persons said to be adversely affected by the alleged misconduct as a kind of interdependent group, such that the law of class actions appropriately may recognize that interdependence by way of mandatory class treatment.[9] For "divisible remedies"—such as plain, old, ordinary damages—the same interdependence does not obtain, because "the distribution of relief to one or more claimants individually" does not "determin[e] in practical effect the application or availability of the same remedy to any other claimant."[10] As a consequence, an opportunity to opt out is required.

5. Speaking to adequate class representation, the ALI *Principles* cast such adequacy in terms of a judicial determination—as among the "necessary conditions" for class treatment—"that there are no structural conflicts of interest," whether between the proposed class and class counsel or among the class members themselves.[11] Recognizing that no class action can realistically ensure a complete alignment of interest in these regards, section 2.07(a)(1) casts disabling "structural" conflicts in terms of "a significant risk that the lawyers for claimants might skew systematically the conduct of the litigation so as to favor some claimants over others on grounds aside from reasoned evaluation of their respective claims or to disfavor claimants generally vis-à-vis the lawyers themselves."

---

7. 417 U.S. 156, 177 (1974) (stating, in connection with a dispute over responsibility for the cost of class notice, that "[w]e find nothing in either the language or history of Rule 23 that gives a court any authority to conduct a preliminary inquiry into the merits of a suit in order to determine whether it may be maintained as a class action."). On the confusion wrought by *Eisen* and the clarification offered in recent lower-court decisions, see Richard A. Nagareda, *Class Certification in the Age of Aggregate Proof,* 84 N.Y.U. L. Rev. 97 (2009).

8. ALI *Principles* at § 2.04(b).

9. *See id.* at § 2.07(c).

10. *Id.* at § 2.04(a).

11. *Id.* at § 2.07(a)(1).

6. The ALI *Principles* elaborate a distinctive law of class action settlements. Notable features here include—among other provisions—greater recognition for settlement classes[12] (including those that encompass future claims)[13] and more rigorous judicial standards for the use of cy pres remedies in class settlements.[14]

Taken together, the ALI *Principles* and the ABA *Guide* thus offer a window on the state of class action law today and the directions for its future.

12. *See id.* at § 3.06 cmt. *a* ("[Section 3.06] does not require a settlement class to satisfy all of the same criteria as a class certified for purposes of litigation. For example, settlement classes should not be subject to a rigorous evidentiary showing that, in a contested trial, common issues would outweigh individualized issues. So long as there is sufficient commonality to establish that the class is generally cohesive, the propriety of a settlement need not depend on satisfaction of a 'predominance' requirement. However, the inability to certify a class for litigation purposes may be important evidence of the lack of leverage by proposed class counsel and thus may suggest the possibility of inadequate representation.").

13. *See id.* at § 3.10 (defining "future claims" and discussing principles for their resolution in class settlements).

14. *See id.* at § 3.07 cmt. *a* ("[Section 3.07] generally permits cy pres awards only when direct distributions to class members are not feasible—either because class members cannot be reasonably identified or because distribution would involve such small amounts that, because of the administrative costs involved, such distribution would not be economically viable. In such circumstances, there should be a presumed obligation to award any remaining funds to an entity that resembles, in either composition or purpose, the class members or their interests.").

PART I

THE ANATOMY OF A CLASS ACTION

PRECERTIFICATION

JOSEPH H. PARK

I. Introduction

Class certification is properly recognized as perhaps the most critical point for class actions. Indeed, as courts and commentators regularly note, the denial of class certification "may sound the 'death knell'" of the class action.[1] The initial period between the filing of a putative class action and the court's ruling on class certification—the precertification period—is also an important phase. Proper consideration and utilization of available precertification procedures can significantly affect how the case will proceed, including the certification decision and even whether the certification issue is considered. A carefully prepared strategy—based on a full consideration and evaluation of case management issues, available procedural tools, and potential pitfalls during the precertification period—can limit the time and costs of the precertification stage while also optimizing prospects for either the grant or denial of class certification.

II. Case Management

A. EFFECTIVE MANAGEMENT OF THE CONDUCT OF CLASS ACTIONS

As in all cases, counsel in a class action are required to participate in Rule 26(f) and Rule 16 conferences. While the initial case management conference and related case management/scheduling orders are important in all cases, their significance is amplified in class actions because of the heightened stakes in class action litigation and the attendant high costs associated with prosecuting and defending class claims. Consequently, class actions generally require more active case management

---

1. *In re Hydrogen Peroxide Antitrust Litig.*, 552 F.3d 305, 310 (3d Cir. 2008) (quoting *Newton v. Merrill Lynch, Pierce, Fenner & Smith, Inc.*, 259 F.3d 154, 162 (3d Cir. 2001)).

both by the courts and by the parties to achieve an efficient and cost-effective resolution of the numerous, complex, and often unique issues associated with class
actions.[2] Careful preparation in advance of the Rule 26(f) and Rule 16 conferences
provides the parties with an opportunity, at an early juncture in the case, to influence the timing of the class certification decision, as well as the scope of permissible activities during the precertification period, including the availability and extent
of any precertification discovery.

In connection with the initial case management conference and proposed case
management/scheduling orders, the parties may address and advocate their respective positions about, *inter alia*: (1) the timing of the class certification motion,
including briefing schedules; (2) whether and to what extent precertification discovery is necessary, including whether discovery will be bifurcated and whether
discovery will be necessary from absent potential class members; (3) coordination
with related cases, including whether the case should be stayed in deference to
earlier filed actions in other jurisdictions; (4) whether it is necessary to appoint
interim class counsel during the precertification period; and (5) whether potential
dispositive motions, particularly those raising questions of law, should be heard
prior to the class certification motion. Resolution of these and related case management issues identified in Rules 16(c)(2) and 26(f) will assist the court and the parties in laying a concrete road map for the precertification phase of the class action.

Express authority for a court's active management of class actions can be found
not only in Rule 16 (setting forth the court's authority to issue scheduling and case
management orders), but also in Rule 23(d), which specifically empowers the court
to issue orders that:[3]

- Determine the course of proceedings or prescribe measures to prevent
  undue repetition or complication in presenting evidence or argument;
- Require the giving of appropriate notices to some or all class members to
  protect the class members and fairly conduct the action;

---

2. *See generally* MANUAL FOR COMPLEX LITIGATION (FOURTH) § 21 (2004):

Because the stakes and scope of class action litigation can be great, class actions often require
closer judicial oversight and more active judicial management than other types of litigation. Class
action suits present many of the same problems and issues inherent in other types of complex
litigation. The aggregation of a large number of claims and the ability to bind people who are not
individual litigants tend to magnify those problems and issues, increase the stakes for the named
parties, and create potential risks of prejudice or unfairness for absent class members. This imposes
unique responsibilities on the court and counsel. Once class allegations are made, decisions such
as whether to settle and on what terms are no longer wholly within the litigants' control. Rather,
the attorneys and named plaintiffs assume responsibilities to represent the class. The court must
protect the interests of absent class members, and Rule 23(d) gives the judge broad administrative
powers to do so, reflecting the equity origins of class actions.

3. FED. R. CIV. P. 23(d)(1)(A)–(D).

- Impose conditions on the representative parties or on intervenors; and
- Require that the pleadings be amended to eliminate allegations about representation of absent persons and that the action proceed accordingly.

Importantly, Rule 23(d)(1)(E) provides a "catchall" provision, authorizing the court to issue orders to "deal with similar procedural matters." This provision is interpreted broadly and is often cited as authority for many orders not specifically enumerated in Rule 23 or elsewhere.[4] Under the broad authority granted by Rule 23(d)(1), courts can issue a wide-ranging variety of orders in aid of the effective management of class actions.[5]

B. PLEADING PRACTICE

The rules applicable to civil actions generally apply to class actions, including the pleading standards set forth in Rules 8 and 9.[6] Class action complaints are subject to additional pleading requirements, however, as they must also contain factual allegations as to the prerequisites for class actions set forth in Rule 23(a)—numerosity, commonality, typicality, and adequacy of representation—as well as one or more of the grounds for class certification under Rule 23(b): (1) the potential risk of inconsistent results in separate actions; (2) the need for classwide injunctive relief; and/or (3) the predominance of common questions of fact or law and the superiority of class actions over separate actions.[7] Local rules should also be consulted, as some local rules include specific provisions applicable to class actions, including required allegations, information to be included in case management statements, the Internet posting of case filings, and motion filing deadlines.[8] Additional requirements are imposed on securities class actions subject to the Private Securities Litigation Reform Act, including stricter pleading requirements, a certification accompanying the complaint, and early publication of class notice.[9]

---

4. *County of Suffolk v. Long Island Lighting Co.*, 907 F.2d 1295, 1304 (2d Cir. 1990).

5. *See generally* 5 JAMES WM. MOORE ET AL., MOORE'S FEDERAL PRACTICE §§ 21.140–23.145 (3d ed. 1999).

6. FED. R. CIV. P. 8, 9.

7. FED. R. CIV. P. 23(a)(1)–(4), 23(b)(1)–(3); *In re Am. Med. Sys., Inc.*, 75 F.3d 1069, 1079 (6th Cir. 1996) (conclusory allegations reciting Rule 23 requirements inadequate; "[T]here must be an adequate statement of basic facts to indicate that each requirement of the rule is fulfilled."); *Ziedman v. J. Ray McDermott & Co.*, 651 F.2d 1030, 1038 (5th Cir. 1981) (conclusory allegation regarding numerosity of class and impracticability of joinder insufficient); *Stambaugh v. Kansas Dep't of Corr.*, 151 F.R.D. 664 (D. Kan. 1993) ("Conclusory allegations of discrimination on a class-basis are not enough."). *But see Doe v. Charleston Area Med. Ctr., Inc.*, 529 F.2d 638, 645 (4th Cir. 1975) (speculative allegation regarding class size adequate where only relief sought was injunctive and declaratory relief); *Clark v. State Farm Mut. Auto. Ins. Co.*, 231 F.R.D. 405, 407 (C.D. Cal. 2005) (motion to strike class action allegations denied where class action allegations were conclusory).

8. *See, e.g.*, C.D. CAL. L.R. 23-1, 23-2; N.D. CAL. L.R. 3-4, 3-7, 16-9, 23-1, 23-2; D. UTAH L.R. 23-1; S.D.N.Y. L.R. 4; N.D. TEX. L.R. 23.1, 23.2.

9. 15 U.S.C. §§ 77z-1, 78u-4.

Just as class action complaints must comply with general pleading requirements, class action complaints are subject to attack by motions filed pursuant to Rule 12, including motions to dismiss, motions for judgment on the pleadings, motions for more definite statement, and motions to strike.[10] Thus, the Supreme Court's recent rulings in *Bell Atlantic Corp. v. Twombly*[11] and *Ashcroft v. Iqbal*,[12] rejecting the traditional Rule 12(b)(6) standards in *Conley v. Gibson*,[13] apply to motions to dismiss in class actions. Relying on the new "plausibility" standard under *Twombly/ Iqbal*, courts are likely to show an increased willingness to dismiss class actions at the pleadings stage.[14] The impact of *Twombly/Iqbal* may be short-lived, however, if pending legislation is enacted to overturn those decisions and codify the *Conley* standard for motions to dismiss: "A court shall not dismiss a complaint . . . unless it appears beyond doubt that the plaintiff can prove no set of facts in support of the claim which would entitle the plaintiff to relief."[15]

1. Jurisdictional and Standing Issues

Among the issues most frequently raised by Rule 12 motions are jurisdictional issues, including subject matter jurisdiction, standing, and mootness.

Class actions must comply with the jurisdictional requirements applicable to all federal actions. Thus, federal courts must have subject matter jurisdiction over the action, whether based on federal question or diversity.[16] In that regard, Rule 23 is a procedural rule that governs the conduct of class actions in federal court and does not create subject matter jurisdiction where none exists.[17] In enacting the Class

---

10. FED. R. CIV. P. 12(b), (c), (e), (f). *See Muniz-Rivera v. United States*, 326 F.3d 8 (1st Cir. 2003) (dismissal under Rule 12(b)(1)); *Doe v. Unocal Corp.*, 248 F.3d 915 (9th Cir. 2001) (dismissal under Rule 12(b)(2)); *Miller v. Champion Enters., Inc.*, 346 F.3d 660 (6th Cir. 2003) (dismissal under Rule 12(b)(6)); *Clark v. McDonald's Corp.*, 213 F.R.D. 198 (D.N.J. 2003) (motion under Rule 12(e)); *Neilson v. Union Bank of Cal., N.A.*, 290 F. Supp. 2d 1101 (C.D. Cal. 2003) (motion to strike under Rule 12(f)).

11. 550 U.S. 544 (2007).

12. 129 S. Ct. 1937, 1950 (2009).

13. 355 U.S. 41, 45–46 (1957).

14. *See, e.g., In re Toshiba HD DVD Mktg. and Sales Practices Litig.*, MDL No. 1956, 2009 WL 2940081 (D.N.J. Sept. 11, 2009) (relying on *Iqbal*, dismissed MDL consolidated complaint); *DeBlasio v. Merrill Lynch & Co., Inc.*, 2009 U.S. Dist. LEXIS 64848 (S.D.N.Y. July 29, 2009) (dismissal of securities class action under Rules 9(b) and 12(b)(6)); *Wright v. General Mills, Inc.*, 2009 U.S. Dist. LEXIS 90576 (S.D. Cal. Sept. 30, 2009) (granting motion to dismiss, with leave to amend, class action against General Mills of misleading consumers on labeling of granola bars). *But see Siracusano v. Matrixx Initiatives, Inc.*, 585 F.3d 1167 (9th Cir. 2009) (applying *Twombly* and reversing grant of motion to dismiss securities class action); *Fowler v. UPMC Shadyside*, 578 F.3d 203 (3d Cir. 2009) (applying *Iqbal* and reversing dismissal of employment class action).

15. H.R. 4115, 111th Cong. (2009).

16. 28 U.S.C. §§ 1331, 1332(a).

17. FED. R. CIV. P. 82; *Cramer v. Florida*, 117 F.3d 1258, 1264 n.16 (11th Cir. 1997).

Action Fairness Act (CAFA) of 2005, however, Congress has significantly expanded the availability of diversity jurisdiction in the class action context.[18]

Constitutional Article III standing is also a jurisdictional prerequisite for the maintenance of a class action, as well as for class certification—injury in fact, causation, and redressability.[19] Accordingly, at least one of the named plaintiffs must have standing as to each claim asserted against each defendant in a class action.[20] Likewise, the proposed representative plaintiffs must also have standing for the type of relief sought, e.g., for prospective injunctive relief.[21] Where the only named plaintiff lacks standing, the court must dismiss the action.[22]

Even where a named plaintiff has standing at the outset of the case, that plaintiff may lose standing during the pendency of the case if the plaintiff's claims become moot. Generally, when a named plaintiff's claim becomes moot prior to class certification, the entire action is dismissed.[23] If a named plaintiff's claim becomes moot after a class is certified, however, the entire action is not rendered moot because the class "acquire[s] a legal status separate from the interest asserted by [the named plaintiff]."[24] Courts generally have held that a putative class action need not be

---

18. *See* Pub. L. 109-2, 119 Stat. 4 (2005) (codified at 28 U.S.C. §§ 1332, 1335, 1453, 1603, 1711–1715). The Class Action Fairness Act is separately discussed in detail in Chapter 10, "The Class Action Fairness Act of 2005."

19. *Steel Co. v. Citizens for a Better Env't*, 523 U.S. 83, 102 (1998); *Prado-Steiman v. Bush*, 221 F.3d 1266, 1279–80 (11th Cir. 2000) ("[B]efore undertaking any formal typicality or commonality review, the district court must determine that at least one named class representative has Article III standing to raise each class subclaim.").

20. *See O'Shea v. Littleton*, 414 U.S. 488, 494 (1974) ("[I]f none of the named plaintiffs purporting to represent a class establishes the requisite of a case or controversy with the defendants, none may seek relief on behalf of himself or any other member of the class."); *Cent. States Se. & Sw. Areas Health & Welfare Fund v. Merck-Medco Managed Care, LLC*, 504 F.3d 229, 241 (2d Cir. 2007) (stating that there must be at least one plaintiff with standing as to each defendant named in the action); *Griffin v. Dugger*, 823 F.2d 1476, 1483 (11th Cir. 1987) ("[A] claim cannot be asserted on behalf of [the] class unless at least one named plaintiff has suffered the injury that gives rise to that claim.").

21. *See, e.g., Bates v. United Parcel Serv. Inc.*, 511 F.3d 974, 985 (9th Cir. 2007) ("Standing must be shown with respect to each form of relief sought, whether it be injunctive relief, damages, or civil penalties."); *Wooden v. Bd. of Regents of Univ. Sys. of Ga.*, 247 F.3d 1262, 1284 (11th Cir. 2001); *Elizabeth v. Montenez*, 458 F.3d 779, 784–85 (8th Cir. 2006).

22. *See Lierboe v. State Farm Mut. Auto. Ins. Co.*, 350 F.3d 1018, 1023 (9th Cir. 2003) (entire action required to be dismissed where named plaintiff lacked standing at the outset of the case); *Foster v. Ctr. Twp. of LaPorte County*, 798 F.2d 237, 244–45 (7th Cir. 1986) (same).

23. *Brown v. Phila. Hous. Auth.*, 350 F.3d 338, 343 (3d Cir. 2003) ("[W]hen claims of the named plaintiffs become moot before class certification, dismissal of the action is required."); *Greif v. Wilson, Elser, Moskowitz, Edelman & Dicker, LLP*, 258 F. Supp. 2d 157, 159–61 (E.D.N.Y. 2003) (same).

24. *Sosna v. Iowa*, 419 U.S. 393, 401–02 (1975); *Carroll v. United Compucred Collections, Inc.*, 399 F.3d 620, 624–25 (6th Cir. 2005).

dismissed and may continue to be maintained where the named plaintiff's claim becomes moot while a class certification motion is pending.[25]

Among the exceptions to the mootness rule is the "relation-back" doctrine, which is generally applied in cases with "inherently transitory claims" that are "capable of repetition, yet evading review."[26] Under the relation-back doctrine, the certification of a class is deemed to "relate back" to the filing of the complaint, thereby permitting the class action to proceed notwithstanding the mootness of the representative plaintiff's claim. Some courts have also applied the relation-back doctrine to permit a named plaintiff with a moot claim to move for class certification where the plaintiff's claim is rendered moot by a precertification offer of judgment under Rule 68.[27] The application of the relation-back doctrine has been extended to such cases to address the danger that defendants may use offers of judgment to "pick off" named plaintiffs at an early stage, which "would frustrate the objectives of class actions" and "invite waste of judicial resources."[28]

2. Failure to State a Claim

Although the named plaintiff in a putative class action seeks to prosecute the claims of a class as a member and representative of the proposed class, the named plaintiff is also asserting his or her own individual claim. Thus, as with any individual action, the named plaintiff's claims can be, and often are, tested by motions to dismiss for failure to state a claim under Rule 12(b)(6) on any number of potentially applicable grounds, e.g., lapsing of statute of limitations, failure to allege a required element of a claim, failure to exhaust administrative remedies, and failure to plead with the specificity required under Rule 9(b). If a court dismisses the named plaintiff's claims prior to certification, courts will dismiss the complaint, rendering the class certification issue moot.[29]

Class claims can also be the subject of a Rule 12(b)(6) motion to dismiss or a Rule 12(f) motion to strike the class allegations in a complaint.[30] Often brought

---

25. *Susman v. Lincoln Am. Corp.*, 587 F.2d 866, 869–71 (7th Cir. 1978); *Lusardi v. Xerox Corp.*, 975 F.2d 964, 975 (3d Cir. 1992).

26. *County of Riverside v. McLaughlin*, 500 U.S. 44, 51–52 (1991) ("Some claims are so inherently transitory that the trial court will not have even enough time to rule on a motion for class certification before the proposed representative's individual interests expire."); *Gerstein v. Pugh*, 420 U.S. 103, 110 n.11 (1975) (relation-back doctrine is an exception to the mootness rule, which applies when a claim is "capable of repetition, yet evading review").

27. *Weiss v. Regal Collections*, 385 F.3d 337 (3d Cir. 2004).

28. *Deposit Guar. Nat'l Bank v. Roper*, 445 U.S. 326, 339 (1980) (discussing danger of named plaintiffs being "picked off"); *Weiss*, 385 F.3d at 344 ("As sound as is Rule 68 when applied to individual plaintiffs, its application is stained when an offer of judgment is made to a class representative.").

29. *McDuffy v. Worthmore Furniture, Inc.*, 380 F. Supp. 257 (E.D. Va. 1974).

30. Some courts address the striking of class allegations under Rule 23(d)(1)(D) rather than Rule 12(f). *Markey v. La. Citizens Fair Plan*, No. Civ. A 06-5473, 2008 U.S. Dist. LEXIS 106051, *5–6 (E.D. La. Dec. 30, 2008) (striking class allegations under Rule 23(d)(1)(D) instead of Rule 12(f)). Rule 23(d)(1)(D) authorizes

together or in the alternative,[31] motions to dismiss and/or strike class claims generally raise class certification issues—that the class claims should be stricken/dismissed because the complaint, on its face, demonstrates that one or more of the requirements for class certification under Rule 23(a) or 23(b) cannot be met.[32] Courts generally look upon such motions with disfavor, however, often concluding that class certification issues should be addressed in connection with a motion for class certification, after the parties have had the opportunity to undertake at least some discovery.[33] As one court concluded, "dismissal of class allegations at the pleading stage should be rarely done and . . . the better course is to deny such a motion because the shape and form of a class action evolves only through the process of discovery."[34] In those instances where a defendant makes a preemptive motion to deny class certification based on the pleadings and before discovery, courts generally decide such motions under the Rule 12(b) standard applicable to motions to dismiss.[35]

C. PRECERTIFICATION DISCOVERY ISSUES

An important case management issue in class actions that should be addressed at the outset is precertification discovery, particularly since discovery in class actions

the court to issue orders that "require that the pleadings be amended to eliminate allegations about representation of absent persons and that the action proceed accordingly." FED. R. CIV. P. 23(d)(1)(D).

31. *See, e.g., Thorpe v. Abbott Labs., Inc.,* 534 F. Supp. 2d 1120 (N.D. Cal. 2008).

32. *Robinson v. Wal-Mart Stores, Inc.,* 254 F.R.D. 396, 402 (S.D. Miss. 2008) ("In sum, the Court finds that because the class action proposed by Plaintiffs in their Amended Complaint can not be certified under Rule 23(b), they have failed to 'state a claim to relief that is plausible on its face' and, therefore, their class action should be dismissed."); *John v. Nat'l Sec. Fire & Cas. Co.,* 501 F.3d 443, 445 (5th Cir. 2007) ("Where it is facially apparent from the pleadings that there is no ascertainable class, a district court may dismiss the class allegation on the pleadings."); *Bessette v. Avco Fin. Servs., Inc.,* 279 B.R. 442, 450 (D.R.I. 2002) (proper to dismiss class allegations if the plaintiff does not allege facts sufficient to make out a class).

33. *See, e.g., Bryant v. Food Lion, Inc.,* 774 F. Supp. 1484, 1495 (D.S.C. 1991) (denial of motion to dismiss class allegations in complaint because discovery is usually necessary to determine class certification issue); *Inter-modal Rail Employees Ass'n v. Atchison, Topeka, & Santa Fe Ry. Co.,* 80 F.3d 348, 353 (9th Cir. 1996), *vacated on other grounds,* 520 U.S. 510 (1997) (improper to dismiss class claim under Rule 12(b)(6) before answer or discovery); *Gillibeau v. City of Richmond,* 417 F.2d 426, 432 (9th Cir. 1969) ("[C]ompliance with Rule 23 is not to be tested by a motion to dismiss for failure to state a claim."); *Clark v. McDonald's Corp.,* 213 F.R.D. 198, 205 n.3 (D.N.J. 2003) ("A defendant may move to strike class action allegations prior to discovery in those rare cases where the complaint itself demonstrates that the requirements for maintaining a class action cannot be met.").

34. *In re Wal-Mart Stores, Inc., Wage & Hour Litig.,* 505 F. Supp. 2d 609, 615 (N.D. Cal. 2007) (quotations omitted).

35. *Blihovde v. St. Croix County,* 219 F.R.D. 607, 614 (W.D. Wis. 2003) ("When there has been no discovery and the defendants challenge class certification on the basis of the allegations in the complaint only, the proper standard is the same as a motion to dismiss for failure to state a claim."); *Picus v. Wal-Mart Stores, Inc.,* 256 F.R.D. 651 (D. Nev. 2009) (granting motion to deny class certification applying Rule 12(b)(6) standards).

raises issues unique to class actions.[36] Among the questions that may need to be addressed, depending on the nature and facts of the case, are the following:

- Is precertification discovery necessary?
- Should discovery be bifurcated?
- May defendants take discovery from unnamed class members?
- May defendants conduct discovery as to the named plaintiffs' finances?

In dealing with these and other discovery-related issues, courts have great latitude and discretion in authorizing or limiting precertification discovery.[37] Where it is apparent that the certification can be decided without the need for discovery, courts will deny requests for precertification discovery as "it would be a waste of the parties' and judicial resources to conduct discovery on class certification."[38] In most cases, however, courts generally permit some discovery as to matters pertaining to class certification issues.[39] Indeed, some courts have found it to be an abuse of discretion to deny certification-specific discovery.[40]

Assuming that precertification discovery is deemed to be appropriate or necessary, a frequent issue that arises is whether discovery should be bifurcated by limiting precertification discovery to certification issues while deferring merits discovery until after the certification decision. "Generally, discovery into certification issues pertains to the requirements of Rule 23 and tests whether the claims and defenses are susceptible to class-wide proof; discovery into the merits pertains to the strength or weaknesses of the claims or defenses and tests whether they are likely to succeed."[41] Whether discovery should be bifurcated is left to the sound discretion of the court.[42]

---

36. For a more detailed discussion on this subject, *see* Chapter 6.A, "Discovery from Class Members."

37. *Heerwagen v. Clear Channel Commc'ns*, 435 F.3d 210, 233–34 (3d Cir. 2006); *Miles v. Merrill Lynch & Co. (In re Initial Pub. Offering Sec. Litig.)*, 471 F.3d 24, 41 (2d Cir. 2006) (district court has discretion to set parameters of discovery relevant to class certification and the scope of hearing on motion for class certification "to ensure that a class certification motion does not become a pretext for a partial trial of the merits."); *Stewart v. Winter*, 669 F.2d 328, 331 (5th Cir. 1982); *Kamm v. Cal. City Dev. Corp.*, 509 F.2d 205, 209 (9th Cir. 1975).

38. *Walls v. Wells Fargo Bank, N.A. (In re Walls)*, 262 B.R. 519, 524 (Bankr. E.D. Cal. 2001); *see also* MANUAL FOR COMPLEX LITIGATION (FOURTH) § 21.14 (2004) ("Discovery may not be necessary when claims for relief rest on readily available and undisputed facts or raise only issues of law (such as a challenge to the legality of a statute or regulation).").

39. *Bryant*, 774 F. Supp. at 1484, 1495; *Stewart*, 669 F.2d at 328, 331; *see also supra* note 33.

40. *See, e.g., Mills v. Foremost Ins. Co.*, 511 F.3d 1300, 1309–11 (11th Cir. 2008) (abuse of discretion to decide whether class could be certified based on the pleadings); *Yaffe v. Powers*, 454 F.2d 1362, 1364 (1st Cir. 1972) (abuse of discretion to dismiss class action without permitting certification-related discovery).

41. MANUAL FOR COMPLEX LITIGATION (FOURTH) § 21.14 (2004).

42. *See Washington v. Brown & Williamson Tobacco Corp.*, 959 F.2d 1566, 1571 (11th Cir. 1992) (for efficiency/fairness purposes, courts can limit discovery to certification issues and defer merits discovery); *see also* MANUAL FOR COMPLEX LITIGATION (FOURTH) § 11.213 (2004) ("The court should ascertain what discovery on class questions is needed for a certification ruling and how to conduct it efficiently and

The primary justification for bifurcated discovery is judicial efficiency and economy—merits discovery needlessly delays the certification decision and, in the event that certification is denied, may be unnecessary.[43] Frequently, however, disputes arise as to whether specific proposed discovery relates to "merits" or "class" discovery, often requiring judicial intervention. Additionally, because facts relating to the merits can sometimes play an important role in the certification decision, "[a]rbitrary insistence on the merits/class discovery distinction sometimes thwarts the informed judicial assessment that current class certification practice emphasizes."[44]

Recognizing the potential for issues relating to bifurcated discovery, the Advisory Committee note to the 2003 amendments to Rule 23 makes the following comment:

> In this sense, it is appropriate to conduct controlled discovery into the "merits," limited to those aspects relevant to making the certification decision on an informed basis. Active judicial supervision may be required to achieve the most effective balance that expedites an informed certification determination without forcing an artificial and ultimately wasteful division between "certification discovery" and "merits" discovery.[45]

Issues concerning whether discovery will be bifurcated and whether specific proposed precertification discovery will be permitted as "class" or "merits" discovery must be determined on a case-by-case basis, analyzing the particular facts and issues presented in particular cases, including the cost burdens on the parties.[46]

Occasionally, defendants seek precertification discovery from unnamed proposed class members to obtain evidence relevant to determining, *inter alia*, the existence of common issues.[47] Courts have the discretion to permit precertification discovery from absent class members. Nevertheless, courts generally do not encourage discovery from absent class members and allow it only when it is not unduly

---

economically. Consider also staying other discovery if resolution of the certification issue may obviate some or all further proceedings. Discovery may proceed concurrently if bifurcating class discovery from merits discovery would result in significant duplication of effort and expense to the parties.").

43. MANUAL FOR COMPLEX LITIGATION (FOURTH) § 21.14 (2004).

44. *Id.*; *see also* FED. R. CIV. P. 23, advisory committee note (2003) ("[D]iscovery in aid of the certification decision often includes information required to identify the nature of the issues that actually will be presented at trial.").

45. FED. R. CIV. P. 23, advisory committee note (2003); *see also* 3 HERBERT B. NEWBERG & ALBA CONTE, NEWBERG ON CLASS ACTIONS: A MANUAL FOR GROUP LITIGATION AT FEDERAL AND STATE LEVELS § 7:8 (4th ed. 2002) [hereinafter NEWBERG] ("Discovery bifurcation will often be counterproductive in delaying the progress of the suit for orderly and efficient adjudication.").

46. *See Nat'l Org. for Women, Farmington Valley Chapter v. Sperry Rand Corp.*, 88 F.R.D. 272 (D. Conn. 1980).

47. *Berenson Co., Inc. v. Faneuil Hall Marketplace, Inc.*, 103 F.R.D. 635, 637 (D. Mass. 1984); *see also* MANUAL FOR COMPLEX LITIGATION (FOURTH) § 21.14 (2004).

burdensome and only upon a particularized showing of need.[48] Where some discovery from absent and unnamed class members is permitted, courts should impose limitations to minimize time, costs, and burdens on such members.[49]

An additional precertification issue arises from defendants' attempts to discover information concerning the named plaintiffs' finances. The justification for such discovery is that the named plaintiffs' ability to fund the costs involved in prosecuting class actions is relevant to whether they are adequate representatives of the proposed class.[50] There is a split of authority on whether such discovery is relevant and permissible. Some courts permit such discovery, finding that the named plaintiffs' financial resources are a relevant consideration in determining whether the plaintiffs would adequately represent the class.[51] Others courts deem such discovery irrelevant and prohibit defendants' attempts to obtain such discovery.[52] Other courts have noted that the ability to finance the litigation is relevant, but that it is the class counsel's ability to fund the litigation, not the named plaintiffs', that is relevant to the issue of whether representation is adequate.[53]

---

48. *Berenson Co.*, 103 F.R.D. at 637 (authorizing precertification discovery from absent class members where information sought was relevant to certification issue, the requests are made in good faith and are not unduly burdensome, and the information is not available from the proposed representative); *see also Mehl v. Canadian Pac. Ry.*, 216 F.R.D. 627, 631 (D.N.D. 2003) (precertification discovery from absent unnamed class members "not generally encouraged due to its potential for harassment and due to concerns regarding its practicality"); *Baldwin & Flynn v. Nat'l Safety Assocs.*, 149 F.R.D. 598, 600 (N.D. Cal. 1993) ("Defendants must have leave of court to take depositions of members of a putative class, other than the named class members—after first showing that discovery is both necessary and for a purpose other than taking undue advantage of class members.").

49. MANUAL FOR COMPLEX LITIGATION (FOURTH) § 21.14 (2004):

> If precertification discovery of unnamed class members is appropriate, the court should consider imposing limits beyond those contemplated by the Federal Rules of Civil Procedure. Such limits might include the scope, subject matter, number, and time allowed for depositions, interrogatories, or other discovery directed to class representatives or unnamed class members, and might limit the period for completing certification-related discovery. If some merits discovery is permitted during the precertification period, consider limits that minimize the time and effort involved, such as requiring the use of questionnaires or interrogatories rather than depositions, and consider limiting discovery to a certain number or a sample of proposed class members.

50. *See McGowan v. Faulkner Concrete Pipe Co.*, 659 F.2d 554, 559–60 (5th Cir. 1981).

51. *Id.*; *In re ML-Lee Acquisition Fund II*, 149 F.R.D. 506, 508–09 (D. Del. 1993); *In re One Bancorp Sec. Litig.*, 134 F.R.D. 4, 8, n.3 (D. Me. 1991).

52. *Sanderson v. Winner*, 507 F.2d 477, 479–80 (10th Cir. 1974); *Klein v. Checker Motors Corp.*, 87 F.R.D. 5, 6 (N.D. Ill. 1979).

53. *See, e.g., Rand v. Monsanto Co.*, 926 F.2d 596, 599 (7th Cir. 1991); *Wolgin v. Magic Marker Corp.*, 82 F.R.D. 168, 175 (E.D. Pa. 1979); MANUAL FOR COMPLEX LITIGATION (FOURTH) § 21.141 (2004) ("Precertification inquiries into the named parties' finances or the financial arrangements between the class representative and their counsel are rarely appropriate, except to obtain information necessary to determine whether the parties and their counsel have resources to represent the class adequately.").

D. PRECERTIFICATION COMMUNICATIONS
WITH UNNAMED PROPOSED CLASS MEMBERS[54]

Courts have long recognized that while class actions "serve an important function in our system of civil justice," they also present "opportunities for abuse."[55] In particular, certain direct communications by parties and their counsel with unnamed members of a proposed class can be improper, unseemly, and abusive. For example, plaintiffs' counsel might engage in improper in-person solicitation of potential class members.[56] On the other hand, defendants or their counsel might engage in misconduct by seeking to dissuade potential class members from participating in a class action or to undermine their cooperation with or confidence in class counsel through the use of false, incomplete, or misleading information.[57] The primary abuses are those communications "that mislead or otherwise threaten to create confusion and to influence the threshold decision whether to remain in the class."[58]

To deal with the potential for abuse, under Rule 23, "a district court has both the duty and the broad authority to exercise control over a class action and to enter appropriate orders governing the conduct of counsel and parties."[59] Such authority is not without limits, however, as the court's discretion is "bounded by the relevant provisions of the Federal Rules."[60] In the context of orders restricting or prohibiting communications with putative class members, the court's discretion is subject to the parties' freedom of speech rights under the First Amendment.[61]

In *Gulf Oil v. Bernard*,[62] the Supreme Court recognized the power of district courts to regulate the parties' and counsel's precertification communications with putative class members but held that the issuance of an order imposing a blanket prohibition on all precertification communications with putative class members,

---

54. For a detailed discussion of this subject, *see* Chapter 2, "Ethical and Practical Issues of Communicating with Members of a Class."

55. *Gulf Oil Co. v. Bernard*, 452 U.S. 89, 100 (1981).

56. *Waldo v. Lakeshore Estates, Inc.*, 433 F. Supp. 782, 790 (E.D. La. 1977) ("the heightened susceptibilities of nonparty class members to solicitation amounting to barratry as well as the increased opportunities of the parties or counsel to 'drum up' participation in the proceeding."), *appeal dismissed without published opinion*, 579 F.2d 642 (5th Cir. 1978). *But see Foltz v. U.S. News & World Report, Inc.*, 106 F.R.D. 338 (D.D.C. 1984) (proper for named plaintiffs in antitrust action to solicit contributions to defray costs).

57. *In re Sch. Asbestos Litig.*, 842 F.2d 671, 682 n.23 (3d Cir. 1988) (compiling cases).

58. *Id.* at 683.

59. *Gulf Oil*, 452 U.S. at 100.

60. *Id.*

61. *See Zauderer v. Office of Disciplinary Counsel*, 471 U.S. 626 (1985); *In re Sch. Asbestos Litig.*, 842 F.2d at 680 ("Orders regulating communications between litigants . . . also pose a grave threat to first amendment freedom of speech. Accordingly, a district court's discretion to issue such orders must be exercised within the bounds of the First Amendment and the Federal Rules.") (citing *Gulf Oil*, 452 U.S. at 100).

62. 452 U.S. 89 (1981).

without specific findings supporting such a prohibition, was an abuse of discretion.[63] In so holding, the Supreme Court stated:

> [A]n order limiting communications between parties and potential class members should be based on a clear record and specific findings that reflect a weighing of the need for a limitation and the potential interference with the rights of the parties. . . . [S]uch a weighing—identifying potential abuses being addressed—should result in a carefully drawn order that limits speech as little as possible, consistent with the rights of the parties under the circumstances.[64]

In applying *Gulf Oil*, courts have generally taken a case-by-case, fact-specific approach to deciding whether to restrict specific precertification communications with putative class members. As the decision of the court to restrict such communications is discretionary, subject to *Gulf Oil*, where "it is clear the defendant is attempting to engage in conduct which would undermine the purpose of the rule," gag orders may still be proper.[65] Most courts, however, "are reluctant to restrict communications between the parties or their counsel and potential class members, except when necessary to prevent [actual or threatened] serious misconduct."[66]

Generally, in the absence of an applicable court order or rule, defendants and their counsel are free to engage in precertification communications with potential class members in the ordinary course of business, including settlement discussions—so long as they do not "give false, misleading, or intimidating information, conceal material information, or attempt to influence the decision about whether to request exclusion from a class."[67] Where a party has engaged in abusive conduct in connection with communications with a putative class member, courts often order the offending party to cure any miscommunication or require prior notice of future communications.[68]

---

63. Prior to the *Gulf Oil* decision, it was common practice for federal courts to use gag orders or rules based on the model rule and order included in an earlier edition of the *Manual for Complex Litigation* requiring prior judicial approval of all communications with putative class members, a prior restraint on speech. Subsequent to *Gulf Oil*, the model rule and order were withdrawn from the *Manual for Complex Litigation*. *See* 5 NEWBERG §§ 15:7, 15:9.

64. *Gulf Oil*, 452 U.S. at 101–02.

65. *See Burrell v. Crown Cent. Petroleum, Inc.*, 176 F.R.D. 239, 243 (E.D. Tex. 1997).

66. MANUAL FOR COMPLEX LITIGATION (FOURTH) § 21.12 (2004); *Williams v. Chartwell Fin. Servs., Ltd.*, 204 F.3d 748, 759 (7th Cir. 2000); *Great Rivers Coop. v. Farmland Indus.*, 59 F.3d 764, 766 (8th Cir. 1995) (actual or threatened misconduct of serious nature required).

67. MANUAL FOR COMPLEX LITIGATION (FOURTH) § 21.12 (2004); *EEOC v. Mitsubishi Motor Mfg. of Am., Inc.*, 102 F.3d 869, 870 (7th Cir. 1996) (recognizing both parties' right to precertification communications with putative class members); *Resnick v. Am. Dental Ass'n*, 95 F.R.D. 372, 377 (N.D. Ill. 1982) (ordinary course of business communications).

68. MANUAL FOR COMPLEX LITIGATION (FOURTH) § 21.12 (2004); *Mitsubishi Motor Mfg.*, 102 F.3d at 870–71 (requirement for prior notice to prevent future misconduct); *Haffer v. Temple Univ.*, 115 F.R.D. 506, 512 (E.D. Pa. 1987) (notice to correct improper communications).

E. TIMING OF CERTIFICATION: "AT AN EARLY PRACTICABLE TIME"

Prior to the 2003 amendments to the rule, Rule 23(c)(1)(A) directed courts to decide the class certification issue "as soon as practicable." Under the 2003 amendments, the "as soon as practicable" language was changed to "at an early practicable time."[69] As explained in the Advisory Committee notes to the 2003 amendments, this modification was made to give courts more flexibility in the timing of the class certification decision because "[t]he 'as soon as practicable' exaction neither reflects prevailing practice nor captures the many valid reasons that may justify deferring the certification decision."[70]

Although Rule 23 does not provide any specific deadline for the filing of a motion for class certification, some district courts do impose a deadline pursuant to local rules. For example, in the Central District of California, the District of Utah, and the Eastern District of Louisiana, motions for class certification are required to be filed within 90 days of service of a class action complaint.[71] An unintended failure to strictly comply with such local rules will not necessarily result in the denial of class certification, as these courts are generally lenient in dealing with a party's failure to seek class certification in a timely manner.[72] Additionally, because a 90-day time limit may conflict with Rule 23(c)(1)'s directive that the court determine the certification issue "[a]t an early practicable time," local rules imposing such deadlines may be unenforceable.[73] Nevertheless, prudence dictates that if a party anticipates that it will be unable to comply with any local rules that impose a time limit for the filing of a class certification motion, relief from such rules should be timely sought.

---

69. FED. R. CIV. P. 23(c)(1)(A).

70. FED. R. CIV. P. 23, advisory committee note (2003) (citing THOMAS E. WILLGING, LAURAL L. HOOPER & ROBERT L. NIEMIC, EMPIRICAL STUDY OF CLASS ACTIONS IN FOUR FEDERAL DISTRICT COURTS: FINAL REPORT TO THE ADVISORY COMMITTEE ON CIVIL RULES, at 26–36 (Federal Judicial Center 1996) [hereinafter FJC STUDY] (In cases where motions to dismiss and motions to certify were filed, 60 to 80 percent of the time, rulings on motions to dismiss preceded the certification decision.)).

71. See, e.g., Cottone v. Blum, 571 F. Supp. 437, 440–41 (S.D.N.Y. 1983) (dismissal for failure to move for certification within 60 days per local rules); C.D. CAL. L.R. 23-3 (within 90 days of service of class action complaint); D. UTAH L.R. 23-1(d) (same); E.D. LA L.R. 23.1(b) (same); N.D. TEX. L.R. 23.2 (same).

72. See Gray v. Greyhound Lines, 545 F.2d 169, 173 n.11 (D.C. Cir. 1976); Brown v. J.P. Allen Co., 79 F.R.D. 32 (N.D. Ga. 1978) (where no prejudice to defendant, failure to comply with local rule not determinative). But see Carroll v. Blinken, 99 F.R.D. 166 (S.D.N.Y. 1983) (dismissal of class action for unjustified four-week delay in filing motion for class certification).

73. Slanina v. William Penn Parking Corp., 106 F.R.D. 419, 422 (W.D. Pa. 1984) (unnecessary to strictly comply with local rule requirement that class certification motion be filed within 90 days of filing); FED. R. CIV. P. 83(a)(1) ("A local rule must be consistent with—but not duplicate—federal statutes and rules adopted under 28 U.S.C. §§ 2072 and 2075 . . .").

Although an early resolution of the certification question is generally desirable,[74] the actual timing depends on the specific facts and circumstances of each case, many of which can and should be addressed by the parties and the court early in the case.[75] For example, whether precertification discovery is necessary and the extent and scope of such discovery will dictate how much time the parties will need before a certification motion can be filed.[76] Whether discovery is bifurcated into "class" and "merits" discovery, the physical volume of the information produced during discovery, whether statistical analysis is necessary to support or oppose certification, and similar discovery-related considerations will impact the timing of the certification decision.

An additional consideration is whether there are threshold issues or potentially dispositive issues that can be raised by a motion under Rule 12 or 56.[77] Most courts are in agreement that a district court is free to rule on dispositive motions prior to deciding the certification issue—Rule 23(c)(1)'s "early practicable time" standard does not preclude district courts from ruling on dispositive merits issues prior to class certification.[78] But where a class action seeks money damages, certification must precede any determination of the merits to prevent "one-way intervention"— where absent class members have the ability to opt out of any class action where there has been an adverse merits determination.[79]

As the timing of the certification decision is generally up to the discretion of the court,[80] based on the facts and circumstances in each case, one commentator has observed:

---

74. *See Bertrand ex rel. Bertrand v. Maram*, 495 F.3d 452, 455 (7th Cir. 2007) (early certification decision necessary to, *inter alia*, avoid mootness problems).

75. *See* FED. R. CIV. P. 23, advisory committee note (2003).

76. *See supra*, part II.B.

77. *See* FJC STUDY at 33 (approximately 30 percent of cases terminated the action as a result of rulings on motions to dismiss or for summary judgment).

78. *See Schweizer v. Trans Union Corp.*, 136 F.3d 233, 239 (2d Cir. 1998); *Floyd v. Bowen*, 833 F.2d 529, 534–35 (5th Cir. 1987); *Miami Univ. Wrestling Club v. Miami Univ.*, 302 F.3d 608, 616 (6th Cir. 2002) ("We have consistently held that a district court is not required to rule on a motion for class certification before ruling on the merits of the case"); *Curtin v. United Airlines, Inc.*, 275 F.3d 88, 92 (D.C. Cir. 2001) (court has discretion to resolve individual claims, which may obviate need to address class issues); *Wade v. Kirkland*, 118 F.3d 667, 670 (9th Cir. 1997); *see also* BARBARA J. ROTHSTEIN & THOMAS E. WILLGING, MANAGING CLASS ACTION LITIGATION: A POCKET GUIDE FOR JUDGES at 8 (Federal Judicial Center 2009) (Rule 23 permits courts to rule on motions to dismiss or for summary judgment before ruling on class certification; "Given the flexibility in the rules, the most efficient practice is to rule on motions to dismiss or for summary judgment before addressing class certification.").

79. *See, e.g., Am. Pipe & Constr. Co. v. Utah*, 414 U.S. 538, 547–49 (1974); *Hudson v. Chicago Teachers Union*, 922 F.2d 1306, 1317 (7th Cir. 1991).

80. *Philip Morris Inc. v. Nat'l Asbestos Workers Med. Fund*, 214 F.3d 132, 134–36 (2d Cir. 2000) (district court has discretion regarding timing of certification decision, but it should occur before trial on merits); *Chavez v. Illinois State Police*, 251 F.3d 612, 629–30 (7th Cir. 2001) (better policy is to rule on certification before ruling on merits, but it is not error to rule on merits before certification).

Initial class rulings may be made before, after, or simultaneously with the disposition of other motions. Accordingly, class rulings have been made before, contemporaneously with, and following disposition of a defendant's motion to dismiss for failure to state a cause of action, lack of jurisdiction, lack of standing of the plaintiff, or improper venue. So also, initial class rulings have been made at various times in relation to motions for transfer of venue, consolidation under 28 U.S.C.A. § 1407, abstention or stay of proceedings, preliminary injunction, amendment of the complaint, a three-judge court, approval of a settlement, voluntary dismissal of the entire litigation, and motions for summary judgment.[81]

Although the timing of the certification decision is generally left to the court's discretion, it is still the court's obligation to make the determination at an "early practicable time." Thus, one court has held that a district court could not deny a class certification motion on the basis that the plaintiff failed to timely move for class certification because the court itself had the onus of considering the issue.[82] Similarly, another court has rejected the proposition that the district court need not rule on certification until a party moves for class certification.[83] In fact, a court may act on its own initiative in deciding whether to certify a class.[84] A court may not, however, act on its own initiative to expand an individual complaint into a class action.[85]

III. Multiple Cases with Similar Issues and Multidistrict Litigation Proceedings

Frequently, a class action pending in one federal jurisdiction is only one of many identical or similar actions pending in various jurisdictions throughout the country arising out of the same or similar set of facts and claims.[86] A court facing such a situation will have a number of ways of potentially dealing with competing, conflicting, or overlapping cases, depending on the type of action (class action, consolidated cases, or individual cases) and the jurisdictions in which they are pending (same district, different district, or state court). The possible scenarios that a court can face are many, including one or more of the following:[87]

---

81. 3 Newberg § 7:15.

82. *Trevizo v. Adams*, 455 F.3d 1155, 1161 (10th Cir. 2006).

83. *Bieneman v. City of Chicago*, 838 F.2d 962, 963 (7th Cir. 1988).

84. *McGowan v. Faulkner Concrete Pipe Co.*, 659 F.2d 554, 559 (5th Cir. 1981) ("The trial court has an independent obligation to decide whether an action was properly brought as a class action, even where neither party moves for a ruling on class certification.").

85. *Newsom v. Norris*, 888 F.2d 371, 380–82 (6th Cir. 1989) (vacating district court order converting an individual action into a class action and certifying the class).

86. For a more detailed discussion on this issue, *see* Chapter 12, "Multidistrict Litigation."

87. Manual for Complex Litigation (Fourth) § 21.25 (2004).

- Multiple cases with similar class allegations, each of which might be appropriately certified under Rule 23, but which may overlap or conflict if more than one is certified;
- Cases alleging a nationwide class and cases seeking multistate or single state class certification pending in different courts at the same time;
- Cases filed as class actions in federal and state courts relating to the same type of transactions and involving some or all of the same parties;
- Cases filed by the same lawyers seeking to represent an overlapping or duplicative class of plaintiffs in order to obtain the most favorable forum;
- Cases filed by different lawyers competing for the fastest and most favorable rulings on class certification and appointment as class counsel;
- Multiple individual actions or other forms of aggregate litigation pending in state or federal courts, raising the same issues and involving some or all of the same parties; or
- Prior unsuccessful class certification efforts in state or federal courts.

Whether courts and parties face one, or a combination, of the above scenarios, the critical issue is effective case management and coordination. Counsel should become familiar with the options available to the court in dealing with the situation and formulate a strategy based on an evaluation of the pros and cons as to each of these options in order to effectively advocate for the course of conduct that would best further the clients' interests.

Among the options and procedural mechanisms available to a court to manage situations involving multiple related actions are the following:[88]

- Where related federal actions are pending in the same district, consider whether the cases can or should be consolidated before the same judge under Rule 42 for pretrial proceedings and, if appropriate, for trial.[89]
- Where related federal actions are pending in different districts, consider whether the cases can or should be consolidated in one court: (1) through transfers under 28 U.S.C. § 1404(a) or 1406; or (2) by transfer to the Judicial Panel on Multidistrict Litigation under 28 U.S.C. § 1407.[90]
- Where related federal actions are not capable of being consolidated in one district, consider whether the judges, parties, and counsel in the pending cases can coordinate proceedings in the related actions by, *inter alia*: (1) specially assigning a judge to the cases under 28 U.S.C. §§ 292 through 294; (2) designating a lead case and staying all other cases pending conclu-

---

88. *See generally* 3 NEWBERG §§ 9:13–9:37; MANUAL FOR COMPLEX LITIGATION (FOURTH) §§ 20, 21 (2004).
89. MANUAL FOR COMPLEX LITIGATION (FOURTH) § 21.11 (2004).
90. *Id.* §§ 21.12–21.133.

sion of the lead case; (3) holding joint telephonic hearings or conferences; (4) appointing joint experts under Federal Rule of Evidence 706 or special masters under Rule 53; (5) avoiding duplicative discovery; (6) clarifying class definitions; and (7) staying actions pending conclusion of another federal action.[91]

- Where there are related state and federal actions, consider whether the state court proceeding(s) can be removed under the class action or "mass action" provisions of CAFA.[92]
- Where there are related state and federal actions, consider whether coordination of the various proceedings is feasible by, *inter alia*, (1) jointly deferring certification decisions and holding a joint certification hearing; (2) designating a court, jurisdiction, or state as the lead on certain proceedings; (3) staying cases until the conclusion of designated cases; (4) holding joint hearings on pretrial motions using coordinated briefs; (5) jointly appointing special masters or court-appointed experts; (6) jointly appointing lead counsel, committees of counsel, or liaison counsel; (7) coordinating pretrial discovery with the maintenance of joint document depositories, coordinated document productions, joint depositions, and coordinated discovery rulings; and (8) conducting joint comprehensive settlement discussions.[93]

Where coordination is not feasible or efforts to coordinate have failed, federal courts can stay or dismiss their actions where certain conditions exist warranting the federal court's deference to parallel state actions.[94] Alternatively, as a measure of last resort, federal courts may enjoin parallel state proceedings. The ability of a federal court to enjoin a state court action, however, is subject to the Anti-Injunction Act, which prohibits federal courts from enjoining a state court action "except as expressly authorized by Act of Congress, or where necessary in aid of its jurisdiction or to protect or effectuate its judgments."[95] Nevertheless, federal courts on occasion have enjoined parallel or duplicative state court proceedings under the All Writs Act,[96] and as necessary under the "in aid of its jurisdiction or to protect or effectuate its judgments" exception to the Anti-Injunction Act.[97]

---

91. *Id.* § 20.14.

92. 28 U.S.C. § 1332(d); *see also* Chapter 10, "The Class Action Fairness Act of 2005," and Chapter 11, "Mass Actions Under the Class Action Fairness Act."

93. MANUAL FOR COMPLEX LITIGATION (FOURTH) § 20.313 (2004).

94. *Id.* § 210.32.

95. 28 U.S.C. § 2283.

96. 28 U.S.C. § 1651.

97. *See, e.g.*, *Carlough v. Am.-Chem Products, Inc.*, 10 F.3d 189 (3d. Cir. 1993); *In re "Agent Orange" Prod. Liab. Litig.*, 996 F.2d 1425 (2d Cir. 1993).

ETHICAL AND PRACTICAL ISSUES OF COMMUNICATING WITH MEMBERS OF A CLASS[1]

SCOTT J. ATLAS

I. Introduction

Courts and commentators have long been concerned with the potential for abuse inherent in the class action method of litigating claims. These concerns are of particular import in the area of communications with class members.[2] As the Third Circuit noted, "[m]isleading communications to class members concerning the litigation pose a serious threat to the fairness of the litigation process, the adequacy of representation and the administration of justice generally."[3] Similarly, the Eleventh Circuit cautioned that "[u]nsupervised, unilateral communications with the plaintiff class sabotage the goal of informed consent by urging exclusion on the basis of a one-sided presentation of the facts, without opportunity for rebuttal. The damage from misstatements could well be irreparable."[4]

The rules governing communications with class members offer little definitive guidance to the courts with respect to the permissible scope and content of such communications. Broad principles derived from First Amendment and due process rights establish the outer limits of courts' ability to limit communications. Within these boundaries, however, courts have considerable discretion to regulate

---

1. This chapter was adapted from a paper prepared by Carl Jordan and Vanessa Griffith of Vinson & Elkins, L.L.P., and is an updated version of an article published by Mr. Atlas and Juanita E. Mantz, "Let's Talk—The Ethical and Practical Issues of Communicating with Members of a Class," ABA Section of Litigation, Class Actions (2004). Thanks to Giana Ortiz for her assistance in updating this article.

2. *See, e.g.*, MANUAL FOR COMPLEX LITIGATION (FOURTH) § 21.12, at 320 (2004) ("Direct communications with class members, however, whether by plaintiffs or defendants, can lead to abuse.").

3. *In re Sch. Asbestos Litig.*, 842 F.2d 671, 680 (3d Cir. 1988).

4. *Kleiner v. First Nat'l Bank of Atlanta*, 751 F.2d 1193, 1203 (11th Cir. 1985).

both court-authorized notice and party-initiated communications. This chapter provides an overview of the substantive principles governing communications with class members and the means by which courts attempt to control, and if necessary remedy, the effects of misleading communications with class members on the integrity of the class litigation.

II. Communications by the Parties to the Class Members in Rule 23 Class Actions

A large and complex body of law has developed around the issue of communications by lawyers and the named parties with potential and actual class members. The cases in this area reflect the difficulty of applying general principles in the highly fact-specific contexts typically at issue when a party seeks to communicate with class members. Moreover, despite the breadth of discussion addressing this issue both in the courts and academia, courts continue to wrestle with the complex interplay among the needs to comply with ethical rules, advise class members to facilitate their informed decision making, prevent abuses and dissemination of misinformation, and protect the parties' rights to freedom of expression.

In this area, there are two fundamental principles that courts must reconcile when facing the question of what constitutes permissible communications to class members. On the one hand, courts have long been concerned with the potential for abuse inherent in the class mechanism.[5] They have sought to regulate the means by which lawyers communicate with class members to ensure that applicable ethical rules are followed and that the class receives only accurate and objective information. At the same time, the parties frequently have a real need to communicate with class members, and attempts to impinge on this need must be tempered by the limits of courts' authority under Rule 23 and by First Amendment concerns.[6] And while the Supreme Court's 1981 seminal opinion in *Gulf Oil Co. v. Bernard*[7] prescribes some general guidelines for the regulation of communications with class members, the lower courts continue to struggle with the application of *Gulf Oil* to particular circumstances.

---

5. *E.g., In re Sch. Asbestos Litig.*, 842 F.2d at 680; *Kleiner*, 751 F.2d at 1203; *see also, e.g., Waldo v. Lakeshore Estates, Inc.*, 433 F. Supp. 782, 790 (E.D. La. 1977) (noting the "heightened susceptibilities of nonparty class members to solicitation amounting to barratry as well as the increased opportunities of the parties or counsel to 'drum up' participation in the proceeding"), *appeal dismissed without published opinion*, 579 F.2d 642 (5th Cir. 1978).

6. *E.g., Jackson v. Papa John's USA, Inc.*, No. 1:08-CV-2791, 2009 U.S. Dist. LEXIS 23325, at *4 (N.D. Ohio Mar. 10, 2009); *Longcrier v. HL-A Co., Inc.*, 595 F. Supp. 2d 1218, 1226 (N.D. Ala. 2008).

7. 452 U.S. 89 (1981).

A. A HISTORICAL PERSPECTIVE

Before 1981, courts looked primarily to the guidance offered in the *Manual for Complex Litigation* (*Manual*) when faced with the question of whether to permit communications with class members. The *Manual* advocated the position that because class actions were susceptible to abuse, courts should take an active role in preventing such abuse by regulating communications with the class.[8] The *Manual* was primarily concerned with solicitation of clients, solicitation of funds, solicitation of agreements by actual and potential class members who were not formal parties to the action to pay fees and expenses, and solicitation by defendants of class members' requests to opt out where applicable.[9] The *Manual* proposed both a local rule and a model order severely limiting the rights of lawyers to communicate with class members, both of which were widely used. Approximately ten districts adopted a version of the proposed rule, and many more courts entered orders similar to the *Manual*'s model order in which communications with the class were restricted.[10] These gag rules and orders were challenged by many parties seeking to communicate with potential and actual class members. The primary ground for challenge was that the prohibition violated the First Amendment. The majority of these challenges failed. Some courts determined that even though the ban constituted a prior restraint on expression, it was justified by the compelling governmental interest in protecting the judicial process, the parties, and the class members from misrepresentations.[11] Other courts simply bypassed the constitutional issues.[12] Until the decisions by the Fifth Circuit and the Supreme Court in *Gulf Oil*, gag orders were the rule rather than the exception.[13]

B. *GULF OIL CO. V. BERNARD*

The seminal case addressing the extent to which courts can limit class counsel's communication with potential class members is *Gulf Oil*.[14] The case arose from a conciliation agreement between the Equal Employment Opportunity Commission and Gulf involving allegations of race and sex discrimination at Gulf's Port

---

8. MANUAL FOR COMPLEX LITIGATION § 1.41 (1977).

9. *Id.*

10. *See, e.g., Coles v. Marsh*, 560 F.2d 186, 186–89 (3d Cir. 1977); *Nat'l Org. for Women, Inc.* (*NOW*) *v. Minn. Mining & Mfg. Co.*, 18 F.E.P. Cas. (BNA) 1176, 1178 (D. Minn. 1977); *Chrapliwy v. Uniroyal, Inc.*, 12 F.E.P. Cas. (BNA) 1661, 1662–64 (N.D. Ind. 1976).

11. *See, e.g., NOW*, 18 F.E.P. Cas. (BNA) at 1178; *Waldo*, 433 F. Supp. at 793. *But see Zarate v. Younglove*, 86 F.R.D. 80 (C.D. Cal. 1980) (rejecting a blanket communications ban because the potential harm did not outweigh the interest in facilitating the class action).

12. *E.g., Halverson v. Convenient Food Mart, Inc.*, 458 F.2d 927 (7th Cir. 1972).

13. 5 HERBERT B. NEWBERG & ALBA CONTE, NEWBERG ON CLASS ACTIONS: A MANUAL FOR GROUP LITIGATION AT FEDERAL AND STATE LEVELS § 15:7 to 15:9 (4th ed. 2002) [hereinafter NEWBERG].

14. *See Bublitz v. E.I. Du Pont de Nemours & Co.*, 196 F.R.D. 545, 547 (S.D. Iowa 2000) (noting that *Gulf Oil* set forth the broad principles governing limitations on communications with potential class members).

Arthur, Texas, refinery.[15] As part of the agreement, Gulf agreed to offer back pay to the alleged victims of discrimination, based on an agreed formula.[16] In accordance with the agreement, Gulf sent notice to the eligible individuals that included a statement of the amount available to each person in return for the execution of a release of all discrimination claims.[17] The notice also requested that the individual refrain from discussing the notice with others, although any questions could be directed to the company, which would then arrange for an interview with the EEOC.[18]

In the meantime, *Gulf Oil* was filed as a class action under Title VII and 42 U.S.C. § 1981 on behalf of all present and former African American employees and rejected applicants.[19] The proposed class included many of the individuals who were then receiving settlement offers from Gulf under the conciliation agreement.[20] Class counsel consisted of three lawyers from the NAACP Legal Defense and Education Fund and two other lawyers, presumably in private practice.[21]

Shortly after the class action was filed, Gulf filed a motion in district court seeking to limit communications by class counsel to class members.[22] In particular, Gulf alleged that at a meeting of 75 class members, class counsel recommended that they reject the release offered by Gulf and return any checks they had already received as they could secure twice that amount by participating in the class litigation.[23] The trial court granted Gulf's motion, entering an order prohibiting all communications concerning the case from the parties or their counsel to both prospective and actual class members.[24] The court subsequently modified the order to exclude from the ban attorney-client communications initiated by the client, communications in the ordinary course of business, and communications by Gulf involving the conciliation agreement.[25] The court also stated that if a party, without receiving prior court approval, communicated with a class member on the basis of a claimed constitutional right to do so, then the party must file a summary of the communication with the court within five days.[26] Notably, in fashioning its

---

15. 452 U.S. 89, 91.
16. *Id.*
17. *Id.*
18. *Id.* at 91 n.1.
19. *Id.* at 92.
20. *Id.*
21. *Id.* at 92 n.3.
22. *Id.* at 92.
23. *Id.* at 92–93.
24. *Id.* at 93.
25. *Id.* at 95.
26. *Id.*

order the district court expressly relied on the recommendations contained in the *Manual for Complex Litigation*.[27]

In accordance with the court's order, the plaintiffs submitted to the court for approval a proposed notice to prospective class members.[28] The notice urged the class to confer with a lawyer before signing the releases from Gulf and contained the names and addresses of class counsel.[29] The court delayed ruling on the motion until after the expiration of the 45-day period in which individuals were required to respond to Gulf's settlement offer.[30] The result of the court's delay was to preclude the named plaintiffs and their lawyers from communicating with prospective class members before their deadline for deciding whether to accept Gulf's settlement offer. On appeal to the Fifth Circuit and, ultimately, to the U.S. Supreme Court, the plaintiffs argued that the limitations imposed by the district court exceeded the court's power under Rule 23 and were unconstitutional under the First Amendment.[31]

The Fifth Circuit, en banc, reversed, concluding that the district court's order was an unconstitutional prior restraint of protected expression.[32] Specifically, the court held that the order was overbroad and unjustified in the absence of a particularized showing of need.[33] However, 8 of the 22 judges in the majority, in a special concurrence, opined that the court unnecessarily reached the constitutional issue since the order exceeded the trial court's authority under Rule 23.[34]

The Supreme Court agreed with the concurring judges that the constitutional issue need not be reached.[35] The Court held that the order was an abuse of the trial court's Rule 23 discretion to control class actions and enter appropriate orders governing the conduct of counsel and parties. The Court recognized that the trial court's order precluding communications by class counsel unfairly interfered with class counsel's rights to notify potential class members about the action and to develop the case before certification. Accordingly, the Court held that

> an order limiting communications between parties and potential class members should be based on a clear record and specific findings that reflect a weighing of the need for a limitation and the potential interference with the rights of the parties. Only such a determination can ensure that the court is furthering, rather than hindering, the policies embodied in the Federal Rules of Civil Procedure, especially

---

27. *Id.* at 93.
28. *Id.* at 96–97.
29. *Id.* at 97.
30. *Id.*
31. *Id.*
32. 619 F.2d 459, 466–78 (5th Cir. 1980), *aff'd*, 452 U.S. 89.
33. *Id.*
34. *Id.* at 481.
35. *Gulf Oil*, 452 U.S. at 99, 101–02 n.15.

Rule 23. In addition, such a weighing—identifying the potential abuses being addressed—should result in a carefully drawn order that limits speech as little as possible, consistent with the rights of the parties under the circumstances.[36]

Despite the Court's express refusal to rest its opinion on constitutional grounds, the implications of the holding in *Gulf Oil* are significant. As shown below, courts have liberally construed *Gulf Oil*, and its holding cannot be overlooked in any situation where counsel for any party seeks to communicate with class members during any phase of the litigation.

C. COMMUNICATIONS BY CLASS COUNSEL AND REPRESENTATIVE PARTIES

Gulf Oil eliminated many of the structural obstacles previously in place that restricted representative plaintiffs and their counsel from communicating with class members and prospective class members. However, communications with class members are still subject to considerable oversight and regulation by the courts. For example, courts retain considerable discretion under 23(d)(2) to enter appropriate orders in order to manage class communications. Furthermore, party-initiated communications are still subject to review by the court, and corrective action may be required. Moreover, state laws and ethical rules that restrict or prohibit client solicitation may place further limits on communications with class members.[37]

1. The Impact of Gulf Oil on Court Regulation of Communications by Class Counsel

Since *Gulf Oil*, several courts have applied its analysis to communications by class counsel with class members. Moreover, despite the apparent breadth of the Court's holding, several courts subsequently have nonetheless restricted the plaintiffs' rights to communicate with class members. In *Rossini v. Ogilvy & Mather, Inc.,*[38] for example, the Second Circuit upheld communication restrictions imposed by the trial court on both parties. *Rossini*, a sex discrimination lawsuit, involved an order entered by the trial judge requiring court approval of virtually all oral and written communications between the parties and the potential class members.[39] The court entered this order after each party complained about communications by the other. Specifically, the plaintiffs criticized the defendant for circulating a questionnaire among its female employees shortly after the commencement of litigation, and the defendant protested the propriety of a meeting at which the named plaintiff discussed the pending suit. The judge concluded that both parties' conduct was

---

36. *Id.* at 101–02 (footnotes omitted).

37. *Id.* at 104 n.21 ("We also note that the rules of ethics properly impose restraints on some forms of expression.").

38. 798 F.2d 590 (2d Cir. 1986).

39. *Id.* at 601.

improper and posed a threat of "possible chilling of the rights of the potential class members . . . seeming to pressure any of them unduly to opt-out of the class . . . or . . . creating confusion."[40]

Two years later, the plaintiffs moved to vacate the order. The judge modified the order to include only written communications, but left the substance intact. The Second Circuit determined that the order was not an abuse of the judge's discretion primarily because the judge made specific findings, as required by *Gulf Oil*, that the order was necessary.[41] The appellate court also noted that while the order was potentially broader than necessary to curb the abuses found by the trial court, in the absence of a complaint as to its breadth at the time the order was entered, the order did not exceed the trial court's authority.[42]

In *Hoffman v. United Telecommunications, Inc.*,[43] a Kansas district court held that the principles of law enumerated in *Gulf Oil* apply equally to EEOC direct enforcement actions. *Hoffman* was a Title VII lawsuit in which the EEOC intervened. The plaintiffs and the EEOC sought to send a letter and questionnaire to all current and former employees of the defendant, as well as all applicants for employment. Relying on *Gulf Oil*, plaintiffs argued that the proposed communication was necessary to "uncover specific instances of sex discrimination and verify the information found in defendants' records."[44]

Defendants opposed plaintiffs' request on numerous grounds, including that it was a mere fishing expedition since plaintiffs had no rational basis for contacting the proposed women other than their having worked or applied for work at some point with one of the defendants.[45] Defendants further objected to the content of the letter and questionnaire.[46] Finally, defendants argued that *Gulf Oil* did not apply to this suit because it was not a class action proceeding under Rule 23.[47]

The court held that EEOC direct enforcement actions are subject to *Gulf Oil*. The court noted that in representative actions, the EEOC acts both in vindication of the public interest and on behalf of individual claimants. As a consequence, the EEOC acted as "'a de facto class representative.'"[48] However, the court then found that the communication requested by the plaintiffs "may pose a substantial threat to the business operations of the defendants and to the working relationships of their employees."[49] Specifically, the court was concerned that the notice bore the

---

40. *Id.* at 602 (quoting the trial court's findings in support of its order).
41. *Id.*
42. *Id.*
43. 111 F.R.D. 332 (D. Kan. 1986).
44. *Id.* at 333–34.
45. *Id.* at 333.
46. *Id.*
47. *Id.* at 334–35.
48. *Id.* at 335 (quoting *Harris v. Amoco Prod. Co.*, 768 F.2d 669 (5th Cir. 1985)).
49. *Id.*

official seal and letterhead of the EEOC and thus carried the appearance of government sanction; that it described the case only from the plaintiffs' point of view; that it, at least implicitly, solicited claims; and that it implied that a recovery would be obtained.[50] The court took issue with the questionnaire's requests for subjective opinions in addition to factual information.[51] For these reasons, the court refused to permit the plaintiffs to disseminate the proposed letter and questionnaire.[52] Notably, however, the court refused to grant the defendants' motion for a protective order that would have completely restricted the plaintiffs' rights to communicate with nonparties. The court held that such an order would violate *Gulf Oil* unless the defendants had compelling reasons, supported in the record, showing why the plaintiffs should be prohibited from conduct that arguably is necessary for investigation and trial preparation.[53]

Not all courts agree that communications by class counsel to potential class members must be objective and neutral. *Babbitt v. Albertson's, Inc.*[54] was an employment discrimination case brought under Title VII and California's equivalent statute. Counsel for the named plaintiffs sent a letter to all prospective class members, which stated in part:

> Our law firm has filed a statewide class action against Albertson's. The named plaintiffs, six of your co-workers, charge Albertson's with giving better training, jobs, hours and promotions to white males, while women and Hispanics get the lower-paid and dead-end departments and jobs. If we win this suit, we expect to change Albertson's discriminatory practices, and get money damages for women and Hispanic employees. This firm recently won a similar lawsuit against Lucky stores in Northern California which resulted in more promotions and job opportunities for blacks and women.
>
> The federal court ordered Albertson's to give us the addresses of everyone who might be included in this case. We are writing to you because you might have suffered from employment discrimination at Albertson's.
>
> We would like to hear from you especially if you have been denied any of the following: training, full-time status, additional hours, favorable job assignments, night crew work, or promotion to any managerial positions . . . . If you have information regarding such discrimination, please fill out and return the enclosed questionnaire or call us at 1-800-568-7441. There will be no charge for consulting with us.
>
> We would also like to hear from you if an Albertson's attorney or representative has contacted you about your discrimination claims. We advise you that you do not

---

50. *Id.* at 335–36.
51. *Id.* at 336.
52. *Id.*
53. *Id.* at 336–37.
54. 1993 WL 150300 (N.D. Cal. Mar. 31, 1993).

have to talk to Albertson's attorneys or other representative about your claims of discrimination. Albertson's may attempt to use your statements against you in this lawsuit. IT IS ILLEGAL FOR ALBERTSON'S TO RETALIATE AGAINST YOU.[55]

The letter was accompanied by an "intake form" requesting that recipients provide their name, Social Security number, sex, race, date of hire, first position held, subsequent positions held, and similar information.[56]

The defendant challenged the letter as misleading and deceptive, particularly with respect to the court's role in the mass mailing, the status of the lawsuit, and the nature of the claims involved. In addition, the California district court noted that the letter was not objective or neutral in tone, did not state that the purpose of the letter was to gather information necessary to obtain class certification, and did not inform the recipients that no response was required. Notwithstanding these concerns, the court held as an initial matter that there was no requirement that the communication be objective. The court distinguished the letter from class certification notices sent in accordance with 23(c)(2), which must present the case as objectively as possible in order to satisfy due process concerns.[57] The court dismissed the holding in *Hoffman* as irrelevant because it did not involve a Rule 23 lawsuit, and the court apparently disregarded the *Hoffman* court's express reliance on *Gulf Oil*'s Rule 23 analysis. The court concluded that although the plaintiffs' statements were "slanted," they did not constitute factual misrepresentations and, therefore, should not be restricted. However, the court did find that potential class members could possibly believe that the class had already been certified or that they needed to respond to the letter and, therefore, corrective notice would have been appropriate but for the passage of time since the letter was mailed.[58]

In both *Rossini* and *Hoffman*, the key consideration was that the party seeking to restrict communications was able to establish the potential for abuse. While the record in *Rossini* is somewhat unclear, the *Hoffman* case illuminates some types of risks that must be proven before a court will prohibit communication or regulate its content. In the absence of such a showing, courts properly deny attempts to restrain communications. For example, in *Sunbird Air Services, Inc. v. Beech Aircraft Corp.*,[59] the court denied the defendants' motion to require advance review of communications by plaintiffs with potential class members because of the dearth of evidence indicating the likelihood of misleading communications. The sole reason proffered by the defendants in support of their motion was that "without such an opportunity to review communications before mailing, [defendant] could only learn of

---

55. *Id.* at *2.
56. *Id.*
57. *Id.* at *4.
58. *Id.* at *8.
59. 1990 WL 252131 (D. Kan. Oct. 30, 1990).

objectionable or improper communications after they were disseminated."[60] The court dismissed this argument as insufficient to justify restrictions on speech and found defendants' allegations—that misrepresentations were likely—to be speculative and unsupported in the record. Accordingly, the defendants' motion was denied.[61]

2. Precertification Communications with Class Members

In addition to the limits placed on communications by Rule 23, at the outset of class litigation, class counsel is immediately faced with the task of assembling a sufficient number of interested parties to support certification without running afoul of ethical rules that prohibit solicitation. Communications by nonlawyers with actual or potential class members are not subject to any ethical restrictions.[62] Thus, some of the organizational activities can be delegated to the lead plaintiffs. However, for obvious reasons, this may be an ineffective and inefficient method of communicating with potential class members and informing them of the possibility of class litigation. Accordingly, class counsel must carefully navigate among the applicable ethical and disciplinary rules, state regulation of barratry and similar activities, and the limits of commercial speech protections.

Virtually every state imposes restrictions on lawyers' abilities to solicit clients.[63] Notwithstanding the frequently onerous language of ethical rules, the Supreme Court held in 1977 that lawyer advertising and solicitation are protected forms of commercial speech.[64] In the decades following this decision, the courts have gradually and consistently expanded First Amendment commercial speech rights for lawyers.[65] However, in *Went For It, Inc. v. Florida Bar*,[66] the Court held for the first time that the state may restrict truthful, nondeceptive advertising. While the impact of *Went For It* on state regulation of client solicitation is beyond the scope of this chapter, it is clear that state regulation of client solicitation is a serious consideration for all class counsel seeking to communicate with class members before the class is certified.

Of course, "disciplinary rules governing the legal profession cannot punish activity protected by the First Amendment, and . . . the First Amendment protection survives even when the lawyer violates a disciplinary rule he swore to obey when

---

60. *Id.* at *2.

61. *Id.* at *2–3.

62. *See* 5 NEWBERG, *supra* note 13, § 15:6.

63. *See Zauderer v. Office of Disciplinary Counsel*, 471 U.S. 626, 674 (1985) (noting that "[a]lmost every State restricts an attorney's ability to accept employment resulting from unsolicited legal advice" (O'Connor, J., concurring in part and dissenting in part)).

64. *Bates v. State Bar of Ariz.*, 433 U.S. 350, 363 (1977).

65. *E.g.*, *Shapero v. Ky. Bar Ass'n*, 486 U.S. 466 (1988); *In re RMJ*, 455 U.S. 191 (1982).

66. 515 U.S. 618 (1995).

admitted to the practice of law."[67] Yet these words may prove cold comfort when a lawyer must evaluate whether to engage in a communication that may be protected by the First Amendment but may violate state law or disciplinary rules. Courts have resolved this issue by distinguishing between communications that constitute solicitation and those that merely provide notice. For example, in *Goerke v. Commercial Contractors & Supply Co.*,[68] the court responded to the plaintiff's fears in this regard by noting that "plaintiff need only make certain that any communications in which he engages are directed toward the provision of notice, rather than toward active solicitation of individuals to join in the present litigation."[69]

3. Postcertification Communications with the Class

Gulf Oil's reasoning applies equally to restrictions imposed on plaintiffs' counsel postcertification. For example, in *Domingo v. New England Fish Co.*,[70] the Ninth Circuit reviewed communication restrictions imposed by the trial court on the named plaintiffs and their counsel after the court had certified a class and determined that the employer had discriminated against the class. At that point in the litigation, only the damages phase remained. The trial court, without making any of the specific findings required by *Gulf Oil*, prohibited the plaintiffs' counsel from privately interviewing back-pay claimants, limited the ability of plaintiffs and counsel to assist class members in filing claims, and refused to identify plaintiffs' counsel in the notice to class members.[71]

On appeal, the Ninth Circuit vacated the prohibitive order primarily because the trial court failed to make the specific factual findings required by *Gulf Oil*. The court rejected the defendant's argument that *Gulf Oil* was inapplicable because *Gulf Oil* involved a precertification restriction. The court explained:

> The abuses at which communications restrictions are aimed arise from the fact that the class representative and his counsel may have interests that are in conflict with those of the class members. . . . It is hard to identify any conflict of interest that might have existed between plaintiffs' counsel and class members during the time at issue here. [Defendant's] liability had already been determined. Because the class had already been certified, class members who did not present their claims would be barred by res judicata from ever obtaining relief. Class members' only interest was in presenting their claims to the court in the best possible light. Plaintiffs' counsel, whatever their motives, had the same interest.[72]

---

67. *Gentile v. State Bar of Nev.*, 501 U.S. 1030, 1054 (1991).

68. 600 F. Supp. 1155, 1161 (N.D. Ga. 1984).

69. *See also Dolan v. Project Constr. Corp.*, 725 F.2d 1263, 1268 (10th Cir. 1984); *Hoffman-La Roche, Inc. v. Sperling*, 493 U.S. 165 (1989).

70. 727 F.2d 1429 (9th Cir.), *modified on other grounds*, 742 F.2d 520 (9th Cir. 1984).

71. *Domingo*, 727 F.2d at 1439.

72. *Id.* at 1441.

D. COMMUNICATIONS BY THE PARTY OPPOSING THE CLASS

1. Before Litigation

Prospective defendants are free to communicate with potential class members until the class action has actually been filed. Because Rule 23(e), which requires court approval of class action settlements, is inapplicable, the defendant may attempt to settle grievances and obtain releases of liability from potential class members before class claims are asserted in court.[73] Moreover, the defendant is always entitled to communicate with potential class members in the ordinary course of business.

The Ninth Circuit has extended protection to class action defendants who sent pre-suit settlement demand letters.[74] In *Sosa v. DIRECTV*, DIRECTV, upon learning of widespread signal theft, initiated suit against certain vendors selling the equipment necessary to "unscramble" the DIRECTV signal and thereby allow users to gain unauthorized access.[75] In the course of that lawsuit, DIRECTV obtained lists of names and addresses of individuals who had purchased the unscrambling equipment.[76] The letters demanded return of the equipment and payment of an undisclosed settlement sum to DIRECTV.[77] Some of the allegedly "innocent" recipients of this letter, rather than hire a lawyer to defend them against DIRECTV, paid DIRECTV thousands of dollars in settlement.[78] These innocent recipients formed the *Sosa* class, alleging that the demand letters constituted a violation of the federal anti-racketeering statute.[79] The Ninth Circuit held that restrictions on pre-suit demand letters may impair the right of access to the courts protected by the First Amendment and that to impose RICO treble damages on the recipient of such letters would raise substantial First Amendment problems.[80] The appeals court affirmed the decision to dismiss Sosa's class action for failure to state a claim.[81] The court also noted in dicta that pre-suit settlement demands are typical and efficient;[82] that many states protect such prelitigation communica-

---

73. *See Weight Watchers of Phila., Inc. v. Weight Watchers Int'l, Inc.*, 455 F.2d 770, 773 (2d Cir. 1972) ("[W]e are unable to perceive any legal theory that would endow a plaintiff who has brought what would have been a 'spurious' class action under former Rule 23 with a right to prevent negotiation of settlements between the defendant and other potential members of the class who are of a mind to do this; it is only the settlement of the class action itself without court approval that [Rule] 23(e) prohibits.").

74. *Sosa v. DIRECTV, Inc.*, 437 F.3d 923, 932–33 (9th Cir. 2006).

75. *Id.* at 926.

76. *Id.*

77. *Id.*

78. *Id.*

79. *Id.* at 927.

80. *Id.* at 936.

81. *Id.* at 942.

82. *Id.* at 936.

tions by statute;[83] and that the same reasoning had been adopted by the majority of other circuits.[84]

2. Before Class Certification

As a general rule, defendants are free to communicate with absent class members in the "ordinary course of business" so long as the court does not have in place a local rule or standing order prohibiting such communications. Several courts have held that before certification, ethical rules prohibiting communications with represented parties do not apply.[85] Nonetheless, defendants should ensure that communications, even at this stage, do not interfere with what has been termed "an incipient fiduciary relationship between class counsel and the class he or she is seeking to represent."[86]

Before certification, the collection of putative-class-member declarations may be acceptable. In *Kerce v. West Telemarketing Corp.*, a district court declined to strike employee declarations, finding that "there is nothing improper about [an employer] gathering facts to support its defense."[87] However, in collecting such declarations, defense counsel should not "engage[ ] in conduct that would reasonably be expected to mislead and deceive the prospective plaintiffs concerning the nature, purposes and implications of their participation in the declaration process."[88] Additionally, in cases where the defendant and the class member enjoy a past or potential future employment relationship, the risk is high that the communication will have a coercive effect.[89]

3. Solicitation of Exclusions and Individual Settlements

Although there may be circumstances where defendants are free to communicate with class members before class certification, the court will carefully scrutinize any conduct that reasonably appears aimed at soliciting opt-outs from the litigation. This applies whether the contact is made before class certification or after

---

83. *Id.* (citing CAL. CIV. CODE § 47(b)).

84. *Id.* at 937 (citing *Primetime 24 Joint Venture v. Nat'l Broad. Co.*, 219 F.3d 92, 100 (2d Cir. 2000); *Glass Equip. Dev., Inc. v. Besten, Inc.*, 174 F.3d 1337, 1343–44 (Fed. Cir. 1999); *McGuire Oil Co. v. Mapco, Inc.*, 958 F.2d 1552, 1560 (11th Cir. 1992); *CVD, Inc. v. Raytheon Co.*, 769 F.2d 842, 850–51 (1st Cir. 1985); *Coastal States Mktg., Inc. v. Hunt*, 694 F.2d 1358, 1367–68 (5th Cir. 1983)).

85. *Cada v. Costa Line, Inc.*, 93 F.R.D. 95, 98 (N.D. Ill. 1981); *see also Longcrier*, 595 F. Supp. 2d at 1226. *But see Dondore v. NGK Metals Corp.*, 152 F. Supp. 2d 662, 665 (E.D. Pa. 2001) (holding the "mere initiation of a class action" prohibits defense counsel from contacting or interviewing potential class members).

86. *Knuth v. Erie-Crawford Dairy Coop. Ass'n*, 463 F.2d 470 (3d Cir. 1972); *see also* 5 NEWBERG, *supra* note 13, § 15:14, at 55. *But cf. Weight Watchers of Phila., Inc.*, 455 F.2d at 773.

87. 575 F. Supp. 2d 1354, 1366 (S.D. Ga. 2008).

88. *Longcrier*, 595 F. Supp. 2d at 1227 (striking 245 declarations from putative class members where the defense lawyers had misled the potential plaintiffs into thinking the declarations were "surveys," while the data being collected might in reality compromise or waive the declarants' right to participate in the class action suit).

89. *Ojieda-Sanchez v. Bland Farms*, 600 F. Supp. 2d 1373, 1379–80 (S.D. Ga. 2009).

certification, but before the conclusion of the opt-out period. Similarly, attempts by a defendant to obtain settlements, releases, or affidavits of no interest will also be closely examined and perhaps even denied effect if later challenged.

The leading case addressing the propriety of communications between opposing counsel and class members is *Kleiner v. First National Bank of Atlanta*.[90] *Kleiner* was a class action filed by borrowers challenging a bank's lending practices. Most of the class members had ongoing relationships with the bank, and some were dependent on the bank for future financing. In response to the litigation, the defendant's loan officers initiated an active campaign of soliciting class members to opt out of the class. The campaign was highly successful, which the court viewed as indicative of the coercive nature of the defendant's actions. The trial court ruled that the opt-out requests were voidable and imposed sanctions on the defendant and its counsel.[91]

On appeal, the Eleventh Circuit affirmed the district court's order with the exception of the order disqualifying the bank's in-house counsel. The court relied on both Rule 23 guidelines as set forth in *Gulf Oil* and free-speech principles. The court held that the trial court had discretion under Rule 23 to prohibit the bank's efforts to encourage opt-outs and noted that the defendant's contacts with class members raised particularly noteworthy problems of class action management. Specifically, the court opined that it was essential that the class members receive accurate and impartial information regarding the status, purposes, and effects of the lawsuit and that "[u]nsupervised, unilateral communications with the plaintiff class sabotage the goal of informed consent by urging exclusion on the basis of a one-sided presentation of the facts, without opportunity for rebuttal."[92] The court noted that the defendant's interest in communicating with the plaintiffs was not to facilitate informed consent or to provide valuable information, but rather to minimize the defendant's liability by making the class as small as possible. This was especially problematic in light of the ongoing financial relationship between the defendant and the plaintiffs and the inherently coercive nature of that relationship.

The court rejected the bank's argument that its overtures to class members were protected First Amendment speech. The court assumed that the defendant's speech was protected under the First Amendment, but only to the limited extent afforded commercial speech. Notwithstanding this limited protection, an order limiting communications is permissible where it is well-grounded and issued with

---

90. 102 F.R.D. 754 (N.D. Ga. 1983), *aff'd as modified*, 751 F.2d 1193 (11th Cir. 1985); *Cobell v. Norton*, 212 F.R.D. 14, 20–21 (D.D.C. 2002) (applying *Kleiner* and issuing restrictive order, holding that defendants' mailing of statements of account to individual class members that had the effect of extinguishing the rights of those class members without first seeking court approval was improper).

91. *Kleiner*, 102 F.R.D. at 775–76.

92. *Kleiner*, 751 F.2d at 1203.

a heightened sensitivity toward free-speech concerns.[93] In light of these principles, the court held that the trial court's order did not violate the First Amendment because the harm was great, the order was narrowly drawn to avoid suppressing speech unnecessarily, less onerous alternatives were not available, and the order was of short duration.[94] However, more than just the potential for abuse is required to support the issuance of a protective order under *Gulf Oil*.[95]

Similar attempts by defendants to encourage class members to opt out of the litigation have been consistently criticized by the courts. In *Hampton Hardware, Inc. v. Cotter & Co.*,[96] for example, a customer-owned wholesaler of hardware was sued by a class of its customers. Shortly after the lawsuit was filed and before a class was certified, the defendant sent three letters urging the potential class members not to participate in the lawsuit. For example, one of the letters stated:

> While we believe that Cotter will win this case for many reasons, it is important that you understand the enormous potential cost to your Company due to this class action. Your team in Chicago will spend thousands of hours on this lawsuit, pulling old documents, reconstructing records, traveling to Dallas and explaining the service charge policy and how your Company operates. . . . What can you do to avoid this waste of time and money? Decide not to participate in this lawsuit. Under the law you may be given the opportunity to join the class. By refusing to join the class, you save your Company time and expenses which ultimately will be returned to you in the form of your patronage dividend.[97]

The other two letters were similar in content and tone.

As a threshold matter, the court quickly concluded that the letters were precisely the type of misleading communications that warranted court intervention.[98] The court noted that "[t]he fact that the defendant and potential class members are involved in an on-going business relationship further underscores the potential for coercion."[99] In addition, given that the obvious purpose of the letters was to reduce participation in the lawsuit, the court concluded that the communications undermined the policies expressed in Rule 23 in favor of resolving such disputes in a single lawsuit.[100] Based on its conclusion that the defendant had improperly communicated with the prospective class, the court entered an order prohibiting

---

93. *Id.* at 1205.

94. *Id.* at 1206–07.

95. *Basco v. Wal-Mart Stores, Inc.*, No. CIV.A.00-3814, 2002 WL 272384, at *3–4 (E.D. La. Feb. 25, 2002) (holding that a court cannot issue an order without evidence that a potential for serious abuse exists); MANUAL FOR COMPLEX LITIGATION (FOURTH) § 21.12, at 321 (2004).

96. 156 F.R.D. 630 (N.D. Tex. 1994).

97. *Id.* at 631.

98. *Id.* at 632.

99. *Id.* at 633 (citing *Kleiner*, 751 F.2d at 1202).

100. *Id.*

the defendant and its lawyers from contacting the potential class "in any manner with regard to the instant litigation."[101]

The court faced a somewhat different scenario in *In re Potash Antitrust Litigation*.[102] There, a defendant in a class action sent a letter to class members who were also its customers shortly after the notice of class certification was disseminated. The letter urged the customers to read the notice carefully and to consult with their own lawyer or class counsel. The letter expressed the defendant's inability, under the law, to influence its customers' opt-out decisions.[103] The plaintiffs complained that the letter was an attempt to solicit opt-outs and violated the ethical prohibition on communicating with represented parties.[104] The court disagreed. Specifically, the court stated that the letter "was not a covert expression, nor was it coercive, abusive or fundamentally misleading."[105] The court did hold, however, that by commenting on the merits, the defendant "pushes the envelope of proper comment."[106] Moreover, the intent of Rule 23, to provide the class with the "best notice practicable," would be frustrated if, following issuance of the certification notice, the parties were at liberty to freely comment on the merits of the suit.[107] Yet despite the court's concern with the impact of the letters, it refused to issue a gag order and instead required that the defendants file with the court, for in camera inspection, all written communications with the class.[108] Notably, the court failed to address the merits of the plaintiffs' claim that the letter was a violation of the prohibition on communications with represented parties.

At least two courts have held that communications by defendants with prospective class members do not constitute improper misrepresentations where the communication merely omits certain facts rather than affirmatively misrepresents facts. For example, in *O'Neil v. Appel*,[109] the defendant corporation sent a letter to its shareholders in which it discussed a shareholder class action recently filed against the company. The letter implied that because of the lawsuit, the company— which was in bankruptcy proceedings at the time—would be unable to obtain crucial financing and would "in all likelihood liquidate."[110] The court held that

---

101. *Id.* at 635.
102. 896 F. Supp. 996 (D. Minn. 1995).
103. *Id.* at 919.
104. *Id.*
105. *Id.* at 920.
106. *Id.*
107. *Id.*
108. *Id.* at 921.
109. 1:94-CV-97, 1995 WL 351371 (W.D. Mich. Mar. 21, 1995).
110. *Id.* at *1.

although the letter did not provide a complete picture of the company's financial health, these omissions did not make the letter misleading.[111]

4. After Class Certification

Once a class is certified, class counsel is deemed to have an attorney-client relationship with each class member. Accordingly, communications by the opposing party are governed by the applicable ethical rules, which invariably require that such communications go through class counsel. In addition to these limitations, courts typically give greater scrutiny to communications with class members by opposing counsel than they do to communications by class counsel. Most courts agree that the restrictions placed by *Gulf Oil* on courts' ability to regulate communications apply in the context of defense communications, as well as communications by class counsel.[112] Nonetheless, defendants should carefully evaluate any proposed communications with class members to ensure that such communications will withstand court scrutiny.

In *In re School Asbestos Litigation*,[113] the Third Circuit addressed the propriety of the trial court's order restricting a captive association's communication with class members. During the course of the class action, an association that included the class action defendants as members distributed a booklet entitled "What You Should Know about Asbestos in Buildings" to school officials, state and federal officials, and building owners.[114] Many, but not all, of the recipients were class members. The trial judge entered an order requiring that in all communications relating to asbestos in school buildings, the association disclose its affiliation with the defendant manufacturers and its involvement in the litigation. The Third Circuit vacated the order. While affirming the lower court's power to limit the association's direct communications with members of the plaintiff class, the appellate court held that the order as written exceeded the court's authority because it applied to all public communications by the association regardless of whether the communications targeted class members.[115]

Some courts have restricted communications between parties opposing the class and the class members on the sole basis that such communications created or had the potential to create ethical conflicts. In *Gulf Oil*, the Court recognized that "the rules of ethics properly impose restraints on some forms of expression."[116]

---

111. *Id.* at *2; *see also Cohen v. Apache Corp.*, No. 89-CV-0076 (PNL), 1991 WL 1017 (S.D.N.Y. 1991) (holding that omissions in a defendant's communication with shareholder class members did not constitute misrepresentations of material fact).

112. *E.g., Kleiner,* 751 F.2d at 1203.

113. 842 F.2d 671 (3d Cir. 1988).

114. *Id.* at 675.

115. *Id.* at 683.

116. 452 U.S. at 104 n.21 (citing Model Code of Professional Responsibility DR 7-104 (1980)).

Accordingly, in *Tedesco v. Mishkin*,[117] the court held that a communication by a defendant, sent under a codefendant's signature and containing statements that were "materially false and misleading in several respects," violated Model Code of Professional Responsibility Rule 7-104. The court permitted the plaintiff to send out a letter correcting misrepresentations made in the defendant's letter and enjoined the defendant from further communicating with class members concerning the lawsuit. The court recognized that free-speech concerns are implicated when communications are prohibited, but stressed that in this particular case the prohibition was justified by the likelihood of serious abuses.[118]

Similarly, in *Haffer v. Temple University*,[119] the court concluded that certain statements by the defendant's employees violated Rule 7-104 and held that under Rule 23, such statements could be prohibited and corrective notices issued. *Haffer* was a class action brought under Title IX in which the plaintiffs charged that Temple unlawfully deterred women from participating in the school's intercollegiate athletics program. During the course of litigation, class counsel began meeting with class members to discuss the lawsuit. While these meetings were being scheduled, a lawyer for the university and a university employee who was also a named defendant developed and disseminated a memorandum to the student athletes that had the effect of discouraging them from speaking with class counsel.[120] The court found that the letter, in addition to containing numerous misrepresentations, violated the ethical prohibition on contact with represented individuals.[121]

The court in *Resnick v. American Dental Association*[122] likewise concluded that communications between the defendant and class members were barred under the Code of Professional Responsibility. In *Resnick*, the plaintiffs sought a protective order prohibiting the defendant from any communications with class members regarding the litigation. The court rejected the defendant's argument that *Gulf Oil* prohibits such an order absent a clear showing of abuse. The court stated that the principles set forth in *Gulf Oil* "obviously do not apply to protect communications to class members by opposing counsel."[123]

E. COMMUNICATIONS BY THIRD PARTIES

Third parties often seek to communicate with potential or actual class members. In the typical situation, the third party, either an individual who opted out of the suit or a lawyer representing opt-out plaintiffs, communicates with class members

---

117. 629 F. Supp. 1474 (S.D.N.Y. 1986).
118. *Id.* at 1484 (citing *Gulf Oil*, 452 U.S. at 104 n.21).
119. 115 F.R.D. 506 (E.D. Pa. 1987).
120. *Id.* at 509.
121. *Id.* at 511.
122. 95 F.R.D. 372 (N.D. Ill. 1982).
123. *Id.* at 376.

in an attempt to solicit opt-outs from the class action. As with defendants who encourage exclusion from the class, this conduct has serious implications for the integrity of the class action process and raises difficult questions with respect to the extent to which courts can regulate the conduct of these third parties.

For example, in *Georgine v. Amchem Products Inc.*,[124] the plaintiffs filed a class action complaint seeking damages resulting from asbestos exposure contemporaneously with a motion for class certification and to approve a settlement agreement.[125] Shortly thereafter, the court certified an opt-out class and eventually approved settlement of the matter. After approval, the court authorized notice to the class that contained a provision for opting out of the settlement. In response, the court received 236,323 requests for exclusion, less than 5 percent of which were made on the opt-out form provided with the notice.[126]

After the opt-out period closed, the parties filed a joint motion requesting that the court establish a second notice and opt-out period for class members who had requested exclusion from the settlement. According to the movants, this drastic remedy was needed to "remedy the adverse effects of an allegedly massive campaign, launched by lawyers who oppose the settlement, to solicit opt-outs through purportedly misleading mass mailings and advertisements targeted to absent class members."[127] The particular action sought was the creation of a second notice and opt-out period and the issuance of an injunction requiring any notices from the third-party lawyers to contain a "Disclosure Statement." The court granted the first request and denied the second.[128]

In reviewing the notices and letters mailed and published by the third-party lawyers, the court identified two primary concerns with the documents. First, they contained false or misleading statements about the class members' prospects of receiving compensation. Second, they failed to disclose that the authors and senders of the letters had a "strong pecuniary interest" in soliciting the opt-out.[129] Accordingly, the court concluded that these "unilateral communications with class members by various lawyers were misleading and made it unlikely that class members who received these communications or were informed of their contents made an informed choice to exclude themselves from the class."[130]

The court faced a similar dilemma in *Superior Beverage Co. v. Owens-Illinois, Inc.*[131] The class representatives in that case sought an order barring communication

---

124. 160 F.R.D. 478 (E.D. Pa. 1995).
125. *Id.* at 486.
126. *Id.*
127. *Id.* at 489.
128. *Id.* at 490–94.
129. *Id.* at 490.
130. *Id.*
131. No. 83 C 512, 1988 WL 87038 (N.D. Ill. Aug. 16, 1988).

with unnamed class members by individual plaintiffs who had opted out of the class action and filed separate lawsuits. Specifically, the class representatives sought to prohibit these individual plaintiffs and their counsel from soliciting class members to opt out, soliciting legal representation of class members, and soliciting fees and expenses from those members. The class representatives additionally sought to bar all communication with class members without prior court approval.[132] The court agreed that under Rule 23(d) it had substantial discretion to regulate the conduct of parties and their counsel. It noted that such an order might be necessary to prohibit counsel from communicating with adverse parties. However, there was no indication that the interests of the unnamed class members were adverse to the interests of the individual plaintiffs. Moreover, the unnamed class members were sophisticated businesses that were capable of protecting their own interests. Accordingly, the court held that a protective order barring such communications was unnecessary.[133]

F. REMEDIES

Courts have considerable authority under Rule 23(d)(2) to require corrective notices or to enter other curative orders as the court deems necessary to remedy improper communications.[134] As noted above at part II.A., before *Gulf Oil*, courts prevented abusive conduct by the parties by instituting prior restraints on communications, whether by local rule, standing order, or specific orders issued at the outset of the class action. However, after *Gulf Oil*, such anticipatory prohibitions are, for the most part, no longer employed. As a consequence, courts frequently find themselves in the difficult position of attempting to remedy misconduct after it occurs and after it has had an undesirable effect on the class.

In virtually every case in which a court has concluded that a party—whether it be class counsel, the named plaintiffs, defendants, or defense counsel—communicated improperly with the class, the court has entered an order prohibiting or limiting such communications in the future.[135]

---

132. *Id.* at *1.

133. *Id.* at *2.

134. *See, e.g., Jackson*, 2009 U.S. Dist. LEXIS 23325, at *6–7 (noting that a party seeking authorization for corrective notice must show that the communication was "in some way coercive, misleading, or improper").

135. *See, e.g., Romano v. SLS Residential, Inc.*, 253 F.R.D. 292 (S.D.N.Y. 2008) (ordering a corrective notice when defendants—against their counsel's advice—contacted plaintiffs directly and disseminated false information about the suit); *Cobell*, 212 F.R.D. at 20–21 (prohibiting defendants from contacting any class members without prior court authorization); *In re Potash Antitrust Litig.*, 896 F. Supp. at 921 (requiring defendants to submit to the court and plaintiffs copies of proposed communications with class members); *Hampton Hardware*, 156 F.R.D. at 635 (prohibiting all communication by defendant with class members regarding litigation); *Resnick*, 95 F.R.D. at 376–77 (same).

Increasingly, however, courts are being more creative and more aggressive in their efforts to remedy what they perceive to be the harmful effects of the improper communication.[136] Recently, a district court excluded information gained in violation of the attorney-client relationship and ordered the disqualification and replacement of counsel.[137] In addition to standard orders limiting or prohibiting communications, the remedial orders most frequently used by courts are corrective notices, voiding of opt-outs, and contempt. Of these three, corrective notices are by far the most common.

1. Standard for Remedial Orders

Remedial orders issued under Rule 23(d) do not require a finding of actual harm. Rather, all that is required is a showing of a "likelihood of serious abuses."[138] However, this finding must be based on a clear record and specific findings.[139] In light of this requirement, it is advisable that the court hold an evidentiary hearing. At a minimum, the court will have to consider documentary evidence and affidavits submitted by the parties.[140] In addition, should the court conclude that a remedy is warranted, it should impose the minimum remedy necessary to correct the effects of the improper conduct.[141]

2. Corrective Notice

Corrective notice is generally considered the appropriate remedy when a party is found to have engaged in coercive communications aimed at influencing class members' decision to participate in the litigation. Corrective notice was ordered in *Shores v. Publix Super Markets, Inc.*[142] to remedy the effects of communications that the court viewed as "intended to discourage class members from participation in the lawsuit." *Shores* involved a class certified under 23(b)(2) alleging that Publix engaged in a pattern and practice of discrimination against women. The class consisted of all female employees in Florida and South Carolina who were employed by Publix during a specified time period. The court was primarily concerned with internal communications distributed by Publix to its employees at the workplace,

---

136. *See Jackson*, 2009 U.S. Dist. LEXIS 23325, at *6; *Ralph Oldsmobile, Inc. v. Gen. Motors Corp.*, No. 99 Civ. 4567, 2001 WL 1035132, at *7 (S.D.N.Y. 2001) (ordering curative notices be sent at the expense of party at fault); *Hammond v. City of Junction City*, 167 F. Supp. 2d 1271, 1293 (D. Kan. 2001) (ordering party at fault to pay lawyers' fees and costs incurred by opposing party to file protective orders); *In re McKesson HBOC, Inc. Sec. Litig.*, 126 F. Supp. 2d 1239, 1247 (N.D. Cal. 2000) (ordering printing and mailing costs of curative notice to be paid by party at fault).

137. *See Hammond*, 167 F. Supp. 2d at 1293 (excluding evidence gained from improper communications and disqualifying plaintiffs' counsel and their firm because of improper communications).

138. *In re Sch. Asbestos Litig.*, 842 F.2d at 683 (citing *Gulf Oil*, 452 U.S. at 104).

139. *Gulf Oil*, 452 U.S. at 104.

140. *See In re Sch. Asbestos Litig.*, 842 F.2d at 681.

141. *Coles*, 560 F.2d at 189; *Georgine*, 160 F.R.D. at 502.

142. 69 Empl. Prac. Dec. ¶ 44,478, 1996 WL 859985 (M.D. Fla. Nov. 25, 1996).

including a monthly newsletter, an electronic mail publication, and a video. In one video, the director of media relations for Publix stated:

> Even if Publix is found liable in court, which we believe is unlikely, each member of the class will still have to prove the merits of her case on an individual basis to receive any payment. In a case represented by the same attorneys against Safeway Stores class members averaged $250 each before taxes, while their lawyers collected 2.5 million dollars.[143]

Another Publix publication quoted its lawyer as stating that "the law requires individual 'mini-trials' for each class member seeking damages . . . [which] could clog the courts for years."[144]

The court was concerned that since this information had been provided to the employees at the workplace, there was little opportunity for them to objectively analyze its content. Furthermore, the communications were disseminated by the very managers accused of discrimination. The court concluded that Publix's statements "clearly imply that it would be futile, and possibly detrimental to participate in the class. Under these circumstances, the likely coercive [effect] on class members is great."[145] To remedy the allegedly harmful effects of Publix's communications, the court directed Publix to disseminate a curative notice and to refrain from direct communications with class members about the litigation except managerial class members where necessary to discuss acts and omissions for which Publix could be liable.

The notice directed by the court was presented in a question-and-answer format that consisted of following questions:

1. Who is a member of the class?
2. What is the lawsuit about?
3. What are plaintiffs asking for?
4. How will the case proceed?
5. What do I have to do?
6. What is the Union's role in this lawsuit[?]
7. What about the things I hear at work?
8. Which lawyers am I supposed to talk to?
9. What happens if I already signed something for Publix?
10. Where can I get more information? [and]
11. How will this affect my job?[146]

Publix was required to post the notice in every store next to the time clock as well as in employee lounges, attach a copy to every paycheck, send a copy to

---

143. *Id.* at *2.
144. *Id.*
145. *Id.* at *3.
146. *Id.* at *5–7.

the last known address of former employees, and include a copy in the monthly newsletter.[147]

Several other courts have ordered corrective notice under similar circumstances.[148] Notably, at least one court has held that despite the impropriety of a defendant's contacts with class members, corrective notice was unnecessary because the notice of class certification had yet to be issued. In *Hampton Hardware*,[149] the defendant impermissibly sought to influence the class members' view of the litigation, but did so before the court certified the class. The court entered an order restricting future communications, but refused to require distribution of a corrective notice. The court noted that there was little evidence of actual harm from the defendant's letter and, therefore, any notice would be premature and potentially confusing.[150] Further, the court reasoned that, in the event a class was certified, the court-approved notice to class members would be sufficient to provide the requisite objective information regarding the class action.[151]

3. Opt-Out Nullification

Another type of remedy employed by courts attempting to ameliorate the effects of improper contacts with class members is the voiding of opt-outs. Or, as the *Georgine* court stated in ordering this remedy, "I will restore to the members who originally filed timely exclusion requests the opportunity to make a new independent decision to opt out of the class."[152] That court determined that plaintiffs' lawyers who were not participating in the class action materially impacted class members' opt-out decisions through an aggressive publicity campaign disparaging the proposed settlement. To remedy the effects of this campaign, the court voided all previously filed opt-outs and ordered a curative notice sent to all class members who had opted out.[153] The court further ordered that the notice to be mailed to these individuals should contain a statement describing the reasons for the new opt-out period. The court rejected arguments by the third-party lawyers against invalidation of the opt-out requests of individuals whose opt-outs were submitted on court-approved notices or those who opted out on the advice of counsel. The court opined that because it was impossible to determine the precise reason why

---

147. *Id.*

148. *E.g., Haffer*, 115 F.R.D. at 512 (directing defendant to issue curative notice based on the finding that defendant had impeded class counsel's ability to communicate with class members); *Tedesco*, 629 F. Supp. at 1484–85 (corrective notice ordered after defendant improperly communicated with class members); *Impervious Paint Indus., Inc. v. Ashland Oil*, 508 F. Supp. 720, 723 (W.D. Ky. 1981) (same), *appeal dismissed without opinion*, 659 F.2d 1081 (6th Cir. 1981).

149. 156 F.R.D. at 635.

150. *Id. But see Ralph Oldsmobile*, WL 1035132, at *7 (ordering curative notice for improper precertification communications).

151. *Hampton Hardware*, 156 F.R.D. at 635.

152. 160 F.R.D. at 502.

153. *Id.* at 501.

any particular class member chose to be excluded, and because the notice process had been so "broadly subverted," it was a necessary caution that each and every class member be given the chance to "reaffirm her decision to opt out . . . ."[154]

Several other courts have likewise found nullification of opt-outs to be the only effective means to remedy improper contacts with class members. In *Kleiner*, for example, after concluding that the defendants' opt-out campaign had been successful, the court ruled that the opt-outs were voidable.[155]

4. Contempt

In *In re Federal Skywalk Cases*,[156] the court held that defendants who made unauthorized contact with members of the class without notifying class counsel could be held in contempt. *Federal Skywalk* was a class action filed in federal court over the collapse of two skywalks at a hotel. At the same time, a class action was filed against the same defendants in state court concerning the same disaster. The defendants obtained state court approval of a tentative settlement. Immediately thereafter, the defendants disseminated the settlement notice to the state court class members and held a press conference discussing the settlement.[157] Many of the state court class members were also members of the federal suit who had not opted out of that action.[158] The federal court found that the defendants had attempted an "end-run" around the court's supervisory authority over the class action and, based on their improper conduct, held them in contempt of court.[159]

III. Communications "In the Ordinary Course of Business"

Courts routinely exclude from orders restricting or prohibiting communications with class members any communications made "in the ordinary course of business."[160] However, courts offer little guidance on precisely what types of communications qualify for this exception.

---

154. *Id.* at 503.

155. 102 F.R.D. at 775–76; *see also Impervious Paint Indus.*, 508 F. Supp. at 721–22, 724 (noting that "if these class members did, in fact, make a free and unfettered decision in choosing to withdraw, then they will do so again"); *In re Fed. Skywalk Cases*, 97 F.R.D. 370, 378 (W.D. Mo. 1983); *Sommers v. Abraham Lincoln Fed. Sav. & Loan Ass'n*, 79 F.R.D. 571, 577 n.4 (E.D. Pa. 1978).

156. 97 F.R.D. at 370.

157. *Id.* at 374–75.

158. *Id.* at 376.

159. *Id.* at 377, 379.

160. *E.g.*, *Babbitt v. Albertson's, Inc.*, No. C-92-1883 SBA (PJH), 1993 WL 128089, at *3 (N.D. Cal. Jan. 28, 1993); *Resnick*, 95 F.R.D. at 377; *see also* MANUAL FOR COMPLEX LITIGATION (FOURTH) § 21.33, at 391 (2004).

Contacts with class members regarding the class action are not considered "in the ordinary course of business."[161] Thus, as a practical matter, defendants and their lawyers may need to obtain authorization from either the court or class counsel to contact class members, including those needed for its defense.

It is important to note that defendants in corporate and securities class action litigation have the right to communicate with shareholders during the pendency of the lawsuit.[162] Typically, these communications are presented in annual and quarterly reports to stockholders.[163] However, communications in the form of letters sent directly to shareholders or printed in newspapers are also generally considered to be within the company's rights.[164]

IV. Conclusion

Class action litigation is pervaded by questions relating to the permissible scope and content of communications with class members. Class members rely on these communications, whether in the form of official notices from the court or unofficial contacts from the parties or their lawyers, to make informed choices about their participation in the litigation. Accordingly, courts have recognized the importance of communications in the class action litigation scheme and have aggressively sought to protect class members from any actual or perceived improprieties. Thus, parties seeking to communicate with class members may not rely solely on First Amendment protections and instead must be ready to defend any communications to class members against claims that they disseminated misleading information, violated ethical rules of conduct, or otherwise jeopardized the integrity of the class action.

---

161. *Bernard v. Gulf Oil Co.*, 596 F.2d 1249, 1262 (5th Cir. 1979), *aff'd in part, rev'd in part on other grounds*, 619 F.2d 459 (5th Cir. 1980) (en banc), *aff'd*, 452 U.S. 89 (1981).

162. *See generally* 5 NEWBERG, *supra* note 13, § 15:14, at 55.

163. *E.g., Cohen*, 1991 WL 1017, at *1.

164. *E.g., O'Neil*, 1995 WL 351371, at *1; 5 NEWBERG, *supra* note 13, § 15:14, at 55 & n.2 (citing a newspaper advertisement purchased by a defendant in a class action lawsuit and used to clarify management's position on the pending litigation).

Table 1: Quick Reference for Communication with a Class by Counsel

	By Class/Plaintiffs' Counsel	By Defense Counsel	By Third Parties
Pre-suit Communication	*Gulf Oil* applies; consult ethical and disciplinary rules.[165]	Rule 23 not applicable; prelitigation settlement demands.[166]	
Precertification Communication	*Gulf Oil* applies; consult ethical and disciplinary rules.[167]	Acceptable in the ordinary course of business and/or when not reasonably expected to mislead and deceive the prospective plaintiffs.[168]	Lead plaintiff's conduct not regulated.[169]
Postcertification Communication	*Gulf Oil* applies.[170]	Standard ethical rules and *Gulf Oil* apply.[171]	

---

165. *See* part II.C.1–2 *supra*.
166. *See* part II.D.1 *supra*.
167. *See* part II.C.1–2 *supra*.
168. *See* part II.D.2 *supra*.
169. *See* part II.C.2 *supra*.
170. *See* part II.C.3 *supra*.
171. *See* part II.D.4 *supra*.

CLASS DEFINITION

MADELEINE FISCHER

I. Introduction

An implicit requirement for class certification is that an identifiable class must exist.[1] The class definition provides the measuring stick against which other requirements of Rule 23 are evaluated. The Supreme Court has said that many of the explicit requirements of Rule 23 are designed to "protect absentees by blocking unwarranted or overbroad class definitions."[2] Thus, the class definition and the explicit requirements work in tandem: for example, a good definition may demonstrate numerosity and commonality and set the standard for typicality, while a poor definition may expose problems with these and other required elements. The Fifth Circuit has gone so far as to say that if the absence of an ascertainable class is facially apparent from the pleadings, a district court may dismiss the class allegation on the pleadings.[3]

The most significant function of a precise class definition is the protection of both absent putative class members and defendants. Judgment in a class action suit binds all parties including absent class members, whether the judgment favors the class or the defendants.[4] Because of this res judicata effect, a proper class definition should leave no doubt as to who is a class member and who is not. A proper definition identifies (1) who is entitled to relief; (2) who is bound by the judgment; and (3) who is entitled to notice in a Rule 23(b)(3) action.[5] Do not make the court

---

1. *Oshana v. Coca-Cola Co.*, 472 F.3d 506, 513 (7th Cir. 2006), *cert. denied*, 551 U.S. 1115 (2007).
2. *Amchem Prods., Inc. v. Windsor*, 521 U.S. 591, 620 (1997).
3. *John v. Nat'l Sec. Fire & Cas. Co.*, 501 F.3d 443, 445 (5th Cir. 2007).
4. *Dafforn v. Rousseau Assocs., Inc.*, No. 75-74, 1976 WL 1358, at *1 (N.D. Ind. July 27, 1976).
5. MANUAL FOR COMPLEX LITIGATION (FOURTH) § 21.222 (2004).

guess at the definition.[6] A precise definition that meets all requirements may save counsel from a rebuke such as the following:

> The Court rejects any suggestion that plaintiffs' Motion for Class Certification compels the undersigned to scrutinize the vast universe of all possible class definitions . . . to ascertain whether any of them might pass Rule 23 muster, then select the broadest one that satisfies all Rule 23 prerequisites. The Rule 23 inquiry is not an exercise in determining whether it is theoretically possible to construct a class definition as to which class certification might be justified. Plaintiffs have delineated a particular class definition in their Motion, and it is that singular definition that is being evaluated here.[7]

II. Ascertainability Requirement

The class definition requirement is often phrased in terms of ascertainability, i.e., does the class definition contain objective criteria by which to categorically identify class members?

In order to satisfy ascertainability, the class definition should not contain subjective criteria; it should not depend upon a determination of the merits; it should be administratively feasible; and it should not be overly broad so as to potentially include people who have not been injured by the defendant's conduct.

A. SUBJECTIVITY

A definition that incorporates the state of mind of class members is subjective and thus inadequate. For example, in *Zapka v. Coca-Cola Co.*,[8] the named plaintiff alleged that the Coca-Cola Corporation misrepresented that bottled Diet Coke and fountain Diet Coke contained the same ingredients, when in fact fountain Diet Coke contained saccharin. By drinking fountain Diet Coke, the named plaintiff unwittingly consumed saccharin, a nonnutritive sweetener she wanted to avoid because of fear over its health effects. She proposed the following class definition:

> All individuals who consumed Diet Coke from the fountain, deceived by the marketing practices employed by Coca-Cola Company into believing that fountain Diet Coke does not contain saccharin.

The district court held that the definition was inadequate because it was contingent on the state of mind of putative class members—each person would have to be examined as to what advertising they saw and whether they were deceived.

---

6. *Scaggs v. N.Y. State Dep't of Educ.*, No. 06-799, 2009 WL 890587, at *3 (E.D.N.Y. Mar. 31, 2009) ("The court agrees in principle with defendants' argument that neither they nor the court should have to guess at plaintiffs' intentions.").

7. *Fisher v. Ciba Specialty Chems. Corp.*, 238 F.R.D. 273, 300 (S.D. Ala. 2006).

8. No. 99-CV-8238, 2000 WL 1644539 (N.D. Ill. Oct. 27, 2000).

In *Wallace v. Chicago Housing Authority*,[9] current and former residents of public housing in Chicago brought suit against the Chicago Housing Authority contending that they were harmed by the Authority's discriminatory actions, policies, and practices. Plaintiffs proposed the creation of two subclasses:

1

Residents who left public housing with Housing Choice Vouchers before October 1, 1999 who subsequently moved on or after October 1, 1999 into segregated neighborhoods.

2

Residents who left public housing with Housing Choice Vouchers before October 1, 1999 who moved into segregated neighborhoods, *and* who have subsequently attempted to move on or after October 1, 1999, but who due to the Defendants' policies and practices, failed to make another move.

The district court found that the first subclass was sufficiently identified by objective criteria, namely, the dates of members' initial relocation from public housing, the dates of subsequent moves using vouchers, and the demographics of the neighborhoods into which they moved. However, the district court found that the second subclass contained an inherently subjective element. Specifically, to determine class membership in the second subclass required an inquiry into whether the individuals failed to move "due to" the Authority's policies, or whether there was some other reason they did not move. Accordingly, the district court held that the second subclass definition was ineligible for class certification.

B. MERITS-BASED

If a court must make a determination on the merits in order to decide who is a class member, the definition does not satisfy ascertainability. The United States Supreme Court held in *Eisen v. Carlisle & Jacquelin* that "nothing in either the language or history of Rule 23 . . . gives a court any authority to conduct a preliminary inquiry into the merits of a suit in order to determine whether it may be maintained as a class action."[10]

In *Xiufang Situ v. Leavitt*,[11] Medicare beneficiaries with dual eligibility for Medicaid brought a class action for an injunction against the U.S. Secretary of Health and Human Services over various alleged deficiencies in the shifting of their prescription drug coverage from Medicaid to the Medicare Part D program. Plaintiffs proposed the following class definition:

---

9. 224 F.R.D. 420 (N.D. Ill. 2004).

10. 417 U.S. 156, 177 (1974). This maxim has perhaps eroded in some contexts, but remains the rule where class definitions are concerned. *See In re Initial Pub. Offering Sec. Litig.*, 471 F.3d 24 (2d Cir. 2006).

11. 240 F.R.D. 551 (N.D. Cal. 2007).

All full benefit dually eligible Medicare beneficiaries who are unable to receive the full benefits of Medicare Part D prescription drug coverage and/or the Low Income Subsidy program due to the actions or failure to act of the Secretary of Health and Human Services.

The district court agreed with the defendant that the definition was improper because it was impossible to determine whether a dual eligible beneficiary was a member of the class without determining the merits of the claim, i.e., the Secretary's obligations under the law. The district court rewrote the definition to focus on the issues actually alleged in the complaint rather than the amorphous "actions or failure to act" by the Secretary. The court-authored definition, which was far more precise and did not require merits-based determinations, read:

All full benefit dually eligible Medicare beneficiaries who have not received the full benefits of Medicare Part D prescription drug coverage or the Low Income Subsidy program because of one or more of the following: (1) the Secretary did not follow all auto-enrollment requirements after the beneficiary failed to enroll in a plan of his or her choice; (2) at the time benefits were sought, the beneficiary's Part D plan had not been informed by the Secretary of the beneficiary's enrollment in the plan or of his or her entitlement to the Low Income Subsidy; or (3) the beneficiary was listed by the Secretary as a member of more than one Part D plan or as a member of the incorrect Part D plan after the beneficiary elected to change plans.[12]

A proposed class definition that rests on the paramount liability question cannot be objective, nor can the class members be presently ascertained. When the class definition depends upon a conclusion of liability, the trial court has no way of determining whether a given person is a member of the class until liability is decided. This is sometimes called a "fail-safe" class because it requires a resolution of the ultimate liability issue in favor of the plaintiffs that is only binding on the class if favorable. Conversely, if the liability determination is in favor of the defendant, the class will be found never to have existed.[13]

In *Dafforn v. Rousseau Associates, Inc.*,[14] for instance, the district court refused to certify a class of homeowners who had been charged "illegal" brokerage fees because the class definition depended on a finding that the defendants' fees were illegal. As the court explained, if the trier of fact determined that the defendants' fees were not illegal, there would be no class members against whom res judicata would apply, allowing homeowners to bring individual suits to retry the same issues. The court thus refused to certify the proposed class.

---

12. *Id.* at 558–59.

13. *Adashunas v. Negley*, 626 F.2d 600, 604 (7th Cir. 1980); *Indiana State Emp. Ass'n Inc. v. Indiana State Highway Comm'n*, 78 F.R.D. 724, 725 (S.D. Ind. 1978).

14. 1976 WL 1358.

Not all cases apply the fail-safe prohibition strictly. For example, the Fifth Circuit in *Mullen v. Treasure Chest Casino, LLC*[15] upheld a definition of a class of former employees of a floating casino who suffered respiratory illness "caused or exacerbated by the defective ventilation system." In response to the defendant's complaint that membership in the class was contingent upon proof of causation, the Fifth Circuit replied that it was good enough that the class members were linked by a common complaint and the fact that the class was defined with reference to an ultimate issue of causation did not prevent certification.

C. ADMINISTRATIVE FEASIBILITY

A class definition may be objective and independent of the merits, but may still be deficient if its application is not administratively feasible. An excellent example of such a case is *Fisher v. Ciba Specialty Chemicals Corp.*[16] There the plaintiffs claimed their property values had been diminished by contamination from a nearby chemical manufacturing plant. They sought certification of a class of all individuals who owned "non-income-producing property" within a 2.1-mile radius of the plant as of August 25, 2003.

The district court held that it would be easy enough to determine who owned property within the geographic boundary set by the definition. However, whether or not a particular parcel of land was or was not income-producing would require the collection of evidence as to numerous property owners concerning uses of their property in August 2003 and whether the property was actually yielding or was intended to yield income at that time. Mini-trials would have to be conducted just to determine whether property owners were class members. "The massive administrative burdens inherent in such an endeavor counteract the efficiency gains that the Rule 23 mechanism is intended to capture. This defect constitutes a separate, independent ground for denying class certification here."[17]

In *Adair v. Johnston*,[18] the district court refused to certify a class of policyholders of whole-life insurance policies covered by ERISA and issued by a particular life insurance company. The court noted that the life insurance company had issued over half a million whole-life policies and that there was no easy way to determine whether any particular policy was part of an ERISA plan without doing a fact-intensive individualized analysis of each. The administrative burden in determining class membership rendered class certification inappropriate.

---

15. 186 F.3d 620 (5th Cir. 1999).
16. 238 F.R.D. at 273.
17. *Id.* at 302.
18. 221 F.R.D. 573 (M.D. Ala. 2004).

D. OVERLY BROAD

A class definition that includes many people who have not been injured by the defendant's conduct will be deemed overly broad and insufficient. Such was the fate of the class definition proposed in *Oshana v. Coca-Cola Co.*,[19] another case of alleged deceit by the soft drink company over inclusion of saccharin in fountain Diet Coke.

In an effort to avoid the problems of the class definition proposed in the *Zapka* case (defeated by its reference to class members' subjective feeling of having been deceived), the plaintiff in *Oshana* defined the class merely as anyone who had purchased a fountain Diet Coke from March 12, 1999, forward. The Seventh Circuit decided that that definition was far too broad because it "could include millions who were not deceived."[20] The definition, while objective, independent of the merits, and administratively feasible, was defective:

> Some people may have bought fountain Diet Coke *because* it contained saccharin, and some people may have bought fountain Diet Coke *even though* it had saccharin. Countless members of Oshana's putative class could not show any damage, let alone damage proximately caused by Coke's alleged deception.[21]

A narrowly tailored class definition avoids issues of standing and ripeness often entailed in an overly broad definition. However, a class definition is not defectively overbroad merely because it contains *some* uninjured individuals—indeed, that is often the case at the outset when many class members are unknown. As pointed out by the Seventh Circuit in *Kohen v. Pacific Investment Management Co.*,[22] if a class definition is so broad that it sweeps within it people who *could not* have been injured by the defendant's conduct, it is too broad. In the same case, the Seventh Circuit maintained that a class should not be certified if the definition makes it apparent that it contains a *great many* uninjured people, "if only because of the *in terrorem* character of a class action."[23]

---

19. 472 F.3d at 506.

20. *Id.* at 514.

21. *Id.* (emphasis in original).

22. 571 F.3d 672, 677 (7th Cir. 2009) (Posner, J.).

23. *Id.* at 677–78. The court explained the *in terrorem* effect as follows: "When the potential liability created by a lawsuit is very great, even though the probability that the plaintiff will succeed in establishing liability is slight, the defendant will be under pressure to settle rather than to bet the company, even if the betting odds are good." *Id.* at 678 (citations omitted).

III. Subclasses[24]

Rule 23(c)(5) allows a class to be divided into subclasses. Each subclass must independently meet all of the requirements of Rule 23.[25] This includes, of course, the requirement of an adequate definition. This was well-illustrated in *LaBauve v. Olin Corp.*,[26] a case involving alleged mercury pollution from a chemical plant. The plaintiffs there defined three subclasses according to the pollution pathway: an air subclass, a surface water subclass, and a groundwater subclass. The district court found that the air subclass had been adequately defined, but that the surface water and groundwater subclasses had not. Only the air subclass was certified.

Subclasses are used to separate groups with different or conflicting interests. They can assist in making a class more manageable and sometimes can overcome obstacles that would defeat certification if all members were lumped together in a single class. These concerns are often addressed retrospectively, rather than at the outset, because conflicts may not exist initially but may develop or become apparent as the case is litigated.

In *Boucher v. Syracuse University*,[27] seven women lacrosse players and one woman softball player brought suit against the university claiming it violated Title IX in its treatment of women's sports versus men's sports. The district court certified a class of women lacrosse players only finding that there could be a conflict between lacrosse players and softball players since the university had finite resources and the university might achieve compliance by elevating one sport over the other. The Second Circuit agreed that a conflict existed but held that rather than limiting the class and excluding softball players, the district court should have certified two subclasses, one for each sport.

In cases involving the laws of different states, dividing the case into subclasses according to state may make the case more manageable and overcome problems of predominance. Thus, in *Saltzman v. Pella Corp.*,[28] a consumer fraud case, the district court specified subclasses for each of six states. The *Manual for Complex Litigation*, however, cautions that such an approach is appropriate when the law of

---

24. For additional information regarding subclasses, *see* Chapter 27, "Management Techniques and Devices for Segmenting Aggregate Litigation."

25. Fed. R. Civ. P. 23(b)(5); *Johnson v. Am. Credit Co. of Ga.*, 581 F.2d 526, 532 (5th Cir. 1978); *Recinos-Recinos v. Express Forestry, Inc.*, 233 F.R.D. 472 (E.D. La. 2006); *LaBauve v. Olin Corp.*, 231 F.R.D. 632, 662 (S.D. Ala. 2005).

26. 231 F.R.D. at 632, 662.

27. 164 F.3d 113 (2d Cir. 1999).

28. 257 F.R.D. 471 (N.D. Ill. 2009).

only a few jurisdictions applies.[29] The applicability of multiple different state laws usually precludes certification of nationwide class actions.[30]

In *Casale v. Kelly*,[31] the district court made a creative distinction between subclasses under Rule 23(c)(5) and "case-management subclasses" as a management tool under Rule 23(d)'s general provisions allowing a court to make orders to determine the course of proceedings and prevent undue repetition or complication in presenting evidence. There, the plaintiffs sought certification of a class of people harmed by enforcement of New York City's loitering law after the law had been declared unconstitutional. The court held that, if there were a true conflict among class members or if their claims were divergent and nonoverlapping, the case would have to proceed under Rule 23(c)(5), and all requirements would have to be met for each separate subclass. However, the court held that if neither conflict nor divergence were present, the court could create case-management subclasses that would not have to be examined for commonality, numerosity, typicality, or adequacy of representation.[32]

IV. Issue Classes[33]

Rule 23(c)(4) provides that when appropriate, an action may be brought or maintained as a class action with respect to particular issues. The interpretation of this provision has led to a split among the circuits.

In an influential decision written by Judge Posner, the Seventh Circuit confronted the question of whether the issue of liability could be split from the issue of damages. The case, *In re Rhone-Poulenc Rorer, Inc.*,[34] involved a proposed nationwide class of hemophiliacs who had been infected with HIV through blood products manufactured by the defendants. The district court held that predominance could not be satisfied as to proximate cause, injury, and damages, but certified an issue class regarding negligence and breach of fiduciary duty. The Seventh Circuit, without direct reference to Rule 23(c)(4), decertified on several grounds, one of which was Judge Posner's contention that the proposed separation of the negligence issue was "inconsistent with the principle [of the Seventh Amendment] that the findings of one jury are not to be reexamined by a second, or third, or nth jury."[35]

---

29. MANUAL FOR COMPLEX LITIGATION (FOURTH) § 22.634 (2004).

30. *See, e.g.*, Castano v. Am. Tobacco Co., 84 F.3d 734, 741 (5th Cir. 1996), and *In re Vioxx Prods. Liab. Litig.*, 239 F.R.D. 450 (E.D. La. 2006).

31. 257 F.R.D. 396 (S.D.N.Y. 2009).

32. *Id.* at 409.

33. *See also* Chapter 28, "Creative Application of Rule 23(c)(4): How Issue Certification Interacts with the Requirements of Rule 23(b)(3)."

34. 51 F.3d 1293 (7th Cir. 1995).

35. *Id.* at 1303. It should be noted that since this decision Judge Posner has stated that not all bifurcations of liability from damage issues in class actions pose a constitutional problem. In *Carnegie v. Household*

Subsequently, the Fifth Circuit in *Castano v. American Tobacco Co.*[36] reversed a district court's certification of multiple "core liability issues" in a nationwide class action suit brought by smokers against tobacco companies. In a significant footnote, the Fifth Circuit held that issue classes could not be used to create predominance as to any cause of action:

> A district court cannot manufacture predominance through the nimble use of subdivision (c)(4). The proper interpretation of the interaction between subdivisions (b)(3) and (c)(4) is that a cause of action, as a whole, must satisfy the predominance requirement of (b)(3) and that (c)(4) is a housekeeping rule that allows courts to sever the common issues for a class trial . . . Reading rule 23(c)(4) as allowing a court to sever issues until the remaining common issue predominates over the remaining individual issues would eviscerate the predominance requirement of rule 23(b)(3); the result would be automatic certification in every case where there is a common issue, a result that could not have been intended.[37]

The Fifth Circuit reversed class certification for lack of predominance, among other grounds.[38]

The Ninth Circuit holds a different view. In *Valentino v. Carter-Wallace, Inc.*,[39] that court stated, albeit in dicta, that even if common issues do not predominate over individual issues as to the entire action, Rule 23(c)(4) permits isolation of common issues and certification of those issues. The Second Circuit strongly agrees with the Ninth Circuit as expressed in *In re Nassau County Strip Search Cases.*[40] There the Second Circuit reasoned that the language and structure of Rule 23 require that a court first identify common issues and only then apply a predominance analysis. The Fourth Circuit has also aligned itself with this view in *Gunnells v. Healthplan Services, Inc.*[41]

In *In re General Motors Corp. Dex-Cool Products Liability Litigation*,[42] the plaintiffs complained that General Motors breached express warranties in the owner's manuals that accompanied their various vehicles by installing Dex-Cool, an engine coolant, that allegedly damaged their engines. The class was defined as all consumers who purchased GM cars during the years 1995 to 2004, but plaintiffs

---

Int'l, Inc., 376 F.3d 656 (7th Cir. 2004), Judge Posner wrote that a court could try the question of whether the defendant violated RICO without the encumbrance of causation or damage issues. He specifically referenced tools available to district judges to deal with individual damage issues, including "bifurcating liability and damage trials with the same or different juries." *Id.* at 662.

36. 84 F.3d at 734.

37. *Id.* at 746.

38. *See also Norwood v. Raytheon Co.,* 237 F.R.D. 581, 589 (W.D. Tex. 2006), and *In re Am. Commercial Lines, LLC,* No. 00-252, 2002 WL 1066743, at *13 (E.D. La. May 28, 2002).

39. 97 F.3d 1227, 1234 (9th Cir. 1996).

40. 461 F.3d 219 (2d Cir. 2006).

41. 348 F.3d 417 (4th Cir. 2003).

42. 241 F.R.D. 305 (S.D. Ill. 2007).

requested that only two issues be determined for the class: (1) whether Dex-Cool was incompatible with the intake manifold gasket that was factory-installed in certain specified vehicles; and (2) whether Dex-Cool was incompatible with the cooling system in certain other vehicles.

The district court rejected the notion that the concept of predominance should be relaxed in a class certified for determination of an issue rather than a claim. The court, while sympathetic to concerns about how to manage a rising tide of mass tort litigation, "conclude[d] that an expansive approach to class certification under Rule 23(c)(4)(A) is supported neither by the text of Rule 23 nor the binding precedent of this Circuit."[43] Citing *Rhone-Poulenc*, the court noted, "Rule 23(c)(4)(A) does not create, in addition to the three types of class actions enumerated in Rule 23(b), a fourth type, the 'issue' class action."[44]

Whether an issue class is appropriate in any case can only be determined by looking to the law of the particular circuit.

---

43. *Id.* at 314.
44. *Id.*

NUMEROSITY, COMMONALITY, AND TYPICALITY[1]

RUTH A. BAHE-JACHNA

I. Introduction

Three of the four prerequisites for class certification under Rule 23(a) are addressed in this chapter: numerosity (23(a)(1)), commonality (23(a)(2)), and typicality (23(a)(3)). The fourth Rule 23(a) prerequisite, adequacy, is addressed in Chapter 3.C, "Adequacy Requirements."

II. Numerosity

Rule 23(a)(1) provides that a class action is maintainable only if "the class is so numerous that joinder of all members is impracticable." Courts routinely note that "[i]mpracticable does not mean impossible."[2] The "numerosity requirement reflects the general theory behind class action lawsuits which is to permit a large group of individuals whose interests are sufficiently related to bring one lawsuit, instead of many lawsuits, so as to conserve judicial resources and increase judicial access."[3] Although this requirement is commonly referred to as numerosity (as this

---

1. John J. Elliott, an associate in the litigation group in Greenberg Traurig's New York office, assisted in the preparation of these materials.

2. *Robidoux v. Celani*, 987 F.2d 931, 935–36 (2d Cir. 1993); *see also Harris v. Palm Springs Alpine Estates, Inc.*, 329 F.2d 909, 913–14 (9th Cir. 1964); *Adver. Specialty Nat'l Ass'n v. FTC*, 238 F.2d 108, 119 (1st Cir. 1956); *Goldstein v. N. Jersey Trust Co.*, 39 F.R.D. 363, 367 (S.D.N.Y. 1966) (impracticable does not mean "'incapable of being performed' or 'infeasible'"); 7A Charles A. Wright, Arthur R. Miller & Mary K. Kane, Federal Practice and Procedure § 1762, at 159 (2d ed. 1986); 3B James Wm. Moore, Moore's Federal Practice ¶ 23.05[3], at 23-156 (2d ed. 1992).

3. *Safran v. United Steelworkers of Am., AFL-CIO*, 132 F.R.D. 397, 401 (W.D. Pa. 1989).

chapter does), the key consideration is in fact one of impracticability of joinder, not the number of putative class members. Thus courts take several factors into account when determining if "joinder of all members is impracticable" and have refrained from setting a bright-line rule for the minimum number of class members sufficient to meet the standard. As the United States Supreme Court stated, the "numerosity requirement requires examination of the specific facts of each case and imposes no absolute limitations."[4]

Whether joinder of all members of the putative class is practicable depends not merely on the number of class members but also on consideration of the "judicial economy arising from the avoidance of a multiplicity of actions, geographic dispersion of class members, financial resources of class members, the ability of claimants to institute individual suits, and requests for prospective injunctive relief which would involve future class members."[5] The weight given to each of these factors varies in proportion to the number of members of the putative class. That is, the more members in the putative class, the less need there is for the court to examine the other factors.[6]

A. CLASS SIZE

The most important factor in determining numerosity is class size. It is generally accepted that "[w]hen class size reaches substantial proportions . . . the impracticability requirement is usually satisfied by the numbers alone."[7] The Second, Third, and Eleventh Circuits have held, and a leading commentary argues, that the impracticability of joinder "is presumed at a level of 40 members."[8] This is not uniform across all circuits, however; the Tenth Circuit explicitly rejected this presumption, stating that "there is 'no set formula to determine if the class is so numerous that it should be so certified.'"[9] Classes as small as 13 defendants have

---

4. *Gen. Tel. Co. of the Nw., Inc. v. EEOC*, 446 U.S. 318, 330 (1980); *see also Moskowitz v. Lopp*, 128 F.R.D. 624, 628 (E.D. Pa. 1989) ("No magic number exists satisfying the numerosity requirement").

5. *Robidoux*, 987 F.2d at 936.

6. *In re Am. Med. Sys., Inc.*, 75 F.3d 1069, 1079 (6th Cir. 1996).

7. *Id.*

8. *Consol. Rail Corp. v. Town of Hyde Park*, 47 F.3d 473, 483 (2d Cir. 1995); *see also Cox v. Am. Cast Iron Pipe Co.*, 784 F.2d 1546, 1553 (11th Cir. 1986); *Stewart v. Abraham*, 275 F.3d 220, 226–27 (3d Cir. 2001) ("[G]enerally if the named plaintiff demonstrates that the potential number of plaintiffs exceeds 40, the first prong of Rule 23(a) has been met."); 1 Herbert B. Newberg & Alba Conte, Newberg on Class Actions: A Manual for Group Litigation at Federal and State Levels § 3:5 (4th ed. 2002).

9. *Trevizo v. Adams*, 455 F.3d 1155, 1162 (10th Cir. 2006) (affirming denial of certification of 84-member class) (quoting *Rex v. Owens ex rel. State of Okla.*, 585 F.2d 432, 436 (10th Cir. 1978)).

been certified,[10] while classes with more than 300 putative members have been denied.[11]

Although a plaintiff need not allege the precise number of class members, the plaintiff does carry the burden of providing facts or demonstrating circumstances to show a reasonable estimate of class size, and a class cannot be certified where the class size is based upon speculation.[12] However, where only injunctive or declaratory relief is sought, some courts have held that the numerosity requirement is relaxed so that even speculative or conclusory allegations regarding numerosity are sufficient to permit class certification.[13]

---

10. *Dale Elecs., Inc. v. R.C.L. Elecs., Inc.*, 53 F.R.D. 531 (D.N.H. 1971); *see also Manning v. Princeton Consumer Disc. Co., Inc.*, 390 F. Supp. 320, 324 (E.D. Pa. 1975) (14 members), *aff'd*, 533 F.2d 102 (3d Cir. 1976); *Cypress v. Newport News Gen. & Nonsectarian Hosp. Ass'n*, 375 F.2d 648, 653 (4th Cir. 1967) (18 members); *but see Jones v. Firestone Tire & Rubber Co., Inc.*, 977 F.2d 527, 534 (11th Cir. 1992) (finding that fewer than 21 individuals is generally inadequate).

11. *Minersville Coal Co. v. Anthracite Exp. Ass'n*, 55 F.R.D. 426 (M.D. Pa. 1971); *see also Marcial v. Coronet Ins. Co.*, 880 F.2d 954, 957 (7th Cir. 1989) (plaintiffs failed to satisfy numerosity requirement for proposed class of 400 to 600 policyholders).

12. *Muro v. Target Corp.*, 580 F.3d 485, 492–93 (7th Cir. 2009) (affirming denial of class certification where plaintiff "made no showing of the numerosity" of her proposed class); *Vega v. T-Mobile USA, Inc.*, 564 F.3d 1256, 1267–68 (11th Cir. 2009) (noting that while "plaintiff need not show the precise number of members in the class," because the "record is utterly devoid of any showing" of class size, the class would be decertified (quoting *Evans v. U.S. Pipe & Foundry Co.*, 696 F.2d 925, 930 (11th Cir. 1983)); *Turnage v. Norfolk S. Corp.*, 307 F. App'x 918, 919-23, 2009 WL 140479, at *1 (6th Cir. 2009) (finding that the "evidence of numerosity was too speculative to merit certification"); *Arreola v. Godinez*, 546 F.3d 788, 797–98 (7th Cir. 2008) (certifying class based on testimony establishing a class of at least 350 members); *Pederson v. La. State Univ.*, 213 F.3d 858, 868–69 (5th Cir. 2000) (reversing district court and certifying class in Title IX case, finding that evidence supported conclusion that "numerous future female LSU students will desire to try out for varsity soccer and fast-pitch softball"); *Robidoux*, 987 F.2d at 935–36 (reversing district court and finding that plaintiffs submitted sufficient evidence to establish numerosity); *Makuc v. Am. Honda Motor Co., Inc.*, 835 F.2d 389, 394–95 (1st Cir. 1987) (affirming denial of class certification where two years of discovery established that one person was injured and that "plaintiff's contention as to the size of the class was purely speculative"); *Zeidman v. J. Ray McDermott & Co.*, 651 F.2d 1030, 1040 (5th Cir. 1981) (same); *Gevedon v. Purdue Pharma*, 212 F.R.D. 333, 337–38 (E.D. Ky. 2002) (holding, in a products liability case, that the total sales volume of the product in question is not in itself sufficient proof of numerosity); *Osterberg v. Bd. of Tr. of State Employees' Ret. Sys.*, 722 F. Supp. 415 (N.D. Ill. 1989) (denying certification of class alleging unlawful denial of disability benefits during high-risk pregnancy; court could not "take judicial notice of the fact" that, absent any other evidence, the number of women who would suffer a disabling pregnancy was "so large as to make joinder impracticable"); *Waldman v. Electrospace Corp.*, 68 F.R.D. 281, 285 (S.D.N.Y. 1975) (finding class composed of purchasers of stock or convertible debentures over a four-year period did not meet numerosity requirement merely because of evidence showing a substantial increase in number of shares outstanding and decrease in number of debenture holders of record).

13. *See, e.g., Sueoka v. United States*, 101 F. App'x 649, 653, 2004 WL 1042541, at *2 (9th Cir. 2004) (overruling district court and finding numerosity as to subclass seeking injunctive and declaratory relief, relying on a "reasonable inference arising from plaintiffs' other evidence that the number of unknown and future members of proposed subclass . . . is sufficient to make joinder impracticable"); *Jack v. Am. Linen Supply Co.*, 498 F.2d 122, 124 (5th Cir. 1974) (noting that "[t]he alleged class . . . include[d] unnamed, unknown

B. OTHER FACTORS

The remaining factors revolve around the practicality of joinder. As the Seventh Circuit has noted, it "ordinarily is not difficult to ascertain if a class approach would be useful to avoid the practical problems of trying to join many named plaintiffs or otherwise clog the docket with numerous individual suits. Except for the class approach many might never receive any redress for the wrong done them."[14] Cases have taken account of the location of the class members,[15] whether the class

---

future . . . [members] who will be affected by . . . discriminatory policies, and joinder of unknown individuals is certainly impracticable"); *Doe v. Charleston Area Med. Ctr., Inc.*, 529 F.2d 638, 645 (4th Cir. 1975) ("Where 'the only relief sought for the class is injunctive and declaratory in nature . . . ,' even 'speculative and conclusory representations' as to the size of the class suffice as to the requirement of many." (quoting *Doe v. Flowers*, 364 F. Supp. 953, 954 (N.D. W. Va. 1973), *aff'd mem.*, 416 U.S. 922 (1974))); *Leszczynski v. Allianz Ins.*, 176 F.R.D. 659, 39 Fed. R. Serv. 3d 908 (S.D. Fla. 1997) (conditionally granting certification and noting that where only injunctive or declaratory relief is pled, numerosity is relaxed so that even speculative or conclusory allegations are sufficient); *Clarkson v. Coughlin*, 145 F.R.D. 339, 348 (S.D.N.Y. 1993) (certifying subclass of seven deaf or hearing-impaired female inmates because alleged problems were systemic throughout prison and because "the composition of the prison population is inherently 'fluid'"); *Goodnight v. Shalala*, 837 F. Supp. 1564 (D. Utah 1993) ("[W]hen injunctive relief is the only relief requested, even speculative or conclusory representations regarding numerosity will suffice to permit class certification."). The reason for this relaxed standard is that "the defendant will not be prejudiced if the plaintiff proceeds on a class action basis, as opposed to an individual basis, because the requested relief generally will benefit not only the claimant but all other persons subject to the practice under attack." *Weiss v. York Hosp.*, 745 F.2d 786, 808 (3d Cir. 1984).

14. *Eggleston v. Chicago Journeymen Plumbers' Local Union No. 130, U.A.*, 657 F.2d 890, 895 (7th Cir. 1981).

15. *See, e.g., Turnage*, 307 F. App'x at 919–23, 2009 WL 140479, at *1 (affirming denial of class certification where "every potential plaintiff in this case lives within a three-mile radius"; further, "[r]egardless of the actual number of plaintiffs in this case, their proximity to each other and the discrete and obvious nature of the harm make identifying and contacting them relatively easy"); *Mullen v. Treasure Chest Casino, LLC*, 186 F.3d 620, 624–25 (5th Cir. 1999) (affirming district court's finding of numerosity for 100- to 150-person class where "the district court reasonably inferred from the nature of the putative class members' employment that some of them would be geographically dispersed"); *Baltimore v. Laborers' Int'l Union of N. Am.*, No. 93-1810, 1995 WL 578084, at *1 (4th Cir. Oct. 2, 1995) (affirming district court's determination that numerosity was not met where "the members probably reside within an established jurisdictional boundary"); *Robidoux*, 987 F.2d at 936 (finding district court abused discretion in denying class certification on numerosity grounds where "the potential class members are distributed over the entire area of Vermont"); *Kilgo v. Bowman Transp., Inc.*, 789 F.2d 859, 878 (11th Cir. 1986) (affirming district court's finding of numerosity for 31-person class and noting that the "certified class also includes applicants from a wide geographical area"); *Andrews v. Bechtel Power Corp.*, 780 F.2d 124, 131–32 (1st Cir. 1985) (affirming district court's denial of class certification where "members of the subclass came from the same small geographic area"); *Garcia v. Gloor*, 618 F.2d 264, 267 (5th Cir. 1980) (affirming district court's finding that numerosity was not satisfied where the 33 class members "all lived in a compact geographical area"); *Alvarado Partners, L.P. v. Mehta*, 130 F.R.D. 673, 675 (D. Colo. 1990) (granting class certification of 33-person defendant class where class members "are dispersed throughout the country. Thus, joinder is rendered much more difficult for all parties.").

members have been identified or are unknown,[16] and the ability and potential willingness of class members to institute individual actions.[17] For instance, the Second Circuit affirmed a finding of numerosity where, after considering the factors above, it determined that "[j]oinder of all claims into one proceeding would be expensive, time-consuming, and logistically unfeasible" where 650 class members were spread across the United States.[18]

III. Commonality and Typicality

The commonality requirement of Rule 23(a)(2) provides that a class may not be certified unless "there are questions of law or fact common to the class." Rule 23(a)(3) addresses typicality and provides that a class may not be certified unless "the claims or defenses of the representative parties are typical of the claims or defenses of the class." As the Supreme Court has noted, the

> commonality and typicality requirements of Rule 23(a) tend to merge. Both serve as guideposts for determining whether under the particular circumstances maintenance of a class action is economical and whether the named plaintiff's claim and

16. *See, e.g., Baltimore v. Laborers' Int'l Union*, 1995 WL 578084, at *1 (affirming district court's determination that numerosity was not met where "[t]he majority of the members of the proposed class were identified"); *Liberty Lincoln Mercury, Inc. v. Ford Mktg. Corp.*, 149 F.R.D. 65, 74 (D.N.J. 1993) (noting that factors relevant to numerosity include "ease of identifying members and determining addresses, ease of service on members if joined, [and] geographical dispersion"); *Andrews*, 780 F.2d at 131–32 (affirming district court's denial of class certification and noting that "where class members can be easily identified, joinder is more likely to be practicable"); *Garcia*, 618 F.2d at 267 (affirming district court's finding that numerosity was not satisfied where the 31 class members' "identity and addresses were readily ascertainable").

17. For example, courts have considered it relevant that the size of the claim or the economic condition of the class members made it unlikely that individual suits would be pursued. *See, e.g., Robidoux*, 987 F.2d at 936 (finding district court abused discretion in denying class certification on numerosity grounds where the class members were "economically disadvantaged, making individual suits difficult to pursue"); *Swanson v. Am. Consumer Indus., Inc.*, 415 F.2d 1326, 1333 n.9 (7th Cir. 1969) (reversing denial of class certification and noting that "[e]ven if the class were limited to 40 stockholders . . . that is a sufficiently large group to satisfy Rule 23(a) where the individual members of the class are widely scattered and their holdings are generally too small to warrant undertaking individual actions"). Similarly, courts have found numerosity despite small class size where class members feared retaliation if they brought suit individually. *See, e.g., Mullen*, 186 F.3d at 624–25 (affirming district court's finding of numerosity for 100- to 150-person class where it could be "reasonably presumed that those potential class members still employed by [defendant] might be unwilling to sue individually or join a suit for fear of retaliation at their jobs"); *Slanina v. William Penn Parking Corp.*, 106 F.R.D. 419, 423–24 (W.D. Pa. 1984) (finding numerosity for 25-person class where "Plaintiffs have indicated fears of reprisal and retaliation from the Defendants should the Plaintiffs be forced to pursue this matter individually"); *Deposit Guar. Nat'l Bank v. Roper*, 445 U.S. 326, 339 (1980) ("Where it is not economically feasible to obtain relief within the traditional framework of a multiplicity of small individual suits for damages, aggrieved persons may be without any effective redress unless they may employ the class-action device.").

18. *In re Drexel Burnham Lambert Group, Inc.*, 960 F.2d 285, 290 (2d Cir. 1992).

the class claims are so interrelated that the interests of the class members will be fairly and adequately protected in their absence.[19]

Each factor, however, serves a discrete purpose. "Commonality examines the relationship of facts and legal issues common to class members, while typicality focuses on the relationship of facts and issues between the class and its representatives."[20] Stated differently, the "commonality requirement is said to be met if plaintiffs' grievances share a common question of law or of fact."[21] Typicality, by contrast, requires that the claims of the class representative(s) be typical of those of the class and is "'satisfied when each class member's claim arises from the same course of events, and each class member makes similar legal arguments to prove the defendant's liability.'"[22] Each of these two requirements is examined separately.

A. COMMONALITY STANDARDS

The commonality standard is low, as it only requires "one common issue the resolution of which will advance the litigation."[23] A common issue "is one that can be resolved for each class member in a single hearing, such as the question of whether an employer engaged in a pattern and practice of unlawful discrimination against a class of its employees."[24] The common question "may be either of law or of fact."[25] Conversely, a question is not common if its resolution "turns on a consideration of the individual circumstances of each class member."[26] Note that "even though

---

19. *Gen. Tel. Co. v. Falcon*, 457 U.S. 147, 158 n.13 (1982); *see also Mace v. Van Ru Credit Corp.*, 109 F.3d 338, 341 (7th Cir. 1997) (noting that the "typicality and commonality requirements of the Federal Rules ensure that only those plaintiffs or defendants who can advance the same factual and legal arguments may be grouped together as a class."); *Baby Neal ex rel. Kanter v. Casey*, 43 F.3d 48, 56 (3d Cir. 1994) ("The concepts of commonality and typicality are broadly defined and tend to merge.").

20. *Dukes v. Wal-Mart, Inc.*, 509 F.3d 1168, 1184 n.12 (9th Cir. 2007); *see also Piazza v. Ebsco Indus., Inc.*, 273 F.3d 1341 (11th Cir. 2001) (noting that "[t]raditionally, commonality refers to the group characteristics of the class as a whole, while typicality refers to the individual characteristics of the named plaintiff in relation to the class").

21. *Armstrong v. Davis*, 275 F.3d 849, 868–69 (9th Cir. 2001) (citing *Baby Neal ex rel. Kanter*, 43 F.3d at 56).

22. *Marisol A. ex rel. Forbes v. Giuliani*, 126 F.3d 372, 376 (2d Cir. 1997) (quoting *In re Drexel Burnham Lambert Group*, 960 F.2d at 291).

23. *Sprague v. Gen. Motors Corp.*, 133 F.3d 388, 397 (6th Cir. 1998); *see also In re Schering Plough Corp. ERISA Litig.*, 589 F.3d 585, 597 n.10 (3d Cir. 2009) (noting that "[i]t is well established that only one question of law or fact in common is necessary to satisfy the commonality requirement, despite the use of the plural "questions" in the language of Rule 23(a)(2)" (citing *In re "Agent Orange" Prod. Liab. Litig.*, 818 F.2d 145, 166–67 (2d Cir. 1987) and *Weiss*, 745 F.2d at 808–09 (3d Cir. 1984))).

24. *Thorn v. Jefferson-Pilot Life Ins. Co.*, 445 F.3d 311, 319 (4th Cir. 2006) (citing 7A Charles A. Wright, Arthur R. Miller & Mary K. Kane, Federal Practice and Procedure § 1763 (3d ed. 2005)).

25. *In re "Agent Orange" Prod. Liab. Litig.*, 818 F.2d at 166–67.

26. *Id.*

individual factual circumstances may be present among class members, the commonality requirement is satisfied where it is alleged that the defendants have acted in a uniform manner with respect to the class."[27]

Commonality was thus found where employees of a subprime mortgage lender allegedly misrepresented loans to borrowers using a standardized sales pitch.[28] Similarly, the question whether defendants conspired to decrease competition was sufficient to find commonality in an antitrust action, notwithstanding any differences in how the conspiracy actually manifested in the market.[29] But where a class action was brought for breach of contract and each class member entered into a separate contract with the defendant, the Sixth Circuit found commonality lacking. It held that "[p]roof that [defendant] had contracted to confer vested benefits on one [class member] would not necessarily prove that [defendant] had made such a contract with a different [class member]."[30]

B. TYPICALITY STANDARDS

Typicality "entails an inquiry whether 'the named plaintiff's individual circumstances are markedly different or . . . the legal theory upon which the claims are based differs from that upon which the claims of other class members will perforce be based.'"[31] The goal is to ensure that the named plaintiffs have incentives that align with those of absent class members, so that the absentees' interests will be fairly represented.[32] Factual differences are no bar to a finding of typicality as long as "the claim arises from the same event or practice or course of conduct that gives rise to the claims of the class members, and if it is based on the same legal theory."[33] It is a general standard and "refers to the nature of the claim or defense of the class representative, and not to the specific facts from which it arose or the relief sought."[34]

---

27. *Int'l Molders' & Allied Workers' Local Union No. 164 v. Nelson*, 102 F.R.D. 457, 462 (N.D. Cal. 1983) (citing *Alliance to End Repression v. Rochford*, 565 F.2d 975, 979 (7th Cir. 1977)).

28. *In re First Alliance Mortgage Co.*, 471 F.3d 977 (9th Cir. 2006).

29. *In re Fine Paper Antitrust Litig.*, 82 F.R.D. 143 (E.D. Pa. 1979), *aff'd*, 685 F.2d 810 (3d Cir. 1982).

30. *Sprague*, 133 F.3d at 398; *see also Hudson v. Delta Air Lines, Inc.*, 90 F.3d 451 (11th Cir. 1996) (finding commonality lacking where impact of alleged fraud not uniform across class).

31. *Hassine v. Jeffes*, 846 F.2d 169, 177 (3d Cir. 1988) (quoting *Eisenberg v. Gagnon*, 766 F.2d 770, 786 (3d Cir. 1985)).

32. *Baby Neal ex rel. Kanter*, 43 F.3d at 58.

33. *Hoxworth v. Blinder, Robinson & Co.*, 980 F.2d 912, 923 (3d Cir. 1992) (citing *Grasty v. Amalgamated Clothing & Textile Workers Union*, 828 F.2d 123, 130 (3d Cir. 1987)); *see also De La Fuente v. Stokely-Van Camp, Inc.*, 713 F.2d 225, 232 (7th Cir. 1983) (affirming certification of a class challenging a farmworker recruitment system even though some of the named plaintiffs had not worked for the defendant company during the disputed years and even though it was not clear that all plaintiffs had worked in the specific employment situation as the named plaintiffs).

34. *Weinberger v. Thornton*, 114 F.R.D. 599, 603 (S.D. Cal. 1986).

The Supreme Court directly addressed typicality in *General Telephone Co. of Southwest v. Falcon*, where it reversed certification of a class of Mexican Americans challenging hiring and promotion actions on typicality grounds. The Court found that the plaintiff had not shown a pervasive discriminatory policy or practice that resulted in all of the injuries the class allegedly suffered. Thus, the named plaintiff need not have the same injury as the class members in order to prove typicality, but the named plaintiff must demonstrate that all of the alleged injuries—to the named plaintiff and the class members alike—arose from the same practice.[35] Such a showing is particularly important in civil rights cases.[36]

The Fourth Circuit engaged in a lengthy discussion of typicality in *Deiter v. Microsoft Corp.*[37] Several consumers brought an antitrust class action against Microsoft, alleging that they overpaid for Microsoft's operating system software because of Microsoft's alleged monopoly power. The district court certified a class of individual consumer purchasers, but did not include in the class consumers who bought at least 250 licenses for the operating system under the terms of Microsoft's Enterprise Program.[38]

The Fourth Circuit affirmed the decision, relying principally on the differences in how individual consumers and Enterprise customers purchased the software and how those differences implicated the plaintiffs' burden of proof under antitrust law. Although the named plaintiffs purchased operating system software "either on-line or by telephone, paying the fixed prices that Microsoft posted as part of its offer to sell," the Enterprise customers "did not purchase on-line or by telephone, nor did they pay prices established in advance by Microsoft."[39] They paid unique negotiated prices for a slightly different product, "three-year deals that included upgrades for the software."[40] The crucial distinction was how these differences interacted with antitrust law:

> [W]ith respect to the Enterprise deals, the plaintiffs would have to define and prove a relevant market and then injury to competition in *that* market. . . . [E]vidence would be required to demonstrate how Microsoft's monopoly powers caused Enterprise customers to be overcharged in *negotiated* deals involving bundles of products otherwise sold in two different markets. Because of these factual dissimilarities as to market injury to competition, and causation, the district court's conclusion that there would be a substantial gap between what plaintiffs proved for their individual

---

35. *Falcon*, 457 U.S. at 157–59.

36. *See, e.g., D.S. ex rel. S.S. v. New York City Dep't of Educ.*, 255 F.R.D. 59, 71 (E.D.N.Y. 2008); *Jones v. GPU, Inc.*, 234 F.R.D. 82, 97 (E.D. Pa. 2005).

37. 436 F.3d 461 (4th Cir. 2005).

38. *Id.* at 465.

39. *Id.* at 467–68.

40. *Id.* at 468.

cases and what would be required proof for the Enterprise customers' claims was a reasonable one.[41]

One of the more frequent challenges to typicality is the assertion of defenses that are unique to the named plaintiff. As the Third Circuit has said, "[i]t is well established that a proposed class representative is not 'typical' under Rule 23(a)(3) 'if the representative is subject to a unique defense that is likely to become a major focus of the litigation.'"[42] The "challenge presented by a defense unique to a class representative" is that "the representative's interests might not be aligned with those of the class, and the representative might devote time and effort to the defense at the expense of issues that are common and controlling for the class."[43]

C. COMMONALITY AND TYPICALITY TREATED SIMILARLY

Despite their distinct functions, courts frequently merge their commonality and typicality analysis. For example, in *Marisol A. ex. rel. Forbes v. Giuliani*, the Second Circuit considered whether class certification was appropriate where a class of children alleged that New York child welfare officials deprived them of child welfare services.[44] Eleven children charged that defendants violated a panoply of federal and state laws while they were in the child welfare system through "inadequate training and supervision of foster parents, the failure to properly investigate reports of suspected neglect and abuse, unconscionable delay in removing children from abusive homes, and the inability to secure appropriate placements for adoption."[45] The defendants argued that because each named plaintiff challenged a different aspect of the child welfare system, and because "no single plaintiff (named or otherwise) is affected by each and every legal violation alleged in the complaint," the class lacked both commonality and typicality. The Second Circuit did not conduct a separate analysis of the commonality and typicality requirements. Instead, it considered whether the various statutory provisions created standards for a "single scheme for the delivery of child welfare services . . . standards that the defendants

---

41. *Id.* (emphasis in original).

42. *In re Schering Plough Corp.*, 589 F.3d at 598 (quoting *Beck v. Maximus*, 457 F.3d 291, 301 (3d Cir. 2006)).

43. *Beck*, 457 F.3d at 297; *see also Gary Plastic Packaging Corp. v. Merrill Lynch, Pierce, Fenner & Smith, Inc.*, 903 F.2d 176, 180 (2d Cir. 1990) ("[T]here is a danger that absent class members will suffer if their representative is preoccupied with defenses unique to it."); *Hanon v. Dataproducts Corp.*, 976 F.2d 497, 508 (9th Cir. 1992) (same); *J.H. Cohn & Co. v. Am. Appraisal Assocs.*, 628 F.2d 994, 999 (7th Cir. 1980) ("[T]he presence of even an arguable defense peculiar to the named plaintiff or a small subset of the plaintiff class may destroy the required typicality of the class . . . The fear is that the named plaintiff will become distracted by the presence of a possible defense applicable only to him so that the representation of the rest of the class will suffer." (internal citations omitted)).

44. 126 F.3d 372 (2d Cir. 1997).

45. *Id.* at 377.

are alleged to have violated in a manner common to the plaintiff class."[46] The court affirmed class certification, noting that while the "high level of abstraction" of the claims "stretches the notions of commonality and typicality, [the court] cannot say that these claims are so unrelated that their aggregation necessarily violates Rule 23."[47] The court did, however, require that the district court engage in "rigorous analysis of the plaintiffs' legal claims and factual circumstances" to create subclasses that would appropriately match each discrete legal claim to those named plaintiffs aggrieved under each claim and determine the subclass definition for each.[48]

Similarly, in *Vega v. T-Mobile USA, Inc.*, the Eleventh Circuit found that the same issues that precluded a finding of commonality also precluded typicality.[49] A former employee brought two claims, for unpaid wages and unjust enrichment, arising from defendant's alleged failure to pay sales commissions on the sale of certain cellular telephone contracts. The court treated the unpaid wages claim as a claim for breach of contract and found that commonality was lacking because he had not "alleged in his complaint the existence of a common contract under which [defendant] employed all class members."[50] The elements of a breach of contract claim would be different for each class member and depended on

> when a given employee was hired, what the employee was told (and agreed to) with respect to compensation rules and procedures at the time of hiring, the employee's subjective understanding of how he would be compensated . . . and when and how any pertinent part of the employee's compensation agreement or understanding thereof may have changed during the course of that employee's tenure [with defendant].[51]

The unjust enrichment claim suffered the same fate, as "there [was] no evidence that the circumstances under which [defendant] accepted a benefit from each of the putative class members . . . were common."[52]

The court's typicality analysis was much the same. It noted that because the plaintiff did not allege a common contract among all class members, the claims "are not typical of the class's for many of the same reasons as the class fails for lack of commonality."[53] The court also noted, though, that the typicality claim failed even if it treated one particular document as a common contract because the plaintiff was not similarly situated to the other class members. The document had

---

46. *Id.*
47. *Id.*
48. *Id.* at 378–79.
49. 564 F.3d 1256 (11th Cir. 2009).
50. *Id.* at 1272.
51. *Id.*
52. *Id.* at 1274.
53. *Id.* at 1276.

different compensation terms for various specific positions within the defendant company. Thus, the compensation program for the plaintiff, applicable to retail sales representatives, was not "typical of class members from other business units or channels . . . all of whom were subject to divergent compensation rules and procedures."[54]

The differences between commonality and typicality are best appreciated where a court finds one but not the other. Such was the case in *In re Schering Plough Corp. ERISA Litigation*,[55] where the Third Circuit found that commonality was easily met, but remanded the case to the district court for a closer scrutiny of the typicality requirement.

In *Schering Plough*, the plaintiffs brought four breach of fiduciary duty claims against Schering-Plough under ERISA. They alleged that defendant breached its fiduciary duties by allowing employees to invest in an individual account plan that was composed "primarily of shares of Schering-Plough common stock."[56] The stock lost much of its value, and plaintiffs asserted that defendants had a "role in and knowledge of the alleged causes of the decline."[57]

The Third Circuit found that commonality was "clearly satisfied." The common questions included

> whether defendants were fiduciaries; whether defendants breached their duties to the Plan by failing to conduct an appropriate investigation into the continued investment in Schering-Plough stock; whether defendants breached their duties by continuing to invest in Schering-Plough stock and in continuing to offer the Schering-Plough Stock Fund; whether the defendants in supervisory roles failed in their monitoring of the Investment Committee Defendants; whether defendants failed to retain independent fiduciaries; and whether the Plan suffered losses as a result of defendants' breaches.[58]

The court found that typicality, however, was a closer question. Preliminarily, it stated that the standard for typicality "properly focuses on the similarity of the legal theory and legal claims; the similarity of the individual circumstances on which those theories and claims are based; and the extent to which the proposed representative may face significant unique or atypical defenses to her claims."[59] There was no doubt that the one remaining plaintiff had brought a claim "identical to those of the class she [sought] to represent."[60] Further, the factual basis for her claim was the same, in that it arose from "defendants' conduct, [plaintiff's]

---

54. *Id.* at 1277.
55. 589 F.3d 585 (3d Cir. 2009).
56. *Id.* at 591.
57. *Id.* at 592.
58. *Id.* at 597.
59. *Id.* at 597–98.
60. *Id.* at 599.

participation in the Plan, and her investment in Schering-Plough stock."[61] Plaintiff had an issue, though, because she had signed a separation agreement that "included a general release and a covenant not to sue. As a result, she may be subject to unique defenses that could become a focus of the litigation, rendering her atypical and making class certification inappropriate."[62] Thus, the court remanded the action to the district court so it could make a determination of whether the separation agreement rendered plaintiff atypical, or if the class members had also signed a release and covenant not to sue.

---

61. *Id.*
62. *Id.*

ADEQUACY REQUIREMENTS

MADELEINE FISCHER

I. Introduction

Adequacy of representation is essential to the maintenance of a class action because the judgment conclusively determines the rights of absent class members.[1] The adequacy requirement thus has constitutional dimensions because the choice of representatives "implicates the due process rights of all members who will be bound by the judgment."[2] Adequacy is never presumed: it is up to the plaintiff to demonstrate it.[3]

II. Considerations for Class Representative

To meet the adequacy requirement, the class representative must have no significant conflicts of interest with other class members and must zealously represent the class. The requirements of typicality and adequacy of representation overlap to a large degree. If typicality of claims is absent, then the class representative has an inherent conflict of interest with the class because he or she has no incentive to vigorously pursue the class claims.[4]

A. CONFLICTS

The Supreme Court addressed conflicts between class representatives and absent class members in the landmark case of *Amchem Products v. Windsor*.[5] There, the plaintiffs proposed a massive class action settlement of all present and future claims against CCR, a conglomeration of defendants who manufactured asbestos-containing

---

1. *Hansberry v. Lee*, 311 U.S. 32 (1940); *Dierks v. Thompson*, 414 F.2d 453, 456 (1st Cir. 1969).
2. *Berger v. Compaq Computer Corp.*, 257 F.3d 475, 481 (5th Cir. 2001).
3. Id.
4. *Gen. Tel. Co. v. Falcon*, 457 U.S. 147, 157 n.13 (1982).
5. 521 U.S. 591 (1997).

products. The district court certified a single class consisting of people who had not yet filed lawsuits for asbestos-related injuries against CCR but who had been themselves occupationally exposed or had a family member who had been occupationally exposed to asbestos attributable to a CCR product. The Third Circuit reversed class certification, and the Supreme Court agreed to hear the case. The Supreme Court's primary holding was that settlement-only classes must meet the same rigorous standards for class certification as any other proposed class. In the process of reaching this conclusion, the Court focused in part on the adequacy of representation requirement.

The complaint identified nine class representatives, half of whom claimed current asbestos-related diseases and half of whom had not yet manifested disease. The Supreme Court explained the conflict that the representatives had with other class members as follows:

> [N]amed parties with diverse medical conditions sought to act on behalf of a single giant class rather than on behalf of discrete subclasses. In significant respects, the interests of those within the single class are not aligned. Most saliently, for the currently injured, the critical goal is generous immediate payments. That goal tugs against the interest of exposure-only plaintiffs in ensuring an ample, inflation-protected fund for the future.[6]

The court hinted that these conflicts might have been ameliorated through subclassing, pointing out that, as structured, each representative was meant to serve the interests of the class as a whole rather than a separate constituency. The court further observed that when differences among class members are such that subclasses should be established, no authority permits proceeding as a single group "on the basis of consents by members of a unitary class, some of whom happen to be members of the distinct subgroups."[7] Because of the conflicts between class representatives and various elements within the single class, the Supreme Court held that the adequacy of representation requirement was not met.

On the other hand, if a conflict is not fundamental, it will not defeat adequacy. In *Gunnells v. Healthplan Services, Inc.*,[8] purchasers and beneficiaries of a multi-employer health care plan brought suit against the plan's claims administrator. The district court certified the class. On interlocutory appeal to the Fourth Circuit, the administrator argued that adequacy was not met because the interests of employer class members conflicted with those of employee class members who might want to sue their employers for unpaid medical bills resulting from the collapse of the plan.

---

6. *Id.* at 626.

7. *Id.* at 627 (quoting *In re Joint E. and S. Dist. Asbestos Litig.*, 982 F.2d 721, 742–43 (1992), *modified on reh'g sub nom. In re Findley*, 993 F.2d 7 (1993)).

8. 348 F.3d 417 (4th Cir. 2003).

The Fourth Circuit rejected the idea of a conflict as hypothetical and speculative. The court pointed out that, to date, no employee had filed any such claim and the statute of limitations now barred such claims. Further, even if an employee could bring a claim against his or her employer, that would not be a conflict that went to the heart of the litigation. Both employers and employees shared the same interest in establishing the liability of the administrator and had the same factual and legal positions. Thus, all class representatives were adequate.

B. ZEAL/COMPETENCE

An adequate class representative must be willing and able to take an active role in the litigation to protect the interests of absent class members. The Fifth Circuit in *Berger v. Compaq Computer Corp.* wryly observed, "Class action lawsuits are intended to serve as a vehicle for capable, committed advocates to pursue the goals of the class members through counsel, not for capable, committed counsel to pursue their own goals through those class members."[9]

Courts vary in the degree of knowledge and vigor required of an adequate class representative. Some circuits appear to minimize or skip over altogether any such elements and formulate the adequacy standard for representatives solely as an absence of conflicts.[10] The Fifth Circuit emphasizes the willingness and ability of the representative to take an active role in and control the litigation and to protect the interests of absentees.[11] Not surprisingly, district courts in the Fifth Circuit have issued a number of opinions that appear to demand more of class representatives.

In *Kase v. Salomon Smith Barney, Inc.*,[12] a district court judge in the Southern District of Texas questioned the adequacy of a representative who did not participate in many of the strategic decisions of the case and allowed counsel to pursue the case at counsel's discretion. Although a class representative is entitled to rely on the professional judgment of qualified class counsel, the court criticized the fact that the representative had not shown an inclination to take the active role in monitoring class counsel's activities that it believed were required of a class representative.

And in *Ogden v. AmeriCredit Corp.*,[13] a district court judge from the Northern District of Texas also found the representative inadequate for similar reasons. The representative's deposition demonstrated that she had been involved in the

---

9. *Berger*, 257 F.3d at 484; *see also Kelley v. Mid-Am. Racing Stables, Inc.*, 139 F.R.D. 405, 409 (W.D. Okla. 1990) ("The upshot of this requirement is that the class's attorney may not become a de facto plaintiff.").

10. *New Directions Treatment Servs. v. City of Reading*, 490 F.3d 293, 313 (3d Cir. 2007); *Andrews v. Bechtel Power Corp.*, 780 F.2d 124, 130 (1st Cir. 1985); *Baffa v. Donaldson, Lufkin & Jenrette Sec. Corp.*, 222 F.3d 52, 61 (2d Cir. 2000) (decrying "harsh" application of knowledge standard).

11. *Horton v. Goose Creek Indep. Sch. Dist.*, 690 F.2d 470, 484 (5th Cir. 1982).

12. 218 F.R.D. 149 (S.D. Tex. 2003).

13. 225 F.R.D. 529 (N.D. Tex. 2005).

planning stages of the litigation and knew that a large amount of money had been lost, but in many other areas she had little or no knowledge beyond what was fed to her by counsel. The representative then failed to appear at the class certification hearing and failed to notify defendants in advance that she would not be attending the hearing. The court found her later-submitted affidavit to be an unpersuasive explanation for her absence. The court concluded that "[i]nstead of demonstrating her willingness and ability to act as a class representative, . . . Ogden has instead shown that she lacks the requisite degree of zeal necessary for the great responsibility that she seeks to assume."[14]

Other courts are more lenient and apply an adequacy standard tailored to the facts and theory of the case. For example, in an antitrust case, class representatives were not expected to understand complex economic theories or have an expert's knowledge of the market.[15] And, in a class action challenging enforcement of New York City's loitering law, it was not surprising that one class representative had a history of mental illness and another had spent time in jail for drug use.[16] The district court found the representatives adequate and deemed the assault on their qualifications by the defense "disrespectful and blatantly self-serving."[17] Further, in a case involving low-skilled laborers suing an employer for failure to pay overtime, the class representative's inability to speak fluent English and therefore inability to supervise class counsel did not disqualify him.[18] There the court explained:

> [E]ven though Nunez arguably lacks the ability effectively to supervise class counsel, a rigid application of this requirement is inappropriate where, as here, the class comprises relatively low-skilled laborers. Such inflexibility runs counter to a principal objective of the class action mechanism—to facilitate recovery for those least able to pursue an individual action.[19]

If the class representatives are found inadequate, a court has several options. The court may simply dismiss the action for failure to meet all of the requirements of Rule 23.[20] The court may dismiss the class allegations only and continue with the case for the sole benefit of the named representative.[21] The court may resolve disqualifying conflicts by creating subclasses.[22] Or, the court may correct the situation by appointing a new qualified representative.[23]

---

14. *Id.* at 537.
15. *Natchitoches Parish Hosp. Serv. Dist. v. Tyco Int'l, Ltd.*, 247 F.R.D. 253, 265 (D. Mass. 2008).
16. *Casale v. Kelly*, 257 F.R.D. 396 (S.D.N.Y. 2009).
17. *Id.* at 412.
18. *Noble v. 93 Univ. Place Corp.*, 224 F.R.D. 330 (S.D.N.Y. 2004).
19. *Id.* at 344.
20. *See, e.g., Rainy Lake One Stop v. Marigold Foods*, 195 F.3d 430, 436–37 (8th Cir. 1999).
21. *See, e.g., Savino v. Computer Credit*, 164 F.3d 81, 86–87 (2d Cir. 1998).
22. *McMahon Books, Inc. v. Willow Grove Assocs.*, 108 F.R.D. 32, 36 (E.D. Pa. 1985).
23. *Ford v. U.S. Steel Corp.*, 638 F.2d 753, 762 (5th Cir. 1981).

III. Appointment of Class Counsel

Adequacy of class counsel was treated by case law as a part of the adequacy of representation requirement of Rule 23(a)(4) until 2003. In that year, Rule 23 was amended and subdivision (g) was added. Subdivision (g) is entirely devoted to class counsel. Under Rule 23(g)(4) the duty of class counsel is to fairly and adequately represent the interests of the class.

Rule 23(g)(1) mandates that the district court appoint class counsel unless a statute directs otherwise. *In re Cree, Inc. Securities Litigation*[24] provides an example of a statutory exception. The case asserted claims under the Private Securities Litigation Reform Act, which provides that lead plaintiffs select and retain counsel to represent the class subject to the approval of the court. The court looked to the factors in Rule 23(g)(1)(A) for guidance in its decision to approve of the lead plaintiff's counsel choice.

Under Rule 23(g)(3), before certification a court may, but is not required to, appoint interim counsel to act on behalf of the putative class. In *Webb v. Onizuka*,[25] the district court denied without prejudice a motion by the putative class representative who was appearing pro se to have himself appointed as interim counsel. The court cited a pending motion to dismiss for lack of subject matter jurisdiction as a matter to be decided first. Even were that obstacle overcome, the court expressed doubts as to whether a pro se plaintiff would ever be appointed to represent a certified class.[26]

When only one applicant seeks appointment as counsel, the court may appoint the applicant only if the applicant is adequate under the considerations of Rule 23(g)(1) and 23(g)(4).

IV. Selection of Class Counsel

In the selection of class counsel, Rule 23(g)(1)(A) sets four mandatory factors that the court must consider

- the work counsel has done in identifying or investigating potential claims in the action;
- counsel's experience in handling class actions, other complex litigation, and the types of claims asserted in the action;
- counsel's knowledge of the applicable law; and
- the resources counsel will commit to representing the class.

---

24. 219 F.R.D. 369 (M.D.N.C. 2003).
25. No. 08-487, 2009 WL 1687492 (D. Haw. June 15, 2009).
26. *See also Ransom v. U.S. Postal Serv.*, 170 F. App'x 525 (10th Cir. 2006) (unpublished).

Rule 23(g)(1)(B) permits the court to flexibly consider "any other matter pertinent to counsel's ability to fairly and adequately represent" the class.

In *Harrington v. City of Albuquerque*,[27] the district court held that the new subdivision 23(g) carried a presumption that lawyers who represent the party applying for class certification will be appointed as class counsel, because invariably those are the only lawyers who have done any work in identifying or investigating potential claims in the action—one of the mandatory factors that the court must consider. In *Harrington*, the counsel seeking appointment and representing the putative class representatives was The National Right to Work Legal Defense Foundation. The court also found that the Foundation met the other three mandatory considerations: (1) the Foundation had represented plaintiffs in similar cases; (2) the Foundation had played a significant role in shaping the law applicable to the case; and (3) the Foundation had resources that most other lawyers would be unable to muster.

A case in which counsel was found inadequate is *Kay v. Wells Fargo & Co.*[28] In *Kay*, the court found that all the requirements of class certification were met except that counsel for the class representatives had unnecessarily delayed taking discovery. The court conditioned class certification upon the plaintiff publicizing notice calculated to invite other counsel to compete for class representation pursuant to Rule 23(g).

V. Is Adequacy of Counsel a Requirement for Class Certification?

With the advent of Rule 23(g), there is a division of case law as to whether adequacy of counsel, formerly considered as part of Rule 23(a)(4)'s adequacy of representation requirement, continues to be a prerequisite to class certification. In the *Harrington* case, the district court expressly stated that it is not, because Rule 23(g) provides that the court shall appoint class counsel after the class has been certified. Some cases now separate the counsel inquiry from the general adequacy inquiry.[29] Others continue to analyze adequacy of counsel as a certification prerequisite and implicit in the adequacy of representation requirement of Rule 23(a)(4).[30]

---

27. 222 F.R.D. 505, 519–20 (D.N.M. 2004).

28. 247 F.R.D. 572 (N.D. Cal. 2007).

29. *See Prater v. Ohio Educ. Ass'n*, No. C2041077, 2008 WL 2566364 (S.D. Ohio June 26, 2008); *Velez v. Majik Cleaning Serv., Inc.*, No. 03-8698, 2005 WL 106895 (S.D.N.Y. Jan. 19, 2005).

30. *Cunningham Charter Corp. v. Learjet, Inc.*, No. 07-233, 2009 WL 1119494 (S.D. Ill. Apr. 27, 2009); *Bibo v. Fed. Exp., Inc.*, No. 07-2505, 2009 WL 1068880 (N.D. Cal. Apr. 21, 2009).

NONMONETARY RELIEF

MARCY HOGAN GREER

I. Introduction

In order for a court to certify a class, the proposed class must satisfy all the threshold requirements for certification under Rule 23(a)—numerosity, commonality, typicality, and adequacy—and it must be suitable for certification under at least one of the three categories of class actions set forth in Rule 23(b)(1) through (3).[1]

There are significant jurisprudential and practical differences among the categories of Rule 23(b). Most significant is the fact that (b)(1) and (b)(2) classes are mandatory, meaning that class members are not entitled to notice or the opportunity to "opt out" or exclude themselves from the binding effect of the litigation.[2] But considering that each of these three categories "builds on the same four prerequisites" of Rule 23(a), "it is not surprising that . . . a proposed class action may often qualify under two or all three functional class categories, which considerably overlap."[3] With a few exceptions, (b)(1) and (b)(2) classes generally address equitable remedies, while (b)(3) classes are used to recover monetary relief.[4]

II. Requirements for (b)(1) and (b)(2) Classes

In order to certify a (b)(1)(A) or (b)(2) class, proponents must demonstrate that the class members have similar interests that make classwide equitable relief an appropriate resolution.[5] Under Rule 23(b)(1), certification is appropriate if individual

---

1. There are actually four types of class actions, because Rule 23(b)(1) actually defines two different types of class actions. *See* FED. R. CIV. P. 23(b)(1)(A) and (B); *see also* sections II.A and II.B, *infra*.

2. *See* section III, *infra*.

3. 2 HERBERT B. NEWBERG & ALBA CONTE, NEWBERG ON CLASS ACTIONS: A MANUAL FOR GROUP LITIGATION AT FEDERAL AND STATE LEVELS § 4:1, at 4 (4th ed. 2002) [hereinafter NEWBERG].

4. *See* Chapter 14, "The Special Role of 23(b)(2) Classes."

5. *Amchem Prods. Inc. v. Windsor*, 521 U.S. 591, 614 (1997).

litigation either would create incompatible varying standards of conduct or would create individual adjudications that would be dispositive of awards that other class members could seek.[6]

A. RULE 23(B)(1)(A)

A Rule 23(b)(1)(A) class can be certified only in limited circumstances. First, a court can certify a (b)(1)(A) class if "there is a palpable risk the defendant will be placed in a position of being incapable of complying with one judgment without violating the terms of another."[7] But it is not enough merely to show that different courts might reach different results on similar claims.[8]

Additionally, a growing number of courts have concluded that a (b)(1)(A) class is inappropriate where the class seeks monetary damages.[9] For example, in *Langbecker v. Electronic Data Systems Corp.*,[10] the Fifth Circuit analyzed Federal Rule of Civil Procedure 23(b)(1)(A) and instructed trial courts to "consider the extent to which the due process concerns inherent in *Allison*[11] apply to a (b)(1)(A) class and whether a (b)(1)(A) class can be maintained if damages are the primary remedy sought."[12] District courts following *Langbecker* have held that because of the

---

6. Under Rule 23(b)(1), a class can only be certified where the prosecution of separate actions by or against individual members of the class would create a risk of:

(A) inconsistent or varying adjudications with respect to individual class members that would establish incompatible standards of conduct for the party opposing the class; or

(B) adjudications with respect to individual class members that, as a practical matter, would be dispositive of the interests of the other members not parties to the individual adjudications or would substantially impair or impede their ability to protect their interests[.]

Fed. R. Civ. P. 23(b)(1)(A), (B).

7. *Compaq Computer Corp. v. Albanese*, 153 S.W.3d 254, 262 (Tex. App.—Beaumont 2004, no pet.) (reversing (b)(1)(A) certification under analogous Texas rule).

8. *E.g., Cunningham Charter Corp. v. Learjet, Inc.*, 258 F.R.D. 320, 330–31 (S.D. Ill. 2009) (where breach of warranty claim sought substantial damages for class members, certification under (b)(1)(A) was properly denied); *Spann v. AOL Time Warner, Inc.*, 219 F.R.D. 307, 321–22, 31 Employee Benefits Cas. (BNA) 2883 (S.D.N.Y. 2003) (certification denied in ERISA action where class members sought damages because defendant was not obligated to treat all class members alike in recalculating pension benefits, and claims were otherwise subject to individual issues, including unique defenses, although court noted that certification might be appropriate if the request were solely for declaratory relief); *Smith v. Brown & Williamson Tobacco Corp.*, 174 F.R.D. 90, 99 (W.D. Mo. 1997) (potential for recovery by some class members, but not others, does not justify application of (b)(1)(A)).

9. Newberg § 4:1, at 14–16 (collecting cases). *But see In re A.H. Robins Co.*, 880 F.2d 709 (4th Cir. 1989) (Rule 23(b)(1)(A) can be used for classes seeking damages), *abrogated on other grounds, Amchem*, 521 U.S. at 618–19.

10. 476 F.3d 299, 318 (5th Cir. 2007).

11. In *Allison v. Citgo Petroleum Corp.*, the Fifth Circuit was concerned with cases where the procedural safeguards of notice and opt-out are necessary because the "monetary relief being sought is less of a group remedy and instead depends more on varying circumstances and merits of each class member's case." 151 F.3d 402, 413 (5th Cir. 1998).

12. *Langbecker*, 476 F.3d at 318 (citing *Allison*, 151 F.3d 402).

"individual-specific nature of the plaintiffs' claims for compensatory and puni-tive damages," Rule 23(b)(1)(A) does not apply to claims for monetary damages.[13] Although this interpretation of the rule lacks "textual support from the language of the rule itself,"[14] the due process concerns inherent in using a mandatory class vehicle—i.e., without a notice requirement or the ability to opt out—may counsel in favor of the limited interpretation.[15] As a result of these uncertainties as to the scope of this provision, courts rarely certify classes pursuant to Rule 23(b)(1)(A).

B. RULE 23(B)(1)(B)

A (b)(1)(B) class is generally appropriate only where there are multiple claimants to a limited fund. "A limited fund exists when a fixed asset or piece of property exists in which all class members have a preexisting interest, and an apportionment or determination of the interests of one class member cannot be made without affect-ing the proportionate interests of other class members similarly situated."[16] This provision is typically used when, in the absence of a classwide remedy, claimants suing individually would be prejudiced by exhaustion of the limited fund.[17] Rule 23(b)(1)(B) permits class claimants to be aggregated in one action to recover on a per capita or other basis against that limited fund.

In *Ortiz v. Fibreboard Corp.*,[18] the Supreme Court set forth three demanding criteria for approval of a Rule 23(b)(1)(B) limited fund settlement class. First, the proponents of such a class must demonstrate to the court through extrinsic evi-dence that the defendant's funds or fixed assets are in fact limited; this element cannot be satisfied by a stipulation of the parties.[19] Second, the terms of the set-tlement agreement must be such that the implementation of the settlement will exhaust the defendant's limited fund.[20] Finally, the terms of the settlement must provide for a fair and equitable distribution of the fund among class members.[21]

---

13. *See, e.g., Caruso v. Allstate Ins. Co.*, No. 06-2613 Section "R" (5), 2007 U.S. Dist. LEXIS 56760, at *12–15 (E.D. La. Aug. 3, 2007) (rejecting class certification under (b)(1)(A) in breach of contract suit seek-ing monetary damages (quoting *Allison*, 151 F.3d at 421)).

14. NEWBERG § 4:5, at 18–19.

15. *See* section III, *infra; see also* Chapter 14, "The Special Role of 23(b)(2) Classes" (discussing due pro-cess concerns with using (b)(2) mandatory classes to adjudicate damages claims).

16. NEWBERG § 4:9, at 33–35.

17. *Ortiz v. Fibreboard Corp.*, 527 U.S. 815, 842 (1999).

18. *Id.* at 838–41, 848.

19. *Id.* at 838–39, 841, 848; *see also St. Louis Sw. Ry. Co. v. Voluntary Purchasing Groups*, 929 S.W.2d 25, 32–33 (Tex. App.—Texarkana 1996, no writ) ("[T]here is nothing other than the broad assertion of a lim-ited fund to be found in the record. Thus, the trial court had nothing before it which would permit it to reasonably reach even a preliminary conclusion that a limited fund existed.").

20. *Ortiz*, 527 U.S. at 838–39.

21. *Id.*

Because the global asbestos settlement in *Ortiz* failed these three tests, the Court invalidated the (b)(1)(B) limited fund settlement.[22]

The Supreme Court's 1999 decision in *Ortiz*, and the standards the Court articulated in that decision, have made it extremely difficult to negotiate and consummate settlements under the Rule 23(b)(1)(B) class provision. Subsequent to *Ortiz*, very few class action settlements have been formulated under the limited fund theory.

In light of the significant restrictions on classes under this subsection of the rule, (b)(1)(A) and (b)(1)(B) class categories have proved to be of limited utility both in litigation classes and as structural bases for settling parties in a classwide settlement.

C. RULE 23(B)(2)

Rule 23(b)(2) permits certification where "the party opposing the class has acted or refused to act on grounds that apply generally to the class, so that final injunctive relief or corresponding declaratory relief is appropriate respecting the class as a whole . . . ."[23] The purpose of the (b)(2) class and its requirement of cohesion is markedly different from the purpose and function of the (b)(3) class.

The (b)(2) class action was adopted for cases in which injunctive or declaratory relief is needed to remedy classwide wrongs.[24] According to the Advisory Committee notes to Rule 23, subdivision (b)(2) is "intended to reach situations where a party has taken action or refused to take action with respect to a class, and final relief of an injunctive nature or of a corresponding declaratory nature, settling the legality of the behavior with respect to the class as a whole, is appropriate."[25]

"Subdivision (b)(2) was added to [the Federal Rules] in 1966 primarily to facilitate the bringing of class actions in the civil rights area" because it was unclear whether a class action seeking injunctive or declaratory relief as to illegal discrimination was proper.[26] Before the adoption of (b)(2), the class action rule made no reference to declaratory relief, resulting in "some uncertainty whether a class action seeking one of those remedies was an appropriate device for vindicating civil rights."[27] Subsection (b)(2) became popular with public interest lawyers who used

---

22. *Id.*

23. FED. R. CIV. P. 23(b)(2).

24. *Holmes v. Cont'l Can Co.*, 706 F.2d 1144, 1155 n.8 (11th Cir. 1983).

25. FED. R. CIV. P. 23 advisory committee note (1966).

26. *Kincade v. Gen. Tire & Rubber Co.*, 635 F.2d 501, 506 n.6 (5th Cir. 1981) (quoting 7A CHARLES A. WRIGHT, ARTHUR R. MILLER & MARY K. KANE, FEDERAL PRACTICE AND PROCEDURE § 1775, at 470–71 (2d ed. 1986) [hereinafter WRIGHT, MILLER & KANE]).

27. *In re Monumental Life Ins. Co.*, 365 F.3d 408, 417 n.16 (5th Cir. 2004) (quoting WRIGHT, MILLER & KANE at 470).

this tool to provide relief to indigent and minority persons who otherwise could not obtain effective redress for civil rights–type injuries.[28]

The key to (b)(2) classes is "cohesiveness."[29] The prototypical (b)(2) homogeneous class does not contain individual fact issues.[30] Consequently, Rule 23(b)(2) requires a rigorous analysis of "cohesiveness" and is "premised on an assumption of homogeneity."[31] Cohesiveness means that the class members must be "bound together through 'preexisting or continuing legal relationships' or by some significant common trait such as race or gender."[32] Under Rule 23(b)(2), if there are disparate factual circumstances and if there is no "uniform group remed[y]," no class can be certified.[33] Put another way, "[a] class action may not be certified under Rule 23(b)(2) if relief specifically tailored to each class member would be necessary to correct the allegedly wrongful conduct of the defendant."[34]

1. Declaratory Relief

Section (b)(2) applies where the defendant's actions make appropriate "final injunctive relief or *corresponding* declaratory relief."[35] "Declaratory relief 'corresponds' to injunctive relief when [1] as a practical matter it affords injunctive relief or [2] serves as a basis for later injunctive relief."[36] Declaratory relief does not "correspond" to injunctive relief when it merely provides a basis for damages.[37] Professor Charles Alan Wright explains this distinction:

> A request for a declaration that a particular patent is invalid or that a statute is unconstitutional would qualify as "corresponding declaratory relief" because the

---

28. *Compaq Computer Corp. v. Lapray*, 135 S.W.3d 657, 664 (Tex. 2004).

29. *Allison*, 151 F.3d at 413.

30. *Id.* ("[T]he (b)(2) class is, by its very nature, assumed to be a homogenous and cohesive group with few conflicting interests among its members.").

31. *Lapray*, 135 S.W.3d at 670 (certification reversed for failure to rigorously analyze whether the class was cohesive).

32. *Barnes v. Am. Tobacco Co.*, 161 F.3d 127, 143 n.18 (3d Cir. 1998).

33. *See, e.g., Allison*, 151 F.3d at 414–15; *Barnes*, 161 F.3d at 143 (failure to certify class because of individual issues); *In re Rezulin Prods. Liab. Litig.*, 210 F.R.D. 61, 75 (S.D.N.Y. 2002) (no cohesion because there was no groupwide injury).

34. 5 JAMES WM. MOORE ET AL., MOORE'S FEDERAL PRACTICE § 23.43(2)(b), at 23-196 (3d ed. 2005); *see also Barnes*, 161 F.3d at 143.

35. FED. R. CIV. P. 23(b)(2) (emphasis added).

36. FED. R. CIV. P. 23 advisory committee note (1966).

37. 7A WRIGHT, MILLER & KANE § 1775, at 462–63; *see also Goldberg v. Winston & Morrone, P.C.*, No. 95 Civ. 9282 (LAK), 1997 WL 139526, at *3 (S.D.N.Y. Mar. 26, 1997) ((b)(2) class for a declaratory judgment that defendant's collection letters violated federal statute failed because the declaratory relief did not as a practical matter afford injunctive relief under (b)(2)); *Benfield v. Mocatta Metals Corp.*, No. 91 Civ. 8255 (LJF), 1993 WL 148978, at *5 (S.D.N.Y. May 5, 1993) (requested declaration "would merely provide a basis for an award of money damages"); *see also Sarafin v. Sears, Roebuck & Co.*, 446 F. Supp. 611, 615 (N.D. Ill. 1978) (the "effect of [the requested] declaration would be to provide the foundation for later damages claims, not injunctive relief. Therefore [plaintiff]'s suggested procedure is not a proper use of Rule 23(b)(2).").

resulting judicial directive would have the effect of "enjoining" the enforcement of the patent or the statute. *On the other hand, an action seeking a declaration that certain conduct constitutes a breach of contract would not qualify under Rule 23(b)(2) because the effect simply is to lay the basis for a damage award rather than injunctive relief.*[38]

For example, in *Goldberg v. Winston & Morrone, P.C.*,[39] the plaintiff sought certification of a (b)(2) class for a declaratory judgment that the defendant's collection letters violated the Fair Debt Collection Practices Act (FDCPA). The court denied certification because the declaratory relief did not "correspond" to injunctive relief under either prong of the Advisory Committee's test. First, the court held that the declaratory judgment was not the basis for later injunctive relief under (b)(2) because by statute, violations of the FDCPA cannot serve as the basis for injunctive relief for private plaintiffs. Second, the court held that the declaratory judgment did not as a practical matter afford injunctive relief under (b)(2):

> A determination that [Defendant] violated the FDCPA in this case would not afford injunctive relief in a practical sense, as [Defendant] could continue to engage in similar practices free of the risk of contempt. It would risk only future suits for statutory damages.[40]

Similarly, in *Benfield v. Mocatta Metals Corp.*,[41] the court held:

> Plaintiffs' request for a declaration that defendants' conduct constitutes a breach of contract does not qualify as a request for "corresponding declaratory relief" under the Rule because such a declaration would not have the effect of an injunction, but rather, would merely provide a basis for an award of money damages.[42]

2. Injunctions

A major issue arises in (b)(2) classes with respect to the rule's applicability to cases involving money damages. When the primary goal of the class claim is the recovery of damages rather than equitable relief, then the class is not properly certified under Rule 23(b)(2).[43] The Supreme Court has yet to weigh in on the issue directly, although it has expressed concerns about the necessity of providing opt-out rights

---

38. 7A WRIGHT, MILLER & KANE § 1775, at 462–63 (emphasis added).

39. 1997 WL 139526, at *3.

40. *Id.*

41. 1993 WL 148978, at *5; *see also Sarafin*, 446 F. Supp. at 615 ("[Plaintiff] seeks a declaration that Sears' conduct violated the Truth in Lending Act. The effect of such a declaration would be to provide the foundation for later damage claims, not injunctive relief. Therefore [plaintiff]'s suggested procedure is not a proper use of Rule 23(b)(2).").

42. *Benfield*, 1993 WL 148978, at *5.

43. *See Maldonado v. Ochsner Clinic Found.*, 493 F.3d 521, 525 (5th Cir. 2007) (where equitable relief would be meaningless, the "situation leaves monetary claims for retrospective damages predominant . . . .").

to class members as a matter of due process—especially when damages are sought.[44] In the absence of Supreme Court guidance, the various circuit courts of appeals are wrestling with the dividing line between (b)(2) and (b)(3) classes when it comes to claims for monetary damages.[45] Another issue on which the courts are divided involves claims for medical monitoring, as some of the states that have recognized such a claim treat monitoring as equitable relief, suitable for (b)(2) certification, while others consider monitoring to be a claim for money damages, and so findings of predominance and superiority are required.[46]

III. Notice, Opt-Out, and Other Due Process Considerations

As noted, Rule 23(b)(1) and (b)(2) are typically referred to as "mandatory" classes because the rule does not allow for class members to opt out of the class. With a few exceptions, these (b)(1) and (b)(2) class actions are generally used to afford equitable remedies, such as injunctions or declaratory judgments, but not monetary relief.

Until 2003, members of a (b)(1) or (b)(2) litigation class did not receive notice of the action. The class action rule has recently been amended to permit the district court, in its discretion, to issue notice to class members of such classes.[47] In contrast, class members of a (b)(3) class are always entitled to notice and the opportunity to opt out.[48] Regardless of the class type, all class members must receive notice of any proposed settlement when the settlement is offered to the court for final approval.[49]

Finally, in a (b)(3) class, unlike (b)(1) and (b)(2) classes, absent class members have the right to enter their appearance through counsel without having to satisfy the requirements for intervention.[50]

---

44. *See, e.g., Ortiz*, 527 U.S. at 847–48 (1999); *Ticor Title Ins. Co. v. Brown*, 511 U.S. 117, 121 (1994) (per curiam); *Phillips Petroleum Co. v. Shutts*, 472 U.S. 797, 812 (1985); *Mullane v. Cent. Hanover Bank & Trust Co.*, 339 U.S. 306, 313 (1950); *see also* Chapter 30, "Other Due Process Challenges to the Class Device."

45. For a detailed discussion of this issue, *see* Chapter 14, "The Special Role of 23(b)(2) Classes."

46. *See* Chapter 15, "Medical Monitoring Classes."

47. FED. R. CIV. P. 23(c)(2)(A) ("Notice. For (b)(1) or (b)(2) Classes. For any class certified under Rule 23(b)(1) or (b)(2), the court may direct notice to the class.").

48. FED. R. CIV. P. 23(c)(2)(B)(i)–(vii); *see also Eisen v. Carlisle & Jacquelin*, 417 U.S. 156, 176 (1974) ("[N]otice to identifiable class members is not a discretionary consideration to be waived in a particular case. It is, rather, an unambiguous requirement of Rule 23.").

49. FED. R. CIV. P. 23(e)(1) ("The court must direct notice in a reasonable manner to all class members who would be bound by the proposal.").

50. NEWBERG § 4:1, at 5 (citing FED. R. CIV. P. 23(c)(2)).

PREDOMINANCE AND SUPERIORITY

RAND P. NOLEN

I. Introduction

Before certifying any class, a district court is required to conduct a rigorous analysis of the Rule 23 prerequisites.[1] At the certification stage, the trial court does not determine the merits of the plaintiffs' claim, but can consider the merits of the case to the degree necessary to determine whether the requirements of Rule 23 will be satisfied.[2] In order to sustain the burden of establishing the propriety of class certification, the plaintiff must satisfy all four threshold Rule 23(a) requirements—numerosity, commonality, typicality, and adequacy of representation—and at least one Rule 23(b) requirement, such as showing that a class action is superior to other available methods for the fair and efficient adjudication of the controversy.[3] While subdivisions (b)(1) and (b)(2) provide for the bringing of a class action based on the type or effect of the relief being sought, Rule 23(b)(3) only authorizes a class action when justified by the presence of predominating common questions of law or fact and a determination that the class action is superior to other available methods for resolving the dispute fairly and efficiently.[4] The twin requirements of

---

1. *Castano v. Am. Tobacco Co.*, 84 F.3d 734, 740 (5th Cir.1996).

2. *Gen. Tel. Co. v. Falcon*, 457 U.S. 147, 160 (1982).

3. *See* FED. R. CIV. P. 23; *Amchem Prods. Inc. v. Windsor*, 521 U.S. 591, 613–14 (1997); *O'Sullivan v. Countrywide Home Loans, Inc.*, 319 F.3d 732, 737–38 (5th Cir. 2003).

4. FED. R. CIV. P. 23(b)(3) (Under Rule 23(b)(3), a class action is appropriate where the questions of law or fact common to the members of the class predominate over any questions affecting only individual members and the class action is superior to other available methods for the fair and efficient adjudication of the controversy. The matters pertinent to the findings include: (1) the interest of members of the class in individually controlling the prosecution or defense of separate actions; (2) the extent and nature of any litigation concerning the controversy already commenced by or against members of the class; (3) the desirability or undesirability of concentrating the litigation of the claims in the particular forum; (4) the difficulties likely to be encountered in the management of a class action).

Rule 23(b)(3) are known as predominance and superiority.[5] A Rule 23(b)(3) action is appropriate when the actual interests of the parties can be served best by settling their differences in a single action.[6]

II. The Predominance Requirement[7]

"The predominance inquiry . . . is 'far more demanding' than Rule 23(a)'s commonality requirement."[8] The predominance inquiry "tests whether proposed classes are sufficiently cohesive to warrant adjudication by representation."[9] Issues common to the class must predominate over individual issues.[10] The distinction is significant and should not be overlooked. "Rule 23(a)(2)'s commonality element requires that the proposed class members share at least one question of fact or law in common with each other."[11] Rule 23(b)(3)'s predominance element "requires that common issues predominate over issues affecting only individual class members."[12] "In order to meet the predominance requirement of Rule 23(b)(3), a plaintiff must establish that 'the issues in the class action that are subject to generalized proof, and thus applicable to the class as a whole, . . . predominate over those issues that are subject only to individualized proof.'"[13] Because the predominance requirement is more demanding than the commonality requirement under Rule 23(a), a court must deny certification where individual fact issues are abundant.[14]

Unfortunately, Rule 23(b)(3) does not specify precisely what the word "predominate" means,[15] and the case law does not provide any sort of checklist test for determining the sufficiency of the common questions necessary to comply with the rule.[16] Given that the "nature of the evidence that will suffice to resolve a question determines whether the question is common or individual,"[17] it follows

---

5. *In re Hydrogen Peroxide Antitrust Litig.*, 552 F.3d 305, 310–11 (3d Cir. 2008).

6. *See Clark v. Bonded Adjustment Co.*, 204 F.R.D. 662 (E.D. Wash. 2002).

7. For a more detailed discussion of the predominance questions in the context of specific types of class actions, *see* Chapters 17.A through 17.G, "Consumer Actions and Fraud/Reliance-Based Torts," "Antitrust," "Exposure Torts," "Oil and Gas Royalty Classes," "Employment Cases," "Insurance Class Actions," and "Securities Class Actions.

8. *Amchem*, 521 U.S. 623–24.

9. *Id.* at 621.

10. *In re Prudential Ins. Co. Am. Sales Practice Litig.*, 148 F.3d 283, 313–14 (3d Cir. 1998).

11. *In re Warfarin Sodium Antitrust Litig.*, 391 F.3d 516, 527–28 (3d Cir. 2004).

12. *Id. Cf. Danvers Motor Co. v. Ford Motor Co.*, 543 F.3d 141, 148 (3d Cir. 2008) ("[W]here an action is to proceed under Rule 23(b)(3), the commonality requirement is subsumed by the predominance requirement." (internal quotation marks omitted)).

13. *Rutstein v. Avis Rent-A-Car Sys., Inc.*, 211 F.3d 1228, 1233 (11th Cir. 2000).

14. *Moore v. PaineWebber, Inc.*, 306 F.3d 1247, 1252 (2d Cir. 2002).

15. *Minnesota v. U.S. Steel Corp.*, 44 F.R.D. 559, 569 (D. Minn. 1968).

16. *Dirks v. Clayton Brokerage Co. of St. Louis Inc.*, 105 F.R.D. 125, 132 (D. Minn. 1985).

17. *Blades v. Monsanto Co.*, 400 F.3d 562, 566 (8th Cir. 2005).

that "a district court must formulate some prediction as to how specific issues will play out in order to determine whether common or individual issues predominate in a given case."[18] Thus, the predominance inquiry obligates a court to consider the manner in which a trial on the merits would be conducted if a class were certified.[19] The inquiry necessarily "entails identifying the substantive issues that will control the outcome, assessing which issues will predominate, and then determining whether the issues are common to the class, a process that ultimately prevents the class from degenerating into a series of individual trials."[20]

Despite the fact that common questions must be present for certification, those questions need not be dispositive of the entire action in order for certification to be proper.[21] When one or more of the central issues in the action predominates, the action can be maintained pursuant to Rule 23(b)(3) even though other significant issues may have to be tried separately.[22] For example, predominance may be found even in cases where damages have to be determined individually.[23] However, if the central issues in the case require the separate adjudication of each class member's individual claim or defense, a Rule 23(b)(3) action is almost always not appropriate.[24]

III. The Necessity of Superiority

The second requirement that must be satisfied before an action may be brought under Rule 23(b)(3) is superiority.[25] The superiority requirement obligates the court to determine whether "a class action is superior to other available methods for fairly

---

18. *In re New Motor Vehicles Can. Exp. Antitrust Litig.*, 522 F.3d 6, 20 (1st Cir. 2008).

19. *See Bell Atl. Corp. v. AT&T Corp.*, 339 F.3d 294, 302 (5th Cir. 2003).

20. *Id.* (quotation marks and citation omitted).

21. *See Lockwood Motors, Inc. v. Gen. Motors Corp.*, 162 F.R.D. 569, 580 (D. Minn. 1995).

22. *Green v. Wolf Corp.*, 406 F.2d 291, 301 (2d Cir. 1968) ("The effective administration of 23(b)(3) will often require the use of the 'sensible device' of split trials."); *see also* Chapter 28, "Creative Application of Rule 23(c)(4): How Issue Certification Interacts with the Requirements of Rule 23(b)(3)."

23. *Heastie v. Cmty. Bank of Greater Peoria*, 125 F.R.D. 669, 676 (N.D. Ill. 1989) (common questions of fact that predominated in consumer's action against a bank under the Illinois Consumer Fraud Act despite the fact that damage determinations would entail individual factual questions).

24. *See, e.g., Klay v. Humana, Inc.*, 382 F.3d 1241 (11th Cir. 2004) (district court abused its discretion by certifying breach-of-contract claims against health-maintenance organizations because individualized issues of fact would most likely predominate); *McCracken v. Best Buy Stores, L.P.*, 248 F.R.D. 162 (S.D.N.Y. 2008) (Common questions of law or fact did not predominate over individual issues in suit by consumers against retailer based upon alleged misrepresentations as to a magazine subscription promotion. Retailer's liability under a breach-of-contract theory was contingent upon the specific oral representations made by individual sales employees to each consumer.); *In re St. Jude Med., Inc.*, 522 F.3d 836 (8th Cir. 2008) (district court improperly certified a products liability class involving heart valves because information on which the treating doctors based their actions in utilizing the valves would vary with each individual doctor).

25. FED. R. CIV. P. 23(b)(3).

and efficiently adjudicating the controversy."[26] The superiority requirement "reflects a broad policy of economy in the use of society's difference-settling machinery."[27]

Rule 23(b)(3) provides a nonexhaustive list of four factors pertinent to determining superiority.[28] The first matter for consideration identified in Rule 23(b)(3)(A) is the interest individual members may have in controlling the prosecution or defense of their rights in separate actions.[29]

The second matter identified in Rule 23(b)(3)(B) asks the court to analyze the "extent and nature of any litigation concerning the controversy already commenced by or against members of the class."[30] In the Ninth Circuit's decision in *Kamm v. California City Developments Co.*, the plaintiffs brought a putative class action for claims arising out of the defendants' land promotion scheme.[31] Before the plaintiffs filed suit, the California Attorney General and the Real Estate Commissioner of California had brought an action against four of the five defendants, in which a permanent injunction and final judgment on a settlement agreement had been entered.[32] The prior settlement agreement called for offers of restitution of principal payment to certain purchasers as well as an agreement that defendant would use its "best efforts to establish and implement a program to settle future disputes," including but not limited to filing quarterly reports with the Attorney General with the names of complainants, the general nature of the complaints, and the disposition.[33] Defendants were further enjoined from engaging in the fraudulent conduct that had given rise to the suit, and the state court retained jurisdiction over the matter. Under those circumstances, the Ninth Circuit upheld the district court's dismissal of the class complaints for lack of superiority because (1) significant relief had been realized already through the state court action, which included restitution, a permanent injunction, and the defendant's agreement to establish a program to settle future disputes; (2) a class action would duplicate and potentially negate aspects of the state action; (3) the state court retained jurisdiction; and (4) individual claimants still retained the ability to press their own claims and seek damages.[34] The *Kamm* court's analysis illustrates the factual and legal inquiry necessary to determine the superiority or inferiority of the class device in the face of prior litigation.

---

26. *Id.*

27. *Berley v. Dreyfus & Co.*, 43 F.R.D. 397, 398 (S.D.N.Y. 1967).

28. FED. R. CIV. P. 23(b)(3); *see also Amchem*, 521 U.S. at 623–24.

29. FED. R. CIV. P. 23(b)(3)(A); *see also Boca Raton Cmty. Hosp. v. Tenet Healthcare Corp.*, 238 F.R.D. 679, 700 (S.D. Fla. 2006).

30. FED. R. CIV. P. 23(b)(3)(B).

31. 509 F.2d 205 (9th Cir. 1975).

32. *Id.* at 207–08.

33. *Id.* at 208.

34. *Id.* at 212.

The third matter the court should consider under Rule 23(b)(3)(C) is the desirability of having the litigation concerning the controversy concentrated in one forum.[35] This too requires extensive analysis by the court of the particular facts and circumstances of the individual case.[36]

The fourth matter that is described in Rule 23(b)(3)(D) that requires consideration by the court is its evaluation of the management difficulties likely to be encountered if the action is continued as a class suit.[37] The court's focus is not on the convenience or burden of a class action suit in and of itself, but on the relative advantages of a class action suit over whatever other forms of litigation might be realistically available to the plaintiffs.[38]

---

35. FED. R. CIV. P. 23(b)(3)(C).

36. *See, e.g., Sweet v. Pfizer*, 232 F.R.D. 360, 372–73 (C.D. Cal. 2005) (plaintiffs alleged products case against drug company, and court considered appropriateness of consolidating cases in a single forum).

37. FED. R. CIV. P. 23(b)(3)(D).

38. *See In re Managed Care Litig.*, 209 F.R.D. 678, 692 (S.D. Fla. 2002) (noting that this consideration "requires the Court to determine whether there is a better method of handling the controversy other than through the class action mechanism"); *Carnegie v. Mut. Sav. Life Ins. Co.*, No. CV-99-S-3292-NE, 2002 U.S. Dist. LEXIS 21396, at *76–77 (N.D. Ala. Nov. 1, 2002) ("It is only when management difficulties make a class action less fair and efficient than some other method, such as individual interventions or consolidation of individual lawsuits, that a class action is improper." (quoting HERBERT B. NEWBERG & ALBA CONTE, NEWBERG ON CLASS ACTIONS § 4:32, at 4-125 (3d ed. 1992))).

CERTIFICATION HEARINGS AND DECISIONS

STEVEN F. GRIFFITH, JR.[1]

I. Introduction

This chapter addresses class certification hearings and decisions. Federal Rule of Civil Procedure 23 governs the process by which federal courts decide whether to allow a proceeding to continue as a class action. The sections of the Rule that are particularly applicable to this chapter are, first, 23(c)(1)(A), providing "[a]t an early practicable time after a person sues or is sued as a class representative, the court must determine by order whether to certify the action as a class action." Second, Rule 23(c)(1)(C) provides, "An order that grants or denies class certification may be altered or amended before final judgment." Finally, Rule 23(f) states, "A court of appeals may permit an appeal from an order granting or denying class-action certification under this rule if a petition for permission to appeal is filed with the circuit clerk within 14 days after the order is entered. An appeal does not stay proceedings in the district court unless the district judge or the court of appeals so orders."[2]

There has been considerable variety in circuit and state court interpretation of both Rule 23 and the Supreme Court holdings regarding the certification process. Major points of contention have been the evidentiary standard and the treatment of expert testimony at the certification stage. However, recently, cases relying on the 2003 Amendments to Rule 23 have produced some movement toward a common ground. That said, it is still incumbent upon practitioners to confirm

---

1. The author wishes to thank Sarah K. Casey, Esq. and Rosita R. Strehle for their wonderful assistance with the writing of this chapter.
2. FED. R. CIV. P. 23.

their own court precedent and local rules and practices when preparing for a class action certification hearing.

II. The Hearing Requirement

There is nothing in Rule 23 that mandates, recommends, or even describes a class certification hearing. Instead, case law illustrates the current jurisprudential stance on classification hearings. The general rule is that no hearing is required by Rule 23, but one is appropriate in most instances to ensure a full record.[3]

The nature and scope of the class to be certified determine whether a full evidentiary hearing is necessary. In some circumstances, the certification hearing may consist only of argument regarding the Rule 23 requirements, and the court may rely chiefly on stipulations and affidavits submitted by the parties.[4] The consensus is that a full evidentiary hearing is necessary when it is not possible to resolve the class certification issue by the pleadings alone.[5] Within this general outlook, the circuit courts have developed their own standards. For example, the Second Circuit has not mandated an evidentiary hearing, but finds that "the district judge must receive enough evidence, by affidavits, documents, or testimony, to be satisfied that each Rule 23 requirement has been met."[6] The Fifth Circuit maintains that the district court should "ordinarily" conduct an evidentiary hearing,[7] and that it *must* conduct one "when there is any doubt about the issue, even when counsel fails to move for such a hearing."[8] An evidentiary hearing is only unnecessary when there are clear grounds for denial of class certification.[9] The Eleventh Circuit utilizes a different standard, providing that the failure to hold an evidentiary hearing "does not require reversal unless the parties can show that the hearing, if held, would have affected their rights substantially."[10] Finally, the Fourth Circuit does not require an evidentiary hearing, but it notes, "[i]t is seldom, if ever, possible to resolve class repre-

---

3. MANUAL FOR COMPLEX LITIGATION (FOURTH) § 21.21 (2004).

4. *Id.*

5. *See Int'l Woodworkers v. Chesapeake Bay Plywood Corp.*, 659 F.2d 1259, 1267–68 (4th Cir. 1981); *Morrison v. Booth*, 730 F.2d 642, 643–44 (11th Cir. 1984); *see also Gen. Tel. Co. v. Falcon*, 457 U.S. 147, 160 (1982) ("Sometimes the issues are plain enough from the pleadings to determine whether the interests of the absent parties are fairly encompassed within the named plaintiff's claim, and sometimes it may be necessary for the court to probe behind the pleadings before coming to rest on the certification question.").

6. *In re Initial Pub. Offering Sec. Litig.*, 471 F.3d 24, 41 (2d Cir. 2006).

7. *Merrill v. S. Methodist Univ.*, 806 F.2d 600, 608–09 (5th Cir. 1986) (citing *King v. Gulf Oil Co.*, 581 F.2d 1184, 1186 (5th Cir. 1981)).

8. *Morrison*, 730 F.2d at 643–44 (interpreting Fifth Circuit precedent) (citing *Satterwhite v. City of Greenville*, 578 F.2d 987, 993 n.7 (5th Cir. 1978)).

9. *Id.*

10. *Grayson v. K Mart Corp.*, 79 F.3d 1086, 1099 (11th Cir. 1996).

sentation questions from the pleadings, and where facts developed during discovery proceedings are inadequate, an evidentiary hearing should be held."[11]

Counsel should check their respective circuit case law to assess where along the spectrum the circuit falls and any relevant nuances it may have adopted. In addition, if litigation is taking place in state court, there may be additional statutes, rules, and practices that may pertain to class certification proceedings.[12]

III. Conduct of the Hearing

A. BURDEN OF PROOF

The party seeking to certify a class bears the burden of proof.[13] As discussed elsewhere in this book, there are essentially five Rule 23 requirements that must be proved. First, Rule 23(a) requires proof of (1) numerosity, (2) commonality, (3) typicality, and (4) adequacy.[14] Second, Rule 23(b) requires that the proposed class fit within one of those subsections:

(1) prosecuting separate actions by or against individual class members would create a risk of:

(A) inconsistent or varying adjudications with respect to individual class members that would establish incompatible standards of conduct for the party opposing the class; or

(B) adjudications with respect to individual class members that, as a practical matter, would be dispositive of the interests of the other members not parties to the individual adjudications or would substantially impair or impede their ability to protect their interests;

(2) the party opposing the class has acted or refused to act on grounds that apply generally to the class, so that final injunctive relief or corresponding declaratory relief is appropriate respecting the class as a whole; or

(3) the court finds that the questions of law or fact common to class members predominate over any questions affecting only individual members, and that a class action is superior to other available methods for fairly and efficiently adjudicating the controversy.[15]

---

11. *Int'l Woodworkers*, 659 F.2d at 1268.

12. *See* section IV, *infra*, for more information.

13. *See Caridad v. Metro-North Commuter R.R.*, 191 F.3d 283, 291 (2d Cir. 1999); *Castano v. Am. Tobacco Co.*, 84 F.3d 734 (5th Cir. 1996).

14. Fed. R. Civ. P. 23(a).

15. Fed. R. Civ. P. 23(b).; *see also* Chapter 2, "Ethical and Practical Issues of Communicating with Members of a Class."

The failure of one element precludes certification.[16] That the party seeking certification bears the burden is clear; it is what kind of burden it must carry that is relatively unsettled. When it comes to the evidentiary standard that the moving party must meet and the extent to which the court may consider the merits of the action in its analysis, there is no straightforward answer.

B. RIGOROUS ANALYSIS OF CERTIFICATION REQUIREMENTS

The Supreme Court last ruled on the standards governing certification decision making in 1982.[17] In its last proclamation on the issue, *General Telephone Co. of the Southwest v. Falcon*, the Court reversed the court of appeals' judgment affirming the class certification order and remanded for additional proceedings.[18] The Court found that the plaintiff in the Title VII class action had not satisfied the Rule 23 requirements. The Court quoted a Fifth Circuit Title VII concurring opinion that had advocated for more precise pleadings because "without reasonable specificity the court cannot define the class, cannot determine whether the representation is adequate, and the employer does not know how to defend."[19] In *Falcon*, the Supreme Court held that a class action may only be certified "if the trial court is satisfied, after a rigorous analysis, that the prerequisites of Rule 23(a) have been satisfied" and that the district court failed "to evaluate carefully" these requirements.[20] The Court's guidance has proved to be at best ambiguous, and at worst contentious.

Courts have had a difficult time reconciling the "rigorous analysis" message with the Court's earlier ruling in *Eisen v. Carlisle & Jacquelin*,[21] which admonished courts not to delve into the merits of a potential class action suit at the certification stage:

> We find nothing in either the language or history of Rule 23 that gives a court any authority to conduct a preliminary inquiry into the merits of a suit in order to determine whether it may be maintained as a class action. Indeed, such a procedure contravenes the Rule by allowing a representative plaintiff to secure the benefits of a class action without first satisfying the requirements for it.[22]

---

16. *See Heaven v. Trust Co. Bank*, 118 F.3d 735, 737 (11th Cir. 1997); *Ansari v. N.Y. Univ.*, 179 F.R.D. 112 (S.D.N.Y. 1998).

17. *See Falcon*, 457 U.S. at 147.

18. *Id.*

19. *Id.* (quoting *Johnson v. Georgia Highway Express, Inc.*, 417 F.2d 1122, 1126 (5th Cir. 1969) (Godbold, J., concurring), *overruled by Griffin v. Dugger*, 823 F.2d 1476 (11th Cir. 1987). Judge Godbold went on to lament the danger to class members who would be bound by the judgment if the class were too broad because some jurists operated under the belief that "all will be well for surely the plaintiff will win and manna will fall on all members of the class." *Johnson*, 417 F.2d at 1127).

20. *Falcon*, 457 U.S. at 160–61.

21. 417 U.S. 156, 177 (1974).

22. *Id.* The Court also noted that a preliminary determination of the merits could prejudice the defendant since it is devoid of the traditional civil trial safeguards.

In *Eisen*, the district court had conducted a preliminary hearing on the merits and determined that the plaintiff was more than likely to prevail on his claims, and it therefore ordered that the defendant bear 90 percent of the cost of notice to the class members.[23] The Court was very clear that this premature merits prediction was unacceptable.

Of course, the evidence regarding the certification requirements often overlaps with the merits of an action, and in some cases, that overlap has made inroads upon the "rigorous analysis" standard. For instance, *Eisen* influenced the language in the Second Circuit's decision in *Caridad v. Metro-North*, finding that "class certification would not be warranted absent *some showing* that the challenged practice is causally related to a pattern of disparate treatment."[24] District courts picked up on the "some showing" standard, and the Second Circuit was left to rehabilitate the evidentiary standard seven years later in *In re Initial Public Offering Securities Litigation*.[25]

In its later statement on the issue, the Second Circuit clarified

(1) that a district judge may not certify a class without making a ruling that each Rule 23 requirement is met and that a lesser standard such as "some showing" for satisfying each requirement will not suffice, (2) that all evidence must be assessed as with any other threshold issue, (3) that the fact that a Rule 23 requirement might overlap with an issue on the merits does not avoid the court's obligation to make a ruling as to whether the requirement is met, although such a circumstance might appropriately limit the scope of the court's inquiry at the class certification stage.[26]

The Second Circuit clarified that the *Eisen* prohibition against consideration of the merits was made in the context of an analysis of the merits that did not involve a Rule 23 requirement; the admonishment simply did not apply in cases where the court may need to look to the merits to determine a certification requirement.[27] The Second Circuit did not, however, throw caution to the wind in advocating for a more stringent analysis. It still recognized that a court must tread carefully into merits: "To avoid the risk that a Rule 23 hearing will extend into a protracted mini-trial of substantial portions of the underlying litigation, a district judge must be accorded considerable discretion to limit both discovery and the extent of the hearing on Rule 23 requirements."[28]

---

23. *Id.* at 177.

24. 191 F.3d at 292 (emphasis added).

25. 471 F.3d 24, 27 (2d Cir. 2006).

26. *Id.*

27. *Id.* at 34 ("Unfortunately, the statement in *Eisen* that a court considering certification must not consider the merits has sometimes been taken out of context and applied in cases where a merits inquiry either concerns a Rule 23 requirement or overlaps with such a requirement.").

28. *Id.* at 41.

As *In re Initial Public Offering* indicates, there has been a recent movement to make the certification process more stringent. The judicial debate has resulted in some circuits proclaiming a preponderance of the evidence standard and eschewing any lesser burden that may have been used in the past.[29] Other courts have expressed similar sentiments, recognizing the importance of a "rigorous analysis," the danger of allowing avoidance of the merits to trump the Rule 23 requirements, and at the same time, the need to limit a court's foray into the merits of an action at the certification stage.[30] This tension is not new, and courts will most likely continue to struggle with it.[31]

C. THE 2003 AND 2009 AMENDMENTS TO RULE 23

There are three 2003 amendments that are applicable to class certification hearings. First, the provision that a class certification "may be conditional" was deleted from Rule 23(c)(1)(C). The court retains the power to alter or amend the class certification, but the Advisory Committee eliminated the conditional language because "[a] court that is not satisfied that the requirements of Rule 23 have been met should refuse certification until they have been met."[32] As noted by the Sec-

---

29. *Teamsters Local 445 Freight Div. Pension Fund v. Bombardier Inc.*, 546 F.3d 196, 202 (2d Cir. 2008) ("Today, we dispel any remaining confusion and hold that the preponderance of the evidence standard applies to evidence proffered to establish Rule 23's requirements."); *see also Alaska Elec. Pension Fund v. Flowserve Corp.*, 572 F.3d 221, 228 (5th Cir. 2009); *In re Hydrogen Peroxide Antitrust Litig.*, 552 F.3d 305, 320 (3d Cir. 2008) ("Rule 23 findings must be made by a preponderance of the evidence.").

30. *See, e.g., Love v. Turlington*, 733 F.2d 1562, 1564 (11th Cir. 1984) ("While it is true that a trial court may not properly reach the merits of a claim when determining whether class certification is warranted, this principle should not be talismanically invoked to artificially limit a trial court's examination of the factors necessary to a reasoned determination of whether a plaintiff has met her burden of establishing each of the Rule 23 class action requirements."); *Szabo v. Bridgeport Machs., Inc.*, 249 F.3d 672, 676 (7th Cir. 2001) ("Before deciding whether to allow a case to proceed as a class action, therefore, a judge should make whatever factual and legal inquiries are necessary under Rule 23 . . . where it is not possible to evaluate impending difficulties without making a choice of law, and not possible to make a sound choice of law without deciding whether Bridgeport authorized or ratified the dealers' representations—then the judge must make a preliminary inquiry into the merits.").

31. *See, e.g., Prof'l Adjusting Sys. of Am., Inc. v. Gen. Adjustment Bureau, Inc.*, 64 F.R.D. 35, 38 (S.D.N.Y. 1974) ("Enough must be laid bare to let the judge survey the factual scene on a kind of sketchy relief map, leaving for later view the myriad of details that cover the terrain. But to find its way, the Court must know something of the commonality of action or frustration that binds the class."); *Heerwagon v. Clear Channel Commc'ns*, 435 F.3d 219, 232 (2d Cir. 2006), *overruled on other grounds by Teamsters Local 445 Freight Div.*, 546 F.3d 196 ("Some overlap with the ultimate review on the merits is an acceptable collateral consequence of the "rigorous analysis" that courts must perform when determining whether Rule 23's requirements have been met, so long as it does not stem from a forbidden preliminary inquiry into the merits.").

32. FED. R. CIV. P. 23 advisory committee note (2003). The text of 23(c)(1)(C) was "An order that grants or denies class certification may be conditional, and may be altered or amended before the decision on the merits." It now reads: "An order that grants or denies class certification may be altered or amended before final judgment."

ond Circuit, this change is an attempt to make the court's analysis of certification issues more stringent.[33]

Second, Rule 23(c)(1)(A) no longer mandates that the certification decision be made "as soon as practicable"; it now reads "at an early practicable time."[34] The Committee recognized the "many valid reasons that may justify deferring the initial certification decision."[35] The Second Circuit found the allowance of additional time another indication that the court was to strengthen its analysis of class certification issues.[36] The Advisory Committee itself commented on the "merits" debate, recognizing that the court may indeed need prehearing case development in order to look to the merits as they relate to the Rule 23 requirements:

> Although an evaluation of the probable outcome on the merits is not properly part of the certification decision, discovery in aid of the certification decision often includes information required to identify the nature of the issues that actually will be presented at trial. In this sense it is appropriate to conduct controlled discovery into the "merits," limited to those aspects relevant to making the certification decision on an informed basis.[37]

Third, the 2003 Amendments included newly created Rule 23(c)(1)(b), which states in relevant part, "[a]n order that certifies a class action must define the class and the class claims, issues, or defenses . . ." The Third Circuit has interpreted this change to require "more specific and more deliberate treatment of the class's issues, claims and defenses" than was common in earlier practice.[38] Demanding more specific information in the certification order implies a more "rigorous analysis" at the certification stage. A lack of uniformity still exists, however, and it is unclear whether and to what extent the 2003 amendments have altered past court decisions.[39]

---

33. *In re Initial Pub. Offering*, 471 F.3d at 39.

34. FED. R. CIV. P. 23.

35. FED. R. CIV. P. 23 advisory committee note (2003) (citing THOMAS E. WILLGING, LAURAL L. HOOPER & ROBERT J. NIEMIC, EMPIRICAL STUDY OF CLASS ACTIONS IN FOUR FEDERAL DISTRICT COURTS: FINAL REPORT TO THE ADVISORY COMMITTEE ON CIVIL RULES 26–36 (Federal Judicial Center 1996)).

36. *In re Initial Pub. Offering*, 471 F.3d at 39.

37. FED. R. CIV. P. 23 advisory committee note (2003).

38. *Wachtel v. Guardian Life Ins. Co. of Am.*, 453 F.3d 179, 185 (3d Cir. 2006).

39. *See, e.g., In re Cardizem CD Antitrust Litig.*, 200 F.R.D. 297, 321–22 (E.D. Mich. 2001) (In analyzing the 23(b) requirements, the court stated, "[a]t the class certification stage, it is not necessary to identify specific benchmarks or methodology to ascertain the amount of damages. It is sufficient to note at this stage that there are methodologies available, and that Rule 23(c)(1) and (d) provide ample flexibility to deal with individual damages issues that may develop") (citing *In re NASDAQ Mkt. Makers Antitrust Litig.*, 169 F.3d 493, 522 (S.D.N.Y. 1996)). As noted before, 23(c)(1) has been revised to no longer include the statement that a class certification may be conditional. To what extent the flexibility the court refers to is diminished by this change is unclear.

Only one change occurred with the 2009 Amendments. Rule 23(f) was amended to allow a party 14 days after an order granting or denying class certification to file a petition for permission to appeal with the circuit clerk. This amendment is effective as of December 1, 2009.

IV. Class Action Experts

Some courts allow expert testimony on whether or not Rule 23 requirements have been met.[40] Recently, the Third Circuit has included the evaluation of expert testimony as part of the required "rigorous analysis" when it bears on certification, rather than merits, issues.[41] In *In re Hydrogen Peroxide Antitrust Litigation*, the court stated, "[e]xpert opinion with respect to class certification, like any matter relevant to a Rule 23 requirement, calls for rigorous analysis. It follows that opinion testimony should not be uncritically accepted as establishing a Rule 23 requirement merely because the court holds the testimony should not be excluded . . . ."[42]

Interestingly, a district court in Georgia heard testimony from class action expert Herbert Newberg.[43] The defendants filed a motion to strike the testimony of Professor Newberg because it contained legal conclusions. The court denied the motion, indicating that it would only consider the factual opinions of Professor Newberg and disregard his legal conclusions.[44]

The federal courts are split on whether the trial judge can resolve conflicts between experts' testimony at the certification stage. The vast majority of courts will settle factual disputes in order to determine whether Rule 23 requirements have been met. For example, the Eighth Circuit has stated that district courts may be required to resolve the disputes of experts.[45] Similarly, the First Circuit held that the district court was entitled to look beyond the pleadings when determining the class certification issues, including a consideration of both parties' expert reports.[46] The Seventh Circuit has rejected a district court's reasoning that expert conflict was enough to justify certification, and held instead that the court should resolve such disputes at this stage:

---

40. *See, e.g., In re Polymedica Corp. Sec. Litig.*, 432 F.3d 1, 6 (1st Cir. 2005); *see also* Chapter 13, "*Daubert* Challenges in Class Certification."

41. *In re Hydrogen Peroxide Antitrust Litig.*, 552 F.3d at 323.

42. *Id.*

43. *In re Domestic Air Transp. Antitrust Litig.*, 137 F.R.D. 677, 682 n.2 (N.D. Ga. 1991). Herbert Newberg is the author of *Newberg on Class Actions*.

44. The court went on to note that the only legal conclusions of Professor Newberg to which it would refer would be those found in his treatise *Newberg on Class Actions*.

45. *Blades v. Monsanto Co.*, 400 F.3d 562, 575 (8th Cir. 2005).

46. *In re Polymedica Corp.*, 432 F.3d at 6.

[A] district judge may not duck hard questions by observing that each side has some support, or that considerations relevant to class certification also may affect the decision on the merits. Tough questions must be faced and squarely decided, if necessary by holding evidentiary hearings and choosing between competing perspectives.[47]

Equally controversial is the degree to which courts must determine the admissibility and reliability of expert testimony at the certification stage. This analysis overlaps with the discussion of the *Daubert* standard, which will be further addressed in Chapter 13, but we will include a word about it here.

Lax treatment of expert testimony developed in part from the same sentiment that diluted the evidentiary standard after *Eisen*. Courts appeared reluctant to delve into the merits of the actions and therefore took a lackadaisical stance regarding expert testimony. A California district court stated, "At this early stage, robust gatekeeping of expert evidence is not required; rather, the court should ask only if expert evidence is 'useful in evaluating whether class certification requirements have been met.'"[48] But other courts have rallied around a higher standard just as they had in regard to the evidentiary standard. The Second Circuit, at the same time it recanted its earlier evidentiary standard of "some showing," overruled its previous holding that expert testimony was sufficient to establish class certification requirements as long as it met the low standard of not being "fatally flawed."[49]

A growing trend counsels that trial courts should make reliability determinations in the context of deciding certification. Regardless of the credentials of the expert, the court should not blindly follow his or her conclusions on Rule 23 requirements. The court should analyze the testimony as it would any other factual evidence and weigh any conflict between the parties' experts. However, the court must be careful to only proceed into the merits of the action to the extent that they bear on a Rule 23 requirement.[50]

V. Interlocutory Appeals[51]

Rule 23(f) governs appeals of class action certification decisions:

---

47. *West v. Prudential Sec., Inc.*, 282 F.3d 935, 938 (7th Cir. 2002) (citing *Szabo v. Bridgeport Machs., Inc.*, 249 F.3d 672 (7th Cir. 2001)); *see also Issacs v. Sprint Corp.*, 261 F.3d 679 (7th Cir. 2001).

48. *Ellis v. Costco Wholesale Corp.*, 240 F.R.D. 627, 635 (N.D. Cal. 2007) (quoting *Dukes v. Wal-Mart, Inc.*, 222 F.R.D. 189, 191 (N.D. Cal. 2004)).

49. *In re Initial Public Offering*, 471 F.3d at 42 (overruling *In re Visa Check/Mastermoney Antitrust Litig.*, 280 F.3d 124 (2d Cir. 2001)).

50. *In re Hydrogen Peroxide Antitrust Litig.*, 552 F.3d at 324 ("That weighing expert opinions is proper does not make it necessary in every case or unlimited in scope.").

51. *See also* Chapter 5, "Interlocutory Appeals."

A court of appeals may permit an appeal from an order granting or denying class-action certification under this rule if a petition for permission to appeal is filed with the circuit clerk within 10 days after the order is entered. An appeal does not stay proceedings in the district court unless the district judge or the court of appeals so orders.[52]

These appeals are not automatic; it is within the discretion of the court of appeals whether to allow an interlocutory appeal. Circuit courts generally will not allow interlocutory review if the decision granting or denying certification centered on case-specific facts.[53] Frequently, as the cases cited in this chapter illustrate, an appeal turns on issues of evidentiary standards or merits analysis.

If an appeal is granted, the standard of review is abuse of discretion, "[p]rovided that the district court has applied the proper legal standards in deciding whether to certify a class."[54] If an incorrect legal standard has been used, the issue is reviewed de novo.[55] It is not clear whether the abuse of discretion standard may be used only for the court's overall certification decision or also for the court's rulings on each of the six requirements.[56] However, courts routinely apply the standard to the individual conclusions.[57]

It is interesting to note that on appeal, the court will examine not only the evidence available to the lower court, but also available "facts developed at the trial of the plaintiffs' individual claims."[58]

VI. Particular State Laws Governing Certification Hearings[59]

When litigating in state court, it is important to note that there may be additional or different requirements as to class certification hearings found in that state's class action statutes, rules, case law, and local practices. While many states' cer-

---

52. FED. R. CIV. P. 23(f). Effective December 1, 2009, absent contrary congressional action, 23(f) will allow 14 days to file the appeal.

53. *Prado-Steiman ex rel. Prado v. Bush*, 221 F.3d 1266, 1275–76 (11th Cir. 2000) ("We reiterate, however, that a class certification decision which 'turns on case-specific matters of fact and district court discretion'—as most certification decisions indisputably do—generally will not be appropriate for interlocutory review" (quoting FED. R. CIV. P. 23 advisory committee note (2003))).

54. *Caridad*, 191 F.3d at 291. *See also Mullen v. Treasure Chest Casino, LLC*, 186 F.3d 620, 624 (5th Cir. 1999); *Jenkins v. Raymark Indus., Inc.*, 782 F.2d 468, 472 (5th Cir. 1986).

55. *In re Initial Pub. Offering*, 471 F.3d at 32.

56. *Id.*

57. *Id.*

58. *E. Texas Motor Freight Sys., Inc. v. Rodriguez*, 431 U.S. 395, 406 n.12 (1977); *see also Merrill*, 806 F.2d at 607–08.

59. Part III of this book contains a state-by-state analysis of the ways in which each state has applied, modified, or rejected the class action model of Federal Rule of Civil Procedure 23.

tification requirements are based on Federal Rule of Civil Procedure 23, there are differences both between state law and federal law and among the states.

Some state laws may require a certification hearing. For example, both Louisiana's and Iowa's class action statutes mandate a certification hearing, and the Pennsylvania statute has been interpreted by the courts to so require as well.[60]

State courts also differ in their view of the moving party's burden at the certification stage. The Pennsylvania Supreme Court has stated its view that the burden is "not a heavy one. It is the strong and oft-repeated policy of this Commonwealth that, in applying the rules for class certification, decisions should be made liberally and in favor of maintaining a class action."[61] While the Michigan Supreme Court has not classified the burden as a light one, it has stated that "the federal 'rigorous analysis' requirement does not necessarily bind state courts."[62]

The state courts tend to follow the prevailing federal stance as to class action experts. For instance, the Colorado Court of Appeals quoted *In re Hydrogen Peroxide Antitrust Litigation* in holding that a court must not blindly accept an expert's testimony as establishing a Rule 23 requirement.[63] Despite the relative federal/state alignment, however, it certainly still behooves a practitioner to check the local court precedent before proceeding.

Many states also have distinct rules regarding the appeals of certification orders. For instance, the Missouri Western District Court of Appeals lists the circumstances the court is to consider when determining whether to grant an interlocutory appeal on a certification order:

1. Whether the trial court's denial of class status would effectively end the litigation and any realistic chance that individual claims could be prosecuted.
2. Whether the trial court's grant of class status would put substantial pressure on the defendant to settle without regard to the merits of the case.
3. Whether an interlocutory appeal of the trial court's class action determination would facilitate the development of the law pertaining to class actions.
4. Whether the trial court's order granting or denying class certification is clearly erroneous.

---

60. LA. CODE CIV. PROC. ANN. art. 592(A)(3)(a) (2009) ("No motion to certify an action as a class action shall be granted prior to a hearing on the motion. Such hearing shall be held as soon as practicable . . . ."); IOWA R. CIV. P. 1.262(1) (2009) ("[T]he court shall hold a hearing and determine whether or not the action is to be maintained as a class action."); *Baldassari v. Suburban Cable TV Co., Inc.*, 808 A.2d 184, 188 (Pa. 2002) (citing PA. R. CIV. P. 1707); *Volpe v. Union Fid. Life Ins. Co.*, 507 A.2d 1250 (Pa. 1986) ("The very language of the above-cited rule dictates that, in all class actions, a hearing to determine certification is required.").

61. *Baldassari*, 808 A.2d at 189.

62. *Henry v. Dow Chem. Co.*, 484 Mich. 483 (2009).

63. *Jackson v. Unocal Corp.*, No. 09CA0610, 2009 WL 2182603, at *8 (Colo. Ct. App. July 23, 2009) (vacating the district court's certification order because it was an abuse of discretion for the court to not weigh conflicting expert testimony).

5. Whether there are any other special circumstances sufficient to justify an interlocutory appeal.[64]

In addition to what may amount to substantive differences in these statutes and Rule 23, there may also be procedural differences in the time for filing for an appeal. For example, New Mexico state courts allow 10 days for the filing of a certification order appeal, while, as of December 1, 2009, Rule 23 allows 14 days.[65] Local court rules may also affect both timing and other logistical particulars of any appeal.

VII. Conclusion

The party moving for certification bears the burden of proof at the certification hearing. While it is still unsettled as to what exactly Rule 23 demands of courts at the certification stage, recent court opinions have more strongly aligned the federal courts with the "rigorous analysis" standard advocated by the U.S. Supreme Court in *Falcon*, although there continues to be concern over balancing a "rigorous analysis" of the Rule 23 requirements and abstaining from a preliminary hearing on the merits. Despite a recent confluence among the federal courts, state statutes and state court rules pertaining to class actions contribute to a lack of uniformity in this area of the law. Potential differences in circuit and/or local laws and requirements often exacerbate the differences in conducting hearings and certification outcomes across the country.

---

64. Mo. Ct. App. W.D. R. 40.
65. *See, e.g.*, N.M. Ann. State Ct. R. art. 2, R. 12-203A.

INTERLOCUTORY APPEALS

MICHAEL S. TRUESDALE

I. Introduction

Unlike the run-of-the-mill rulings in a typical case, the Federal Rules of Civil Procedure specifically allow for interlocutory appeals of orders "granting or denying class-action certification."[1] Rule 23(f) reflects a recognition that, while many class action suits present issues no more worthy of immediate review than many other interlocutory rulings, the consequences of a class certification ruling justified the expansion of opportunities to obtain interlocutory review.[2] For example, an order denying certification in a consumer-related case may compel individual plaintiffs to proceed to final judgment on the merits of a claim before they can challenge the certification ruling, even though the value of the individual claims may be much smaller than the litigation costs. On the other side, an order granting certification "may force a defendant to settle rather than incur the costs of defending a class action and run the risk of potentially ruinous liability."[3] Rule 23(f) addresses the concerns on both ends of the spectrum by establishing a low-cost mechanism by which discretionary review may be granted in cases presenting issues worthy of review.[4]

In addition to the procedures set forth in Rule 23(f), appellate review of interlocutory rulings made in class actions may be available under statute as well. For example, the Class Action Fairness Act of 2005 provides means for seeking interlocutory review of an order remanding a removed class action.[5] And other statutes governing interlocutory appeals, including 28 U.S.C. § 1292(b), may allow review

---

1. FED. R. CIV. P. 23(f).
2. FED. R. CIV. P. 23(f), advisory committee note ¶ 2 (1998).
3. Id.
4. Id.
5. See 28 U.S.C. § 1453(c)(1).

of interlocutory orders in class action cases that do not give rise to an appeal otherwise available under Rule 23(f).[6]

II. Overview of Applicable Rules

A. RULE 23(F)

Prior to 1998, the Federal Rules of Civil Procedure did not provide for interlocutory appeals of class certification orders.[7] The 1998 amendments added subdivision 23(f) to allow such appeals. Save for an amendment effective December 1, 2009, which extends the time for appeal from 10 to 14 days, the subdivision has since been unchanged. Rule 23(f) now states:

> Appeals. A court of appeals may permit an appeal from an order granting or denying class action certification under this rule if a petition for permission to appeal is filed with the circuit clerk within 14 days after the order is entered. An appeal does not stay proceedings in the district court unless the district judge or the court of appeals so orders.[8]

Rule 23(f) was promulgated pursuant to the authority conferred by 28 U.S.C. § 1292(e).[9] Upon the adoption of Rule 23(f), Federal Rule of Appellate Procedure 5 was also modified "to establish the procedure for petitioning of leave to appeal under this subdivision (f)."[10]

While Rule 23(f) confers the right to seek interlocutory review of an order granting or denying class certification, the failure to raise an interlocutory challenge does not preclude a postjudgment challenge to the certification ruling.[11]

---

6. *See Richardson Elecs., Ltd. v. Panache Broad. of Pa., Inc.*, 202 F.3d 957, 959 (7th Cir. 2000) (explaining that "district judges should not, and we shall not, authorize appeal under 28 U.S.C. § 1292(b) when appeal might lie under Rule 23(f)").

7. *See, e.g., Armstrong v. Martin Marietta Corp.*, 138 F.3d 1374, 1378 n.1 (11th Cir. 1998) ("The district court's denial of class certification is an interlocutory order, not reviewable as of right until after the entry of final judgment.").

8. FED. R. CIV. P. 23(f).

9. *See* 28 U.S.C. § 1292(e) ("The Supreme Court may prescribe rules, in accordance with section 2072 of this title, to provide for an appeal of an interlocutory decision to the courts of appeals that is not otherwise provided for under subsection (a), (b), (c), or (d)."). In *Bolin v. Sears, Roebuck & Co.*, 231 F.3d 970, 972–74 (5th Cir. 2000), the Fifth Circuit rejected a constitutional separation of powers challenge to the delegation of rulemaking authority under 28 U.S.C. 1292(e), holding that Rule 23(f), prescribed thereunder, did not allow the judiciary to expand its jurisdiction, and did not alter what may be reviewed by a federal court, only when matters may be reviewed.

10. FED. R. CIV. P. 23(f), advisory committee note ¶ 6 (1998).

11. *See Molski v. Green*, 307 F.3d 1155, 1170 n.19 (9th Cir. 2002).

B. APPELLATE REVIEW OF REMAND ORDERS UNDER THE CLASS ACTION FAIRNESS ACT

The Class Action Fairness Act of 2005 (CAFA) significantly expanded federal court jurisdiction over class action lawsuits, in part by allowing for the removal to federal court of state-filed class actions under certain circumstances. While typically a district court order remanding a removed case is not subject to appellate review,[12] CAFA expanded the federal appellate court's jurisdiction to allow appeals from orders granting or denying motions to remand class actions to the state courts from which they were removed.[13]

Until recently, section 1453(c)(1) provided that an "application [must be] made to the court of appeals *not less than 7 days* after entry of the order."[14] That provision, read literally, meant that an application made to the court of appeals within seven days of the order would be premature, and that any such application may be made at any time no sooner than seven days after the entry of the order.[15] Various courts concluded that such an interpretation would be illogical and inconsistent with the legislative intent and thus construed the section as requiring an application to be filed "no more than 7 days after the entry of the order."[16] In fact, the Advisory Committee on Appellate Rules noted that the "no more than 7 days" language "was clearly a drafting error."[17] At the recommendation of the Advisory Committee, Congress amended the statute from "not less than 7 days" to "not more than 10 days."[18] This amendment took effect on December 1, 2009.

Appeals accepted under section 1453(c)(1) must be completed no later than 60 days after the date on which the appeal was filed, unless procedures for extending the period are satisfied; if a final judgment in the appeal is not concluded in that time period, the appeal shall be denied.[19]

---

12. *See* 28 U.S.C. § 1447(d).

13. 28 U.S.C. § 1453(c)(1).

14. *Id.* (emphasis added).

15. *See, e.g., Amalgamated Transit Union Local 1309, AFL-CIO v. Laidlaw Transit Servs., Inc.,* 435 F.3d 1140, 1145–46 (9th Cir. 2006).

16. *Id.; see also Pritchett v. Office Depot, Inc.,* 420 F.3d 1090, 1093 n.2 (10th Cir. 2005) ("We believe [the 'not less than 7 days' provision] to be a typographical error.").

17. Letter from Judge Lee Rosenthal, Chair, Standing Committee on Rules of Practice and Procedure, to Judge Carl E. Stewart, Chair, Advisory Committee on Appellate Rules (May 13, 2008, rev. June 20, 2008), at 2–3, *available at* http://www.uscourts.gov/rules/jc09-2008/2008-09-Appendix-B.pdf.

18. *Id.*

19. 28 U.S.C. §§ 1453(c)(3)–(4).

III. Issues Under Rule 23(f)

A. TYPES OF ORDERS SUBJECT TO REVIEW

1. Orders Granting/Denying Class Action Certification

By its terms, Rule 23(f) allows an appeal of an order "granting or denying class action certification."[20] This provision has included orders conditionally certifying a class pursuant to former Rule 23(c)(1)(C).[21] To trigger Rule 23(f), the order must be set out in a separate document rather than a minute entry.[22]

2. Appeal from Rulings Following Initial Certification Ruling

Once a certification decision has been made, various methods exist to alter the district court's ruling. A party may seek reconsideration of the ruling, or to decertify a class, or to renew a request to certify a class that was not certified. Disposition of these various challenges to an initial ruling may have different appellate consequences.

A Rule 23(f) appeal may be taken from an order denying a motion for reconsideration or a motion to decertify a class if the motion is filed within the time period in which to appeal the initial certification ruling.[23] Such motions have been analogized to post-judgment motions under Federal Rule of Civil Procedure 59 and toll the time for taking an appeal until they are ruled upon.[24] In contrast, no interlocutory appellate rights will attach to the denial of a motion for reconsideration or to decertify a class filed outside the 14-day period in which a Rule 23(f) appeal may be taken.[25]

Whether successive motions for certification "retrigger" the Rule 23(f) period depends upon the posture at the time they are urged. For example, plaintiffs in a Title VII case obtained certification on disparate impact claims but not on disparate treatment claims.[26] Thereafter, the court decertified the disparate treatment class. They subsequently filed a renewed motion for recertification of the disparate impact claims, and after that motion was denied, they filed a second renewed

---

20. Fed R. Civ. P. 23(f).

21. See, e.g., Robinson v. Texas Auto. Dealer Assoc., 387 F.3d 416, 420 (5th Cir. 2004) (allowing appeal from order conditionally certifying class). But see Liles v. Del Campo, 350 F.3d 742 (8th Cir. 2003) (denying leave to appeal conditional class certification order, noting that additional steps remained before the district court would finally approve class certification and any settlement, with an interlocutory appeal causing unnecessary delay and depletion of the limited assets available for resolving class claims). The conditional certification language of Rule 23(c)(1)(C) was omitted in the 2003 amendments to Rule 23. See Fed. R. Civ. P. 23 advisory committee note ¶ 6 (2003).

22. See, e.g., Theriot v. ASW Well Serv., Inc., 951 F.2d 84, 87 (5th Cir. 1992).

23. See Blair v. Equifax Check Servs., Inc., 181 F.3d 832, 837 (7th Cir. 1999).

24. Id.

25. Gary v. Sheahan, 188 F.3d 891, 892 (7th Cir. 1999).

26. See Carpenter v. Boeing Co., 456 F.3d 1183 (10th Cir. 2006).

motion for certification of the disparate treatment claims as well as the disparate impact claims. After the second renewed motion was denied, plaintiffs sought to appeal pursuant to Rule 23(f). The court of appeals concluded that neither of the rulings on the renewed motions constituted an order "granting or denying certification," and neither changed the status of the class. As a result, neither triggered a new period for filing a Rule 23(f) appeal.

A district court order granting a motion to decertify a class filed outside the ten-day time period provided by Rule 23(f) constitutes an order giving rise to appeal under Rule 23(f) by the party aggrieved by the alteration.[27] Similarly, an order on a motion to clarify an earlier class may give rise to a Rule 23(f) appeal if the order does more than merely clarify the prior certification order and instead substantially alters the certification ruling. Under such circumstances, the order in response to the motion to clarify can constitute an order granting or denying certification from which a Rule 23(f) appeal may be taken.[28]

3. Orders Striking Class Action Allegations
An order striking class action allegations does not constitute an order granting or denying class certification and thus cannot be challenged by an interlocutory appeal taken pursuant to Rule 23(f).[29]

4. Appeals from Multifarious Orders
When an appeal is taken from a district court's order that does more than grant or deny class certification, only the portion of the order addressing certification may be reviewed in a Rule 23(f) appeal.[30] An exception arises when the related order has a bearing on the certification issue, such as when a summary judgment ruling substantially narrows the scope of the class and certification is denied based in part on the absence of numerosity.[31]

5. Class Actions from Specialized Courts
Though rules applicable to certain specialized courts may authorize class actions, Rule 23(f) only authorizes appeals from orders granting or denying class action

---

27. *Gary,* 188 F.3d at 893 (7th Cir. 1999).

28. *Glover v. Standard Fed. Bank,* 283 F.3d 953 (8th Cir. 2001).

29. *In re Ingram Barge Co.,* 517 F.3d 246, 247 (5th Cir. 2008).

30. *See McKowan Lowe & Co., Ltd. v. Jasmine, Ltd.,* 295 F.3d 380, 389–90 (3rd Cir. 2002) (district court denied class certification and granted summary judgment, holding claims asserted on behalf of class were time barred; court of appeals declined to address summary judgment ruling during the Rule 23(f) appeal); *see also Vega v. T-Mobile USA, Inc.,* 564 F.3d 1256 (11th Cir. 2009) (on a Rule 23(f) interlocutory appeal, "our jurisdiction is limited to review of the district court's class certification decision, and, therefore, we do not address the district court's denial of T-Mobile's motion for summary judgment."); *DeLeon-Granados v. Eller & Sons, Trees, Inc.,* 497 F.3d 1214, 1218 n.1 (11th Cir. 2007) (declining to review statute of limitations order issued contemporaneously with certification ruling, noting that the jurisdiction conferred by Rule 23(f) does not extend to that separate order).

31. *Cliff v. Payco Gen. Am. Credits, Inc.,* 363 F.3d 1113 (11th Cir. 2004).

certification "under this rule"—i.e., Rule 23 of the Federal Rules of Civil Procedure. Thus, certification rulings in class actions proceeding under other provisions, such as under the Fair Labor Standards Act, do not invoke interlocutory appellate rights under Rule 23(f).[32] Nor does Rule 23(f) apply to actions brought before the Court of Federal Claims[33] or classes certified pursuant to the rules of the Court of International Trade.[34] The Eleventh Circuit has held that Rule 23(f) does not provide for interlocutory appellate review by the court of appeals of a certification ruling made in class actions brought in bankruptcy court under bankruptcy rules,[35] particularly in light of the rights to appeal bankruptcy rulings to district court afforded by the Bankruptcy Code, 28 U.S.C. § 158(a).

B. FACTORS RELEVANT TO DECISION WHETHER TO GRANT REVIEW

1. Advisory Committee

The 1998 notes of the Advisory Committee identified the scope of discretion to grant permission to appeal, factors relevant to that decision, and the power of the courts of appeals to define criteria for granting review. Initially, the Committee explained that an "[a]ppeal from an order granting or denying class certification is permitted in the sole discretion of the court of appeals" and noted further that courts of appeals are given "unfettered discretion whether to permit the appeal, akin to the discretion exercised by the Supreme Court in acting on a petition for certiorari."[36]

The Committee made an analogy between Rule 23(f) and the provision for permissive appeal on certification by a district court pursuant to 28 U.S.C. § 1292(b), noting two significant differences. First, an appeal pursuant to Rule 23(f) need not be certified by the district court. Second, a party seeking to appeal pursuant to Rule 23(f) is not constrained to show the existence of controlling questions of law as to which there are substantive ground for difference of opinion and that an immediate appeal from the order may materially advance the ultimate termination of the case.[37]

The Committee recognized that permission to grant or deny leave to appeal may be based on any consideration the courts of appeals find persuasive, anticipating that leave would be most often granted "when the certification decision turns on a novel or unsettled question of law, or when, as a practical matter, the decision on certification is likely dispositive of the litigation."[38] The Committee anticipated

---

32. *See Baldridge v. SBC Commc'ns*, 404 F.3d 25 (5th Cir. 2005).

33. *See Christopher Vill., L.P. v. United States*, 15 F. App'x 922, 2001 WL 1646762 (Fed. Cir. 2001) (Rule 23(f) does not apply to certification rulings under the rules of the Court of Federal claims).

34. *Stone Container Corp. v. United States*, 229 F.3d 1345, 1355 (Fed. Cir. 2000) (noting that the rules of the Court of International Trade do not provide for interlocutory appellate review of certification rulings).

35. *See Chrysler Fin. Corp. v. Powe*, 312 F.3d 1241 (11th Cir. 2002).

36. FED. R. CIV. P. 23(f), advisory committee note ¶ 1 (1998).

37. *Id.*

38. *See id.*, ¶ 3.

that the courts of appeals would develop standards for granting review that would reflect "the changing areas of uncertainty in class litigation."[39]

2. Factors Adopted by the Circuit Courts of Appeal

Many circuits have announced factors similar to those set forth in the Advisory Committee notes. The following subsections highlight some of the different approaches used in various circuits.

a. Seventh Circuit

Guided by the reasons set forth by the Rules Advisory Committee for adopting Rule 23(f), the Seventh Circuit, in *Blair v. Equifax Check Services, Inc.*,[40] set forth three circumstances under which review of an order granting or denying certification would be appropriate: (1) if the denial of certification effectively terminates the case; (2) if the grant of certification so generates insurmountable pressure to settle; and (3) when the case will lead to a clarification of a fundamental issue of law. A party seeking to appeal under the first two circumstances must also make some showing that the ruling at issue is questionable in light of the district court's discretion and the governing standard of review.[41]

Since its decision in *Blair*, the Seventh Circuit has granted leave to appeal in cases in which certification generated insurmountable pressure to settle[42] and when issues raised by petitions allowed for a clarification of law.[43]

---

39. *See id.*, ¶ 2.

40. 181 F.3d at 834.

41. *Id.* at 835.

42. *See, e.g., Issacs v. Sprint Corp.*, 261 F.3d 679, 681 (7th Cir. 2001) (granting review when certification order and corresponding case management plan necessarily placed undue pressure on the defendants to settle regardless of the merits); *Szabo v. Bridgeport Machs., Inc.*, 249 F.3d 672, 675 (7th Cir. 2001) (noting that the certification order transformed a $200,000 dispute into a $200,000,000 "bet-the-company" case such that it would likely induce settlement even if the position of the class were weak; concluding that the size of the dispute as well as problems with the certification ruling gave rise to a "prime occasion" for review); *In re Bridgestone/Firestone, Inc.*, 288 F.3d 1012, 1015 (7th Cir. 2002) (aggregated claims made settlement nearly inevitable).

43. *See Jefferson v. Ingersoll Int'l Inc.*, 195 F.3d 894, 897 (7th Cir. 1999) (addressing an issue "in which the legal question is important, unresolved, and has managed to escape resolution by appeals from final judgments."); *see also In re Household Int'l Tax Reduction Plan*, 441 F.3d 500 (7th Cir. 2006) (granting leave to appeal novel issue that could advance the development of law governing class action); *West v. Prudential Sec., Inc.*, 282 F.3d 935 (7th Cir. 2002) (granting review of a certification ruling presenting a novel question of law—a "substantial extension" of the then existing fraud-on-the-market doctrine); *Carnegie v. Household Int'l, Inc.*, 376 F.3d 656, 658 (7th Cir. 2004) ("[T]he more novel the issue presented by the appeal and so the less likely that the district court's resolution of it will stand, the more important the resolution of the issue is either to the particular litigation or to the general development of class action law, and the more likely the prompt resolution of the issue is to expedite the litigation and prevent a coercive settlement, the stronger the case for allowing the appeal."); *Allen v. Int'l Truck & Engine Corp.*, 358 F.3d 469, 470 (7th Cir. 2004) ("The parties' comprehensive submissions show not only that immediate review would promote the development of the law governing questions that have escaped resolution on appeal from final decisions, but also that the district court committed an error best handled by a swift remand. It is better to act

b. First Circuit

In its first Rule 23(f) appeal, *Waste Management Holdings, Inc. v. Mowbray*,[44] the First Circuit set forth the same three factors articulated in *Blair* as guiding its decision to grant leave to appeal: (1) the denial of class status effectively ends the case; (2) the grant of certification generates an irresistible pressure to settle; and (3) the appeal will lead to the clarification of a fundamental issue of law. However, it altered the third element by limiting it to cases "in which an appeal will permit the resolution of an unsettled legal issue that is important to the particular litigation as well as important in itself and likely to escape effective review if left hanging until the end of the case."[45] The court also left open its discretion to grant or deny review in other circumstances. In subsequent cases, the court has granted review of decertification rulings that would effectively cause a party to abandon claims[46] and of certification orders that created irresistible settlement pressure on defendants, even when the orders would likely survive review.[47]

The First Circuit has also analyzed three factors warranting review of a defendant class action: "(i) denial of certification effectively disposes of the litigation because the plaintiff's claim would only be worth pursuing as against a full class of defendants; or (ii) an interlocutory appeal would clarify an important and unsettled legal issue that would likely escape effective end-of-case review; or (iii) an interlocutory appeal is a desirable vehicle either for addressing special circumstances or for avoiding manifest injustice."[48] As in a plaintiff class action, the party seeking review under the first factor must also demonstrate some error in the certification order.

c. Eleventh Circuit

After noting reasons weighing against frequent interlocutory appeals of class certification rulings, the Eleventh Circuit, in *Prado-Steiman v. Bush*,[49] set forth nonexhaustive factors to guide review of Rule 23(f) applications. First the reviewing court should consider whether the certification order would likely constitute the death knell for either party.[50] Second, the court should consider whether the petitioner has shown a substantial weakness in the class certification decision likely reflecting an abuse of discretion (e.g., the district court's use of the wrong standard). This factor should be evaluated on a sliding scale, such that the stronger the showing of

---

summarily on this interlocutory matter than to delay the proceedings during full-dress appellate review." (citation omitted)).

44. 208 F.3d 288, 293–94 (1st Cir. 2000).

45. *Id.* at 294.

46. *Smilow v. Sw. Bell Mobile Sys., Inc.*, 323 F.3d 32, 37 n.4 (1st Cir. 2003).

47. *Tardiff v. Knox County*, 365 F.3d 1 (1st Cir. 2004).

48. *Tilley v. TJX Cos.*, 345 F.3d 34, 38–39 (1st Cir. 2003).

49. 221 F.3d 1266 (11th Cir. 2000).

50. *Id.* at 1274.

an abuse, the more the factor should favor review. Third, the court should consider, as set forth in *Mowbray*, whether the case presents an unsettled legal issue important to the particular litigation, as well as important in itself. Fourth, the court should consider the nature and status of the litigation, recognizing that some cases will be in a better pretrial posture for interlocutory appellate review than others. Finally, the court should consider whether future actions (e.g., impending settlements, bankruptcy risks, related cases) may make immediate appeal more or less appropriate.

d. Fourth Circuit

The Fourth Circuit adopted the Eleventh Circuit's *Prado-Steiman* five-factor "sliding scale" test to govern consideration of petitions filed pursuant to Rule 23(f).[51] It explained that where a certification order is "manifestly erroneous and virtually certain to be reversed on appeal," it is less critical that the issue involved be of general importance or that the certification order constitute a "death knell" for either party, recognizing that judicial resources could be preserved by the prompt correction of the error.[52] In fact, when decertification is a "functional certainty," that fact alone may be sufficient to justify interlocutory review.[53] However, when the "weakness of the certification order is less substantial, a stronger showing on other factors may be required to support review."[54]

e. Third Circuit

The Third Circuit identified the following nonexclusive factors as guiding the decision whether to grant review pursuant to Rule 23(f).[55] It determined that review would be appropriate if it would (1) allow the court to address the possible case-ending effect of an imprudent class certification decision (the decision is likely dispositive of the litigation); (2) allow the court to address an erroneous ruling; or (3) facilitate development of the law on class certification.[56]

---

51. *Lienhart v. Dryvit Sys., Inc.*, 255 F.3d 138 (4th Cir. 2001).

52. *Id.* at 145.

53. *Id.* at 146.

54. *Id.* (granting leave to appeal, noting that "under the sliding scale approach we have adopted, review is appropriate without regard to the other factors in order to avoid the judicial diseconomy entailed in allowing a class certification which is clearly infirm to be litigated to final judgment only to face vacatur on appeal").

55. *Newton v. Merrill Lynch, Pierce, Fenner & Smith, Inc.*, 259 F.3d 154 (3d Cir. 2001).

56. *Id.*; *see also Hagan v. Rogers*, 570 F.3d 146, 157–78 (3d Cir. 2009) (noting nonexclusive factors to guide discretion to exercise jurisdiction that favor review "when denial of certification would effectively terminate a litigation, create excessive pressure to settle, or reach a novel or unsettled question of law"); *In re Hydrogen Peroxide Antitrust Litig.*, 552 F.3d 305, 322 (3d Cir. 2008) (noting that "one important reason for granting interlocutory appeals under [Rule 23(f)] is to address 'novel or unsettled questions of law' . . .").

f. Second Circuit

The Second Circuit has also adopted factors to consider when deciding whether to grant review under which a party seeking leave to appeal must show: "(1) that the certification order will effectively terminate the litigation and there has been a substantial showing that the district court's decision is questionable, or (2) that the certification order implicates a legal question about which there is a compelling need for immediate resolution."[57] The Second Circuit recognizes that orders that will almost certainly result in reversal are prime candidates for interlocutory review; however, issues that would at most result in modification of a class or depend on future fact-finding would be less appropriate for review. A novel legal question will be more likely reviewed if it is fundamentally important and likely to otherwise evade appellate review.[58]

g. D.C. Circuit

The D.C. Circuit set forth three factors, derived from the Advisory Committee notes, to guide review of Rule 23(f) applications: (1) when a questionable certification ruling generates a "death knell" situation for either party; (2) when the decision generates "an unsettled and fundamental issue of law relating to class actions . . . that is likely to evade end-of-the-case review"; and (3) when the ruling is manifestly erroneous.[59] In another case, the court explained that certain requests for declaratory and injunctive relief could not create situations generating "death knell" settlement pressures on the defendant.[60]

h. Sixth Circuit

The Sixth Circuit explained that in considering Rule 23(f) appeals, it would "eschew any hard-and-fast test in favor of a broad discretion to evaluate relevant factors that weigh in favor of or against an interlocutory appeal."[61] Parties invoking the "death knell" factor as supporting review must demonstrate why a plaintiff could

---

57. *In re Sumitomo Copper Litig.*, 262 F.3d 134, 139 (2d Cir. 2001); *see also Teamsters Local 445 Freight Div. Pension Fund v. Bombardier Inc.*, 546 F.3d 196, 197 (2d Cir. 2008) (court agreed to hear appeal "to consider whether the district court applied the correct standard of proof—the preponderance of the evidence standard—to this decision.").

58. *In re Sumitomo Copper Litig.*, 262 F.3d at 140. Shortly after the *Sumitomo Copper Litigation* ruling, the Second Circuit granted review in *In re Visa Check/Mastermoney Antitrust Litigation*, 280 F.3d 124, 132 n.3 (2d Cir. 2001). Citing *Sumitomo*, the court explained that "interlocutory jurisdiction was appropriate to resolve the uncertainty regarding the proper standard for evaluating expert opinions at the class certification stage, and to address the questions of predominance and manageability in light of individualized damage issues that emerge in tying cases." *See also Hevesi v. Citigroup Inc.*, 366 F.3d 70, 76 (2d Cir. 2004) (applying the *Sumitomo* factors to grant the petition of certain defendants and deny the petition of others).

59. *In re Lorazepam & Clorazepate Antitrust Litig.*, 289 F.3d 98, 105 (D.C. Cir. 2002); *see also In re James*, 444 F.3d 643 (D.C. Cir. 2006) (declining to review certification ruling for failing to satisfy the *Lorazepan* standards).

60. *In re Veneman*, 309 F.3d 789, 794 (D.C. Cir. 2002).

61. *In re Delta Air Lines*, 310 F.3d 953, 959 (6th Cir. 2002).

not proceed in an individual capacity or what potential expenses or liabilities await a defendant. They must also demonstrate "some likelihood of success in overturning the class certification decision."[62]

Also appropriate for review are cases raising novel or unsettled questions, with the factor weighing more heavily in favor of review when the question relates not only to the particular case but to class action litigation generally.[63]

The court also referred to the weakness of the district court's decision, i.e., the likelihood of the petitioner's success on appeal, particularly when the issue may evade appellate review absent an interlocutory appeal. Finally, the court noted as relevant the posture of the case before the district court. If a court indicates it will reexamine the certification ruling after discovery, such a fact may militate against review.

i. Fifth Circuit

The Fifth Circuit has relied on the criteria set forth in the Advisory Committee notes as guiding the decision whether to grant leave to appeal certification rulings. In a recent case, the court granted leave to appeal, discussing the comments to Rule 23(f) and explaining that the certification ruling gave rise to unsettled questions of law and that settlement pressures were "particularly acute."[64]

j. Ninth Circuit

The Ninth Circuit has explained that "[t]he Committee Notes provide the essential guidelines for determining when interlocutory review is appropriate under rule 23."[65] In doing so, it explained, "Review of class certification decisions will be most appropriate when: (1) there is a death-knell situation for either the plaintiff or defendant that is independent of the merits of the underlying claims, coupled with a class certification decision by the district court that is questionable; (2) the certification decision presents an unsettled and fundamental issue of law relating to class actions, important both to the specific litigation and generally, that is likely to evade end-of-the-case review; or (3) the district court's class certification decision is manifestly erroneous."[66]

k. Tenth Circuit

The Tenth Circuit has also adopted the standards set forth by the Rules Advisory Committee, not as exclusive factors, but as guides. First, it observed appellate review is generally appropriate in death-knell cases.[67] Second, review is appropriate

---

62. *Id.* at 960.

63. *Id.*

64. *Regents of the Univ. of Cal. v. Credit Suisse First Boston (USA), Inc.*, 482 F.3d 372, 379–80 (5th Cir. 2007).

65. *Chamberlan v. Ford Motor Co.*, 402 F.3d 952, 959 (9th Cir. 2005).

66. *Id.*

67. *Vallario v. Vandehey*, 554 F.3d 1259, 1263 (10th Cir. 2009).

when an issue will facilitate the development of the law.[68] To invoke this basis for seeking review, the certification decision must involve an unresolved issue of law relating to class actions that is likely to evade end-of-the-case review that is not only significant to the case but to class action law generally. The goal advanced by this standard may be met without regard to the prospects for showing error in the ruling because case law may be developed by judgments affirming the district court as well as judgments reversing the district court. The merits of the certification ruling, however, give rise to the third standard, in which review may be appropriate when the certification decision is manifestly erroneous. To satisfy this standard, deficiencies in the certification order must be both significant and readily ascertainable, taking into account the district court's discretion in matters of class certification.[69]

C. ISSUES THAT MAY BE RAISED IN RULE 23(F) APPEALS

Rule 23(f) does not expressly identify what issues may be considered in an appeal from an order granting or denying class action certification; rather, it merely authorizes an appeal "from an order granting or denying class action certification" under Rule 23. The following describes categories of issues courts have considered or declined to consider in the course of Rule 23(f) appeals.

1. Class Certification Ruling

By its terms, Rule 23(f) authorizes an appeal of an order granting or denying class action certification.[70] Pursuant to that rule, courts have reviewed the sufficiency with which a certification order complies with the requirements of Rule 23(c)(1)(B) in defining the class, the class claims, issues, or defenses.[71]

2. Subject Matter Jurisdiction/Standing

Appellate courts have recognized that because subject matter jurisdiction is a prerequisite to class certification, a court may confirm its jurisdiction in the scope of a Rule 23(f) appeal.[72] If the record on appeal is inadequate to determine the amount in controversy in a case removed to federal court on diversity grounds,

---

68. *Id.*

69. *Id.* at 1263–64.

70. FED. R. CIV. P. 23(f).

71. *See Wachtel v. Guardian Life Ins. Co. of Am.*, 453 F.3d 179 (3d Cir. 2006) (holding that Rule 23(c)(1)(B) requires that the text of the order or an incorporated opinion include (1) a readily discernible, clear, and precise statement of the parameters defining the class or classes to be certified, and (2) a readily discernible, clear, and complete list of the claims, issues, or defenses to be treated on a class basis; *see also Beck v. Maximus, Inc.*, 457 F.3d 291 (3d Cir. 2006) (vacating certification order and remanding with instructions to reconsider certification issues and set forth its reasoning).

72. *See Lindsay v. Gov't Employees Ins. Co.*, 448 F.3d 416 (D.C. Cir. 2006).

the appellate court may remand in order to satisfy its obligation to inquire into its own jurisdiction.[73]

As a component of jurisdiction, standing is a threshold issue properly reviewable on a Rule 23(f) class certification appeal.[74] While Rule 23(f) appeals may only address issues of certification and none other, standing goes to the constitutional power of the federal court to entertain an action. Because federal courts have a duty to determine whether standing exists, even when not raised by the parties, standing is an inherent prerequisite to the class certification inquiry. Thus, despite the narrow scope of a Rule 23(f) appeal, standing may be raised in an appeal relating to a certification order.[75] Further, when a named plaintiff does not have a claim or otherwise lacks constitutional standing, that plaintiff may not seek relief on its own behalf or on behalf of a class.[76]

Courts have differentiated between standing in the constitutional sense and standing to assert antitrust claims.[77] Because the court's jurisdiction does not turn on antitrust standing, challenges to antitrust standing may not be raised in an interlocutory appeal under Rule 23(f).[78]

The authority to address subject matter jurisdiction may not give rise to the assertion of pendent jurisdiction over issues of abstention unless the abstention issue is inextricably intertwined with, or necessary to ensure meaningful review of, the class certification decision.[79] However, the propriety of exercising supplemental jurisdiction over state law claims has been addressed in the course of a Rule 23(f) appeal.[80]

---

73. *See Samuel-Bassett v. Kia Motors Am., Inc.,* 357 F.3d 392, 294–95 (3d Cir. 2004).

74. *See Bertulli v. Indep. Ass'n of Cont'l Pilots,* 242 F.3d 290, 293 (5th Cir. 2001); *Cole v. Gen. Motors Corp.,* 484 F.3d 717, 721 (5th Cir. 2007).

75. *Bertulli,* 242 F.3d at 294; *see also Rivera v. Wyeth-Ayerst Labs.,* 283 F.3d 315, 319 (5th Cir. 2002) (vacating certification order and dismissing case when plaintiff lacked constitutional standing).

76. *See Rivera,* 283 F.3d at 319; *see also Lierboe v. State Farm Mut. Auto. Ins. Co.,* 350 F.3d 1018 (9th Cir. 2003) (holding that when sole named plaintiff does not have a claim, the party cannot seek relief on its own behalf or on behalf of a class).

77. *See In re Lorazepan,* 289 F.3d at 107.

78. *Id.* at 107–08.

79. *See Poulos v. Caesars World, Inc.,* 379 F.3d 654 (9th Cir. 2004) (addressing issues of subject matter jurisdiction as threshold matter, but dismissing for lack of jurisdiction issues raised in primary jurisdiction abstention motions).

80. *See De Asencio v. Tyson Foods, Inc.,* 342 F.3d 301 (3d Cir. 2003). In *De Asencio,* plaintiffs obtained certification of an opt-in class pursuant to the Fair Labor Standards Act, and thereafter sought certification of state law claims. On appeal of the certification of the state law claims, the Third Circuit addressed objections to the assertion of supplemental jurisdiction over the state law claims and concluded that the district court did not exercise sound discretion in granting supplemental jurisdiction over the state law actions.

3. Merits of the Case

Courts widely recognize that the merits of the case are not subject to review during a Rule 23(f) appeal.[81] But merits-related issues may be subject to consideration on a Rule 23(f) appeal insofar as they implicate the decision to certify a class.[82] Under such circumstances, any overlap is only coincidental.[83] However, the line between what may be appropriately considered as relevant to certification and what constitutes an impermissible inquiry into the merits is not always as clear.

The Fifth Circuit recently decertified an appeal in a securities fraud case, concluding that the plaintiffs could not invoke the fraud-on-the-market presumption to satisfy loss causation absent a showing that a corrective disclosure actually moved the market, and thus, common issues would not predominate.[84] The dissent complained that proof of loss was not related to the certification inquiry, and thus, that the majority's focus on loss causation during the Rule 23(f) appeal reflected a drastic departure from the prior scope of such interlocutory appeals, which prohibited such a consideration of the merits unrelated to the requirements of Rule 23.[85]

4. Rulings Striking Expert Testimony

The fact that threshold legal rulings may be relevant to the certification does not transform all evidentiary rulings made in the certification process into matters to be reviewed on appeal. For example, on appeal of certification, a court may lack jurisdiction to review a motion to strike plaintiff's expert witness tendered in support of the certification motion, even though the court may have jurisdiction to evaluate whether the expert evidence supports certification. The certification ruling may turn on whether the expert evidence supported the ruling, but that issue involves an entirely different inquiry than whether a motion to strike should have been denied.[86]

---

81. See, e.g., Pickett v. Iowa Beef Processors, 209 F.3d 1276, 1279 (11th Cir. 2000) ("Rule 23(f) provides for our jurisdiction over interlocutory appeals from a district court's order granting class certification, and we limit our discussion to that issue. We do not address the merits of Plaintiffs' claims.").

82. See, e.g., Langbecker v. Elec. Data Sys. Corp., 476 F.3d 299, 307 (5th Cir. 2007) (recognizing that federal courts cannot assess the merits at the discovery stage, but explaining that a "district court's threshold legal rulings are essential to its conclusion that this case may be maintained as a class action").

83. See Regents of the Univ. of Cal., 482 F.3d at 380–81.

84. See Oscar Private Equity Invs. v. Allegiance Telecom, Inc., 487 F.3d 261, 271 (5th Cir. 2007).

85. Id. at 278.

86. See In re Visa Check/Mastermoney, 280 F.3d at 132 n.4; see also Bell v. Ascendant Solutions, Inc., 422 F.3d 307, 314 (5th Cir. 2005) (declining to consider exclusion of expert report and evaluating remainder of record in reviewing certification ruling).

D. PROCEDURES FOR RULE 23(F) APPEALS

1. When to File

A petition for permission to appeal under Rule 23(f) must be filed with the circuit clerk within 14 days after the order is entered.[87] The calculation of the 14-day period is subject to Federal Rule of Civil Procedure 6(a), which now includes intermediate Saturdays, Sundays, and legal holidays, but if the last day is a Saturday, Sunday, or legal holiday, the period continues to run until the end of the next day that is not a Saturday, Sunday, or legal holiday.[88] Several circuits have held that the 14-day period is strict and mandatory.[89]

2. What Triggers/Tolls the 14-day Period

The 14-day period is triggered by the entry of an order granting or denying certification. A motion seeking relief from the certification order tolls the time for filing an appeal if the motion is filed with the 14-day period for taking an appeal. Thus, if a party files a motion for reconsideration or a motion to decertify a class within 14 days of the entry of the class order, such motion will toll the time period for taking an appeal.[90] The 14-day period will begin to run upon the denial of such motion.

If a party files a motion for reconsideration or seeking decertification outside the 14-day period for perfecting an appeal, the motion will not toll the running of the appellate deadlines, and no Rule 23(f) appeal may be taken from the denial of such a motion.[91] Similarly, the denial of a motion to clarify filed outside the 14-day period gives rise to no appellate remedy under Rule 23(f).[92] The timeliness may not be circumvented by requesting a district court to vacate an order and re-enter it merely to restart the appellate deadlines.[93]

---

87. FED. R. CIV. P. 23(f).

88. FED. R. CIV. P. 6(a)(2); *see also Shin v. Cobb County Bd. of Educ.*, 248 F.3d 1061, 1065 (11th Cir. 2001); *Blair*, 181 F.3d at 837; *Lienhart*, 255 F.3d at 142 n.1; *In re Veneman*, 309 F.3d at 793.

89. *In re DC Water & Sewer Auth.*, 561 F.3d 494 (D.C. Cir. 2009); *Gutierrez v. Johnson & Johnson Co.*, 523 F.3d 187, 192 (3d Cir. 2008) (both decided under previous version of the rule, which specified a ten-day period).

90. *See McNamara v. Felderhof*, 410 F.3d 277, 281 (5th Cir. 2005); *Shin*, 248 F.3d 1061; *Blair*, 181 F.3d at 837; *Gary*, 188 F.3d at 892.

91. *See, e.g., McNamara*, 410 F.3d 277 (treating plaintiff's amended trial plan as motion for reconsideration of denial of certification; however, since the amended trial plan was filed more than ten days after certification was denied (the deadline under the previous version of the rule), the denial of reconsideration did not re-trigger the Rule 23(f) appellate period).

92. *In re DC Water & Sewer Auth.*, 561 F.3d 494.

93. *See Jenkins v. BellSouth Corp.*, 491 F.3d 1288 (11th Cir. 2007). In *Jenkins*, the court dismissed an appeal from an untimely motion for reconsideration. On remand, the district court vacated and then reentered its order denying reconsideration in order to trigger anew the Rule 23(f) deadlines. The court of appeals dismissed the subsequent appeal, holding that the district court lacked the authority to circumvent the ten-day deadline for seeking appellate review under such circumstances.

The Tenth Circuit has held that the deadline in Rule 23(f) is not subject to an extension of time.[94]

3. How to Appeal (What and Where to File)

Federal Rule of Appellate Procedure 5 sets forth the procedures for requesting permission to appeal.[95] It requires that a petition for permission to appeal "be filed with the circuit clerk with proof of service on all other parties to the district court action."[96] It also sets forth the required contents of the petition and other technical requirements. While Rule 5(a) adopts the 14-day time period contained in Rule 23(f) as the deadline for filing a petition,[97] Rule 5 separately sets forth a 10-day deadline for filing an answer or cross-petition.[98]

4. Effect of a Rule 23(f) on Trial Court Proceedings

By the terms of Rule 23(f), "an appeal does not stay proceedings in the district court unless the district judge or the court of appeals so orders."[99] The 1998 Notes of the Rules Advisory Committee further state that "[a] stay should be sought first from the trial court. If the trial court refuses a stay, its action and any explanation of its views should weigh heavily with the court of appeals."[100]

5. Standard of Review Applied on Appeal

Appeals pursuant to Rule 23(f) focus on the order granting or denying certification. A district court's decision to grant or deny certification is reviewed for an abuse of discretion.[101] An abuse of discretion will be found in several circumstances. First, a district court abuses its discretion if it relies upon an improper factor in making the certification ruling.[102] Second, a district court abuses its discretion if it omits a substantial element from its review. Finally, a district court abuses its discretion if it commits a clear error of judgment in weighing the correct mix of factors.[103] An

---

94. *Delta Airlines v. Butler*, 383 F.3d 1143, 1145 (10th Cir. 2004).

95. *See* FED. R. APP. P. 5.

96. *Id.* at 5(a)(1).

97. *See* FED. R. APP. P. 5(a)(2) ("The petition must be filed within the time specified by the statute or rule authorizing the appeal or, if no such time is specified, within the time provided by Rule 4(a) for filing a notice of appeal."). Rule 23(f) contains the 14-day period. Because the deadlines for perfecting an appeal under Rule 23(f) arise from the Federal Rules of Civil Procedure rather than the Federal Rules of Appellate Procedure, those deadlines are subject to the calculation rules found in Federal Rule of Civil Procedure 6 rather than Federal Rule of Appellate Procedure 26. *See Lienhart*, 255 F.3d at 142 n.1; *Blair*, 181 F.3d at 837; *In re Veneman*, 309 F.3d at 793.

98. FED. R. APP. P. 5(b)(2) ("A party may file an answer in opposition or a cross-petition within 10 days after the petition is served.").

99. FED. R. CIV. P. 23(f).

100. FED. R. CIV. P. 23(f), advisory committee note ¶ 5 (1998).

101. *In re Wells Fargo Home Mortgage Overtime Pay Litig.*, 571 F.3d 953 (9th Cir. 2009).

102. *Id.*

103. *Id.*

abuse of discretion standard governs both the ultimate determination on certification and the district court's ruling that individual Rule 23 requirements have been met.[104] The district court's factual determinations are reviewed for clear error, while its legal determinations are reviewed de novo for clear error.[105] Finally, a district court's order granting certification is accorded "noticeably more deference" than an order denying certification.[106]

---

104. *In re Flag Telecom Holdings, Ltd. Sec. Litig.*, 574 F.3d 29, 34 (2d Cir. July 22, 2009); *In re Initial Pub. Offering Sec. Litig.*, 471 F.3d 24, 31–32 (2d Cir. 2006).

105. *In re Initial Pub. Offering*, 471 F.3d at 40–41.

106. *In re Salomon Analyst Metromedia Litig.*, 544 F.3d 474, 480 (2d Cir. 2008).

DISCOVERY FROM CLASS MEMBERS

BRADLEY S. WOLFF
MOLLY PRODGERS KING
ERNESSA M. BRAWLEY

I. Introduction

Discovery from named, representative plaintiffs in class actions is allowed just as in any civil litigation.[1] When it comes to discovery from unnamed, nonrepresentative class members, however, requests for discovery are often opposed. This section addresses discovery from these unnamed class members in federal and state courts.

Discovery from absent class members is neither expressly allowed nor expressly forbidden by the federal rules. A few courts have held that discovery from class members is forbidden since it is not expressly permitted in the rules.[2] Most courts, however, looking to Rule 23(d), permit discovery from absent class members when certain criteria are met. The courts note "the inevitable tension" in such discovery because of the conflict between "the competing interests of the absent class members in remaining passive and the defendant in having the ability to ascertain necessary information for its defense."[3] On the other hand, "[o]ne of the principal advantages of class actions over massive joinder or consolidation would be lost if all class members were routinely subjected to discovery."[4] Generally, such discovery is disfavored.[5]

---

1. *See Dellums v. Powell*, 566 F.2d 167, 187 (D.C. Cir. 1977); *Wainwright v. Kraftco Corp.*, 54 F.R.D. 532 (N.D. Ga. 1972).

2. *See Wainwright*, 54 F.R.D. 532; *Fischer v. Wolfinbarger*, 55 F.R.D. 129 (W.D. Ky. 1971).

3. *Redmond v. Moody's Investor Serv.*, No. 92 Civ. 9161 (WK), 1995 U.S. Dist. LEXIS 6277 (S.D.N.Y. 1995) (internal citations omitted).

4. Manual for Complex Litigation (Fourth) § 21.41 (2004).

5. *Kline v. First W. Gov't Sec.*, No. 83-1076, 1996 U.S. Dist. LEXIS 3329 (E.D. Pa. 1996).

Courts generally consider some or all of the following questions in deciding whether to permit or deny specific discovery from absent class members:

- Is the requested information necessary for trial preparation and "correct adjudication of the principal suit"?
- Are the discovery devices being used to take unfair advantage of the absent class members?
- Is the information sought relevant to the decision of common questions?
- Is the information readily available to the defendant or the representative parties?
- Are the requests made in good faith?
- Are the requests unduly burdensome or overly broad?
- Do the requests require assistance of technical and legal advice?

These criteria were developed primarily in cases decided in the Court of Appeal for the Seventh and D.C. Circuits[6] and are discussed below in sections II.G and II.L, respectively.

The burden is on the defendant to demonstrate the meritorious nature of its requests.[7] Because of the intrusive nature of depositions, "the burden confronting the party seeking deposition testimony should be more severe than that imposed on the party requesting permission to use interrogatories."[8]

Where allowed, class action suits are also filed in state courts. Most states have enacted class action legislation identical or substantially similar to Federal Rule of Civil Procedure 23(d) and, accordingly, these state courts look to federal decisions to guide them.[9] States that treat discovery from absent class members differently are discussed in section III.

---

6. *Dellums,* 566 F.2d at 187; *Clark v. Universal Builders, Inc.,* 501 F.2d 324 (7th Cir. 1974); *Brennan v. Midwestern United Life Ins. Co.,* 450 F.2d 999 (7th Cir. 1971).

7. *Clark,* 501 F.2d 324, discussed *infra* in section II.G.1.

8. *Groth v. Robert Bosch Corp.,* No. 1:07-cv-962, 2008 U.S. Dist. LEXIS 52328 (W.D. Mich. 2008), *citing Clark,* 501 F.2d 324; *see also In re FedEx Ground Package Sys., Inc.,* 3:05-MD-527 RM (MDL-1700), 2007 U.S. Dist. LEXIS 16205 (N.D. Ind. 2007).

9. Alabama: *Reynolds Metals Co. v. Hill,* 825 So. 2d 100, 104 n.1 (Ala. 2002); Alaska: *Int'l Seafoods of Alaska, Inc. v. Bissonette,* 146 P.3d 561 (Alaska 2006); Arizona: *Johnson v. Svidergol,* 757 P.2d 609, 611 (Ariz. Ct. App. 1988); Arkansas: *Fraley v. Williams Ford Tractor & Equip. Co.,* 339 Ark. 322 (1999); California: See discussion *infra* in section III; Colorado: *State v. Buckley Powder Co.,* 945 P.2d 841, 844 (Colo. 1997); Connecticut: *McNerney v. Carvel,* No. CV00579244, 2001 Conn. Super. LEXIS 619 (2001); Delaware: *O'Malley v. Boris,* No. Civ.A. 15735, 2001 WL 50204, at *3 (Del. Ch. 2001); Florida: *In re Rules of Civil Procedure,* 391 So. 2d 165 (Fla. 1980); Georgia: *Sta-Power Indus. Inc. v. Avant,* 134 Ga. App. 952 (1975); Hawaii: *Sheehan v. Grove Farm Co.,* 114 Haw. 376 (Ct. App. 2005); Idaho: *O'Boskey v. First Fed. Sav. & Loan Ass'n of Boise,* 739 P.2d 301 (Idaho 1987); Illinois: *Avery v. State Farm Mut. Auto. Ins. Co.,* 216 Ill. 2d 100 (2005); Indiana: *Hefty v. Certified Settlement Class,* 680 N.E.2d 843 (Ind. 1997); Iowa: See discussion *infra* in section III; Kansas: *Dragon v. Vanguard Indus.,* 277 Kan. 776 (Kan. 2004); Kentucky: *Lamar v. Office of Sheriff,* 669 S.W.2d 27 (Ky. Ct. App. 1984); Louisiana: *Banks v. N.Y. Life Ins. Co.,* 722 So. 2d 990 (La. 1998); Maine: *Millett v. Atl. Richfield Co.,* 2000 Me. 178 (2000); Maryland: See discussion *infra* in section III; Massachusetts:

II. Illustrative Cases Concerning Discovery from Class Members in Federal Courts

The following are illustrative cases, organized by federal circuit, either permitting or denying discovery from absent class members.

A. FIRST CIRCUIT

1. Discovery Permitted

The court in *M. Berenson Co. v. Faneuil Hall Marketplace, Inc.*[10] permitted discovery from unnamed class members as long as defendants adhered to the following guidelines:

> discovery is available, at least when the information requested is relevant to the decision of common questions, when the interrogatories or document requests are tendered in good faith and are not unduly burdensome, and when the information is not available from the representative parties.[11]

2. Discovery Denied

In a succinct conclusion, without much discussion of its reasons, the court in *Bonilla v. Trebol Motors Corp.*[12] denied discovery of class members where the defendant had made no showing of any need. Further, the court precluded any discovery relative to individual reliance on misrepresentations and discovery on individual

Aspinall v. Philip Morris Cos., No. 98-6002-H, 2005 Mass. Super. LEXIS 642 (2005); see discussion below, *infra*; Michigan: See discussion *infra* in section III; Minnesota: *Glen Lewy 1990 Trust v. Inv. Advisors, Inc.*, 650 N.W.2d 445 (Minn. Ct. App. 2002); Mississippi: See discussion *infra* in section III; Missouri: *Hale v. Wal-Mart Stores, Inc.*, 231 S.W.3d 215 (Mo. Ct. App. 2007); Montana: *USF&G Co. v. Rodgers*, 267 Mont. 178 (1994); Nebraska: *Blankenship v. Omaha Pub. Power Dist.*, 195 Neb. 170 (1976); Nevada: *Nelson v. Heer*, 122 P.3d 1252, 1253 (Nev. 2005); New Hampshire: *Cantwell v. J & R Props. Unltd., Inc.*, 155 N.H. 508 (2007); New Jersey: *Beegal v. Park W. Gallery*, 394 N.J. Super. 98 (2007); New Mexico: *Ferrell v. Allstate Ins. Co.*, 144 N.M. 405 (2008); New York: *Ray v. Marine Midland Grace Trust Co.*, 316 N.E.2d 320 (N.Y. 1974); North Carolina: *Scarvey v. First Fed. Sav. & Loan Ass'n*, 552 S.E.2d 655 (N.C. Ct. App. 2001); North Dakota: See discussion *infra* in section III; Ohio: *State ex rel. Davis v. Pub. Emples. Ret. Bd.*, 855 N.E.2d 444 (Ohio 2007); Oklahoma: *Burgess v. Farmers Ins. Co.*, 2006 Okla. 66 (2006); Oregon: *Newman v. Tualatin Dev. Co.*, 287 Or. 47 (1978); Pennsylvania: *Pa. Orthopaedic Soc'y v. Independence Blue Cross*, 2005 Pa. Super. 344 (2005); Rhode Island: *Kedy v. A.W. Chesterton Co.*, 946 A.2d 1171 (R.I. 2008); South Carolina: *Gardner v. Newsome Chevrolet-Buick*, 304 S.C. 328 (1991); South Dakota: *Trapp v. Madera Pac.*, 390 N.W.2d 558 (S.D. 1986); Tennessee: *Walker v. Sunrise Pontiac-GMC Truck, Inc.*, 249 S.W.3d 301 (Tenn. 2008); Texas: See discussion *infra* in section III; Utah: *Plumb v. State*, 809 P.2d 734 (Utah 1990); Vermont: *Salatino v. Chase*, 2007 Vt. 81 (2007); Virginia: See discussion *infra* in section III; Washington: *Pickett v. Holland Am. Line-Westours, Inc.*, 35 P.3d 351 (Wash. 2001); West Virginia: *Love v. Georgia-Pacific Corp.*, 214 W. Va. 484 (2003); Wisconsin: See discussion *infra* in section III; Wyoming: *Blount v. Laramie*, 510 P.2d 294 (Wyo. 1973).

10. 103 F.R.D. 635 (D.C. Mass. 1984).
11. *Id.* at 637 (citing *Dellums*, 566 F.2d at 187).
12. No. 92-1795, 1997 U.S. Dist. LEXIS 4370 (D.C.P.R. 1997).

sophistication. Finally, the court denied any discovery as to plaintiffs' personal tax returns or other financial information.

B. SECOND CIRCUIT

1. Discovery Permitted

In a Securities Act of 1933 class action, *In re Warner Chilcott Securities Litigation*,[13] the court permitted defendants to seek discovery from at least 30 absent class members. Defendants sought to serve narrow document requests and take short depositions of the absent class members who attended the presentations at issue in order to establish a defense that those class members had actual knowledge of certain facts that plaintiffs alleged were not disclosed. The court found that defendants' requested discovery was necessary for their defense, narrowly tailored, and would not impose undue burden on the absent class members and, accordingly, granted their request for discovery.

In *Krueger v. New York Telephone Co.*,[14] six former employees brought a class action alleging age discrimination under the Age Discrimination in Employment Act (ADEA),[15] and unlawful interference with pension rights under ERISA.[16] The plaintiffs sought to maintain a collective opt-in action for the ADEA claims. Plaintiffs moved for authorization to proceed on behalf of the 162 "consent signers" with respect to the ADEA claims. The court permitted depositions of consent signers to the ADEA portion of the case. The court found first that defendants needed the discovery for purposes of trial of the issues common to the class. The would-be deponents participated in evaluations and appraisals of other class members and, accordingly, such depositions would address classwide liability issues. The court found there was no meaningful evidence that defendants were attempting to harass the absent class members. The intended deponents were evaluatees whose observations and experiences were relevant to the allegations that defendants administered its evaluations of employees in a way that impermissibly discriminated against older employees and, therefore, they were properly the subject of defendants' discovery.

The defendants further sought to serve interrogatories on all 162 class members in the form of a questionnaire. The plaintiffs sought a protective order and, alternatively, sought to reduce the interrogatories to a sample of the class. The court permitted the interrogatories to the entire class, finding that the defendants "face difficulty participating in settlement negotiations without a reasonable basis

---

13. No. 06 Civ. 11515 (WHP), 2008 U.S. Dist. LEXIS 7613 (S.D.N.Y. 2008).
14. 163 F.R.D. 446 (S.D.N.Y. 1995).
15. 29 U.S.C. § 621 *et seq.* (ADEA).
16. 29 U.S.C. § 1001 *et. seq.* (ERISA).

on which to measure their potential exposure."[17] The court did restrict some of the items on the questionnaire regarding educational background, spousal information, and the like, as overbroad and burdensome.

The court in *Redmond v. Moody's Investor Service*[18] was faced with an employment discrimination case where plaintiffs contended they were denied advancement on the basis of race. The defendant submitted a proposed deposition list that included several absent class members. The court denied this request, finding it unduly burdensome. However, the court noted there was some basis for interrogatories and document requests to be served because the defendant was entitled to determine whether the experiences of nonrepresentative class members would confirm or rebut the claims of classwide discrimination. Accordingly, the court ordered counsel to "attempt to agree on the proper scope and wording of interrogatories and document requests to be propounded."[19]

New Castle v. Yonkers Contracting Co.[20] was an antitrust class action alleging price-fixing in the sale of asphalt. Defendants subpoenaed several absent class members for deposition. The court found that the request for 20 depositions was "finite" and "certainly identifiable," and each class member specifically authorized the litigation.[21] The court was further persuaded by defendants' contention that they would be unable to disprove the claim of fraudulent concealment if they could not have discovery from the absent class members. However, the court did restrict the discovery relating to damages to that necessary to defend against plaintiffs' claim of an antitrust injury. The court further ordered that defendants would have to explain what general information they expected each witness to provide and how it would assist them in their defense. It further cautioned defendants that they should make every effort to finish the depositions as quickly as possible.

2. Discovery Denied

In *Teachers' Retirement System of Louisiana v. ACLN Ltd.*,[22] plaintiffs claimed violations of the Securities Exchange Act of 1934, claiming that defendant issued allegedly false audit reports. The court denied defendant's request to depose a subset of absent class members in order to test the lead plaintiff's assertion that the "market" attributed the audit reports to defendant. The court first noted that the "fraud-on-the-market" theory is predicated on the understanding that individual investors in an impersonal market may be unaware of particular information.[23]

---

17. *Krueger*, 163 F.R.D. at 451–52.
18. No. 92 Civ. 9161 (WK), 1995 U.S. Dist. LEXIS 6277.
19. *Id.* at *4–5.
20. No. 88 Civ. 2952 (CES), 1991 U.S. Dist. LEXIS 11232 (S.D.N.Y. 1991).
21. *Id.* at *5.
22. No. 01 Civ. 11814 (LAP), 2004 U.S. Dist. LEXIS 25927 (S.D.N.Y. 2004).
23. *Id.* at *29.

In other words, misleading statements will defraud purchasers of stock even if the purchasers do not directly rely on the misstatements.[24] The court was not satisfied that defendant had explained how discovery sought from the absent class members would sever the link between the alleged misrepresentation and either the price received or the decision to trade at a fair market price.[25] Further, discovery of the named plaintiff appeared to be sufficient. The court invited defendant to reapply for discovery if the completed discovery of the named plaintiff was insufficient.

The court in *McCarthy v. Paine Webber Group*[26] denied defendants' proposed questionnaire as it was primarily a "proof of claim" form. The proposed form asked questions about class members' reliance on a confidential memorandum and other documents. The court reasoned that "[t]o require class members to complete and return the questionnaire on the condition that failure to do so would result in the member's dismissal from the Class has the effect of requiring the class member to opt into the Class."[27] The court concluded that such was contrary to the opt-out policy of Rule 23.

Dubin v. E.F. Hutton Group,[28] involved a class action relating to defendants' alleged sale of unregistered securities to employees in violation of section 5 of the Securities Act of 1933. Defendants sought an order compelling absent class members to answer interrogatories concerning their employment, their employment negotiations, and details of the method of dissemination of the "Equity Ownership Plan" information. The court denied the motion, holding that circumstances surrounding the specific employees' decisions to accept employment presented individual questions. Further, defendants' own words revealed that the sought discovery was "intended to determine whether individual class members are properly included within the class."[29] This was in direct contravention of the rule precluding discovery intended to reduce the class size.

One of the first cases in the Second Circuit to address discovery from absent class members was *Robertson v. National Basketball Ass'n*.[30] The defendants sought discovery (interrogatories and requests to produce) in three broad areas: bargaining history, reasonableness of the restraints, and fact and amount of damages.[31] The court was satisfied that the requisite showing of relevance and need had been met

---

24. *Id.* (citing *Basic Inc. v. Levinson*, 485 U.S. 224 (1988)).

25. *Id.* at *30 (citing *Basic*, 485 U.S. at 248).

26. 164 F.R.D. 309 (D.C. Conn. 1995).

27. *Id.* at 312.

28. 88 Civ. 0876 (PKL), 1992 U.S. Dist. LEXIS 107 (S.D.N.Y. 1992).

29. *Id.* at *12.

30. 67 F.R.D. 691 (S.D.N.Y. 1975).

31. *Id.* at 700.

for the first two areas of inquiry. However, the court declined to allow the defendants to discover information relating to damages.

C. THIRD CIRCUIT

1. Discovery Permitted

Interrogatories and requests to produce were permitted in *Easton & Co. v. Mutual Benefit Life Insurance Co.*[32] This case involved plaintiffs' claims that several defendants knowingly disseminated inaccurate and misleading written statements regarding defendant life insurance company's guarantee of interest payments on bonds and the investment risks associated with the bonds. The instructions in the interrogatories conveyed that class members would risk dismissal of their claims if they failed to respond or if their responses were insufficient. Plaintiffs claimed that the discovery requests, which focused on reliance of the class members upon the alleged misrepresentations, were irrelevant to the decision of common questions. The court noted that a presumption of causation arises in "fraud on the market" claims. However, this presumption is rebuttable and, therefore, the court found the requests relevant to the determination of common questions. The court did order the defendants to exclude the warning that failure to respond would result in dismissal. The court further ordered the defendants to streamline the requests so that they did not seek information on matters already known to defendants.

In *McMahon Books, Inc. v. Willow Grove Associates,*[33] the court granted in part and denied in part plaintiffs' motion for a protective order to prevent defendants from obtaining discovery from absent class members. This case involved a class action brought on behalf of tenants of a mall against the owners and operators of the mall. The plaintiffs alleged defendants overcharged them for utilities, taxes, and maintenance charges through a fraudulent scheme. The court noted that in securities fraud class actions, common liability issues typically are tried first and then, if necessary, individual issues such as reliance and damages are tried separately. The court said that although discovery on individual issues should be postponed until after the common issues are decided, defendants "nevertheless, are entitled to some discovery from the class members at this stage of the proceeding."[34] Because it was not clear what representations were made to what class members, the court permitted defendants' discovery "of the full spectrum of those representations in preparation of their case on liability."[35] However, the court granted plaintiffs' motion for protective order with respect to defendants' interrogatories relating to individual issues, such as each class member's understanding of the terms of documents

---

32. Nos. 91-4012 (HLS), 92-2095 (HLS), 1994 U.S. Dist. LEXIS 12308 (D.N.J. 1994).
33. No. 84-3861, 1986 U.S. Dist. LEXIS 23637 (E.D. Pa. 1986).
34. *Id.* at *6.
35. *Id.* at *7.

received from defendants; complaints each class member made to defendants about excessive charges; and each class member's business experience generally and in situations similar to the lease agreement at issue.

2. Discovery Denied

In *In re Lucent Technologies Inc. Securities Litigation*,[36] the district court affirmed the magistrate's denial of defendant's requested discovery from 41 named, non-lead plaintiffs. The discovery sought information relevant to plaintiffs' allegations within the lawsuit, the plaintiffs' investment history and practices with defendant, and the plaintiffs' securities litigation history. The court concluded that the 41 nonlead, nonrepresentative plaintiffs should be treated as passive class members and thus not subject to discovery. The court noted that discovery from 41 members included within a class of thousands would not meaningfully aid the defendant.[37]

The court in *Gunter v. Ridgewood Energy Corp.*[38] granted plaintiffs' motion for a protective order precluding defendants from taking discovery of absent class members. Although the court found the requests were not abusive or made in bad faith (members were sophisticated investors) and the information could not be obtained from the class representatives or defendants, the requests did not address a common issue. The requests focused on individual reliance; however, individual reliance did not need to be proven at the liability stage for claims brought under the Securities and Exchange Act of 1934. The requests, therefore, did not address a common issue for these claims.

A defendant's motion for discovery was denied in *Kline v. First Western Government Securities, Inc.*[39] *Kline* involved a class action securities fraud claim brought on behalf of investors who purchased forward contracts in government securities through one of the defendants. Plaintiffs claimed that written materials issued by this and other defendants contained material misrepresentations and omitted material facts in their description of the investment program. One of the defendants sought to serve interrogatories and requests to produce relevant to reliance and whether the class members had a reasonable expectation of economic gain. The court denied the defendant's request because its proposed discovery dealt with individual, not common, questions, such as damages. The court further noted that some of the requests were sufficiently complicated so as to require the assistance of an accountant or a lawyer before responding. Considering the size of the class, this level of complexity would make answering the requests impractical. Finally, the court pointed out that other requests were impermissibly overbroad—for example, seeking tax returns for an eight-year span.

---

36. 00 CV 621 (JAP), 2002 U.S. Dist. LEXIS 24973 (D.N.J. 2002).
37. *Id.*
38. 95-438 (WW), 1996 U.S. Dist. LEXIS 22298 (D.N.J. 1996).
39. 83-1076, 1996 U.S. Dist. LEXIS 3329 (E.D. Pa. 1996).

D. FOURTH CIRCUIT

1. Discovery Permitted

In *Alexander v. Burrus, Cootes & Burrus*,[40] the defendant accountants raised the affirmative defenses of statute of limitations and nonreliance against each of the 3,500 class members in response to the class action allegations. The accountants sought to propound discovery on all class members and, further, requested the depositions of 439 class members with claims of $5,000 or more. The district court permitted the interrogatories and allowed the defendants to use contact information furnished by plaintiffs to mail their interrogatories to class members at defendants' expense. The Fourth Circuit Court of Appeals affirmed.

E. FIFTH CIRCUIT

1. Discovery Permitted

The court in *Transamerican Refining Corp. v. Dravo Corp.*[41] permitted the defendants to take discovery of absent class members. The class action involved plaintiffs who contended they purchased specialty steel piping material from defendants on a cost-plus basis, but that those cost-plus purchases amounted to a kickback scheme. Plaintiffs sought to recover the overpayments and damages. The court found the proposed interrogatories clear, concise, and limited primarily to the defendants' defenses and the plaintiffs' claims. They were not misleading or confusing, and they would impact common issues at trial. Such inquiries included whether the class members actually purchased specialty steel on a cost-plus basis; from whom the purchases were made; the actual amount of each purchase; and for which specific projects each purchase was made. The court found equally pertinent the issues of whether the absent class members relied upon the alleged fraudulent misrepresentations or fraudulent concealments. As to defendants' affirmative defenses of waiver, ratification, estoppel, accord and satisfaction, and release, the court found it appropriate for defendants to inquire regarding whether absent class members received credits from suppliers, whether they passed on the alleged overcharged costs, and whether they received restitution or had given releases for their claims. However, the court found that interrogatories propounded on 6,000 absent class members would be unduly burdensome and, accordingly, ordered defendants to identify and serve 50 absent class members with the interrogatories.[42]

2. Discovery Denied

The court denied defendant's motion for permission to serve written interrogatories on all class members in *In re Corrugated Container Antitrust Litigation*,[43]

---

40. 24 Fed. R. Serv. 2d (Callaghan) 1313 (4th Cir. 1978) (per curiam) (unpublished opinion).

41. 139 F.R.D. 619 (S.D. Tex. 1991).

42. *Id.* at 622.

43. No. MDL 310, 1981 U.S. Dist. LEXIS 11004 (S.D. Tex. 1981).

concluding that the information sought could be "more efficiently and accurately obtained" from other sources.[44] The court noted that a by-product of the proposed detailed interrogatories would likely be to eliminate a large number of small purchasers who would be unable to answer the interrogatories or unwilling to expend the time, effort, and legal fees necessary to do so.

F. SIXTH CIRCUIT

1. Discovery Denied

In *Groth v. Robert Bosch Corp.*,[45] the plaintiffs in a putative class action, on behalf of a class of retirees, alleged breach of a collective bargaining agreement allegedly guaranteeing lifetime health care benefits. Defendant sought depositions of absent class members to discover the financial status and health situation of each deponent. Defendant argued that these depositions were relevant to the question of whether defendant's proposed increase in health care premiums to its retirees would cause them irreparable harm. The court, recognizing that the burden is more stringent upon a defendant seeking deposition testimony, found that the deposition subpoenas were "extremely burdensome, both in the scope of the documents demanded and in the intrusive nature of the interrogation."[46] Further, defendant made no showing of particularized need, as Sixth Circuit jurisprudence does not impose a high burden upon plaintiffs to establish irreparable harm in these kinds of cases.[47]

The district court in *Serrano v. Cintas Corp.*[48] affirmed the magistrate's grant of plaintiffs' motion to quash defendant's deposition subpoenas of absent class members. The magistrate judge had serious doubts as to whether defendant's requested depositions would provide anything of benefit. The court noted that the unnamed class members were not hired based on reviews of their employment applications and that defendant already had all of the applications of those unnamed class members. The court affirmed the magistrate's decision on the grounds that the depositions were unnecessary.[49]

In *Hawkins v. Holiday Inns, Inc.*,[50] the court followed *Fischer v. Wolfinbarger*[51] and *Wainwright v. Kraftco Corp.*,[52] discussed in section K, and found that absent "class members are not 'parties' and are not therefore subject to the normal dis-

---

44. *Id.* at *2.
45. No. 1:07-CV-962, 2008 U.S. Dist. LEXIS 52328.
46. *Id.* at *4.
47. *Id.* at *4–5.
48. 04-40132, 2007 U.S. Dist. LEXIS 66553 (E.D. Mich. 2007).
49. *Id.* at *8.
50. C-72-217, 1977 U.S. Dist. LEXIS 17175 (W.D. Tenn. 1977).
51. 55 F.R.D. 129.
52. 54 F.R.D. 532.

covery rules."[53] The court considered defendant's interrogatories to be "obtuse and vexatious" and found it difficult to believe many of the class members would be willing or able to fully respond,[54] and so it denied defendant's application to serve the discovery.

Fischer v. Wolfinbarger was a class action brought by purchasers of stock. One of the defendants moved for an order requiring each of more than 3,000 claimants who had filed proofs of claim to answer certain interrogatories. The interrogatories sought information already contained in the proofs of claim; information relating to persons from whom the securities were purchased; the nature of the representations; printed information read in connection with the purchase; and the like. Denying the request, the court held that such requests to all class members were improper, as a class action is designed for the situation in which "the class is so numerous that joinder of all members is impracticable."[55] It is not intended, the court reasoned, "that members of the class should be treated as if they were parties plaintiff, subject to the normal discovery procedures, because if that were permitted, then the reason for the rule would fail."[56]

G. SEVENTH CIRCUIT

1. Discovery Permitted

A landmark Seventh Circuit opinion laid the foundation for many decisions not only in the Seventh Circuit but in other circuits as well. *Brennan v. Midwestern United Life Insurance Co.*[57] involved allegations of violation of section 10(b) of the Securities Exchange Act of 1934 and, specifically, that defendant aided and abetted the fraudulent conduct of a dealer in securities. The plaintiff sought damages for herself and others who never received delivery of stock that they had purchased from the dealer. The court enforced a stricter standard of discovery from absent class members to avoid the risk that absent class members would not be misled or confused.

The trial court granted defendant's motion to serve interrogatories and requests to produce documents to the named plaintiff and each of the 535 members of the class and further instructed counsel for the named plaintiff and the defendant to agree on the form of the interrogatories to be submitted. Although counsel for the named plaintiff reminded the absent class members that responses were required, some failed to respond. The trial court stated it would dismiss with prejudice the claims of such persons who had not yet responded. Again, counsel for the named plaintiff reminded the absent class members to comply with discovery. Absent class

---

53. *Hawkins*, 1977 U.S. Dist. LEXIS 17175, at *4.
54. *Id.* at *5–6.
55. 55 F.R.D. at 132.
56. *Id.*
57. 450 F.2d 999.

members missed the trial court's deadline to show cause why their claims should not be dismissed and, as a result, the court granted defendant's motion to dismiss the claims of the nonresponding members with prejudice. The court of appeals affirmed, finding that the district court had "valid reasons" to order discovery in the case.[58] The requests were directed at obtaining information relating to certain defenses raised by defendant in the principal trial. The court found nothing to suggest such discovery was used as a tactic to take undue advantage of the class members or as a strategy to reduce the number of claimants.[59]

The court in *In re FedEx Ground Package System, Inc.*[60] held that the same standards of *Brennan* and *Clark v. Universal Builders, Inc.*,[61] below, applied in precertification cases. *In re FedEx* centered around plaintiffs' main contention that FedEx was treating them as independent contractors when they were actually employees. Defendant served document and deposition requests to absent class members. Applying *Brennan* and *Clark*, the court denied the deposition of two absent class members and permitted the defendant to take the deposition of one formerly named representative.

The court first acknowledged that the burden is more severe when deposition testimony from absent class members is sought and that "[m]ere relevance and helpfulness do not constitute a need."[62] The court held that defendant failed to articulate the need for the depositions of two class members. However, the court did allow the deposition of one class member to be taken because the would-be deponent had been a named plaintiff for over two years and was suddenly dropped because the parties learned that he did not have any employment relationship with FedEx. As a consequence, his situation was unique, and defendant was permitted to depose him. The court found a substantial need was shown; plaintiffs appeared to have deliberately changed his circumstances so as to hide behind *Brennan* and *Clark*; and the court noted that FedEx did not appear to be seeking his testimony to harass absent class members—nor would the deposition be unduly burdensome under the circumstances.[63]

The court in *Hammond v. Trans World Airlines, Inc.*[64] granted, but restricted, the requested discovery. The plaintiffs in *Hammond* alleged ERISA violations and common law breach of contract claims. Defendants sought leave from the court to serve discovery upon absent class members. The court found that defendants had demonstrated a need for the proposed discovery because, in order to prepare a

---

58. *Id.* at 1005.
59. *Id.*
60. 2007 U.S. Dist. LEXIS 16205.
61. 501 F.2d 324.
62. *In re FedEx Ground Package Sys., Inc.*, 2007 U.S. Dist. LEXIS 16205, at *22.
63. *Id.* at *26.
64. No. 89 C 8398, 1991 U.S. Dist. LEXIS 6868 (N.D. Ill. 1991).

defense, defendants might need information regarding the reactions of the absent class members to a letter about the termination of the retirement plan, and releases signed by some of the absent class members when they received lump sum checks. Defendants intended to assert the letter and the signed releases as part of their defenses.

Although some of the proposed interrogatories were appropriate, some were held to be unduly burdensome and beyond what was reasonably necessary to prepare a defense.[65] The court concluded by reminding counsel that the "class members should be informed that their claims could be dismissed if they fail to respond to the permitted discovery."[66]

In *Long v. Trans World Airlines, Inc.*,[67] the parties agreed that discovery on damages was appropriate; however, they disagreed on whether a sampling method would be used to limit discovery from the 3,000 class members. The plaintiffs argued that consultation and drafting of discovery responses would consume at least eight hours per class member, or more than 24,000 lawyer hours total. Defendant argued, on the other hand, that each member may be differently situated with respect to damages. The court held that the sampling method would be appropriate, finding that defendant "has no 'right' to an individualized determination of damages for each plaintiff; the desire for accuracy must be balanced against other factors such as the burdens of discovery in relation to the size of the individual claims."[68]

2. Discovery Denied

Another landmark decision from the Seventh Circuit Court of Appeals is *Clark v. Universal Builders, Inc.*[69] *Clark* involved a class of African American citizens who purchased newly constructed houses in Chicago and claimed they were exploited and made to pay prices far in excess of the amounts white persons paid for comparable residences, all in violation of the 13th and 14th Amendments. Plaintiffs appealed from the district court, *inter alia*, the dismissal with prejudice of class members who failed to answer interrogatories or to appear for depositions. The Seventh Circuit agreed and reversed the trial court and remanded.

The court of appeals first noted that there was no attempt by the trial court to reach a determination as to whether the information sought by the interrogatories was "necessary, or whether the interrogatories were a mere stratagem to diminish class membership."[70] The interrogatories would have required the assistance

---

65. *Id.* at *10.
66. *Id.* at *11.
67. 761 F. Supp. 1320 (N.D. Ill. 1991).
68. *Id.* at 1327.
69. 501 F.2d 324.
70. *Id.* at 340.

of technical and legal advice; certain questions pertained to allegations that were proved at trial through expert witnesses; and some interrogatories sought information on matters already known to the defendants. Accordingly, the court found that "in view of the substantive nature of the questions propounded we do not believe that defendants could have met the burden of demonstrating the meritorious nature of their request."[71] The court disapproved of the attempt to depose the class members because of the burdens of the deposition process—"namely, the passive litigants are required to appear for questioning and are subject to often stiff interrogation by opposing counsel with the concomitant need for counsel of their own."[72] Accordingly, the court said the burden on a party seeking deposition testimony of absent class members to demonstrate need should be more severe.[73]

In *Rogers v. Baxter International, Inc.*,[74] the court denied defendants' motion for leave to serve interrogatories on 14,511 class members. The case involved an ERISA class action that challenged defendants' decision to continue to offer company stock as a plan investment option. The court first held that one interrogatory, seeking information concerning the size and composition of class members' overall investment portfolio, was improper because defendants failed to adequately establish how plaintiff's theory of failure to diversify so as to minimize the risk of large losses implicated the participants' entire asset portfolio.[75] Additional interrogatories requested information regarding the materials or advice on which class members relied in deciding to invest in the fund during the class period. However, the court did not agree that class discovery regarding individual issues of reliance was necessary for defendants' trial preparation. Further, even if individual detrimental reliance would be relevant to the representative fiduciary misrepresentation claim, discovery regarding such issue was not necessary at that time, as proof of such common questions focuses primarily on defendants' conduct, not the actions of individual participants.[76]

In *Feldman v. Motorola, Inc.*,[77] plaintiffs alleged defendants misrepresented material facts concerning the continuing growth and profitability of defendant Motorola, Inc. The court had previously granted defendants' motion to compel from the *named* plaintiffs their brokerage account statements. In addition, four of the six named plaintiffs had been deposed. Two named plaintiffs, however, made no such production and refused to appear for deposition. In lieu of compliance, they submitted a notice of their withdrawal as class representatives and a subsequent

---

71. *Id.*
72. *Id.* at 341.
73. *Id.*
74. 04 C 6476, 2007 U.S. Dist. LEXIS 74268 (N.D. Ill. 2007).
75. *Id.* at *13.
76. *Id.* at *18.
77. 90 C 5887, 1992 U.S. Dist. LEXIS 20586 (N.D. Ill. 1992).

motion for protective order because they were no longer class members. Despite defendants' skepticism about the motivations of the named plaintiffs who seemingly sought to abdicate their responsibilities as class representatives in order to avoid discovery orders, the court granted plaintiffs' motion for a protective order.[78]

The court denied defendants' motion to compel in *Halling v. Hobert & Svoboda, Inc.,*[79] as it found defendants failed to meet their burden under *Brennan.*[80] The class action alleged that defendants violated section 10(b) of the Securities Exchange Act, various state statutes, and common law. Plaintiffs alleged that an offering of more than $2.5 million of limited partnership interests contained material omissions and misrepresentations. Defendants served interrogatories and requests to produce individually to each of the 40 absent class members. In their motion to compel, defendants attempted to satisfy the "necessity" requirement by arguing that information about the actual tax benefits received by class members was relevant to the issue of damages. The court disagreed, finding that tax benefits were irrelevant to the proper measure of damages in the event of liability.[81]

The defendants also argued that information about individual differences related to reliance would be relevant to the issue of liability, speculating that some of the plaintiffs would have invested even knowing of the alleged misrepresentations and omissions in the offering memorandum. The court, however, found this case to be a "fraud on the market" case, where the reliance of the investor on the integrity of the market is *presumed*. The court then held that speculation otherwise was "insufficient to satisfy the threshold burden of demonstrating the necessity required to justify discovery of absent class members."[82]

In *In re Burlington Northern, Inc.,*[83] the district court denied the defendant's motion to depose class members where the defendant already had the information it sought from those depositions. The court held that the defendant, through Equal Employment Opportunity Commission investigatory and conciliatory procedures, had gained access to information concerning the charges of plaintiffs even before the commencement of the class action.[84] Accordingly, the court found that the defendant "failed to establish the requisite actual need to depose class members."[85] The court further noted the "particularly onerous burden" on the would-be

---

78. *Id. But see In re FedEx Ground Package Sys., Inc.,* 2007 U.S. Dist. LEXIS 16205, discussed at note 60 and 62, *supra.*

79. 87-C-912, 1989 U.S. Dist. LEXIS 18115 (E.D. Wis. 1989).

80. 450 F.2d 999.

81. *Halling,* 1989 U.S. Dist. LEXIS 18115, at *8.

82. *Id.* at *10.

83. Nos. 374, 78 C 269, 1980 U.S. Dist. LEXIS 10884 (N.D. Ill. 1980).

84. *Id.* at *5.

85. *Id.* at *6.

deponents,[86] as the class members would be required to obtain counsel and members still employed by the defendant might be discouraged from participating.[87]

H. EIGHTH CIRCUIT

1. Discovery Permitted

In re Airline Ticket Commission Antitrust Litigation[88] involved a class action against domestic airlines' travel agent commissions. Discovery on the liability issues was completed, and the defendants sought specific information from the class regarding damages.[89] The court concluded that the defendants' discovery requests were in part necessary, involving information not otherwise available.[90] The court even allowed discovery of information that seemed irrelevant on its face, but would allow the defendants to sufficiently establish the record.[91]

2. Discovery Denied

In *Hanson v. Acceleration Life Insurance Co.*,[92] the court addressed the defendants' request to send discovery along with the class notice in an insurance fraud case. The defendants sought to send specific interrogatories and document requests to all class members who chose not to opt out.[93] Despite finding some of the information relevant, the court declined to grant the request because the defendants' need did not "outweigh" the concerns to the class.[94] In reviewing the discovery topics, the court concluded that the absent class members could "become overwhelmed and confused by defendants' requests for information, and the reliability of their responses may be questionable."[95] However, the court found that discovery topics could be revisited upon a determination of liability.[96] Defendants also requested the depositions of some absent class members on the issue of reliance, but the court deemed the testimony unnecessary.[97]

Evanson v. Union Oil Co.[98] involved a class suing an oil company for failure to provide competitive oil prices. The defendants filed a motion to compel absent class members to respond to 25 interrogatories addressing various topics. The court concluded that the defendants' interrogatories would require individualized responses

---

86. *Id.*
87. *Id.* at *7.
88. 918 F. Supp. 283 (D. Minn. 1996).
89. *Id.* at 286.
90. *Id.* at 287–88.
91. *Id.* at 288.
92. Civ. No. 3:97CV-152, 1999 U.S. Dist. LEXIS 23298 (D.N.D. 1999).
93. *Id.* at *3.
94. *Id.* at *7.
95. *Id.*
96. *Id.* at *6.
97. *Id.* at *10–11.
98. No. 4-75-Civ. 671, 1979 U.S. Dist. LEXIS 10682 (D. Minn. 1979).

from the plaintiffs, lacking the element of commonality required for discovery in a class action.[99] Relying on precedent in other circuits, the court found that the requests lacked the requisite need and relevance as well.[100]

A district court acknowledged the discretionary nature of permitting discovery of absent class members in its decision in *Morgan v. United Parcel Service of America, Inc.*[101] Plaintiffs filed a protective order to prevent the defendants from deposing absent class members in this employment discrimination class action.[102] Ultimately, the court found that defendants failed to demonstrate that the absent plaintiffs possessed additional information unknown to the named plaintiffs.[103] Stating that the burden on the defendants was "heavy to justify asking questions by interrogatories and even heavier to justify depositions," the court refused to allow the discovery.[104] The court did not permanently foreclose defendants' requests if defendants could satisfy their burden in the future.[105]

I. NINTH CIRCUIT

1. Discovery Denied

Kops v. Lockheed Martin Corp.[106] involved a variety of questions regarding whether discovery was obtainable from absent class members. The court found "a party seeking discovery from unnamed class members must obtain a court order before propounding the discovery."[107] Next, the court placed the burden on the defendants to show the need for the discovery. Finally, the court set forth the factors for determining whether the discovery was necessary:

> Specifically, a party seeking discovery from absent class members must establish the following conditions: (1) that the information sought must be necessary to trial of issues affecting the class as a whole (rather than issues relating to individual claims); (2) that the information sought must not be readily obtainable from other sources; and (3) that the discovery must not be unduly burdensome, and must not have been demanded for an improper purpose (*e.g.*, to harass the absent class members, or to force them to opt out of the class).[108]

---

99. *Id.* at *4–5.
100. *Id.*
101. Case No. 4:94-CV-1184 (CEJ), 1998 U.S. Dist. LEXIS 20197 (D. Mo. 1996).
102. *Id.* at *2.
103. *Id.* at * 4–5.
104. *Id.* at *4.
105. *Id.* at *5.
106. Case No. CV 99-6171-MRP, 2003 U.S. Dist. LEXIS 8568 (C.D. Cal. 2003).
107. *Id.* at *4.
108. *Id.*

In its conclusion, the court granted plaintiffs' motion, which restricted defendants' access to discovery from named plaintiffs only.[109] The court found that the defendants failed to address the factors necessary to impose such discovery on absent class members.[110]

Cornn v. United Parcel Service, Inc.[111] was a class action lawsuit filed by all nonexempt hourly California employees of UPS in certain departments. The allegations stemmed from UPS's alleged mismanagement of its electronic bookkeeping system.[112] Defendant UPS requested the depositions of 1,000 absent class members, which was denied by special master because UPS failed to show the depositions were necessary.[113] Subsequently, UPS sought to depose a smaller group of absent class members, which was denied as well. UPS filed an objection to the special master's decision to deny the discovery. The district court reviewed the record and denied UPS's request to take the depositions of absent class members, but allowed UPS to utilize questionnaires and interrogatories as a less burdensome alternative.[114]

On The House Syndication, Inc. v. Federal Express Corp.[115] involved a class of plaintiffs suing Federal Express. Federal Express sought discovery from absent class members to ascertain the viability of certain defenses and setoff rights.[116] Despite the fact defendants' discovery was specifically tailored to particular relevant topics, the court found the discovery inappropriate.[117] The court found that the defendants had not demonstrated the appropriate need to obtain discovery from absent members, analyzing the issue under tests utilized in both the Eleventh and Seventh Circuits.[118]

McPhail v. First Command Financial Planning, Inc.[119] was filed by a group of plaintiffs alleging that defendants violated the Securities Exchange Act. Defendants propounded requests for production of documents, requests for admissions, and interrogatories upon absent class members.[120] Relying on the *Clark* factors enunciated by the Seventh Circuit, the court determined defendants had not sufficiently carried the burden to show the "practical effect" of obtaining discovery

---

109. *Id.* at *6.
110. *Id.*
111. No. C03-2001 TEH, 2006 U.S. Dist. LEXIS 69196 (N.D. Cal. 2006).
112. *Id.* at *2.
113. *Id.*
114. *Id.* at *15.
115. 203 F.R.D. 452 (S.D. Cal. 2001).
116. *Id.* at 453.
117. *Id.* at 457–58.
118. *Id.* at 456.
119. 251 F.R.D. 514 (S.D. Cal. 2008).
120. *Id.* at 516.

from absent class members.[121] Specifically, the court found that the defendants had not stated the purpose for the discovery, had not shown it was necessary, and failed to convince the court the absent class members could respond to the discovery without the assistance of counsel.[122]

J. TENTH CIRCUIT

1. Discovery Permitted

Schwartz v. Celestial Seasonings, Inc.[123] was a class action suit involving shareholders who sued on the basis of securities violations. Once the class was certified, defendant sought to include a questionnaire in the class notice to obtain additional information regarding a damages determination.[124] The court considered several factors in deciding whether to allow the unnamed class members to receive the discovery:

1. whether the questions were common to both sides;
2. whether the defendant sought the information in good faith;
3. whether the questionnaire imposed an undue burden on the class members;
4. whether the defendant had other access to the information;
5. whether the questionnaire contained clear and concise requests; and
6. whether the questionnaire was necessary.[125]

Upon consideration of these factors, the court allowed the defendant to include a concise questionnaire with the class notice.[126]

2. Discovery Denied

Gardner v. Awards Marketing Corp.[127] was filed on behalf of class members participating in the retail sale of petroleum products for the period known as the Gold Stamps strike. The defendants sought to propound interrogatories upon between 600 and 700 individuals and/or firms.[128] The discovery primarily centered on the issue of damages. The court recognized its discretionary role in permitting the defendants the ability to seek discovery[129] and rejected the proposed interrogatories to absent class members because it would be an "undue burden of the class,

---

121. *Id.* at 518.
122. *Id.*
123. 185 F.R.D. 313 (D. Colo. 1999).
124. *Id.* at 315.
125. *Id.* at 316–17.
126. *Id.* at 320.
127. 55 F.R.D. 460 (D. Utah 1972).
128. *Id.*
129. *Id.* at 462.

unnecessary, and unjustifiably dilatory."[130] The court noted that it would allow discovery only upon a strong showing of necessity or the likelihood of material need.[131]

K. ELEVENTH CIRCUIT

1. Discovery Permitted

Luna v. Del Monte Fresh Produce[132] involved a class action suit filed by immigrant workers on Georgia farmland during the harvest season. Noting a general presumption against discovery from absent class members, the court reviewed the defendants' request for specific plaintiffs' deposition testimony. The court allowed defendants to take the depositions of opt-in plaintiff class members, but concluded that discovery from the other class members was inappropriate because those plaintiffs had not affirmatively opted in to class membership.[133]

2. Discovery Denied

Wainwright v. Kraftco Corp.[134] is frequently cited for the court's decision to deny defendants' request for discovery from unnamed members. The plaintiffs filed suit against milk companies for an alleged conspiracy to eliminate milk sale competition throughout the state.[135] Defendants sent an initial set of interrogatories to over 160 plaintiffs. Many plaintiffs failed to respond to the discovery, and defendants moved to dismiss the claims of all the class members who failed to respond.[136] The court observed that unnamed class members are not parties to a class action suit and concluded that the "usefulness of Rule 23 would end if class members could be subjected to Rule 33 and forced to spend time, and perhaps engage legal counsel, to answer detailed interrogatories."[137]

Cooper v. Pacific Life Insurance Co.[138] involved a class of persons suing on annuity contracts and investment accounts purchased with Pacific Life Insurance Company. After certification, Pacific Life wanted to send a questionnaire to the class members along with the class notice,[139] seeking information regarding individual matters, such as whether the class members had relied on any representations of the company.[140] Finding no appellate precedent, the court looked to the test

---

130. *Id.*
131. *Id.* at 463.
132. No. 1:06-CV-2000-JEC, 2007 U.S. Dist. LEXIS 36893 (N.D. Ga. 2007).
133. *Id.* at *24.
134. 54 F.R.D. 532.
135. *Id.* at 533.
136. *Id.*
137. *Id.* at 534.
138. Civ. No. CV203-131, 2005 U.S. Dist. LEXIS 16465 (S.D. Ga. 2005).
139. *Id.* at *4.
140. *Id.*

employed by the courts in *Clark* and *Dellums v. Powell*.[141] Without endorsing either test, the court concluded that the defendants failed to show necessity for serving absent class members with the questionnaire.[142]

Collins v. International Dairy Queen[143] involved a class action of over 3,000 franchisees with antitrust claims against the franchisor. The defendants sought information regarding plaintiffs' net economic loss and coercion in purchasing foods.[144] After reviewing cases that have granted and denied discovery requests, the court employed a balancing test to determine whether the defendants were entitled to this discovery. The court denied the discovery, finding that defendants had not demonstrated a need for damages discovery from absent class members before resolution of the liability issues.[145]

L. D.C. CIRCUIT

1. Discovery Permitted

In *Dellums v. Powell*,[146] the court addressed a number of factors relevant in determining whether to allow discovery in class action cases. After an adverse trial result, defendants argued several grounds for a new trial, including that they had been precluded from obtaining discovery from the unnamed class members.[147] The court rejected this argument and described circumstances where such discovery might be obtainable. In order to gain access to absent class members, the party seeking discovery had to demonstrate that

1. the information sought is relevant to the decision of common questions;
2. the discovery is requested in good faith and not unduly burdensome; and
3. the information is not available from the representative parties.[148]

These factors are heavily relied on in the D.C. Circuit and other circuits for discovery among absent case members.[149]

In a later related opinion, the *Dellums* court found that "discovery against absent class members 'can be a tactic to take undue advantage of the class members . . . and further that Rule 23 of the Federal Rules contemplates that absentee parties shall remain the passive beneficiaries of class suits, [therefore] courts have

---

141. *Id.* at *6 (citing *Clark*, 501 F.2d 324); *see also Dellums*, 566 F.2d 167.

142. *Id.* at *9.

143. 190 F.R.D. 629 (M.D. Ga. 1999).

144. *Id.* at 632.

145. *Id.* at 633.

146. 566 F.2d 167.

147. *Id.* at 187.

148. *Id.*

149. *See Aspinall*, 2005 Mass. Super. LEXIS 642, at *2–3, for a detailed analysis of each of the *Dellums* factors.

found it necessary to restrict availability of discovery against absentees to those instances in which a need can be shown.'"[150] In this opinion, the court dismissed the claim of a class member who failed to respond to discovery as a sanction.[151] In reaching its conclusion, the court found that the named class member should have fully participated in discovery, given the restrictive ability to gain such information from unnamed class members.[152]

In *Disability Rights Council of Greater Washington v. Washington Metropolitan Area Transit Authority*,[153] plaintiffs sued the Transit Authority for failure to provide sufficient services to disabled people. Each of the class members had previously submitted a description of his or her experiences in writing.[154] In weighing the discovery options, the court reasoned that since the statements could be relied upon at future stages of the litigation, some additional discovery was necessary. As a result, the court exercised its discretion to allow the defendants to interview the unnamed plaintiffs and choose 20 plaintiffs to be formally deposed.[155] Additionally, the court placed a restriction on the length of the depositions and provided the defendants an opportunity to request further depositions upon a showing of need.[156]

In *United States v. Trucking Employers, Inc.*,[157] African American and Spanish-surnamed individuals filed a class action lawsuit under Title VII for discrimination in the trucking industry.[158] Plaintiffs propounded interrogatories upon the class of defendant trucking companies. The court stated "when the circumstances of the case justify such action," discovery may be sought from absent class members.[159] Plaintiffs' discovery requests involved information that the named defendants did not possess. The court found it would be impossible for the plaintiffs to proceed on the common issues at trial without this discovery.[160] In addition, the court concluded that the discovery would not be unduly burdensome and was sufficiently narrow to allow a response by the unnamed defendants.[161]

---

150. *Dellums*, 566 F.2d at 231, 236.
151. *Id.*
152. *Id.*
153. Civ. A. No. 04-498 (HHK/JMF), 2006 U.S. Dist. LEXIS 63424 (D.D.C. 2006).
154. *Id.* at *4.
155. *Id.*
156. *Id.*
157. 72 F.R.D. 101 (D.D.C. 1976).
158. *Id.* at 103.
159. *Id.* at 104.
160. *Id.* at 105.
161. *Id.*

2. Discovery Denied

Recently, in *Barham v. Ramsey*,[162] the D.C. Circuit used the *Dellums* factors to deny discovery from class members in an action involving plaintiffs arrested after a demonstration. Defendants argued that propounding discovery upon the plaintiffs would be necessary for a fair trial.[163] The court first acknowledged that discovery of absent class members may be necessary in some instances.[164] However, in denying the requests here, the court concluded defendants had no need to seek discovery from plaintiffs because, among other things, "liability has all but been decided."[165] The court reviewed each of the defendants' proposed interrogatories and found the information unnecessary and readily available through the representative parties.[166]

III. Discovery from Class Members in State Courts

As noted in the overview, most states have class action rules similar to the federal rule and follow the same jurisprudence concerning discovery from absent class members.[167] Several states, including California, Iowa, Maryland, Michigan, Mississippi, North Dakota, Texas, Virginia, and Wisconsin, do not follow the federal class action rules.

California provides for specific types of information that may be obtained from an unnamed class member. The California Rules of Court provide that an absent class member may be deposed (in written, oral, or documentary form) unless a protective order is sought.[168] Interrogatories, however, are not allowed unless a court order is obtained.[169] Courts consider several factors in determining whether to ultimately allow depositions or interrogatories, including

1. the timing of the request;
2. the subject matter to be covered;
3. the materiality of the information being sought;
4. the likelihood that class members have such information;
5. the possibility of reaching factual stipulations that eliminate the need for such discovery;

---

162. 246 F.R.D. 60 (D.D.C. 2007).
163. *Id.* at 63.
164. *Id.*
165. *Id.*
166. *Id.* at 65.
167. *See supra* note 9.
168. CAL. R. CT. 3.768(a) & (b) (2009); *see also* Chapter 33, "California."
169. CAL. R. CT. 3.768(c).

6. whether class representatives are seeking discovery on the subject to be covered; and

7. whether discovery will result in annoyance, oppression, or undue burden or expense for the members of the class.[170]

Virginia is not a class action state and has no class action statute.[171] Mississippi only acknowledges equitable class actions, and the discovery rules of Rule 23 do not apply.[172]

Iowa and North Dakota are the only two states that adhere to the Uniform Class Action Act.[173] These states address the issue of discovery from absent class members by nearly identical rules of civil procedure, which are similar to the predominant common law federal analysis:[174]

> Discovery may be used only on order of the court against a member of the class who is not a representative party or who has not appeared. In deciding whether discovery should be allowed the court shall consider, among other relevant factors, the timing of the request, the subject matter to be covered, whether representatives of the class are seeking discovery on the subject to be covered, and whether the discovery will result in annoyance, oppression, or undue burden or expense for the member of the class.[175]

By statute, class actions in Texas do not consider unnamed class members to be parties for the purpose of discovery.[176] However, general discovery rules as to

---

170. CAL. R. CT. 3.768 (2009); *Nat'l Solar Equip. Owners' Ass'n v. Grumman Corp.*, 235 Cal. App. 3d 1273, 1283 (1991); *Spoon v. Superior Court*, 130 Cal. App. 3d 735, 740 (1982).

171. *See Nationwide Mut. Ins. Co. v. Hous. Opportunities Made Equal, Inc.*, 259 Va. 8 (2000) (citing *W.S. Carnes, Inc. v. Bd. of Supervisors*, 478 S.E.2d 295, 300 (Va. 1996) (reciting that "Virginia is not a class-action state, and 'an individual or entity does not acquire standing to sue in a representative capacity by asserting the rights of another, unless authorized by statute to do so.'")); *see also Heirs of Roberts v. Coal Processing Corp.*, 235 Va. 556 (1988) (sustaining defendants' motion on the ground that class actions are impermissible in actions at law in Virginia); Chapter 33, "Virginia."

172. *USF&G Ins. Co. v. Walls*, No. 2002-IA-00185-SCT, 2004 Miss. LEXIS 657, at *4 (Miss. 2004) ("The comment to Mississippi Rule 23 was meant to convey our reluctance to adopt the elaborate mechanisms of the class action, since 'few procedural devices have been the subject of more widespread criticism and more sustained attack—and equally spirited defense—than practice under Federal Rule 23 and its state counterparts.'"); *see also* MISS. R. CIV. P. 23 cmt. n.1; Chapter 33, "Mississippi."

173. Thomas D. Rowe, Jr., *State and Foreign Class-Action Rules and Statutes: Differences from and Lessons for Federal Rule 23*, 35 W. ST. U. L. REV. 101, 123 (2008); *see also* Chapter 33, "Iowa" and "North Dakota."

174. *Ritter, Laber & Assocs. v. Koch Oil, Inc.*, 605 N.W.2d 153 (N.D. 2000).

175. IOWA R. CIV. P. 1.269 (2009); *see also* N.D. R. CIV. P. 23(j)(1).

176. TEX. R. CIV. P. 42(f); *see also* Chapter 33, "Texas."

nonparties still apply.[177] In Maryland, discovery of unnamed class members may only be conducted upon motion.[178] In Michigan, absent class members are treated like nonparties for purposes of discovery, but may be treated as parties if ordered by the court.[179]

---

177. *Sw. Ref. Co. v. Bernal*, 960 S.W.2d 293 (Tex. App.—Corpus Christi 1997). *But see Tracker Marine, L.P. v. Ogle*, 108 S.W.3d 349 (Tex. App.—Houston [14th Dist.] 2003, no pet.); *E & V Slack, Inc. v. Shell Oil Co.*, 969 S.W.2d 565 (Tex. App.—Austin 1998, no pet.); *Vinson v. Texas Commerce Bank—Houston Nat'l Ass'n*, 880 S.W.2d 820 (Tex. App.—Dallas 1994, no writ) (finding that if forced to proceed as a class action, the defendant would not have the benefit of discovery from class members and, therefore, could only speculate about who in the proposed class had not been paid during the time period the defendant allegedly converted proceeds from oil and gas production).

178. MD. R. CIV. P. 2-231(g) (2009); *see also* Chapter 33, "Maryland."

179. MICH. GEN. CT. R. 3.501(G) (2009); *see also* Chapter 33, "Michigan."

TRIALS

MICHAEL J. MUELLER
JASON M. BEACH

I. Introduction

Class actions are not often tried; accordingly, there is a dearth of authority about class action trials compared to what is available for the more common and conventional individual trial. This chapter addresses the special challenges inherent in such trials, covering both problems of proving class claims and of crafting appropriate jury instructions.

II. Balance Between Individual and Classwide Proof

A hallmark of a class action is its representative nature. In other words, a class action is a litigation construct in which a class representative seeks redress not only for his or her personal claims, but also for the claims of absent class members who have not been made a party by service of process. A class action's representative nature, however, generally does not alter class representatives' burden to prove each element of every claim, not only for themselves, but also for each class member. This makes sense because judgments in class actions generally are intended to bind absent class members. Therefore, counsel often experiences tension between *individual* proof for a representative's claims and the additional, perhaps even different, *class* proof required to establish a case for the class or subclass represented.

A. BURDENS REMAIN THE SAME, BUT EVIDENCE MUST BRIDGE THE GAP FROM A CLASS REPRESENTATIVE'S CLAIM TO THE CLASS MEMBERS' CLAIMS

The class action device does not "alter the required elements which must be found to impose liability and fix damages (*or the burden of proof thereon*) or the identity of the substantive law."[1] The Rules Enabling Act, 28 U.S.C. § 2072, supports this proposition for federal class actions.[2] As the United States Court of Appeals for the Fifth Circuit explained in *Cimino v. Raymark Industries, Inc.*:

> This Circuit has . . . explained that the meaning of liability for antitrust purposes does not change simply because a trial is bifurcated under FED. R. CIV. P. 42(b). In *Response of Carolina, Inc. v. Leasco Response, Inc.*, 537 F.2d 1307 (5th Cir. 1976), this court stated that there was no basis in law or logic to give liability different meanings depending upon the trial procedure used. *Id.* at 1321. The *Leasco* opinion explained that bifurcation in no way diminishes the requirement that a plaintiff show some evidence that a violation caused him injury before a defendant is found liable.
>
> * * * *
>
> Just as the meaning of liability does not vary because a trial is bifurcated, the requisite proof also *in no way hinges upon whether or not the action is brought on behalf of a class under Rule 23*. It is axiomatic that a procedural rule cannot abridge, enlarge, or modify any substantive right . . . . Consequently, *this court has no power to define differently the substantive right of individual plaintiffs as compared to class plaintiffs.*[3]

Although the burdens of proof remain unaffected by the class action device, a class action trial will create a tension not present in non-class litigation. Plaintiffs' counsel, for example, must "effectively bridge[ ] the gap between the individual claim that, most likely, started the case, and the other class members who have the same interests and the same or similar injuries."[4] Conversely, defense counsel not only must attack the merits of the class representative's claim, but also must try to

---

1. *Cimino v. Raymark Indus., Inc.*, 151 F.3d 297, 312 (5th Cir. 1998) (emphasis added).

2. The Rules Enabling Act states, in pertinent part:

    (a) The Supreme Court shall have the power to prescribe general rules of practice and procedure and rules of evidence for cases in the United States district courts (including proceedings before magistrate judges thereof) and courts of appeals.

    (b) Such rules shall not abridge, enlarge or modify any substantive right. All laws in conflict with such rules shall be of no further force or effect after such rules have taken effect.

28 U.S.C. § 2072. *See Amchem Prods., Inc. v. Windsor*, 521 U.S. 591, 613 (1997) ("Rule 23's requirements must be interpreted in keeping with Article III constraints, and with the Rules Enabling Act.").

3. 151 F.3d at 312 (internal quotation marks omitted). Just as a class representative's proof might not demonstrate liability for the entire class, injuries to unnamed putative class members cannot inversely cure a named plaintiff's lack of standing. *See, e.g., Warth v. Seldin*, 422 U.S. 490, 502 (1975); *Jenson v. IPEX USA, Inc.*, No. C08-0016MJP, 2008 WL 5062657, at *5 (W.D. Wash. Oct. 7, 2008) ("[A] plaintiff may not use the procedural device of a class action to bootstrap himself into standing he lacks under the express terms of the substantive law." (internal quotation marks omitted)); *German v. Fed. Home Loan Mortgage Corp.*, 885 F. Supp. 537, 548 (S.D.N.Y. 1995) (same).

4. 97 AM. JUR. PROOF OF FACTS 3d § 28 (2009); *Williams v. Mohawk Indus., Inc.*, 568 F.3d 1350, 1358 (11th Cir. 2009) (identifying issue of "how the class will prove causation and injury and whether those elements will be subject to class-wide proof").

show how proof of a class representative's claim cannot establish the claim for the entire class or subclass.

B. BUILDING—AND BURNING—BRIDGES TO CLASSWIDE PROOF

"Merely because the court has certified a class does not ensure that the case will go to trial."[5] A federal trial court can alter or amend a class certification order at any time before final judgment pursuant to Rule 23(c)(1)(C).[6] For this purpose, the concept of "final judgment" is a pragmatic one.[7] Similarly, the initial certification of a "collective action," another form of representative action created by Congress for private claims under various employment laws, also is conditional.[8] The conditional nature of representative actions is unsurprising because "class actions often present extraordinarily complex factual and legal scenarios, such that a complete list of the claims, issues, or defenses appropriate for class treatment may be difficult to discern or articulate at the time of certification."[9]

A court may redefine or subdivide the original class to conform to the proof presented at trial.[10] Indeed, the court may even decertify the class if the proofs

5. *Anderson v. Boeing Co.*, No. 02-CV-0196-CVE-FHM, 2006 WL 2990383, at *1 (N.D. Okla. Oct. 18, 2006) (decertifying class after conclusion of merits discovery).

6. *Gen. Tel. Co. v. Falcon*, 457 U.S. 147, 160 (1982) (trial judge is free to modify certification order in light of subsequent developments in the litigation); *In re Integra Realty Res., Inc.*, 354 F.3d 1246, 1261 (10th Cir. 2004) ("[A] trial court overseeing a class action retains the ability to monitor the appropriateness of class certification throughout the proceedings and to modify or decertify a class at any time before final judgment."); *Boucher v. Syracuse Univ.*, 164 F.3d 113, 118 (2d Cir. 1999) ("But under Rule 23(c)(1), courts are required to reassess their class rulings as the case develops." (citations and internal quotation marks omitted)); *Richardson v. Byrd*, 709 F.2d 1016, 1019 (5th Cir. 1983) ("[T]he district court is charged with the duty of monitoring its class decisions in light of the evidentiary development of the case."); *see also* 5 JAMES WM. MOORE ET AL., MOORE'S FEDERAL PRACTICE, § 23.87 (3d ed. 1997) [hereinafter MOORE'S] (citing *Int'l Union of Elec. Salaried, Mach. & Furniture Workers v. Unisys Corp.*, 155 F.R.D. 41, 47 (E.D.N.Y 1994) and *Kuehner v. Heckler*, 778 F.2d 152, 163 (3d Cir. 1985)).

7. An Advisory Committee note to Rule 23 explains that the "final judgment concept is pragmatic. It is not the same as the concept used for appeal purposes, but it should be flexible, particularly in protracted litigation." FED. R. CIV. P. 23 advisory committee note (2003).

8. *See, e.g.*, *Morgan v. Family Dollar Stores, Inc.*, 551 F.3d 1233, 1261 (11th Cir. 2008), *cert. denied*, 130 S. Ct. 59 (2009); *Thiessen v. Gen. Elec. Capital Corp.*, 267 F.3d 1095, 1102–05 (10th Cir. 2001) (discussing extensively the two-step process for actions brought under 29 U.S.C. § 216(b)); *see also* Chapter 17.E, "Employment Cases."

9. *Wachtel v. Guardian Life Ins. Co. of Am.*, 453 F.3d 179, 186 n.8 (3d Cir. 2006).

10. *See, e.g.*, *Bates v. United Parcel Serv., Inc.*, 511 F.3d 974, 983 (9th Cir. 2007) (noting trial court modified composition of the class post-trial); 5 MOORE'S § 23.87 (citing *Becher v. Long Island Lighting Co.*, 172 F.R.D. 28, 30–31 (E.D.N.Y. 1997) (previously-certified subclass description was amended by dividing class in two)); *Watson v. Fort Worth Bank & Trust*, 798 F.2d 791, 797 (5th Cir. 1986) (after all evidence at trial in action alleging discrimination by bank against applicants and employees based on race, trial court decertified a class and created two classes because no common question of law or fact existed between applicants and employees), *vacated and remanded on other grounds*, 487 U.S. 977 (1988); *Penk v. Or. State Bd. of Higher Educ.*, 816 F.2d 458, 467 (9th Cir. 1987) (after six months of trial in gender-based discrimination class action, redefining the plaintiff class was not an abuse of discretion).

at trial show that certification never was, or no longer is, appropriate.[11] An Advisory Committee note to Rule 23 specifically observes that "[d]ecertification may be warranted in light of further proceedings."[12]

While discovery and other pretrial proceedings should help determine before trial whether redefinition or decertification is appropriate, the tension between individual and classwide proofs will remain throughout trial. Counsel therefore must decide how best to structure the trial. For a class action trial, "a court [with the help of counsel] must devise a plan of adjudication."[13] In fact, "[a]n increasing number of courts require a party requesting class certification to present a "trial plan" that describes the issues likely to be presented at trial and tests whether they are susceptible to class-wide proof."[14] In *Hohider v. United Parcel Service, Inc.*, the United States Court of Appeals for the Third Circuit recently held that the failure of a trial court to properly address such trial planning issues justified decertification.[15] Therefore, counsel should begin thinking about trial structure and the relation of individualized and classwide proofs as early as possible.[16] "If there is no realistic

---

11. *See, e.g., Forehand v. Fla. State Hosp.*, 89 F.3d 1562, 1566–67 (11th Cir. 1996) (affirming district court's decertification of class six years after bench trial); *see also Carnegie v. Household Int'l, Inc.*, 376 F.3d 656, 661 (7th Cir. 2004) ("Rule 23 allows district courts to devise imaginative solutions to problems created by the presence in a class action litigation of individual damages issues," including "decertifying the class after the liability trial and providing notice to class members concerning how they may proceed to prove damages."); *Key v. Gillette Co.*, 782 F.2d 5, 7 (1st Cir. 1986) (affirming decertification of class after bench trial); *Stastny v. S. Bell Tel. & Tel. Co.*, 628 F.2d 267, 275–76 (4th Cir. 1980) ("[T]he court must be prepared under Rule 23(c)(1) to alter or amend [the class ruling] if the course of trial on the merits reveals the impropriety of class action maintenance."); *White Indus., Inc. v. Cessna Aircraft Co.*, 657 F. Supp. 687, 716 (W.D. Mo. 1986) (where class certification is found to be improvident because the requirements of Rule 23 cannot be met, the court must decertify "even if the finding is not made until during or at the time of conclusion of the trial on the merits"), *aff'd*, 845 F.2d 1497 (8th Cir. 1988) (affirming decertification because individual questions of fact predominated over common questions); *see also Penk*, 99 F.R.D. at 516 ("If the evidence at trial indicates that a class action is not in fact appropriate [because of commonality and typicality problems], the court will not hesitate to decertify."); *Reynolds v. Sheet Metal Workers, Local 102*, 702 F.2d 221, 226 (D.C. Cir. 1981) ("[C]lass certification problems are constantly subject to reconsideration as the facts develop at trial.").

12. FED. R. CIV. P. 23 advisory committee note (2003).

13. 3 HERBERT B. NEWBERG & ALBA CONTE, NEWBERG ON CLASS ACTIONS: A MANUAL FOR GROUP LITIGATION AT FEDERAL AND STATE LEVELS § 9:60 (4th ed. 2002) [hereinafter NEWBERG].

14. FED. R. CIV. P. 23 advisory committee note (2003).

15. No. 07-1689, 2009 WL 2183267, at *22 (3d Cir. Jan. 16, 2009) ("[D]eferral of [trial planning] analysis post class certification was an abuse of discretion."). In contrast, "[t]o demonstrate the manageability of the class action, the district court [may] outline[ ] a trial plan based, in large part, on how other courts have handled similarly large and complex class action suits." *Dukes v. Wal-Mart, Inc.*, 509 F.3d 1168, 1190 (9th Cir. 2007).

16. *See McNamara v. Felderhof*, 410 F.3d 277, 280 (5th Cir. 2005) (noting that class plaintiff's counsel attempted to submit a "trial plan" *after* trial court's denial of class certification to address court's concerns).

means of proof, many resources will be wasted setting up a trial that plaintiffs cannot win."[17]

One method used by courts to devise a plan for management of remaining individual issues is severance of issues and separate trials under Rule 23(d)[18] and Rule 42(b).[19] This may be accomplished by structuring trials in sequential segments to determine designated issues or claims, narrowing and limiting issues for jury determination, or deferring such proceedings pending the exhaustion of other procedures as directed by the court.[20]

One issue is how to address individual proofs regarding damages. Plaintiffs' counsel may "aggregate class proof of damages, together with the potential use of cy pres or escheat distributions of an aggregate class recovery."[21] Ultimate individual questions may be susceptible to adjudication on a common basis, and the creation of subclasses may be available for this purpose where appropriate.[22] Additionally, plaintiffs' counsel may attempt to have the court authorize a class recovery distribution to class members on some per capita, average, or formula basis, accompanied by an automatic distribution without the need for individual proof of claims.[23] "Aggregate class recovery proofs are becoming a recognized means

---

17. *In re New Motor Vehicles Can. Exp. Antitrust Litig.*, 522 F.3d 6, 29 (1st Cir. 2008) (remanding case and noting that "the district court must still ensure that the plaintiffs' presentation of their case will be through means amenable to the class action mechanism").

18. Rule 23(d) provides:

> (1) In General. In conducting an action under this rule, the court may issue orders that:
>   (A) determine the course of proceedings or prescribe measures to prevent undue repetition or complication in presenting evidence or argument;
>   (B) require—to protect class members and fairly conduct the action—giving appropriate notice to some or all class members of:
>   (i) any step in the action;
>   (ii) the proposed extent of the judgment; or
>   (iii) the members' opportunity to signify whether they consider the representation fair and adequate, to intervene and present claims or defenses, or to otherwise come into the action;
>   (C) impose conditions on the representative parties or on intervenors;
>   (D) require that the pleadings be amended to eliminate allegations about representation of absent persons and that the action proceed accordingly; or
>   (E) deal with similar procedural matters.
> (2) Combining and Amending Orders. An order under Rule 23(d)(1) may be altered or amended from time to time and may be combined with an order under Rule 16.

19. "For convenience, to avoid prejudice, or to expedite and economize, the court may order a separate trial of one or more separate issues, claims, crossclaims, counterclaims, or third-party claims. When ordering a separate trial, the court must preserve any federal right to a jury trial." FED. R. CIV. P. 42(b); *see also* NEWBERG § 9:66.

20. NEWBERG § 9:66.

21. *Id.* at § 9:62.

22. *Id.*

23. *Id.*; *see also* Chapter 30, "Other Due Process Challenges to the Class Device."

of proceeding in class adjudications, provided such means of proof are able to be developed in the particular circumstances and otherwise comply with applicable evidentiary rules."[24] Generally, individual issues regarding damages will not prevent class action litigation from proceeding.[25]

Mathematical averaging, however, can be problematic if it masks individualized issues and avoids the factual analysis necessary to meet a plaintiff's evidentiary burdens.[26] For example, in *Bell Atlantic Corp. v. AT&T Corp.*,[27] the United States Court of Appeals for the Fifth Circuit analyzed whether individualized issues regarding the amount of damages for each class member would predominate if the case were certified and proceeded to the merits phase. The Fifth Circuit agreed with the lower court that certification was improper, but based its opinion on the plaintiffs' improper use of averages.[28] The court explained that the plaintiffs proposed to calculate damages for the members of each subclass according to a formula using nationwide averages.[29] The plaintiffs' proposed methodology, however, did not allow for examination of the "variegated" and individualized inquiries necessary to evaluate each class member's damages.[30] Because numerous factors would have affected the amount of damages, if any, suffered by a given class member, class certification was improper.[31]

---

24. NEWBERG § 9.62; *see also* Chapter 18, "Statistical Sampling as a Basis for Extrapolating Liability and/or Damages."

25. *See, e.g., Klay v. Humana, Inc.*, 382 F.3d 1241, 1259–60 (11th Cir. 2004) (holding "where damages can be computed according to some formula, statistical analysis, or other easy or essentially mechanical methods, the fact that damages must be calculated on an individual basis is no impediment to class certification" (internal citations omitted)).

26. *See, e.g., In re Hydrogen Peroxide Antitrust Litig.*, 552 F.3d 305, 324 (3d Cir. 2008) (vacating class certification order on ground that the district court did not undertake the necessary rigorous analysis of the parties' experts' opinions and remanding with the direction that the district court should resolve the dispute between the experts whether impact was susceptible to classwide proof); *Bell Atl. Corp. v. AT&T Corp.*, 339 F.3d 294, 304 (5th Cir. 2003); *Newton v. Merrill Lynch, Pierce, Fenner & Smith, Inc.*, 259 F.3d 154, 166 (3d Cir. 2001) ("The ability to calculate the aggregate amount of damages does not absolve plaintiffs from the duty to prove each investor was harmed by the defendants' practice.").

27. 339 F.3d at 304.

28. *Id.* at 303.

29. *Id.* at 304.

30. *Id.*

31. *Id.* at 304–05. The *Bell Atlantic* decision is only one of many decisions that criticize using averages when they mathematically mask individualized issues. *See Piggly Wiggly Clarksville, Inc. v. Interstate Brands Corp.*, 100 F. App'x 296, 300 (5th Cir. 2004) (finding use of averages improper when a large number of independent factors affecting damages suffered by each class member existed and could not be approximated, thus precluding class certification); *Broussard v. Meineke Disc. Muffler Shops, Inc.*, 155 F.3d 331, 342–43 (4th Cir. 1998) (finding need to calculate damages will defeat predominance when the issue requires separate mini-trials of an overwhelmingly large number of individual claims); *Windham v. Am. Brands, Inc.*, 565 F.2d 59, 68 (4th Cir. 1977); *Plekowski v. Ralston Purina Co.*, 68 F.R.D. 443, 454–55 (M.D.

C. ARE THE CLASS REPRESENTATIVE'S CLAIMS REALLY REPRESENTATIVE?

One problem that may arise before or during trial is that proof of the named plaintiff's case may potentially limit the ability of other class members to recover.[32] Such a limitation can occur when the evidence shows that class representatives are not typical of the class, thus preventing a bridge between individualized and classwide proof. For example, in *Broussard v. Meineke Discount Muffler Shops, Inc.*, the issue of tolling of the statute of limitations for each plaintiff's claims depended on individualized determinations that were not typical, but rather were unique to each franchisee.[33]

Linkage problems between a class representative's claim and those of the class also can occur when there are "conflicts of interest between named parties and the class they seek to represent."[34] "[A] class representative must be part of the class and possess the same interest and suffer the same injury as the class members."[35] Therefore, the class representative's personal claim must not be inconsistent with the claims of other members of the class.[36]

A class that is "no more than a hodgepodge of factually as well as legally different plaintiffs that should not have been cobbled together for trial" hopefully will not become apparent for the first time on the eve of, or during, trial.[37] Nevertheless, class defense counsel should highlight at trial all aspects of a class representative's factual circumstances that limit his ability to translate individual proof to classwide proof.

D. BURDENS WHEN CONFRONTING MULTIPLE JURISDICTIONS' LAWS

Another issue that may present a problem with bridging an individual proof to classwide proof occurs in multistate class actions where the laws of many jurisdictions control.[38] As discussed above, a court may structure a jury trial, including a multijurisdiction class trial, "in the most efficient and economical way possible, as

---

Ga. 1975) (noting that class damages should not be based on a system of averaging); *Ralston v. Volkswagenwerk, A.G.*, 61 F.R.D. 427, 432–33 (W.D. Mo. 1973) (same).

32. 2 ROBERT L. HAIG ET AL., BUSINESS AND COMMERCIAL LITIGATION IN FEDERAL COURTS § 16.13 (2d ed. 2005).

33. 155 F.3d 331, 342–43.

34. *Amchem*, 521 U.S. at 625 (citing *Falcon*, 457 U.S. at 157–58).

35. *Id.* at 625–26 (internal quotation marks omitted).

36. *See, e.g.*, *Valley Drug Co. v. Geneva Pharm., Inc.*, 350 F.3d 1181, 1189–92 (11th Cir. 2003) (finding class representatives inadequate where their economic interests and objectives conflicted substantially with those of absent class members); *Penn. Dental Ass'n v. Med. Serv. Ass'n of Pa.*, 745 F.2d 248, 263 (3d Cir. 1984) (refusing to certify class containing dentists who did and did not participate in a challenged dental fee program, because of "inherent conflicts" between the two groups).

37. *Broussard*, 155 F.3d at 343.

38. For a more detailed discussion of the issue, *see* Chapter 24, "Multistate Class Actions and Choice of Law."

long as the substance of the right to have the jury determine the facts at issue is ultimately preserved."[39] Therefore, a court may "bifurcate or otherwise structure a segmented jury trial, give interim instructions after each segment, use special jury interrogatories and request special verdicts from the jury for each segment, and finally, reach nonjury findings and mold the final verdict based on the special jury verdicts rendered on the underlying facts at issue."[40] However, in such cases, class counsel will bear the duty to "parse the various elements of proof to show violations in each [applicable] jurisdiction under each liability theory."[41]

Class plaintiffs' counsel have presented, and courts have rejected, radical trial plans seeking to resolve these individual proof issues in a class setting.[42] To illustrate, courts have rejected trial plans that relied upon the following: a fictional composite of the class;[43] expert testimony addressing individualized issues in the aggregate, such as group models using statistical methods;[44] affidavits or

---

39. NEWBERG § 9:68.

40. *Id.*

41. *Id.*

42. For more in-depth treatment of this subject, see Byron G. Stier, *Resolving the Class Action Crisis: Mass Tort Litigation as Network*, 2005 UTAH L. REV. 863, 884 (2005), which collects and summarizes many of the cases cited here.

43. *Thorn v. Jefferson-Pilot Life Ins. Co.*, 445 F.3d 311, 327 (4th Cir. 2006) (discussing danger of having to "defend against a fictional composite without the benefit of deposing or cross-examining the disparate individuals behind the composite" (internal quotation marks omitted)); *Broussard*, 155 F.3d at 344–45 (rejecting plaintiffs' proposed "perfect plaintiff," and stating that "plaintiffs portrayed the class at trial as a large, unified group that suffered a uniform, collective injury. And [the defendant] was often forced to defend against a fictional composite without the benefit of deposing or cross-examining the disparate individuals behind the composite creation."); *In re Paxil Litig.*, 212 F.R.D. 539, 548 (C.D. Cal. 2003) ("[A] class trial on liability without any reference to [defendant's defenses] runs 'the real risk . . . of a composite case being much stronger than any plaintiff's individual action would be . . . [thus] permitt[ing] plaintiffs to strike [defendants] with selective allegations, which may or may not have been available to individual named plaintiffs.'" (quoting *O'Connor v. Boeing N. Am., Inc.*, 197 F.R.D. 404, 415 (C.D. Cal. 2000) (internal quotation marks omitted))).

44. The United States Court of Appeals for the Fifth Circuit has held:

A contemplated "trial" of the 2,990 class members without discrete focus . . . cannot focus upon such issues as individual causation, but ultimately must accept general causation as sufficient, contrary to Texas law. "[P]opulation-based probability estimates do not speak to a probability of causation in any one case; the estimate of relative risk is a property of the studied population, not of an individual's case." This type of procedure does not allow proof that a particular defendant's asbestos "really" caused a particular plaintiff's disease. . . . This is the inevitable consequence of treating discrete claims as fungible claims.

[T]he procedures here . . . comprise something other than a trial . . . It is called a trial, but is not.

In re Fibreboard Corp., 893 F.2d 706, 711–12 (5th Cir. 1990) (certain internal quotation marks omitted); *see also Cimino*, 151 F.3d at 300 (reversing judgment based on extrapolation of average of 160 verdicts to other plaintiffs with same disease).

questionnaires for the purposes of trial;[45] and abstract examinations of a defendant's conduct or generic causation.[46] Such trial plans may deny due process to defendants.[47]

Additionally, trial plans that attempt to grapple with individual issues by empanelling separate juries for class action litigation may violate the 7th Amendment. Specifically, if separate juries decide commingled factual questions in the class action context, a subsequent jury may run the risk of reexamining a previous jury's findings, thus violating a plaintiff or defendant's 7th Amendment right to a jury trial.[48]

45. *See, e.g., Barnes v. Am. Tobacco Co.*, 161 F.3d 127, 145–46 (3d Cir. 1998) (discussing use of questionnaire in possible certification case to prove causation of individualized injuries); *Arch v. Am. Tobacco Co.*, 175 F.R.D. 469, 489 n.21 (E.D. Pa. 1997) (holding that use of questionnaires to establish injury and causation violated defendant's due process rights); *Guillory v. Am. Tobacco Co.*, No. 97 C 8641, 2001 WL 290603, at *9 (N.D. Ill. Mar. 20, 2001) (stating that inability to individually probe into the peculiarities of each class member's case would deny the opportunity to prepare a defense); *Hoyte v. Stauffer Chem. Co.*, No. 98-3024-CI-7, 2002 WL 31892830, at *56 (Fla. Cir. Ct. 2002) (holding pervasive individual issues could not be solved by questionnaires).

46. *In re Hanford Nuclear Reservation Litig.*, 292 F.3d 1124, 1129 (9th Cir. 2002) (discussing bifurcation of discovery regarding generic and individual causation); *Patterson v. Mobil Oil Corp.*, 241 F.3d 417, 419 (5th Cir. 2001) (stating that "effort to decide" only defendant's conduct "would be no more than the trial of an abstraction—for which subclassing and bifurcation is no cure"); *In re "Agent Orange" Prod. Liab. Litig.*, 818 F.2d 145, 165 (2d Cir. 1987); *Blain v. SmithKline Beecham Corp.*, 240 F.R.D. 179, 185 (E.D. Pa. 2007) ("In mass tort cases, courts have routinely refused to certify common questions of general causation."); *Estate of Mahoney v. R.J. Reynolds Tobacco Co.*, 204 F.R.D. 150, 157 (S.D. Iowa 2001) ("No one seriously doubts the general premise that smoking causes lung cancer. . . . [A] plaintiff must necessarily eliminate all other risk factors as possible causes of his lung cancer."); *Neenan v. Carnival Corp.*, 199 F.R.D. 372, 377 (S.D. Fla. 2001) (in class action regarding the inhalation of fecal fumes, court "would drown in a rogue wave of highly case-specific factual issues" (internal quotation marks omitted)); *Barreras Ruiz v. Am. Tobacco Co.*, 180 F.R.D. 194, 195, 197 (D.P.R. 1998) (denying class certification based on first phase trial on defendant's conduct and noting that plaintiffs' approach "suggests a nearly cavalier attitude towards the complexity of the class they propose"); *Arch*, 175 F.R.D. at 488 ("Unless it is proven that cigarettes always cause or never cause addiction, the resolution of the general causation question accomplishes nothing for any individual plaintiff." (internal quotation marks omitted)).

47. *Gartin v. S&M NuTec LLC*, 245 F.R.D. 429, 442 (C.D. Cal. 2007) ("Since the class is likely to be so large and varied, as discussed above, Defendant's due process rights may be affected like those of the defendant in *Fibreboard*. Accordingly, due process concerns weigh against certification of the class."); *Broussard*, 155 F.3d at 352 ("Without respect for law[,] neither the class action device nor the jury system can serve the important functions for which they were intended."); *Fibreboard*, 893 F.2d at 711 (rejecting trial plan and noting that problems "find expression in defendants' right to due process"); *Nelson v. Adams USA, Inc.*, 529 U.S. 460, 465 (2000) ("The Federal Rules of Civil Procedure are designed to further the due process of law that the Constitution guarantees."); *In re Repetitive Stress Injury Litig.*, 11 F.3d 368, 373 (2d Cir. 1993) ("'The systemic urge to aggregate litigation must not be allowed to trump our dedication to individual justice, and we must take care that each individual plaintiff's—and defendant's—cause not be lost in the shadow of a towering mass litigation.'" (quoting *In re Brooklyn Navy Yard Asbestos Litig.*, 971 F.2d 831, 853 (2d Cir. 1992))).

48. *Gasoline Prods. Co. v. Champlin Ref. Co.*, 283 U.S. 494, 499–500 (1931) (holding that 7th Amendment requires that related issues of fact be decided by one jury, not reexamined by second jury); *Allison v. Citgo Petroleum Corp.*, 151 F.3d 402, 419–20 (5th Cir. 1998) ("[T]o manage the case, the district court faced the likelihood of bifurcated proceedings before multiple juries. This result . . . increased the probability

To illustrate, a first jury trial verdict regarding an issue, such as fraud, might be reexamined by a second jury looking into what each class member saw, knew, and/or relied upon. Plaintiffs' counsel therefore must propose a workable trial plan that shows how to try the class action without violating defendants' rights.[49]

E. REPRESENTATIVE ACTION ANALOGS

The tension between individual proof versus classwide proof also can be seen in actions under the Fair Labor Standards Act (FLSA), which have become one of the most prevalent alternative forms of group actions in the past decade. The FLSA allows one or more employees to pursue an action along with "other employees similarly situated."[50] A collective action under a statutory scheme such as the FLSA (or under the Age Discrimination in Employment Act of 1967 (ADEA[51])) affords plaintiffs the advantage of lower individual costs to vindicate rights by pooling resources, and the judicial system purportedly benefits by efficient resolution in one proceeding of common issues of law and fact.[52]

---

that successive juries would pass on issues decided by prior ones, introducing potential Seventh Amendment problems and further decreasing the superiority of the class action device."); *Cimino*, 151 F.3d at 312 ("[T]he applicability of the Seventh Amendment is not altered simply because the case is a Rule 23(b)(3) class action."); *id.* at 319 (stating that "causation must be determined as to 'individuals, not groups,'" and that "the Seventh Amendment gives the right to a jury trial to make that determination"); *Castano v. Am. Tobacco Co.*, 84 F.3d 734, 750–51 (5th Cir. 1996) ("The Seventh Amendment entitles parties to have fact issues decided by one jury, and prohibits a second jury from reexamining those facts and issues. . . . Comparative negligence, by definition, requires a comparison between the defendant[]s and the plaintiff's conduct. . . . At a bare minimum, a second jury will rehear evidence of the defendant's conduct. . . . In such a situation, the second jury would be impermissibly reconsidering the findings of a first jury. The risk of such reevaluation is so great that class treatment can hardly be said to be superior to individual adjudication."); *In re Rhone-Poulenc Rorer, Inc.*, 51 F.3d 1293, 1297, 1303 (7th Cir. 1995) (stating that "judge must not divide issues between separate trials in such a way that the same issue is reexamined by different juries"); *In re Live Concert Antitrust Litig.*, 247 F.R.D. 98, 149 n.47 (C.D. Cal. 2007) ("Bifurcation is limited by the Seventh Amendment to the extent that the Seventh Amendment generally entitles parties to have facts decided by one jury and prohibits a second jury from reexamining those facts."(internal quotation marks omitted)).

49. *See* FED. R. CIV. P. 23 advisory committee note (2003) (discussing class action trial plan); *Zinser v. Accufix Research Inst., Inc.*, 253 F.3d 1180, 1189 (9th Cir. 2001) ("Because [plaintiff] seeks certification of a nationwide class for which the law of forty-eight states potentially applies, she bears the burden of demonstrating a suitable and realistic plan for trial of the class claims." (internal quotation marks omitted)), *amended by* 273 F.3d 1266 (9th Cir. 2001); *Barreras Ruiz*, 180 F.R.D. at 195, 197 (rejecting plan that called for "defendant-conduct-only" class trial and then additional trials for individual issues, and stating that proposed trial plan "suggests a nearly cavalier attitude towards the complexity of the class [plaintiffs] propose"); *Gartin*, 245 F.R.D. at 439 (citing *Zinser* and stating that "variances in state law may overwhelm common issue of fact and destroy predominance.").

50. 29 U.S.C. § 216(b); *see also* Chapter 17.E, "Employment Cases."

51. Section 7(b) of the ADEA incorporates enforcement provisions of the FLSA, 29 U.S.C. § 201, and provides that the ADEA shall be enforced using certain of the powers, remedies, and procedures of the FLSA. *Hoffmann-La Roche Inc. v. Sperling*, 493 U.S. 165, 167 (1989).

52. *See generally Sperling*, 493 U.S. at 167 (addressing collective actions under the ADEA).

In a number of respects, an FLSA "collective action" functions like a class action under Rule 23, and FLSA claims often are accompanied by parallel Rule 23 claims under state laws or other federal statutes. In theory, the FLSA provides a mechanism for the efficient resolution of the claims of multiple plaintiffs that involve common factual issues on the basis of representative proof.[53] Rather than trying many individual employees' claims that present common factual and legal questions separately, a court may resolve them collectively on the basis of evidence that is representative of the whole.[54]

F. PRACTICAL CONSIDERATIONS FOR CLASS ACTION TRIALS

The bridge from individual to classwide proof can be difficult to cross. However, there are several techniques counsel can use when conducting a class action trial to address burden of proof issues. For example, when examining a witness, defense counsel will want to establish that the witness's knowledge is limited to her particular circumstances (either by job, or geographically, or in whatever other way would make a difference to the substantive claim). This will help to underscore the individualized nature of her evidence and perhaps distance her from the class she represents. Defense counsel also can "summarize" prior, differing testimony by having the witness admit that she is saying something that varies from an earlier witness or witnesses. Additionally, demonstrative charts can be used throughout the trial to remind the jury how varied the admitted evidence is. To the extent plaintiffs' counsel uses experts to establish class proof, defense counsel should seek admissions that any formulaic, statistical, or averaging techniques do not necessarily answer injury or causation issues for *every* class member and have the expert identify certain categories of class members that must be excluded. Conversely, plaintiffs' counsel should emphasize the supposed broad similarity of what each witness says when compared to prior witnesses. A useful technique is to employ the same simple examination script repeatedly. Such repetition will highlight similarities and ensure that the jury starts to tire of hearing the same questions and

---

53. There is, however, an important procedural distinction between a FLSA collective action under § 216(b) and a class action under Rule 23. Pursuant to the collective action provision of the FLSA, "[n]o employee shall be a party plaintiff to any such action unless he gives his consent in writing to become such a party and such consent is filed in the court in which such action is brought." 29 U.S.C. § 216(b). Therefore, in the FLSA context, a plaintiff must affirmatively join the lawsuit or "opt in," whereas under Rule 23(b)(3), a claimant must affirmatively "opt out" of the class action in order to preserve any individual claims that he or she might have. *See, e.g., Johnson v. Big Lots Stores, Inc.*, 561 F. Supp. 2d 567, 572–73 (E.D. La. 2008). Therefore, unlike opt-in collective actions under § 216(b), a district court's decision to certify a Rule 23(b) class binds all the class members. *Morgan*, 551 F.3d 1233 n.36.

54. *See Mooney v. Aramco Servs. Co.*, 54 F.3d 1207, 1212–14 (5th Cir. 1995) (discussing similarities between collective action under the FLSA § 216(b) standard and Rule 23 class actions), *abrogated on other grounds by Desert Palace, Inc. v. Costa*, 539 U.S. 90 (2003).

answers, and illustrates that the testimony of the class representatives *is* the same as the presumed testimony of absent class members.

III. Jury Charge

"It now seems settled in the lower federal courts that class action plaintiffs may obtain a jury trial on any legal issues they present."[55] However, "[j]urors are not experts in legal principles; to function effectively, and justly, they must be accurately instructed in the law."[56] This is especially true in the class action context, where trials can be lengthy and issues complex. Indeed, class actions may depart from traditional trial models,[57] making the fact-finding function of the class action jury—or several juries—even more intricate. Therefore, copying pattern instructions wholesale, to the extent they exist or adequately address the issues in your particular case, may waste valuable tactical opportunities both before and during a class action trial. For example, lawyers not only can introduce jury instruction concepts to the venire during the voir dire, they also can, and often should, weave key instruction issues into opening statements, witness examinations, and closing arguments.

This section analyzes the following aspects of class action jury instructions: rules governing jury instructions; the role of choice of law, in particular the difficulties presented in multistate class actions; the proper use of pattern, or model, jury instructions; the benefits of preliminary instructions; the jury instruction conference; getting objections on the record; interim instructions; final instructions; and practical instruction considerations.

A. THE PROCEDURE

In federal courts, jury instructions are addressed by Federal Rule of Civil Procedure 51.[58] Rule 51 applies with equal force to class jury trials, but may be altered by local rule or court order. Generally, however, "[a]t the close of the evidence or at any earlier reasonable time that the court orders, a party may file and furnish to every other party written requests for the jury instructions it wants the court to give."[59] After the close of the evidence, a party may "file requests for instructions on issues that could not reasonably have been anticipated by an earlier time that the court

---

55. *Ross v. Bernhard*, 396 U.S. 531, 541–42 (1970).

56. *Carter v. Kentucky*, 450 U.S. 288, 302 (1981).

57. MANUAL FOR COMPLEX LITIGATION (FOURTH) § 21.50 (2004).

58. Certain other types of instructions, however, are not governed by Rule 51, such as "preliminary instructions to a venire and cautionary or limiting instructions delivered in immediate response to events at trial." *See* 9 MOORE'S § 51.02 (footnote omitted) (citing cases).

59. FED. R. CIV. P. 51(a)(1).

set for requests; and . . . with the court's permission, file untimely requests for instructions on any issue."[60]

After the submission of any proposed instructions, the trial judge "must inform the parties of its proposed instructions and proposed action on the requests before instructing the jury and before final jury arguments."[61] The trial court also "must give the parties an opportunity to object on the record and out of the jury's hearing before the instructions and arguments are delivered."[62] The judge is allowed to charge or instruct the jury at any time before the jury is discharged.[63]

Counsel also should examine relevant local rules for jury instructions. Although a court's procedural rules generally may govern the timing of jury instructions, trial judges often are given great latitude in this respect. For example, a local rule or judge may request the submission of proposed jury instructions before the trial commences. A pretrial deadline creates a risk that the requested instructions will inadequately address unanticipated issues that arise at trial.[64] To the extent a pretrial submission is required, a party should request the opportunity to modify, supplement, or withdraw any instructions at the close of the evidence.

B. CHOICE OF LAW

Although granting or denying instructions is tested under federal law in diversity cases, a jury instruction's substance is determined by the substantive law of the jurisdiction's laws that apply to the underlying dispute (e.g., state law in a diversity case).[65] Thus, class counsel must understand the legal foundations for each claim to draft proper and effective jury instructions. In the context of multistate or nationwide class actions, this task can present certain procedural and practical difficulties when developing jury instructions. For example, to prevent the certification of a class, defense counsel often will have argued that applying the laws of the various states would present "insuperable obstacles" in trying the case if it proceeded to trial.[66] A leading commentator has analogized as follows:

> Although the comparison obviously is inexact, one can appreciate the magnitude of the trial judge's task by imagining a first-year law student who, instead of a course

---

60. FED. R. CIV. P. 51(a)(2)(A)–(B).

61. FED. R. CIV. P. 51(b)(1).

62. FED. R. CIV. P. 51(b)(2). Objections to jury instructions are addressed in subsection III.I.

63. FED. R. CIV. P. 51(b)(3).

64. 9 MOORE'S § 51.11[2].

65. *See, e.g.,* ROBERT S. HUNTER, FEDERAL TRIAL HANDBOOK: CIVIL § 71:1 (2007) (citing *Smith v. Mill Creek Court, Inc.,* 457 F.2d 589, 592 (10th Cir. 1972)).

66. *In re Ford Motor Co. Bronco II Prod. Liab. Litig.,* 177 F.R.D. 360, 368–69 (E.D. La. 1997); *In re Am. Med. Sys. Inc.,* 75 F.3d 1069, 1085 (6th Cir. 1996) (holding that differing state laws pose an "impossible task of instructing a jury on the relevant law"); *Chin v. Chrysler Corp.,* 182 F.R.D. 448, 458 (D.N.J. 1998) (finding that jurors would be overwhelmed by multistate jury instructions); *Walsh v. Ford Motor Co.,* 807 F.2d 1000, 1017 (D.C. Cir. 1986).

in contracts, is required simultaneously to enroll in fifty courses, each covering the contract law of a single state, and to apply each body of law correctly on the final examination. Another way to appreciate the dimension of the task is to consider that fifty opinions are more than most appellate judges write in a year.[67]

The court in *Chin v. Chrysler*[68] hinted at the enormity and impracticality of applying the laws of multiple jurisdictions. In rejecting a motion for class certification, the court stated, "Plaintiffs essentially ask the Court to certify this class on the basis of mere promises that a manageable litigation plan can be designed in this case for five causes of action under the law of 52 jurisdictions as the litigation progresses."[69] The court specifically discussed the difficulties this presented in creating jury instructions. Plaintiffs have the burden of analyzing state law variations and submitting sample jury instructions and special verdict forms reflecting those variations. Plaintiffs must explain to the court "how their multiple causes of action could be presented to a jury for resolution in a way that fairly represents the law of the 50 states while not overwhelming jurors with hundreds of interrogatories and a verdict form as large as an almanac."[70] In *Chin*, the plaintiffs did not meet this burden, and this failure contributed in large part to the court's refusal to certify the proposed class.

If a class has been certified, then the trial judge at least has made a preliminary determination that any issues arising from the application of various states' laws would not undermine the goals and efficiencies of the class action device. The difficulty counsel therefore must confront is preparing jury instructions that will be helpful to the jury and manageable for the court. The challenges in crafting workable jury instructions for some multistate class actions has led to the decertification of a number of class actions. The charge conference thus provides defense counsel an opportunity to remind the court—regularly—of the practical problems a certified class may present with regard to charging a jury.

For example, in *In re American Medical Systems, Inc.*,[71] the Sixth Circuit decertified a nationwide class of persons who were implanted with certain defective or malfunctioning prostheses. Included in the Sixth Circuit's reasoning for decertifying the class was the difficulty in providing a sufficient jury instruction on negligence. The court stated, "If more than a few of the laws of the fifty states differ, the district judge would face an impossible task of instructing the jury on the relevant law."[72]

---

67. Arthur R. Miller & David Crump, *Jurisdiction and Choice of Law in Multistate Class Actions After Phillips Petroleum Co. v. Shutts*, 96 Yale L.J. 1, 64 (1986) (footnote omitted).

68. 182 F.R.D. at 459.

69. *Id.* at 459.

70. *Id.* at 458 (quoting *In re Ford Motor Co. Ignition Switch Prods. Liab. Litig.*, 174 F.R.D. 332, 349 (D.N.J. 1997)).

71. 75 F.3d at 1069.

72. *Id.* at 1085.

A similar concern led to the Seventh Circuit's decertification of a plaintiff class of hemophiliacs who had been exposed to HIV-contaminated blood products in the case of *In re Rhone-Poulenc Rorer, Inc.*[73] A primary concern of the court was the creation of a jury instruction that could satisfactorily merge the negligence standards of all 50 states and the District of Columbia.[74] The court used the term "esperanto" to describe this type of composite jury instruction.[75] The court explained the term using the following hypothetical: a single jury would be instructed with law that is not the law of any particular jurisdiction.[76] This jury then would decide whether an industry was negligent based on a composite instruction that attempts to meld and harmonize the negligence laws of approximately 51 jurisdictions.[77] A possible result would be that one jury would "hurl the industry into bankruptcy."[78] The Seventh Circuit did note, however, that some general negligence principles that were common to all jurisdictions could be gleaned and that the jurisdictional variations in negligence law might not be outcome determinative.[79] Therefore, special care must be taken when crafting the jury instructions for class actions involving the laws of various jurisdictions to address manageability and prevent jury confusion.

C. PRECISION WITH PATTERN INSTRUCTIONS

In many jurisdictions, word-for-word use of approved pattern jury instructions is the prevailing practice, which is often beneficial to lawyers and judges because it provides consistency and helps to insulate against reversible error on appeal. Pattern instructions also assist jurors because they generally are developed to provide brief statements of the law stated in simple, objective terms that are understandable to laypersons. Although jury instructions in complex civil litigation, as with any other case, are highly specific to the issues of a particular matter, class action jury instructions present additional challenges that generally are not captured by pattern instructions. For example, most of the federal circuit courts have created pattern jury instructions for civil cases, but counsel will find that there is a lack of information on jury instructions regarding the class aspects of litigation. For instance, although many class action lawsuits have been filed under the FLSA, this

---

73. 51 F.3d at 1293.

74. *Id.* at 1300.

75. *Id.* The court may have chosen the term "esperanto" to describe the ad hoc nature of such an instruction "because the term esperanto refers to artificial language created by combining commonly known words of various European languages." Pamela M. Madas, *To Settlement Classes and Beyond: A Primer on Proposed Methods for Federalizing Mass Tort Litigation*, 28 Seton Hall L. Rev. 540, 546 n.39 (1997). Ms. Madas's article presents an in-depth treatment of the issue in this section and many of the cases cited here.

76. *In re Rhone-Poulenc*, 51 F.3d at 1300.

77. *Id.*

78. *Id.*

79. *Id.*

is not reflected in the pattern jury instructions developed by the Fifth and Eleventh Circuits for FLSA claims.[80]

To the extent that such instructions exist, class counsel should not blindly accept pattern instructions simply because they are required or standard. Rather, independent research is key to ensure that pattern jury instructions are current and are a good fit for a particular case. Additionally, even though trial judges generally have wide discretion in creating jury instructions,[81] careful investigation must be conducted to determine the extent to which a particular judge adheres to pattern instructions. Many judges use the pattern jury instructions as a starting point. Knowledge of how closely a judge follows pattern instructions will help to inform just how much latitude class counsel may be given and how much ultimate success class counsel may have in prevailing upon a judge to accept nonconforming instructions.

For class action litigation, the real battle arises when a judge adds language instructing the jury on balancing individual claims with establishing elements for the entire class. When counsel is defending against a class of plaintiffs that should not, in their opinion, have been certified, then defense counsel may continually seek to remind the court of the ramifications of a class certification. The jury instructions submitted by defense counsel therefore may include the phrase "and all class members" each time the plaintiff is mentioned. Doing so will underscore that the elements of the claim must be met for the named plaintiff *and* for all members of the class. Plaintiffs' lawyers, in contrast, may attempt to draft jury instructions that skirt the issue of the burden to prove the claim for the members of the class apart from the named plaintiffs.

D. PRELIMINARY JURY INSTRUCTIONS

Similar to the road-mapping techniques used in writing legal briefs, counsel should supply jurors with the legal and factual framework they need to understand the law and evaluate evidence. A jury is much more likely to focus on key facts and legal concepts if they are told what those facts and concepts are at the beginning of a trial. Preliminary jury instructions therefore are a good way to orient a jury and tell them not only what to expect and listen for, but also how to process and evaluate what they hear. Many courts have pattern preliminary instructions that

---

80. *See* Rachel Geman & Ellen C. Kearns, *Evidence and Jury Instructions in FLSA Actions*, ALI-ABA Course of Study (Feb. 2007).

81. *See Stuart Park Assoc. Ltd. P'ship v. Ameritech Pension Trust*, 51 F.3d 1319, 1323 (7th Cir. 1995) ("The crafting of jury instructions is largely a matter within the district court's discretion."); *May v. Ark. Forestry Comm'n*, 993 F.2d 632, 637 (8th Cir. 1993) ("Jury instructions are generally committed to the sound discretion of the district judge, and the district judge is entitled to a great deal of deference in his or her formulation.").

should provide a good starting point. Again, however, class counsel should not assume that preliminary pattern instructions will correctly or adequately address the unique facts and circumstances of each case. Topics to be included in preliminary instructions may include those addressed in the following subsections.

1. Preliminary Statement of Legal Principles and Factual Issues

The Manual for Complex Litigation encourages preliminary instructions to summarize the key factual issues, including any undisputed or stipulated facts and the parties' main contentions.[82] A class action trial presents no reason to depart from this advice. Most importantly, plaintiffs' counsel will want the jury to know that the case is a class action, although only some of the class members will testify. Defense counsel will want to emphasize that the testimony that the jury will hear will not be representative of the absent class members and thus plaintiffs will not be able to prove their class claims.

Preliminary instructions also should explain the core legal issues—for example, the elements of the claims and any defenses. It is important that the court emphasize that the preliminary instructions do not address all the factual issues or legal principles. Instead, the final instructions given at the end of the case will govern the jurors' deliberations. The court may elect to give the preliminary instructions before opening statements, which gives counsel the opportunity to incorporate the instructions into their presentations. The court may, however, choose to deliver preliminary instructions after opening statements or give supplemental preliminary instructions at that time.[83] Counsel should inquire in advance how the court will address preliminary instructions so that they can be tailored and opening statements prepared accordingly.

2. Comment about the Class Action Device

Because jurors may not understand the class action procedure or how it affects the trial they are about to hear, preliminary instructions are a good opportunity to orient the jury. Some counsel will wait until final jury instructions to focus on "class instructions." This wastes a valuable opportunity to educate the jury. Preliminary instructions can provide a way to give the class action device understandable context and help to avoid any notions the jury may have about the progress of class litigation. For example, plaintiffs' counsel may want a jury to know that the court already has certified a class action and that not all class members are required to appear in court. Defense counsel may want the jury to know that the court's class certification is still subject to the jury's verdict, which will depend upon the proofs they hear on the class issues.

---

82. Manual for Complex Litigation (Fourth) § 12.432 (2004).
83. *Id.*

An example of a class action orientation instruction is produced below. It is taken from jury instructions in the matter of *Smith v. Behr Process Corp.*[84] While the class orientation instruction was delivered as a final jury instruction, it also is well-suited for a preliminary instruction. Note how the third paragraph of the instruction set forth below references the class proof issues addressed in section II above. The fourth and fifth paragraphs of the instruction then attempt to address any inference that a juror may make due to certification of the class.

> This type of case is known as a "class action," in which the named plaintiffs represent themselves and a large number of unnamed persons or entities who purchased and applied the two Behr products—Super Liquid RawHide (Nos. 12 or 13) and Natural Seal Plus (Nos. 80 or 92) on their wood surfaces.
>
> A "class action" is a form of a lawsuit designed to permit the claims of a large group of persons, too numerous to be individual participants, to be tried through an action by named plaintiffs, called "class representatives." Each of the basic claims made by the plaintiffs personally is likewise made on behalf of each of the class members.
>
> Without the use of a class action, most people's claims would not be large enough to permit them to economically obtain relief through legal action, and the courts would be flooded with numerous similar cases. A class action permits persons who have similar claims to prosecute those claims together, since the same proof applies to all the claims. The Court has certified the class procedure for use in this case.
>
> You should not concern yourself with the appropriateness of this case being certified as a class action since that is a matter for this court to determine. Nor should your verdict be influenced by any consideration of which or how many class members may make claims in the event your verdict is for the plaintiffs or whether any particular class member would or would not qualify for compensation.
>
> The fact that this is a class action in no way indicates whether or not the claims made on behalf of the plaintiffs or the represented class have merit. Your consideration of the facts and your verdict should not therefore be influenced in any regard merely because the litigation is presented in the form of a class action. Other than as I instruct you, you are not to draw any conclusions or reach any preconceptions, one way or another, by virtue of this being a class action.[85]

In another example, the United States District Court for the District of Kansas gave a class action orientation instruction in *In re Universal Service Fund Telephone Billing Practices Litigation*, an antitrust case against AT&T for telephone billing.[86] While the jury instructions in the *Universal* case do not include the helpful lan-

---

84. No. 98-2-00635-4 (Wash. Super. Ct. Grays Harbor County Aug. 18, 2000).
85. *Jury Instructions and Judgment on Verdict in Consumer Fraud/Warranty/Contract Class Actions*, 22 No. 2 CLASS ACTION REPORTS, at 4 (Apr. 2001), *available at* http://www.westlaw.com.
86. No. 02-MD-1468-JWL (D. Kan. Nov. 19, 2008).

guage regarding the impact of class certification on the jury's deliberations, they do include a helpful instruction regarding absent class members. Instruction No. 11, in relevant part, stated:

> As I mentioned to you at the outset, this case is proceeding as a class action. A class action procedure allows the filing of one lawsuit by a representative or a small number of representatives on behalf of a whole group of plaintiffs who have similar claims. The procedure is intended to avoid having multiple plaintiffs filing separate identical lawsuits in different courts and trying the same case multiple times before different judges. Thus, it avoids duplication of effort and expense. Your verdict here will be binding on all class members.
>
> * * * *
>
> You should not construe the physical absence of any class member in any way as lack of concern or interest on his or her part as to the outcome of the litigation. It is the very purpose of the class action procedure to avoid having to bring a representative from each class member here, and, therefore, the absence of class members from this trial should not be construed against the class in any way.[87]

FLSA collective actions also benefit from a preliminary explanation of their classlike aspects to a jury. In particular, a jury should be instructed about how it must balance proof going to an individual employee's claim and the representative proof required for the claims of the other similarly situated employees. From a defense counsel's perspective, a jury is more likely to notice holes in the evidence if it understands what the full evidence must be and how it is to be weighed with respect to the class. To illustrate, jury instructions proposed by defense counsel in the case of *De Asencio v. Tyson Foods, Inc.*[88] addressed the burden of proof as it related to the absent class members. The proposed instruction stated, in relevant part:

> [This] case is a class action lawsuit. This means that the court has allowed other employees at Tyson's New Holland chicken processing facility to pursue their claims collectively with the seven named plaintiffs. These other employees going beyond the named plaintiffs are entitled to prevail on their claims only if they establish that they are all similarly situated to each other.
>
> In order to establish that all of the employees are similarly situated, the plaintiffs must provide evidence that all of the employees joined in this suit were commonly affected by a single decision, policy or plan. It is not enough that only some of the employees joined in this suit were affected by the decision, policy or plan. Moreover, the evidence presented by plaintiffs at this trial must be representative. Representative evidence is evidence that gives you reason to believe that the testimony provided by the employee witnesses at trial would also be true for those employees who did not testify. Moreover, the plaintiffs must also provide a sufficient amount

---

87. Jury instructions available online, at PACER, http://pacer.psc.uscourts.gov.
88. No. 00-CV-4294 (E.D. Pa. June 2, 2006) (defendant's proposed jury instructions).

of employee testimony for you to infer that the testimony would represent all of the employees joined in this lawsuit.

Use of a special jury verdict form that identifies the need for "representative evidence" can reinforce for the jury the burden that plaintiffs' counsel must carry to prove the class claims. The *De Asencio* Jury Verdict Form is included at the end of this chapter.

3. The Conduct and Schedule of the Trial

The judge also "should inform the jurors of the anticipated course of the trial from opening statements to verdict, the methods for presenting evidence, and the procedure for raising and resolving objections."[89] Explanation may be needed for the frequent excusal of the jury when the judge must address matters with class counsel outside of the jury's presence, as this practice may be confusing and frustrating for jurors. Additionally, it usually is helpful to introduce court personnel and identify any equipment that will be used during the course of the trial.[90] Because class action cases may be especially protracted, estimated trial length might be a helpful communication to jurors, as well as the daily trial schedule.

4. Limiting Juror Conduct to Prevent a Mistrial

The judge should instruct the jury not to discuss the case or to communicate with the participants in the trial.[91] This can be especially important during meal recesses when judges, jurors, lawyers, and witnesses may find themselves at the same restaurants. Additionally, jurors must be warned against exposure to publicity and attempts at independent fact-finding, such as viewing the scene of some occurrence or undertaking experiments or research.[92] With the ease of free-flowing information on the Internet and smartphones, and the widely publicized nature of many class actions, jurors may be more tempted to "Google" the parties or issues, or "Twitter" about the progress of the case, including the jury's deliberations. A preliminary instruction that jurors not engage in such communications while they are serving as jurors is advisable.

5. Pretrial Procedures and the Functions and Duties of the Jury

In addition to the issues addressed above regarding preliminary instructions, preliminary instructions should concisely describe the various discovery tools used during the pretrial stage of the litigation—for example, depositions, document production, interrogatories, and admissions.[93] This information will be helpful when class counsel introduces the evidence, and it explains how the parties learned the

---

89. MANUAL FOR COMPLEX LITIGATION (FOURTH) § 12.432 (2004).
90. *Id.*
91. *Id.*
92. *Id.*
93. *Id.*

facts of the case.[94] The judge also should describe the jury's role as a fact finder, the burdens of proof (individual and class proof, as explained above), assessing the credibility of witnesses, the nature of the evidence (including circumstantial evidence and the purpose of the rules of evidence), and the jurors' need to rely on their recollection of testimony (including any instructions regarding the permissibility of note-taking or questions to the judge).[95]

E. INTERIM INSTRUCTIONS

Developments during trial may require additional instructions to the jury.[96] Such instructions may arise, for example, due to evidentiary objections and rulings during trial. Some judges prefer to address certain motion in limine issues when they arise, which also may necessitate the need for interim instructions. Pursuant to Federal Rule of Evidence 105, "[w]hen evidence which is admissible as to one party or for one purpose but not admissible as to another party or for another purpose is admitted, the court, upon request, shall restrict the evidence to its proper scope and instruct the jury accordingly." The judge may repeat such limiting instructions at the close of trial.[97] Counsel should be advised that when they contemplate offering such evidence, they should raise the issue promptly, perhaps before trial, and submit proposed instructions.[98]

The judge also may give instructions at any point when they might be helpful to the jury.[99] Explaining applicable legal principles may be more helpful when the issue arises than if they are deferred until the close of trial. But counsel should be permitted to comment or object before an instruction is given.[100] Similar to the recommendations regarding preliminary instructions, the judge should inform the jury that these are only interim explanations and that the final, complete instructions on which they will base their verdict will come at the close of trial.[101] If the parties are presenting their evidence according to a prescribed sequence, the interim instructions also should be structured appropriately.[102]

F. JURY INSTRUCTION CONFERENCE

Federal Rule of Civil Procedure 51 does not specifically require a jury instruction conference, but it does provide that counsel will have the opportunity to make

---

94. *Id.*
95. *See id.*
96. *Id.* at § 12.433.
97. *Id.*
98. *Id.*
99. *Id.*
100. *Id.*
101. *Id.*
102. *Id.*

objections to the instructions with the jury not present.[103] Courts appear to construe this aspect of Rule 51 to mean that an actual jury instruction conference, in some form, will occur.[104] Whether in chambers or in the courtroom with the jury excused, jury instruction conferences are especially appropriate for class actions due to the complex jury instruction issues that can arise, such as charging the jury on the laws of multiple jurisdictions.

Wherever the jury instruction conference is held, however, a court reporter should be present to ensure that a proper record is made should any aspect of the jury instructions be appealed.[105] Also, if the judge modifies a pattern instruction or if counsel believes a non-pattern instruction should be given, the justifications for the pattern departures, along with the departures themselves, should be made part of the record.[106] This will ensure that a reviewing court has the proper context and the benefit of counsel's arguments as part of the record on any appeal.[107]

During the jury instruction conference, after hearing arguments from class counsel regarding whether the jury should be charged with a certain instruction, the court may note on its copy of each of the instructions whether it will be given.[108] The court's copy of the instructions, with the notations, generally will be made part of the record. It is important, however, that class counsel makes his or her own copy of the "given" and "refused" instructions.[109] This will help to ensure that counsel has a reference point when the judge reads the final instructions to the jury.[110] It is not unheard of for a judge to read an instruction that was not among those marked "given" or for the judge to skip or rephrase an instruction, in whole or in part.[111]

G. PRACTICAL CONSIDERATIONS

What form should proposed jury instructions take? Judges likely will be more comfortable with counsel's proposed instructions when they have a familiar look and feel. Familiarity may be created by using certain pattern instructions, which is addressed in section III.C above. Additionally, creating a comfort level can be achieved with strategic formatting. Obtain copies of previous instructions the judge has used, or any published format for instructions. Adapt any proposed instruc-

---

103. FED. R. CIV. P. 51(b)(2).

104. HUNTER, *supra* note 65, at § 71:5.

105. *See* C. Barry Montgomery & Bradley C. Nahrstadt, *What Must Be Proven: Link Trial Presentation to Jury Instructions*, FOR THE DEFENSE, June 2006, at 15, *available at* http://www.willmont.com/files/FTD-0606-MontgomeryNahrstadt.pdf.

106. *Id.*

107. *Id.*

108. *Id.*

109. *Id.*

110. *Id.* at 16.

111. *Id.*

tions to his or her format. Another helpful tool for class jury instructions is a table of contents. A table of contents is especially beneficial at the jury instructions conference when counsel are advocating the inclusion of their proposed instructions.

H. FINAL INSTRUCTIONS

The time to submit proposed final instructions generally will be governed by local rule, specific written order of the court (i.e., a pretrial order), or oral directive from the judge during trial. If proposed jury instructions are submitted before the close of the evidence, developments during the trial may require submitted instructions to be revised, supplemented, or deleted.[112] Some judges may provide counsel with the entire charge they propose to give and then hold a jury instruction conference to consider counsel's objections and requests.[113]

Final instructions may be given before or after closing arguments.[114] Although jury instructions traditionally have been given after closing arguments, there are advantages to giving the bulk of the instructions before argument.[115] At a minimum, class counsel likely will know before closing arguments what final instructions will be given by the court.[116] This may provide structure to closing arguments.[117] Closing arguments are the last opportunity class counsel will have to provide a conceptual overlay to help the jury understand how the law, as instructed by the judge, will apply to the facts shown at trial.

Some judges allow jurors to have copies of the jury instructions to use during their deliberations.[118] Some judges do not allow jurors to have copies of the jury instructions during the judge's oral charge in an attempt to focus the jury's attention on the delivery.[119] In contrast, other judges permit the jurors to follow the text in hard copy or on a monitor, or at least give them a brief topical outline to follow as the instructions are given.[120] The oral charge, transcribed by the court reporter, should be complete and not merely refer to writings that the jury may be given.[121] To the extent variations exist between the oral and written charges, the oral charge controls and should govern the jury's deliberations.[122] If your proposed charge is lengthy or the issues in your class action are especially complex, consider requesting your judge to allow some of the techniques discussed above, as jurors may quickly

---

112. *See* Manual for Complex Litigation (Fourth) § 12.434 (2004).
113. *Id.*
114. *Id.* (citing Fed. R. Civ. P. 51).
115. *Id.*
116. *Id.*
117. *Id.*
118. *Id.*
119. *Id.*
120. *Id.*
121. *Id.*
122. *Id.*

tune out a judge who merely reads from a jury instruction script.[123] To the extent applicable, jurors also should have any special verdict forms or interrogatories for use during deliberations. *The Manual for Complex Litigation* recommends the use of special verdict forms and interrogatories for complex trials such as class actions.[124]

In federal court, after the judge has given all instructions, and before the jury retires, counsel are entitled to record any objections to the charge outside the presence of the jury.[125] Objections and the grounds must be stated distinctly or be deemed waived.[126] The judge can deliver corrective or supplemental instructions before the jury's deliberations begin.[127] Careful attention must be given to any rules regarding objections for class actions being litigated in state court to ensure that a proper record is made.

I. GETTING OBJECTIONS ON THE RECORD

In federal court, "[a] party who objects to an instruction or the failure to give an instruction must do so on the record, stating distinctly the matter objected to and the grounds for the objection."[128] Timing of jury instruction objections also is key:

> An objection is timely if: (a) a party objects at the opportunity provided under Rule 51(b)(2); or (b) a party was not informed of an instruction or action on a request before that opportunity to object, and the party objects promptly after learning that the instruction or request will be, or has been, given or refused.[129]

IV. Conclusion

The trial of a class action requires that counsel and judges exercise ingenuity. Traditional methods of proof must be adapted to the class context, and standard jury instructions often need to be changed. Attention to these differences will enable counsel to handle class action trials more effectively for the courts and their clients.

---

123. *Id.* Some judges have experimented with providing jurors with a tape recording of the charge for use during their deliberations.

124. *Id.* at § 12.451.

125. *Id.* at § 12.434; *see also* FED. R. CIV. P. 51(b)(2).

126. MANUAL FOR COMPLEX LITIGATION (FOURTH) § 12.434 (2004); FED. R. CIV. P. 51(c)(1).

127. MANUAL FOR COMPLEX LITIGATION (FOURTH) § 12.451 (2004).

128. FED. R. CIV. P. 51(c)(1).

129. FED. R. CIV. P. 51(c)(2)(A)–(B).

IN THE UNITED STATES DISTRICT COURT
FOR THE EASTERN DISTRICT OF PENNSYLVANIA

MELANIA FELIX DE ASENCIO, MANUEL A.   :   CIVIL ACTION
GUTIERREZ, ASELA RUIZ, EUSEBIA RUIZ,   :
LUIS A. VIGO, LUZ CORDOVA, and   :
HECTOR PANTAJOS, on behalf of themselves :
and all other similarly situated individuals

FILED

vs.

JUN 2 1 2006

TYSON FOODS, INC.   MICHAEL E. KUNZ, Clerk 294
By_____JP_____Dep. Clerk

JURY VERDICT FORM

I.   Work

1.   Have the plaintiffs provided representative evidence that the following activities are "work"?

    Donning and washing at the beginning of   YES _____   NO ___✓___
    the shift

    Doffing and washing before going to meal   YES _____   NO ___✓___
    break

    Donning and washing when returning from   YES _____   NO ___✓___
    meal break

    Doffing and washing at the end of the   YES _____   NO ___✓___
    shift

2.   If you answered "yes" to any part of Question 1, how many total minutes each day does it reasonably take to perform all of the activities that you determined are "work"? _____

3.   Have the plaintiffs provided representative evidence that Tyson Foods required them to arrive at the beginning of the shift or end of the meal breaks before the product got to their station, such that they were "engaged to wait"? YES _____   NO ___✓___

4.   If you answered "yes" to Question 3, how many total minutes each day was a typical plaintiff required to arrive at the line before the first product arrived at his/her station? _____ (Your answer should *not* double-count any part of answer No. 2.)

II. **PAYMENT OF EXTRA MINUTES AND**
     WHETHER REMAINING MINUTES ARE *DE MINIMIS*

5.   (Answer the following question *only* if you answered "yes" to Question 1 or Question 3, or both.)

     Have the plaintiffs provided representative evidence that they have not received full compensation for their work activities?

     > YES _____ (A "yes" answer means Tyson Foods did not provide enough "extra minutes" of paid time to fully compensate for the daily activities that you determined are "work".)

     > NO _____ (A "no" answer means Tyson Foods provided enough "extra minutes" of paid time to fully compensate for the daily activities that you determined are "work".)

6.   (Answer the following question *only* if you answered "yes" to Question 5.)

     Has Tyson Foods proven by a preponderance of the evidence that any uncompensated "work" time in First Processing is *de minimis*?

     > YES _____ (A "yes" answer means that no further compensation is owed to plaintiffs who worked in these departments.)

     > NO _____ (A "no" answer means that further compensation is owed to plaintiffs who worked in these departments.)

7.   (Answer the following question *only* if you answered "yes" to Question 5.)

     Has Tyson Foods proven by a preponderance of the evidence that any uncompensated "work" time in Debone and Further Processing is *de minimis*?

     > YES _____ (A "yes" answer means that no further compensation is owed to plaintiffs who worked in these departments.)

     > NO _____ (A "no" answer means that further compensation is owed to plaintiffs who worked in these departments.)

Signature of Foreperson: _____

DATE: ___6/21/06___

SETTLEMENTS

LINDA S. MULLENIX

I. Introduction

The reality in most American class litigation is that class actions are rarely if ever tried to a jury.[1] It is very difficult to find reported evidence of class actions that have been tried to jury verdicts in American courts. In class actions that survive both trial and appellate orders certifying a class action, almost all are settled before trial. Indeed, a substantial jurisprudence and academic literature supports the conclusion that a court's class certification decision is the seminal event in the class litigation process because the court's affirmative decision to certify a class places considerable pressure on defendants to settle the action.[2]

This chapter discusses class action settlements and addresses (1) the role of settlement in ordinary and class action litigation[3] and the historical development of the settlement class concept; (2) due process requirements for the binding effect

---

1. *See, e.g.,* the view of federal district judge Jack Weinstein of the Federal District Court for the Eastern District of New York, who has commented:

> Concentration of individual damage suits in one forum can lead to formidable problems, but the realities of litigation should not be overlooked in theoretical musings. Most tort cases settle, and the preliminary maneuverings in litigation today are designed as much, if not more, for settlement purposes than for trial. Settlements of class actions often result in savings for all.

Quoted in *In re Sch. Asbestos Litig.*, 789 F.2d 996, 1009 (3d Cir. 1986).

2. *See, e.g., Newton v. Merrill Lynch, Pierce, Fenner & Smith, Inc.*, 259 F.3d 168 n.8 (3d Cir. 2001) (discussion of so-called "settlement blackmail" as a consequence of a court's decision to certify a class); *Castano v. Am. Tobacco Co.*, 84 F.3d 734, 746 (5th Cir. 1996) (same); *In re Rhone-Poulenc Rorer, Inc.*, 51 F.3d 1293, 1298 (7th Cir. 1995); *Ruiz v. Am. Tobacco Co.*, 180 F.R.D. 194, 198 (D.P.R. 1998); *In re Dow Corning Corp.*, 211 B.R. 545, 585 (E.D. Mich. 1997) (same). *But cf.* Allan Kanner & Tibor Nagy, *Exploding the Blackmail Myth: A New Perspective on Class Action Settlements*, 57 BAYLOR L. REV. 681 (2005) (disagreeing with the hypothesis that class certification exerts undue pressure on class action defendants to settle litigation).

3. Practicing lawyers recognize that settling class action litigation differs greatly from settling traditional two-party litigation. *See, e.g.,* Aashish Y. Desai, *The Confirmation Process for Class Action Settlements Is Far More Complex than in Traditional Litigation*, 31 L.A. LAW. (Aug. 2008).

of settlement orders and the possibility of subsequent collateral attack against settlements; (3) possible types of settlement classes; (4) ethical problems inherent in class action settlements and potential abuses; (5) forces that militate in the negotiation of a settlement; (6) parties and fiduciaries involved in the settlement process; (7) substantive terms of a settlement; (8) procedural rules and standards governing the finalization of settlements; and (9) implications of the Class Action Fairness Act of 2005[4] for class action settlements.

Within the last decade, the U.S. Supreme Court and Congress have turned their attention to problems involved in class action settlements, setting forth judicial and statutory principles to guide current class action settlements. In its last two pronouncements dealing with class action litigation, the Court has twice addressed problems of "settlement classes" in two landmark cases.[5]

Additionally, Congress also entered the debate over class action settlements through provisions in the Class Action Fairness Act of 2005 (CAFA) that set forth procedural and substantive requirements for class action settlements. These CAFA settlement provisions generally are intended to protect consumers involved in consumer class actions by facilitating fair and just resolution of their claims through negotiated settlement.

II. The Role of Settlement in Ordinary and Class Action Litigation, and the Historical Development of the Settlement Class Concept

It is a fixed and often-repeated principle of American jurisprudence that the law prefers and encourages settlement of disputes, rather than litigation. This principle applies with equal force in "ordinary" or traditional two-party litigation and in complex, aggregate litigation such as class action litigation.[6] Class action settle-

---

4. Pub. L. No. 109-2, § 3, 119 Stat. 4, 5–9 (codified at 28 U.S.C. §§ 1332(d), 1453, and 1711–1715 (2006)) [hereinafter CAFA]. *See generally* John Beisner & Jessica Davidson Miller, *The Class Action Fairness Act: Cleaning Up the Class Action Mess*, 6 CLASS ACTION LITIG. REP. 104, 104 (2005); Stephanie Fiereck, *Class Action Reform: Be Prepared to Address New Notification Requirements*, 6 CLASS ACTION LITIG. REP. 333, 333 (2005) (noting that CAFA was "promoted as a business-backed initiative"); Jennifer Gibson, *New Rules for Class Action Settlements: The Consumer Class Action Bill of Rights*, 39 LOY. L.A. L. REV. 1103 (2006); Robert H. Klonoff & Mark Herrmann, *The Class Action Fairness Act: An Ill-Conceived Approach to Class Settlements*, 80 TUL. L. REV. 1695 (2006); Richard A. Nagareda, *Aggregation and Its Discontents: Class Settlement Pressure, Class-Wide Arbitration, and CAFA*, 106 COLUM. L. REV. 1872 (2006); Scott Nelson & Brian Wolfman, *A Section-by-Section Analysis of the Class Action "Fairness" Act*, 6 CLASS ACTION LITIG. REP. 365, 372 (2005) ("The Class Action Fairness Act marks the first major success of the Bush administration's efforts to enact pro-defendant civil justice legislation."); and Lewis Powell III, *Class Settlement of Mass Tort Cases*, 7 SEDONA CONF. J. 259 (2006) (commentary on CAFA settlement provisions).

5. *Ortiz v. Fibreboard Corp.*, 527 U.S. 815 (1999); *Amchem Prods., Inc. v. Windsor*, 521 U.S. 591 (1997).

6. There are other mechanisms for accomplishing aggregate litigation, in addition to class action litigation. These include the creation of a multidistrict litigation (an MDL) pursuant to statute, 28 U.S.C.

ments, however, have presented an array of challenging jurisprudential and practical problems for federal and state courts. Foremost among these problems are the jurisprudential authority for settlement classes and the due process protections for absent class members involved in the underlying litigation. These two concerns have formed the nub of the debate over settlement classes in the United States.

Class action settlements are largely governed by provisions of the 1966 amended rule,[7] although the 1966 rule provided scant guidance for class action settlements.[8] Various issues relating to settlement classes did not percolate through American jurisprudence until the 1990s. The emergence of the phenomenon of mass tort litigation, as a discrete type of litigation, propelled a heated judicial debate over the legitimacy of so-called settlement classes.

By the late 1980s and early 1990s several federal judges, exercising their managerial powers under Federal Rule of Civil Procedure 23(d),[9] began to authorize the certification of class actions for the purposes of settlement only. These judges found some authority to certify settlement-only classes in Rule 23(c), which permitted the certification of conditional or provisional classes.[10]

The concept of the settlement class is distinct from a litigation class, and courts distinguish between the two. A so-called litigation class is a proposed class action that a court must certify at the outset of the litigation, and the class is certified for

---

§ 1407, or mass joinder of claims pursuant to Federal Rule of Civil Procedure 42(a). Settlement of aggregate litigation outside the class action context is not subject to the rules and procedures for class action settlements. Most notably, aggregate litigation that is resolved outside the class action context is not subject to the more stringent due process requirements that apply to class action settlements. This fact has led to criticism of the resolution of complex litigation and aggregate claims that are not resolved through the auspices of a class action.

7. Federal Rule of Civil Procedure 23 was amended in 1997 to add 23(f), a means of interlocutory review of class certification orders. Rule 23 was amended again in 1998 and 2003. The 1998 amendment to Rule 23 added a new subsection (f), which provided for interlocutory appeal of court orders either granting or denying class certification. See FED. R. CIV. P. 23(f). In 2003, Congress amended the class action rule to add new provisions 23(g), governing standards for appointment of counsel in a proposed class action, and 23(h), governing standards for the award of attorney fees in class actions. The 2003 amendments also included revisions to subsection (e), the most relevant provision of the rule dealing with class action settlements. Finally, as of December 2007, all Federal Rules of Civil Procedure were modified and amended to conform to English plain language standards, and consequently the current version of Rule 23 reflects the revisions of the plain language project.

8. Indeed, Rule 23(e), which pertains to class action settlements, did not actually or specifically use the term "settlement" until it was amended in 2003. The 1966 version of Rule 23(e) read in its entirety: "A class action shall not be dismissed or compromised without the approval of the court, and notice of the proposed dismissal or compromise shall be given to all members of the class in such manner as the court directs."

9. This Rule enumerates various judicial powers and orders that a judge may issue in the management of a class action.

10. The Rule 23(c) language permitting conditional class certification was eliminated from the rule as part of the 2003 amendments. Notwithstanding the elimination of provision for conditional class certification, federal courts have largely ignored this limitation and continue to certify conditional classes.

the purpose of trial.[11] A litigation class must satisfy each of the requirements of Rule 23(a) and (b) in order to proceed to trial.

Settlement-only classes, however, are provisionally certified for a very different purpose and in many cases do not have to meet all of the same exacting standards of litigation classes.[12] There is a general understanding among all the parties and the court that a settlement class will not be litigated at trial. Instead, the final certification of a settlement class occurs when the parties present the settlement to the court for approval in a fairness hearing. Thus, the final certification of a settlement class occurs at the back end of the settlement process, and not at the outset of the litigation (which would occur if the proposed action were a litigation class).

The purpose of certifying a class for settlement purposes only, then, is to encourage the lawyers on all sides of the litigation to meet and negotiate a settlement prior to a lengthy or contested class certification process. However, in certifying a class conditionally for settlement purposes, the court is *not* signaling that a proposed class action is suitable for final certification under Rule 23 standards; the court will make that determination only after the parties accomplish a settlement.

These efforts by federal judges in the 1980s and 1990s to resolve mass tort litigation through the device of settlement-only certification inspired a heated controversy about whether there was jurisprudential authority for the proposition that a class could be certified for settlement purposes only.[13] Some federal courts concluded that the equitable roots of class action litigation and precedent supported the concept of settlement class certification:

> The hallmark of Rule 23 is the flexibility it affords to the courts to utilize the class device in a particular case to best serve the ends of justice for the affected parties and to promote judicial efficiencies. Temporary settlement classes have proved to be quite useful in resolving major class action disputes. While their use may still be controversial, most courts have recognized their utility and have authorized the parties to seek to compromise their differences, including class action issues through this means.[14]

Notwithstanding the endorsement of the settlement class concept by an increasing number of federal courts during the early 1990s, settlement-only classes inspired spirited criticism from many quarters in this same period. Objectors con-

---

11. *See* MANUAL FOR COMPLEX LITIGATION (FOURTH) § 21.611 (2004) ("Issues Relating to Cases Certified for Trial and Later Settled").

12. *Id.* at § 21.612 ("Issues Relating to Cases Certified and Settled at the Same Time").

13. *See, e.g., In re A.H. Robins Co.*, 880 F.2d 709 (4th Cir. 1989) (describing the controversy over settlement-only classes in detail, and surveying various federal court decisions discussing the problem, including *In re Bendectin*, 102 F.R.D. 239, 240 (S.D. Ohio 1984) (grant of certification for settlement purposes only)).

14. *In re A.H. Robins*, 880 F.2d at 740 (citing *Weinberger v. Kendrick*, 698 F.2d 61, 72–73 (2d Cir. 1982)); *see also In re Mid-Atlantic Toyota Antitrust Litig.*, 564 F. Supp. 1379, 1388–90 (D. Md. 1983) (same); *In re First Commodity Corp. of Boston*, 119 F.R.D. 301, 306–08 (D. Mass. 1987) (same).

tended that no provision of Rule 23 specifically authorized judges to certify settlement classes and that such authority had to be cobbled together from various other nonspecific provisions in the rule. Moreover, the first edition of the Federal Judicial Center's *Manual for Complex Litigation* strongly disapproved of settlement classes.[15]

More importantly, objectors contended that the certification of settlement-only classes provided inadequate protection of the interests of absent class members who, without notice of the pending action and scant judicial oversight, would have no idea plaintiff and defense lawyers were bargaining away their interests in settlement negotiations.[16] Settlement classes, then, implicated important and worrisome due process issues relating to the conduct of parties involved in such settlement efforts.

In 1995, the Court of Appeals for the Third Circuit identified the core problem relating to the use of settlement classes:

> But their use [settlement classes] has not been problem free, provoking a barrage of criticism that the device is a vehicle for collusive settlements that primarily serve the interests of defendants—by granting expansive protection from law suits—and of plaintiff's counsel—by generating large fees gladly paid by defendants as a quid pro quo for finally disposing of many troublesome claims.[17]

By the late 1990s, the dispute over settlement classes focused on the issue of whether certification standards for settlement classes could be more relaxed because the action would never be tried.[18] Supporters of settlement classes argued

---

15. MANUAL FOR COMPLEX LITIGATION (1st ed. 1969). The second, third, and fourth editions of the MANUAL endorse the concept of the settlement class. *See* MANUAL FOR COMPLEX LITIGATION (FOURTH) §§ 21.6 (settlements) and 22.9 (mass tort settlement) (2004).

16. *See generally* Roger C. Cramton, *Individualized Justice, Mass Torts, and "Settlement Class Actions": An Introduction*, 80 CORNELL L. REV. 811, 826–35 (1995) (discussing problems of adequacy of representation in class containing claimants with future injuries); *see also* John C. Coffee, Jr., *Class Action Accountability: Reconciling Exit, Voice, and Loyalty in Representative Litigation*, 100 COLUM. L. REV. 370 (2000).

17. *In re Gen. Motors Corp. Pick-Up Truck Fuel Tank Prods. Liab. Litig.*, 55 F.3d 768, 789 (3d Cir. 1995). The Third Circuit, in a lengthy decision authored by Judge Carl Becker that canvasses all arguments relating to the problem of settlement classes, ultimately endorsed the concept of the settlement class:

> We acknowledge that settlement classes, conceived of either as provisional or conditional certifications, represent a practical construction of the class action rule. Such construction affords considerable economies to both the litigants and the judiciary and is also fully consistent with the flexibility integral to Rule 23. A number of other jurisdictions have already accepted settlement classes as a reasonable interpretation of Rule 23 and have thereby achieved these substantial benefits. Although we appreciate the concerns raised by the device, we are confident that they can be addressed by the rigorous applications of the Rule 23 requisites by the courts at the approval stages . . . . For these reasons, we hold that settlement classes are cognizable under Rule 23.

55 F.3d at 794.

18. *See id.* Judge Becker contended that settlement classes were permissible under the Rule, but had to satisfy all the requirements for class certification as a litigation class. The Supreme Court two years later would modify the Third Circuit's conclusion in *Amchem*, 521 U.S. 591.

that certification requirements should be different and more relaxed in the settlement context. Opponents of the settlement class argued that Rule 23 did not authorize relaxation of certification standards, and that the application of such relaxed standards jeopardized the due process rights of absent class members.

The debate over the legitimacy of settlement classes became so contentious that by the late 1990s, the federal Advisory Committee on Civil Rules—in response to this heated debate—proposed an amendment to Rule 23(b) that would have added a new provision specifically providing for a settlement class.[19] This proposed addition of a new (b)(4) class category would have expressly authorized settlement class certification, in conjunction with a motion by settling parties, "even though the requirements of subdivision (b)(3) might not be met for purposes of trial."[20]

The Advisory Committee on Civil Rules never acted on its proposal to codify a new Rule 23(b)(4) provision authorizing settlement classes because the Supreme Court resolved the issue and validated the legitimacy of settlement classes in its 1997 decision in *Amchem Products, Inc. v. Windsor*.[21] Noting that all federal circuit courts had recognized the utility of Rule 23(b)(3) settlement classes, the Supreme Court further noted that the federal courts were then divided on the extent to which courts needed to apply the Rule 23 criteria for class certification to settlement classes. The Court resolved this dispute by holding that a settlement class needed to satisfy all the same requirements for certification as would a proffered litigation class, except for the manageability requirement of Rule 23(b)(3)(D):

> Confronted with the request for settlement-only class certification, a district court need not inquire whether the case, if tried, would present intractable management problems, see FED. R. CIV. P. 23(b)(3)(D), for the proposal is that there be no trial. But other specifications of the rule—those designed to protect absentees by blocking unwarranted or overbroad class definitions—demand undiluted, even heightened, attention in the settlement context. Such attention is of vital importance, for a court asked to certify a settlement class will lack the opportunity, present when a case is litigated, to adjust the class, informed by the proceedings as they unfold.
>
> And, of overriding importance, courts must be mindful that the rule as now composed sets the requirements they are bound to enforce.[22]

In addition, the Supreme Court also held that in assessing class certification, a federal court could take into account the substantive and procedural fairness

---

19. *See* Proposed Amendment of FED. R. CIV. P. 23(b), 117 S. Ct. No. 1 CXIX, CLIV to CLV (Aug. 1996) (Request for Comment), noted by the U.S. Supreme Court in *Amchem*, 521 U.S. at 619.

20. *Id.* For a discussion of the proposed Rule 23(b)(4) settlement class, *see* Linda S. Mullenix, *The Constitutionality of the Proposed Rule 23 Class Action Amendments*, 39 ARIZ. L. REV. 615 (1997).

21. 521 U.S. at 619–20.

22. *Id.* at 620.

of the underlying settlement.[23] Two years after its *Amchem* decision, the Supreme Court reiterated its endorsement of settlement classes in *Ortiz v. Fibreboard Corp.*,[24] an asbestos settlement class accomplished under Rule 23(b)(1)(B).[25]

A decade after the Supreme Court's landmark decisions in *Amchem* and *Ortiz* that ratified and approved the concept of the settlement class, settlement classes are now a fixed feature of the American class action landscape. With the legitimacy of settlement classes no longer in doubt, judicial and legislative attention in the ensuing decade has shifted to the due process rights and adequate representation of differing class members' interests in settlement classes.[26] Thus, in the 21st century, the focus of judicial concern with regard to settlement classes has shifted to ensuring adequate representation of absent class members in order to give binding effect to a settlement order.

III. Due Process Requirements for the Binding Effect of Settlement Orders and the Possibility of Subsequent Collateral Attack Against Settlements

Class action litigation is a form of representational litigation; that is, the class members are not actually present to represent their own personal interests. In representational litigation, the vast majority of class members are not actually present to communicate with the class lawyers, supervise the development of the litigation, participate in decision making or negotiations, or authorize settlement terms. Consequently, to protect absent class members from self-dealing or collusion by the lawyers handling the dispute, class action litigation is imbued with various due process protections.[27]

The array of due process protections that adhere in class litigation are not deemed necessary in traditional litigation, where the party-plaintiff is actually present to protect his or her own interests in the litigation.[28] Therefore, many of

---

23. *Id.* at 619–20.

24. 527 U.S. 815.

25. In both *Amchem* and *Ortiz* the Supreme Court repudiated approval of the settlement classes, although on different grounds in each case. The Court found a lack of adequate representation in both the *Amchem* and *Ortiz* settlement classes.

26. *See generally* MANUAL FOR COMPLEX LITIGATION (FOURTH) § 21.612 (2004) (identifying recurring issues raised by settlement classes, including conflicts of interest, future claimants, administration of claims procedures, and attorney fee applications).

27. Both the 5th and 14th amendments to the United States Constitution contain identical due process clauses, which protect citizens from the deprivation "of life, liberty, or property without due process of law." The 5th Amendment constrains the federal government, and the 14th Amendment constrains state governments, from such due process violations. *See* U.S. CONST. amends. V, XIV.

28. *See* MANUAL FOR COMPLEX LITIGATION (FOURTH) § 13.14 (2004) (noting that ordinarily settlement does not require judicial review and approval in traditional litigation).

the rules, standards, and requirements in class litigation have no counterpart in traditional litigation, where the parties are the guardians of their own interests.

Rule 23 and jurisprudence construing the rule have articulated various types of due process protections. For example, class action litigation typically involves the early and active intercession of a judicial officer to oversee and manage the class action. In contrast, in traditional litigation, a judge may not meet the litigants until the day of trial. In class action litigation, a judge must make a determination, as early as possible, that the proposed class action is suitable to be maintained as a class action.[29] In traditional litigation, the parties do not have to seek prior approval of a judge to proceed. The proposed class action must satisfy the threshold requirements for certification,[30] including an assessment by the judge of the adequacy of representation by the proposed class counsel and class representatives.[31] Moreover, the judge must appoint class counsel based on criteria set forth in the rule.[32] In traditional litigation, a judge does not assess the adequacy of representation at any time of the proceedings.

Judges are vested with a broad array of managerial powers to supervise class actions and are encouraged to actively supervise such litigation,[33] whereas in traditional litigation a judge will not typically be actively involved in the development or trial of the case. In damage class actions that a court certifies pursuant to Rule 23(b)(3), the rule requires that class members receive notice of the action and the opportunity to "opt out" or exclude themselves from the class.[34] Hence, notice and the right to opt out are additional due process protections that distinguish class litigation from traditional litigation.

Finally, Rule 23(e) also requires that a court approve any class action settlement in order for the action to be settled, compromised, or dismissed.[35] The 2003 amended settlement provision requires notice of the settlement to class members, as well as a fairness hearing before a judge. The requirements of notice, hearing,[36] and judicial approval are all intended to provide additional layers of due process protections to absent class members. In contrast, litigants in a traditional litigation may negotiate and consummate a settlement and dismiss their action, without any oversight from a court.

---

29. FED. R. CIV. P. 23(c)(4)(A).
30. FED. R. CIV. P. 23(a)(1)–(4).
31. FED. R. CIV. P. 23(a)(4).
32. FED. R. CIV. P. 23(g) (as amended in 2003).
33. FED. R. CIV. P. 23(d).
34. FED. R. CIV. P. 23(c)(2)(B).
35. FED. R. CIV. P. 23(e).
36. *Id.* The dual requirements of notice and a hearing were added as amendments to Rule 23(e) in 2003. The 2003 amendments to Rule 23 for the first time indicated that this provision applied to class action settlements, in addition to other efforts to compromise or dismiss a class action.

Ensuring adequate representation for absent class members in class litigation and settlements is the due process linchpin for a binding judgment in such litigation.[37] The Supreme Court has long recognized that in absence of adequate representation, class action judgments are not binding on class members.[38] In *Amchem* and *Ortiz*, the Court indicated that federal courts cannot approve settlement classes that fail to satisfy the adequacy requirement for class certification. The asbestos claimants in those cases included both currently impaired and nonimpaired claimants (designated "future" claimants). In *Ortiz*, the asbestos claimants included class members whose claims were insured by different policies applicable to different time periods.

In both asbestos settlements, the differences among the class members' claims created intraclass conflicts of interest, yet the lawyers negotiated the settlements simultaneously for all class members. The Court concluded that the intraclass conflicts of interest among the asbestos claimants were not resolved with appropriate structural assurances of due process to protect those differing interests.[39] Consequently, both the *Amchem* and *Ortiz* settlements failed. As a result, the Supreme Court held that the lack of adequacy of representation among the competing claimants in the *Amchem* and *Ortiz* settlements required rejection of both settlements.

In the wake of the Supreme Court's discussion of adequacy in *Amchem* and *Ortiz*, the Court of Appeals for the Second Circuit had to determine whether two Vietnam veterans suffering from cancer could collaterally attack the *"Agent Orange"* settlement approved by a New York court in 1984.[40] At the time of the *"Agent Orange"* settlement, the two veterans had not manifested illness and did not recover any damages from the Agent Orange fund. When the veterans manifested illness nearly 20 years later, they sought to recover damages from Dow Chemical, one of the defendants in the original *"Agent Orange"* litigation. Dow Chemical argued that the final settlement order in *"Agent Orange"* was res judicata and barred the veterans from suing Dow Chemical. Citing *Amchem* and *Ortiz*, the veterans argued that as nonimpaired "future claimants," they were not adequately represented at the time the lawyers negotiated and the court approved the *"Agent Orange"* settlement.

---

37. *See Ortiz*, 527 U.S. at 856–57; *Amchem*, 521 U.S. at 627.

38. *See Hansberry v. Lee*, 311 U.S. 32 (1940) (no binding res judicata effect to class judgment in absence of adequate class representation in the prior litigation). Since the Supreme Court's decision in *Hansberry*, federal courts have permitted collateral attacks against class action judgments based upon due process and adequate representation concerns. *See, e.g., Van Gemert v. Boeing Co.*, 590 F.2d 433, 440 n.15 (2d Cir. 1978), *aff'd* 444 U.S. 472 (1980) (a "[j]udgment in a class action is not secure from collateral attack unless the absentees were adequately and vigorously represented.").

39. *Ortiz*, 527 U.S. at 832, 856; *Amchem*, 521 U.S. at 627.

40. *See Stephenson v. Dow Chemical Corp.*, 273 F.3d 249, 251 (2d Cir. 2001), *aff'd in part, vacated in part*, 539 U.S. 111 (2003).

The Second Circuit Court of Appeals, in *Stephenson v. Dow Chemical Corp.*,[41] agreed with the two veterans and held that pursuant to *Amchem* and *Ortiz* (as well as other Supreme Court precedent), a lack of adequacy of representation in a settlement provided a class member with a subsequent basis to collaterally attack a settlement:

> Res judicata generally applies to bind absent class members except where to do so would violate due process. Due process requires adequate representation "at all times" throughout the litigation, notice "reasonably calculated . . . to apprise interested parties of the pendency of the action," and an opportunity to opt out.[42]

The court's decision in *Stephenson* is highly significant for the negotiation and consummation of settlement classes. It is perhaps fair to suggest that class action settlements today are negotiated and consummated in the shadow of the *Stephenson* decision, with the knowledge that a poorly structured settlement may be subject to subsequent collateral attack and possibly undone.

Generally, plaintiffs and defendants in settlement seek a global resolution of all class members' claims, and defendants especially seek finality and immunity from future litigation. To the extent that *Stephenson* authorizes subsequent collateral attack against class action settlements—even 20 years after a settlement—its doctrine places settlement classes in future jeopardy and undermines the value of finality.

Clearly, it is not in the interests of plaintiffs, defendants, or the judicial system for class action settlements to be subsequently invalidated. Therefore, ensuring adequate representation at the time of the negotiation and approval of a settlement is absolutely crucial to preserving the settlement from collateral attack. Ensuring

---

41. *Id.* at 261 (citing *Phillips Petroleum Co. v. Shutts*, 472 U.S. 797 (1985)). In *Stephenson*, the Second Circuit held that class members in the 1984 *"Agent Orange"* settlement could collaterally attack that settlement for lack of adequate representation. For commentary on the court's decision in *Stephenson* and the requirement of adequacy of representation in litigation and settlement classes, *see generally* Debra Lyn Bassett, *The Defendant's Obligation to Ensure Adequate Representation in Class Actions*, 74 U. Mo. Kan. City L. Rev. 511 (2006); Kevin R. Bernier, Note, *The Inadequacy of Broad Collateral Attack: Stephenson v. Dow Chemical Company and Its Effects on Class Action Settlements*, 84 B.U.L. Rev. 1023, 1037–44 (2004); David A. Dana, *Adequacy of Representation After* Stephenson: *A Rawlsian/Behavorial Economics Approach to Class Action Settlements*, 55 Emory L.J. 279 (2006); Linda S. Mullenix, *Taking Adequacy Seriously: The Inadequate Assessment of Adequacy in Litigation and Settlement Classes*, 57 Vand. L. Rev. 1687 (2004); Richard A. Nagareda, *Administering Adequacy in Class Representation*, 82 Tex. L. Rev. 287 (2003); Patrick Wooley, *Shutts and the Adequate Representation Requirement*, 74 U. Mo. Kan. City L. Rev. 765 (2006).

42. *Stephenson*, 273 F.3d at 260. The Second Circuit's decision in *Stephenson* was appealed to the U.S. Supreme Court where an eight-Justice Court split evenly in a per curiam decision that allowed the Second Circuit's decision to stand as precedent in the Second Circuit only. *See Dow Chem. Co. v. Stephenson*, 539 U.S. 111 (2003). *See generally* Gregory M. Wirt, *Missed Opportunity:* Stephenson v. Dow Chemical Co. *and the Finality of Class Action Settlements*, 109 Penn. St. L. Rev. 1297 (2005).

adequate representation and other due process protections to absent class members is one of the central concerns in class settlement in the United States today.

IV. Possible Types of Settlement Classes

As indicated above, in order for a court to approve a settlement class, the court must also certify that the class meets the requirements for certification. Hence, a settlement class must satisfy all the threshold requirements for certification under Rule 23(a), including numerosity, commonality, typicality, and adequacy. In addition, settlement classes must be suitable for certification under at least one of the three categories of class actions delineated in Rule 23(b)(1) through (3).[43]

The settling parties will determine which class category applies to their settlement, and this determination may depend on an array of legal, strategic, and logistical concerns. The class category under which the settlement is consummated has consequences for final judicial approval and implementation of the settlement, as the class categories have different requirements. In addition, each of these class categories presents different problems for the settling parties, the claimants, and the courts.

There are significant jurisprudential and practical differences among the three categories of class actions. The Rule 23(b)(1) and (b)(2) class categories[44] are so-called mandatory classes and do not permit class members to opt out of the class. With a few exceptions discussed below, these (b)(1) and (b)(2) class actions generally embrace equitable remedies, such as injunctions or declaratory judgments, but not monetary relief. Any settlement under the (b)(1) and (b)(2) provisions is binding on all class members. In the settlement context, class members in a (b)(1) or (b)(2) settlement will be bound by the agreement that the court approves.

Until 2003, members of a (b)(1) or (b)(2) litigation class did not receive notice of the action. The class action rule has been amended to permit notice to such class members, at the court's discretion, and this new provision applies equally to

---

43. There are actually four types of class actions, because Rule 23(b)(1) embraces two types of class actions. *See* FED. R. CIV. P. 23(b)(1)(A) and (B).

44. Rule 23(b) provides:

> (b) Types of Class Actions. A class action may be maintained if Rule 23(a) is satisfied and if:
> (1) prosecuting separate actions by or against individual class members would create a risk of:
> (A) inconsistent or varying adjudications with respect to individual members that would establish inconsistent standards of conduct for the party opposing the class; or
> (B) adjudications with respect to individual class members that, as a practical matter, would be dispositive of the interests of the other members not parties to the individual adjudications or would substantially impair or impede their ability to protect their interests;
> (2) the party opposing the class has acted or refused to act on grounds that apply generally to the class, so that final injunctive relief or corresponding declaratory relief is appropriate respecting the class as a whole . . . .

settlement classes.[45] Moreover, all class members, without regard to the category of the class action, must receive notice of a proposed settlement when the settlement is offered to the court for final approval.[46]

In contrast, the Rule 23(b)(3) class is generally understood to be the appropriate class category for the resolution of monetary damage claims.[47] Notice to class members, which includes the opportunity to opt out, is required for (b)(3) damage class actions.[48] Since 2003, if parties to a dispute seek judicial approval of a damage class settlement under the (b)(3) provision, then the parties must afford class members a second notice that informs the class members of the terms of the settlement, and a renewed opportunity to opt out.[49]

As indicated above, the types of remedies available to (b)(1) and (b)(2) classes generally differ from the monetary relief available in a (b)(3) class. Conventionally, the (b)(1)(A) and (b)(2) categories are appropriate for classwide injunctive and declaratory relief. In order to certify a (b)(1)(A) or (b)(2) litigation or settlement class, proponents must demonstrate that the class members have homogeneous interests that make classwide equitable relief an appropriate resolution. Moreover, a majority of courts that have considered the matter have concluded that the Rule 23(b)(1)(A) class category is not suitable for the recovery of monetary damages. In class action practice, courts rarely certify classes pursuant to the Rule 23(b)(1)(A) provision and even more rarely approve (b)(1)(A) as an appropriate basis for a settlement class.

Rule 23(b)(1)(B) is known as the "limited fund" class action, on the theory that where a defendant's assets constitute a limited fund, claimants suing individually would be prejudiced (in absence of a classwide remedy) by exhaustion of the limited fund at some point. Hence, the Rule 23(b)(1)(B) category permits all class claimants to be aggregated in one action, to recover on a per capita or some other basis against that limited fund.

---

45. FED. R. CIV. P. 23(c)(2)(A) ("Notice. *For (b)(1) or (b)(2) Classes*. For any class certified under Rule 23(b)(1) or (b)(2), the court may direct notice to the class.").

46. FED. R. CIV. P. 23(e)(1) ("The court must direct notice in a reasonable manner to all class members who would be bound by the proposal.").

47. Rule 23(b)(3) provides that a class action may be maintained under this provision if "[t]he court finds that the questions of law or fact common to class members predominate over any questions affecting only individual members, and that a class action is superior to other available methods for fairly and efficiently adjudicating the controversy." Rule 23(b)(3) enumerates four factors that courts may evaluate in assessing whether a proposed class action satisfies the predominance and superiority requirements. *See* FED. R. CIV. P. 23(b)(3)(A)–(D).

48. FED. R. CIV. P. 23(c)(2)(B)(i)–(vii).

49. FED. R. CIV. P. 23(e)(4) ("[I]f the class action was previously certified under Rule 23(b)(3), the court may refuse to approve a settlement unless it affords a new opportunity to request exclusion to individual class members who had an earlier opportunity to request exclusion but did not do so.").

Until recently, federal courts had limited experience with limited fund settlement classes, and Rule 23(b)(1)(B) classes were rarely certified.[50] The Supreme Court's 1999 decision in *Ortiz* set forth the definitive analysis of limited fund class action settlements (which particular issue was before the Supreme Court).

In *Ortiz*, the Supreme Court articulated three sweeping criteria for approval of a Rule 23(b)(1)(B) limited fund settlement class. First, the proponents of such a class must demonstrate to the court, through extrinsic evidence, the existence of the defendant's limited funds.[51] The Court rejected the proponents' offer of the existence of the limited fund by the stipulation of the parties.[52] Second, the terms of the settlement agreement must be such that the implementation of the settlement will exhaust the defendant's limited fund.[53] And third, the terms of the settlement must provide for a fair and equitable distribution of the fund among class members.[54] Because the global asbestos settlement in *Ortiz* failed these three tests, the Court invalidated the (b)(1)(B) limited fund settlement.[55]

The Supreme Court's decision in *Ortiz*, and the standards the Court articulated in that decision, have made it extremely difficult to negotiate and consummate settlements under the Rule 23(b)(1)(B) class provision. Subsequent to *Ortiz*, very few class action settlements have been formulated under the limited fund theory. Consequently, Rule 23(b)(1)(A) and (b)(1)(B) class categories have proved to be of limited utility for settling parties as the structural basis for a classwide settlement agreement.

Class action settlements, therefore, usually are structured as Rule 23(b)(2) equitable relief classes or Rule 23(b)(3) damage classes. Settlements pursued under these provisions often entail substantial problems. To certify and approve a Rule 23(b)(2) settlement class, the proponents must demonstrate the cohesiveness or homogeneity of the class members, the suitability of the requested equitable relief, and that an injunction or declaratory judgment is the predominant form of relief in the settlement. Conventionally, Rule 23(b)(2) classes are not suitable for the recovery of damages. However, a conflicting body of jurisprudence has emerged during the last decade that would permit the recovery of some monetary damages in Rule 23(b)(2) actions where those damages are "incidental" to the predominant equitable relief.[56] This jurisprudence has engendered a spirited debate concerning

---

50. *But see In re Orthopedic Bone Screw Prod. Liab. Litig.*, 176 F.R.D. 158 (E.D. Pa. 1997) (pre-*Ortiz* limited fund settlement class approved by court).

51. 527 U.S. at 838, 848.

52. *Id.* at 839, 841.

53. *Id.* at 838–39.

54. *Id.*

55. *Id.* at 841, 848–61.

56. For a discussion of this controversy, the conflicting federal court opinions, and the problem of "category creep," *see generally* Linda S. Mullenix, *No Exit: Mandatory Class Actions in the New Millennium and the Blurring of Categorical Imperatives*, 2003 U. CHI. LEGAL F. 177 (2003); *see also* Chapter 14, "The Special Role of 23(b)(2) Classes."

what types of damages are "incidental" to the equitable relief requested and what tests courts should apply to evaluate such claims.

The Rule 23(b)(3) category, then, is the category pursuant to which most settling parties structure their damage class action settlements. A Rule 23(b)(3) settlement, however, entails adherence to a different set of requirements than the so-called mandatory classes, and Rule 23(b)(3) settlements often are more complicated than settlements under the other rule provisions.

Unlike class settlements under the (b)(1) or (b)(2) provisions, Rule 23(b)(3) settlement classes may embrace class members with heterogeneous claims or interests. Because Rule 23(b)(3) damage class actions tend to be more sprawling and less cohesive than other types of settlement classes, securing judicial approval for a Rule 23(b)(3) settlement generally is more complicated and demanding. After the Supreme Court's decisions in *Amchem* and *Ortiz*, the settling parties must provide structural assurances of due process protections to class members with differing interests. To satisfy such due process concerns, a settlement may have to provide for subclasses, as well as independent, separate counsel for those subclasses. In addition, a Rule 23(b)(3) settlement class may require multiple rounds of notice and opportunities to the class to opt out. Because notice is not optional in (b)(3) settlement classes, the cost of complying with notice requirements is an additional and substantial cost in most damage settlement classes.

Moreover, the settlement of damage class actions involves complicated issues and problems in administering the settlement. Settlements that are consummated and approved under Rule 23(b)(1) and (b)(2) tend to be of a self-executing nature, because the remedies in these actions typically are injunctions or declaratory judgments. Apart from continuing judicial oversight, there is little interaction with class members involved in (b)(1) or (b)(2) settlements. In contrast, Rule 23(b)(3) damage settlements are not self-executing, but instead involve extensive post-settlement administration.

Thus, assuming that a proposed Rule 23(b)(3) settlement secures judicial approval (discussed below in section VI), damage class settlements typically implicate complicated damage models, administrative mechanisms to locate claimants and administer and distribute damages, administrative or judicial mechanisms for challenge and appeal of damage awards, default procedures for unclaimed damages such as cy pres distributions, involvement of special masters or other similar surrogates, and continuing judicial oversight.

Parties who desire to settle a class action will, at some point, have to determine the structural class category that will govern the class settlement. A variety of factors, discussed below, will guide parties in this consideration. However, before a court may approve a settlement, it must be satisfied that the proposed settlement comports with the requirements for class certification under an appropriate Rule 23(b) class category.

V. Ethical Problems Inherent in Class Action Settlements and Potential Abuses

There is a sizeable literature on the ethical problems entailed in class action litigation.[57] At the beginning or front end of such litigation, class actions present an array of challenging issues relating to improper solicitation of clients, client referral, and fee-sharing arrangements. During the development of a class action, problems of adequate representation permeate every aspect of case development, including but not limited to communications with class members, discovery and development of evidence and witnesses, financing the class action, and conflicts among class members' interests.

Although class litigation generally is imbued with many ethical challenges, a significant universe of discrete ethical challenges emerges when parties to class litigation decide to settle their dispute. Although the ethical challenges during settlement are intertwined with ordinary professional responsibility duties, the class settlement process has been a central object of concern and scrutiny for courts and commentators.[58]

Courts and commentators have identified many underlying reasons why ethical tensions are inherent in class action settlements. As indicated above, class actions are representational litigation, and therefore class counsel and the class representatives are nominally the guardians for the interests of absent class members. But as many commentators have documented, class action litigation presents unique opportunities for self-dealing and collusion among parties to the dispute.[59] In traditional litigation, a plaintiff is actually present to monitor the actions of his or her own lawyer and to agree or disagree to a proposed settlement after reasoned discussion with counsel.[60] If the plaintiff is unhappy or dislikes the terms of a

---

57. *See generally* JACK B. WEINSTEIN, INDIVIDUAL JUSTICE IN MASS TORT LITIGATION (1995); Jack B. Weinstein, *Ethical Dilemmas in Mass Tort Litigation*, 88 Nw. U. L. REV. 469 (1994) (lengthy survey of ethical problems in mass tort class litigation); MANUAL FOR COMPLEX LITIGATION (FOURTH) § 13.24 (2004) ("Ethical Considerations"); *see also* Chapter 32, "Ethical Issues in Class Actions."

58. *See generally* Howard M. Downs, *Federal Class Actions: Diminished Protection for the Class and the Case for Reform*, 73 NEB. L. REV. 646 (1994); Note, *Abuse in Plaintiff Class Action Settlements: The Need for a Guardian During Pretrial Settlement Negotiations*, 84 MICH. L. REV. 308, 316–20 (1985).

59. Professor John C. Coffee has written extensively concerning problems of self-dealing and collusion in class action litigation and class action settlements. *See, e.g.,* John C. Coffee, *Class Wars: The Dilemma of the Mass Tort Class Action*, 95 COLUM. L. REV. 1343 (1995); John C. Coffee, *The Regulation of Entrepreneurial Litigation: Balancing Fairness and Efficiency in the Large Class Action*, 54 U. CHI. L. REV. 877 (1987); John C. Coffee, *Understanding the Plaintiff's Attorney: The Implications of Economic Theory for Private Enforcement of Law Through Class Actions and Derivative Actions*, 86 COLUM. L. REV. 669 (1986).

60. *See In re Masters Mates and Pilots Pension Plan*, 957 F.2d 1020, at 1025–26 (2d Cir. 1992) (voluntary dismissal by stipulation of all the parties); MANUAL FOR COMPLEX LITIGATION (FOURTH) § 13.14 (2004) ("Ordinarily, settlement does not require judicial review and approval. Many of the exceptions to the rule,

settlement, the client can instruct the lawyer to reject the settlement or restructure it on more favorable terms.

In class settlements, however, class members typically do not learn of a settlement until after class counsel has negotiated the terms with the opposing parties, at which point the class members usually have no opportunity to contribute to the design of the settlement, to change terms of the settlement, or to meaningfully object to the settlement. Indeed, if a class member is part of a mandatory Rule 23(b)(1) or (b)(2) class, that class member may not opt out or exit the class, but will be bound by the settlement if the court approves it.

Class counsel and their defense adversaries understand these dynamics of class settlements and further understand that class counsel enjoys almost unfettered discretion to negotiate and fashion a class settlement on behalf of absent class members. The dynamics of class settlement also are closely intertwined with attorney fee awards in such litigation.[61] Although some federal courts adhere to a so-called lodestar[62] methodology for the determination of fee awards,[63] the prevailing standard in most federal courts is to award plaintiffs' counsel a percentage of the common benefit fund given to the class.[64] Such percentage awards typically are in the 25 percent range, but can be as high as 40 percent of the fund. Because American damage class actions frequently involve millions of dollars in damages, attorney fee awards consequently are commensurate with the size of the class recovery.

Given the relative size of a monetary damage class and the prospect of a percentage fee award, class action lawyers may have a disincentive to incur massive expenses in developing the class litigation through discovery and trial. If the counsel for the class can settle the class early in the litigation, counsel will still reap a percentage of the class recovery (often millions of dollars in attorney fees) with a minimum of effort and expenditure. Correlatively, defense counsel understand that it may be to class counsel's own advantage to settle early, which provides leverage to defendants to offer cheap settlements early in the litigation. In this scenario, both plaintiff and defense counsel win: class counsel recoups a signifi-

---

however, are of particular relevance to complex litigation. The Federal Rules require court approval of settlements in class actions . . . .").

61. *See* FED. R. CIV. P. 23(h), which now governs court approval of attorney fees in class actions. Rule 23(h) was added to the class action rule in 2003. Rule 23(h) authorizes the court to approve an attorney's fee petition and authorizes the courts to use various methodologies, including the "percentage of the benefit fund" approach or the lodestar methodology. These two methodologies were the prevailing standards for the award of attorney fees used by federal courts prior to 2003, and the 2003 amendment was intended to codify existing practice.

62. The lodestar calculation determines a reasonable number of hours worked multiplied by a reasonable hourly rate. *See* Chapter 8, "Attorney Fee Awards and Incentive Payments."

63. *See* MANUAL FOR COMPLEX LITIGATION (FOURTH) § 14.122 (2004) ("Lodestar Fee Awards").

64. *Id.* at § 14.121 ("Percentage Fee Awards").

cant fee without much effort and expense, and the defense secures an economical settlement for its client.

The economics of class litigation, then, encourage some degree of conscious or unconscious collusion between class counsel and the defendants; this is especially pertinent in Rule 23(b)(3) settlement classes. Class settlement presents significant ethical challenges because class counsel have a strong self-interest in negotiating on behalf of a quick settlement to receive attorney fees, which may induce them to be less than vigorous in negotiating a large common fund award for the class members.

Moreover, the ultimate source of attorney fees presents another ethical dilemma.[65] If an attorney fee award is to come out of the class fund, this further diminishes class counsel's advocacy on behalf of individual class members' interests. Therefore, some courts have determined that attorney fee awards need to be discussed separate and apart from negotiations over the class fund. However, in class litigation, defendants frequently know the limit of their offer in settlement, and it is a matter of indifference to the defendants how that ultimate settlement cost is divided between the class and their lawyers. In this scenario, even the separation of fee negotiations from the class fund is inadequate to discourage a disadvantageous financial impact on the class.

These inherent forces in damage class action settlements also contributed to the rise of dubious settlement offers, most notably controversial devices such as "coupon settlements" prevalent during the late 1990s.[66] Rather than return compensatory damages to class members, these settlements instead awarded class members with coupons entitling the class member to future discounts on the defendant's goods or services. Logically, defendants favored coupon settlements for many reasons, not the least of which was that redemption rates on settlement coupons typically were very low. Initially, coupons awarded in these settlements had limited use and were not transferable, causing critics to label coupon settlements as worthless. Coupon settlements generated a veritable firestorm of criticism among class action opponents,[67] and ultimately led to restrictions on such settlements in the Class Action Fairness Act of 2005.[68]

---

65. See id. at § 13.24 (discussion of ethical problems relating to negotiations regarding attorney fees).

66. See generally J. Brendan Day, Comment, My Lawyer Went to Court and All I Got Was This Lousy Coupon! The Class Action Fairness Act's Inadequate Provision for Judicial Scrutiny Over Proposed Coupon Settlements, 38 SETON HALL L. REV. 1085 (2008); Steven B. Hantler & Robert E. Norton, Coupon Settlements: The Emperor's Clothes of Class Actions, 18 GEO. J. LEGAL ETHICS 1343 (2005); Christopher R. Leslie, The Need to Study Coupon Settlements in Class Action Litigation, 18 GEO. J. LEGAL ETHICS 1395 (2005); Christopher R. Leslie, A Market-Based Approach to Coupon Settlements in Antitrust and Consumer Class Action Litigation, 49 U.C.L.A. L. REV. 991 (2002).

67. See generally Leslie, The Need to Study Coupon Settlements in Class Action Litigation, supra note 66.

68. Discussed infra at notes 137–47.

Rule 23(b)(3) damage class actions may give rise to other ethical dilemmas for lawyers seeking to settle these classes. Because Rule 23(b)(3) embraces the possibility of class members with heterogeneous or differing claims and interests, class counsel must ensure that the interests of all class members receive adequate representation. The Supreme Court in *Amchem* and *Ortiz* conclusively indicated that class representatives cannot simultaneously represent the interests of class members with conflicting interests. Thus, counsel must provide structural assurances of due process, which may involve the creation of subclasses with independent counsel.

In addition to ethical problems relating to conflicts of interest and attorney fees, class litigation also raises complex problems concerning the bounds of permissible communications with class members,[69] the possibility of agreements that foreclose class counsel from undertaking subsequent representation,[70] and the failure to submit offers to class representatives.[71]

In considering these inherent tensions presented by the prospect of class action settlements, many commentators have pointed out that the central ethical question in class action settlements is, "Who is guarding the guardians of the class?" The Supreme Court and the lower federal courts have located the answer to this question in the requirement of adequate representation during the course of representation, including especially the settlement process.

A. FORCES THAT MILITATE IN THE NEGOTIATION OF A SETTLEMENT

Parties involved in class litigation may pursue settlement at any time during the development of the litigation. The defendant or defendants typically will determine whether settlement negotiations will occur, although the plaintiffs generally will seek settlement from their initiation of litigation.

Whether a defendant will settle a class action depends on a variety of commercial, legal, and strategic factors. Defense counsel, in consultation with the client, will make a reasoned decision whether it is in the client's best interests to litigate or settle a pending class action, which largely may be a business decision. This conversation will include a valuation of the class claims, transactional costs of developing a class defense, and a concomitant risk assessment of proceeding to trial versus settling the class claims at some point. In addition, a defendant's assessment of a settlement strategy also will take into account less tangible but nonetheless real factors, such as reputational value or good will. A defendant may choose to settle a class action early in order to stanch negative media publicity about a company's products and to preserve a reputation of integrity within the marketplace.

---

69. *See* MANUAL FOR COMPLEX LITIGATION (FOURTH) §§ 13.24, 21.3, 21.6 (2004); *see also* Chapter 2, "Ethical and Practical Issues of Communicating with Members of a Class."

70. *See* MANUAL FOR COMPLEX LITIGATION (FOURTH) § 13.24 (2004).

71. *Id.*

The defense counsel's role in settlement will be governed by the client's decision to settle the litigation rather than to litigate. Any decision to settle a class action is the client's decision, not counsel's decision.[72] In addition, the client's insurer and reinsurers may play a role in the client's decision to enter settlement negotiations, because the client's liability exposure in excess of claim coverage is another consideration affecting whether to proceed with a classwide settlement.

When a defendant makes the decision to settle rather than to litigate the class claims, the defendant typically will have a range of values—often informed by its insurance coverage—within which the defendant is willing to settle on behalf of the class claims. This range of settlement values will inform both the plaintiff's and defendant's settlement negotiations.

Defendants have different approaches to settlement in class litigation. Some defendants have a "no settlement" philosophy, in which case these defendants will aggressively oppose class certification and will proceed with classwide discovery and trial. Other defendants will choose to settle class litigation at a very early stage, particularly if the defendant believes that the litigation amounts to a nuisance or strike suit that can be settled for a small amount with plaintiffs. In between these extreme approaches, defendants may choose to aggressively contest class certification and await a court's decision to certify a class. If the court certifies the class, the defendant may at that point capitulate and enter into settlement negotiations.[73]

The timing of when parties choose to enter settlement negotiations may have consequences for the settlement itself. As discussed above, an early and quick settlement may prove efficacious for the class counsel and the defendant, but may result in a weak settlement for class members. If class counsel can successfully convince a court to certify the class, the strategic equities shift to the plaintiff's advantage and the defendant's disadvantage. As indicated above, a court's decision to certify a class effectively exerts, for many defendants, an enormous pressure to settle the case.[74]

However, some defendants may choose not to enter settlement negotiations after a court certifies the class, but may instead choose to proceed with discovery and fact development of the case. If the parties proceed with class discovery,

---

72. This is required by all codes of professional responsibility. This rule for class action settlements is the same rule for traditional litigation, where the decision to settle is the client's decision, and not the attorney's decision.

73. As indicated above, a defendant may also choose to challenge a certification determination through an interlocutory appeal. If successful on appeal, the plaintiff in all likelihood will abandon the class action. On the other hand, if the appellate court affirms the class certification, the defendant may at this point enter into settlement negotiations or proceed with classwide discovery.

74. This leverage is characterized as "settlement blackmail" by some courts and commentators.

this process will provide them with additional information concerning the relative strengths and weaknesses of each side's positions in the litigation.

If the plaintiff's development of discovery evidence (including fact and expert witness testimony) supports a strong plaintiff's case on behalf of the class, this will militate in favor of the defendant settling the litigation and will provide the plaintiff with a strong bargaining position in settlement negotiations. On the other hand, if the defense's development of evidence is strong, this may militate against settlement or provide the defendant with a strong bargaining position in settlement negotiations. If either side's development of the case proves weak, this also may militate in favor of entering settlement negotiations, albeit in a weaker negotiation posture.

Apart from timing considerations, an array of factors will inform class and defense counsel concerning whether and under what circumstances to settle. The factors that determine a decision to settle class litigation are the same as those that inform the decision to settle a traditional litigation, although the magnitude of these factors may be exponentially increased by the scope of class litigation. In short, the stakes of class litigation are greatly increased compared to traditional litigation, and the increased stakes exert tremendous pressure on both sides to negotiate a reasonable settlement.

Hence, counsel on both sides of the litigation will consider the size and geographic dispersion of the class, and the nature of the underlying claims. The parties will assess the remedies requested, and attempt to value the costs of such remedies, including injunctive relief and compensatory damages. If class counsel has pleaded punitive damages as an element of relief, the litigants will assess the possible exposure to such damages, and the valuation of such damages. The litigants also will assess what law will apply to resolve the claims, and whether in certain types of class actions—such as nationwide products liability actions—applicable law problems will complicate resolution of the action.

Counsel also will assess the transaction costs of settling the case at different stages of the proceeding, including the costs and expenses of prosecuting interlocutory appeals, engaging in discovery, and staging a trial. Discovery is perhaps the most expensive component of litigation, embracing such mechanisms as interrogatories, document production, depositions, physical and mental exams, and inspection of facilities. In large-scale class litigation, the prospect of substantial discovery expenses may induce either side of the litigation to seek settlement to avoid these costs.

In determining whether to settle a class action, the parties additionally will assess forum considerations, such as the venue of a possible trial, the disposition of juries in similar cases, the likelihood of success on the merits of the class claims if the case is taken to trial, the temperament of the presiding judge, and the experience and skill of opposing counsel. At some point in the litigation, a court may have ordered the parties to engage in mediation. If prior mediation failed, this process will have informed the litigants of the negotiation posture of each side, the relative strengths and weaknesses of their claims and defenses, and the level of tolerance for compromise. Counsel also may assess the court's record in settling class actions and the substantive provisions of prior settlements in the jurisdiction.

When the parties reach a decision to settle a class, the positions of the litigants may be modified in significant ways. It is conventionally recognized that when defendants decide to settle a class action, their goal is to accomplish what class action attorneys label "global peace." Global peace for defendants consists of a classwide binding judgment that will completely foreclose subsequent litigants from bringing an individual case against the defendant on the class claims. In addition, defendants also seek to foreclose any subsequent class litigation on the same claims.

To accomplish this goal, defendants in negotiating settlements often prefer and insist that the class action be settled on a mandatory class action basis—that is, pursuant to Rule 23(b)(1) or (b)(2). As discussed above, a Rule 23(b)(1) or (b)(2) settlement class judgment is mandatory and binding on all class members, which settlement forecloses any class members from suing the defendant in the future. Corporate defendants sometimes disfavor Rule 23(b)(3) class settlements, which permit claimants to opt out of the class and pursue individual litigation.

A defendant's insistence on settlement through the mandatory class action mechanism creates problems for structuring class settlements, particularly when the underlying class is an action for damages, which must be certified under Rule 23(b)(3). Hence, the structural form of the settlement agreement and the class category under which the settlement will be offered to the court for final approval often are points of contention in settlement negotiations.

It is not uncommon for a class counsel to originally plead a class action as a Rule 23(b)(3) action, but then to agree to settle the action with the defendant as a Rule 23(b)(1) or (b)(2) class. This type of concession raises complications where the settling parties seek certification of a damage class action under the Rule 23(b)(1) or (b)(2) provisions. Because the court ultimately will have to certify the settlement class as part of the final approval of the settlement, the structural basis for the settlement may raise jurisprudential problems at the time of the final settlement approval.

In addition, the defendant's desire to accomplish global peace through a class action settlement also results in the defendant's insistence on certain types of provisions in the settlement agreement that will insulate the defendant from future litigation and liability. Many of these provisions have proven controversial in current class action settlements. Among these provisions are (1) complete and global releases of any and all claims related to the underlying class litigation; (2) class action waivers; and (3) "exploding" provisions. A class action waiver provision basically works as a bar that prevents class claimants from suing the defendant in another subsequent class action. "Exploding" or "blow-up" provisions in Rule 23(b)(3) settlements provide that if a certain percentage of class members opt out,[75] then the settlement agreement "explodes" or is invalidated.

In addition to the structural format in which the class will be settled, all settling parties have an interest in the nature and scope of settlement remedies. To this end, defendants obviously have an interest in minimizing the scope of their financial exposure to the class, while class counsel have a countervailing interest in maximizing recovery to the class. In this regard, plaintiffs may favor a compensatory damage fund, a punitive damage fund, or some form of injunctive relief, which may be valued in monetary terms. Such real measures of damages will assist class counsel in justifying a request for an attorney fee award based on the value of the settlement to the class.

In turn, defendants often will negotiate for nonmonetary equivalents, such as coupon settlements or injunctive relief in which the defendant is required to modify or change a course of conduct. In addition, defendants have an interest in the disposition of unclaimed funds in monetary settlements—sometimes negotiating for a return of unclaimed class proceeds to the defendant, or for a cy pres reversion of such funds to charitable organizations. The settling parties may have an interest in designating cy pres beneficiaries or may agree to leave the designation of cy pres beneficiaries to the discretion of the court.

Finally, all settling parties have interests in determining which party will be allocated costs relating to payment of attorney fees and expenses relating to the implementation of the settlement, including but not limited to the costs of serving notice (or multiple notices), expenses of claim administration, and costs of private vendors or special masters. These matters will be subject to negotiation and either allocated to the class itself or shifted to the defendant.

B. ACTORS AND FIDUCIARIES INVOLVED IN THE SETTLEMENT PROCESS

A number of different actors will be involved in the settlement process, and many serve in fiduciary roles as guardians or protectors of the interests of absent class members. Among the actors who may be involved in class action settlement are (1) the plaintiff's class and defense counsel, (2) the class representatives, who are the nominal plaintiffs, (3) judicial magistrates or special masters, (4) the presiding judge, (5) objectors, (6) governmental agencies, and (7) commercial notice and settlement administration vendors. In addition to these actors, expert witnesses may be utilized in the settlement process to assist in the formulation of settlement terms, or to provide testimonial evidence in support of final approval of a proposed settlement.

---

75. The percentage that will trigger the settlement to be negated or explode is typically low, usually at 10 percent or more of class members who opt out.

1. The Role of Class and Defense Counsel

Class counsel and their counterpart defense counsel play the central role in negotiating the terms of the settlement. Class counsel function under a professional responsibility duty to zealously represent the interests of the class, and some courts have suggested that because class actions are representational litigation, class counsel have a fiduciary duty to absent class members.[76] However, absent class members are not actual parties to the litigation, and class action jurisprudence is unclear concerning who the client is, particularly before a class is formally certified by a court. One line of authority suggests that the attorneys represent only the individual class representatives prior to certification of the class (on the theory that there is no class until the court certifies the class). Another line of authority suggests that class counsel's fiduciary duties to the class attach as soon as the lawyer files the complaint in the form of a class action.

The determination of who the client is in a class action, and when one becomes a class member entitled to undiluted, zealous representation, has direct relevance for the obligations of the lawyer in the settlement context. This is especially problematic in situations where a court does not certify the class at the outset of the litigation (or provisionally certifies the class), but defers the final certification decision until the parties have reached a settlement. In this scenario, critics have argued that in absence of a final certified class, class counsel have no class clients and therefore can negotiate unfettered from the fiduciary duties conferred by the formalism of class certification.

While there are conflicting opinions between the courts, the better view seems to be that the attorney-client relationship between class members and class counsel is established when the litigation is filed as a class action. At that point, the obligations and duties to zealously represent the interests of absent members attach. In the class action settlement context, these duties include a settlement on the most favorable terms to the class as a whole. Class counsel may not bargain the interests of class members against each other or negotiate less favorable terms for some segment of the class. In addition, class counsel may not negotiate different terms for the actual class representatives, although it is permissible to seek a relatively modest bonus for persons who serve in this capacity.

Although class counsel is under a duty of professional responsibility to advocate on behalf of the entire class in settlement negotiations, the inertia of self-interest often competes with this duty. As discussed above, the attorneys' interest in maximizing attorney fees while minimizing labor and transaction costs often encourages class counsel to settle quickly and on less advantageous terms for the class. In addition, once the defendant has signaled interest in settling the class,

---

76. MANUAL FOR COMPLEX LITIGATION (FOURTH) § 21.541 (2004) ("The Role of Class Counsel in Settlement").

plaintiffs' counsel may willingly concede defendant-favoring settlement terms such as releases, waivers, and costs and expenses. And, as indicated above, class counsel may accede to a defendant's demands that the class be settled on a mandatory basis, even though class action jurisprudence may not support such class certification.

Unlike class counsel, defense counsel have no fiduciary relationship to absent class members. However, in the dynamics of class litigation, the defendant's own self-interests often align to secure certain settlement provisions that serve to protect the interests of class members. One of the defendant's primary goals—in addition to achieving global peace—is to ensure that a class settlement is final, binding, and insulated from future collateral attack. To secure the invulnerability of the class settlement, then, it is in the defendant's interest to ensure that all due process is accorded to absent class members. This means that cautious defendants will want to ensure that adequacy of representation is accomplished by both the class counsel and the class representatives and that adequate notice and an opportunity to be heard is afforded to absent class members. In addition, defense counsel may also attempt to ensure that substantive and procedural fairness is accorded during the settlement approval process before the court.

2. The Role of the Class Representatives

The class representatives are the nominal plaintiff-parties to the litigation. Although it is possible to have a single person serve in the capacity of class representative, most class actions name more than one class representative. The class representatives serve as fiduciaries for the interests of absent class members and are supposed to protect class members against the potential for attorney self-dealing and collusion.[77] Before a class action may be certified, the court must assess whether the class representatives are capable of adequately representing the interests of absent class members.

If the class is certified at the outset, the court will assess the representative's adequacy by evaluating whether the class representative knows and understands the nature of class litigation, the representative's role in protecting the interests of the absent class members, the representative's willingness and ability to serve in this capacity, and the representative's financial obligations to the class. In addition, the court will evaluate whether the class representative has the ability to act independently of class counsel and to oversee decision making in the development of the litigation. The court also will assess whether the class representatives have any conflicts of interest with absent class members.[78]

---

77. *Id.* at § 21.642 ("Role of the Class Representative in Settlement").

78. *See* Nancy Morawetz, *Bargaining, Class Representation, and Fairness*, 54 OHIO ST. L. REV. 13 (1993).

A court's assessment of the class representatives becomes somewhat more complicated when the class is not certified at the outset of the litigation, but rather at the time a settlement is offered to the court. In this situation, the court is faced with making a retroactive determination whether the class representative performed his or her duties in protecting the interests of absent class members and did not accede to attorney self-dealing. The court will evaluate the adequacy of the class representative at the time of the final settlement hearing and will receive testimony and evidence relating to the class representative's role in the litigation and the settlement.

In reality, class representatives play a small role in the class action settlement process. At one end of a continuum, class counsel may not consult with the class representatives at all during the process of negotiating a settlement, in which case the class representatives serve as little more than figureheads for the litigation and the settlement. However, most class counsel now communicate with their class representatives during the progress of settlement negotiations, and in varying degrees will keep the class representatives informed of the development of the settlement terms. As the nominal plaintiffs and clients in the litigation, the class representatives ultimately must give consent to the settlement.

Although the class representatives are fiduciaries for the interests of absent class members, it is arguable whether class representatives have the actual ability or knowledge to protect those interests. Very few attorneys actively involve their class representatives in the development of the litigation or in settlement negotiations. Instead, settlement terms are often presented to the client after the terms have been negotiated by counsel. As such, the fiduciary role of the class representatives often remains more a theoretical aspiration than an accomplished fact.

3. The Role of Judicial Magistrates or Special Masters

In addition to life-tenured district judges, the federal judicial system provides for a system of magistrate judges to handle certain civil and criminal matters.[79] One of the purposes of the magistrate system is to relieve federal judges from repetitive and routine matters that may be expeditiously handled by a magistrate judge instead. This referral of routine matters to magistrates, in turn, alleviates the dockets of federal judges to preside over actual trials.

In complex litigation, magistrate judges often assist district judges with certain aspects of the litigation, such as pretrial motion practice, pleading matters, and discovery.[80] In class action litigation, a district judge may request that the magistrate make preliminary findings on a class certification motion. In addition, a

---

79. *See* 28 U.S.C. § 636(b)(1); Fed. R. Civ. P. 53(f) and 72. *See also* Manual for Complex Litigation (Fourth) § 11.53 (2004).

80. *See also* Chapter 31, "Use of Special Masters in Connection with Class Proceedings."

federal judge may request that the magistrate meet and confer with the parties to oversee settlement negotiations.[81]

Where a federal judge has involved a magistrate in pending class litigation from the outset, the magistrate may develop an in-depth understanding of the parties to the dispute, the nature and strength of the claims and defenses, the risks entailed in litigating the dispute, and the settlement posture of the parties. Thus, the magistrate may be well-positioned to mediate a settlement among the parties and help craft the settlement for presentation to the court for final approval. In some instances, a judge may request that the magistrate evaluate preliminary approval of the settlement. In their role as judicial officers presiding over some portion of class litigation, magistrates then serve as additional fiduciaries protecting the interests of absent class members. In the final analysis, however, the federal judge must conduct the fairness hearing and issue the final order approving the class.

The Federal Rules of Civil Procedure also provide for the appointment of special masters.[82] Special masters are court-appointed persons with special expertise, and they are generally assigned a specific task by the court. Special masters are required to report to the court upon completion of the assigned task.[83] Judges occasionally appoint special masters to assist during the development of a class action settlement, particularly if the settlement requires a specialized task, such as an accounting or a damage model. Special masters typically will consult with parties to the litigation to obtain information necessary to complete the master's task.

4. The Role of the Presiding Judge

The presiding judge in class action litigation serves as an additional guardian of the interests of absent class members, and assumes the role of protecting class members from self-dealing by class counsel and possible collusion with the defendant.[84] The judge, then, serves as one of the primary bulwarks against bad deals.[85] As indicated above, the class action rule (and precedents interpreting the rule) provides judges with a variety of standards to ensure the due process protection of absent class members.

Thus, a judge's early supervision of class litigation provides an important measure of judicial oversight as the class litigation proceeds. The class certification process is one means by which the judge can assess the adequacy of representation

---

81. Manual for Complex Litigation (Fourth) § 21.644 (2004) ("Role of Special Magistrate Judges, Special Masters, and Other Judicial Adjuncts in Settlement").

82. Fed. R. Civ. P. 53; see also Manual for Complex Litigation (Fourth) §§ 11.52 and 21.644 (2004); see also Chapter 31, "Use of Special Masters in Connection with Class Proceedings."

83. Fed. R. Civ. P. 53(b), (f).

84. Manual for Complex Litigation (Fourth) § 21.61 (2004) ("Judicial Role in Reviewing a Proposed Class Action Settlement").

85. See Jack B. Weinstein & Karin S. Schwartz, Notes from the Cave: Some Problems of Judges in Dealing with Class Action Settlements, 163 F.R.D. 369 (1995); see also Chapter 32, "Ethical Issues in Class Actions."

at the outset of the litigation.[86] Judicial supervision of communications with class members is another means for controlling or sanctioning abusive class tactics.[87]

Presiding judges also play a substantial role in assuring due process protection of absent class members through application of the requirements of Rule 23(e),[88] which relates to class action settlements. No class action may be settled, compromised, or dismissed without approval of the court. As will be discussed below, a proposed settlement must be evaluated during a so-called fairness hearing before the judge.[89] The judge must make a determination on record evidence whether the class may be certified for final approval and whether the terms of the settlement are fair, adequate, and reasonable.[90]

Some federal judges, in varying degrees, also may participate in settlement negotiations with the parties in order to assist in brokering a settlement.[91] The extent

---

86. FED. R. CIV. P. 23(a)(1)–(4).

87. *See generally Gulf Oil Co. v. Bernard*, 452 U.S. 89 (1981) (permissible communications with class members); *Kleiner v. First Nat'l Bank*, 751 F.2d 1193, 1209–11 (11th Cir. 1985) (defendants violated court order limiting communications with class members; sanctions issued against defense counsel); MANUAL FOR COMPLEX LITIGATION (FOURTH) §§ 21.322–.323 and 21.33 (2004) (sections dealing with problems relating to communications with class members pre- and post–class certification); *see also* Chapter 2, "Ethical and Practical Issues of Communicating with Members of a Class."

88. Rule 23(e) in its entirety states:

(e) Settlement, Voluntary Dismissal, or Compromise. The claims, issues, or defenses of a certified class may be settled, voluntarily dismissed, or compromised only with the court's approval. The following procedures apply to a proposed settlement, voluntary dismissal, or compromise:

(1) The court must direct notice in a reasonable manner to all class members who would be bound by the proposal.

(2) If the proposal would bind class members, the court may approve it only after a hearing and on finding that it is fair, adequate, and reasonable.

(3) The parties seeking approval must file a statement identifying any agreement made in conjunction with the proposal.

(4) If the class action previously was certified under Rule 23(b)(3), the court may refuse to approve a settlement unless it affords a new opportunity to request exclusion to individual class members who had an earlier opportunity to request exclusion but did not do so.

(5) Any class member may object to the proposal if it requires court approval under this subdivision (e); the objection may be withdrawn only with the court's approval.

It should be noted that the provisions of Rule 23(e) apply only to classes that have been certified by the court, but not to class actions that are filed and not certified. Thus, plaintiff's attorneys may withdraw a class action without court approval before the action has been certified, and other provisions of Rule 23(e), such as notice requirements, do not apply.

89. FED. R. CIV. P. 23(e)(2). Prior to 2003, there was no requirement for a fairness hearing in the rule. The requirement of a hearing was added as part of the 2003 amendments to Rule 23. As a matter of practice, most courts routinely conducted fairness hearings prior to making a determination to finally approve a proposed settlement.

90. *Id.* Federal courts have articulated different standards to guide the determination of whether a proposed settlement is "fair, adequate, and reasonable." Hence, these standards vary across the federal circuits.

91. *See* MANUAL FOR COMPLEX LITIGATION (FOURTH) § 13.11 (2004).

of judicial involvement depends on the temperament of the individual judge, with some federal judges playing a more activist role in shaping class action settlements than others. In extreme cases, some federal judges have offered the litigants previews of their potential ruling on the merits of class claims and defenses to serve as an inducement to settlement.[92] However, such judicial involvement in settlement negotiations is highly controversial and not the norm among federal judges.[93]

5. The Role of Objectors

Objectors to class action settlements often play an important role as guardians of the interests of absent class members.[94] There are various types of objectors who may appear during the settlement process. Rule 23(e)(5) specifically indicates that any class member may object to a settlement proposal if the settlement requires approval under Rule 23(e). Some objectors, then, may be members of the class who, upon learning of the terms of the settlement, retain independent counsel or appear pro se to file objections with the court as part of the Rule 23(e) fairness hearing.

In addition to class members, persons extraneous to the class action—that is, non-class members—may raise objections to a proposed settlement. There are at least two types of "professional objectors" who frequently appear in class litigation to object to settlements.[95] One group consists of public interest and other lobbying groups, who may have an interest in the litigation but are not part of the class defined in the class definition. Examples of such professional objectors are entities such as Public Citizen, which has assumed the role of public guardian of class action settlements. Frequently, interest groups such as Public Citizen will raise an array of due process procedural objections to a proposed settlement, or criticisms of the substantive terms of the agreement.

Another group of so-called "professional objectors" have less laudatory goals and consequently less savory reputations in the settlement process.[96] Settling parties have a heightened interest in obtaining court approval of their agreement, and therefore the appearance of objectors always threatens the parties' carefully crafted agreement. Armed with this knowledge, some objectors file weakly based objec-

---

92. *See id.*

93. *See* D. MARIE PROVINE, FED. JUDICIAL CTR., SETTLEMENT STRATEGIES FOR FEDERAL DISTRICT JUDGES 28 (1986).

94. *See generally* Edward Brunet, *Class Action Objectors: Extortionist Free Riders or Fairness Guarantors,* 2003 U. CHI. LEGAL F. 403 (2003); Theodore Eisenberg & Geoffrey Miller, *The Role of Opt-Outs and Objectors in Class Action Litigation: Theoretical and Empirical Issues,* 57 VAND. L. REV. 1529 (2004); Robert B. Gerard & Scott A. Johnson, *The Role of the Objector in Class Action Settlements: A Case Study of the General Motors Truck "Side Saddle" Fuel Tank Litigation,* 31 LOY. L.A. L. REV. 409 (1998); Mike Absmeier, Note, *The Professional Objector and Revised Rule 23: Protecting Voice Rights while Limiting Objector Abuse,* 24 REV. LITIG. 609 (2005); *see also* MANUAL FOR COMPLEX LITIGATION (FOURTH) § 21.643 (2004) ("Role of Objectors in Settlement").

95. Absmeier, *supra* note 94, at 613–25 (describing types of objectors and objections).

96. MANUAL FOR COMPLEX LITIGATION (FOURTH) § 21.643 (2004). The *Manual* notes that "[a] challenge for the judge is to distinguish between the meritorious objections and those advanced for improper purposes." *Id.*

tions to settlement proposals in the hope of being compensated by the settling parties to withdraw their objections.

These types of objectors are sometimes characterized as nuisance objectors,[97] because settling parties often are willing to pay these objectors for the nuisance value of their challenges. The settling parties may agree to pay off the objectors with a side deal or to designate some role for the objecting attorneys in the future administration of the settlement fund, which will return a financial benefit to these objectors. Thus, when nuisance objectors appear to challenge a class settlement, the settling parties may either reach an agreement with these objectors or defend against their challenges at the court's fairness hearing, which may prove costly and jeopardize the settlement.

Courts have developed other rules, standards, and procedures relating to the role of objectors in class action settlements. The Supreme Court has held that an objector does not need to formally intervene in a class action in order to bring a subsequent appeal challenging the settlement if the court approves it.[98] However, such an objector must appear at the fairness hearing and present the objector's challenges at that time in order to have standing to appeal approval of the settlement.[99]

In addition, the 2003 amended Rule 23(e) now provides that "the parties seeking approval must file a statement identifying any agreement made in connection with the proposal."[100] This provision was added to the rule to address the problem of so-called "side deals" negotiated by the parties but undisclosed to the class members or court.[101] Presumably, this new provision will capture any agreements made with nuisance objectors to withdraw their objections prior to the final fairness hearing in return for either payment or some compensatory role in administering the settlement.

6. The Role of Governmental Agencies

Generally, unless a governmental agency is a party to a class action, governmental agencies have no role in class action settlements. However, CAFA confers on governmental agencies an oversight role by virtue of the provision that requires

---

97. *See, e.g.,* Absmeier, *supra* note 94, at 613.

98. *Devlin v. Scarletti,* 536 U.S. 1 (2002).

99. *Id.*

100. FED. R. CIV. P. 23(e)(3).

101. There are many different types of "side deals" or "side agreements" that heretofore might be negotiated among parties to a settlement, but not disclosed to the court or class members. Common types of side agreements include so-called Mary Carter agreements, sharing agreements, most-favored-nation clauses, and tolling agreements. For a description of these types of side agreements, *see* MANUAL FOR COMPLEX LITIGATION (FOURTH) § 13.23 (2004) ("Side Agreements"). As indicated *supra,* the problem with many of these side agreements is nondisclosure to the class members and the court. All such side deals must now be disclosed to the court at the time of the fairness hearing.

notice to all relevant governmental agencies of a proposed settlement.[102] It is not yet settled law concerning which governmental agencies need to be supplied with notice of a settlement pursuant to CAFA. However, this oversight role applies to any governmental agency with a regulatory or protective role over citizens within the state or agency's jurisdiction. Theoretically, then, the state attorney generals of all 50 states would need notice of a nationwide class action settlement, and if the settlement implicated federal regulatory concerns, the U.S. attorney general and regulatory agency director would need notice as well.

CAFA additionally specifies that a federal court may not approve a settlement for at least 90 days after notice is given to the relevant governmental agencies.[103] Hence, federal and state agencies have a three-month window in which to review a proposed settlement and to appear as objectors to a proposed settlement. Thus, CAFA has conferred a guardian role on governmental agencies with regard to class action settlements as protectors of citizens within their jurisdictions. This CAFA governmental notice provision, therefore, provides a powerful protective mechanism for absent class members in large-scale class settlements.

7. The Role of Commercial Notice and Claim Administration Vendors

Another set of important—but largely overlooked—actors in the settlement process are commercial notice and settlement administration vendors. In large-scale or nationwide class litigation, the attorneys rarely perform the tasks relating to crafting class notice, distributing class notice, or administering claims that the court approves as part of the settlement. These tasks are often accomplished by commercial vendors who have developed expertise in crafting notice to comply with legal requirements, as well as developing claims forms and administrative structures to handle claims processing.

In negotiating a class settlement, the settling parties will reach agreements about the nature and scope of class notice, the allocation of the costs of notice, and which commercial vendors will supply notice. In addition, the settling parties typically negotiate which commercial vendors will administer class remedies.

Because many settlement agreements in large-scale class litigation specify commercial vendors to implement notice and claims administration, the parties may interview several candidates for these tasks. During the settlement process, commercial vendors may make suggestions to the settling parties concerning how the

---

102. CAFA, *supra* note 4, at § 1715 ("Notifications to Appropriate Federal and State Officials"). Section 1715(a)(2) defines an appropriate state official to be "the person in the State who has primary regulatory or supervisory responsibility with respect to the defendant, or who licenses or otherwise authorizes the defendant to conduct business in the State, if some or all of the matters alleged in the class action are subject to regulation by that person."

103. *Id.* at § 1715(d).

vendor will identify class members and construct a program to accomplish the best practicable notice under the circumstances. The vendors also may suggest to the settling parties various ways to structure and implement claims administration.

When commercial vendors are involved in the settlement process, they frequently will supply an expert report or affidavit detailing the notice campaign and claims administration to be included with materials in support of final approval of the settlement. At the final fairness hearing, the settling parties will offer the commercial vendors' reports to the court for approval.

8. The Role of Expert Witnesses

Expert witnesses have various roles throughout class litigation, some of which apply especially to the settlement process.[104] Thus, expert witnesses may play a role in crafting a settlement agreement or in supporting the proposed settlement during the court's final fairness hearing. Settling parties may retain expert witnesses to review the settlement and offer opinion testimony concerning the suitability for class certification, the substantive fairness and adequacy of the terms of the agreement, the feasibility of a settlement damage model, or the suitability of the proposed notice and claims administration program. Class counsel also may offer expert testimony in support of the attorney fee petition to convince the court that class counsel's fee request is within reasonable ranges for similar types of class settlements.

Objectors also may retain expert witnesses to support their challenges to settlement terms. In addition—although this is somewhat rare—the presiding judge may choose to appoint his or her own experts to assist in evaluating the substantive and procedural fairness of a proposed settlement.[105]

C. SUBSTANTIVE TERMS OF A SETTLEMENT

Class settlement agreements typically include an array of substantive terms and procedural provisions. Because settlement agreements embody a negotiated compromise between the plaintiff and defendant(s), both parties influence the content and expression of the settlement agreement.

A settlement agreement typically sets forth an explanation of the facts underlying the litigation and the claims asserted by the plaintiff as a consequence. The settlement will recite that the parties have reached agreement to settle the dispute

---

104. *See generally* William W. Schwartzer & Joe S. Cecil, *Management of Expert Evidence*, in FED. JUDICIAL CTR., REFERENCE MANUAL ON SCIENTIFIC EVIDENCE 39 (2d ed. 2000); MANUAL FOR COMPLEX LITIGATION (FOURTH) § 11.48 (2004).

105. *See* FED. R. EVID. 706; MANUAL FOR COMPLEX LITIGATION (FOURTH) § 11.51 (2004); *see generally* JOE S. CECIL & THOMAS E. WILLGING, FED. JUDICIAL CTR., COURT-APPOINTED EXPERTS: DEFINING THE ROLE OF EXPERTS APPOINTED UNDER FEDERAL RULE OF EVIDENCE 706 (1993).

in order to avoid the cost and expense of protracted litigation, but that in settling, the defendant does not concede liability for any of the acts alleged by the plaintiffs. This descriptive analysis may include a balanced discussion of the relative strengths and weaknesses of each side of the litigation (claims and defenses) and the risk assessment that induced the parties to forgo the risks of litigation and settle their dispute.

The settlement will contain a description of the class and who the members of the class are, often delimited by certain dates or other conditions. The settlement will set forth legal and equitable remedies afforded by the agreement, including any equitable remedies and compensatory or punitive damages. If the settling parties have agreed on a lump settlement fund, the agreement will set forth the amount of the common benefit fund. If the settlement agreement includes cy pres remedies, the proposal will set forth the nature of the cy pres relief and the way in which the cy pres relief will be administered.

The agreement will contain a provision indicating the amount of attorney fees and the source of payment of those attorney fees. If the class representatives have been awarded a bonus or incentive payment for their service as class representatives, the settlement agreement will indicate those amounts.

The settlement will include any releases of future claims by class members, as well as other provisions such as class action waivers. The agreement also may contain a provision for the invalidation of the agreement if a certain percentage of class members elect to opt out of a Rule 23(b)(3) class.

The settlement agreement will set forth provisions relating to notice to class members and may include detailed information concerning not only the content of the notice, but how notice will be implemented to satisfy constitutional due process requirements. The settlement agreement may contain information about claims administration, including the processes for such administration, as well as any commercial vendor retained to perform these functions.

VI. Procedural Rules and Standards Governing the Judicial Approval of Settlements

A. THE TWO-STEP FINAL APPROVAL PROCESS: PRELIMINARY AND FINAL APPROVAL OF CLASS ACTION SETTLEMENT

As indicated above, Rule 23(e) requires judicial approval for proposed class action settlements. Judicial scrutiny of settlement proposals serves the important function of ensuring due process protections for absent class members and providing the jurisprudential basis for a binding judgment.

Judicial approval of a proposed settlement is a two-step process: a preliminary approval of a proposed class action settlement, followed by a final fairness hearing and judicial approval of the settlement. In some instances, if the case is presented for both class certification and settlement approval, the certification process and preliminary approval process can be combined.

B. PRELIMINARY APPROVAL OF A PROPOSED CLASS ACTION SETTLEMENT

The first step in the judicial approval process consists of a preliminary fairness review by the court, where the settling parties must submit the proposed settlement and supporting materials to the court for preliminary approval. The settling parties carry the burden of proof to convince the court that the proposed settlement is within the range of possible approval. A judge may request that counsel supply the court with additional information to evaluate the proposed settlement, particularly if a settlement is proposed very early in the litigation where there has been minimal development of the case.[106] Thus, counsel may be asked to furnish detailed information that will support a valuation of the settlement, including information concerning (1) the likelihood of success at trial; (2) the likelihood of class certification; (3) the status of competing or overlapping actions; (4) a claimant's damages and value of claims; (5) the total present value of monetary and nonmonetary terms; (6) attorney fees; (7) the cost of litigation; and (8) the defendant's ability to pay.[107]

1. Criteria for Evaluating a Proposed Settlement

The court will evaluate three components of the settlement: (1) whether the proposed class is suitable for final certification as under Rules 23(a) and (b); (2) whether the substantive and procedural terms of the settlement are "fair, adequate, and reasonable"; and (3) whether the court should approve class counsel's fee award.

Regarding the first component, the judge must make at least a preliminary determination that the settlement class satisfies the threshold requirements of Rule 23(a) for numerosity, commonality, typicality, and adequacy. The judge also must determine that the settlement class is suitable for certification pursuant to at least one of the subsections of Rule 23(b). However, if the settlement class is proposed under Rule 23(b)(3), then the class action does not have to satisfy the requirement of manageability, because the action will not be tried. In considering preliminary class certification, the judge also must assess whether the action needs to be divided into subclasses and whether the court needs to appoint independent counsel to represent those subclasses.

In order to issue a preliminary approval of a settlement class, the judge also must make an initial determination that the substantive terms of the proposed settlement are fair, adequate, and reasonable. The standards for assessing whether

---

106. MANUAL FOR COMPLEX LITIGATION (FOURTH) § 21.632 (2004).
107. *Id.* at § 21.631.

a proposed settlement is fair, adequate, and reasonable vary across the numerous federal district courts.[108] However, several federal circuits have articulated standards that govern judicial settlement approval within those individual circuits, and the Federal Judicial Center has distilled general principles from this evolving common law. Hence, the Center notes:

> A number of factors are used to apply those criteria and evaluate a proposed settlement. Deciding which factors apply and what weight to give them depends on a number of variables: (1) the merits of the substantive class claims, issues, or defenses; (2) whether the class is mandatory or opt-out; and (3) the mix of claims that can support individual litigation, such as personal injury claims, and claims that are only viable within a class action, such as small economic loss claims. A class involving small claims may provide the only opportunity for relief and pose little risk that the settlement terms will sacrifice the interests of individual class members. A class involving many claims that can support individual suits—ranging from claims of severe injury or death to relatively slight harms, as for example a mass torts personal-injury class—might require more scrutiny by the court to fairness.[109]

Furthermore, the Federal Judicial Center has distilled, from common law standards applied by federal courts, several factors that may bear on review of a settlement, which include

> 1. the advantages of the proposed settlement versus the probable outcome of a trial on the merits of liability and damages as to the claims, issues, or defenses of the class and individual class members;
>
> 2. the probable time, duration, and cost of trial;
>
> 3. the probability that the class claims, issues, or defenses could be maintained through trial on a class basis;
>
> 4. the maturity of the underlying substantive issues, as measured by the information and experience gained through adjudicating individual actions, the development of scientific knowledge, and other factors that bear on the probable outcome of a trial on the merits;
>
> 5. the extent of participation in the settlement negotiations by class members or class representatives and by a judge, a magistrate judge, or a special master;
>
> 6. the number and force of objections by class members;
>
> 7. the probable resources and ability of the parties to pay, collect, or enforce the settlement compared with enforcement of the probable judgment predicted under above paragraph 1 or 4;

---

108. For illustrations of judicial assessment of the fairness of proposed settlements, *see, e.g., Wal-Mart Stores, Inc. v. Visa U.S.A., Inc.*, 396 F.3d 96 (2d Cir. 2005) (approving settlement); *Staton v. Boeing Co.*, 327 F.3d 938 (9th Cir. 2003) (rejecting settlement); *Molski v. Gleich*, 318 F.3d 937 (9th Cir. 2003) (rejecting settlement); *Reynolds v. Beneficial Nat'l Bank*, 288 F.3d 277 (7th Cir. 2002) (reversing and remanding approval of class action settlement).

109. MANUAL FOR COMPLEX LITIGATION (FOURTH) § 21.62 (2004) ("Criteria for Evaluating a Proposed Settlement").

8. the effect of the settlement on other pending actions;

9. similar claims by other classes and subclasses and their probable outcome;

10. the comparison of the results achieved for individual class or subclass members by the settlement or compromise and the results achieved or likely to be achieved for other claimants pressing similar claims;

11. whether class or subclass members have the right to request exclusion from the settlement, and, if so, the number exercising that right;

12. the reasonableness of any provisions for attorney fees, including agreements on the division of fees among attorneys and the terms of any agreements affecting the fees to be charged for representing individual claimants or objectors;

13. the fairness and reasonableness of the procedure for processing individual claims under the settlement;

14. whether another court has rejected a substantially similar settlement for a similar class; and

15. the apparent intrinsic fairness of the settlement terms.[110]

In addition, the Federal Judicial Center has suggested that

[i]n determining the weight accorded these and other factors, courts have examined whether

- other courts have rejected similar settlements for competing or overlapping classes;
- the named plaintiffs are the only class members to receive monetary relief or are to receive relief that is disproportionately large (differentials are not necessarily improper, but may call for judicial scrutiny);
- the settlement amount is much less than the estimated damages incurred by members of the class as indicated by preliminary discovery or other objective measures, including settlements or verdicts in individuathe settlement was completed at an early stage of the litigation without substantial discovery and with significant uncertainties remaining;
- nonmonetary relief, such as coupons or discounts, is unlikely to have much, if any, market or other value to the class;
- significant components of the settlement provide illusory benefits because of strict eligibility conditions;
- some defendants have incentives to restrict payment of claims because they may reclaim residual funds;
- major claims or types of relief sought in the complaint have been omitted from the settlement;
- particular segments of the class are treated significantly differently from others;
- claimants who are not members of the class (*e.g.*, opt outs) or objectors receive better settlements than the class to resolve similar claims against the same defendants;

---

110. *Id.*

- attorney fees are so high in relation to the actual or probable class recovery that they suggest a strong possibility of collusion;
- defendants appear to have selected, without court involvement, a negotiator from among a number of plaintiffs' counsel; and
- a significant number of class members raise apparently cogent objections to the settlement. (The court should interpret the number of objectors in light of the individual monetary stakes involved in the litigation. When the recovery for each class member is small, the paucity of objections may reflect apathy rather than satisfaction. When the recovery for each class member is high enough to support individual litigation, the percentage of class members who object may be an accurate measure of the class' sentiments toward the settlement. However, an apparently high number of objections may reflect an organized campaign, rather than the sentiments of the class at large. A similar phenomenon is the organized opt-out campaign.)[111]

2. Procedures for Reviewing a Proposed Settlement

The judge may preliminarily approve a settlement class based on submissions by the parties or objectors, or may appoint a special master to assist the court in such an evaluation. The judge may hold an evidentiary hearing with witness testimony. The judge also may rely on preliminary assessments by a magistrate judge or special master. In addition, the court may rely on expert witness testimony in support of the valuation of a settlement.

The court may hear from objectors during this phase of preliminary approval. If the judge has concerns about the structure or the terms of the settlement, he or she may raise these reservations during a hearing on preliminary approval. Such concerns might include questions about preferential treatment for members of the class or the class representatives; the need for subclasses; inadequate compensation to class members; and excessive attorney fees.[112] The judge may withhold preliminary approval and request the parties to resume negotiations.[113]

The judge may offer views on the settlement agreement, but may not rewrite provisions of the settlement. If the judge conducts preliminary conferences with the settling parties, he or she may offer views that encourage the parties to change and modify provisions of the settlement agreement, prior to serving notice to the class of the settlement terms.[114]

If, after initial scrutiny, the court is satisfied that the class may be certified and that the terms of the settlement tentatively are fair, adequate, and reasonable, the court will then order that formal notice of a Rule 23(e) hearing be given to class

---

111. *Id.*
112. *Id.* at § 21.632.
113. *Id.*
114. *Id.* at § 21.61 ("Judicial Role in Reviewing Proposed Class Action Settlement").

members.[115] The notice of the fairness hearing should alert class members of their opportunity to retain separate counsel, to appear at the fairness hearing, to submit objections to the court, or to opt out of the action if the class is certified as a Rule 23(b)(3) action.[116] The 2003 amendments to the class action have afforded class members a second opportunity to opt out of the class at this point, although very few courts have actually granted a second opt-out right under Rule 23(e)(3).[117]

3. Discovery and Fairness Issues

Parties to a settlement will have access to all materials developed during the course of the litigation, and these materials may be used in support of a judicial determination that a proposed settlement is fair, adequate, and reasonable. Parties should make discovery materials accessible in order to evaluate the relative strengths of the claims on the merits as part of the fairness assessment. However, at times objectors may seek discovery relating to the settlement in order to frame or refine objections to the settlement, based on underlying documentation or strategy.

Courts generally have not granted objectors unlimited access to discovery materials in order to present objections to settlements.[118] Courts generally do not favor granting objectors access to discovery because doing so tends to delay the settlement process and may be used for illegitimate purposes, such as to leverage an attorney fee award to an objector's attorney. Hence, some courts will countenance discovery to an objector only upon a showing of need.

The Federal Judicial Center has advised that courts should monitor post-settlement discovery by objectors and limit such discovery to information that will assist an objector in evaluating the fairness of the settlement.[119] Generally, courts have not permitted discovery into the settlement negotiation process unless the objector is able to make some preliminary showing of collusion or other improper behavior by the settling parties.[120]

4. Statement Requirement

In addition to presenting to the court evidence in support of the proposed class action settlement, the settling parties are now required under Rule 23(e)(2) to

---

115. *Id.* at § 21.633.

116. *See* FED. R. CIV. P. 23(e)(1), (4), (5).

117. *See, e.g., Denney v. Deutsche Bank AG*, Nos. 05-1275CVL, 05-1279CV, 05-1287CV, 2006 WL 845727, at *12 (2d Cir. Mar. 31, 2006) (court denied second opt-out); *Hicks v. Morgan Stanley & Co.*, No. 01 Civ. 10071 (RJH), 2005 U.S. Dist. LEXIS 24890, at *17 (S.D.N.Y. Oct. 24, 2005) (same); *In re Visa Check/ Mastermoney Antitrust Litig.*, 297 F. Supp. 2d 503, 518 (E.D.N.Y. 2003) (same). *But see Nilsen v. York County*, 382 F. Supp. 2d 206, 210 (D. Me. 2005) (granting second opt-out).

118. *See In re Lorazapram & Clorazepate Antitrust Litig.*, 205 F.R.D. 24, 26 (D.D.C. 2001) (objectors to a settlement class do not have absolute right to discovery; court may in its discretion permit discovery to assist court in determining whether settlement is fair, adequate, and reasonable).

119. MANUAL FOR COMPLEX LITIGATION (FOURTH) § 21.643 (2004).

120. *Id.; see Bowling v. Pfizer*, 143 F.R.D. 141, 153 & n.10 (S.D. Ohio 1992).

submit a statement that identifies any agreement made in connection with the settlement, including all agreements "that, although seemingly separate, may have influenced the terms of the settlement by trading away possible advantages for the class in return for advantages for others." If the settling parties have any doubts about whether some "side agreement" needs to be disclosed to the court, the Advisory Committee note to Rule 23(e)(2) indicates that such doubts should be resolved in favor of disclosure.

The purpose of this disclosure statement relating to side agreements obviously is intended to allow the court to assess the course of dealings that resulted in the settlement, in order to adequately represent and protect the interests of absent class members.

C. CLASS SETTLEMENT NOTICE

As indicated above, when a court has determined to preliminarily certify a class settlement for approval, the court also will approve notice to be sent to class members relating to final approval of the class action. If the settlement class is a Rule 23(b)(3) class, then the required notice under Rule 23(c)(2) and Rule 23(e) may be combined in one process.

The notice should inform class members of a description of the litigation, the forum in which the settlement has been preliminarily approved, and the underlying claims and defenses, as well as proposed attorney fees awarded in the litigation. The notice should inform class members of the terms of the tentative settlement and give notice of the upcoming fairness hearing, including the time and place of the hearing. Class members should be informed that they may present views on the settlement, either in person or through counsel.

The notice of settlement also should inform prospective objectors of their right to opt out or to file written objections by a specified date in advance of the final fairness hearing, as well as to give notice to the court's clerk if the objector intends to appear at the hearing.

D. FINAL FAIRNESS HEARING

Once notice has been served to the class and a fairness hearing set, the court will conduct a final fairness hearing. When a court determines to finally approve a class action settlement, it must issue an order of final approval. Typically, this order sets forth the court's findings of fact and conclusions of law relating to the court's approval of the settlement. Therefore, a court will desire to have an adequate factual and evidentiary record upon which to make its findings and conclusions. "The record and findings must demonstrate to a reviewing court that the judge has made the requisite inquiry and has considered the diverse interests and the requisite factors in determining the settlement's fairness, reasonableness, and adequacy."[121]

The court's assessment of the proposed settlement agreement initially is based on submissions by the settling parties in support of their agreement.[122] As indicated above, since the 2003 amendment to Rule 23, the settling parties are now required to disclose to the court any side agreements negotiated as part of the settlement.[123] The court also may hear evidence from any objectors to the settlement, court-appointed experts, or the preliminary opinions of a magistrate judge.

Typically, the court will receive written submissions from interested parties, including objectors, and then will conduct a formal evidentiary hearing, which may be brief or last several days.[124] Often the court will separate its consideration of class counsel's fee petition until after the court has determined whether to give final approval to the settlement agreement.

The Federal Judicial Center has suggested that in reviewing proposed class action settlements, judges must adopt the role of a skeptical client and critically examine the class certification elements, settlement terms, and proposed procedures, because typically there is no client with the motivation, knowledge, or resources to protect the interests of the class.[125] The Judicial Center describes the judge's role:

> To determine whether a proposed settlement is fair, reasonable, and adequate the court must examine whether the interests of the class are better served by the settlement than further litigation. Judicial review must be exacting and thorough. The task is demanding because the adversariness of litigation is often lost after the agreement to settle. The settling parties frequently make a joint presentation of the benefits of the settlement without significant information about any drawbacks. If objectors do not emerge, there may be no lawyers or litigants criticizing the settlement or seeking to expose flaws or abuses. Even if objectors are present, they may simply seek to be treated differently than the class as a whole, rather than advocating for classwide interests.[126]

The Federal Judicial Center also has identified at least ten potential abuses of class action settlements that courts need to be wary of when evaluating proposed settlements. These potential abuses include (1) conducting "reverse auctions"; (2) granting class members illusory nonmonetary benefits, such as coupon settlements, while granting substantial monetary attorney fee awards; (3) filing or

---

121. Manual for Complex Litigation (Fourth) § 21.635 (2004).

122. *Id.* at § 21.631.

123. Fed. R. Civ. P. 23(e)(2); Manual for Complex Litigation (Fourth) § 21.631 (2004).

124. *See, e.g., In re Silicone Gel Breast Implant Prods. Liab. Litig.*, No. CV 92-P-10000-S, 1994 WL 578353 (N.D. Ala. Sept. 1, 1994) (testimony from breast implant recipients during three days of testimony).

125. *Id.*

126. *Id.*

voluntarily dismissing class allegations for strategic purposes; (4) imposing strict eligibility conditions or cumbersome claims procedures on class members, particularly if unclaimed benefits revert to the defendants; (5) treating similarly situated class members differently; (6) releasing claims against parties who did not contribute to the settlement; (7) releasing claims of parties who received no compensation in the settlement; (8) setting attorney fees based on a very high valuation ascribed to nonmonetary relief awarded to the class (such as an injunction, medical monitoring, or coupons); (9) assessing class members for attorney fees in excess of the amount of damages awarded to each member; and (10) settlement of individual claims to extract an unreasonably high benefit for potential class representatives and their attorneys.[127]

The judge's final approval of a settlement will be guided by the particular set of factors articulated in that jurisdiction for assessing the fairness, reasonableness, and adequacy of the settlement, as delineated above.

VII. Implications of the Class Action Fairness Act of 2005 for Class Action Settlements

Through the Class Action Fairness Act of 2005,[128] Congress created new federal jurisdiction for class actions[129] and a new removal provision to enable defendants to remove state class actions into federal court.[130] The jurisdictional provisions of CAFA are beyond the scope of this chapter.[131] However, it may be noted that CAFA has had an impact on the forum in which class actions are now litigated, with more cases removed into federal court or initiated there as a matter of first filing.[132] Consequently, greater numbers of class actions are subject to CAFA's provisions relating to class settlement. In addition, there is anecdotal evidence that

---

127. *Id.*

128. CAFA, *supra* note 4.

129. 28 U.S.C. § 1332(d).

130. *Id.* at § 1453.

131. *See generally* Anna Andreeva, *Class Action Fairness Act of 2005: The Eight Year Saga Is Finally Over,* 59 MIAMI L. REV. 385 (2005); Joseph M. Callow Jr., *The Class Action Fairness Act of 2005: An Overview and Analysis,* 52 FED. LAW. 26 (2005); Anthony Rollo & Gabriel A. Crowson, *Mapping the New Class Action Frontier—A Primer on the Class Action Fairness Act and Amended Rule 23,* 59 CONSUMER FIN. L.Q. REP. 11 (2005); David F. Herr & Michael C. McCarthy, *The Class Action Fairness Act of 2005—Congress Again Wades into Complex Litigation Management,* 228 F.R.D. 673 (2005); Georgene M. Vairo, *Class Action Fairness Act of 2005: With Commentary and Analysis* (2005).

132. *See* EMERY G. LEE III & THOMAS E. WILLGING, THE IMPACT OF THE CLASS ACTION FAIRNESS ACT OF 2005 ON THE FEDERAL COURTS: FOURTH INTERIM REPORT TO THE JUDICIAL CONFERENCE ADVISORY COMMITTEE ON CIVIL RULES (Federal Judicial Center 2008); THOMAS E. WILLGING & EMERY G. LEE III, THE IMPACT OF THE CLASS ACTION FAIRNESS ACT OF 2005 ON THE FEDERAL COURTS: THIRD INTERIM REPORT TO THE JUDICIAL CONFERENCE ADVISORY COMMITTEE ON CIVIL RULES (Federal Judicial Center 2007); THOMAS E. WILLGING & EMERY G. LEE III, THE IMPACT OF THE CLASS ACTION FAIRNESS ACT OF 2005: SECOND INTERIM REPORT TO THE JUDICIAL CONFERENCE ADVISORY COMMITTEE ON CIVIL RULES (Federal Judicial Center 2006); *see also* THOMAS E. WILLGING & SHANNON R. WHEATMAN,

some state court judges are adhering to CAFA requirements relating to class action settlements in state court, even though these jurisdictions are not subject to CAFA's provisions.

CAFA contains four central provisions relating to class action settlements: (1) coupon settlements;[133] (2) protection against loss by class members;[134] (3) protection against discrimination based on geographic location;[135] and (4) required notifications to appropriate federal and state officials.[136]

A. COUPON SETTLEMENTS

Critics of class action abuse lobbied Congress to include provisions in CAFA to address the problems of worthless coupons or coupons of such little value that few class members were incentivized to redeem those coupons. Consequently, the award of attorney fees under section 1712 (the provision addressing coupon settlements) is subject to the court's approval,[137] upon a hearing to determine that the settlement is fair, adequate, and reasonable to class members.[138] At their discretion, courts may seek the assistance of expert witness testimony to provide information on the actual value of coupons that class members redeem.[139]

CAFA links the redemption of coupons to the award of attorney fees. Thus, in a class action that awards class members coupons—if the value of coupons is used to determine an attorney fee award—then the portion of any attorney fee award that is attributable to the award of coupons is required to be based on the value to class members of the coupons actually redeemed.[140]

However, if a portion of the class recovery of the coupons is not used to determine the attorney fees, then the fee award shall be based upon the amount of time the attorney reasonably expended working on the action.[141] In approving an attorney fee request under section 1712, the court also shall include an appropriate attorney fee for obtaining equitable relief, such as an injunction.[142] In addition, nothing in section 1712 prohibits the court from applying the lodestar/multiplier methodology to determine a fee award in a coupon settlement.[143] In class action settlements that

---

FED. JUDICIAL CTR., ATTORNEY CHOICE OF FORUM IN CLASS ACTION LITIGATION: WHAT DIFFERENCE DOES IT MAKE? (2006).

133. 28 U.S.C. § 1712.

134. *Id.* at § 1713.

135. *Id.* at § 1714.

136. *Id.* at § 1715.

137. Class action attorney fees also are subject to the requirements of Rule 23(h).

138. 28 U.S.C. § 1712(e).

139. *Id.* at § 1712(d).

140. *Id.* at § 1712(a).

141. *Id.* at § 1712(b)(1).

142. *Id.* at § 1712(b)(2).

143. *Id.*

combine both coupons and equitable relief, courts are instructed to combine both methodologies: redemption rates as well as time reasonably expended on the action.[144]

Finally, courts may order that the settlement agreement provide for a cy pres distribution of unclaimed coupons to charitable or governmental entities, as the parties agree.[145] If unclaimed coupons are awarded on a cy pres basis, they may not be used to calculate the attorney fees.[146]

Clearly, the thrust of the CAFA provisions relating to coupon settlements is to create a serious disincentive to the parties to offer coupons as a form of class relief.[147] To date, CAFA seems to have accomplished its intended effect, with settlement parties largely eschewing conventional coupon settlements in their settlement agreements.

B. PROTECTION AGAINST LOSS BY CLASS MEMBERS

Another class action abuse CAFA intends to address is how class members may, through the terms of the settlement agreement, be obligated to pay class counsel fees at a net loss to the class member. In some notorious class settlements, attorney fee sums paid to class counsel have exceeded the recovery returned to the class member; hence, some class members have suffered a negative loss as a consequence of being a member of a class action.[148] This negative loss situation is particularly acute where the classwide relief is equitable, and there is no monetary recovery to individual class members.

To this end, section 1713 provides simply that "[t]he court may approve a proposed settlement under which any class member is obligated to pay sums to class counsel that would result in a net loss to the class member only if the court makes a written finding that nonmonetary benefits to the class member substantially outweigh the monetary loss."[149]

C. PROTECTION AGAINST DISCRIMINATION BASED ON GEOGRAPHY

The jurisdictional provisions of CAFA are intended to authorize nationwide or multistate class actions of significant national interest in the federal courts. In multistate or national class actions, class counsel and the class representatives may be

---

144. *Id.* at § 1712(c).

145. *Id.* at § 1712(e).

146. *Id.*

147. *See* Andrew McGuiness & Richard Gottlieb, *New Class Action Law Contains Pitfalls for Defendants,* 28 CHI. LAW. 60 (2005) (commenting on coupon settlement provisions in CAFA); *see also* Guy V. Amoresano & Michael R. McDonald, *Class Litigants Face Tougher Forum: Will Closer Scrutiny by Federal Judges Curb Costs?,* 180 N.J.L.J. 282 (2005) ("[C]oupon settlements will be increasingly less attractive for the plaintiffs' bar and potential defendants."). *But cf.* Day, *supra* note 66.

148. *See, e.g., Kamilewicz v. Bank of Boston,* 100 F.3d 1348, 1349 (7th Cir. 1996) (Easterbrook, J., dissenting from denial of rehearing en banc; class member received award of $2.19, but $91.33 deducted from class member's bank account for attorney's fees).

149. 28 U.S.C. § 1713.

drawn from one location and may file their action in a particular forum. In order to guard against the forum favoring one group of class members over another based on geographic location, CAFA prohibits such geographic discrimination: "The court may not approve a proposed settlement that provides for the payment of greater sums to some class members than to others based solely on the basis that the class members to whom the greater sums are to be paid are located in closer geographic proximity to the court."[150]

D. NOTIFICATIONS TO APPROPRIATE FEDERAL AND STATE OFFICIALS

As indicated above, CAFA has introduced an oversight role for federal and state governmental officials as a consequence of the new mandatory notice provisions.[151] CAFA's provisions for notice to governmental officials are lengthy and highly detailed.

In essence, however, the CAFA settlement notice provisions require that not later than ten days after the parties file a proposed settlement with the court, each defendant in a settlement proposal must serve upon appropriate state officials of each state in which a class member resides, and the appropriate federal official, a notice of the proposed settlement.[152] The statute sets forth a detailed description of the required information that the notice must contain in order to inform appropriate officials of the terms of the settlement.[153]

---

150. *Id.* at § 1714.
151. *See id.* at § 1715.
152. *Id.* at § 1715(b).
153. *Id.* at § 1715(b)(1)–(8), which includes:

> (b) In general.—Not later than 10 days after a proposed settlement of a class action is filed in court, each defendant that is participating in the proposed settlement shall serve upon the appropriate State official of each State in which a class member resides and the appropriate Federal official, a notice of the proposed settlement consisting of—
> (1) a copy of the complaint and any materials filed with the complaint and any amended complaints (except such materials shall not be required to be served if such materials are made electronically available through the Internet and such service includes notice of how to electronically access such material);
> (2) notice of any scheduled judicial hearing in the class action;
> (3) any proposed or final notification to class members of–
>   (A) (i) the members' rights to request exclusion from the class action; or
>   (ii) if no right to request exclusion exists, a statement that no such right exists; and
>   (B) a proposed settlement of a class action;
> (4) any proposed or final class action settlement;
> (5) any settlement or other agreement contemporaneously made between class counsel and counsel for the defendants;
> (6) any final judgment or notice of dismissal;
> (7) (A) if feasible, the names of class members who reside in each State and the estimated proportionate share of the claims of such members to the entire settlement to that State's appropriate State official; or

CAFA provides appropriate state and federal officials with 90 days in which to review a proposed settlement and to make a determination whether the officials will appear and raise objections concerning the settlement.[154] A court may not issue an order approving a settlement within this time window.

If a defendant does not comply with the CAFA provisions relating to notice to appropriate officials, the consequences can be extreme for the noncomplying defendant. The statute specifies that if notice is not provided, then a class member may refuse to comply with a settlement, and may choose not to be bound by a settlement agreement.[155]

Hence, in order to secure the binding effects of a settlement, CAFA incentivizes defendants to comply with CAFA's notice provisions or forfeit that binding effect as to some or all members of the class. Even more important, the CAFA notice provisions encourage settling parties to craft better settlements in order to avoid lengthy challenges by governmental agencies that might undermine or invalidate the settlement. It should be noted, though, that the CAFA notice requirements impose an additional cost on the defendants of supplying notice to governmental officials, which in turn may inspire further expenses in responding to any challenges to the settlement that are raised by governmental officials after notice of the settlement.

E. EFFECTS OF CAFA ON CLASS ACTION SETTLEMENTS

CAFA has been in effect for approximately five years, but very few class actions subject to CAFA have progressed through the settlement stage. Instead, most litigation in federal court relating to CAFA has centered on CAFA's original and removal jurisdiction provisions. Therefore, it will take additional time for courts to be confronted with interpreting and applying the CAFA settlement requirements and for standards to be developed under these provisions.

Anecdotally, it appears that settling parties are eschewing coupon settlements because of CAFA's link between such settlements and attorney fees. In addition, practicing lawyers are highly cognizant of CAFA's new notice requirements, and defendants are especially concerned with determining which governmental officials are "appropriate" for notice based on the nature of the class settlement.

    (B) if the provision of information under subparagraph (A) is not feasible, a reasonable estimate of the number of class members residing in each State and the estimated proportionate share of the claims of such members to the entire settlement; and

       (8) any written judicial opinion relating to the materials described under subparagraphs (3) through (6).

154. *Id.* at § 1715(d).
155. *Id.* at § 1715(e).

ATTORNEY FEE AWARDS AND INCENTIVE PAYMENTS

CLIFFORD H. WALSTON

I. Introduction

Class actions present unique issues in the award of attorney fees. As the Supreme Court has noted, "Courts have struggled to formulate the proper measure for determining the 'reasonableness' of a particular fee award."[1] Great care should be taken in any practitioner's request for fees because awards of attorney fees have come under increased scrutiny in the judicial and political arenas. The issue originates from two competing judicial doctrines. The first is grounded in quantum meruit and unjust enrichment in the sense that absent class members should not be unjustly enriched by the efforts of the class representative who retains class counsel to achieve a benefit for all.[2] Absent class members, therefore, should compensate class counsel for their efforts through an award of fees from the common fund.[3] The second reflects the reality that in making a claim for fees on the common fund, class counsel cease to act in a fiduciary capacity representing the interests of the class and become claimants against the fund representing their own interests.[4]

Thus, the trial court assumes the fiduciary role for the benefit of the absent class members to ensure that any distribution reasonably compensates counsel for their contributions made in securing the common fund for the class. The court's review of the attorney fees component of a settlement agreement is an essential

---

1. *Pennsylvania v. Del. Valley Citizens' Council for Clean Air*, 478 U.S. 546, 562 (1986).

2. MANUAL FOR COMPLEX LITIGATION (FOURTH) § 14.12 (2004).

3. 4 WILLIAM RUBENSTEIN, ALBA CONTE & HERBERT B. NEWBERG, NEWBERG ON CLASS ACTIONS: A MANUAL FOR GROUP LITIGATION AT FEDERAL AND STATE LEVELS § 14:6 (4th ed. 2002 and Supp. 2009) [hereinafter NEWBERG].

4. *Court Awarded Attorneys' Fees, Report of the Third Circuit Task Force* (Oct. 8, 1985), 108 F.R.D. 237, 251.

part of its role as guardian of the interests of class members.[5] To properly fulfill its Rule 23(e) duty, a court must not cursorily approve the attorney fees provision of a class settlement or delegate that duty to the parties.[6] Even when the district court finds the settlement agreement to be untainted by collusion, fraud, or other irregularities, the court must thoroughly review an attorney fee award.[7]

In doing so, courts employ both the hourly-based lodestar method and the percentage-of-the-common-fund method of determining a reasonable fee. In either method, the party requesting attorney fees bears the burden of demonstrating entitlement to the fees through documentation of its efforts in the litigation.[8] As a result, accurate time records detailing the efforts of counsel have become paramount in any request for attorney fees, regardless of the methodology utilized in calculating the fee award and regardless of any contingency fee nature of the underlying representation. Simply put, keeping accurate and detailed records of counsel's efforts in the litigation is the single most important step practitioners can take to ensure reasonable compensation for the tremendous efforts often associated with litigating class claims. Without such records, the likelihood of a substantial award of attorney fees is extremely low, despite the efforts and contributions of counsel in achieving a benefit for the class.[9]

II. Source of Fee Award

Although the "American Rule" generally requires a litigant to bear the cost of its own representation, the U.S. Supreme Court has established the "common-fund exception," which allows a court to award attorney fees to a party whose litigation efforts directly benefit others.[10] This is particularly applicable in the class action context when a fund is established for the benefit of members of a class by the efforts of counsel through settlement or a verdict. In such a situation, it is appropriate for the trial court to shift the costs associated with establishment of the fund to those who enjoy its benefit through an award of attorney fees that reasonably compensate counsel for the efforts associated with creation of the fund.[11]

---

5. *Strong v. BellSouth Telecomm., Inc.*, 137 F.3d 844, 850 (5th Cir. 1998).

6. *In re High Sulfur Content Prod. Liab. Litig.*, 517 F.3d 220, 228 (5th Cir. 2008).

7. *Strong*, 137 F.3d at 850.

8. *Hensley v. Eckerhart*, 461 U.S. 424, 437 (1983).

9. For examples of the detail necessary for a reviewing court to conduct an adequate review of that attorneys' fee award, *see In re Enron Corp. Sec., Derivative & ERISA Litig.*, 586 F. Supp. 2d 732 (S.D. Tex. 2008), and *In re Copley Pharm., Inc.*, 50 F. Supp. 2d 1141 (D. Wyo. 1999), *aff'd*, 232 F.3d 900 (10th Cir. 2000). The Fifth Circuit described *Copley* as "a helpful model for other district courts." *In re High Sulfur Content*, 517 F.3d at 233.

10. *Chambers v. NASCO, Inc.*, 501 U.S. 32, 45 (1991); *Alyeska Pipeline Serv. Co. v. Wilderness Soc'y*, 421 U.S. 240, 259 (1975).

11. *Alyeska Pipeline Serv. Co.*, 421 U.S. at 257.

Most often, courts utilize the percentage-of-the-fund method in common-fund cases,[12] although the lodestar method is also appropriate in common-fund cases in certain jurisdictions.[13]

In addition, many federal statutes include fee-shifting provisions permitting a court to assess the costs and attorney fees of a prevailing party against another litigant.[14] These statutes provide an incentive for the public to enforce certain federal statutes, particularly if the potential relief is purely injunctive or nominal.[15] To determine a reasonable fee pursuant to a fee-shifting statute, federal courts employ the lodestar method.[16]

III. Determining Reasonable Attorney Fees in Common-Fund Cases

The common-fund exception to the American Rule permits courts to grant an award of reasonable costs and attorney fees from the common fund.[17] The method for determining that award, however, varies by jurisdiction and is a constantly shifting landscape. Some jurisdictions, such as the Third Circuit, prefer to calculate an award based upon a percentage of the recovery of the fund because "it allows courts to award fees from the fund in a manner that rewards counsel for success and penalizes it for failure."[18] Others, such as the Second Circuit, permit an award based on either a percentage or a lodestar basis, although the trend is toward utilization of the percentage method in nonstatutory fee-shifting cases.[19] The Second Circuit disfavors application of the lodestar method because it is perceived to disincentivize early settlements, tempts lawyers to run up their hours, and requires courts to engage in a "gimlet-eyed review of line-item fee audits."[20] Yet other circuits, notably the Fifth Circuit, currently utilize solely the lodestar

---

12. *See, e.g., Gottlieb v. Barry*, 43 F.3d 474, 482 (10th Cir. 1994) (recognizing "the more recent trend has been toward utilizing the percentage method in common fund cases"); *In re Am. Bank Note*, 127 F. Supp. 2d 418, 431 (S.D.N.Y. 2001) ("Although the law in the Circuit has not been uniform, the trend of the district courts in this Circuit is to use the percentage of the fund approach to calculate attorneys' fees.").

13. *In re High Sulfur Content*, 517 F.3d at 228 (stating that "[t]his circuit requires district courts to use the 'lodestar method' to 'assess attorneys' fees in class action suits'" in a common fund case).

14. 4 Newberg § 14:1 (citing Manual for Complex Litigation (Third), § 24.11 at 186–87 (1995)).

15. *Id.* at § 14:3.

16. *City of Burlington v. Dague*, 505 U.S. 557, 562 (1992).

17. Manual for Complex Litigation (Third) § 24.11 (1995).

18. *In re AT&T Corp. Sec. Litig.*, 455 F.3d 160, 164 (3d Cir. 2006) (internal citations and quotations omitted).

19. *Wal-Mart Stores, Inc. v. Visa U.S.A. Inc.*, 396 F.3d 96, 121 (2d Cir. 2005); *In re Merrill Lynch Tyco Research Sec. Litig.*, 249 F.R.D. 124, 136 (S.D.N.Y. 2008).

20. *In re Merrill Lynch Tyco Research*, 249 F.R.D. at 136.

approach, although courts in the circuit have employed the percentage-of-the-fund method in the past.[21]

A. PERCENTAGE-OF-THE-FUND METHOD

There is no general rule on what constitutes a reasonable percentage for an award of attorney fees from a common fund. Courts, however, are directed to "do their best" to award counsel the "market price for legal services" taking into consideration certain factors.[22] The Ninth Circuit has established a benchmark of 25 percent that may be utilized by a court in common-fund class action settlements so long as the court also considers any "special circumstances" of the case that would dictate a higher or lower award.[23] Indeed, most awards appear to fall in the range of 20 to 33 percent; however, many exceptions exist.[24] Generally, 50 percent is the maximum fee that is considered reasonable.[25] By contrast, in so-called megafund cases, the trend is to set a lower percentage award for attorney fees based on the rationale that a smaller percentage of such a large fund would reasonably compensate the counsel involved.[26] In such cases, the percentage award of the fund attributable to fees generally range from 10 to 25 percent and can often include a staggered percentage of recovery that declines as the size of the fund increases.[27]

In establishing an appropriate percentage, courts are directed to look at a number of factors that generally fall into five categories: (1) issues related to counsel, including the time and labor expended together with the skill and efficiency of counsel; (2) issues related to the litigation, including its complexity, duration, and risk; (3) the size of the fund created and the number of persons benefited; (4) results and awards in similar cases; and (5) other factors, including public policy concerns and the presence or absence of objections by members of the class.[28] These factors are subjective in nature and give a court wide latitude in establishing the reasonable percentage. However, the Seventh Circuit has consistently rejected the "degree of success" of the litigation as a standard on which to base an award of

---

21. *In re High Sulfur Content*, 517 F.3d at 228 (stating that "[t]his circuit requires district courts to use the 'lodestar method' to 'assess attorneys' fees in class action suits'"). *But see* 4 NEWBERG § 14:6 nn. 12–13 (identifying several Fifth Circuit cases from the 1990s utilizing the percentage method).

22. *In re Synthroid Mktg. Litig.*, 264 F.3d 712, 718 (7th Cir. 2001).

23. *In re Ventro Corp. Sec. Litig.*, 226 F. App'x 711, 711 (9th Cir. 2007).

24. 4 NEWBERG § 14:6.

25. *Id.* at n.8.

26. *In re Synthroid Mktg. Litig.*, 325 F.3d 974, 975 (7th Cir. 2003).

27. *See* 4 NEWBERG § 14:6; *In re Synthroid Mktg. Litig.*, 325 F.3d at 975, 980 (rejecting a 10 percent absolute cap in megafund cases and applying a staggered percentage of recovery based upon market forces); *In re Currency Conversion Fee Antitrust Litig.*, MDL No. 1409, Cause No. M 21-95, ___ F.R.D. ___, 2009 WL 3415155 at *19 (S.D.N.Y. 2009) (upholding an award of attorney fees of 15.25 percent and reviewing numerous awards in megafund cases ranging from 15 to 20 percent).

28. *Gunter v. Redwood Energy Corp.*, 223 F.3d 190, 195 (3d Cir. 2000); *Goldberger v. Integrated Res., Inc.*, 209 F.3d 43, 50 (2d Cir. 2000).

attorney fees in the common-fund context, presumably because the degree of success is already subsumed in the size of the fund and does not reflect its preferred market-based approach.[29]

Practitioners requesting an award of attorney fees predicated on a percentage basis would be wise to explain to the court in great detail their efforts and contributions in achieving the common fund, being sure to distinguish their efforts from those of other groups such as governmental agencies.[30] In doing so, counsel should focus on the complexities of the case and any potential unique or novel issues. In addition, counsel should be familiar with the range of awards in similar cases with similar-sized common funds, as this seems to be a key factor in trial courts' analyses of the issues. Finally, in at least two jurisdictions, the Second and Third Circuits, courts are also required to conduct a lodestar analysis as a "cross check" on the percentage-of-fund recovery method to ensure its fairness,[31] thereby memorializing the observations of researchers that awards of attorney fees tend to generally result in similar awards regardless of whether the percentage-of-the-common-fund or lodestar method is utilized.

B. LODESTAR METHOD AND THE *JOHNSON* FACTORS

Two competing hourly-based methodologies were developed in the 1970s by the Third and Fifth Circuits in attempts to provide a framework for trial courts to determine the reasonableness of fee requests.[32] The first, developed by the Third Circuit, was the lodestar method, which sought to calculate a fee award based on a reasonable hourly rate multiplied by a reasonable number of hours worked.[33] This lodestar was then adjusted upward or downward based on case-specific considerations such as the "contingent nature of success" and the "quality of the attorneys' work."[34] The Fifth Circuit soon followed with a competing method in *Johnson v. Georgia Highway Express, Inc.*, that sought a more flexible approach that did not "reduce the calculation of a reasonable fee to mathematical precision," but instead required a court to evaluate 12 factors, most of which are highly subjective, in arriving at a reasonable fee.[35] In theory, a court utilizing the lodestar method was expected to consider fewer variables than a district court utilizing the *Johnson* method. In practice, however, both methods considered substantially the same set of factors, just at different points in time. Indeed, the two methods have largely

---

29. *Sutton v. Bernard*, 504 F. 3d 688, 693 (7th Cir. 2007); *In re Synthroid Mktg. Litig.*, 264 F.3d at 718.

30. *In re AT&T Corp.*, 455 F.3d at 165–66.

31. *Id.* at 164; *Wal-Mart Stores*, 396 F.3d at 123.

32. For a history of attorney fee jurisprudence, *see* the Second Circuit's discussion in *Arbor Hill Concerned Citizens Neighborhood Ass'n v. County of Albany*, 522 F.3d 182, 186–90 (2d Cir. 2008).

33. *Lindy Bros. Builders, Inc. v. Am. Radiator & Standard Sanitary Corp.*, 487 F.2d 161 (3d Cir. 1973).

34. *Id.* at 168.

35. 488 F.2d 714 (5th Cir. 1974) (declining to limit fee award to amount stipulated in attorney-client agreement), *abrogated on other grounds by Blanchard v. Bergeron*, 489 U.S. 87, 92–93 (1989).

collapsed into one, with the Fifth Circuit now characterizing its approach as the "lodestar-fee and *Johnson* analysis."[36]

C. CALCULATION OF THE LODESTAR

A district court using this method first sets the lodestar by multiplying the reasonable number of hours expended by a reasonable hourly rate.[37] In calculating the reasonable number of hours expended, courts will scrutinize the lawyers' time records and other documentation to eliminate unnecessary and unproductive work and any efforts relating to nonlegal work.[38]

The party seeking attorney fees is charged with the burden of showing the reasonableness of the hours billed and with proving that it exercised billing judgment, which requires documentation of the hours charged and of the hours written off as unproductive, excessive, or redundant.[39] Failure to meet this burden may result in a "reduction of the award by a percentage intended to substitute for the exercise of billing judgment."[40] In addition, "[i]f more than one attorney is involved, the possibility of duplication of effort along with the proper utilization of time should be scrutinized. The time of two or three lawyers in a courtroom or conference when one would do may be obviously discounted."[41] This scrutiny highlights the importance of detailed record keeping. In preparing detailed, contemporaneous time records, a practitioner can provide the court with the necessary understanding of the nature of the work performed in support of the fee request.

The reasonable hourly rate is generally regarded as the market rate for the forum in which the litigation is pending, regardless of the actual billing rates of the lawyers engaged in the litigation.[42] According to the forum rule, courts should generally utilize the hourly rates employed in the district in which the reviewing court sits in calculating the reasonable hourly rate.[43] In order to establish the reasonable hourly rate for the forum, litigants often utilize affidavits from other lawyers who practice in the district, as well as hourly-rate surveys.[44] "The evidence to support an hourly rate entails more than an affidavit of the attorney performing the work, but must also address the rates actually billed and paid in similar lawsuits."[45]

---

36. *McClain v. Lufkin Indus., Inc.*, 519 F.3d 264, 284 (5th Cir. 2008).

37. *Blum v. Stenson*, 465 U.S. 886, 888 (1984); *Lindy Bros. Builders*, 487 F.2d at 168–69.

38. *Hensley*, 461 U.S. at 434.

39. *Saizan v. Delta Concrete Prods. Co., Inc.*, 448 F.3d 795, 799 (5th Cir. 2006).

40. *Id.*

41. *Abrams v. Baylor Coll. of Med.*, 805 F.2d 528, 535 (5th Cir. 1986).

42. *Blum*, 465 U.S. at 895–96; *Simmons v. N.Y. City Transit Auth.*, 575 F.3d 170, 174–75 (2d Cir. 2009).

43. *Simmons*, 575 F.3d at 174.

44. *See, e.g., Saizan*, 448 F.3d at 756, 780–81.

45. *Watkins v. Input/Output, Inc.*, 531 F. Supp. 2d 777, 784 (S.D. Tex. 2007).

To compensate for the delay in receiving fees often associated with contingency fee cases, courts have approved of the use of current billing rates.[46] In addition, an issue that often arises in the lodestar calculation is how to account for paralegals and contract lawyers. Class counsel often hire contract lawyers and use paralegals to perform certain tasks throughout the course of litigation and seek compensation for that time based upon the billing rate of the paralegal or contract lawyer as opposed to the actual cost. Objectors often argue that class counsel should be reimbursed the actual cost of the contract lawyer as an expense. Courts have generally resolved this issue in favor of class counsel, permitting them to recover the higher billing rate for paralegals and contract lawyers.[47]

D. ADJUSTMENTS TO THE LODESTAR

As noted, the *Johnson* court posited 12 factors (derived directly from the American Bar Association Code of Professional Responsibility) to be considered in calculating a reasonable attorney fee:

1. the time and labor required;
2. the novelty and difficulty of the questions;
3. the skill required;
4. the preclusion of other employment by the lawyer;
5. the customary fee;
6. whether the fee is fixed or contingent;
7. time limitations imposed by the client or the circumstances;
8. the amount involved and the results obtained;
9. the experience, reputation, and ability of the lawyers;
10. the undesirability of the case;
11. the nature and length of the professional relationship with the client; and
12. awards in similar cases.[48]

Based on one or more *Johnson* factors, the court may apply a multiplier to adjust the lodestar up or down if the *Johnson* factor has not already been accounted for in the lodestar.[49] "[T]he district court must be careful . . . not to double count a *Johnson* factor already considered . . . when it determines the necessary adjustments."[50] Generally, "'novelty and complexity of the issues,' 'the special skill and experience of counsel,' the 'quality of the representation,' and 'the results obtained' from the litigation are presumably already encompassed in the lodestar and therefore should

---

46. *Missouri v. Jenkins*, 491 U.S. 274, 283–84 (1989).

47. *In re Enron Corp.*, 586 F. Supp. 2d at 782–86.

48. *Johnson*, 488 F.2d at 717–19; *see also Hensley*, 461 U.S. at 430 n.3.

49. *Strong*, 137 F.3d at 850; *In re Fender*, 12 F.3d 480, 487 (5th Cir. 1994).

50. *Shipes v. Trinity Indus.*, 987 F.2d 311, 320 (5th Cir. 1993).

generally not be used to enhance the award."[51] "Enhancements based upon these factors are only appropriate in rare cases supported by specific evidence in the record and detailed findings by the courts."[52]

Courts enhance such a fee award by applying a multiplier to the lodestar. The common range for multipliers is generally from one to four,[53] although larger multipliers have been awarded.[54] In order to support a request for a multiplier of the lodestar, a practitioner would be wise to cull case data and secondary sources[55] to provide the reviewing court with examples of multipliers in similar cases.

IV. Determining Reasonable Attorney Fees in Statutory Fee-Shifting Cases

In an effort to provide access to legal representation and to encourage citizens to enforce certain laws as private attorney generals, more than 200 federal statutes provide for fee shifting to successful litigants.[56] These statutes encourage enforcement of areas of the law normally reserved for governmental action, such as civil rights, environmental protection, and employment discrimination.[57] In statutory fee-shifting cases, federal courts utilize the lodestar method to calculate reasonable attorney fees.[58] As discussed in greater detail above, the lodestar method seeks to derive a reasonable fee by multiplying a reasonable hourly rate by a reasonable

51. *In re Enron Corp.*, 586 F. Supp. 2d at 785–86.

52. *Walker v. U.S. Dep't of Housing and Urban Dev.*, 99 F.3d 761, 771 (5th Cir. 1996) (internal quotations omitted).

53. *See, e.g., In re Prudential Ins. Co. Am. Sales Practice Litig. Agent Actions*, 148 F.3d 283, 341 (3d Cir. 1998) ("[M]ultiples ranging from one to four are frequently awarded in common fund cases when the lodestar method is applied.") (quoting 3 NEWBERG § 14.03 at 14-5); *see also Vizcaino v. Microsoft Corp.*, 290 F.3d 1043, 1051 n.6 (9th Cir. 2002) (citing to the accompanying appendix that reviewed 24 attorney fees awards in class actions and found that 20 of the 24 awards (83 percent) contained a multiplier that fell within the range of one to four); *In re Enron Corp.*, 586 F. Supp. 2d at 798–99 (reviewing various sources indicating that a multiplier of 4.5 was the average award in cases over $100 million).

54. *In re Cardinal Health*, 528 F. Supp. 2d 752, 768 (S.D. Ohio 2007) (award of 18 percent and multiplier of six); *In re Rite Aid Corp. Sec. Litig.*, 362 F. Supp. 2d 587, 590 (E.D. Pa. 2005) (awarding a 25 percent fee award and finding the resulting multiplier of 6.96 reasonable); *In re Charter Commc'ns, Inc. Sec. Litig.*, No. 4:02-CV-1186 CAS, 2005 WL 4045741 (E.D. Mo. June 30, 2005) (20 percent of $146,250,000 settlement fund and multiplier of 5.6); *Roberts v. Texaco, Inc.*, 979 F. Supp. 185, 198 (S.D.N.Y. 1997) (16.66 percent of $115 million common fund and multiplier of 5.5); *In re RJR Nabisco, Inc. Sec. Litig.*, No. 88 Civ. 7905, 1992 WL 210138 (S.D.N.Y. Aug. 24, 1992) (awarding 30 percent of $72.5 million with multiplier of six).

55. *See, e.g.,* Stuart J. Logan, Jack Moshman & Beverly C. Moore, Jr., *Attorney Fee Awards in Common Fund Class Actions*, 24 CLASS ACTION REP. 169 (Mar.–Apr. 2003).

56. 4 NEWBERG § 14:3; John F. Vargo, *The American Rule on Attorney Fee Allocation: The Injured Person's Access to Justice*, 42 AM. U. L. REV. 1567, 1576 (1993).

57. *See, e.g.,* Civil Rights Act of 1964, 42 U.S.C. § 2000a-3(b); Clean Air Act, 42 U.S.C. § 7604(d); Age Discrimination Act of 1967, 29 U.S.C. § 626(b).

58. *Dague*, 505 U.S. at 562.

number of hours for the work performed.[59] However, a battleground has emerged as to whether this lodestar is subject to enhancement for certain factors such as the contingency nature of the engagement or superior results being obtained by the lawyers representing the successful litigants, i.e., several of the *Johnson* factors.[60]

In analyzing this issue, the Supreme Court applied the lodestar method in *City of Burlington v. Dague*[61] and held that any enhancement to the lodestar to account for the contingent risk of a case is improper. Specifically, the Court stated that the lodestar already encompasses the contingent risk associated with the case "either in the higher number of hours expended to overcome the difficulty [of establishing the merits of the claim], or in the higher hourly rate of the attorney skilled and experienced enough to do so."[62] Enhancing the lodestar amount to reflect the contingent risk of the case would result in double counting of this factor.[63] Thus, the Supreme Court has established a "strong presumption" that the unadjusted lodestar amount represents the "reasonable" fee.[64]

With the door to fee enhancement based upon contingent risk seeming closed, the debate has shifted to enhancements based upon the quality and success of the legal representation. The Supreme Court has instructed lower courts to end their calculation after computing the time-rate lodestar amount and to apply a multiplier or enhancement to the time-rate lodestar only in "rare" and "exceptional" cases; however, the Court has not provided much guidance into what circumstances qualify as "rare" or "exceptional."[65] Some courts, such as the Sixth and Eleventh Circuits, have permitted fee enhancements predicated on the success of the litigation in the past.[66]

However, the Eleventh Circuit recently revisited the issue in a rather extraordinary opinion in *Kenny A. v. Perdue*.[67] In that case, Judge Carnes provided a detailed review of the history of Supreme Court precedent on fee-shifting enhancement jurisprudence, ultimately concluding that it is clearly improper for a court to enhance the lodestar amount in recognition of "superior results" obtained by counsel.[68] The rationale for Judge Carnes's position appears to be threefold. First, the "quality of the representation" is often already reflected in the high hourly

---

59. *Blum*, 465 U.S. at 888; *Lindy Bros. Builders*, 487 F.2d at 168–69.

60. *See, e.g., Kenny A. v. Perdue*, 532 F.3d 1209, 1239–40 (11th Cir. 2008) (discussing the Sixth Circuit's position in *Grier v. Sundquist*, 372 F.3d 784 (6th Cir. 2004)), *cert. granted*, 129 S. Ct. 1907 (2009).

61. 505 U.S. at 567.

62. *Id.* at 562.

63. *Id.* at 563.

64. *Id.* at 562.

65. *Del. Valley Citizens' Council*, 478 U.S. at 565.

66. *See Grier*, 372 F.3d at 784; *Norman v. Hous. Auth. of Montgomery*, 836 F.2d 1292, 1302 (11th Cir. 1988); *NAACP v. City of Evergreen*, 812 F.2d 1332, 1337 (11th Cir. 1987).

67. 532 F.3d 1209 (11th Cir. 2008), *cert. granted*, 129 S. Ct. 1907 (2009).

68. *Id.* at 1236.

rates requested by the lawyers (which, in *Perdue*, were awarded without any reduction as requested by class counsel), and an upward adjustment is only justified when the applicant can show that the result "was superior to that one reasonably should expect in light of the hourly rates charged and that the success was exceptional."[69] Second, the statutory purpose behind fee-shifting provisions is to provide adequate access to representation, not "to provide representation that will win plaintiffs more than a correct application of substantive and remedial law entitles them to receive."[70] Third, Judge Carnes took the position that there is no such thing as a "superior result," and no justification for an enhancement of a fee can exist on that basis.[71]

> To put it in an either-or manner, superb results are either what a fair application of the law produces, which means that they are not truly "superb," or they are results that exceed what the law allows and for that reason are beyond the purpose of the fee-shifting statutes. Those statutes are designed to provide a reasonable fee for a reasonable result, not an extraordinary fee for a result that goes beyond what the law would provide if the claims were litigated to their correct conclusion on the merits. Look at it this way. A merits-exceeding result for plaintiffs must be the product of one, or some combination, of the following factors: superior lawyering by plaintiffs' counsel, bad lawyering by defendants' counsel, poor decision making by the court, or dumb luck.[72]

Nevertheless, the court in *Perdue* ultimately affirmed the district court's fee enhancement based upon the "superior results" obtained by counsel because of prior Eleventh Circuit precedent in *Norman v. Housing Authority of Montgomery* and *NAACP v. City of Evergreen* that the panel was obligated to follow, despite its conclusion that the precedent was "wrong and conflict[ed] with relevant Supreme Court decisions."[73]

The Supreme Court granted certiorari, heard oral argument, and issued its opinion on April 21, 2010. Despite having the opportunity to provide meaningful guidance on the issue, the Court failed to do so. Instead, it merely reversed the lower courts, stating that statutory fee enhancements were appropriate in "rare" and "exceptional" circumstances, but the Court declined to elaborate on what exactly constituted such circumstances. Based upon the current landscape, therefore, it appears fee enhancements in statutory fee-shifting cases are largely inappropriate. Counsel requesting an award of attorney fees under a fee-shifting statute would be wise to factor in the contingency risk, complexity, and success of

---

69. *Id.* at 1222 (quoting *Blum*, 465 U.S. at 899 (internal quotations omitted)).
70. *Id.* at 1230.
71. *Id.* at 1230–31.
72. *Id.*
73. *Id.* at 1238 (citing *Norman*, 836 F.2d 1292, and *Evergreen*, 812 F.2d 1332).

the representation in the requested hourly rate used to compute the lodestar in the first instance, rather than request an enhancement of the fee award based upon the same factors.

V. Incentive Payments for Class Representatives

Generally, named plaintiffs are eligible for reasonable incentive payments for their participation in the pursuit of claims on behalf of the class.[74] In theory, these payments compensate the representative for his or her time and effort expended in support of the class, although courts have expressed a concern that these payments could serve as an inducement to entice a representative to support a marginal settlement.[75]

> [E]xcessive payments to named class members can be an indication that the agreement was reached through fraud or collusion. Indeed, if class representatives expect routinely to receive special awards in addition to their share of the recovery, they may be tempted to accept suboptimal settlements at the expense of class members whose interests they are appointed to guard.[76]

Therefore, the district court must evaluate their awards individually, using relevant factors, including the actions the plaintiff has taken to protect the interests of the class, the degree to which the class has benefited from those actions, the amount of time and effort the plaintiff expended in pursuing the litigation, and the reasonable fear of workplace retaliation, if any.[77]

Incentive payments are often relatively modest, most falling in the $5,000 to $25,000 range,[78] although some incentive payments have exceeded that amount.[79]

---

74. *Staton v. Boeing Co.*, 327 F.3d 938, 977 (9th Cir. 2003).

75. *Adderley v. Nat'l Football League Players Ass'n*, No. C-07-00943 WHA, 2009 WL 4250792 at *8 (N.D. Cal. 2009).

76. *Staton*, 327 F.3d at 977.

77. *Id.* (citing *Cook v. Niedert*, 142 F.3d 1004, 1016 (7th Cir. 1998)).

78. *See, e.g., In re Mego Fin. Corp. Sec. Litig.*, 213 F.3d 454, 463 (9th Cir. 2000) (approving incentive awards of $5,000 each to the two class representatives of 5,400 potential class members in a settlement of $1.725 million); *In re U.S. Bancorp Litig.*, 291 F.3d 1035, 1038 (8th Cir. 2002) (approving $2,000 incentive awards to five named plaintiffs out of a class potentially numbering more than 4 million in a settlement of $3 million); *Cook*, 142 F.3d at 1016 (approving, in the context of a recovery of more than $14 million, an incentive payment of $25,000 to one named plaintiff who "spent hundreds of hours with his attorneys and provided them with 'an abundance of information'"); *In the Matter of Cont'l Ill. Sec. Litig.*, 962 F.2d 566, 571–72 (7th Cir. 1992) (upholding a district court's rejection of a proposed $10,000 award to a named plaintiff "for his admittedly modest services"); *In re SmithKline Beecham Corp. Sec. Litig.*, 751 F. Supp. 525, 535 (E.D. Pa. 1990) (approving $5,000 awards for one named representative of each of nine plaintiff classes involving more than 22,000 claimants in a settlement of $22 million).

79. *See, e.g., Van Vranken v. Atl. Richfield Co.*, 901 F. Supp. 294, 300 (N.D. Cal. 1995) (approving an incentive award of $50,000 in a case involving an award of more than $76 million); *In re Dun & Bradstreet*

Large and disproportionate incentive payments, however, will draw added scrutiny from the court and result in either a reduction of the award or remand for reconsideration.[80]

VI. Conclusion

There can be little debate that awards of attorney fees in class actions have come under tremendous scrutiny. Given the responsibilities placed upon the trial court in its role as a fiduciary in reviewing any such award, counsel requesting attorney fees bear a significant burden in providing the court with the necessary evidence and legal authority to support such an award. More often than not, a request for attorney fees will be met with skepticism from the trial court, the court of appeals, or both. As a result, accurate, contemporaneous time records detailing the efforts of counsel coupled with relevant examples of fee awards in similar cases will be essential to any successful request for attorney fees, regardless of the methodology utilized in calculating the fee award. Without detailed record keeping, the likelihood of a substantial award of attorney fees is extremely low, despite the efforts and contributions of counsel in achieving a benefit for the class.

Credit Servs. Customer Litig., 130 F.R.D. 366, 374 (S.D. Ohio 1990) (approving incentive payments of $55,000 to two class representatives and $35,000 to three class representatives in a case with a total award of $18 million).

80. *See, e.g., Staton,* 327 F.3d at 977 (remanding for reconsideration of proposed incentive payments totaling $890,000 to 29 class representatives, averaging more than $30,000 per class representative, in a settlement of approximately $6.5 million); *See, e.g., Van Vranken,* 901 F. Supp. at 300 (reducing the requested award from $100,000 to $50,000 in a case involving an award of more than $76 million).

CHAPTER 9

CLAIMS ADMINISTRATION

DAVID HOLLAND

I. An Introduction to the Class Action Settlement Administration Process

While every class action settlement administration process is different, there are certain aspects most settlements have in common. This is especially true within certain practice areas: there are similarities common to securities settlements that differ from antitrust, consumer, or labor and employment settlements. This chapter will guide the newcomer to class action settlement administration through the process, and discuss some typical differentiators across practice areas.

A. PRE-SETTLEMENT CONSULTATION

The settlement administration process can—and often does—begin before a lawsuit is settled. Settlement administrators often serve as consultants, as well as fulfillment specialists. Prior to finalizing the settlement agreement, the parties to a lawsuit frequently consult with administrators on details of the feasibility or practicality of the settlement structure.

This consultation may be formal. For example, an administrator with the necessary resources may provide the parties and the court with an expert opinion on the effectiveness of a notice program or even design the notice program. As an example of informal consultation, an administrator may provide suggestions as to the structure or timeline for a claims or distribution process.

One of the most common topics during pre-settlement consultation is the claims filing rate. As counsel prepares for the settlement of a class action lawsuit and the subsequent administration, the defendant company, counsel for both sides, and the settlement administrator alike want to determine the likely claims filing rates. The information is useful to the parties in structuring a claims program that will receive a judge's approval, preparing to fund a settlement account, and assisting the administrator's planning.

There is no perfect way to predict claims filing rates for any particular settlement, but there are certain factors that allow for relatively accurate estimates. The following factors have an effect on the eventual claims filing rate:

- Case type
- Unpaid (earned) media attention
- Type and value of benefits
- Class demographics
- Type and scope of notice program and claim form design
- Claim process structure

Taking these factors into account, an experienced administrator can make a reasonable estimate as to the percentage of class members likely to file claims under a settlement. Through pre-settlement consultation, the parties are able to discuss such issues up front. And by considering potential pitfalls early and addressing them in the settlement agreement, the parties can avoid costly and time-consuming issues later in the process.

II. Class Data Management

Class data management is an integral (if overlooked) aspect of class action settlement administration that overarches all other processes. The class member database is used to enable and support all other processes: notification, claims processing, call center, and fund distribution. An administrator creates a custom database from one or more files containing any class member lists available. The administrator refines, or "cleanses," the data according to standard processes or agreed-upon criteria.

This processing of class member data benefits settlement administration in many ways.

- Normalizing data into a single format and layout, even when received from multiple sources in different formats and layouts, allows for simplified processing later in the administration process—e.g., for address look-ups.
- Performing de-duplication processing on the mailing list helps ensure that class members do not unnecessarily receive multiple notices, and that the mailing is as cost-effective as possible.
- Reviewing and processing records according to any settlement-specific criteria helps ensure that only class records are left in the database, thus avoiding the expense and confusion of sending notice to non–class members.
- Acquiring the most up-to-date addresses from the U.S. Postal Service helps ensure that the notice program is carried out accurately and that notices are received.

These processes take time, and the more data sources involved or data manipulation to be accomplished, the longer they take. The parties should involve their administrator as early as possible and set realistic timelines. Allow for sampling of the mailing list to ensure that all required processing has been conducted accurately.

III. Notification

With respect to notification, Rule 23(c)(2)(B) of the Federal Rules of Civil Procedure clearly states, "For any class certified under Rule 23(b)(3), the court must direct to class members the best notice that is practicable under the circumstances, including individual notice to all members who can be identified through reasonable effort."

Rule 23 requires that certain information be included in the notice. At minimum, it must "clearly and concisely state in plain, easily understood language":

- the nature of the action;
- the definition of the class certified;
- the class claims, issues, or defenses;
- that a class member may enter an appearance through a lawyer if the member so desires;
- that the court will exclude from the class any member who requests exclusion;
- the time and manner for requesting exclusion; and
- the binding effect of a class judgment on members under Rule 23(c)(3).

The Class Action Fairness Act of 2005 brought additional requirements to the parties. Not only must they notify potential class members of actions and settlements, but within ten days of filing a settlement, defendants must identify the appropriate federal and state officials and provide them with key information regarding the class action:

- The complaint and amended complaints filed
- Notice of any scheduled hearings
- Proposed or final notification to the class, including proposed settlement opt-out rights
- Proposed or final settlement agreement
- Agreements between class counsel and defense counsel
- Written judicial opinions regarding class notification, the settlement agreement, judgment, or dismissal
- If feasible, class member names and the proportionate share of their claims
- If feasible, a reasonable estimate of each state's class members and the proportionate share of their claims

The notification process can take several forms, with one major determinant of the form being whether class members are known up front. In some types of settlements, such as insurance settlements, for example, the defendants frequently have a relatively complete list of class members because they have had direct and documented contact with them. In others, such as indirect purchaser antitrust or consumer settlements, the identities of very few class members may be known up front because the defendants have had little to no contact with them. These varying circumstances make either direct or media-based notice more practicable.[1]

Regardless of the media selected to transmit the notice, it is essential that the parties consider the audience when drafting notice language. Rule 23(c)(2) requires that class action notices be written in "plain, easily understood language." Plain language is "more than just simplified language, or the elimination of legalese, jargon and complex language. Plain language is an approach to communicating based on who the audience is, and how best to deliver an understandable message."[2] Plain language takes into account factors such as font choices, font size, and readability level. Some examples of the presentation of information in notice materials by plain language principles include organizing information from the general to the more specific, using a table of contents, and placing the content into a question-and-answer format.

Legal requirements require not only that notice be provided in understandable language, but that any paid media notice plans be designed and implemented according to accepted and accredited methodologies used in the fields of advertising and media planning. *Daubert v. Merrell Dow Pharmaceuticals*[3] and *Kumho Tire Co. v. Carmichael*[4] require experts to employ the "same level of intellectual rigor that characterizes the practice of an expert in the relevant field."[5]

Direct notice is a form by which the parties (typically through an administrator) directly contact identified class members. This is most frequently accomplished through traditional mail. The parties have numerous options in the format of direct, mailed notice, ranging from simple postcards to complex packages containing multiple documents and forms. An administrator generally formats the notice text and claim form and selects paper sizes to ensure reasonable printing and mailing costs.

---

1. *See also* Chapter 20.C, "Reality Check: The State of New Media Options for Class Notice."

2. Katherine Kinsella, Plain Language Primer for Class Action Notice (2009), *available at* http://www.kinsellamedia.com (adapted and expanded from an earlier version published in 3 CLASS ACTION LITIG. REP. (BNA) 688–91 (Oct. 25, 2002)); *see also* Chapter 20.B, "The Plain Language Toolkit for Class Action Notice."

3. 509 U.S. 579 (1993).

4. 526 U.S. 137 (1999).

5. *Id.* at 141.

A primary challenge when dealing with notification of class members by direct mail is a poor-quality list. In addition to certain class members simply having never been on the list, there are also typically class members found on the list whose mailing addresses have changed, who are included in exact or (more problematically) not-exact duplicate, or whose information was not completely or properly captured in the creation of the list. An administrator or vendor can take certain steps up front to improve the quality of the mailing list, such as comparing the addresses with National Change of Address information, identifying and removing duplicate records, and formatting addresses to meet postal standards.

Rates of undeliverable mail vary across settlements, based largely on the age of the mailing list and the demographics of the class. To expect 10 percent of mail to be returned is a reasonable assumption, but with certain types of settlements, that number may exceed 25 percent. Some of the undeliverable notices are returned with a forwarding address from the U.S. Postal Service. For other undeliverable notices, administrators or vendors have certain options available, depending on the administrative procedures agreed to by the settling parties, to attempt to identify current addresses for the class members whose notices are returned.

E-mail notice is an increasingly attractive option when practicable. It has the appeal of being a fast and inexpensive way of communicating with the class. However, as with traditional mailed notice, e-mail notice to class members is subject to certain limitations. Like first-class mail, e-mail notice is only as effective as the quality of the list used. Many people use multiple e-mail addresses (one for work, one or more for various aspects of their personal lives) or switch from one address to another; moreover, e-mail lacks the resources of traditional mail that enable address updates. Tracking tools have been developed to quantify undeliverable e-mail—and even to identify specifically which e-mailed notices were not delivered or opened—but any follow-up must be done by other means.

Among the categories of undeliverable e-mail that can be tracked throughout notification are "hard bounces" and "soft bounces." An e-mail that is rejected by the addressee's domain is called a hard bounce. This is common when a person has moved and no longer has an address issued by an Internet service provider (ISP). This may occur if a person deletes an e-mail account, if the address was not correct as sent, if the account was canceled for lack of use, or if the addressee has left an employer (which then deleted the account). If the ISP itself no longer exists, this also triggers a hard bounce. With a soft bounce, a server recognizes that an e-mail address exists, but cannot deliver e-mail to it. Some possible reasons are that the e-mail account is full or that the recipient uses an e-mail server that requires the active download of e-mail messages and has not yet done so.

E-mail can also be undelivered or unopened if it is considered unwanted e-mail, or spam. Spam has become so great a problem that Congress has passed laws against sending it and an entire industry devoted to filtering spam from reaching the addressee has arisen. However, the CAN-SPAM Act of 2003 (Controlling the Assault of Non-Solicited Pornography and Marketing) also affects the way parties and settlement administrators design and disseminate e-mail notice, and spam filters have had the unintended side effect of screening out e-mail such as class notices.

Media-based notice, also known as published notice, is a form by which the parties—typically through an administrator or through a firm that specializes in placing notice—carry out a program to reach unidentified class members through media such as print, online, television, or radio advertisements, or press releases.

The differing needs of settlements causes media-based notice programs to vary widely in scope (and cost). Indirect purchaser antitrust or consumer settlements typically have relatively expansive programs, while securities and labor and employment settlements are more likely to have one or a few small newspaper advertisements as their sole media-based notice.

Parties can engage firms to conduct two very different levels of services related to media notification. One of these levels is that of media placement: the firm engaged arranges for ad placement in the publications identified by the parties in the settlement agreement. A notice expert provides a broader and higher-level set of services. The notice expert designs the notification plan so that it meets the legal requirements of the settlement and any court order and withstands collateral attacks. He or she is willing and able to submit affidavits and testify in court to the adequacy of the plan.

IV. Claims, Exclusion, and Objection Processing

A. EXCLUSIONS AND OBJECTIONS

Class members typically have one to three months from the beginning of the notice process to make any necessary decisions regarding their rights and options under the proposed settlement—although sometimes they may have significantly longer, particularly to file their claims. Among the rights a class member may exercise are the right to opt out of the settlement (sometimes referred to as exclusion) and the right to object to the settlement.

In most settlements, class members are instructed to forward objections to the parties and the court; therefore, objections received by the settlement administrator are logged and immediately forwarded to the parties and the court for review. However, the administrator often processes exclusions, both in the forms of a preprinted opt-out form disseminated as part of the notice package or a letter or other writing prepared by the class member. The administrator is responsible for logging the receipt of the exclusion, the relevant dates (postmark date, receipt date, or both), and whether the exclusion meets the criteria set forth in the settlement agreement. Any valid exclusion is noted in the class database to ensure that the now former class member does not receive settlement benefits when they are distributed.

B. CLAIMS PROCESSING

Most settlements incorporate some degree of claims processing, much of which takes place during this several-month phase of administration. However, different types of settlements, values of awards, and allotted budgets for administration greatly affect the specific processes that define a settlement administration program's claims process.

Generally, the settlement administrator receives claim forms submitted by class members and logs the receipt of that form into each respective class member's existing record within that particular settlement's database. Such a database record typically originates from either the initial mailing data or, in the case of what are called "self-identifiers," from a potential class member who was not a part of the initial mailing, but identified him or herself as a possible class member through a phone call or other correspondence. This linking of the form to the database record is typically done through the use of identifiers, such as preprinted bar codes, which can be scanned upon receipt of the form and tied to an identification number associated with the claimant's database information, thus indicating that the claim has been received.

Occasionally, documentation of receipt of a claim form is the only processing required. This is typically true of settlements with relatively small benefit amounts or no variation of benefit amounts between class members. As a fictional example, all class members who return claim forms in a certain consumer settlement may receive a $5 coupon toward a future purchase of the defendant's product. In this example, there is no additional information required of the claimant for processing or validation, as long as the claimant is a class member and returned his or her properly completed claim form on time.

More often, at least some level of data capture and analysis is required as a part of claims processing. The details of any such work are largely determined by the settlement at hand: it may relate to confirming a class member's hours worked, the review of purchase documentation, the review of product damage, or any number of other possibilities. Some claim forms require class members to select from among options, while others require narrative descriptions of situations or attachments of various types of supporting documentation.

In the administration of certain settlements, online claims submission and validation are increasingly popular and effective methods of processing claims. While claim processes that require certain types of documentation do not lend themselves to an online process, many simpler claims processes work well on such a platform.

Some percentage of claims received cannot be accepted in their submitted form. Such forms can be broadly categorized as being either technically deficient or incomplete. Technically deficient claims are those that, while containing the necessary information to process the claim, fail to meet some stated requirement. Examples of technically deficient claims include those that are unsigned, are signed by someone other than the listed class member, or are submitted after the deadline. The settlement administrator can identify who submitted the claim and any other claim information, but the claim is not deemed technically compliant. Incomplete claims simply lack the information required to process the claim. An example of such a claim could be one in which a class member failed to submit any of the required purchase information, and thus no calculation of award could be made.

A "cure" process is often built into an administration plan to address some or all of these deficiencies. On a rolling basis or all at once, according to its own standards and expertise or according to guidelines developed by or with the parties, the settlement administrator categorizes claims into appropriate categories and notifies the claimants of their deficiencies, offering a window of opportunity to cure the deficiency. The letters used in this process often must be at least approved, if not written, by the parties. Those claimants who do not cure their deficient claims generally are not offered a second chance and do not receive whatever settlement benefits would have resulted from the claims.

Because of these tremendous disparities between claims processes in different settlements, the cost and time required for claims processing varies dramatically. A settlement administrator can help assess such issues prior to settlement to ensure that the parties do not write unrealistic processes into the settlement agreement and are not surprised later in the process.

As discussed in section I.A, "Pre-Settlement Consultation," most parties are interested in predicting claims filing rates. The involvement of claims filing services in claims administration can dramatically affect both claims filing rates and processes. Claims filing services are companies that assist businesses or consumers in the preparation and filing of claims in return for a fee, most often a percentage of the eventual settlement award. Especially in settlements with unidentified class members, claims filing services can generate substantially higher claims rates through their marketing efforts than would otherwise exist.

With these claims filed through a business on behalf of class members, however, come additional issues for consideration. The parties and administrator must determine how to handle forms signed by the service, correspondence regarding the claims, and requests to change the class members' addresses to that of the service. Even the issue of distribution is complicated by claims filing services, as the parties and administrator must determine when or whether it is permissible to disseminate payments to a claims filing service instead of the class member. These issues are best addressed by the parties in the settlement agreement itself, long before claims begin arriving.

V. Class Member Communication

Throughout the notification and claims processing stages, class members communicate with the parties and administrator. The parties and administrator often work together to funnel these communications through selected media and to selected personnel to ensure a consistent, organized response. Traditionally, the media through which settlement communications would be handled were telephone and mail. However, as more options are available to more people, websites, e-mail, and other media have become increasingly common. What's more, with an increasingly diverse population, some or all of these communication media are made available in multiple languages.

The centerpiece of class member communication remains the toll-free telephone number. While counsel on one or both sides occasionally lists their own telephone numbers in the notice materials, by far the most common telephone option for class members is the toll-free number (most often maintained by an administrator, as it is not an efficient use of time or expense for counsel to deal directly with any significant number of class members). The end-users' toll-free number experience has evolved with technology, as more robust interactive voice response (IVR) systems have become practical and acceptable in the industry. Even when live customer service representatives (CSRs) are a part or all of the telephone support provided in the administration of a settlement, the level of expertise and experience of the CSRs can vary greatly across settlement types to meet specific needs, ranging from lawyers to entry-level personnel.

IVR systems are the various menus of prerecorded messages that a caller hears (and in many cases, responds to) either before or instead of reaching a CSR. Once primarily static messages, the functionality of IVR systems has improved to the point that often they are used instead of CSRs. In addition to informational front-end messaging, IVR systems frequently incorporate features such as notice request systems and question-and-answer menus.

Through various systems that accomplish similar ends, callers can not only request that a notice be mailed to them, but have their addresses identified through an automated process. Through this feature, callers speak their telephone numbers, and voice recognition software does a "reverse address lookup" to identify the caller and his or her listed address. If the system identifies the correct name and address, the caller simply confirms the information, as opposed to providing it him or herself. More traditional methods of accomplishing this end include the caller leaving a simple voicemail with his or her name and address, with the administrator or a vendor later transcribing all such information to carry out notice requests.

IVR systems reduce the cost of call center operations by reducing or eliminating the need for CSRs and ensure that the information provided to class members is standardized. While not an appropriate solution in every settlement, an IVR-only telephone system can be effective in relatively straightforward settlements in which class members have few options. Conversely, a claims-made settlement with a multipart notice package, numerous options for a class member to consider, and multiple forms from which to choose may not be a good option for an IVR-only system.

Live interaction with class members is an integral part of the administration of many settlements. Regardless of the clarity of the notification, some class members will not understand the situation, will have questions about the settlement, or will need basic assurances. For an example of the last, a common question from class members across settlements is "Am I being sued?" Scripting that is written or approved by the parties allows an administrator to provide explanatory information on each point of the settlement terms, the class members' options, or the claim form.

Class member communication takes other forms, as well. In addition to the traditional form of U.S. mail, settlement administrators increasingly offer e-mail or other online question-and-answer options. Across all available media, the keys to class member communication remain constant. When written according to plain language principles and consistent in content and tone with media notice, long-form notice, settlement websites, and other communications, an administrator's class member communication scripting can help class members navigate an unfamiliar topic, understand their options, and make informed decisions.

With each live or one-to-one written communication, however, the parties must take into account the potential risk. A printed notice is a single communication, carefully crafted and reviewed for accuracy, disseminated to a broad audience. With the attention dedicated to its development, the risk of a significant error within it is small. Each communication, however, increases the risk of an error being introduced to class members. Even with preapproved scripting, a CSR could misinterpret a question or simply provide misinformation.

Partly because of the need to deal with any such situations that should arise, the parties should ensure that an administrator has effective and thorough tracking mechanisms to link any outgoing communications to class members. Call recordings, archived e-mails, and copies of outbound mail are all examples of such mechanisms, each made more effective by being directly linked to the file associated with the corresponding class member. Should a problem arise from a miscommunication or mistake, it can often be mitigated through a timely and thorough investigation of the situation and an authoritative, corrective response.

VI. Award Calculation and Distribution

The process for calculating and distributing settlement benefits varies greatly based upon the settlement design, often dictated largely by the settlement type and subject matter. In addition, settlement benefits themselves may take any number of forms. The most typical is a payment, but benefits may also be in the form of coupons, vouchers, products, or procedural changes by the defendant.

When the benefit is a payment, the process typically follows one of two basic designs. One is a set settlement fund with benefits calculated on a pro rata basis. In such examples, all claims must be submitted, reviewed, and verified prior to calculations being made or checks being printed and mailed to any claimants. The fund is a set amount to be split, either equally or often proportionately, among all claimants with valid claims.

The second common design for allocating settlement funds is through set per-claim amounts, where what one class member receives has no effect on the amount another class member receives. For example, each class member may receive $5 for each proof of purchase of Product X submitted with his or her claim form. In this situation, each class member will receive the benefit for each proof of purchase submitted, regardless of how many other class members submit claims of their own. In such settlements, a rolling distribution process is possible, as there is no required cutoff for calculations to take place prior to distribution.

In settlements where distributions involve checks, funds can be placed into the appropriate distribution account. In these situations, an administrator of the parties, either with in-house resources or through a vendor, uses the distribution file to print and mail checks. For distributions with a large number of checks to be mailed, vendors are typically used.

For several months after distribution, the administrator (or party that handled the distribution) typically handles routine administration, including reissuing checks to class members who have lost or accidentally discarded their benefits, or, in cases when the original class member is deceased or otherwise incapable of cashing his or her own benefits, reissuing checks in the name of an appropriately documented representative.

For settlements in which the distribution takes the form of benefits other than checks, the distribution process may be very similar, or it can be entirely different. Printed coupons or vouchers are no more (and in many cases, less) complex to print and mail than checks. Some settlements include relatively long-term processes, however, such as ongoing voucher and redemption programs or additional settlement death benefit management programs. These benefit programs often carry on for years after the settlement administration is otherwise complete.

Cy pres programs are another increasingly common aspect of settlements that are tied to the distribution phase of administration, but carry on past the initial payment dates. In class action settlements, cy pres programs are a means of redistributing unclaimed settlement benefit funds, typically to charities or schools. Therefore, these programs do not begin, as a practical matter, until after the primary distribution is complete and settlement funds are accounted for.

VII. Project Reporting and Wrap-Up

Throughout the administration of a settlement, documentation of key aspects of the settlement (most of which are described above) allows an administrator to manage day-to-day activities, the parties to maintain oversight of the process, and eventually the court to make an informed decision as to whether to grant final approval. In most settlements, the administrator will provide regular statistical reporting, as well as one or more affidavits or declarations regarding its activities. Sometimes this may be a single affidavit prior to the fairness hearing; at other times, there may be one affidavit for each major stage in administration—notification, distribution, and so on.

Establishing a plan and timeline for an orderly project wrap-up at the outset of an administration program helps alleviate drawn-out, expensive conclusions to settlements. With numerous parties involved—as well as possibly hundreds of thousands or even millions of printed and published materials in the public eye—closing down a settlement administration process is not as easy as the flip of a switch. It is therefore important to consider in advance such issues as document and data retention, call center and website messaging or closedown, and ongoing class member communication processes.

PART II

SPECIAL ISSUES IN CLASS ACTIONS

THE CLASS ACTION FAIRNESS ACT OF 2005

MARCY HOGAN GREER
PAUL L. PEYRONNIN

I. Introduction

Congress passed the Class Action Fairness Act of 2005 (CAFA or the Act)[1] on February 17, 2005, and it was signed into law by President George W. Bush on February 18, 2005. CAFA is codified at 28 U.S.C. §§ 1332(d), 1453, and 1711–1715 and was made applicable to "any civil action commenced on or after" February 18, 2005.[2]

The statute was passed as a response to the perception of several members of Congress that the class action device has been abused, particularly in the state court system, and that such abuses "(A) harmed class members with legitimate claims and defendants that have acted responsibly; (B) adversely affected interstate commerce; and (C) undermined public respect for our judicial system."[3] The Senate Judiciary Committee Report that explains the legislation is pointed:

> One key reason for the[ ] problems [with our existing class action system] is that most class actions are currently adjudicated in state courts, where the governing rules are applied inconsistently (frequently in a manner that contravenes basic fairness and due process considerations) and where there is often inadequate supervision over litigation procedures and proposed settlements.[4]

The stated purposes of the Act are to "(1) assure fair and prompt recoveries for class members with legitimate claims; (2) restore the intent of the framers of the

---

1. Pub. L. No. 109-2, 119 Stat. 4 (codified at 28 U.S.C. §§ 1332(d), 1453, and 1711–15 (2005)) [hereinafter CAFA].

2. *Id.* at § 9.

3. *Id.* at § 2(a)(2).

4. S. Rep. No. 109-14, at 4 (2005), *reprinted in* 2005 U.S.C.C.A.N. 3 [hereinafter S. Rep. 109-14].

United States Constitution by providing for Federal court consideration of inter-state cases of national importance under diversity jurisdiction; and (3) benefit society by encouraging innovation and lowering consumer prices."[5]

The foundational premise of CAFA is that massive, multistate class actions are of national importance and the state courts are ill-suited to handle them.[6] CAFA thus expands federal jurisdiction to cover a wide range of class actions that were previously beyond the reach of the federal courts by changing the diversity and removal rules for these cases. To accomplish this result, CAFA has three principal components. The first set of provisions, known as the "consumer class action bill of rights,"[7] establishes new procedural and substantive standards applicable to class action settlements. Some of these standards duplicated existing practice under the Federal Rules of Civil Procedure, but others—such as limitations on attorney fees in coupon settlements and requirements for notification of government officials whenever a class action settlement is initiated—were new.

The second, in some ways more significant, set of provisions significantly modified traditional principles of statutory diversity jurisdiction and supplies both original federal jurisdiction for, and removal of, state-law-based class actions that previously could be filed only in state courts. Fundamentally, CAFA makes the ordinary requirement of "complete diversity" of citizenship inapplicable to class actions and provides for federal jurisdiction when some class members and some defendants are from different states. It also eliminates the earlier jurisdictional limitation that the claims of class members could not be aggregated to meet the "amount-in-controversy" requirement and provides for federal jurisdiction when the total amount in controversy in a class action exceeds $5 million. The effect is to allow most class actions with classes or defendants including citizens of more than one state to be filed in, or removed by defendants to, federal court.

The third component of CAFA directed the Judicial Conference of the United States to conduct a comprehensive review of class action settlements and attorney fee awards and make recommendations for improvements and best practices in this area of class action law.[8]

II. Background of the Statute

As a number of courts have observed, "[i]n enacting CAFA, Congress was respond-ing to what it perceived as abusive practices by plaintiffs and their lawyers in litigat-

---

5. CAFA at § 2(b).
6. *See generally* S. REP. 109-14, at 13–27.
7. *Id.* at 5.
8. CAFA at §§ 6(a) and (b).

ing major interstate class actions in state courts . . . ."[9] To address these perceived harms, Congress provided for "[f]ederal court consideration of interstate cases of national importance under diversity jurisdiction."[10]

CAFA has been controversial, to say the least:

> Some of the political and social implications of [CAFA] are hard to miss. That statute, after all, resulted from years of intense lobbying (on both sides of the aisle by interest groups associated with both plaintiffs and defendants), partisan wrangling, and following two successful filibusters, fragile compromises. Not only does CAFA mark a sharp break from the nearly uniform history of congressional contraction of diversity jurisdiction. The scope of putative class actions that, at the end of the day, the statute brings within the subject matter jurisdiction of the federal courts is very broad. Those facts—coupled with the legislation's place in a trio of "tort reform" measures sought by the Bush administration, and with unrelenting attacks on lawyers in general and plaintiffs' lawyers in particular—help to understand why some critics regard the compromises as insufficient and the ultimate legislation as inimical to the interests of numerous groups of potential litigants.[11]

Many courts have relied upon the Senate Judiciary Committee Report,[12] which contains a detailed and substantial analysis of the purposes of each provision of CAFA, for elucidation. Several courts have expressed the view that this legislative history is not persuasive authority because it is not the history of the passage of CAFA, but instead is a retrospective assessment of the Act issued ten days after CAFA was enacted:

> The problem with relying solely on CAFA's legislative history is that the portion that supports burden-shifting "does not concern any text in the bill that eventually became law . . . . But when legislative history stands by itself, as a naked expression of 'intent' unconnected to any enacted text, it has no more force than an opinion poll of legislators—less, really, as it speaks for fewer. Thirteen Senators signed this report and five voted not to send the proposal to the floor. Another 82 Senators did not express themselves on the question; likewise 435 Members of the House and one President kept their silence."[13]

---

9. *Amoche v. Guar. Trust Life Ins. Co.*, 556 F.3d 41, 47 (1st Cir. 2009) (quoting CAFA at § 2(a), 119 Stat. 4, 4 (2005) (codified as a note to 28 U.S.C. § 1711)).

10. *Luther v. Countrywide Home Loans Servicing, LP*, 533 F.3d 1031, 1034 (9th Cir. 2008).

11. Stephen B. Burbank, *Fairness to Whom? Perspectives on the Class Action Fairness Act of 2005*, 15 U. Pa. L. Rev. 1439, 1441 (June 2008).

12. S. Rep. 109-14.

13. *Morgan v. Gay*, 471 F.3d 469, 473 & n.2 (3d Cir. 2006) (quoting *Brill v. Countrywide Home Loans, Inc.*, 427 F.3d 446, 448 (7th Cir. 2005)); *see also Caruso v. Allstate Ins. Co.*, 469 F. Supp. 2d 364, 370 (E.D. La. 2007). *But see Saab v. Home Depot U.S.A., Inc.*, 469 F.3d 758, 759-60 (8th Cir. 2006) (quoting S. Rep. 109-14 in interpreting the scope of appellate review).

Senator Patrick Leahy and others published their minority views as part of the report. According to Senator Leahy, "at the insistence of the Republican leadership, this bill was rushed through the Judiciary Committee and then forced through the Senate without amendment."[14]

The judicial trend seems to be moving toward reliance upon the report to help discern the reasons for certain provisions of CAFA. Although it was not printed until after CAFA was fully enacted, the report "was *submitted* to the Senate on February 3, 200[5]—while that body was considering the bill."[15] Further, large portions of the 2005 Senate Report were also contained in a 2003 Senate Report on the subject.[16]

A widely held view is that the statute is not a model of clarity. It has been described as "confusing," "clumsy," and having "cryptic text," and the mass action provision in particular has been severely criticized:

> CAFA's mass action provisions present an opaque, baroque maze of interlocking cross-references that defy easy interpretation, even though they are contained in a single paragraph of the amended diversity statute . . . . [T]o resolve the current dispute, we are tasked with plotting the proper route through this statutory labyrinth.[17]

Against that backdrop, we review the elements and judicial interpretations of CAFA's provisions.

III. Overview

The most significant provisions of CAFA are as follows.

A. EXPANDED DIVERSITY JURISDICTION AND REMOVAL

- CAFA widens federal diversity jurisdiction for many class actions. Diversity is judged by any class member's citizenship (whether a named plaintiff or not) being different from any defendant's.

---

14. S. Rep. 109-14, at 79 ("Additional Views of Senator Patrick Leahy") (informing that "[t]he Republican leadership's timetable was so short that there was no opportunity to prepare a Committee report before final passage"); *see also id.* at 82, 84 ("Minority Views of Senators Leahy, Kennedy, Biden, Feingold, and Durbin") ("Before even considering S. 5, the Committee and the full Senate should have insisted on receiving objective and comprehensive data justifying such a dramatic intrusion into state court prerogatives.").

15. *Lowery v. Ala. Power Co.*, 483 F.3d 1184, 1206 n.50 (11th Cir. 2007).

16. *See* S. Rep. 108-123 (2003).

17. *Lowery*, 483 F.3d at 1198–99; *see also Abrego Abrego v. Dow Chem. Co.*, 443 F.3d 676, 681–82 (9th Cir. 2006) (describing the wording of 28 U.S.C. § 1332(d)(11)(a) as "clumsy" and further noted that meshing the mass action provisions with the rest of § 1332 is "far from straightforward").

- The minimum amount in controversy is now $5 million, but that calculation permits aggregation of the claims of all plaintiffs, not just the named plaintiff(s).[18]
- 28 U.S.C. § 1453(b) permits a defendant to remove unilaterally without obtaining the consent of other defendants and without respect to whether there is an in-state defendant.
- Federal jurisdiction is also available for "mass actions" that do not necessarily meet the CAFA definition of "class action," but for purposes of removal are "deemed to be a class action removable under" the class action provisions of the statute "if it otherwise meets th[ose] provisions . . . ."[19]
- However, this expanded jurisdiction is subject to a number of exceptions designed to ensure that small, purely local controversies are permitted to proceed in the state courts.[20]

B. DELAYED REMOVAL OPTIONS

- The new Act increases the chances of a removal occurring long after the case has been pending in state court. The one-year limitation on diversity removals contained in 28 U.S.C. § 1446(b) is eliminated in CAFA cases by section 1453(b).[21]

C. SETTLEMENT

- The "Consumer Class Action Bill of Rights" appearing at sections 1711–1715 sets forth conditions on settling class actions in federal court. In settlements involving coupons, only the value of redeemed coupons will be considered for determining contingent attorney fees.[22]
- In settlements calling for noncash benefits (such as coupons), the court must convene a hearing and make written findings on whether the settlement is "fair, reasonable, and adequate" for the class members, taking into account certain standards.[23]
- Section 1715 requires class action defendants to notify appropriate state and federal regulators before completing any settlement and allow them 90 days to intervene.[24]

---

18. 28 U.S.C. § 1332(d) (as amended) and 28 U.S.C. § 1453 (newly enacted).

19. 28 U.S.C. § 1332(d)(11)(A).

20. *Preston v. Tenet Health Sys. Mem'l Med. Ctr., Inc.*, 485 F.3d 793, 803 (5th Cir. 2007) (*Preston I*) (citing *Hart v. FedEx Ground Package Sys., Inc.*, 457 F.3d 675, 682 (7th Cir. 2006)); *see also Preston v. Tenet Health Sys. Mem'l Med. Ctr., Inc.*, 485 F.3d 804, 810 (5th Cir. 2007) (*Preston II*).

21. 28 U.S.C. § 1453(b).

22. *Id.* § 1712.

23. *Id.* § 1712(e).

24. *Id.* § 1715.

D. APPEALS

- Unlike traditional remand orders, which are barred from appellate review,[25] a decision on a CAFA remand is subject to a discretionary interlocutory appeal if a petition is filed within ten days after the order.[26]
- The court of appeals must consider the entire appeal and reach a decision within 60 days from the date the court accepts review—a time period that includes full briefing and argument.[27]

IV. Implementation of CAFA—Early Interpretations of the Statute

A. EFFECTIVE DATE

Following the enactment, initial judicial review focused on whether particular cases would be subject to CAFA. That question is addressed in the last section of the Act, section 9, which provides that "[t]he amendments made by this Act shall apply to *any civil action commenced on or after the date of enactment of this Act.*"[28] As this relatively simple pronouncement should indicate, the Act applies to class actions filed on or after Friday, February 18, 2005. It does not apply to actions already pending on that date.

Many circuits have assumed that state law governs the question of when an action is "commenced" for purposes of CAFA—including whether a post-CAFA amendment to a state court class action that was filed prior to the effective date of CAFA is a re-"commencement" of the action that could trigger its removal provisions[29]—but the question is not settled.[30]

1. Definition of "Commenced"

Early on, defendants tested the effective date provision by attempting to remove cases that were pending before February 18, 2005, asserting that a civil action is commenced on the date it is removed, not the date it was originally filed in state court. These efforts to remove already pending cases were largely unsuccessful, but the principles of interpreting CAFA are useful for other cases going forward.

---

25. *Id.* § 1447(d).

26. *Id.* § 1453(c)(1).

27. *Id.* § 1453(c)(2).

28. Pub. L. No. 109-2, § 9 (emphasis added).

29. *Schorsch v. Hewlett-Packard Co.*, 417 F.3d 748, 750–51 (7th Cir. 2005); *Plubell v. Merck & Co.*, 434 F.3d 1070, 1071 (8th Cir. 2006); *Bush v. Cheaptickets, Inc.*, 425 F.3d 683, 686 (9th Cir. 2005); *see also Admiral Ins. Co. v. Abshire*, 574 F.3d 267, 273 (5th Cir. 2009); *Wright v. Am. Bankers Life Assur. Co. of Fla.*, 586 F. Supp. 2d 464 (D.S.C. 2008).

30. *Springman v. AIG Mktg., Inc.*, 523 F.3d 685, 687–88 (7th Cir. 2008).

In the leading case, *Pritchett v. Office Depot, Inc.*,[31] the Tenth Circuit held that the language of the statute, the presumption that removal provisions are to be narrowly construed, the legislative history, and considerations of public policy all pointed to the same conclusion: "removal to federal court does not 'commence' an action for the purposes of the Class Action Fairness Act of 2005 . . . ."[32]

Presented with a slightly different fact pattern, the Fifth Circuit reached a similar result in *Patterson v. Dean Morris, L.L.P.*,[33] in which class actions were commenced in Louisiana state court one day prior to enactment of CAFA when the plaintiffs fax-filed their complaints, as permitted by Louisiana law. They failed, however, to pay the required court fees at that time, but paid them once they were notified of the oversight.[34] The court of appeals concluded that plaintiffs' failure to initially pay the fees did not affect the commencement date of suits under Louisiana law for the purpose of deciding whether CAFA provided a basis for federal jurisdiction and agreed that the case should be remanded to state court.[35]

The Ninth Circuit likewise held, in *Bush v. Cheaptickets, Inc.*,[36] that a consumer class action "commenced," for purpose of determining the applicability of federal removal jurisdiction under CAFA, on the date that the action was filed in California state court, rather than on the date the action was removed to federal court or on the date that service of process was perfected; California law determined when the action was initiated or commenced under CAFA, and California law provided that a lawsuit commenced when it was filed.

2. Amended Pleadings

Some decisions have allowed amendments to pleadings to restart the CAFA removal clock. For instance, in the seminal case of *Braud v. Transport Service Co. of Illinois*,[37] the Fifth Circuit declared that an amendment of a complaint to add a new defendant after the effective date of CAFA constituted the "commencement" of a new suit, under both Louisiana and federal law,[38] as would permit removal by the newly joined defendant to federal court under CAFA. Although the initial action was filed in state court prior to the effective date of CAFA, the addition of a new defendant changed the character of the litigation, so as to make it substantially a new suit.[39] The *Braud* court limited its holding to changes that added new defendants, noting

---

31. 420 F.3d 1090 (10th Cir. 2005).

32. *Id.* at 1097.

33. 448 F.3d 736, 740 (5th Cir. 2006).

34. *Id.*

35. *Id.* at 740–41.

36. 425 F.3d at 686–87.

37. 445 F.3d 801, 803–04 (5th Cir. 2006).

38. As noted above, the decision as to when a case is "commenced" for purposes of CAFA is a matter of state law.

39. *Braud,* 445 F.3d at 804.

that it did not "decide when or whether the addition of new claims to a pre-CAFA case provides a new removal window."[40]

In *Admiral Ins. Co. v. Abshire*,[41] the Fifth Circuit addressed this open question. After the effective date of CAFA, plaintiffs amended their complaint to add class allegations, make a claim for attorney fees, and "resurrect[ ]" claims that had previously been made in the decades-old lawsuit. The Fifth Circuit held that the amendment did not commence a new suit under Louisiana and/or federal law, as would permit removal to federal court under CAFA, because the initial action was filed in state court prior to the effective date of CAFA and the purported class comprised only individuals or successors of individuals who were already parties to the suit.[42]

Similarly, in *Phillips v. Ford Motor Co.*,[43] the court of appeals held that, as to state court consumer fraud class actions against automobile manufacturers, post-CAFA amendments to the complaint to add or substitute named plaintiffs did not constitute the commencement of new actions, so as to permit removal. The amendments at issue related back under governing state law because the new complaints arose out of the same transaction or occurrence set up in the original complaints.[44] The court noted that a routine amendment to a complaint filed prior to the effective date of CAFA does not commence a new suit, so as to render the action removable under CAFA.[45]

However, in *Jones v. Sears Roebuck & Co.*,[46] the Fourth Circuit held that an amended complaint that presented new claims "premised on conduct and occurrences that are readily distinct from the allegations of" the prior complaint did not relate back to the pre-CAFA complaint under West Virginia law, and thus commenced a new suit covered by CAFA.

Courts appear to be more lenient when evaluating the impact of actual notice to a proper defendant. For example, the court in *Dinkel v. General Motors Corp.*[47] held that late service upon the removing defendants, which had the effect of commencing a Kansas class action lawsuit as to them after the effective date of CAFA, rendered the entire lawsuit properly removable by those defendants under CAFA.

---

40. *Id.* at 808 n.16; *see also Hall v. State Farm Mut. Auto. Ins. Co.*, 215 F. App'x 423, 428 (6th Cir. 2007) (finding that, under Michigan law, substitution of new named plaintiff effected a "commencement" of a new action for purposes of CAFA). *But see McAtee v. Capital One, F.S.B.*, 479 F.3d 1143, 1145, 1148 (9th Cir. 2007) (substitution of a named defendant for a previously pled "Doe" defendant did not commence a new action under CAFA).

41. 574 F.3d at 273.

42. *Id.* at 278–79.

43. 435 F.3d 785, 787–88 (7th Cir. 2006).

44. *Id.*

45. *Id.* at 786.

46. 301 F. App'x 276, 289–90 (4th Cir. 2008).

47. 400 F. Supp. 2d 289, 293 (D. Me. 2005).

In *Springman v. AIG Marketing, Inc.*,[48] the court deemed a fraud suit against a company that processed insurance to have been commenced when the company was substituted as a defendant in place of its affiliate in the claimant's state court class action—not years earlier when its affiliate was originally sued. Therefore, the entire action was removable pursuant to CAFA, which became effective after the class action was initiated, but before the company was added as a defendant.[49] The claimant's unexcused, almost three-year delay in seeking substitution after discovering that he had sued the wrong party was particularly important to the court's relation-back analysis.[50]

Marshall v. H&R Block Tax Services[51] did not involve a formal pleadings amendment, but the district court's post-CAFA decertification of the defendant class left H&R Block as the only defendant, greatly expanding its liability to the class. The Seventh Circuit concluded that "from the standpoint of the original claim, the expansion of potential liability was a surprise," and "the change in the scope of the plaintiffs' claim" did not relate back to the original claim.[52]

3. Change to Class Definition

Other cases have considered whether CAFA applied to a changed class definition. In *Knudsen v. Liberty Mutual Insurance Co.*,[53] the plaintiffs brought a state court class action against an insurer, alleging systematic underpayment of automobile and worker's compensation insurance claims. The case was originally filed prior to the effective date of CAFA and was thus not removable under the Act, but the court reasoned that the state court's post-CAFA expansion of the class definition to include insureds under policies issued by all of the insurer's affiliates and subsidiaries constituted the commencement of a new action, rendering the suit removable under CAFA even though the insurer remained the only named defendant.[54]

The reasoning in *Knudsen* can be contrasted with *Schorsch v. Hewlett-Packard Co.*,[55] where the Seventh Circuit held that a change to the class definition occurring after the Act's effective date did not constitute the commencement of a new action so as to permit removal. Plaintiffs had brought a state court class action against the manufacturer of drum kits for printers prior to the effective date of

---

48. 523 F.3d at 690.

49. *Id.*

50. *Id.* at 689.

51. 564 F.3d 826, 827 (7th Cir. 2009).

52. *Id.* at 829.

53. 435 F.3d 755 (7th Cir. 2006), *vacating Knudsen v. Liberty Mut. Ins. Co.*, 405 F. Supp. 2d 916 (N.D. Ill. 2005).

54. *Id.* (observing that the expansion amounted to the assertion of new claims against the insurer, i.e., claims arising under the subsidiaries' policies did not relate back to the original complaint under the applicable state law, since the insurer was not responsible for adjusting all demands for payment of all of its subsidiaries' policies).

55. 417 F.3d 748.

CAFA. After CAFA became effective, they expanded the class definition from purchasers of drum kits to purchasers of all printer consumables that contained the same chip; the court concluded that this change did not present a new claim or add a new defendant, because, from the outset, the key to the litigation was the chip in the drum kits.[56]

The issue appears to boil down, as a practical matter, to notice—"whether the allegations of the pre-CAFA complaint sufficiently placed [the defendant] on notice of the claims against it" in the post-CAFA expansion.[57] In *In re Safeco Insurance Co. of America*,[58] the Seventh Circuit navigated the lines between *Knudsen* and *Schorsch* in a case where a change in the class definition was also claimed to have expanded Safeco's liability through the addition of claims based on the alleged conduct of its affiliates. The court disagreed, finding instead that the key claim against Safeco—challenging its use of a computer program to systematically underpay auto claims—had been inherent from the pre-CAFA inception of the suit and thus the action was not properly removed: "workaday changes to class definitions do not create new litigation for CAFA purposes."[59]

B. EFFECTIVE DATE FOR SETTLEMENTS

Significantly, the effective date provision applies to all of the changes made by CAFA, including the provisions on settlements,[60] which presumably could have been applied to future settlements in pending actions without raising concerns about unfair retroactivity. Applying the removal and jurisdictional provisions to previously filed actions, by contrast, would have been far more disruptive of settled expectations.

Because the drafters of the Act chose a uniform, bright-line approach to the effective date for all provisions of the new law, settlements of class actions in federal courts may be subject to two different sets of procedures, depending on the date of filing of the action. Thus, the "effective date" provision appears relatively clear as it applies to the jurisdictional and removal provisions, but may prove to be an ongoing source of complication for settlements.

V. *Jurisdictional Provisions*

CAFA's provisions for original jurisdiction and removal jurisdiction over multistate class actions are some of its most important features. Under the law as it stood before CAFA's passage, class actions raising federal claims could be brought in or

---

56. *Id.* at 750.
57. *In re Safeco Ins. Co. of Am.*, 585 F.3d 326, 333 (7th Cir. 2009).
58. *Id.* at 333–34.
59. *Id.*
60. CAFA at § 9.

removed to federal court by virtue of the grant of federal question jurisdiction in 28 U.S.C. § 1331. However, most class actions raising state law claims could reach federal court only if they satisfied the requirements for diversity jurisdiction under 28 U.S.C. § 1332. Section 1332 posed two significant obstacles to federal jurisdiction over such class actions—the "complete diversity" rule, which requires that *all* plaintiffs be diverse in citizenship from *all* defendants—and the amount-in-controversy requirement.

The complete diversity requirement is judge-made law,[61] while the amount-in-controversy is purely statutory. Both serve as significant limitations on the diversity jurisdiction that federal courts may exercise, but neither originates in the constitutional delegation of federal power under Article III of the Constitution.[62] Congress was well within its constitutional authority under Article III to expand diversity jurisdiction as long as there is "minimal diversity" between some plaintiffs and some defendants, and it was not required to impose any amount-in-controversy requirements on the exercise of this jurisdiction.[63]

In CAFA, Congress dipped into the Article III reservoir of authority and significantly broadened the existing framework for federal jurisdiction in the specific context of class actions. To accomplish this purpose, CAFA amended both the diversity statute[64] and the removal laws[65] to provide for federal jurisdiction—at the election of either the plaintiff or any defendant—over class actions that do not satisfy the traditional complete diversity and amount-in-controversy requirements.

A. "CLASS ACTION"

The first requirement of the statute is that the case be a "class action."[66] CAFA defines a class action as follows:

> [T]he term "class action" means any civil action filed under rule 23 of the Federal Rules of Civil Procedure or similar State statute *or rule of judicial procedure authorizing an action to be brought by 1 or more representative persons as a class action.*[67]

The legislative history indicates that this definition "is to be interpreted liberally. Its application should not be confined solely to lawsuits that are labeled 'class

---

61. *See Strawbridge v. Curtis*, 3 Cranch 267, 2 L. Ed. 435 (1806); *see also Owen Equip. & Erection Co. v. Kroger*, 437 U.S. 365, 375 (1978).

62. *E.g., Newman-Green, Inc. v. Alfonzo-Larrain*, 490 U.S. 826, 829 n.1 (1989) ("The complete diversity requirement is based on the diversity statute, not Article III of the Constitution.").

63. This is not to suggest that there may not be legitimate constitutional challenges to CAFA's federalization of state class actions, but they would not find support in Article III.

64. 28 U.S.C. § 1332.

65. *Id.* at § 1441 *et seq.*

66. There is a statutory alternative for a mass action that does not necessarily meet the CAFA standard for class actions. *See* section VIII; *see also* Chapter 11, "Mass Actions Under the Class Action Fairness Act."

67. 28 U.S.C. § 1332(d)(1)(B) (emphasis added).

actions' by the named plaintiff or the state rulemaking authority."[68] Not surprisingly, the emphasized phrase has spawned some litigation in cases where aggregated claims are brought without expressly invoking a class action rule or statute.

For example, in *In re Katrina Canal Litigation Breaches (Louisiana v. AAA Insurance)*,[69] the state of Louisiana filed a class action—in which both the state and numerous Louisiana citizens were class members—against certain insurance companies based on claims that the defendants had failed to pay covered claims following Hurricanes Katrina and Rita. Louisiana was a claimant in its own right because it had been assigned certain proceeds under the insurance policies under a state-funded relief program, known as the Road Home Program, that provided money to Louisiana homeowners to rebuild homes damaged by the hurricanes.[70] The defendants removed under CAFA, and Louisiana sought remand, which was denied.[71] On appeal, Louisiana contested that it had not filed the case as a class action under CAFA and that it was not a "citizen" for purposes of diversity.[72] The Fifth Circuit rejected both arguments and instead held that the state of Louisiana's deliberate inclusion of private litigants in its class action lawsuit rendered the suit removable under CAFA and resulted in the waiver of any sovereign immunity the state otherwise might have from removal to federal court.[73]

Going one step further, in *Louisiana ex rel. Caldwell v. Allstate Insurance Co.*,[74] the state of Louisiana and a number of private law firms filed a *parens patriae* action[75] against a number of insurance companies, global consultants, and software companies claiming an antitrust conspiracy to fix prices of repair services used in connection with adjusting homeowners claims arising out of Hurricane Katrina.[76] The Louisiana attorney general asserted claims under the Louisiana Monopolies Act and sought treble damages and injunctive relief.[77] However, this time, Louisiana did not use the words "class action" or invoke Louisiana's class action analog in seeking relief.[78] The defendants removed under CAFA, claiming that the suit was a representative action for damages allegedly incurred by an iden-

---

68. S. Rep. 109-14, at 35.

69. 524 F.3d 700, 702 (5th Cir. 2008).

70. *Id.* at 702–03.

71. *Id.* at 702.

72. *Id.* at 705.

73. *Id.* at 706, 711.

74. 536 F.3d 418 (5th Cir. 2008).

75. "*Parens patriae* means literally 'parent of the country.'" *Alfred L. Snapp & Son, Inc. v. Puerto Rico*, 458 U.S. 592, 600 (1982); *see also Mormon Church v. United States*, 136 U.S. 1, 57 (1890). It is derived from the "royal prerogative" retained by the King of England, a collection of "powers and duties [that] were said to be exercised by the King in his capacity as 'father of the country.'" *Hawaii v. Standard Oil Co.*, 405 U.S. 251, 257 (1972).

76. *Caldwell*, 536 F.3d at 422.

77. *Id.* at 422–23.

78. *Id.* at 424.

tifiable group of people that could only proceed as a class action.[79] Alternatively, they claimed the suit was properly removed as a mass action under CAFA.[80] Reasoning that the real parties of interest were the Louisiana policyholders and that the attorney general sought to collect damages on behalf of these individuals, the district court concluded that the action must be viewed as a class action lawsuit rather than a pure enforcement action and thus removal under CAFA was appropriate.[81] The Fifth Circuit agreed that CAFA jurisdiction was available, although it concluded that the case was more properly characterized as a mass action and declined to decide whether it qualified as a class action.[82] Like the district court, it looked to "the substance of the action and not only at the labels that the parties may attach."[83] Because the attorney general was acting in a representative capacity on behalf of the insureds, CAFA's jurisdictional requirements were satisfied.[84]

In *Missouri ex rel. Koster v. Portfolio Recovery Associates, Inc.*,[85] a district court in Missouri reached a different conclusion, based in large part on Judge Southwick's dissent in *Caldwell*.[86] In that case, Missouri filed an action based on the defendants' "allegedly deceptive and unfair collection practices," seeking injunctive relief, civil penalties, and restitution under a Missouri statute prohibiting these practices.[87] The court distinguished *Caldwell* because in the case presented, Missouri did not have to join as parties the consumers who would benefit from the restitution in order to recover; instead, the statute at issue provided that any restitution would be paid as a lump sum to the state, which would then distribute it to the injured consumers.[88]

Another jurisdictional wrinkle arises when state law prevents the putative class claim from being brought on behalf of a class. In *Bonime v. Avaya, Inc.*,[89] the plaintiff brought a putative class action in New York district court alleging violations of the Telephone Consumer Protection Act (TCPA)[90] and asserted CAFA as the basis for federal jurisdiction. The district court dismissed the case for lack of jurisdiction because New York law did not permit a private action under the TCPA to be brought as a class action, and so CAFA could not supply the jurisdictional base

---

79. *Id.* at 423.
80. *Id.* at 430.
81. *Id.* at 429–30.
82. *Id.* at 430.
83. *Id.* at 424 (citing *Grassi v. Ciba-Geigy*, 894 F. 2d 181, 185 (5th Cir. 1990)).
84. *Id.* at 430.
85. ___ F. Supp. 2d ___, 2010 WL 675153, at *4–5 (E.D. Mo. Feb. 24, 2010).
86. *Id.* (citing *Caldwell*, 536 F.3d at 433–36 (Southwick, J., dissenting)).
87. *Id.* at *1.
88. *Id.* at *3.
89. 547 F.3d 497, 497, 500 (2d Cir. 2008).
90. 47 U.S.C. § 227(b)(1)(C) (TCPA).

for the case.[91] The court of appeals agreed that the state court limitation on class actions applied and so CAFA jurisdiction was lacking.[92]

A related question is whether denial of class certification is fatal to CAFA jurisdiction.[93] An earlier version of CAFA passed by the House (but not the Senate) in 2003 would have provided that if a federal court denied class certification in a case where federal jurisdiction depended on the new class action jurisdiction/removal provisions, the court was required to dismiss the action.[94]

As enacted, CAFA contains no such provision. Presumably, because diversity jurisdiction depends on the facts at the time of filing and is not affected by subsequent events,[95] the district court would retain jurisdiction over an action brought in or removed to federal court under the Act even if it were to later deny class certification or define the class in a way that evades CAFA's jurisdiction.[96] Such a result is consistent with the legislative history of CAFA, confirming that "[c]urrent law" not altered by CAFA "is also clear that, once a complaint is properly removed to federal court, the federal court's jurisdiction cannot be 'ousted' by later events."[97] Of course there may be situations where the class allegations are so facially frivolous that CAFA would not be implicated. Judge Richard Posner provided the colorful example of a plaintiff suing a fish tank distributor on behalf of himself and a class of 1,000 goldfish, which would presumably fail to qualify under CAFA even if the claims were otherwise viable and the amount in controversy exceeded $5 million.[98]

---

91. *Bonime,* 547 F.3d at 499 ("'Bonime may not assert a class action for statutory damages under the TCPA in New York state and therefore may not utilize CAFA to establish diversity jurisdiction.'" (quoting *Bonime v. Avaya, Inc.,* No. 06 CV 1630, 2006 U.S. Dist. LEXIS 91964, at *3 (E.D.N.Y. Dec. 20, 2006))).

92. *Id.* at 501.

93. *Coll. of Dental Surgeons of P.R. v. Conn. Gen. Life Ins. Co.,* 585 F.3d 33, 42 (1st Cir. 2009) (noting an "open question" as to whether a subsequent denial of certification would "divest the district court of CAFA jurisdiction").

94. *Lewis v. Ford Motor Corp.,* ___ F. Supp. 2d ___, CA No. 090164, 2010 WL 27409 (W.D. Pa. Jan. 5, 2010).

95. *Grupo Dataflux v. Atlas Global Group, LP,* 541 U.S. 567 (2004).

96. *See, e.g., Vega v. T-Mobile USA, Inc.,* 564 F.3d 1256, 1268 n.12 (11th Cir. 2009) (even if class is later narrowed by certification decision to fewer than 100 claimants, that development would not divest the court of CAFA jurisdiction: "jurisdictional facts are assessed at the time of removal; and post-removal events (including non-certification, decertification, or severance) do not deprive federal courts of subject matter jurisdiction."); *see also* James Wm. Moore et al., Moore's Federal Practice § 23.63(2)(a) (3d ed. 2009) [hereinafter Moore's]. *But see Ronat v. Martha Stewart Living Omnimedia, Inc.,* No. 05-520-GPM, 2008 U.S. Dist. LEXIS 91814, at *20–24 (S.D. Ill. Nov. 12, 2008) (remanding to state court after denying class certification because "it is clear to this Court that CAFA does not provide a basis for subject matter jurisdiction after a court denies class certification").

97. S. Rep. 109-14, at 70 (2005), *reprinted in* 2005 U.S.C.C.A.N. 3, 66.

98. *Cunningham Charter Corp. v. Learjet, Inc.,* 592 F.3d 805, 806 (7th Cir. 2010).

In *Lewis v. Ford Motor Co.*,[99] the district court denied plaintiff's motion to remand after denying certification and ordering the class allegations stricken from a plaintiff's complaint that had been removed pursuant to CAFA. The court concluded that CAFA's legislative history reflected "a [c]ongressional intent to allow cases which were originally filed as class actions and met the CAFA requirements to continue in federal court even after certification is denied."[100] The court further explained that federal courts had the "'discretion to handle Rule 23-ineligible cases appropriately.'"[101]

Shortly after the *Lewis* decision, the Seventh Circuit spoke to the issue as well. In *Cunningham Charter Corp. v. Learjet*,[102] the district court denied certification and remanded the case to state court, concluding that the certification ruling eliminated the sole basis for its subject matter jurisdiction under CAFA. The Seventh Circuit reversed, holding that federal jurisdiction under CAFA does not depend upon certification.[103] In so holding, it joined the Eleventh Circuit's ruling in *Vega v. T-Mobile USA, Inc.*,[104] and "vindicate[d] the general principle that jurisdiction once properly invoked is not lost by developments after a suit is filed . . . ."[105]

The question is an open one in the Ninth Circuit. In *United Steel, Paper & Forestry, Rubber Manufacturing Energy, Allied Industrial & Service Workers International Union AFL-CIO, CLC v. ConocoPhillips Co.*,[106] the district court had noted that "[t]he Ninth Circuit has never addressed this question" and concluded that CAFA jurisdiction was lacking because "there is 'no reasonably foreseeable possibility' that a class will be certified." On appeal, the Ninth Circuit reversed the decision on class certification and so did not reach this issue.[107]

B. BURDEN OF PROOF

As in traditional diversity cases, the party seeking to remove a case under CAFA bears the burden to establish the jurisdictional prerequisites under CAFA.[108]

---

99. 2010 WL 27409, at *4–5.

100. *Id.* at *9.

101. *Id.* at *8 (quoting 149 Cong. Rec. S16, 102–03, daily ed. Dec. 9, 2003 (statement of Sen. Christopher Dodd)).

102. 592 F.3d at 805–06.

103. *Id.* at 806–07.

104. 564 F.3d 1256. *Lewis* also discussed *Vega*, explaining that the operative footnote from the opinion "does not provide a circuit court's decision on the continuing jurisdiction question, it implies that the Eleventh Circuit Court of Appeals would align with lower courts holding that once jurisdiction is established under CAFA, it continues throughout the life of the case." *Lewis*, 2010 WL 27409, at *6.

105. *Cunningham*, 592 F.3d at 807.

106. 593 F.3d 802, 805–06 (9th Cir. 2010).

107. *Id.* at 810.

108. *See, e.g., Amoche*, 556 F.3d at 48; *Blockbuster, Inc. v. Galeno*, 472 F.3d 53, 58 (2d Cir. 2006); *Morgan*, 471 F.3d 469; *Strawn v. AT&T Mobility LLC*, 530 F.3d 293, 298 (4th Cir. 2008) (collecting cases); *Smith v. Nationwide Prop. & Cas. Ins. Co.*, 505 F.3d 401, 404–05 (6th Cir. 2007); *Spivey v. Vertrue, Inc.*, 528 F.3d

C. MINIMAL DIVERSITY UNDER CAFA

For purposes of the "complete diversity" requirement in traditional diversity class actions, *all* named class representatives and *all* defendants had to be citizens of different states. If any named plaintiff and any named defendant were from the same state, the action could not be filed in or removed to federal court.[109]

The CAFA amendments to section 1332(d) vest the federal courts with "minimal diversity" jurisdiction (subject to certain important exceptions discussed below) over putative class actions with 100 or more putative class members in which more than $5 million is in controversy, so long as any member of the putative plaintiff class is a citizen of a state different from that of any defendant, or any class member or defendant is a foreign state or a citizen or subject to a foreign state. The minimal diversity provision is reminiscent of the federal interpleader statute.[110]

Thus, under CAFA, the claims of a Native American landowners class and a medical monitoring class could be prosecuted in federal court though complete diversity was lacking.[111] Likewise, diversity jurisdiction existed over private cause of action under the TCPA,[112] which permits private persons to bring suit "in an appropriate court of . . . State," where action was removed under CAFA and independent basis for jurisdiction existed under that statute, as both the amount-in-controversy requirement and the minimal diversity requirements are met.[113]

The minimal diversity requirement of CAFA was also satisfied in *Blockbuster, Inc. v. Galeno*,[114] in a class action alleging deceptive business practices, by the complaint's averment that "thousands" of "New York customers" were class members, even though the complaint did not aver that any particular New York resident was a New York citizen and thus diverse from the defendant corporation.

In *McMorris v. TJX Cos.*,[115] the court held that the minimal diversity of citizenship requirements were satisfied in suit by a putative class of Massachusetts "residents," against Massachusetts-based defendants, considering that "residency" did not equate with "citizenship," and therefore averments of residency were not dispositive of the issue.

982, 986 (7th Cir. 2008); *Hartis v. Chicago Title Ins. Co.*, No. 09-1105, 2009 U.S. App. LEXIS 5372, at *8 (8th Cir. Mar. 13, 2009); *Lowdermilk v. U.S. Bank Nat'l Ass'n*, 479 F.3d 994 (9th Cir. 2007); *Miedema v. Maytag Corp.*, 450 F.3d 1322 (11th Cir. 2006).

109. *See Strawbridge*, 3 Cranch 267, 2 L. Ed. 435; *Supreme Tribe of Ben-Hur v. Cauble*, 255 U.S. 356 (1921).

110. 28 U.S.C. § 1335(a)(1).

111. *Ponca Tribe of Indians of Okla. v. Cont'l Carbon Co.*, 439 F. Supp. 2d 1171 (W.D. Okla. 2006).

112. Telephone Consumer Protection Act of 1991, § 3(a), 47 U.S.C. § 227(b)(3).

113. 28 U.S.C. §§ 1332(d), 1441(a); *Kavu, Inc. v. Omnipak Corp.*, 246 F.R.D. 642 (W.D. Wash. 2007).

114. 472 F.3d at 59.

115. 493 F. Supp. 2d 158 (D. Mass. 2007).

1. Determining Citizenship

In most cases, citizenship is determined as it was prior to CAFA. For example, the citizenship of corporations continues to be governed by section 1332(c)(1), which provides that incorporated companies are deemed to be citizens of both the state of incorporation and the state where they have their principal place of business.[116] However, a corporation cannot use the fact of its dual citizenship to establish minimal diversity.[117]

CAFA also statutorily changes the "citizenship" of unincorporated associations for purposes of its jurisdictional inquiry. Section 1332(d)(10) provides that "an unincorporated association shall be deemed to be a citizen of the State where it has its principal place of business and the State under whose laws it is organized."[118] This language represents a departure from the ordinary rule that the citizenship of an unincorporated association is determined by reference to all of its members.[119] Several courts have considered this CAFA provision in the context of a limited liability company, concluding that, based on the language of section 1332(d)(10), a limited liability company should be treated as a citizen of the states under whose laws it is organized and/or in which it has its principal place of business, rather than looking to the citizenship of its owners.[120]

2. Timing of Citizenship

CAFA provides that the citizenship of the plaintiffs must be determined as of the date the complaint (or amended complaint) is filed or when the "other paper" first giving a right to removal is received.[121] There is no statutory provision setting the snapshot in time for deciding a defendant's citizenship, but the legislative history indicates that the removal rules in effect prior to CAFA should continue in effect where the statute makes no change.[122] As a result, the general rule that citizenship be determined as of the date of the complaint "should continue to apply to defendants."[123]

---

116. 28 U.S.C. § 1332(c)(1); see also The Hertz Corp. v. Friend, 559 U.S. ___, 130 S. Ct. 1181 (2010) (holding that the "principal place of business" of a corporation is the location of its "nerve center" or headquarters).

117. Johnson v. Advance Am., Cash Advance Ctrs. of S.C., Inc., 549 F.3d 932, 936 (4th Cir. 2008) ("Because Advance America has South Carolina citizenship, it cannot carry its burden of demonstrating that the citizenship of the South Carolina class members is different from its own." (emphasis in original)).

118. 28 U.S.C. § 1332(d)(10).

119. Carden v. Arkoma Assocs., 494 U.S. 185, 196–97 (1990) (limited partner is not a citizen, so courts must look to citizenship of its members to determine citizenship of entity); see also Ferrell v. Express Check Advance of SC LLC, 591 F.3d 698, 703 (4th Cir. 2010); see also Abrego Abrego, 443 F.3d at 684.

120. Ferrell, 591 F.3d at 704–05; Dunham v. Coffeyville Res., L.L.C., No. 07-1186-JTM, 2007 WL 3283774, at *4 (D. Kan. Nov. 6, 2007); Sundy v. Renewable Envtl. Solutions, L.L.C., No 07-5069-CV-SW-ODS, 2007 WL 2994348 (W.D. Mo. Oct. 10, 2007).

121. 28 U.S.C. § 1332(d)(7).

122. S. Rep. 109-14, at 36.

123. Moore's, § 23.63(b).

D. AMOUNT-IN-CONTROVERSY REQUIREMENT

The $75,000 amount-in-controversy requirement of section 1332(a) has also historically proven to be a formidable hurdle to the removal of class actions because the claims of class members could not be aggregated to satisfy the jurisdictional amount in diversity cases.[124] Under the Supreme Court's decision in *Zahn v. International Paper Co.*,[125] all class members had to have claims exceeding $75,000 for a class action to be removable on diversity grounds. After *Zahn*, Congress conferred on the district courts "supplemental jurisdiction over all other claims that are so related to the claims in the action within [their] original jurisdiction that they form part of the same case or controversy . . . ."[126] The circuit courts of appeals divided as to whether section 1367 overruled *Zahn*. In 2005—notably after CAFA was adopted—the Supreme Court finally resolved that split in *Exxon Mobil Corp. v. Allapattah Services, Inc.*,[127] concluding that "[i]f the [district] court has original jurisdiction over a single claim in the complaint, it has original jurisdiction over [the] 'civil action' within the meaning of section 1367(a) even if the civil action over which it has jurisdiction comprises fewer claims than were included in the complaint."[128] The Court observed that CAFA had likewise statutorily abrogated *Zahn* in cases under its ambit, but held that the statute had no bearing on the case presented because it originated prior to the effective date of CAFA.[129]

1. Elements of Recovery

When the class claims are for damages, the amount in controversy includes all forms of recoverable damages "exclusive of interest and costs."[130] This language is similar to the traditional diversity amount-in-controversy requirement of section 1332(a), and the CAFA courts have interpreted the provision in a similar fashion. As explained below in sections V.D.2 and 3, the determination of the actual damages in dispute can be complicated.

Punitive damages are included in the amount in controversy if they are available under applicable law based on the allegations and claims asserted.[131] However, at least one court has held that exemplary damages should not be counted in

---

124. *See Snyder v. Harris*, 394 U.S. 332 (1969).

125. 414 U.S. 291 (1973).

126. 28 U.S.C. § 1367(a).

127. 545 U.S. 546 (2005).

128. *Id.* at 559.

129. *Id.* at 571–72.

130. 28 U.S.C. § 1332(d)(2).

131. *See, e.g., Kaufman v. Allstate N.J. Ins. Co.*, 561 F.3d 144, 151–52 (3d Cir. 2009) (including punitive damages in determination of amount in controversy); *Guglielmino v. McKee Foods Corp.*, 506 F.3d 696, 700–01 (9th Cir. 2007) (CAFA's amount-in-controversy requirement excludes only "interest and costs," and therefore calculation includes actual and exemplary damages and attorney fees if requested).

determining the amount in controversy when contract claims, totaling less than the CAFA minimum, would not support an award for punitive damages under governing Tennessee law, and the plaintiffs had expressly disclaimed any punitive damages.[132] Statutory liquidated damages are also included in calculating the jurisdictional amount where the basis for their recovery is alleged and the allegations would support the right to this relief.[133]

Attorney fees are also included if they are recoverable from the defendant.[134] However, many courts require an affirmative showing that such fees are recoverable, such as a statutory right to recovery.[135] The Third Circuit has referred to the Federal Judicial Center's study on median percentage recoveries in calculating an appropriate amount of fees for purposes of this inquiry.[136]

2. Determining the Amount in Controversy

A removing defendant need not confess liability in order to show that the amount in controversy exceeds the $5 million removal threshold under CAFA.[137] The jurisdictional amount must be "either stated clearly on the face of the [removing] documents before the court, or readily deducible from them . . . ."[138] As noted above in section V.B, the federal courts have consistently placed the burden of proving that a case meets CAFA's jurisdictional requirements on the party invoking CAFA jurisdiction—which is typically the removing defendant. They have divided rank when it comes to determining what level of proof is required to meet that burden. Several different approaches have generally emerged.

When a state court pleading alleges an amount in controversy that exceeds the jurisdictional minimum, the statute is considered to be "presumptively satisfied"—

---

132. *See Smith*, 505 F.3d at 408 (automobile owner's state-court breach of contract class action alleging automobile insurer's failure to cover post-repair loss of value was not removable under CAFA because it failed to meet the amount-in-controversy threshold); *see also Trahan v. U.S. Bank Nat'l Ass'n*, No. C 09-03111, 2009 WL 4510140, at *3–5 (N.D. Cal. Nov. 30, 2009) (explaining that punitive damages and attorney fees are typically considered in determining amount in controversy, but declining to consider them in that case because plaintiffs' ability to seek such damages was speculative at best on the claims asserted).

133. *Bartnikowski v. NVR, Inc.*, 307 F. App'x 730, 735 (4th Cir. 2009).

134. *Frederico v. Home Depot*, 507 F.3d 188, 199 (3d Cir. 2007).

135. *E.g., Hartis*, 2009 U.S. App. LEXIS 5372, at *8–9 (only "'statutory attorney fees count toward the jurisdictional minimum calculation'" (quoting *Rasmussen v. State Farm Mut. Auto. Ins. Co.*, 410 F.3d 1029, 1031 (8th Cir. 2005)); *Lowdermilk*, 479 F.3d at 1000 (where underlying state law provided for payment of fees, those fees are included in the amount in controversy).

136. *In re Rite Aid Corp. Sec. Litig.*, 396 F.3d 294, 303 (3d Cir. 2005) (relying upon expert affidavit from Professor John C. Coffee referencing attorney fee studies and surveys conducted by the Federal Judicial Center).

137. *Spivey*, 528 F.3d at 986 (quoting *Brill v. Countrywide Home Loans, Inc.*, 427 F.3d at 449).

138. *Lowery*, 483 F.3d at 1211.

meaning the removing party has discharged its burden "unless it appears to a 'legal certainty' that the plaintiff cannot actually recover that amount."[139]

If the complaint instead either fails to specify an amount in controversy or is "unclear" or "ambiguous" as to the total at stake, the removing defendant must prove, to a "reasonable probability"—or on a preponderance of the evidence basis— that the jurisdictional threshold is met.[140] Notably, the Third Circuit has instead used the "legal certainty" test where the plaintiff had provided "no useful information with which to calculate the amount in controversy," but the underlying facts were not in dispute.[141] Applying it to the facts presented, the court concluded that removal was appropriate because it did "not appear to a *legal certainty* that Frederico cannot recover the jurisdictional amount."[142]

Finally, where the state court pleading disclaims that the amount in controversy meets the jurisdictional standard or specifically pleads an amount below the minimum, the party "'seeking removal must prove with legal certainty that CAFA's jurisdictional amount is met.'"[143] These decisions follow the lead of the seminal diversity case, *St. Paul Mercury Indemnity Co. v. Red Cab Co.*,[144] giving effect to the principle that if a plaintiff "does not desire to try his case in the federal court, he may resort to the expedient of suing for less than the jurisdictional amount, and though he would be justly entitled to more, the defendant cannot remove."

The Eighth Circuit has eschewed the tripartite standard and stated that "a party seeking to remove under CAFA must establish an amount in controversy by a preponderance of the evidence regardless of whether the complaint alleges an amount below the jurisdictional minimum."[145]

As is the case with traditional diversity, the CAFA courts have held that events occurring after removal to reduce the amount in controversy do not divest a federal court of jurisdiction.[146] However, post-removal affidavits may be used to clarify what is really in controversy when the complaint is ambiguous.[147]

---

139. *Guglielmino*, 506 F.3d at 699. Although *Guglielmino* was not a CAFA case, its outline of the three approaches has been cited in CAFA decisions. *See, e.g., Bell v. The Hershey Co.*, 557 F.3d 953, 957–58 (8th Cir. 2009).

140. *Amoche*, 556 F.3d at 43, 50 (noting that the "reasonable probability" test "uses different nomenclature from, but we believe is substantially the same as, the standards adopted by several circuits"); *Smith*, 505 F.3d at 404–05; *Bell*, 557 F.3d at 957–58; *Abrego Abrego*, 443 F.3d at 683 (using preponderance standard in CAFA cases where amount in controversy is not stated in pleading); *Miedema*, 450 F.3d 1322. The Eleventh Circuit later lamented that it was "at a loss as to how to apply the preponderance burden meaningfully." *Lowery*, 483 F.3d at 1210.

141. *Frederico*, 507 F.3d at 198.

142. *Id.* at 199 (emphasis in original).

143. *Guglielmino*, 506 F.3d at 699 (quoting *Lowdermilk*, 479 F.3d at 1000); *Morgan*, 471 F.3d at 471.

144. 303 U.S. 283, 294 (1938).

145. *Bell*, 557 F.3d at 958.

146. *Amoche*, 556 F.3d at 51.

147. *Id.* at 51–52.

3. Types of Permissible Proof

Despite liberal pleading requirements, evidence of the amount in controversy must not be speculative.[148] For example, when a defendant offered no support as to the size of the prospective class and made questionable assumptions regarding each class member's recovery, it failed to meet its burden of proving the $5 million jurisdictional minimum under CAFA.[149] Similarly, the Fourth Circuit rejected an attempt by the removing defendant in a Fair Labor Standards Act case to substantiate the amount in controversy with extrapolated calculations based on an assumption that each member of the plaintiff class worked an average of five hours of overtime per week.[150]

The Ninth Circuit likewise concluded that the defendant's "numbers are weak" when it had to assume that all class members would be entitled to the maximum damages available under the governing law in order to arrive at a number exceeding the $5 million threshold.[151] The court was also openly skeptical of the defendant's use of a class list from another case "that had not been vetted or certified" and apparently contained errors.[152] It concluded that, "[u]ntil the parties are able to more definitively ascertain the potential size of the class or the extent of the damages, we cannot base our jurisdiction on Defendant's speculation and conjecture."[153]

The types of proof used to satisfy this burden necessarily vary depending on the circumstances of the case and the standard to which the removing party is held.[154] Examples of different species of proof that have been suggested or accepted by the courts include the following:

- Statistical analyses involving a sampling of the defendant's credit insurance certificates to give a "rough sense for the class size."[155]
- Evidence of market share and revenues from the geographic region covering the class.[156]
- The approximately 4,000 unsolicited faxes sent by the defendant in alleged violation of the TCPA multiplied by the potential for treble damages to arrive at an amount in controversy of $6 million.[157]

---

148. *Thomas v. Bank of Am. Corp.*, 570 F.3d 1280, 1283 (11th Cir. 2009).

149. *Atteberry v. Esurance Ins. Servs., Inc.*, 473 F. Supp. 2d 876, 877 (N.D. Ill. 2007).

150. *Bartnikowski*, 307 F. App'x at 735–37.

151. *Lowdermilk*, 479 F.3d at 1001.

152. *Id.* at 1001–02.

153. *Id.* at 1002.

154. *See* section V.D.2, *supra.*

155. *Amoche*, 556 F.3d at 52.

156. *Id.*

157. *Gene & Gene LLC v. Biopay LLC*, 541 F.3d 318, 324–25 (5th Cir. 2008).

- Proof that approximately 58,800 AT&T customers were enrolled in a road-side assistance program after the free trial period had expired and were charged $2.99 per month for the service when the claim was that AT&T wrongfully automatically enrolled customers in an unwanted service to extract a fee.[158]
- When citizenship is implicated, a plaintiff class defined to include only "citizens" of a state is effective to limit the plaintiffs' side of the diversity equation to that state.[159]

Some courts are more willing to extrapolate the amount in controversy from assumptions based on the facts alleged in the complaint. In one decision, the Third Circuit divided the $5 million threshold by the amount of damages sought by the named plaintiff to posit that the class size was 2,233 individuals, which was well within the "tens of hundreds of thousands" of class members alleged in the complaint.[160] The Fourth Circuit similarly credited the district court's finding that the amount in controversy was met when the defendant had closed a factory where over 2,000 employees had worked and dividing the jurisdictional amount across the potential class of former workers led it to conclude that each plaintiff "would need to recover a little over $2,000 per person to exceed the $5 million requirement."[161] However, many courts have not been willing to extrapolate from individual circumstances to determine the amount in controversy.[162]

The Eleventh Circuit has expressed a much more limited view of the scope of permissible evidence. In *Lowery v. Alabama Power Co.*, the court held that the complaint and/or removal papers constitute the "limited universe of evidence available" and that if that record is insufficient to permit a court to conclude that removal was proper, then it must remand: "The absence of factual allegations pertinent to the existence of jurisdiction is dispositive and, in such absence, the existence of jurisdiction should not be divined by looking to the stars."[163] Nor would it countenance the defendant's attempt to adduce further proof through jurisdictional discovery: "The defendants' request for discovery is tantamount to an admission that

---

158. *Strawn*, 530 F.3d at 299.

159. *Johnson*, 549 F.3d at 937–38 (rejecting minimal diversity based on theory that some of class members could be citizens of states other than South Carolina when plaintiff had limited class definition to South Carolina citizens).

160. *Frederico*, 507 F.3d at 199 (3d Cir. 2007).

161. *Lanier v. Norfolk S. Corp.*, 256 F. App'x 629, 632 n.1 (4th Cir. 2007).

162. *Amoche*, 556 F.3d at 52 (refusing to extrapolate an estimate of the amount in controversy for a 13-state class from a figure representing only one state's experience by multiplying by 13 because "[t]hat sum is not reliable").

163. *Lowery*, 483 F.3d at 1214–15. The court did note some "limited circumstances" under which a defective notice might be "effectively amended" by additional evidence, such as the post-removal receipt of a paper that provides sufficient grounds for removal. *Id.* at 1214 n.66.

the defendants do not have a factual basis for believing that jurisdiction exists. The natural consequence of such an admission is remand to state court."[164]

What these cases show is that the federal circuit courts are demanding legitimate, defensible proof of the amount in controversy and expect removing defendants to marshal proof from within their own records to support their theories. Further, that evidence is subject to cross-examination by the courts; although they are willing to accept statistical analyses and extrapolation in lieu of mathematically certain proof, those calculations must be based on solid grounding; they will not permit assumptions and presumptions to fill in any gaps. As one court put it, "[w]e reach our decision to affirm the district court['s remand order] not unmindful of the difficulty that CAFA defendants face in demonstrating that the amount in controversy is met when plaintiffs have left their damages unspecified."[165] However, that court and others around the country have found a mitigating benefit in the knowledge that CAFA permits "[s]uccessive attempts at removal . . . where the grounds for removal become apparent only later in the litigation," and the statute eliminates the one-year limit for doing so:

> [The defendant's] removal of this case at the earliest possible date was understandable, given the removal statute's requirement that a defendant file a notice of removal within thirty days of his receipt of the first removable document . . . . It is not unfair that [the defendant] wait until the class allegations are more fully developed before attempting to remove, if there is a later basis for removal, especially now that class actions under CAFA are exempt from the removal statute's one-year time limit.[166]

Although decisions like *Bartnikowski v. NVR*[167] and *Amoche v. Guarantee Trust Life Insurance Co.*[168] may provide arguments for delaying removal until the amount-in-controversy facts are sufficiently well-developed, it would seem more prudent to utilize the 30-day removal window of section 1446(b) and later invoke the successive removal option, rather than counting on section 1453(b) to effectively expand the 30-day period for removal under section 1446(b), which is left intact.

---

164. *Id.* at 1217–18; *cf. Preston II*, 485 F.3d at 821 ("At this preliminary stage, it is unnecessary for the district court to permit exhaustive discovery capable of determining the exact class size to an empirical certainty.").

165. *Bartnikowski*, 307 F. App'x at 739.

166. *Amoche*, 556 F.3d at 53 (citation omitted); *see also Bartnikowski*, 307 F. App'x at 739.

167. 307 F. App'x at 739.

168. 556 F.3d at 47.

VI. CAFA's Exceptions

Not all CAFA cases that have been properly removed will remain in federal court. Although the new jurisdictional provisions for class actions are very broad, they do not give the federal courts unlimited authority to entertain state law classes; there are a number of exceptions built into the statute. Some of these exceptions are quite complicated, and the courts have differed as to whether they are jurisdictional or merely procedural. As a general matter, however, these exceptions are intended to keep the following kinds of cases out of federal court: class actions that involve both class members and defendants who mostly are citizens of the forum state; class actions against state government defendants; class actions with fewer than 100 class members; and shareholder class actions or derivative suits based on state corporation law.

A. BURDEN OF PROOF

As noted above in section V.B, the federal courts have ascribed the burden of proving the elements of federal jurisdiction in section 1332(d) to the removing party. The burden of proving CAFA's exceptions, however, is on the party seeking to remand to state court or otherwise to convince the federal court to abstain from exercising jurisdiction under CAFA, regardless of the status of that party.[169] All of the circuit courts that have addressed the issue have concluded that once CAFA jurisdiction has been established, the burden shifts to the party objecting to federal jurisdiction to show that the CAFA exceptions apply.[170]

B. MANDATORY ABSTENTION

Section 1332(d)(4) sets out two types of circumstances in which a federal court is required to decline jurisdiction under CAFA. These exceptions—known as the "home state" and "local controversy" exceptions—are "'designed to draw a delicate balance between making a federal forum available to genuinely national litigation and allowing the state courts to retain cases when the controversy is strongly linked to that state.'"[171]

Under section 1332(d)(4), a federal court "shall decline to exercise jurisdiction" over a class action if two-thirds of all class members are citizens of the forum state and either all "the primary defendants" are citizens of the same state or at least

---

169. *See, e.g., Preston II,* 485 F.3d at 813 (where codefendant was the only party moving for remand, that party bore the burden of showing that one of the CAFA exceptions applied).

170. *See, e.g., Grimsdale v. Kash N' Karry Food Stores, Inc. (In re Hannaford Bros. Customer Data Sec. Breach Litig.),* 564 F.3d 75, 78 (1st Cir. 2009); *Kaufman,* 561 F.3d at 153; *Frazier v. Pioneer Ams. LLC,* 455 F.3d 542, 546 (5th Cir. 2006); *Hart,* 457 F.3d at 679–82; *Serrano v. 180 Connect, Inc.,* 478 F.3d 1018, 1021–22, 1023 (9th Cir. 2007); *Evans v. Walter Indus., Inc.,* 449 F.3d 1159, 1165 (11th Cir. 2006).

171. *Preston I,* 485 F.3d at 803 (quoting *Hart,* 457 F.3d at 682).

one defendant from whom "significant relief" is sought and whose conduct is a "significant basis" of the claims asserted is a citizen of the forum state. In the latter instance, however, mandatory abstention is required only if the "principal injuries" were suffered in the forum state or the relevant conduct by the defendants occurred there, and no other "similar" class actions have been filed within the past three years.[172] Together these provisions allow some class actions to proceed in state court where a substantial majority of the class and one or more significant defendants are citizens of the forum state. They are reserved for application in "a narrow category of truly localized controversies . . . ."[173]

1. The "Home State" Exception

Section 1332(d)(4)(B)—labeled the "Home State Exception"—triggers mandatory abstention if two-thirds or more of the proposed plaintiffs, and "the primary defendants," are citizens of the state in which the action was originally filed.[174]

a. Determining the Citizenship of the Putative Class Members

The two-thirds citizenship requirement for putative class members has proved to be a formidable task in many cases. CAFA provides that this determination is to be made as of the date the complaint or amended complaint is filed or the "other paper" giving a right to removal is received.[175]

The Fifth Circuit has written on the subject in a pair of cases involving wrongful death and personal injury claims against a hospital having patients who died or were injured in the aftermath of Hurricane Katrina. The court construed the home state and local controversy exceptions, both of which "require[ ] the court to make an objective factual finding regarding the percentage of the class members that were citizens of Louisiana at the time of filing of the class petition."[176] In doing so, the court explored the line between showing mere residency and citizenship—which is required for purposes of the CAFA exception.

In the first case, the plaintiffs "made no effort to provide citizenship data," instead offering an affidavit from the director of medical records attesting that 242 of the 299 patients at the facility during the storm had Louisiana addresses.[177] The court held that this proof did not satisfy the plaintiffs' burden to prove that more than two-thirds of the class members were *citizens* of Louisiana, stating that this requirement cannot be presumed—at least in Louisiana, considering the

---

172. 28 U.S.C. § 1332(d)(4)(A)(ii).
173. *Preston II*, 485 F.3d at 812 (quoting *Evans*, 449 F.3d at 1164).
174. 28 U.S.C. § 1332(d)(4)(B).
175. *Id.* at § 1332(d)(7).
176. *Preston II*, 485 F.3d at 811.
177. *Preston I*, 485 F.3d at 798.

displacement of so many citizens in the aftermath of Hurricane Katrina.[178] The court also dismissed the plaintiffs' attempt to prove citizenship through census data and voter turnout records—which they claimed showed that the displaced residents intended to return to Louisiana—as being too general to permit legitimate conclusions about the class members.[179] Although the Fifth Circuit acknowledged that "the quality and quantity of the evidence" necessary to prove this exception will necessarily "vary from case to case based on the class definition and underlying facts," it nonetheless required the movant to "make some minimal showing of the citizenship of the proposed class at the time that suit was filed."[180]

The plaintiffs in the second decision fared better, as they submitted eight affidavits from class members evidencing their intent to return to New Orleans, which the court found "unequivocally evince[d] the intent of these plaintiffs not to change their domicile."[181] Although these affidavits represented only a fraction of the class, the court permitted that "evidentiary standard for establishing the domicile of more than one hundred plaintiffs must be based on practicality and reasonableness."[182] Considering the logistical difficulties of obtaining this proof and the underlying circumstances of the storm, the district court was within its discretion to accept these affidavits as representative of the class as a whole: "The sheer magnitude of this shared catalyst formed an adequate backdrop for the district court's extrapolation that the reasons offered by the affiants for not immediately returning home . . . were probably representative of many other proposed class members."[183]

In re Sprint Nextel Corp.[184] represents another attempt to wrestle with the two-thirds citizenship requirement, this time in the context of a putative class action against a cell phone provider accused of imposing artificially high prices for text messaging services in violation of Kansas' consumer protection statute. The plaintiffs sought remand under the home-state exception, but failed to submit any proof of citizenship.[185] The district court nonetheless concluded that the two-thirds requirement was satisfied because the class was defined to include only Kansas cell phone numbers and billing addresses.[186] The Seventh Circuit characterized its deduction as "[s]ensible guesswork, based on a sense of how the world works, but

---

178. *Id.* at 801–02 ("CAFA does not permit the courts to make a citizenship determination based on a record bare of any evidence showing class members' intent to be domiciled in Louisiana.").

179. *Id.* at 802 (concluding that the "census data is too general to contradict an assertion that two-thirds of the patients were not domiciled in the area at the relevant time").

180. *Id.*

181. *Preston II*, 485 F.3d at 815–16.

182. *Id.* at 816.

183. *Id.* at 817.

184. 593 F.3d 669, 670–71 (7th Cir. 2010).

185. *Id.* at 673.

186. *Id.*

guesswork nonetheless" and held that the court should not have "draw[n] conclusions about the citizenship of class members based on things like their phone numbers and mailing addresses."[187] The court appreciated the difficulties in establishing citizenship for a class of potentially hundreds of thousands of plaintiffs, and suggested that the following might satisfy the requirement:

- Proof of domicile from a representative sample, such as affidavits or survey responses of a sufficient size to extrapolate;[188] or
- Changing the class definition to include only "citizens" of Kansas.

Other cases have addressed how to determine the denominator of the two-thirds requirement. For instance, *In re Hannaford Bros. Co. Customer Data Security Breach Litigation*,[189] a class action against grocery stores in Florida involving only Florida citizens and Florida causes of action, qualified for remand under the home state exception to CAFA, although persons who were not Florida citizens also did business at those stores in Florida. In upholding the remand, the First Circuit rejected the grocery store's argument that the term "members of all proposed plaintiff classes in the aggregate" required consideration of other class actions arising from similar facts.[190] According to the First Circuit, neither the statute's construction nor the legislative history could justify consideration of other class actions outside the four corners of the complaint to increase the denominator of the two-thirds fraction under CAFA.[191]

b. Primary Defendants

On the defense side, the focus of the home state exception[192] is on identifying the primary defendants. There is yet scant case law to assist in determining what factors are relevant to a determination of "primacy," or the appropriate approach to analyzing this issue. The following commentary from Senate Report No. 109-14 is illuminating:

> [T]he Committee intends that "primary defendants" be interpreted to reach those defendants who are the real "targets" of the lawsuit—*i.e.*, the defendants that would be expected to incur most of the loss if liability is found. Thus, the term "primary defendants" should include any person who has substantial exposure to significant portions of the proposed class in the action, particularly any defendant that

---

187. *Id.* at 674.

188. The court posited that, while statistical science typically requires a 95 percent confidence level, "any number greater than 50 percent would have allowed the district court to conclude that the plaintiffs had established the citizenship requirement by a preponderance of the evidence." *Id.* at 675–76 (citing *Ethyl Corp. v. EPA*, 541 F.2d 1, 28 n.58 (D.C. Cir. 1976) (en banc)).

189. 564 F.3d at 76.

190. *Id.* at 79–81.

191. *Id.* at 79–80; *accord In re Sprint Nextel Corp.*, 593 F.3d at 672.

192. 28 U.S.C. § 1332(d)(4)(B).

is allegedly liable to the vast majority of the members of the proposed classes (as opposed to simply a few individual class members).[193]

Federal courts have divined various ways to ascertain the distinction between "primary" and "secondary," and most have ultimately concluded that "primary defendants" are those directly liable to the plaintiffs, as opposed to those defendants liable under theories of vicarious liability or joined for purposes of contribution or indemnity.[194] A primary defendant is one "(1) who has the greater liability exposure; (2) is most able to satisfy a potential judgment; (3) is sued directly, as opposed to vicariously . . . ; (4) is the subject of a significant portion of the claims asserted by plaintiffs; or (5) is the only defendant named in one particular cause of action."[195]

One decision out of the Western District of Louisiana has observed that "whether a putative class seeks significant relief from an in-state defendant includes not only an assessment of how many members of the class were harmed by the defendant's actions, but also a comparison of the relief sought between all defendants and each defendant's ability to pay a potential judgment."[196] This is a fact-intensive analysis, and the case law generally allows discovery. Nonetheless, it is the plaintiffs who will have the burden of proof, and the case law (and Senate commentary) indicates that, unlike removal statutes in general, CAFA's provisions are to be construed broadly in favor of removal and federal jurisdiction.

2. The "Local Controversy" Exception

So long as the two-thirds citizenship requirement is met as to the putative class members, mandatory abstention can apply even if only one of the defendants is a citizen of the forum state under section 1332(d)(4)(A). However, the local controversy exception contains a number of additional requirements when less than all of the primary defendants are forum residents. The Senate Report explains that "[t]his provision is intended to respond to concerns that class actions with a truly local focus should not be moved to federal court under [CAFA] because state courts have a strong interest in adjudicating such disputes."[197] However, Congress also "intended the local controversy exception to be a narrow one, with all doubts resolved 'in favor of exercising jurisdiction over the case.'"[198] The first require-

---

193. S. REP. 109-14, at 43.

194. *Kitson v. Bank of Edwardsville*, Civ. No. 06-528-GPM, 2006 WL 3392752, at *5 (S.D. Ill. Nov. 22, 2006).

195. *Brook v. UnitedHealth Group, Inc.*, No. 06-CV-12954(GBD), 2007 WL 2827808, at *5 (S.D.N.Y. Sept. 27, 2007).

196. *Robinson v. Cheetah Transp.*, Civ. A. No. 06-0005, 2006 WL 468820, at *3 (W.D. La. Feb. 27, 2006).

197. S. REP. 109-14, at 39.

198. *Evans*, 449 F.3d at 1163 (quoting S. REP. 109-14, at 42).

ment of section 1332(d)(4)(A) mirrors the two-thirds citizenship requirement of the home state exception and is interpreted accordingly. The other considerations are discussed below.

a. Significant Relief/Significant Basis Test

Under this exception, the in-state defendant must be one from whom "significant relief is sought" and "whose alleged conduct forms a significant basis for the claims asserted by the proposed plaintiff class."[199] Courts interpreting the "significant relief" provision have used the same general standard: "significant relief" is implicated "when the relief sought against that defendant is a significant portion of the entire relief sought by the class."[200] As stated by one district court, this inquiry involves an assessment of how many members of the class were harmed by the in-state defendant's actions, as well as a comparison of the relief sought against each defendant, and each defendant's ability to pay a potential judgment.[201]

The Tenth Circuit has concluded that a "defendant from whom significant relief is *sought*" does not mean a "defendant from whom significant relief may be *obtained*."[202] To the contrary—"[t]here is nothing in the language of [CAFA] that indicates Congress intended district courts to wade into the factual swamp of assessing the financial viability of a defendant as part of this preliminary consideration . . . ."[203] Thus, district courts are not required to consider a local defendant's ability to pay a potential judgment.

The "significant conduct" element of section 1332(d)(4)(A)—inquiring whether the conduct of a local defendant is a "significant basis for the claims"—often merges into the inquiry of whether significant relief is sought against a local defendant. For example, in *Evans v. Walter Industries, Inc.*,[204] the Eleventh Circuit blended the inquiries into a "Significant Defendant Test" and applied a single standard to both prongs. A district court divined the following considerations in assessing both inquiries: "(1) whether the product was sold outside of the locality; (2) whether the injury incurred was specific to the locality; [and] (3) whether the class as a whole seeks relief against the local defendant" in deciding whether the "significant basis"/"significant relief" prong has been met.[205]

---

199. 28 U.S.C. § 1332(d)(4)(A).

200. *Evans*, 449 F.3d at 1167; *Cooper v. R.J. Reynolds Tobacco Co.*, 586 F. Supp. 2d 1312, 1317–18 (M.D. Fla. 2008) (finding "significant relief" requirement not met where only Florida defendant, Liggett, had a market share of 1.2 percent to 5 percent); *Robinson*, 2006 WL 468820.

201. *Robinson*, 2006 WL 468820, at *3.

202. *Coffey v. Freeport McMoran Copper & Gold*, 581 F.3d 1240, 1245 (10th Cir. 2009) (emphasis added).

203. *Id.*

204. 449 F.3d at 1166; *see also Ava Acupuncture P.C. v. State Farm Mut. Auto. Ins. Co.*, 592 F. Supp. 2d 522 (S.D.N.Y. 2008).

205. *Eakins v. Pella Corp.*, 455 F. Supp. 2d 450, 452–53 (E.D.N.C. 2006) (citing S. Rep. 109-14, at 40).

The Third Circuit's analysis of the "significant basis" prong in *Kaufman v. Allstate New Jersey Insurance Co.*[206] likewise echoes the "significant relief" analysis described above. In that case, the court held that satisfaction of the "significant basis" prong requires "at least one local defendant whose alleged conduct forms a significant basis for all the claims asserted in the action."[207] The court clarified, however, that this requirement does not mean that every proposed class member must have a claim against the local defendant.[208] Although the quantity of claims asserted against the local defendant can be important, it is not determinative.[209] Instead, the court must compare the local defendant's alleged conduct to the alleged conduct of all defendants still parties to the suit.[210] In making that determination, the court suggested that district courts consider the following factors:

> 1) the relative importance of each of the claims to the action; 2) the nature of the claims and issues raised against the local defendant; 3) the nature of the claims and issues raised against all the Defendants; 4) the number of claims that rely on the local defendant's alleged conduct; 5) the number of claims asserted; 6) the identity of the Defendants; 7) whether the Defendants are related; 8) the number of members of the putative classes asserting claims that rely on the local defendant's alleged conduct; and 9) the approximate number of members in the putative class.[211]

For example, in *Bond v. Veolia Water Indianapolis, LLC*,[212] a public utility that was organized under Delaware law but provided water service in an Indiana city was a citizen of both Indiana and Delaware for purposes of CAFA, and thus, remand to state court was warranted under CAFA's local controversy, home state controversy, and interests of justice exceptions in actions challenging the frequency with which water usage meters were read; the proper focus was on the nerve center of the utility itself, which was in the city, not the headquarters of its parent.

In yet another application of the local controversy rule, the conduct of an out-of-state window manufacturer's local distributor did not form a significant basis of purchasers' products liability claims, and thus the purchasers' state court action against the distributor and manufacturer did not fall within CAFA's local contro-

---

206. 561 F.3d at 154–55.

207. *Id.* at 155. The court noted the general rule that citizenship be determined as of the date suit is filed, but indicated that the local controversy rule requires consideration of post-filing changes as to the local defendant: "Applying the exception when no local defendant remains in the action . . . would not comport with the exception's focus on discerning local controversies based, in part, on the presence of a significant local defendant." *Id.* at 153.

208. *Id.* at 155.

209. *Id.* at 155–56.

210. *Id.* at 156–57; *see also Ava Acupuncture*, 592 F. Supp. 2d at 531–32 (comparing alleged conduct of and claims asserted against all defendants to determine whether there was a significant local defendant).

211. *Kaufman*, 561 F.3d at 157 n.13.

212. 571 F. Supp. 2d 905 (S.D. Ind. 2008).

versy exception where the windows were not sold exclusively in the state, the injury resulting from the defect was not specific to the state, and there was no showing that the class as a whole had a cause of action against the local distributor.[213]

b. In-State Injuries or Related Conduct

The next requirement of the local controversy exception is that the "principal injuries resulting from the alleged conduct or any related conduct of each defendant were incurred in the State in which the action was originally filed."[214] The drafters provided an example of class action for property damages allegedly resulting from a chemical leak at a local manufacturing plant.[215] Courts have interpreted the provision accordingly. For example, where the principal injuries claimed by a class were the contamination of real property and the need to monitor class members for future adverse health effects allegedly related to exposure to the contaminants released by the defendants, the in-state injury requirement was met.[216]

In another factual presentation, allegations that the named plaintiff and putative class members lived in Ohio, that the defendants failed to refund premiums and to charge proper interest rates in Ohio, and that the challenged loans and accompanying insurance policies were issued in Ohio were sufficient to show that the injuries occurred in Ohio.[217]

In *Kaufman*,[218] the defendant asserted that this requirement could only be satisfied if the principal injuries *and* the related conduct by the defendant both occurred in the forum state. The Third Circuit rejected this contention, holding that the plain language of the statute—which stated the two alternatives in the disjunctive—negated that argument and thus the principal injuries provision was met.[219]

c. Consideration of Other Class Actions

The fourth prong of the local controversy exception requires the federal court to consider whether "during the 3-year period preceding the filing of that class action, no other class action has been filed asserting the same or similar factual allegations against any of the defendants on behalf of the same or other persons."[220] In the drafters' view, "if a controversy results in the filing of multiple class actions, it is a strong signal that those cases may not be of the variety that this

---

213. *Eakins*, 455 F. Supp. 2d 450.

214. 28 U.S.C. § 1332(d)(4)(A)(i)(III).

215. S. REP. 109-14, at 40.

216. *Anderson v. Hackett*, 646 F. Supp. 2d 1041, 1049–50 (S.D. Ill. 2009) ("In short, the injuries alleged by Plaintiffs are exactly the sort Congress had in mind when it fashioned this element of the local controversy exception." (citing S. REP. 109-14, at 40, 2005, *reprinted in* U.S.C.C.A.N. 38)).

217. *Am. Gen. Fin. Servs. v. Griffin*, 685 F. Supp. 2d 729, 735 (N.D. Ohio 2010).

218. 561 F.3d at 158.

219. *Id.*

220. 28 U.S.C. § 1332(d)(4)(A)(ii).

exception is intended to address."[221] A second purpose of this requirement (which is also contained in the discretionary abstention provision discussed below at section VI.C) is "to ensure that overlapping or competing class actions or class actions making similar factual allegations against the same defendant that would benefit from coordination are not excluded by the Local Controversy Exception and thus placed beyond the coordinating authority of the Judicial Panel on Multidistrict Litigation."[222]

3. Is Remand Under These Provisions Waivable?

It is not clear whether these mandatory provisions can be waived or if a remand request can be made outside of the 30-day statutory period.[223] A district court has opined that the mandatory remand provision of section 1332(d) "deals not with whether the court has jurisdiction, but rather . . . whether the right circumstances exist to prevent the court from exercising its jurisdiction."[224] On appeal to the Seventh Circuit, the court did not expressly decide the issue but held that plaintiffs could invoke the mandatory remand provisions outside of the usual 30-day window for removal if facts developed during discovery supported such a remand.[225] Two more recent cases have indicated that that the abstention exceptions are jurisdictional and thus not subject to waiver.[226]

C. DISCRETIONARY ABSTENTION

In addition to the home state and local controversy exceptions, which require federal courts to decline jurisdiction when their elements are demonstrated, CAFA also contains a discretionary abstention provision. Under section 1332(d)(3), a federal court is permitted to decline jurisdiction where the primary defendants and between one-third and two-thirds of the class members are citizens of the forum state and other pragmatic "interests of justice" factors weigh in favor of resolution by a state court.[227] As the Fifth Circuit has described it, "§ 1332(d)(3) provides a

---

221. S. Rep. 109-14, at 40.

222. *Id.* at 40–41.

223. *See* 28 U.S.C. § 1446(b).

224. *In re FedEx Ground Package Sys.*, No. 03:05-MD-527 RM, 2006 U.S. Dist. LEXIS 1219, at *25 (N.D. Ind. Jan. 13, 2006).

225. *Hart*, 457 F.3d at 681–82; *see also Kitson*, 2006 WL 3392752, at *5 ("The Court notes that in *Hart*, though the Seventh Circuit did not address the precise issue of waiver of the right to seek abstention under CAFA, the court specifically held that a plaintiff has the right to seek abstention not only at the time that the case is removed under CAFA but later in the case as well, if ongoing discovery reveals the necessity of abstention.").

226. *See Preston II*, 485 F.3d at 812 n.2 (addressing discretionary abstention provision and stating that a court may sua sponte review whether it has subject matter jurisdiction); *see also Martin v. Lafon Nursing Facility of the Holy Family, Inc.*, 548 F. Supp. 2d 268, 279 n.45 (E.D. La. 2008) (citing *Preston II* and dismissing as "without merit" defendant's argument that plaintiff waived the right to seek remand pursuant to the discretionary abstention provision of CAFA).

227. 28 U.S.C. § 1332(d)(3).

discretionary vehicle for district courts to ferret out the 'controversy that uniquely affects a particular locality to the exclusion of all others.'"[228]

In deciding whether to exercise its power to decline jurisdiction, the court must consider the "interests of justice" and "the totality of the circumstances," including whether the claims involve matters of national interest, whether they involve the application of the law of states other than the forum state, whether the class action was pleaded in an effort to avoid federal jurisdiction, whether there is a "distinct nexus" between the case and the forum state, whether the number of class members who are citizens of the forum state is substantially greater than the number of citizens of other states, and whether similar class actions have been brought within the past three years.[229] Because the factors are designed to be individualized and flexible it is, not surprisingly, difficult to draw many rules of guidance from the application of this exception.

For example, in *Preston v. Tenet Health System Memorial Medical Center (Preston II)*,[230] the Fifth Circuit alternatively analyzed the plaintiffs' request to remand under the discretionary abstention provision of CAFA, analyzing each factor and concluding that the case "symbolizes a quintessential example of Congress' intent to carve-out exceptions to CAFA's expansive grant of federal jurisdiction when our courts confront a truly localized controversy."[231]

Likewise, in *Martin v. Lafon Nursing Facility of the Holy Family, Inc.*,[232] another action involving allegations of negligence and wrongful death at a New Orleans nursing home in the wake of Hurricane Katrina, the court found that a discretionary declination of jurisdiction was warranted because the claims involved matters of local interest; the only claims asserted were state law claims; a distinct nexus existed between Louisiana and the class members, the harm, and the defendants; and it appeared that at least one-third of the class members were Louisiana citizens.

The court in *Ava Acupuncture P.C. v. State Farm Mutual Automobile Insurance Co.*[233] considered whether a class action brought by claimants and their assignees against insurers and their lawyers alleging fraudulent failure to pay statutorily mandated no-fault medical benefits as a result of their use of unqualified and

---

228. *Preston II*, 485 F.3d at 812 (quoting *Evans*, 449 F.3d at 1164).

229. *Id.*

230. *Id.* at 822–24.

231. *Id.* at 823.

232. 548 F. Supp. 2d at 278–79. The court also declined jurisdiction under the home state and local controversy exceptions, finding that the plaintiff had proven by a preponderance of the evidence—through the use of questionnaires filled out by 52 putative class members—that two-thirds of the potential class members were Louisiana citizens. *Id.* at 275, 277. The court's decision to decline jurisdiction under the discretionary abstention provision was an additional basis for remanding. *Id.* at 279.

233. 592 F. Supp. 2d 522.

illegal special investigation units fell within CAFA's local controversy exception, and thus was subject to removal, even though it was very likely that two-thirds of all class members were state residents and that principal injuries were suffered in the state, no other similar class action had been brought against defendants, and two of three insurers and their law firm were state residents, where nearly all claim denials in question came from a foreign insurer, and the vast majority of relief sought was from a foreign insurer.

A district court's balancing of the discretionary abstention factors can be reviewed on appeal either if it dismisses a case originally filed in federal court (in which case its decision is appealable under section 1291) or if it remands a case that was removed by a defendant (in which case the permissive appeal provisions of section 1453 apply).

D. STATE ACTION EXCEPTION

Although CAFA only requires "minimum diversity"—i.e., that one plaintiff is a citizen of a state that is diverse from one defendant—a state (including a political subdivision or "arm" of the state) is not considered to be a "citizen of a State" for purposes of traditional diversity. There is a long line of diversity cases in which the presence of a state as a legitimate party defeated or destroyed diversity.[234] These cases have interpreted the requirement that plaintiffs and defendants be "citizens of different States"[235] to exclude the states themselves (and their political subdivisions, arms, agents, and instrumentalities).[236] Further, federal courts are generally barred by the 11th Amendment from hearing state law claims against either state governments or state government officials.[237]

CAFA has integrated these principles into section 1332(d)(5), which excludes application of the statute to any suit where "the primary defendants are States, State officials, or other *governmental entities against whom the district court may be foreclosed from ordering relief*" (emphasis added). This provision is an attempt to codify the 11th Amendment to the U.S. Constitution, which prohibits a state from being sued in federal court without its consent and to give effect to other

---

234. *E.g., Frazier*, 455 F.3d at ("[I]t is long-settled that a state has no citizenship for § 1332(a) diversity purposes." (citing *Cory v. White*, 457 U.S. 85, 87 (1982))).

235. 28 U.S.C. § 1332(a)(1).

236. There is a potential wrinkle in the fact that the traditional diversity statute uses the term "citizens of different states," while CAFA employs a slightly different terminology—"any member of a class of plaintiffs is a citizen of a State different *from any defendant*." *Compare* 28 U.S.C. § 1332(a)(1) *with id.* at § 1332(d)(2)(A) (emphasis added). Further, subparts (b)(2)(B) and (C) of CAFA reiterate the "citizen" qualifier, *see* 28 U.S.C. § 1332(d)(2)(B) and (C), which might be argued to evidence an intention that the term "any defendant" in § 1332(d)(2)(A) is meant to include not only "citizens of" states, but the states themselves. As noted above, § 1332(d)(5) would appear to obviate any concern in this regard.

237. *See Pennhurst State Sch. & Hosp. v. Halderman*, 465 U.S. 89 (1984).

governmental immunities from suit.[238] It has been characterized as the "state-action exemption," and the Senate Report issued after the passage of CAFA indicates that the purpose of this provision was to "prevent states, state officials, or other governmental entities from dodging legitimate claims by removing class actions to federal court and then arguing that the federal courts are constitutionally prohibited from granting the requested relief."[239] In the Fifth Circuit, the burden of proving this exception would appear to be on the party contesting jurisdiction.[240] Because the provision is grounded in the 11th Amendment, the analysis of whether the defendant is an arm or instrumentality of the state for purposes of the government-defendant exception to CAFA presumably turns on similar considerations.

E. LIMITED SCOPE EXCEPTION

A non–federal question class action is not subject to the new provisions for diversity jurisdiction or removal if the total number of class members is less than 100.[241] Noting that class actions can "involve as few as 21 class members," the drafters of CAFA made clear that this provision is to permit class actions with relatively few members to remain in state court.[242] Like the other exceptions to CAFA, this provision is intended to be a narrow one.[243]

The courts are in conflict as to whether this requirement is a prerequisite or an exception to jurisdiction. The Ninth and Eleventh Circuits have concluded that the 100 claimants provision is part of the jurisdictional threshold,[244] while the Fifth Circuit treats it as an exception.[245] As one court has characterized it, "[t]his is more than a formalistic dispute, as the removing party has the burden to establish jurisdictional requirements, and the party seeking remand has the burden to prove exceptions."[246]

---

238. The provision appears to be designed to encompass all forms of governmental immunity, including 11th Amendment and sovereign immunity for both state and federal governmental entities.

239. S. REP. 109-14, at 42, *reprinted in* 2005 U.S.C.C.A.N. 3.

240. *Frazier*, 455 F.3d at 546 ("We hold that plaintiffs [seeking remand] have the burden to show the applicability of the § 1332(d)(3)–(5) exceptions when jurisdiction turns on their application."). Although the Fifth Circuit characterized this provision as an "exception" to CAFA jurisdiction in *Frazier*, other courts have treated it as a jurisdictional prerequisite. *See, e.g.*, *Serrano*, 478 F.3d at 1020 & n.3; *Hart*, 457 F.3d at 679.

241. 28 U.S.C. § 1332(d)(5)(B).

242. S. REP. 109-14, at 42 & n.127.

243. *Id.* at 42.

244. *Serrano*, 478 F.3d at 1020 ("As a threshold matter, CAFA applies to 'class action' lawsuits where the aggregate number of members of all proposed plaintiff classes is 100 or more persons."); *Miedema*, 450 F.3d at 1327 n.4 (CAFA's jurisdictional provision "does not apply to a class action in which 'the number of members of all proposed plaintiff classes in the aggregate is less than 100.'").

245. *Frazier*, 455 F.3d at 546.

246. *PHLD P'ship v. Arch Specialty Ins. Co.*, 565 F. Supp. 2d 1342, 1344 n.1 (S.D. Fla. 2008) (citing *Miedema*, 450 F.3d at 1328, and *Evans*, 449 F.3d at 1164).

F. SECURITIES AND CORPORATE LAW CARVE-OUTS

The Act excludes from its coverage certain actions involving securities and corporate governance claims.[247] The district court lacks federal jurisdiction over claims that are solely limited to (1) "covered" securities as defined under the Securities Act of 1933 ("'33 Act")[248] and the Securities Exchange Act of 1934 ("'34 Act");[249] (2) relating to a company's internal affairs or corporate governance arising under the laws of the state that governs it; or (3) relating to certain rights, duties, and obligations relating to or created by certain securities under the '33 Act.[250] These exceptions attempt to "avoid disturbing in any way the federal vs. state court jurisdictional lines already drawn in the securities litigation class action context by the enactment of the Securities Litigation Uniform Standards Act of 1988" and to exempt from CAFA's original jurisdiction "those class actions that solely involve claims that relate to matters of corporate governance arising out of state law."[251]

The first of these exceptions is designed to prevent a collision with jurisdiction over certain types of securities actions. They exclude "covered securities" defined under section 16(f)(3) of the '33 Act and section 28(f)(5)(E) of the '34 Act. For purposes of this exception, "covered securities" as defined by the '33 Act are "securities that are traded nationally or listed on a regulated national exchange."[252]

Section 1332(d)(9)(B), which is sometimes referred to as the "Delaware carve-out," applies to actions that solely involve claims relating to "the internal affairs or governance of a corporation or other form of business enterprise and that arise[ ] under or by virtue of the laws of the State in which such corporation or business enterprise is incorporated or organized."[253] The effect of this exclusion is to prevent shareholder derivative actions or other representative actions involving state corporation law issues from being entirely federalized.[254]

The third exception—for claims "that relate[ ] to the rights, duties (including fiduciary duties), and obligations relating to or created by or pursuant to any security (as defined under section 2(a)(1) of the Securities Act of 1933 and the regulations issued thereunder"[255]—is also a narrow exception. In *Estate of Pew v. Cardarelli*,[256] the plaintiffs brought a putative class action against an issuer of

---

247. *Estate of Pew v. Cardarelli*, 527 F.3d 25, 30 (2d Cir. 2008).

248. 15 U.S.C. §§ 78p(f)(3) & 25(f)(5)(E).

249. 15 U.S.C. § 78bb(f)(5)(E).

250. 28 U.S.C. § 1332(d)(9).

251. S. Rep. 109-14, at 45.

252. *Estate of Pew*, 527 F.3d at 34 (citing 15 U.S.C. §§ 77r(b), 77p(f)(3), 78bb(f)(5)(E)); *see also Davis v. Chase Bank U.S.A., N.A.*, 453 F. Supp. 2d 1205, 1209 (C.D. Cal. 2006) (credit card agreements, bills, and finance charges held not to be securities and so not covered by this carve-out).

253. 28 U.S.C. § 1332(d)(9)(B); *see also* 28 U.S.C. § 1453(d)(2).

254. *See* S. Rep. 109-14, at 45.

255. 28 U.S.C. § 1332(d)(9)(C).

256. 527 F.3d at 26.

securities and its auditor, alleging that officers of the issuer failed to disclose that the company was insolvent in marketing its securities and seeking relief under New York's consumer fraud statute.[257] The case was removed under CAFA, and in seeking remand, the plaintiffs invoked section 1332(d)(9)(C), asserting that "rights . . . relating to . . . any security" "includes the right to bring any cause of action that relates to a security."[258] The Second Circuit rejected this argument because, in its view, such a construction would "defeat any limitation intended by the use of the term" and render section 1332(d)(9)(A) superfluous.[259] Although the certificates at issue were undisputedly "securities" under CAFA, the suit did not relate to the "obligations" or "rights" created under those securities. Instead, the court characterized the suit as "a state-law consumer fraud action alleging that [the issuer] fraudulently concealed its insolvency when it peddled the Certificates," which was not covered by the exception.[260] The Second Circuit noted that the legislative history of this exception indicated that the exemption was "'intended to cover disputes over the meaning of the terms of a security.'"[261]

By contrast, in *Indiana State District Council of Laborers and Hod Carriers Pension Fund v. Renal Care Group, Inc.*,[262] the district court granted the motion to remand under this exception. The case, filed as a shareholder class action in a Tennessee state court, involved claims under Delaware law for breach of fiduciary duty and self-dealing in connection with a pending corporate merger.[263] The defendants removed the case to federal court under CAFA, and the plaintiffs sought remand, asserting that the breach of fiduciary duty claim fell within one of the carve-outs under CAFA, making the case nonremovable.[264] The court rejected the defendants' argument that the provision was ambiguous, instead concluding that "any class action solely based upon breach of fiduciary duty in connection with a security is, itself, a 'carve out'" from CAFA.[265] As a result the exception applied, and the case was remanded.[266]

Although CAFA does not directly address the matter through an exception, the removal changes wrought by the Securities Litigation Uniform Standards Act of 1998 (SLUSA)[267] and CAFA have created an uneven landscape for removal of

---

257. *Id.* at 31.
258. *Id.*
259. *Id.*
260. *Id.* at 31–32.
261. *Id.* at 33 (quoting S. Rep. 109-14, at 45).
262. No. Civ. 3:05-0451, 2005 WL 2000658 (M.D. Tenn. Aug. 18, 2005).
263. *Id.* at *1.
264. *Id.*
265. *Id.*
266. *Id.*
267. *See Merrill Lynch, Pierce, Fenner & Smith, Inc. v. Dabit*, 547 U.S. 71, 81–83 (2006).

'33 Act claims, and currently a circuit split exists as to the impact of CAFA on the '33 Act's non-removal provision.[268]

G. ADDITIONAL EXCEPTIONS

Attempts to engraft additional exceptions onto CAFA through jurisprudential means have thus far not met with much success. For example, in *Massey v. Shelter Life Insurance Co.*,[269] the defendants argued that the court should dismiss the class action on the basis of comity, and the court declined to do so. Instead, it explained that "the plain language of [CAFA] reveals" that "Congress has determined that class action suits such as this one are most appropriately considered in federal courts [because] one of the three purposes of [CAFA] is to 'restore the intent of the framers of the United States Constitution by providing for Federal court consideration of interstate cases of national importance under diversity jurisdiction.'"[270]

VII. Removal Procedures Under CAFA

The removal provisions of CAFA are coextensive with the original jurisdiction provisions, so any class action that fits within the new diversity provisions can be removed to federal court.[271] The CAFA removal provisions for class actions generally incorporate the standard removal requirements and procedures set forth in sections 1441 and 1446,[272] with a couple of important exceptions that significantly expand the possibility of removal, discussed below.

Like other removals under section 1446, the defendant must effect the removal within "thirty days after the receipt by the defendant, through service or otherwise, of a copy of the initial pleading" evidencing a right of removal.[273] However, if the case is not removable at the time it is initially filed, it may be removed if a notice of removal is filed within 30 days after receipt of "an amended pleading,

---

268. *Compare Katz v. Gerardi*, 552 F.3d 558, 561–63 (7th Cir. 2009) (CAFA's broad removal provision trumps the antiremoval provisions of Securities Act of 1933), and *New Jersey Carpenters Vacation Fund v. HarborView Mortgage Loan Trust 2006-4*, 581 F. Supp. 2d 581, 587–88 (S.D.N.Y. 2008), *with Luther*, 533 F.3d at 1034 ("CAFA's general grant of the right of removal of high-dollar class actions does not trump § 22(a)'s specific bar to removal of cases arising under the Securities Act of 1933."); *cf. Estate of Pew*, 527 F.3d at 32 (construing CAFA and SLUSA together "confirms an overall design to assure that the federal courts are available for all securities cases that have national impact . . . without impairing the ability of state courts to decide cases of chiefly local import or that concern traditional state regulation of the state's corporate creatures."); *see also* Chapter 17.G, "Securities Class Actions."

269. No. 05-4106-CV-NKL, 2005 WL 1950028, at *2 (W.D. Mo. 2005).

270. *Id.* (quoting CAFA at § 2).

271. *See* 28 U.S.C. § 1453.

272. 28 U.S.C. §§ 1441, 1446.

273. 28 U.S.C. § 1446(b).

motion, order or other paper from which it may first be ascertained that the case is one which is or has become removable . . . ."[274]

It is not clear whether the 30-day removal clock begins to tick from service on the first defendant or on the removing defendant, which creates some uncertainty. It can be persuasively argued that CAFA's elimination of the requirement that all defendants consent to the removal and the principle in *Murphy Bros., Inc. v. Michetti Pipe Stringing*[275] that defendants cannot be required to take action until they are served with process compel the conclusion that the relevant trigger is service upon the removing defendant. However, as a general proposition, whether the 30-day period to file (or join) a notice of removal begins to run upon service on the first-served or last-served defendant is still an open question in some circuits.[276]

CAFA also eliminates the statutory "outside-window" for traditional diversity removals under section 1446(b). In section 1453(b), Congress made clear that "the 1-year limitation under section 1446(b) shall not apply" to CAFA removals.[277] Considering that proof of damages and the size and geographic scope of the class are often developed late in the case, extending the removal deadline may now afford options for seeking a federal forum even in cases that have substantially progressed in state court. As noted in section V.D.3 above, many courts are taking refuge in this provision in remanding CAFA cases to state court if the facts are not sufficiently well-developed to support federal jurisdiction.

Section 1453 of Title 28 also eliminates other obstacles that have precluded traditional diversity removals. For example, a case that meets the jurisdictional requirements defined above can be removed even though one of the defendants is a resident of the forum state.[278]

Additionally, the statute removes the judge-made requirement that all defendants consent to the removal.[279] However, if the removing party joins independent grounds for subject matter jurisdiction and removal—such as traditional diversity or federal question jurisdiction—it must comply with the unanimous consent rule in order to preserve that alternative jurisdictional basis.[280]

Like traditional removals, CAFA permits removal of the entire case, not just the claims against a given defendant. Thus, when a new defendant was added after

---

274. *Id.* As explained above, the one-year limitation on diversity removals in § 1446(b) does not apply to CAFA removals. 28 U.S.C. § 1453(b).

275. 526 U.S. 344, 347–48 (1999).

276. *See, e.g., United Steel, Paper & Forestry, Rubber Mfg. Energy, Allied Indus. & Serv. Workers v. Shell Oil Co.,* 549 F.3d 1204, 1208 (9th Cir. 2008).

277. 28 U.S.C. § 1453(b).

278. *Id.*

279. *Id.*

280. *See Coll. of Dental Surgeons,* 585 F.3d at 37 n.1.

the effective date of the statute, that defendant properly removed the entire case—including those defendants who had been sued before CAFA became effective.[281]

Only defendants may remove a case under CAFA; a party joined as a defendant solely to a counterclaim does not have the right to remove under the statute.[282]

VIII. Mass Actions

The statute also contains a provision for federal jurisdiction over mass actions, which do not necessarily meet the CAFA definition of "class action" but for purposes of federal jurisdiction are "deemed to be a class action removable under" the class action provisions of the statute "if it otherwise meets th[ose] provisions . . . ."[283] Mass actions are addressed in greater detail in Chapter 11, "Mass Actions Under the Class Action Fairness Act."

Mass actions are treated as class actions under CAFA when they otherwise satisfy the conditions of the statute and therefore are removable when the aggregate amount in controversy exceeds $5 millionin claims, minimal diversity is present, the action involves monetary claims of 100 or more plaintiffs, and the plaintiffs' claims involve common questions of law or fact.[284]

A mass action is defined by CAFA as

> any civil action (except a civil action within the scope of section 1711(2)) in which monetary relief claims of 100 or more persons are proposed to be tried jointly on the ground that the plaintiffs' claims involve common questions of law or fact, *except that jurisdiction shall exist only over those plaintiffs whose claims in a mass action satisfy the jurisdictional amount requirements under subsection (a)*.[285]

CAFA's definition of a mass action may encompass a number of different kinds of cases, but particularly those allowed under certain state procedures for joinder and

---

281. *Lowery,* 483 F.3d at 1196–98.

282. *Palisades Collections, LLC v. Shorts,* 552 F.3d 327, 336–38 (4th Cir. 2008); *see also Progressive W. Ins. Co. v. Preciado,* 479 F.3d 1014, 1017–18 (9th Cir. 2007) (CAFA did not enable a counterclaim defendant who was the original plaintiff to remove to federal court). *But see Deutsche Bank Nat'l Tr. Co. v. Weickert,* 638 F. Supp. 2d 826, 829 (N.D. Ohio 2009) (adopting dissent from *Palisades* and concluding that "CAFA expanded removal authority to include parties added as counterclaim defendants to a class action by authorizing removal by 'any defendant,'" which term includes a counterclaim defendant (citing *Palisades,* 552 F.3d at 339 (Niemeyer, J., dissenting))).

283. 28 U.S.C. § 1332(d)(11)(A).

284. *Id.* ("For purposes of [28 U.S.C. § 1332(d)] and section 1453 [CAFA's removal provisions], a mass action shall be deemed to be a class action removable under paragraphs (2) through (10) if it otherwise meets the provisions of those paragraphs."). It is not clear whether a mass action can be filed originally in federal court. *See Lowery,* 483 F.3d at 1200 n.41.

285. 28 U.S.C. § 1332(d)(11)(B)(i) (emphasis added). The current amount-in-controversy threshold is $75,000. *See* 28 U.S.C. § 1332(a).

consolidation cases, in which large numbers of nominally distinct individual claims are tried together, with an impact on defendants similar to that of a class action.

A. NUMEROSITY REQUIREMENT

The statutory requirement that the claims of "100 or more persons are proposed to be tried jointly" has been the subject of several mass action challenges. The statute provides that there is no federal jurisdiction under the Act over a mass action if it is the result of a defendant's motion for joinder;[286] thus, a defendant cannot obtain federal jurisdiction over individual claims filed against it in state court by obtaining consolidation in state court and then removing the case as a "mass action" or to aggregate the amounts in controversy from multiple suits once removed.[287] However, when an otherwise suitable mass action is artificially divided into multiple state court actions for the evident purpose of avoiding CAFA, the Sixth Circuit has found the amount-in-controversy requirement to be met by aggregating the splintered suits.[288] Moreover, if the state court pleading names over 100 plaintiffs with similar claims, and it is "facially apparent" that they will exceed $5 million in the aggregate, CAFA's mass action provision is satisfied, and the removing defendant's stated intention to seek severance in federal court should not defeat CAFA jurisdiction.[289]

B. THE ROLE OF THE INDIVIDUAL AMOUNT IN CONTROVERSY

The interaction of the aggregate amount-in-controversy requirement with the individual amount-in-controversy requirement of section 1332(a) remains unclear. In *Abrego Abrego v. Dow Chemical Co.*,[290] the Ninth Circuit Court of Appeals noted that meshing the mass action provisions with the rest of section 1332 is "far from straightforward," and ultimately remanded the case (which satisfied the aggregate amount in controversy) because the defendant did not establish that even one plaintiff satisfied the $75,000 jurisdictional amount requirement of section 1332(a).

---

286. 28 U.S.C. § 1332(d)(11)(B)(ii).

287. *Tanoh v. Dow Chem. Co.*, 561 F.3d 945, 950, 953 (9th Cir. 2009).

288. *Freeman v. Blue Ridge Paper Prods., Inc.*, 551 F.3d 405, 407 (6th Cir. 2008) ("If such pure structuring permits class plaintiffs to avoid CAFA, then Congress's obvious purpose in passing the statute—to allow defendants to defend large interstate class actions in federal court—can be avoided almost at will, as long as state-law permits suits to be broken up on some basis."); *id.* at 409 (limiting its holding to cases "where there is no colorable basis for dividing up the sought-for relief into separate time periods, other than to frustrate CAFA"); *see also Proffitt v. Abbott Labs.*, No. 2:08-CV-148, 2008 U.S. Dist. LEXIS 72467, at *7–12 (E.D. Tenn. Sept. 23, 2008) (aggregating amounts in controversy from multiple class actions based on the same antitrust conspiracy that were divided into one-year periods for the apparent purpose of circumventing CAFA).

289. *Cooper*, 586 F. Supp. 2d at 1315–16, 1320–22.

290. 443 F.3d at 681–82.

The Eleventh Circuit Court of Appeals also discussed the matter, quoting a portion of the Senate Judiciary Committee Report for guidance.[291] However, it ultimately left the issue unresolved and held instead:

> Because . . . the defendants have not established the $5,000,000 aggregate amount in controversy, we need not decide today whether the $75,000 provision might yet create an additional threshold requirement that the party bearing the burden of establishing the court's jurisdiction must establish at the outset, *i.e.*, that the claims of at least one of the plaintiffs exceed $75,000.[292]

C. OTHER LIMITATIONS

In addition, the mass action provision contains other, seemingly more straightforward, limitations. First, the law does not permit federal jurisdiction over mass actions involving an "event or occurrence" that took place within the forum state and caused injury in that state and contiguous states.[293]

Second, a mass action does not include state attorney general actions—or, in the words of the Act, civil actions in which "all of the claims in the action are asserted on behalf of the general public (and not on behalf of individual claimants or members of a purported class) pursuant to a state statute specifically authorizing such action."[294]

Third, the Act provides that mass actions do not include claims that are consolidated for pretrial purposes only.[295] Such claims, of course, would not meet the basic definition of a mass action anyway because they are not proposed to be tried jointly.

Finally, as with class actions, the mass action provision is subject to mandatory and discretionary abstention provisions.[296]

The mass action provisions may prove to have relatively little effect. They can be evaded by simply not joining more than 99 individual claims. Moreover, to the extent one purpose of the Act is to bring state court class actions into federal court where they may be subject to more stringent certification requirements, that purpose will not necessarily be served by removal of a mass action. In such a case, the plaintiffs will not need to seek certification because it was never intended to be a class action, and the federal court will have to address the individual claims of all

---

291. *Lowery*, 483 F.3d at 1206 (quoting S. Rep. 109-14, at 47, *reprinted in* 2005 U.S.C.C.A.N. 3, 44).

292. *Id.* at 1206–07.

293. 28 U.S.C. § 1332(d)(11)(B)(ii)(I). The conditions under which there is federal jurisdiction over such "mass accident claims" are set forth in 28 U.S.C. § 1369.

294. 28 U.S.C. § 1332(d)(11)(B)(ii)(III).

295. *Id.* at § 1332(d)(11)(B)(ii)(IV).

296. *Id.* at § 1332(d)(11)(A) ("For purposes of this subsection and section 1453, a mass action shall be deemed to be a class action removable under paragraphs (2) through (10) if it otherwise meets the provisions of those paragraphs."); *see also* sections VI.B and C, *supra*.

of the mass action plaintiffs regardless of whether the case could qualify for class certification under Rule 23.[297]

IX. Appeals

A decision on CAFA jurisdiction is subject to a discretionary interlocutory appeal if a petition for review[298] is filed not more than ten days after the order.[299] The ten-day limit was added by amendment effective December 1, 2009.[300] Once an appeal is accepted by the circuit court, it must be resolved within 60 days or it is deemed to be denied.[301]

According to the Senate Report, CAFA's appeal provision was an integral piece of the legislation:

> The purpose of this provision is to develop a body of appellate law interpreting the legislation without unduly delaying the litigation of class actions. As a general matter, appellate review of orders remanding cases to state court is not permitted, as specified by 28 U.S.C. 1447(d). New subsection 1453(c) provides discretionary appellate review of remand orders under this legislation but also imposes time limits.[302]

The review provisions of section 1453(c) do not apply to all class actions, but rather "are limited to class actions brought under CAFA . . . ."[303]

Assuming that there is appellate jurisdiction under CAFA, other related legal issues may be raised on appeal.[304] In fact, the U.S. Supreme Court decided an important issue of diversity jurisdiction—holding that the "principal place of business"

---

297. Indeed, by providing that mass actions are exempt from being transferred for multidistrict litigation proceedings unless the plaintiffs seek class certification, 28 U.S.C. § 1332(d)(11)(C), CAFA discourages plaintiffs in a mass action from seeking class certification after removal.

298. Federal Rule of Appellate Procedure 5(a) governs appeals "within the court of appeals' discretion." Fed. R. App. P. 5(a)(1). This rule governs CAFA appeals under 28 U.S.C. § 1453(c)(1). *See Main Drug, Inc. v. Aetna U.S. Healthcare, Inc.*, 475 F.3d 1228, 1229–30 (11th Cir. 2007) (collecting cases).

299. 28 U.S.C. § 1453(c)(1).

300. Pub. L. 111-16, § 6(2) (2009). The prior language said "not less than 7 days," which was generally understood to be a typographical error, as Congress has at all times intended a short deadline, not a "cooling period." S. Rep. 109-14, at 42, *reprinted in* 2005 U.S.C.C.A.N 3.

301. *See* 28 U.S.C. § 1453(c)(4); *see also Hart*, 457 F.3d at 678–79 (60-day period begins to run from the date the appeal is accepted by the circuit court, not the date the petition is filed (collecting cases)).

302. S. Rep. 109-14, at 49; *see also Wallace v. La. Citizens Prop. Ins. Corp.*, 444 F.3d 697, 700 (5th Cir. 2006) (relying on this Senate Report for its statement that "the legislative history of CAFA also indicates that § 1453(c)(1) was enacted to ensure expeditious review of remand decisions in class action suits brought under the new legislation").

303. *Saab v. Home Depot U.S.A., Inc.*, 469 F.3d 758, 759–60 (8th Cir. 2006); *see also Wallace*, 444 F.3d at 700.

304. *Alvarez v. Midland Credit Mgmt., Inc.*, 585 F.3d 890, 894 (5th Cir. 2009) ("We recognize that § 1453(c) does not limit our discretionary appellate jurisdiction to matters unique or peculiar to CAFA.").

of a corporation[305] was the location of its "nerve center" or headquarters—in a CAFA appeal.[306] The Court in *Hertz Corp. v. Friend* also rejected a challenge to its own jurisdiction, holding that CAFA's reference to appellate review in the "courts of appeals" did not preclude the Supreme Court from exercising jurisdiction over a CAFA appeal.[307]

The Seventh Circuit has concluded that it was "free to consider any potential error in the district court's decision, not just a mistake in application of the Class Action Fairness Act,"[308] and other circuits have followed its lead.[309] Appellate jurisdiction under CAFA has also been held to permit review of collateral orders, such as a decision to grant or deny attorney fees in connection with the removal under 28 U.S.C. § 1447(c).[310]

However, when considering the strict time limits placed on the circuit courts by CAFA to conclude these appeals and the congressional purpose of the appeal provision to develop interpretational law, it is noteworthy that several have refused to exercise their discretionary appellate review for issues that are not unique to CAFA.[311]

Other factors that bear on the discretionary decision to grant review include (1) the importance of the CAFA issue;[312] (2) the importance of non-CAFA issues (although to a lesser degree);[313] (3) the novelty and uncertainty of the question presented;[314] (4) whether the question appears to have been correctly decided or is "at least fairly debatable";[315] (5) the consequences of delaying the decision until

---

305. *See* 28 U.S.C. § 1332(c)(1).

306. *Hertz*, 559 U.S. ___, 130 S. Ct. 1181.

307. *Id.* at *5 (concluding that the history of general grants of certiorari review "provides particularly strong reasons *not* to read § 1453(c)'s silence or ambiguous language as modifying or limiting our pre-existing jurisdiction.").

308. *Brill*, 427 F.3d at 451–52.

309. *E.g.*, *Coffey*, 581 F.3d at 1247.

310. *Admiral Ins. Co.*, 574 F.3d at 280.

311. *Alvarez*, 585 F.3d at 894 (where unique CAFA issue had been originally presented in petition for permission to appeal, but had not been briefed on merits, the Fifth Circuit concluded that its original permission "was improvidently granted"); *Coll. of Dental Surgeons*, 585 F.3d at 38; *Coffey*, 581 F.3d at 1247–48 (declining to exercise appellate jurisdiction over issues involving the Comprehensive Environmental Response, Compensation and Liability Act that were not particular to CAFA). For a more detailed discussion of the appellate courts' considerations and standards for granting interlocutory review, *see* Chapter 5, "Interlocutory Appeals."

312. *Coll. of Dental Surgeons*, 585 F.3d at 38.

313. *Id.*; *Estate of Pew*, 527 F.3d at 29.

314. *Coll. of Dental Surgeons*, 585 F.3d at 38 ("[U]ncertainty is also a factor that cuts in favor of an affirmative exercise of discretion; to warrant immediate appeal, the question presented usually will be unsettled." (citing *Bullard v. Burlington N. Santa Fe Ry. Co.*, 535 F.3d 759, 761 (7th Cir. 2008))); *Estate of Pew*, 527 F.3d at 29.

315. *Coll. of Dental Surgeons*, 585 F.3d at 38 ("If, on the face of the materials presented, it seems likely that the district court decided the question correctly, the need for immediate review is lessened.").

final resolution of the case;[316] (6) whether the appeal presents a "serious jurisdictional issue[ ]";[317] (7) the likelihood of recurrence;[318] (8) whether the decision is "sufficiently final to position the case for intelligent review";[319] and (9) "a balance of relevant harms."[320] None of these factors is considered to be dispositive or required—the decision is ultimately committed to the discretion of the reviewing court.[321]

As with other types of remand orders, CAFA decisions are reviewed de novo.[322] However, evidentiary findings that support the decision on remand are reviewed for clear error.[323] Because the statute expressly grants this avenue of appellate relief, an appellant need not seek a stay of the remand order in order to preserve its appeal.[324]

X. CAFA Settlements

In addition to its jurisdictional and removal sections, CAFA adds a new chapter to Title 28 of the United States Code setting forth a number of requirements applicable to the settlement of class actions in federal courts.[325] Some of the new requirements were wholly or largely duplicative of existing practice under Rule 23, while others represent substantial changes. All of the provisions are applicable only to class actions, narrowly defined as cases filed in federal court under Rule 23 or filed as class actions in state court and removed to federal court.[326]

A. COUPON SETTLEMENTS

During the legislative process for the enactment of CAFA, great attention was focused on "coupon settlements," or settlements in which class members receive coupons, often of dubious value, while class counsel receive cash payouts as reimbursement for their attorney fees. Both courts and commentators have criticized

---

316. *Id.* ("A particularly important factor is whether the question is likely to evade effective review if left for consideration only after final judgment.").

317. *Id.*

318. *Id.*

319. *Id.* at 38–39 (citing *Amoche*, 556 F.3d 41, as an example of a CAFA case with an insufficiently developed record to justify premature removal).

320. *Id.* at 39.

321. *Id.* (stating that the court's discretion "is not cabined by rigid rules . . . [b]ut the factors we have identified will, in the majority of cases, serve as buoys to mark channels of inquiry").

322. *Luther*, 533 F.3d at 1033.

323. *E.g., Coffey*, 581 F.3d at 1246 (review of trial court's decision on principal place of business is for clear error).

324. *Estate of Pew*, 527 F.3d at 28.

325. *See also* Chapter 7, "Settlements."

326. 28 U.S.C. § 1711(2).

such settlements, for example where a car manufacturer offers the class members discount coupons for the purchase of its new cars, as being of no value to the class members, who must purchase a new car from the defendant in order to receive any value, while the class counsel receive cash payouts. As a result, CAFA contains a provision that addresses both aspects of coupon settlements—their overall fairness and the determination of attorney fees when the class receives coupons.[327]

1. What Are Coupon Settlements?

CAFA does not define the term "coupon." Courts can thus decide to employ it broadly or narrowly. Coupon settlements are typically considered to be a form of in-kind compensation that requires a future business transaction between the class members and the defendant.[328] Courts tend to consider in-kind compensation to be worth less than cash of the same nominal value.

According to the legislative debates and transcripts, a universally accepted meaning of "coupon" is a voucher "redeemable for discounts off future purchases from the defendant."[329] Coupon *could* also include

- other types of noncash relief that requires class members to take affirmative action to receive the benefit of the coupon, such as redeeming the certificates for cash; or
- other noncash relief given without the need for affirmative action, such as free cellular phone minutes to cell phone customer class members and extended warranties to product owner class members.[330]

Coupon settlements are those that require class members to receive a discount from the defendant that only has value if the class member makes an additional purchase from the defendant. Therefore, where class members received vouchers for free cellular phones from the defendant that required no additional purchase by the class member, the settlement was not a coupon as Congress had intended that term to mean.[331]

---

327. 28 U.S.C. § 1712.

328. *Synfuel Tech., Inc. v. DHL Express (USA), Inc.*, 463 F.3d 646, 654 (7th Cir. 2006) (mentions CAFA, but is not a CAFA case).

329. *See* Jennifer Gibson, *New Rules for Class Action Settlements: The Consumer Class Action Bill of Rights*, 39 Loy. L.A. L. Rev. 1103, 1110 & nn. 37 & 38 (Oct. 2006) (citing S. Rep. 109-14, at 15–20, *reprinted in* 2005 U.S.C.C.A.N. 3, 15–20 ("citing numerous cases that include voucher, discounts, and coupons as within the provisions of coupon settlements")), *available at* http://llr.lls.edu/volumes/v39-issue3/docs/v.pdf.

330. Gibson, *supra* note 329, at 1110 (noting that it is "less clear" as to whether these definitions would constitute coupon settlements). A prior version of CAFA would have applied to all settlements "under which the class members would receive noncash benefits or would otherwise be required to expend funds in order to obtain part or all of the proposed benefits." *Id.* at 1110 n.39.

331. *Perez v. Asurion Corp.*, No. 06-20734-CIV, 2007 WL 2591180, at *2 (S.D. Fla. Sept. 6, 2007).

2. Fairness Aspects of Coupon Settlements

As to the basic fairness of coupon settlements, CAFA provides that a court may approve a class action settlement involving coupons "only after a hearing to determine whether, and making a written finding that, the settlement is fair, reasonable, and adequate for class members."[332] Of course, Rule 23 already provides for this same review; indeed, this standard has been applied by federal courts to class action settlements for many years.

Section 1712(e) goes beyond existing law in one minor respect: it explicitly provides that a court has discretion to require that in a coupon settlement, some portion of the value of unclaimed coupons be distributed to charity, and it forbids an award of attorney fees based on the value of the contribution of unclaimed coupons. It may be doubtful that this provision would materially change the terms of any settlement that a court would have approved under Rule 23 before the passage of CAFA.[333] Some judges, however, may exercise their discretion to add such cy pres provisions to settlements that they would otherwise have approved, and the statute may also encourage parties to include such provisions in more settlements.

Coupon settlements are not prohibited per se, but the statutory provision highlights Congress's view that these settlements are especially suspect, and as a result, some courts have interpreted this provision as imposing a heightened level of scrutiny in reviewing coupon settlements.[334] In *True v. American Honda Motor Co.*,[335] the court summarized the criticisms of such settlements as follows:

> The Court acknowledges the wide range of judicial and scholarly criticism of coupon settlements . . . and concurs that such settlements are generally disfavored. This is due to three common problems with coupon settlements: "they often do not provide meaningful compensation to class members; they often fail to disgorge ill-gotten gains from the defendant; and they often require class members to do future business with the defendant in order to receive compensation."

Congress did not, however, prohibit coupon settlements. In certain cases, such a settlement may be appropriate and in fact the best form of consideration under the circumstances.[336] "A court's inquiry does not therefore end with a determination

---

332. 28 U.S.C. § 1712(e).

333. *Cf.* S. REP. 109-14, at 31 ("The Committee wishes to make clear that nothing in Section 1712 is intended to change current law regarding the circumstances under which an award of attorneys' fees is appropriate.").

334. *See, e.g., Synfuel Tech.*, 463 F.3d at 654; *Figueroa v. Sharper Image Corp.*, 517 F. Supp. 2d 1292, 1321 (S.D. Fla. 2007); *see also* S. REP. 109-14, at 27 (noting that provision requires "greater scrutiny of coupon settlements").

335. No. EDCV 07-0287-VAP, 2010 WL 707338, at *12 (C.D. Cal. Feb. 26, 2010) (quoting *Figueroa*, 517 F. Supp. 2d at 1302, and collecting cases).

336. *See id.* (citing *In re Mexico Money Transfer Litig.*, 267 F.3d 743, 748–49 (7th Cir. 2001), as an example of a coupon settlement that passed muster under pre-CAFA law).

that a proposed settlement is a coupon settlement; it must discern if the value of a specific coupon settlement is reasonable in relation to the value of the claims surrendered."[337]

3. Coupon Settlements and Attorney Fees

The provisions regarding the award of attorney fees in coupon cases, by contrast, work an important change in existing law. New section 1712(a) sets forth the basic rule that in a coupon settlement, "the portion of any attorney's fee award to class counsel that is attributable to the award of the coupons shall be based on the value to class members of the coupons that are redeemed."[338] In other words, lawyers will no longer be able to receive fees based on the gross amount of coupons awarded, or even upon predictions of how many coupons will be redeemed. Any percentage-based fee can be awarded only on the basis of the value of coupons actually redeemed.[339]

If a settlement utilizes both coupons and a cash payment, the situation is governed by section 1712(b), which provides that "if . . . a portion of the recovery of the coupons is not used to determine the attorney's fee to be paid to class counsel, any attorney's fee award shall be based upon the amount of time class counsel reasonably expended working on the action."[340] Courts will undoubtedly face some difficulty in dealing with this provision, but it appears to mean that part of the fee can be based on the value of the coupons redeemed, while the fee for the cash

---

337. Id.

338. 28 U.S.C. § 1712(a).

339. The Act further provides that expert testimony on the value to class members of the coupons that are redeemed is admissible in the discretion of the court, 28 U.S.C. § 1712(d), but the basic standard under the Act will still be actual redemption, not redemption rates as predicted by experts. See True, 2010 WL 707338, at *16–17 (criticizing expert's projections of coupon utilization as based on prior versions of the settlement and "several assumptions flawed as a matter of logic or law").

340. 28 U.S.C. § 1712(b). The Senate Judiciary Committee Report states that

> [i]n some cases, the proponents of a class settlement involving coupons may decline to propose that attorney's fees be based on the value of the coupon-based relief provided by the settlement. Instead, the settlement proponents may propose that counsel fees be based upon the amount of time class counsel reasonably expended working on the action. Section 1712(b) confirms the appropriateness of determining attorneys' fees on this basis in connection with a settlement based in part on coupon relief.

S. Rep. 109-14, at 30. Thus, it was the judiciary committee's intent to allow the exclusive use of the lodestar method even when part of the relief provided is in the form of a coupon. Moreover, "nothing in . . . section [§ 1712(b)] should be construed to prohibit using the 'lodestar with multiplier' method of calculating attorney's fees." Id. However, when coupons make up a portion of the settlement, "the fees must be 'time based' and not 'value based' unless the 'redeemed value' of the coupons awarded is used." John Kolinski, The Class Action Fairness Act of 2005, 80 Fla. B.J. 18, 20 (Apr. 2006); see also Perez, 2007 WL 2591180 (section 1712(b) interpreted to mean that district court may use lodestar method to calculate a reasonable attorney fee award in cases involving "coupon"; lodestar compensates counsel based on the time reasonably expended rather than the value of the class's recovery).

portion of the settlement should be determined on the basis of the lodestar calculation—i.e., the reasonable number of hours expended times a reasonable rate[341]—together with a multiplier if the court deems it appropriate.[342]

In cases where a settlement involves both coupons and injunctive relief, the Act provides that any portion of the fee attributable to coupons shall be calculated on the basis of the coupons actually redeemed, while any fee attributable to the equitable relief shall be determined on the lodestar basis together with a multiplier if the court deems it appropriate.[343]

Finally, under CAFA, federal courts may order that the settlement agreement provide for a cy pres distribution of unclaimed coupons to charitable or governmental entities, if the parties agree.[344] However, unclaimed coupons awarded on a cy pres basis may not be used to calculate the attorney fees.[345]

4. Other Protections for Class Members

New section 1713 provides that a court may approve a settlement in which class members incur out-of-pocket losses to compensate class counsel "only if the court makes a written finding that nonmonetary benefits to the class member substantially outweigh the monetary loss."[346] This provision was designed to limit the number of situations in which attorney fees might exceed the recovery provided to the class members and, in doing so, avoid the prospect that class members might be liable for more fees to class counsel than they can recover under the settlement.[347]

New section 1714 prohibits class settlements that provide payment of greater amounts to some class members "solely on the basis that the class members to whom the greater sums are to be paid are located in closer geographic proximity to the court."[348] However, settlements that require class members to pay class counsel out of pocket are very rare. Under Rule 23—even without these new statutes—such

---

341. *See* Chapter 8, "Attorney Fee Awards and Incentive Payments."

342. Section 1712(c) applies when the attorney fees are based partly on coupons issued and partly on an injunction granted for the benefit of the class members.

> [I]f a proposed settlement provides for both coupon and equitable relief, then the portion of the award that is a contingent fee based on the value of the coupons must be calculated based on the value of redeemed coupons, and the portion not based on the value of coupons should be based on the time spent by class counsel on the case.

S. REP. 109-14, at 31. The use of the lodestar method with a multiplier is also sanctioned under § 1712(c).

343. 28 U.S.C. § 1712(c).

344. *Id.* at § 1712(e).

345. *Id.*

346. *Id.* at § 1713.

347. *See, e.g., Kamilewicz v. Bank of Boston,* 100 F.3d 1348, 1349 (7th Cir. 1996) (Easterbrook, J., dissenting from denial of rehearing en banc; class member received award of $2.19, but $91.33 deducted from class member's bank account for attorney fees).

348. 28 U.S.C. § 1714.

settlements would be highly unlikely to be approved as fair unless the class received significant nonmonetary benefits.

B. NOTIFICATIONS TO FEDERAL AND STATE OFFICIALS

In a major departure from existing practice, the Act adds section 1715, which requires that notice of any settlement of a class action in federal court be provided to "appropriate" federal and state officials. This provision was "intended to combat the 'clientless litigation' problem by adding a layer of independent oversight to prohibit inequitable settlements."[349] An example of this provision in action is *True v. American Honda Motor Co.*,[350] where the state of Texas intervened and objected to the settlement, a group of 12 state attorneys general filed an amicus brief further criticizing it, and these official statements were instrumental in defeating final approval of a proposed nationwide settlement.

For all settlements, the Attorney General of the United States is an "appropriate [f]ederal official."[351] In cases involving regulated financial institutions, the federal officials who must be notified also include the federal official having primary regulatory authority over the institutions at issue (e.g., the FDIC).[352]

The term "appropriate [s]tate official" means either a state official who has regulatory authority over the defendant or the matters at issue in the case, or, if there is no such official, the attorney general of any state in which any class member lives.[353] "Some states regulate obscure subjects, [and] identifying the regulators may not be easy."[354] Therefore research must be conducted to determine if the defendant's business operation is regulated in any of the various states where a class member may reside. The default value appears to be the state's attorney general: "If some class members reside in states where the company does not do business and therefore is not subject to regulation, then notice would be given to those states' attorneys general."[355] Thus, "[i]f the company at issue were a toy manufacturer which is not licensed by a particular regulatory body, then notice would have to be given to the state attorney general for each state where plaintiffs reside."[356] One prudent approach is to provide notice to all relevant attorneys general *and* to any state officials with primary regulatory authority. In large, multistate cases, it is

---

349. S. REP. 109-14, at 34.

350. 2010 WL 707338, at *1–2, 21–23.

351. 28 U.S.C. § 1715(a)(1)(A).

352. *Id.* ar § 1715(a)(1)(B).

353. *Id.* at § 1715(a)(2).

354. *See* Robert H. Klonoff & Mark Herrmann, *The Class Action Fairness Act: An Ill-Conceived Approach to Class Settlements*, 80 TUL. L. REV. 1695, 1708 (2006).

355. S. REP. 109-14, at 34.

356. *Id.*

best to err on the side of sending multiple notices to the U.S. Attorney General, the relevant states' attorneys general, and possible regulators.[357]

The notice to be provided must be sent no more than ten days after a proposed settlement is filed in federal court, and it must include (1) the complaint; (2) notice of any scheduled hearing; (3) copies of notices to class members informing them of opt-out rights and/or of the settlement; (4) copies of the settlement itself and any side agreements; (5) copies of any (proposed) final orders or judgments; (6) "if feasible," a list of the class members and the estimated proportionate shares of the settlement they will receive (or a reasonable estimate); and (7) copies of related judicial opinions.[358] In addition, the notice must, to the extent possible, inform the appropriate state officials of the identities and/or numbers of class members residing in their states.[359] Responsibility for providing the required notice falls on "each defendant."[360] Failure to provide the required notice means class members may choose not to be bound by the settlement,[361] and the court may give final approval of a settlement until 90 days after the appropriate state and federal officials have been served with notice.[362] However, CAFA does not specify nor require the attorney general or other appropriate federal officials to do anything with the notices received.

It is advisable for defendants to provide the court with a summary of the CAFA Notice Packet that they plan to distribute to the appropriate state official for preapproval. The court's preapproval of the CAFA Notice Packet could defeat a class member's argument that proper CAFA notification was not served on the necessary regulatory officials. Section 1715(e)(2) provides that "[a] class member may not refuse to comply with or be bound by a settlement agreement or consent decree . . . if the notice required . . . was directed to the appropriate Federal official and to *either* the State attorney general *or* the person that has primary regulatory, supervisory, or licensing authority over the defendant."[363] Two authors have noted that, based on the plain language of section1715(e)(1), when a state attorney general has been served, a class member is precluded from challenging the adequacy of

---

357. *See, e.g., First State Orthopedics v. Concentra, Inc.*, 534 F. Supp. 2d 500, 508 & n.9 (E.D. Pa. 2007) (finding compliance with § 1715 when defendant sent notices to 53 state attorneys general and 31 additional state regulators); *Fresco v. Auto Data Direct, Inc.*, No. 03-61063-CIV, 2007 WL 2330895, at *7 (S.D. Fla. Mar. 14, 2007) (finding compliance with § 1715 when notice was sent to the U.S. Attorney General and the attorneys general of all 50 states and the District of Columbia, Guam, Puerto Rico, and the U.S. Virgin Islands, as well as to the department of motor vehicles officials in all 50 states and the District of Columbia).

358. 28 U.S.C. § 1715(b).

359. *Id.* at § 1715(b)(7).

360. *Id.* at § 1715(b).

361. *Id.* at § 1715(e).

362. *Id.* at § 1715(d).

363. *Id.* at § 1715(e)(2) (emphasis added).

the settlement proposal based upon improper CAFA notification.[364] In addition, because it may be difficult to identify each of the states in which the class members reside, defendants are well advised to notify an official in *every* state.[365]

C. REQUIRED PROCEDURE FOR PRE–CLASS CERTIFICATION SETTLEMENTS[366]

STEP 1. Parties stipulate to a temporary settlement class for purposes of settlement only. The defendant agrees to the entry of a ruling that the class be certified if the settlement is approved. If the settlement fails, the defendant's stipulation is withdrawn.

STEP 2. Parties prepare and submit a joint stipulation of settlement to the court for preliminary approval consisting of the essential terms of the agreement, including the amount of settlement and form of payment. "[I]n the context of a case in which the parties reach a settlement agreement prior to class certification, courts must peruse the proposed compromise to ratify both the proprietary of the certification and the fairness of the settlement."[367]

STEP 3. The court determines whether the proposed class meets the requirements of Rule 23. "[A] party seeking class certification must demonstrate the following prerequisites: (1) the class is so numerous that joinder of all members is impracticable, (2) there are questions of law or fact common to the class, (3) the claims or defenses of the representative parties are typical of the claims or defenses of the class, and (4) the representative parties will fairly and adequately protect the interests of the class."[368]

STEP 4. The court directs the parties to distribute notices of the settlement hearing combined with notice of opportunity for exclusion from the action (Opt-Out Notice) under Rule 23(c)(2). Notice is given by way of mail, publication, or both.

STEP 5. Per the New CAFA Amendments, and not later than ten days after a proposed settlement of class action is filed in court, each defendant is required to serve upon the appropriate federal and state officials.

STEP 6. The court conducts a fairness hearing pursuant to CAFA and Federal Rule 23(e) to determine if the settlement is fair, reasonable, and adequate to the class members prior to approving the settlement. The burden is on

---

364. Klonoff & Herrmann, *supra* note 354, at 1709; Gibson, *supra* note 329, at 1128–29.

365. Gibson, *supra* note 329, at 1128–29.

366. Unless otherwise noted, the information in this section is derived from HERBERT B. NEWBERG & ALBA CONTE, NEWBERG ON CLASS ACTIONS: A MANUAL FOR GROUP LITIGATION AT FEDERAL AND STATE LEVELS, ch. 11, "Settlement of Class Actions" (4th ed. 2002 & 2008 update).

367. *Staton v. Boeing Co.*, 327 F.3d 938, 952 (9th Cir. 2003).

368. *Acosta v. Trans Union, LLC*, 243 F.R.D. 377, 383 (C.D. Cal. 2007).

the proponents of the agreement to establish that the settlement agreement, including the proposed attorney fee, is fair to the class. Presumably, this is the stage where the determination is made regarding the existence of a coupon settlement.

STEP 7. Any party with standing to object (such as state agencies served with notice of the settlement) may do so in the fairness hearing. Typically, objectors register their written objection to the court and serve the same on counsel for the parties before a specific date prior to the settlement hearing.

STEP 8. The court either approves or disapproves the settlement. If the court approves the settlement, it will then issue an order no earlier than 90 days after the appropriate state officials for all states involved are served.

STEP 9. The settlement has preclusive effect for all class members that did not opt out—assuming their state official was properly served.[369]

---

369. *See* 28 U.S.C. § 1715(e).

MASS ACTIONS UNDER THE CLASS ACTION FAIRNESS ACT

JAMES L. BERNARD
JILL A. KRAUSS

I. Introduction

As defined by the Class Action Fairness Action of 2005 (CAFA),[1] a "mass action" is a civil action that provides a federal forum for the monetary relief claims of 100 or more persons so long as the parties are "minimally diverse," the aggregated value of the claims exceeds $5 million, and those claims "involve common questions of law or fact." CAFA mass actions expand federal diversity jurisdiction by allowing both defendants to remove to and plaintiffs to bring actions in federal court by virtue of the concept of minimal diversity in which only one class member is diverse from any one defendant. Thus, CAFA mass actions permit a party who cannot establish the "complete diversity" required by a traditional class action to gain access to federal court.

The party seeking CAFA mass action jurisdiction has the burden of establishing that the action meets the amount-in-controversy, numerosity, and commonality requirements noted above. That party must also show that the suit does not fall into one of several categories of actions excluded from the definition of a mass action. Under CAFA, an action cannot be categorized as a mass action when (1) all claims arise from a local, isolated event with no significant interstate effects, (2) the claims are joined by motion of a defendant, (3) the claims are brought on behalf of the general public, and (4) the claims were only consolidated for pretrial proceedings.

Once a party has established federal jurisdiction under the mass action provisions, the opposing party seeking to remand the action to state court has the burden to demonstrate that one of the CAFA exceptions applies. CAFA's mandatory

---

1. Pub. L. No. 109-2, 119 Stat. 4 (codified at 28 U.S.C. §§ 1332(d), 1453, and 1711–1715 (2005)).

and discretionary exceptions are intended primarily to ensure that actions with a purely local focus (i.e., those with but one or a few out-of-state parties) remain in state court. Under CAFA, a district court may decline jurisdiction in the interests of justice if between one-third and two-thirds of the class members are citizens of the state where the action was brought. A district court *must* remand an action to state court, however, if either the local controversy, home state, or corporate governance exception applies.

II. Mass Action Section of CAFA

A. BURDEN OF ESTABLISHING FEDERAL JURISDICTION

1. CAFA Maintains Traditional Burden on Party Seeking Federal Jurisdiction
All circuits that have considered this issue have followed this construction.

a. Second Circuit

DiTolla v. Doral Dental IPA of New York, LLC[2] (holding that the appellants failed to meet their burden of demonstrating that their claim satisfies CAFA's amount-in-controversy requirement).

Blockbuster, Inc. v. Galeno[3] (recognizing the "long standing judicial rules placing the burden on the defendant" to establish federal jurisdiction).

b. Third Circuit

Morgan v. Gay[4] (rejecting defendant's argument that the party seeking remand bears the burden, noting the well-established proposition that the party seeking removal carries the jurisdiction-proving burden and stating "[u]nder CAFA, the party seeking to remove the case to federal court bears the burden to establish that the amount in controversy requirement is satisfied").

c. Sixth Circuit

Smith v. Nationwide Property & Casualty Insurance Co.[5] (noting that "CAFA does not alter the fact that the removing defendant has the burden of demonstrating, by a preponderance of the evidence, that the amount in controversy requirement has been met").

---

2. 469 F.3d 271, 277 (2d Cir. 2006).
3. 472 F.3d 53, 58 (2d Cir. 2006).
4. 471 F.3d 469, 473 (3d Cir. 2006).
5. 505 F.3d 401, 404 (6th Cir. 2007).

d. Seventh Circuit

Hart v. FedEx Ground Package System, Inc.[6] (affirming remand and stating "[w]hen a party seeks removal, it must present evidence of federal jurisdiction once the existence of that jurisdiction is fairly cast into doubt").

Brill v. Countrywide Home Loans, Inc.[7] (rejecting defendant's contention that CAFA reassigns the burden of persuasion to the proponent of remand, stating "[w]hichever side chooses federal court must establish jurisdiction").

e. Ninth Circuit

Abrego Abrego v. Dow Chemical Co.[8] (holding that the party seeking federal jurisdiction bears the burden and finding that "[t]he legal context in which the 109th Congress passed CAFA into law features a longstanding, near-canonical rule that the burden on removal rests with the removing defendant.").

f. Eleventh Circuit

Thomas v. Bank of America Corp.[9] (affirming the district court's remand because the defendants failed to show that the amount in controversy and size of the class met CAFA requirements by a preponderance of evidence).

Lowery v. Alabama Power Co.[10] (acknowledging a unique tension in applying the fact-weighing standard (a preponderance) to the fact-free context of pleadings and examining the history of that standard in the Eleventh Circuit).

Evans v. Walter Industries, Inc.[11] (noting "CAFA does not change the traditional rule that the party seeking to remove the case to federal court bears the burden of establishing federal jurisdiction").

2. CAFA Shifts the Burden to the Party Opposing Federal Jurisdiction

Several district courts, however, have suggested that the party opposing federal jurisdiction must establish lack of jurisdiction.

Garcia v. Boyar & Miller P.C.[12] (stating that when prima facie requirements of amount in controversy and minimal diversity under CAFA are met, the party who objects to removal based on a statutory exception must show that the exception applies).

---

6. 457 F.3d 675, 682 (7th Cir. 2006).
7. 427 F.3d 446, 447 (7th Cir. 2005).
8. 443 F.3d 676, 684 (9th Cir. 2006).
9. 570 F.3d 1280, 1283 (11th Cir. 2009).
10. 483 F. 3d 1184, 1204–05 (11th Cir. 2007).
11. 449 F.3d 1159, 1164 (11th Cir. 2006).
12. 3:06-CV-1936-D, 2007 WL 1556961, at *2 (N.D. Tex. May 30, 2007).

Dinkel v. General Motors Corp.[13] (citing legislative history to support shifting the burden of proof onto the party opposing removal).

Natale v. Pfizer, Inc.[14] (stating that "[u]nder the [Class Action Fairness] Act, the burden of [proof] is on the party opposing removal to prove that remand is appropriate.").

B. BURDEN OF REMAND

1. *The Party Seeking Remand Must Show One of CAFA's Exceptions Applies*

All circuit courts addressing this issue agree that party seeking remand has the burden to demonstrate that one of CAFA's exceptions requires remand.

a. Fifth Circuit

Preston v. Tenet Health Systems Memorial Medical Center, Inc.[15] (adopting the rule that once federal jurisdiction has been established under CAFA, the objecting party bears the burden of proof as to the applicability of any express statutory exception under the local controversy and home state exceptions).

b. Seventh Circuit

Hart v. FedEx Ground Package System, Inc.[16] (concluding that "the party seeking to take advantage of the home-state or local exception to CAFA jurisdiction has the burden of showing that it applies.").

c. Ninth Circuit

Serrano v. 180 Connect, Inc.[17] (concluding that "the party seeking remand bears the burden to prove an exception to CAFA's jurisdiction.").

d. Eleventh Circuit

Evans v. Walter Industries, Inc.[18] (holding that when a party seeks to avail itself of an express statutory exception to federal jurisdiction granted under CAFA, "the party seeking remand bears the burden of proof with regard to that exception.").

2. *Legislative History*

The Senate Report states that the party seeking remand bears the burden: "If a purported class action is removed pursuant to these jurisdictional provisions, the

---

13. 400 F. Supp. 2d 289, 295 (D. Me. 2005).

14. 379 F. Supp. 2d 161, 168 (D. Mass. 2005), *aff'd*, 424 F.3d 43 (1st Cir. 2005).

15. 485 F.3d 804, 813 (5th Cir. 2007).

16. 457 F.3d at 680.

17. 478 F.3d 1018, 1021–22 (9th Cir. 2007).

18. 449 F.3d at 1164.

named plaintiff(s) should bear the burden of demonstrating that the removal was improvident."[19]

3. The Standard for Deciding the Propriety of Removal

a. The Facts of the Case at the Time Motion to Remand Is Filed Determine If Removal Is Proper
   If the facts as they exist at the time of removal meet the requirements of fedral jurisdiction, removal was proper.

   Lowery v. Alabama Power Co.,[20] stating that [i]n assessing whether removal was proper . . . the district court has before it only the limited universe of evidence available when the motion to remand is filed, *i.e.*, the notice of removal and accompanying documents. If that evidence is insufficient to establish that removal was proper or that jurisdiction was present, neither the defendants nor the court may speculate in an attempt to make up for the notice's failings.

b. Post-Removal Events May Divest the District Court of CAFA Jurisdiction
   Garcia v. Boyar & Miller P.C.[21] (stating that although post-removal events (such as the addition of a nondiverse party in a non-CAFA removal) can divest the court of CAFA subject matter jurisdiction, no bright-line test will determine whether the court maintains jurisdiction).

4. CAFA and Post-Removal Jurisdictional Discovery

a. The Decision to Allow Discovery Is Left to the Discretion of the District Court
   i. Ninth Circuit
   Abrego Abrego v. Dow Chemical Co.[22] (noting that courts are not required to allow jurisdictional discovery and emphasizing that district courts must be given the discretion to balance the need for information with the time pressures imposed by the removal statutes).

   ii. Second Circuit
   Anwar v. Fairfield Greenwich Ltd.[23] (granting defendants' request for post-removal discovery on the issue of jurisdiction in a diversity case, finding that *Lowery* conflicts with Second Circuit precedent and emphasizing a court's "'considerable latitude' in supervising the development of 'facts pertinent to jurisdiction'").

---

19. S. Rep. No. 109-14, at 42 (2005).
20. 483 F.3d at 1214–15.
21. 2007 WL 1556961, at *2.
22. 443 F.3d at 691–92.
23. No. 09 Civ. 0118 (VM) (THK), 2009 WL 1181278, at *3 (S.D.N.Y. May 1, 2009).

b. Post-Removal Discovery Is Not Allowed

i. Eleventh Circuit

Lowery v. Alabama Power Co.,[24] stating

[p]ost-removal discovery for the purpose of establishing jurisdiction in diversity cases cannot be squared with the delicate balance struck by Federal Rules of Civil Procedure 8(a) and 11 and the policy and assumptions that flow from and underlie them. . . . The defendants' request for discovery is tantamount to an admission that the defendants do not have a factual basis for believing that jurisdiction exists. The natural consequence of such an admission is remand.

C. MASS ACTION REQUIREMENTS

1. The Statute

28 U.S.C. § 1332(d)(11)(A): "For purposes of this subsection and section 1453, a mass action shall be deemed to be a class action removable under paragraphs (2) through (10) if it otherwise meets the provisions of these paragraphs."

28 U.S.C. § 1332(d)(11)(B):

As used in subparagraph (A), the term "mass action" means any civil action (except a civil action within the scope of section 1711 (2)) in which monetary relief claims of 100 or more persons are proposed to be tried jointly on the ground that the plaintiffs' claims involve common questions of law or fact, except that jurisdiction shall exist only over those plaintiffs whose claims in a mass action satisfy the juris-dictional amount requirements under subsection (a).

2. Specific Elements: The Amount in Controversy

a. Two Amount-in-Controversy Requirements

The federal diversity jurisdiction statute, 28 U.S.C. § 1332(a), requires that a plaintiff's claim involve at least $75,000. The mass action provision of CAFA, 28 U.S.C. § 1332(11)(B)(1), requires that a mass action satisfy that amount. However, the amount in controversy required by CAFA at 28 U.S.C. § 1332(d)(2) is $5 million. With respect to mass actions, it is unclear whether both provisions apply, which would require each individual plaintiff to satisfy the $75,000 amount *and* require the aggregate amount at issue to exceed $5 million.

i. Eleventh Circuit

Lowery v. Alabama Power Co.[25] (stating that if the statute were read to require each of the 100 plaintiffs to meet the $75,000 requirement, $5 million aggregate requirement would be rendered "mere surplusage").

---

24. 483 F. 3d at 1215–18.

25. *Id.* at 1204–05.

ii. Ninth Circuit

Abrego Abrego v. Dow Chemical Co.[26] (holding that removal is improper in part because the defendant did not establish that even *one* plaintiff satisfied the $75,000 jurisdictional requirement of section 1332(a) applicable to mass actions by virtue of section 1332(d)(11)(B)(i)).

b. Establishing the Amount in Controversy

In considering the requisite $5 million threshold necessary for federal CAFA jurisdiction, courts generally require the party seeking federal jurisdiction to establish the amount by a preponderance of the evidence. Only if it is *legally certain* the claims at issue will not reach the $5 million threshold will the court remand the case.

Courts require preponderance to establish the amount in controversy and legal certainty to reject the amount in controversy.

i. Third Circuit

Frederico v. Home Depot[27] (where there is a factual dispute over the amount in controversy involved, the preponderance of evidence standard applies; however, "when relevant facts are not in dispute or findings have been made," the legal certainty test controls).

ii. Sixth Circuit (District)

Brown v. Jackson Hewitt, Inc.[28] (stating that "the removing defendant must meet a preponderance burden for all issues, including punitive damages, attorneys' fee and injunction-related costs").

iii. Seventh Circuit

Brill v. Countrywide Home Loans, Inc.[29] ("The question is not what damages the plaintiff will recover, but what amount is 'in controversy' between the parties . . . Once the proponent of jurisdiction has set out the amount in controversy, only a 'legal certainty' that the judgment will be less forecloses federal jurisdiction.").

iv. Eighth Circuit (District)

Wood v. Teris, LLC[30] (stating "the party invoking federal jurisdiction must prove the requisite amount-in-controversy by a preponderance of the evidence").

---

26. 443 F.3d at 689.
27. 507 F.3d 188, 194 (3d Cir. 2007).
28. No. 1:06-CV-2632, 2007 WL 642011, at *4 (N.D. Ohio Feb. 27, 2007).
29. 427 F.3d at 448–49.
30. No. 05-1011, 2006 WL 2091865, at *1 (W.D. Ark. Jul. 26, 2006).

v. Ninth Circuit

Abrego Abrego v. Dow Chemical Co.[31] (noting "[w]here the complaint does not specify the amount of damages sought, the removing defendant must prove by a preponderance of the evidence that the amount in controversy requirement has been met").

vi. Tenth Circuit (District)

Plummer v. Farmers Group, Inc.[32] (concluding that "the face of the Amended Petition and the Notice of Removal show by at least a preponderance of the evidence that the amount in controversy far exceeds the $5,000,000 requirement").

Courts require some reasonable basis for the amount in controversy (i.e., damages based on speculation are insufficient).

DiTolla v. Doral Dental IPA of New York, LLC[33] (finding that a complaint seeking an accounting of an alleged misappropriation of funds scheme that did not assert the amount of money involved failed to establish the amount in controversy).

Miedema v. Maytag Corp.[34] (finding that the defendant failed to establish the amount in controversy by a preponderance of evidence where the amount claimed to be at stake was "merely a guess" based on arbitrary and unfounded assumptions).

Bartnikowski v. NVR, Inc.[35] (finding that where "[d]efendant's offer of proof relies entirely on its speculative calculation of damages, which in turn relies on an unsupported assumption and an undefined, ambiguous term, the Court finds that Defendant has failed to show by a preponderance of the evidence that the amount in controversy, exclusive of interest and costs, exceeds $5,000,000.").

Courts will look to the complaint, notice of removal, contract, and so on to determine whether the amount-in-controversy requirement is met by a reasonable probability.

Lowery v. Alabama Power Co.[36] (noting that because expectation damages are the default measure of damages, "a court may look to the contract and deter-

---

31. 443 F.3d at 683.

32. 388 F. Supp. 2d 1310, 1317–18 (E.D. Okla. 2005).

33. 469 F.3d at 276–77.

34. 450 F.3d 1322, 1331–32 (11th Cir. 2006).

35. No. 1:07CV00768, 2008 WL 2512839, at *6 (M.D.N.C. 2008), *aff'd*, 307 F. App'x 730 (4th Cir. 2009).

36. 483 F.3d at 1215 n.66.

mine what those damages would be" in order to evaluate whether the amount-in-controversy requirement has been met).

Home Depot, Inc. v. Rickher[37] (explaining that the party must demonstrate "reasonable probability that the stakes exceed the minimum").

3. Specific Elements: The Numerosity Requirement

a. Determining Numerosity
Most circuits will look to the plaintiff's complaint to ensure that at least 100 plaintiffs are involved.

Cooper v. R.J. Reynolds Tobacco Co.[38] (numerosity requirement is determined by the number of plaintiffs "proposed to be jointly" in the complaint; defendant's intent to sever claims is irrelevant).

b. Aggregation of Claims
Where plaintiffs file separate complaints, courts may aggregate claims to meet the 100-plainitff requirement.

Freeman v. Blue Ridge Paper Products, Inc.[39] (stating that "where recovery is expanded, rather than limited, by virtue of splintering of lawsuits for no colorable reason, the total of such identical splintered lawsuits may be aggregated").

Tanoh v. Dow Chemical Co.[40] (refusing to consolidate, for removal purposes, the claims of "seven different groups of plaintiffs" who "allege[d] the same injuries in the same court" because plaintiffs did not divide their claims in order to expand their recovery and finding that "the decision to try claims jointly and thus qualify as a 'mass action' under CAFA should remain . . . with plaintiffs").

4. Specific Elements: The Commonality Requirement

CAFA "creates efficiencies in the judicial system by allowing overlapping and 'copy cat' cases to be consolidated in a single federal court, places the determination of more interstate class action lawsuits in the proper forum—the federal courts."[41]
Accordingly, courts will interpret the commonality requirement liberally.

Nesbit v. Unisys Corp.[42] (noting that "[a] sufficient nexus is established if the claims or defenses of the class and the class representative arise from the same event or pattern or practice and are based on the same legal theory" and finding

---

37. No. 06-8006, 2006 WL 1727749 (7th Cir. May 22, 2006).
38. 586 F. Supp. 2d 1312, 1320 (M.D. Fla. 2008).
39. 551 F.3d 405, 409 (6th Cir. 2008).
40. 561 F.3d 945, 954 (9th Cir. 2009).
41. S. REP. No. 109-14, at 5 (2005).
42. No. 2:05-CV-528-MEF, 2006 WL 2480071, at *4 (M.D. Ala. Aug. 25, 2006).

typicality absent where the claims of each individual class member arise under markedly different factual circumstances).

5. Mass Action Exceptions

The following situations will not be found to be mass actions (28 U.S.C. 1332(d) (11)(B)(ii) ("[T]he term 'mass action' shall not include any civil action in which . . . .")).

a. The "Single Occurrence" Exception

Statutory Text: "[A]ll of the claims in the action arise from an event or occurrence in the State in which the action was filed, and that allegedly resulted in injuries in that State or in States contiguous to that State."[43]

This provision applies "only to a truly local single event with no substantial interstate effects. The purpose of this exception was to allow cases involving environmental torts . . . to remain in state court if both the event and the injuries were truly local, even though there are some out-of-state defendants."[44]

> *Cooper v. R.J. Reynolds Tobacco Co.*[45] (finding that the single occurrence exception does not apply to products liability cases in which numerous plaintiffs filed multiple suits against tobacco companies because "the sale of a product to different people does not qualify as an event").

> *Galstadi v. Sunvest Communities USA, LLC*[46] (denying plaintiff's motion to remand and agreeing with defendant's position that the provision applies to "an event or occurrence" in the singular and finding that because the fact alleged sales to numerous parties over a period of approximately one and one-half years, the single occurrence exception was inapplicable).

b. The "Motion by Defendant" Exception

Statutory Text: "[T]he claims are joined upon a motion of a defendant."[47]

> *Duenas v. Dole Food Co.*[48] (explaining that defendants cannot establish the 100-person threshold by moving to join plaintiffs' claims, and rejecting the notion that "plaintiffs cannot artificially splinter their actions to avoid jurisdictional thresholds").

> *Tanoh v. Dow Chemical Co.*[49] (finding no difference, for the purposes of this exception, whether defendants formally moved to consolidate claims or

---

43. 28 U.S.C. § 1332(d)(11)(B)(ii)(I).
44. S. Rep. No. 109-14, at 47 (2005).
45. 586 F. Supp. 2d at 1316–17.
46. 256 F.R.D. 673, 676 (S.D. Fla. 2009).
47. 28 U.S.C. § 1332(d)(11)(B)(ii)(II).
48. No. CV 09-215-CAS (VBKx), 2009 WL 666802, at *3 (C.D. Cal. Mar. 9, 2009).
49. 561 F.3d at 954.

whether they informally urged the court to treat claims as though consolidated for removal and stating that defendant's request "precisely fits the statutory limitation," thus precluding removal).

c. The "General Public" Exception

Statutory Text: All of the claims in the action are asserted on behalf of the general public (and not on behalf of individual claimants or members of a purported class) pursuant to a state statute specifically authorizing such action.[50]

Breakman v. AOL[51] (rejecting defendant's assertion of federal jurisdiction by noting that the statute under which the case was brought authorizes a suit to be brought on behalf of the general public for unlawful trade practices and that even the defendant concedes that the case "falls squarely within the definitional exclusion of 'mass action'").

d. Exception for Claims Consolidated Solely for Pretrial Proceedings

Statutory Text: "[T]he claims have been consolidated or coordinated solely for pretrial proceedings."[52]

Tanoh v. Dow Chemical Co.[53] (noting that this provision reinforces the conclusion that "Congress intended to limit the numerosity component of mass actions quite severely by including only actions in which the trial itself would address the claims of at least one hundred plaintiffs").

D. OTHER PROVISIONS REGARDING MASS ACTIONS

1. Venue Transfers Limited for Mass Actions

Statutory Text: "Any action(s) removed to Federal court pursuant to this subsection shall not thereafter be transferred to any other court pursuant to section 1407, or the rules promulgated thereunder, unless a majority of the plaintiffs in the action requests transfer pursuant to section 1407."[54]

Thorne v. Wyeth[55] (finding that judge did not abuse his discretion by reversing magistrate judge's decision denying defendants' motion for leave to amend their notice of removal to assert diversity jurisdiction).

However, the limitation on venue transfers will not apply "(I) to cases certified pursuant to rule 23 of the Federal Rules of Civil Procedure; or (II) if plaintiffs

---

50. 28 U.S.C. § 1332(d)(11)(B)(ii)(III).
51. 545 F. Supp. 2d 96, 101 (D.D.C. 2008).
52. 28 U.S.C. § 1332(d)(11)(B)(ii)(IV).
53. 561 F.3d at 954.
54. 28 U.S.C. § 1332(d)(11)(c)(i).
55. 06-3123 (DSD/JJG), 2007 WL 2122158 (D. Minn. Jul. 19, 2007).

propose that the action proceed as a class action pursuant to rule 23 of the Federal Rules of Civil Procedure."[56]

2. Tolling the Statute of Limitations on a Mass Action

Statutory Text: "The limitations periods on any claims asserted in a mass action that is removed to Federal court pursuant to this subsection shall be deemed tolled during the period that the action is pending in Federal court."[57]

III. CAFA Exceptions Applicable to Mass Actions

A. GENERALLY

All circuits that have considered this issue agree that the party seeking remand bears the burden of showing that one of the CAFA exceptions applies.

The overall purpose of the CAFA exceptions is to ensure that "where appropriate, state courts can adjudicate certain class actions that have a truly local focus."[58]

1. First Circuit

In re Hannaford Bros. Customer Data Security Breach Litigation[59] (holding "that the burden is on the plaintiff to show that an exception to jurisdiction under CAFA applies").

2. Third Circuit

Kaufman v. Allstate New Jersey Insurance Co.[60] (resolving the question of first impression in the Third Circuit and concluding "that once CAFA jurisdiction has been established, the burden shifts to the party objecting to federal jurisdiction to show that the local controversy exception should apply").

3. Fifth Circuit

Frazier v. Pioneer Americas LLC[61] (holding that "plaintiffs have the burden to show the applicability of the §§ 1332(d)(3)–(5) exceptions when jurisdiction turns on their application").

4. Seventh Circuit

Hart v. FedEx Ground Package System, Inc.[62] (concluding that "the party seeking to take advantage of the home-state or local exception to CAFA jurisdiction has the burden of showing that it applies").

---

56. 28 U.S.C. § 1332(d)(11)(c)(i)(ii).
57. 28 U.S.C. § 1332(d)(11)(d).
58. S. Rep. No. 109-14, at 28 (2005).
59. 564 F.3d 75, 78 (1st Cir. 2009).
60. 561 F.3d 144, 153 (3d Cir. 2009).
61. 455 F.3d 542, 546 (5th Cir. 2006).
62. 457 F.3d at 680.

5. Ninth Circuit

Serrano v. 180 Connect, Inc.[63] (concluding that "the party seeking remand bears the burden to prove an exception to CAFA's jurisdiction").

6. Eleventh Circuit

Evans v. Walter Industries, Inc.[64] (holding that when a party seeks to avail itself of an express statutory exception to federal jurisdiction granted under CAFA, "the party seeking remand bears the burden of proof with regard to that exception").

B. CAFA'S DISCRETIONARY JURISDICTION EXCEPTION: 28 U.S.C.A. 1332(D)(3)

Statutory Text:

A district court may, in the interests of justice and looking at the totality of the circumstances, decline to exercise jurisdiction under paragraph (2) over a class action in which greater than one-third but less than two-thirds of the members of all proposed plaintiff classes in the aggregate and the primary defendants are citizens of the State in which the action was originally filed based on consideration of–

(A) whether the claims asserted involve matters of national or interstate interest;

(B) whether the claims asserted will be governed by laws of the State in which the action was originally filed or by the laws of other States;

    (i) S. Rep. 109-14 at 37 (2005) provides that "if the federal court determines that multiple state laws will apply to aspects of the class action, that determination would favor having the matter heard in the federal court system, which has a record of being more respectful of the laws of the various states in the class action context."

(C) whether the class action has been pleaded in a manner that seeks to avoid Federal jurisdiction;

    (i) S. Rep. 109-14 at 37 explains that "[t]he purpose of this inquiry is to determine whether the plaintiffs have proposed a 'natural class'—a class that encompasses all of the people and claims that one would expect to include in a class action, as opposed to proposing a class that appears to be gerrymandered solely to avoid federal jurisdiction by leaving out certain potential class members or claims."

(D) whether the action was brought in a forum with a distinct nexus with the class members, the alleged harm, or the defendants;

    (i) S. Rep. 109-14 at 37 provides that "[t]his factor is intended to take account of a major concern that led to this legislation—the filing of lawsuits in out-of-the-way 'magnet' state courts that have no real relationship to the controversy at hand."

---

63. 478 F.3d at 1021–22.
64. 449 F.3d at 1164.

(E) whether the number of citizens of the State in which the action was originally filed in all proposed plaintiff cases in the aggregate is substantially larger than the number of citizens from any other State, and the citizenship of the other members of the proposed class is dispersed among a substantial number of States; and

(F) whether, during the 3-year period preceding the filing of that class action, 1 or more other class actions asserting the same or similar claims on behalf of the same or other persons have been filed.

   (i) S. Rep. 109-14 at 38 explains that "[t]he purpose of this factor is efficiency and fairness: to determine whether a matter should be subject to federal jurisdiction so that it can be coordinated with other overlapping or parallel class actions."

For cases brought in a defendant's home state in which between one-third and two-thirds of the class members were citizens of that state, federal jurisdiction would also exist; however, a federal judge would have the discretion, in the interests of justice, to decline to exercise that jurisdiction based on consideration of six factors designed to help assess whether the claims at issue are indeed local in nature.[65]

The district may decline to exercise its jurisdiction of a class action in which one-third to two-thirds of the class members are citizens of the state in which the action was brought.

Preston v. Tenet Health System Memorial Medical Center, Inc.[66] (finding that movant must satisfy the one-third citizenship requirement prior to the district court considering the additional statutory factors in deciding whether to remand; section 1332(d)(3) "provides a discretionary vehicle for district courts to ferret out the controversy that uniquely affects a particular locality to the exclusion of all others.").

C. CAFA'S MANDATORY JURISDICTION EXCEPTIONS: THE LOCAL CONTROVERSY AND HOME STATE EXCEPTIONS IN 28 U.S.C.A. 1332(d)(4)

Generally: Cases that are particularly local in nature *must* be remanded to the state court under the local controversy exception. Cases involving controversies that are somewhat local in nature *may* be remanded to state courts subject to the district court's discretion as set out above. (Cases involving controversies that are somewhat local in nature *may* be remanded to state courts subject to the district court's discretion as set out above in subsection B and as required by 28 U.S.C.A 1332(d)(3)).

---

65. S. Rep. No. 109-14, at 38 (2005).
66. 485 F.3d at 812.

1. The Local Controversy Exception: 28 U.S.C. § 1332(d)(4)(A)

This section is "intended to ensure that state courts can continue to adjudicate truly local controversies in which some of the defendants are out-of-state corporations."[67]

Statutory Text:

A district court shall decline to exercise jurisdiction under paragraph (2)
(i) over a class action in which—
(I) greater than two-thirds of the members of all proposed plaintiff classes in the aggregate are citizens of the State in which the action was originally filed;
(II) at least 1 defendant is a defendant—
(aa) from whom significant relief is sought by members of the plaintiff class;
(bb) whose alleged conduct forms a significant basis for the claims asserted by the proposed plaintiff class;
(cc) who is a citizen of the State in which the action was originally filed; and
(III) principal injuries resulting from the alleged conduct of each defendant were incurred in the State in which the action was originally filed;
(ii) during the 3-year period preceding the filing of that class action, no other class action has been filed asserting the same or similar factual allegations against any of the defendants on behalf of the same or other persons.

The Senate committee clarified that this is a very narrow exception not to become a jurisdictional loophole. In applying this criterion, courts are to construe the factors narrowly to ensure that overlapping competing class actions against the same defendant receive that benefit of coordination that federal courts provide.[68]

The following four requirements must be satisfied for this exception: (1) the class must be primarily local in that more than two-thirds of class members must be residents of the state in which the action was filed; (2) at least one real defendant who is allegedly responsible for significant relief must be local; (3) the principal injuries must have occurred in the state where the suit was brought; and (4) no other similar class actions can have been filed against any of the defendants by the same classes in the preceding three years.

a. "Primarily Local" Requirement

Generally courts reject evidence of residency as sufficient to establish citizenship of the class (the "primarily local" requirement). However, courts may allow plaintiff discovery to establish this requirement and may relax the standard.

---

67. S. Rep. No. 109-14, at 28 (2005).
68. S. Rep. No. 109-14, at 39–41 (2005).

i. Strict Standard

(a) Fifth Circuit (District)
Martin v. Lafon Nursing Facility of the Holy Family[69] (finding that plaintiff seeking removal did not meet burden of establishing the local controversy exception where she offered no evidence of citizenship).

ii. Relaxed Standard

(a) Sixth Circuit (District)
Ford Motor Credit Co. v. Jones[70] (finding citizenship requirement for a local controversy established where plaintiff showed that all plaintiffs were Ohio residents).

(b) Seventh Circuit (District)
Kitson v. Bank of Edwardsville[71] (holding that the plaintiff's list establishing residency created a rebuttable presumption of citizenship that was not rebutted and thus was sufficient for the citizenship requirement).

(c) Eleventh Circuit
Evans v. Walter Industries, Inc.[72] (rejecting extrapolation from sample of potential class members where lawyer reviewed 10,118 potential plaintiffs and determined that half were class members and that 93.8 percent of those class members were residents of Alabama, because there was no indication of the selection process for the sample and no basis on which to determine whether conclusions were reliable).

b. Significant Relief/Significant Defendant

i. Eleventh Circuit
Evans v. Walter Industries, Inc.[73] (noting that courts have found significant relief against a defendant when "the relief sought against the defendant is a significant portion of the entire relief sought by the class" and finding insufficient evidence to compare the relief sought against a particular defendant to the overall relief sought in the case).

ii. Fourth Circuit (District)
Eakins v. Pella Corp.[74] (noting the Senate Report illustrated insignificant relief where the relief sought against one defendant was "small change compared to what they were seeking from" another defendant).

---

69. 06-5108, 2007 WL 162813, at *3 (E.D. La. Jan. 18, 2007).
70. 1:07 CV 728, 2007 WL 2236618, at *3 (N.D. Ohio Jul. 31, 2007).
71. Civ. No. 06-528-GPM, 2006 WL 3392752, at *6, 13 (S.D. Ill. Nov. 22, 2006).
72. 449 F.3d at 1166.
73. *Id.* at 1167.
74. 455 F. Supp. 2d 450, 453 (E.D.N.C. 2006).

iii. Sixth Circuit (District)

Nichols v. Progressive Direct Insurance Co.[75] (comparing the overall magnitude of the relief sought to that being sought from the local defendant).

iv. Fifth Circuit (District)

Caruso v. Allstate Insurance Co.[76] (finding that defendant insurer was significant defendant as the third largest homeowner insurer in Louisiana).

c. "Principal Injuries"

i. Seventh Circuit (District)

Kitson v. Bank of Edwardsville[77] (interpreting the state of "principal injuries" to be the state where the chief or primary violation of legal rights incurred).

ii. Fourth Circuit (District)

Eakins v. Pella Corp.[78] (listing the following factors as relevant in evaluating the significance of the defendant to determine whether the local controversy exception warrants remand: "whether the alleged defective product was sold outside the locality, whether the injury incurred was specific to the locality, and whether the class as a whole seeks relief against the local defendant.").

iii. Senate Report 109-14

Senate Report 109-14 at 40 (2005) says that by "principal injuries,"

[the] Committee means that all or almost all of the damage caused by the defendants' alleged conduct occurred in the state where the suit was brought. The purpose of this criterion is to ensure that this exception is used only where the impact of the misconduct alleged by the purported class is localized.

d. No "Copycat" Litigation

No other similar class actions have been filed against any of the defendants by the same classes in the preceding three years.

2. The Home State Exception: 28 U.S.C.A. 1332(d)(4)(B)

Statutory Text: "A district court shall decline to exercise jurisdiction under paragraph (2) [if] two-thirds or more of the members of all proposed plaintiff classes in the aggregate, and the primary defendants, are citizens of the State in which the action was originally filed."

Two-thirds of all defendants and plaintiffs are citizens of the State in which the action was brought and the defendants are "primary."

---

75. 06-146-DLB, 2007 WL 1035014, at *3 (E.D. Ky. Mar. 31, 2007).

76. 469 F. Supp. 2d 364, 369 (E.D. La. 2007).

77. 2006 WL 3392752, at *13.

78. 455 F. Supp. 2d at 453.

a. "Members of All Proposed Plaintiff Classes"

i. First Circuit

In re Hannaford Bros. Customer Data Security Breach Litigation[79] (finding that courts are not required, but may choose, to look outside "the four corners of the complaint" in order to identify "all proposed plaintiff classes in the aggregate").

b. "Primary Defendants"

Courts have emphasized the difference in language between significant defendant under the local controversy exception and the primary defendant requirement under the home state exception. Generally, a primary defendant is viewed as more important than a significant defendant.

Primary defendant should be interpreted to reach those defendants that "would be expected to incur most of the loss if liability is found."[80]

i. Second Circuit (District)

Brook v. UnitedHealth Group, Inc.[81] (noting that courts have taking various approaches with respect to what constitutes a primary defendant, including one: (1) who has the greater liability exposure; (2) is most able to satisfy a potential judgment; (3) is sued directly (rather than vicariously); (4) is the subject of a significant portion of the claims asserted by plaintiffs; (5) is the only defendant named in one particular cause of action).

ii. Fifth Circuit

Caruso v. Allstate Insurance Co.[82] (noting that primary means first in importance, chief, and main and thus must be of more importance than a significant defendant).

iii. Eleventh Circuit (District)

Cooper v. R.J. Reynolds Tobacco Co.[83] (finding no statutory definition for a "primary defendant" and finding that the defendant tobacco company with a small market share could not be labeled the "primary defendant").

3. *The Corporate Governance Exception: 28 U.S.C.A. 1332(d)(9)*

Statutory Text:

[CAFA jurisdiction] shall not apply to any class action that solely involves a claim—

---

79. 564 F.3d at 78.

80. S. Rep. No. 109-14, at 43 (2005).

81. 06 CV 12954 (GBD), 2007 WL 2827808, at *5 (S.D.N.Y. Sept. 27, 2007).

82. 469 F. Supp. 2d at 369.

83. 586 F. Supp. 2d at 1318.

(A) concerning a covered security as defined under 16(f)(3) of the Securities Act of 1933 (15 U.S.C. 78p(f)(3)) and section 28(f)(5)(E) of the Securities and Exchange Act of 1934 (15 U.S.C. 78bb(f)(5)(E));

(B) that relates to the internal affairs or governance of a corporation or other form of business enterprise and that arises under or by virtue of the laws of the State in which such corporation or business enterprise is incorporated or organized;

(C) that relates to the rights, duties (including fiduciary duties), and obligations relating to or created by or pursuant to any security (as defined under section 2(a)(1) of the Securities Act of 1933 (15 U.S.C. 77b(a)(1)) and the regulations issued thereunder).

New Jersey Carpenters Vacation Fund v. Harborview Mortgage Loan Trust[84] (finding that CAFA overrides the Security Act's antiremoval provision because the case involves exactly the type of case CAFA was concerned about—a large, nonlocal securities class action dealing with a matter of national importance).

IV. Section 1453(B) Removal of Class Actions Under CAFA

Statutory Text:

(b) In General.— A class action may be removed to a district court of the United States in accordance with section 1446 (except that the 1-year limitation under section 1446(b) shall not apply), without regard to whether any defendant is a citizen of the State in which the action is brought, except that such action may be removed by any defendant without the consent of all defendants.

V. Ancillary Issues Not Addressed by the Statute

A. ORIGINAL JURISDICTION OVER MASS ACTIONS

1. *Fourth Circuit*

Lanier v. Norfolk Southern Corp.[85] ("For the district court to have original jurisdiction over a class action under CAFA, the proponent of removal must show minimal diversity, and it must be clear from the face of the complaint that the amount in controversy exceeds $5 million.").

---

84. 581 F. Supp. 2d 581, 588–89 (S.D.N.Y. 2008).
85. 256 F. App'x 629, 631 (4th Cir. 2007).

2. Ninth Circuit

Serrano v. 180 Connect, Inc.[86] (stating that once "the prerequisites of § 1332(d)(5) are satisfied, CAFA vests federal courts with 'original' diversity jurisdiction . . . .").

Abrego Abrego v. Dow Chemical Co.[87] (noting that, while on its face CAFA vests the district courts with original jurisdiction, Congress's use of the word "removable" in section 1332(d)(11)(A) "blurs what had previously been a clear distinction between jurisdiction and removal statutes, and thus obscures the reach of jurisdiction over mass actions.").

B. DENIAL OF CLASS CERTIFICATION AND MASS ACTIONS UNDER CAFA

District courts have generally held that denial of class certification will not preclude the court from exercising CAFA jurisdiction.

1. Second Circuit (District)

Falcon v. Philips Electronics North America Corp.[88] (holding that plaintiffs do not automatically lose subject matter jurisdiction under CAFA upon denial of plaintiffs' class certification motion).

2. Fifth Circuit (District)

Garcia v. Boyar & Miller P.C.[89] ("Class certification is neither a requirement for removal nor a prerequisite for federal jurisdiction under CAFA.").

3. Seventh Circuit (District)

Genenbacher v. CenturyTel Fiber Co. II, LLC[90] (holding that "[t]he denial of class certification is an interlocutory order that may be altered or amended . . . Because the class claims are not finally resolved, they remain part of this case, and this Court retains jurisdiction until a final judgment can be entered . . . .").

4. Ninth Circuit (District)

Arabian v. Sony Electronics Inc.[91] (finding that plaintiffs are unable to claim CAFA jurisdiction because "there is no 'reasonably foreseeable possibility' that a class of FX computer purchasers will be certified in the future of this action").

C. WHEN AN ACTION HAS COMMENCED FOR CAFA PURPOSES

All circuits that have addressed this issue agree that state law controls.

---

86. 478 F.3d at 1020–21.
87. 443 F.3d at 681–82.
88. 489 F. Supp. 2d 367, 368 (S.D.N.Y. 2007).
89. 2007 WL 1556961, at *5.
90. 500 F. Supp. 2d 1014, 1017 (C.D. Ill. 2007).
91. 05CV1741 WQH (NLS), 2007 WL 2701340, at *5 (S.D. Cal. Sept. 13, 2007).

Fifth Circuit: *Braud v. Transport Service Co.*[92] (agreeing with the "countless courts of appeals that have examined the issue and unanimously held that when a lawsuit is initially 'commenced' for purposes of CAFA is determined by state law").

Sixth Circuit: *Smith v. Nationwide Property & Casualty Insurance Co.*[93] (noting that "state law applies to determine when a matter is 'commenced' for purposes of the application of CAFA").

Eighth Circuit: *Plubell v. Merck & Co., Inc.*[94] (noting that CAFA only applies to class actions commenced on or after February 28, 2005, and that "state law determines when a suit is commenced in state court").

Ninth Circuit: *Bush v. Cheaptickets, Inc.*[95] (noting that CAFA's "'commenced' language surely refers to when the action was originally commenced in state court").

Eleventh Circuit: *Tmesys, Inc. v. Eufaula Drugs, Inc.*[96] ("[T]he consensus among circuits is that state law determines when an action is commenced for purposes of CAFA.").

D. CAFA AND SUPPLEMENTAL JURISDICTION

The legislative history of CAFA suggests that supplemental jurisdiction remains a potential independent basis for federal jurisdiction, regardless of whether the action satisfies the mass action requirements.

CAFA "is in no way intended to abrogate 28 USC 1367 or to narrow current jurisdictional rules in any way. Thus, if a federal court believed it to be appropriate, the court could apply supplemental jurisdiction in the mass action context as well."[97]

---

92. 445 F.3d 801, 803 (5th Cir. 2006).
93. 505 F.3d at 405.
94. 434 F.3d 1070, 1071 (8th Cir. 2006).
95. 425 F.3d 683, 686 (9th Cir. 2005).
96. 462 F.3d 1317, 1319 (11th Cir. 2006).
97. S. Rep. No. 109-14, at 48 (2005).

MULTIDISTRICT LITIGATION

THOMAS C. GALLIGAN, JR.
RICHARD J. ARSENAULT

I. Introduction

The rules and procedures applied in complex cases grew out of less complex times. One might wonder if law schools' educational focus on the individual case and its resolution has not rigidly shaped our thinking in a way that makes it more difficult for us to contemplate complex litigation and how it might be best resolved. That is, are we stuck in the paradigm of the individual case, even when it no longer efficiently fits the needs of modern-day mass litigation? Some of the legal vehicles lawyers, litigants, and our courts travel in today include consolidation[1] and the subject of this book, class actions.[2] Another is multidistrict litigation (MDL). An MDL may include class actions, but it need not itself involve a class, and quite commonly does not. It is the MDL, some of the practical issues it presents, its promise, and its limitations that we will address in this chapter. We will consider the current MDL landscape: what works, what doesn't, and why. We will discuss the advantages and disadvantages of participating in the process. We will explore whether litigants should embrace the MDL procedure or avoid it like the plague. We will also provide a statistical report card and see what, when, where, and how MDL litigation is being processed.

The litigation we studied in law school arose in simpler times. Torts, for example, involved one person whose actions allegedly damaged the interests of another, usually in a way that an objective person could physically observe.[3] In this one-on-one world, the court heard the case of one against one, at trial and on appeal.

---

1. *See* Fed. R. Civ. P. 42(a).
2. *See* Fed. R. Civ. P. 23.
3. *See generally* Thomas C. Galligan, Jr., *The Risks of and Reactions to Underdeterrence in Torts*, 70 Mo. L. Rev. 691 (2005).

In the United States, this litigation most frequently occurred in state court, but might arise in federal court if there was diversity of citizenship and the jurisdictional amount was satisfied. If the parties settled, they did so by talking to one another, albeit usually through their lawyers, who met with the clients individually and conducted face-to-face conversations about rights, options, and resolutions. Interestingly, in the embryonic stages of corporate litigation, Wall Street presumed that a lawyer's job was to settle disputes in the "conference room," not in the "courtroom."[4] That business model, however, was short-lived.

Since the onset of the Industrial Age, followed by what we might call the Information Technology Age, things have changed. For the last 100 years, while one-on-one lawsuits arising from a single incident have still been common, the world that lawyers and courts increasingly face has evolved into a landscape where a corporate defendant's actions have the potential to injure not one or a few, but literally thousands. Mass production has created mass torts. In this new world, often many plaintiffs seek recovery from a single defendant or, in other instances, multiple defendants. Moreover, particularly in the field of toxic tort and pharmaceutical litigation, individuals may not yet have an observable or manifest injury, but instead may have an increased risk of suffering adverse consequences in the future. Issues arise regarding whether it is possible to settle future, unknown claims. Some of these individuals may not even be aware of the potential risk.

The attorney-client relationship has likewise evolved. Plaintiff lawyers who handle mass torts may only infrequently meet face-to-face with their clients and not until and unless there is an important reason to do so. Much of their communication is by telephone or e-mail. The advent of modern technology facilitates plaintiffs' counsel's ability to represent large numbers of claimants in a single or coordinated proceeding. In fact, plaintiff firms that handle mass torts typically form strategic alliances with other firms and divide key responsibilities of managing large caseloads. The clients benefit from the collective strength and clout these groups provide. Costs per claimant decrease because they are typically shared among larger groups of plaintiffs so each individual pays less. In many instances, these strategic alliances are the only litigation model that can shoulder the invest-

---

4. MALCOLM GLADWELL, OUTLIERS: THE STORY OF SUCCESS 124 (2008):

The old-line Wall Street law firms had a very specific idea about what it was that they did. They were corporate lawyers. They represented the country's largest and most prestigious companies, and "represented" meant they handled the taxes and the legal work behind the issuing of stocks and bonds and made sure their clients did not run afoul of federal regulators. They did not do litigation; that is, very few of them had a division dedicated to defending and filing lawsuits. As Paul Cravath, one of the founders of Cravath, Swaine and Moore, the very whitest of the white-shoe firms, once put it, the lawyer's job was to settle disputes in the conference room, not in the courtroom. "Among my classmates at Harvard, the thing that bright young guys did was securities work or tax," another white-shoe partner remembers. "Those were the distinguished fields. Litigation was for hams, not for serious people. Corporations just didn't sue each other in those days."

ment required to take on complex and expensive litigation that is defended by well-funded corporate defendants.

The efficiencies derived from processing the cases of many plaintiffs in a single proceeding are matched by magnified risks for both sides. From the plaintiff's viewpoint, early adverse rulings in mass tort litigation can cause the entire litigation to quickly fall into a downward spiral. Preemption defenses, *Daubert*[5] scrutiny, *Lone Pine* orders,[6] motions in limine, and dispositive motions, along with evolving pleading standards[7] all pose daunting obstacles that can impose litigation fatigue and, in some instances, the civil death penalty (dismissal with prejudice) on hundreds or thousands of plaintiffs' cases with a single ruling. On the defense side, a corporate defendant must bring all its resources to bear when the stakes are raised from the one-on-one case to a mass tort case that could deal the defendant's business a significant blow or even drive the company into bankruptcy. Regardless of the merits of the case, the costs of litigation alone constitute a substantial burden that can drive a defendant to settlement. It is a David versus Goliath dynamic where a corporate defendant's formidable resources are brought to bear on loosely organized and often competing groups of plaintiff lawyers that form temporary (and often strained) alliances to combat the national mega–law firms that routinely service the world's largest and most powerful corporations. Even the court's role has evolved—judges, who formerly primarily focused on serving as independent arbiters of the fact-finding mission and application of controlling legal principles, must become administrators and case managers when handling mass tort cases.

II. Statutory Basis

In the 1960s, after the U.S. government successfully prosecuted electrical equipment manufacturers for antitrust violations, over 1,800 separate private damages actions were filed in 33 federal district courts. These cases presented what seemed like overwhelming case management challenges. However, through the remarkable work of the Coordinating Committee for Multiple Litigation of the U.S. District Courts, the relevant judges and lawyers successfully conducted joint pretrial proceedings, and all the cases were resolved. This stellar success in coordinated discovery became the inspiration for the creation of a regime to deal with such cases in

---

5. *Daubert v. Merrell Dow Pharm., Inc.*, 509 U.S. 579, 113 S. Ct. 2786 (1993).

6. *Lore v. Lone Pine Corp.*, No. L-33606-85 1985, N.J. Super. LEXIS 1626 (1986). A Lone Pine Order requires that a plaintiff substantiate his cause of action before embarking on a costly lawsuit with numerous defendants and lawyers. *Id.* at *4.

7. *See, e.g., Ashcroft v. Iqbal*, 556 U.S. ___, 129 S. Ct. 1937, 1950 (2009); *Bell Atl. Corp. v. Twombly*, 550 U.S. 544, 556 (2007).

the future. That regime was the U.S. Judicial Panel on Multidistrict Litigation (the MDL Panel) and its authority to transfer cases for pretrial proceedings.[8]

The critical statutory section (which Congress enacted in 1968) is 28 U.S.C. § 1407. The MDL Panel itself consists of seven federal district and circuit court judges, no two of whom may be from the same circuit. The Chief Justice of the U.S. Supreme Court appoints the Panel members.[9] Except for the rule that no two judges may come from the same circuit, the Chief Justice's appointment authority is unlimited; however, Chief Justice Rehnquist instituted a procedure under which the members served in staggered definite terms, the maximum of which is seven years. Chief Justice Roberts has continued this practice.[10] Before that, the MDL Panel judges served indefinite terms at the pleasure of the Chief Justice.[11]

The Panel may transfer cases then pending in different districts and involving one or more common questions of fact to another single district for coordinated or consolidated pretrial proceedings.[12] The concurrence of four of the seven Panel judges is necessary for transfer.[13] Notably, in order to be eligible for transfer, the case must be pending in federal court. Thus, the MDL process does not apply to cases pending in state court, although creative federal judges have found ways of encouraging voluntary coordination with state court judges.[14]

Critically, the Panel may transfer a case to any other district in the nation. It is not limited in its transfer power to a district in which the claim may initially have been brought. Put slightly differently, the Panel is not constrained by the limits and criteria of 28 U.S.C. § 1404, the more general transfer of venue statute. Thus, the normal venue rules and venue transfer rules that apply in the simpler one-on-one litigation model do not govern in an MDL. Likewise, the deference accorded a plaintiff's choice of forum in one-on-one litigation carries no weight in an MDL, at least for pretrial proceedings.

III. Considerations for Transfer

What litigation actually gets MDL consolidation and why? The statute provides that the Panel shall transfer a relevant case when it determines that transfer will be for

---

8. *See, e.g.,* H.R. REP. No. 90-1130 (1968), *reprinted in* 1968 U.S.C.C.A.N. 1898, at *1900.

9. 28 U.S.C. § 1407(d).

10. For an informative overview see John G. Heyburn II, *A View from the Panel: Part of the Solution,* 82 TUL. L. REV. 2225, 2228 (2008).

11. Gregory Hansel, *Extreme Litigation: An Interview with Judge Wm. Terrell Hodges, Chairman of the Judicial Panel on Multidistrict Litigation,* 19 ME. B.J. 16, 19–20 (2004).

12. 28 U.S.C. § 1407(a).

13. *Id.* at § 1407(d).

14. Federal/state committees were established in a number of MDLs including *In re Propulsid Prod. Liab. Litig.,* MDL No. 1355 (E.D. La. 2001), *In re Vioxx Prods. Liab. Litig.,* MDL No. 1657, and *In re Baycol Prods. Liab. Litig.,* MDL No. 1431 (8th Cir. 2010).

the convenience of parties and witnesses and will promote the just and efficient conduct of such actions.[15] Thus, the three transfer considerations are (1) existence of common questions of fact; (2) convenience of the parties and witnesses; and (3) justice and efficiency.[16] One commentator has stated:

> In practice, the Panel applies standards more detailed than those of the statute to determine if transfer will, in fact, achieve the purposes of the statute. These factors include, but are hardly limited to:
>
> 1. Convenience of counsel;
> 2. Convenience of witnesses;
> 3. Minimizing of duplicative discovery;
> 4. Possibility of conflicting rulings;
> 5. Number of actions and pendency of at least one action in the proposed transferee district;
> 6. Progress of discovery at the time of proposed transfer;
> 7. Docket conditions;
> 8. Familiarity of transferee judge with issues raised;
> 9. Availability of judicial resources;
> 10. Number of actions pending in district; and
> 11. Size of litigation.
>
> Agreement by all parties that transfer is appropriate may increase the likelihood that cases will be transferred and consolidated. Opposition by all parties will not, however, defeat consolidation and transfer.[17]

The initiate will note that these factors are different from the Rule 23 factors courts consider in determining whether or not to certify a class action. MDL transfer is a lower hurdle than certification of a class action. Of course, class actions may be transferred as part of an MDL,[18] and once individual cases are transferred

---

15. 28 U.S.C. § 1407(a).

16. One commentator has noted:

An examination of the opinions issued by the MDL Panel indicates that there is considerable overlap among these requirements and that they are not given equal weight in deciding transfer applications. Often the panel's opinion will merely conclude that common questions of fact exist without further examination of the common factual issues and their relation, if any, to the consolidated actions. It should be noted that in a situation in which the claimants in various actions have asserted differing legal theories, transfer still is possible if there are common factual questions. If the actions have only legal questions in common, the statutory requirement is not literally satisfied, and the panel may not order consolidation of the actions.

Desmond T. Barry, Jr., *A Practical Guide to the Ins and Outs of Multidistrict Litigation*, 64 Def. Couns. J. 58, 59 (1997).

17. David F. Herr & Nicole Narotzky, *The Judicial Panel's Role in Managing Mass Litigation*, in ALI-ABA Course of Study, Mass Litigation 249 (2008) (footnote omitted).

18. *See, e.g., Hilao v. Estate of Marcos*, 103 F.3d 767 (9th Cir. 1996).

and consolidated the transferee court may decide to certify all or some of the cases as a class action if the Rule 23 prerequisites are also met.

The transfer may be made based on motion of the parties or by the Panel on its own initiative. Transfer by the Panel itself, without motion, is usually limited to "tag-along" cases. Those are cases already pending in a district that have common factual questions with an action that has already been transferred. Such a development may be quite a surprise to the lawyer who was not previously notified. One commentator has described that surprise as follows:

> Imagine you are minding your own business and litigating a case in federal court. Opening your mail one day, you find an order—from a court you have never heard of—declaring your case a "tag-along" action and transferring it to another federal court clear across the country for pretrial proceedings. Welcome to the world of multidistrict litigation.[19]

Actually, in the hypothetical case, the surprised lawyer would have an opportunity to object to the transfer under Rule 7.4 of the Rules of Procedure of the Judicial Panel on Multidistrict Litigation. All of the rules are available on the MDL Panel's website, http://www.jpml.uscourts.gov/. Other helpful resources available to the practitioner include *The Manual for Complex Litigation (Fourth)* (2004), which is published by the Federal Judicial Center.[20]

Naturally, the Panel may decline transfer. Since 1968 there have been 669 litigations docketed encompassing 6,571 actions in which transfer has not occurred, either because the Panel denied it or because the motion was withdrawn.[21] By contrast, over the same period, the Panel has docketed 216,809 actions in which it has granted transfer.[22] Thus, the evidence is clear that the Panel is more likely to transfer than to decline to do so. In one recent case, *In re Reglan/Metoclopramide Products Liability Litigation*,[23] plaintiffs in ten pending actions (most of whom were represented by common counsel)[24] sought certification as an MDL and transfer, while the plaintiff in a single eleventh action opposed transfer. The common issue

---

19. Hansel, *supra* note 11.

20. Available free online at http://www.fjc.gov/public/home.nsf/pages/470. West publishes an annotated version. Useful treatises include Paul D. Rheingold, Mass Tort Litigation (1996) and Richard L. Marcus & Edward F. Sherman, Complex Litigation: Cases and Materials on Advanced Civil Procedure (4th ed. 2004).

21. U.S. Judicial Panel on Multidistrict Litig., Statistical Analysis of Multidistrict Litigation 2009, http://www.jpml.uscourts.gov/Statistics/JPML_Statistical_Analysis_of_Multidistrict_Litigation_2009.pdf, at 74 [hereinafter Statistical Analysis].

22. *Id.* at 3.

23. 622 F. Supp. 2d 1380 (U.S.J.P.M.L. 2009).

24. *Id.* at 1381 n.3.

involved whether a drug, metoclopramide, caused neurological injuries. In refusing to transfer the Panel said:

> [W]e are not persuaded that Section 1407 centralization would serve the convenience of the parties and witnesses or further the just and efficient conduct of this litigation at the present time. The eleven actions at issue do share factual issues as to whether the drug metoclopramide causes neurological injuries (principally, tardive dyskinesia). But there is no single common defendant, and some entities, such as Baxter Healthcare Corp., are named in only one or two actions. Moreover, several of the actions appear to be substantially advanced (five were commenced in either 2006 or 2007). Metoclopramide litigation has a lengthy history, and the record indicates that a significant amount of the common discovery has already taken place. The proponents of centralization have failed to convince us that any remaining common questions of fact among these actions are sufficiently complex and/or numerous to justify Section 1407 transfer at this time. Alternatives to transfer exist that may minimize whatever possibilities there might be of duplicative discovery and/or inconsistent pretrial rulings.[25]

Thus, while there was a significant common factual issue, the MDL Panel concluded that there were no common defendants and the cases were essentially too far along to significantly benefit from the MDL process.

In addition to the 216,809 actions transferred from a different home district, 106,449 actions that were originally filed in the transferee district were included in MDLs.[26] Thus during its 40 years of existence, the MDL process has involved a total of 323,258 actions.[27] As of the end of September 2009, there were more MDL actions (47,030 involving 24 separate MDLs) pending in the Eastern District of Pennsylvania than anywhere else.[28] However, there were more discrete MDL proceedings (52) pending in the Southern District of New York than in any other district.[29] Whether this number speaks more to the convenience of witnesses and evidence, the expertise of the respective judges, or the location of the lawyers involved is a matter of conjecture. The actions that the Panel has processed include securities actions, antitrust actions, intellectual property actions, mass disaster cases, product liability cases, labor and discrimination actions, environmental actions, insurance cases, and qui tam actions.[30]

---

25. *Id.* at 1381.
26. STATISTICAL ANALYSIS at 4.
27. *Id.*
28. *Id.* at 8, 15.
29. *Id.* at 14–15.
30. *See* Herr & Narotzky, *supra* note 17.

IV. Selection of Transferee Court

The judge to whom the Panel transfers cases can have a critical effect on the ultimate outcome of the cases and thus can be a subject of some contention before the Panel.[31] In selecting the transferee district, the Panel necessarily considers some of the same factors that it considers in deciding whether to transfer, as well as others.[32] Since the action may be transferred to a venue in which it could not have originally been brought, the choices of potential venues and judges are unlimited, and each party will advocate for the forum it perceives as most favorable to its position.

The MDL transferee judge's crucial role in settlement heightens the interest of both sides in his or her selection. In complex litigation, courts are authorized and expected to take an active role in shepherding the case to resolution. The *Manual for Complex Litigation (Fourth)* states that effective judicial management of complex litigation is "active," "substantive," "timely," "continuing," "firm but fair," and "careful."[33] Those characteristics are particularly apropos regarding settlement. The *Manual* encourages the trial judge "at each conference" of the parties to "explore the settlement posture of the parties and the techniques, methods, and mechanisms that may help resolve the litigation short of trial."[34] The *Manual* dedicates an entire section to a trial judge's role in the settlement process,[35] and advocates various techniques, such as firm trial dates, reference to magistrate judges or another judge for settlement negotiations (to alleviate the appearance of partiality), required attendance at settlement conferences, confidential discussions with the judge, appointment of special masters, and other strategies. Available devices may include settlements where claimants opt in to a settlement, which avoids the due process issues that may arise with opt-out settlements involving unnamed and unknown individuals.

If the parties are not satisfied with the Panel's decision, what are the appellate options? Review of a Panel decision ordering transfer is only by extraordinary writ in the court of appeals for the circuit in which the transferee court[36] is located, and there is no review of a decision denying MDL status.[37] The Panel may separate any claim, cross-claim, counterclaim, or third-party claim and remand any of such

---

31. *See generally* Steve Korris, *Under Pressure, Attorneys Shop for Judges in MDL Hearings*, MADISON/ST. CLAIR RECORD, Jan. 17, 2007, *available at* http://www.madisonrecord.com/news/189157-under-pressure-attorneys-shop-for-judges-in-mdl-hearings.

32. *See* Herr & Narotzky, *supra* note 17.

33. MANUAL FOR COMPLEX LITIGATION (FOURTH) § 10.13 (2004).

34. *Id.* at § 11.214.

35. *Id.* at §§ 13.1–.15.

36. The court to which an action is transferred under 28 U.S.C. § 1407 is referred to as the "transferee" court, and the court from which the action is transferred is called the "transferor" court.

37. 28 U.S.C. § 1407(e).

claims to the originating court before the remainder of the action is remanded, but this is rarely done.[38]

V. Management by the Transferee Court

Once the Panel has transferred a case, it is assigned an MDL number and name. All counsel involved in any MDL are expected to familiarize themselves with the *Manual for Complex Litigation* and be prepared to suggest procedures that will facilitate the just, speedy, and inexpensive resolution of the litigation. To assist the court in identifying any problems of recusal or disqualification, counsel are often asked to identify all companies affiliated with the parties and all counsel associated with the litigation. Usually lawyers admitted to practice in good standing in any U.S. District Court are admitted pro hac vice in the MDL transferee court, and the association of local co-counsel is generally not required.

A. COMMITTEES AND LEAD COUNSEL

Upon transfer, the transferee court normally appoints a plaintiffs' steering committee (PSC) and, in cases involving multiple defendants, a defense steering committee (DSC). Most courts request applications for lead and liaison counsel appointments. Typically, a PSC is put together with some combination of lead counsel and/or executive committee and liaison counsel, while a DSC may consist of representatives of those defendants with the most serious exposure to liability, or, in the case of different categories of defendants, one or more representatives from each category. If categories of defendants appear to have conflicts of interest, the court may appoint separate DSCs for each category. There is usually considerable competition to become a member of the relevant committee because it will give the lawyer a leadership role in the subsequent proceedings. It may also entitle the leadership counsel on the plaintiff's side to increased fees for providing a common benefit to all plaintiffs involved. Not being a member of the relevant committee necessarily means that the lawyer will not have a seat at the primary table where many decisions about the conduct of the litigation are considered, debated, and made.

The roles, responsibilities, and obligations regarding these positions vary from court to court. Many courts note that the main criteria for an appointment are (1) the willingness and ability to commit to a time-consuming process; (2) the ability to work cooperatively with others; (3) professional experience in this type of litigation; and (4) access to sufficient resources to advance the litigation in a timely manner. For the lawyer accustomed to the one-on-one mode of litigation and being directly and solely responsible for representing his or her client, the

---

38. *Id.* at § 1407(a).

role of a committee member may be a difficult adjustment. The lawyer may feel particularly uncomfortable in this role with its possible ethical implications under the one-on-one model. Of course, even though the lawyer in an MDL may play an unfamiliar and challenging role, the lawyer still must exercise his or her best efforts to represent the clients' interest, including keeping them fully informed of developments and their associated rights. One court has referred to the failure to do so as contributing to the "common detriment" of the MDL.[39] Being a member of the committee imposes a great burden of communication and responsibility not merely to a lawyer's individual client or clients but also to other lawyers and their clients. As a committee member, the lawyer's role resembles the role of class counsel in a class action, who represents many absent class members whom he does not know and may never meet. Of course, unlike the class action lawyer, the committee member does not represent other lawyers' clients who are also in the MDL even though the committee member's actions and decisions may affect those lawyers and their clients.

PSCs require counsel with a variety of skill sets and an ability to overcome differences in personal litigation styles and approaches. Unlike their defense counterpart, which, in single-defendant cases, is likely a single large firm with access to the variety of resources in a single cohesive package, the PSC is often a collection of small plaintiff firms forced to work with each other by virtue of the judge's appointments rather than by choice. The appointed PSC firms have likely already engaged in some significant disagreements with each other to get the PSC appointment, and may have never worked together before. Some lawyers will do the research and brief writing, others will develop experts, others will take depositions, others will focus on the science, others will manage documents, others will focus on the trial, and so on. It is a challenge to organize a PSC so that it can quickly operate effectively against an opponent or opponents who usually start from a more easily unified position.

Most MDL transferee courts establish mechanisms for dissenting opinions. For example, in *In re Medtronic, Inc., Sprint Fidelis Leads Product Liability Litigation*,[40] Judge Richard Kyle issued an order early in the case specifically providing that any counsel for any plaintiff who disagreed with plaintiffs' lead counsel or who had individual or divergent positions could present written and oral arguments, and otherwise act separately on behalf of their clients as appropriate, provided that in doing so they did not repeat arguments, questions, or actions of the plaintiffs' lead counsel.

---

39. *In re Guidant Corp. Implantable Defibrillators Prods. Liab. Litig.*, MDL No. 05-1708, Order Sanctioning Counsel (D. Minn. 2009).

40. MDL No. 08-1905, Order No. 4 (D. Minn. June 4, 2008).

What is the dynamic that allows an MDL to function? From the defense point of view, consolidation in an MDL is desirable because it allows the defendant to achieve efficiencies of scale by litigating pretrial issues in all cases in a single forum and obtaining uniform rulings that govern all cases rather than litigating individual cases over and over with a hodgepodge of results. The downside for the defendant, of course, is the potential for failure in the event of adverse rulings, although this potential is somewhat mitigated since, unlike the class action, the transfer and consolidation is for pretrial proceedings only. On the defense side, a new dynamic is emerging, with defendants hiring a variety of large experienced defense firms to serve in different discrete capacities, such as local counsel, litigation counsel, settlement counsel, and coordination counsel.

From the plaintiffs' point of view, for an MDL to enjoy success, it needs critical mass. It needs to be the place where the majority of the litigation is taking place. If the serious action is in state court (and cannot be removed because of lack of diversity), the MDL can only hope to be the tail that wags the dog. The All Writs Act[41] versus the Anti-Injunction Act[42] tension often comes into play when the federal MDL and significant state litigation on the same subject matter are proceeding at the same time. Under the All Writs Act, federal courts "may issue all writs necessary or appropriate in aid of their respective jurisdictions and agreeable to the usages and principles of law."[43] However, this power is limited by the Anti-Injunction Act, which bars federal courts from enjoining state courts unless that action is "expressly authorized by Acts of Congress, or where necessary in aid of jurisdiction, or to protect or effectuate its judgments."[44] Parallel state and federal litigation sometimes peacefully coexist. Sometimes the MDL dominates through a combination of diplomacy and All Writs power. Sometimes the MDL is marginalized by the lack of litigation volume before it. Therefore, in light of this reality, in addition to other considerations associated with selecting a PSC, an important factor to consider is whether a lawyer candidate has a large inventory of clients and whether that lawyer has strategic alliances with other counsel, as well as a significant number of referral counsel. These circumstances often are instrumental in ensuring that an MDL enjoys widespread support, cooperation, and participation. The traditional antagonism between mass tort lawyers and lawyers representing small numbers of clients, between state and federal courts, between advertising lawyers and non-advertising lawyers, can all be more successfully addressed when the PSC is composed of lawyers who represent large numbers of clients, have a large number of referral lawyers, and are well-respected by both the bench and bar.

---

41. 28 U.S.C. § 1651.
42. 28 U.S.C. § 2283.
43. 28 U.S.C. § 1651.
44. *Id.* at § 2238.

The candidate must, of course, also have the resources, willingness, and availability to commit to the time-consuming challenges presented by an MDL.

B. DISCOVERY

After appointing committees, the court will consider processes and a time line for organizing and conducting the pretrial discovery. Here again, technology has created challenges. The Internet and electronic methods of communication have exponentially complicated traditional discovery. In an MDL proceeding, the challenge is often magnified because of the volume of documents and number of participants involved in the various electronic communications. Courts are increasingly called upon to review documents to determine whether attorney-client privileges have been appropriately raised. When the number of relevant documents reaches into the millions, it takes enormous resources to review the documents and determine which are responsive to what requests, which are nonresponsive, and which are privileged. Obviously, depending on your perspective, there may be a bias toward nonproduction. If delay is strategically desirable, this process creates welcome opportunities. MDL jurists are often faced with the task of deciding how to review hundreds of thousands of pages where privileges have been claimed. If this task is delegated to a special master, the costs can be significant. In *In re Vioxx Products Liability Litigation*,[45] for example, a special master was appointed and incurred over $400,000 in fees and expenses in reviewing approximately 2,500 representative documents over the course of three months. These costs were paid equally by both sides. In anticipation of these privilege-related disputes, courts might consider orders setting forth an appropriate method of organizing documents to be submitted for in camera review and consider establishing practical guidelines for the creation of a detailed privilege log that identifies the individuals that wrote and received the documents and explains their relationship to the document and to the party asserting the privilege.

C. SETTLEMENT

As the case proceeds, the court may make significant rulings on the qualifications of experts, on summary judgment, and on a variety of potentially outcome-determinative motions including Rule 12(b)(6) motions. But perhaps most significantly, the transferee court can be the catalyst for and oversee the settlement process. As noted, some of the parties may object when the judge takes on the role of dispute resolution administrator in addition to retaining the traditional role as arbiter. Settlement is usually the ultimate result in most MDLs and courts are ready to assist. In the next section, we will explore issues that arise in the settlement context.

---

45. MDL No. 1657 (E.D. La. 2007).

VI. Selected Settlement Issues

An MDL often explores settlement options.[46] Naturally, not all actions in the MDL must settle. And, if there are class actions involved in the MDL, there may be opt-out provisions involved that will not result in total resolution of all disputes. Still, defense interests normally will seek to resolve as many of the potential claims arising out of the underlying allegedly injurious conduct as possible. Realistically, an inability to resolve a sufficient number of involved cases may jeopardize any settlement. Thus, tension may arise between plaintiffs' counsel who want to settle and those who do not. Whether resolution is through a class or mass tort, voluntary opt-in mechanism, an important consideration must be dealing with those who seek to undermine any global resolution for their independent financial gain. The parties must anticipate the actions of lawyers with large inventories of cases who may seek to leverage those inventories for preferential treatment. Such attempts may be exercised through wholesale opt-outs or a boycott of the settlement with corresponding demands for "most favored nation status" (i.e., settlement of those cases at a premium above any other going rate). Conversely, some counsel (sometimes referred to as professional objectors) typically represent a small number of clients or even just a single client and may threaten delays in obtaining any necessary court approval or appeals in the hope of enhancing the recovery of their clients for reasons unrelated to the merits of their claims.

During settlement negotiations, the plaintiffs' lawyer who is not on the PSC may feel especially left out. To address this concern, PSC members need to fully and ably communicate what is transpiring in the settlement negotiations. Without full transparency from the PSC, other plaintiffs' lawyers cannot know whether their clients' interests as a whole are being fairly represented and may suspect that the PSC members are negotiating in their own best interests. One is reminded of the Irishman, Michael Collins, who negotiated the peace treaty after the Irish Rebellion that resulted in the creation of the Irish Free State and Northern Ireland. Upon his return home he was hailed as a hero by some and by others called a traitor; the resulting civil war cost Collins his life.

Why do cases often settle in MDLs? One reason is that the incentives to avoid the risk of trial increase exponentially as the stakes increase with large numbers of claimants. For similar reasons, class action trials are "quite rare."[47] Empirical studies of class actions confirm both the practical reasons behind low trial rates and the efficacy of class settlements. "[C]lass actions remove a large number of claims

---

46. *See generally* RICHARD A. NAGAREDA, MASS TORTS IN A WORLD OF SETTLEMENT (2007); David Marcus, Review, *Some Realism about Mass Torts*, 75 U. CHI. L. REV. 1949 (2008) (reviewing NAGAREDA, *supra*).

47. Marc Galanter, *The Vanishing Trial: An Examination of Trials and Related Matters in Federal and State Courts*, 1 J. EMPIRICAL LEGAL STUD. 459 (2004) (citing Janet Cooper Alexander, *Do the Merits Matter? A Study of Settlements in Securities Class Actions*, 43 STAN. L. REV. 497, 567 (1991)).

from the possibility of being tried individually and replace them with a much smaller number of cases in a category that very rarely eventuates in a trial."[48] As trial rates in general plummet, it should be no surprise that trial rates for mass actions likewise have decreased. Scholars argue that the "rate of trials may reflect changing strategies by *defendants* as well as by plaintiffs."[49] Defendants understand the advantage of eliminating large pools of liability quickly and permanently. The uncertainty of litigation often creates the most heartburn on Wall Street. Empirical studies also challenge the notion that "class settlement can be vehicles for collusion between defendant and class counsel."[50] To the contrary, research shows that class settlements are actually associated with lower fees,[51] without reducing amounts awarded to aggrieved parties. Without question, "the low trial rate in class actions reflects the high stakes that such cases represent for defendants."[52] But it also reflects a confluence of factors that may benefit parties specifically and the justice system as a whole.

The media attention that high-profile MDL litigation receives also provides an incentive to conclude litigation without any potentially problematic conduct being placed under a public microscope. Furthermore, the enormous cost associated with pretrial activity places a premium on early resolution.[53]

The attempt to ultimately resolve all controversies arising from the relevant conduct or actions can add other federalism tensions in the MDL. As noted, and by definition, MDLs are limited to claims that are pending in federal court. Claims that are pending in state court are not subject to the federal MDL process (although some states have similar schemes for consolidating and coordinating claims pending in their state courts) because, unless they are removable, they are not subject to federal jurisdiction. At the same time, the defendant in the MDL may desire to settle all pending claims against it that arise out of the relevant action or conduct— both those pending in the MDL and those pending in state court. And the parties may be before a federal judge in the MDL who very much wants to get the litigation resolved and who realizes that will not happen unless the parties can settle the state cases that are not a part of the MDL.

In this federalism quandary, the court and the parties may consider the certification of a class for settlement purposes of all persons affected by the defendants'

---

48. *Id.* at 487.

49. *Id.* (italics in original).

50. Theodore Eisenberg & Geoffrey P. Miller, *Attorney Fees in Class Action Settlements: An Empirical Study*, 1 J. EMPIRICAL LEGAL STUD. 27, 67 (2004).

51. *Id.* at 28.

52. Galanter, *supra* note 47 at 487.

53. In the *Vioxx* litigation, as of December 31, 2005, Merck & Co. had a reserve of $685 million solely for its future legal defense costs. During 2006, the company spent $500 million in the aggregate in defense costs. As of December 31, 2006, Merck's reserves were $858 million. Merck & Co., Inc. 10-K, Feb. 28, 2007.

actions or conduct.[54] If certifiable, a class action may encompass all plaintiffs, including those in state court cases. In anticipation of the possibility of global settlement, one device MDL judges have employed to deal with counsel not before them is the creation of a federal-state liaison committee to interact with the cases pending in state court. As noted, courts also employ opt-in settlement agreements that avoid some of the due process issues that arise with class settlements.

While on the subject of global resolution, a slight tangent is apt. The federalism issues raised above have been impacted by the Class Action Fairness Act of 2005. The Act[55] greatly expands federal jurisdiction in class actions, requiring only that there be minimal diversity (between one plaintiff and one defendant) and that at least $5 million be in dispute.[56] Since federal jurisdiction is expanded, the reach of the MDL Panel understandably increases when class actions are involved.

VII. Lexecon Inc. v. Milberg Weiss Bershad Hynes & Lerach

But what happens when the cases are not dismissed, disposed of by summary judgment, or settled? May the transferee court try the case? Between 1968 and 1998 a practice developed by which transferee judges transferred cases permanently to themselves under 28 U.S.C. § 1404(a). By the end of September 1995, self-transfer had occurred in 279 out of the 39,228 cases transferred and terminated as of that date.[57] Section 1407(a) states, in part, that "[e]ach action so transferred shall be remanded by the panel at or before the conclusion of such pretrial proceedings to the district from which it was transferred unless it shall have been previously terminated . . . ."[58] Was the self-transfer process consistent with the words of the statute? The U.S. Supreme Court considered the issue in *Lexecon Inc. v. Milberg Weiss Bershad Hynes & Lerach*,[59] and in an opinion by Justice Souter, held that the transferee judge lacked the statutory authority to use the transfer of venue statute to self-transfer. The proper course was for the Panel to remand the cases as section 1407(a) required. After *Lexecon*, some commentators have claimed that its holding limits the effectiveness of the MDL process as a means to resolve complex litigation

---

54. *See* Chapter 7, "Settlements."

55. Pub. L. No. 109-2, 119 Stat. 4 (codified at 28 U.S.C. §§ 1332(d), 1453, and 1711–15 (2005)); *see also* The Multiparty, Multiforum Trial Jurisdiction Act of 2002, Pub. L. No. 107-273, § 11,020, 116 Stat. 1758, 1826–29 (codified at 28 U.S.C. §§ 1369, 1391, 1441, 1697, 1785), which eliminates the need for complete diversity in a case involving the death of at least 75 people in a single accident at a discrete location. Further discussion of the Act can be found in Chapter 10, "The Class Action Fairness Act of 2005."

56. 28 U.S.C. § 1332(d).

57. *Lexecon Inc. v. Milberg Weiss Bershad Hynes & Lerach*, 523 U.S. 26, 33 (1998).

58. 28 U.S.C. § 1407(a).

59. 523 U.S. 26; *see also* Benjamin W. Larson, Case Comment, Lexecon Inc. v. Milberg Weiss Bershad Hynes & Lerach: *Representing the Plaintiff's Choice of Forum*, 74 NOTRE DAME L. REV. 1337 (1999).

and have called for reform. Congress has considered legislation to give transferee courts the power *Lexecon* denied them.[60]

In response to *Lexecon*, courts and lawyers have found various ways to avoid its effect. Courtney Silver has itemized a number of these methods, including (1) moving in the original district court for transfer to the MDL transferee court under section 1404; (2) party consent to venue or trial in the transferee court; (3) agreement stipulating to be bound by bellwether cases; (4) dismissing and refiling in the transferee court; (5) moving to transfer back to the transferee court under section 1404 or 1406 after the Panel remands; and (6) intercircuit or intracircuit assignment of the transferee judge.[61] However, she points out that there are significant limitations on all of the *Lexecon* antidotes.

Even if *Lexecon* hampered the operation of the MDL as a resolution vehicle, the success of the MDL to resolve actions is exceptional. As noted, as of September 30, 2009, there were 323,258 actions that had been part of MDLs.[62] On that same date 88,000 were pending, which meant that 235,258 had been either terminated or remanded. Of that number, 223,126 were terminated by the transferee court. Only 11,737 were remanded by the Panel, while 395 were reassigned to transferor courts within the transferee district. That meant that only 12,132 were not terminated by the transferee court. Of all the MDL cases since 1968 that were not pending as of September 30, 2008, about 95 percent were terminated by the transferee court.

VIII. Bellwether Trials

What is it in the MDL landscape that is conducive to global settlements? Is it the fact that it allows the tort to mature in a single cohesive venue? And why is it important for the litigation to mature? If a mass tort has not yet "matured," cases typically do not have a predictable range of values. Lacking a history of trials and individual settlements, true case values are unknown. Conversely, as the *Manual for Complex Litigation* explains, in a mature mass tort, most of the relevant evidence has been discovered, appellate review of novel legal issues has been completed, and a full cycle of trial strategies has been explored.[63] The mature mass tort has had a sufficient number of trials or settlements to provide instructive guidance for resolving other similarly situated cases.

One case management strategy that is routinely employed when there has been insufficient activity to evaluate the issues and corresponding value of claims is setting several individual cases for trial as "bellwether trials." These are also some-

---

60. *See generally* Courtney E. Silver, Note, *Procedural Hassles in Multidistrict Litigation: A Call for Reform of 28 U.S.C. § 1407 and the Lexecon Result*, 70 OHIO ST. L.J. 455 (2009).

61. *Id.* at 468–75.

62. STATISTICAL ANALYSIS at 4.

63. MANUAL FOR COMPLEX LITIGATION (FOURTH) § 22.314 (2004).

times referred to as "test," "representative," or "instructive" trials. The key to successful bellwether trials is that they must be fairly representative of the range of other cases; otherwise, the entire process is undermined.[64] In part, the function of bellwether trials is to educate both the parties and the court regarding the types of cases pending in a coordinated proceeding. The hope is that bellwether trials will provide helpful information regarding the value of various case categories as well as strengths and weaknesses of the claims, and potentially establish a structure for future settlement dialogue. Even if they do not lead to settlements, an indirect benefit of bellwether trials is that they can streamline subsequent trials through the experience gained in connection with motions in limine, *Daubert* rulings, and other pretrial activity.

The bellwether trial process can also provide assistance regarding class certification motion practice to the extent it presents an opportunity to actually see what issues are common and whether the common issues predominate. For any judge wrestling with the decision of whether to certify a class, trying several bellwether trials can be instructive. In addition to providing real context to a variety of rulings that will have to be made, these trials will give the court a clear sense regarding manageability issues and, more particularly, whether a trial plan is workable.

The bellwether selection process is critical—it is a "garbage in, garbage out" dynamic. Obviously, the process should be designed so that the cases that are selected provide reliable data regarding key issues. For years, our courts have experimented with various selection procedures. The pendulum has swung from the extremes of random selection versus allowing the parties to select, with a variety of blended options in between. Cases where the parties are likely to dismiss the results as being case-specific aberrations with no broader instructive value should not be selected.

So what, if any, downside is there to bellwether trials? In a mass tort involving thousands of cases, how informative can trying just a few cases really be? How many need to be tried for results that may be predictive for future cases? Some argue that unless a statistically significant sample is tried, the results are meaningless. Many variations can affect case outcome, such as where the case is being tried, the personality of the particular plaintiff involved, the particular case-specific fact pattern, the talent of the specific trial counsel, the strength of the particular presentation, and the judge who tries the case. Results can be so varied that they lose instructive value. Additionally, a handful of early results can be misleading. Large verdicts may unreasonably raise plaintiffs' expectations, and losses may embolden the defense.

If nothing else, bellwether trials certainly help identify issues. They compel litigants to prepare and test their trial packages. They give the court a preview

---

64. *Id.* at § 22.315.

of what issues will arise. Everyone gets exposure to how witnesses will perform, what experts are necessary, what evidence will be required, and how juries respond to the presentations. A bellwether trial provides an opportunity to develop case themes and educate both trial counsel and the court on how best to try these cases. It lets everyone know what the price of admission will be, that is, the cost to try a case. And it helps determine the economic viability of conducting trials. If properly orchestrated, bellwether trials unquestionably improve the prospects of global resolution and assist in developing efficient trial plans for subsequent litigation. Thus, the concept has achieved general acceptance by both the bench and bar.

In the *Vioxx* MDL, one of the court's first priorities was to assist the parties in selecting and preparing certain test cases to proceed as bellwether trials. The MDL transferee court conducted six such bellwether trials. Some suggest that these bellwether trials were a significant catalyst for the $4.85 billion settlement.

IX. Attorney Fees in MDLs—The Vioxx Example

Once a settlement is within striking distance, the parties, of course, have to wrestle with what procedure will be employed to effectuate the settlement. Will it be through a class action or a voluntary opt-in arrangement? In the *Vioxx* MDL, class certification was denied early in the litigation and thus the parties elected the latter. Additionally, the *Vioxx* settlement program contemplated the court overseeing certain specific aspects of the administration of the settlement proceedings, including appointing a fee allocation committee, allocating a percentage of the settlement proceeds to a common benefit fund, and approving a cost assessment to make recommendations concerning an appropriate distribution of common benefit fees. Common benefit fees are those fees set aside for lawyers who have provided services in the MDL that have benefited plaintiffs as a whole.

A particularly difficult issue arose in *Vioxx* concerning private contingent fee arrangements between individual plaintiff lawyers and their clients—a separate issue from common benefit fees. After the parties had bound themselves to the resolution program, Judge Fallon sua sponte issued an order capping contingent fee arrangements for all lawyers representing claimants in the *Vioxx* global settlement at 32 percent plus reasonable costs.[65] Many of the private contingency fee contracts called for a 40 percent fee. This reduction therefore represented a 25 percent reduction in fees that most plaintiffs' counsel expected to receive and upon which they relied in pursuing and funding the litigation. Judge Fallon concluded that he had authority to issue such an order based on several sources.

---

65. Order and Reasons, Aug. 27, 2008, *In re Vioxx Prods. Liab. Litig.*, MDL No. 1657, Rec. Doc. 15722, at 20–21 (Aug. 27, 2008), *available at* http://vioxx.laed.uscourts.gov/Orders/o&r082708.pdf.

The first source cited by Judge Fallon was Rule 23, which specifically grants district courts the power to regulate fees in class actions. While acknowledging that an MDL is distinct from a class action, Judge Fallon held that the similarities between the two warranted the treatment of the MDL as a "quasi-class action" with concomitant authority to review contingency fee contracts for reasonableness.

Second, Judge Fallon pointed to the court's inherent authority to exercise ethical supervision over lawyers who appear before him. Although Judge Fallon did not find that any ethical breach had occurred, he expressed concern over the public's perception of the settlement, which involved tens of thousands of plaintiffs and billions of dollars. He also felt that the *Vioxx* plaintiffs might need special protection because, in his view, most were "elderly and in poor health."[66]

Last, Judge Fallon pointed to certain terms of the settlement agreement voluntarily entered into by the parties as an additional source of authority. Although the agreement did not address capping of private contingent fee arrangements, other language in the agreement granted the court authority to oversee certain aspects of the administration of the settlement. The court explained that unlike a traditional settlement agreement that the parties execute without the assistance of the court, the parties in *Vioxx* clearly contemplated that the *Vioxx* court would be involved in the administration of the settlement agreement.

Judge Fallon's ruling capping contingent fees was challenged by several plaintiff lawyers.[67] On reconsideration, Judge Fallon modified certain aspects of his ruling, but left intact his decision that he had authority to cap contingent fees in

---

66. *Id.* at 12.

67. One group argued:

Although the MDL statute has been in force since 1968, until Judge Weinstein's 2006 decision in the *Zyprexa* MDL, [*In re Zyprexa Prods. Liab. Litig.*, 424 F. Supp. 2d 488 (E.D.N.Y. Mar. 28, 2006)] no court had changed percentages set in private contingency fee agreements in a non-class action MDL. Judge Frank followed Judge Weinstein and made a similar ruling in the *Guidant* MDL in 2008. [*In re Guidant Corp. Implantable Defibrillators Prods. Liab. Litig.*, MDL No. 05-1708, 2008 WL 682174 (D. Minn. Mar. 7, 2008)]. Judge Frank later increased the amount of the cap in *In re Guidant Corp. Implantable Defibrillators Prods. Liab. Litig.*, MDL No. 05-1708, 2008 WL 389606 (D. Minn. Aug. 21, 2008). When this Court issued its original Order and Reasons on August 27, 2008, (Rec. Doc. 15722) it was only the third district court to rule on the issue. (*In re Silicone Gel Breast Implant Prods. Liab. Litig.*, MDL No. 926, 1994 WL 114580 (N.D. Ala. Apr. 1, 1994), cited by the Court in its Order and Reasons, was a class action.) No court of appeal has taken a position on the controlling question of law. (The ruling on *Zyprexa* has been appealed, briefed and orally argued. The Second Circuit, however, has not yet ruled, and if it did, its ruling would not obviate the need for a definitive decision on this issue from the Fifth Circuit.) This judicially-created doctrine is in its nascent stage of development. As explained in the Order and Reasons, it relies for support on 1) analogy to class action procedure; 2) notions of inherent and equitable authority; and 3) wording in the MDL statute providing that the Judicial Panel on Multidistrict Litigation may transfer cases only when transfer will "promote the just and efficient conduct of such actions." [28 U.S.C. § 1407(a)] Accordingly, there is substantial room for good faith difference of opinion on the legality of this new doctrine.

a non–class action MDL. This ruling may affect how plaintiff lawyers evaluate whether to undertake MDL litigation in the future.

X. Conclusion

The 21st century lawyer must become conversant with the MDL process as a potential tool for resolving complex disputes. And, in becoming familiar with the MDL device, lawyers must adjust their philosophies and notions of how cases are litigated and how they get concluded. The MDL is a far cry from the traditional one-on-one dispute resolution model with which we all began our study of law. What role it will continue to play, and with what efficacy, remains to be seen.

Complex litigation provides an opportunity for creative thinking and requires strategic coordination. MDLs, if properly managed, can provide one option for processing our 21st century needs while still preserving fundamental principles of equity, justice, and fairness.

Memorandum in Support of the Vioxx Litigation Consortium's Motion for Certification Under 28 U.S.C. § 1292(b) and For Alternative Final Judgment Under Rule 54(b), and For Stay Pending Appeal, *In re Vioxx Prods. Liab. Litig.*, MDL No. 1657, Rec. Doc. 22132, at 3–4 (Aug. 13, 2009).

DAUBERT CHALLENGES IN CLASS CERTIFICATION

DANIEL M. MCCLURE

I. Introduction

Does *Daubert* apply to expert testimony at the class certification stage? While a few courts have explicitly embraced that view, the strong trend is toward a more critical analysis of expert opinions offered at the class certification stage, which has been referred to by some practitioners as a *"Daubert*-light" approach. This chapter will assess that trend, which is an outgrowth of the requirement now imposed by most courts for a "rigorous analysis" of whether all class certification requirements are met in deciding a class motion.

Whether or not the courts have fully embraced *Daubert* at the class certification stage, the issue for the practitioner remains whether to file a motion to exclude expert testimony under *Daubert* or whether instead to attack expert testimony in the response to a class certification motion. The answer for the practitioner must surely be that a questionable expert opinion that bears on class certification must be challenged at the class certification stage. Whether to do so by a full-blown *Daubert* motion to exclude or within the class action hearing and briefing itself is a strategic decision that will depend upon a variety of factors that will be discussed in this chapter.

II. The Daubert *Rule 702 Standard*

The Supreme Court's decision in *Daubert v. Merrell Dow Pharmaceuticals, Inc.*[1] was a seminal event requiring courts to serve as the "gatekeepers" to questionable expert testimony. *Daubert* went further than the traditional minimalist standard

---

1. 509 U.S. 579 (1993).

for the admissibility of expert testimony that a scientific opinion must merely be "generally accepted" in the relevant scientific community, set out in earlier precedent under *Frye v. United States*.[2] *Daubert* required that scientific testimony be both (1) reliable and (2) relevant.[3] It also provided a nonexclusive list of factors to be considered in weighing the reliability of any expert opinion.[4] The *Daubert* standard has now been imported into Federal Rule of Evidence 702, as amended following the *Daubert* decision. Rule 702 now requires that "a witness qualified as an expert by knowledge, skill, experience, training, or education, may testify thereto in the form of an opinion or otherwise, if (1) the testimony is based upon sufficient facts or data, (2) the testimony is the product of reliable principles and methods, and (3) the witness has applied the principles and methods reliably to the facts of the case."[5]

In *Kumho Tire Co., Ltd., v. Carmichael*,[6] the Court clarified that the *Daubert* standards applied not only to scientific experts, but also to experts who testify based on "technical" or "other specialized" knowledge. The *Daubert* standards have now been broadly applied outside of purely scientific expert opinion testimony, including testimony by economists, other "soft"-science experts, and technical experts. The effect of *Daubert*, of course, has been to add another phase to the litigation process, the filing of "*Daubert* motions" as an almost routine pretrial practice to challenge expert testimony. Many docket control orders now routinely provide for pretrial deadlines for the filing of *Daubert* motions, so that courts may decide the admissibility of expert testimony well in advance of trial.

III. The Effect of the Evolving Class Certification Standards

The issue of whether to conduct a *Daubert* hearing in connection with class certification has been raised in recent years because of the evolving trend in the federal courts (as well as state courts) to conduct a more searching inquiry at the class certification stage of whether the plaintiff can satisfy all of the required elements of class certification under Rule 23 (and similar state rules). As the courts have moved more toward a "rigorous analysis" of whether class certification standards have been met, the scrutiny given to expert witnesses has also increased.[7]

For many years courts often decided class certification based upon the pleadings, purporting to follow the Supreme Court's admonition in *Eisen v. Carlisle & Jacquelin* that the federal courts may not "conduct a preliminary inquiry into the

---

2. 293 F. 1013 (1923).

3. 509 U.S. at 590.

4. *Id.* at 593–95.

5. FED. R. EVID. 702.

6. 526 U.S. 137 (1999).

7. *See also* Chapter 4, "Certification Hearings and Decisions."

merits of a suit in order to determine whether it may be maintained as a class action."[8] Most courts have now recognized that *Eisen* was misinterpreted and that at least some factual inquiry into the merits issues is necessary to determine whether class certification standards have been met.[9] The Fifth Circuit has said: "*Eisen* did not drain Rule 23 of all rigor. A district court still must give full and independent weight to each Rule 23 requirement, regardless of whether that requirement overlaps with the merits."[10] The Second Circuit agreed:

> With *Eisen* properly understood to preclude consideration of the merits only when a merits issue is unrelated to a Rule 23 requirement, there is no reason to lessen a district court's obligation to make a determination that every Rule 23 requirement is met before certifying a class just because of some or even full overlap of that requirement with a merits issue.[11]

Lower courts have followed the Supreme Court's later admonition in *General Telephone Co. of the Southwest v. Falcon*[12] that class certification is proper only "if the trial court is satisfied, after a rigorous analysis, that the prerequisites" of Rule 23 have been met. Most courts have now held that the district court must look beyond the pleadings and pierce the pleadings, look to how the case will actually be tried, and assess whether the merits issues at trial are capable of determination by class action as opposed to individual actions.[13] The Fourth Circuit observed:

> If it were appropriate for a court simply to accept the allegations of a complaint at face value in making class action findings, every complaint asserting the requirements of Rule 23(a) and (b) would automatically lead to a certification order, frustrating the district court's responsibilities for taking a "close look" at relevant matters, for conducting a "rigorous analysis" of such matters, and for making "findings" that the requirements of Rule 23 have been satisfied.[14]

Most courts now hold that a "rigorous analysis" must be conducted with respect to each of the requirements for class certification under Rule 23—numerosity, commonality, typicality, adequacy, predominance, and superiority (including

---

8. 417 U.S. 156, 177 (1974).

9. *In re Hydrogen Peroxide Antitrust Litig.*, 552 F.3d 305, 316–18 (3d Cir. 2008); *In re New Motor Vehicles Can. Exp. Antitrust Litig.*, 522 F.3d 6, 24 (1st Cir. 2008) ("It is a settled question that some inquiry into the merits at the class certification stage is not only permissible but appropriate to the extent that the merits overlap the Rule 23 criteria.").

10. *Oscar Private Equity Invs. v. Allegiance Telecom, Inc.*, 487 F.3d 261, 268 (5th Cir. 2007).

11. *In re Initial Pub. Offerings Sec. Litig.* (*IPO*), 471 F.3d 24, 41 (2d Cir. 2006).

12. 457 U.S. 147, 161 (1982).

13. *See Szabo v. Bridgeport Machs., Inc.*, 249 F.3d 672, 675 (7th Cir. 2001); *Oscar*, 487 F.3d at 268; *Hydrogen Peroxide*, 552 F.3d at 316–18; *IPO*, 471 F.3d at 41; *Newton v. Merrill Lynch, Pierce, Fenner & Smith, Inc.*, 259 F.3d 154, 166–69 (3d Cir. 2001).

14. *Gariety v. Grant Thornton, LLP*, 368 F.3d 356, 365 (4th Cir. 2004) (citations omitted).

manageability).[15] There is "no reason to doubt" that the Supreme Court's "rigorous analysis" language "applies with equal force to all Rule 23 requirements, including those set forth in Rule 23(b)(3)."[16]

IV. Application of Daubert at the Class Certification Stage

Until the Seventh Circuit's recent opinion in *American Honda Motor Co. v. Allen*,[17] relatively few cases and no circuit courts have expressly held that a full *Daubert* gatekeeper analysis is required at the class certification stage.[18] Of those that did, one rationale was that, because the Federal Rules of Evidence apply to proceedings under Rule 23, *Daubert*, now incorporated in Rule 702, must also apply.[19] By contrast, many courts have declined to conduct a full *Daubert* analysis at the class certification stage.[20] One reason given by some courts for not allowing full-blown *Daubert* challenges at the class stage is that the rules of evidence are generally more relaxed at the class stage and the gatekeeper function of *Daubert* was intended to prevent jurors from being influenced by unreliable opinions so that the need for *Daubert* protection is significantly reduced when the judge alone hears the evidence.[21]

In its recent opinion in *American Honda*, the Seventh Circuit became the first circuit court to expressly permit full *Daubert* motions to exclude class certification experts. The Seventh Circuit ruled that when deciding motions for class certification supported by expert testimony, district courts "must conclusively rule on the admissibility of an expert opinion prior to class certification . . . [where] that opinion is essential to the certification decision."[22] The court added that "the district

---

15. *See supra* note 13.

16. *IPO*, 471 F.3d at 33 n.3.

17. 606 F.3d 813 (7th Cir. 2010).

18. *See, e.g., Rhodes v. E.I. Du Pont de Nemours & Co.*, No. 6:06-CV-00530, 2008 WL 2400944 at *10–12 (S.D. W. Va. June 11, 2008) (holding that class expert opinions must meet *Daubert* standards); *Srail v. Vill. of Lisle*, 249 F.R.D. 544, 557–64 (N.D. Ill. 2008) (applying *Daubert* to determine admissibility of expert opinions at class certification stage, but denying *Daubert* motion).

19. *See, e.g., Reed v. Advocate Health Care*, No. 1:06CV03337, 2009 WL 3146999 at *21 (N.D. Ill. Sept. 28, 2009).

20. *In re Wal-Mart Stores Inc. Wage & Hour Litig.*, No. C 06-2069 SBA, 2008 WL 413749, at *14 (N.D. Cal. Feb. 13, 2008) ("it is not necessary . . . to engage in a full-fledged *Daubert* analysis at the class certification stage"); *Ammons v. La-Z-Boy Inc.*, No. 1:04-CV-67 TC, 2008 WL 5142186, at *13 (D. Utah Dec. 5, 2008); *In re Katrina Canal Breaches Consol. Litig.*, No. 05-4182, 2007 WL 3245438, at *12 (E.D. La. Nov. 1, 2007) (refusing to undertake full *Daubert* analysis before class certification but performing Rule 702 review "limited to the opinion's reliability and relevance to the requirements of class certification under Rule 23").

21. *In re FedEx Ground Package Sys., Inc. Employment Practices Litig.*, MDL 1700, 2007 U.S. Dist. LEXIS 76798 at *10–11 (N.D. Ind. Oct. 15, 2007) (employing a "substantially relaxed Rule 702 analysis" to experts at the class stage).

22. *Am. Honda*, 606 F.3d at 814.

court must perform a full *Daubert* analysis before certifying the class if the situation warrants."[23] Because the district court did not completely resolve at the class certification stage whether the expert report was admissible in its entirety before granting plaintiffs' motion for class certification, the Seventh Circuit vacated the district court's order certifying the class and the denial of Honda's motion to strike the expert report.[24]

Regardless of whether a full *Daubert* analysis is required at the certification stage, the developing trend in the case law is to more carefully scrutinize class certification experts and subject their opinions to "rigorous analysis."[25] For example, in *Blades v. Monsanto Co.*,[26] the Eighth Circuit affirmed a denial of class certification based on the district court's rejection of the plaintiffs' expert opinions—even though the district court denied the defendants' motion to strike the expert under *Daubert* and chose to analyze (and reject) the expert's opinion at the class certification stage.[27]

The sequence of opinions by the Ninth Circuit in *Dukes v. Wal-Mart*[28] illustrates the inconsistent approach of the courts in deciding whether to apply *Daubert* at the class certification stage. In the initial Ninth Circuit opinion in *Dukes*, the court held that it need not apply *Daubert* at the class certification stage and rejected the defendant's attack on the plaintiff's expert, holding, "Accordingly, the district court was not required to apply *Daubert* at the class certification stage."[29] However, on rehearing (*Dukes II*), the court withdrew its prior opinion and deleted those *Daubert* comments. Instead, the Ninth Circuit appeared to assume that *Daubert* would be applicable, but held that the defendant had not made a true *Daubert* challenge and instead had attacked the persuasiveness of the expert's opinion as opposed to the reliability of the expert's methodology.[30] On rehearing, the en banc

---

23. *Id.* at 816.

24. *Id.* at 819.

25. *Lewis v. Ford Motor Co.*, No. 09-164, 2009 U.S. Dist. LEXIS 65845 at *5 (W.D. Pa. 2009) (undertaking a "rigorous analysis" of expert report on motion to exclude defendant's expert prior to class certification hearing).

26. 400 F.3d 562, 569–70 (8th Cir. 2005).

27. *Id.*

28. 474 F.3d 1214 (9th Cir. 2007).

29. *Id.* at 1227.

30. 509 F.3d 1168, 1179 (9th Cir. 2007), *rehearing en banc granted*, 556 F.3d 919 (9th Cir. 2009), *aff'd*. Citing the *Dukes v. Wal-Mart* substituted opinion, a subsequent federal district court in California struck a defense expert's testimony by employing "a lower *Daubert* standard" to analyze admissibility of the expert testimony at the class certification hearing. *In re First Am. Corp. ERISA Litig.*, No. SACV 07-01357-JVS, 2009 WL 928294 (C.D. Cal. 2009). The court held that instead of satisfying the "full rigors of the *Daubert* analysis," it must only be shown that an expert's opinion was "relevant and useful in evaluating whether class certification requirements have been met." *Id.* at *1.

court indicated that *Daubert* challenges are generally best left to the merit stages of the class litigation.[31]

Other courts have moved away from a highly deferential approach to expert testimony to a more critical assessment of expert testimony at the class certification stage. The evolution of standards in the Second Circuit is illustrative. The Second Circuit initially set a very low bar for accepting an expert at the class stage in *In re Visa Check/MasterMoney Antitrust Litigation*,[32] where it held that "[a] District Court must insure that the basis of the expert opinion is not so flawed that it would be inadmissible as a matter of law."[33] The Second Circuit also held that district courts "may not weigh conflicting expert evidence or engage in statistical dueling of experts."[34] Rather, "[t]he question for the district court at the class certification stage is whether the plaintiffs' expert evidence is sufficient to demonstrate common questions of fact warranting certification of the proposed class, not whether the evidence will ultimately be persuasive."[35] Part of the rationale for the Second Circuit's approach was its view of the *Eisen* prohibition of considering the merits. However, five years later, the Second Circuit shifted its position regarding the appropriate standards for adjudicating a motion for class certification and for assessing expert testimony in that context in *In re Initial Public Offerings Securities Litigation (IPO)*.[36] In *IPO* the Second Circuit held that *Eisen* did not prohibit a consideration of the merits during the class certification stage. The Second Circuit then "disavow[ed] the suggestion in *Visa Check* that an expert's testimony may establish a component of a Rule 23 requirement simply by not being fatally flawed."[37] Instead, *IPO* held that a court must resolve factual disputes, including conflicting expert testimony, before applying the Rule 23 legal standard.[38]

A leading recent case that presented a balanced approach to the application of *Daubert* at class certification is the Third Circuit's opinion in *In re Hydrogen Peroxide Antitrust Litigation*.[39] The district court had denied the defendant's motion to exclude the opinion of the plaintiff's econometrics expert under *Daubert*, holding

---

31. *Dukes v. Wal-Mart Stores, Inc.*, ___ F.3d ___, Nos. 04-16688 & 04-16720, 2010 WL 1644259, at *23 (9th Cir. Apr. 26, 2010) (stating that district court's role at class certification stage is "to make factual determinations regarding evidence as it relates to common questions of fact or law but not to decide which parties' evidence is ultimately more persuasive as to liability.").

32. 280 F.3d 124 (2d Cir. 2001).

33. *Id.* at 135.

34. *Id.*

35. *Id.*

36. 471 F.3d 24.

37. *Id.* at 42.

38. Lower courts in the Second Circuit, following *IPO*, have held that "the proper role for a *Daubert* inquiry at the class certification stage remains limited by *Rule 23* itself . . . . [T]his Court's *Daubert* inquiry is limited to whether or not the [expert reports] are admissible to establish the requirements of Rule 23." *In re NYSE Specialists Sec. Litig.*, No. 03 Civ. 8264 (RWS), 2009 U.S. Dist. LEXIS 53255, at *23 (S.D.N.Y. 2009).

39. 552 F.3d 305.

that "because the evidence is here offered for the limited purpose of class certification, our inquiry is perhaps less exacting than it might be for evidence to be presented at trial."[40] That ruling denying the *Daubert* motion was not challenged by the defendants on appeal. But the Third Circuit emphasized that whether or not the expert testimony was excluded under *Daubert*, that would not be the end of the inquiry. Expert testimony should not be "uncritically accepted as establishing a Rule 23 requirement."[41] Instead, "a district court's conclusion that an expert's opinion is admissible does not necessarily dispose of the ultimate question—whether the district court is satisfied, by all of the evidence and arguments including all relevant expert opinion, that the requirements of Rule 23 have been met."[42] The Third Circuit emphasized that, as with all Rule 23 requirements, "[e]xpert opinion with respect to class certification . . . calls for rigorous analysis."[43] The Third Circuit also emphasized that when there are opposing expert opinions, weighing conflicting expert testimony is not only "permissible" at the certification hearing, but "it may be integral to the rigorous analysis Rule 23 demands."[44] The Third Circuit reversed class certification because the district court had applied a too-relaxed standard for certification and had refused to resolve disputes between plaintiffs' and defendants' experts.[45] The Seventh Circuit has adopted the same approach requiring a rigorous analysis of expert opinion and warning that failure to resolve disputes between experts "amounts to a delegation of judicial power to the plaintiffs, who can obtain class certification just by hiring a competent expert."[46]

V. A Practitioner's Dilemma: Whether to File a Daubert Motion

Because the case law is not settled as to whether a full or limited *Daubert* review of expert opinions is permitted—much less required—at the class certification stage, the practitioner is left to struggle with the question of how best to challenge expert testimony at the class certification stage. Because there is no doubt that unchallenged expert testimony may have a decisive impact on the class certification decision, the practitioner cannot leave questionable expert testimony unchallenged. Moreover, because the trend of the courts is to apply greater scrutiny and rigorous

---

40. *Id.* at 315 (quoting *In re Hydrogen Peroxide Antitrust Litig.*, 240 F.R.D. 163, 170 (E.D. Pa. 2007), *rev'd* 552 F.3d 305 (3d Cir. 2008)).
41. *Id.* at 323.
42. *Id.* at 315 n.13.
43. *Id.* at 323.
44. *Id.*
45. *Id.* at 322, 325.
46. *Am. Honda*, 606 F.3d 813; *see also West v. Prudential Sec., Inc.*, 282 F.3d 935, 938 (7th Cir. 2002).

analysis to expert opinions at the class certification stage, the best strategy is to affirmatively attack questionable expert opinions at the class certification stage.

Whether and to what extent an actual *Daubert* motion should be filed to exclude expert testimony will depend upon several factors. First, the practitioner must consider how flawed the expert opinion is and whether the opinion truly fails to meet *Daubert*'s reliability standards—as opposed to being merely unpersuasive, which goes instead to its weight. Second, the practitioner must consider the case law in the particular jurisdiction as to whether *Daubert* challenges are permitted or prohibited at the class certification stage.

Several factors argue for filing the *Daubert* motion before the class hearing. First, a stand-alone motion focuses the court's attention on the questionable expert opinion and forces a ruling on that issue. Second, if the motion to exclude is successful, it has a potentially big payoff in later defeating class certification, as well as possibly later on the merits. Third, even if a *Daubert* motion is denied, it provides an opportunity to identify for the court weaknesses in the opinions of the plaintiffs' experts, which the court is likely to weigh in deciding the class certification issue itself later. The *Daubert* motion would lay the groundwork for the ultimate rejection of the expert's opinion at the class hearing.

On the other hand, there are strategic factors that argue against filing a formal *Daubert* motion as a vehicle to attack expert opinions before the class hearing. First, *Daubert* motions are expensive for the parties, as well as time-consuming for the court and the parties. Second, if the court determines that *Daubert* exclusion is not required, there may be a tendency of the court to feel that the expert issue has already been resolved and that it should not be reconsidered later in deciding the certification motion. Third, the *Daubert* motion places a spotlight on supportable opinions of the opposing expert, which—if they are able to withstand *Daubert*—may well become increasingly more persuasive to the court. Unless there are strong arguments to undercut the opposing expert's opinions, the *Daubert* motion may have the unintended effect of showcasing the expert's opinions and persuading the court that the plaintiff may have a good case on the merits, as well as meeting certification standards.

The strategic alternative to filing a full *Daubert* motion to exclude the expert is simply to challenge the expert opinion and testimony as part of the opposition to a class certification motion (in the case of a defendant) or as an element of the attack on defendant's experts as part of the affirmative motion for class certification (in the case of a plaintiff). The relative advantages and drawbacks of waiting to attack the expert opinions in the class certification hearing and briefing stage are essentially the flip side of the same factors to be considered in deciding whether to file a formal *Daubert* motion. First, if *Daubert* is not well recognized at the class stage in the particular jurisdiction's practice, it may be better to wait for the class hearing and briefing to address expert opinion issues. Second, if the issues go more to the persuasiveness of the opinions than to the pure admissibility of the opinions, and if there are opposing experts on the issues, then the expert issues may be best reserved for class certification briefing and hearing.

Regardless of which approach is used, there can be no doubt that attacks on expert testimony, whether by full *Daubert* motion or by other means, is an effective and necessary strategy when expert testimony is offered by either side at the class certification stage.

VI. Conclusion

In the Seventh Circuit, *Daubert* motions are now expressly allowed at the class certification stage. Elsewhere, the evolving trend appears to be to apply a modified *Daubert* analysis at the class certification stage focusing on the Rule 23 requirements. In short, the courts will not uncritically accept expert testimony and will engage in a rigorous analysis of expert testimony. Some may apply the *Daubert* relevance and reliability standards to a limited degree, while others actually resolve differences between competing expert opinions to the extent necessary to determine whether the requirements of Rule 23 are met.

THE SPECIAL ROLE OF 23(B)(2) CLASSES

JEFFREY M. GRANTHAM
C. PATRICK BODDEN

I. Introduction

A claim seeking class action certification must meet the initial requirements set forth in Rule 23(a) (typicality, numerosity, commonality, and adequacy of representation). Rule 23(b) sets forth three subcategories of class actions with varying attributes and requirements.[1] These different types of class actions are categorized on the basis of the type of relief being sought.[2]

Under Rule 23(b)(1), certification is appropriate if individualized litigation either would create incompatible varying standards of conduct or would create individualized adjudications that would be dispositive of awards that other class members could seek.[3] Rule 23(b)(2)—dealt with in detail in this chapter—is intended for cases where the defendant has acted in a way generally applicable to the class and, accordingly, injunctive or declaratory relief is an appropriate remedy.[4]

Rule 23(b)(3) certification requires that the class action be superior to other methods of adjudication because common questions of law or fact predominate over questions affecting individual members. Rule 23(b)(3) class actions include claims involving money damages.[5]

---

1. Fed. R. Civ. P. 23.

2. *See Allison v. Citgo Petroleum Corp.*, 151 F.3d 402, 412 (5th Cir. 1998).

3. Fed. R. Civ. P. 23; *see also Amchem Prods. v. Windsor*, 521 U.S. 591, 614 (1997).

4. For certification under Federal Rule of Civil Procedure 23(b)(2), a class may be maintained if "the party opposing the class has acted or refused to act on grounds that apply generally to the class, so that final injunctive relief or corresponding declaratory relief is appropriate respecting the class as a whole." Fed. R. Civ. P. 23.

5. *Id.*

Rule 23(b)(2) differs substantively and procedurally from 23(b)(3) litigation in ways that make 23(b)(2) certification attractive to plaintiffs' lawyers. In recent years, courts have grappled with the degree to which claims seeking Rule 23(b)(2) certification may also seek to include monetary damages. In contrast to bringing a (b)(2) claim seeking monetary damages, plaintiffs sometimes seek certification under both (b)(2) and (b)(3), claiming that the defendant's conduct warrants both injunctive or declaratory relief and monetary damages. The circuits have drafted two contrasting approaches to hybrid (b)(2) classes. The first approach—originally espoused by the Fifth Circuit—uses a bright-line test to determine certification; the second approach—first adopted by the Second Circuit—uses an ad hoc balancing test to determine whether certification under (b)(2) is appropriate.

We now look at the mandatory nature of (b)(2) class actions by contrasting (b)(2) notice requirements with those of (b)(3). Next, we will examine the types of relief afforded by litigation under (b)(2). Lastly, we will examine the varying circuit court precedents involving hybrid (b)(2) and (b)(3) claims.

II. Are Mandatory Classes Ever Appropriate?

Rule 23(b)(2) was incorporated into the Federal Rules of Civil Procedure in 1966 to assist in civil rights class actions.[6] Although the ambit of the rule was not limited to the civil rights arena, employment-based discrimination and other civil rights claims provided the most frequent bases for early (b)(2) certifications. However, in recent years, plaintiffs' lawyers have sought (b)(2) certification in a variety of areas, including antitrust, ERISA, life insurance, and tort actions.

Certification under 23(b)(2) is referred to as mandatory because class members are only allowed to opt out of litigation at the court's discretion.[7] In class actions certified under Rules 23(b)(1) and 23(b)(2), the court may provide "appropriate" notice to class members.[8] If a judge elects to give such notice, the notice need not provide class members with the ability to opt out. Accordingly, participation in these class actions is mandatory because the judge's discretion governs the ability of class members to opt out of the litigation. In practice, notice and opt-out rights are often limited under a Rule 23(b)(2) action.[9]

---

6. *Amchem*, 521 U.S. at 614 ("Civil rights cases against parties charged with unlawful, class-based discrimination are prime examples [for certification under Rule 23(b)(2)]."). The Advisory Committee provides a litany of civil rights cases where 23(b)(2) certification is appropriate. *See* FED. R. CIV. P. 23 advisory committee note (1966).

7. *See* FED. R. CIV. P. 23 advisory committee note (1966); *see also Jenkins v. United Gas Corp.*, 400 F.2d 28, 34 n.14 (5th Cir. 1968).

8. FED. R. CIV. P. 23(c)(2)(a).

9. *See, e.g., Palmigiano v. Sundlun*, 59 F.3d 164 (Table), 1995 U.S. App. LEXIS 15794 (1st Cir. June 27, 1995) (per curiam) (where a class member was prohibited from opting out of a (b)(2) class action because only equitable relief was sought); *DeBoer v. Mellon Mortgage Co.*, 64 F.3d 1171, 1175–76 (8th Cir. 1995)

In contrast, Rule 23(b)(3) certification affords class members the right to decline to join the class. The Advisory Committee notes that

> interests of the individuals in pursuing their own litigations may be so strong [under 23(b)(3)] as to warrant denial of a class action altogether . . . [T]he court is required to direct notice to the members of the class of the right of each member to be excluded from the class upon his request.[10]

The rights involved in Rule 23(b)(3) litigation are great because they relate to the individual compensatory damages that a plaintiff could expect to recover.[11] Due process requires the court to afford class members the right to opt out of claims seeking predominantly money damages.[12]

Rule 23(b)(2) actions are mandatory because they are intended to seek injunctive relief that relates to the class as whole—such as ceasing a polluting discharge or refraining from a discriminatory employment practice. By mandating that class members join the action, the courts are allowing litigation to proceed in the most efficient, manageable manner. In contrast, the monetary damages available under (b)(3) certification involve constitutional rights of litigants that courts are unwilling to compromise by aggregate suits. The damages that a class seeks are a determining factor of which type of certification the class receives.

III. Damages Versus Injunctive/Declaratory Relief

The different categories of class actions found in 23(b) are classified according to the type of relief that each category provides. The (b)(2) class action was adopted for cases in which injunctive or declaratory relief is needed to remedy classwide wrongs.[13] Civil rights cases contain the prototypical (b)(2) scenarios. The Supreme Court has stated that "[c]ivil rights cases against parties charged with unlawful class-based discrimination are prime examples" of candidates for (b)(2) certification.[14]

(allowing (b)(2) certification to include a damages claim with limited notice and no opt-out rights); *Jordan v. Wolke*, 75 F.R.D. 696, 699 (E.D. Wis. 1977) (stating that (b)(2) notice does not require individual mailings and that the mandatory notice is not applicable to (b)(2) claims).

10. FED. R. CIV. P. 23 advisory committee note (1966).

11. *See Hansberry v. Lee*, 311 U.S. 32, 42 (1940) (noting "failure of due process only in those cases where it cannot be said that the procedure adopted fairly insures the protection of the interests of absent parties who are to be bound by it" (citations omitted)).

12. *Phillips Petroleum Co. v. Shutts*, 472 U.S. 797, 811–12 (1985) (holding that in claims for money damages, courts should provide, at a minimum, absent class members both notice and an opportunity to be heard).

13. *Holmes v. Cont'l Can Co.*, 706 F.2d 1144, 1155 n.8 (11th Cir. 1983).

14. *Amchem*, 521 U.S. at 614; *see also Comer v. Cisneros*, 37 F.3d 775, 796 (2d Cir. 1994) (stating that discrimination cases seeking injunctive relief "are the 'paradigm' of 23(b)(2) class action cases").

Rule 23(b)(2) is intended to certify classes in cases where injunctive or declaratory relief is appropriate for the class as a whole. The goal of (b)(2) remedies is "either to make a declaration about or enjoin the defendant's actions affecting the class as a whole."[15] According to the Advisory Committee notes to Rule 23, subdivision (b)(2) is "intended to reach situations where a party has taken action or refused to take action with respect to a class, and final relief of an injunctive nature or of a corresponding declaratory nature, settling the legality of the behavior with respect to the class as a whole, is appropriate."[16] Accordingly, in (b)(2) claims, individual hearings are not necessary.[17]

Money damages are not precluded from (b)(2) actions, and the Advisory Committee leaves open the possibility of equitable relief. However, the Advisory Committee notes that (b)(2) does not extend to cases where appropriate relief is either "exclusively or predominantly" money damages.[18] To the chagrin of judges, the Advisory Committee does not provide courts guidance by defining predominance.

Monetary damages must not predominate over the injunctive or declaratory relief sought in a (b)(2) claim.[19] However, some monetary damages are allowed. A (b)(2) claim must seek injunctive relief as its primary source of relief; however, the circuits disagree to what extent monetary damages are permitted.

IV. Hybrid Classes

Courts have struggled with whether class action claims seeking monetary damages are certifiable under Rule 23(b)(2). Although not prohibiting these hybrid (b)(2) class actions, the Supreme Court has questioned whether (b)(2) class actions seeking compensatory damages can be properly certified.[20] These concerns derive from constitutional questions involving both the 7th Amendment and due process rights. Seventh Amendment concerns focus on the reexamination clause and the trial by jury clause.

The reexamination clause states, "[N]o fact tried by jury, shall be otherwise re-examined in any Court of the United States, than according to the rules of common law."[21] Commentators favoring hybrid classes suggest that hybrid class actions will not run afoul of the 7th Amendment if specific factual findings are

---

15. *Thorn v. Jefferson-Pilot Life Ins. Co.*, 445 F.3d 311, 330 (4th Cir. 2006).

16. FED. R. CIV. P. 23 advisory committee note (1966).

17. *Id.*

18. *Id.*

19. *Thorn*, 445 F.3d at 332.

20. *See, e.g., Ticor Title Ins. Co. v. Brown*, 511 U.S. 117, 121 (per curiam) (1994) (writing that there is "at least a substantial possibility" that "a constitutional right to opt out of such actions" would mean that class actions seeking money damages "can only be certified under Rule 23(b)(3)").

21. U.S. CONST. amend. VII.

not reexamined by subsequent juries.[22] The trial by jury clause guarantees the right to a trial by jury "in Suits at common law."[23] Unwilling or ignorant class members' right to recover damages could be jeopardized in a (b)(2) action seeking compensatory damages. By not providing notice and opt-out rights, a hybrid (b)(2) class could potentially try an issue that would limit an un-notified or unwilling class member's right to recover damages.

Notice and opt-out rights provide a significant difference between (b)(2) and (b)(3) certification. When the plaintiff seeks damages on behalf of a class, due process and Rule 423(b)(3) require that the class members be given notice and the opportunity to exclude themselves from the class, preserving their rights to bring individual actions. Because notice and opt-out rights are not provided in a (b)(2) class, plaintiffs have a freer hand than they do in (b)(3) litigation.

The Fifth Circuit and the Second Circuit have adopted contrasting tests to determine to what degree monetary damages are allowed in Rule 23(b)(2) class actions. The Fifth Circuit first adopted the "incidental damages" test in *Allison v. Citgo Petroleum Corp.*,[24] and although the court has since revised the *Allison* standard, *Allison* is the forebear to standards adopted in the Fourth, Sixth, Seventh, and Eleventh Circuit Courts. Below we set forth the *Allison* standard and analyze its progeny by circuit court. Afterward, we analyze the Second Court's contrasting precedent from *Robinson v. Metro-North Commuter Railroad Co.*,[25] and we likewise analyze cases in the Second and Ninth Circuits. Lastly, we look to the First, Third, Eighth, Tenth, and District of Columbia Circuit Courts, which have yet to make a definitive choice between either the *Allison* or *Robinson* standards.

A. *ALLISON* AND ITS PROGENY: THE INCIDENTAL DAMAGES TEST

1. Fifth Circuit

The Fifth Circuit first definitively addressed hybrid (b)(2) claims in *Allison v. Citgo Petroleum Corp.* The court's decision is the genesis of the incidental damages test that many circuits endorse in some form or fashion. In *Allison*, claimants sought certification under (b)(2) and/or (b)(3) to bring a claim on "behalf of black employees and applicants for employment alleging that Citgo engaged in class-wide racial discrimination with respect to general hiring, promotion, compensation, and training policies at its manufacturing facilities in Lake Charles, Louisiana."[26] Ultimately, the court denied certification of a 23(b)(2) class action because the

---

22. *See, e.g.*, Jon Romberg, *The Hybrid Class Action as Judicial Spark: Managing Individual Rights in a Stew of Common Wrong*, 29 J. MARSHALL L. REV. 231, 233 (2006) (discussing the constitutional concerns over hybrid claims).

23. U.S. CONST. amend. VII.

24. 151 F.3d 402.

25. 267 F.3d 147 (2d Cir. 2001).

26. *Allison*, 151 F.3d at 407.

court felt that in this circumstance, "[t]he claims for injunctive relief, declaratory relief, and any equitable or incidental monetary relief cannot be litigated in a class action bench trial (in the same case prior to certification of any aspects of the pattern-or-practice claim) without running afoul of the Seventh Amendment."[27] The court looked to 23(b)(2) class actions and attempted to determine to what degree monetary claims can join claims for injunctive and declaratory relief in a (b)(2) class action.

Seeing the Advisory Committee's notes stating that monetary damages cannot predominate over the request for injunctive relief, the court decided to adopt a test that would discern whether the claims for damages predominated.[28] The court held that "monetary relief predominates in (b)(2) class actions unless it is incidental to requested injunctive or declaratory relief."[29] If the damages are merely "incidental" to the injunctive or declaratory relief sought, certification under Rule 23(b)(2) is permissible.[30] *Allison* proceeds to define incidental damages as "damages that flow directly from liability to the class as a whole on claims forming the basis of the injunctive or declaratory relief."[31]

Because the complaints in *Allison* involved highly individualized claims for back pay, front pay, and compensatory and punitive damages, the court determined that the district court did not err in denying (b)(2) certification.[32] The Fifth Circuit was careful to note that monetary damages themselves are not precluded by (b)(2) class actions, and past Fifth Circuit decisions allowed monetary damages in the form of back pay as an equitable relief claim.[33] However, for monetary damages to be incidental, the damages should be calculable by an objective, classwide standard.[34] Moreover, these damages should be generally applicable to the class as a whole so as not to require additional hearings to resolve individual claims.[35]

The Fifth Circuit revisited the *Allison* standard in *In re Monumental Life Insurance Company*.[36] *In re Monumental* involved claimants who alleged that the defendant engaged in discriminatory pricing of its insurance policies based upon race.[37] Claimants sought certification under (b)(2) seeking both an injunction to prevent the defendant from engaging in discriminatory practices and compensatory dam-

---

27. *Id.* at 425 (citations omitted).

28. *Id.* at 411.

29. *Id.* at 415.

30. *Id.*

31. *Id.* at 425.

32. *Id.* at 417; *see also Jenkins v. Raymark Indus.*, 782 F.2d 468, 471–72 (5th Cir. 1986) ("The district court has wide discretion in deciding whether or not to certify a proposed class.").

33. *Allison*, 151 F.3d at 415.

34. *Id.*

35. *Id.*

36. *Bratcher v. Nat'l Standard Life Ins. Co. (In re Monumental Life Ins. Co.)*, 365 F.3d 408 (5th Cir. 2004).

37. *Id.* at 412.

ages related to being overcharged on life insurance premiums.[38] The district court ruled that the claims seeking monetary relief would predominate at trial; accordingly, certification under 23(b)(2) was inappropriate.

The Fifth Circuit reversed and remanded, determining that the district court misapplied the *Allison* test. Before finding whether the monetary damages will predominate at trial, the court must determine whether the class as a whole is properly seeking injunctive relief. In this regard, the court stated, "[t]he question whether the proposed class members are properly seeking such relief is antecedent to the question whether that relief would predominate over money damages."[39] Thus, the incidental damages test developed two parts. First, the court must determine whether the class as a whole is properly seeking declaratory or injunctive relief.[40] Second, the court must then determine—using the incidental damages approach— whether the claim for monetary damages will predominate at trial.[41]

Because the record indicated that a sufficient number of class members could still be paying discriminatory insurance premiums, the *In re Monumental* court determined that the class as a whole could properly be seeking injunctive relief.[42] After reconsidering the case, the district court found that only a small minority of litigants would benefit from an injunction. Accordingly, the district court ruled that the class as a whole would not benefit from injunctive relief and denied (b)(2) certification.

Adding further to *Allison*, the Fifth Circuit now requires a majority of the (b)(2) class to face future harm for certification to be appropriate. In *Maldonado v. Ochsner Clinic Foundation*, the Fifth Circuit stated that "Rule 23(b)(2) certification is also inappropriate when the majority of the class does not face future harm."[43] In *Maldonado*, plaintiffs were uninsured medical patients who received treatment from the Ochsner Clinic.[44] The plaintiffs alleged that the defendant charged unreasonable rates for its medical services to uninsured patients.[45] When the court ruled, the Clinic had already instituted new voluntary pricing policies that provided uninsured patients with discounts.[46] Accordingly, the court ruled that an injunction would be meaningless because said injunction would not provide relief

---

38. *Id.* at 412–13.

39. *Id.* at 416.

40. *Id.*

41. *Id.*

42. *Id.*

43. 493 F.3d 521, 525 (5th Cir. 2007); *see also Bolin v. Sears, Roebuck & Co.*, 231 F.3d 970, 978 (5th Cir. 2000) (recognizing that classes who are mainly "individuals who do not face further harm" are not appropriately certifiable under (b)(2)).

44. 493 F.3d at 523.

45. *Id.*

46. *Id.*

to the class.[47] Rather, with the absence of any real possibility of prospective relief, the court of appeals concluded that monetary damages related to reimbursements would predominate at trial.[48]

District courts in the Fifth Circuit have applied *Allison* in a variety of situations.[49] For example, a Louisiana district court denied class certification in *Xavier v. Belfor Group USA, Inc.*[50] because of the predominance of monetary damages. In *Xavier*, the defendant, Belfor Group USA, Inc., was engaged in reconstruction projects related to Hurricane Katrina. Plaintiff employees alleged that the defendant forced its employees to work overtime without compensation in violation of Fair Labor Standards Act (FLSA).[51] The court provided an extensive review of the damages claim for past pay, and, applying the *Allison* standard, determined that recovery for damages should be "concomitant with, not merely consequential to, class-wide injunctive or declaratory relief."[52] Because the plaintiffs' claims for monetary relief did not flow directly from a possible finding of liability on the injunctive claim, the court ruled that monetary damages would predominate at trial.[53]

2. Fourth Circuit

The Fourth Circuit has elected to follow the Fifth Circuit's *Allison* approach. In *Thorn v. Jefferson-Pilot Life Ins. Co.*, plaintiffs alleged that the defendant and its corporate predecessors discriminated against African Americans by charging higher premiums on insurance policies than the premiums paid by Caucasian customers.[54] Plaintiffs sought certification under both (b)(2) and (b)(3), which the district court denied. The district court denied the (b)(2) certification because it felt that the plaintiffs' requested remedy was merely a predicate for monetary damages.[55] Because the defendant in *Thorn* had declared all insurance premiums "paid up" and was no longer charging premiums, the plaintiffs could not benefit from

---

47. *Id.* at 525.

48. *Id.*

49. *See, e.g., Owner Operator Indep. Drivers Ass'n v. FFE Transp. Servs.*, 245 F.R.D. 253, 256–57 (N.D. Tex. 2007) (plaintiff truck drivers denied (b)(2) certification because damages arising from contractual disputes would be determined on an individualized basis and these individual issues would predominate at trial); *DeHoyos v. Allstate Corp.*, 240 F.R.D. 269, 285 (W.D. Tex. 2007). In *DeHoyos*, the court ruled that (b)(2) certification was appropriate where minority customers alleged formulaic, incidental damages ranging from $50 to $150. *Id.* at 284. The court also denied opt-out rights to claimants. *Id.; see also Burrell v. Crown Cent. Petroleum, Inc.*, 197 F.R.D. 284, 290 (E.D. Tex. 2000) (holding, in the face of (b)(2) certification of a Title VII claim seeking (b)(2) certification, that any claim seeking compensatory and punitive damages would necessarily involve individualized adjudications and not be incidental to the injunctive relief sought).

50. 254 F.R.D. 281, 284–85 (E.D. La. 2008).

51. *Id.* at 285.

52. *Id.* at 288.

53. *Id.*

54. 445 F.3d at 314.

55. *Id.*

an injunction prohibiting the defendant from charging discriminatory premiums in the future.[56]

Therefore, the initial request for the injunction was moot, so the plaintiffs put forth another argument for (b)(2) certification.[57] Plaintiffs argued both that the monetary claims for reimbursement were equitable in nature and that (b)(2) certification is authorized if the relief sought is equitable as applied to the class as a whole.[58] The court rejected these arguments by stating that "certification under Rule 23(b)(2) is improper when the predominant relief sought is not injunctive or declaratory, even if the relief is equitable in nature."[59]

The opinion noted the twin requirements to Rule 23(b)(2) certification: "[(1)] that the defendant acted on grounds applicable to the class and [(2)] that the plaintiff seeks predominantly injunctive or declaratory relief."[60] Even if (b)(2) certification was authorized for claims seeking predominantly equitable relief, the plaintiffs failed to show that their reimbursement claims were equitable—rather than legal—in nature.[61] In affirming the district court ruling, the Fourth Circuit held that denial under (b)(2) was proper "because Appellants' requested relief was not predominantly injunctive or declaratory in nature."[62]

Applying *Thorn*, the District Court of Maryland set forth a fairly straightforward (b)(2) analysis in *Bulmash v. Travelers Indemnity Co.*[63] In *Bulmash*, the plaintiff sought to recover statutory interest on personal injury protection claims that Travelers paid late, and she sought class certification under (b)(2) and (b)(3) for similarly situated customers of Travelers' insureds residing in Maryland.

After ruling that *Bulmash* had met the requirements for 23(a), the district court moved to its (b)(2) analysis.[64] Citing *Thorn*, the court stated both that (b)(2) does not cover cases where the primary claim is for damages and that the goal of (b)(2) litigation is to remedy the class as a whole.[65] As such, the court rejected the claimants' request for certification.[66] First, the court noted that the plaintiff's primary claim was for individual—rather than collective—damages, even though the damages were easily calculated pursuant to statute.[67] Second, the nature of the damages may require individual hearings for each claimant, thereby allowing

---

56. *Id.* at 330–31 (citations omitted).
57. *Id.* at 331.
58. *Id.*
59. *Id.*
60. *Id.* at 330.
61. *Id.* at 332.
62. *Id.*
63. 257 F.R.D. 84, 86 (D. Md. 2009).
64. *Id.* at 89.
65. *Id.*
66. *Id.* at 90.
67. *Id.*

individual damages to predominate at trial.[68] As such, the court ruled that denial of class certification based on Rule 23(b)(2) was appropriate.[69]

3. Sixth Circuit

The Sixth Circuit has adopted the most rigid approach to class action certification by indicating that any (b)(2) action that involves compensatory damages is not appropriate for class certification.[70] Taking the *Allison* standard to an extreme, the Sixth Circuit's seminal ruling is found in *Reeb v. Ohio Department of Rehabilitation & Correction, Belmont Correctional Institution*.[71] In *Reeb*, female corrections officers alleged that their employer discriminated on the basis of sex. The plaintiffs sought compensatory and punitive damages as their remedies.[72] Applying the balancing approach espoused by the Second Circuit in *Robinson v. Metro-North Commuter Railroad*, the district court certified the (b)(2) class based on its determination that the damages would be relatively simple to determine.[73]

Reversing the district court, the Sixth Circuit in *Reeb* ruled that the damages related to Title VII required individualized adjudication because the court would need to adjudicate the degree of damages suffered by each class member.[74] The Sixth Circuit determined that *Allison* was the more appropriate precedent to provide instruction.[75] Applying that construct, the court of appeals concluded that individualized adjudications would predominate, making (b)(2) certification inappropriate.[76]

The *Reeb* court concluded that "individual compensatory damages are not recoverable by a Rule 23(b)(2) class."[77] Although claims seeking back pay as an equitable remedy are allowed in a (b)(2) claim, the court noted that the claim at issue here sought individual compensatory damages. *Reeb* does not foreclose the possibility of recovery of monetary damages by way of an equitable remedies claim, but plaintiffs must meet a higher burden than the incidental damages test espoused by *Allison*. Specifically, claimants seeking (b)(2) certification should not seek any compensatory damages.

---

68. *Id.*

69. *Id.*

70. *See* Carol V. Gilden, *The Evolving Use of Rule 23(b)(2) in Hybrid Class Actions Seeking Monetary Damages: A Hybrid Approach*, in CLASS ACTION LITIGATION 2007: PROSECUTION & DEFENSE STRATEGIES 209 (PLI Course Handbook Series No. 11372, 2007) (discussing the rigidity of *Reeb v. Ohio Dep't of Rehab. & Corr., Belmont Corr. Inst.*, 435 F.3d 639 (6th Cir. 2006)).

71. 435 F.3d at 640.

72. *Id.*

73. *Id.* at 642.

74. *Id.* at 651.

75. *See id.* at 648 (discussing *Coleman v. GMAC*, 296 F.3d 443 (6th Cir. 2002)).

76. *Id.* at 651.

77. *Id.*

The Sixth Circuit has recently applied the *Reeb* decision in *Serrano v. Cintas Corp.*[78] to deny (b)(2) certification where the plaintiffs were seeking front pay, back pay, and punitive damages in addition to injunctive relief. In analyzing the request for (b)(2) certification, the court decided that "even if Plaintiffs had met all the requirements of Rule 23(a), the Court finds that Rule 23(b)(2) certification is not appropriate under the current circumstances."[79] Noting that (b)(2) certification is only available where monetary relief is incidental to the injunctive relief sought, the court ruled that the requests for all monetary damages (e.g., punitive) would require individualized adjudications.[80]

4. Seventh Circuit

In *Jefferson v. Ingersoll International Inc.*,[81] the Seventh Circuit was the first circuit court to agree with *Allison*. Like *Allison*, *Ingersoll* involved a Title VII pattern-or-practice case. In *Ingersoll*, the plaintiffs alleged that the defendant engaged in race-based discrimination when reviewing employment applications. The plaintiffs sought an injunction to change the defendant's hiring practices, and the district court certified the class action under (b)(2).[82] The defendant appealed, allowing the court to question whether (b)(2) certification was proper because the plaintiffs also sought compensatory and punitive damages.[83]

Judge Easterbrook—writing the opinion of the court—explained that pattern-or-practice cases historically were certified under (b)(2). When (b)(2) was first promulgated, Title VII cases entitled plaintiffs to only equitable relief.[84] Because awards resulting from (b)(2) claims historically provided plaintiffs "injunctive or corresponding declaratory relief with respect to the class as a whole," Title VII cases naturally aligned with (b)(2) litigation.[85] However, the Civil Rights Act of 1991 provided plaintiffs the right to seek compensatory and punitive damages in Title VII cases.[86] Therefore, the court needed to reconsider whether (b)(2) certification was appropriate for such claims seeking compensatory and punitive damages.[87]

After weighing the constitutional considerations of a (b)(2) action, the court adopted the *Allison* approach. It explained that "[i]f Rule 23(b)(2) ever may be used when the plaintiff class demands compensatory or punitive damages, that step would be permissible only when monetary relief is incidental to the equitable

---

78. 106 Fair Empl. Prac. Cas. (BNA) 154, *7 (E.D. Mich. Mar. 31, 2009).
79. *Id.* at *31.
80. *Id.*
81. 195 F.3d 894 (7th Cir. 1999).
82. *Id.* at 896.
83. *Id.*
84. *Id.*
85. *Id.*
86. *Id.*
87. *Id.* at 896–97.

remedy."[88] The court suggested that it is possible to bifurcate the claim—certifying the claim for the injunction under (b)(2) and certifying the claim for damages under (b)(3).[89] However, it observed that because plaintiffs may now seek compensatory and punitive damages in Title VII actions, the balance has tilted towards (b)(3)—rather than (b)(2)—certification for such civil rights claims.[90] Thus, the Seventh Circuit reversed the district court opinion and adopted the *Allison* standard.

The Seventh Circuit reaffirmed its *Ingersoll* decision in *Lemon v. International Union of Operating Engineers, Local No. 139*.[91] *Lemon* sets forth the *Allison* test as adopted by the Seventh Circuit. Plaintiffs—racial minorities and women—alleged that International Union discriminated against them when administering an employment referral service. Without the benefit of the decision in *Ingersoll*, the district court certified the action as a (b)(2) class action.[92]

Upon reversing the district court's certification of the class as a (b)(2), *Lemon* instructed the district court to choose one of three options.[93] First, the district court could certify the entire action as a (b)(3) class; however, the plaintiffs would need to overcome predominance questions relating to damages[94] and notice and opt-out rights would have to be provided to the class.[95] Second, the district court could issue a divided certification, using a (b)(2) certification for equitable relief claims and (b)(3) certification for damages, with only the (b)(3) claim requiring predominance, notice, and opt-out rights.[96] Lastly, the district court could certify the claim using (b)(2), but the court would have to require notice and opt-out rights in exercising its plenary powers afforded under Rules 23(d)(2) and 23(d)(5).[97]

The *Lemon* court applied the *Allison* test, ruling that the claims for damages—compensatory and punitive—were not incidental to the equitable relief sought. Thus, (b)(2) certification was not appropriate for the class, unless the district court used its plenary power to provide notice and opt-out rights.[98]

District courts in the Seventh Circuit have dealt with hybrid 23(b)(2) claims since *Ingersoll* and *Lemon*. In *Vulcan Golf, LLC v. Google Inc.*,[99] plaintiffs were owners of certain Internet domain names. Plaintiffs alleged that the defendant would

---

88. *Id.* at 898.
89. *Id.* at 899.
90. *Id.* at 898.
91. 216 F.3d 577, 579 (7th Cir. 2000).
92. *Id.* at 579–80.
93. *Id.* at 581–82.
94. *Id.* at 581.
95. *Id.*
96. *Id.* at 581–82.
97. *Id.* at 582.
98. *Id.*
99. 254 F.R.D. 521, 523 (N.D. Ill. 2008).

register deceptively similar domain names in a hope to profit off of the plaintiffs' domain names.[100] The court denied (b)(2) certification on two grounds.[101] First, it noted that (b)(2) is based on the presumptive homogeneity of the class, but that the particular facts relevant to each plaintiff would affect the adjudication or remedy.[102] Also, monetary relief must be incidental to the injunctive relief that is sought.[103] Although the plaintiffs argued that monetary relief could be calculated according to a rigid formula, the district court noted that the plaintiffs failed to show how such calculations could be made.[104]

Occasionally, claimants will seek (b)(2) certification for claims that seek punitive damages but do not seek compensatory damages. In *Palmer v. Combined Insurance Co.*,[105] the plaintiff sued defendant employer alleging pattern-or-practice gender discrimination. The plaintiff sought class certification for all female employees working for Combined Insurance after a certain date.[106] Palmer sought injunctive relief and punitive damages; however, she did not seek compensatory damages.[107]

The defendant argued that punitive damages correlated directly to compensatory damages and, therefore, punitive damages would not be available if compensatory damages were not sought. The district court noted, however, that *Allison* had held that punitive damages do not require proof of individualized harm.[108] The district court also stated that punitive damages are meant to punish, not compensate.[109] Because the plaintiff sought only punitive damages and injunctive relief, the court could not relate the punitive damages to compensation.[110] Rather, the court determined that an award of punitive damages could be incidental to injunctive relief by further incentivizing the defendant to correct the alleged bad behavior.[111] Thus, the court allowed (b)(2) certification.[112] Following *Ingersoll*, the district court nevertheless decided to provide notice and opt-out rights to class members to protect due process rights.[113]

---

100. *Id.* at 523.
101. *Id.* at 535–36.
102. *Id.* at 535.
103. *Id.* at 535–36.
104. *Id.* at 536.
105. 217 F.R.D. 430, 433 (N.D. Ill. 2003).
106. *Id.* at 436.
107. *Id.*
108. *Id.* at 438.
109. *Id.*
110. *Id.* at 438–39.
111. *Id.* at 439–40.
112. *Id.*
113. *Id.* at 440.

5. Eleventh Circuit

When confronted with a hybrid (b)(2) claim, the Eleventh Circuit first adopted the *Allison* approach in *Murray v. Auslander*.[114] In this case, disabled Floridians alleged that they were denied benefits under Medicaid for which they were eligible. After the district court certified the (b)(2) class, the defendant appealed the certification. The circuit court noted that plaintiffs' claims were primarily aimed at obtaining injunctive and declaratory relief; however, the plaintiffs also sought compensatory damages for pain and suffering.[115] Citing *Allison*, the court noted that monetary relief is allowable under (b)(2) claims so long as monetary relief does not predominate.[116] The court then decided to adopt *Allison* and determined that the plaintiffs' claims for damages were necessarily individualized and not a group remedy.[117] Accordingly, these claims would need to be adjudicated separately and would, therefore, predominate at trial.[118] The court ruled (b)(2) certification to be improper under these circumstances.[119]

Cooper v. Southern Co.[120] presented the Eleventh Circuit with an opportunity to address (b)(2) certification in a pattern-or-practice employment discrimination case. In *Cooper*, plaintiff employees brought suit against their employer, claiming the employer engaged in racial discrimination in promotions and compensation. The plaintiffs sought injunctive relief, back pay, compensatory damages, and punitive damages.[121] The plaintiffs sought class certification for past and present African American employees.[122]

After the district court denied class certification, the court of appeals was presented with the question of whether (b)(2) certification was proper since the plaintiffs sought compensatory and punitive damages. The plaintiffs argued that the district court should have certified the class with respect to injunctive and equitable relief only.[123] However, they sought certification for both present and former employees.[124] Because former employees could not benefit from the injunction, they could not be adequately represented by the class.[125] For former employees who were class members, compensatory and punitive damages would play a larger

---

114. 244 F.3d 807, 808 (11th Cir. 2001).
115. *Id.* at 809.
116. *Id.* at 812.
117. *Id.*
118. *Id.* at 812–13.
119. *Id.* at 813.
120. 390 F.3d 695, 702 (11th Cir. 2004) (overruled in part on other grounds).
121. *Id.*
122. *Id.* at 703.
123. *Id.* at 712.
124. *Id.* at 721.
125. *Id.*

role in the trial than injunctive relief.[126] Moreover, the court held that "'complex, individualized determinations' necessary to fix the appropriate level of individual damage awards in this case are exactly the type that *Murray* and *Allison* make clear should not be considered incidental to the claims for injunctive and declaratory relief."[127]

Eleventh Circuit district courts have applied *Murray* on numerous occasions. In *Hicks v. Client Services*,[128] plaintiff debtor sued a debt collection service for violating the Fair Debt Collection Practices Act (FDCPA). The plaintiff sought (b)(3) and (b)(2) certification on behalf of all Floridians who fell victim to similar violations of the FDCPA by the defendant.[129] Although the court granted (b)(3) certification, the court denied the (b)(2) class.[130] It ruled that the FDCPA only provides for monetary relief and does not provide for injunctive relief.[131] Accordingly, monetary damages could not be incidental to the injunctive relief.[132]

Not all district court decisions have consistently applied *Murray* and *Allison*. In *Agan v. Katzman & Korr, P.A.*,[133] the district court issued a puzzling ruling. The court considered plaintiff's argument for both (b)(3) certification and a hybrid (b)(2) claim. While the court granted the (b)(3) certification, it denied (b)(2) certification because "the Court finds that declaratory relief is not merely incidental to monetary damages."[134] This ruling seemingly misapplied the *Allison* and *Murray* rulings, which had provided that monetary relief must be incidental to the injunctive relief sought rather than the opposite.

B. ROBINSON AND ITS PROGENY: THE AD HOC APPROACH

1. Second Circuit

The Second Circuit's decision in *Robinson v. Metro-North Commuter Railroad*[135] was the first circuit decision to reject the *Allison* standard. In *Robinson*, African American employees brought a pattern-or-practice claim of discrimination against their employer as a Title VII claim. The district court applied the *Allison* standard and thereby denied (b)(2) certification because the plaintiffs sought compensatory damages that were not incidental to the injunctive relief sought.[136] In reviewing the *Allison* standard, the Second Circuit noted that by adopting a standard that

---

126. *Id.*

127. *Id.*

128. No. 07-61822-CIV, 2008 U.S. Dist. LEXIS 101129, at *1–2 (S.D. Fla. Dec. 11, 2008).

129. *Id.* at *3–4.

130. *Id.* at *26, *27.

131. *Id.* at *27; *see also* 15 U.S.C.S. § 1692.

132. *Hicks*, 2008 U.S. Dist. LEXIS 101129, at *27.

133. 222 F.R.D. 692, 700–02 (S.D. Fla. 2004).

134. *Id.* at 702.

135. 267 F.3d at 154.

136. *Id.*

allows no more than mere incidental damages, the district foreclosed the possibility of a (b)(2) class that includes any compensatory or punitive damages even if the plaintiffs are primarily seeking injunctive relief.[137]

The court rejected the *Allison* standard and held that "a district court must 'consider[ ] the evidence presented at a class certification hearing and the arguments of counsel,' and then assess whether (b)(2) certification is appropriate in light of 'the relative importance of the remedies sought, given all of the facts and circumstances of the case.'"[138] This ad hoc standard chose functionalism over formalism, and the decision provided courts considering (b)(2) certification with a standard different from *Allison*.

The *Robinson* standard provides that a court considering certification of a (b)(2) class should

> at a minimum, satisfy itself of the following: (1) even in the absence of a possible monetary recovery, reasonable plaintiffs would bring the suit to obtain the injunctive or declaratory relief sought; and (2) the injunctive or declaratory relief sought would be both reasonably necessary and appropriate were the plaintiffs to succeed on the merits.[139]

The test provides significantly more latitude to district courts seeking to certify a hybrid (b)(2) claim than *Allison*. However, the court noted that in the case of "[i]nsignificant or sham requests for injunctive relief," courts "should not provide cover for (b)(2) certification of claims that are brought essentially for monetary recovery."[140]

The Second Circuit reaffirmed the *Robinson* decision in *Parker v. Time Warner Entertainment Co.*[141] In reversing a district court decision that had applied the *Allison* standard prior to Second Circuit's *Robinson* decision, the Second Circuit applied the ad hoc approach in a consumer-protection case. The Second Circuit also provided more guidance to the district courts about how to apply the ad hoc approach.

In *Parker*, Parker—a subscriber to Time Warner's cable television service—alleged both that Time Warner had failed to disclose that Time Warner would sell subscribers' information to third parties and that Time Warner had failed to provide subscribers with an opportunity to opt out.[142] Parker alleged that Time Warner's actions violated the Cable Act, and Parker sought statutory damages, actual damages, punitive damages, attorney fees, and an injunction to prevent future viola-

---

137. *Id.* at 163.
138. *Id.* at 164 (quoting *Hoffman v. Honda of Am. Mfg., Inc.*, 191 F.R.D. 530, 536 (S.D. Ohio 1999)).
139. *Id.*
140. *Id.*
141. 331 F.3d 13, 15 (2d Cir. 2003).
142. *Id.*

tions of the Cable Act.[143] The magistrate court looked at possible (b)(2) certification and issued a Report and Recommendation stating, among other things, that (b)(2) certification was not proper because monetary damages would predominate over injunctive relief at trial.[144] Using the *Allison* approach, the district court adopted the magistrate court's recommendations and provided (b)(2) certification for the injunctive relief claim only.[145]

The Second Circuit remanded the case to the district court to reconsider (b)(2) certification by applying the *Robinson* standard.[146] The court noted that "[t]he *Robinson* ad hoc approach requires a district court to have detailed information about the circumstances surrounding the certification issue, and indeed, favors a class certification hearing prior to decision of a Rule 23(b)(2) certification motion."[147] The court also noted that the district court likely could find that the claim for injunctive relief was insignificant, and, therefore, that any (b)(2) certification would be inappropriate.[148] Providing guidance to lower courts, *Parker* expounds on *Robinson* by noting that the courts likely should conduct "at least minimal class discovery" to determine whether the facts will allow a (b)(2) certification.[149]

The Second Circuit district courts have embraced the *Robinson* approach.[150] In *United States v. City of New York*,[151] a district court was faced with a pattern-or-practice discrimination case. Under auspices of section 706 and 707 of Title VII, the U.S. Attorney General, the Vulcan Society, and various individuals brought suit against the City of New York claiming that certain examinations used in firefighter examinations had a disparate impact among black and Hispanic applicants. The plaintiffs also argued that because the city had known of the disparate impact, the discrimination was intentional.[152] Considering (b)(2) certification, the court looked first to whether, in the absence of the monetary claims, the plaintiffs would bring their case for injunctive relief.[153] Second, the court determined whether injunctive relief would be both reasonably necessary and appropriate were the plaintiffs to prevail.[154] The court ruled that the plaintiffs would have brought their claims even in the absence of monetary relief, and—presuming that the plaintiffs

---

143. *Id.*

144. *Id.* at 16.

145. *Id.*

146. *Id.* at 18–19.

147. *Id.* at 20–21.

148. *Id.* at 20.

149. *Id.* at 21.

150. *See, e.g., Foti v. NCO Fin. Sys.*, No. 04 Civ. 00707, 2008 U.S. Dist. LEXIS 16511 (S.D.N.Y. Feb. 19, 2008) (certifying a (b)(2) hybrid claim, the court wrote that "monetary damages would be so *de minimis* that the value of the injunction to the plaintiffs clearly outweighs any potential financial recompense").

151. 258 F.R.D. 47, 52 (E.D.N.Y. May 11, 2009).

152. *Id.* at 53–54.

153. *Id.* at 66.

154. *Id.*

were to win on the merits of their case—injunctive relief would be an appropriate remedy.[155]

Jermyn v. Best Buy Stores, L.P.[156] provides another example of a Second Circuit district court applying the *Robinson* standard. In *Jermyn*, the consumer plaintiff alleged that the defendant deceptively advertised a price-match guarantee even though the company encouraged its employees not to honor requests for price matching.[157] Seeking injunctive relief and monetary damages, the plaintiff sought certification under (b)(2).[158] The defendant argued that (b)(2) certification was not appropriate because the plaintiff sought money damages not incidental to the injunctive relief.[159] Siding with the plaintiff, the Court held that *Robinson* does not provide credence to such incidental damages arguments.[160] Instead, the question is whether injunctive relief was the primary motivation for bringing the suit.[161] Using *Robinson*, the court attempted to determine the motivation of the plaintiff.[162] The court found that, because the plaintiff only suffered $180 in damages, the evidence suggested that the plaintiff brought suit to obtain injunctive relief.[163]

2. Ninth Circuit

Like the Second Circuit, the Ninth Circuit has declined to follow the *Allison* approach to hybrid (b)(2) claims. The Ninth Circuit's first case addressing hybrid (b)(2) claims was *Molski v. Gleich*.[164] In this case, plaintiff consumers brought suit against the defendant—an owner of gas stations and mini-markets—alleging denial of access to public accommodations in violation of the Americans with Disabilities Act.[165] The district court certified a mandatory class under Rule 23(b)(2) and approved a consent decree whereby the defendant was required to construct certain accommodations for the plaintiffs and pay specified damages in exchange for the class forgoing any claim to statutory and actual damages.[166]

The defendant urged the circuit court to adopt *Allison* and argued that the damages were not incidental to the injunctive relief sought.[167] Although the court agreed that the damages were not incidental to the relief sought, the circuit court

---

155. *Id.* at 66–67.
156. 256 F.R.D. 418 (S.D.N.Y. 2009).
157. *Id.* at 424.
158. *Id.* at 433.
159. *Id.*
160. *Id.* at 434.
161. *Id.*
162. *Id.*
163. *Id.*
164. 318 F.3d 937, 941 (9th Cir. 2003).
165. *Id.*
166. *Id.*
167. *Id.* at 949.

ultimately concluded that a bright-line rule resembling that espoused in *Allison* would nullify the district court's historical discretion when analyzing class certification.[168] The court also expressed concern that *Allison*'s standard would prevent many traditional pattern-or-practice (b)(2) claims from coming to the fore.[169] Accordingly, the incidental/nonincidental distinction was not relevant to the Court's calculus in determining (b)(2) certification. The Ninth Circuit has explicitly continued to reject the incidental damages approach.[170]

Instead, the court decided to adopt a similar standard to that in *Robinson*. The court determined that the correct approach is to "examine the specific facts and circumstances of each case."[171] To determine whether the monetary damages would predominate at trial, courts should look to the intent of the plaintiffs bringing suit.[172] In sum, the *Molski* test allows certification under (b)(2) only if "the claim for monetary damages" is "secondary to the primary claim for injunctive or declaratory relief."[173]

Applying this new standard, the court in *Molski* held that monetary damages would not predominate at trial and that the district court acted within its discretion in certifying the (b)(2) claim.[174] The *Molski* court also referenced *Ingersoll*, stating that to survive constitutional scrutiny the claim should provide notice and opt-out rights like those required in a (b)(3) action.[175]

In 2010, the Ninth Circuit reversed the *Molski* approach in *Dukes v. Wal-Mart Stores, Inc.*[176] In a typical pattern-or-practice discrimination claim, the plaintiffs in *Dukes* brought a discrimination claim against Walmart as employer alleging sex discrimination under Title VII of the 1964 Civil Rights Act.[177] The plaintiffs alleged that women working in Walmart's stores are "(1) paid less than men in comparable positions, despite having higher performance ratings and greater seniority, and (2) receive fewer—and wait longer for—promotions to in-store management positions."[178] The plaintiffs sought (b)(2) certification for all women employed by Walmart after December 26, 1998.[179] The district court certified the (b)(2) class with respect to injunctive relief, declaratory relief, and back pay, and, although a notice and opt-out class was created with respect to punitive damages claims,

---

168. *Id.* at 950.
169. *Id.*
170. *Id.*
171. *Id.*
172. *Id.*
173. *Id.* at 947.
174. *Id.* at 950.
175. *Id.* at 949.
176. 04-16688, 04-16720, 2010 U.S. App. LEXIS 8576 (9th Cir. Cal. Apr. 26, 2010).
177. *Id.* at *5.
178. *Id.*
179. *Id.* at *3.

the punitive damages claims were certified under (b)(2) as well.[180] On appeal, Walmart alleged that the district court should not have certified the (b)(2) class because monetary claims predominate over claims for injunctive relief.[181]

In conducting its analysis, the Ninth Circuit cited *Merriam-Webster's Collegiate Dictionary*'s definition of "'predominant' as 'having superior strength, influence, or authority: prevailing.'"[182] The court then determined that the subjective test in *Molski* is an incomplete method for determining whether monetary damages will predominate. In other words, the subjective intent of plaintiffs will not show a district court whether monetary damages will predominate at trial. However, the Ninth Circuit also critiqued the *Allison* approach.[183] The court noted a qualitative difference between "incidental" monetary damages and damages that would predominate at trial. The court reasoned that the *Allison* approach would fail to certify (b)(2) claims where monetary damages were more than merely incidental to the injunctive relief but still failed to predominate.[184] Accordingly, the court decided: "To the extent *Molski* required the district court to inquire only into the intent of the plaintiffs and focus primarily on determining whether reasonable plaintiffs would bring suit to obtain injunctive or declaratory relief even in the absence of a possible monetary recovery . . . it is overruled."[185]

The Ninth Circuit then established that district courts should employ a case-by-case approach to determine the effect of monetary claims on the litigation. In analyzing the (b)(2) claims, the district courts should consider "whether [the claim (1)] introduces new and significant legal and factual issues, [(2)] whether it requires individualized hearings, and [(3)] whether its size and nature—as measured by recovery per class member—raise particular due process and manageability concerns would all be relevant, though no single factor would be determinative."[186] Using this standard, the court examined punitive damages claims and determined that said claims might predominate.[187] Accordingly, the court remanded the decision to certify a (b)(2) class with respect to punitive damages.[188]

Although the district court used its discretion both to require that the plaintiffs have adequate notice and also to allow plaintiffs to opt out of the litigation, the district court did not determine whether the final relief was predominantly monetary.[189] The circuit court reasoned that allowing opt-out rights and notice

---

180. *Id.* at *3–4.
181. *Id.* at *122.
182. *Id.* at *124.
183. *Id.* at *125–26.
184. *Id.* at *126.
185. *Id.* at *126–27.
186. *Id.* at *127.
187. *Id.* at *141.
188. *Id.*
189. *Id.* at *140–41.

does not alleviate the concern of whether to certify the class under (b)(2) or (b)(3). When including punitive damages in the (b)(2) claim, the circuit court noted the district court should consider that (1) liability will be decided by a jury instead of a judge, (2) punitive damages introduce a new and substantial factual issue, (3) the size of punitive damages could be large, and (4) the punitive damages in this instance do not require individualized punitive damages determinations.[190] The circuit court declined to make a final determination with respect to certifying the punitive damage claim under (b)(2) because it felt that the district court should rule on the issue first.

In sum, the Ninth Circuit has adopted a multifaceted balancing test to determine whether monetary damages will predominate at trial. Adoption of this approach separates the Ninth Circuit from the more rigid test of the Fifth Circuit, but still provides clear factors for the district courts to weigh.

V. No Clear Standard—Other Circuit Courts

A. FIRST CIRCUIT

Although most circuits have adopted an approach to hybrid (b)(2) and (b)(3) claims, the First Circuit has only addressed hybrid (b)(2) claims at the district court level. *Ramirez v. DeCoster*[191] provides an example of a district court in the First Circuit adopting *Allison*. In *Ramirez*, former and current employees alleged racial discrimination by its employer, DeCoster Egg Farms. The workers sought both (b)(2) and (b)(3) certification of a class including all DeCoster employees of Mexican descent who worked after 1988.[192] Among the various types of relief, the workers sought compensatory damages, punitive damages, and "a permanent injunction enjoining DeCoster 'from maintaining a policy of discrimination against Mexicans.'"[193]

In undertaking a (b)(2) analysis, the court decided to follow the incidental damages test set forth in *Allison*.[194] The court determined that the claims were predominantly monetary in nature.[195] The court noted that the only injunction that the plaintiffs sought was to prevent the employer from discriminating against its current employees, and only one of the class members was a current employee.[196] As such, injunctive relief would not benefit the class as a whole; therefore, the focus of the class claim was for compensatory and punitive damages.[197] The court

---

190. *Id.* at *141–44.
191. 194 F.R.D. 348, 351 (D. Me. 2000).
192. *Id.* at 351–52.
193. *Id.* at 352.
194. *Id.*
195. *Id.*
196. *Id.*
197. *Id.*

left open the possibility that a claim for back pay, which would be an equitable remedy, would be certifiable under (b)(2), but the plaintiffs had failed to request back pay in their claim.[198]

B. THIRD CIRCUIT

While the Third Circuit has addressed hybrid claims, it has not adopted one standard for analyzing certification of hybrid claims under (b)(2). Instead, the Third Circuit has ruled that both the *Allison* and *Robinson* approaches are correct when undertaking a (b)(2) analysis; moreover, the court has left open the possibility that other approaches to (b)(2) analysis are also correct.[199]

In *Barabin v. Aramark Corp.*,[200] the Third Circuit reviewed an interlocutory appeal from African American employees alleging racial discrimination by the employer defendant. Plaintiffs' claim requested compensatory and punitive damages along with injunctive relief. The plaintiffs sought class certification for all African Americans employed over a certain time frame by the defendant and its corporate predecessors.[201]

Seeing that the Third Circuit had not adopted an approach to hybrid (b)(2) claims, the district court applied the *Allison* standard and denied certification.[202] The plaintiffs sought review of the district court's denial of both (b)(2) and (b)(3) certification. The district court had ruled that the injunctive relief sought was, at best, a secondary claim to the monetary damages.

In conducting a review of the (b)(2) request, the Third Circuit noted that the decisions in *Molski* and *Allison* required some form of the incidental damages test.[203] The court also referenced *Robinson* in stating that (b)(2) certification would prevent unnamed plaintiffs from opting out of the litigation and, therefore, that class cohesion is necessary.[204] The Third Circuit recited the rationale of the district court in applying the *Allison* standard and found no error.[205]

Because the court referenced conflicting circuit court opinions favorably when finding no error in the district court's approach, a district court within the Third Circuit is not prohibited from using *Molski* or *Robinson* standards in a (b)(2) analysis. However, because the Third Circuit specifically allowed the *Allison* standard in adjudicating (b)(2) certification, the district courts under its authority have gravi-

---

198. *Id.*
199. *See infra* notes 206 and 219.
200. No. 02-8057, 2003 U.S. App. LEXIS 3532, at *2–3 (3d Cir. Jan. 24, 2003).
201. *Id.* at *2.
202. *Id.* at *6.
203. *Id.* at *4 (citing *Allison*, 151 F.3d at 415).
204. *Id.* (citing *Robinson*, 267 F.3d at 163–66).
205. *Id.* at *6–7 (citation omitted).

tated toward the *Allison* approach.[206] In fact, one district court has predicted the adoption of the *Allison* test by the Third Circuit.[207]

In *Hohider v. UPS*[208]—a decision later reversed by the Third Circuit—the district court applied the *Allison* standard and granted, in part, certification for a (b)(2) claim that included monetary damages. Plaintiffs alleged discrimination by employer defendant and sought relief under the Americans with Disabilities Act.[209] Plaintiffs sought a variety of injunctions and monetary relief.[210] Considering *Barabin*, the court applied the *Allison* standard to determine whether (b)(2) certification was appropriate.[211] After stating that back pay and other forms of equitable relief were allowable under (b)(2), the court granted (b)(2) certification to the class with respect to claims seeking injunctive relief, equitable relief in the form of back pay, and other incidental damages.[212] Because the claimants sought real injunctive relief related to current policies of the defendant, the court distinguished other cases where the requested injunctive relief was illusory.[213] However, the court would not provide (b)(2) certification with respect to compensatory, punitive, and other nonincidental damages that the plaintiffs also sought.[214] Instead, it limited the recovery of monetary damages to equitable relief and other incidental damages.[215]

On appeal, the Third Circuit reversed the district court's certification of the (b)(2) class, finding numerous errors in the lower court's reasoning.[216] The appeals court noted that, even if the district court were correct in certifying the (b)(2) claim with regard to injunctive and declaratory relief, certifying the claim with respect to back pay claims was inappropriate.[217] The district court only determined that back pay could be nonincidental, rather than determining that the claims actually were nonincidental.[218] The Third Circuit ruled that "before moving forward with certification, it [is] necessary for the court to determine whether plaintiffs' back-pay request actually conforms with the requirements of Rule 23, including Rule

---

206. *See, e.g., Gaston v. Exelon Corp.*, 247 F.R.D. 75 (E.D. Pa. 2007) ("[A]lthough our Court of Appeals has not adopted the *Allison* standard, it has ruled that a district court does not err by applying it." *Id.* at 86–87.).

207. *Pichler v. UNITE*, 228 F.R.D. 230, 256 (E.D. Pa. 2005) (writing that with the Third Circuit in *Barabin* "[e]ssentially restating (albeit in shorthand) the bright-line approach, this statement suggests that the Court of Appeals will join the Fifth, Seventh, and Eleventh Circuits when an appropriate case reaches it").

208. 243 F.R.D. 147 (W.D. Pa. 2007), *rev'd*, 574 F.3d 169 (3d Cir. 2009).

209. 243 F.R.D. at 153.

210. *Id.* at 154.

211. *Id.* at 242.

212. *Id.* at 244.

213. *Id.*

214. *Id.*

215. *Id.*

216. *See generally Hohider*, 574 F.3d 169.

217. *Id.* at *101–02.

218. *Id.*; *see also Hohider*, 243 F.R.D. at 242.

23(b)(2)'s monetary-predominance standard."[219] The court remanded and instructed the district court to determine whether the class was certifiable under (b)(2) using either *Allison*'s incidental damages test or *Robinson*'s ad hoc test.[220] As a result, the Third Circuit currently allows its district courts to use either *Robinson* or *Allison* to govern its (b)(2) analysis.[221]

C. EIGHTH CIRCUIT

To date, the Eighth Circuit has not adopted either the *Allison* or the *Robinson* approach. However, since the *Allison* and *Robinson* decisions, district courts in the Eighth Circuit have addressed hybrid (b)(2) claims generally under the *Allison* approach. *Nelson v. Wal-Mart Stores, Inc.*[222] provides a good example of such a hybrid (b)(2) claim. Plaintiffs—African American truck drivers—sued Wal-Mart, alleging racially discriminatory practices in hiring truck drivers.[223] The plaintiffs sought class certification for two separate classes of African American job applicants.[224] After ruling that the plaintiffs satisfied the 23(a) requirements, the court addressed the (b)(2) and (b)(3) claims.[225] In doing so, it described the necessity of notice and opt-out rights in a (b)(3) claim.[226] However, the court noted that monetary damages should not predominate at trial in a (b)(2) claim.[227] The court decided that it should follow the *Allison* approach, noting that "the weight of authority holds that money damages predominate when they are not incidental to declaratory and injunctive relief, *i.e.*, when the damages do not 'flow directly from liability to the class as a whole on the claims forming the basis of the injunctive or declaratory relief.'"[228] In effect, the district court decided to apply the *Allison* test because more circuit courts had adopted *Allison* than *Robinson*.[229]

In applying the *Allison* test, the district court looked at the different types of monetary damages that the plaintiffs brought.[230] Referencing *Allison*, the court noted that the plaintiffs' claims for back pay are allowable under (b)(2).[231] Because plaintiffs sought punitive damages but not compensatory damages, the court was forced to consider whether punitive damages can predominate under (b)(2) if these

---

219. *Hohider*, 574 F.3d at 202.
220. *Id.* at 203.
221. *Id.*
222. 245 F.R.D. 358 (E.D. Ark. 2007).
223. *Id.* at 362, 365.
224. *Id.* at 365.
225. *Id.* at 373.
226. *Id.* at 373–74.
227. *Id.* at 374.
228. *Id.* (citing *Allison*, 151 F.3d at 415).
229. *See id.* at 374 n.128.
230. *Id.* at 374–75.
231. *Id.*

damages do not accompany a compensatory damages claim.[232] Noting that the Eighth Circuit allows plaintiffs to seek punitive damages without seeking compensatory damages, the court analyzed whether the claim for punitive damages was either an individualized remedy or classwide relief.[233] The court ruled that the claim for punitive damages would require individualized adjudication because the harm that punitive damages are meant to punish occurs in an individualized manner[234] and concluded that punitive damages would predominate at trial.[235] The court also refuted the plaintiffs' arguments that notice and opt-out rights allow (b)(2) claims to proceed even if these claims seek nonincidental monetary damages; citing a prior Eighth Circuit Court decision, the court determined that "'the privilege to opt-out of the action should be operable only when the class action is maintainable under [Rule 23(b)(3)] alone.'"[236] The court ruled that, according to the Eighth Circuit's decision in *DeBoer v. Mellon Mortgage Co.*, a plaintiff can only obtain opt-out rights in a (b)(3) action.[237]

D. TENTH CIRCUIT

The Tenth Circuit has not yet adopted either the *Allison* or *Robinson* approach. However, both standards were applied in the district court decision of *Atwell v. Gabow*,[238] where (b)(2) certification was denied. Plaintiffs sued the defendant hospital alleging pattern-or-practice discrimination against nonwhite employees.[239] The plaintiffs— seeking (b)(2) certification—brought claims for lost wages, punitive damages, pain and suffering, emotional distress, and injunctive relief.[240] Following *Robinson*, the district court overlooked plaintiffs' assertions that the primary relief sought was injunctive, concluding that the claim for injunctive relief seemed "contrived" because the plaintiffs merely sought an injunction stating that defendant's actions were unlawful.[241] The court noted that injunctive relief should be specific to meet the muster of a (b)(2) claim.[242] Applying *Allison*, the court ruled that the damages sought by the plaintiffs did not flow from the claims for injunctive relief.[243] Applying

---

232. *Id.* at 375–78.
233. *Id.* at 375–76.
234. *Id.* at 378.
235. *Id.*
236. *Id.* (citing *DeBoer*, 64 F.3d at 1175).
237. *Id.*; *see also DeBoer*, 64 F.3d 1171 (8th Cir. Minn. 1995).
238. 248 F.R.D. 588 (D. Colo. 2008).
239. *Id.* at 589–90.
240. *Id.* at 590.
241. *Id.* at 595–96.
242. *Id.* at 596.
243. *Id.*

a standard claimed to be that of *Robinson*, the court stated that the injunctive relief was merely incidental to the damages claims.[244]

Clark v. State Farm Mutual Automobile Insurance Co.[245] is another example of a court seeming to use both *Allison* and *Robinson* (b)(2) analysis in considering a hybrid (b)(2) claim. In *Clark*, the plaintiff customers sued State Farm, alleging that the company failed to provide a legal minimum amount of insurance to customer plaintiffs.[246] The claimants sought both injunctive relief to reform the insurance policies and monetary damages.[247] Noting that there is no clear (b)(2) standard within the Tenth Circuit, the court determined that the plaintiffs would not have sought injunctive relief unless it related to a claim for monetary damages.[248] Because the amount of damages was individualized, the court could not rule the damages incidental.[249] Accordingly, the court declined to certify under (b)(2).[250]

In an earlier case involving a hybrid (b)(2) claim, plaintiffs in *Robinson v. Sears, Roebuck & Co.*[251] sought both compensatory and punitive damages in a pattern-or-practice claim against an employer defendant. The court looked to *Allison* and determined that the monetary damages requested were not incidental to the injunctive relief sought.[252] However, it decided to adopt the Seventh Circuit's *Lemon* and *Ingersoll* standards to certify the (b)(2) claim.[253] The court noted that the Seventh Circuit provides for (b)(2) certification of claims seeking monetary damages if the court uses its discretionary power to provide notice and opt-out rights to the class members.[254] Thus, the court certified the (b)(2) class seeking compensatory and punitive damages but afforded the class members these due process rights.[255]

E. DISTRICT OF COLUMBIA CIRCUIT

The District of Columbia Circuit Court of Appeals remains unwilling to follow the *Allison* and *Robinson* approaches in determining whether money damages predominate.[256] Rather, the D.C. Circuit has so far avoided choosing between *Allison* and *Robinson* by using an a priori approach when confronted with hybrid (b)(2) claims.

---

244. *Id.* at 596–97.
245. 245 F.R.D. 478 (D. Colo. 2007).
246. *Id.* at 480.
247. *Id.* at 485.
248. *Id.* at 487.
249. *Id.*
250. *Id.*
251. 111 F. Supp. 2d 1101, 1105 (E.D. Ark. 2000).
252. *Id.* at 1126.
253. *Id.* at 1127.
254. *Id.*
255. *Id.* at 1127–28.
256. *See Richards v. Delta Air Lines, Inc.*, 453 F.3d 525, 531 n.8 (D.C. Cir. 2006) (noting the *Allison*-*Robinson* split between the circuit courts).

Eubanks v. Billington[257] involved a suit from two class members seeking to opt out of a settlement agreement to a (b)(2) claim. This settlement agreement was to provide the plaintiffs—African American employees of the Library of Congress—with back pay for alleged discrimination that took place during their employment.[258] However, class members, pursuant to the settlement agreement, were to acknowledge payment for all monetary claims, excepting attorney fees, costs, and interest.[259] The class counsel agreed with the defendant's counsel not to advocate for opt-out rights for class members.[260]

The court began by admitting that the rationale for (b)(2) certification begins to deteriorate in the presence of monetary damages.[261] Accordingly, the court held that it is permissible for a district court to allow opt-out rights in a (b)(2) claim where both injunctive and monetary relief is sought.[262] The court reasoned that "the need to protect the rights of individual class members may necessitate procedural protections beyond those ordinarily provided under (b)(1) and (b)(2)."[263] *Eubanks* provides that when a (b)(2) claim seeks both monetary and injunctive relief, the district court has two choices.[264] First,

> [a] court may conclude that the assumption of cohesiveness for purposes of injunctive relief that justifies certification as a (b)(2) class is unjustified as to claims that individual class members may have for monetary damages. In such a case, the court may adopt a "hybrid" approach, certifying a (b)(2) class as to the claims for declaratory or injunctive relief, and a (b)(3) class as to the claims for monetary relief, effectively granting (b)(3) protections including the right to opt out to class members at the monetary relief stage.[265]

In the alternative, a district court may determine "that the claims of particular class members are unique or sufficiently distinct from the claims of the class as a whole, and that opt-outs should be permitted on a selective basis."[266] Unlike the Fifth and Second Circuits, the D.C. Circuit, in *Eubanks*, did not address the question of whether monetary damages will predominate at trial. Rather, *Eubanks* provides district courts with loose guidance to consider the due process rights of class members.

---

257. 110 F.3d 87, 88 (D.C. Cir. 1997).
258. *Id.* at 88.
259. *Id.* at 90.
260. *Id.*
261. *Id.* at 95.
262. *Id.* at 94.
263. *Id.* at 95.
264. *Id.* at 96.
265. *Id.*
266. *Id.*

Thomas v. Albright[267] presented the D.C. Circuit with a race discrimination claim involving employees of the U.S. Department of State. The circuit court determined that the district court abused the discretion that *Eubanks* provides.[268] In considering certification of a (b)(2) claim seeking compensatory damages, the district court should first look to whether an "assumption of [class] cohesiveness" inherent to (b)(2) claims is challenged by individuals' monetary claims.[269] If it determines that the class is not cohesive, the court should certify the claim using a hybrid (b)(2)–(b)(3) approach.[270] Finally, the court should provide opt-out rights in limited circumstances if the particular claims of the class members are distinct from the claims of the class as a whole.[271] In other words, district courts should consider using both (b)(2) and (b)(3) certification before considering certification of a (b)(2) claim where defendants are allowed to opt out.[272]

In re Veneman[273] presented the D.C. Circuit with a standard pattern-or-practice discrimination claim. Plaintiffs alleged that the U.S. Department of Agriculture used racially discriminatory practices when awarding subsidies and loans through its farm programs.[274] The plaintiffs sought class certification for Native Americans who claimed that they had been discriminated against.[275] The plaintiffs sought a hybrid (b)(2)–(b)(3) certification, whereby the court would certify the equitable claims under (b)(2) and the monetary claims under (b)(3).[276] The district court decided to certify the (b)(2) claim for equitable relief only and determined that it did not have enough of a factual record to rule on the (b)(3) claim.[277] The defendant appealed, alleging that the district court must first look to whether claims for money damages would predominate over those for equitable relief before certifying a (b)(2) claim that is solely for equitable relief.[278]

Considering whether partial certification is allowable, the circuit court noted that the district court only certified the (b)(2) claim with respect to equitable relief.[279] The court also noted that district courts are allowed to certify particular claims "where appropriate" under Rule 23(c)(4).[280] To determine whether certification of a particular claim is appropriate, a district court must consider (1) the due

267. 139 F.3d 227 (D.C. Cir. 1998).
268. *Id.* at 233.
269. *Id.* at 234 (citing *Eubanks*, 110 F.3d at 96).
270. *Id.* at 234–35.
271. *Id.* at 235.
272. *See id.* at 234–35.
273. 309 F.3d 789 (D.C. Cir. 2002).
274. *Id.* at 791–92.
275. *Id.* at 791.
276. *Id.* at 793.
277. *Id.*
278. *Id.* at 795.
279. *Id.*
280. *Id.*

process rights of absent class members and (2) whether the absent class members will be bound by the judgment.[281] Although the court thought it premature to opine on the district court's ruling, *In re Veneman* provides district courts with more guidance concerning hybrid (b)(2) claims. The court denied the defendant's petition because it determined that the questions required to resolve certification were unbriefed and that the issue would be resolved upon appellate review.

VI. Conclusion

In seeking to certify claims, plaintiffs find the mandatory nature of (b)(2) certification less onerous than the opt-out and notice rights that accompany (b)(3) claims. However, constitutional concerns have forced the circuit courts of appeal to address limitations on (b)(2) claims seeking monetary damages. The circuit courts disagree about which method best addresses (b)(2) claims that seek monetary damages. Although use of the *Allison* standard is more prevalent among circuit and district court decisions, *Robinson* provides courts with a functional alternative. Until the U.S. Supreme Court decides the issue for all, the different circuit courts of appeal will continue to fashion particular standards governing (b)(2) certification for their respective circuits, and the district courts will wade through the decisions for guidance.

---

281. *Id.*

MEDICAL MONITORING CLASSES

MARCY HOGAN GREER
MADELEINE FISCHER[1]

I. Introduction

An independent cause of action, a mere remedy, or an unviable claim—"medical monitoring" means different things in different settings. But for purposes of this chapter, medical monitoring refers to a unique legal claim that is becoming increasingly more difficult to certify.

Medical monitoring claims typically seek a monitoring program comprising medical tests and services.[2] The program aims to detect latent injuries that may develop as a result of some tortious act or event so that a plaintiff can seek early treatment and minimize long-term health effects.[3] Medical monitoring first emerged as a legal remedy a quarter-century ago in the landmark case *Friends for All Children, Inc. v. Lockheed Aircraft Corp.*[4]

Friends for All Children arose from a tragic incident in Ho Chi Minh City at the close of the Vietnam War.[5] A U.S.-bound aircraft carrying Vietnamese war orphans crashed shortly after takeoff, killing many orphans and attendants.[6] The survivors allegedly suffered from a neurological development disorder due to the decompression of the aircraft's cabin and the impact of the crash itself.[7] They sought an

---

1. The authors wish to thank Tina C. Longoria, associate at Fulbright & Jaworski L.L.P., for her invaluable assistance in preparing this chapter.

2. *Leib v. Rex Energy Operating Corp.*, No. 06-CV-802-JPG-CJP, 2008 U.S. Dist. LEXIS 102847, at *34–35 (S.D. Ill. Dec. 19, 2008) (citing *In re Fosamax Prods. Liab. Litig.*, 248 F.R.D. 389, 395 (S.D.N.Y. 2008)).

3. *Id.*; *see also Bower v. Westinghouse Elec. Corp.*, 522 S.E.2d 424, 429 (W. Va. 1999).

4. 746 F.2d 816 (D.C. Cir. 1984). Despite its nomenclature, "medical monitoring" is not a medical term.

5. *Id.* at 818.

6. *Id.* at 819.

7. *Id.*

injunction ordering the aircraft manufacturer to provide funding for medical diagnosis and treatment of the disorder.[8] After noting several reasons that made such extraordinary relief appropriate in this case, the D.C. Circuit upheld an injunction requiring the manufacturer to create a medical monitoring fund for the survivors.[9] It reasoned that the crash "exposed [them] to the risk of serious brain damage" and that the need for monitoring was clear.[10] The D.C. Circuit concluded that "even in the absence of physical injury [a plaintiff] ought to be able to recover the cost for the various diagnostic examinations proximately caused by [a defendant's] negligent action."[11] For the D.C. Circuit, medical monitoring relief represented a means of making the survivors whole.[12]

Since *Friends for All Children*, medical monitoring has expanded in response to new situations presenting alleged needs for medical screening and testing, particularly in cases involving pharmaceuticals, medical devices, and exposure to toxic substances. But the claim has remained controversial. Indeed, courts still regard medical monitoring as a "novel" and "non-traditional" legal remedy decades after its creation.[13]

In the context of class actions, a number of courts throughout the country have refused to certify medical monitoring classes because the individual questions inherent in exposure cases tend to predominate over questions common to the class members. In fact, the U.S. Supreme Court has noted that the "call for caution" in certifying mass exposure classes is implicated most where "individual stakes are high and disparities among class members great."[14] In 2005, the Eighth Circuit Court of Appeals in *In re St. Jude Medical, Inc.*[15] observed that "proposed medical monitoring classes suffer from cohesion difficulties" and underscored a growing trend across the country when it recognized that a number of courts have denied certification of such classes.[16] *In re St. Jude* and other recent cases[17] have explored a number of reasons for this national trend.

---

8. *Id.* at 822.

9. *Id.* at 823.

10. *Id.* at 825–26.

11. *Id.* at 825.

12. *Id.* at 826.

13. *See Badillo v. Am. Brands, Inc.*, 16 P.3d 435, 438 (Nev. 2001).

14. *Amchem Prods., Inc. v. Windsor*, 521 U.S. 591, 624–25 (1997).

15. *In re St. Jude Med., Inc. Silzone Heart Valve Prods. Liab. Litig.*, 425 F.3d 1116 (8th Cir. 2005).

16. *Id.* at 1122 (citing *Ball v. Union Carbide Corp.*, 385 F.3d 713, 727–28 (6th Cir. 2004); *Zinser v. Accufix Research Inst., Inc.*, 253 F.3d 1180, 1195–96, amended, 273 F.3d 1266 (9th Cir. 2001); *Barnes v. Am. Tobacco Co.*, 161 F.3d 127, 143–46 (3d Cir. 1998); *Boughton v. Cotter Corp.*, 65 F.3d 823, 827 (10th Cir. 1995)).

17. *See, e.g., In re St. Jude Med., Inc.*, 522 F.3d 836 (8th Cir. 2008) (same case considered under Rule 23(b)(3)); *Fosamax*, 248 F.R.D. at 396, 400 & n.11 ("The inherently individualized nature of the proximate cause inquiry is a major reason why class certification has been denied in nearly every pharmaceutical products liability medical monitoring case to date."); *Sanders v. Johnson & Johnson, Inc.*, No. CIV 03-2663, 2006 WL 1541033 (D.N.J. June 2, 2006) (use of medical product Intergel); *Wyeth, Inc. v. Gottlieb*, 930 So.

II. Aspects of Medical Monitoring Claims That Present Challenges to Class Certification

A. NATIONWIDE MEDICAL MONITORING CLASSES

State law distinctions prevent class treatment in many putative nationwide mass exposure classes seeking medical monitoring relief. Although medical monitoring appeared to be gaining traction through the mid-1990s, a majority of the states now either reject the theory of recovery in the absence of a physical injury or do not recognize an independent tort claim for medical monitoring.[18] Several courts have expressed concern that medical monitoring claims stretch the bounds of state tort law. For example, the Supreme Court of Michigan concluded that medical monitoring claims "would require both a departure from fundamental tort principles and a cavalier disregard of the inherent limitations of judicial decision-making."[19]

The U.S. Supreme Court weighed in on the issue in a Federal Employers' Liability Act (FELA) case in *Metro-North Commuter R.R. Co. v. Buckley*.[20] There the Court declined to recognize a medical monitoring claim brought by a pipe fitter against his employer after substantial exposure to asbestos. Specifically, the Court held

---

2d 634 (Fla. Dist. Ct. App. 2006) (use of drug Prempro); *In re Prempro Prods. Liab. Litig.*, 230 F.R.D. 555 (E.D. Ark. 2005) (use of drug Prempro). *But see Meyer ex rel. Coplin v. Fluor Corp.*, 220 S.W.3d 712 (Mo. 2007) (finding that common questions predominated over individual questions in medical monitoring class and reversing the circuit court's denial of certification).

18. *See, e.g., Sinclair v. Merck & Co.*, 948 A.2d 587, 595–96 (N.J. 2008) (rejecting monitoring claim in pharmaceutical products case); *Lowe v. Philip Morris USA, Inc.*, 183 P.3d 181, 187 (Or. 2008) (rejecting monitoring claim in absence of current physical injury as failing to state a claim for negligence); *Paz v. Brush Engineered Materials, Inc.*, 949 So. 2d 1, 5–6 (Miss. 2007) ("[I]t would be contrary to current Mississippi law to recognize a claim for medical monitoring allowing a plaintiff to recover medical monitoring costs for mere exposure to a harmful substance without proof of current physical or emotional injury from that exposure."); *Henry v. Dow Chem. Co.*, 701 N.W.2d 684, 701 (Mich. 2005); *Wood v. Wyeth-Ayerst Labs.*, 82 S.W.3d 849, 856–59 (Ky. 2002); *Hinton v. Monsanto Co.*, 813 So. 2d 827 (Ala. 2001); *Norwood v. Raytheon Co.*, 414 F. Supp. 2d 659, 665–68 (W.D. Tex. 2006) ("I[n] light of the foregoing, it appears likely that the Texas Supreme Court would follow the recent trend of rejecting medical monitoring as a cause of action."); *Duncan v. Nw. Airlines, Inc.*, 203 F.R.D. 601, 614 (W.D. Wash. 2001) (applying Washington law); *Badillo*, 16 P.3d at 440; *Anello v. Shaw Indus., Inc.*, No. 95-30234-FHF, 2000 WL 1609831 (D. Mass. Mar. 31, 2000); *Ball v. Joy Mfg. Co.*, 755 F. Supp. 1344, 1372 (S.D. W. Va. 1990), *aff'd*, 958 F.2d 36 (4th Cir. 1991) (applying Virginia law); *Carroll v. Litton Sys., Inc.*, No. B-C-88-253, 1990 WL 312969, at *51 (W.D.N.C. Oct. 29, 1990) (applying North Carolina law), *aff'd in part, rev'd in part*, 47 F.3d 1164 (4th Cir. 1995); *Purjet v. Hess Oil V.I. Corp.*, No. 1985/284, 1986 WL 1200, at *4 (D.V.I. Jan. 8, 1986) (applying Virgin Islands law). The Louisiana Supreme Court recognized medical monitoring in *Bourgeois v. A.P. Green Indus., Inc.*, 716 So. 2d 355 (1998). The following year the Louisiana legislature modified the law to provide that "[d]amages do not include costs for future medical treatment, services, surveillance, or procedures of any kind unless such treatment, services, surveillance, or procedures are directly related to a manifest physical or mental injury or disease." LA. CIV. CODE ANN. art. 2315 (2010).

19. *Henry*, 701 N.W.2d at 701.

20. 521 U.S. 424 (1997).

that a plaintiff who is negligently exposed to a carcinogen, but who is without symptoms of any disease, cannot recover money damages for emotional distress or for medical monitoring costs "unless, and until, he manifests symptoms of a disease."[21] The opinion discussed the policies for and against a judicially created claim for medical monitoring and concluded that eliminating the requirement of a manifest physical injury would be unwise, at least in the context of a full-blown lump-sum damages claim:

> [T]ens of millions of individuals may have suffered exposure to substances that might justify some form of substance-exposure-related medical monitoring. . . . And that fact, along with uncertainty as to the amount of liability, could threaten both a "flood" of less important cases (potentially absorbing resources better left available to those more seriously harmed) and the systemic harms that can accompany "unlimited and unpredictable liability" (for example, vast testing liability adversely affecting the allocation of scarce medical resources).[22]

Nonetheless, the Court did not close the door to medical monitoring claims entirely, indicating that it remained open to the possibility of a court-supervised monitoring fund as an alternate remedy. The reality that medical monitoring claims are not cognizable in a majority of states presents a formidable initial hurdle for any nationwide medical monitoring class action. Moreover, differences in the legal requirements in jurisdictions that recognize medical monitoring further exacerbate the challenges in seeking a nationwide class. Some jurisdictions view medical monitoring as an independent cause of action,[23] while others consider medical monitoring to be a form of damages.[24] Still others regard medical monitoring relief as essentially injunctive.[25] The courts that recognize medical monitoring are further split regarding the requirement of a manifest physical injury.

Many American jurisdictions allow medical monitoring recovery as a component of damages only when a plaintiff has suffered a "manifest physical injury."[26] But state law may differ on what qualifies as a manifest physical injury. A line of cases involving allegations of cellular and subcellular or "mitochondrial" injury demonstrates this divergence. In these cases, plaintiffs have attempted to satisfy the "present" or "manifest" physical injury requirement by arguing that exposure to a hazardous substance caused them injury in the form of asymptomatic cellular and subcellular changes. Many, but not all, courts have rejected the notion that cellular changes that do not manifest in clinically observable symptoms or disease

---

21. *Id.* at 427.
22. *Id.* at 442 (citations omitted).
23. *See, e.g., Redland Soccer Club, Inc. v. Dep't of Army,* 696 A.2d 137 (Pa. 1997).
24. *See, e.g., Ayers v. Jackson,* 525 A.2d 287 (N.J. 1987).
25. *See, e.g., Friends for All Children,* 746 F.2d 816.
26. *See supra* note 18.

can constitute physical injuries that would entitle plaintiffs to monitoring relief.[27] For example, the court in *In re Rezulin Products Liability Litigation* concluded that such claims presented "problems of proof and resource allocation" and that "any recovery would be a windfall" if based on claims for injuries that do not produce any disease or clinically observable injuries.[28] Similarly, in rejecting a claim based on alleged exposure to radioactive material and brought under the federal Price-Anderson Atomic Energy Act,[29] the Ninth Circuit reasoned as follows:

> [N]ot every alteration of the body is an injury. Thinking causes synapses to fire and the brain to experience tiny electric shocks; fear stimulates the production of chemicals associated with the fight-or-flight response. All life is change, but all change is not injurious. Adopting plaintiffs' interpretation of bodily injury would render the term surplusage, as every exposure to radiation would perforce cause injury.[30]

The variances in state law produced by the lack of uniform approach to this issue further exacerbate the difficulties in certifying nationwide monitoring classes.

Beyond variances involving the manifest physical injury requirement, the elements of a medical monitoring claim can vary by state in those jurisdictions where

---

27. For example, in *In re Rezulin Products Liability Litigation*, Judge Kaplan concluded that subcellular mitochondrial damage allegedly caused by the drug Rezulin was not a manifest physical injury under either Texas or Louisiana law. 361 F. Supp. 2d 268, 273–76 (S.D.N.Y. 2005); *see also Paz v. Brush Engineered Materials, Inc.*, 555 F.3d 383, 398–99 (5th Cir. 2009) ("sub-clinical and sub-cellular changes, which none of the parties dispute," from exposure to beryllium-containing products were not "physical injur[ies]" compensable injuries under Mississippi law (citing *Paz v. Brush Engineered Materials, Inc.*, 949 So. 2d 1 (Miss. 2007))); *Dumontier v. Schlumberger Tech. Corp.*, 543 F.3d 567, 571 (9th Cir. 2008) (alleged subcellular damage), *cert. denied*, ___ U.S. ___, 129 S. Ct. 1329 (2009); *Rainer v. Union Carbide Corp.*, 402 F.3d 608 (6th Cir. 2005) (alleged chromosome damage did not constitute a "present physical injury" under Kentucky law); *Parker v. Wellman*, 230 F. App'x 878, 880–83 (11th Cir. Apr. 18, 2007) (personal injury claims based on beryllium exposure where only "sub-clinical, cellular, or sub-cellular injuries"—unaccompanied by any "identifiable physical disease, illness, or impairing symptoms"—were alleged). *But see Werlein v. U.S.*, where, in case involving exposure to trichloroethylene and other chemicals, court denied defendant's summary judgment, stating:

> Based on the record before it, this Court cannot rule as a matter of law that plaintiffs' alleged injuries are not "real" simply because they are subcellular. The effect of volatile organic compounds on the human body is a subtle, complex matter. It is for the trier of fact, aided by expert testimony, to determine whether plaintiffs have suffered present harm.

746 F. Supp. 887 (D. Minn. 1990), *vacated in part on other grounds*, 793 F. Supp. 898, 901 (D. Minn. 1992).

28. 361 F. Supp. 2d at 275.

29. This Act creates a private right of action for claims for "bodily injury" arising out of a "nuclear incident." 42 U.S.C. §§ 2014(q), (hh).

30. *Dumontier*, 543 F.3d at 570. In this case, the plaintiffs had presented expert evidence that "radiation always 'damage[s] the DNA or other important cellular components.'" *Id.* at 571 (internal quotations and citations omitted). But as demonstrated by the above quotation, the Ninth Circuit rejected the plaintiffs' claims that this subcellular damage—in the absence of "pain or interference with bodily functions"—was a "bodily injury" for purposes of the Price-Anderson Atomic Energy Act. *Id.*

it is recognized in any form.[31] Accordingly, a court facing a nationwide medical monitoring class would have to deal with the myriad variations in the tort laws of the 50 states. This factor alone is often cited as grounds for denying class certification.[32] As the Fifth Circuit recognized in decertifying a nationwide class of tobacco plaintiffs:

> We find it difficult to fathom how common issues could predominate in this case when variations in state law are thoroughly considered. . . . [b]ecause we must apply an individualized choice of law analysis to each plaintiff's claims, the proliferation of disparate factual and legal issues is compounded exponentially . . . . In short, the number of uncommon issues in this humongous class action, with perhaps as many as a million class members, is colossal.[33]

Ultimately, the lack of uniformity among states would appear to rule out a nationwide medical monitoring class.

B. OTHER OBSTACLES TO CERTIFICATION

In those jurisdictions that recognize medical monitoring to detect potential or latent injuries, the named plaintiff faces a potentially difficult task of convincing a judge that the proposed class action satisfies the criteria set out in Federal Rule of Civil Procedure 23(a) or a state counterpart. Even those jurisdictions that have recognized such claims are increasingly hesitant to certify monitoring classes because of the highly individualized and variant circumstances that typically give rise to such a claim.[34] A recent decision of Judge Keenan in the *In re Fosamax* multidistrict litigation explains why such claims are difficult to certify, as discussed further below.[35]

---

31. Generally, however, plaintiffs are required to prove (1) exposure greater than normal (2) to a proven hazardous substance (3) caused by the defendant's negligence, where (4) plaintiff has a significantly increased risk of contracting a serious latent disease as a proximate result of the exposure, (5) a monitoring procedure exists that makes early detection of the disease possible, (6) the monitoring regime is different from that normally recommended in the absence of exposure, and (7) the regime is reasonably necessary according to contemporary scientific principles. *See, e.g.*, *Redland Soccer Club*, 696 A.2d at 145–46.

32. *Castano v. Am. Tobacco Co.*, 84 F.3d 734, 742 & n.15 (5th Cir. 1996).

33. *Id.* at 743 n.15.

34. *See, e.g.*, *Rink v. Cheminova, Inc.*, 203 F.R.D. 648, 660 (M.D. Fla. 2001) (denying certification where pleadings were too vague to support such relief); *Sanders*, 2006 WL 1541033, at *5–6 (striking class allegations and refusing to certify monitoring class because of individualized fact questions unique to each class member); *Wyeth*, 930 So. 2d at 643 (reversing certification of monitoring class of plaintiffs who took hormone replacement therapy because individual issues, including differences in ingestion, time periods of exposure, and levels of awareness of existing studies, precluded finding of predominance); *Guillory v. Am. Tobacco Co.*, No. 97C8641, 2001 WL 290603, at *5–9 (N.D. Ill. Mar. 20, 2001) (denying certification of monitoring claims on multiple bases, including the lack of typicality, predomination of individual exposure and causation issues, and manageability problems with so many particularized claims).

35. *In re Fosamax* involved a suit against Merck & Co., Inc. brought by plaintiffs who took Fosamax, a prescription drug for treating osteoporosis and other bone disorders. *In re Fosamax*, 248 F.R.D. at 390. The *Fosamax* plaintiffs claimed that the drug caused them to either develop a condition known as osteonecrosis

1. Class Definition Problems[36]

At the outset, medical monitoring plaintiffs may face difficulties in crafting a proper class definition. For instance, in *In re Fosamax*, the proposed class definitions did not (1) set specific dosage or duration limitations on class membership; (2) attempt to screen out persons with unique risk factors for the alleged condition, ONJ;[37] or (3) specify the duration of the proposed monitoring program.[38] The court recognized that even if the plaintiffs had attempted a more narrow class definition, "[s]everal decisions denying class certification in pharmaceutical products liability and medical monitoring cases have found that class membership is not feasibly ascertainable where it hinges on myriad medical factors individual to each class member."[39] Courts also recognize that medical monitoring classes can be overly broad and reject certification for this reason.[40]

Efforts to encompass every possible class member also often lead to a class definition that is too vague and indefinite to allow a ready determination of class

---

of the jaw (ONJ) or to suffer a considerably increased risk of developing the condition. The putative class representatives sought to have Merck establish and fund a medical monitoring regimen to detect ONJ under Federal Rule of Civil Procedure 23(b)(3). *Id.* They asked Judge Keenan to certify three statewide classes of all current and former Fosamax users who had not yet been diagnosed with ONJ. *Id.* The court denied their bid for certification, citing a number of different failures to satisfy the class action requirements, as explained above.

36. For an additional discussion of the class definition requirement, *see* Chapter 3.A, "Class Definition."

37. *Id.*

38. *Fosamax*, 248 F.R.D. at 397.

39. *Id.*; *see id.* at 396 ("Lower courts almost unanimously have rejected class certification in pharmaceutical products liability actions . . . .").

40. *See, e.g., Lockheed Martin Corp. v. Superior Court*, 63 P.3d 913 (Cal. 2003), where the California Supreme Court rejected class certification of a proposed medical monitoring class of people exposed to contaminated groundwater beneath the city of Redlands, California. The class was defined as persons who had been exposed "at levels at or in excess of the dose equivalent of the M.C.L. (Maximum Contaminant Level), or in excess of the safe dose where there is no MCL" "for some part of a day, for greater than 50% of a year, for one or more years from 1955 to the present" within specified geographical boundaries. *Id.* at 920, 921. The California Supreme Court found this definition overly broad:

> As defendants emphasize, that all plaintiffs exposed to Redlands water received identical *dosages* of any toxic chemicals it contained is unlikely. On the one hand, duration of exposure to polluted water will vary among class members, as the class would include numerous people who lived in Redlands for a relatively short period of time during the more than 40-year class period. On the other hand, as the Court of Appeal observed, severity of exposure among class members may vary according to the amount of water they used.
>
> Examination of the instant record reveals that plaintiffs have not provided substantial evidence that they are in a position to resolve possible dosage issues with common proof. Each class member's actual toxic dosage would remain relevant to some degree even if plaintiffs' "minimum dosage" liability theory ultimately were to prove viable.

Id. at 1109.

membership.[41] For example, in *In re Paxil Litigation*,[42] the plaintiffs sought to certify various subclasses (including a medical monitoring subclass) of persons who had used the antidepressant medication Paxil and who had suffered "severe" withdrawal symptoms. No definition was given for what constituted "severe" symptoms. The district court elaborated on the many problems caused by such a vague definition:

> With the possible exception of the proffered class representatives, the putative class members can neither be identified nor its total size estimated.
>
> This inability to ascertain which particular plaintiffs belong in the class gives rise to several problems. For example, it makes it difficult for the Court to determine whether requirements such as numerosity and typicality are met.
>
> Due process concerns abound as well. Since many Paxil users cannot know if they will be part of the class at this time, the Court doubts that those users can be provided notice adequate to allow them to make an informed decision whether to opt out.
>
> Certifying the Plaintiffs in the manner proposed by their counsel might also hamper settlement efforts. As vaguely defined, the class size may include only a handful of individuals, or possibly, many thousands of persons. . . .
>
> As an initial matter then, certification must fail because Plaintiffs have not met their burden of defining proper classes for the Court's consideration.[43]

In short, vague and indefinite class definitions pose questions about each individual plaintiff's circumstances that cannot be determined on a classwide basis. And when a class definition requires a mini-trial or administrative burden to determine each person's class membership, class certification is generally inappropriate.[44] *In re Paxil Litigation* also demonstrates that an imprecise class definition

---

41. *See, e.g., Rink*, 203 F.R.D. 648. Here, the plaintiffs sought to certify a medical monitoring subclass of all individuals within a certain geographic area in Florida "who were exposed to malathion-based insecticide during the Medfly Eradication Program from June 1997 through October 1998." *Id.* at 659. The court found that the definition was overly broad and said that the plaintiffs had

> failed to define the proposed subclass with sufficient precision or specificity to allow for determination of its members. . . . [A]bsent further limiting language, it is conceivable that every citizen present in the geographic area during the spraying period might claim to be a part of the class having been "exposed" to the spraying in one fashion or another.

Id. The court also noted that "[s]uch a vague class definition portends significant manageability problems for the court." *Id.* at 660.

42. 212 F.R.D. 539 (C.D. Cal. 2003).

43. *Id.* at 545–46 (citations omitted).

44. *See, e.g., Middleton v. Arledge*, No. CIV.A. 3:06-CV-303WH, 2008 WL 906525, *9–10 (S.D. Miss. Mar. 31, 2008) (class certification denied in part because of the administrative burden created by a factual and legal review of each purported class member's claims to determine class membership); *In re Vioxx Prods.*

creates difficulties in determining whether the other Rule 23(a) requirements are met as well. Finally, class definition difficulties are not limited to situations where terms and phrases are vague and not objectively defined.

A definition that employs objective criteria may end up defining a monitoring class that depends upon a determination of the merits of the plaintiffs' suit. This situation is sometimes called a "fail-safe class"[45] because it requires a resolution of the ultimate liability issue in favor of the plaintiffs—but if the judgment is in favor of the defendants, the class will be found never to have existed. When the class definition depends upon a conclusion of liability, the trial court has no way of determining whether a given person is a member of the class until liability is decided. Further, if the defendant is found liable, the litigation comes to an end. But if the defendant is not liable, that finding eradicates the class and prevents the proposed class members from being bound by the judgment. It also means that the class was certified improperly because the class did not in fact exist.[46]

2. The Intertwined Dilemmas of Standing, Adequate Representation, and Res Judicata

In medical monitoring cases, plaintiffs with existing injuries sometimes pursue monitoring relief on behalf of others without existing injuries on the theory that these exposure-only class members will very likely develop some future injury. Several difficulties flow from this particular scenario.

Standing requires that a plaintiff has suffered an "injury in fact," meaning that there is a concrete, particularized, and actual or imminent invasion of a legally

---

Liab. Litig., No. MDL 1657, 2008 WL 4681368, *10 (E.D. La. Oct. 21, 2008); *Perez v. Metabolife Int'l, Inc.*, 218 F.R.D. 262, 269 (S.D. Fla. 2003) ("A court should deny class certification where the . . . number of individualized determinations required to determine class membership becomes too administratively difficult."); *Fisher v. Ciba Specialty Chems. Corp.*, 238 F.R.D. 273, 301 (S.D. Ala. 2006) ("A court should deny class certification . . . where the number of individualized determinations required to determine class membership becomes too administratively difficult." (citations omitted)); *Crosby v. Soc. Sec. Admin.*, 796 F. 2d 576, 580 (1st Cir. 1986) (certification improper because class members were "impossible to identify prior to individualized fact-finding and litigation").

45. *See, e.g., Intratex Gas Co. v. Beeson*, 22 S.W.3d 398, 408 (Tex. 2000).

46. *See, e.g., In re Paxil Litig.*, 212 F.R.D. at 545 ("A second problem with the Plaintiffs' class certification proposal is that it defines classes in a manner making the actual composition only determinable at the conclusion of all proceedings."); *Ostler v. Level 3 Commc'ns, Inc.*, No. IP 00-0718-C H/K, 2002 WL 31040337 (S.D. Ind. Aug. 27, 2002) ("Where such a decision on the merits of a person's claim is needed to determine whether a person is a member of a class, the proposed class action is unmanageable virtually by definition."); *Nudell v. Burlington N. Santa Fe Ry. Co.*, No. A3-01-41, 2002 WL 1543725 (D.N.D. July 11, 2002) ("[E]ven accepting that the definition might not lead to the classic failsafe class, it still too closely identifies the class definition with a merits determination, in that class membership depends on resolution of many predicate factual issues related at least in part, to the ultimate questions in the case. . . . Obviously, notice to class members is a virtual impossibility under these circumstances, since they cannot be identified."); *Adashunas v. Negley*, 626 F.2d 600, 604 (7th Cir. 1980); *Ind. State Employees Ass'n v. Ind. State Highway Comm'n*, 78 F.R.D. 724, 725 (S.D. Ind. 1978); *Dunn v. Midwest Buslines, Inc.*, 94 F.R.D. 170, 172 (E.D. Ark. 1982).

protected interest.[47] In the context of a class action, the U.S. Supreme Court has made clear that named plaintiffs who represent a putative class "must allege and show that they personally have been injured, not that injury has been suffered by other, unidentified members of the class to which they belong and which they purport to represent."[48] If the named plaintiff lacks standing, she may not seek relief on behalf of herself or any other member of the class.[49]

Because the plaintiff must allege the same injury as the putative class members, a plaintiff who alleges a manifest physical injury arguably lacks standing to assert a medical monitoring claim on behalf of those who only suffer an alleged increased risk of experiencing adverse health conditions in the future. The issues implicated by standing can also impact the adequacy of class representatives in medical monitoring cases. In some cases, a named plaintiff suffering from a present physical injury might not vigorously pursue a medical monitoring regime on behalf of a class because the plaintiff needs treatment, not monitoring.[50] In fact, in *Amchem Products, Inc. v. Windsor*, the Supreme Court found a disabling conflict of interests between members of a proposed settlement class who had manifesting injuries—who would presumably want payments for their medical expenses presently—with the "future injury" claimants who would presumably prefer to maintain funds to pay their bills if the injuries manifest.[51] However, if a plaintiff alleges that the defendant's product causes an array of health problems, the plaintiff suffering one condition arguably still has an incentive to seek monitoring for other conditions that have yet to develop.[52]

Finally, proposing such a class has possible adverse ramifications on any future injury claims of the monitoring claimants.[53] "Res judicata may preclude [exposure only] class members from later litigating personal injury claims that could have been brought in the earlier action."[54] Claim preclusion concerns also arise when a plaintiff only asserts claims based on a potential future injury. The U.S. District Court for the Southern District of Illinois described a major concern implicated when a plaintiff seeks purely injunctive relief in the form of a court-supervised

---

47. *See Lujan v. Defenders of Wildlife*, 504 U.S. 555, 560 (1992); *see also Lewis v. Casey*, 518 U.S. 343, 349 (1996).

48. *Simon v. E. Ky. Welfare Rights Org.*, 426 U.S. 26, 40 n.20 (1976) (internal quotations and citation omitted).

49. *O'Shea v. Littleton*, 414 U.S. 488, 494–95 (1974).

50. *See, e.g., Leib*, 2008 U.S. Dist. LEXIS 102847, at *28 ("It is true that a plaintiff may be an inadequate class representative if her interest in immediate medical treatment competes with other class members' interest in medical monitoring for future problems.").

51. 521 U.S. at 623–26 (holding that an inherent intraclass conflict between the actual-injury plaintiffs and the future-injury plaintiffs precluded certification).

52. *See Leib*, 2008 U.S. Dist. LEXIS 102847, at *29.

53. *See In re Fosamax*, 248 F.R.D. at 401.

54. *Id.* (citation omitted).

medical monitoring fund: "A judgment on that claim would not prevent a class member from later bringing a personal injury lawsuit seeking damages, although the class member may be bound by issues actually determined in the class action and may be unable to recover for services received from the medical monitoring fund."[55]

3. Typicality, Predominance, and Superiority

In *Fosamax*, Judge Keenan determined that (1) the class representatives did not satisfy the typicality requirement of Rule 23(a); (2) individual questions of fact and law predominated over common ones; and (3) class treatment of the monitoring claims would not be a superior means of adjudicating them.[56] Regarding typicality, he stressed that "almost every element of a medical monitoring claim will require highly individualized proof of each class members' medical condition and the circumstances of their use of Fosamax."[57] The court further noted that a single element of medical monitoring claims, proving the defendant's negligence, could foreclose certification.[58]

Other elements of a monitoring claim may also require individual determinations, particularly the proximate cause inquiry—i.e., ascertaining whether a person's risk of contracting a serious latent disease has been significantly increased. Indeed, determining an individual's risk is often keyed to individual factors of level of exposure, duration of exposure, and individual characteristics including other risk factors for contracting the disease. In those circumstances, a plaintiff's risk of contracting a serious latent disease cannot be determined on a classwide basis.[59] Numerous courts have refused to certify medical monitoring claims based on their determinations that the causation inquiry necessary to determine each plaintiff's eligibility to receive such tests is too inherently individual to be tried in the aggregate.[60]

---

55. *Leib*, 2008 U.S. Dist. LEXIS 102847, at *27–28.

56. 248 F.R.D. at 397. Judge Keenan noted that Rule 23(a)'s numerosity and commonality requirements are relatively easy to satisfy. *Id*. at 398.

57. *Id*. at 399.

58. *Id*. at 399 n.10 ("Other courts in pharmaceutical products liability cases have found that the individual issues enmeshed in proving negligence weighs heavily against certification.").

59. *See id*. at 399–400 ("A plaintiff cannot prevail by proving that, in general, Fosamax could cause a significant increase in the risk of ONJ in some users. . . . A court could not decide whether any class member's ingestion of Fosamax caused him or her to suffer a significant increase in the risk of ONJ without considering . . . individual factors."); *Barnes*, 161 F.3d at 145 ("[P]laintiffs cannot prove causation by merely showing that smoking cigarettes causes cancer and other diseases," but "must demonstrate that defendants' [acts] caused each individual plaintiff to have a significantly increased risk of contracting serious latent diseases thereby demonstrating the need for medical monitoring.").

60. *See, e.g., In re St. Jude (Silzone)*, 425 F.3d at 1122–23 (medical monitoring inappropriate for class certification because determination as to whether class members require diagnostic tests depends on individualized inquiry including plaintiff's medical history, among other factors); *Ball*, 385 F.3d at 727–28 (denial of class certification was not abuse of discretion because medical monitoring claims raised extensive

Because of these types of individualized inquiries, predominance represents one of the most difficult hurdles for medical monitoring claims. For example, in the *Fosamax* decision, Judge Keenan concluded that the individualized questions central to whether class members were entitled to recovery predominated over any common questions.[61] He also noted that class members might be subject to individual defenses, such as comparative negligence and assumption of risk, that would require individualized assessments of each plaintiff's knowledge of Fosamax and its risks at the time he or she took it.[62] Such particularized factual determinations required plaintiff-by-plaintiff adjudication, precluding class certification.[63]

Where predominant individual issues would "do little to increase the efficiency of the litigation," class certification is inappropriate.[64] But efficiency gains *can* be captured through consolidation of medical monitoring cases for pretrial proceedings.[65]

For similar reasons, class treatment of medical monitoring claims often fail the superiority requirement of Rule 23(b)(3) where it applies.[66] As a prerequisite for a medical monitoring program in those states acknowledging it, the plaintiffs must demonstrate that the monitoring regime is different from that which would be recommended in the absence of exposure.[67] A class representative would therefore need to demonstrate that class members would be better served by participating in a mass program than by receiving individualized treatment by a physician of their own choosing. Put another way, the class proponents must prove that the class members will prefer the proposed monitoring program to one designed specifically for each member.[68] In some cases, "[c]lass members may wish to seek a monitoring program that is tailored, under the advice of their own physicians, to their individ-

---

individual issues); *Barnes*, 161 F.3d at 146 (class certification is inappropriate for a medical monitoring claim, as it would require consideration of facts and circumstances unique to each person); *Zehel-Miller v. Astrazeneca Pharms., LP*, 223 F.R.D. 659, 664 (M.D. Fla. 2004) (same); *Perez*, 218 F.R.D. at 266 (same); *In re Baycol Prods. Litig.*, 218 F.R.D. 197, 211–13 (D. Minn. 2003) (same); *In re Rezulin Prods. Liab. Litig.*, 210 F.R.D. 61, 73 (S.D.N.Y. 2002).

61. *In re Fosamax*, 248 F.R.D. at 401.

62. *Id.* at 401–02.

63. *Id.*

64. *In re St. Jude Med. Inc.*, 522 F.3d at 841.

65. *See In re Fosamax*, 248 F.R.D. at 404.

66. As noted, medical monitoring relief is characterized differently in different jurisdictions. In those states that consider monitoring to be injunctive, certification is typically sought under Rule 23(b)(2). *See* Chapter 14, "The Special Role of 23(b)(2) Classes." Conversely, where monitoring claims are considered to be damage claims, the proposed class must satisfy Rule 23(b)(3), which requires findings of predominance and superiority. *See* Chapter 3.E, "Predominance and Superiority."

67. *See In re Prempro*, 230 F.R.D. at 571 (in denying nationwide medical monitoring class action, court described a "key element[ ] generally required by states recognizing medical monitoring relief" as being that "a monitoring procedure exists that makes early detection of disease possible, and that this procedure is different from the health monitoring normally recommended in the absence of exposure.").

68. *See In re Fosamax*, 248 F.R.D. at 402.

ual preferences and unique medical histories."[69] Further, in pursuing their claims individually, plaintiffs may be able to seek damages for medical expenses already incurred and mental distress.[70] On the other hand, certifying a monitoring class can raise many tough issues, such as the feasibility of providing notice to everyone in the class and the res judicata ramifications for those who fail to opt out.

Medical monitoring plaintiffs may also run into related practical problems. What if there is no specific test that will with precision detect or predict a disease before it becomes apparent to the patient's health care provider? Monitoring should lead to a treatment that, if instituted, would improve health care outcomes. But if these tests and treatments are not reliable or readily available, monitoring may ultimately produce no benefit. And how is the benefit to be measured? The value of medical tests once accepted as standard for early detection of disease, such as mammograms, may be questioned as medical technology evolves and epidemiological studies challenge their usefulness. In some cases, the costs of establishing who falls into the monitoring class could exceed the costs of the actual monitoring.

Finally, leaving the development of medical programs for "a more cautious case-by-case approach" that is supported by scientific authority and focused on the particular factual circumstances of the individual plaintiffs may be the best method for resolving the claims.[71]

III. Medical Monitoring Classes That Have Been Certified

The courts that have considered certification of monitoring classes have used different provisions of Rule 23(b) to support their decisions. For example, in *In re Telectronics Pacing Systems, Inc.*,[72] the court, under both Rule 23(b)(1)(A) and (b)(3), certified a class of patients who had pacemakers containing an allegedly defective lead. After a number of patients with implanted pacemakers suffered failure of the devices due to lead fracture, the pacemaker manufacturer took steps to control the situation. The manufacturer recalled all unimplanted leads. Then, with FDA approval, the manufacturer sent a "Dear Doctor" letter advising physicians

---

69. *Id.*; *see also Leib*, 2008 U.S. Dist. LEXIS 102847, at *37:

[P]roposed class members are likely to want to consult with their own physicians about the risks and benefits of diagnostic tests to be performed on them in light of their own health backgrounds instead of leaving it to the class representatives and the Court to make those medical decisions for them.

70. *See In re Fosamax*, 248 F.R.D. at 402.

71. *See id.*; *see also In re Propulsid Prods. Liab. Litig.*, 208 F.R.D. 133, 147 (E.D. La. 2002) (in denying class certification of a medical monitoring program for users of the drug Propulsid, Judge Fallon stated, "This raises the issue of the role of the courts in such an instance. Stated succinctly, the question is whether the courts should lead the scientific community in an area of medical science."); *In re Baycol*, 218 F.R.D. at 212.

72. 172 F.R.D. 271 (S.D. Ohio 1997).

that their patients who had pacemakers should be given fluoroscopic screening every six months to detect lead fractures before they could cause injury.[73] The manufacturer agreed to pay the reasonable, unreimbursed expenses for the screenings and any lead extraction (consistent with certain patient management guidelines).[74] The district court concluded that the proposed class was "an ideal candidate" for certification under Rule 23(b)(1)(A) because "separate adjudications would impair [the defendant's] ability to pursue a single, uniform medical monitoring program" and "[a]ny judicially imposed modification of th[e] program would affect all class members" in the same way.[75] The court also certified the monitoring class[76] under Rule 23(b)(3) based on its determination that the primary defense to the class claims—that the FDA-approved monitoring program was amply sufficient to detect and prevent injuries—was common to all class members and that the individual claims were sufficiently small that it would be difficult for class members to pursue individual actions.[77] The court rejected the defendant's claim that the class would be unmanageable in light of state law variations because the defendant had already "acknowledge[d] that all implantees require medical monitoring" and the remaining issues as to whether the existing program was adequate and should be continued surmounted any problems that might be raised by such variations.[78]

Likewise, in *Olden v. LaFarge Corp.*, the Sixth Circuit affirmed a class of monitoring plaintiffs under both Rule 23(b)(2) and (b)(3) where 3,600 homeowners alleged personal injuries and property damages stemming from the release of toxins from a large cement plant.[79] The court of appeals concluded that the thrust of the plaintiffs' claims for medical monitoring was proving "[w]hether the defendant's negligence caused *some* increased health risk and . . . whether it tended to cause the class minor medical issues"—determinations that could likely be made for the entire class.[80] As a result, the court concluded that individual damage determinations would not predominate over common allegations of harm.[81] With respect to the (b)(2) class, the court concluded that the plaintiffs were legitimately seeking

---

73. *Id.* at 277.

74. *Id.*

75. *Id.* at 284–85 (citing *Boggs v. Divested Atomic Corp.*, 141 F.R.D. 58, 67 (S.D. Ohio 1991)).

76. In observing that some states permit monitoring claims in the absence of a present physical injury, while others do not have such a requirement, *see supra* note 18, the court certified two monitoring subclasses—collecting together in one subclass the claimants from states that permit such claims and another from those states that do not allow the claims. *Id.* at 287.

77. *Id.* at 286–87.

78. *Id.* at 287.

79. 383 F.3d 495, 496 (6th Cir. 2004).

80. *Id.* at 508.

81. *Id.*

an injunction against further pollution, thus supporting class treatment under this provision as well.[82]

Other courts have "divided over whether Rule 23(b)(2) or Rule 23(b)(3) is the appropriate vehicle for certifying a mass tort class for medical monitoring."[83] The key lies in determining whether damages are the primary type of relief sought.[84] Because courts have been reluctant to certify 23(b)(3) claims, class proponents may be more inclined to frame their claims under 23(b)(2) as predominately seeking a court-supervised monitoring program.[85]

Indeed, plaintiffs have had their most consistent success in obtaining class certification when they seek a court-administered fund and the fund is categorized as injunctive relief.[86] For example, the U.S. District Court for the Eastern District of Pennsylvania conditionally certified a medical monitoring class of Fen-Phen users seeking a medical monitoring and research fund under Rule 23(b)(2) in *In re Diet Drugs Products Liability Litigation*.[87] However, the district court recognized that the defendant raised issues such as affirmative defenses that "should be further explored."[88] It concluded that if these issues "destroy[ed] cohesion or deprive[d] the parties of their constitutional right to due process, then the court [would] exclude parts of the class or decertify the class in its entirety accordingly."[89]

Likewise, in *Gates v. Rohm & Haas Co.*,[90] the class members sought both personal injury and other relief based on exposure to pollutants in their drinking water. The court certified the medical monitoring class for settlement purposes because it sought relief based solely on the increased risk of injury as a result of the exposure.[91] Any individual differences in medical histories, lifestyles, and property uses were determined not to affect causation analysis for purposes of liability because many of the claims were based on the allegation that a minimum level of exposure triggered a heightened risk of cancer.[92]

In contrast, the U.S. District Court for the Eastern District of Louisiana in *In re Propulsid Products Liability Litigation* refused to certify a claim seeking a court-supervised medical monitoring program under Rule 23(b)(2) after determining

82. *Id.* at 510–11.

83. 32-22P JAMES WM. MOORE, MOORE'S FEDERAL PRACTICE—CIVIL 22.74 Medical Monitoring Class Actions (3d ed. 2009) (citations omitted).

84. *See id.; Barnes*, 161 F.3d at 142–44.

85. *See Barnes*, 161 F.3d at 132.

86. *See id.*

87. No. 98-20626, 1999 U.S. Dist. LEXIS 13228 (E.D. Pa. Aug. 26, 1999).

88. *Id.* at *32.

89. *Id.* at *36.

90. 248 F.R.D. 434 (E.D. Pa. 2008).

91. *Id.* at 443.

92. *Id.*

that the plaintiff's monetary claims predominated.[93] *In re Propulsid* demonstrates that courts will scrutinize plaintiffs' attempts to characterize the relief sought as injunctive in an attempt to get around Rule 23(b)(3)'s requirements.

Even under Rule 23(b)(2), plaintiffs must still meet Rule 23(a)'s stringent requirements. And Rule 23(b)(2) still requires the medical monitoring class to be "cohesive."[94] This reality, in combination with courts' inclination to characterize claims for monitoring relief as seeking personal injury damages, suggests that medical monitoring claims will continue to be difficult at best to certify for class treatment. Even under Rule 23(b)(2), plaintiffs cannot escape the fact that medical monitoring claims on the whole "present too many individual questions of fact particular to each class member's claim."[95]

IV. Conclusion

This chapter has discussed a few of the many reasons that singly or collectively have caused courts to be reluctant to certify medical monitoring claims. For the reasons explained above, medical monitoring classes certainly face a host of obstacles in obtaining certification. The fact that only a minority of states currently recognize claims for medical monitoring in the absence of a physical injury means that nationwide classes will almost undoubtedly fail. And even in those states that do afford this relief, the courts have increasingly refused to certify medical monitoring claims for class treatment because of the highly individualized issues inherent in proving them. Courts that have certified these claims have credited the common issue of whether the exposure has led to an increased risk of harm as paramount to any individualized issues of damages from particularized harm.

---

93. 208 F.R.D. at 145. In addition to a court-supervised trust fund to finance a medical monitoring program, the plaintiff sought restitution of all money acquired from the sale of the drug to class members, compensatory and punitive damages, pre- and post-judgment interest, costs, and attorney fees. *Id.* at 144. The *Propulsid* court distinguished *In re Diet Drugs* on the grounds that the federal government had already recommended various forms of medical monitoring there. *Id.* at 146. It also criticized that court's decision to certify a class before the plaintiffs had even briefed the issue of varying state law. *Id.* at 147.

94. *See Barnes*, 161 F.3d at 143 (affirming decertification of a class of cigarette smokers seeking medical monitoring under Rule 23(b)(2) and recognizing that a (b)(2) class must be cohesive; *see also In re Diet Drugs*, 1999 U.S. Dist. LEXIS 13228, at *25.

95. *In re Fosamax*, 248 F.R.D. at 391.

BANKRUPTCY AND CLASS ACTIONS

VAN A. CATES

I. Bankruptcy Jurisdiction in General

Section 1334(b) of Title 28 of the United States Code provides that "the district courts shall have original but not exclusive jurisdiction of all civil proceedings arising under title 11 or arising in or related to cases under title 11."[1] Pursuant to 28 U.S.C. § 157(a), most, if not all, district courts refer "any or all proceedings arising under title 11 or arising in or related to a case under title 11 . . . to the bankruptcy judges for the district."[2]

If the bankruptcy court has jurisdiction under 28 U.S.C. § 1334, the next issue is whether the suit is a "core" or "non-core" proceeding. A nonexclusive list of core proceedings is set forth in 28 U.S.C. § 157(b)(2) and includes, among other things, matters concerning the administration of the estate and counterclaims by the estate against persons filing claims against the estate.[3] Generally, core matters include (1) those matters "arising under" Title 11, that is, those asserting rights created by the Bankruptcy Code itself, and (2) those matters "arising in" a bankruptcy case.[4] Although courts have not precisely defined what matters fall within the "arising under" and "arising in" jurisdiction, courts have made it clear that proceedings involving substantive bankruptcy rights and the integrity of the bankruptcy courts fall within this core jurisdiction.[5] As stated by the bankruptcy court for the Southern District of Texas in *In re Cano*:

---

1. 28 U.S.C. § 1334(b).

2. 28 U.S.C. § 157(a); *see also, e.g., In re Cano*, 410 B.R. 506, 545 (Bankr. S.D. Tex. 2009) (the Southern District of Texas's General Order of Reference refers all matters over which the district court has bankruptcy jurisdiction to the bankruptcy judges, and the bankruptcy judges operate as a unit of the district court with authority to adjudicate all matters that fall within the district's bankruptcy jurisdiction).

3. 28 U.S.C. § 157(b)(2).

4. *See id.; see also In re Nat'l E. Corp.*, 391 B.R. 663, 668–69 (Bankr. D. Conn. 2008).

5. *In re Cano*, 410 B.R. at 545.

Generally, a matter arises under title 11 if it, "by its nature, could arise only in the context of a bankruptcy case." *Matter of Wood*, 825 F.2d at 97 [(5th Cir. Miss. Aug. 26, 1987)] ("If the proceeding is one that would arise only in bankruptcy, it is also a core proceeding . . ."); *Geruschat v. Ernst & Young LLP* (*In re Seven Fields Dev. Corp.*), 505 F.3d 237, 260 (3d Cir. 2007) ("[C]laims that 'arise in' a bankruptcy case are claims that by their nature, not their particular factual circumstances, could only arise in the context of a bankruptcy case.") (quoting *Stoe v. Flaherty*, 436 F.3d 209, 218 (3rd Cir. 2006)); *In re Southmark*, 163 F.3d at 930. [(5th Cir. Tex. Jan. 11, 1999)][6]

For example, bankruptcy courts have subject matter jurisdiction to enforce court orders and to protect important debtor rights created by the Bankruptcy Code pursuant to the "arising in" and "arising under" jurisdictional grants under 28 U.S.C. § 1334.[7]

Non-core matters are those "related to" the debtor's bankruptcy case, that is, those whose outcome could conceivably affect the bankruptcy estate.[8] Most courts view the "related to" standard expansively by requiring only that the outcome of the proceeding "could conceivably have any effect" on the bankruptcy estate.[9] Certainty or likelihood that the suit will have an effect on the bankruptcy estate is not required.[10] As stated by the District Court judge in *Bank United v. Manley*:

> The conceivable limits of bankruptcy jurisdiction, therefore, must embrace matters beyond those simply affecting the estate. Proceedings affecting a debtor's rights, liabilities, options, or freedom of action are also valid proceedings cognizable by bankruptcy courts when they arise under the Bankruptcy Code. To contend otherwise strips the debtor of certain authorized (and perhaps implied) causes of action, and eliminates specific grants of jurisdiction.[11]

Other courts require a *direct* effect upon either the assets of the estate or their distribution to creditors, and state that any overlap between the bankrupt's affairs and another dispute is insufficient to provide jurisdiction unless its resolution also affects the bankruptcy estate or the allocation of its assets among creditors.[12] A bankruptcy judge may hear a non-core proceeding and make proposed findings of

---

6. *Id.*

7. *Id.* at 546.

8. *In re Nat'l E. Corp.*, 391 B.R. at 669.

9. *See In re G.S.F. Corp.*, 938 F.2d 1467, 1475 (1st Cir. 1991); *Pacor, Inc. v. Higgins*, 743 F.2d 984, 994 (3d Cir. 1984); *A.H. Robbins Co. v. Piccinin*, 788 F.2d 994, 1002 n.11 (4th Cir. 1986); *Matter of Wood*, 825 F.2d 90, 93 (5th Cir. 1987); *Robinson v. Mich. Consol. Gas Co.*, 918 F.2d 579, 583–84 (6th Cir. 1990); *In re Dogpatch U.S.A., Inc.*, 810 F.2d 782, 786 (8th Cir. 1987); *In re Fietz*, 852 F.2d 455, 457 (9th Cir. 1988); *In re Gardner*, 913 F.2d 1515, 1518 (10th Cir. 1990); *In re Lemco Gypsum, Inc.*, 910 F.2d 784, 788 (11th Cir. 1990).

10. *In re Cannon*, 196 F.3d 579, 858 (5th Cir. 1999).

11. 273 B.R. 229, 243 (N.D. Ala. 2001).

12. *Home Ins. Co. v. Cooper & Cooper, Ltd.*, 889 F.2d 746, 749 (7th Cir. 1989).

fact and conclusions of law to the district court, but only the district court judge may enter a final order or judgment.[13]

A bankruptcy judge's determination of whether a proceeding is core or non-core does not affect the bankruptcy court's power to hear the case. Rather, it affects the form of the bankruptcy court's disposition, that is, whether it is final and appealable to the district court, or a report and recommendation to be reviewed by the district court.[14]

II. Bankruptcy Jurisdiction for Class Actions in Particular

Rule 7023 of the Federal Rules of Bankruptcy Procedure (the Bankruptcy Rules) incorporates Rule 23 of the Federal Rules of Civil Procedure in bankruptcy court adversary proceedings, but rules of procedure cannot expand the subject matter jurisdiction of the bankruptcy courts over class actions.[15] As explained below, there is a split in authority as to the extent to which bankruptcy courts can exercise jurisdiction over class action litigation.

Section 1334(e)(1) of Title 28 provides that the district court (and the bankruptcy court for the district) in which a case under Title 11 is commenced or pending shall have exclusive jurisdiction of all property of the estate "wherever located."[16] While there appears to be a split of authority as to the application of 28 U.S.C. § 1334(e)(1) to class actions, it has been stated that there is no doubt that a bankruptcy court has authority over class claims filed against a single debtor.[17] Some courts hold that bankruptcy courts can only exercise jurisdiction over class members if their bankruptcy petitions were filed in the same specific district as that of the named plaintiff.[18] These courts reason that since "property of the estate" includes causes of action, the legal claims that underlie the class complaint

---

13. 28 U.S.C. § 157(c)(1); *see also In re Mullarkey*, 536 F.3d 215, 221 (3d. Cir. 2008).

14. *In re Mullarkey*, 536 F.3d at 222.

15. *Bank United*, 273 B.R. at 250.

16. 28 U.S.C. § 1334(e)(1).

17. *In re Cano*, 410 B.R. at 550 (citing *In re Am. Reserve Corp.*, 840 F.2d 487 (7th Cir. 1988); *Birting Fisheries, Inc. v. Lane* (*In re Birting Fisheries, Inc.*), 92 F.3d 939 (9th Cir. 1996); *In re Charter Co.*, 876 F.2d 866 (11th Cir. 1989); *Reid v. White Motor Corp.*, 886 F.2d 1462 (6th Cir. 1989); *In re Craft*, 321 B.R. 189 (Bankr. N.D. Tex. 2005)).

18. *Cline v. First Nationwide Mortgage Corp.* (*In re Cline*), 282 B.R. 686, 696 (W.D. Wash. 2002) (no jurisdiction exists over members of proposed class whose bankruptcy "homes" are outside the representative plaintiff's district); *In re Williams*, 244 B.R. 858, 866–68 (S.D. Ga. 2000) (dismissing claims of putative class members who filed their bankruptcy petitions outside the Southern District of Georgia while allowing class claims of debtors who commenced their bankruptcy cases within the district to proceed); *In re Beck*, 283 B.R. 163 (Bankr. E.D. Pa. 2002) (Chapter 7 debtor class action on behalf of nationwide debtor class stricken to the extent that the debtor sought to recover on behalf of debtors in other districts).

may only be decided by the court that adjudicates the debtor's or class member's bankruptcy case and the court will not exercise jurisdiction over out-of-district class members that are subject to the jurisdiction of other courts.[19] Another set of courts holds that class claims may proceed at least as to bankruptcy cases filed within the state in which the court sits.[20] Yet another set of courts holds that bankruptcy courts have jurisdiction to certify a nationwide class action for violations of the Bankruptcy Code under certain circumstances, despite the fact that such an order will impact bankruptcy cases pending in other states, circuits, and district courts.[21] Among other things, these courts note that the text of certain venue provisions supports the notion that 28 U.S.C. § 1334(e) does not preclude "outside" district courts from exercising original nonexclusive jurisdiction under 28 U.S.C. § 1334(b) over numerous bankruptcy proceedings.[22]

The seminal case allowing class actions in bankruptcy court is *In re American Reserve Corp.*, which held that a creditor may file a class proof of claim against the debtor on behalf of similarly situated creditors.[23] In so holding, the court reasoned that 11 U.S.C. § 501 did not preclude the filing of proofs of claims by the class representative, which is the agent for the missing class members.[24] As for the practical considerations of pursuing class actions in bankruptcy court, the *Reserve* court observed:

> The bankruptcy forum, as a mandatory collective proceeding, serves this purpose without the overlay of the class action. Substantively, the class action permits the aggregation and litigation of many small claims that otherwise would lie dormant. At least in principle, the class action provides compensation that cannot be achieved in any other way; although the costs of litigation may consume much of the benefit, the device still serves a deterrent function by ensuring that wrongdoers bear the costs of their activities.[25]

---

19. *In re Cline*, 282 B.R. at 696.

20. *See, e.g., Coggin v. Sears, Roebuck & Co. (In re Coggin)*, 155 B.R. 934 (Bankr. E.D.N.C. 1993) (class action was certified comprised of Chapter 7 debtors with cases pending in the Eastern and Middle districts of North Carolina).

21. *Bank United*, 273 B.R. at 229 (class claims asserted by Chapter 13 debtor did not have to be pursued separately only in judicial district in which each class member's bankruptcy case was pending (home courts), but could be prosecuted together in the Northern District of Alabama where claims invoked substantive right under the Bankruptcy Code that would potentially affect each debtor or each debtor's estate); *In re Noletto*, 244 B.R. 845 (Bankr. S.D. Ala. 2000) (core nature of the proceedings cannot be changed by the fact that the suit is not connected to bankruptcy cases over which the judges in the district had control).

22. *In re Collett*, 297 B.R. 321, 324 (Bankr. S.D. Ga. 2003); *see also In re Cano*, 410 B.R. at 554–55 ("§ 1334's language is clear. District Courts have subject matter jurisdiction over nationwide class actions, including those brought by debtors.").

23. 840 F.2d 487.

24. *Id.* at 493.

25. *Id.* at 489.

Today, the class action is commonplace in bankruptcy court, from both the creditor standpoint and the debtor-plaintiff standpoint.[26]

III. Venue for Bankruptcy Class Actions

As stated above, 28 U.S.C. § 1334(e) gives district courts exclusive jurisdiction over all property, wherever located, of the debtor as of the commencement of the case and property of the estate.[27] However, control over property of the estate is distinct from determining whether rights in a lawsuit are meritorious.[28] Numerous venue and jurisdiction provisions mandate that a court other than the home court adjudicate suits involving property of the estate.[29] For example, 28 U.S.C. § 1409 mandates that certain adversary proceedings be filed "only in the district court for the district in which the defendant resides."[30] As courts should generally avoid statutory interpretations that render other statutory provisions superfluous,[31] it follows that elevating the exclusive jurisdiction provided in section 1334(e) over venue provisions would render them meaningless and unworkable and should be avoided.[32] Additionally, the removal provisions of 28 U.S.C. § 1452(a)[33] may also trump the exclusive jurisdiction of the bankruptcy courts under section 1334(e) under certain circumstances:

> For example, "A" may file state court lawsuit against "B" in Illinois. If "B" then files for bankruptcy in Texas, the state court lawsuit may be removed to federal court. However, § 1452 requires the lawsuit to be removed to the federal court in Illinois, not the Bankruptcy Court in Texas.[34]

In summary, venue statutes should be consulted to determine the appropriate venue for bankruptcy class actions.

---

26. *See, e.g., In re Beck*, 283 B.R. 163 (Chapter 7 debtor files class action on behalf of nationwide debtor class).

27. 28 U.S.C. § 1334(e).

28. *In re Cano*, 410 B.R. at 553.

29. *Id.*

30. 28 U.S.C. § 1409(b).

31. *In re Noletto*, 244 B.R. at 849.

32. *In re Cano*, 410 B.R. at 553; *see also In re Noletto*, 244 B.R. at 853.

33. 28 U.S.C. § 1452(a) provides, "A party may remove any claim or cause of action in a civil action . . . to the district court for the district where such civil action is pending, if such district court has jurisdiction of such claim or cause of action under section 1334 of this title."

34. *In re Cano*, 410 B.R. at 554.

IV. Bankruptcy Class Action Requirements

Bankruptcy Rule 7023 incorporates Rule 23 of the Federal Rules of Civil Procedure in bankruptcy court adversary proceedings, and Bankruptcy Rule 9014 provides that Bankruptcy Rule 7023 applies to "any stage" in contested matters. It follows that the two-step process outlined in Rule 23 for determining whether class certification is appropriate must be met before a bankruptcy class action is certified and allowed to proceed.[35] First, the bankruptcy court must engage in a "rigorous analysis" to confirm that the four elements of numerosity, commonality, typicality, and adequacy of representation provided in Rule 23(a) are met.[36] Second, assuming the requirements of Rule 23(a) are met, the bankruptcy court must confirm that the action is maintainable by falling within one of the three kinds of actions maintainable under Rule 23(b)(1), (2), or (3). An action is maintainable under Rule 23(b)(1) when there is either a risk of prejudice from separate actions establishing incompatible standards of conduct or the judgment in an individual lawsuit might adversely impact other class members.[37] An action is maintainable under Rule 23(b)(2) when the defendant "has acted or refused to act on grounds generally applicable to the class, thereby making appropriate final injunctive relief or corresponding declaratory relief with respect to the class as a whole."[38] An action is maintainable under Rule 23(b)(3) if questions of law or fact common to the class predominate over questions affecting individual members, and the court decides that a class is superior to other methods available for adjudicating the controversy.[39] In other words, the determination of whether class certification is appropriate will be handled very similarly to how they are determined in federal district courts.[40] The state and federal case law applicable to Rule 23 found elsewhere in this book should be consulted on Rule 23 issues.

---

35. *In re Montano*, 398 B.R. 47, 53 (Bankr. D.N.M. 2008).

36. *Id.*

37. *Id.*; *see also* FED. R. CIV. P. 23(b)(1).

38. *In re Montano*, 398 B.R. at 53; FED. R. CIV. P. 23(b)(2).

39. *In re Montano*, 398 B.R. at 53; FED. R. CIV. P. 23(b)(3).

40. One exception should be noted. The procedures for appealing an order granting or denying certification under Rule 23(f) do not govern appeals of bankruptcy court certification orders pursuant to Bankruptcy Rule 7023. *See generally* Chapter 5, "Interlocutory Appeals."

CONSUMER ACTIONS AND FRAUD/RELIANCE-BASED TORTS

PETER H. MASON

JOSHUA D. LICHTMAN

ERIC A. HERZOG

I. Introduction

This chapter explores manageability and predominance concerns that often arise in the area of consumer class actions. Broadly defined, consumer actions include any litigation intended to protect or vindicate the rights of members of the public who purchase goods and services. Consumer actions are a major part of the litigation landscape and provide fertile ground for class action litigation. Consumer class actions surface in virtually every industry and cover a wide range of products and business practices, from defective computers to complex financial instruments.

Among the most frequently asserted types of claims advanced in consumer cases are fraud and negligent misrepresentation; breach of contract; breach of warranty; defective design; and violation of state consumer protection statutes. As discussed below, each of these claims can present potential challenges to parties seeking class certification. For example, in common law fraud actions, satisfying the required element of predominant common issues is often a major hurdle to the certification of a class of consumers because there may be great divergence within a putative class on such matters as (1) what specific representations were made to or received by a given class member and (2) the extent to which reliance on such statements may be shown. In many instances, courts have found that class treatment is unwarranted because common questions of fact and law do not predominate.

Whether there is sufficient commonality among putative class members is often the decisive inquiry in determining whether a court will certify a class of consumers. The predominance requirements of Rule 23(b)(3) are familiar.[1]

- Under Rule 23(b)(3), "common questions must 'predominate over any questions affecting only individual members,' and class resolution must be 'superior to other available methods for the fair and efficient adjudication of the controversy.'"[2]
- "The Rule 23(b)(3) predominance inquiry tests whether proposed class members are sufficiently cohesive to warrant adjudication by representation."[3]
- "Class-wide issues predominate if resolution of some of the legal or factual questions that qualify each class member's case as a genuine controversy can be achieved through generalized proof, and if these particular issues are more substantial than the issues subject only to individualized proof."[4]

This chapter will address the application of these principles in consumer class actions and other actions involving fraud and reliance claims.

II. Fraud Actions Generally

In a typical common-law fraud case, a plaintiff must show that he or she received the defendant's alleged misrepresentation and relied on it.[5] Because proof often varies among individuals concerning what representations were received and the degree to which the representations were relied on, fraud cases often are unsuitable for class treatment.[6]

The Advisory Committee notes to Rule 23(b)(3) state, in part:

It is only where . . . predominance exists that economies can be achieved by means of the class-action device. In this view, a fraud perpetrated on numerous persons by the use of similar misrepresentations may be an appealing situation for a class action, and it may remain so despite the need, if liability is found, for separate determination of the damages suffered by individuals within the class. On the other hand, although having some common core, a fraud case may be unsuited for treatment as a class action if there was material variation in the representations made or in the kinds or degrees of reliance by the persons to whom they were addressed.[7]

---

1. *See also* Chapter 3.E, "Predominance and Superiority."
2. *Hanlon v. Chrysler Corp.*, 150 F.3d 1011, 1022 (9th Cir 1998) (quoting FED. R. CIV. P. 23(b)(3)).
3. *Amchem Prods., Inc. v. Windsor*, 521 U.S. 591, 616 (1997).
4. *Moore v. PaineWebber, Inc.*, 306 F.3d 1247, 1252 (2d Cir. 2002).
5. *In re St. Jude Med., Inc.*, 522 F.3d 836, 838 (8th Cir. 2008).
6. *Id.*
7. FED. R. CIV. P. 23(b)(3), advisory committee note (1966 amendment).

Along these lines, the Second Circuit has held that

> [t]o recover for a defendant's fraudulent conduct, even if that fraud is the result of a common course of conduct, each plaintiff must prove that he or she personally received a material misrepresentation, and that his or her reliance on this misrepresentation was the proximate cause of his or her loss. Fraud actions must therefore be separated into two categories: fraud claims based on uniform misrepresentations made to all members of the class and fraud claims based on individualized misrepresentations. The former are appropriate subjects for class certification because the standardized misrepresentations may be established by generalized proof. Where there are material variations in the nature of the misrepresentations made to each member of the proposed class, however, class certification is improper because plaintiffs will need to submit proof of the statements made to each plaintiff, the nature of the varying material misrepresentations, and the reliance of each plaintiff upon those misrepresentations in order to sustain their claims.[8]

Hence, in the context of fraud actions, although the common-issue requirement is "readily met in certain cases alleging consumer . . . fraud,"[9] the presence of individualized issues regarding the necessity of proving reliance may preclude a finding of predominance.[10] Indeed, because reliance raises individual issues, such as credibility and state of mind, class certification is generally inappropriate where reliance is an issue.[11]

As illustrated in *McLaughlin v. American Tobacco Co.,* "proof of misrepresentation—even widespread and uniform misrepresentation—only satisfies half the equation; the other half, reliance on the misrepresentation, cannot be subject to general proof."[12] In *McLaughlin,* the plaintiffs contended that reliance could be proved on a classwide basis because the defendant cigarette companies marketed their light cigarettes in a consistent, singular, uniform fashion.[13] The court determined, however, that "[i]ndividualized proof [was] needed to overcome the possibility that a

---

8. *Moore,* 306 F.3d at 1253 (citing *Grainger v. State Sec. Life Ins. Co.,* 547 F.2d 303, 307 (5th Cir. 1977) ("The key concept in determining the propriety of class action treatment is the existence or nonexistence of material variations in the alleged misrepresentations."); *cf. In re First Alliance Mortgage Co.,* 471 F.3d 977, 990 (9th Cir. 2006) ("Class treatment has been permitted in fraud cases where, as in this case, a standardized sales pitch is employed.").

9. *Amchem,* 521 U.S. at 625.

10. *See, e.g., McLaughlin v. Am. Tobacco Co.,* 522 F.3d 215 (2d Cir. 2008).

11. *See, e.g., Basic, Inc. v. Levinson,* 485 U.S. 224, 242 (1988); *Moore,* 306 F.3d at 1249, 1253; *Binder v. Gillespie,* 184 F.3d 1059, 1064 (9th Cir. 1999); *Patterson v. Mobil Oil Corp.,* 241 F.3d 417, 419 (5th Cir. 2001) ("Claims for money damages in which individual reliance is an element are poor candidates for class treatment, at best."); *Castano v. Am. Tobacco Co.,* 84 F.3d 734, 745 (5th Cir. 1996) (A "fraud class action cannot be certified when individual reliance will be an issue."); *Bradberry v. John Hancock Mut. Life Ins. Co.,* 222 F.R.D. 568, 571–72 (W.D. Tenn. 2004); *Van West v. Midland Natl. Life Ins. Co.,* 199 F.R.D. 448, 454 (D.R.I. 2001); *Adams v. Kansas City Life Ins. Co.,* 192 F.R.D. 274, 278–79 (W.D. Mo. 2000).

12. 522 F.3d at 223.

13. *See id.*

member of the purported class purchased Lights for some reason other than the belief that Lights were a healthier alternative . . . ."[14] The court held that smokers of light cigarettes could have elected to purchase such cigarettes "for any number of reasons, including a preference for the taste and a feeling that smoking Lights was cool."[15] Accordingly, the court found that reliance was "too individualized to admit of common proof."[16]

Similarly, the Eighth Circuit in *In re St. Jude Med., Inc.,* observed that that case "exemplifies the difficulty with class treatment of cases alleging fraud or misrepresentation."[17] In that case, the recipients of certain prosthetic heart valve implants sued "[a]fter a clinical study showed that patients implanted with the valve experienced an increased risk of paravalvular leakage."[18] The district court certified the class of patients under Rule 23(b)(3), and the appellate court reversed. The Eighth Circuit found that the defendant presented evidence that a number of implant patients did not receive any material representation about the heart valve. Critical to the court's decision was the following evidence:

> Two of the five named plaintiffs . . . testified that they did not remember hearing anything about the unique qualities of the Silzone valve. . . . On the other hand, one named plaintiff . . . testified that her doctor told her that the Silzone valve would be better because it would reduce the risk of infection. . . . Whether each plaintiff even received a representation from St. Jude about the efficacy of the heart valve is likely to be a significant issue in each case of alleged liability.

> Evidence of representations made to the treating physicians also illustrates the predominance of individual issues concerning representations and reliance. Physicians learned about St. Jude's heart valve in different ways. One doctor heard about the valve from a senior partner, another discovered it at a cardiology conference, and a third learned about the valve from a St. Jude sales representative and a St. Jude advertisement. . . . Whether the information on which physicians based their actions ultimately can be traced to a representation by St. Jude undoubtedly will vary by individual physician. Even where the present record does contain evidence that a physician eventually talked to a St. Jude representative or read Silzone promotional materials, those physicians assert that they did not rely on the representations by St. Jude in deciding to recommend the Silzone valve to their patients. . . . Any trial thus would require physician-by-physician inquiries into each doctor's sources of information about the valve, and the credibility of any physician's denial that he relied on St. Jude's statements.[19]

---

14. *Id.*
15. *Id.* at 225 (internal quotations and citation omitted).
16. *Id.*
17. 522 F.3d at 838.
18. *Id.* at 837.
19. *Id.* at 838–39.

The court found that "given the individual issues necessarily involved in determining liability and the requested relief of medical monitoring and damages, we think it is clear that the common issues do not predominate over individual issues that must be litigated to resolve the plaintiffs' claims."[20]

One way to overcome the individualized nature of reliance is through a presumption of reliance. A presumption of reliance is more likely to be found appropriate in fraud cases where plaintiffs primarily have alleged omissions of material facts.[21] In addition, in some jurisdictions, an inference of reliance may arise when it is shown that the same alleged misrepresentations "have actually been communicated to each member of a class[.]"[22]

Courts "usually hold that an action based on substantially . . . oral rather than written misrepresentations cannot be maintained as a class action" because in such cases typically "each plaintiff heard a slightly different, individualized sales pitch."[23] As one court summarized:

> Defendant argues, and the overwhelming weight of authority shows, that cases involving sales through non-uniform oral presentations and issues of reliance are generally unsuited for class certification. Courts considering these issues usually hold that individualized issues predominate over common questions, where there is no evidence of a uniform course of conduct in sales presentations, and necessary factual determinations include what statements were made or not made to each class member, whether the class member relied on those representations, and whether that reliance was reasonable, given other factors including background knowledge, understanding of the transaction, and receipt of documents. This is true both for insurance sales cases and other cases involving common law fraud claims.[24]

In *Moore v. PaineWebber, Inc.*,[25] plaintiffs argued commonality was established by PaineWebber's "centralized marketing scheme" to sell universal life insurance policies as a retirement plan. Plaintiffs showed that the "scheme" was carried out insofar as PaineWebber trained the brokers and made standardized marketing materials and "three different telephone scripts" available to them.[26] The *Moore* court nonetheless held that each plaintiff would still have to individually prove "that he or she personally received a material misrepresentation" because the existence of

---

20. *Id.* at 841.

21. *See, e.g.*, Binder, 184 F.3d at 1063; *In re Mercedes-Benz Tele Aid Contract Litig.*, 257 F.R.D. 46, 74–75 (D.N.J. 2009).

22. *Mirkin v. Wasserman*, 5 Cal. 4th 1082, 1093–95 (1993).

23. *Simon v. Merrill Lynch, Pierce, Fenner & Smith, Inc.*, 482 F.2d 850, 882–83 (5th Cir. 1973); *see also Gilbert v. Woods Mktg., Inc.*, 454 F. Supp. 745, 750 (D. Minn. 1978); *Moore*, 306 F.3d at 1249.

24. *Bradberry*, 222 F.R.D. at 571–72.

25. 306 F.3d at 1250–51.

26. *Id.* at 1252–56.

the "scheme" did not establish that "the individual misrepresentations made were uniform."[27] It denied certification based upon evidence that there were "material variations in the [brokers'] sales pitches" and that "the telephone scripts . . . varied significantly."[28] Similarly, the court in *Van West v. Midland National Life Insurance Co.*[29] denied certification because "the evidence regarding what agents and brokers may have told particular class members will vary, [so] determining whether [they] falsely represented that premiums would vanish becomes a matter of individualized proof rather than a common question."

III. Fraud Actions Under State Consumer Protection Acts

In contrast with claims of common law fraud, actions alleging fraudulent business practices under the respective states' consumer protection statutes are often more amenable to class treatment because many such acts

> do not explicitly require the traditional elements of common law fraud and negligent misrepresentation claims, such as reliance, intent, injury, and damages. This allows lawyers to argue that proof of such basic elements is unnecessary and that plaintiffs should be able to receive a monetary award for a misleading advertisement, even if they never saw it.[30]

While all 50 states have enacted one or more statutes to protect consumers, the elements necessary to bring private lawsuits under such statutes vary widely from state to state. For example, while recognizing private rights of action, at least eight states (Alabama, Alaska, Georgia, Kentucky, Louisiana, Mississippi, Montana, and Virginia) do not permit consumers to assert class actions to enforce that state's consumer protection statute.

In abandoning traditional requirements such as reliance, certain state consumer protection acts have thereby "significantly reduced the showing necessary to certify a case as a class action."[31] For example, to state a claim under the California Unfair Competition Law (UCL) based on false advertising or promotional practices, "it is necessary only to show that members of the public are likely to be deceived."[32]

---

27. *Id.* at 1255–56.

28. *Id.* at 1252–53, 1255–56.

29. 199 F.R.D. at 454.

30. Victor E. Schwartz & Cary Silverman, *Common-Sense Construction of Consumer Protection Acts*, 54 KAN. L. REV. 1 (2006), *available at* http://www.law.ku.edu/publications/lawreview/pdf/schwartz.pdf.

31. Sheila B. Scheuerman, *The Consumer Fraud Class Action: Reining in Abuse by Requiring Plaintiffs to Allege Reliance as an Essential Element*, 43 HARV. J. ON LEGIS. 1, 7 (2006).

32. *In re Tobacco II Cases*, 46 Cal. 4th 298, 312 (2009) (internal quotations and citation omitted); CAL. BUS. & PROF. CODE § 17200 *et seq.*

The fraudulent business practice prong of the UCL has been understood to be distinct from common law fraud. A [common law] fraudulent deception must be actually false, known to be false by the perpetrator and reasonably relied upon by a victim who incurs damages. None of these elements are required to state a claim for injunctive relief under the UCL.[33]

In *In re Tobacco II Cases*, the California Supreme Court held that the plain language of the UCL supported the conclusion that only the representative plaintiff is required to meet the UCL's standing requirements.[34] Accordingly, absent class members on whose behalf a private UCL action is prosecuted need *not* show on an individualized basis that they have "lost money or property as a result of the unfair competition."[35]

Similarly, a New Jersey federal court certified a class of car buyers seeking relief under the New Jersey Consumer Fraud Act (NJCFA), explaining the key differences between common law fraud and violations of the New Jersey statute as follows:

> The distinction between the proof of reliance required at common law and the less-rigorous "causal nexus" standard applicable to NJCFA claims is best explained by examining the precise nature of the "ascertainable loss" at issue in this case. Plaintiffs do not allege that, but for the alleged misrepresentations, they would not have purchased their vehicles. Nor do they contend that analog Tele Aid service would have been available after 2007 if not for Mercedes's alleged misconduct; AT&T stopped providing analog service because the FCC rule change removed the requirement that it do so, not because of any statement made by Mercedes. Plaintiffs simply claim that they did not get what they paid for—that because of Mercedes's alleged wrongdoing, they did not know that the Tele Aid systems in their automobiles would become useless long before the vehicles aged to such a degree that they were no longer drivable. Therefore, Plaintiffs will not need to prove at trial that each individual class member relied on Mercedes statements relating to Tele Aid when purchasing their vehicles. To the contrary, Plaintiffs can establish the necessary "causal nexus" between their ascertainable loss and the alleged misrepresentations simply by proving with respect to the class as a whole that, had Mercedes disclosed the existence of the FCC rule change and the fact that analog service would no longer be available after 2007, that disclosure would have effectively warned potential purchasers of vehicles equipped with analog-only Tele Aid systems that those systems would soon be rendered obsolete.[36]

Because state consumer protection acts vary in their scope and requirements, a close examination of the statutory language and case law thereunder is critical

---

33. *In re Tobacco II Cases*, 46 Cal. 4th at 312 (internal quotations and citation omitted).
34. *Id.* at 315; *see also* Cal. Bus. & Prof. Code §§ 17203 & 17204.
35. *Id.* at 320.
36. *In re Mercedes-Benz Tele Aid Contract Litig.*, 257 F.R.D. at 75.

to determining whether a particular business practice affecting consumers may justify class treatment.

IV. The Impact of Choice of Law Issues in Multistate Consumer Actions

Given that a number of consumer fraud actions seek certification of multistate or nationwide classes, choice of law problems often arise because of variations among state laws.[37] These choice of law issues frequently lead courts to find proposed class actions to be unmanageable where the laws of multiple states would have to be applied to putative class members' claims.[38] Some courts, however, have found that class treatment in consumer fraud actions was warranted despite the fact that putative class members were located in multiple states.[39]

V. Summary of Issues to Consider Regarding Predominance in Fraud Actions

In the context of consumer fraud class actions (grounded either in common law or statutory theories), the following is a summary of issues to consider in determining whether common issues may or may not predominate in a given case:

- Did each putative class member purchase the same product/service for the same purpose?
- Has there been a common misrepresentation or omission of material fact made in connection with the product/service at issue? If so, what was the source of the misrepresentation/omission?
- How was the product/service marketed/sold?

---

37. For a more detailed analysis of the multistate class and choice of law issues, *see* Chapter 24, "Multistate Class Actions and Choice of Law."

38. *See, e.g.,* In re Bridgestone/Firestone, Inc. Tires Prods. Liab. Litig., 288 F.3d 1012 (7th Cir. 2002) (reversing certification because class claims would be adjudicated under the law of many jurisdictions, and finding that a single nationwide class was not manageable); *Castano*, 84 F.3d at 741 ("In a multi-state class action, variations in state law may swamp any common issues and defeat predominance."); *In re Grand Theft Auto Video Game Consumer Litig.*, 251 F.R.D. 139, 161 (S.D.N.Y. 2008) (decertifying settlement class where there were numerous differences in the requirements of the underlying state laws applicable to the claims of the class members); *Lewis Tree Serv. v. Lucent Techs., Inc.*, 211 F.R.D. 228, 235–37 (S.D.N.Y. 2002) ("[T]he class requires that the law of at least fifty jurisdictions be applied."); *Barbara's Sales, Inc. v. Intel Corp.*, 879 N.E.2d 910, 918 (Ill. 2007) ("These substantial differences in the states' laws are the varying degrees to which the law allows a private right of action and class actions, the limitations periods, what constitutes a violation, what form of scienter is required, what form of reliance is required, and damages.").

39. *See, e.g.,* In re Mercedes-Benz Tele Aid Contract Litig., 257 F.R.D. at 46 (resolving choice of law issues in favor of class certification); *Mooney v. Allianz Life Ins. Co.*, 244 F.R.D. 531 (D. Minn. 2007) (applying Minnesota law to the claims of non-Minnesota class members).

- • Were there common sales materials/documents?
- • Were any oral representations made at the point of sale?
- • Did class members enter into any contracts?
- Does the plaintiff need to show actual deception, or is proof of a practice that was merely likely to deceive sufficient?
- Reliance:
  - • Who must prove reliance, if anyone? The class representative only? All class members?
  - • Is there any basis for a presumption of reliance (e.g., fraud on the market in securities cases or in common-law fraud cases where plaintiffs have primarily alleged omissions)?
- Is the plaintiff seeking certification of a multistate class? If so, do choice-of-law issues present significant manageability problems?

VI. Product Liability Claims Brought Under the Consumer Protection Laws

Putative class actions are often filed in cases involving alleged defects in products sold to consumers. Resolution of whether common questions of fact or law predominate in such cases tends to vary depending on (1) the theory of liability asserted and (2) the type of relief sought. Specifically, common issues are far less likely to be found to predominate where claims are asserted on tort theories (such as negligence or strict products liability) rather than on contractual warranty theories. Similarly, where the claims alleged or relief sought is of a type that would require proof of actual property damage or personal injury to the putative class members, courts are far less likely to find that commonly triable issues predominate.

Further, even in cases where plaintiffs have attempted to limit the scope of their claims or the relief sought, presumably either to attempt to minimize apparent individual issues or because the named plaintiffs themselves had not suffered the types of injuries that could support tort claims, courts have in some instances denied class certification based on a determination that some or all of the putative class members could not establish valid claims under the substantive law. In contrast, other courts have found this issue to present a "merits" question that does not bar certification where the trial would turn on the predominant common issue of proof of the alleged defect.

For example, in *Hicks v. Kaufman & Broad Home Corp.*,[40] plaintiff homeowners alleged that the concrete slab foundations under their homes were "inherently defective" because the builder had constructed them using a product known as fibermesh, which was "more prone" to cracking than welded wire mesh. Plain-

---

40. 89 Cal. App. 4th 908, 911–12 (2001).

tiffs asserted claims against the builder for strict liability, negligence, and breach of express and implied warranties.[41] However, plaintiffs sought as damages only the cost to repair or replace the allegedly defective concrete foundations, and expressly disclaimed seeking recovery for personal injury or consequential property damages.[42]

The trial court denied class certification. The court of appeal reversed in part, concluding that common issues predominated on the claims for breach of express and implied warranty because the alleged "inherent defect" could be proved in common and the only individualized issue as to those claims would be proof of the amount needed to repair or replace the foundation.[43] However, the court held that common issues did not predominate as to plaintiffs' tort causes of action and therefore affirmed the denial of certification as to those claims.

Having found that "the question whether an inherently defective product is presently functioning as warranted goes to the remedy for the breach, not proof of the breach [of warranty] itself,"[44] the court in *Hicks* therefore held that the class should have been certified with respect to breach of warranty claims because (1) "the existence of a common inherent defect was a question of fact common to the class," and (2) whether the fibermesh had already failed did not preclude certification because it was a remedy issue.[45]

In contrast, *Hicks* affirmed the denial of class certification as to plaintiffs' tort claims for strict liability and negligence. The court explained that those causes of action "do not provide a remedy for defects" that have caused personal injury, as defects "causing only economic damage" (i.e., the cost to repair or replace an inherently defective foundation) would support only contract or warranty claims.[46] Accordingly, to recover under the tort claims each class member would have to come forward and prove (1) that the fibermesh had actually malfunctioned; (2) that their home had suffered "specific damage"; and (3) "that such damage was caused by cracks in the foundation, not some other agent."[47] Therefore, the court held that commonly triable issues would not predominate as to the product liability and negligence claims, given the substantial individual inquiry required to decide these issues with respect to each putative class member.[48]

---

41. *Id.*
42. *Id.* at 912–13.
43. *Id.* at 913.
44. *Id.* at 917–18.
45. *Id.* at 918–19, 923.
46. *Id.* at 919–21, 923 (citing *Aas v. Superior Court*, 24 Cal. 4th 627 (2000)).
47. *Id.* at 924.
48. *Id.*

In *Ronat v. Martha Stewart Living Omnimedia, Inc.*,[49] plaintiffs alleged that one of the models of the Martha Stewart brand of glass top patio tables was prone to "spontaneously shatter during ordinary use" and therefore asserted class action claims for unjust enrichment, breach of implied warranty, and for damages, restitution, and injunctive relief under the Illinois Consumer Fraud and Deceptive Practices Act. The court denied certification, holding that the class was not ascertainable, and/or common issues would not predominate. The court stated it could not certify a class defined to include all purchasers because it would include many purchasers whose tables had not shattered; but, it also found that, if the class was limited to those whose tables had shattered, there would then be no way to identify class members.[50] In so doing, the court combined its predominance assessment with analysis of the substantive law, rejecting plaintiffs' argument that they could prove all of the tables were inherently defective because it was "substantially certain" that each would spontaneously shatter during its "useful life," concluding that there would be no way to prove on a classwide basis that every instance of a table shattering was "spontaneous," rather than having been caused by something else.[51]

A somewhat contrary result was reached in *Hewlett-Packard Co. v. Superior Court*.[52] There, plaintiffs alleged that certain Hewlett-Packard (HP) computers were manufactured with defective inverters that could cause the display screens to dim and that HP knew of, but failed to disclose, this defect.[53] Based on these allegations, plaintiffs asserted claims for breach of express warranty, unjust enrichment, and violations of California's UCL and Consumers Legal Remedies Act (CLRA).[54] It was undisputed that the dim displays could be caused by other factors besides a defective inverter, such as liquid spills, customer abuse, and software incompatibility. It was also undisputed that (1) HP used multiple inverters from different suppliers; (2) not all of them would fail; and (3) determining which type of inverter was used in any given computer required that the display screen be disassembled and the inverter itself inspected.[55]

The trial court certified the class, and HP appealed, arguing that *Daugherty v. American Honda*[56] barred plaintiffs' warranty claims because the inverter defects were alleged to have manifested only after the warranty period. HP further argued that common issues would not predominate because plaintiffs had alleged only

---

49. Civ. No. 05-520-GPM, 2008 U.S. Dist. LEXIS 91814 (S.D. Ill. 2008).
50. *Id.* at *17–19.
51. *Id.*
52. 167 Cal. App. 4th 87 (2008).
53. *Id.* at 89–90.
54. *Id.* at 90 (citing CAL. BUS. & PROF. CODE § 17200 and CAL. CIV. CODE § 1750).
55. *Id.*
56. 144 Cal. App. 4th 824 (2006).

that the inverter "would likely fail and cause the screens to dim and darken some-time before the end of the notebook's 'useful life,'" but not necessarily during the warranty period, and that most putative class members also could not assert valid breach of warranty claims.[57] The court rejected this argument, holding that *Daugherty* involved a substantive merits issue that "was not a proper consideration at the class certification state."[58]

The court explained that "whether or not the alleged defects occurred during the warranty period does not affect a finding of community of interest in the present case."[59] Specifically, the court concluded that "whether the inverters were defective is appropriate for a joint trial with common proof."[60] It also stated that "if the jury finds that the inverters were defective, then each plaintiff would not need to separately prove that his or her inverter was defective, only that he or she had a computer that contained that type of inverter," which would not present a substantial individual issue for trial.[61]

Similarly, class certification was granted in *Joseph v. General Motors Corp.* in an action arising out of plaintiffs' allegations that design defects in the model engine utilized in certain Cadillacs caused them to suffer "unexpected stalling, hesitation, surging and poor fuel economy."[62] Plaintiffs asserted that GM knew of, but failed to disclose (and, indeed, actively concealed) these alleged defects in its marketing and that it issued warranties knowing it could not honor them and repair the defective vehicles. Based on these allegations, plaintiffs sought certification of a Colorado class with respect to claims for negligence, strict products liability, fraud, breach of express and implied warranties, and violation of the Magnuson-Moss Warranty–Federal Trade Commission Improvement Act.[63] The court certified the class as to all causes of action. It concluded that common issues relating to whether the engine was defectively designed (and, if so, whether it caused "characteristic operational problems" and caused the engine to be unreasonable dangerous) represented the "core" of plaintiffs' action against GM.[64] Accordingly, while acknowledging that there were what it characterized as "some" questions that would require individual-ized proof (such as whether the alleged design defects caused the claimed damages, reliance by class members, and the amount of damages), the court nevertheless concluded that the common questions predominated because of the "common nucleus of operative facts" upon which the case would turn.[65]

---

57. *Hewlitt-Packard*, 167 Cal. App. 4th at 95.

58. *Id.*

59. *Id.* at 96.

60. *Id.*

61. *Id.*

62. 109 F.R.D. 635, 637 (D. Colo. 1986).

63. 15 U.S.C. §§ 2301–2312.

64. *Id.* at 641–42.

65. *Id.*

VII. Consumer Form Contract and Statutory Violation Cases

Numerous courts have found that actions arising out of form contracts with consumers are amenable to class action treatment, holding that common issues relating to the meaning or validity of contract terms or as to company practices in interpreting or implementing such contracts present predominant common issues, irrespective of the need for individual damages analyses. In reaching these results, several courts have held that the common issues predominated even as to fraud or statutory deceptive practices claims, where the claims were based on alleged omissions from the form contracts, because in those circumstances the claim could still be proved in common since the class would not need to present evidence of individual affirmative representations that may have differed between class members.

For example, in *McGhee v. Bank of America*,[66] plaintiffs sued three different banks, alleging that they made mortgage loans under which the borrower's monthly payments included, in addition to principal and interest, amounts impounded by the banks and then released at their discretion to pay taxes and insurance. Plaintiffs asserted the banks acted improperly by commingling the impounded funds, and failing to pay interest on the impounded funds. The trial court denied class certification, and the court of appeal reversed.

The appellate court held that common issues predominated because the impound provisions were all contained in preprinted form deeds of trust that appeared to be contracts of adhesion.[67] It commented that actions involving alleged contracts of adhesion "present ideal cases for class adjudication" because (1) the agreements are "uniform," (2) "all members of the class will share a common interest in the interpretation of [that] agreement," and (3) "the same principles of interpretation apply to each contract."[68]

The court rejected the defendants' argument that proving the deeds of trust were contracts of adhesion would in and of itself constitute a predominant individual issue (requiring examination of the borrowers' relative bargaining power, their alternatives, and their knowledge of such alternatives). Instead, it held that plaintiffs could use bank witnesses to establish that they had such power that the "trust deed is adhesive as to virtually all members of the class," in which case plaintiffs would "not need to elicit testimony from each borrower."[69]

The same disposition to certify class actions based on form contracts was found in *Dupler v. Costco Wholesale Corp.*[70] In that case, plaintiffs alleged breach of contract and unjust enrichment based on Costco's alleged policy to "backdate"

---

66. 60 Cal. App. 3d 442 (1976).
67. *Id.* at 448–49.
68. *Id.* at 449.
69. *Id.*
70. 249 F.R.D. 29 (E.D.N.Y. 2008).

memberships that were renewed after their expiration date (e.g., if a membership was due to expire on March 31, and the member paid the one-year renewal fee in June, the renewal period would expire the next March 31 rather than in June). The court found that common questions predominated because all putative class members were subject to the same membership agreement and Costco's alleged backdating practice would either be valid or improper across the board as to all members.[71] In so doing, the court commented that "claims arising out of form contracts" and, more specifically, claims for breach of such contracts, "are particularly appropriate for a class action treatment."[72]

Numerous courts have applied similar rationales to certify classes alleging claims asserting violations of the Fair Debt Collection Practices Act (FDCPA),[73] which arise from standardized writings or other debt collection practices, notwithstanding the presence of individualized damages issues. For instance, in *Brink v. First Credit Resources*,[74] the defendant purchased plaintiff's outstanding (but time-barred) credit card debt; then, in a form mailing, the defendant (1) stated it had purchased the debt, (2) advised the recipient he or she was "approved" for a new credit card (with "no finance charge" and "low monthly payments"), but (3) limited the amount of credit it would offer to the amount of the plaintiff's outstanding debt, and (4) conditioned the new credit upon the plaintiff's agreement to reaffirm his or her otherwise time-barred debts. Plaintiff alleged claims under the FDCPA based on the allegedly improper debt collection practice and upon the alleged misrepresentations in the form letter. The court held that common issues predominated, as the claims arose from the mailing of the standard credit card solicitation, and that any individualized inquiry necessary to calculate damages did not preclude certification.[75]

In addition, classes were certified in *Labbate-D'Alauro v. GC Services Limited Partnership*[76] and *Leone v. Ashwood Financial, Inc.*,[77] both of which arose out of allegations that the defendants used form debt collection letters that violated the FDCPA because they were allegedly improperly harassing and misleading (*Labbate*) or because they contained a false threat of litigation, as the debts at issue were so small the defendant would not actually have sued to collect (*Leone*). Labbate rejected the defendant's argument that common issues did not predominate because some of the class members received additional collection telephone calls

---

71. *Id.* at 37.

72. *Id.* at 37, 46 (citing *Flanigan v. Allstate Ins. Co.*, 242 F.R.D. 421, 428 (N.D. Ill. 2007); *In re Tri-State Crematory Litig.*, 215 F.R.D. 660, 692 (N.D. Ga. 2003)).

73. 15 U.S.C. § 1692.

74. 185 F.R.D. 567, 569 (D. Ariz. 1999).

75. *Id.* at 572.

76. 168 F.R.D. 451 (E.D.N.Y. 1996).

77. 247 F.R.D. 343 (E.D.N.Y. 2009).

or other letters, holding that "the claims of individual class members do not have to match precisely" and that the conduct at issue was sufficiently standardized to support certification, as all of the class members had received both of the two identical letters upon which the claims were based.[78] Common issues were similarly found to predominate in *Leone*, because the claims of all class members were based on "substantially similar" collection letters, and the "overarching question" was whether those letters violated the FDCPA.[79]

Actions alleging violations of the Truth in Lending Act (TILA)[80] have resulted in less consistent class certification decisions, depending largely upon the remedy sought. For example, common issues were found to predominate in *Hickey v. Great Western Mortgage Corp.*,[81] where plaintiff alleged (on behalf of a nationwide class) that Great Western failed to include two fees imposed by a lawyer at the time of closing of a mortgage refinance (for delivery and discharge/release of prior encumbrance fees) in the "finance charge" section of its truth-in-lending disclosures, instead including them in the "amount financed" figure. Based on this allegation, plaintiff asserted claims for violation of TILA (seeking recovery of actual and/or statutory damages) and also for violation of California's UCL.[82] The court certified the class as to the TILA claim only, concluding that it could not decide on the record presented whether California's consumer protection law could be applied to the claims of non-California class members.[83] As to the TILA claim, the court held that common issues predominated because the claim arose from "standardized conduct" and that most of the asserted "individualized" issues (e.g., whether the challenged fees were included in the "amount financed" or "finance charge" categories) were either readily decided with classwide proof or, to the extent subject to individual proof, presented a "simple ministerial task."[84] The court also held that differences in individual cases concerning damages would not bar certification, in part because TILA authorized recovery in class actions of statutory damages that would likely dwarf the relatively small amounts of individual "actual damages," eliminating the need for significant individualized damages inquiry.[85]

In contrast, certification was denied in *Andrews v. Chevy Chase Bank*.[86] In that case, plaintiffs alleged that the bank's disclosure statement failed to make sufficiently clear that the "teaser" interest rate on their adjustable mortgage was applicable only for the first month of the loan, rather than fixed for the first five

---

78. *Labbate*, 168 F.R.D. at 456, 458.
79. *Leone*, 247 F.R.D. at 352–53.
80. 15 U.S.C. §§ 1601–1667.
81. 158 F.R.D. 603, 606 (N.D. Ill. 1994).
82. *Id.*
83. *Id.* at 612–13.
84. *Id.*
85. *Id.* at 611–12.
86. 545 F.3d 570 (7th Cir. 2008).

years.[87] Plaintiffs asserted a putative class action for violation of TILA, but the only remedy sought was rescission of the subject loans.[88] The court denied certification, in part based on its conclusion that individual issues would swamp any common issues relating to the existence of a TILA violation in determining whether any particular loan could be rescinded, as that would depend on highly individualized factors, such as whether the borrower was in position to return the principal amount of the loan and whether "unwinding" the transaction could be safely accomplished without the bank losing its security interest in the property.[89]

Predominance issues arose in a case presenting a somewhat unusual combination of standardized contracts and alleged statutory violations in *In re Universal Services Fund Telephone Billing Practices Litigation*.[90] In that case, plaintiffs alleged that defendants AT&T and Sprint conspired with nonparty MCI to overcharge their customers to recoup the phone companies' contributions to the federal Universal Service Fund (USF) program, so as to create a "secret profit center" for themselves.[91] Specifically, plaintiffs alleged that the FCC, which was authorized by statute to administer the USF program, had set contribution rates, but that the phone companies illegally conspired to bill their respective customers for USF "surcharges" that were several percentage points higher than the rates set by the FCC.[92] Plaintiffs sought to certify a nationwide class of long-distance business customers and a California class of residential customers with respect to their antitrust conspiracy claim, and, as to their breach of contract claims, sought to certify separate classes consisting of customers of AT&T (against AT&T) and Sprint (against Sprint).[93] The court held that common issues predominated as to both the conspiracy and breach of contract claims and certified both classes.[94]

As to the conspiracy claim, the court noted that the primary issues necessarily revolved around the defendants' conduct and, thus, would be subject to common proof (namely, whether they conspired to fix USF surcharges at supracompetitive levels and "the effect of the alleged conspiracy on their respective surcharge rates").[95] The court acknowledged that in order to prove their antitrust claims, the plaintiffs would have to show, in addition to a violation of antitrust law, the elements of impact and damages.[96] However, the court concluded that these issues did not prevent certification, crediting plaintiffs' expert economist's assertions that

---

87. *Id.* at 572.
88. *Id.*
89. *Id.* at 577.
90. 219 F.R.D. 661 (D. Kan. 2004).
91. *Id.* at 663–64.
92. *Id.* at 664.
93. *Id.*
94. *Id.* at 666–67 and 673–79.
95. *In re Universal Servs. Fund*, 219 F.R.D. at 666, 673.
96. *Id.* at 673.

(1) plaintiffs could demonstrate the impact of the alleged conspiracy on a class-wide basis, in that it had caused all AT&T and Sprint customers to pay higher USF fees than they otherwise would have been charged; and (2) that plaintiffs could provide "a potentially feasible method for proving damages on a class-wide basis."[97]

As to the breach of contract claim, the court held that common issues predominated because both AT&T and Sprint utilized standard form contracts and, therefore, the dispositive question would be whether their USF fund recovery practices (subject to common proof) breached those standard contract terms.[98]

In *Lazar v. Hertz Corp.*, plaintiff alleged that when he returned rental cars without refilled gas tanks, Hertz imposed a refueling charge that exceeded federal regulations capping the resale price of gasoline.[99] Based on this allegation, he asserted putative class claims for price-fixing, breach of the implied duty of good faith and fair dealing, and fraud. The trial court denied class certification, but the court of appeal reversed and ordered the class certified.

Hertz's refueling charge was based on a standard, preprinted form contract that each customer was required to sign, which provided, in essence, that if the customer's rental rate did not include gasoline and they returned the car with less gas than when rented, then the customer "shall pay an additional charge determined by [Hertz] for refueling service."[100] Plaintiff alleged that Hertz set its refueling charges without regard to the amount of gasoline actually used or Hertz's refueling costs (i.e., gasoline and labor costs).[101] However, the evidence reflected that Hertz set refueling charges based on the prevailing retail price of gasoline in the particular location where the car was returned.[102] Nevertheless, the court held that common issues predominated.

The court identified as common questions of law and fact whether Hertz disclosed to renters (1) that failure to refill the gas tank would result in a substantial premium over the maximum legal price of gasoline or (2) that the refueling charge bore no relationship to Hertz's costs for gas or labor. The court held that there was no individualized issue of reliance because the alleged omission was contained in a standard contract provided to all class members, so that it could be inferred that all class members who rented cars had relied on the alleged misrepresentation.[103]

Other consumer cases that have been certified as class actions involve alleged statutory violations that courts have found subject to classwide proof. For instance,

---

97. *Id.* at 673–77.

98. *Id.* at 667, 679 (citing, among others, *Winkler v. DTE, Inc.*, 205 F.R.D. 235, 243 (D. Ariz. 2001) (rejecting argument that individual issues would predominate breach of contract claim where standard form contracts were at issue)).

99. 143 Cal. App. 3d 128 (1983).

100. *Id.* at 135.

101. *Id.*

102. *Id.* at 136.

103. *Id.* at 140 (citing *Occidental Land v. Superior Court*, 18 Cal. 3d 355, 363 (1976)).

in *Medrazo v. Honda of North Hollywood*, plaintiff alleged that when she purchased her motorcycle it did not have attached a "hang tag" (required by the California Vehicle Code) listing the Manufacturer's Suggested Retail Price and the dealer's additional charges for transportation and optional equipment.[104] Plaintiff asserted claims under California's Unfair Business Practices Act and its CLRA.[105] The trial court denied class certification, holding that common issues did not predominate. The court of appeal reversed and ordered the class certified.

Defendant argued that common issues did not predominate because the manufacturer put hang tags on some of its motorcycles, so it was impossible to know without individual inquiry (1) if putative class members purchased motorcycles without hang tags and/or (2) if the failure to attach a hang tag was the fault of the manufacturer or the dealer. The court held that even if those issues would require individualized proof, they did not predominate over issues common to the class. The court premised its analysis on the fact that "predominance is a comparative concept, [so that] the necessity for class members to individually establish eligibility and damages does not mean individual questions predominate."[106]

In *Coleman v. General Motors Acceptance Corp.*,[107] plaintiffs asserted that GMAC's retail finance policies, as implemented by the auto dealers with whom it contracted, caused African American consumers to pay higher average finance charges than similarly situated white consumers, in violation of the Equal Credit Opportunity Act (ECOA). After the Sixth Circuit held that individualized issues related to plaintiffs' claims for damages were a fatal bar to class certification,[108] plaintiffs amended their complaint to seek only declaratory and injunctive relief.[109] Given this amendment, the court found that plaintiffs would not be required to make the same showing of predominance that they would have been required to make under Rule 23(b)(3) if they were still seeking damages.[110] Instead, the plaintiffs needed to establish only that GMAC had acted on grounds generally applicable to the class, such that there were substantial common questions of law or fact.[111] The court found that plaintiffs had met this burden by asserting that GMAC used a standard credit pricing policy throughout the United States, "which authorizes the imposition by GMAC dealers of purely subjective finance charges on credit applicants in a manner unrelated to their creditworthiness, and which results in an unlawful discriminatory impact," and that plaintiffs asserted that this policy was susceptible

---

104. 166 Cal. App. 4th 89 (2008).
105. *Id.* at 93.
106. *Id.* at 99–100 (citing *Sav-On Drug Stores, Inc. v. Superior Court*, 34 Cal. 4th 319, 334 (2004)).
107. 220 F.R.D. 64, 67–68 (M.D. Tenn. 2004).
108. *Coleman v. Gen. Motors Acceptance Corp.*, 296 F.3d 443, 449 (6th Cir. 2002).
109. *Coleman*, 220 F.R.D. at 68.
110. *Id.* at 85–86.
111. *Id.* at 70–71, 85–86.

to common proof.[112] Accordingly, the court held that "common declaratory and injunctive remedies will settle the legality of the behavior with regard to the class as a whole," noting that "the Sixth Circuit has observed that application of the Rule 23(b)(2) form is particularly appropriate when class-wide discrimination is alleged, because 'the common claim is susceptible to a single proof and subject to a single injunctive remedy.'"[113]

A number of courts have addressed predominance issues in claims arising out of allegedly standardized provisions in insurance policies. For example, in *Steinberg v. Nationwide Mutual Insurance Co.*,[114] plaintiff sought certification of a national class of Nationwide insureds who had submitted claims under their automobile policies that provided, in part, that if the auto was damaged, Nationwide would "pay for the loss less your declared deductible." Plaintiff alleged that Nationwide breached class members' policies based on its standard practice to deduct from the amounts paid for repairs not only the deductible, but also a so-called "betterment charge," which it did not define in the policy, but was presumably intended as a rough measure of the added value that the newly repaired vehicle would have above its pre-damage condition.[115] The court certified a national class, holding that common issues predominated because (1) all class members had "substantively identical or similar form agreements with Nationwide"; (2) Nationwide had engaged in a "common course of conduct" in taking the "betterment" deductions; and (3) the "central issue" was whether the "uniform" policy language permitted it to take such deductions.[116] The court rejected Nationwide's argument that common issues would not predominate because of the need to apply the substantive law of the 46 separate states where it had sold policies and because the policy language was not identical in all states.[117] The court held that these arguments did not defeat predominance because the key policy language was substantially the same in all states and that there were "no material differences" in the various states' breach of contract elements or in their "contract interpretation principles."[118] Moreover, to the extent that there were slight variations in contract interpretation principles between the various states, the court held that they fell into four groups that could be easily managed.[119]

In *Lebrilla v. Farmers Group, Inc.*, plaintiffs alleged that an insurer's practice of using replacement parts not manufactured by the original equipment manufacturer

112. *Id.* at 85–87.
113. *Id.* at 86 (citing *Senter v. Gen. Motors Corp.*, 532 F.2d 511, 525 (6th Cir. 1976)).
114. 224 F.R.D. 67, 70 (E.D.N.Y. 2004).
115. *Id.*
116. *Id.* at 73–74, 77.
117. *Id.* at 76–78.
118. *Id.*
119. *Id.*

(OEM) violated policy terms requiring it to repair or replace damaged vehicles with "like kind and quality" parts.[120] Plaintiffs sued for declaratory and injunctive relief under California's consumer protection laws (UCL and CLRA). The trial court denied plaintiffs' motion for class certification, but the court of appeal reversed and ordered the class certified.

Plaintiffs identified two common issues: (1) whether Farmers had a "practice" to specify that non-OEM replacement parts met the policy's "like kind and quality" standard, and (2) whether each class member's vehicle was repaired pursuant to that policy.[121] Plaintiffs argued that common issues would predominate because these issues were subject to common proof and because each of the policies was identical, so a declaration of the insureds' rights under the policy would apply classwide.[122] Further, plaintiffs argued that they could establish (through expert testimony) that non-OEM parts were not "like kind and quality" through classwide proof, without requiring examination of individual parts.[123]

The California appellate court noted that the issue of whether non-OEM replacement parts could be shown to be uniformly not of "like kind and quality" to OEM parts had been raised in numerous lawsuits around the country, resulting in a split of authority.[124] Courts in Illinois, Florida, Pennsylvania, and Mississippi had certified classes, holding that the propriety of using non-OEM parts could be tested with classwide proof. In contrast, courts in Tennessee, Alabama, Washington, Texas, Maryland, Massachusetts, and Ohio had denied certification, finding this to be an individual issue. In discussing the various out-of-state authorities, the California court synthesized as the critical issue whether "like kind and quality" should be regarded as involving comparison to the damaged part's original condition or to its age, condition, and extent of use as of the time of the repair; if the latter, then individualized evaluations would be needed.[125] The California court concluded that "like kind and quality" concerned "only a part's material and suitability, not its age or extent of use," and, therefore, the determination that non-OEM replacement parts could *never* be of "like kind and quality" could be adjudicated on a classwide basis with common proof and without regard to the specific age and condition of any particular part being replaced.[126]

Finally, a number of cases have certified classes asserting claims (on varying legal theories) based on allegations that purchasers of title insurance did not receive discounted rates to which they were allegedly entitled pursuant to the rate

---

120. 119 Cal. App. 4th 1070 (2004).
121. *Id.* at 1075.
122. *Id.* at 1075–76.
123. *Id.* at 1076.
124. *Id.* at 1077–82.
125. *Id.* at 1080–81.
126. *Id.* at 1082–83.

manuals filed with applicable state regulatory agencies. For example, in *Slapikas v. First American Title Insurance Co.*,[127] plaintiffs alleged that First American failed to adhere to provisions in its rate manual requiring that purchasers of title insurance in connection with home mortgage refinances receive premium discounts if title insurance had been issued on the property in the last three or ten years.[128] Based on this allegation, plaintiffs asserted claims for breach of contract, fraud, unjust enrichment, and violation of the Pennsylvania Unfair Trade Practices and Consumer Protection Law.[129] The court certified a class as to all causes of action, holding that common issues predominated because issues related to the "legal and factual interpretation of the Rate Manual will apply to each member of the class."[130] The court also noted that numerous other courts had certified similar classes.[131]

A similar rationale was applied in *Hoving v. Lawyers Title Insurance Co.*[132] In that case, the plaintiff sought certification of a multistate class action asserting a single cause of action for unjust enrichment, based on the allegation that the insurer had charged full premiums instead of the discounted premiums allegedly required to be charged under the applicable rate manuals to customers who were refinancing mortgage loans made within the last two years.[133] Finding that there was no material difference in the elements of an unjust enrichment claim under the various states' law, and that the defendant was allegedly engaged in a "systematic scheme" (reflected in standard instructions issued by the company to agents) to overcharge for title insurance in violation of the applicable rate manual, the court held that common issues predominated because "a jury could conclude that the defendant was unjustly enriched no matter what the particular facts of the individual borrower's case."[134] However, the court denied certification because the named plaintiff was not a qualified class representative.[135]

VIII. Other Issues Impacting Predominance

Even where consumers may be able to establish a defendant's liability through the use of common proof, the respective amounts of damage incurred by putative class

---

127. 250 F.R.D. 232 (W.D. Pa. 2008).
128. *Id.* at 233–34.
129. 73 PA. STAT. ANN. §§ 201–207.
130. *Slapikas*, 250 F.R.D. at 244–47.
131. *Id.* at 233 (citing, among others, *Mitchell-Tracey v. United Gen. Ins. Co.*, 237 F.R.D. 551 (D. Md. 2006); *In re Coordinated Title Ins. Cases*, 784 N.Y.S.2d 919 (N.Y. Sup. 2004)).
132. 256 F.R.D. 555 (E.D. Mich. 2009).
133. *Id.* at 558–61.
134. *Id.* at 569–70.
135. *Id.* at 566, 571.

members may vary widely. Such individual damages questions are often not on their own sufficient to defeat class certification in consumer cases, but such issues may be a relevant consideration in certification proceedings.[136]

Likewise, a defendant's statute of limitations defense may also require individualized inquiry, especially where consumers have purchased a product at different times during a given class period.[137]

IX. Conclusion

As demonstrated above, consumer and fraud-based claims present unique challenges when it comes to the predominance and superiority provisions of Rule 23(b)(3). Whether a class can be certified and maintained through trial is often difficult to predict. The extent to which the representation or allegedly wrongful conduct is uniform or standardized as to all class members is usually the key factor courts consider in deciding whether to certify these types of classes.

---

136. *See, e.g., In re Cmty. Bank of N. Va. & Guar. Nat'l Bank of Tallahassee Second Mortgage Loan Litig.,* 418 F.3d 277, 306 (3d Cir. 2005); *Buetow v. A.L.S. Enters.,* 259 F.R.D. 187, 192–93 (D. Minn. 2009) ("The fact that damages will need to be assessed on an individualized basis does not, in and of itself, require the denial of a class certification motion. However, the need for detailed and individual factual inquiries concerning the appropriate remedy . . . still weighs strongly against class certification" (internal quotations and citation omitted)); *Osborne v. Subaru of Am., Inc.,* 198 Cal. App. 3d 646, 657 (1988); *Sav-On Drug Stores,* 34 Cal. 4th at 335.

137. *See, e.g., Barnes v. Am. Tobacco Co.,* 161 F.3d 127, 149 (3d Cir. 1998) ("[D]etermining whether each class member's claim is barred by the statute of limitations raises individual issues that prevent class certification."); *Buetow,* 259 F.R.D. at 192–93.

ANTITRUST

LAYNE KRUSE
DAN PIROLO

I. Introduction

Antitrust class actions pose special challenges to courts and parties addressing the predominance and superiority elements of class certification under Rule 23(b)(3). While class issues related to liability or damages are treated much as in other class actions, courts must wrestle with an added element in antitrust claims—the element of antitrust injury or impact. Related to damages, but a component of a plaintiffs' liability case, antitrust impact remains an element that courts and parties struggle with at the class certification phase. This is particularly true in light of the admonition that "the fact that a case is proceeding as a class action does not in any way alter the substantive proof required to prove up a claim for relief."[1]

II. Predominance Concerns in Antitrust Actions

Courts have indicated that individualized questions as to the calculation of class members' damages alone will not suffice to defeat predominance at the class certification phase. For example, in *In re Scrap Metal Antitrust Litigation*,[2] the Sixth Circuit affirmed the certification of a class in which the defendants had argued that damages could not be calculated on a classwide basis. The court rebuffed defendants on appeal, finding that defendants "erroneously assume that the issue of damages must predominate."[3] Instead, the court concluded that proof of conspiracy as a common question predominated over other issues, and that "[e]ven where there are individual variations in damages, the requirements of Rule 23(b)(3) are satisfied if the plaintiffs can establish that the defendants conspired

---

1. *Alabama v. Blue Bird Body Co*, 573 F.2d 309, 327 (5th Cir. 1978).
2. 527 F.3d 517 (6th Cir. 2008).
3. *Id.* at 535.

to interfere with the free-market pricing structure."[4] Where damages issues will require individual proof, some courts have embraced limited certification of a class for liability purposes, and conducted separate individual trials where necessary on damages issues.[5] However, some courts have also denied class certification on the basis that separate "mini-trials" on damages issues would threaten to overwhelm the benefits of class certification on liability issues, counseling against certification under both the predominance and superiority requirements of Rule 23(b)(3).[6]

On the other hand, courts routinely deny class certification on predominance grounds in cases that require individualized proof on liability issues.[7] No liability issue is under more scrutiny during class certification than antitrust impact or injury.[8] The U.S. Supreme Court has explained that claimants "must prove antitrust injury, which is to say injury of the type the antitrust laws were intended to prevent and that flows from that which makes defendants' acts unlawful."[9] In other words, the alleged injury "should reflect the anticompetitive effect either of the violation or of anticompetitive acts made possible by the violation."[10] Several courts have allowed plaintiffs to satisfy the predominance requirement by merely demonstrating that they plan to prove antitrust impact at trial using common

---

4. *Id.*; *see also, e.g., Bogosian v. Gulf Oil Corp.*, 561 F.2d 434, 456 (3d Cir. 1977) (holding that "the necessity for calculation of damages on an individual basis should not preclude class determination when the common issues which determine liability predominate"); *In re Carbon Black Antitrust Litig.*, 2005-1 Trade Cas. (CCH) ¶ 74,695, at 101,360 (D. Mass. 2005) (holding that "the need for individualized determinations of the putative class members' damages does not, without more, preclude certification of a class under Rule 23(b)(3)"); *In re Mercedes-Benz Antitrust Litig.*, 213 F.R.D. 180, 190 (D.N.J. 2003) ("There is ample authority that the need for individualized damages calculations should not automatically preclude class certification.").

5. *See, e.g., In re Linerboard Antitrust Litig.*, 305 F.3d 145, 163 (3d Cir. 2002) ("'Many courts faced with similar circumstances have certified class status with the expectation that individual questions concerning fraudulent concealment can be resolved at a later damages phase.'"); *In re Vitamins Antitrust Litig.*, 209 F.R.D. 251, 268 (D.D.C. 2002) (holding that common issues may predominate with respect to conspiracy and impact elements and that individualized damages could be determined later using separate proceedings).

6. *See, e.g., In re Beef Indus. Antitrust Litig.*, MDL No. 248, 1986 U.S. Dist. LEXIS 24731 (S.D. Tex. June 3, 1986) (holding that the "issue of damages does not lend itself to such a mechanical calculation, but requires separate 'mini-trials' of an overwhelming large number of individual claims"); *see also Bell Atl. Corp. v. AT&T Corp.*, 339 F.3d 294, 307 (5th Cir. 2003) (finding individualized nature of damages determination prevented plaintiffs from satisfying the predominance requirement); *In re Fresh Del Monte Pineapples Antitrust Litig.*, No. 1:04-MD-1628 (RMB), 2008 U.S. Dist. LEXIS 18388, at *33–36 (S.D.N.Y. 2008) (denying class certification where plaintiffs failed to offer a "reliable methodology for determining damages to the class").

7. *See, e.g., Rodney v. Nw. Airlines*, 146 F. App'x 783, 787 (6th Cir. 2005) (finding individualized questions would predominate where proof of liability depended on evidence specific to more than 50 airline routes); *Nichols v. Mobile Bd. of Realtors*, 675 F.2d 671, 679 (5th Cir. 1982); *Blue Bird Body*, 573 F.2d at 328.

8. *See, e.g., Blue Bird Body*, 573 F.2d at 320 (holding that the key inquiry is whether injury is "an issue common to the class and subject to generalized proof, or . . . an issue unique to each class member").

9. *Brunswick Corp. v. Pueblo Bowl-O-Mat, Inc.*, 429 U.S. 477, 489 (1977).

10. *Id.*

evidence.[11] Similarly, in an antitrust conspiracy case, some courts have held that common proof of the alleged conspiracy is sufficient to satisfy the predominance requirement.[12] Other courts, however, have imposed more stringent requirements on plaintiffs at the class certification phase.[13] The Third Circuit, for example, requires that plaintiffs offer common proof of more than merely a common conspiracy; rather, plaintiffs must demonstrate that classwide issues will predominate over individual issues with respect to (1) violation of the applicable antitrust law; (2) fact of injury or impact; and (3) the amount of damages.[14]

A recent prominent example from the Third Circuit is *In re Hydrogen Peroxide Antitrust Litigation*.[15] In that case, the district court certified a Rule 23(b)(3) class of purchasers of hydrogen peroxide and related chemical products, noting that the plaintiffs only needed to make a "threshold" showing to satisfy the predominance requirement.[16] Because the district court found that plaintiffs had an "intention" to try the case in a manner that satisfied the predominance requirement, it certified the class.[17] On appeal, the Third Circuit vacated the decision. The appellate court emphasized that "[antitrust] impact often is critically important for the purpose of evaluating Rule 23(b)(3)'s predominance requirement because it is an element of the claim that may call for individual, as opposed to common, proof."[18] Because the district court required only a "threshold" showing, the appellate court concluded that it had failed to conduct the "rigorous analysis" required under Rule 23(b)(3) and remanded the case for more complete consideration.[19]

---

11. *See, e.g., In re Wellbutrin SR Direct Purchaser Antitrust Litig.*, No. 04-5525, 2008 U.S. Dist. LEXIS 36719, at *31–38 (E.D. Pa. 2008) (finding predominance requirement fulfilled where plaintiffs provided a "colorable method" to establish a common antitrust impact); *Natchitoches Parish Hosp. Serv. Dist. v. Tyco Int'l*, 247 F.R.D. 253, 269–74 (D. Mass. 2008) (focusing on plaintiffs' "proposed methodologies to prove classwide antitrust liability").

12. *See, e.g., In re Urethane Antitrust Litig.*, 251 F.R.D. 629, 635 (D. Kan. 2008) (holding that conspiracy is a common issue that predominates over other issues); *Hyland v. HomeServices of Am.*, No. 1:07CV527, 2008 U.S. Dist. LEXIS 90892, at *29 (W.D. Ky. 2008) (same); *accord Se. Mo. Hosp. v. C.R. Bard, Inc.*, No 1:07CV0031, 2008 U.S. Dist. LEXIS 71841, at *18 (E.D. Mo. 2008) (holding that predominance is satisfied because establishing a violation of the antitrust laws requires scrutiny of defendant's conduct).

13. *See, e.g., In re K-Dur Antitrust Litig.*, MDL No. 1419, 2008 U.S. Dist LEXIS 71771, at *35 (D.N.J. 2008) (denying class certification because plaintiffs could not demonstrate that the antitrust injury element was susceptible to common proof); *California v. Infineon Techs. AG*, No. C 06-4333, 2008 U.S. Dist LEXIS 81251, at *45 (N.D. Cal. 2008) (denying class certification where proof of impact would vary according to market conditions); *Stand Energy Corp. v. Columbia Gas Transmission Corp.*, Civ. A 2:04-0867, 2008 U.S. Dist. LEXIS 63913, at *39–60 (S.D.W. Va. 2008) (denying class certification where plaintiffs relied on proof of multiple conspiracies).

14. *Danvers Motor Co. v. Ford Motor Co.*, 543 F.3d 141, 148–49 (3d Cir. 2008); *see also In re Hydrogen Peroxide Antitrust Litig.*, 552 F.3d 305, 311–12 (3d Cir. 2008).

15. 552 F.3d 305.

16. *See id.* at 308–09 (describing district court holding).

17. *Id.* at 321.

18. *Id.* at 311.

19. *Id.* at 315–21.

Similarly, the Third Circuit clarified the application of the predominance requirement under Rule 23(b)(3) to antitrust claims in *American Seed Co. v. Monsanto Co.*[20] The plaintiff in *American Seed* argued that it could establish a presumption of classwide antitrust impact through the use of common proof.[21] After examining the opinions of the plaintiff's expert, the district court concluded that the expert had not demonstrated the validity of his theory of impact by comparing the theoretical results generated by the expert's theory to actual data made available by defendants in discovery.[22] The district court denied class certification, and the Third Circuit affirmed, holding that the putative class must support its proposed presumption of antitrust impact with "some additional amount of empirical evidence."[23]

There are no "hard and fast rules" for determining what type of antitrust claims are appropriate for class certification under Rule 23(b)(3), and the analysis of each case will turn on "unique facts."[24] However, courts have found that some types of cases are more susceptible to class certification than others. For example, horizontal price-fixing cases involving products that are discrete and fungible are commonly cited as appropriate candidates for class certification.[25] However, class treatment is often inappropriate when injury or impact can be shown only on an individual basis, such as when the claim requires examination of local market conditions, or when there is wide variation in pricing practices, individual buyer-seller negotiations, or unique and customized products.[26]

---

20. 271 F. App'x 138 (3d Cir. 2008).

21. *Id.* at 140.

22. *Id.* at 140–41.

23. *Id.* at 141.

24. *Blue Bird Body*, 573 F.2d at 316.

25. *Paper Sys. v. Mitsubishi Corp.*, 193 F.R.D. 601, 612 (E.D. Wis. 2000) (price-fixing cases often certified); *In re Commercial Tissue Prods.*, 183 F.R.D. 589, 595 (N.D. Fla. 1998) (same); *In re Potash Antitrust Litig.*, 159 F.R.D. 682, 693 (D. Minn. 1995) ("A mere allegation of price-fixing will not satisfy Rule 23(b)'s predominance requirement. However, as a general rule in antitrust price-fixing cases, questions common to the members of the class will predominate over questions affecting only individual members.").

26. *See, e.g.*, *Heerwagen v. Clear Channel Commc'ns*, 435 F.3d 219, 229 (2d Cir. 2006) (affirming denial of class certification because individualized questions as to each geographic market would predominate); *Blades v. Monsanto Co.*, 400 F.3d 562, 572 (8th Cir. 2005) (holding that "highly individualized" local markets and variation in prices precluded satisfaction of predominance requirement); *Reed v. Advocate Health Care*, No. 06 C 3337, 2009 U.S. Dist. LEXIS 89576 (N.D. Ill. 2009) (denying class certification in an alleged nurse wage-fixing conspiracy since individual issues predominate); *In re Indus. Diamonds Antitrust Litig.*, 167 F.R.D. 374, 384 (S.D.N.Y. 1996) (finding that common issues predominate with respect to a class of purchasers of products with list prices, but denying class certification to class of purchasers without list prices because of variation in pricing practices); *Butt v. Allegheny Pepsi Cola Bottling Co.*, 116 F.R.D. 486, 490–92 (E.D. Va. 1987) (denying class certification where individualized proof would be required by customer, transaction, and products); *In re Agric. Chems. Antitrust Litig.*, No. 94-40216, 1995 U.S. Dist. LEXIS 21075 (N.D. Fla. Oct. 23, 1995) (variation in "particular mix of product and service that is purchased by the customer"); *In re Beef Indus. Antitrust Litig.*, MDL No. 248, 1986 U.S. Dist. LEXIS 24731 (variation on geographic pricing).

EXPOSURE TORTS

RICHARD W. MARK
LAURIE STRAUCH WEISS[1]

I. Introduction

Federal Rule of Civil Procedure 23 provides for various types of class actions, and the type most frequently invoked by mass tort plaintiffs is the "opt-out" class under Rule 23(b)(3). To certify a class under Rule 23(b)(3), plaintiffs must show, in addition to the four familiar requirements of Rule 23(a),[2] that common issues predominate and that the class action is a superior vehicle for prosecuting the action.

A survey of case law reveals that the "predominance" requirement presents a major hurdle to prosecuting mass exposure torts as class actions. Attempts to use the class action device for such claims frequently fail because courts tend to conclude that common legal or factual questions do not predominate over causation issues—even small variations in the amount or timing of exposure, for example—that affect individual class members. The fact-specific analysis required to assess predominance defies extracting a general rule or pattern.[3] Environmental pollution from an identified source has elements of time, geography, and individual dose that defeat class action treatment in some cases, but not others.[4] Class treatment of personal injury claims arising from mass market products and pharmaceuticals is generally rejected because of factual variations among class members.[5] Efforts to fit claims to the class action form by limiting the relief sought to injuries

---

1. The authors thank Emily Green, associate at Orrick, Herrington & Sutcliffe, LLP, Adam Zimmerman, formerly associated with Orrick, Herrington & Sutcliffe, LLP, and Ilene Albala, summer law clerk at Orrick, Herrington & Sutcliffe, LLP, for their assistance in preparing this chapter.

2. Those requirements are numerosity, commonality, typicality, and adequacy of representation. *See* FED. R. CIV. P. 23(a).

3. *See infra* section IV.

4. *See infra* section IV.A.

5. *See infra* sections IV.B and IV.C.

that do not require individualized proof beyond an objectively determined amount of damage (e.g., a consumer action) have had mixed success.[6] Some courts find that the limitation eliminates the noise of individual issues.[7] Other courts reject the truncation precisely because it leaves individual injury claims that arise from many of the same alleged facts as the economic injury for later litigation.[8] There are exposure tort cases resolved by certifying a settlement class (where agreement among the parties may avoid due process questions that would be insurmountable if actually litigated) and others that reject that approach.[9] When a mass exposure occurs in a single event and so diminishes individual distinctions of time and dosage, courts sometimes certify a class and other times do not.[10] Overall, the class action is not a procedure used easily to manage exposure tort litigation.

II. Original Intent: Rule 23 Was Not Expected to Manage Exposure Torts

Rule 23 was comprehensively revised in 1966 and the Advisory Committee note accompanying that work anticipates that mass torts will generally not be suited to class treatment.[11] The Advisory Committee expected that application of (b)(3) would turn on case-specific facts, and that the class device could be used in cases "in which a class action would achieve economies of time, effort, and expense, and promote uniformity of decision as to persons similarly situated, without sacrificing procedural fairness or bringing about other undesirable results."[12] The note goes on to state that "a fraud perpetrated on numerous persons by the use of similar misrepresentations may be an appealing situation for a class action" even if separate liability determinations for class members are required.[13] On the other hand:

> A "mass accident" resulting in injuries to numerous persons is ordinarily not appropriate for a class action because of the likelihood that significant questions, not only of damages but of liability and defenses of liability, would be present, affecting the individuals in different ways. In these circumstances an action con-

---

6. *See infra* section IV.D.

7. *See, e.g., Nafar v. Hollywood Tanning Sys., Inc.*, No. 06-CV-3826 (DMC), 2008 WL 3821776 (D.N.J. Aug. 12, 2008).

8. *See, e.g., In re Teflon Prods. Liab. Litig.*, 254 F.R.D. 354 (S.D. Iowa 2008).

9. *See infra* section IV.E.

10. *Compare In re Train Derailment Near Amite La.*, No. MDL 1531, 2006 WL 1561470 (E.D. La. May 24, 2006) (granting class certification), *with Braud v. Transp. Servs. of Ill.*, Nos. 05-1898, 06-891, 05-1977, 05-5557, 2009 WL 2208524 (E.D. La. July 23, 2009) (denying class certification).

11. *See* FED. R. CIV. P. 23, subdivision (b)(3) advisory committee note (1966).

12. *Id.*

13. *Id.*

ducted nominally as a class action would degenerate in practice into multiple law-suits separately tried.[14]

An exposure tort (if that term even had currency in 1966) represents the paradigm of a claim that the Advisory Committee believed "ordinarily" would fail as a (b)(3) class action.

III. The Supreme Court's Decision in Amchem

In the years after the 1966 revision, litigation of exposure torts evolved and the class action procedure was used as a way to manage large numbers of claims, frequently via the device of a settlement class.[15] The U.S. Supreme Court examined that practice in its landmark 1997 ruling in *Amchem Products, Inc. v. Windsor.*[16] If in 1966 the Advisory Committee believed that predominance presented a prohibitively high hurdle for mass torts to surmount on the way to class certification, *Amchem* confirmed as much.[17] The case involved workers who had been exposed to asbestos, and the matter was to be settled on a class basis.[18] The Third Circuit, however, decertified the class, and plaintiffs sought review in the Supreme Court.[19]

The Supreme Court affirmed the decertification, rejecting the use of the (b)(3) class procedure even though the parties were trying to effectuate a global settlement and would not be litigating claims on a class basis.[20] Even in that context, the Court emphasized that the requirements for class certification had to be met and, for the type of class at issue, the courts could not skip past the predominance requirement under 23(b)(3).[21]

In analyzing predominance, the *Amchem* Court noted that the circumstances of liability and injury varied considerably among class members.[22] In emphasizing the underlying questions "undermining class cohesion" in the case, the Court cited the Third Circuit's statement that

> [c]lass members were exposed to different asbestos-containing products, for different amounts of time, in different ways, and over different periods. Some class

---

14. *Id.*
15. *See* Thomas E. Willging, Laural L. Hooper & Robert L. Niemic, Empirical Study of Class Actions in Four Federal District Courts: Final Report to the Advisory Committee on Civil Rules 61–62 (Federal Judicial Center 1996), *available at* http://www.fjc.gov/public/pdf.nsf/lookup/rule23.pdf/$File/rule23.pdf (noting large number of settlement classes in districts studied).
16. 521 U.S. 591 (1997).
17. *See id.*
18. *Id.* at 597.
19. *Id.*
20. *Id.* at 603, 612.
21. *Id.* at 619–20.
22. *Id.* at 624.

members suffer no physical injury . . . while others suffer from lung cancer . . . .
Each has a different history of cigarette smoking, a factor that complicates the causation inquiry.[23]

Because of these differences among members in the exposure class, the Court concluded that common questions of law or fact concerning, for example, the conduct
of defendants at relevant points in time, would not predominate over questions
affecting only individual members of the class.[24] The Court did not shut the door
on use of class actions in exposure torts, suggesting that some of the problems with
the single, comprehensive *Amchem* class might be avoided through creating narrow
subclasses.[25] That was left, however, as a largely theoretical possibility. The Court
cited to the 1966 Advisory Committee note and voiced skepticism over the prospect
of mass tort claims in general meeting the (b)(3) predominance requirement.[26]

Analysis of predominance always brings up the due process question at the core
of the class action device: while courts and parties crave efficiency, would presentation of the plaintiffs' claim en masse be functionally equivalent to proving each
class member's claim; *and* does the defendant facing the mass have a fair opportunity to litigate all material issues that could deny any individual class member's
claim? Until and unless those due process concerns are satisfied—viz., if a party
were to succeed in laying a foundation that there are no material differences in
causation questions among plaintiffs claiming personal injury from exposure to
allegedly harmful agents—exposure torts will continue to be generally unsuitable
for class action treatment.

IV. Case Examples

Court treatment of the predominance issue in exposure torts is shown in the
following case summaries. These are provided as illustrative examples, without
intending to present a complete or comprehensive review of all cases touching on
the issue. The cases have been grouped into categories for convenient review, but
the boundaries between them are not rigid. While a class certification application
touches on many factors and denial of certification may rest on multiple flaws, the

---

23. *Id.* (citing *Georgine v. Amchem Prods., Inc.*, 83 F.3d 610, 626 (3d Cir. 1996)).

24. *Id.* at 623–24.

25. *Id.* at 636 (Breyer, J., concurring in part and dissenting in part). However, the Court then goes on
to say that subclasses can also create problems: "These differences might warrant subclasses, though subclasses can have problems of their own. 'There can be a cost in creating more distinct subgroups, each with
its own representation . . . . [T]he more subclasses created, the more severe conflicts bubble to the surface
and inhibit settlement . . . .'" *Id.* (quoting JACK B. WEINSTEIN, INDIVIDUAL JUSTICE IN MASS TORT LITIGATION 66
(1995)).

26. *Id.* at 625 (majority opinion).

cases included here explicitly reference (b)(3) and the predominance question in their analyses.

A. ENVIRONMENTAL EXPOSURE

Cases involving release of an agent from a point into air or water, resulting in a mass of individual exposures in a relatively confined geography, are sometimes proposed for class action treatment. Although the defendant's conduct leading to the release in such a case could involve adjudication of common questions, whether such questions predominate over those affecting the exposed individuals will depend on particular facts. These include cases where the mass exposure occurs in a single event (such as a factory explosion) and where the exposure occurs over a longer period (as in groundwater contamination).

Thus, in *Burkhead v. Louisville Gas & Electric Co.*,[27] where a utility's power plant allegedly spread contaminants over the local geography and caused property damage, the court denied (b)(3) certification, finding that causation and damage questions were individualized for each property. To prove their trespass claim, for example, the plaintiffs would have had to show an intrusion or encroachment that unreasonably interfered with their possessory use of property.[28] Plaintiffs submitted no evidence from which they proposed to show liability on a classwide basis.[29] Although the emissions in that case came from one point, the geographic dispersal of proposed class members made for variation in the circumstances of individual exposure.[30] Plaintiffs' attempt to make the existence of property damage the predominant question—by proposing a class definition limiting membership to those "whose property was damaged by noxious odors, fallout, pollutants and contaminants which originated from [the defendant's] facility"—failed because it blended the class determination with the merits.[31]

A compact time frame for the emission will not necessarily support a predominance finding. A court denied certification of a class of workers all allegedly injured in a single incident of a chemical plant fire, finding even in that temporally compact setting that each individual plaintiff suffered different alleged periods

---

27. 250 F.R.D. 287 (W.D. Ky. 2008); *see also Cochran v. Oxy Vinyls LP*, No. 3:06CV-364-H, 2008 WL 4146383 (W.D. Ky. Sept. 2, 2008) (rejecting (b)(3) certification for property owner class claiming damage from industrial plant emissions); *Rowe v. E.I. DuPont de Nemours & Co.*, Nos. 06-1810 (RMB), 06-3080 (RMB), 2008 WL 5412912 (D.N.J. Dec. 23, 2008) (rejecting (b)(3) certification for proposed medical monitoring class for individuals exposed to factory emissions in air and water); *Turner v. Murphy Oil USA, Inc.*, 234 F.R.D. 597 (E.D. La. 2006) (rejecting (b)(3) certification of common law tort claims for property damage attributable to hurricane-caused oil spill).

28. *Burkhead*, 250 F.R.D. at 300.

29. *Id.* at 299, 300.

30. *Id.* at 293, 295.

31. *Id.* at 293–94.

and magnitudes of exposure and suffered different alleged symptoms as a result, and that many sought damages for emotional and other intangible injuries.[32]

A multidistrict litigation alleging personal injury and property damage from exposure to the gasoline additive methyl tertiary butyl ether (MTBE) provides an illustration of a court certifying some (b)(3) subclasses and rejecting others in an environmental exposure case.[33] In *In re Methyl Tertiary Butyl Ether ("MTBE") Products Liability Litigation*,[34] the court concluded that the predominance requirement was *not* satisfied with respect to the subclass claiming for personal injuries from MTBE exposure resulting from defendants' release of gasoline from a pipeline because the proximate cause element could not be proved on a classwide basis. On the other hand, the court concluded that the predominance requirement was satisfied by two subclasses asserting tort claims based on contamation of real property and water sources from the same release.[35] The court concluded that the subclass members' property damage claims arose out of a single event and liability could be resolved by a jury with a single decision that applied to both subclasses.[36]

The Seventh Circuit approved certification in *Mejdrech v. Met-Coil Systems Corp.*,[37] a case involving the factory leak of a noxious solvent into the groundwater affecting the homes of 1,000 nearby property owners where the issue for class treatment was limited to whether unlawful contamination occurred and whether such contamination reached residents' properties. The court acknowledged that case law involving the class certification of such cases was slim.[38] Certification was approved only because of the strict limitation on the issues to be resolved on a representative basis.[39]

The Sixth Circuit similarly approved class treatment of a limited issue in *Olden v. LaFarge Corp.*,[40] a case involving 3,600 homeowners alleging personal injuries and property damages stemming from the release of toxins from a large cement plant. The thrust of the plaintiffs' claims for medical monitoring was proving

---

32. *Steering Comm. v. Exxon Mobil Corp.*, 461 F.3d 598, 602–03 (5th Cir. 2006); *see also Bradford v. Union Pac. R.R. Co.*, No. 05-CV-4075, 2007 WL 2893650 (W.D. Ark. Sept. 28, 2007) (rejecting (b)(3) certification, even with subclasses, for personal injury and property damage claims allegedly caused by train derailment and consequent fire and explosions); *Snow v. Atofina Chems., Inc.*, No. 01-72648, 2006 WL 1008002 (E.D. Mich. Mar. 31, 2006) (rejecting (b)(3) certification for personal injury, medical monitoring, and economic loss all allegedly attributed to chemicals emitted as a result of a plant explosion).

33. *In re Methyl Tertiary Butyl Ether ("MTBE") Prods. Liab. Litig.*, 241 F.R.D. 435 (S.D.N.Y. 2007).

34. *Id.* at 449.

35. *Id.* at 447–48.

36. *Id.* ("Courts have repeatedly drawn distinctions between proposed classes involving a single incident or single source of harm and proposed classes involving multiple sources of harm occurring over time. The former warrant certification, while the latter do not.").

37. 319 F.3d 910, 911 (7th Cir. 2003).

38. *Id.* at 910–11.

39. *Id.* at 912.

40. 383 F.3d 495, 496 (6th Cir. 2004).

"[w]hether the defendant's negligence caused *some* increased health risk and . . . whether it tended to cause the class minor medical issues"—determinations that could likely be made for the entire class.[41] The court concluded that individual damage determinations would not predominate over common allegations of harm.

B. EXPOSURE VIA MASS MARKET PRODUCTS

Personal injury claims are resistant to (b)(3) class certification—as *Amchem* shows—because variations in the time and level of individual exposures overwhelm common issues that may exist simply because the alleged injury is traceable to a common product. Even before *Amchem*, courts rejected applications to certify (b)(3) classes of cigarette smokers. The Fifth Circuit's *Castano v. American Tobacco Co.*[42] ruling is illustrative. Questions that affected individuals in the proposed nationwide class included the varying tort standards under the state laws governing different claims; the different products used; the different time periods; and the different knowledge of class members.[43] Because "these factual differences impact[ ] the application of legal rules such as causation, reliance, comparative fault, and other affirmative defenses," class certification failed.[44]

Similar factors of individual variation have precluded class certification in claims based on exposure to formaldehyde emissions from emergency housing units;[45] exposure to pesticides;[46] exposure to x-ray radiation from radar equipment;[47] and exposure to allegedly contaminated peanut butter.[48]

C. PHARMACEUTICALS

Class treatment is sometimes sought for claims of personal injury from pharmaceuticals. Logically, the analysis should track that for other consumer products, and a review of cases confirms that inference. The circumstances of individual exposure and injury tend to preclude a conclusion that common issues relating to the product predominate in the litigation.

The multidistrict products liability case involving the painkiller Vioxx presents a typical case.[49] The plaintiffs in this action moved to certify a class to litigate claims for personal injuries and wrongful death allegedly caused by a prescription pain

---

41. *Id.* at 508 (emphasis in original).
42. 84 F.3d 734 (5th Cir. 1996).
43. *Id.* at 741–44, 742 n.15.
44. *Id.* at 742 n.15.
45. *In re FEMA Trailer Formaldehyde Prods. Liab. Litig.*, No. MDL 071873, 2008 WL 5423488, at *22–23 (E.D. La. Dec. 29, 2008).
46. *Fisher v. Ciba Specialty Chems. Corp.*, 238 F.R.D. 273, 305–15 (S.D. Ala. 2006).
47. *Norwood v. Raytheon Co.*, 237 F.R.D. 581, 600–03 (W.D. Tex. 2006).
48. *In re Conagra Peanut Butter Prods. Liab. Litig.*, 251 F.R.D. 689, 696–702 (N.D. Ga. 2008).
49. *In re Vioxx Prods. Liab. Litig.*, 239 F.R.D. 450 (E.D. La. 2006).

relier.[50] The district court denied the application for several reasons, including the class's failure to satisfy Rule 23(b)(3).[51] Regarding that section of the rule, the court noted the following as creating issues among individuals and precluding a conclusion that common issues predominated: the putative class members' claims would be governed by substantive laws of their respective jurisdictions; the package insert and label changed several times during the period when class members received Vioxx, and liability would turn on individual knowledge and individual interactions with prescribing physicians; and the class members would have distinct medical histories and causation issues.[52]

In re Prempro Products Liability Litigation[53] is another example of a case in which the court denied certification. The case involved a drug prescribed for post-menopausal women.[54] Plaintiffs sought class certification for a consumer protection class and a medical monitoring class; neither class was certified.[55] Plaintiffs argued that questions of law and fact were common to the classes, as the defendant engaged in a marketing campaign designed specifically to increase the drug's sales, and this marketing campaign constituted uniform deception.[56] The court disagreed and reasoned that questions of fact in *Prempro* were diverse, as liability depended upon factors including when each individual took the drug, what advertising each individual saw, and what knowledge, if any, the individual had before seeing the advertisement.[57]

The majority of courts have denied or decertified class action treatment in drug and medical device cases involving dispersed mass torts, and only a few courts

---

50. *Id.* at 453.

51. *Id.* at 460–63.

52. *Id.* at 460–62; *see also In re Fosamax Prods. Liab. Litig.*, 248 F.R.D. 389, 399 (S.D.N.Y. 2008) (denying (b)(3) certification in action seeking medical monitoring based on exposure to a drug to treat osteoporosis; case would be dominated by issues requiring individualized proof of each class member's medical condition and circumstances of their use of drug); *Blain v. SmithKline Beecham Corp.*, 240 F.R.D. 179 (E.D. Pa. 2007) (denying (b)(3) certification in an action alleging that the prescription drug Paxil could cause suicide or suicidality in children because the causation issues were all individualized); *Sanders v. Johnson & Johnson, Inc.*, No. 03-2663 (GEB), 2006 WL 1541033 (D.N.J. June 2, 2006) (denying (b)(3) certification in an action for injuries from use of Intergel, a product used "on the peritoneal surfaces following surgical procedures," because common factual issues did not predominate over individual issues concerning each class member's medical history, understanding of the product, and physician-patient relationship). It is worth noting that Merck, the manufacturer of Vioxx, eventually entered into a $4.85 billion non–class action settlement agreement in 2007 where claims were to be evaluated on an individual basis. Merck Agreement to Resolve U.S. Vioxx Product Liability Lawsuits, http://www.merck.com/newsroom/press_releases/corporate/2007_1109.html (last visited May 8, 2010).

53. 230 F.R.D. 555 (D. Ark. 2005).

54. *Id.* at 557.

55. *Id.* at 558.

56. *Id.* at 566.

57. *Id.* at 567.

have certified classes.[58] *In re Telectronics Pacing Systems Inc.*[59] (decided pre-*Amchem*) provides an example of class certification being granted. Plaintiffs brought claims against the manufacturer of a heart pacemaker.[60] The class was originally certified, then decertified, and finally certified again.[61] *Telectronics* differs from other, unsuccessful attempts at class treatment because the court certified ten subclasses, each tailored to a particular state and claims under that state's law.[62] "[B]y creating subclasses based upon causes of actions and providing class representatives whose home state's law recognizes the cause of action represented in the subclass, Plaintiffs have remedied the problem which made the original class representatives atypical—namely representing absent class members whose claims differed from their own."[63] Notably, the court did not certify all the proposed subclasses: the court refused to certify a punitive damages subclass as it "failed to take into account adequately the multiple variations in the law of punitive damages."[64]

D. CLAIMS TO RECOVER ECONOMIC LOSS

In some cases, plaintiffs have tried to make the class action device a better fit for their case by voluntarily cutting out the issues that breed individual questions. The theory is that plaintiffs can avoid individual questions of causation and damages if the claim is limited to economic loss, such as a fraud claim to recover the price paid for the product. Such a claim ought to appear more like the type of fraud claim the 1966 Advisory Committee hypothesized as attractive for class action treatment. Courts, however, have generally not taken to this approach. The claim being proved is generally viewed as the same one that would support relief for personal injuries, and courts do not like to section off relief that could otherwise be awarded on the facts proved. Gerrymandering the claim in this way also tends to create problems in meeting the 23(a) class action predicates.

In re Teflon Products Liability Litigation[65] provides an example. This multidistrict litigation involved allegations that the maker of nonstick cookware made false, misleading, and deceptive representations about product safety.[66] Certification under (b)(3) was denied for several reasons including the predominance of

---

58. *In re Telectronics Pacing Sys. Inc.*, 172 F.R.D. 271 (S.D. Ohio 1997); *In re Diet Drugs Prods. Liab. Litig.*, No. 98-20626, 1999 WL 673066 (E.D. Pa. Aug. 26, 1999) (conditionally certifying a medical monitoring class under Rule 23(b)(2), which, unlike 23(b)(3), does not contain a predominance requirement).

59. 172 F.R.D. 271.

60. *Id.* at 276–77.

61. *Id.* at 278, 295.

62. *Id.* at 278–95.

63. *Id.* at 281.

64. *Id.* at 294.

65. 254 F.R.D. 354.

66. *Id.* at 357.

individual issues relating to when the cookware was purchased.[67] The plaintiffs also attempted to eliminate individual issues by abandoning original claims for medical monitoring and expressly disavowing any current claims for personal injury.[68] That, however, worked against the application for class certification because the abandonment resulted in the conclusion that the proposed representatives failed to satisfy Rule 23(a)'s requirement for adequate representation of class member interests.[69] While the representatives could waive their own claims, it was not appropriate for them to bind absent class members to that waiver.[70]

The district of New Jersey reached a different conclusion in litigation involving tanning salons.[71] In *Nafar v. Hollywood Tanning Systems, Inc.*, plaintiffs brought a class action alleging violation of the New Jersey Consumer Fraud Act (NJCFA), fraud, unjust enrichment, and breach of warranty, and sought certification under (b)(3).[72] The claims were premised on sale of tanning memberships by defendants who allegedly failed to disclose that any exposure to ultraviolet rays increases the risk of cancer and who made other claimed misrepresentations.[73] Plaintiff excluded personal injury damages from the claim.[74] The court certified the class, concluding that the common factual and legal issues under the NJCFA would predominate over individual questions.[75] Unlike the *Teflon* court, the *Nafar* court was not troubled by the representatives' abandonment of the personal injury claims.

In contrast to the tanning salon case, the district court in Massachusetts, dealing with a pharmaceutical claim under the NJCFA, denied class certification.[76] In *In re Neurontin Marketing & Sale Practices Litigation*, plaintiffs alleged improper marketing of Neurontin for off-label uses and sought economic damages only.[77] The court rejected class certification under (b)(3), ruling that determination of

---

67. *Id.* at 365, 370.

68. *Id.* at 358, 366–67.

69. *Id.* at 368.

70. *Id.* at 367. *Krueger v. Wyeth, Inc.*, No. 03CV2496 JLS (AJB), 2008 WL 481956 (S.D. Cal. Feb. 19, 2008), is a similar holding in the context of a prescription drug. Plaintiffs sought (b)(3) certification for a class defined as all California consumers damaged by purchasing Premarin, Prempro, and/or Premphase, between January 1995 and January 2003. *Id.* at *1. The class failed Rule 23(a)'s adequacy of representation requirement: "In the present action, Plaintiff leaves the class open to those who have suffered personal injuries, while stating she does not seek to pursue personal injury damages claims. As a result, the Court finds that Plaintiff Krueger is an inadequate class representative under the current class definition." *Id.* at *4.

71. *Nafar*, 2008 WL 3821776.

72. *Id.* at *1.

73. *Id.*

74. *Id.*

75. *Id.* at *5–6.

76. *In re Neurontin Mktg. & Sale Practices Litig.*, 244 F.R.D. 89 (D. Mass. 2007).

77. *Id.* at 91, 93–103.

which prescriptions were caused by the alleged fraud would require individualized evidence and determination.[78]

Litigation over the antidepressant Paxil further illustrates the possibility of different outcomes. In *In re Paxil Litigation*,[79] the Central District of California rejected plaintiffs' fashioning several different class certification arguments, including an attempt to attach a plea for economic damage from purchasing Paxil to a claim for an injunction to stop the allegedly deceptive advertising. The court rejected that attempt to obtain monetary relief under the rubric of 23(b)(2), and rejected the application for certification under 23(b)(3) for additional reasons.[80] On the other hand, an Illinois state court approved a settlement class in *Hoorman v. SmithKline Beecham Corp.*,[81] where the relief was limited to economic loss from purchasing Paxil for minors. In assessing litigation risk as a justification for the compromise settlement, the state court noted the federal court rejection of class certification as evidence that the manufacturers have strong defenses "and a successful outcome for the plaintiffs was anything but certain."[82]

E. SETTLEMENT CLASSES

Even after *Amchem*, courts continue to certify settlement classes. After all, *Amchem* did not categorically eliminate settlement classes: it only reminded courts that even in the settlement context, a court had to analyze the certification application according to the standards of (b)(3), and the litigants' desire to settle could not obscure the conflicting interests among class members.[83]

Gates v. Rohm & Haas Co.[84] reflects one post-*Amchem* example. This ruling involved proposed settlement classes of plaintiffs seeking (1) medical monitoring and (2) damages for diminution in property value based on exposure to drinking water pollutants allegedly generated and released by defendants.[85] The court certified the proposed classes because both sought relief based on exposure alone.[86] With respect to the medical monitoring class, individual differences in medical histories, lifestyles, and property uses would not affect causation analysis for purposes of liability because many of the claims were based on the allegation that

---

78. *Id.* at 111–13.

79. 218 F.R.D. 242, 247–48 (C.D. Cal. 2003).

80. *Id.* at 247–50.

81. No. 04-L-715, 2007 WL 1591510 (Ill. Cir. Ct. May 17, 2007).

82. *Id.* at ¶ 9 & n.2 (citing several published decisions denying class certification in other Paxil litigation).

83. *Amchem*, 521 U.S. at 619–20.

84. 248 F.R.D. 434 (E.D. Pa. 2008).

85. *Id.* at 437.

86. *Id.* at 443.

a minimum level of exposure triggered a heightened risk of cancer.[87] As for the property damage class, the common question of whether there was exposure dominated individual issues concerning the amount of exposure or amount of diminution in property value.[88]

Exhibiting a little more analytical flexibility than in *Gates*, *Bell v. DuPont Dow Elastomers, LLC*[89] certified a settlement class alleging nuisance, negligence and/or gross negligence, trespass, and strict liability claims and seeking damages for personal injury and property damage. All of these injuries were allegedly caused by emissions into the air from defendant's plant.[90] On that record, the court found that the common issues of fact and law predominated over any individual issues and concluded that class certification was appropriate.[91]

Two transportation accident litigations provide examples of opposite conclusions on roughly similar facts. The fact that one case featured a settlement class while the other remained a contested putative class action appears outcome determinative. Both cases involved environmental releases of chemicals, one the result of a train derailment[92] and the other a tractor-trailer accident.[93] The court in *In re Train Derailment Near Amite Louisiana* granted certification under (b)(3) for a settlement class.[94] It cited the common issues of defendant's conduct as weighing in favor of certification.[95] More significant, however, the court concluded that plaintiffs' theory of compensable injuries—"fear and fright and evacuation/inconvenience"—were general and allowed for class disposition.[96] Indeed, the claims stopped at that theory because individual causation of injury from the exposure could not be established.[97] The court in *Braud v. Transport Services of Illinois*, however, recognized the unifying factors of source, timing, and legal theories, but rejected certification under (b)(3) because "defendants' conduct, while common, is but a minor part of each potential class member's case."[98] The court concluded that issues of individual causation and injury attributable to the exposure precluded class treatment.[99]

---

87. *Id.*

88. *Id.*

89. No. 3:07-CV-581-H, 2009 WL 1917081 (W.D. Ky. July 1, 2009).

90. *Id.* at *1.

91. *Id.* at *3; *see also Donaway v. Rohm & Haas Co.*, No. 3:06-CV-575-H, 2009 WL 1917083 (W.D. Ky. July 1, 2009) (reaching same conclusion for a settlement class).

92. *In re Train Derailment Near Amite La.*, 2006 WL 1561470.

93. *Braud*, 2009 WL 2208524.

94. 2006 WL 1561470, at *17–18.

95. *Id.* at *10.

96. *Id.* at *11.

97. *Id.*

98. 2009 WL 2208524, at *13.

99. *Id.* at *11–13.

V. Conclusion

Despite the demonstrated difficulty of obtaining class certification for exposure torts, courts continue to face applications for that relief. Although the case reports suggest that relief will usually be denied, each case ultimately turns on its own facts. By carefully considering the language of the rule and the standards it embodies, how that standard applies to a claim, and the fundamental requirements of due process, an application may credibly be made for class relief—even if it is ultimately unsuccessful.

OIL AND GAS ROYALTY CLASSES

MARK D. CHRISTIANSEN

I. General Backdrop of Oil and Gas Class Action Royalty Litigation

For more than 15 years, oil- and gas-producing states, such as Texas, Oklahoma, New Mexico, and Colorado, have experienced a proliferation of lawsuits by royalty owner counsel who have sought to assert royalty underpayment claims on behalf of proposed fieldwide, statewide, multistate, and nationwide classes of royalty owners. In determining whether those proposed classes can properly be certified for disposition of royalty claims on a classwide basis, the elements of manageability and predominance have proven to be very significant.

Counsel for royalty owner plaintiffs often describe suits over alleged underpayments of oil and gas royalties as simple "accounting lawsuits," in which the use of a common accounting system to pay all of the royalty owners of a particular defendant company makes class action treatment appropriate. The defense counsel usually respond by pointing to the fact that the overriding considerations affecting the validity of royalty underpayment claims under the substantive laws of the states have little to do with the defendant's accounting practices and systems. Rather, they note that the factors emphasized by the courts to determine legal liability on the claims in royalty cases vary from well to well, property to property, and owner to owner, such that it is not possible to conduct a fair and proper trial of those claims on a classwide basis.

The courts have reached mixed decisions when presented with the above arguments. With the increasing efforts to obtain class certification in oil and gas cases over the past 15 years, it has become apparent that certain venues and courts are more receptive than others to the certification of large royalty owner classes. Since counsel for plaintiff royalty owners control venue selections, they usually choose to file their proposed class actions in forums that have already shown a receptiveness to the use of class action procedure in oil and gas cases. As a consequence, when totaling the number of cases in which class certification has been granted or denied, it should be noted that a disproportionate number of the cases were likely filed in the venues that had already approved class action procedure in large oil and gas cases.

Moreover, unlike class action litigation directed toward most other areas of business and industries, the debate over the use of the class action device in oil and gas royalty lawsuits has at times included a political component.[1] Where the use or nonuse of class action procedure becomes a significant local political issue in a state or locale, concerns arise as to whether that environment will complicate the normal process under which the outcome in particular circumstances is to be based upon the law and the facts.

The following decisions are examples of both rulings that have certified classes in royalty lawsuits and rulings in which class certification has been denied.

II. Examples of Cases in Which Royalty Classes Were Certified

In *Rudman v. Texaco, Inc.*,[2] the plaintiff royalty owners in two unitized oil and gas fields[3] alleged that the defendants underpaid royalties on production that Texaco sold to itself or an affiliate. In affirming most[4] of the district court's order granting class certification, the court of appeals found that the fundamental issues raised by the plaintiffs were (1) whether the defendant's secondary recovery unit organization and its operator owed a fiduciary duty to the royalty owners, and (2) if so, whether the unit and operator breached that duty. The court concluded that the question of damages and the question of legal liability were not so intertwined in the case as to make them impossible to separate.

The court gave little weight to defendants' assertion that the varying provisions of the oil and gas leases and division order documents created individualized questions that precluded class certification, and instead simply noted that the evidence submitted in support of class certification showed that "the sundry provi-

---

1. *See Questions and Answers with Terry Stowers*, OKLAHOMAN, Apr. 16, 2008, http://newsok.com/article/3230560/1208311168. In that article, one of the leaders of a royalty owner and landowner association refers to the public debate over the possible curtailment of class action procedure in the state, alludes to those proposals as being adverse to class action royalty lawsuits, and advises that "[o]ur mission is not only to educate the legislators, but to report back to royalty owners whether their legislators are truly representing them."

2. 70 O.B.J. 2631 (Okla. App. 1999—#92,012) (not for publication).

3. The procedure for unitization of oil and gas fields for secondary recovery operations in Oklahoma is generally set forth in OKLA. STAT. tit. 52, § 287.1 *et seq.* (2000).

4. The court of appeals did direct the district court to remove from the class those royalty owners who took payment of their royalties "in kind" (rather than in monetary form) as well as royalty owners whose royalties were paid exclusively by working interest owners other than the unit organization or Texaco or any entity related to or affiliated with Texaco or the unit.

sions for payment set forth in the leases and division orders were disregarded [by the defendants]."[5]

In *Freeman v. Great Lakes Energy Partners, L.L.C.*,[6] the lower court had certified a class of royalty owners with respect to the plaintiffs' assertions that the defendant had artificially manipulated the price upon which their royalties were calculated. The appellate court found that the common questions of law and fact concerned "defendants' common course of conduct with respect to plaintiffs, including whether certain deductions taken by defendants in calculating royalties were improper and whether defendants artificially manipulated the royalty calculations as a result of self-dealing transactions."[7] The court affirmed the granting of class certification.

The North Dakota Supreme Court in *Ritter, Laber & Associates, Inc. v. Koch Oil, Inc.*[8] was presented with a class of some 6,000 royalty and leasehold interest owners in some 2,300 wells, involving assertions that Koch's measurement of crude oil by hand gauging led to inaccurate measurements and to the defendant acquiring more oil than it paid for. The class asserted claims for conversion and unjust enrichment and for an accounting for the years 1975 through 1988. Koch appealed the order granting class certification under Rule 23 of the North Dakota Rules of Civil Procedure.

The court observed that "[h]ere, all the proposed class members are owners of oil interests, the only commodity is oil, the only transaction is selling oil, the only buyer is Koch, and the only means of measuring the oil is hand-gauging."[9] The court held that, although individual issues might be present in the case, individual issues did not defeat or preclude a finding that common questions predominated in the case.[10]

While it concluded that "[m]ost of the [district] court's findings are affirmable,"[11] the appellate court found that the district court erred in its analysis of both the "common interest" factor under Rule 23(c)(1)(A) and the "inconsistent standards" factor under Rule 23(c)(1)(B).[12] The court cited with approval the following statements in *Werlinger v. Champion Healthcare Corp.*:

> Here, the main premise of the district court's finding seems to be that results could differ among the plaintiffs if their claims were adjudicated individually. This is not a risk of incompatible standards. Generally, different results in actions for money

---

5. *Id.*

6. 12 A.D.3d 1170 (N.Y. App. Div. 2004).

7. *Id.* at 1171.

8. 2000 N.D. 15, 605 N.W.2d 153.

9. *Id.* ¶ 24, at 159.

10. *Id.* ¶ 27, at 160.

11. *Id.* ¶ 31, at 160.

12. *Id.*

damages do not qualify as incompatible standards. . . . Courts reason a defendant is not subject to incompatible standards merely through the risk of being found liable to some plaintiffs and not to others.[13]

The court concluded that it was error for the trial court to find that the incompatible standards factor had been met on the basis that multiple lawsuits might cause varying results as to monetary damages. The case was remanded for a reevaluation of the Rule 23(c)(1) factors based upon the correct standards described by the appellate court.

In *Bice v. Petro-Hunt, L.L.C.*,[14] the district court had certified a class of royalty owners and overriding royalty interest owners under oil and gas leases in the Little Knife Field located in three counties in North Dakota. The plaintiffs alleged that Petro-Hunt had underpaid royalties by inappropriately deducting costs and expenses associated with compressing and treating the produced gases, charging for excess depreciation and alleged improper charges as to risk capital. They also asserted that Petro-Hunt was obligated to pay for processed gas returned and consumed at central tank batteries.

In determining whether to affirm the certification of the class, the court found that the "[p]laintiffs' main theory of recovery is that defendants have a duty as operators under the oil and gas leases to produce the first marketable product."[15] With regard to Petro-Hunt's assertion that differing lease provisions, contract terms, and statutory provisions left the case unsuitable for class treatment, the appellate court held:

> The similarity in [Petro-Hunt's] treatment of owners regardless of individual lease terms strongly suggests there are common lease terms or, if not, that differing lease terms are similar in import or treated as being common or similar in import. In light of the parties' assertions about similar treatment, we are unable to conclude the trial court was not justified in determining that common questions of law or fact predominate.[16]

As a final example of the royalty owner lawsuits in which courts have granted class certification, the case of *SEECO, Inc. v. Hales*[17] involved an appeal of the certification of a class of some 3,000 royalty owners. The royalty owners asserted claims for actual and constructive fraud, breach of oil and gas leases, breach of

---

13. 1999 ND 173, ¶ 55, 598 N.W.2d 820, 834.

14. 2004 ND 113, 681 N.W.2d 74.

15. *Id.* ¶ 17, at 80.

16. *Id.* ¶ 19, at 80. For a discussion of the flaws in the argument of class action plaintiff counsel that "if the defendant treated the class members the same in certain respects, the courts are at liberty to ignore rules of substantive law that would otherwise mandate individualized treatment of the rights and claims of each claimant," *see* Mark Christiansen, *Class Actions Pushed to the Extreme: Will Class Action Plaintiff Lawyers Be Permitted to Re-Zone Our Courts for Tract Housing?* 24 J. Land Resources & Envtl. L. 77 (2004).

17. 954 S.W.2d 234 (Ark. 1997).

the duty to market, breach of the duty of good faith and fair dealing, violation of Arkansas statutes governing penalties for fraudulently withholding oil and lease payments, unjust enrichment, tortious interference with contractual relations, civil conspiracy, and violation of Arkansas statutes requiring the calculation of royalties on a weighted-average price.

On appeal, SEECO asserted that common questions of law and fact did not predominate over questions affecting individual class members and that class action procedure was not the superior method for adjudicating the controversy. However, the court found as follows:

> What is alleged in the case at hand is a single course of fraudulent conduct perpetrated by the appellants and directed at the royalty owners, with each plaintiff depending on the same facts and legal arguments for recovery. The issue of fraudulent scheme is central to the instant case and a common starting point for all class members.[18]

The court found that individual issues associated with proof of reliance or fraudulent concealment did not override the common question presented by the alleged fraudulent scheme. The court affirmed the granting of class certification.

III. Examples of Cases in Which Royalty Classes Were Denied

Texas courts have issued a number of decisions rejecting attempts to litigate royalty claims on a classwide basis. In *Union Pacific Resources Group, Inc. v. Neinast*,[19] the trial court certified a royalty owner class with respect to claims that the lessee had breached the implied covenant under the class members' oil and gas leases to diligently market production. The court of appeals found that "[o]f all prerequisites to class certification, predominance is one of the most stringent."[20] The court observed that, among other considerations, "predominance is determined by: identifying the substantive issues that are dispositive of the litigation; assessing which issues will predominate; and determining whether these predominating issues are actually common to the class."[21] The court noted, citing *Southwest Refining Co. v. Bernal*,[22] that the important purpose of the predominance requirement is to "prevent class-action litigation when the sheer complexity and diversity of the individual issues would overwhelm or confuse a jury or severely compromise a party's ability to present viable claims or defenses."[23]

---

18. *Id.* at 240.
19. 67 S.W.3d 275 (Tex. App. 2001).
20. *Id.* at 281 (citing *Sw. Ref. Co. v. Bernal*, 22 S.W.3d 425, at 433 (Tex. 2000)).
21. *Id.*
22. 22 S.W.3d at 434.
23. *Neinast*, 67 S.W.3d at 281.

The court of appeals found that the trial court erred in concluding that an implied covenant to reasonably market production was necessarily present in every oil and gas lease, and instead recognized that a lease-by-lease evaluation would be required in order to determine whether such an implied covenant was present. The court further found that the task of "[d]etermining the best reasonably attainable price under same or similar circumstances necessarily contemplates a fact specific, location-by-location inquiry for each lease."[24] The court reversed the order granting class certification.

The case of *Union Pacific Resources Group, Inc. v. Hankins*[25] involved UPRG's appeal of the district court's order certifying a class of royalty owners with respect to claims for alleged breach of implied covenant to diligently market production and unjust enrichment, and seeking accounting and injunctive relief. In addressing UPRG's contention that the granting of class certification would deny its substantive, contractual, and constitutional rights, the court stated in part as follows:

> The class action is a procedural device intended to advance judicial economy by trying claims together that lend themselves to collective treatment; however, it is not meant to alter the parties' burdens of proof, right to a jury trial, or the substantive prerequisites to recovery under a particular cause of action. "Procedural devices may not be construed to enlarge or diminish any substantive rights or obligations of any parties to any civil action." Essentially, convenience and economy must yield to a fair and impartial trial. Basic to the right to a fair trial is that each party have the opportunity to adequately and vigorously present any material claims and defenses.[26]

While recognizing the above principles, the court found that UPRG's assertions did not call for the reversal of the class certification order within the context of this lawsuit.

The court of appeals further found that the trial court appropriately understood the claims, defenses, relevant facts, and substantive law in certifying the class and assessed the nature of the case as follows:

> Here, the predominant issues concern whether the appellants underpaid royalties to the class members through their alleged common scheme of inter-affiliate conveyances at indexed prices. The fact that damage issues may have to be computed individually for different class members does not preclude class certification. These damages may be determined through proof-of-claim forms, individual damage hearings or other manageable means.[27]

---

24. *Id.* at 284.
25. 51 S.W.3d 741 (Tex. App. 2001), *rev'd*, 111 S.W.3d 69 (Tex. 2003).
26. 51 S.W.3d at 749.
27. *Id.* at 754.

The court affirmed the certification of the class, observing that class action procedure is the superior method for adjudicating claims when the benefits of such procedure outweigh any difficulties that may arise in the management of the class.[28]

The Supreme Court of Texas granted review and reversed the court of appeals.[29] It explained that not one of the 11 issues identified in the trial court as common issues both "'inheres in the complaint of all class members' and is 'subject to generalized proof.'"[30] Thus, it reversed the court of appeals' judgment without considering other challenges to the certification prerequisites.[31]

In *Stirman v. Exxon Corporation*,[32] Exxon appealed the certification of a multistate class a suit by royalty owners that alleged that Exxon had breached the implied covenant to market that was alleged to be a part of all of the underlying oil and gas leases. The Fifth Circuit found that the district court had failed to take into account the significant variations in the different state's laws regarding the extent and scope of any implied covenant to market production.[33] It additionally found that the lower court had failed to conduct the type of rigorous analysis required on the issue of whether a class action was a superior method for adjudicating the controversy, and reversed the order granting class certification.[34]

The Texas Court of Appeals in *Enron Oil & Gas Company v. Joffrion*[35] was again presented with the appeal of a district court order certifying a class of approximately 300 royalty owners with respect to claims for alleged breach of express and implied covenants under the oil and gas leases. In assessing the predominance requirement, the court stated:

> The test for predominance is not whether common issues outnumber uncommon issues, but whether common or individual issues will be the subject of most of the litigants' and court's efforts. If, after common issues are resolved, presenting and resolving individual issues is likely to be an overwhelming or unmanageable task for a single jury, then common issues do not predominate. Ideally, a judgment in favor of the unnamed plaintiffs should decisively settle the entire controversy, and all that should remain is for other class members to file proofs of claim.[36]

After applying those standards to the royalty claims presented in the case, the court found that it was improper to certify the subject class.

---

28. *Id.*
29. *See Hankins*, 111 S.W.3d 69.
30. *Id.* at 74.
31. *Id.* at 75.
32. 280 F.3d 554 (5th Cir. 2002).
33. *Id.* at 564.
34. *Id.* at 566.
35. 116 S.W.3d 215 (Tex. App. 2003).
36. *Id.* at 221.

While the preceding examples involved the reversal of trial court orders granting class certification, there are many instances in which trial courts have denied
class certification on grounds similar to those reflected in the above appellate decisions. One of the key Oklahoma cases in which class certification was denied in a
royalty owner lawsuit is the case of *Gillespie v. Amoco Production Co.*[37] In the *Gillespie* case, the plaintiffs alleged that the defendant had improperly factored into
gas royalty payments certain types of costs and fees, including compression, dehy-
dration, gathering, marketing, and transportation costs. At the conclusion of a
class certification evidentiary hearing on the plaintiffs' motion for certification of
a nationwide class, the court found in part as follows:

> The individual issues predominate and I find that certification is not a superior
> form of adjudicating this controversy. . . . It is the opinion of this Court that instead
> the most efficient way and the most cost effective way to adjudicate the claims of
> these royalty owners is for these Plaintiffs, and any other interested owners, to pur-
> sue this matter as a joint action.[38]

The plaintiffs in *Gillespie* subsequently filed a new motion for class certification asking the court to at least certify a statewide class of royalty and overriding
royalty owners from whom Amoco had deducted post-production costs, limited in
time frame to the five-year statute of limitations period for actions on a written
contract under Oklahoma law. In its later order, the court again denied the plaintiffs' second motion for class certification, finding in part as follows:

> [T]he ultimate question of law posed by each plaintiff and each proposed class
> member is the same: did Amoco breach the subject leases by improperly deducting
> certain costs from royalty payments? As demonstrated by the Oklahoma Supreme
> Court's opinion in *Mittelstaedt v. Santa Fe Minerals, Inc.*, 954 P.2d 1203 (Okla.
> 1998), the differences in the facts underlying each plaintiff's and each proposed
> class member's claim affect the answer to that question.[39] Indeed, Amoco's liability

---

37. No. CIV-96-063-M (E.D. Okla. Mar. 5, 1997).

38. *See* Transcript of Class Certification Hearing in *Gillespie v. Amoco Prod. Co.*, No. CIV-96-063-M.

39. The court quoted in a footnote certain portions of the Oklahoma Supreme Court's decision in *Mittelstaedt*, including the Oklahoma Supreme Court's recitation of the facts that must be shown in order for
certain marketing-related costs to be deducted from royalty payments, with that court stating, at the end
of the recitation of those factual showings, the following: "Thus, in some cases a royalty interest may be
burdened with post-production costs, and in other cases it may not be." The court in *Gillespie* also quoted
the finding in *Mittelstaedt* that "[p]ost-production costs must be examined on an individual basis to determine if they are within the class of costs shared by a royalty interest." *Mittelstaedt v. Santa Fe Minerals,
Inc.*, 1998 OK 7, 954 P.2d 1203, 1205, 1208. On December 3, 2009, the U.S. District Court for the Western
District of Oklahoma, upon the motion and urging of Marathon Oil Company, found that it needed to
receive guidance from the Oklahoma Supreme Court as to the state law issue of what the term "market-

as to a particular plaintiff or proposed class member depends upon facts and circumstances unique to that plaintiff or proposed class member.[40]

A similar ruling was reached by the state district court in Latimer County, Oklahoma, in early 1998 in the case of *Barnaby v. Marathon Oil Company.*[41]

In the subsequent state court lawsuit of *Watts v. Amoco Production Co.,*[42] the plaintiffs asked the district court to certify a class of royalty owners and unleased mineral owners in a seven-county area of Oklahoma. In opposing this subsequent effort to obtain class certification, Amoco cited to the state district court the prior federal court decision in *Gillespie,* denying class certification in that prior royalty owner action. In likewise denying the plaintiffs' motion for class certification, the state district court in *Watts* cited the federal court's decision in *Gillespie* and stated that, while the decision in *Gillespie* was not binding on the state district court, "this Court chooses to agree with the holding in *Gillespie* and apply it to this case."[43]

On September 14, 2004, the Oklahoma Court of Appeals affirmed the district court's denial of class certification in the *Watts* case, and stated in part as follows:

> [T]he propriety of deducting [post-production costs from royalty payments] involves an individualized inquiry of the factors discussed in *Mittelstaedt v. Santa Fe Minerals, Inc.,* 1998 OK 7, 954 P.2d 1203, making this issue unsuitable for class action disposition. The need for individualized inquiry is further evident by the need to examine each of thousands of sales in deciding whether Amoco received the best market price for the gas *vis-à-vis* the costs incurred to prepare the gas for introduction into the pipeline. . . .

---

able" means under the prior *Mittelstaedt* decision before the federal court rules on the plaintiffs' motion seeking certification of a statewide royalty owner class. *See Hill v. Marathon Oil Co.,* No. CIV-08-37-R (W.D. Okla. Dec. 3, 2009). At the time this chapter was submitted for publication, the parties were in the process of presenting to the court their final positions as to how the state law questions to be certified to the Oklahoma Supreme Court should be stated.

40. See Order, at 6–7, *Gillespie v. Amoco Prod. Co.,* No. CIV-96-063-M (E.D. Okla. Jan. 11, 1999).

41. Case No. C-96-40 (Dist. Ct. Latimer County, Okla.). The court in *Barnaby* granted certification of a limited statewide class in a royalty cost deduction lawsuit, consisting only of royalty owners covered by certain specific types of royalty provisions. That class certification ruling was announced in late 1997 after a two-day class certification hearing. However, when the Oklahoma Supreme Court's decision in *Mittelstaedt* was issued in January of 1998, the district court granted Marathon's motion for reconsideration of its grant of class certification and vacated its late 1997 ruling. The district court found that the legal standards announced in *Mittelstaedt* rendered it improper to grant the royalty owner class described by the court in its late 1997 pronouncement.

42. 75 O.B.J. 2459 (Okla. App. 2004—#98,782, Petition for certiorari denied Jan. 24, 2005) (not for publication).

43. *See Watts v. Amoco Prod. Co.,* Case No. C-2001-73, Order at 2 (Dist. Ct. Pittsburg County, Okla. Dec. 26, 2002). The district court also stated in its initial ruling that it was adopting the detailed proposed findings and conclusions submitted by Amoco, which contained additional bases for rejecting the request for class certification. *Id.*

In the instant case, we agree with the trial court that the requirements of typicality, predominance, and superiority cannot be met under the record given the individualized inquiry to resolve the two central issues.[44]

In the later case of *Rees v. BP America Production Co.*,[45] different plaintiff counsel attempted yet another class action royalty lawsuit against BP (successor in interest to Amoco). In finding that the royalty owner plaintiff in *Rees* was bound by the prior denial of class certification in the *Watts* case, the Oklahoma Court of Appeals held:

> ¶11 [W]e hold Rees, as an unnamed member of the proposed class in *Watts*, is bound by the Court's ruling denying certification to the proposed class . . . . Any other result would allow plaintiffs to continue filing broad class actions against BP until a trial court grants class certification, rendering ineffective the previous denials of other courts. . . .
>
> ¶12 In addition, Rees or any other class member may seek certification of a narrower class, provided he is able to present a good faith argument the proposed circumscription of the class obviates individual inquiry of the factors set forth in *Mittelstaedt v. Santa Fe Minerals, Inc.*, 1998 OK 7, 954 P.2d 1203. Rees has not presented such an argument supporting the class proposed in his petition. Instead, he argues the scope of his claim is narrower than that in Watts because he has not asserted a fraud claim. The Court's denial of certification in *Watts* was based on the need for individualized inquiries as to the propriety of deducting post-production costs from royalties, not on the individual issues posed by fraud. Eliminating a fraud claim does not sufficiently narrow the issues to obviate individual inquiry of the *Mittelstaedt* factors.[46]

A final example of a case in which certification was denied, and the denial was affirmed on appeal, is the case of *Mayo v. Kaiser-Francis Oil Company*.[47] The Oklahoma Court of Appeals in *Mayo* upheld the district court's refusal to certify a proposed class of royalty owners that included both royalty owners who had contractual privity with the defendant under oil and gas leases and royalty owners who had no contractual privity, but who were entitled to be paid royalties by the defendant under provisions of the Oklahoma Statutes.

---

44. See pages 3–4 of the Oklahoma Court of Appeals' Sept. 14, 2004 decision in *Watts v. Amoco Prod. Co.*, Case No. 90,404, slip op. at 3–4 (Ok. Ct. App. Sept. 14, 2004).

45. 2009 OK Civ. App. 37, 211 P.3d 910 (2008).

46. *Id.* ¶¶ 11, 12, at 912–13.

47. 1998 OK Civ. App. 94, 962 P.2d 657.

EMPLOYMENT

WYNDALL A. IVEY
DICK SEMERDJIAN
SARAH BRITE EVANS

I. Introduction

According to an ongoing study by the Federal Judicial Center regarding the impact of the Class Action Fairness Act of 2005, labor and employment class actions account for an increasing share of the class actions filed in federal district courts.[1] Labor and employment class actions constituted almost one-quarter of all class actions identified in 2001, and almost one-half of all class actions identified by 2007.[2] State courts are seeing a similar pattern; for example, in California, employment class actions represented nearly 30 percent of all class action cases filed in state courts between 2000 and 2006 and grew from 29 cases in 2000 to 120 cases in 2005—an overall increase of more than 300 percent.[3]

Manageability and predominance issues arise in employment class actions. Collective actions brought under the Fair Labor Standards Act (FLSA) are designed to mostly avoid these issues until the second judicial inquiry following notice to the employees affected and return of their opt-in forms. On the other hand, class actions involving state labor claims can be combined with FLSA claims to require an analysis of manageability and predominance issues at an earlier stage.

Other employment claims, especially employment discrimination claims, create unique predominance and manageability concerns. Rule 23(b)(2) of the Federal

---

1. EMERY G. LEE III & THOMAS E. WILLGING, THE IMPACT OF THE CLASS ACTION FAIRNESS ACT OF 2005 ON THE FEDERAL COURTS, FOURTH INTERIM REPORT 3–4 (Federal Judicial Center 2008), *available at* http://www.fjc.gov/public/pdf.nsf/lookup/cafa0408.pdf/$file/cafa0408.pdf.

2. *Id.*

3. HILARY HEHMAN, ADMIN. OFFICE OF THE COURTS, FINDINGS OF THE STUDY OF CALIFORNIA CLASS ACTION LITIGATION, 2000–2006, FIRST INTERIM REPORT, MARCH 2009, at 5, *available at* http://www.courtinfo.ca.gov/reference/documents/class-action-lit-study.pdf.

Rules of Civil Procedure was specifically designed to facilitate discrimination class actions by eliminating some of these concerns, but the only available remedy in these claims is injunctive relief. Certification of discrimination claims under Rule 23(b)(3) is far more difficult, especially because the predominance requirement is difficult to satisfy where harassment evidence is purely anecdotal.

II. Collective/Representative Action Under FLSA

A. THE FAIR LABOR STANDARDS ACT GENERALLY

The Fair Labor Standards Act of 1938[4] established a national minimum wage for the first time and guaranteed time and a half for overtime in certain jobs.[5] It applies to employees engaged in interstate commerce or employed by an enterprise engaged in commerce or in the production of goods for commerce,[6] unless the employer can claim an exemption from coverage.

The FLSA allows an employee to recover unpaid minimum wages and overtime compensation, as well as to redress retaliatory discharge through a private civil action to enforce FLSA provisions.[7] An employee may bring an FLSA claim on the employee's own behalf and on behalf of any "similarly situated" employees. Specifically, section 216(b) of the FLSA provides that an FLSA action

> may be maintained against any employer . . . in any Federal or State court of competent jurisdiction by any one or more employees for and [on] behalf of himself or themselves and other employees similarly situated.[8]

An employee who seeks to become a member of a claim brought under the FLSA must opt in to the class by filing consent in writing.[9] FLSA actions are distinguishable from traditional class actions because federal courts generally hold that FLSA collective actions need not comply with the Rule 23 class action requirements.[10]

B. CERTIFYING FLSA REPRESENTATIVE ACTIONS

Generally, the certification process for FLSA collective actions proceeds in two stages.[11] A judge first evaluates the collective action at "the notice stage," where

---

4. June 25, 1938, ch. 676, § 1, 52 Stat. 1060.

5. 29 U.S.C. §§ 206, 207.

6. 29 U.S.C. § 203(s).

7. 29 U.S.C. §§ 206, 207, 215(a)(2), 215(a)(3), 216.

8. 29 U.S.C. § 216(b).

9. Id.

10. See, e.g., La Chapelle v. Owens-Illinois, Inc., 513 F.2d 286, 299 (5th Cir. 1975) (holding that "[t]here is a fundamental, irreconcilable difference between the class action described by Rule 23 and that provided for by FLSA § 16(b).").

11. A few courts have employed a separate approach, employing the elements set forth in Rule 23 to the extent those elements do not conflict with section 216 (i.e., numerosity, commonality, typicality, and ade-

the district court uses its discretion to authorize conditional notification of similarly situated employees to allow them to opt into the lawsuit. In the second stage, which is usually triggered by an employer's motion for decertification, the district court has a much thicker record than it had at the notice stage and can therefore make a more informed factual determination of similarity. This second stage is less lenient, and the plaintiff bears a heavier burden.

1. A "Similarly Situated" Analysis Is Used in FLSA Representative Actions

The first step under the two-tiered approach considers whether the proposed class should be given notice of the action,[12] and initially analyzes whether the class is "similarly situated," rather than whether common claims predominate. At the first stage, plaintiffs bear the burden of showing that they and the proposed class are similarly situated for purposes of section 216(b).[13] The term "similarly situated" is not defined under the FLSA, but the majority of courts, including four circuit courts, have adopted a two-tiered case-by-case approach.[14] Because the court generally has a limited amount of evidence before it, the initial determination is usually made under a fairly lenient standard and typically results in conditional class certification.[15] Courts have held that conditional certification requires only that "plaintiffs make substantial allegations that the putative class members were subject to a single illegal policy, plan or decision."[16]

Once discovery is complete and the case is ready to be tried, the party opposing class certification may move to decertify the class, which is the second step of the tiered process.[17] The court then must make a factual determination regarding

---

quacy of representation). *See, e.g., Garcia v. Elite Labor Serv., Ltd.*, 95 C 2341, 1996 WL 559958, at *2 (N.D. Ill. 1996); *Shushan v. Univ. of Colo.*, 132 F.R.D. 263, 265 (D. Colo. 1990). This approach is rarely utilized, because "in contrast to class actions under Rule 23, members of the FLSA representative action 'opt in'; therefore, the stricter Rule 23 test is irrelevant and unnecessary because, at this stage, the potential class is uncertain and self selective." *Garza v. Chicago Transit Auth.*, 00 C 438, 2001 WL 503036, at *2 (N.D. Ill. 2001).

12. *Leuthold v. Destination Am., Inc.*, 224 F.R.D. 462, 467 (N.D. Cal. 2004); *Pfohl v. Farmers Ins. Group*, CV03-3080 DT (RCX), 2004 WL 554834, at *2 (C.D. Cal. 2004); *Kane v. Gage Merch. Servs., Inc.*, CV03-3080 DT (RCX), 138 F. Supp. 2d 212, 214 (D. Mass. 2001), citing *Mooney v. Aramco Servs. Co.*, 54 F.3d 1207, 1214 (5th Cir. 1995); *see Reeves v. Alliant Techsystems, Inc.*, 77 F. Supp. 2d 242, 246 (D.R.I. 1999).

13. 29 U.S.C. § 216(b); *see also Romero v. Producers Dairy Foods, Inc.*, 235 F.R.D. 474, 481 (E.D. Cal. 2006).

14. *See, e.g., Thiessen v. Gen. Elec. Capital Corp.*, 267 F.3d 1095, 1102–03 (10th Cir. 2001); *Hipp v. Liberty Nat'l Life Ins. Co.*, 252 F.3d 1208, 1219 (11th Cir. 2001); *Mooney*, 54 F.3d at 1213–14; *Comer v. Wal-Mart Stores, Inc.*, 454 F.3d 544, 546 (6th Cir. 2006). Other options include the incorporation of the requirements of Rule 23 of the current Federal Rules of Civil Procedure or the incorporation of the requirements of the pre-1966 version of Rule 23 for "spurious" class actions. *Romero*, 235 F.R.D. at 481.

15. *Pfohl*, 2004 WL 554834, at *2 (C.D. Cal. 2004); *Kane*, 138 F. Supp. 2d at 214; *Reeves*, 77 F. Supp. 2d at 246.

16. *Kane*, 138 F. Supp. 2d at 214; *see also Sperling v. Hoffmann-La Roche, Inc.*, 118 F.R.D. 392, 406 (D.N.J. 1988).

17. *Kane*, 138 F. Supp. 2d at 214; *Reeves*, 77 F. Supp. 2d at 247.

the propriety and scope of the class and must consider the following factors: (1) the disparate factual and employment settings of the individual plaintiffs; (2) the various defenses available to the defendants with respect to the individual plaintiffs; and (3) fairness, procedure, and manageability.[18] Should the court determine on the basis of the complete factual record that the plaintiffs are not similarly situated or for any reason that a class is improper, then the court may decertify the class and dismiss the opt-in plaintiffs without prejudice.[19]

2. Manageability Can Be Analyzed at Either Phase

Although plaintiffs in FLSA cases appear individually and not as a class, courts nevertheless consider whether proceeding collectively is manageable. The district court must assess this factor in light of "the fundamental purpose of 29 U.S.C. § 216(b): (1) to lower costs to the plaintiffs through the pooling of resources; and (2) to limit the controversy to one proceeding which efficiently resolves "'common issues of law and fact that arose from the same alleged activity.'"[20]

Manageability issues are expressly raised as part of the third factor considered during the second phase, although they may also be considered in the first phase as well.[21] When considered in the first phase, courts have done so as part of their "duty to determine whether the matter before it is an appropriate case for collective treatment."[22] Thus, courts' discretion to send out notice to potential members of a collective action is based on principles of orderly case management, but this focus does not mandate that district courts send out notice when it appears that an FLSA case will be unmanageable as a collective action.[23]

Courts have also taken case management into account at the first stage "because a collective action is simply a procedural device aimed at facilitating, in an efficient and cost effective way, the adjudication of numerous claims in one action."[24] Manageability is easily shown where representative plaintiffs can show that there is a

---

18. *Hipp*, 252 F.3d at 1218; *Pfohl*, 2004 WL 554834, at *2–3 (citing *Thiessen*, 267 F.3d at 1103); *see also Reeves*, 77 F. Supp. 2d at 247.

19. *Kane*, 138 F. Supp. 2d at 214 (citing *Reeves*, 77 F. Supp. 2d at 247).

20. *Moss v. Crawford & Co.*, 201 F.R.D. 398, 410 (W.D. Pa. 2000).

21. *Saleen v. Waste Mgmt., Inc.*, Civ. No. 08-4959 (PJS/JJK), 2009 WL 1664451, at *8 (D. Minn. 2009); *Jimenez v. Lakeside Pic-N-Pac, L.L.C.*, 1:06-CV-456, 2007 WL 4454295, at *2 (W.D. Mich. Dec. 14, 2007).

22. *Saleen*, 2009 WL 1664451, at *8 (citing *West v. Border Foods, Inc.*, Civ. No. 05-2525 (DWF/RLE), 2006 WL 1892527, at *7 (D. Minn. 2006) (noting that "neither the remedial purposes of the FLSA, nor the interests of judicial economy, would be advanced if we were to overlook facts which generally suggest that a collective action is improper"); and *Basco v. Wal-Mart Stores, Inc.*, Civ. A. 00-318, 2004 WL 1497709, at *7 (E.D. La. July 2, 2004) ("While it is true that th[e] 'lesser' standard should not preclude certification, and 'similarly situated' does not mean identically situated, plaintiffs have failed in their burden to demonstrate identifiable facts or legal nexus that binds the claims so that hearing the cases together promotes judicial efficiency.")).

23. *Id.* (citing *Hoffmann-La Roche Inc. v. Sperling*, 493 U.S. 165, 170–72 (1989)).

24. *Id.*

single decision, policy, or plan that adversely affects a group of similarly situated employees.[25] Manageable collective action classes have also been found where all potential plaintiffs worked or currently work at the same location.[26]

On the other hand, manageability is not shown in cases in which there is considerable variation in the reasons plaintiffs and the putative collective action members were not compensated for, for example, working through meal breaks.[27] If such variation is shown at the initial stage, courts can decide that the "case would not be more orderly and sensibly managed as a nationwide collective action."[28]

When considered in the second phase, manageability issues are addressed in a similar manner. Thus, where factual questions regarding off-the-clock claims vary widely, a claim would be unduly burdensome to manage collectively.[29] Where the off-the-clock and overtime claims involved individual plaintiffs from nearly every state, working in dozens or hundreds of stores and under hundreds of managers, a collective action was deemed to be unmanageable as well.[30] Where "no single decision, policy, or plan" is at issue, a collective action FLSA claim has been determined to "present[ ] enormous manageability problems."[31]

3. FLSA Collective Action Procedures Also Apply to ADEA Claims and Equal Pay Act Claims

FLSA's section 216(b) provision applies to statutory claims other than FLSA claims. Section 216(b) also applies to discrimination cases under the Age Discrimination in Employment Act (ADEA).[32] Specifically, the ADEA incorporated the FLSA's requirement of 29 U.S.C. § 216(b).[33]

---

25. *Id.*

26. *Bouaphakeo v. Tyson Foods, Inc.*, 564 F. Supp. 2d 870, 897–98 (N.D. Iowa 2008); *Owens v. S. Hens, Inc.*, Civ. A. No. 2:07CV28-KS-MTP, 2008 WL 723923, at *3 (S.D. Miss. 2008) (noting all potential plaintiffs "are all employees at a single facility"); *Freeman v. Wal-Mart Stores, Inc.*, 256 F. Supp. 2d 941, 945 (W.D. Ark. 2003) (refusing to permit notice to employees at every Walmart store in the country); *Sheffield v. Orius Corp.*, 211 F.R.D. 411, 413 (D. Or. 2002) (noting "dissimilarities among the putative class members extend to geography, work sites, and payment systems").

27. *Saleen*, 2009 WL 1664451, at *9.

28. *Id.* (citing *Basco*, 2004 WL 1497709, at *5 (noting that "[t]o create a collective action class, including the cost associated with that when a Court is convinced that there is insufficient support for the same prior to certification would be an exercise in futility and wasted resources for all parties involved")).

29. *Lawrence v. City of Phila., Pa.*, 03-CV-4009, 2004 WL 945139, at *2 (E.D. Pa. 2004).

30. *Smith v. T-Mobile USA, Inc.*, CV 05-5274 ABC (SSx), 2007 WL 2385131, at *8 (C.D. Cal. 2007).

31. *Basco*, 2004 WL 1497709, at *8; *see also Mielke v. Laidlaw Transit, Inc.*, 313 F. Supp. 2d 759, 764 (N.D. Ill. 2004) (declining to certify collective action given the absence of a uniform policy, disparate factual and employment settings, and likelihood that case would not be resolved summarily).

32. 29 U.S.C. § 626(b).

33. *Id.*

The Equal Pay Act[34] was enacted as an amendment to the FLSA.[35] "As part of the FLSA, the [Equal Pay Act] utilizes the FLSA's enforcement mechanisms and employs its definitional provisions,"[36] including section 216(b).

4. FLSA Claims Plus State Law Class Actions

Many states have labor laws that parallel the FLSA provisions and allow independent actions to address their violations. Because state labor laws can govern employment issues, plaintiffs often seek to bring a state law employment class claim pursuant to Federal Rule of Civil Procedure 23 at the same time they bring their FLSA collective action claim. Recently, one court noted the "recent phenomenon" of the "'explosion' of hybrid lawsuits involving both state and FLSA claims."[37]

Obviously, the two types of claims are different and distinct. Unlike the procedure set out in 29 U.S.C. § 216(b), Rule 23 class certification of state law labor claims requires notice to all potential class members that they must affirmatively decline to join ("opt out" of) the lawsuit if they do not want to be class members.[38]

A district court has authority to exercise supplemental jurisdiction over non-federal claims arising from the same case or controversy as the federal claim.[39] Some courts hold that the FLSA and state labor law claims arise from the same controversy and share a common nucleus of operative fact, as the same acts are alleged to violate parallel federal and state laws. The exercise of supplemental jurisdiction is discretionary and "reflects the understanding that, when deciding whether to exercise supplemental jurisdiction, 'a federal court should consider and weigh in each case, and at every stage of the litigation, the values of judicial economy, convenience, fairness, and comity.'"[40]

---

34. 29 U.S.C. § 206(d).

35. *See Nw. Airlines, Inc. v. Transp. Workers Union*, 451 U.S. 77, 79 n.1 (1981); *Frasier v. Gen. Elec. Co.*, 930 F.2d 1004, 1007 (2d Cir. 1991).

36. *Anderson v. State Univ. of N.Y.*, 169 F.3d 117, 119 (2d Cir. 1999), *vacated on other grounds*, 528 U.S. 1111.

37. *Ellis v. Edward D. Jones & Co.*, 527 F. Supp. 2d 439, 459 n.19 (W.D. Pa. 2007).

38. FED. R. CIV. P. 23(c)(2)(B) ("For any class certified under Rule 23(b)(3), the court must direct to class members the best notice practicable under the circumstances . . . that the court will exclude from the class any member who requests exclusion, stating when and how members may elect to be excluded"); *In re Veneman*, 309 F.3d 789, 792 (D.C. Cir. 2002) ("[C]ertification pursuant to Rule 23(b)(3), however, comes with certain procedural requirements: Because members of a class seeking substantial monetary damages may have divergent interests, due process requires that putative class members receive notice and an opportunity to opt out.").

39. 28 U.S.C. § 1367.

40. *City of Chicago v. Int'l Coll. of Surgeons*, 522 U.S. 156, 173 (1997) (quoting *Carnegie-Mellon Univ. v. Cohill*, 484 U.S. 343, 350 (1988)).

Despite their confusing semantic similarities, the differences between class actions and collective actions are great.[41] Plaintiffs in class actions certified under Rule 23 are generally class members unless they opt out, while under section 216(b), plaintiffs must opt in to become a member of the collective action. As a result, courts are split on whether it is appropriate to exercise supplemental jurisdiction over the Rule 23 class action.[42] Some courts have declined to certify a Rule 23 class action for state labor law claims in an FLSA collective action on the grounds that collective FLSA actions are inherently incompatible with Rule 23 state law, opt-out class actions and would undermine Congress's intent in implementing an opt-in requirement for FLSA actions.[43]

Other courts have allowed the two actions to coexist and have explicitly rejected the argument that the incompatibility of the two provisions bars the state action.[44] In those cases, the analysis of whether Rule 23's requirements are satisfied proceeds as it would in a typical class action.

---

41. *See Lugo v. Farmer's Pride Inc.*, Civ. A. No. 07-CV-00749, 2008 WL 638237, at *2 (E.D. Pa. Mar. 7, 2008) ("Class actions and collective actions can often be confused with each other."); *Salazar v. Agriprocessors, Inc.*, 527 F. Supp. 2d 873, 877 (N.D. Iowa 2007) ("At the outset, it is crucial to note the distinction between a FLSA *collective* action and a Rule 23 *class* action. The distinction is sometimes blurred."). *See generally* Charles A. Wright, Arthur R. Miller & Mary K. Kane, Federal Practice and Procedure § 1807 at 468–77 (3d ed. 2005 & Supp. 2007) (stating the differences between Rule 23 class actions and FLSA collective actions).

42. *See, e.g., De Asencio v. Tyson Foods, Inc.*, 342 F.3d 301, 312 (3d Cir. 2003) (finding district court abused its discretion in exercising supplemental jurisdiction over state law class claims because the size of the class was too big and the state law claims involved different legal issues than FLSA claims); *Neary v. Metro. Prop. & Cas. Ins. Co.*, 472 F. Supp. 2d 247, 251–252 (D. Conn. 2007) (recognizing the incompatibility between section 216(b) and Rule 23, but ultimately declining to exercise supplemental jurisdiction because the state law class claims, involving all 50 states, predominated over the FLSA claim). *But see Goldman v. RadioShack Corp.*, Civ. A. 2:03-CV-0032, 2003 WL 21250571 (E.D. Pa. 2003) (citing efficiency concerns in deciding to exercise supplemental jurisdiction over class claim for violation of Pennsylvania wage and hour statute).

43. *De Asencio*, 342 F.3d 301; *Otto v. Pocono Health Sys.*, 457 F. Supp. 2d 522 (E.D. Pa. 2006); *Moeck v. Gray Supply Corp.*, 03-1950 (WGB), 2006 WL 42368 (D.N.J. 2006) (stating "to circumvent the opt-in requirements and bring unnamed parties into federal court by calling upon state statutes similar to the FLSA would undermine Congress' intent to limit these types of claims to collective actions"); *Leuthold*, 224 F.R.D. at 470 (denying motion to certify Rule 23 class for state law claims because "maintaining the suit exclusively as a FLSA conditional class action is superior to certifying an additional state law class under Rule 23(b)(3)").

44. *See, e.g., Garcia v. Tyson Foods, Inc.*, 255 F.R.D. 678, 689–90 (D. Kan. 2009) (finding no conflict of interest); *Guzman v. VLM Inc.*, 07-CV-1126 (JG)(RER), 2008 WL 597186 (E.D.N.Y. 2008) (stating "there is no reason that FLSA's collective action procedure is incompatible with maintaining a state law class action over the same conduct."); *Torres v. Gristede's Operating Group*, 04 Civ. 3316 (PAC), 2006 WL 2819730 (S.D.N.Y. 2006) (certifying both FLSA action and class action for violation of New York labor law without discussing supplemental jurisdiction issues); *Scott v. Aetna Servs.*, 210 F.R.D. 261 (D. Conn. 2002) (allowing state law claims of potential class members who were not included in the FLSA action).

III. Employment Discrimination Claims

The Civil Rights Act of 1964[45] was a landmark piece of legislation in the United States that outlawed racial segregation in schools, public places, and employment. Title VII of the Act prohibits discrimination by covered employers on the basis of race, color, religion, sex, or national origin[46] and forms the basis of both Rule 23(b)(2) and Rule 23(b)(3) class actions.

Rule 23(a)(2) requires plaintiffs to demonstrate the existence of questions of law and fact that are common to the class, and subsection (b)(3) of Rule 23 requires plaintiffs to demonstrate that these common questions predominate over questions that affect only individual plaintiffs.

In employment cases analyzed under Rule 23 involving a claim that an employer's policy and practices violated labor law, the key question for class certification is whether there is a consistent employer practice that could be a basis for consistent liability.[47] Thus, where the employer has a uniform policy that is uniformly applied, predominance is established.[48]

A. RULE 23(B)(2) EMPLOYMENT DISCRIMINATION CLASS ACTIONS

A Rule 23(b)(2) class may be maintained when "the party opposing the class has acted or refused to act on grounds that apply generally to the class, so that final injunctive relief or corresponding declaratory relief is appropriate respecting the class as a whole."[49] Rule 23(b)(2) certification is generally limited to class actions "[w]hen the main relief sought is injunctive or declaratory, and the damages are only 'incidental. . . .'"[50] A class action under Rule 23(b)(2) has been described as a "uniquely appropriate procedure" in civil rights cases, which generally involve an allegation of discrimination against a group as well as the violation of rights of particular individuals.[51]

---

45. Pub. L. No. 88-352, 78 Stat. 241.

46. 42 U.S.C. §§ 2000e *et seq.*

47. *Kamar v. Radio Shack Corp.*, 254 F.R.D. 387, 398–99 (C.D. Cal. 2008).

48. *See, e.g., In re Wells Fargo Home Mortgage Overtime Pay Litig.*, 527 F. Supp. 2d 1053, 1071 (N.D. Cal. 2007) (certifying class where plaintiffs demonstrated that Wells Fargo's policy and practice related to compensation was uniform for all putative class members); *Kurihara v. Best Buy Co., Inc.*, C 06-01884 MHP, 2007 WL 2501698, at *9–10 (N.D. Cal. 2007) (predominance requirement satisfied where plaintiff provided substantial evidence of the existence of a company-wide policy even if in practice there are deviations from the policy).

49. FED. R. CIV. P. 23(b)(2).

50. *In re Allstate Ins. Co.*, 400 F.3d 505, 507 (7th Cir. 2005). *See also Cooper v. Southern Co.*, 390 F.3d 695, 721 (11th Cir. 2004) (citing the Advisory Committee's note to Rule 23, which explains that certification under section (b)(2) is not proper in "cases in which the appropriate final relief relates exclusively or predominantly to money damages." (1966)).

51. *See United States v. New York City Bd. of Educ.*, 487 F. Supp. 2d 220, 236 (E.D.N.Y. 2007) and *Moeller v. Taco Bell Corp.*, 220 F.R.D. 604 (N.D. Cal. 2004), both quoting 7A CHARLES A. WRIGHT, ARTHUR R. MILLER

By its terms, Rule 23(b)(2) requires that the defendant's actions or inactions must be based on grounds generally applicable to all class members. While Rule 23(b)(2) contains no predominance requirement, Rule 23(b)(2) classes must be cohesive.[52] Rule 23(b)(2) authorizes an inquiry into the relationship between the class, its injuries, and the relief sought, and courts have interpreted the rule to require that a class must be amenable to uniform group remedies.[53] Relevant considerations in determining what relief is appropriate are whether "(1) even in the absence of a possible monetary recovery, reasonable plaintiffs would bring the suit to obtain the injunctive or declaratory relief sought"; and whether "(2) the injunctive or declaratory relief sought would be both reasonably necessary and appropriate were the plaintiffs to succeed on the merits."[54]

This, in turn, requires that the remedy be manageable on a classwide basis.[55] Courts generally require that the class be sufficiently cohesive so that any classwide injunctive relief can satisfy the limitations of Federal Rule of Civil Procedure 65(d)—namely, the requirement that it state its terms specifically and describe in reasonable detail the act or acts restrained or required. Consequently, they will usually refuse to certify a Rule 23(b)(2) class if relief specifically tailored to each class member would be necessary to correct the allegedly wrongful conduct of the defendant.[56]

B. RULE 23(B)(3) CERTIFICATION IS MORE DIFFICULT FOR DISCRIMINATION CLAIMS

Monetary damages can be recovered in employment discrimination claims,[57] but those actions must proceed to class certification under Rule 23(b)(3). An employment discrimination claim is based upon either a disparate treatment or a disparate impact theory,[58] but either basis requires a corporate-wide practice or policy in order for a class to be certified. Disparate treatment claims normally involve individualized discriminatory motives, while pattern-or-practice disparate treatment claims must establish that intentional discrimination was the defendant's

---

& Mary K. Kane, Federal Practice and Procedure § 1776 (3d ed. 2005).

52. *See Lemon v. Int'l Union of Operating Eng'rs*, 216 F.3d 577, 580 (7th Cir. 2000) (explaining that "Rule 23(b)(2) operates under the presumption that the interests of the class members are cohesive and homogeneous such that the case will not depend on adjudication of facts particular to any subset of the class nor require a remedy that differentiates materially among class members"); *Barnes v. Am. Tobacco Co.*, 161 F.3d 127, 143 (3d Cir. 1998) (noting that "[w]hile 23(b)(2) class actions have no predominance or superiority requirements, it is well established that the class claims must be cohesive").

53. *Shook v. El Paso County*, 386 F.3d 963, 973 (10th Cir. 2004).

54. *Robinson v. Metro-North Commuter R.R.*, 267 F.3d 147, 164 (2d Cir. 2001).

55. *Shook v. Board of County Comm'rs*, 543 F.3d 597, 612 (10th Cir. 2008).

56. *Id.*

57. In addition to back pay and front pay, Title VII authorizes the recovery of compensatory and punitive damages. *See* 42 U.S.C. § 1981a(a)(1).

58. *See Hazen Paper Co. v. Biggins*, 507 U.S. 604, 610 (1993).

"standard operating procedure."[59] Disparate impact claims are concerned with whether employment policies or practices that are neutral on their face and were not intended to discriminate have nevertheless had a disparate effect on the protected group.[60]

In making the determination as to predominance, of utmost importance is whether the discrimination is an issue common to the class and subject to generalized proof or whether it is instead an issue unique to each class member. Where the discrimination claims are individualized as opposed to standardized, courts will generally find a lack of predominance and manageability as to the proposed class.[61] Without statistical evidence to prove classwide, company-wide discrimination, predominance is difficult to show in either disparate impact or disparate treatment cases.[62] "[I]f generalized proof of impact is . . . improper, then the district court must carefully consider whether this requirement of individual proof does not defeat the class certification on either predominance or manageability grounds."[63]

In employment discrimination class actions, the factor of manageability is ordinarily satisfied so long as common issues predominate over individual issues. For example, courts have found that a class that involved 1.5 million female employees of Walmart was manageable. In that case—described as "the largest class certified in history"—manageability was of utmost importance.[64] The management plan there described by the district court involved two stages: in stage one, the plaintiffs would attempt to prove that Walmart engaged in a pattern and practice of discrimination against the class via its company-wide employment policies, and stage two was left for punitive damages proof.[65]

Other courts have created other strategies for case management if the other class action prerequisites are fulfilled: they have bifurcated liability and damage trials; appointed a magistrate judge or special master to preside over individual damages proceedings; decertified the class after the liability trial and provided

---

59. *Int'l Bhd. of Teamsters v. United States*, 431 U.S. 324, 336 (1977).

60. *See Griggs v. Duke Power Co.*, 401 U.S. 424, 432 (1971) (stating that an employer's "good intent" is irrelevant to a disparate impact claim). "The doctrine seeks the removal of employment obstacles, not required by business necessity, which create built-in headwinds and freeze out protected groups from job opportunities and advancement." *EEOC v. Joe's Stone Crab, Inc.*, 220 F.3d 1263, 1274 (11th Cir. 2000) (internal quotation marks and citation omitted).

61. *Williams v. Mohawk Indus., Inc.*, 568 F.3d 1350, 1358 (11th Cir. 2009) (citing *Alabama v. Blue Bird Body Co.*, 573 F.2d 309, 320 (5th Cir. 1978)).

62. *Puffer v. Allstate Ins. Co.*, 255 F.R.D. 450 (N.D. Ill. 2009).

63. *Williams*, 568 F.3d at 1358 (citing *Blue Bird Body*, 573 F.2d at 324).

64. *Dukes v. Wal-Mart, Inc.*, 509 F.3d 1168, 1190 (9th Cir. 2007).

65. *Id.* at 1191 n.16. The court did not approve nor disapprove the trial court's proposed plan. The court stated that "there are a range of possibilities—which may or may not include the district court's proposed course of action—that would allow this class action to proceed in a manner that is both manageable and in accordance with due process, manageability concerns present no bar to class certification here." *Id.* at 1191.

notice to class members concerning how they may proceed to prove damages; or created subclasses.[66]

C. HYBRID CLASS ACTIONS TO RECOVER MONETARY DAMAGES AND SECURE INJUNCTIVE RELIEF

Rule 23(b)(2) certification "does not extend to cases in which the appropriate final relief relates exclusively or predominantly to money damages."[67] Circuits are split on whether hybrid class actions seeking both monetary and injunctive relief can proceed.[68] Some circuits have adopted the "incidental damages" standard[69] and others have opted for a more discretionary, "ad hoc balancing" approach.[70]

Under the incidental damages standard, "monetary relief predominates in (b)(2) class actions unless it is incidental to requested injunctive or declaratory relief,"[71] meaning that the damages that flow directly from liability to the class as a whole form the basis of the injunctive or declaratory relief and should be capable of computation by means of objective standards and not dependent in any significant way on the intangible, subjective differences of each class member's circumstances.

In the ad hoc balancing approach, the question becomes whether the positive weight or value to the plaintiffs of the injunctive or declaratory relief sought is predominant even though compensatory or punitive damages are also claimed, and class treatment would be efficient and manageable, thereby achieving an appreciable measure of judicial economy.[72]

IV. Conclusion

Manageability and predominance issues arise in unique ways in employment class actions as a result of the specialized method(s) that are used to litigate employment claims. Collective actions brought under the FLSA are designed to mostly avoid these issues until the second judicial inquiry following notice to the employees affected and return of their opt-in forms. On the other hand, class actions involving state labor claims can be combined with FLSA claims to require an analysis of manageability and predominance issues at an earlier stage.

---

66. *Carnegie v. Household Int'l Inc.*, 376 F.3d 656, 661 (7th Cir. 2004).

67. FED. R. CIV. P. 23 advisory committee note (1966).

68. *See* Chapter 14, "The Special Role of 23(b)(2) Classes."

69. This test was set forth by the Court of Appeals for the Fifth Circuit in *Allison v. Citgo Petroleum Corp.*, 151 F.3d 402 (5th Cir. 1998) and has been adopted by the Seventh and Third Circuits. *See Lemon*, 216 F.3d at 581 and *Barabin v. Aramark Corp.*, 02-8057, 2003 WL 355417, at *1, 2 (3d Cir. 2003).

70. These are used by the court of appeals in *Robinson*, 267 F.3d 147, and *Molski v. Gleich*, 318 F.3d 937, 949–50 (9th Cir. 2003).

71. *Allison*, 151 F.3d at 415.

72. *Robinson*, 267 F.3d at 163, 164.

Other employment claims create unique predominance and manageability concerns, especially employment discrimination claims. Federal Rule 23(b)(2) was specifically designed to facilitate discrimination class actions by eliminating some of these concerns, but the only available remedy for these claims is injunctive or other equitable relief. Certification of these discrimination claims under Rule 23(b)(3) is far more difficult, in large part because the predominance requirement is difficult to satisfy—especially where the discrimination or harassment evidence is purely anecdotal.

INSURANCE

RICHARD L. FENTON[1]

I. Introduction

The case law is replete with putative class actions against insurance carriers seeking damages, and often bad-faith liability, based on alleged underpayment of claims. Typically, certification is sought under Rule 23(b)(3).[2] In addition to the requirements of Rule 23(a)—numerosity, commonality, typicality, and adequacy of representation—the court under Rule 23(b)(3) must also find that "the questions of law or fact common to class members predominate over any questions affecting only individual members, and that a class action is superior to other available methods for fairly and efficiently adjudicating the controversy."[3] The matters pertinent to these findings include

(A) the class members' interests in individually controlling the prosecution or defense of separate actions;

(B) the extent and nature of any litigation concerning the controversy already begun by or against class members;

(C) the desirability or undesirability of concentrating the litigation of the claims in the particular forum; and

(D) the likely difficulties in managing a class action.[4]

Subdivision (b)(3) encompasses those cases in which a class action would achieve economies of time, effort, and expense, and promote uniformity of decision

---

1. Mr. Fenton wishes to thank his valued colleagues Steven Levy, Wendy Enerson, Tery Gonsalves, and Mary Mills for their able assistance in the preparation of this chapter.

2. FED. R. CIV. P. 23(b)(3); *see also, e.g., Green v. Occidental Petroleum Corp.*, 541 F.2d 1335, 1339–40 (9th Cir. 1976). Note, however, that there may be circumstances in connection with "limited fund" recoveries where certification under Rule 23(b)(1)(B) is permissible. *See, e.g., Ortiz v. Fibreboard Corp.*, 527 U.S. 815, 834–35 (1999).

3. FED. R. CIV. P. 23(b)(3).

4. *Id.*

as to persons similarly situated, without sacrificing procedural fairness or bring-ing about other undesirable results.[5] This portion of the rule also was expected to be particularly helpful in enabling numerous persons who have small claims that might not be worth litigating in individual actions to combine their resources and bring an action to vindicate their collective rights.[6]

Property and casualty insurance, broadly defined, includes homeowners, auto-mobile, and commercial insurance, including third-party liability insurance. How-ever, for purposes of this chapter, we focus on first-party claims under homeowner and automobile policies, as these claims illustrate some of the recurrent themes that arise in insurance class action litigation.[7] The homeowners insurance context has been a fertile area for controversy in recent years, particularly with the mul-tiple class actions that were filed in the wake of Hurricane Katrina.

II. Homeowner Claims

For the most part, plaintiffs seeking certification of a class of homeowner claim-ants have a heavy burden. At first glance, the class action device might appear attractive. Homeowner's insurance claims are often relatively small, and the class action device is an appealing means for adjudicating claims on a mass basis that otherwise might not justify the cost of litigation. In addition, insurers' increas-ing use of computerized estimation and adjusting software has enabled plaintiffs' counsel to argue that the use or accuracy of these software programs presents com-mon issues that predominate over individualized questions and that individual damage issues may be reduced to a formulaic proposition.

On the other hand, homeowner insurance claims often are highly individu-alized. Property claims are tremendously varied, and notwithstanding the use of software tools, claims adjustment remains a highly individualized process, where the application of electronic tools and claims analysis software requires the exer-

---

5. FED. R. CIV. P. 23(b)(3) advisory committee note (2009).

6. CHARLES A. WRIGHT, ARTHUR R. MILLER & MARY K. KANE, FEDERAL PRACTICE AND PROCEDURE § 1777 (3d ed. 2005).

7. Although life insurance is beyond the focus of this chapter, it bears mention that Rule 23(b)(3) class action litigation in the life insurance context typically involves allegations of improper or misleading sales practices as opposed to claims practices. In such cases, predominance and manageability issues loom large with respect to whether (1) misrepresentations can be established on a common or uniform basis, and (2) whether reliance can be established on a classwide basis. *Compare Moore v. PaineWebber, Inc.*, 306 F.3d 1247, 1255–56 (2d Cir. 2002) (district court did not abuse its discretion in denying class certification, as defendant's brokers did not adopt a materially uniform approach to their sales presentations) *with In re Lutheran Bhd. Variable Ins. Prods. Co. Sales Practices Litig.*, 201 F.R.D. 456 (D. Minn. 2001) (statutory fraud class action certified based on uniform sales practices and absence of actual reliance requirement for statu-tory consumer fraud, but class certification denied on breach of fiduciary duty claim because individual-ized inquiry needed); *see also* Chapter 17.A, "Consumer Actions and Fraud/Reliance-Based Torts."

cise of adjuster judgment and discretion and where the amount of the loss often lies within a range and cannot be calculated with precision. Proof that an insurer breached its contract with one policyholder does not necessarily establish a breach with respect to other policyholders.[8] Even where the damage to property arguably arises out of a common event, such as in Hurricane Katrina, individual adjusting issues may abound.

First is the question of coverage. In Hurricane Katrina, damage to a particular property was sometimes the result of flooding or storm surge, which is not a covered peril under most homeowner policies, and sometimes the result of wind or wind-driven rain, which generally is covered.[9] More often than not, the damage was the result of multiple perils, some of which were covered and some of which were not.[10] That circumstance, in itself, requires individualized inquiry into the cause and origin of the loss and the extent of loss due to a covered peril.

Even where a covered loss is established, no two properties and no two losses are identical. Properties differ in design, construction materials, elevations, and location, and in the nature of the damage itself. Any homeowner who has gone through the process of obtaining multiple repair or remodeling estimates understands that construction cost estimates can vary widely, even for the same damage to the same property. In addition, local market factors can significantly affect repair cost. In the aftermath of Hurricane Katrina, for example, the prices for construction materials and labor in affected areas spiked sharply in the months following the hurricane because of the sharp surge in demand, then tended to fluctuate widely as the market slowly returned to equilibrium. An estimate prepared one week may have contained estimated pricing for materials and/or labor that differed from the prices applicable in the market just a few weeks earlier or a few weeks later. Thus, the question becomes whether the plaintiffs' losses and the

---

8. *See Pollet v. Travelers Prop. & Cas. Ins. Co.*, Civ. A. No. 01-863, 2001 WL 1471724, at *2 (E.D. La. Nov. 16, 2001) (finding action alleging intentional or negligent failure to adequately compensate putative class of insureds for claims arising out of hailstorm failed to meet the predominance requirement due to numerous individualized issues); *Newell v. State Farm Gen. Ins. Co.*, 118 Cal. App. 4th 1094 (2004) (class action cannot be maintained where each insured's right to recover depends upon particular facts of his or her claim); *Comer v. Nationwide Mut. Ins. Co.*, Civ. A. No. 1:05-CV-436, 2006 WL 1066645, at *3-4 (S.D. Miss. Feb. 23, 2006) (denying motion for leave to file amended complaint seeking class action against insurers by homeowners seeking coverage from damages from Hurricane Katrina because no two property owners would have suffered the same loss and each individual claim would require evidence to establish the cause and extent of loss). The question of whether proof of the named plaintiffs' claim will tend to establish the claims of absent class members implicates not only the manageability and predominance factors of Rule 23(b), but also the typicality requirement under Rule 23(a).

9. *Vanderbrook v. Unitrin Preferred Ins. Co. (In re Katrina Canal Breaches Consol. Litig.)*, 495 F.3d 191, 214 (5th Cir. 2007).

10. *See, e.g., Dickerson v. Lexington Ins. Co.*, 556 F.3d 290, 295 (5th Cir. 2009); *Nunez v. Standard Fire Ins. Co.*, Civ. A. No. 7-7457, 2009 WL 799756 (E.D. La. Mar. 24, 2009).

respective adjustment of those losses are sufficiently similar to establish class cohesion or predominance of the common issues.

For example, in *Newell v. State Farm General Insurance Company*,[11] the court affirmed the denial of class treatment for a suit against several insurance carriers for homeowner claims arising out of the Northridge earthquake:

> Even if State Farm and Farmers adopted improper claims practices to adjust Northridge earthquake claims, each putative class member still could recover for breach of contract and bad faith *only* by proving his or her individual claim was wrongfully denied, in whole or in part, and the insurer's action in doing so was unreasonable. Thus, each putative class member's potential recovery would involve an individual assessment of his or her property, the damage sustained, and the actual claims practices employed. In such cases, class treatment is unwarranted.[12]

Similarly, class action treatment for Hurricane Katrina homeowner claims has been almost uniformly rejected in the federal courts, often by way of motion to strike the class allegations on the face of the pleading.[13] In *Aguilar v. Allstate Fire and Casualty Company*,[14] the court held that allegations that defendant had underpaid claims by repeatedly utilizing below-market unit pricing could not be proven on a classwide basis, and reasoned as follows:

> While [defendant's] general internal policies for adjusting claims may arguably be one common issue of fact, demonstrating a wrongful pattern and practice of failing to adjust claims will require an intensive review of the individual facts of each class member's damage claim, including the nature and extent of damage, the timing and adjustment of each class member's claim, how much each class member was paid for his claim and for what damage, and whether that amount was suf-

---

11. 118 Cal. App. 4th 1094.

12. *Id.* at 1103 (citations omitted; emphasis in original).

13. *See, e.g., Jones v. Nat'l Sec. Fire & Cas. Co.*, Civ. A. No. 06-1407, 2006 WL 3228409 (W.D. La. Nov. 3, 2006), *aff'd*, 501 F.3d 443 (5th Cir. 2007). In addition to the trend in homeowner's cases toward striking class allegations on the face of the pleadings, *see, e.g., Cox v. Allstate Ins. Co.*, Civ. A. No. Civ-07-1449, 2009 WL 2591673, at *4–5 (W.D. Okla. Aug. 19, 2009), the medical payments class actions discussed at section IV, *infra*, also evidence a recent trend in class action defense to preemptively attack certification in a preliminary motion designed to obviate expensive class action discovery and related proceedings. Numerous courts have ruled on motions to strike or dismiss medical payments class action allegations on the pleadings. Proponents of such motions argue that, from the face of the pleadings, it is evident that the individualized issues discussed above will predominate, hence there is no basis for the class allegations to proceed. Several courts have in fact granted motions on this basis. *See, e.g., Advanced Acupuncture Clinic v. Allstate Ins. Co.*, Civ. A. No. 07-4925 (JAP), 2008 WL 4056244, at *15 (D.N.J. Aug. 26, 2008), *aff'd on other grounds*, 342 F. App'x 809 (3d Cir. 2009); *Gloria v. Allstate County Mut. Ins. Co.*, Civ. A. No. SA-99-CA-676-PM, 2000 WL 35754563, at *6 (W.D. Tex. Sept. 29, 2000); *Ross-Randolph v. Allstate Ins. Co.*, Civ. A. No. DKC 99-3344, 2001 WL 36042162, at *6–7 (D. Md. May 11, 2001).

14. Civ. A. No. 07-1738, 2007 WL 734809 (E.D. La. Mar. 6, 2007).

ficient and timely. On the face of the pleading, it is clear that those individualized and highly personal issues pertaining to each class member patently overwhelm any arguably common issues rendering the claims inappropriate for class treatment.[15]

A similar note was struck by the court in *In re Katrina Canal Breaches Consolidated Litigation*,[16] where the court—primarily on predominance grounds—struck plaintiffs' class allegations in a class action against multiple carriers claiming systematic underpayment of claims in connection with hurricane losses:

> In addressing the substances of the remaining class claims, this Court finds that they are not suitable for class certification. Plaintiffs have alleged claims for breach of contract, breach of the implied covenant of good faith and fair dealing, violation of Louisiana laws prohibiting bad faith by insurers, and breach of fiduciary duty. These claims inherently require individualized fact-specific inquiries because they depend upon whether the Defendants failed to properly adjust and pay for Hurricane Katrina-related property claims. As persuasively argued by Defendants, this Court would have to delve into individualized inquiries regarding the nature and extent of a property owner's damage, the source of damage (*i.e.*, wind versus flood), the timing and adjustment of claims, the market conditions when that claim was adjusted, whether each class member complied with his post-loss duties, how much each class member was paid and for what damage that payment was made, and whether any supplemental payments were timely and sufficient to satisfy the claim.[17]

Likewise, the court found plaintiffs' bad faith claims inappropriate for class treatment because they would require individualized determination of the reasonableness of each defendant's conduct in connection with each loss, overwhelming any arguably common issues.[18]

Attempts to overcome predominance and manageability issues based on an insurer's use of estimating software to adjust claims have not fared significantly better in the homeowner's context. While the use of estimating software may provide one arguably common issue, it also opens up a host of individualized questions. Insurers who utilize estimating software in the claims process often rely on data supplied by a third-party vendor who provides geographically specific data that is periodically updated to reflect market changes in the price of construction materials. In addition, adjusters may have the ability to override the pricing in the system based on, for example, more current or claim-specific information. Thus, notwithstanding the use of computerized estimating software, analysis of any

---

15. *Id.* at *3.
16. Civ. A. No. 05-4182, 2009 WL 1707923 (E.D. La. June 16, 2009).
17. *Id.* at *6.
18. *Id.* at *7.

given claim may boil down to a claim-by-claim inquiry.[19] As the court observed in *Franceschini v. Allstate Floridian Insurance Company*:[20]

> Plaintiff argues that because Allstate used the same software in determining the awards of all putative class members, common questions of fact are predominant. . . . [T]he fact that Integriclaim software may have been used in determining the compensation received by each member of this putative class is irrelevant to this cause of action and does not create a common legal or factual issue. Each class member would have to present evidence of hurricane damage to their property, the value of the loss, their communications with Allstate regarding this loss, and the payment, if any, received by Allstate. A class action in this case would result in nothing more than a series of mini-trials on insurance coverage and property damage. Therefore, this Court finds that Plaintiff has failed to meet his burden under Rule 23(b)(3).[21]

Picking out particular components of pricing in an attempt to show some kind of systematic underpayment on a common basis is not necessarily a formula for success. The fact that a particular component of the repair cost may have been underpriced does not automatically establish that any given estimate was underpriced. Depending on the policy terms, the insurer's obligation generally is to pay the insured the actual cash value of the damaged property or the amount reasonably necessary to repair or replace the damaged property, which may or may not include a deduction for depreciation. The question, then, is not whether each component of the loss was properly priced, but whether the insurer's payment *as a whole* adequately compensated the policyholder for his loss. Thus, in *Melancon v. State Farm Insurance Company*,[22] class certification was denied on manageability grounds where the plaintiffs alleged that State Farm systematically underpaid general contractor overhead and profit (GCOP) in connection with homeowner claims:

> It is true that plaintiff has a simple trial plan. He intends to stipulate that State Farm's estimate reflects the reasonable cost to repair or replace his property, except

---

19. *See Schafer v. State Farm Fire & Cas. Co.*, Civ. A. No. 06-8262, 2009 WL 2391238, at *7 (E.D. La. Aug. 3, 2009).

20. Civ. A. No. 6:06-CV-1283, 2007 WL 646957 (M.D. Fla. Feb. 27, 2007).

21. *Franceschini*, Civ. A. No. 6:06-CV-1283, Rec. Doc. No. 54 (M.D. Fla. May 30, 2007); *see also Henry v. Allstate Ins. Co.*, No. 07-1738, 2007 WL 2287817, at *5 (E.D. La. Aug. 8, 2007) (striking class allegations and fraud claim regarding the use of computerized software because "proving a questionable pattern and practice of undervaluing claims will require an intensive review of the individualized facts of each class member's damage claim"); *Schafer*, 2009 WL 2391238, at *4 ("[T]o prove liability, Plaintiff would have to determine the accuracy of each line item, *i.e.*, the actual fair market value of each line item on each list," but the plaintiffs failed to provide any expert testimony about how these fair market values could be efficiently calculated on a classwide basis. [Thus,] "the calculation of the fair market value . . . would be an incredibly particularized assessment that would predominate over any common issues.").

22. Civ. A. No. 06-5230, 2008 WL 4691685 (E.D. La. Oct. 22, 2008).

to challenge the percentage of GCOP as insufficient, and he plans to call an expert to establish the proper percentage(s) of GCOP, which he contends is greater than 20%. That is not the end of the case, however, as failing to pay more than 20% GCOP is not *ipso facto* a breach of contract. State Farm's insurance policy does not provide that it will pay every insured the market rate for each item in need of repair. The contract provides that State Farm will pay the insured the **total amount** that is reasonably necessary to repair or replace the property. Therefore, for each class member, the issue is whether the total amount paid, not just a discrete, uniformly applicable component of that payment, was sufficient to satisfy State Farm's contractual obligation.[23]

Payment of GCOP in connection with homeowner's claims has been a frequent area of litigation, and there is a split of authority with respect to class certification. Much of the controversy stems from questions about whether a court can apply a rule of thumb, such as the number of trades involved in the repair, to determine whether GCOP is appropriate in a given claim. Cases where GCOP classes have been certified include *Press v. Louisiana Citizens Fair Plan Property Insurance Company*[24] and *Burgess v. Farmers Insurance Company*.[25] Cases denying certification include *Melancon*,[26] *Samantha Nguyen v. St. Paul Travelers Insurance Company*,[27] and *Allen-Wright v. Allstate Insurance Company*.[28]

III. First-Party Auto Physical Damage Claims

First-party automobile class actions generally have tended to focus either on the estimating process for automobile physical damage or on medical payments for first-party medical payment or PIP coverage.[29] The issues in automobile physical damage cases are similar to those presented in the homeowner's context in terms of the use of the common issues presented by the use of computerized estimating platforms for claim adjustment. A number of class actions in the late 1990s and early 2000s zeroed in on insurers' specification of aftermarket sheet metal parts in automobile repair estimates, fueled in part by a $1.2 billion verdict against State Farm that was ultimately reversed in its entirety by the Illinois Supreme Court. Plaintiffs' theory was that original equipment manufacturer (OEM) parts were of higher quality than non-OEM parts and that by specifying less expensive non-OEM

---

23. *Id.* at *5.

24. 12 So. 3d 392, 396 (La. App. 4th Cir. Apr. 22, 2009).

25. 151 P.3d 92, 93–94, 99–101 (Okla. 2006); *see also Lindquist v. Farmers Ins. Co. Ariz.*, Civ. A. No. CV-06-597, 2008 WL 343299 (D. Ariz. Feb. 6, 2008) (motion to strike class allegations denied).

26. 2008 WL 4691685, at *5.

27. No. 06-4130, 2008 WL 4534395, at *8 (E.D. La. Oct. 6, 2008).

28. Civ. A. No. 7-CV-4087, 2008 WL 5336701, at *5 (E.D. Pa. 2008).

29. "PIP" refers to "personal injury protection" coverage.

parts, the insurer was breaching its obligation to pay for repair or replacement of the damaged property. To avoid predominance problems, plaintiffs in these cases typically asserted that non-OEM parts were "categorically inferior" to OEM parts and that the "categorical inferiority" of non-OEM parts obviated individualized questions about whether the non-OEM parts were in fact of lesser quality than OEM parts.[30] The defendants, by contrast, typically argued that such determinations could not be made without reference to the specific vehicle, parts, repair, etc.

Similarly, a series of first-party claims was also brought for purported "diminished value" claims. The theory of diminished value presupposes that an automobile that has suffered significant collision damage, even if properly repaired, loses value that is not typically compensated in first-party collision claims. That contrasts with third-party insurance claims, where the tortfeasor, and ultimately his liability carrier, is liable in tort if the claimant can establish that the automobile has in fact suffered diminished value as a result of the collision. Again, plaintiffs in these cases typically try to avoid predominance problems by asserting a theory of "inherent diminished value" to the effect that all vehicles that have been repaired suffer a stigma of diminished value, regardless of whether the repairs have fully restored the vehicle. In this regard, they claim that the court need not consider individualized proofs.[31] The claims are attractive for certification because they involve assertion of relatively small dollar thresholds and the use of proposed formulas for determining the amount of diminished value per vehicle. Once again, defendants typically contest that there is any inherent diminished value—much less one that can be determined by applying an across-the-board formula—and that the determination of whether an automobile has suffered diminished value as a result of a collision can only be made on a case-by-case basis. These types of theories—both that injury is categorical and that the amount of damages can be calculated on a formula basis—have been subjected to expert challenges under *Daubert* and analogous state law at the class certification stage because the reliability of the expert's opinion bears directly on the propriety of class certification, although it may also impact the ultimate merits decision.[32]

What both the aftermarket parts class actions and diminished value class actions demonstrate is plaintiffs' use of expert testimony to try to establish common factual propositions—and thereby a predominance of common issues—in circumstances where defendants argue that those same facts must be adjudicated on a case-by-case basis. For example, in *Avery v. State Farm Mutual Automobile Insurance Company*, plaintiffs offered the expert testimony of an automotive engineer who

---

30. *Compare Smith v. Am. Family Mut. Ins. Co.*, 289 S.W.3d 675 (Mo. App. 2009) *with Avery v. State Farm Mut. Auto. Ins. Co.*, 835 N.E.2d 801 (2005).

31. *See Sims v. Allstate Ins. Co.*, 851 N.E.2d 701 (Ill. App. 2006); *Siegle v. Progressive Consumers Ins. Co.*, 788 So. 2d 355 (Fla. App. 2001).

32. *See* Chapter 13, "*Daubert* Challenges in Class Certification."

opined that non-OEM automobile sheet metal parts are "categorically inferior" to their OEM counterparts, while defendants offered testimony and data indicating that many non-OEM parts are equivalent to or exceed OEM parts for quality.[33] In the diminished-value cases, plaintiffs typically contend that all automobiles with more than a minimum threshold of surface damage suffer inherent diminished value, while defendants proffer examples of automobiles that have maintained resale value after repair, notwithstanding the collision damage.

There is significant confusion as to how, and at what stage, the court should address the issue of predominance in these circumstances. Some courts have suggested that plaintiffs may maintain a class action based on generalized expert testimony on the theory that the credibility of the expert and whether the facts at issue can be established as a universal proposition for the class is a "merits" determination that should be left to the jury.[34] On the other hand, defendants would argue that the determination as to whether common issues predominate is a question for the court under Rule 23, to be addressed on a motion for class certification, and is not an issue for the jury. Defendants also argue that there can be no predominance of common issues where the expert's opinion purporting to establish a global fact is itself disputed and subject to legitimate controversy and that a defendant should not be deprived of the opportunity to present evidence on a case-by-case basis as to each putative class member simply because a plaintiffs' expert opines that such proof is not necessary.

While by no means an exhaustive list, other automobile physical damage claims practices that have been the subject of class actions include betterment,[35] i.e., insurer's taking of a deduction from the claimant's recovery where the repair or replacement has enhanced the quality of the vehicle, as where worn tires damaged

---

33. 835 N.E.2d at 815–16.

34. Many courts, both state and federal, have interpreted the U.S. Supreme Court's opinion in *Eisen v. Carlisle & Jacquelin*, 417 U.S. 156 (1974), as prohibiting any inquiry into the credibility of experts on either side at the class certification stage on the ground that such an inquiry would involve a "merits" determination. *See, e.g., In re Visa Check/Mastermoney Antitrust Litig.*, 280 F.3d 124, 136–37 (2d Cir. 2001), *superseded by statute and on other grounds* (affirming certification of antitrust class in part on expert's dubious testimony that injury in fact could be demonstrated on a classwide basis). More recent authorities have questioned this expansive interpretation of *Eisen* and have suggested that the court can and should make findings necessary to establish Rule 23 requirements, notwithstanding that such findings may overlap with merits issues. *See, e.g., Miles v. Merrill Lynch & Co.*, 471 F.3d 24, 33 (2d Cir. 2006) ("[C]areful examination of *Eisen* reveals that there is no basis for thinking that a specific Rule 23 requirement need not be fully established just because it concerns, or even overlaps with, an aspect of the merits."); *Szabo v. Bridgeport Machs., Inc.*, 249 F.3d 672, 675 (7th Cir. 2001) ("The proposition that a district judge must accept all of the complaint's allegations when deciding whether to certify a class cannot be found in Rule 23 and has nothing to recommend it.").

35. *See Steinberg v. Nationwide Mut. Ins. Co.*, 224 F.R.D. 67, 78–79 (E.D.N.Y. 2004) (rejecting defendants' manageability arguments); *see also* Chapter 17.A, "Consumer Actions and Fraud/Reliance-Based Torts."

in an accident are replaced with new tires, and so-called "omitted repair" cases challenging whether insurers' repair estimates systematically omit needed repair processes.[36]

IV. Med-Pay and PIP Class Actions

The key inquiry in actions seeking certification of putative medical payments classes is dependent upon how the issue is construed. Plaintiffs seeking class certification attempt to construe the issue as whether the third-party medical bill review software used by insurers to assist in determining the proper medical payment amounts owed to insureds are generically flawed and result ineluctably in biased payment decisions. If the issue is viewed in this fashion, classwide determination could be appropriate, since a determination that the software itself is inherently biased and flawed could establish some sort of liability on a classwide basis. Such has been the rationale of the courts that have certified medical payments class actions.[37]

On the other hand, a majority of the cases in this context have denied certification. These cases have held that the liability determination does not turn on the efficacy of the software that insurers use to assist in bill review, but instead is based simply on whether the contract has been breached. The contractual promise in these cases, those courts have reasoned, is not to use any sort of bill review methodology, but instead to pay a reasonable amount for the medical bills at issue. Since that is the promise, proof of a flawed methodology will not resolve the issue on a classwide basis, because even if the methodology is flawed that does not mean any particular payment was unreasonable. As a result, each payment for each bill would, to determine liability, need to be assessed on a case-by-case basis, with all evidence as to the reasonableness and/or unreasonableness of any payment taken into account. In turn, that would mean that individualized issues (as to the reasonableness of each payment) would predominate over any common issues (the efficacy of the particular bill review system used), and that in turn means that a class action would be wholly unmanageable, since it would devolve into a series of mini-trials.[38]

---

36. *See Levy v. State Farm Mut. Auto. Ins. Co.*, 150 Cal. App. 4th 1 (4th Dist. 2007).

37. *See, e.g., Sitton v. State Farm Mut. Auto. Ins. Co.*, 63 P.3d 198 (2003); *Strasen v. Allstate Ins. Co.*, Civ. A. No. 99-L-1040 (Cir. Ct. of Madison County, Ill. Sept. 10, 2001).

38. *See, e.g., Gloria*, 2000 WL 35754563, at *9 (dismissing class allegations where plaintiff alleged defendant insurer improperly used computer database to adjust medical bills and stating "issues such as whether a particular provider's charge was reasonable and/or necessary for a particular treatment for a particular injury in a particular location must be determined on an individualized basis. Each putative plaintiff would be required to prove entitlement to benefits under the terms of the policy and that the medical expenses were reasonable and the services were necessary"); *Physical Therapy v. Metlife Auto & Home*, Civ. A. No. 07-3110, 2008 WL 4056225 (D.N.J. Aug. 26, 2008) (finding class action treatment inappropriate in

V. Multistate and Nationwide Class Actions

The superiority and manageability issues inherent in multistate or nationwide class actions, discussed in more detail in Chapter 24, "Multistate Class Actions and Choice of Law," are particularly acute in the context of insurance claims practices class actions. Under the McCarran Ferguson Act,[39] regulation of the business of insurance is relegated to the states, and while there undoubtedly are similarities in the regulatory frameworks applied in the different states, there are significant dissimilarities as well.

In *Avery v. State Farm*,[40] the Illinois Supreme Court reversed a nationwide class action judgment against State Farm based on its specification in automobile repair estimates of parts that were not made by the original automobile manufacturer (non-OEM parts).[41] Concurring in the result, Justice Freeman observed:

> The same shortcomings that caused the Supreme Court to find a constitutional violation in *Shutts*[42] are present in the instant case. As in *Shutts*, there are significant outcome-determinative differences between the law of Illinois and the laws of other states regarding the breach of contract action. For instance, our circuit and appellate courts determined that State Farm's promise to have repairs performed with parts "of like kind and quality" meant "of like kind and quality to OEM parts," a conclusion with which I agree. However, as State Farm observes, courts in other jurisdictions have not so construed the language. . . . Other states have expressly provided by statute or regulation that non-OEM parts may be used in repairs . . . .[43]

---

case alleging defendant insurers underpaid medical bills submitted under automobile insurance policies), *aff'd on other grounds*, 342 F. App'x 809 (3d Cir. 2009); *Ross-Randolph*, 2001 WL 36042162, at *6–7; *Antoine v. Allstate Ins. Co.*, Civ. A. No. 214453 (Md. Cir. Ct. Montgomery County, Dec. 5, 2001).

39. 15 U.S.C. § 1012.

40. 835 N.E.2d at 867.

41. The regulation of non-OEM parts in automobile repair, for example, differs substantially from state to state. For example, Illinois has a disclosure requirement. *See* 215 ILL. COMP. STAT. 5/155.29(d). Alaska does not. *See* ALASKA STAT. §§ 45.45.130, 45.45.150, and 45.45.190. Illinois regulates the quality of non-OEM parts. *See* ILL. ADMIN. CODE tit. 50, § 919.80(d)(5)(C). Alaska, Arizona, Colorado, Kansas, Nevada, Oklahoma, and Washington do not. *See generally* ARIZ. REV. STAT. § 44-1291 *et seq.*; COLO. REV. STAT. § 42-9-101 *et seq.*; KAN. STAT. ANN. § 50-659 *et seq.*; NEV. REV. STAT. § 686A.240 *et seq.*; OKLA. STAT. tit. 15, § 951 *et seq.*, and WASH. REV. CODE § 46.71.005 *et seq.* Illinois does not require the affirmative consent of the insured before non-OEM parts may be used. 815 ILL. COMP. STAT. 308/15. Colorado and Oregon do. *See* COLO. REV. STAT. § 42-9-107; OR. REV. STAT. §§ 746.287(1), 746.292(4)(b). These differences may be outcome determinative, and thereby require a court to interpret and apply the insurance regulations of each state, making class adjudication inefficient and improper.

42. *Phillips Petroleum Co. v. Shutts*, 472 U.S. 797, 821–24 (1985).

43. *Avery*, 835 N.E.2d at 869; see also *In re Jackson Nat'l Life Ins. Co. Premium Litig.*, 183 F.R.D. 217, 223 (W.D. Mich. 1998) (concluding that due process required life insurance sales practice claims be decided under the laws of the states of the absent class members' residence); *Ferrell v. Allstate Ins. Co.*, 150 P.3d 1022 (N.M. Ct. App. 2006), *rev'd on other grounds*, 188 P.3d 1156 (N.M. 2008) (no predominance in class action

Courts considering certification of a multistate class action in the insurance arena must be particularly cognizant of the potential impact a decision may have on the regulatory scheme in the states whose citizens will compose the purported class.

VI. Conclusion

The insurance industry is a frequent target of class action litigation, much of it relating to first-party property and casualty claims. Class certification in such cases often hinges on Rule 23(b)(3) predominance and manageability issues, with the focus being on whether allegedly uniform or systematic claims practices can be said to "predominate" over the individualized nature of each claim, with many courts, particularly in the homeowners insurance area, concluding that the individualized nature of property and casualty claims tend to outweigh any arguably common issues. Given the differences in state regulation of the business of insurance, particular predominance and manageability issues are presented in nationwide or multistate class actions because of the different, and possibly inconsistent, laws and regulations applicable to insurance carriers in different states.

---

challenging imposition of service fees for premium installment payments where differences between statutory definitions of "premium" rendered application of New Mexico law to the non–New Mexico plaintiffs improper).

SECURITIES

HAROLD C. HIRSHMAN
CAMILLE E. BENNETT

I. The Prevalence of Securities Class Actions

In 2009, securities class actions were far and away the most prevalent type of federal class actions.[1] More than 215 federal securities class actions were filed in 2009, which is well above the securities class action filings in 2005 and 2006.[2] Before the current credit crisis, 2006 saw a low of 130 securities cases, the lowest total since the Private Securities Litigation Reform Act (PSLRA) was instituted in 1996.[3] Securities class actions are a coastal phenomenon with the bulk of the cases filed in the Second and the Ninth Circuits, particularly in Los Angeles and New York, but they span every federal circuit.[4] As Professor John Coffee has colorfully said, "In effect [securities class actions] are the 800 pound gorilla that dominates and overshadows other forms of class actions."[5]

---

1. JOHN C. COFFEE JR. & DANIEL WOLF, CLASS CERTIFICATION: DEVELOPMENTS OVER THE LAST FIVE YEARS (2004–2009), at 13 (ABA National Institute on Class Actions, 2009), *available at* http://www.acslaw.org/node/15057 [hereinafter COFFEE & WOLF]; *see also* STEPHANIE PLANCICH & SVETLANA STARYKH, NERA ECONOMIC CONSULTING, RECENT TRENDS IN SECURITIES CLASS ACTION LITIGATION: 2009 YEAR-END UPDATE 1 (2009), *available at* http://www.securitieslitigationtrends.com/Recent_Trends_Report_01.10.pdf (describing surge in federal securities class action filings).

2. *See* PLANCICH & STARYKH, *supra* note 1, at 1–2.

3. *Id.* at 1.

4. *Id.* at 4.

5. John C. Coffee, Jr., *Reforming the Securities Class Action: An Essay on Deterrence and Its Implementation*, 106 COLUM. L. REV. 1534, 1539 (2006).

II. The Beginnings and Efficacy of Securities Class Actions

The actuality is that securities class actions have been controversial almost from their birth, and remain so.[6]

At first blush, it would seem impossible to have a securities fraud class action. Neither the Securities Act of 1933 ('33 Act) nor the Securities Exchange Act of 1934 ('34 Act) mention class actions. In the beginning, private remedies of any kind were severely limited. The '33 Act does provide a remedy for a purchaser in Section 11 if there has been a material misstatement in the offering materials for a security.[7] Section 10(b) of the '34 Act—now the central claim in most securities fraud class actions—merely prohibits the use of deceptive devices in selling securities; it provides no purchaser remedy.[8] Years went by with enforcement of the securities laws in the hands of the SEC. However, in the 1960s, the world changed. The Federal Rules of Civil Procedure were amended in 1966, and private rights of action were endorsed to facilitate enforcement of the securities laws. Although some commentators suggest that the 1966 amendments made little actual difference, as a practical matter the '60s saw the beginning of securities class actions.[9]

That the federal securities laws were not crafted with class actions in mind has had lasting consequences. On its surface, a securities class action under Rule 10b-5, a fraud rule, seems to be a contradiction in terms. We all know that reliance is a critical element of any fraud action. Once a private remedy under the '34 Act had been created via Rule 10b-5, the wizards of the Chicago School solved the reliance problem for the courts through the fiction of the efficient market. This concept obviates the need for each class member to prove reliance on omitted or misstated facts. With it, the 10b-5 class action was on its way via "fraud on the market"—the notion that the market, not the investor, was misled.[10] Once the market is introduced into the equation, with its spongelike ability to assimilate all information, what needs to be shown is that the missing information had a material market impact when it became known—i.e., stock price movement. This impact is then extrapolated backward to the moment when a disclosure was purportedly

---

6. *Compare* Comment, *The Impact of Class Actions on Rule 10b-5*, 38 U. Chi. L. Rev. 337 (1971) *with* Arthur R. Miller, *Of Frankenstein Monsters and Shining Knights: Myth, Reality, and the "Class Action Problem,"* 92 Harv. L. Rev. 664 (1979) *and* Coffee, *supra* note 5; *see also* Donald C. Langevoort, *Basic at Twenty: Rethinking Fraud on the Market*, 2009 Wis. L. Rev. 151, 155–66 (2009).

7. *See* 15 U.S.C. § 77k *et seq.* (2009).

8. *Id.* at § 78a *et seq.*

9. Miller, *supra* note 6, at 664. Miller notes that "the Federal Courts have played a major role in the increase of litigation, particularly by watering down some, although not all, of the common law fraud requirements for claims under Rule 10b-5." *Id.* at 673.

10. *See The Impact of Class Actions on Rule 10b-5, supra* note 6, at 345–52; *see also Basic, Inc. v. Levinson*, 485 U.S. 224, 244–45 (1988).

required. However, the idea of the efficient market has fallen into some academic disrepute, given the recent widespread demonstration of the fallibility of the market. This crucial element of a securities class action is now under attack, as Professor Donald Langevoort has recently explained.[11]

The efficacy of securities class actions has been questioned since at least 1971. Early critics saw them as economic blackmail. Their view was that actual perpetrators of the claimed fraud were generally indemnified by the entities that employed them, and so it was likely that the present shareholders of a company would have to pay for the sins of past company agents and employees:

> [C]ompensation for defrauded investors is often paid, indirectly, by innocent shareholders of the defendant corporation. If the corporation is a defendant, or if it indemnifies its executives, any recovery will decrease the equity of existing shareholders. If compensation is desirable, it is difficult to see why, especially in a large public corporation, it should be achieved at the shareholder's expense. . . .

> The final benefit alleged to result from expanded liability under 10b-5 is deterrence of securities fraud. This is acknowledged to be the principal objective of the Act. But the crucial question—which has never been addressed empirically—is whether and how well the current state of 10b-5 law serves the deterrence goal.[12]

This problem persists. Professor Coffee wrote in 2006:

> But do these massive penalties achieve much of value—let alone approach optimal deterrence? Not necessarily. Deterrence works best when it is focused on the culpable, but there is little evidence that securities class actions today satisfy this standard. Rather, because the costs of securities class actions—both the settlement payments and the litigation expenses of both sides—fall largely on the defendant corporation, its shareholders ultimately bear these costs indirectly and often inequitably.[13]

Notwithstanding issues of efficacy, faced with the presumption of fraud-on-the-market, it was standard practice until a few years ago simply to concede that a class existed under Rule 10b-5. Kermit Roosevelt noted, "A recent empirical survey of class actions in four federal districts over a two-year period found that a (b)(3) class was certified in 94% to 100% of the securities cases."[14] But the world has changed. Now, according to Professor Coffee, "[f]or better or worse it is today clear that the tide has turned against class certification, and new barriers have arisen across a variety of contexts where formerly class certification had seemed relatively

---

11. Langevoort, *supra* note 6, *passim*.

12. *The Impact of Class Actions on Rule 10b-5, supra* note 6, at 370.

13. Coffee, *supra* note 5, at 1536.

14. Kermit Roosevelt, III, *Defeating Class Certification In Securities Fraud Actions*, 22 Rev. Litig. 405, 406–07 (relying on Thomas W. Willing, et al., *An Empirical Analysis of Rule 23 to Address the Rulemaking Challenges*, 71 N.Y.U. L. Rev. 79, 88–90 (1996)).

certain."[15] This comment is certainly true of the securities laws, and the cases discussed in the next sections are both symptoms and causes of this change.

III. Current Issues

In recent years, a series of judicial developments has reinvigorated the issue of whether a class action is the most appropriate vehicle to resolve securities claims. The district courts in many circuits are now enjoined to avoid cursory conclusions on the various elements necessary to determine class certification and not to forget the historic injunction against mini-trials contained in *Eisen v. Carlisle & Jacquelin*.[16] There must be a fully independent weighing of each Rule 23 requirement, even if there is an overlap with the merits. Exactly how these standards will play out in reality, i.e., what a weighing of the merits means, is as yet unknown.

The standards are only the beginning of the story; the rest of the story is what issues are fair game at the class certification hearings. Issues that were normally reserved for trial, loss causation and market efficiency, are now fair game at the class certification stage.[17] The question of market efficiency critical to the class-wide presumption of reliance has received renewed attention. As a practical matter, economic experts will now be featured players in securities class action certification hearings. Courts will be called on to apply the preponderance of evidence standard when they weigh two contrary expert opinions.

The Fifth Circuit has gone the furthest in permitting challenges to certification in *Oscar Private Equities Investments v. Allegiance Telecom, Inc.*[18] As yet, no other circuit has adopted *Oscar*; however, *Oscar*-like concerns are reverberating through the class action world. For instance, the Second and Third Circuits have accepted the preponderance of evidence standard of class certification, which *Oscar* enunciated.[19]

Five cases are critical to understanding the current securities litigation landscape: *In re Initial Public Offering Securities Litigation; In re PolyMedica Corp. Securities Litigation; Oscar; Wachtel v. Guardian Life Insurance Company of America;* and *In re Constar International Securities Litigation*, each of which will be addressed below.

---

15. COFFEE & WOLF, *supra* note 1, at 5.

16. 417 U.S. 156, 177–78 (1974); *see also* COFFEE & WOLF, *supra* note 1, at 6.

17. *See* COFFEE & WOLF, *supra* note 1, at 6–7; *see also* Chapter 4, "Certification Hearings and Decisions."

18. 487 F.3d 261 (5th Cir. 2007).

19. *In re Hydrogen Peroxide Antitrust Litig.*, 552 F.3d 305, 320 (3d Cir. 2008); *Teamsters Local 445 Freight Div. Pension Fund v. Bombardier, Inc.*, 546 F.3d 196, 202 (2d Cir. 2008).

A. *IN RE INITIAL PUBLIC OFFERING SECURITIES LITIGATION:* THE SECOND CIRCUIT RESOLVES IMPORTANT ISSUES

In reversing the district court's class certification of six focus cases out of 310 consolidated class actions in *In re Initial Public Offering Securities Ligitation (In re IPO)*,[20] Judge Newman, speaking for the court, raised issues that he considered "surprisingly unsettled":[21] the standards governing district courts in adjudicating a motion for class certification. These issues included whether a definitive ruling must be made as to each Rule 23 requirement; whether evidence is to be assessed; whether the appropriate standard to evaluate a plaintiff's evidence is "weak" or "fatally flawed"; and how Rule 23 requirements that overlap with aspects of the merits are to be handled.[22] The district court judge, Judge Shira Scheindlin, had concluded that weighing competing expert reports was inappropriate at the class certification stage.[23] The Second Circuit disagreed, vacating the initial class certification and remanding the case, and resolved for the Second Circuit all of the "surprisingly unsettled" issues.[24]

The Second Circuit determined that *Eisen*'s statement about not reaching merits issues was limited to merits issues that did not implicate required class action determinations. "The point is that the Supreme Court was not faced with determination of any particular Rule 23 requirement or requirement that overlapped with the merits."[25] Judge Newman noted that outside of the securities law context, now–Chief Judge Easterbrook of the Seventh Circuit in *Szabo v. Bridgeport Machines, Inc.*[26] admonished that "a judge should make whatever factual and legal inquiries are necessary," even if it required a preliminary assessment of the merits.[27] Judge Newman noted that *Szabo* has been followed in the Third and Fourth Circuits.[28]

The Second Circuit concluded that a definitive ruling must be made on all Rule 23 requirements, that "some showing" is insufficient, that evidence must be assessed, and that overlap with the merits "does not avoid the court's obligation to make a ruling as to whether the requirement is met."[29] The court also focused on the necessity of showing that plaintiff lacked knowledge of the specific omissions at issue and had not known, when trading, that the price was affected by the

---

20. 471 F.3d 24 (2d Cir. 2006).

21. *Id.* at 26.

22. *Id.* at 24.

23. *In re Initial Pub. Offering Sec. Litig.*, 227 F.R.D 65 (S.D.N.Y. 2004).

24. *In re Initial Pub. Offering*, 471 F.3d at 27.

25. *Id.* at 34.

26. 249 F.3d 672, 676 (7th Cir. 2001).

27. *In re Initial Pub. Offering*, 471 F.3d at 34.

28. *Id.*

29. *Id.* at 27.

manipulator.[30] The Second Circuit cautioned that, if ascertaining an individual purchaser's intent is required, this individualized determination likely dooms class certification.[31] On remand, the case settled and so there was no opportunity to see if Judge Scheindlin could meet the Second Circuit's requirements and certify a litigation class. At a minimum, *In re IPO* means an increased burden on plaintiffs on a host of factors at the class certification stage.

B. *POLYMEDICA* AND *OSCAR*: THE FUTURE OF THE FRAUD-ON-THE-MARKET PRESUMPTION OF RELIANCE

In 1988, the Supreme Court gave its imprimatur to securities class actions based on the fraud-on-the-market theory with its decision in *Basic, Inc. v. Levinson*.[32] *Basic* would be important for the unanimous opinion alone, which articulates the standard for assessing materiality, but it was the 4–2 opinion on reliance, authored by Justice Blackmun, that was momentous for class actions under Section 10(b) and Rule 10b-5 of the '34 Act. The opinion was frank about what was at stake: because reliance is an element of Rule 10b-5 claims, "[r]equiring proof of individualized reliance from each member of the proposed plaintiff class effectively would have prevented respondents from proceeding with a class action, since individual issues then would have overwhelmed the common ones."[33] To avoid this outcome, the district court had applied the "fraud-on-the-market theory," which created a "presumption of reliance."[34] As described by *Basic*, quoting from a Third Circuit opinion, *Peil v. Speiser*[35]:

> The fraud on the market theory is based on the hypothesis that, in an open and developed securities market, the price of a company's stock is determined by the available material information regarding the company and its business. . . . Misleading statements will therefore defraud purchasers of stock even if the purchasers do not directly rely on the misstatements. . . . The causal connection between the defendants' fraud and the plaintiffs' purchase of stock in such a case is no less significant than in a case of direct reliance on misrepresentations.[36]

Oddly, for such a momentous holding, *Basic* sidestepped the question whether the theory supporting the rebuttable presumption was intellectually well-founded: *"Our task, of course, is not to assess the general validity of the theory, but to consider*

---

30. *Id.* at 43 (citing *Gurary v. Winehouse*, 190 F.3d 37, 45 (2d Cir. 1999) and *DeMaria v. Andersen*, 319 F.3d 170, 175 (2d Cir. 2003)).

31. *Id.* at 44 (relying on *Simer v. Rios*, 661 F.2d 655, 669 (7th Cir. 1981)).

32. 485 U.S. 224. The decision was followed by a substantial increase in securities class actions. *See* Langevoort, *supra* note 6, at 179.

33. *Basic*, 485 U.S. at 242.

34. *Id.* at 245.

35. 806 F.2d 1154, 1160–61 (3d Cir. 1986).

36. *Basic*, 485 U.S. at 241–42 (quoting *Peil*, 806 F.2d at 1160–61).

whether it was proper for the courts below to apply a rebuttable presumption of reliance, supported in part by the fraud-on-the-market theory."[37] It emphasized the practical advantages of the presumption of reliance instead, and its consonance with legislative intent.[38]

Commentators over the two decades since have pointed out that the majority did not seem to understand the theory it approved.[39] The opinion careens between the language of "information efficiency" and that of (much more controversial) "value efficiency."[40] *Basic* in fact disclaims any particular view of market efficiency: "By accepting this rebuttable presumption, we do not intend conclusively to adopt any particular theory of how quickly and completely publicly available information is reflected in market price."[41] It may well be that the majority was agnostic as to the foundations for the presumption. By 1988, the "efficient market hypothesis" already had some two decades of academic life behind it, long enough to have developed serious critics and come under serious attack.[42] *Basic* avoids the fray, with enduring consequences for the courts left to interpret it.

Commentators quickly moved in to shore up the intellectual foundations of the fraud-on-the-market presumption, explaining that the majority had, without naming it, implicitly adopted the so-called semi-strong form of the efficient market hypothesis.[43] To help determine whether the market in which a stock traded was efficient (the predicate for entitlement to the presumption of reliance), many courts adopted a list of factors from a district court case, *Cammer v. Bloom*.[44] These factors have endured for 20 years despite recent serious criticism; part of the movement to a heavier burden on plaintiffs is the decline of the *Cammer* factors, many of which are relatively easy to show, in favor of data-heavy events studies and similar expert analysis.

---

37. *Id.* at 242 (emphasis added).

38. *Id.* at 246–47.

39. John R. Macey & Geoffrey P. Miller, *Good Finance, Bad Economics: An Analysis of the Fraud-on-the-Market Theory*, 42 STAN. L. REV. 1059, 1077 (1990); Langevoort, *supra* note 6, at 158–60.

40. Langevoort, *supra* note 6, at 159. On "informational" vs. "fundamental value" efficiency, *see* Lynn A. Stout, *The Mechanisms of Market Inefficiency: An Introduction to the New Finance*, 28 J. CORP. L. 635, 639–41 (2003); *In re PolyMedica Corp. Sec. Litig.*, 432 F.3d 1, 14–17 (1st Cir. 2005).

41. *Basic*, 485 U.S. at 249 n.28.

42. *See* Donald C. Langevoort, *Taming the Animal Spirits of the Stock Market: A Behavioral Approach to Securities Regulation*, 97 Nw. U. L. REV. 135, 136 & n.4 (2002) (collecting literature).

43. Macey & Miller, *supra* note 39, at 1076–79; *see also* Daniel R. Fischel, *Efficient Capital Markets, The Crash, and the Fraud on the Market Theory*, 74 CORNELL L. REV. 907, 917–22 (1989).

44. 711 F. Supp. 1264 (D.N.J. 1989). These factors include:

(1) the stock's average trading volume; (2) the number of securities analysts that followed and reported on the stock; (3) the presence of market makers and arbitrageurs; (4) the company's filing eligibility; and (5) empirical facts showing a cause and effect relationship between unexpected corporate events or financial releases and an immediate response in the stock price.

Id. at 1286–87.

Two recent opinions—*In re PolyMedica Corp. Securities Litigation*[45] and *Oscar Private Equity Investments v. Allegiance Telecom, Inc.*[46]—show where *Basic* is going in a less plaintiff-friendly world. Both put significant extra pressure on the predicate for the presumption of reliance: namely, that the market is efficient. Plaintiffs must be prepared to make a significant investment in expert testimony to demonstrate entitlement to that presumption to clear the bars set by the First and Fifth Circuits.

PolyMedica announced a standard for determining whether a market was efficient for purposes of applying the fraud-on-the-market presumption of investor reliance: "an efficient market is one in which the market price of the stock *fully* reflects *all* publicly available information."[47] It reached this conclusion in rejecting a lesser standard articulated in a lower court opinion that was a tour de force in its own right, by a well-known jurist and torts professor, senior judge Robert E. Keeton.

Judge Keeton went back to *Basic*, and took its theoretical agnosticism at face value. Evaluating plaintiffs' contention that the market for PolyMedica stock had been efficient during the proposed class period (which he characterized as a question of fact),[48] he propounded a reading of *Basic* that openly rejected the gloss of academic commentary. Based upon statements in *Basic* that the presumption was being adopted because "*most* publicly available information is reflected in market price";[49] "market professionals *generally* consider *most* publicly announced material statements about companies, thereby *affecting* stock market prices";[50] and finally that the *Basic* court did "not intend conclusively to adopt any particular theory of how quickly and completely publicly available information is reflected in market price,"[51] Judge Keeton concluded:

> Considering the three statements together, I conclude that an "efficient" market in the context of the "fraud on the market" theory is not one in which a stock price rapidly reflects all publicly available information. Rather, the "efficient" market required for "fraud on the market" presumption of reliance is simply one in which "market professionals generally consider most publicly announced material statements about companies, thereby affecting stock market prices."[52]

Acknowledging that this definition differed from that of "academic economists," Judge Keeton dismissed this difference as irrelevant: "Where legal prece-

---

45. 432 F.3d 1.
46. 487 F.3d 261.
47. 432 F.3d at 14 (emphasis added).
48. *In re PolyMedica Corp. Sec. Litig.*, 224 F.R.D. 27, 42 (D. Mass. 2004), *rev'd*, 432 F.3d 1 (1st Cir. 2005).
49. *Basic*, 485 U.S. at 247 (emphasis added).
50. *Id.* at 247 n.24 (emphasis added).
51. *Id.* at 249 n.28.
52. *In re PolyMedica Corp.*, 224 F.R.D. at 41.

dent is available, I follow it, not economic or academic literature. . . . [I]t is plain in *Basic* that the Court did not want to adopt the 'economic' or 'academic' definition of efficient market."[53]

Plain in *Basic* or not, this reading threatened to devastate the post-*Basic*/fraud-on-the-market equilibrium in which the class-enabling presumption of reliance for 10b-5 claims is balanced by a defendant's opportunity to show lack of semi-strong market efficiency. The First Circuit reversed and replaced Judge Keeton's more plaintiff-friendly standard with a hurdle that is harder for plaintiffs to clear. The appellate court's first move was to declare that the question of market efficiency was—insofar as it was a question of "the formulation of the proper standard for efficiency"—a "purely legal question" subject to de novo review.[54] From there, the court moved to the history of the efficient market hypothesis: "The efficient market hypothesis began as an academic attempt to answer the following question: Can an ordinary investor beat the stock market . . . ?"[55] If the market is efficient, "the answer is 'no,'" because "an ordinary investor who becomes aware of publicly available information cannot make money by trading on it because the information will have already been incorporated into the market by arbitrageurs."[56] The court's discussion includes references to many of the high points of the academic literature[57] (including one to Eugene Fama, the father of market efficiency) as well as a summary of the weak, semi-strong, and strong forms of the efficient market hypothesis.[58]

In short, the *PolyMedica* court moved decisively back to the academic roots of the fraud-on-the-market hypothesis and to the standard reading of *Basic* derived from those roots. It noted that the definition rejected by Judge Keeton—i.e., "[m]ost cases define an 'efficient' market as a market in which prices incorporate rapidly or promptly all publicly available information"—was, as PolyMedica urged, the one "overwhelmingly favor[ed]" by other courts.[59] Pointing to other statements in *Basic* in which the majority had suggested that the "efficient market" absorbs "all publicly available information"[60] or even just "all the information available" in setting a security's price,[61] the First Circuit settled on a definition of market efficiency drawn from this language.

---

53. *Id.*

54. *In re PolyMedica Corp.*, 432 F.3d at 4. Whether a particular market was efficient, once the proper definition of efficiency was applied to it, is a mixed question of fact and law according to the First Circuit, not a question of fact as Judge Keeton had declared. *Id.* at 4–5 & n.9.

55. *Id.* at 8.

56. *Id.* at 9–10 (quotation omitted).

57. *Id.* at 8–16.

58. *Id.* at 10.

59. *Id.* at 12.

60. *Id.* at 10.

61. "[T]he market is acting as the unpaid agent of the investor, informing him that given all the information available to it, the value of the stock is worth the market price," and "the market price of shares

Because of the instability of *Basic*'s analysis of the theoretical underpinnings of the fraud-on-the-market hypothesis, this formulation, using *Basic*'s language, had another potential pitfall that the First Circuit was determined to squelch at the outset. Language suggesting that "the market price" reflects all available information naturally implies that the stock is "correctly" priced by the fully informed market—that the market "responds to information not only quickly *but accurately*, such that market prices mirror the best possible estimates, in light of all available information, of the actual economic values of securities in terms of their expected risks and returns."[62] This view, known as "fundamental value efficiency," is especially controversial.[63] The *PolyMedica* plaintiff complained that the "fully reflects" formulation would require him "to prove that the market price 'correctly' reflects a stock's fundamental value"; the First Circuit said, not so.[64] "Fully reflect" could indicate an endorsement of fundamental value efficiency, but it could also mean only that the market was "informationally efficient"—that "prices respond so quickly to new information that it is impossible for traders to make trading profits on the basis of that information."[65] This "informational efficiency" was the efficient-market concept endorsed by the First Circuit: "[F]or purposes of establishing the fraud-on-the-market presumption of reliance, investors need only show that the market was informationally efficient."[66]

Finally, the *PolyMedica* court turned to the question of how "informational efficiency" was to be shown at the class certification stage. How much evidence was enough? Here, the court left the issue to the discretion of the trial court with the admonition that "basic facts" were all that was required and "the district court must evaluate the plaintiff's evidence of efficiency critically without allowing the defendant to turn the class-certification proceeding into an *unwieldy* trial on the merits."[67] As to what factors the district court should employ, the court said that while the *Cammer* factors relied on by Judge Keeton "were relevant to the issue of market efficiency," they were "not exhaustive."[68]

On remand, the case was assigned to Judge William G. Young, Judge Keeton having retired from the bench. Judge Young denied class certification, concluding in a detailed opinion that plaintiff had failed to show that the market for Poly-

---

traded on well-developed markets reflects all publicly available information, and hence, any material misrepresentations." *Id.* at 11 (quoting *Basic*, 485 U.S. at 244, 246).

62. *Id.* at 14–15 (quotation omitted; emphasis in original).

63. *See, e.g.*, Fischel, *supra* note 43, at 919–20.

64. *In re PolyMedica Corp.*, 432 F.3d at 15.

65. *Id.* at 14 (quotation omitted).

66. *Id.* at 16. The court did add, though, that "[e]vidence bearing on a stock's fundamental value may be relevant to the efficiency determination . . . ." *Id.*

67. *Id.* at 17 (emphasis in original).

68. *Id.* at 18.

Medica stock was efficient during the class period.[69] Plaintiff's expert relied exclusively on the *Cammer* factors; the opinion illustrates the decline of the *Cammer* factors in favor of new approaches to demonstrating market efficiency that require costly analysis. The court agreed that some of the *Cammer* factors were probative, but others were not.[70] The fifth and, in the court's view, most important factor—a cause-and-effect relationship, over time, between unexpected corporate events or financial releases and an immediate response in stock price—was where plaintiff's expert had faltered. Plaintiff's expert had chosen five days to analyze; defendant's expert criticized this selection as rudimentary and unscientific, which was quoted at length in the opinion:

> [Y]ou went and searched for the largest price drops. That's not a scientific study. A scientific study is one where you draw a sample and then you compare a test statistic from that sample to another sample . . . . All you did was went and picked the largest stock price drops and said, oh, gee, that just shows that it's informationally efficient. You picked five days out of about 160 trading days. What you should do is look at all 160 trading days and do a scientific study to see if there's a difference between the news days and the non-news days. And if you would have done that you would have found that there wasn't any difference between them . . . .[71]

Judge Young agreed with this assessment: "To approach usefulness, an analysis should statistically compare all news days with all non-news days."[72] The court additionally agreed that the ability of the market to respond "quickly" to new information was highly relevant to the "informational efficiency" standard articulated by the First Circuit,[73] and concluded that defendants' showing that short selling PolyMedica stock was difficult during the class period rebutted plaintiffs' weak showing of market efficiency.[74] Noting the "significant role of arbitrageurs" toward information efficiency "widely acknowledged in academic commentary,"

---

69. *In re PolyMedica Corp.*, 453 F. Supp. 2d 260 (D. Mass. 2006).

70. For instance, trading volume (here, high) was probative of market efficiency, but the court questioned whether the second and third factors—number of securities analysts and market makers—were useful in the absence of any accepted standard by which to judge how many securities analysts or market makers were enough. *Id.* at 266–68. The court further noted the criticism of the market maker factor as irrelevant since they "generally do not analyze and disseminate information about the stock." *Id.* at 267–68 & n.6 (quotation omitted).

71. *Id.* at 269.

72. *Id.* at 270.

73. The decline and fall of the efficient market theory as a whole is hinted at as well; at one point, Judge Young used an example from behavioral finance as to how it was possible that investors with different assessments of a stock's worth could keep it from ever obtaining the "new equilibrium every time new information is released" contemplated by the notion of information efficiency, and added, "Because the notion of information efficiency upon which the fraud-on-the-market presumption rests is crumbling under sustained academic scrutiny, the future of securities fraud class action litigation—dependent on this presumption—may be in jeopardy." *Id.* at 272 & n.10.

74. *Id.* at 278.

the court approved defendant's analysis, which proffered evidence of a high short interest average; number of days it took to cover a short sale (indicative of difficulty in finding shares to short); high transaction costs for selling the stock short; and evidence of "violations of put-call parity" (described in some detail by the court).[75] Finally, defendant's expert also submitted "several statistical analyses" showing that PolyMedica stock "exhibited positive serial correlation," rather than following the "random walk" pattern characteristic of informationally efficient stocks.[76]

In sum, as illustrated by the decision on remand, the First Circuit's decision in *PolyMedica* appears—under the guise of reinforcing the status quo—to have raised the bar for plaintiffs seeking certification of 10b-5 classes. While no one would bother to contest that some stocks—Exxon, for instance—trade in an information- ally efficient market, for many others the answer is not so obvious. Costly expert analyses are the only way to show what the First Circuit requires.

The Fifth Circuit's decision in *Oscar* is on its face even more startling. Appar- ently turning *Basic*'s presumption of reliance on its head, it requires the plaintiff to establish loss causation as a predicate for class certification based on the fraud-on- the-market doctrine. *Oscar* was a 2–1 decision with a vigorous dissent and has not to date been endorsed by any other appellate court. As with *PolyMedica*, however, the result of the opinion is to require a more refined demonstration of market effi- ciency as the price of admission for *Basic*'s presumption of reliance.

The company defendant in *Oscar*, Allegiance Telecom, was a telecommunica- tions provider (which, as the majority opinion notes, was part of an industry suf- fering as a whole during the proposed class period in 2001).[77] Plaintiffs alleged that Allegiance's "line-installation count" had been misrepresented in a series of quar- terly announcements in 2001 and that when the count was finally restated, the stock had dropped.[78] Defendants contended that the restatement was the result of a new billing system, not fraud, and that the restatement in any event did not cause the stock to drop.[79]

The opinion is explicit about what it is doing, and the motives behind it:

> We now require more than proof of a material misstatement; we require proof that the misstatement *actually moved* the market. That is, the plaintiff may recover under the fraud on the market theory if he can prove that the defendant's non-disclosure

---

75. *Id.* at 273.

76. In PolyMedica's case, the news that affected its stock price continued to affect its stock price over a period of time; a stock whose price responds promptly to new information should only see the impact of that information for one day. *Id.* at 277–78.

77. *Oscar*, 487 F.3d at 262–63.

78. *Id.* at 263.

79. *Id.*

materially affected the market price of the security. Essentially, we require plaintiff to establish loss causation in order to trigger the fraud-on-the-market presumption.[80]

. . . .

Given the lethal force of certifying a class of purchasers of securities enabled by the fraud-on-the-market doctrine, we now in fairness insist that such a certification be supported by a showing of loss causation that targets the corrective disclosure appearing among other negative disclosures made at the same time.[81]

Oscar's loss causation requirement is not easily squared with *Basic*'s formulation of the fraud-on-the-market presumption of reliance as a rebuttable presumption. The *Oscar* majority urged that *Basic*'s statement that the presumption could be rebutted "by 'any showing that severs the link between the alleged misrepresentation and . . . the price received (or paid) by the plaintiff'" supported their loss causation requirement,[82] but as the dissent pointed out, the majority's rule imposed a burden on the *plaintiff* where *Basic* and which had imposed one on the *defendant*—the burden of establishing that the presumption should not apply by coming forward with a "showing that sever[ed] the link" between misrepresentation and market price.[83]

Ultimately, however, *Oscar* finds firmer ground by explaining that the loss causation requirement going to the efficient-market demonstration that *is* plaintiff's responsibility under *Basic* is also the predicate for the presumption of reliance: "[L]oss causation speaks to the semi-strong efficient market hypothesis on which classwide reliance depends . . . ."[84] "The assumption that every material misrepresentation will move a stock in an efficient market is unfounded, at least as market efficiency is presently measured."[85] A stock that trades in an otherwise efficient market may also trade in a market that is *in*efficient as to the particular type of information alleged to have been misrepresented: "First, it might be that even though the market for the defendant's shares has been demonstrated efficient by the usual indicia, the market is actually inefficient with respect to the particular type of information conveyed by the material misrepresentation . . . . Thus, our approach gives effect to information-type inefficiencies, recognizing that 'the market price of a security will not be uniformly efficient as to all types of information.'"[86] Further:

A second possible explanation for a misrepresentation's failure to move the market is that the market was strong-form efficient with respect to that type of information,

80. *Id.* at 265 (footnotes and quotation omitted; emphasis in original).
81. *Id.* at 262.
82. *Id.* at 265.
83. *Id.* at 273–74 (Dennis, J., dissenting).
84. *Id.* at 269.
85. *Id.*
86. *Id.* (quoting Macey & Miller, *supra* note 39, at 1083).

i.e., due to insider trading, the restated line count was reflected by the stock price well before the 4Q01 corrective disclosure. Both explanations resist application of the semi-strong efficient-market hypothesis, the theory on which the presumption of classwide reliance depends. This court honors both theory and precedent in requiring plaintiffs to demonstrate loss causation before triggering the presumption of reliance.[87]

Thus, *Oscar* does *PolyMedica* one better in requiring not merely a showing of "informational efficiency" but a showing of informational efficiency *specifically linked* to the misrepresentation alleged by the plaintiff. While it is not always the case that multiple items of negative news are released by a company simultaneously, only some of which are alleged to have corrected prior misrepresentations, it is very often the case. Like *PolyMedica*, *Oscar* imposes a more demanding (and more costly) regime of expert analysis on plaintiffs:

> When multiple negative items are announced contemporaneously, mere proximity between the announcement and the stock loss is insufficient to establish loss causation.
>
> . . . .
>
> [T]he plaintiffs must, in order to establish loss causation at this stage, offer some empirically-based showing that the corrective disclosure was more than just present at the scene. . . . At least when multiple negative items are contemporaneously announced, we are unwilling to infer loss causation without more.[88]

Whether there is, for practical purposes, a difference between *PolyMedica* and *Oscar* remains to be seen. *PolyMedica*'s requirement of a showing that the market "fully" reacts to "all" publicly available information perforce includes a showing that it reacts to the complained-of misleading information—what *Oscar* requires in the showing of loss causation.

The *Oscar* requirement that plaintiff prove that the misstatement caused the loss has not been followed to date by other federal appellate courts, and the Second Circuit, in *In re Salomon Analyst Metromedia Litigation*,[89] refused to require such a showing. Instead the Second Circuit requires that a statement be material. If the statement is material, then the defendants have the burden of rebutting the claim of materiality. In both circuits, experts will be crucial. On remand, the district court denied certification in *Oscar* and in *Fener v. Belo Corp.*,[90] a different panel of the Fifth Circuit enforced *Oscar*'s rule and made it clear that any plaintiff who

---

87. *Id.* at 269–70.
88. *Id.* at 271 (footnote omitted).
89. 544 F.3d 474, 483 (2d Cir. 2008).
90. 579 F.3d 401 (5th Cir. 2009).

seeks class certification without expert analysis that isolates the effect of the supposed fraud on the security's price does so at his or her peril.[91]

C. WACHTEL AND THE NEED FOR A TRIAL PLAN

Although not a securities class action, *Wachtel v. Guardian Life Insurance Company of America*[92] is an important precedent that, as yet, has only had limited reach outside of the Third Circuit. By its terms, in the Third Circuit, it will apply to securities law claims, and requires an explanation of how plaintiff will demonstrate efficiency, materiality, and damages, all of which would then be tested at the class certification stage.

Plaintiffs' ERISA claim was that Health Net, though required to use valid databases, used an invalid database.[93] The district court had certified a class. Defendants appealed pursuant to Rule 23(f). The case turned on the significance of the 2003 amendments to Rule 23, in particular subdivision (c)(1)(B), which provides that "an order certifying a class action must define the class and the class claims, issues, or defenses."[94] The Third Circuit concluded that "the plain text of the subdivision, especially when considered in light of the text and structure of parallel provisions in Rule 23, indicate that Rule 23(c)(1)(B) requires District Courts to include in class certification orders a clear and complete summary of those claims, issues, or defenses subject to class treatment."[95] This is essentially the same conclusion Judge Newman reached in *In re IPO*. To the Third Circuit, it was self-evident that a clear and complete summary would shed light on a district court's numerosity, commonality, typicality, and predominance analysis. The Third Circuit supported its analysis by citing the Advisory Committee notes to Rule 23(c)(1)(A) dealing with the timing of class certification.[96] The Advisory Committee cited the practice in some courts of requiring a party requesting certification to present a "trial plan."[97] The Third Circuit endorsed this requirement so that the district courts would have the context for determining the claims, issues, and defenses.

With the increasing focus on the class certification hearings, the trial plan becomes critical. It is the only way to test issues of market efficiency, damage causation, and the tracing required under '33 Act Section 11 cases. Although the practice has not yet spread, more and more courts will likely mandate that the parties provide a trial plan to help them scrutinize the requirements of Rule 23 and to

---

91. *See id.* at 409–10.
92. 453 F.3d 179 (3d Cir. 2006).
93. *Id.* at 182.
94. *Id.* at 184.
95. *Id.*
96. *Id.* at 186 (citing FED. R. CIV. P. 23(c)(1)(A) advisory committee note (2003)).
97. *Id.*

avoid reversal as in *Wachtel*. Rule 23 specifically provides for courts to issue orders "to determine the course of the proceedings."[98]

D. *IN RE CONSTAR*: PLAINTIFFS RETREAT TO SECTION 11

As '34 Act claims have come under increasing pressure, plaintiffs have turned to Section 11 of the '33 Act, although there are serious limitations on such claims, since they apply only to offerings of securities. Where such claims can be brought, however, class certification under Section 11 poses far fewer issues than in a Rule 10b-5 suit, because reliance and market efficiency are not issues. In *In re Constar International Securities Litigation*,[99] plaintiffs successfully beat back an effort to bring a reliance requirement to Section 11 claims. The Third Circuit explained why it felt the opinion of defendant's expert was irrelevant:

> [R]eliance is *not* an element under § 11 . . . As the District Court noted, because reliance is not an element under § 11, "the conduct of the defendants, not the knowledge of the plaintiffs, is determinative" of materiality. . . . The crucial questions are: "[W]as there a misrepresentation? And, if so, was it objectively material?". . . . Since reliance is irrelevant in a § 11 case, a § 11 case will never demand individualized proof as to an investor's reliance of knowledge (except where more than twelve months have passed since the registration statement became effective). Further, because a misrepresentation is material if a reasonable investor would have considered a fact important, the effect of a material misrepresentation is felt uniformly across the class of investors, regardless of whether the market is efficient. Since this is an objective standard, materiality is not determined, as Dr. Jarrell contends, by the "mix of information" available to each individual plaintiff.[100]

The Second Circuit, following settled law, had explained in *In re IPO* that "the market for IPO shares is not efficient."[101] The expert's hypothesis was that, in an inefficient market, one has to know why an investor bought the new issues. The court rejected this theory in favor of a reasonable investor test, without confronting the thorny question of how to prove what was important to a "reasonable investor" in a new issue.[102] Materiality as reflected by the market's response to a piece of information is an academically accepted hypothesis for testing the importance of a piece of information. Some omissions in a prospectus are obviously material—for instance, that a company's only product, a new drug, has failed to meet certain FDA-prescribed tests. The significance of other information is less obvious. Say, for

---

98. FED. R. CIV. P. 23(d)(1)(A).
99. 585 F.3d 774 (3d Cir. 2009).
100. *Id.* at 784 (citations omitted; emphasis added).
101. 471 F.3d at 57.
102. *In re Constar*, 585 F.3d at 777.

instance, that a company's backlog is overstated by 10 percent or less.[103] The Third Circuit does not explain how to prove what the reasonable investor would deem important in an inefficient market.

The Third Circuit did suggest that market efficiency might be pertinent to the predominance requirement of Rule 23(b)(3), but was particularly skeptical of the defendants' contentions in this regard because the case was brought under Section 11, and the defendants' expert had not "addressed the effect of market efficiency on the predominance requirement in a § 11 class certification."[104] It remains to be seen whether another expert economist can meet the challenge thrown down by the Third Circuit.

IV. Numerosity, Commonality, Typicality, and Adequacy of Representation

Turning to the standard Rule 23(a) factors, numerosity is simply not a significantly contested issue for a widely traded security. Commonality is also generally not significant because the challenged statement or omission is usually either contained in a prospectus or was made by company officials in earnings conference calls or press releases. Commonality in essence is subsumed by the requirement that the statement be material. Typicality is also of limited significance, except perhaps in Section 11 cases if the purchaser is a sophisticated party, or for nonequity securities in inefficient markets, where the plaintiff has done its own independent valuation and analysis. Discovery in this type of case may lead to the conclusion that what initially appeared to be a material fact was in fact irrelevant to the actual investment decision.

Adequacy of representation is also rarely a factor, since a very significant number of the pending securities cases are brought by law firms that specialize in such litigation. Courts find that representatives of these firms are well qualified to handle securities litigation.

V. Options for Removal of '33 Act Claims

'34 Act claims are within the exclusive jurisdiction of the federal courts.[105] However, the '33 Act provides for concurrent state jurisdiction, and contains an "anti-removal" provision, Section 22(a): "[n]o case arising under this subchapter and brought in any State court of competent jurisdiction shall be removed to any court

---

103. *See, e.g., Schultz v. TomoTherapy,* Nos. 08-CV-314-SLC, 08-CV-342-SLC, 2009 U.S. Dist. LEXIS 116749 (W.D. Wis. Dec. 14, 2009).

104. *In re Constar,* 585 F.3d at 782, 785–86.

105. 15 U.S.C. § 78aa.

of the United States."[106] The heightened pleading standards of the PSLRA (which are applicable only to '34 Act claims) renewed plaintiffs' interest in '33 Act claims and state law securities claims; Congress responded with the Securities Litigation Uniform Standards Act of 1998 (SLUSA).[107] The removal changes wrought by SLUSA and the Class Action Fairness Act of 2005 (CAFA) have created an uneven landscape for removal of '33 Act claims, and currently a circuit split exists as to the impact of CAFA on the '33 Act's nonremoval provision.

SLUSA amended the nonremoval provision of the '33 Act to provide that "covered class actions" (generally speaking, class actions involving securities traded on national exchanges) that were "based upon the statutory or common law of any State or subdivision thereof" and brought in state court were removable and thereafter subject to dismissal.[108] Although Congress's intent was likely to foreclose "covered" class actions from being litigated in state court altogether,[109] taken on its face the amendment did not change the nonremovability of '33 Act claims—it prohibited removal only of "covered class actions" based on state law.[110] District courts divided on whether the statutory language should be read as written (forbidding removal) or according to apparent legislative intent (allowing removal).[111]

CAFA created a new complication by amending the federal removal statutes to permit the removal of class actions with minimal diversity.[112] As to class actions brought solely under the '33 Act that meet CAFA removal standards, CAFA and Section 22(a) of the '33 Act are in conflict. To date, the Ninth and the Seventh Circuits have split on which statute trumps the other. In *Luther v. Countrywide Home Loans Servicing LP*,[113] the Ninth Circuit forbade removal, holding that the conflict was governed by the rule that a more "specific" statute, the '33 Act (a "statute dealing with a narrow, precise, and specific subject") trumps a later statute, CAFA, "covering a more generalized spectrum."[114] Hence, CAFA's "general grant" of removal must yield to the '33 Act's rule covering the "narrow subject of securities cases."[115]

---

106. 15 U.S.C. § 77v(a).

107. *See Merrill Lynch, Pierce, Fenner & Smith, Inc. v. Dabit,* 547 U.S. 71, 81–83 (2006).

108. 15 U.S.C. § 77p(b), (c); *id.* at § 77r(b) (covered securities).

109. *See* Matthew O'Brien, *Choice of Forum in Securities Class Actions: Confronting "Reform" of the Securities Act of 1933,* 28 REV. LITIG. 845, 863–65 (2009); *see also Brody v. Homestore, Inc.,* 240 F. Supp. 2d 1122, 1123–24 (C.D. Cal. 2003) (discussing legislative history).

110. *See* 15 U.S.C. § 77p(b), (c).

111. *Compare Brody,* 240 F. Supp. 2d 1122 (denying motion to remand) *with Zia v. Med. Staffing Network, Inc.,* 336 F. Supp. 2d 1306 (S.D. Fla. 2004) (granting motion to remand); *see also* O'Brien, *supra* note 109, at 865–67.

112. Roughly speaking, under CAFA, if any plaintiff is diverse from any defendant, and the amount in controversy exceeds $5 million, a class action is removable to federal court. 28 U.S.C. § 1332(d); *see also* Chapter 10, "The Class Action Fairness Act of 2005."

113. 533 F.3d 1031 (9th Cir. 2008).

114. *Id.* at 1034.

115. *Id.*

This analysis was resoundingly rejected by the Seventh Circuit in *Katz v. Gerardi.*[116] According to Chief Judge Easterbrook, "[t]he canon favoring preservation of specific statutes arguably affected by newer, but more general, statutes works when one statute is a subset of the other"—e.g., if CAFA "dealt with all civil suits."[117] But Section 22(a) "includes all securities actions—single-investor suits as well as class actions, small class actions as well as large multi-state ones."[118] CAFA, "by contrast, covers only large, multi-state class actions," hence the "specific law/general law" distinction did not apply.[119] Since CAFA specifically excludes certain securities class actions from removal, it followed that "[o]ther securities class actions are removable if they meet the [CAFA] requirements."[120]

VI. Other Issues

Other issues may bedevil securities class actions in the coming years. Consider the allegations in *In re IPO* that the market was rigged because many investors bought or were induced to purchase by special payments. Those people should be excluded from the class, but how are they identified? Does this necessary weeding out make the class unmanageable? The need for an elaborate factual analysis doomed the class in *Newton v. Merrill Lynch.*[121] Or consider the prevalence of quantitative trading and trading models that are triggered by small price movements. Should such "investors" be swept under the rubric of the "reasonable investor"? To date the courts have not grappled with these issues in the Section 11 or Rule 10b-5 context.

When Sears announced that it had fired senior executives for untruth, Sears stock plummeted.[122] Was that drop caused by a material fact that had been hidden or because Sears had bad management? Mismanagement does not support a securities claim.[123] The court was unwilling to sort out the matter on a motion to dismiss, but after *Oscar* and *Fener*, courts would have to address this issue at the class certification hearing.

As countless commentators have noted, securities cases are very rarely tried. Since 1996, Riskmetrics has counted eight cases that have gone to verdict and

116. 552 F.3d 558 (7th Cir. 2009).

117. *Id.* at 561.

118. *Id.*

119. *Id.* at 561–62.

120. *Id.* at 562. The same conclusion was reached by the district court in *N.J. Carpenters Vac. Fund v. Harborview Mortgage Loan Trust 2006-4*, 581 F. Supp. 2d 581 (S.D.N.Y. 2008), bolstered by CAFA's legislative history expressing a "strong preference that interstate class actions should be heard in a Federal court," and the analogous reasoning of the Second Circuit in *Cal. Pub. Employees' Retirement Sys. v. WorldCom, Inc.*, 368 F.3d 86 (2d Cir. 2004).

121. 259 F.3d 154, 190–91 (3d Cir. 2001).

122. *See In re Sears, Roebuck and Co. Sec. Litig.*, 291 F. Supp. 2d 722, 725 (N.D. Ill. 2003).

123. *Santa Fe Indus., Inc. v. Green*, 430 U.S. 462, 479 (1977).

seven other cases where trial began—out of the approximately 3,000 securities class actions filed. It is an often noted truism that certifying a class has an *in terrorem* effect:

> When the potential liability created by a lawsuit is very great, even though the probability that the plaintiff will succeed in establishing liability is slight, the defendant will be under pressure to settle rather than to bet the company, even if the betting odds are good.[124]

Some of this effect may be lessened under the regime envisioned by *In re IPO*, *PolyMedica*, *Oscar*, and *Wachtel*, because more of these issues will be faced at the class certification hearing and with the possibility of appellate review.

VII. Conclusion

The times are changing. Behavioral economics is on the rise in academia.[125] It poses a direct challenge to the efficient market with its claim that there is a great deal of herd instinct at work in securities trading. Whenever everyone begins to run for the exit at the same time, valuation or other problems ensue (hence the prohibition on yelling "Fire" in a crowded theater). In the absence of mandated continuous disclosure, in the present SEC regime, periodic disclosure is the norm, as Judge Easterbrook has reminded us in *Gallagher v. Abbott Laboratories*.[126] In this regime, crowds are always waiting to exit every quarter as earnings are announced. Is the market's response on that day really the best test of the importance of a new piece of information?

The efficient market hypothesis has also received a significant blow with the mass destruction in value of subprime mortgage securities and the meltdown of value in the stock market itself. Just how far this reevaluation will go, no one can say. However, the Fifth Circuit has expressed significant skepticism about the efficient market hypothesis, both in its *Oscar* opinion and in *Regents of the University of California v. Credit Suisse, First Boston (USA), Inc.*[127] Whether the Second Circuit and Ninth Circuit will follow suit remains to be seen.

For the defendant's lawyer there is new hope that certification can be avoided or challenged on an early appeal. Rule 26(f) provides a means of challenging certification that simply did not exist for most of the history of class securities litiga-

---

124. *Kohen v. PIMCO*, 571 F.3d 672, 678 (7th Cir. 2009).

125. Stephen J. Choi & A. C. Pritchard, *Behavioral Economics and the SEC*, 56 Stan. L. Rev. 1, 2 (2003); Gregory Mitchell, *Why Law and Economics' Perfect Rationality Should Not Be Traded for Behavioral Law and Economics' Equal Incompetence*, 91 Geo L.J. 67 (2004).

126. 269 F.3d 806, 808 (7th Cir. 2001).

127. 482 F.3d 372 (5th Cir. 2007).

tion. Judge Easterbrook, in *Blair v. Equifax Check Services, Inc.*,[128] explained how important appeals are to the development of class action law:

> [A]n appeal may facilitate the development of the law. Because a large proportion of class actions settles or is resolved in a way that overtakes procedural matters, some fundamental issues about class actions are poorly developed. . . . When an appellant can establish that such an issue is presented, Rule 23(f) permits the court of appeals to intervene.[129]

All of the class actions that form the bulk of this chapter were Rule 26(f) appeals. Securities class action law is developing, and the possibility of challenging certification in the securities realm is no longer dormant, but how securities class actions will evolve is an open question.

---

128. 181 F.3d 832 (7th Cir. 1999).
129. *Id.* at 835.

STATISTICAL SAMPLING AS A BASIS FOR EXTRAPOLATING LIABILITY AND/OR DAMAGES

PETER A. ANTONUCCI[1]

I. Introduction

One particularly controversial issue arises at the intersection of class actions and the use of statistical sampling as evidence of classwide harm or damages. No majority rule has emerged on whether statistical sampling can be used in class actions to prove liability or damages. Most cases addressing the issue contain scant analysis. Those courts that do allow statistical sampling generally emphasize its efficiency, while courts rejecting it typically do so on due process grounds or because they conclude that doing so impermissibly permits the class to shift the burden of proof. Certain types of cases, such as those involving antitrust or employment discrimination, are generally regarded as being more receptive to statistical sampling than others, but jurisprudence on this issue is still relatively nascent.[2] Regardless, while statistical sampling may appear to present an appealing means of bringing data before the court, it cannot be allowed to usurp individual proof requirements or to trump the applicability of the 7th Amendment.

---

1. Lauren Harrison, an associate in the litigation group in Greenberg Traurig's New York office, assisted in the preparation of these materials.

2. Statistical sampling has been used outside the class action context, but this evaluation focuses on its use in class actions both as a means to justify certification and to obtain a judgment based on a jury verdict where plaintiffs attempted to prove liability or damages with statistical or survey-type evidence.

II. Courts Allowing Statistical Sampling

Some courts have been amenable to the use of statistical sampling as evidence of liability and/or damages. The Eastern District of New York has expressly noted that "[t]he use of statistical evidence and methods in the American justice system to establish liability and damages is appropriate, particularly in mass injury cases."[3] In support, the court noted that statistical sampling has been accepted in va wide variety of cases, including cases where plaintiffs seek redress for antitrust violations, employment discrimination, consumer fraud, copyright infringement, patent-law violations, or Medicare reimbursement.[4]

Other courts have demonstrated judicial receptiveness to statistical sampling, both within and outside the class action context.[5] For instance, in *Long v. Trans World Airlines, Inc.,*[6] a class of flight attendants sued their employer for failure to provide designated-rights letters under the Airline Deregulation Act, after the flight attendants had gone on strike and were not rehired. The flight attendants won summary judgment on the issue of liability.[7] On the damages issue, the flight attendants requested that discovery proceed on a sampling basis, arguing that full-blown discovery from the entire class was unnecessary and unduly burdensome.[8] The defendant countered that the "presence of individual issues entitle[d] it to discovery from each plaintiff."[9] The court held for the flight attendants, allowing statistical sampling on the issue of damages.[10] In so holding, the court cited various authorities supporting aggregate class recoveries, which eliminate the need for individual damage proofs.[11] It rejected the defendant's arguments that it had a

---

3. *In re Simon II Litig.,* 211 F.R.D. 86, 150 (E.D.N.Y. 2002) (citing *In re Chevron U.S.A., Inc.,* 109 F.3d 1016, 1019–20 (5th Cir. 1997)), *vacated on other grounds,* 407 F.3d 125 (2d Cir. 2005).

4. *Id.* at 149–50.

5. *See, e.g., EEOC v. Joe's Stone Crab, Inc.,* 220 F.3d 1263, 1274 (11th Cir. 2000) (Title VII sex discrimination); *Ratanasen v. Cal. Dep't of Health Services,* 11 F.3d 1467, 1470 (9th Cir. 1993) (audit of overcharging and fraud against the government); *Long v. Trans World Airlines, Inc.,* 761 F. Supp. 1320, 1324 (N.D. Ill. 1991) (labor); *State of Georgia v. Califano,* 446 F. Supp. 404, 409 (N.D. Ga. 1977) (reimbursement for Medicaid); *N.J. Welfare Rights Org. v. Cahill,* 349 F. Supp. 501 (D.N.J. 1972) (welfare rights), *aff'd,* 483 F.2d 723 (3d Cir. 1973); *In re Coordinated Pretrial Proceedings in Antibiotics Antitrust Actions,* 333 F. Supp. 278 (S.D.N.Y. 1971) (antitrust), *mandamus denied,* 449 F.2d 119 (2d Cir. 1971); *Rosado v. Wyman,* 322 F. Supp. 1173 (E.D.N.Y. 1970) (challenge to New York social services law), *aff'd,* 402 U.S. 991 (1971); *Bell v. Farmers Ins. Exch.,* 9 Cal. Rptr. 3d 544, 577–78 (Ct. App. 2004) (labor); *In re Visa Check/Mastermoney Antitrust Litig.,* 192 F.R.D. 68, 79 (E.D.N.Y. 2000) (antitrust), *aff'd,* 280 F.3d 124 (2d Cir. 2001).

6. 761 F. Supp. at 1322.

7. *Id.*

8. *Id.* at 1323.

9. *Id.*

10. *Id.*

11. *Id.* at 1324–26 (explaining that "courts have approved various methods of discovering and determining damages in class actions on the basis of classwide, rather than individualized proof of damages, and the use of statistics and representative samples are one such legitimate method").

right to an individualized determination of the damages for each class plaintiff.[12] The court held that although the defendant was entitled to an accurate estimation of damages, damages in class actions (like other cases) need not be determined with 100 percent accuracy.[13] The need for accuracy must be balanced against other factors, including the burdens imposed by discovery.[14] With this balance in mind, the court found it appropriate to allow statistical sampling and extrapolation of damages on a classwide, aggregate basis.[15]

In *Bell v. Farmers Insurance Exchange*, the class plaintiffs were current and former claims representatives working for Farmers Insurance.[16] The claims representatives brought a class action suit against Farmers for unpaid overtime compensation.[17] Farmers challenged the plaintiffs' aggregation of class damages: the plaintiffs had proposed to determine damages for the entire class via random statistical sampling and extrapolation.[18] The California Court of Appeal rejected Farmers' argument, allowing the plaintiffs' statistical sampling.[19] The court reasoned that statistical sampling does not dispense with proof of damages, but rather simply offers a different method of proof: inference from membership in the class substitutes for individual evidence and testimony from each class plaintiff.[20] Although the court acknowledged a significant weakness of statistical sampling and extrapolation—it necessarily yields an average figure that will overestimate or underestimate the right to relief of individual plaintiffs—the court held that this weakness may be outweighed by the benefits of statistical sampling.[21] In particular, drawing inferences from statistical sampling can often promote conservation of judicial resources and mitigate the deterring effect that the cost of litigation would otherwise pose to small claimants.[22] Moreover, the court explained that the problem of awarding damages to plaintiffs who did not deserve them was not particular to statistical sampling and is inherent in all class actions.[23]

Certain class actions may lend themselves to statistical sampling. For example, in modern products liability cases, the technological developments of recent decades may play an important role in justifying the use of statistical evidence.

---

12. *Id.* at 1327.

13. *Id.*

14. *Id.* at 1323–24, 1327 n.7 (citing 2 Herbert B. Newberg, Newberg on Class Actions 355 (2d ed. 1985)).

15. *Id.* at 1329.

16. 9 Cal. Rptr. at 549.

17. *Id.*

18. *Id.* at 571.

19. *Id.* at 571–79.

20. *Id.* at 574.

21. *Id.* at 574–75.

22. *Id.* at 575.

23. *Id.* at 574.

According to at least one court favoring the use of statistical sampling, the recent evolution in economic systems for communication, data compilation, and retrieval has augmented the potential for mass injury.[24] Using new chemical compounds and processes, manufacturers now mass-produce goods for consumption by millions.[25] Where numerous consumers are injured by these products, an argument has been forwarded that adjudicatory tools "must allow fair, efficient, effective, and responsive resolution of the injured masses' claims."[26] Plaintiffs would argue that this potential for mass injury results in an increased need for statistical evidence that can be extrapolated to very large classes.[27]

III. Courts Rejecting Statistical Sampling Methodology

Other courts have rejected the use of statistical sampling as a means of proving liability or damages in class actions.[28] In *McLaughlin v. American Tobacco Co.*, the plaintiffs proposed to prove damages on a classwide basis and then set up a claims process for individual plaintiffs.[29] The plaintiffs, cigarette users, claimed they were deceived into believing that "light" cigarettes were not as dangerous as regular cigarettes.[30] The plaintiffs proposed to estimate the percentage of class members who were defrauded through statistical methods and then calculate a damages figure on an estimate of the average loss per plaintiff.[31] The Second Circuit rejected this attempt as a "disconnect" that violated both due process and the Rules Enabling Act, which provides that the federal rules of procedure cannot be used to "abridge, enlarge, or modify any substantive right."[32] Numerous courts throughout the country are in accord with *McLaughlin*.[33]

---

24. *Simon II*, 211 F.R.D. at 151; *see also generally* Deborah R. Hensler & Mark A. Peterson, *Understanding Mass Personal Injury Litigation: A SocioLegal Analysis*, 59 BROOK L. REV. 961 (1993).

25. *Simon II*, 211 F.R.D. at 151.

26. *Id.*

27. *Id.*

28. *See, e.g., McLaughlin v. Am. Tobacco Co.*, 522 F.3d 215, 231 (2d Cir. 2008); *Cimino v. Raymark Indus., Inc.*, 151 F.3d 297, 316 (5th Cir. 1998); *Arch v. Am. Tobacco Co.*, 175 F.R.D. 469, 493 (E.D. Pa. 1997).

29. 522 F.3d at 231.

30. *Id.* at 220.

31. *Id.* at 231.

32. *Id.*

33. *See, e.g., Shuette v. Beazer Homes Holdings Corp.*, 124 P.3d 530, 545 (Nev. 2005) (involving claims for construction defects to homes; court held that evidence on liability and damages as to each individual's home differed, proving that there was no reasonable basis on which "to extrapolate to all of the houses the property damage, and causes therefor, pertaining to the inspected houses"); *see also In re Genetically Modified Rice Litig.*, 251 F.R.D. 392 (E.D. Mo. 2008) (claims of damage caused by genetically modified rice, traces of which contaminated the U.S. rice supply; putative class representatives proposed to show market injury and aggregate damages and damages per hundredweight on a classwide basis, to be followed by a claims process to determine individual producers' damages based on the producer's quantity of rice); *Rollins, Inc. v. Warren*, 653 S.E.2d 794, 799–800 (Ga. Ct. App. 2007) (finding abuse of discretion in certifying breach

Cases rejecting statistical sampling often show a particular aversion to statistical evidence in certain types of class actions. Typically, courts show this increased hesitancy to allow statistical sampling and extrapolation where the underlying cause of action is inherently particularized to each individual plaintiff. For instance, statistical sampling is often viewed as problematic in cases where each individual has to prove breach of contract and damages,[34] or in fraud cases where individual reliance is required.[35] Several courts, including *McLaughlin*, have emphatically said no to statistical sampling evidence in personal injury suits.[36] However, even in courts that reject statistical sampling in certain cases—e.g., breach of contract and fraud—statistical sampling may find more support in cases where statistics are essentially the only means of proving liability or damages, such as cases involving antitrust or disparate impact discrimination.[37]

The pervasive rationale underlying decisions rejecting statistical evidence is that the class device does not trump the requirement that plaintiffs must show individual proof of causation and damages.[38] As one court explained, proof of injury "is in no way lessened by reason of being raised in the context of a class action."[39] Another court reasoned similarly, holding that the class action mechanism "does

---

of contract claim against a pest control company based on statistical sampling evidence). As the Georgia Court of Appeal explained:

> [E]ven if this statistical data is accurate, a general finding of incompleteness in 66 to 98 percent of the sampled documentation does not answer the question of whether any one particular Orkin customer in Georgia out of thousands failed to receive adequate reinspection services in one or more of the approximately eleven years covered by the class period.

34. *See, e.g., Shuette,* 124 P.3d at 544–45. As with statistical sampling in general, though, there is no clear rule on whether statistical sampling is appropriate in breach-of-contract class actions. Section IV of this chapter discusses the split among courts on this issue.

35. *See, e.g., Castano v. Am. Tobacco Co.,* 84 F.3d 734, 745 (5th Cir. 1996) (class may not be properly certified if individual reliance is an issue). *But see Fortis Ins. Co. v. Kahn,* 299 Ga. App. 319, 324–26 (Ga. Ct. App. 2009) (claims included breach of statutory duty and breach of contract and fraud, among others, and still court rejected appellant's argument that trial court erred in certifying class where each claim would require individual proof holding that "minor variations in amount of damages . . . do not destroy class when the legal issues are common" because "where damages can be computed according to . . . statistical analysis . . . the fact that damages must be calculated on an individual basis is no impediment to class certification" (citing *Klay v. Humana, Inc.,* 382 F.3d 1241 (11th Cir. 2004)).

36. *See, e.g., Cimino,* 151 F.3d at 316 (rejecting district court's use of 160 sample cases and five categories of disease to extrapolate damages to 2,128 other asbestos cases on numerous grounds, including the 7th Amendment right to jury trial and the Texas substantive requirement that damages be proved by "individuals, not groups"); *Arch,* 175 F.R.D. at 493 (rejecting plaintiffs' proposal to use statistical sampling to award classwide damages in a tobacco lawsuit, concluding that the "degree of injury" for each class member "would necessarily entail an individual inquiry").

37. See discussion *supra* section II.

38. *See, e.g., Shuette,* 124 P.3d at 545.

39. *Bell Atl. Corp. v. AT&T Corp.,* 339 F.3d 294, 302 n. 52 (5th Cir. 2003).

not alter the required elements which must be found to impose liability and fix damages."[40]

Indeed, federal courts routinely acknowledge that a defendant's right to a jury trial requires proof of individual damages.[41] In *Basco v. Wal-Mart Stores, Inc.*, Walmart objected to the plaintiffs' use of statistical evidence of classwide damages.[42] In reaching its determination, the court rejected plaintiffs' attempt to "cure the individualized nature" of their claims by employing statistical analysis.[43] In so doing, the court emphasized that plaintiffs' reliance on a representational method to determine damages would deprive defendants of their right to have a jury determine liability and damages as to each plaintiff.[44] Thus, the court rejected any attempt by plaintiffs to employ statistics to cure the individualized nature of their breach of contract cause of action.[45]

As the Fifth Circuit has remarked, "[T]he applicability of the Seventh Amendment is not altered simply because the case is [a] . . . class action."[46] Numerous other federal courts have likewise refused to certify classes employing statistical sampling damage models (or required decertification) because such procedures were found to violate due process rights and the right to jury trial.[47] Many state courts have reached the same conclusion.[48]

---

40. *Cimino*, 151 F.3d at 312.

41. *See, e.g., McLaughlin*, 522 F.3d at 231 ("Roughly estimating the gross damages to the class as a whole and only subsequently allowing for the processing of individual claims would inevitably alter the defendants' substantive right to pay damages reflective of their actual liability."); *Cooper v. Southern Co.*, 390 F.3d 695, 722 (11th Cir. 2004) ("[W]e agree with the district court that substantial limitations in the plaintiffs' statistical evidence rendered the form of proof wholly insufficient to show that any pattern or practice of discrimination disparately affected the plaintiffs' class, or for that matter, that the defendants had a general policy of discrimination."), *overruled on other grounds, Ash v. Tyson Foods, Inc.*, 546 U.S. 454, 457 (2006) (per curiam); *Ridgeway v. Burlington N. Santa Fe Corp.*, 205 S.W.3d 577, 585 (Tex. App.—Fort Worth 2006) (aggregated damages model using statistical evidence could not support class certification because it would improperly shift burden of proof to defendants and would not eliminate individualized liability issues (collecting cases)).

42. 216 F. Supp. 2d 592, 598–99 (E.D. La. 2002).

43. *Id.*

44. *Id.* at 604.

45. *Id.* at 603.

46. *Cimino*, 151 F.3d at 312.

47. *See, e.g., Bell Atl. Corp.*, 339 F.3d at 304 (where numerous factors would affect amount of damages, if any, suffered by the individual class members, plaintiffs' proposed formula was not workable and certification was properly denied); *Basco*, 216 F. Supp. 2d 592, 603–04 (E.D. La. 2002) (refusing to certify a class in an employment case despite plaintiffs' attempt to determine the number of hours the class members worked "off-the-clock" at Walmart through statistical sampling).

48. *See, e.g., Alix v. Wal-Mart Stores, Inc.*, 838 N.Y.S.2d 885 (N.Y. Sup. Ct. 2007) (refusing to substitute statistical sampling for individualized proof where "facts and circumstances surrounding the allegedly unpaid work vary substantially from associate to associate"), *aff'd*, 868 N.Y.S.2d 372 (N.Y. App. Div. 3d Dep't 2008); *Cutler v. Wal-Mart Stores, Inc.*, 927 A.2d 1, 11–15 (Md. App. 2007) (upholding decision of circuit court that no implied contract common to the class existed, thus the alleged breaches would give

IV. Case Study: Statistical Sampling in Breach of Contract Class Actions

As with statistical sampling in general, no clear rule has emerged on whether statistical sampling is acceptable in the context of a breach of contract class action. Two cases illustrate different approaches and different results.

In *Rollins, Inc. v. Warren*, the plaintiffs asserted a breach of contract claim against a pest control company, claiming the company failed to provide termite reinspections that it had contractually promised.[49] Plaintiffs sought damages for services not performed.[50] Plaintiffs also claimed that company representatives had forged customer signatures on reinspection records.[51] The trial court certified the class.[52] In reversing the certification order, the appellate court held that whether the company forged a signature of any particular customer is "a highly particularized and fact-specific inquiry."[53]

Put another way, the generalized evidence offered by the plaintiffs would not resolve whether any particular company representative forged reinspection records in his or her file or whether any particular customer failed to receive proper annual reinspection services for his or her property. In *Rollins*, the statistical evidence upon which the plaintiffs and the trial court placed heavy emphasis reflected that the 389 sampled customer termite files were incomplete between 66 and 98 percent of the time. Thus, even if this statistical data was accurate, a general finding of incompleteness in 66 to 98 percent of the sampled documentation would not have answered the question of whether any one particular customer out of thousands failed to receive adequate reinspection services in one or more of the approximately 11 years covered by the class period.[54] The court of appeals further opined that the statistical evidence would not address or resolve whether the class members had fulfilled their affirmative contractual obligations to the pest control company.[55] Based on this reasoning, the court held that the trial court had abused its discretion in granting class certification.[56]

---

rise); *Ridgeway*, 205 S.W.3d at 585 (aggregated damages model using statistical evidence could not support class certification because it would improperly shift burden of proof to defendants and would not eliminate individualized liability issues (collecting cases)).

49. 653 S.E.2d at 796.
50. *Id.* at 796.
51. *Id.*
52. *Id.*
53. *Id.* at 799.
54. *Id.* at 799–800.
55. *Id.* at 800.
56. *Id.*

In *Iliadis v. Wal-Mart Stores, Inc.*, New Jersey's highest court reached the opposite conclusion.[57] In *Iliadis*, the class action concerned various breach of contract claims by employees against Walmart.[58] Both sides engaged statistical experts.[59] Walmart argued that plaintiffs' statistical expert reports would prevent it from fully exploring its defenses and challenging the individual class members' claims.[60] In holding that class certification was warranted and that common questions of law and fact predominated over any individualized questions, the court opined:

> We are confident that the Law Division will properly employ its broad, equitable authority and sound discretion to manage the instant litigation and appropriately address the important concerns of both parties in respect of the permissible uses of statistical extrapolation, evidentiary redundancy, and any other procedural, administrative, and evidentiary issues that may arise.[61]

V. Conclusion

Rollins and *Iliadis* illustrate the divisive nature of the statistical sampling issue. Although both cases concerned breach of contract claims—which conceptually are necessarily particularized to each class plaintiff—the two courts took opposite approaches in determining how this inherent particularity bore on the need for individualized evidence. Courts like *Rollins* rejecting statistical evidence tend to emphasize the highly individualized and fact-based inquiry that arises from the individual plaintiffs' claims. These courts hold that the need for individualized evidence is not outweighed by any benefit gained from statistical sampling. On the other hand, courts allowing statistical sampling, such as *Iliadis*, often take the exact same types of inherently particularized claims, but de-emphasize the need for individualized evidence. In the end, whether statistical evidence can be used in class actions involving fact-intensive, particularized claims will ultimately depend on the jurisdiction.

---

57. 922 A.2d 710 (N.J. 2007).
58. *Id.* at 714.
59. *Id.* at 715.
60. *Id.* at 717–18.
61. *Id.* at 727.

AGGREGATION OR STACKING OF PENALTIES OR PUNITIVE MEASURES

JULIAN W. POON
THEANE EVANGELIS KAPUR
BLAINE H. EVANSON[1]

I. Introduction

While the class action device has many benefits, in some circumstances it can create perverse results. One such circumstance is a class action that aggregates statutory penalties, even minimum statutory damages, across a large plaintiff class, which can result in an enormous judgment against the defendant—several multiples beyond what the enacting legislature ever could have intended. Aggregated penalties thus have the potential to distort the underlying legislative scheme, force defendants to settle meritless lawsuits, and result in a punishment that is grossly disproportionate to the reprehensibility of the defendant's conduct. Aggregated penalties arise when plaintiffs file a class action lawsuit seeking statutory damages on behalf of hundreds or thousands of putative class members. Examples of statutes that allow for statutory damages include the Fair and Accurate Credit Transactions Act (FACTA),[2] the Fair Credit Reporting Act (FCRA),[3] the Truth in Lending Act (TILA),[4] the Telephone Consumer Protection Act (TCPA),[5] and state waiting-time penalty statutes.[6] Many of these statutes allow individuals to recover statutory damages ranging from $100 to $1,000 even if no actual harm is alleged.

---

1. The authors wish to thank Vaughn A. Blackman and Elizabeth R. Doisy for their invaluable assistance in preparing this chapter.
2. 15 U.S.C. § 1681c(g).
3. *Id.* at § 1681–1681x.
4. *Id.* at § 1640.
5. 47 U.S.C. § 227.
6. *See, e.g.,* CAL. LAB. CODE § 203; OR. REV. STAT. § 652.150.

For example, in *Price v. Lucky Strike Entertainment, Inc.*, the proposed plaintiff class of approximately 33,000 members could have collected damages between $3.3 million and $33 million for a FACTA violation, even though plaintiffs alleged no actual damages.[7] The court denied certification, holding it could not put a company out of business for failing to remove expiration dates from credit card receipts when no actual harm was alleged.[8] As in *Price*, aggregated statutory damages may force many defendant companies into bankruptcy.

Faced with potentially crushing liability in such cases, defendants often see no choice but to settle. But there are important ways in which defendants can challenge, limit, and control otherwise excessive awards of aggregated penalties in class action lawsuits. First, defendants can use such penalties as a sword in opposing class certification. Either in their opposition to a plaintiff's motion for class certification or in their own preemptive motion to preclude class certification, defendants can argue that, given such penalties, the class should not be certified because it would not meet the requirements of Federal Rule of Civil Procedure 23 (or the analogous state law or other rule governing class actions). Class actions involving aggregated penalties fail to satisfy Rule 23's superiority requirement for a number of reasons. For one, aggregation results in damages that are disproportionate to any actual harm suffered and often apply even when there has been no such harm. And crippling damages are possible even when the defendant has substantially complied with the statute. In addition, there is potential for abuse by lawyers seeking to enrich themselves personally. Moreover, statutory penalties often mean that individual class members already have sufficient incentive to bring their own individual actions, without the added incentive of a class action. Finally, Rule 23's predominance requirement often will not be satisfied, especially when the statutory penalties are predicated on a finding that the defendant has acted willfully. After all, due process requires an individualized inquiry into the circumstances surrounding the harm each class member allegedly suffered and its relationship to any punitive award.

Second, defendants have strong arguments that such enormous penalties violate due process. The due process clauses of the 5th and 14th amendments to the U.S. Constitution prohibit Congress and the states from imposing civil penalties that are disproportionate to the underlying offense. This principle was elaborated upon through a series of Supreme Court cases in the early 20th century, holding that a statutory penalty violates due process when it is "so severe and oppressive as to be wholly disproportioned to the offense and obviously unreasonable."[9] Later, in *BMW of North America, Inc. v. Gore*,[10] the Court set forth three guideposts for

---

7. No. CV 07-960-ODW(MANx), 2007 WL 4812281, at *4–5 & n.4 (C.D. Cal. Aug. 31, 2007).

8. *Id.*

9. *E.g., St. Louis, I.M. & S. Ry. Co. v. Williams*, 251 U.S. 63, 67 (1919).

10. 517 U.S. 559, 575 (1996).

determining whether a punitive award is so excessive that it violates due process. These due process limitations may offer some hope to defendants seeking to cabin the exorbitant liability created by aggregating statutory penalties, and defendants can and should consider raising and preserving due process arguments at various stages throughout the litigation.

II. Why Combining Class Actions and Statutory Damages Is Problematic

Some courts have rejected due process challenges to aggregated penalties, noting that if every individual in a class action filed his own lawsuit, "the sum of actual damages suffered by a class of plaintiffs [would] be the same regardless of whether their claims are prosecuted as a single class action or as a myriad of individual suits."[11] In the abstract, it is true that if every plaintiff pursued his own lawsuit, the aggregated damages would be the same (the number of plaintiffs multiplied by the statutory damages). But this ignores the fact that the potent combination of statutory damages and the class action procedure creates a double incentive for plaintiffs' class action lawyers to file suit; imposes enormous pressure on defendants to settle even relatively meritless or overblown claims; and results in a gross disproportionality between the reprehensibility of defendant's alleged misdeeds and the damages imposed.

A. AN UNNECESSARY DOUBLE INCENTIVE FOR PLAINTIFFS TO FILE SUIT

The combination of minimum statutory penalties and the class action mechanism "distorts the purpose of both statutory damages and class actions,"[12] because they both aim to encourage plaintiffs to file suit for small claims that otherwise would not be brought because of the costs of litigation. And when the two are combined in a single lawsuit, the result is grossly excessive penalties that are completely out of proportion to any actual damages and that punish defendants far in excess of what the legislature intended when it enacted the statutory penalty.[13] Essentially, the class treatment

> turn[s] the per-customer statutory damages in the [statute] into a hammer so heavy as to be beyond any plausible account of the underlying remedial scheme. . . .

---

11. *In re Napster, Inc. Copyright Litig.*, No. C MDL-00-1369 MHP, C 04-1671 MHP, 2005 WL 1287611, at *11 (N.D. Cal. June 1, 2005). *See also Phillips Randolph Enters. LLC v. Rice Fields*, No. 06 C 4968, 2007 WL 129052, at *3 (N.D. Ill. Jan. 11, 2007); *Murray v. Cingular Wireless II, LLC*, 242 F.R.D. 415, 420–21 (N.D. Ill. 2005).

12. *Parker v. Time Warner Entm't Co.*, 331 F.3d 13, 22 (2d Cir. 2003).

13. Richard A. Nagareda, *Aggregation and Its Discontents: Class Settlement Pressure, Class-Wide Arbitration, and CAFA*, 106 COLUM. L. REV. 1872, 1878 (2006).

Because Congress already had set the remedial scheme to make claims worthwhile on a disaggregated basis, that scheme did not plausibly tolerate class certification.[14]

The double incentive leads to awards for statutory penalties that are often grossly out of proportion to the alleged misconduct and do not reflect the kind of penalty Congress intended to impose for violations of the statute at issue. While an award of $100 or $1,000 against a defendant company could be a fair and sufficient punishment for a technical violation, an award that pushes the company toward the brink of bankruptcy or serious financial ruin would in most circumstances be unfair and excessive in light of the conduct committed by the defendant company. This is especially true when the company did not intentionally violate the statute or did not cause any real actual harm.

B. BLACKMAIL SETTLEMENTS

Staggering aggregated penalties in class actions also "create[ ] a potentially enormous aggregate recovery for plaintiffs, and thus an *in terrorem* effect on defendants, which may induce unfair settlements."[15] Commentators have argued that "[c]ombining the litigation incentives of statutory damages and the class action in one suit, . . . creates the potential for absurd liability, . . . over-deterrence,"[16] a windfall to plaintiff's lawyers,[17] and double counting.[18]

Several noted jurists, including Henry Friendly and Richard Posner, have discussed this effect and have likened the immense pressure to settle class actions with such high potential exposure as "blackmail."[19] Blackmail settlements gen-

---

14. *Id.* at 1903. For example, in 1974, Congress amended TILA to limit the amount of damages plaintiffs can recover in a class action. The Report of the Senate Committee on Banking, Housing, and Urban Affairs stated that TILA should not subject defendants "to enormous penalties for violations which do not involve actual damages and may be of a technical nature." *Watkins v. Simmons & Clark, Inc.*, 618 F.2d 398, 400 n.6 (6th Cir. 1980) (citing S. Rep. No. 93-278, at 14–15 (1973)). Congress expressed a similar concern when it enacted the Portal-to-Portal Act amendments to the FLSA. Congress created an opt-in requirement, 29 U.S.C. § 216(b), for FLSA class actions because of "a dramatic influx of litigation, involving vast alleged liability" against defendant employers. 93 Cong. Rec. 2,087 (1947). Congress "was concerned that employers would face 'financial ruin' and employees would receive 'windfall payments, including liquidated damages.'" *Tomlinson v. Indymac Bank, F.S.B.*, 359 F. Supp. 2d 898, 900 (C.D. Cal. 2005) (quoting 29 U.S.C. § 251(a)(1), (a)(4)).

15. *Parker*, 331 F.3d at 22.

16. Sheila B. Scheuerman, *Due Process Forgotten: The Problem of Statutory Damages and Class Actions*, 74 Mo. L. Rev. 103, 111 (2009).

17. Victor E. Schwartz & Cary Silverman, *Common-Sense Construction of Consumer Protection Acts*, 54 U. Kan. L. Rev. 1, 61 (2005).

18. Nagareda, *supra* note 13. *Cf.* Richard A. Epstein, *Class Actions: Aggregation, Amplification, and Distortion*, 2003 U. Chi. Legal F. 475, 505 ("Combining the two mechanisms thus creates a form of double counting which could easily lead to overdeterrence.").

19. *In re Rhone-Poulenc Rorer, Inc.*, 51 F.3d 1293, 1298–99 (7th Cir. 1995) (Posner, C.J.); Henry J. Friendly, Federal Jurisdiction: A General View 120 (1973). In addition, several prominent legal scholars have detailed the intense pressure defendants feel when facing huge potential liabilities in class actions.

erally occur when defendants face huge potential liabilities and choose to settle instead of litigate the suit, *"even when the plaintiff's probability of success on the merits is slight."*[20]

Defendants often are forced to settle class action lawsuits because of their low tolerance for risk. It is "widely recognized"[21] that defendants in class action lawsuits tend to be risk-averse. Because of pressures such as reputation and stock price,[22] companies cannot assume "the sheer *magnitude* of the risk" to which they are exposed when the outcome of many claims depends on one trial instead of many.[23] When the expected value of a claim is $0, a risk-neutral person will pay nothing to settle the claim, even if the actual award could be as much as $1 million. But if an individual is risk-averse, he so fears the potential loss of $1 million that he is willing to pay some amount of money to settle the claim and avoid the risk, even though the claim's expected value is $0. By aggregating all of the claims into one all-or-nothing gamble, class actions create a huge risk of potential loss, forcing risk-averse defendants to settle them for amounts much larger than the claims, when disaggregated, may actually be worth.[24] Defendants simply do "not wish to roll these dice."[25]

In addition, defendants are forced to settle because class certification can "skew[ ] trial outcomes."[26] Empirical studies show that as the number of plaintiffs

See, e.g., Milton Handler, *The Shift from Substantive to Procedure Innovations in Antitrust Suits—The Twenty-Third Annual Antitrust Review,* 71 COLUM. L. REV. 1, 9 (1971). *But see* Bruce Hay & David Rosenberg, *"Sweetheart" and "Blackmail" Settlements in Class Actions: Reality and Remedy,* 75 NOTRE DAME L. REV. 1377, 1378 (2000).

20. *Blair v. Equifax Check Servs., Inc.,* 181 F.3d 832, 834 (7th Cir. 1999) (emphasis added); *see also, e.g., In Re Gen. Motors Corp. Pick-Up Truck Fuel Tank Prod. Liab. Litig.,* 55 F.3d 768, 784–85 (3d Cir. 1995); *In re Lorazepam & Clorazepate Antitrust Litig.,* 289 F.3d 98, 102 (D.C. Cir. 2002); *see also Coopers & Lybrand v. Livesay,* 437 U.S. 463, 476 (1978) ("Certification of a large class may so increase the defendant's potential damages liability and litigation costs that he may find it economically prudent to settle and to abandon a meritorious defense."); *Vasquez-Torres v. McGrath's Publick Fish House, Inc.,* No. CV 07-1332 AHM (CWx), 2007 WL 4812289, at *7 (C.D. Cal. Oct. 12, 2007) (class treatment "would serve as an invitation for clever attorneys to bludgeon defendants into settlement in order to avoid ruination").

21. Michael E. Solimine & Christine Oliver Hines, *Deciding to Decide: Class Action Certification and Interlocutory Review by the United States Courts of Appeals Under Rule 23(f),* 41 WM. & MARY L. REV. 1531, 1546 n.74 (2000); *see also* Julian W. Poon, Blaine H. Evanson & William K. Pao, *Interlocutory Appellate Review of Class-Certification Rulings Under Rule 23(f): Do Articulated Standards Matter?,* CERTWORTHY (DRI Appellate Advocacy Comm.), Winter 2009, at 8, *available at* http://www.dri.org/ContentDirectory/Public/Newsletters/0010/2009%20Appellate%20Advocacy%20Committee%20Certworthy%20Winter.pdf.

22. Scheuerman, *supra* note 16, at 150.

23. *In re Rhone-Poulenc,* 51 F.3d at 1297 (emphasis in original).

24. Charles Silver, *"We're Scared to Death": Class Certification and Blackmail,* 78 N.Y.U. L. REV. 1357, 1371 (2003).

25. *In re Rhone-Poulenc,* 51 F.3d at 1298.

26. *Castano v. Am. Tobacco Co.,* 84 F.3d 734, 746 (5th Cir. 1996) (citing Kenneth S. Bordens & Irwin A. Horowitz, *Mass Tort Civil Litigation: The Impact of Procedural Changes on Jury Decisions,* 73 JUDICATURE 22 (1989); MANUAL FOR COMPLEX LITIGATION (THIRD) § 33.26 n.1056 (1995); *see also* Steven B. Hantler & Robert

increases, juries become more likely to find fault and also tend to impose higher damages per plaintiff.[27] Defendants settle because of the risk that juries may view their case differently depending on whether the claim is presented alone or in combination with many other similar claims.

III. Challenging and Limiting the Size of Aggregated Statutory Penalties Under Rule 23

Rule 23 provides several grounds for defendants to challenge potentially staggering aggregated statutory penalties. Such penalties undermine the superiority of the class action mechanism and often destroy any predominance of common over individual issues. Moreover, many courts have been receptive to such arguments, holding that Rule 23's superiority requirement is not satisfied and refusing to certify the class when aggregated penalties could impose an excessive financial burden on a defendant company and its shareholders, workers, and neighboring communities.

A. RULE 23 SUPERIORITY

Rule 23(b)(3) requires that a class action be "superior to other available methods for fairly and efficiently adjudicating the controversy."[28] The Advisory Committee notes to Rule 23 state that the superiority requirement allows the court to exercise considerable discretion in deciding whether to certify a class[29] because courts must ensure that class actions are used only in appropriate cases.[30] Indeed, many courts have emphasized that under the superiority analysis, fairness and due process concerns make class actions the exception to the normal rule.[31]

Rule 23(b)(3) provides four criteria to aid courts in determining whether a class action satisfies the superiority requirement:

E. Norton, *Coupon Settlements: The Emperor's Clothes of Class Actions*, 18 GEO. J. LEGAL ETHICS, 1343, 1353 (2005).

27. Bordens & Horowitz, *supra* note 26.

28. FED. R. CIV. P. 23(b)(3).

29. *See Kamm v. Cal. City Dev. Co.*, 509 F.2d 205, 210 (9th Cir. 1975); *Spikings v. Cost Plus, Inc.*, No. CV 06-8125-JFW (AJWx), 2007 U.S. Dist. LEXIS 44214, at *7–8 (C.D. Cal. May 29, 2007); *see also Ratner v. Chem. Bank N.Y. Trust Co.*, 54 F.R.D. 412, 416 (S.D.N.Y. 1972) ("Students of [Rule 23] have been led generally to recognize that its broad and open-ended terms call for the exercise of some considerable discretion of a pragmatic nature.").

30. *Legge v. Nextel Commc'ns, Inc.*, No. CV 02-8676DSF(VNKX), 2004 WL 5235587, at *13 (C.D. Cal. June 25, 2004).

31. *See Blanco v. CEC Entm't Concepts L.P.*, No. CV 07-0559 GPS (JWJx), 2008 WL 239658, at *1 (C.D. Cal. Jan. 10, 2008) (quoting *Legge*, 2004 WL 5235587, at *13); 5 JAMES WM. MOORE ET AL., MOORE'S FEDERAL PRACTICE, § 23.02 (3d ed. 1999).

(A) the class members' interests in individually controlling the prosecution or defense of separate actions; (B) the extent and nature of any litigation concerning the controversy already begun by or against class members; (C) the desirability or undesirability of concentrating the litigation of the claims in the particular forum; and (D) the likely difficulties in managing a class action.[32]

In addition, courts have the discretion to consider, and often do rely on, other factors.[33]

Courts often deny class certification based on a lack of superiority when statutory damages are disproportionate to the actual harm allegedly suffered by members of the putative class. This may be the most common reason for a putative class to fail the superiority requirement. Other factors courts consider are whether the defendant complied with the statute, whether certification might lead to attorney abuse, and whether individual actions are feasible.[34] Determining whether the superiority requirement is satisfied typically requires a case-by-case analysis.[35]

1. Damages Disproportionate to Actual Harm

One of the earliest and most frequently cited decisions rejecting certification of a class seeking sizable aggregated statutory damages is *Ratner v. Chemical Bank New York Trust Co.*,[36] in which Judge Frankel, the principal architect of Rule 23, held that paying the statutory minimum of $100 to each of the 130,000 class members for violations of TILA "would be a horrendous, possibly annihilating punishment, unrelated to any damage to the purported class or to any benefit to defendant, for what is at most a technical and debatable violation . . . ."[37] The court further held that "the allowance of thousands of minimum recoveries like plaintiff's would carry to an absurd and stultifying extreme the specific and essentially inconsistent remedy Congress prescribed as the means of private enforcement."[38]

---

32. FED. R. CIV. P. 23(b)(3).

33. *Price*, 2007 WL 4812281, at *2 (citing *Walco Invs., Inc. v. Thenen*, 168 F.R.D. 315, 337 (S.D. Fla. 1996)).

34. *See Saunders v. Louise's Trattoria*, No. CV 07-1060 SJO (PJWx), 2007 WL 4812287, at *1 (C.D. Cal. Oct. 23, 2007).

35. *See Shroder v. Suburban Coastal Corp.*, 729 F.2d 1371, 1377 (11th Cir. 1984); *Watkins*, 618 F.2d at 402; *Ashby v. Farmers Ins. Co. of Or.*, No. CV 01-1446-BR, 2004 WL 2359968, at *7–8 (D. Or. Oct. 18, 2004); *Wilson v. Am. Cablevision of Kansas City, Inc.*, 133 F.R.D. 573, 577 (W.D. Mo. 1990); *Brame v. Ray Bills Fin. Corp.*, 85 F.R.D. 568, 575 (N.D.N.Y. 1979) (citing *Boggs v. Alto Trailer Sales, Inc.*, 511 F.2d 114, 117 (5th Cir. 1975)).

36. 54 F.R.D. at 414; *see Parker*, 331 F.3d at 26 n.4 (stating that denying class certification "drew major support, if not its origin" from *Ratner*); *Haynes v. Logan Furniture Mart, Inc.*, 503 F.2d 1161, 1164 (7th Cir. 1974) (describing *Ratner* as the "seminal case on denial of class action status"); *Legge*, 2004 WL 5235587, at *16 (describing *Ratner* as an "oft-cited and seminal" case).

37. *Ratner*, 54 F.R.D. at 416.

38. *Id.* at 414.

A number of courts have followed the reasoning in *Ratner*. For example, in *Kline v. Coldwell Banker & Co.*, the Ninth Circuit held that class actions are not superior when the damages would be so great that certification would lead to an "ad absurdum result" and would "shock the conscience."[39] Some courts reason that the class action device is not "superior" when "the defendant's potential liability would be enormous and completely out of proportion to any harm suffered by the plaintiff."[40] Other courts hold that the class action procedure is not superior when damages are "grossly disproportionate to the conduct at issue."[41]

In determining whether damages are disproportionately large, courts often consider the impact of the award on the defendant. Damages can be found disproportionately large when, for example, the amount of damages exceeds the defendant's net worth, putting the defendant out of business.[42] But even if the damages would not put the defendant out of business, courts can still find the exposure to be disproportionately high and therefore deny class certification.[43] In *Hillis v. Equifax Consumer Services, Inc.*, for example, the court denied certification because although the $200 million in potential statutory damages would likely not put the defendant out of business, such a large award was still disproportionate to the defendant's alleged misconduct.[44] Other courts have emphasized, however, that certification is not inappropriate solely because of ruinous damages, "but based on the *disproportionality* of a damage award that has little relation to the harm actually suffered by the class."[45]

Disproportionality is assessed based on the harm that defendant's alleged misconduct has caused plaintiffs, and courts are more likely to deny class certification in cases where there is no *actual* harm to the putative class members (i.e., the violation is only technical in nature).[46] Courts have also held that a slight increase in the risk of harm is insufficient to warrant class certification.[47] For example, in

---

39. 508 F.2d 226, 233–35 (9th Cir. 1974); *see Soualian v. Int'l Coffee & Tea LLC*, No. CV 07-502-RGK (JCx), 2007 WL 4877902, at *3 n.8 (C.D. Cal. June 11, 2007).

40. *London v. Wal-Mart Stores, Inc.*, 340 F.3d 1246, 1255 n.5 (11th Cir. 2003) (citing *Kline*, 508 F.2d at 234–35); *see also Price*, 2007 WL 4812281, at *4.

41. *Dilley v. Acad. Credit, LLC*, No. 2:07CV301DAK, 2008 WL 4527053, at *8–9 (D. Utah Sept. 29, 2008); *Helms v. Consumerinfo.com, Inc.*, 236 F.R.D. 561, 568 (N.D. Ala. 2005).

42. *See, e.g., Leysoto v. Mama Mia I., Inc.*, 255 F.R.D. 693, 697–98 (S.D. Fla. 2009) (damages range from $4.6 million to $46 million, but defendant's net worth is only $40,000); *Dilley*, 2008 WL 4527053, at *9; *Vasquez-Torres*, 2007 WL 4812289, at *7 (damages range from $54.15 million to $541.53 million, but defendant's net worth is only $3.83 million); *Spikings*, 2007 U.S. Dist. LEXIS 44214, at *12 (damages range from $340 million to $3.4 billion, but defendant's net worth is only $316 million).

43. *See, e.g., Hillis v. Equifax Consumer Servs., Inc.*, 237 F.R.D. 491, 507 (N.D. Ga. 2006).

44. *Id.*

45. *Spikings*, 2007 U.S. Dist. LEXIS 44214, at *9 (emphasis added).

46. *See Watkins*, 618 F.2d at 403–04.

47. *See Bateman v. Am. Multi-Cinema, Inc.*, 252 F.R.D. 647, 651 (C.D. Cal. 2008); *Blanco*, 2008 WL 239658, at *2 (distinguishing the potential threat of identity theft from actual harm); *Forman v. Data*

Bateman v. American Multi-Cinema, Inc., the court concluded, in reliance on the superiority requirement, that a slight increase in the risk of identity theft caused by printing a few extra digits of a credit card number did not justify certifying the class.[48]

The lack of any actual harm has been held to preclude certification even in cases where a statute specifies that it is appropriate for class treatment, as does TILA. These courts recognize that Congress did not intend to make class actions mandatory under TILA,[49] and one court even noted that Congress did not intend to allow class actions in most TILA cases.[50] Thus, even when a statute specifically provides for class actions, the Rule 23 analysis still applies as in any other case, and plaintiffs must establish that a class action would be superior to individual lawsuits.[51] As a result, even when damages are capped at $500,000, some courts have denied class certification because the damages are disproportionate when there is no actual harm.[52]

Several courts have pointed to the Advisory Committee notes' statement that class certification should not "bring[ ] about other undesirable results."[53] Putting a company out of business, or forcing layoffs or a significant loss of share value, for a technical violation resulting in no real harm is precisely the kind of undesirable result against which the Advisory Committee warned.[54]

There are many other statutes besides the statutes mentioned above where plaintiffs may encounter difficulty in satisfying the superiority requirement. For example, many states' laws provide for so-called waiting-time penalties for employers' failure to pay final wages in a full and timely manner.[55] If an employer violates the statute, the employer can be assessed penalties equal to the amount of wages owed for each day it fails to pay the employee, for up to 30 days.[56] And when these penalties are aggregated over a class of hundreds or thousands of plaintiffs, employers can incur enormous and staggering statutory penalties. Such damages can be crippling and in many cases would be clearly disproportionate to the harm that

---

Transfer, Inc., 164 F.R.D. 400, 404 & n.3 (E.D. Pa. 1995).

48. 252 F.R.D. at 651.

49. *See Watkins*, 618 F.2d at 402.

50. *See Agostine v. Sidcon Corp.*, 69 F.R.D. 437, 444 (E.D. Pa. 1975).

51. *See Boggs*, 511 F.2d at 117; *Agostine*, 69 F.R.D. at 444.

52. *Shroder*, 729 F.2d at 1378 (holding that "violations may be too technical to form the basis for maintaining a class action under TILA"); *Watkins*, 618 F.2d at 404 (stating that "class certification should be denied only in a case involving technical violations and only where the district court . . . believes that certification is unwarranted").

53. *Price*, 2007 WL 4812281, at *4.

54. *Id.*

55. *See, e.g.*, CAL. LAB. CODE § 203; OR. REV. STAT. § 652.150.

56. *See, e.g.*, CAL. LAB. CODE § 203; OR. REV. STAT. § 652.150.

may have been caused.[57] In many cases, states have enacted waiting-time penalties specifically to encourage individual lawsuits, and therefore class actions aggregating these penalties raise the same concerns addressed in cases brought under statutes such as TILA and FACTA.

Some courts nonetheless have suggested that certification should be allowed unless the legislature expressly prohibits class treatment.[58] These courts have relied on the Supreme Court's decision in *Califano v. Yamasaki* for the proposition that class relief is allowed unless Congress expressly restricts it,[59] reasoning that, because many statutes, such as the FCRA, do not restrict class action relief, class action claims are available under those statutes.[60] But many courts have squarely rejected this notion,[61] holding that *Califano* applies only if a class is otherwise certifiable under the requirements of Rule 23.[62] Finally, some plaintiffs have argued that potential damages are not excessive where a defendant would suffer the same ruinous damages from summing up the damages awarded in individual suits.[63] But this argument may prove too much because, as at least one court has explained, it suggests that each member of the class would bring an individual action.[64]

2. Defendant's Substantial Compliance with the Statute

The next factor weighing against class certification is the defendant's substantial compliance with the statute. Courts recognize that one of the purposes of class actions is to deter unlawful conduct,[65] and that deterrence is unnecessary when defendants are already in compliance with the relevant statute.[66] Relatedly, courts look at whether the defendant knew of the violation, as statutory damages were

---

57. See *London*, 340 F.3d at 1255 n.5 (citing *Kline*, 508 F.2d at 234–35); see also *Dilley*, 2008 WL 4527053, at *8–9; *Price*, 2007 WL 4812281, at *4; *Helms*, 236 F.R.D. at 568; *Ratner*, 54 F.R.D. at 414.

58. See, e.g., *In re Farmers Ins. Co., FCRA Litig.*, No. CIV-03-158-F, MDL 1564, 2006 WL 1042450, at *10 (W.D. Okla. Apr. 13, 2006); *Ashby*, 2004 WL 2359968, at *8.

59. See, e.g., *In re Farmers Ins. Co.*, 2006 WL 1042450, at *10 (citing *Califano v. Yamasaki*, 442 U.S. 682, 700 (1979)).

60. *Id.*

61. See, e.g., *Azoiani v. Love's Travel Stops & Country Stores, Inc.*, No. EDCV 07-90 ODW (OPx), 2007 WL 4811627, at *5 n.1 (C.D. Cal. Dec. 18, 2007); *Saunders*, 2007 WL 4812287, at *3; *Price*, 2007 WL 4812281, at *5 n.6.

62. *Saunders*, 2007 WL 4812287, at *3.

63. *Id.*

64. *Id.*

65. *Price*, 2007 WL 4812281, at *5.

66. See *Watkins*, 618 F.2d at 402–03 (stating that the class action was unnecessary because the defendant had already complied with the statute); *Blanco*, 2008 WL 239658, at *2 (stating that allowing aggregation of statutory penalties "would be grossly disproportionate to the harm, especially when Defendant immediately rectified this technical problem after the lawsuit was filed"); *Price*, 2007 WL 4812281, at *5 ("immediate action to comply with FACTA . . . upon notice of Plaintiff's Complaint demonstrates Defendant's good faith while precluding future violations and nullifying any specific deterrence benefit that might have derived from class certification in the absence of such compliance").

not meant to punish an "unwary violator."[67] A defendant's compliance with the applicable statute prior to the class certification hearing may make it more likely that the trial court will deny certification.[68]

3. Attorney Abuse

An additional factor weighing against certification is the potential for attorney abuse.[69] Courts recognize that Rule 23(b)(3) class actions are commonly used as a "device for the solicitation of litigation . . . which is clearly an 'undesirable result' which cannot be tolerated."[70] This factor can be particularly weighty when plaintiff's counsel have filed similar class actions with the same representative plaintiff.[71]

4. Individual Class Members' Ability to Bring Their Own Action

Another important consideration is whether the statute provides incentives for individuals to bring their own individual lawsuits. As a general rule, class actions are superior when there are "multiple claims for relatively small individual sums,"[72] and the superiority requirement is therefore met when "a large number of plaintiffs may have been injured, but not to an extent to induce the instigation of individual litigation."[73] In other words, the class action is superior when "no realistic alternative exists."[74]

Courts have found that, in many instances, attorney fees, punitive damages, and payment of costs give individuals sufficient incentive to sue such that individual actions are realistic alternatives to class adjudication. A number of courts have specifically focused on fee-shifting provisions in finding that individual actions are a feasible alternative.[75] For example, FACTA authorizes the recovery of attorney fees and punitive damages, and courts recognize that the litigant-friendly scheme

---

67. *See Shroder*, 729 F.2d at 1377.

68. *See, e.g.*, *Watkins*, 618 F.2d at 402–03; *Blanco*, 2008 WL 239658, at *2; *Price*, 2007 WL 4812281, at *5.

69. *See Najarian v. Avis Rent A Car Sys.*, No. CV 07-588-RGK (Ex), 2007 WL 4682071, at *5 (C.D. Cal. June 11, 2007); *Spikings*, 2007 U.S. Dist. LEXIS 44214, at *16–17.

70. *Rodriguez v. Family Publ'ns Serv., Inc.*, 57 F.R.D. 189, 195 (C.D. Cal. 1972) (quoting *Buford v. Am. Fin. Co.*, 333 F. Supp. 1243, 1251 (N.D. Ga. 1971)).

71. *See, e.g.*, *Saunders*, 2007 WL 4812287, at *2 n.5 (noting that plaintiff's counsel has filed 37 FACTA class actions with Saunders as plaintiff in 11 of the cases); *Price*, 2007 WL 4812281, at *5 (noting that plaintiff's counsel has been involved in at least 20 FACTA cases with Price as plaintiff in six of the cases).

72. *Legge*, 2004 WL 5235587, at *12 (quoting *Local Joint Executive Bd. of Culinary/Bartender Trust Fund v. Las Vegas Sands, Inc.*, 244 F.3d 1152, 1163 (9th Cir. 2001)).

73. *Forman*, 164 F.R.D. at 404 (citing *Green v. Wolf Corp.*, 406 F.2d 291, 296 (2d Cir. 1968)).

74. *Valentino v. Carter-Wallace, Inc.*, 97 F.3d 1227, 1235 (9th Cir. 1996).

75. *See Dilley*, 2008 WL 4527053, at *10; *Hillis*, 237 F.R.D. at 507; *see also Castano*, 84 F.3d at 748 (recognizing that access to attorney fees often leads to finding the class action mechanism is not superior); *Cooper v. Sunshine Recoveries, Inc.*, No. 00CIV8898LTSJCF, 2001 WL 740765, at *5 (S.D.N.Y. June 27, 2001); *Maguire v. Sandy Mac, Inc.*, 145 F.R.D. 50, 53 (D.N.J. 1992). *But see In re Farmers Ins. Co.*, 2006 WL 1042450, at *11.

Congress created in enacting FACTA makes individual actions fully feasible.[76] Consequently, a class action may not be considered to be superior even though some individuals may choose not to pursue their individual claims.[77]

In addition, statutes providing for treble damages may already create sufficient incentives for individuals to bring suit on their own. At least one federal court has found that the minimum recovery of $500 and treble damages authorized under the TCPA[78] give plaintiffs adequate incentives to file an individual lawsuit.[79] However, when a statute specifically provides for class actions, such as TILA, courts are less willing to find that individuals have incentives to sue on their own.[80]

5. De Minimis Recovery

When statutes place a limit on class action statutory damages, individual class members may receive less from the class action than they would have received had they sued on their own. For example, a statute may allow individual plaintiffs to recover statutory damages ranging from $100 to $1,000, but place a limit on class action damages of $500,000.[81] If 600,000 class members seek the $100 minimum, this leaves a recovery of approximately $1 per class member.[82] This aspect of the statute may pose problems under both the superiority and adequacy of representation prongs of Rule 23(b)(3).[83] A procedural mechanism that requires class members to surrender the lion's share of their damages cannot be characterized as superior.[84] Moreover, there is a concern that the class representative may not have adequate incentive to pursue the class action vigorously when the dollar amount he could hope to recover is so small.[85]

Although class actions can generate lesser recoveries, class actions should not be certified when there is "absolute certainty that such recovery will be essentially eliminated altogether."[86] In *Boggs v. Alto Trailer Sales, Inc.*, the Fifth Circuit suggested that a reduction to $42 per plaintiff from a potential award ranging from

---

76. *See Blanco*, 2008 WL 239658, at *1–2; *Price*, 2007 WL 4812281, at *4–6; *Najarian*, 2007 WL 4682071, at *4–5.

77. *Serna v. Big A Drug Stores, Inc.*, No. SACV 07-0276 CJC (MLGx), 2007 U.S. Dist. LEXIS 82023, at *15 (C.D. Cal. Oct. 9, 2007).

78. 47 U.S.C. § 227(b)(3).

79. *Forman*, 164 F.R.D. at 404.

80. *See Agostine*, 69 F.R.D. at 447–48.

81. *See, e.g.*, TILA, 15 U.S.C. § 1640(a)(2)(A), (B).

82. *See Shelley v. Amsouth Bank*, No. CIV.A.97-1170-RV-C, 2000 WL 1121778, at *14–15 (S.D. Ala. July 24, 2000).

83. *See Boggs*, 511 F.2d at 118; *Jones v. CBE Group, Inc.*, 215 F.R.D. 558, 570 (D. Minn. 2003); *Shelley*, 2000 WL 1121778, at *15–16; *Rollins v. Sears, Roebuck & Co.*, 71 F.R.D. 540, 545 (E.D. La. 1976). *But see Jancik v. Cavalry Portfolio Servs., LLC*, No. 06-3104 (MJD/AJB), 2007 WL 1994026, at *11 (D. Minn. July 3, 2007).

84. *See Shelley*, 2000 WL 1121778, at *15–16.

85. *See Jones*, 215 F.R.D. at 570.

86. *See Shelley*, 2000 WL 1121778, at *15.

$100 to $1,000 may alone suffice to warrant denying class certification.[87] And in *Rollins v. Sears, Roebuck & Co.*, the court found that a reduction from $427 to $331 was enough to deny certification of a class action.[88] The *Rollins* court reached this conclusion even after taking into account that class members with higher individual claims may choose to opt out.[89]

B. RULE 23 PREDOMINANCE

Courts have also denied class certification in aggregated statutory damages cases brought under Rule 23(b)(3) because plaintiffs have failed to satisfy the predominance requirement, which mandates that "questions of law or fact common to class members predominate over any questions affecting only individual members."[90] The court must consider all claims, defenses, and related issues to determine whether they can be proven on a classwide basis,[91] and plaintiffs must establish that common issues outweigh individual ones.[92]

1. Due Process Review Necessitates an Individualized Class-Member-by-Class-Member Inquiry

Defendants opposing certification of classes seeking large aggregated statutory penalty awards can argue that the predominance requirement is not satisfied because due process necessitates individual inquiries into each person's damages award. In *State Farm Mutual Auto Insurance Co. v. Campbell*, the Supreme Court held that due process requires that a punitive award "have a nexus to the specific harm suffered by the plaintiff."[93] The Court made clear that such review calls for a fact-specific inquiry that depends on each individual's compensatory damages award and the harm actually suffered by each individual.[94] Several courts of appeals have held that such an individualized inquiry precludes certification of claims for such punitive awards. In *Allison v. Citgo Petroleum Corp.*, for example, the Fifth Circuit denied certification under Rule 23(b)(2), holding that "punitive damages must be reasonably related to the reprehensibility of the defendant's conduct and to the

---

87. *See* 511 F.2d at 118.

88. 71 F.R.D. at 545.

89. *Id.* at 545 n.4.

90. FED. R. CIV. P. 23(b)(3).

91. *See, e.g.*, *Brown v. Am. Honda*, 522 F.3d 6, 20 (1st Cir. 2008); *Wachtel v. Guardian Life Ins. Co. of Am.*, 453 F.3d 179, 185 (3d Cir. 2006); *Castano*, 84 F.3d at 744–45.

92. *See Valentino*, 97 F.3d at 1234.

93. 538 U.S. 408, 422 (2003). *State Farm* involved an award for punitive damages, not statutory penalties, but as discussed below that distinction should not be relevant for purposes of due process review of punitive awards.

94. *Id.* at 423–24; *see also* Sheila B. Scheuerman, *Two Worlds Collide: How the Supreme Court's Recent Punitive Damages Decisions Affect Class Actions*, 60 BAYLOR L. REV. 880, 905 (2008); *see also Cooper v. Southern Co.*, 390 F.3d 695, 721 (11th Cir. 2004); *Lemon v. Int'l Union of Operating Eng'rs*, 216 F.3d 577, 581 (7th Cir. 2000); *Allison v. Citgo Petroleum Corp.*, 151 F.3d 402, 418 (5th Cir. 1998).

compensatory damages awarded to the plaintiffs."[95] The court further stated that recovery of compensatory and punitive damages can vary depending on each class member's individual circumstances.[96] In *Lemon v. International Union of Operating Engineers*, the Seventh Circuit noted that due process review of punitive awards involves "a fact-specific inquiry into that plaintiff's circumstances."[97] And in *Cooper v. Southern Co.*, the Eleventh Circuit concluded that determining the permissible amount of punitive damages "would require detailed, case-by-case fact finding, carefully calibrated for each individual employee."[98] Because any statutory damages award must be in proportion to the actual harm suffered by each individual class member, and because any award of statutory damages to absent class members would be arbitrary and unconstitutional if not based on such individualized review, defendants may be able to successfully argue that common questions do not predominate in cases involving aggregated penalties based on individualized harm. The due process analysis for each claim of statutory damages must be conducted on an individualized, class-member-by-class-member basis—necessarily entailing a comparison, for each class member, of the degree of reprehensibility of the defendant's conduct to the actual harm allegedly suffered by that particular plaintiff.

2. Other Examples of a Lack of Predominance Involving Penalties

In a related context, courts have denied class certification because individual inquiries predominate when a statute, such as the FCRA or FACTA, requires a finding of willfulness.[99] In *Barnett v. Experian Information Solutions*,[100] for example, the plaintiffs alleged that the defendant failed to adopt reasonable procedures to guarantee the accuracy of defendants' consumer credit reports. The court held that the predominance requirement was not met, because "a determination of willfulness [under the FCRA] is itself a fact-bound inquiry . . . [that] examines the totality of the circumstances involved in a consumer's interaction with a credit reporting agency."[101] In *Glatt v. PMI Group Inc.*, the plaintiffs were allegedly forced to obtain mortgage insurance at a high rate because of a poor credit report.[102] Plaintiffs alleged violations of the FCRA because they did not receive proper notice of the

---

95. 151 F.3d at 417.

96. *Id.* at 418.

97. 216 F.3d at 581.

98. 390 F.3d at 721.

99. *See Najarian*, 2007 WL 4682071, at *4; *Barnett v. Experian Info. Solutions*, No. 2:00CV174, 2004 U.S. Dist. LEXIS 28855, at *16 (E.D. Tex. Sept. 30, 2004); *Glatt v. PMI Group Inc.*, No. 2:03-CV-326-FtM-29SPC, 2004 U.S. Dist. LEXIS 28927, at *2–3 (M.D. Fla. Sept. 7, 2004). *But see Williams v. LexisNexis Risk Mgmt. Inc.*, No. 3:06CV241, 2007 WL 2439463, at *6 (E.D. Va. Aug. 23, 2007); *Bruce v. KeyBank Nat'l Ass'n*, No. 2:05-CV-330, 2006 WL 2334846, at *4 (N.D. Ind. Aug. 7, 2006). For examples of statutes, *see* 15 U.S.C. § 1681n; CAL. LAB. CODE § 203; OR. REV. STAT. § 652.150.

100. 2004 U.S. Dist. LEXIS 28855.

101. *Id.* at *16.

102. 2004 U.S. Dist. LEXIS 28927, at *2–3.

adverse action taken against them.[103] The court denied class certification, holding that damages under the FCRA must be determined on an individual basis because plaintiffs can recover different damages depending on whether the defendants' conduct was negligent or willful.[104] Finally, in *Najarian v. Avis Rent A Car System*, the plaintiffs alleged that the defendant willfully violated FACTA by printing prohibited information on receipts.[105] The court found that "willfulness . . . does not give rise to liability independent of individualized factual determinations as to which customers were 'consumers' and which obtained 'receipts' containing Prohibited Information."[106] Thus, plaintiffs could not satisfy the predominance requirement.

IV. Challenging Statutory Damages Before and After Class Certification

Although many courts consider, at the class-certification stage, whether statutory damages are proportional to the actual alleged harm, some courts reject this approach. Judge Easterbrook, in *Murray v. GMAC Mortgage Corp.*, observed that concerns about an unconstitutionally excessive award are best considered after class certification.[107] Delaying consideration of due process concerns until after certification is problematic, however, because defendants are often forced to settle to avoid an intolerably high risk of financial ruin even in cases of questionable or dubious merit.[108] Further, after the case has been settled, the amount of the statutory penalties obviously cannot be reviewed for unconstitutional excessiveness or reduced.[109] Moreover, courts have a duty to resolve questions regarding superiority

---

103. *Id.* at *3; *see* 15 U.S.C. § 1681m.

104. *Glatt*, 2004 U.S. Dist. LEXIS 28927, at *15–16.

105. 2007 WL 4682071, at *4.

106. *Id.*

107. 434 F.3d 948, 954 (7th Cir. 2006); *see also Chakejian v. Equifax Info. Serv. LLC*, 256 F.R.D. 492, 502 (E.D. Pa. 2009); *Beringer v. Standard Parking Corp.*, Nos. 07 C 5027, 07 C 5119, 2008 WL 4390626, at *5 (N.D. Ill. Sept. 24, 2008); *Cicilline v. Jewel Food Stores, Inc.*, 542 F. Supp. 2d 831, 839 (N.D. Ill. 2008); *Harris v. Best Buy Co.*, 254 F.R.D. 82, 90 (N.D. Ill. 2008); *Redmon v. Uncle Julio's of Ill., Inc.*, 249 F.R.D. 290, 297 (N.D. Ill. 2008); *Meehan v. Buffalo Wild Wings, Inc.*, 249 F.R.D. 284, 288 (N.D. Ill. 2008); *Troy v. Red Lantern Inn, Inc.*, No. 07 C 2418, 2007 WL 4293014, at *4 (N.D. Ill. Dec. 4, 2007); *Bernal v. Keybank*, No. 06-C-8, 2007 WL 2050405, at *4 (E.D. Wis. July 11, 2007); *Forrest v. C.M.A. Mortgage, Inc.*, No. 06-C-14, 2007 WL 188979, at *2 (E.D. Wis. Jan. 19, 2007); *Pavone v. Aegis Lending Corp.*, No. 05 C 5129, 2006 WL 2536632, at *6 (N.D. Ill. Aug. 31, 2006); *Bruce*, 2006 WL 2334846, at *3; *Murray v. Sunrise Chevrolet, Inc.*, No. 04 C 7668, 2006 WL 862886, at *5 (N.D. Ill. Mar. 30, 2006); *In re Napster*, 2005 WL 1287611, at *11.

108. *See Vasquez-Torres*, 2007 WL 4812289, at *7; *Serna*, 2007 U.S. Dist. LEXIS 82023, at *17; *see also Leysoto*, 255 F.R.D. at 699.

109. *Vasquez-Torres*, 2007 WL 4812289, at *7; *Serna*, 2007 U.S. Dist. LEXIS 82023, at *17.

and predominance before certifying a class,[110] and to the extent due process concerns militate against a finding of superiority or predominance, addressing these concerns should not be postponed.

A. BEFORE THE CLASS CERTIFICATION STAGE

Defendants may present their due process concerns before plaintiffs file a motion for class certification through a preemptive motion to deny or preclude class certification,[111] a motion to dismiss, a motion to strike, or a motion for judgment on the pleadings.[112] At this stage, defendants generally argue that the court should dismiss the claim for statutory damages because a class award of even the minimum statutory damages would be so disproportionate to any actual harm that may have been suffered as to run afoul of due process. Unreceptive courts have responded that such claims are "premature," and that they will not dismiss a claim "merely because [plaintiff] requested damages in an amount that might hypothetically be excessive."[113] For example, one court held that "it is conceivable that in the future a party with actual harm that is difficult to compute will bring a case seeking statutory damages. In such a case, the actual harm might be very close to the statutory damages. This mere possibility of a constitutional application is enough to defeat a facial challenge to the statute."[114]

Some courts hold that defendants should raise the due process claim after more discovery has taken place or in the context of a motion for class certification, after evidence of the size of the class and the amount of actual and statutory damages has been submitted.[115] Other courts hold that they will not consider due process challenges regarding punitive awards until after the court has rendered a final judgment against the defendant.[116]

---

110. *See, e.g., In re Hydrogen Peroxide Antitrust Litig.,* 552 F.3d 305, 320 (3d Cir. 2008) (district court must "make a definitive determination that the requirements of Rule 23 have been met before certifying a class"); *see also id.* at 319 (noting that the 2003 amendments to Rule 23 "eliminated the language that had appeared in Rule 23(c)(1) providing that a class certification 'may be conditional'").

111. *E.g., Vinole v. Countrywide Home Loans, Inc.,* 571 F.3d 935, 944 (9th Cir. 2009).

112. *See, e.g., Phillips Randolph Enters.,* 2007 WL 129052, at *1.

113. *Arcilla v. Adidas Promotional Retail Operations, Inc.,* 488 F. Supp. 2d 965, 973 (C.D. Cal. 2007).

114. *Harris v. Mexican Specialty Foods, Inc.,* 564 F.3d 1301, 1313 (11th Cir. 2009) (internal citation omitted).

115. *Follman v. Vill. Squire, Inc.,* 542 F. Supp. 2d 816, 821–22 (N.D. Ill. 2007); *Ramirez v. MGM Mirage, Inc.,* 524 F. Supp. 2d 1226, 1232 (D. Nev. 2007); *Arcilla,* 488 F. Supp. 2d at 973.

116. *Parker,* 331 F.3d at 22; *Irvine v. 233 Skydeck, LLC,* 597 F. Supp. 2d 799, 804 (N.D. Ill. 2009); *Ramirez v. Midwest Airlines, Inc.,* 537 F. Supp. 2d 1161, 1169 (D. Kan. 2008); *Centerline Equip. Corp. v. Banner Pers. Serv., Inc.,* 545 F. Supp. 2d 768, 778 (N.D. Ill. 2008); *Troy v. Home Run Inn, Inc.,* No. 07 C 4331, 2008 WL 1766526, at *3 (N.D. Ill. Apr. 14, 2008); *Klingensmith v. Max & Erma's Rests., Inc.,* No. 07-0318, 2007 WL 3118505, at *3 (W.D. Pa. Oct. 23, 2007); *Pirian v. In-N-Out Burgers,* No. SACV061251DOCMLGX, 2007 WL 1040864, at *3 (C.D. Cal. Apr. 5, 2007).

B. POST-JUDGMENT

After the court renders final judgment, the defendant can argue that the award is unconstitutionally excessive because it is disproportionate to the harm plaintiffs actually suffered and ask the court to lower the award to comport with due process. A number of courts have held that the judge can reduce statutory penalties or damages if disproportionate damages have been awarded to the class.[117] One court noted that constitutional limits are best considered after class certification because "[t]hen a judge may evaluate the defendant's overall conduct and control its total exposure."[118] For example, in *Perez-Farias v. Global Horizons, Inc.*, the district court vacated an earlier judgment and reduced the damages award because of due process concerns.[119]

The ratio between the statutory penalties and compensatory damages in any large class action generally should be no higher than 1:1. Although the Supreme Court has established benchmarks of 4:1 and 9:1 for single-plaintiff punitive damages awards, "[w]hen compensatory damages are substantial," then a smaller ratio of 1:1 is the highest allowed by the due process clause,[120] and in determining whether a damage award in a class action is "substantial" (and thus subject to the 1:1 ratio) courts should consider the aggregate class recovery and not the size of the award to each class member.[121] Although courts are divided on when an award is "substantial," a classwide award will usually qualify because class awards are often in the multi-million-dollar range.[122]

V. The Proper Standard for Scrutinizing the Maximum Permissible Amount of Statutory Damages

There are two major lines of Supreme Court cases regarding the due process limits on statutory penalty awards. The first line of cases began in 1909 with *Waters-Pierce Oil Co. v. Texas*, which explicitly dealt with statutory damages.[123] Under this line of cases, a statutory penalty violates due process when it is "so severe and oppressive

---

117. *Murray*, 434 F.3d at 953–54; *see also* cases cited *supra* note 107.

118. *Murray*, 434 F.3d at 954.

119. No. CV-05-3061-RHW, 2009 WL 1011180, at *5–6 (E.D. Wash. Apr. 15, 2009). *Cf. Texas v. Am. Blastfax, Inc.*, 164 F. Supp. 2d 892, 900–01 (W.D. Tex. 2001) (holding it would be "inequitable and unreasonable to award" minimum statutory damages against a small company, and awarding seven cents per violation instead).

120. *State Farm*, 538 U.S. at 425; *Exxon Shipping Co. v. Baker*, 128 S. Ct. 2605, 2634 n.28 (2008).

121. *Exxon Shipping*, 128 S. Ct. at 2634 n.28.

122. In *State Farm*, the Court held that $1 million awarded in compensatory damages was "substantial," and "likely would justify a punitive damages award at or near the amount of compensatory damages." 538 U.S. at 429.

123. 212 U.S. 86, 111 (1909) (establishing "grossly excessive" standard).

as to be wholly disproportioned to the offense and obviously unreasonable," which includes consideration of "due regard for the interests of the public."[124] The second line of cases built upon these earlier cases,[125] extending the reasoning to limit the size of punitive damage awards.[126] Under this line of cases, the Court articulated a more exacting standard of review by setting forth the three well-known guideposts of *Gore*.[127] The Court elaborated on those limits in *State Farm*[128] and *Philip Morris USA v. Williams*.[129]

Courts are not in complete agreement about which line of cases to apply when assessing whether a statutory damage award violates due process. Many courts explicitly apply the *Gore* and *State Farm* due process limitations to statutory damages in class action lawsuits.[130] However, in what one scholar aptly described as "an ironic twist,"[131] a few courts have refused to apply the later due process cases to class actions involving statutory damages.[132] This disagreement is significant for two reasons. First, the earlier line of cases permits consideration of harm to third parties, including the general public,[133] while under *Philip Morris* consideration of

---

124. *St. Louis*, 251 U.S. at 66–67.

125. *See, e.g.*, *Gore*, 517 U.S. at 575 (citing *St. Louis*, 251 U.S. at 66–67); *TXO Prod. Corp. v. Alliance Res. Corp.*, 509 U.S. 443, 454 (1993) (quoting *Waters-Pierce*, 212 U.S. at 111, and *St. Louis*, 251 U.S. at 66–67); *Browning-Ferris Indus. of Vt., Inc. v. Kelco Disposal, Inc.*, 492 U.S. 257, 276 (1989) (citing *St. Louis*, 251 U.S. at 66–67).

126. *TXO Prod.*, 509 U.S. at 458; *Pac. Mut. Life Ins. Co. v. Haslip*, 499 U.S. 1, 18–19 (1991).

127. 517 U.S. at 575 (listing the three guideposts as the reprehensibility of the defendant's conduct; the relationship between the punitive award and the actual or potential harm plaintiff suffered; and the ratio between the punitive award and the civil or criminal penalties authorized in comparable cases).

128. 538 U.S. at 425.

129. 549 U.S. 346, 353–54 (2007).

130. *Parker*, 331 F.3d at 22; *Perez-Farias*, 2009 WL 1011180, at *5; *In re Napster*, 2005 WL 1287611, at *10. In addition, some courts have applied *Gore* and *State Farm* to cases involving statutory damages without explicit discussion of the differences between statutory and punitive damages. *See, e.g.*, *Murray*, 434 F.3d at 953; *Chakejian*, 256 F.R.D. at 502; *Arcilla*, 488 F. Supp. 2d at 972; *Follman*, 542 F. Supp. 2d at 821–22; *Blanco*, 2008 WL 239658, at *2; *Azoiani*, 2007 WL 4811627, at *4; *Troy*, 2007 WL 4293014, at *4; *Price*, 2007 WL 4812281, at *4; *Najarian*, 2007 WL 4682071, at *4; *Pirian*, 2007 WL 1040864, at *3; *White v. E-Loan, Inc.*, No. C 05-02080 SI, 2006 WL 2411420, at *8 (N.D. Cal. Aug. 18, 2006); *ABT Bldg. Prod. Corp. v. Nat'l Union Fire Ins. Co.*, No. 5:01CV100-V, 2005 WL 6124840, at *5 (W.D.N.C. May 31, 2005).

131. Scheuerman, *supra* note 16, at 116.

132. *See, e.g.*, *Centerline Equip.*, 545 F. Supp. 2d at 778 n.6; *Arrez v. Kelly Servs., Inc.*, 522 F. Supp. 2d 997, 1008 (N.D. Ill. 2007); *Accounting Outsourcing LLC v. Verizon Wireless Pers. Commc'n, L.P.*, 329 F. Supp. 2d 789, 808–09 (M.D. La. 2004); *Holtzman v. Caplice*, No. 07 C 7279, 2008 WL 2168762, at *6 (N.D. Ill. May 23, 2008); *Sadowski v. Med1 Online, LLC*, No. 07 C 2973, 2008 WL 489360, at *5 (N.D. Ill. Feb. 20, 2008); *Phillips Randolph Enters.*, 2007 WL 129052, at *2–3. Other cases apply *St. Louis* without discussion. *See, e.g.*, *Ramirez*, 537 F. Supp. 2d at 1169; *Am. Blastfax*, 121 F. Supp. 2d at 1090–91; *Italia Foods Inc. v. Marino v. Enters., Inc.*, No. 07 C 2494, 2007 WL 4117626, at *4 (N.D. Ill. Nov. 16, 2007).

133. *St. Louis*, 251 U.S. at 66–67 (explaining that statutory damages need not be "confined or proportioned to [actual] loss or damages; for, as it is imposed as a punishment for the violation of a public law, the

such harm is barred.[134] This means that the damage award may be much higher under the earlier line of cases because it need only be proportional to the actual damages suffered by society as a whole. Second, the standard of review under the earlier line of cases "is extraordinarily deferential—even more so than in cases applying abuse-of-discretion review."[135] Indeed, courts have required that the statutory damage award "only bear some relationship to the offense's gravity [because] this is *not* a proportionality inquiry."[136]

Courts refusing to apply *Gore* and its progeny to statutory damages raise a number of concerns. First, they note that the *Gore* line of cases refers to punitive damages, not statutory damages.[137] However, these courts ignore the fact that the later line of cases extends the reasoning of the earlier statutory damages cases to punitive damages.[138] They also ignore the fact that courts, including the Supreme Court, have emphasized that due process protections apply to civil penalties generally, not just those expressly labeled as punitive damages.[139] Furthermore, damages that go beyond compensation for actual injury are punitive-in-fact,[140] because the

Legislature may adjust its amount to the public wrong rather than the private injury, just as if it were going to the state").

134. 549 U.S. at 353–54.

135. *Zomba Enters., Inc. v. Panorama Records, Inc.*, 491 F.3d 574, 587 (6th Cir. 2007).

136. *Arrez*, 522 F. Supp. 2d at 1008 (quoting *United States ex rel. Tyson v. Amerigroup Ill., Inc.*, 488 F. Supp. 2d 719, 744 (N.D. Ill. 2007) (emphasis added; internal quotation marks omitted)).

137. *See, e.g., Accounting Outsourcing*, 329 F. Supp. 2d at 809 (holding that because the cases do not explicitly refer to statutory damages, applying their due process limits to statutory damages would "extend the holdings of *Gore* and *Campbell* beyond their intended application").

138. *See supra* note 125.

139. *See State Farm*, 538 U.S. at 416 (due process "prohibits the imposition of grossly excessive or arbitrary punishments on a tortfeasor"); *Gore*, 517 U.S. at 574 n.22 ("[T]he basic protection against 'judgments without notice' afforded by the Due Process Clause is implicated by civil *penalties*." (emphasis in original; internal citation omitted)); *see also United States v. Halper*, 490 U.S. 435, 448 (1989), *overruled on other grounds by Hudson v. United States*, 522 U.S. 93, 101 (1997) ("'[T]he labels affixed either to the proceeding or to the relief imposed . . . are not Controlling and will not be allowed to defeat the applicable protections of federal constitutional law.'" (quoting *Hicks v. Feiock*, 485 U.S. 624, 631 (1988) (alterations in original))). *Cf. Exxon Shipping*, 128 S. Ct. at 2622 (likening federal treble damages statute and state penalty statutes to a punitive damages award, and finding such statutes have a "broadly analogous object"); *Tull v. United States*, 481 U.S. 412, 422 n.7 (1987) ("[T]he remedy of civil penalties is similar to the remedy of punitive damages."); *Gilbert v. DaimlerChrysler Corp.*, 685 N.W.2d 391, 400 n.22 (Mich. 2004) ("While *State Farm* dealt with punitive damage awards, the due process concerns articulated in *State Farm* are arguably at play regardless of the label given to damage awards.").

140. *See, e.g., Halper*, 490 U.S. at 448 ("[A] civil sanction that cannot fairly be said solely to serve a remedial purpose, but rather can only be explained as also serving either retributive or deterrent purposes, is punishment, as we have come to understand the term."); *Fitzgerald Publ'g Co. v. Baylor Publ'g Co.*, 807 F.2d 1110, 1117 (2d Cir. 1986) ("[S]tatutory damages serve two purposes—compensatory and punitive.").

Whether a statute goes beyond compensation for actual injury to become punitive-in-fact may vary by statute. For example, the California Supreme Court has held that the purpose of California Labor Code § 203 is solely "to compel the prompt payment of earned wages," and thus § 203 is punitive in nature.

potential statutory damages are so much greater than actual damages that they "come to resemble punitive damages."[141] This is of particular concern with respect to statutory damages because they "are often[ ] motivated in part by a pseudo-punitive intention to 'address and deter overall public harm.'"[142]

Courts applying the earlier, more deferential standard also note that statutory damages are different from punitive damages because they are assessed by Congress, not juries, and the Supreme Court focused on the bias, passion, and prejudice of juries when holding that due process limits apply to punitive awards.[143] But the Supreme Court has noted that it "is not correct to assume that the safeguards in the legislative process have no counterpart in the judicial process" because juries make decisions through deliberations based on the arguments of adversaries, as does the legislature.[144] In addition, some courts have refused to apply *Gore* to statutory damages, reasoning that they should give deference to legislative determinations of the appropriate amount of damages to be awarded for the violation of a given statute.[145] These courts usually rely on the third *Gore* guidepost, which states that the reviewing court "should accord substantial deference to legislative judgments concerning appropriate sanctions for the conduct at issue."[146] However, the Supreme Court has held that when a penalty is challenged as constitutionally excessive, courts must "engage[ ] in an independent examination of the relevant

---

Oppenheimer v. Sunkist Growers, Inc., 315 P.2d 116, 118 (Cal. 1957); *Murphy v. Kenneth Cole Prods., Inc.*, 155 P.3d 284, 293 (Cal. 2007); *see also Austin v. United States*, 509 U.S. 602, 621 (1993) (stating a "civil sanction that cannot fairly be said *solely* to serve a remedial purpose, but rather can only be explained also as serving either retributive or deterrent purposes, is punishment" (emphasis in original; internal quotation marks and citation omitted)). Similarly, courts have found that FACTA is punitive-in-fact because the purpose "is to require a FACTA defendant to pay for willful violations of the truncation provision, not to compensate the claimants for any actual monetary or physical loss. Said damages are akin to punitive in nature." *Whole Enchilada, Inc. v. Travelers Prop. Cas. Co.*, 581 F. Supp. 2d 677, 704 (W.D. Pa. 2008). *But see Harris*, 564 F.3d at 1313 (explaining that damages provision is not tantamount to a punitive damages provision "[b]ecause the FCRA already contains a punitive damages provision and specifies that statutory damages may only be awarded in lieu of actual damages"). Courts have made similar arguments with respect to the Credit Repair Organizations Act, *Hillis*, 237 F.R.D. at 507 (reasoning "damages sought here are functionally equivalent to statutory penalties"), and the Washington Farm Labor Contract Act, *Perez-Farias*, 2009 WL 1011180, at *4 n.5 (explaining statutory minimum "would necessarily result in a punitive award because the amount of damages would have no relationship to the harm caused by the wrongful conduct").

141. *In re Napster*, 2005 WL 1287611, at *10 (internal citation and quotation marks omitted).

142. *Parker*, 331 F.3d at 27 (Newman, J., concurring) (quoting *Am. Blastfax*, 121 F. Supp. 2d at 1090); *see also DirecTV, Inc. v. Braun*, No. CIV 3:03CV937(SRU), 2004 WL 288805, at *1 (D. Conn. Feb. 9, 2004).

143. *Kenro, Inc. v. Fax Daily, Inc.*, 962 F. Supp. 1162, 1165 (S.D. Ind. 1997).

144. *TXO Prod.*, 509 U.S. at 456–57.

145. *Phillips Randolph Enters.*, 2007 WL 129052, at *2; *Lowry's Reports, Inc. v. Legg Mason, Inc.*, 302 F. Supp. 2d 455, 460 (D. Md. 2004) ("The unregulated and arbitrary use of judicial power that the *Gore* guideposts remedy is not implicated in Congress'[s] carefully crafted and reasonably constrained statute.").

146. *Gore*, 517 U.S. at 583 (internal quotation marks and citations omitted).

criteria"[147] and not give legislatures free rein to violate defendants' due process rights.

Courts have also found that *Gore* is not relevant to statutory damages because damages under a statute provide adequate notice to defendants. They explain, "[a]t the heart of the Court's rulings in [*State Farm* and *Gore*] was the concern that persons receive fair notice regarding the nature and severity of the punishment inflicted upon them" and that defendants receive "fair notice" by virtue of the statute.[148] But other courts have found that "[*Gore*]'s guideposts are applicable even when the defendant has adequate notice of the amount at issue."[149]

Finally, courts reason that statutory damages are reserved for cases where actual damages would be difficult to quantify, such that it would be impossible to meaningfully apply the *Gore* guideposts.[150] For example, the TCPA was created to address "the difficult to quantify business interruption costs imposed upon recipients of unsolicited fax advertisements."[151] However, *State Farm* explicitly recognized that the constitutional limits apply even in cases where "the monetary value" of the harm "might have been difficult to determine."[152]

VI. Conclusion

Aggregated statutory damages present serious problems for defendants in class action lawsuits. The combination of statutory damages and the class action mechanism creates a double incentive for plaintiffs to file suit, increases the potential for blackmail settlements, and often results in grossly disproportionate penalties. The potential for enormous damages has led many courts to recognize the unintended and devastating effect these damages may have on defendants and to deny class certification under the superiority and predominance requirements of Rule 23.

---

147. *Cooper Indus., Inc. v. Leatherman Tool Group, Inc.*, 532 U.S. 424, 435 (2001). *See also Perez-Farias*, 2009 WL 1011180, at *5 ("[A]ny damage award must meet . . . substantive constitutional requirements.").

148. *Accounting Outsourcing*, 329 F. Supp. 2d at 808–09 (M.D. La. 2004) (internal citations omitted).

149. *VF Corp. v. Wrexham Aviation Corp.*, 686 A.2d 647, 661 (Md. Ct. Spec. App. 1996), *aff'd in part and rev'd in part on other grounds by* 715 A.2d 188 (Md. 1998). *See also* Note, *Grossly Excessive Penalties in the Battle Against Illegal File-Sharing: The Troubling Effects of Aggregating Minimum Statutory Damages for Copyright Infringement*, 83 Tᴇx. L. Rᴇv. 525, 542 (2004).

150. *Centerline Equip.*, 545 F. Supp. 2d at 777–78; *Accounting Outsourcing*, 329 F. Supp. 2d at 809; *Native Am. Arts, Inc. v. Bundy-Howard, Inc.*, 168 F. Supp. 2d 905, 914 (N.D. Ill. 2001); *Am. Blastfax*, 121 F. Supp. 2d at 1090–91; *Kenro*, 962 F. Supp. at 1165; *Sadowski*, 2008 WL 489360, at *4.

151. *Kenro*, 962 F. Supp. at 1166.

152. 538 U.S. at 425 (internal quotation marks and citation omitted).

But Rule 23 is only one part of the solution. Courts should also recognize that certifying classes involving aggregated penalties violates a defendant's due process rights.[153] In the meantime, it is advisable for defendants to raise due process objections at every stage of the litigation and assert every possible challenge under Rule 23 to prevent or limit the certification of classes seeking massive aggregated penalty awards.

---

153. The need to attack aggregated penalties under Rule 23 or federal due process principles is all the more important after the Supreme Court's decision in *Shady Grove Orthopedic Assocs. v. Allstate Ins. Co.*, No. 08-1008, 2010 U.S. LEXIS 2929 (U.S. 2010), which held that a New York procedural rule prohibiting class actions seeking penalties does not apply to federal courts sitting in diversity. *Shady Grove* held that because the New York procedural rule conflicts with Rule 23, which "creates a categorical rule entitling a plaintiff whose suit meets the specified criteria to pursue his claim as a class action," Rule 23 governs. *Id.* at *11.

Whether the Court's fractured opinion will be applied to invalidate other similar state rules remains unclear. Defendants in federal class actions should cite Justice Stevens's concurring opinion, which controls because his vote was necessary to the majority and his was the narrowest opinion concurring in the Court's judgment. *See Marks v. United States*, 430 U.S. 188, 193 (1977). In Justice Stevens's view, a federal procedural rule, as applied, can violate the Rules Enabling Act by effectively abridging, enlarging, or modifying a state-created right or remedy. When a federal rule cannot be construed in a way to avoid such an outcome, "federal courts cannot apply the rule." *Shady Grove*, 2010 U.S. LEXIS 2929, at *55. While the New York restriction at issue is not the sort of procedural rule that is sufficiently interwoven with substantive rights to avoid the application of Rule 23, Justice Stevens emphasized that each case must be addressed on its own merits:

> In some instances, a state rule that appears procedural really is not. A rule about how damages are reviewed on appeal may really be a damages cap. A rule that a plaintiff can bring a claim for only three years may really be a limit on the existence of the right to seek redress. A rule that a claim must be proved beyond a reasonable doubt may really be a definition of the scope of the claim. These are the sorts of rules that one might describe as "procedural," but they nonetheless define substantive rights. Thus, if a federal rule displaced such a state rule, the federal rule would have altered the State's "substantive rights."

Id. at *57 n.8.

QUANTIFYING NOTICE RESULTS IN CONSUMER, MASS TORT, AND PRODUCT LIABILITY CLASS ACTIONS— THE *DAUBERT/KUMHO TIRE* MANDATE

KATHERINE KINSELLA[1]

I. Providing the Courts with Quantifiable Notice Results

Federal class action rules require close judicial supervision of class action litigation and, in particular, notice to absent, and often unwitting, class members whose rights are being adjudicated. The Federal Rules require "the best notice that is practicable under the circumstances, including individual notice to all members who can be identified through reasonable effort."[2] *Eisen v. Carlisle & Jacquelin*,[3] as well as subsequent cases,[4] makes clear that this requirement is quite unforgiving, as "[t]here is nothing in Rule 23 to suggest that the notice requirements can be tailored to fit the pocketbooks of particular plaintiffs."[5]

In many Rule 23(b)(3) class actions, and in most product liability, mass tort, and consumer class cases, the members are not readily identifiable. In cases where warranty registrations, e-mail addresses, or claim forms and the like exist, direct

---

1. This chapter was adapted from "Quantifying Notice Results in Class Action Cases—The *Daubert/ Kumho* Mandate," 2 CLASS ACTION LITIG. REP. (BNA) 531 (Jul. 27, 2001).

2. FED. R. CIV. P. 23(c)(2)(B).

3. 417 U.S. 156, 176 (1974).

4. *See, e.g., In re Franklin Nat'l Bank Sec. Litig.*, 574 F.2d 662 (2d Cir. 1978); *In re Nissan Motor Corp. Antitrust Litig.*, 552 F.2d 1088 (5th Cir. 1977); *Walsh v. Ford Motor Co.*, 807 F.2d 1000 (D.C. Cir. 1986).

5. 417 U.S. at 176. While Rule 23 does not require mandatory notice for classes certified under Rule 23(b)(1) and Rule 23(b)(2), questions have been raised regarding the constitutionality of the failure to provide notice to these types of classes. *See* 3 HERBERT B. NEWBERG & ALBA CONTE, NEWBERG ON CLASS ACTIONS: A MANUAL FOR GROUP LITIGATION AT FEDERAL AND STATE LEVELS §§ 8:13, 8:14 (4th ed. 2002). That subject is beyond the scope of this chapter, which concerns only classes certified under Rule 23(b)(3).

mail notice is possible to some percentage of the class. More often, in cases ranging from prescription drugs and asbestos to house siding and breast implants, class members must be reached through media-based notice utilizing magazines, newspapers, TV, radio, and/or the Internet.

Judges and lawyers need a better understanding of how media penetrates demographic audiences, how media is measured, and the reasoning behind media choices in order to properly evaluate the adequacy of media-based notice. Notice experts are often required to provide affidavits and court testimony attesting to the adequacy of the notice. The methodology used to design a notice program and the qualifications of the notice provider are of paramount importance. Indeed, *Daubert v. Merrell Dow Pharmaceuticals, Inc.*[6] and *Kumho Tire Co., Ltd., v. Carmichael*[7] require more rigorous scrutiny of plans using media-based notice to class members who are otherwise unidentifiable.

Notice plans directed to unidentified class members should (1) identify the demographics of class members and establish a target audience; (2) outline the methodology for selecting the media and other plan elements and how they relate to product usage or exposure; and (3) provide results that quantify for the court the adequacy of the notice based upon recognized tools of media measurement.

Without an understanding of these three factors, the court has no firm basis upon which to form an opinion with regard to the adequacy of media-based notice. "I know it when I see it" is no longer a sustainable position.

A. THE ROLE OF PAID ADVERTISING

Each class action requires a notice program tailored to the case. Factors such as the demographics of class members, the distribution of or exposure to a product, the number of readily identifiable class members, the anticipated class size, and whether the class is statewide, regional, or nationwide influence the direction and scope of the notice program.

Although there are many means of communication, under almost all circumstances paid media *must* be the basic component of a notice plan to reach unidentifiable class members because it can be targeted to specific demographic groups, measured by accredited marketing research firms for audience reach and frequency of exposure, and contractually guaranteed to appear on a certain date.

Notice by press release, video, or audio news release, which can result in media coverage that is referred to as "earned" media, is valuable but not certain. Earned media can never provide guaranteed coverage, given the lack of a contract for services, a time frame within which the story must run, and the uncertainty that such critical information as toll-free numbers and other contact information will

---

6. 509 U.S. 579 (1993).

7. 526 U.S. 137 (1999).

be displayed. Notice to third parties who may have contact with class members and public service announcements can also be valuable, but are similarly not guaranteed notice. The court must be satisfied *before* approving a notice program that an adequate percentage of the class will have an opportunity to see the notice.[8]

B. IDENTIFYING A TARGET DEMOGRAPHIC AND SELECTING MEDIA

Individuals within the general population consume media differently based on income, gender, age, education, and other factors. Notice programs therefore must establish a clear demographic target or targets in order to select media to reach a specific audience. How a product was used or an exposure occurred, who used it or was exposed to it, where and over what period of time use or exposure occurred— all of those factors provide critical information in identifying the demographic characteristics and geographic distribution of class members. This research establishes the parameters for identifying and locating class members and shapes the notice program.

In asbestos cases, for example, occupational exposure is the overwhelming source of injury. The period of time that asbestos was in the workplace, the professions that had exposure (for example, building and construction trades, ship-building industries, and naval or merchant mariners), and the latency period for disease manifestation help provide a demographic profile of class members that is predominantly male, blue-collar, and 55 or older. In addition, the widespread use of asbestos insulation in shipbuilding during wartime pinpoints specific geographic areas where enormous numbers of class members are likely to be located years after exposure.

Nationally accredited media and marketing research firms such as Media-Mark Research, Inc. (MRI) and Simmons Market Research Bureau, Inc. (Simmons) provide syndicated data on audience size, composition, and other factors pertaining to major media including broadcast, print, and outdoor advertising. They provide a single-source measurement of major media, products, services,

---

8. In large and important settlements, the biggest press exposure occurs with the announcement of the settlement. It is far more difficult to get earned media coverage during the notice phase after national media coverage of a settlement has occurred. However, advance planning and preparation can turn the early press coverage into a notice advantage.

In conjunction with the press conference announcing the settlement in the Fen-Phen diet drug case (*In re Diet Drugs (Phentermine/Fenfluramine/Dexfenfluramine) Prods. Liab. Litig.*, MDL No. 1203 (E.D. Pa.)), a website and toll-free number were established to make sure that potential class members could get information. The toll-free number and the website provided information about the forthcoming notice process and allowed individuals to register to receive direct notice. Often, however, the announcement of a settlement precedes the notice by many months, leaving potential class members frustrated with their inability to obtain further information. In the diet drug case, over 80,000 potential class members called the toll-free number or logged on to the website as a result of media coverage of the press conference where they were assured that they would get notice at the appropriate time.

and in-depth consumer demographic and lifestyle or psychographic characteristics. These research companies regularly survey consumers nationally through in-person interviews and questionnaires. They also provide demographic profiles of individuals who use a specific service or product, such as cell phone users, home-owners, cigarette smokers, and insurance and prescription drug purchasers. In many instances, product usage by brand or type is also available.

In addition, the media habits of these product users or demographic targets can be further evaluated to determine whether they are light newspaper readers, heavy television viewers, moderate magazine readers, and so forth. Different types of media can be compared for audience penetration and cost. For example, TV penetration of a particular target audience can be compared to that of radio, magazines, and newspapers. In addition, each media vehicle, such as a specific television show, radio program, or magazine, is indexed with respect to its penetration of the target audience. This information is useful in selecting the media for notice and ensures that the media used actually reaches the target audience. It is not adequate notice, for example, if summary notices appear in hundreds of newspapers nationwide when the class comprises less-educated, low-income consumers who are light users of newspapers.

Simmons and MRI also report the readership, as distinct from circulation, of over 220 consumer publications and national newspapers, allowing the estimation of audience reach through a print media schedule. Nielsen Media Research, Inc. and Arbitron provide audience measurements against age and gender demographics that enable television and radio audience estimates to be made. ABC audit statements provide definitive circulation information for print media. Nielsen Online, a service of The Nielsen Company, and comScore, an independent company, both deliver comprehensive, independent measurement and analysis of online audiences, advertising, video, consumer-generated media, mobile devices, commerce, and consumer online behavior. Both Nielsen and comScore have introduced mobile measurement tools as smartphones become more widely used and accepted.

C. MEASURING THE MEDIA-BASED NOTICE

There are a number of ways to measure media penetration. Two of the most basic are *reach* and *frequency*. Reach is the estimated percentage of a target audience reached through a specific media vehicle or combination of media vehicles. Frequency is the estimated average number of times an audience is exposed to an advertising vehicle carrying the message.[9]

Reach and frequency calculations are estimates within a standard margin of error that provide the advertiser—whether Coca-Cola, McDonald's, the Sierra Club,

---

9. For a discussion of reach and frequency, see Jack Sissors & Robert Baron, *Advanced Measurement and Calculations, in* ADVERTISING MEDIA PLANNING 87–116 (2002).

or the court—with a reliable basis upon which to judge penetration of target audiences by media.

Software programs created by the media industry allow reach and frequency estimates to be calculated. Statistical formulas factor out duplication of readership or viewership among the target audience and allow reach and frequency, as well as other media measurements, to be calculated. This allows determination of the *net* audience reach of a media schedule using various kinds of print and broadcast media.

There is no court-mandated reach or frequency standard. In some instances, a 95 percent reach of the target audience with a frequency of three or more exposures is appropriate; in other cases, a lower reach and frequency is adequate. Reach and frequency targets depend upon a number of factors that guide how extensive a paid media program should be within the context of what is reasonable and practicable. Among the factors are the type of relief (injunctive or damages, whether direct or cy pres/fluid recovery), seriousness of the tort, size of the settlement, and percentage of class to be reached through media versus direct mail.

In addition, it is not always reasonable to achieve a high national reach in a nationwide class action when the class members live for the most part in specific geographic areas. For example, in *Richison v. Weyerhaeuser Co.*,[10] five states had 95 percent of the product distribution even though the class was nationwide. National notice was achieved through *Parade* and *USA Weekend* with a nearly 70 percent reach of the targeted audience. Additional media was purchased in the five states, providing reaches from 91.1 percent to 97.5 percent with frequencies of 2.1 to 3.1 exposures.

D. DETERMINING THE ADEQUACY OF NOTICE

When paid media is a notice vehicle, the tools available for measuring the reach and frequency of the media must be used. Reach and frequency estimates are standard methods used by every major advertising and media-buying firm in the country to help select media to reach particular targets, to measure the reach of those targets, and to calculate the average number of opportunities individuals within the target audience had to see the notice.

The use of these tools is not imposing an "advertising standard" on notice programs. The tools are simply providing a measurement of the media's ability to reach class members. These measurements are the calculation of what the media is delivering. There is, moreover, no advertising or media standard for notice programs. Each case is different; consequently, reach and frequency goals will be different. However, the guiding principle is that due process is achieved by reaching a

---

10. No. 005532 (Cal. Super. Ct. San Joaquin County, 1999).

significant percentage of actual or potential class members based on the individual circumstances of the case.

Some people talk of achieving a "legal standard" for notice programs. A notice is deemed adequate if a court approves it. However, without using industry-recognized standards of measurement, courts do not have the expertise to evaluate media-based notice programs. Circulation figures and the number of advertising placements or press articles alone are insufficient guides for assessing whether notice was actually or likely received or seen by absent class members.

USA Today, for example, is often used for stand-alone national class action notice. However, 2009 average daily readership of *USA Today* by those 18 years of age and older is only 3.69 million out of a total 223.5 million adults nationwide. National distribution should not be confused with national notice; less than 1.7 percent penetration of an audience could never be deemed adequate. (*USA Today* is, however, frequently a useful component of a broader national notice program. It may be necessary, but not independently sufficient.)

II. Expert Defense of the Notice Plan: The Role of Reliability and Relevance

In the wake of the Supreme Court's decisions in *Daubert* and *Kumho Tire*, the reliability of a notice expert's testimony should be tested against the standards that have been developed within the media industry for determining whether and to what degree a target audience has been reached and how often. In performing the gatekeeping function of determining the reliability and relevance of the testimony, courts can be expected to reject expert testimony that does not rely on accepted data and methodology.

As expected, the Supreme Court's decisions in *Daubert* and *Kumho Tire* have led to increased scrutiny of expert testimony.[11] A study released by the Federal Judicial Center on the effect of these decisions indicates that judges are far more cautious about admitting expert testimony and more probing about the basis for the expert's reliability.[12]

While *Daubert* addressed scientific expertise, *Kumho Tire* makes clear that the same principles apply to all expert testimony and not just scientific evidence. According to the Court, "*Daubert*'s general holding—setting forth the trial judge's general 'gatekeeping' obligation—applies not only to testimony based on 'scien-

---

11. *Kumho Tire*, 526 U.S. at 141.

12. The study, "Expert Testimony in Federal Civil Trials: A Preliminary Analysis," is available on the Federal Judicial Center's website at http://www.fjc.gov/public/pdf.nsf/lookup/exptesti.pdf/$file/exptesti .pdf. (The Federal Judicial Center is the research arm of the federal courts.)

tific' knowledge, but also to testimony based on 'technical' and 'other specialized' knowledge."[13]

A federal judge performs this gatekeeping function by ensuring that an expert's testimony both rests on a reliable foundation and is relevant to the task at hand. In order to determine reliability, the court must analyze the data and facts upon which the expert relies and the methodology used to support the conclusions; in other words, the court must evaluate whether the testifying expert "employs in the courtroom the same level of intellectual rigor that characterizes the practice of an expert in the relevant field."[14] That showing would likely require evidence that the expert's data and methodology are similar to that used by professionals in the relevant field.[15]

In the wake of *Daubert* and *Kumho Tire*, experts on class action notice who testify to the adequacy of a notice program should be held to the standards of other media professionals, in addition to being knowledgeable about the requirements of Rule 23, its state equivalents, and prior court approval of particular notice programs. Good notice practice dictates that the notice expert provide the court with the necessary tools to judge the adequacy of a media-based notice program, including the breadth of reach and the opportunities class members have to be exposed to the notice. *Daubert* and *Kumho Tire* now make this good practice an imperative.

---

13. *Kumho Tire*, 526 U.S. at 141; *see also* Chapter 13, "*Daubert* Challenges in Class Certification."

14. *Kumho Tire*, 526 U.S. at 152.

15. For a more expansive discussion of the application of *Daubert* and *Kumho*, see Kenneth S. Geller & Michael E. Lackey, Jr., *Supreme Court's* Kumho *Decision a Boon to Public*, LEADER'S PRODUCT LIABILITY LAW AND STRATEGY, Apr. 1999, at 1, *available at* http://www.appellate.net/articles/kumhodecision.asp.

THE PLAIN LANGUAGE TOOLKIT FOR CLASS ACTION NOTICE

KATHERINE KINSELLA[1]

I. Introduction

The Judicial Conference of the United States approved revisions to Rule 23 of the Federal Rules of Civil Procedure prepared by the Conference's Committee on Rules of Practice and Procedure. These revisions went into effect on December 1, 2003. The changes to Rule 23(c)(2) require that class action notices be written in "plain, easily understood language."

II. What Is Plain Language?

The Committee focused entirely on language. However, plain language, or "plain English" as defined by practitioners, is not just simplified language that eliminates legalese, jargon, and complex syntax. It is a marriage of content and format, focusing not just on what is written but how that text appears on a page. It is an approach to communicating with a reader based on who the reader is and how to deliver an understandable message to that individual:

> It is the use of language stripped of archaic forms and vocabulary, aided by design, layout and typography of the text . . . [It] takes into account the empirical research of the past 30 years about how the mind works—how people read and assimilate information.[2]

---

1. This chapter was adapted from "The Plain Language Tool Kit for Class Action Notice," 3 Class Action Litig. Rep. (BNA) 688–91 (Oct. 25, 2002).

2. Cheryl Stephens, Address to the Wills and Estates Section, Canadian Bar Association (Nov. 27, 1990) (internal quotations and citation omitted).

Plain language is also an international movement that seeks to make documents understandable to the general public. Plain language organizations are rewriting laws, regulations, and other public documents in Canada, the United Kingdom, New Zealand, Australia, Sweden, South Africa, and the United States.[3]

In a plain language document, the effective organization, presentation, design, and layout of information are as important as clear and understandable writing. This chapter explores the principles of plain language as it is broadly defined and advocates its use in notice documents. While this chapter focuses on the development of summary notices for publication purposes, the comments have obvious implications for structuring and writing long-form notices as well.

III. Organizing and Formatting the Notice Document

Four basic questions need to be answered before drafting the notice:

- Who is the audience?
- What is the essential information a class member needs to know?
- What is the logical organization or flow of that information?
- How should the information be formatted for ease of access?

A. WHO IS THE AUDIENCE?

The demographics—age, level of education, and the like—of class members are readily ascertainable through consumer research data. Demographics are important in targeting media to reach the class. However, in writing a legal notice, they are important only to a point. In actuality, the education and comprehension levels of class members in consumer, product liability, mass tort, and employment cases vary so widely that notice must be written in the simplest conversational English without legal jargon, complex language, or unwieldy grammatical structures. When the majority of the class is composed of elderly or minimally educated individuals, language as well as document format requires even greater simplification.

B. WHAT IS THE ESSENTIAL INFORMATION
A CLASS MEMBER NEEDS TO KNOW?

Published notice, whether a print ad or a television spot, is a summary of the most important information in the long-form notice. It should not include all the details of the litigation or the settlement. Answering the following questions easily provides the necessary information:

---

3. *See* website information in the references, *infra* note 4.

- What is the litigation about?
- Am I affected by this litigation?
- What is the product and how was it used (if applicable)?
- What are the terms of the settlement (if applicable)?
- What are my rights?
- Do I need to take action?
- How do I get more information?

Examples of information that can be eliminated from the summary notice are the formal case caption as a headline; the names and addresses of the plaintiff and defendant counsel, unless required for a specific communication function; *detailed* instructions on the procedures for opting out or objecting; or the *details* of the settlement and claims process.

C. WHAT IS THE LOGICAL ORGANIZATION OR FLOW OF THAT INFORMATION?

Think in terms of a hierarchy of information. Start with the general and move to the more specific. A question and answer format is the most effective way to guide a reader through the notice information, particularly the long-form notice. Anticipate a reader's questions and organize the information to answer those questions. This suggested structure leads the class member through progressively more detailed information:

- Headline
- Introduction to what the litigation is about
- Class definition
- Sections (legal rights, product description, settlement terms)
- Subsections under legal rights (opting out, objecting)
- Contact information

1. The Headline

Use the headline to alert readers that the notice may affect them. An advertisement has only a few seconds to get the attention of the reader, and research shows that readers read headlines first.

Never use a formal case caption as a headline in any notice to consumers. Potential class members are not perusing newspapers and magazines looking for legal notices that might affect them. The case caption is a reference for the judicial system.

For example, headlines such as "If you have a breast implant . . ." "If you have an asbestos-related disease . . ." or "If you purchased or took prescription diet drugs . . ." target the consumer personally, directly, and quickly.

Headlines should be simple. When necessary, use an overly inclusive headline that encompasses a larger potential audience, and let the class definition provide the parameters of class membership. For example, use this:

If You Own a Home with Cedar Shingles

Please Read This Legal Notice—It May Affect Your Rights

Don't use this:

If You Own a Home as of June 5, 2002, with Real or Simulated Cedar Shingles Manufactured or Sold by Housetop Roofing and Supply Company

Installed after January 1, 1989

Please Read This Legal Notice—It May Affect Your Rights

Unless a product is well known or carries the name of the manufacturer, most consumers will not necessarily know the brand. Putting information that is too specific in the headline can be an impediment to the reader. In the above example, consumers will know if they have cedar shingles, but not necessarily if they are real or simulated and who sold or manufactured them.

2. Subheads

Use subheads to provide additional information. But get the targeting information into the main headline. For example:

If You Purchased or Used an Aerosol Inhaler

Please Read This Legal Notice—It May Affect Your Rights

Inhalers Were Manufactured or Distributed by ABC Corp., XYZ Corp., and Related Companies

In this case, the notice headline provides the essential information to grab the attention of the reader, and the subhead provides additional qualifying information that would have been too complex and confusing if used in the headline.

3. Introduction

The opening paragraphs of the summary notice should orient the reader to the litigation. Include the name of the case and court, the fact that it has been certified, the settlement status, and a general explanation of the claims and relief sought.

4. Notice Text

Use subheads and descriptive headers to break up the document into manageable sections that group related information together. In product liability cases, graphics—such as a picture of the product or the product markings or label—can help class members determine whether they have the product. These are examples of subheadings:

- Am I a Member of the Class?
- What Are My Legal Rights?
- What Is [the product]?
  - What Is Polybutylene (plastic resin) Pipe?
  - What is EIFS (Exterior Insulation & Finish System) Synthetic Stucco?

5. Contact Information

The telephone number, website, and post office box for additional information should not be buried in the text. The prominence of the contact information should be secondary only to the headline.

D. HOW SHOULD THE INFORMATION BE FORMATTED FOR EASE OF ACCESS?

1. Typography and Space

a. Type

There are two kinds of type styles—serif and sans serif. Serif has small strokes at the beginning and ending of each letter, which visually help to link the reader's eye from one letter to another, making the words and sentences easy to read. It is therefore recommended for text. Sans serif type is recommended for headlines and subheads.

An example of serif type is:	**New Century Schoolbook**
An example of sans serif type is:	**Helvetica**

b. Font Size

Font size should be at least 8 point with an ideal font size being between 10 and 12 point. However, there is variation among font types that may require adjustments. What is 12 point in one font may be equivalent to 10 point in another font.

c. Spacing

White space around the notice and between sections is important for readability. The space between lines, or "leading" (pronounced "led-ing"), is also important. A notice using a 6-point font with little leading is a disservice to class members. Once again, a summary notice is a summary, and readable type can be used when less detail is included. Elderly readers may require a larger type size and increased leading.

2. *Paragraphs and Sentences*

Paragraphs should be short. Long blocks of copy discourage reading. Sentences also should be reasonably short, not paragraph length, contrary to what is often the case in legal documents.

3. *Emphasizing Text*

Use bullets, underlining, and/or italics to emphasize key points. *Never use all upper-case type for sentences or paragraphs—it is the most difficult type to read.* Bold, italics, or initial caps are type treatments that are far more readable than all caps. For example, this is harder to read:

IF YOU ARE ONE OF THE PERSONS DESCRIBED ABOVE, YOU MAY BE A MEM-BER OF THE SETTLEMENT CLASS, AND YOU MAY BE ENTITLED TO PARTICIPATE IN AND/OR OBJECT TO THE FAIRNESS, REASONABLENESS, AND ADEQUACY OF THE PROPOSED SETTLEMENT.

Easier to read:

If You Are One of the Persons Described Above, You May Be a Member of the Settlement Class, and You May Be Entitled To Participate In and/or Object To the Fairness, Reasonableness, and Adequacy of the Proposed Settlement.

If you are one of the persons described above, you may be a member of the Settlement Class, and you may be entitled to participate in and/or object to the fairness, reasonableness, and adequacy of the proposed settlement.

If you are one of the persons described above, you may be a member of the Settlement Class, and you may be entitled to participate in and/or object to the fairness, reasonableness, and adequacy of the proposed settlement.

E. SIMPLIFYING THE LANGUAGE—WRITING IN PLAIN ENGLISH

A widespread consensus exists among plain language experts regarding the basic guidelines that make documents accessible and understandable.

1. *Use Short Sentences*

Complex sentences, especially in legal documents, may be traditional, but they are hard to understand. Many legal sentences are paragraph length. Break the definition of complex material into digestible segments and use bullets and other formatting aids.

The following is a class definition that uses all too common legal jargon:

All persons in the United States who purchased or used an aerosol inhaler manufactured or distributed by ABC Corporation, XYZ Corporation, or any of their subsidiaries or Affiliates from September 20, 1997 through July 2, 2002 and their Representatives, successors, assignees and Subrogees.

The following class definition is more readable:

Anyone who purchased or used an aerosol inhaler from September 20, 1997 through July 2, 2002 manufactured or distributed by:

- ABC Corporation,
- XYZ Corporation, or
- related representatives and companies.

To identify the brands or companies that sold these inhalers, go to www.inhaler .com for information.

2. Use Positive Language and Reduce Negatives, Particularly Double Negatives

Positive language communicates a clearer message than negative language. For example, the following two sentences communicate the same message, but the positive language sentence is easier to understand.

Negative
If you fail to timely file a claim, you will not participate in the settlement distribution.

Positive
You must file a claim by the deadline to participate in the settlement distribution.

3. Use Active Voice—Use Passive Voice Sparingly

The active voice eliminates ambiguity and requires fewer words to express a thought. The subject of the sentence performs the action rather than being acted upon.

Passive
A Fairness Hearing will be held by the court on December 12, 2002.

Active
The court will hold a Fairness Hearing on December 12, 2002.

4. Omit Superfluous Words

Pare the sentences down to the essential thought. Replace wordy phrases with simple words. For example:

Instead of	Use
in order to	*to*
subsequent to	*after*
with regard to	*about*

5. Omit Legal Jargon

Words and phrases such as *heretofore, pursuant to, null and void,* and *herein* can be replaced with *before, following, void,* and *here* without losing their meaning in most circumstances.

6. Limit Defined Terms

Sometimes a defined term can be helpful. For example, if there are multiple defendants, using the defined term "Defendants" after they have all been initially identified is simpler and can save repetition and space. In many instances, counsel incorporates defined terms originating in the settlement agreement into the long-form notice and repeats them in the summary notice, even when they are not needed. If the defined terms do not have a specific use in a particular document, do not use them.

7. Eliminate Unnecessary Details

As discussed earlier, think in terms of what the reader needs to know at the summary notice level: What is the litigation about? Am I involved? What are my rights and how do I get complete information?

8. Personalize the Notice by Using Personal Pronouns

Addressing the notice to the reader using "you," especially in the headline, communicates that the message is specifically for that reader. The question and answer format allows personalization with questions like "What Are My Legal Rights?" and "Do I Need to Take Action?"

9. Avoid Nominalization—Make Nouns into Verbs

Nominalization expresses a thought as a noun requiring a supporting verb. When possible, use a verb instead of a noun. For example: "If you made an application . . ." reads better as "If you applied . . .".

10. Eliminate Redundant Information

In a simple, well-written notice, give the information once. Avoid repeating the names of multiple defendants, the website, telephone number, or other information.

11. Use Parallel Constructions

Similar construction should be used in phrases, sentences, and lists. Use the same tense for verbs in a sentence.

The purpose of the notice is to (a) *inform* class members of the litigation, (b) *out-line* the terms of the settlement, (c) *explain* the legal rights of class members, and (d) *provide* telephone and website contact information to request the complete notice.

IV. Conclusion

The purpose of notice is to inform class members of pending litigation and their legal rights. In far too many cases, the summary and long-form notices confuse rather than inform. Plain language documents provide clear and effective communication of complex and important information to individuals with a basic education. Simple, clear writing and effective presentation ensure understanding, promote informed decision-making, and advance due process.[4]

---

4. References for this chapter include WILLIAM STRUNK, JR. & E. B. WHITE, THE ELEMENTS OF STYLE (3d ed. 1979); RICHARD C. WYDICK, PLAIN ENGLISH FOR LAWYERS 25 (4th ed. 1998); U.S. SEC. & EXCH. COMM'N, OFFICE OF INVESTOR EDUC. & ASSISTANCE, A PLAIN ENGLISH HANDBOOK: HOW TO CREATE CLEAR SEC DISCLOSURE DOCUMENTS (1998); Clarity, http://www.clarity-international.net; Northwest Territories Literacy Council, Plain Language Resources and Links, http://www.nwt.literacy.ca/resources/plainlang/resources.htm; Plain English Committee, State Bar of Michigan, http://www.michbar.org/generalinfo/plainenglish/; Plain Language Action and Information Network, http://www.plainlanguage.gov.; Plain Language Association International, http://www.plainlanguagenetwork.org/Legal/index.html; Cheryl Stephens, A Crash Course in Plain Language, http://www.plainlanguagenetwork.org/stephens/intro.html; Cheryl Stephens, What Is Really Wrong with Legal Language?, http://www.plainlanguagenetwork.org/Legal/wills.html.

REALITY CHECK: THE STATE OF NEW MEDIA OPTIONS FOR CLASS NOTICE

KATHERINE KINSELLA
MAUREEN GORMAN

I. Introduction

Reports on emerging technologies, the popularity of mobile devices, and the demise of traditional media dominate media news. Traditional advertising vehicles—television, newspapers, magazines, and radio—appear to have lost their luster. Even banner ads on the Internet, considered until recently to be a dominant new trend in advertising, are under fire.[1]

Evaluating traditional versus new media is an effort to understand, measure, and compare the effectiveness of existing and emerging options. Not surprisingly, new media itself accounts for much of the noise about the demise of traditional media, as start-up business models try to rake advertising and marketing dollars away from media Goliaths by promoting their own venues as attractive alternatives. In addition, "old" media companies are facing the business realities of shifting audiences. Among the results has been uncertainty about the degree to which these traditional choices should be used for the paid media component of class action notice programs.

What are these new media options, and how are people using them? Are new media equivalents rapidly replacing traditional media? And in the class action context, do these new options necessitate a completely different approach to media-based notice programs? This chapter provides practitioners with answers to those questions and others, to help guide future planning and development of class action notice programs.

---

1. Adapted from an article originally published in Class Action Litigation Report, 11 CLAS 187 (Feb. 26, 2010). Copyright 2010 by The Bureau of National Affairs, Inc. (800-372-1033) http://www.bna.com.

II. New Media Options: What Are They and Do They Change the Game?

Identifying class members by demographic characteristics has long been the first step in developing a media-based class action notice program.[2] A notice provider analyzes media usage and selects appropriate media based on demographics of the target audience. Understanding the media usage of the members of a specific class is paramount in designing a strategic and efficient paid media program to reach them. It is important to examine both the strengths and the weaknesses of each media choice in order to select the most appropriate methods for reaching a class. This process and methodology remain the same as new media options are introduced and gain popularity. New media options that have prompted the most interest include the Internet, mobile media, and social media.

A. INTERNET

As a media vehicle, the Internet has existed since 1994,[3] which makes it practically traditional by today's standards. Banner ads and keyword search ads (the "sponsored links" results a user sees at the top of a search engine results list) are used in the class action context in many notice programs, especially those directed at consumers.

Paid Internet advertising is included in a class action media program in cases in which demographics suggest that class members may be effectively reached through it. The notice provider places banner ads in varying sizes on individual sites, portals, and networks. A short and clear ad provides immediate connection to a case website with a single click. But with the thousands of sites that Internet users visit, it is difficult to achieve extensive reach of a target audience through placement of banner ads alone. However, through new and emerging measurement tools, the reach of banner ads can now be measured against a host of demographics, allowing the Internet reach of a paid media notice program to be included in calculations of notice adequacy and increasing the efficiency of advertising via this medium.

Virtually any class action that has an informational website can benefit from keyword search ads, although they do not contribute to the measurable reach of a notice program the way banner ads do. Every major search engine accepts paid key-

---

2. *See* Chapter 20.A, "Quantifying Notice Results in Consumer, Mass Tort, and Product Liability Class Actions—the *Daubert/Kuhmo Tire* Mandate."

3. David Weir, The First Banner Ads, Fifteen Years Later (Oct. 27, 2009), http://industry.bnet.com/media/10004796/the-first-banner-ads-fifteen-years-later/.

word links. This unique form of advertising guarantees that a site will appear near the top of the page when a user searches for targeted keyword terms. Unlike banner ads, which are delivered to specific web pages, keyword search ads require a class member to know what he or she is looking for. They are therefore not notice, but rather are cues to find the website that contains case information and notice materials. These ads are especially useful if a class action certification or settlement generates media coverage beyond paid advertising, as earned media is less likely to contain specific contact information, such as the website or toll-free telephone number, that a summary notice appearing as an advertisement does.

As a now-common component of many contemporary class action notice programs, online banner advertising has matured. However, new and exciting media forms such as mobile devices and social media are evolving. These channels have exhibited explosive growth and much interest recently. But beyond the hype, are these innovations viable for class action notice?

B. MOBILE MEDIA

Mobile devices are those that allow connectivity virtually anytime and anywhere. As a media type, "mobile" is now classified as the seventh mass media, behind print, recordings, cinema, radio, television, and the Internet.[4]

In 1983, the first mobile phone was introduced with only one single function: voice calls to communicate with another phone. Mobile phones have evolved into multifunction devices that support voice calls, text messaging or Short Message Service (SMS), multimedia messaging (MMS), games, Internet access, cameras, videos, music, Bluetooth devices, and navigational systems (GPS). The introduction of high-speed technology and smartphones (integrated phone and PDA devices) is indeed revolutionizing communication.

The prospect of using these devices for class action notice is tantalizing, but currently few options have the potential to significantly broaden the reach of a paid media program.

1. Mobile Internet

Globally, nearly 4.1 billion people have a mobile phone.[5] In the United States alone, there are 234 million mobile subscribers out of a total population of 307 million.

---

4. Michael Martin, How to Get Started with Mobile Marketing (May 6, 2010), http://searchengine land.com/how-to-get-started-with-mobile-marketing-41032.

5. Press Release, Int'l Telecomm. Union, New ITU ICT Development Index Compares 154 Countries, Northern Europe Tops ICT Developments (Mar. 2, 2009), http://www.itu.int/newsroom/press_releases/2009/07.html.

Of these subscribers, nearly 65 million, or 21 percent of the population, are active users of mobile Internet during a 30-day usage period.[6] With the growth of mobile subscribers fueled by smartphones, which speed up and simplify the mobile Internet experience, mobile Internet is forecast to reach 134 million users in the United States in 2013.[7]

Advertising opportunities to reach the mobile Internet audience include mobile web banners, content placement, and searches. These methods permit advertisers to target advertising to mobile phone users by their geographic location, demographic, day of week, and time of day. In December 2009, 62 million unique mobile users visited a mobile website. While Google Search is the leading site, the e-mail portals Yahoo!, Gmail, MSN Hotmail, and AOL Mail hold four of the other positions in the top ten mobile Internet sites. Other mobile destinations accessed via mobile Internet mirror the total Internet in rank, if not size, with social networks, news, weather, and sports sites performing well.[8]

2. Text Messaging

SMS, also known as text messaging, is a mobile communication that has taken the world by storm. This feature allows the exchange of short text messages (maximum of 160 characters) between mobile devices. In 2009, more than 1.5 trillion text messages were sent over carrier networks in the United States, more than doubling the amount from the previous year. This translates to more than 4.1 billion SMS messages being sent daily.[9]

As demonstrated by the chart below, text messaging is the most commonly used mobile data service, used by 63 percent of mobile subscribers.[10] In an average month, U.S. subscribers are actually texting 75 percent more than making phone calls.[11]

---

6. Press Release, comScore, ComScore Reports December 2009 U.S. Mobile Subscriber Market Share (Feb. 8, 2010), http://www.comscore.com/Press_Events/Press_Releases/2010/2/comScore_Reports_December_2009_U.S._Mobile_Subscriber_Market_Share.

7. EMarketer, Getting to Know the Mobile Population (Aug. 25, 2009), http://www.emarketer.com/Article.aspx?R=1007236&Ntt=getting+to+know+the+mobile+population&No=0&xsrc=article_head_sitesearchx&N=0&Ntk=basic.

8. Nielsen Mobile, Mobile Audience Mirrors Total Internet as Search, Email, Social Networking Drive Traffic (Feb. 2, 2010), http://blog.nielsen.com/nielsenwire/online_mobile/mobile-audience-mirrors-total-internet-as-search-email-social-networking-driving-traffic/.

9. Press Release, CTIA—The Wireless Ass'n, CTIA—The Wireless Association® Announces Semi-Annual Wireless Industry Survey Results (Mar. 23, 2010), http://www.ctia.org/media/press/body.cfm/prid/1936.

10. Press Release, comScore, *supra* note 6.

11. The Nielsen Co., In U.S., SMS Text Messaging Tops Mobile Phone Calling (Sept. 22, 2008), http://blog.nielsen.com/nielsenwire/online_mobile/in-us-text-messaging-tops-mobile-phone-calling/.

Mobile Content Usage
3 Months Ending December 2009 vs. 3 Months Ending September 2009
Total U.S. Age 13+

	Share (%) of U.S. Mobile Subscribers		
	Sep-09	Dec-09	Point Change
Total mobile subscribers	100.0%	100.0%	N/A
Sent text message to another phone	61.0%	63.1%	2.1
Used browser	26.0%	27.5%	1.5
Played games	21.4%	21.6%	0.2
Used downloaded apps	16.7%	17.8%	1.1
Accessed social networking site or blog	13.8%	15.9%	2.1
Listened to music on mobile phone	11.7%	12.1%	0.4

Source: comScore MobiLens

Although text messaging appears to have an extraordinary potential to reach consumers with advertising, the Telephone Consumer Protection Act[12] prohibits commercial text messaging unless the consumer has an existing commercial relationship with the advertiser or gives permission to the advertiser to text a message. This prohibition severely limits any consideration of SMS in class action notice plans, with the exception of "short code" messaging, when a consumer consents to receiving a text message. Short code involves an assigned short number that consumers may text to request further information, and has promising applications for class actions.

As has already been done in a few national consumer class actions, a publication notice may include a short code (e.g., "#12345") among the other contact options such as a toll-free number and website address. A class member may then text a keyword (e.g., "drugsettlement") to the short code and receive a text message back with the case website address (e.g., "For complete information visit www.drug settlement.com or call 1-800-123-4567."). While this procedure has the potential to quickly and easily deliver the case information directly to class members, a class member must first be aware of the case to request it. It depends on the class member seeing the summary notice or a news story in traditional media first.

How can we gauge the effectiveness of mobile media as a way of reaching consumers? Consumer surveys such as Nielsen Mobile and comScore M: Metrics, similar to those used for decades to measure traditional media, are evolving to track mobile usage. These reports currently provide insight into consumers' mobile and

---

12. 47 U.S.C. § 227.

offline media usage. They are increasingly more sophisticated in offering details on mobile usage along with behavioral, psychographic, demographic, and product usage information about mobile subscribers, allowing media planners to understand the mobile landscape.

But mobile measurement is still in the formative stages and falls short of providing a complete picture of specifically who is being reached by advertising delivered through the device. More precise electronic measurement of usage through direct device monitoring is still in the future.

C. SOCIAL MEDIA

"Social media" is an umbrella term coined to define the various online activities that bring together media technology and social interaction. Social media such as blogs and social networks offer a variety of user-generated content (UGC), from photo albums and movie reviews to comments on products and services.

In the early years of Internet development, UGC was viewed as a far-off scenario in which entire communities would spring up based on common interests. In those days, Internet users would compose thoughts and comments on their websites in weblogs (blogs). As speed and ingenuity took hold, personal blogs led to the envisioned communities: websites where people congregate to connect to friends and strangers and share everything from thoughts to images to résumés. They began as outlets for niche groups such as college students and mothers, but have ballooned into a sub-media category incorporating people of all ages and walks of life. Social media giant Facebook, for example, started in 2004 as an online community for college students, but as of January 2010 it had grown to over 100 million members in the United States alone, more than 60 percent of which are 25 or older.[13]

Overall, social media use is growing at an astonishing rate, in terms of both the number of users and the amount of time spent on the websites. As of April 2009, as noted in the chart below, users logged almost 300 million minutes on the microblogging site Twitter, compared to just 7 million in 2008. As of December 2009, the average time a U.S. user had spent on Twitter increased 368 percent from December 2008, and the site's unique users hit 18.1 million, an increase of 579 percent over December 2008.[14] Globally, at least 10 percent of all time spent on the Internet is on social media sites.[15]

---

13. Peter Corbett, Facebook Demographics and Statistics Report 2010—145% Growth in 1 Year (Jan. 4, 2010), http://www.istrategylabs.com/2010/01/facebook-demographics-and-statistics-report-2010-145-growth-in-1-year/.

14. Lance Whitney, Twitter, Facebook Use Up 82 Percent (Feb. 22, 2010), http://news.cnet.com/8301-1023_3-10457480-93.html.

15. The Nielsen Co., Global Faces and Networked Places (Mar. 9, 2009), http://blog.nielsen.com/nielsenwire/wp-content/uploads/2009/03/nielsen_globalfaces_mar09.pdf.

Top Ten Social Networking and Blog Sites Ranked by Total Minutes for April 2009 and Their Year-over-Year Percent Growth (U.S., Home and Work)

Site	Apr-08 Total Minutes (000)	Apr-09 Total Minutes (000)	Year-over-Year Percent Growth
Facebook	1,735,698	13,872,640	699
MySpace.com	7,254,645	4,973,919	–31
Blogger	448,710	582,683	30
Tagged.com	29,858	327,871	998
Twitter.com	7,865	299,836	3712
MyYearbook	131,105	268,565	105
LiveJournal	54,671	204,121	273
LinkedIn	119,636	202,407	69
SlashKey	N/A	187,687	N/A
Gaia Online	173,115	143,909	–17

Source: Press Release, Time Spent on Facebook up 700 Percent, but MySpace.com Still Tops for Video, According to Nielsen, Nielsen Online, June 2, 2009, at http://www.nielsen-online.com/pr/pr_090602.pdf.

However, extrapolating the future of individual social media networks is problematic because the wave of popularity may wane quickly. Consider, for example, that while Facebook and Twitter have grown, MySpace, which led the pack by a substantial margin in 2008, dropped off considerably in 2009 and has had to reevaluate its strategy, now focusing efforts to be a social gathering place for music interests.

In addition to social networks, blogs continue to be a growing element of social media. Among active Internet users (those who use the Internet every day or every other day) globally, 73 percent have read a blog and 36 percent think better of companies that have blogs.[16] Thirty-four percent of bloggers write about their opinions of products and brands.[17] These statistics point to why social media has seen such a meteoric rise; it taps into a consumer's emotional need to be heard by giving them the ability to comment.

As social media grows and diversifies, it will have a role to play in class action notification, but there are distinct limitations. Blogs offer opportunities to get in front of narrow, niche audiences, appealing to a specific interest or opinion. Although this is valuable in reaching a very focused audience, blogs can have uncontrolled and controversial content that can be problematic when trying to present neutral notice.

16. Universal McCann, Power to the People—Social Media Tracker Wave 3 (Mar. 2008), http://www.slideshare.net/mickstravellin/universal-mccann-international-social-media-research-wave-3.

17. Id.

While participating in blogs and social networks offers opportunities to communicate with consumers, traditional media such as television or national print publications remain the more efficient media vehicles to reach large mass consumer audiences because of the way ads are delivered. Unlike print media, where each and every reader has an opportunity to see an advertisement, the advertising on social media sites, as with all Internet websites, is delivered to one user at a time. The frequent user of the website will be the most likely to be exposed to the messages, and the most ads are delivered to the heaviest users. For a paid media notice program, sites must be selected based on their ability to reach specific target audience segments. Therefore, the cost of accumulating significant mass audiences on individual sites can be prohibitive.

However, social media—both blogs and social networks—provide interesting opportunities for nonpaid notice. Outreach to bloggers with a press release and a brief explanation of the relevance of a case to the blog's target audience can result in postings explaining the settlement and links to the case website. And social networks have preexisting defined groups that can be quite useful in distributing information about a case. For example, in *The Authors Guild, Inc. v. Google Inc.*,[18] information on the proposed settlement was provided to author and writer groups on the professional networking site LinkedIn.

Social media also offers additional avenues to drive traffic to a case website through individuals—the online equivalent of word of mouth. Many social networks such as Facebook, LinkedIn, and Digg offer ways to share links by simply adding a line of code to a settlement website. Users can click on the links to share the site with their social networks via functions such as a "newsfeed" or "local activity." As their friends and connections see the link, they will also be informed about the settlement and determine whether their rights are affected. This also serves as organic growth to the reach of sites, similar to the pass-along effect of traditional print advertising.

Advertising dollars spent on social media are growing exponentially, nearly 34 percent annually to a projected $3.1 billion by 2014.[19] With membership numbers and spending expanding so significantly, social media can play a role in certain class action notification programs that involve class members heavily engaged in online activity. But it will not be effective without the assistance of traditional media, which still provides the greatest reach of class members in consumer cases.

---

18. No. 05-8136 (S.D.N.Y., filed Sept. 20, 2005).

19. MarketingCharts.com, Forrester: Interactive Marketing to Hit $55b by 2014 (July 10, 2009), http://www.marketingcharts.com/interactive/forrester-interactive-marketing-to-hit-55b-by-2014-9744/.

III. New Media: Customizing Expanded Access to Information

New media options provide an array of choices for gathering and sharing information as well as for watching and listening to entertainment and getting news and other updates. The Internet and mobile media are increasing consumer connections to one another and to businesses trying to serve them. As a result, there are shifts in consumer behavior as media options multiply.

With these increased choices, overall media usage is predicted to reach an all time high in 2010. The U.S. Census Bureau reports the total number of hours spent outside of work with all forms of media exceeds 9.5 hours per person per day.[20] Add to this the use of the Internet at work and of mobile phones in general, and it is evident that opportunities to communicate with consumers are growing dramatically. But does this mean that new media is more effective in reaching various audiences and that traditional media is now less effective and on the verge of extinction? As it turns out, no.

IV. Traditional Media: "The Reports of My Death Are Greatly Exaggerated"

Declines in print circulation and broadcast ratings, along with the emergence of new media outlets and usage patterns, are spawning rumors about the demise of traditional media. But today, people still spend the largest share of their media time with traditional media—particularly television, which accounts for 45.8 percent of all media usage.[21] As of February 2010, 90 percent of television households subscribe to cable or some form of satellite TV,[22] meaning that viewers have hundreds of channels from which to choose. Not only are there more and better programming choices, but new devices like DVRs and smartphones give consumers access to television programs without time or place constraints, further fragmenting specific program audiences. The challenge is now how to effectively deliver advertising messages to those consumers who have the tools to avoid these messages simply by fast-forwarding past them.

But what about the much-discussed impending death of newspapers? Given the financial challenges and declining circulations, many analysts are rightly concerned about the future of the industry.[23] However, an immediate death is

---

20. U.S. CENSUS BUREAU, 2010 STATISTICAL ABSTRACT (TABLE 1094: MEDIA USAGE AND CONSUMER SPENDING: 2004 TO 2012), *available at* http://www.census.gov/compendia/statab/2010/tables/10s1094.pdf.

21. *Id.*

22. The Nielsen Co., Television Audience 2009, updated Feb. 1, 2010, at http://blog.nielsen.com/nielsenwire/wp-content/uploads/2010/04/TVA_2009-for-Wire.pdf.

23. PRICEWATERHOUSECOOPERS, MOVING INTO MULTIPLE BUSINESS MODELS: OUTLOOK FOR NEWSPAPER PUBLISHING IN THE DIGITAL AGE (2009), *available at* http://www.pwc.com/en_GX/gx/entertainment-media/pdf/

not even remotely probable given that so many consumers still turn to their daily newspaper for news and information. While newspaper readership has declined about 13 percent in the past five years, currently 50 percent of all adults still read a newspaper more than 22 times each month.[24] Newspapers remain a tangible, trusted source of information for young and old alike.[25] The heaviest users of newspapers are older adults, and many notice plans, therefore, use newspapers to reach this target audience. More than 50 percent of U.S. adults are 45 and older, and 58 percent of them still read a Sunday newspaper.[26]

Overall, even today, with audiences fragmented by the magnitude of the choices that users have online and on television, the number of readers of Sunday newspapers, approximately 57.8 million, is higher than the number of average daily visitors to any of the top 25 websites or the average number of viewers of the top 25 television shows.

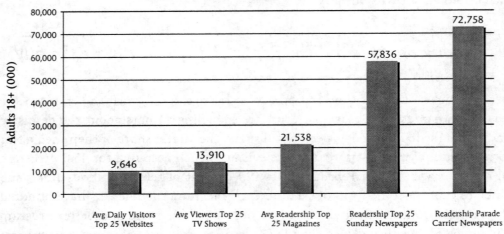

Media Audience Comparison

Source: Website, Magazines, Newspaper and Parade: MRI Doublebase 2009, Television: Nielsen Season Average 2008–2009 Prime Time Live +7

Historically, newspapers have not been as good at reaching young adults, and the biggest decline in newspaper readership is in the 24- to 44-year-old demographic, precisely the group that leads the way in embracing new media. Currently

---

NewsPaperOutlook2009.pdf.

24. Data from Fall 2009 MRI Survey. Mediamark Research & Intelligence (MRI) surveys a large sample of U.S. adults about the media they see and hear and about the products they use. Participants in the survey are identified by age, occupation, income, education, and where they live, among other things. They are asked what magazines and newspapers they read and what TV shows and cable channels they watch, and are asked questions about Internet access and radio formats. Survey data indicate the brands and products they use from among 500 categories and 6,000 consumer brands.

25. Belo Interactive, Online Credibility Survey (2004), http://www.dallasnews.com/sharedcontent/dws/spe/credibility/.

26. MRI Survey, *supra* note 24.

40 percent of this target still reads a Sunday newspaper,[27] so print advertising should continue to be used to reach them in combination with the new media options their demographic has so eagerly espoused. However, the newspaper business models must find ways to appeal to younger audiences that will grow up more comfortable with electronic than print media. Newspapers are evolving to embrace their growing online audiences and to incorporate the distribution of content through social networks and the new wave of devices such as Kindle, iPad, and Android. Time will tell if traditional media will successfully find the key to merging the old with the new.

V. Conclusion: Traditional Media Trumps New Media for Mass Reach

However dazzling, convenient, and fun we find the 24/7 connectivity and speed of the new devices and social networks, media buying is still based on the demographics of specific target audiences and the media those audiences consume. Paid media programs that must reach a wide target audience, particularly in consumer cases, continue to require traditional media components and credible audience measurement. As new media options become available, audiences' attention is divided among the rapidly multiplying media choices and it becomes more difficult for any new media source to reach a significant portion of a target audience. Media sources that provide mass reach, therefore, will become even more valuable in class action notice programs. For now, those mass-reach sources are traditional, reliably measurable media types. While people are certainly using new types of media to get their information, it will take time for their measurement metrics to mature before the courts can rely on them for reach estimates.

New media, however, has a role to play by providing a collection of niches to complement the mass audience reach of traditional media. New media can be expected to evolve in importance over time as new channels are introduced for exposing class members to notice and providing new avenues through which to respond to and access information.

New media options are numerous and growing and each one is taking a slice from other competitors. Consumers, especially younger consumers, "increasingly want their information and their entertainment in the on-demand format of online or on any mobile device"[28] and they will drive the evolution of new media and its measurement. However, even with this explosive growth, these new media types are not likely to eclipse traditional media outlets in the foreseeable future.

---

27. Id.

28. Kathryn Koegel, It's D-Day: The State of Digital Display (May 11, 2009), *available at* http://www.primaryimpact.com/blog/?p=70.

ARBITRATION AND CLASS ACTIONS

THOMAS WERTH THAGARD III
J. ETHAN MCDANIEL
ALEXANDER B. FEINBERG[1]

I. Introduction

Arbitration, as a dispute resolution procedure that quickly and informally resolves individual disputes, can be argued to justify the risk of potentially erroneous and unreviewable results. The expediency and economic efficiency of arbitration, in certain circumstances, is considered more, or at least equally, as important as obtaining a perfectly correct legal decision. To the contrary, however, class action arbitration lacks both of these justifications and offers no inherent benefits of its own.

Indeed, on its face, the consolidation of tens or hundreds of thousands of claims into a single forum that potentially lacks the due process protections of a court of law,[2] res judicata effect, the ability to demand the full faith and credit of subsequent tribunals,[3] and any meaningful appellate review[4] is tantamount to

---

1. The authors wish to give substantial credit to W. Scott Simpson of Ritchey, Simpson & Glick in Birmingham, Alabama, for his editing and input. Mr. Simpson is an Adjunct Professor of Law at Cumberland School of Law where he teaches Alternative Dispute Resolution, among other courses. Much of our exposure to and knowledge of this subject matter arises from our working relationship with Mr. Simpson.

2. While the U.S. Supreme Court has held that court-imposed class action procedures must provide absent class members due process of law (*see, e.g., Phillips Petroleum Co. v. Shutts*, 472 U.S. 797 (1985)), no class arbitration case has reached the high court where the due process issue was properly raised in arbitration and preserved for appeal.

3. Defendants who might wish to consider settling class arbitrations should be wary: the peace purchased through a class arbitration settlement may not be entitled to full faith and credit from a court of law. A subsequent court could well refuse to apply the doctrine of res judicata to the class arbitration settlement, thus allowing absent class members to file later individual cases or even another class action.

4. As shown in detail later in this chapter, appellate review grounds for arbitral proceedings under the Federal Arbitration Act, 9 U.S.C. §§ 1 *et seq.*, are extremely narrow. *Hall St. Ass'n. v. Mattel, Inc.*, 552 U.S.

jurisprudential lunacy. Neither plaintiff nor defendant—not to mention justice—is served if an arbitrator erroneously, yet permanently, decides the fate of such a vast number of claims. Yet, in defiance of good common sense, class arbitration is a reality. And, in fact, before April 27, 2010, when the U.S. Supreme Court rendered its landmark opinion in *Stolt-Nielsen S.A. v. AnimalFeeds International Corp. (Stolt)*,[5] this practice was flourishing.

In order to assist the practitioner with an understanding of this legal Frankenstein, this chapter provides an overview of the class arbitration landscape prior to *Stolt* and examines the recent *Stolt* opinion and its potential implications. Additionally, for those already in or headed to class arbitration, the chapter also discusses how class arbitration is to be conducted and when and what limited appellate review may be available. Finally, the chapter identifies and highlights some legal problems and issues that are unique to class arbitration and, as such, may not be obvious to the everyday lawyer.

II. When Is Class Arbitration Allowed, Who Decides, and How?

If an arbitration agreement expressly permits class arbitration or, alternatively, requires class actions to be brought in court, the terms of the contract should govern. The battle line is drawn, however, when an arbitration agreement is silent on the issue of class arbitration. Generally, the plaintiffs' bar takes the position that a silent arbitration agreement leaves all procedural decisions to the arbitrator, including the possible utilization of class procedures. The proponent of class arbitration argues that if the parties had intended not to allow class arbitration, they would have said so expressly. The party resisting class arbitration typically counters that involuntary or coercive class arbitration fundamentally changes the risks and benefits of the original arbitration agreement and that it never intended to resolve such high-stakes issues without the protections of actual litigation and meaningful appellate review. So how have the courts resolved this hotly contested issue?

A. THE *BAZZLE* PLURALITY ANSWERS NOTHING

1. The Issues Presented

In *Green Tree Financial Corp. v. Bazzle (Bazzle)*,[6] the U.S. Supreme Court was first presented with the issue of whether class arbitration is permissible when the governing arbitration agreement is silent as to class treatment, but the Court failed to resolve it. In *Bazzle*, two sets of consumers, the Bazzles and the Lackeys, filed

---

576, 128 S. Ct. 1396 (2008). An appeal based on legal error or the misapplication of law to facts may not be available.

    5. 559 U.S. ___. 130 S. Ct. 1758 (2010).
    6. 539 U.S. 444, 452 (2003).

separate actions in South Carolina state court against Green Tree, a commercial lender.[7] South Carolina law governed the consumers' contracts with Green Tree, neither of which expressly spoke to whether class arbitration was permissible.[8]

The Bazzles asked the state trial court to certify a class, and that class was certified, but the trial court then compelled arbitration of the class.[9] In the Lackey proceeding, the Lackeys also sought class certification in court.[10] Green Tree successfully sought to compel arbitration, and the arbitrator eventually certified a class and ultimately awarded both statutory damages and attorney fees.[11]

On appeal, the South Carolina Supreme Court ruled "(1) that the arbitration clauses are silent as to whether arbitration might take the form of class arbitration, and (2) that, in that circumstance, South Carolina law interprets the contracts as permitting class arbitration."[12] The Supreme Court of the United States granted certiorari to determine whether the decision of the South Carolina Supreme Court was consistent with the Federal Arbitration Act (FAA).[13]

2. The Fractured Plurality Decision

Despite the straightforward issue presented, the Supreme Court was not able to reach a majority consensus. Four justices—Breyer, Scalia, Souter, and Ginsburg—determined that the arbitrator, and not the court, should determine "whether the contracts forbid class arbitration."[14] In light of this conclusion, these justices opined that the decision of the South Carolina Supreme Court should be vacated and the case remanded because the courts—not the arbitrators—had made the determination, expressly or otherwise, that the arbitration agreements at issue permitted class treatment.[15]

Justice Thomas dissented on the ground that the FAA does not apply to proceedings in state courts, and he would have left undisturbed the South Carolina Supreme Court decision.[16] In his dissenting opinion, Chief Justice Rehnquist, with whom Justices O'Connor and Kennedy joined, stated the view that the FAA does not allow class arbitration where the "contracts do not by their terms [expressly] permit" it.[17] Chief Justice Rehnquist also would have held that this determination should be made by courts, as opposed to an arbitrator.[18]

---

7. *Id.* at 447–49.
8. *Id.* at 447–48.
9. *Id.* at 449.
10. *Id.*
11. *Id.*
12. *Id.* at 447.
13. *Id.; see also* 9 U.S.C. §§ 1 *et seq.*
14. *Bazzle*, 539 U.S. at 454.
15. *Id.*
16. *Id.* at 460 (Thomas, J., dissenting).
17. *Id.* at 455 (Rehnquist, J., dissenting).
18. *Id.*

Justice Stevens's concurrence, which rendered a controlling judgment of the Court, first recognized that, under South Carolina law, class arbitration is permissible if not expressly prohibited by the arbitration agreement.[19] Thus, Justice Stevens believed that remand to the South Carolina Supreme Court was unnecessary, explaining:

> The Supreme Court of South Carolina has held as a matter of state law that class-action arbitrations are permissible if not prohibited by the applicable arbitration agreement, and that the agreement between these parties is silent on the issue. There is nothing in the Federal Arbitration Act that precludes either of these determinations by the Supreme Court of South Carolina.[20]

According to Justice Stevens, the interpretation of the parties' agreement should arguably have been made in the first instance by the arbitrator, rather than the court. However, because the decision to conduct a class action arbitration was correct as a matter of law, and because the petitioner had merely challenged the merits of that decision without claiming that it was made by the wrong decision maker, there was no need to remand the case to correct that possible error.[21]

In its broadest sense, the positions of the justices in *Bazzle* can be summarized as follows: (1) four justices believed that an arbitrator, not a court, should decide whether an arbitration agreement forbids class arbitration; (2) three justices believed that the courts should decide this question, and that the FAA does not permit class arbitration unless the governing arbitration agreement expressly permits it; (3) one justice (Thomas) expressed no opinion on who should resolve this issue, but implicitly recognized that the determination should be made by a court because he would have left South Carolina's ruling undisturbed, consistent with his view that the FAA does not apply in state courts, and (4) one justice (Stevens) believed that the South Carolina Supreme Court's decision that silent arbitration agreements allow class arbitration was correct as a matter of state law and that it was unnecessary to determine who should make that decision particularly since that question was not specifically before the Court.

B. THE RESULTING JUDICIAL DISAGREEMENT OVER *BAZZLE*'S MEANING

As might have been predicted, courts trying to interpret *Bazzle* have reached drastically differing conclusions as to its precedential value and meaning. On one end of the spectrum, the Seventh Circuit, in *Employer's Insurance Co. of Wausau v. Century Indemnity Co.*,[22] observed:

---

19. *Id.* at 454–60 (Stevens, J., concurring).
20. *Id.* at 454–55 (Stevens, J., concurring).
21. *Id.* at 455–60 (Stevens, J., concurring).
22. 443 F.3d 573 (7th Cir. 2006).

Taking these two opinions together, we cannot identify a single rationale endorsed by a majority of the Court. Justice Breyer reasoned that (1) consolidation is a procedural question for the arbitrator; (2) the Supreme Court should not reach the question whether the parties' agreements forbid class arbitration; and (3) remand is required so that the arbitrators can address whether the agreements forbid class arbitration. Justice Stevens, in contrast, reasoned that (1) the South Carolina Supreme Court correctly held as a matter of state law that the parties' agreements do not forbid class arbitration; and (2) remand was not required, because the parties did not argue that the arbitrator, rather than the court, should have decided the appropriateness of class arbitration. The Justices' rationales do not overlap.[23]

As a result, the Seventh Circuit expressly declined to find that *Bazzle* requires the arbitrator to "be the first to interpret the parties' agreements to determine if they allow class certification."[24]

On the other hand, many of the federal circuit courts of appeal directly interpreted *Bazzle* to hold the exact opposite. The Second,[25] Third,[26] Fifth,[27] and Ninth[28] Circuits all construed *Bazzle* as requiring that the arbitrator make the initial determination as to whether class arbitration is allowed.[29] Moreover, other courts interpreted the *Bazzle* plurality decision even more radically, finding that *Bazzle* actually requires class arbitration when the governing arbitration agreement is completely silent on the issue. For example, the Illinois Supreme Court has held that "the United States Supreme Court held in [*Bazzle*] that class may be arbitrated when the agreement between the parties is silent on the question."[30] The Ninth Circuit also seemingly adopted this rationale, regarding *Bazzle* as "an implicit endorsement by a majority of the Court of class procedures as consistent with the Federal Arbitration Act."[31]

C. THE SUPREME COURT RESPONDS WITH *STOLT*

As shown above, *Bazzle* created far more confusion than it purported to resolve. Fortunately, however, some of the confusion generated by *Bazzle* may not persist much longer. The U.S. Supreme Court, in *Stolt*, recently tackled head-on the issue of whether the FAA permits the imposition of class action procedures in a private

---

23. *Id.* at 580.

24. *Id.* at 581.

25. *Stolt-Nielsen S.A. v. AnimalFeeds Int'l Corp.*, 548 F.3d 85, 100 (2d Cir. 2008).

26. *Certain Underwriters at Lloyd's London v. Westchester Fire Ins. Co.*, 489 F.3d 580, 585–87 & n.2 (3d Cir. 2007).

27. *Pedcor Mgmt. Co., Inc., v. Nations Personnel of Tex., Inc.*, 343 F.3d 355, 358–59 (5th Cir. 2003).

28. *Johnson v. Gruma Corp.*, 123 F. App'x 786, 788 (9th Cir. 2005).

29. The Eleventh Circuit also reached the same conclusion in an unpublished, appendix opinion with no precedential value. *Rollins, Inc. v. Garrett*, 176 F. App'x 968, 968 (11th Cir. 2006).

30. *Kinkel v. Cingular Wireless LLC*, 857 N.E.2d 250, 262 (Ill. 2006).

31. *Shroyer v. New Cingular Wireless Servs., Inc.*, 498 F.3d 976, 992 (9th Cir. 2007).

commercial arbitration where the parties' agreement to arbitrate is silent regarding class arbitration.

In *Stolt*, AnimalFeeds filed suit against Stolt-Nielsen, alleging a "global conspiracy to restrain competition in the world market for parcel tanker shipping services in violation of federal antitrust laws."[32] Based on the governing agreements between the parties, Stolt-Nielsen filed a motion to compel arbitration, which was eventually granted.[33] AnimalFeeds then filed a demand for class arbitration.[34] The arbitration panel determined that class arbitration was permissible, even though the arbitration provisions at issue were silent as to class arbitration.[35]

Stolt-Nielsen petitioned the U.S. District Court for the Southern District of New York to vacate the arbitrators' award.[36] That court granted Stolt-Nielsen's petition, holding that the arbitrators acted with manifest disregard of the law in reaching their decision that the governing arbitration agreements allowed for class arbitration when those agreements were silent as to class arbitration.[37] Animal-Feeds appealed, and the Second Circuit reversed, holding that the arbitration panel did not manifestly disregard the law in holding that class arbitration was permissible under the arbitration provisions.[38]

Stolt-Nielsen then filed a petition for a writ of certiorari with the U.S. Supreme Court, arguing that the FAA does not permit the imposition of class action procedures where the agreement is silent.[39] In so doing, the petitioners outlined the inconsistent results stemming from the fractured *Bazzle* plurality decision and invited the Court to set forth a bright-line substantive rule resolving the issue.[40] The Supreme Court ultimately granted certiorari "to decide whether imposing class arbitration on parties whose arbitration clauses are 'silent' on that issue is consistent with the Federal Arbitration Act, 9 U.S.C. § 1 et seq."[41]

The Supreme Court's majority opinion, authored by Justice Alito, began by apparently feigning surprise that *Bazzle* had "baffled" everyone and then immediately attacked the analytic approach of the arbitration panel.[42] The Court quoted

---

32. *Stolt*, 548 F.3d at 87.

33. *Id.*

34. *Id.* at 88.

35. *Id.* at 89.

36. *Id.* at 90.

37. *Id.*

38. *Id.* at 96–97.

39. Petition for Writ of Certiorari at 17–19. *Stolt-Nielsen S.A. v. AnimalFeeds Int'l Corp.*, No. 08-1198, 2009 WL 797583 (U.S. Mar. 26, 2009).

40. *Id.* at 8–15.

41. *Stolt*, 130 S. Ct. at 1764.

42. *Id.* at 1772. Justice Alito filed the majority opinion in which Chief Justice Roberts, Justice Scalia, Justice Kennedy, and Justice Thomas joined. *Id.* at 1763. Justice Ginsburg filed a dissenting opinion in which Justice Stevens and Justice Breyer joined. *Id.* at 1777. Justice Sotomayor took no part in the consideration or decision of the case.

the three grounds advanced by AnimalFeeds in support of construing the arbitration clause to permit class action arbitration:

> (a) the clause is silent on the issue of class treatment and, without express prohibition, class arbitration is permitted under *Bazzle*; (b) the clause should be construed to permit class arbitration as a matter of public policy; and (c) the clause would be unconscionable and unenforceable if it forbade class arbitration.[43]

Justice Alito noted that the arbitrators expressly rejected the first argument and said nothing about the third argument.[44] Rather, "the [arbitration] panel appears to have rested its decision on AnimalFeeds' public policy argument."[45]

The Court took direct issue with the panel's invocation and application of public policy, explaining as a threshold matter that it should have instead proceeded in the following manner:

> Because the parties agreed their agreement was "silent" in the sense that they had not reached any agreement on the issue of class arbitration, the arbitrator's proper task was to identify the rule of law that governs in that situation. Had they engaged in that undertaking, they presumably would have looked either to the FAA itself or to one of the two bodies of law that the parties claimed were governing, *i.e.*, either federal maritime law or New York law. But the panel did not consider whether the FAA provides the rule of decision in such a situation; nor did the panel attempt to determine what rule would govern under either maritime or New York law in the case of a "silent" contract.[46]

Rather than inquiring whether maritime law, New York law, or the FAA contains a default rule under which the arbitration clause may be interpreted, "the panel proceeded as if it had the authority of a common-law court to develop what it viewed as the best rule to be applied in such a situation."[47] In the majority's view, "[t]he conclusion is inescapable that the panel simply imposed its own conception of sound policy . . . and thus exceeded its powers."[48]

Having established that the arbitration panel exceeded its powers, the Court noted that it could, under section 10(b) of the FAA, either direct a rehearing by the arbitrators or decide itself the issue originally submitted to the arbitrators.[49] Justice Alito opined that directing a rehearing was not necessary since "there can be only

---

43. *Id.* at 1768.

44. *Id.*

45. *Id.*

46. *Id.*

47. *Id.* at 1769.

48. *Id.* Interestingly, although the Court did not expressly address the question of whether the manifest disregard of the law standard survived its decision in *Hall Street Associates, L.L.C. v. Mattel*, the Court nevertheless found that the panel acted with manifest disregard of the law in rendering its clause construction award. *Id.* at 1768, n.3.

49. *Id.* at 1770.

one possible outcome on the facts before" the Court.[50] In proceeding, the Court instructed that the parties and the arbitration panel had simply misread *Bazzle*.[51] Instead, "*Bazzle* did not establish the rule to be applied in deciding whether class arbitration is permitted. The decision in *Bazzle* left that question open, and we turn to it now."[52]

The court then examined the effect of the FAA on the issue, recognizing that it "imposes certain rules of fundamental importance, including the basic precept that arbitration is a matter of consent, not coercion."[53] The Court again criticized the arbitration panel's analytical approach, which incorrectly focused on whether the arbitration agreement reflected the parties' intent to *preclude* class arbitration, rather than the parties intended to *permit* it.[54] In fact, the Court found the panel's analysis as "fundamentally at war with the foundational FAA principle that arbitration is a matter of consent."[55]

Thus applying the FAA, the majority set forth the rule that *Bazzle* failed to reach: "[A] party may not be compelled under the FAA to submit to class arbitration unless there is a contractual basis for concluding the party [affirmatively] agreed to do so."[56] More specifically, Justice Alito asserted "[a]n implicit agreement to authorize class-action arbitration . . . is not a term that the arbitrator may infer solely from the fact of the parties' agreement to arbitrate."[57] This must be the case, explained the Court, because class action arbitration fundamentally "changes the nature of arbitration to such a degree that it cannot be presumed the parties consented to it by simply agreeing to submit their disputes to an arbitrator."[58] Therefore:

> consistent with our precedents emphasizing the consensual basis for arbitration, we see the question as being whether the parties agreed to authorize class arbitration. Here, where the parties stipulated that there was "no agreement" on this question, it follows that the parties cannot be compelled to submit their dispute to class arbitration.[59]

D. WHAT QUESTIONS DID *STOLT* FAIL TO ANSWER?

The Supreme Court's opinion did provide one incontrovertible answer—namely, that imposing class arbitration on parties whose arbitration clause is silent on that

---

50. *Id.*
51. *Id.* at 1772.
52. *Id.*
53. *Id.* at 1773.
54. *Id.* at 1775.
55. *Id.*
56. *Id.*
57. *Id.*
58. *Id.* Critically, this analysis is diametrically opposed to the conclusion reached by almost every single AAA arbitration panel that had ever considered the issue prior to *Stolt*.
59. *Id.* at 1776.

issue is inconsistent with the FAA in the absence of other evidence of contractual intent. Nevertheless, the opinion still fails to resolve a variety of key issues concerning class action arbitration.

First, in deciding the question of whether imposing class arbitration on parties whose arbitration clauses are silent, the majority focused primarily on party intent. Notably, however, the Supreme Court provides no direction as to what evidence must actually be shown in the way of intent. The only clear parameter offered is that an agreement to arbitrate a class cannot be inferred solely from the existence of an agreement to arbitrate individual disputes and nothing more. Rather, the Court intentionally avoids the issue in footnote 10 of the opinion, stating, "we have no occasion to decide what contractual basis may support a finding that the parties agreed to authorize class-action arbitration," and thus leaving that question to the lower courts.[60]

Second, the plaintiffs' bar will no doubt take up the Ginsburg dissent's roadmap for narrowing the scope of *Stolt*. Specifically, Justice Ginsburg argues that the majority opinion does not mention and, according to her, must not be intended to apply to "contracts of adhesion presented on a take-it-or-leave-it basis."[61] On this basis, the plaintiffs' bar will most certainly challenge whether the majority opinion applies to consumer contracts. This argument, however, is itself an inference based on "silence." The majority of the Court gave no indication that its opinion should be limited in the manner urged by Justice Ginsburg. Indeed, the age-old principles of arbitration law on which the majority based its holding have been historically and consistently applied in the context of standard-form consumer contracts.[62] As such, this argument faces tremendous obstacles.[63]

Third, *Stolt* did not answer the issue of what rule of law should be applied to interpret party intent. Presumably, courts will continue to look to ordinary state law principles to make such determinations, as they have always been directed to do. However, to the extent that existing or future state law rules conflict with the FAA "rule" of *Stolt*, it is unclear that such state laws can or will control. For example, as set forth in *Bazzle*, South Carolina law allows for class arbitration when

---

60. *Id.* at 1776, n.10.

61. *Id.* at 1783 (Ginsburg, J., dissenting).

62. *See, e.g., Mastrobuono v. Shearson Lehman Hutton, Inc.*, 514 U.S. 52, 57, 68 (1995) (cited in *Stolt* for the proposition that "we have said on numerous occasions that the central or 'primary' purpose of the FAA is to ensure that 'private agreements to arbitrate are enforced according to their terms'").

63. The U.S. Supreme Court recently remanded the Second Circuit's decision in *In re Am. Express Merchants' Litig.*, 554 F.3d 300 (2d Cir. 2009) (*American Express*) for further consideration in light of *Stolt*. *See Am. Express Co. v. Italian Colors Restaurant*, No. 08-1473, 2010 WL 1740528 (U.S. May 3, 2010). In *American Express*, the Second Circuit had previously held that a class action waiver included in an arbitration provision between cardholders and the company was unenforceable. 554 F.3d at 320. While class action waivers are the subject of another chapter in this book—*see* Chapter 22, "Class Action Wavers in Arbitration Provisions"—the *American Express* case will be one of the first cases in which the *Stolt* holding will be applied in the consumer context.

the governing arbitration agreement is silent as to class arbitration.[64] Of course, *Stolt* held that, as a matter of law under the FAA, such a result is impermissible.[65] Accordingly, it remains to be seen how state law will be developed and applied with regard to this issue.

Fourth and finally, the majority did not resolve the split of the circuits on whether arbitrators, rather than courts, should be the first to decide whether a contract permits class arbitration. *Stolt* avoids the question by noting that only four justices—and not the requisite majority—of the Court in *Bazzle* "decided that question."[66] The Court again refused to take a position, stating "we need not revisit that question here because the parties' supplemental agreement expressly assigned this issue to the arbitration panel, and no party argues that this assignment was impermissible."[67] Therefore, this issue remains unsettled.[68]

III. What Is Class Arbitration and How Does It Work?

While *Stolt* will undeniably limit the number of class arbitrations in the future, it is a stretch to say that class arbitration is completely dead. Indeed, it is quite possible that some arbitration agreements will expressly allow for class arbitration and/or some parties have already agreed, or will expressly consent, to it. Accordingly, for the benefit of practitioners, the following is a basic guide to class arbitration with the American Arbitration Association (AAA).

In the wake of *Bazzle*, the AAA promulgated the Supplementary Rules for Class Arbitration (Class Rules), under which the AAA "will administer demands for class arbitrations . . . if (1) the underlying agreement specifies that disputes arising out of the parties' agreement shall be resolved by arbitration in accordance with any of the Association's rules, and (2) the agreement is silent with respect to class claims, consolidation or joinder of claims."[69]

By taking this entrepreneurial step, the AAA has made itself a primary venue for class arbitration. As such, the vast majority of known class arbitrations follow the AAA class procedures, and most of the resulting appellate challenges appear to be decided in the context of the AAA rules. Accordingly, this section outlines the procedures for AAA administration of a class arbitration demand and appellate avenues related to the same.

---

64. *Bazzle*, 539 U.S. at 447.

65. 130 S. Ct. at 1776.

66. *Id.* at 1772.

67. *Bazzle*, 539 U.S. at 447.

68. For those parties who have adopted the American Arbitration Association's Supplementary Rules for Class Arbitration ("Class Rules") in their arbitration agreement, plaintiffs will continue to argue that the arbitrator should decide the question first. *See, e.g., Ex parte Sabrina Johnson*, 993 So. 2d 875 (Ala. 2008).

69. *Id.* It is possible that the AAA will revise this rule in response to the *Stolt* decision.

A. CLAUSE CONSTRUCTION AWARD

Rule 3 of the AAA's Class Rules requires that the arbitrator issue a clause construction award in which he or she initially determines whether a class is permissible under the contract and, presumably, under the applicable state law.[70] Rule 3 provides:

3. Construction of the Arbitration Clause

> Upon appointment, the arbitrator shall determine as a threshold matter, in a reasoned, partial final award on the construction of the arbitration clause, whether the applicable arbitration clause permits the arbitration to proceed on behalf of or against a class (the "Clause Construction Award"). The arbitrator shall stay all proceedings following the issuance of the Clause Construction Award for a period of at least 30 days to permit any party to move a court of competent jurisdiction to confirm or to vacate the Clause Construction Award. Once all parties inform the arbitrator in writing during the period of the stay that they do not intend to seek judicial review of the Clause Construction Award, or once the requisite time period expires without any party having informed the arbitrator that it has done so, the arbitrator may proceed with the arbitration on the basis stated in the Clause Construction Award. If any party informs the arbitrator within the period provided that it has sought judicial review, the arbitrator may still further stay proceedings, or some part of them, until the arbitrator is informed of the ruling of the court.[71]

Interestingly, the plaintiffs' bar always argues that the incorporation of these AAA Class Rules into an arbitration agreement is contractual evidence of the parties' intent to provide for class arbitration. It should be noted, however, the Class Rules themselves make clear that "in construing the applicable arbitration clause, the arbitrator shall not consider the existence of these Supplementary Rules, or any other AAA rules, to be a factor either in favor of or against permitting the arbitration to proceed on a class basis."[72]

It should also be noted, however, that when the governing arbitration agreement at issue incorporates AAA rules, AAA arbitrators have almost always construed the silent agreements to allow for class arbitration. Indeed, upon our last review of the AAA class arbitration docket, of 81 reported AAA clause construction awards in which the meaning of a silent arbitration agreement was determined, 78 found that class arbitration was permissible. Surely, though, *Stolt* will dramatically alter these results going forward.

Equally important to the practitioner, the Class Rules provide for a 30-day stay of further action following entry of the clause construction award to allow judicial review of the award. Despite this rule, courts have taken divergent views as

---

70. *See* AAA Supp. Rules for Class Arbs., *available at* http://www.adr.org/sp.asp?id=21936.
71. AAA Supp. Rules for Class Arbs. 3.
72. *Id.*

to whether they have subject matter jurisdiction to review these clause construction awards. For example, in *Ex parte Sabrina Johnson*, the Alabama Supreme Court allowed for such review under Class Rule 3 subsequent to an arbitrator's ruling that the arbitration agreement does or does not allow for classwide arbitration.[73] Conversely, in *Dealer Computer Services, Inc. v. Dub Herring Ford*,[74] the Sixth Circuit Court of Appeals held that a clause construction award under Class Rule 3 was not "ripe," and therefore, not subject to judicial review under the FAA.[75]

Stolt appears to have decided this issue as well, though—in favor of the AAA rules. Footnote 2 of the decision states: "[T]he [Ginsburg] dissent concludes that the question presented [the appeal of the clause construction award] is not ripe for our review. In doing so, the dissent offers no clear justification for now embracing an argument 'we necessarily considered and rejected' in granting certiorari."[76] Thereafter, the Court explains that the *Stolt* clause construction award was constitutionally ripe for review and that any question regarding prudential ripeness had been waived. Thus, while the "ripeness" door remains cracked to challenge an appeal, very little wiggle room is left.

B. CLASS CERTIFICATION

If the arbitration agreement is construed to allow for class arbitration, the next step with the AAA is class certification. Under Rule 4 of the Class Rules, the arbitrator(s) determine whether a class can be certified in arbitration as follows:

4. Class Certification

(a) Prerequisites to a Class Arbitration

If the arbitrator is satisfied that the arbitration clause permits the arbitration to proceed as a class arbitration, as provided in Rule 3, or where a court has ordered that an arbitrator determine whether a class arbitration may be maintained, the arbitrator shall determine whether the arbitration should proceed as a class arbitration. For that purpose, the arbitrator shall consider the criteria enumerated in this Rule 4 and any law or agreement of the parties the arbitrator determines applies to the arbitration. In doing so, the arbitrator shall determine whether one or more members of a class may act in the arbitration as representative parties on behalf of all members of the class described. The arbitrator shall permit a representative to do so only if each of the following conditions is met:

(1) the class is so numerous that joinder of separate arbitrations on behalf of all members is impracticable;

---

73. 993 So. 2d at 882.
74. 547 F.3d 558, 560 (6th Cir. 2008).
75. *Id.*
76. *Stolt*, 130 S. Ct. at 1767, n.2 (internal citations omitted).

(2) there are questions of law or fact common to the class;

(3) the claims or defenses of the representative parties are typical of the claims or defenses of the class;

(4) the representative parties will fairly and adequately protect the interests of the class;

(5) counsel selected to represent the class will fairly and adequately protect the interests of the class; and

(6) each class member has entered into an agreement containing an arbitration clause which is substantially similar to that signed by the class representative(s) and each of the other class members.

(b) Class Arbitrations Maintainable

An arbitration may be maintained as a class arbitration if the prerequisites of subdivision (a) are satisfied, and in addition, the arbitrator finds that the questions of law or fact common to the members of the class predominate over any questions affecting only individual members, and that a class arbitration is superior to other available methods for the fair and efficient adjudication of the controversy. The matters pertinent to the findings include:

(1) the interest of members of the class in individually controlling the prosecution or defense of separate arbitrations;

(2) the extent and nature of any other proceedings concerning the controversy already commenced by or against members of the class;

(3) the desirability or undesirability of concentrating the determination of the claims in a single arbitral forum; and

(4) the difficulties likely to be encountered in the management of a class arbitration.[77]

Pursuant to Class Rule 5, the arbitrator(s) must issue a written "class determination award" setting forth the determinations made with regard to Class Rule 4.[78]

As with the clause construction award, the arbitrator(s) must stay the arbitration for 30 days after the issuance of a class determination award, and a party may move the court to confirm or vacate the class determination award during this time.

C. RESOLUTION OF THE CLASS CLAIMS

Once a class is certified, the arbitrator(s) have the authority to approve settlements or conduct a hearing on the merits. Under Class Rule 8(a)(3), "[t]he arbitrator may approve a settlement, voluntary dismissal, or compromise that would bind

---

77. AAA Supp. Rules for Class Arbs. 4.
78. AAA Supp. Rules for Class Arbs. 5(a).

class members only after a hearing and on finding that the settlement, voluntary dismissal, or compromise is fair, reasonable, and adequate."[79] Alternatively, the arbitrator(s) can provide a final award on the merits after certification pursuant to Class Rule 7.[80] Again, it appears that either of the determinations under Rules 8(a)(3) or (7) are subject to judicial review.

IV. Special Problems in Class Arbitration

A. EXTRAORDINARILY LIMITED APPELLATE REVIEW

To the extent that the AAA makes judicial review available at the various stages of the class arbitration process, the practitioner must be aware that grounds for such review have been rendered exceedingly narrow. This is especially the case after the U.S. Supreme Court opinion in *Hall Street Associates, L.L.C. v. Mattel, Inc.* (*Hall Street*),[81] in which the Court held that parties cannot contract for expanded judicial review of arbitration awards outside those grounds set forth in the FAA at 9 U.S.C. § 10.[82]

In so doing, the Court held that the grounds for vacatur of an arbitration award set forth in 9 U.S.C. § 10 are "exclusive."[83] Under section 10, a court can vacate an arbitral award only:

(1) where the award was procured by corruption, fraud, or undue means;

(2) where there was evident partiality or corruption in the arbitrators, or either of them;

(3) where the arbitrators were guilty of misconduct in refusing to postpone the hearing, upon sufficient cause shown, or in refusing to hear evidence pertinent and material to the controversy; or of any other misbehavior by which the rights of any party have been prejudiced; or

(4) where the arbitrators exceeded their powers, or so imperfectly executed them that a mutual, final, and definite award upon the subject matter submitted was not made.[84]

In the past, courts generally recognized that an arbitrator's award could also be vacated if the award demonstrated a "manifest disregard of the law."[85] However, after the Court's decision in *Hall Street*, courts have struggled to determine

---

79. AAA Supp. Rules for Class Arbs. 8(a)(1).
80. AAA Supp. Rules for Class Arbs. 7.
81. 552 U.S. 576, 128 S. Ct. 1396.
82. *Id.* at 1401, 1403.
83. *Id.*
84. 9 U.S.C. § 10.
85. *See, e.g., Stolt*, 548 F.3d at 91.

whether "manifest disregard of the law" even survives as a ground for vacatur of an arbitration award.[86] Moreover, *Stolt* failed to resolve whether manifest disregard of the law is a permissible basis to vacate or challenge an arbitration award. Though the majority opinion appears to implicitly acknowledge the continued viability of the manifest disregard standard, the Court emphatically stated it does not "decide whether 'manifest disregard' survives our decision in *Hall Street Associates* . . . as an independent ground for review or as a judicial gloss on the enumerated grounds for vacatur set forth in 9 U.S.C. § 10."[87]

In any event, to the extent that a practitioner is able to obtain judicial review of a clause construction award, he or she must remain mindful that, absent clearly evidenced fraud or corruption, the only clear appellate ground left under the FAA is to show that the arbitrator "exceeded his powers"—a very difficult standard to meet indeed.[88]

B. MULTISTATE CLASSES AND CHOICE OF LAW[89]

Although apparently completely ignored by prior arbitration panels deciding clause construction, it is clear that, in the context of multistate or nationwide class allegations, constitutional due process concerns significantly impact any clause construction analysis.[90] Prior to *Stolt*, the various state courts and federal circuits developed diametrically opposing views on whether class arbitration is allowed under an arbitration agreement that is silent on the issue.[91] Though *Stolt* solved the issue of whether class arbitration is permitted under an arbitration agreement that is silent on the issue, as set forth above, it certainly did not resolve the issues of what contractual evidence is sufficient to prove party intent to submit to class action arbitration and what rules of law govern that intent. Since party intent will, in each instance, be governed by state law, class averments that allege a nationwide or multistate class present significant constitutional hurdles to clause construction.

Class actions, by their very nature, are distinct proceedings because the rights of many parties are litigated by proxy, by a handful of class counsel and named class representatives. Because class members' rights are vindicated or extinguished

---

86. *See id.* (collecting cases).

87. *Stolt*, 130 S. Ct. at 1768, n.3.

88. The practitioner, however, may be able to find additional bases for appellate review under the arbitration laws of the various states.

89. This section is based on the original legal analysis of Lee E. Bains, Jr. and Elizabeth Prim Formby, both of whom practice law at Maynard, Cooper & Gale, P.C. in Birmingham, Alabama.

90. For a detailed discussion of due process concerns with respect to multistate classes, *see* Chapter 24, "Multistate Class Actions and Choice of Law," and Chapter 30, "Other Due Process Challenges to the Class Device."

91. *Compare Med. Ctr. Cars, Inc. v. Smith*, 727 So. 2d 9, 20 (Ala. 1998) (classwide arbitration is not permitted absent an express agreement permitting disposition of claims on that basis) *with Bazzle*, 539 U.S. at 452 (South Carolina's contrary rule).

on a representative basis, class members are entitled to special due process protections, which are unique to class actions. In *Phillips Petroleum Co. v. Shutts (Shutts)*,[92] the U.S. Supreme Court held that whenever state law is in conflict, the due process clause and the full faith and credit clause "require[ ] 'that for a State's substantive law to be selected in a constitutionally permissible manner, that State must have a significant contact or significant aggregation of contacts, creating state interests, such that choice of its law is neither arbitrary nor fundamentally unfair.'"[93] The Supreme Court in *Shutts* warned that applying the law of one state, the forum, to a class when many of the parties did not have contacts with the forum state raised constitutional concerns.[94]

Under this reasoning, the Constitution should also prevent an arbitrator from applying the law of an unrelated state to determine whether the arbitration clause permits class arbitrations. Construing the arbitration clause without considering the law of each state where a subject contract was executed would be "arbitrary [and] fundamentally unfair."[95] This is the case because the law in force at the time the contract is made forms a part of the contract.

Thus, due process requires that the arbitrator, in the clause construction determination, undertake an analysis of the choice-of-law rules of the state in which the arbitration is venued, and then, potentially, an analysis of whether the applicable state law for each of the putative class members permits class arbitration. Obviously, satisfaction of these due process requirements could be an extremely onerous burden in the context of a nationwide class.

C. CLASSWIDE ASSENT WHEN THE GOVERNING AGREEMENT IS UNSIGNED

When a purported agreement to arbitrate is unsigned, additional problems emerge in the class arbitration context.[96] As discussed above, it is a fundamental tenet of arbitration law that "arbitration is a matter of contract and a party cannot be required to submit to arbitration any dispute which he has not agreed so to submit."[97] Indeed, "arbitrators derive their authority to resolve disputes only because the parties have agreed in advance to submit such grievances to arbitration."[98] In

---

92. 472 U.S. 797.

93. *Id.* at 818 (quoting *Allstate Ins. Co. v. Hague*, 449 U.S. 302, 312–13 (1981)).

94. *Id.* at 815–23.

95. *Id.* at 818.

96. The FAA requires arbitration agreements to be in writing, but there is no requirement of a signature. 9 U.S.C. § 2.

97. *Steelworkers v. Warrior & Gulf Navigation Co.*, 363 U.S. 574, 582 (1960).

98. *AT&T Techs., Inc. v. Commc'ns Workers of Am.*, 475 U.S. 643, 649–50 (1986).

light of these principles, many courts have refused to enforce unsigned arbitration provisions generally on the basis of lack of assent.[99]

What seems like an easy concept at first becomes remarkably complex in the class arbitration context when the governing arbitration provision is unsigned. While there is no question that the named class representatives have agreed to arbitrate under the unsigned provision because they have ratified the terms of the provision by instituting the arbitration proceedings, the issue of whether the absent putative class members have assented to arbitration is a difficult one. In such circumstances, it is clear that the arbitrator has jurisdiction over the named plaintiffs. But what about the putative class members the named plaintiffs seek to represent in arbitration—class members who did not sign the arbitration provision and who may or may not have agreed to arbitrate?[100]

Courts around the country have held that the proponent of class arbitration must demonstrate that putative class members have assented to arbitration.[101] When there is no signed arbitration provision (which, under normal circumstances,

---

99. *See, e.g., S. Energy Homes, Inc. v. Godwin*, No. 2:03CV286, 2004 U.S. Dist. LEXIS 29754 (S.D. Miss. Dec. 26, 2004) (home manufacturer could not prove assent to arbitration based on unsigned arbitration agreement in a consumer manual); *Lyles v. Pioneer Hous. Sys., Inc.*, 858 So. 2d 226, 232 (Ala. 2003) (reversing trial court's order to arbitration because the mere fact that an unsigned arbitration agreement was included in a homeowner's manual was insufficient to establish that the homeowner assented to arbitration); *S. Energy Homes, Inc. v. Hennis*, 776 So. 2d 105, 108–09 (Ala. 2000) (explaining that inclusion of an unsigned binding arbitration agreement in a consumer manual was insufficient as a matter of law to prove contract assent because there was no evidence of an offer, acceptance, consideration and mutual assent to the arbitration agreement); *S. Energy Homes, Inc. v. Kennedy*, 774 So. 2d 540, 547 (Ala. 2000) (explaining that when a factual conflict exists in connection with an unsigned arbitration agreement in a consumer manual, the trial court was entitled to find no agreement to arbitrate).

100. Indeed, even the AAA Class Rules imply that an arbitration agreement signed by the parties is a prerequisite to a class arbitration: "[Before certifying any class, the arbitrator must determine that] each class member has entered into an agreement containing an arbitration clause which is substantially similar to that *signed* by the class representative(s) and each of the other class members." AAA Supp. Rules for Class Arbs. 4(a)(6) (emphasis added).

101. *See, e.g., Blythe v. Deutsche Bank AG*, No. 04 Civ. 5867 (SAS), 2005 WL 53281, at *7 n.54 (S.D.N.Y. Jan. 7, 2005) (explaining "defendants in this action have failed to submit any evidence that all putative class members entered into identical agreements containing an arbitration clause. Thus, defendants' motion to compel arbitration and dismiss the complaint in its entirety is inappropriate with respect to the unidentified, putative class members."); *Higgs v. The Warranty Group*, No. C2-02-1092, 2007 U.S. Dist. LEXIS 50063, at *10–11 (S.D. Ohio July 11, 2007) (refusing to compel arbitration of putative class members' claims when the arbitration provision at issue was contained in a warranty because there was no evidence that the putative class members assented to arbitration); *Cross v. Maric College*, No. B184529, 2006 Cal. App. Unpub. LEXIS 5703, at *20–21 (June 29, 2006) (affirming the trial court's order refusing to compel arbitration of putative class members' claims because the party seeking to compel arbitration failed to show that the putative class members had in fact signed the agreement containing the arbitration provision); *Ex parte Green Tree Fin. Corp.*, 723 So. 2d 6, 10 (Ala. 1998) (explaining that plaintiff, the proponent of class arbitration, would have to demonstrate validity of arbitration provision for each putative class member before class arbitration could be appropriate, even when the arbitration provisions at issue were to be signed).

is proof of assent), the evidence of assent must come from the "words and conduct" of the putative class members.[102] It would seem to follow that the words and conduct of the putative class members will have to be evaluated to determine whether they have agreed to arbitrate in the first instance and to determine whether the arbitrator has jurisdiction over any such putative class members.[103]

Moreover, this analysis begs the question of who—the court or the arbitrator—decides whether the words and conduct of each putative class member have manifested assent to arbitration. Surely the task of evaluating the words and conduct of the putative class members cannot belong to the arbitrator, because he or she is without jurisdiction to do anything before the existence of the arbitration agreement between the putative class members and the respondent is established.[104]

Indeed, the *Stolt* opinion lends support for this view:

> To the extent the dissent believes that the question on which we granted certiorari is constitutionally unripe for review, we disagree. The arbitration panel's award means that petitioners must now submit to class determination proceedings before arbitrators who, if petitioners are correct, have no authority to require class arbitration absent the parties' agreement to resolve their disputes on that basis.[105]

These "legalities" are regularly brushed off by the plaintiffs' bar and AAA arbitrators (who argue that the issue can be "fixed" at the opt-out stage), but they present very real risks. Indeed, the possibility exists that an arbitrator could certify a class and reach a determination on the merits or approve a settlement, either of which may be void—or at least unenforceable as to some parties—because the arbitrator arguably never had jurisdiction in the first place. For example, a putative class member who is purportedly bound by a settlement would argue that the arbitrator in question never had jurisdiction over that putative class member because he or she never agreed to arbitrate under the unsigned arbitration provision, leading to unpredictable additional exposure to the settling respondent and no res judicata protections.

---

102. *Santos v. Gen. Dynamics Aviation Servs. Corp.*, 984 So. 2d 658, 661 (Fla. 4th Dist. Ct. App. 2008) ("[W]hen an arbitration agreement is not signed, [the court looks] to a party's words and conduct to determine whether the party assented to the agreement."); 1 THOMAS A. OEHMKE, OEHMKE COMMERCIAL ARBITRATION § 10.2 (3d ed. 2008) (when arbitration provision is unsigned, the conduct of the purported parties to the provision must be analyzed).

103. *See Ex parte Green Tree*, 723 So. 2d at 10 (explaining that plaintiff, the proponent of class arbitration, would have to demonstrate the validity of the arbitration provisions for each putative class member before class arbitration could be appropriate).

104. *AT&T Techs., Inc.*, 475 U.S. at 649–50 (explaining "arbitrators derive their authority to resolve disputes only because the parties have agreed in advance to submit such grievances to arbitration").

105. *Stolt*, 130 S. Ct. at 1767, n.2.

D. PRE-ARBITRATION MEDIATION

Additional issues emerge when the governing arbitration provision requires mediation prior to arbitration. Courts have held that when mediation is a condition precedent to any arbitration, a party cannot compel arbitration under the FAA without first attempting to mediate the dispute. In other words, there can be no arbitration until the condition precedent is satisfied. For instance, in *Kemiron Atlantic, Inc. v. Aguakem International, Inc.*,[106] the Eleventh Circuit affirmed a district court's refusal to compel arbitration because of the failure to satisfy the condition precedent of mediation:

> The FAA's policy in favor of arbitration does not operate without regard to the wishes of the contracting parties. Here, the parties agreed to conditions precedent before arbitration can take place and, by placing those conditions in the contract, the parties clearly intended to make arbitration a dispute resolution mechanism of last resort. Unanue told the court that he did not give any notice to Kemiron that he wanted to mediate the disagreement over the ferric sulfate payment. Hjersted testified that Unanue failed to provide any notice or indication that Aguakem wanted a mediation with respect to the payment dispute. Thus, neither party met the first condition required to invoke the arbitration clause in the Agreement. In fact, the record reveals that Aguakem still has not demanded any mediation or arbitration. *Because neither party requested mediation, the arbitration provision has not been activated and the FAA does not apply.*[107]

Similarly, in *Him Portland v. Devito Builders*,[108] the First Circuit Court of Appeals held that the FAA was not triggered because the parties failed to perform a mediation agreement, which was to be performed before arbitration.[109] As these courts reason, mediation must occur before arbitration because the FAA does not govern mediation.[110]

It is easy to see how a mediation provision complicates the issue of class arbitration. While the named putative class representatives may have mediated prior to invoking arbitration, it must be determined whether each putative class member has mediated his or her claims prior to arbitration. Otherwise, the arbitrator has no jurisdiction over the putative class members because the arbitrator's jurisdiction under the FAA is not triggered until the mediation process has concluded. Because

---

106. 290 F.3d 1287 (11th Cir. 2002).

107. *Id.* at 1291 (emphasis added).

108. 317 F.3d 41, 42 (1st Cir. 2003).

109. *Id.*

110. *Id.; see also Advanced Bodycare Solutions, LLC v. Thione Int'l, Inc.*, 524 F.3d 1235, 1240–41 (11th Cir. 2008) (agreement to mediate is not governed by the FAA).

the issue is jurisdictional, courts have held that the determination of whether mediation has occurred must be made by courts—not arbitrators.[111]

Thus, logically, it would seem that a named plaintiff seeking to arbitrate on behalf of a putative class should be prepared to demonstrate to a court of competent jurisdiction that each person he or she seeks to represent has mediated his or her claims prior to the commencement of arbitration on a putative class basis. While this assertion may seem impossible or impractical, any decision of a tribunal that refuses to acknowledge or deal with this issue is subject to later attack on grounds that the tribunal never had jurisdiction in the first place.

---

111. *Allen v. Apollo Group, Inc.*, No. H-04-3041, 2004 U.S. Dist. LEXIS 26750, at *27 (S.D. Tex. Nov. 9, 2004) (holding that a court, and not an arbitrator, should decide whether mediation agreement should be performed before arbitration); *Him Portland*, 317 F.3d at 42; *Kemiron*, 290 F.3d at 1291.

CLASS ACTION WAIVERS IN ARBITRATION PROVISIONS

JOSEPH B. G. FAY

THOMAS J. SULLIVAN

PAUL D. WELLER

EZRA D. CHURCH[1]

I. Introduction

Parties can agree with potential litigation defendants that they will not litigate disputes on a class basis, notwithstanding the availability of class action procedures in any forum in which a claim might be brought. The enforceability of such "class action waivers" and the legal path through which enforceability is determined have been frequent subjects of judicial decisions. For businesses selling goods or services to a large number of buyers pursuant to the terms of standardized contracts, the validity of class action waivers presents an issue of substantial importance.

Cases addressing class action waivers almost invariably arise in the context of agreements to arbitrate disputes regarding the contractual relationship between buyers and sellers. Such agreements are common in the sale of various types of financial services,[2] but may also be found in a variety of other contexts, such as telephone or television service contracts. Because the potential for class action litigation is strongly present only where there are many similarly situated entities, e.g., many buyers who engaged in similar transactions pursuant to identical or closely similar contracts, class action waivers in arbitration agreements are frequently (but not universally) found in agreements governing consumer transactions.

---

1. The authors, members of Morgan, Lewis's Class Action Working Group, would like to thank all their colleagues at Morgan, Lewis & Bockius LLP who helped them prepare this chapter.

2. See, e.g., Green Tree Fin. Corp. v. Bazzle, 539 U.S. 444 (2003).

II. The Role of Arbitration Statutes

Because class action waiver provisions generally appear in the context of arbitration agreements,[3] the enforceability of such provisions is closely intertwined with statutes governing arbitration. The most prominent of these statutes, the Federal Arbitration Act (FAA),[4] was enacted in 1925, long before the development of modern class action practice. Cases construing the FAA since that time have touched upon a number of issues, including which disputes fall within the purview of the Act, which questions must be resolved with reference to federal or state law, respectively, and who decides particular issues—the court or the arbitral body.[5] In addition to the FAA, almost all states have arbitration statutes, typically modeled in whole or in part on either the Uniform Arbitration Act of 1956 or the Uniform Arbitration Act of 2000. Although the FAA applies in both state and federal courts,[6] the reach of the FAA is necessarily somewhat limited, as a constitutional matter, to maritime transactions and contracts "evidencing a transaction involving commerce."[7] The FAA supersedes state law in these areas and, to the extent state law conflicts with the FAA, the FAA controls.

III. The Application of the Federal Arbitration Act

"[A]rbitration is simply a matter of contract between the parties; it is a way to resolve those disputes—but only those disputes—that the parties have agreed to submit to arbitration."[8] The FAA aims to "ensure judicial enforcement of privately made agreements to arbitrate."[9] The basic command of Section 2 of the FAA provides that a written arbitration provision in a covered contract (involving a maritime transaction or a transaction involving commerce) "shall be valid, irrevocable and enforceable, save upon such grounds as exist at law or in equity for the revocation of any contract."[10]

Although concisely expressed, this basic command has over the years engendered substantial confusion, which has added to the "colorful history" of the

---

3. Although rare, class action waivers do appear in other types of agreements. *See, e.g., Bonanno v. The Quizno's Franchising Co.*, No. 06-02358, 2009 WL 1068744 (D. Colo. Apr. 20, 2009) (discussing a class action waiver in the context of a franchise agreement).

4. 9 U.S.C. § 1 *et seq.*

5. *See also* Chapter 21, "Arbitration and Class Actions."

6. *See, e.g., Southland Corp. v. Keating*, 465 U.S. 1, 2 (1984).

7. 9 U.S.C. § 2.

8. *First Options of Chicago, Inc. v. Kaplan*, 514 U.S. 938, 943 (1995) (citations omitted).

9. *Dean Witter Reynolds Inc. v. Byrd*, 470 U.S. 213, 219 (1985).

10. 9 U.S.C. § 2.

FAA.[11] To put the confusion over Section 2 in context, it is helpful to review briefly the history of the FAA's development.

IV. History of the FAA

A. ARBITRATION IN THE EARLY YEARS

By the early 20th century, arbitration had become a recognized method of dispute resolution in commercial centers such as New York and Chicago, but there was no federal statute that addressed the subject.[12] Many states followed judge-made or statutory arbitration law.[13] A variety of subjects were submitted to arbitration and awards were enforceable at law and equity.[14] Arbitration was conventionally valued as a more informal and less expensive method of dispute resolution than litigation.

Despite the use of voluntary arbitration as a method of dispute resolution, the arbitration process suffered from serious weaknesses that prevented development of a generally recognized and efficient arbitration process.[15] The main weakness was that agreements to arbitrate were not generally enforceable.[16] Arbitration agreements typically did not prevent a party from breaching the agreement to seek redress before a judge instead of through arbitration.[17] Revocation was possible even during arbitration hearings, which not only deprived arbitrators of their power to make an award but also increased the costs to the litigants.[18]

Courts developed various rationales for refusing to compel arbitration. Some federal courts relied on "ouster of jurisdiction" theories to justify a refusal to enforce arbitration agreements.[19] Other federal courts simply refused to follow state arbitration law, where it existed, finding that the issue of the enforceability of arbitration agreements in federal court was governed by general federal law. A reliable method of nonjudicial dispute resolution required a federal law.

1. The Need for the FAA

The passage of the 1920 New York Arbitration Act (the New York Act)[20] marked a significant advance in arbitration law. Under the 1920 New York Act, a written agreement to arbitrate a dispute was valid, enforceable, and irrevocable, except

---

11. *Southland*, 465 U.S. at 35 (O'Connor, J., dissenting).

12. IAN R. MACNEIL, AMERICAN ARBITRATION LAW (1992) at 15 [hereinafter AMERICAN ARBITRATION LAW].

13. *Id.*

14. *Id.* at 19.

15. *Id.*

16. *Id.* at 20–21.

17. *Id.*

18. *Id.*

19. *Id.* at 22–23.

20. 1920 N.Y. Laws ch. 275, § 2.

upon such grounds as might exist at law or equity for the revocation of any contract.[21] The New York Act also provided that a party could petition the court for an order directing that arbitration proceed by giving courts authority to appoint arbitrators where a party failed to do so.[22] However, the need for a federal arbitration act, despite the New York Act, was soon brought into especially sharp focus in *Atlantic Fruit Co. v. Red Cross Line*.[23] The libelant, Atlantic Fruit Company, filed suit in federal court in admiralty to recover money from respondent Red Cross Line allegedly due under a time charter.[24] Red Cross argued that under an arbitration provision in the charter, Atlantic was required to pursue arbitration before suing in federal court.[25] The District Court for the Southern District of New York, however, refused to stay proceedings pending arbitration, holding that it would be inappropriate to apply the new New York Act.[26]

The court recognized that "[t]here was a tendency in the early common law to regard arbitration agreements with extreme disfavor as being contrary to public policy and as ousting the courts of their legitimate jurisdiction" but that there had been a shift in favor of arbitration.[27] Addressing New York law, the court found that in passing the New York Act, "the New York Legislature sought to create no new substantive right, but only to provide in its own courts a new method of procedure for enforcing existing obligations."[28] In the view of the court, arbitration statutes simply created a remedy for the enforcement of the rights created by the parties' agreement.[29] The court added that while a federal court may be required to enforce state substantive rights, "it is not within the power of the state to regulate the procedure and practice of a federal court of admiralty."[30] The court thus concluded that a stay of the proceedings was not proper under the circumstances.

The suggestion of *Atlantic Fruit* was that a federal act would be necessary if arbitration was to be available in the federal courts.[31] Proponents of arbitration, including several members of the American Bar Association (ABA), began working on drafts of model arbitration acts.

In 1921, the ABA Committee on Commerce, Trade and Commercial Law developed drafts of a proposed state arbitration act and a proposed federal act. Patterned on the New York Act, both drafts rejected revocability with respect to present and

---

21. *Id.*
22. *Id.* §§ 3–4.
23. 276 Fed. 319, 320 (S.D.N.Y. 1921).
24. *Id.*
25. *Id.*
26. *Id.* at 324.
27. *Id.* at 321.
28. *Id.* at 323.
29. *Id.*
30. *Id.*
31. AMERICAN ARBITRATION LAW, *supra* note 12, at 85.

future disputes and provided that agreements to arbitrate would be valid, enforceable, and irrevocable, save upon such grounds as exist at law or in equity for the revocation of any contract. Nevertheless, both the draft proposals were incomplete insofar as they lacked provisions for vacating or modifying awards and for witnesses and fees.[32]

In 1922, the Committee revised the draft legislation and the proposals were renamed the Uniform Act for Commercial Arbitration and the United States Arbitration Act, respectively.[33] The Committee's revisions of the draft federal act provided for, among other things, witnesses, confirmation of awards, and grounds for vacating and modifying awards. With the 1922 draft, the ABA's United States Arbitration Act "became a complete and integrated modern arbitration statute."[34] The draft underwent minor revisions in 1923 and was ready for consideration by Congress.[35]

2. The Enactment of the FAA

"One rarely finds a legislative history as unambiguous as the FAA's."[36] The draft, in the form of a bill submitted in December 1923,[37] made its way through Congress with essentially no opposition in 1924. The bill's proponents emphasized the need for arbitration to further the aims of interstate commerce.[38] The hearings emphasized that arbitration would foster the prompt and efficient resolution of disputes.[39] The bill received support from trade associations and several chambers of commerce, as well as from powerful organizations such as the American Farm Bureau Federation.[40] There was a "complete lack of opposition"[41] as it passed through Congress.

On January 24, 1924, the House Judiciary Committee issued a favorable report regarding the bill, summarizing the rationale for the bill, explaining its constitutional basis, and recommending its adoption. The report provided that "[t]he purpose of the bill is to make valid and enforceable agreements for arbitration contained in contracts involving interstate commerce or within the jurisdiction of

---

32. *Id.* at 86.

33. *Id.* at 41.

34. *Id.* at 88.

35. *Id.* at 91.

36. *Southland*, 465 U.S. at 25 (O'Connor, J., dissenting).

37. S. 1005, 68th Cong., 1st Sess. (1923); H.R. 646, 68th Cong., 1st Sess. (1923).

38. AMERICAN ARBITRATION LAW, *supra* note 12, at 92–96 (discussing testimony before joint hearings of congressional subcommittees).

39. Hearings on § 4213 and § 4214 before 41c Subcomms. of the Comms. on the Judiciary, 675th Cong. 2–3 (1924); *see also* David S. Clancy & Matthew M.K. Stein, *An Uninvited Guest: Class Arbitration and the Federal Arbitration Act's Legislative History*, 63 BUS. LAW. 55, 59–60 (Nov. 2007).

40. AMERICAN ARBITRATION LAW, *supra* note 12, at 92.

41. *Id.* at 115.

admiralty, or which may be the subject of litigation in the Federal Courts."[42] The House report explained that the bill provided a "procedure" for the enforcement of arbitration agreements based on the federal control over interstate commerce and admiralty.[43] The report also advised that "[w]hether an agreement for arbitration shall be enforced or not is a question of procedure to be determined by the law court in which the proceeding is brought and not one of substantive law to be determined by the law of the forum in which the contract is made."[44] The House report also explicitly acknowledged the work of the ABA in the drafting of the statute.[45]

On May 24, 1924, the Senate Judiciary Committee issued a favorable report on the bill subject to a few amendments. After some delays, on February 12, 1925, President Calvin Coolidge signed the act that became known as the Federal Arbitration Act.

B. THE FAA'S PROVISIONS

Section 2 is the heart of the FAA. It states the basic principle of the enforceability of arbitration agreements regarding present and future disputes. It provides that in any contract "involving commerce," a written agreement to submit an existing or future dispute to arbitration "shall be valid, irrevocable, and enforceable, save upon such grounds as exist at law or equity for the revocation of any contract."[46] This provision tracks the New York Act of 1920. The final clause of the section has become known as the "savings clause" because it has been interpreted to preserve "generally applicable contract defenses, such as fraud, duress, or unconscionability" from federal preemption.[47]

Sections 3 and 4 implement the command of Section 2 and refer explicitly to the federal courts. Section 3 provides for stay of litigation pending arbitration. It provides that in any suit pending in the federal court, either party may move to compel arbitration and that if the court determines that the dispute is subject to arbitration under a written agreement, it "shall . . . stay the trial of the action until such arbitration has been had in accordance with the terms of the agreement."[48]

Section 4 enforces agreements to arbitrate. It provides that

> a party aggrieved . . . by the alleged failure . . . of another to arbitrate under a written agreement for arbitration may petition any United States district court which,

---

42. H.R. Rep. No. 96, 68th Cong. 1st Sess. at 1–2 (1924).
43. *Id.*
44. *Id.*
45. *Id.*
46. 9 U.S.C. § 2.
47. *Doctor's Assocs., Inc. v. Casarotto*, 517 U.S. 681, 687 (1996).
48. 9 U.S.C. § 3.

save for such agreement, would have jurisdiction . . . for an order directing . . . arbitration in the manner provided for in such an agreement.[49]

If the court is "satisfied that the making of the agreement for arbitration or the failure to comply therewith is not in issue, the court shall make an order directing the parties to proceed to arbitration in accordance with the terms of the agreement."[50]

The remaining sections of the FAA supplement the first four sections. Section 5 provides for the judicial appointment of arbitrators where required.[51] Section 6 deals with application to the courts for arbitration, providing that such applications shall be governed by the rules applying to motions.[52] Section 7 supplements Section 2 by empowering arbitrators to "summon in writing any person to attend before them or any of them as a witness and in a proper case to bring with him" documents and evidence that may be relevant in the case.[53] If a witness refuses to appear, attendance may be compelled by petition to the U.S. district court for the district in which the arbitrators are sitting.[54] Section 8 relates to admiralty cases.[55] Section 9 sets forth the procedures for confirming an arbitration award.[56] Sections 10 through 13 set forth the limited grounds and procedures for modifying and vacating awards.[57] Section 14 provides that the Act does not apply to contracts made prior to January 1, 1926, and Section 15 provides that the Act of State doctrine is inapplicable. Section 16 addresses, *inter alia*, appeals from orders refusing to require arbitration.

C. JUDICIAL INTERPRETATION OF THE FAA

1. The FAA as a Procedural Device

The FAA was originally intended as a procedural device applicable only in the federal courts.[58] The "most important single factor" in understanding Congress's intention in enacting the statute "is the legal background against which it was submitted to Congress."[59] The most significant feature of that legal landscape "was the universal understanding in the period from 1922–1925 that the enforcement and non-enforcement of arbitration agreements and awards . . . were matters of

---

49. *Id.* at § 4.

50. *Id.*

51. *Id.* at § 5.

52. *Id.* at § 6.

53. *Id.* at § 7.

54. *Id.*

55. *Id.* at § 8.

56. *Id.* at § 9.

57. *Id.* at §§ 10–13.

58. AMERICAN ARBITRATION LAW, *supra* note 12, at chs. 11–12 (analyzing in detail transition of FAA as procedural device to substantive law).

59. *Id.* at 109.

remedy."[60] This "forum-remedial" nature of arbitration was a theme advanced by the ABA in the committee hearings before Congress[61] and is adopted in the House report.[62]

There is substantial evidence that the FAA was originally intended only to apply in the federal courts,[63] and none of the state court decisions that immediately followed the enactment of the FAA clearly held that the Act applied to state courts. For example, the Nebraska Supreme Court refused to apply the FAA to a contract dispute.[64] While the defendant argued that the FAA was controlling, the Nebraska court disagreed: "it is well settled in this state that a provision in a contract requiring arbitration, whether of all disputes arising under contract, or only the amount of loss or damages sustained by the parties thereto, will not be enforced . . . ."[65] The confusion over whether the FAA superseded state law continued in state courts for many years. In *Deep South Oil Co. v. Texas Gas Corp.*,[66] a Texas appeals court likewise refused to apply the FAA to a contract dispute. The court held that the FAA did not create substantive rights. Instead, the court viewed the FAA as merely a remedial or procedural statute not binding on state courts.[67]

2. The FAA as Substantive Law

In 1938, the U.S. Supreme Court decided *Erie Railroad Co. v. Tompkins*,[68] holding that federal courts sitting in diversity were bound to follow not only state statutes, but also state rules of decision that were "substantive" rather than "procedural." Following *Erie*, federal courts slowly began to transform the FAA from a procedural statute to a substantive one.[69]

In 1956, the Supreme Court in *Bernhardt v. Polygraphic Co. of America*[70] addressed the issue of whether the FAA applied to diversity of citizenship cases.[71] Disagreeing with the court of appeals over the effect of an arbitration agreement under *Erie*, the Court noted that the dispute in question involved "a right to recover that owes its existence to one of the States, not to the United States."[72] Thus, in diversity cases, the federal court is "in substance, 'only another court of the State.'"[73] The

---

60. *Id.*

61. *Id.* at 109–12.

62. *Id.* at 111.

63. *Id.*

64. *Wilson & Co. v. Fremont Cake & Meal Co.*, 43 N.W.2d 657, 665 (1950).

65. *Id.*

66. 328 S.W.2d 897, 905 (Tex. Civ. App. 1959).

67. *Id.*

68. 304 U.S. 64 (1938).

69. AMERICAN ARBITRATION LAW, *supra* note 12, at 134–40.

70. 350 U.S. 198 (1956).

71. *Id.* at 202.

72. *Id.*

73. *Id.* at 203.

Court reasoned that if a federal court allowed arbitration where the state court would not allow it, the outcome of the litigation might depend on whether the case was brought in state or federal court.[74] The Court went on to discuss the significant "substantive" differences between arbitration and an action commenced in state court.[75] Arbitration, for example, provided no right to a jury trial and a limited right of appeal.[76] Because arbitration affected the substantive rights of the parties, the Court held that if arbitration could not be compelled in state court, it could not be required in federal court.[77]

Ten years later, in *Prima Paint Corp. v. Flood & Conklin Manufacturing Co.*,[78] the Court dealt with the issue of who should resolve a claim of fraud in the inducement of a contract containing an arbitration provision in a diversity case—the court or the arbitrators.[79] Under Section 4 of the FAA, a reviewing court is directed to order arbitration once the court is satisfied that "the making of the agreement for arbitration or the failure to comply [with the arbitration agreement] is not in issue."[80] Applying the FAA, the Court adopted the position that only if a claim is for fraud in the inducement of the arbitration clause itself—an issue that goes to the making of the arbitration contract—could the federal court proceed to decide the issue, as opposed to the arbitrators.[81]

In *Southland Corp. v. Keating*,[82] the Supreme Court completed the transformation of the FAA from a procedural to a substantive statute that controlled state courts and superseded conflicting state law.[83] "In enacting § 2 of the federal Act, Congress declared a national policy favoring arbitration and withdrew the power of the states to require a judicial forum for the resolution of claims which the contracting parties agreed to resolve by arbitration."[84] Citing to its decision in *Moses H. Cone Memorial Hospital v. Mercury Construction Corp.*,[85] the Court reiterated that the FAA "'creates a body of federal substantive law' and expressly stated what was implicit in *Prima Paint*, i.e., that the substantive law the Act created was applicable in state and federal courts."[86]

---

74. *Id.*
75. *Id.*
76. *Id.* at 204–05.
77. *Id.*
78. 388 U.S. 395 (1967)
79. *Id.* at 402.
80. *Id.* at 403 (internal quotations and citation omitted).
81. *Id.* at 403–04.
82. 465 U.S. 1.
83. *Id.* at 10–17.
84. *Id.* at 10.
85. 460 U.S. 1 (1983).
86. *Id.* at 12.

V. The Enforceability of Class Action Waivers in Arbitration

A. THRESHOLD FEDERAL ISSUES

As discussed in detail below, the interpretation of the language of Section 2 of the FAA referring to "grounds . . . for the revocation of any contract" as requiring reference to state contract law has caused such law to assume great importance in analyzing the enforceability of class action waivers in arbitration. However, some overriding federal principles also shape the analysis.

First, to the extent it is contended that an agreement to arbitrate is silent as to whether class arbitration is contemplated, that threshold determination appears to be for the arbitral body rather than the court. This proposition was established in the Supreme Court's plurality opinion in *Green Tree Financial Corp. v. Bazzle.*[87] The recent explosion of class arbitration activity largely follows this decision. In *Bazzle*, the Court considered two South Carolina state court lawsuits brought by home-loan borrowers against Green Tree Financial Corporation. After successfully moving to compel arbitration in each suit, Green Tree found itself defending a class action in arbitration. The trial court confirmed multi-million-dollar class judgments against Green Tree in both actions. The Supreme Court of South Carolina affirmed the judgments, holding that "class-wide arbitration may be ordered when the arbitration agreement is silent if it would serve efficiency and equity, and would not result in prejudice."[88]

The U.S. Supreme Court vacated the decision of the Supreme Court of South Carolina and remanded the cases to the arbitrator, so that the arbitrator rather than the court could decide the issue of whether the arbitration provision permitted class arbitration.[89] In doing so, the Court did not directly address the validity of class arbitration.

Second, just as an agreement to arbitrate federal claims may be invalid if arbitration is inconsistent with the statute creating those claims, even an express waiver of the right to arbitrate claims on a class basis could be invalid if such a waiver were deemed incompatible with the underlying federal right. Courts have to date been hesitant, however, to find in federal statutes a fundamental right to pursue claims under those statutes on a classwide basis.[90]

---

87. 539 U.S. 444 (2003). Since the drafting of this chapter, the Supreme Court decided that a party may not be compelled to submit to arbitration where the agreement is silent on the issue. *See Stolt-Nielsen S.A. v. AnimalFeeds Int'l Corp.,* 559 U.S. ___, 130 S. Ct. 1758 (2010); *see also* Chapter 21, "Arbitration and Class Actions."

88. *Bazzle v. Green Tree Fin. Corp.,* 569 S.E.2d 349, 359–60 (S.C. 2002), *vacated,* 539 U.S. 444 (2003).

89. 539 U.S. at 454. *Bazzle* is a plurality opinion, and the fractured decision is difficult to apply, as evidenced by the number of varying interpretations of the federal and state courts in its wake. *See, e.g.,* Chapter 21, "Arbitration and Class Actions."

90. *See, e.g.,* Gay v. CreditInform, 511 F.3d 369 (3d Cir. 2007) (refusing to find an inherent right to pursue class claims under (*inter alia*) the Credit Repair Organizations Act, 15 U.S.C. § 1679, *et seq.*).

B. THE IMPORTANCE OF STATE LAW

As the law regarding the meaning of the FAA had evolved since 1925, the understanding of the *Erie* doctrine and the importance of class actions for damages also evolved. *Erie*'s construction of the Rules of Decision Act[91] directed federal courts resolving questions of general contract law, in most circumstances, to look to the substantive law of the state in which the federal court was situated. State courts increasingly began to see the ability to proceed on a class basis as an important substantive right, particularly where the individual claims of potential class members involved small sums. These developments have caused state contract principles and state policy regarding class actions to assume paramount importance in analyzing the validity of class action waivers.[92]

As a result of both state and federal courts often looking to state law to determine whether agreements to arbitrate are enforceable, both where the FAA applies and where it does not, the enforceability of class action waivers in agreements to arbitrate has largely become an issue subject to state-by-state analysis. Published opinions on the subject are too numerous to catalog. A majority of the states have weighed in on the subject, with varying results.

Alabama

In *Leonard v. Terminix International Company*,[93] the Alabama Supreme Court found unconscionable a class action waiver where the expense of pursuing the plaintiffs' claim greatly exceeded the claim itself. However, in *Gipson v. Cross Country Bank*,[94] a case involving claims under the Fair Credit Billing Act (FCBA),[95] a federal court applying Alabama law reached a different conclusion. Plaintiff argued that the class action waiver was both inconsistent with federal law (in that it limited remedies otherwise available under the FCBA) and unconscionable under Alabama law. The court rejected the first argument based on its determination that plaintiff had failed to demonstrate that the FCBA was intended to create a nonwaivable right to proceed on a class basis, and it rejected the second argument based on the availability of statutory costs and attorney fees under the FCBA, which the court found distinguished the claims from those asserted in *Leonard*.

---

91. 28 U.S.C. § 1652.

92. The Supreme Court has noted that in most circumstances where the enforceability of an agreement to arbitrate is at issue, "state law, whether of legislative or judicial origin, is applicable *if* that law arose to govern issues concerning the validity, revocability and enforceability of contracts generally." *Perry v. Thomas*, 482 U.S. 483, 492, n.9 (1987); *cf. First Options of Chicago, Inc. v. Kaplan*, 514 U.S. 938, 944 (1995) ("[W]hen deciding whether the parties agreed to arbitrate a certain matter (including arbitrability), courts generally . . . should apply ordinary state-law principles that govern the formation of contracts.").

93. 854 So.2d 529 (Ala. 2002).

94. 294 F. Supp. 2d 1251 (M.D. Ala. 2003), *enforced*, 354 F. Supp. 2d 1278 (M.D. Ala. 2005).

95. 15 U.S.C. § 1666(c).

Alaska

Courts in Alaska do not appear to have addressed specifically whether class action waivers in arbitration agreements are enforceable. The Supreme Court of Alaska has looked to *Restatement (Second) of Contracts* section 208 to evaluate unconscionability.[96]

Arizona

In *Cooper v. QC Financial Service, Inc.*,[97] an action removed to federal court, the court considered whether a class action waiver provision was unconscionable under Arizona law. The court approved the magistrate judge's decision that the class action waiver was procedurally and substantively unconscionable under Arizona law; it supported its decision, in part, by looking to California law and the California Supreme Court's influential decision in *Discover Bank v. Superior Court of Los Angeles*.[98] The class action waiver provision was severed, and defendant's motion to compel arbitration was granted.

Arkansas

In *Magee v. Advance America Servicing of Arkansas, Inc.*,[99] the court looked to Arkansas law to conclude that an arbitration agreement that included a class action waiver was enforceable. The agreement was not unconscionable because it was written in capital letters and bold type, providing fair notice to the plaintiffs.[100] Discussing the class action waiver, the court held that although the waiver clearly benefited the company and not the consumer, a 30-day opt-out provision and the procedural fairness of the arbitration agreement made the waiver acceptable under Arkansas law.[101]

California

The California Supreme Court's decision in *Discover Bank*[102] established a framework for determining whether class action waivers would be regarded as unconscionable, taking into account whether the waiver was found in a contract of adhesion drafted by a party with superior bargaining power, whether the disputes between the parties predictably involved small sums, and whether the party with bargaining power deliberately set out to "cheat large numbers of consumers out of individually small sums of money."[103] The application of the principles of *Dis-*

---

96. *See Vockner v. Erickson*, 712 P.2d 379 (Alaska 1986).

97. 503 F. Supp. 2d 1266 (D. Ariz. 2007).

98. 113 P.3d 1100 (Cal. 2005).

99. No. 6:08-CV-6105, 2009 WL 890991 (W.D. Ark. Apr. 1, 2009).

100. *Id.* at *8.

101. *Id.* at *9.

102. 113 P.3d 1100.

103. *See Shroyer v. New Cingular Wireless Servs., Inc.*, 498 F.3d 976, 983 (9th Cir. 2007) (construing *Discover Bank*).

cover Bank does not inevitably result in the conclusion that class action waivers are unenforceable, but many courts guided by those principles have reached that determination, noting, in particular, that under *Discover Bank* the availability of fees and costs in arbitration is not sufficient to save a class action waiver from a finding of unconscionability.

Colorado

Courts in Colorado have held that class action waivers are not unconscionable.[104] In *Ornelas v. Sonic-Denver T. Inc.*,[105] where both state and federal claims were asserted, the court reached its conclusion without specific reference to Colorado law or the law of any particular state, relying instead on various federal appellate decisions upholding class action waivers.

Connecticut

Courts applying Connecticut law do not appear to have addressed specifically the enforceability of class action waivers. However, Connecticut law of unconscionability has been applied broadly within the framework of arbitration agreements, and such an agreement may be unenforceable due to substantive unconscionability alone.[106] The court in *Williamson v. Public Storage, Inc.*[107] also noted that "an arbitration agreement may be unenforceable if it appears likely that the party seeking to vindicate legal rights will have to pay prohibitive costs."[108]

Delaware

Courts applying Delaware law hold that class action waivers are enforceable.[109] The plaintiff in *Pick v. Discover Financial Services, Inc.* brought a putative class action against a credit card company alleging Truth in Lending Act (TILA) violations.[110] Plaintiff argued that the arbitration clause was unconscionable because, among other things, it contained a class action waiver.[111] Granting the defendant's motion to compel arbitration, the court briefly reasoned that "it is generally accepted that arbitration clauses are not unconscionable because they preclude class actions."[112]

---

104. *See, e.g., Ornelas v. Sonic-Denver T, Inc.*, No. 06-CV-00253-PSF-MJW, 2007 WL 274738 (D. Colo. 2007); *Rains v. Found. Health Sys. Life & Health*, 23 P.3d 1249 (Colo. App. 2001).

105. 2007 WL 274738, at *5–8.

106. *See Williamson v. Pub. Storage, Inc.*, No. 3:03CV1242, 2004 U.S. Dist. LEXIS 3799 (D. Conn. Mar. 4, 2004).

107. *Id.* at *8 (citation omitted).

108. *Id.*

109. *See Pick v. Discover Fin. Servs., Inc.*, No. 00-935, 2001 WL 1180278, at *5 (D. Del. Sept. 28, 2001).

110. *See id.* at *1.

111. *See id.* at *1–2, 4.

112. *Id.; see also Fluke v. Cashcall, Inc.*, No. 08-5776, 2009 WL 1437593, at *4, *6–8 (E.D. Pa. May 21, 2009) ("Under Delaware law, a class-action waiver provision in an arbitration agreement is enforceable."); *Edelist v. MBNA Am. Bank*, 790 A.2d 1249 (Del. Sup. Ct. 2001) (holding that a class action waiver was not unconscionable under Delaware law).

District of Columbia

In *Szymkowicz v. DirecTV, Inc.*,[113] the U.S. District Court for the District of Columbia rejected plaintiff's unconscionability challenge to an arbitration clause that included a class action waiver. Plaintiff relied heavily on California cases hostile to class action waivers, but the court found that the presence of the waiver did not make the arbitration clause unconscionable because plaintiff could not show an absence of meaningful choice along with contract terms unreasonably favorable to one party.[114] The court also analogized to forum selection clauses, which, under the law of the district, are prima facie valid and enforced unless shown by the resisting party to be unreasonable under the circumstances.[115]

Florida

In *Sanders v. Comcast Cable Holdings, LLC*,[116] the U.S. District Court for the Middle District of Florida concluded that an arbitration clause that barred class actions was neither procedurally nor substantively unconscionable under Florida law.[117] Although merely mailed to plaintiff with the monthly cable bills, the class action waiver was not procedurally unconscionable because it appeared in all capital letters and on the third page of the arbitration notice, and plaintiff could opt out within 30 days without adverse consequences.[118] The court also found that the particular facts and circumstances of the case, including the fact that attorney fees were available to prevailing plaintiffs under applicable Florida law, demonstrated that the clause was not substantively unconscionable.[119]

Georgia

Courts applying Georgia law will closely examine class action waivers for unconscionability. In *Jenkins v. First American Cash Advance of Georgia, LLC*,[120] the Eleventh Circuit reversed a district court and held that under Georgia law, a class action waiver in an arbitration agreement was not unconscionable because plaintiff's attorney fees were recoverable such that the plaintiff could vindicate his rights in arbitration.[121] The Eleventh Circuit reached a contrary result in *Dale v. Comcast Corp.*[122] In *Dale*, the court found that under Georgia law, the arbitration agreement was unconscionable, concluding that the unavailability of attorney fees under law applicable in the case made the class action waiver a bar to vindication

---

113.   No. 07-0581, 2007 WL 1424652, at *2–3 (D.D.C. May 9, 2007).
114.   *Id.* at *1–2.
115.   *Id.* at *2.
116.   No. 3:07-CV-918-J-33HTS, 2008 U.S. Dist. LEXIS 2632 (M.D. Fla. Jan. 14, 2008).
117.   *Id.* at *19, *38.
118.   *Id.* at *21.
119.   *Id.* at *32.
120.   400 F.3d 868 (11th Cir. 2005).
121.   *Id.* at 878.
122.   498 F.3d 1216 (11th Cir. 2007).

of plaintiff's claims.[123] The court stated that the enforceability of a class action waiver in an arbitration agreement should be made on a case-by-case basis, and courts should consider

> the fairness of the provisions, the cost to an individual plaintiff of vindicating the claim when compared to the plaintiff's potential recovery, the ability to recover attorney's fees and other costs and thus obtain legal representation to prosecute the underlying claim, the practical effect the waiver will have on a company's ability to engage in unchecked market behavior, and other related public policy concerns.[124]

Hawaii

Courts applying Hawaii law do not appear to have addressed the enforceability of class action waivers. The District Court for the District of Hawaii, in *Branco v. Northwest Bank Minnesota*,[125] held that an arbitration provision was not unconscionable. The circumstances surrounding the agreement did not involve oppression or surprise necessary to find procedural unconscionability.[126] The agreement also did not have "unfair terms that are unreasonably harsh or that favor one of the parties more than should reasonably be expected."[127] Although not applicable to the case before it, the court did note that arbitration agreements that contain provisions "that deprive a party of a statutory right" are unenforceable.[128]

Idaho

Although there do not appear to be any cases addressing class action waivers under Idaho law, the Supreme Court of Idaho has addressed unconscionability in the context of an arbitration clause in an insurance contract.[129] The court held that an arbitration clause in a health insurance policy was not unconscionable because there was no evidence that plaintiff was denied the opportunity to review the policy before applying for insurance coverage and the arbitration clause was not hidden in the terms of the contract.[130] The court also reasoned that the high cost of arbitration was not a basis for invalidating the arbitration agreement, noting that plaintiff would be entitled to attorney fees if she prevailed and expressing skepticism that cost could ever be a proper basis to invalidate an agreement to arbitrate.[131]

---

123. *Id.* at 1222.
124. *Id.* at 1224.
125. 381 F. Supp. 2d 1274 (D. Haw. 2005).
126. *Id.* at 1280.
127. *Id.*
128. *Id.* at 1281.
129. *See Lovey v. Regence Blueshield of Idaho*, 72 P.3d 877 (Idaho 2003).
130. *Id.* at 884.
131. *Id.* at 885.

Illinois

In *Kinkel v. Cingular Wireless LLC*,[132] the Illinois Supreme Court held that an arbitration provision was enforceable, but that a class action waiver included in the provision was unconscionable and severable. The class action waiver was unconscionable "because it is contained in a contract of adhesion that fails to inform the customer of the cost to her of arbitration, and that does not provide a cost-effective mechanism for individual consumers to obtain a remedy for the specific injury alleged in either a judicial or an arbitral form."[133] The court expressly noted that it was not announcing a per se rule against class action waivers, but was requiring a "totality of the circumstances" approach under which it would examine, among other things, the adhesive nature of the agreement, whether the relevant language was conspicuous, the cost of arbitration, the nature of the underlying claim, and alternative venues for relief.[134]

Indiana

In *Furgason v. McKenzie Check Advance of Indiana, Inc.*,[135] the U.S. District Court for the Southern District of Indiana held that an arbitration provision was enforceable, but declined to decide whether class arbitration was required by the agreement.[136] The arbitration provision at issue made reference to class treatment of disputes, but was ultimately ambiguous as to whether class arbitration was permissible.[137] Absent an express provision allowing treatment of disputes, the court could not order class arbitration.[138] The court discussed class action waivers briefly in dicta and expressed skepticism about their enforceability, noting that although class action waivers are not unconscionable on their face, they will frequently deprive plaintiffs of the ability to vindicate their rights.[139]

Iowa

Although there do not appear to be any cases addressing class action waivers under Iowa law, courts considering Iowa law have applied unconscionability rules to arbitration agreements. In *Faber v. Menard*,[140] the Eighth Circuit recognized five factors relevant to determining if an agreement is unconscionable under Iowa law: (1) assent; (2) unfair surprise; (3) notice; (4) disparity of bargaining power; and (5) substantive unfairness.[141] Although the arbitration agreement was acceptable

---

132. 857 N.E.2d 250 (Ill. 2006).
133. *Id.* at 278.
134. *Id.* at 265–75, 278.
135. No. IP00-121-C, 2001 U.S. Dist. LEXIS 2725 (S.D. Ind. Jan. 3, 2001).
136. *Id.* at *32–36.
137. *Id.*
138. *Id.* at *32 (citing *Champ v. Siegel Trading Co.*, 55 F.3d 269, 276–77 (7th Cir. 1995)).
139. *Id.* at *35.
140. 367 F.3d 1048 (8th Cir. 2004).
141. *Id.* at 1053 (citing *Home Fed. Sav. & Loan Ass'n v. Campney*, 357 N.W.2d 613, 618 (Iowa 1984)).

under the first four factors, the court was troubled by the potential substantive unfairness of a fee-splitting provision.[142] The court held that such a provision "may be unconscionable if information specific to the circumstances indicates that fees are cost-prohibitive and preclude the vindication of statutory rights in an arbitral forum."[143] It remanded the case for a factual determination regarding the unconscionability of the fee-splitting provision.[144]

Kansas

In *Wilson v. Mike Steven Motors, Inc.*,[145] the court ruled that an arbitration clause containing a class action waiver was enforceable because it did not preclude vindication of statutory rights under the Kansas Consumer Protection Act. In particular, the court found that plaintiff's argument that the waiver would discourage him from pursing the claim was disingenuous because plaintiff had not originally filed the case as a class action proceeding.[146] The court also held that, in light of Section 2 of the FAA, "[it saw] no way in which a judicially declared public policy prohibition could withstand federal preemption."[147]

Kentucky

In *Eaves-Leanos v. Assurant*,[148] the U.S. District Court for the Western District of Kentucky found that under Kentucky law, an arbitration agreement containing a class action waiver was not procedurally unconscionable where the consumer failed to opt out of the agreement when given the opportunity and the terms of the agreement were included with the credit card billing statements.[149] In addition, the class action waiver did not render the arbitration agreement substantively unconscionable because the cost of arbitrating the claim on an individual basis was not prohibitive.[150]

Louisiana

In *Iberia Credit Bureau Inc. v. Cingular Wireless LLC*,[151] the Fifth Circuit held that an arbitration provision containing a class action waiver was enforceable under Louisiana law. The class action waiver was not unconscionable because the statute under which plaintiffs brought their claim, the Louisiana Unfair Trade Practices

---

142. *Id.*

143. *Id.*

144. *Id.* at 1055.

145. 111 P.3d 1076 (Kan. Ct. App. 2005) (unpublished table decision).

146. *Id.* at *7.

147. *Id.*

148. No. 3:07-CV-18, 2008 U.S. Dist. LEXIS 1460 (W.D. Ky. Jan. 8, 2008).

149. *Id.* at *21.

150. *Id.* at *22.

151. 379 F.3d 159 (5th Cir. 2004).

Act (LUTPA), did not allow for class actions.[152] Moreover, a LUTPA provision allowing the state attorney general to sue on behalf of consumers demonstrated that "the arbitration clause does not leave plaintiffs without remedies or so oppress them as to rise to the level of unconscionability."[153]

Maine

It does not appear that any courts have addressed class action waivers under the law of Maine.

Maryland

"Arbitration provisions providing for the waiver of class actions are routinely enforced in Maryland."[154] In *Walther v. Sovereign Bank*, the Court of Appeals of Maryland (Maryland's highest court) held that a class waiver provision did not render an arbitration agreement unconscionable.[155] The court reasoned that the parties "freely signed" the loan agreement containing the arbitration clause and that the "class action provision was conspicuously presented as part of the arbitration clause."[156] Moreover, state and federal policies in favor of arbitration outweighed the fact that the arbitration agreement may have been somewhat one-sided.[157]

Massachusetts

In *Skirchak v. Dynamics Research Corp.*, the First Circuit held that a class action waiver was invalid under Massachusetts law.[158] Although recognizing that the question of whether a class action is permitted in arbitration is a question of contract interpretation that should be left to an arbitrator, the court nevertheless decided the question because both parties requested that it do so.[159] The court examined the "setting, purpose, and effect" of the agreement and found that it was unconscionable because it was merely included in an e-mail to plaintiff and lacked prominence and clarity to assure that it was knowing and voluntary.[160] Moreover, the state's "statutorily created interest in class actions" was sufficiently strong that the waiver would result in oppression and unfair surprise to the disadvantaged

---

152. *Id.* at 175. *But see Shady Grove Orthopedic Assocs. v. Allstate Ins. Co.*, ___ U.S. ___, 130 S. Ct. 1431 (2010).

153. *Iberia Credit Bureau*, 379 F.3d at 175.

154. *See In re Jamster Mktg. Litig.*, No. 05CV0819 JM(CAB), 2008 WL 4858506, at *4 (S.D. Cal. Nov. 10, 2008) (citing *Snowden v. Checkpoint Check Cashing*, 290 F.3d 631 (4th Cir. 2002)); *Walther v. Sovereign Bank*, 872 A.2d 735 (Md. 2005); *Doyle v. Fin. Am.*, 918 A.2d 1266 (Md. Ct. Spec. App. 2007).

155. 872 A.2d at 751.

156. *Id.*

157. *See id.*

158. 508 F.3d 49 (1st Cir. 2007). *See also Feeney v. Dell, Inc.*, 908 N.E.2d 753 (Mass. 2009) (holding that a class action waiver was unenforceable in a case brought under the Massachusetts Consumer Protection Act).

159. *Skirchak*, 508 F.3d at 56 (citing *Bazzle*, 539 U.S. 444).

160. *Id.*

party.[161] Rejecting California's presumption against class action waivers, the court reiterated the fact-dependent nature behind findings of unconscionability under Massachusetts law.[162] The court found that the waiver could be severed, and the parties were sent to arbitration.[163]

Michigan

In *Adler v. Dell, Inc.*,[164] a court rejected the plaintiff's unconscionability challenge to an arbitration provision containing a class action waiver because plaintiff was provided with the terms of the agreement on several occasions, was a lawyer rather than an unsophisticated customer, had many options for purchase, and could not show that the costs of arbitration were prohibitive.[165]

Minnesota

Minnesota courts apparently have not directly addressed the unconscionability of a class action waiver in an arbitration clause.[166] However, courts have applied Minnesota's unconscionability rules to arbitration clauses more generally. In *Siebert v. Amateur Athletic Union of the U.S., Inc.*, the U.S. District Court for the District of Minnesota held that an arbitration clause was not unconscionable under Minnesota law—it was not a contract "such as no man in his senses and not under delusion would make on the one hand, and as no honest and fair man would accept on the other."[167] The court did indicate that "an arbitration clause which imposes too heavy a financial burden may be unconscionable," citing as relevant considerations arbitration costs and plaintiffs' financial ability to pay them.[168]

Mississippi

There appear to be no cases addressing the enforceability of class action waivers under Mississippi law. However, the Mississippi Supreme Court has applied the doctrine of unconscionability to arbitration provisions in *Equifirst Corp. v. Jackson*,[169] where the court recognized that Mississippi law will invalidate arbitration agreements that are either procedurally or substantively unconscionable.[170] Rejecting

---

161. *Id.* at 60.

162. *Id.* at 61.

163. *Id.* at 62.

164. No. 08-CV-13170, 2008 WL 5351042 (E.D. Mich. Dec. 18, 2008).

165. *Id.* at *32–34; *see also Francis v. AT&T Mobility LLC*, No. 07-CV-14921, 2009 U.S. Dist. LEXIS 12578, at *27–28 (E.D. Mich. Feb. 18, 2009) (citing *Adler* and finding that a class action waiver was not substantively unconscionable).

166. *See McGinnis v. T-Mobile USA, Inc.*, No. C08-106Z, 2008 U.S. Dist. LEXIS 65779, at *14 (W.D. Wash. Oct. 30, 2008) ("[The] parties have cited no Minnesota cases where the court has ruled on the unconscionability of a class action waiver in an arbitration clause.").

167. 422 F. Supp. 2d 1033, 1041 (D. Minn. 2006).

168. *Id.*

169. 920 So. 2d 458, 463–64 (Miss. 2006).

170. *Id.* at 463–64.

plaintiff's unconscionability claims, the court determined that plaintiffs' lack of awareness concerning the arbitration provision was not dispositive, considering their burden to read the agreement they signed and the fact that the arbitration agreement was conspicuous and clear.[171]

Missouri

Missouri law will enforce class action waivers if they are not procedurally and substantively unconscionable. In *Pleasants v. American Express Company*,[172] the Eighth Circuit held that a class action waiver was enforceable against a plaintiff bringing claims under TILA.[173] The court held that the class action waiver was not substantively or procedurally unconscionable under the circumstances.[174] The waiver was presented in conspicuous all-caps font.[175] Moreover, the plaintiff could vindicate her rights without the class action mechanism because costs and attorney fees could be awarded under TILA's remedial provision.[176]

Montana

There appear to be no cases applying Montana law to class action waivers. In *Ticknor v. Choice Hotels International, Inc.*,[177] the Ninth Circuit applied Montana contract law to an arbitration clause included in a franchise agreement. Under Montana law, a court must decide whether the contract is one of adhesion, and if it is, "the provision will not be enforced against the weaker contracting party if it is (1) not within the party's reasonable expectations, or (2) if within those expectations, it is unduly oppressive, unconscionable, or against public policy."[178] The Ninth Circuit found that the arbitration agreement was unconscionable, relying principally on the fact that the agreement unequally burdened the "weaker party," requiring plaintiff to submit claims to arbitration while allowing the defendant to bring claims in federal or state court.[179]

Nebraska

Limited authority on class action waivers under Nebraska law indicates that courts will likely enforce waivers that are not procedurally and substantively unconscionable. In *Schreiner v. Credit Advisors, Inc.*,[180] the court discussed the issue in the process of determining that an arbitration agreement was enforceable. Although the

---

171. *Id.*
172. 541 F.3d 853 (8th Cir. 2008).
173. *Id.* at 855.
174. *Id.* at 858–59.
175. *Id.*
176. *Id.*
177. 265 F.3d 931 (9th Cir. 2001).
178. *Id.* at 939.
179. *Id.* at 940.
180. No. 8:07CV78, 2007 WL 2904098 (D. Neb. Oct. 2, 2007).

agreement was silent on the issue, plaintiff argued that arbitration would improperly preclude a class action.[181] The court held that where an arbitration agreement is silent on class actions, the question is for the arbitrator to decide.[182] In dicta, the court suggested that if an express class action waiver existed, it would likely be enforced so long as it was clear and easy to read, and the cost of arbitration was not so high as to prevent the plaintiff from vindicating his rights.[183]

Nevada

The U.S. District Court for the Central District of California, in *Lux v. Good Guys, Inc.*,[184] held that an arbitration agreement and class action waiver were not unconscionable under Nevada law. Noting that Nevada law will not invalidate contracts unless they are both procedurally and substantively unconscionable and emphasizing that "adhesion contracts are not per se unenforceable," the court found that plaintiff "had a meaningful opportunity to agree to the terms of the agreement," and there was "no evidence of oppression or surprise to support a finding of procedural unconscionability."[185] Moreover, when viewed in the context of the entire agreement, the class action waiver was not so one-sided that it was substantively unconscionable.[186]

New Hampshire

It appears there are no cases addressing class action waivers under New Hampshire law.

New Jersey

Courts applying New Jersey law will examine class action waivers under a multi-factor analysis.[187] Although the appellate court in *Homa v. American Express Co.*[188] remanded for a determination of whether the class action waiver at issue was unconscionable, the court listed the following factors as relevant to the determination: the public interest in the class action as a mechanism for consumers to pursue statutory rights, whether the waiver is in an adhesive contract, whether the setting is such that potential claims will generally involve small damage amounts, the parties' relative bargaining positions, a consumer's ability to obtain representation, the lawsuit's complexity, and the availability of attorney fees and statutory multipliers.

---

181. *Id.* at *7.
182. *Id.*
183. *Id.* at *7–8.
184. No. SACV 05-300, 2005 U.S. Dist. LEXIS 35567 (C.D. Cal. June 27, 2005).
185. *Id.* at *4–5.
186. *Id.* at *5.
187. *See Homa v. Am. Express Co.*, 558 F.3d 225, 231 (3d Cir. 2009).
188. *Id.* at 228–31 (citing *Muhammad v. County Bank of Rehoboth Beach*, 912 A.2d 88 (N.J. 2006); *Delta Funding Corp. v. Harris*, 912 A.2d 104, 115 (N.J. 2006)).

New Mexico

The New Mexico Uniform Arbitration Act provides that arbitration clauses waiving class actions are unenforceable.[189] However, the New Mexico Supreme Court has suggested that Section 2 of the FAA may preempt the statute.[190] Independent of the statutory provision, the New Mexico Supreme Court has held that class action waivers are unconscionable, at least in cases where the plaintiff seeks a small damages award.[191] The court in *Fiser v. Dell Computer Corp.*[192] reasoned that a class action waiver is substantively unconscionable because "[b]y preventing customers with small claims from attempting class relief and thereby circumscribing their only economically efficient means for redress, Defendant's class action ban exculpates the company from wrongdoing." Although the arbitration agreement was not procedurally unconscionable, the court's finding was justified given "such an overwhelming showing of substantive unconscionability."[193] Because the waiver was not severable, the entire arbitration provision was unenforceable.[194]

New York

Under the law of New York, courts will presume that class action waivers are enforceable.[195]

North Carolina

In *Tillman v. Commercial Credit Loans, Inc.*,[196] the North Carolina Supreme Court found that an arbitration agreement was unenforceable, based in part on an unconscionable class action waiver.[197] The court noted that the class action waiver contained within the arbitration agreement "affect[ed] the unconscionability analysis in two specific ways."[198] First, the class action waiver "contribute[d] to the financial inaccessibility of the arbitral forum because it deter[red] potential plaintiffs from bringing and attorneys from taking cases with low damage amounts in the

---

189. *See* N.M. STAT. ANN. § 44-7A-5 (West 2008).

190. *See Fiser v. Dell Computer Corp.*, 188 P.3d 1215, 1219 (N.M. 2008).

191. *See id.* at 1218–22.

192. *Id.* at 1221.

193. *Id.*

194. *Id.* at 1222.

195. *See Nayal v. HIP Network Servs. IPA, Inc.*, No. 08 Civ. 10170, 2009 WL 1560187, at *6 (S.D.N.Y. May 28, 2009) ("[C]ourts applying New York law, however, have uniformly held that class action waivers are not unconscionable" (providing multiple citations to state cases)); *Ranieri v. Bell Atl. Mobile*, 304 A.D.2d 353 (N.Y. App. Div. 2003) ("[G]iven the strong public policy favoring arbitration and the absence of a commensurate policy favoring class actions, we are in accord with authorities holding that a contractual proscription against class actions, such as contained in the Agreements, is neither unconscionable nor violative of public policy." (citations omitted)).

196. 655 S.E.2d 362, 370 (N.C. 2008).

197. *See id.* at 373.

198. *See id.*

face of large costs that cannot be shared with other plaintiffs."[199] Second, the class action waiver contributed to the overall one-sidedness of the arbitration agreement, as the right to pursue class actions would benefit only plaintiffs.[200] Thus, the court held that "the provisions of the arbitration clause, taken together"—and including the class action waiver—"render[ed] [the arbitration clause] substantively unconscionable because the provisions [did] not provide plaintiffs with a forum in which they [could] effectively vindicate their rights."[201]

North Dakota

Courts applying North Dakota law will enforce class action waivers so long as they are not both procedurally and substantively unconscionable. In *Strand v. U.S. Bank National Association ND*,[202] the Supreme Court of North Dakota determined that a class action waiver in an arbitration agreement was valid. Although the credit card company's inclusion of the waiver in a "bill stuffer" included with the customer's monthly statement was procedurally unconscionable, the agreement was not substantively unconscionable because, the court concluded, class actions are a procedural right and not a substantive remedy—substantive rights such as fees and costs would still be available in arbitration.[203] Because the arbitration agreement provided for advancement of fees and costs and an award of attorney fees, the court found that enforcement of the class action waiver would not leave plaintiff without an effective remedy.[204]

Ohio

In *Howard v. Wells Fargo Minnesota*,[205] the U.S. District Court for the Northern District of Ohio rejected a plaintiff's challenge to an arbitration agreement containing a class action waiver, holding that the plaintiff had not satisfied her burden of showing that the arbitration agreement, including the class action waiver, "was so unfair or one-sided as to be adhesive and unconscionable."[206] The court disagreed with plaintiff's argument that the waiver was unconscionable because "potential litigants and their lawyers would be discouraged from pursuing their statutory rights individually because their costs would exceed the remedy."[207] Distinguishing the case from a costly antitrust action, the court found that although the statutory damages available to the plaintiff were only a few hundred dollars and there was no provision for attorney fees, the arbitration agreement had an

---

199. *Id.*
200. *See id.*
201. *Id.*
202. 693 N.W.2d 918 (N.D. 2005).
203. *Id.* at 927.
204. *Id.*
205. No. 1:06CV2821, 2007 U.S. Dist. LEXIS 70099 (N.D. Ohio Sept. 21, 2007).
206. *Id.* at *12.
207. *Id.* at *13–14.

exception that allowed her to pursue her rights in small claims court and avoid prohibitive costs.[208]

Oklahoma

In 2006, Oklahoma enacted legislation barring enforcement of class action waivers in the arbitration context.[209] The statute itself only applies "to the extent permitted by federal law."[210] In a case predating the statute, the U.S. District Court for the Eastern District of Oklahoma held that a class action waiver contained in an arbitration provision was not unconscionable.[211] The court provided little analysis of the issue, simply noting that such provisions are "a common feature of consumer arbitration agreements, and numerous courts have recognized that they are valid and fully enforceable."[212]

Oregon

In *Chalk v. T-Mobile USA, Inc.*,[213] the Ninth Circuit applied Oregon law and held that a class action waiver was unconscionable.[214] Although not procedurally unconscionable, the court concluded that the provision was substantively unconscionable based upon Oregon state court cases indicating that class action waivers involving small claims are impermissible.[215] The class action waiver prevented individuals from vindicating their rights, because the small value of the individual claims covered in the arbitration agreement created a disincentive to litigate separately.[216] The court also reasoned that the provision was inherently one-sided or unilateral in effect because "[i]t [could] hardly be imagined that T-Mobile or its suppliers would ever want or need to bring a class action against T-Mobile's customers."[217] Because the arbitration agreement prohibited severance of the waiver provision, the entire agreement was unenforceable.[218]

Pennsylvania

In *Gay v. CreditInform*,[219] the Third Circuit addressed, *inter alia*, whether class action waiver provisions were enforceable when viewed under Pennsylvania law. Plaintiff Gay brought an action in the Eastern District of Pennsylvania claiming

---

208. *Id.*
209. *See* OKLA. STAT. ANN. tit. 12, § 1880(B) (West 2009).
210. *Id.*
211. *See Edwards v. Blockbuster, Inc.*, 400 F. Supp. 2d 1305, 1309 (E.D. Okla. 2005).
212. *Id.*
213. 560 F.3d 1087 (9th Cir. 2009).
214. *Id.* at 1090.
215. *Id.* at 1097 (citing *Vasquez-Lopez v. Beneficial Or., Inc.*, 152 P.3d 940 (Or. Ct. App. 2007)).
216. *Id.* at 1096.
217. *Id.* at 1095–96.
218. *Id.* at 1098.
219. 511 F.3d 369.

that defendants had violated both the federal Credit Repair Organizations Act[220] and the Pennsylvania Credit Services Act.[221] Plaintiff also sought class certification. The district court ordered arbitration on an individual basis, thereby enforcing the class action waiver provision in plaintiff's arbitration agreement.

Turning first to Virginia law (pursuant to a choice of law clause in the arbitration agreement) and then to Pennsylvania law, the court concluded that under either body of law the class action waiver provision was not unconscionable and therefore would be enforced. As to Pennsylvania, the court held that despite two Pennsylvania Superior Court decisions pointing to a contrary result, Section 2 of the FAA as construed in *Perry v. Thomas*[222] required enforcement of the class action waiver. The court of appeals reasoned that the relevant Pennsylvania cases effectively held that "an agreement to arbitrate may be unconscionable simply because it is an agreement to arbitrate," and that such decisions could not be the basis for invalidating an agreement to arbitrate under Section 2 of the FAA.[223]

The subsequent Third Circuit decision in *Homa*[224] appears to contradict the reasoning in *Gay*, although applying New Jersey law.[225] Most recently, a case from the U.S. District Court for the Eastern District of Pennsylvania treated *Homa* as if it also implicitly overruled *Gay*, citing *Homa* for the proposition that the FAA does not preempt state unconscionability case law, but failing to provide a competing citation to *Gay*.[226]

Rhode Island
It appears that there are no cases addressing class action waivers under Rhode Island law.

South Carolina
There appear to be no cases directly addressing the enforceability of class action waivers under South Carolina law, but an opinion from the U.S. District Court for the District of South Carolina favorably references a magistrate judge's report on the issue.[227] Although the court ultimately remanded the case to state court based on the magistrate's alternative recommendation that the court lacked jurisdiction under the Class Action Fairness Act, the opinion nonetheless provides insight into how South Carolina law might apply class action waivers.[228] The magistrate in

---

220. 15 U.S.C. § 1679 *et seq.*

221. 73 PA. STAT. ANN. § 2181 *et seq.* (West 1993).

222. 482 U.S. 483.

223. *Gay*, 511 F.3d at 395.

224. 558 F.3d at 229.

225. *Id.* at 228–30.

226. *Fluke*, 2009 WL 1437593, at *4.

227. *See Holden v. Carolina Payday Loans, Inc.*, No. 4:08-182-TLW-TER, 2008 WL 4198587, at *16 (D.S.C. Sept. 5, 2008).

228. *Id.*

Holden v. Carolina Payday Loans, Inc. found that an arbitration agreement including a class action waiver was enforceable, rejecting plaintiff's argument that the class action waiver rendered the arbitration agreement substantively unconscionable because "without the class action vehicle, [the plaintiff would] be unable to maintain her legal representation given the small amount of damages."[229] Plaintiff's argument was deemed unfounded because the South Carolina statute under which the plaintiff brought her claims provided for recovery of attorney fees, and the arbitration agreement between the parties provided for advancement of the arbitration costs.[230]

South Dakota

Courts applying South Dakota law will likely enforce class action waivers unless they are clearly unconscionable. In *Dumanis v. Citibank (S.D.)*,[231] the court concluded that under South Dakota law, an arbitration provision containing a class action waiver was neither procedurally nor substantively unconscionable.[232] The arbitration clause was not procedurally unconscionable because it was adopted in accordance with the parties' previous agreement, and plaintiff had the opportunity to opt out.[233] The court also concluded that the arbitration agreement was not substantively unconscionable because plaintiff was entitled to attorney fees if he succeeded on his statutory claims.[234]

Tennessee

In *Pyburn v. Bill Heard Chevrolet*,[235] a Tennessee court applied a vindication of statutory rights analysis to determine whether the unavailability of class action relief rendered an arbitration agreement unenforceable. Although the agreement did not contain an express class action waiver, the court and parties assumed that class treatment would be unavailable in arbitration.[236] The court found that plaintiff could effectively vindicate his Tennessee Consumer Protection Act (TCPA) claims through arbitration regardless of whether class action relief was unavailable.[237] The court noted that even if the "Tennessee Legislature specifically intended on providing class action relief under the TCPA, the Supremacy Clause of the Federal Constitution would preclude [the court] from invalidating an arbitration agreement otherwise enforceable under the FAA simply because a plaintiff cannot maintain a

---

229. *Id.* at *16.
230. *See id.*
231. No. 07-CV-6070, 2007 U.S. Dist. LEXIS 81586 (W.D.N.Y. Nov. 2, 2007).
232. *Id.* at *9.
233. *Id.*
234. *Id.* at *9–10.
235. 63 S.W.3d 351 (Tenn. Ct. App. 2001).
236. *See id.* at 354–55, 364.
237. *Id.* at 364.

class action."[238] The court also found that the arbitration contract as a whole was not unconscionable.[239] Even though the arbitration agreement was adhesive, it was enforceable because it clearly laid out the terms, and it was not beyond the reasonable expectation of an ordinary person.[240]

Texas

In *Pedcor Management Co. v. Nations Personnel of Texas, Inc.*,[241] the Fifth Circuit addressed whether a district court could compel class arbitration when there was no express provision regarding class actions in the arbitration agreement. The court declined to address the question under Texas law, holding that the question of whether an arbitration provision allows for class arbitration is for the arbitrator, not the court.[242] Generally, Texas law will enforce arbitration clauses and their particular provisions so long as they are not substantively or procedurally unconscionable.[243]

Utah

Utah has enacted legislation intended to bolster the enforceability of class action waivers, in open-ended as well as closed-ended consumer credit contracts.[244] For each type of consumer credit contract, the statutes provide that "a creditor may contract with the debtor . . . for a waiver by the debtor of the right to initiate or participate in a class action related to the . . . consumer credit contract," so long as the creditor discloses the waiver to the debtor and prints the waiver in the contract in bold type or all-capital letters.[245] In *Homa*, the Third Circuit (analyzing Utah law) cited the legislation for the proposition that class action waivers in consumer credit agreements are not unconscionable in Utah.[246]

Vermont

There do not appear to be any cases addressing class action waivers under the law of Vermont. The test for unconscionability "is whether, in the light of the general commercial background and commercial needs of the particular trade or case, the clauses involved are so one-sided as to be unconscionable under the circumstances existing at the time of the making of the contract."[247] The principle of

---

238. *Id.* at 365.

239. *Id.* at 360.

240. *Id.*

241. 343 F.3d 355 (5th Cir. 2003).

242. *Id.* at 359 (citing *Bazzle*, 539 U.S. 444).

243. *See Carter v. Countrywide Credit Indus., Inc.*, 362 F.3d 294 (5th Cir. 2004) (holding that an arbitration clause between an employer and employee was not unconscionable).

244. *See* Utah Code Ann. § 70C-4-105 (West 2008); *see id.* at § 70C-3-104.

245. *Id.* at § 70C-4-105(1)–(2); *see id.* at § 70C-3-104(1)–(2).

246. 558 F.3d at 227.

247. Vt. Stat. Ann. tit. 9A, § 2-302 (2009); *Wilk Paving, Inc. v. Southworth-Milton, Inc.*, 649 A.2d 778, 783 (Vt. 1994).

unconscionability "is one of prevention of oppression and unfair surprise" and "not of disturbance of allocation of risks because of superior bargaining power."[248]

Virginia

Under Virginia law, a class action waiver is unconscionable only if both substantive and procedural unconscionability are shown.[249] The court in *Gay* looked to Virginia law (pursuant to a choice of law provision in the arbitration agreement) and concluded that a class action waiver was not in that context unconscionable and thus did not render the arbitration agreement unenforceable.[250] As to procedural unconscionability, the court reasoned that the plaintiff failed to provide "a basis for finding that inequality was 'so gross as to shock the conscience.'"[251] Even if the plaintiff lacked the power to negotiate for the removal of the arbitration clause, the court noted that the plaintiff simply could have forgone the defendant's credit repair services, and elected to employ a different company providing the same services.[252] The court reasoned that the class action waiver was not substantively unconscionable because the plaintiff retained the "full range of substantive rights" created by the statutes under which the plaintiff brought her claims.[253] Similarly, a case from the U.S. District Court for the Eastern District of Virginia held that a class action waiver was enforceable, although providing no analysis of the issue.[254] The court also held that such questions are generally left to the arbitrator, but that it could decide the issue because the class action waiver expressly stated that the "validity" of the waiver was for a court to resolve.[255]

Washington

In *Lowden v. T-Mobile USA, Inc.*,[256] the Ninth Circuit invalidated an arbitration agreement because it contained a class action waiver that was substantively unconscionable under Washington law.[257] Relying on a virtually indistinguishable state case, *Scott v. Cingular Wireless*,[258] the court found that the waiver improperly functioned to exculpate the defendant from liability—the small nature of the claims at issue meant that a class-based remedy was the only way to vindicate the plaintiff's

---

248. *See* VT. STAT. ANN. tit. 9A, § 2-302 (2009); *Colgan v. Agway, Inc.*, 553 A.2d 143, 146–47 (Vt. 1988).
249. *See Gay*, 511 F.3d 369.
250. *See id.* at 391–92.
251. *Id.* at 391.
252. *See id.* at 391 n.15.
253. *See id.* at 391–92.
254. *Freeman v. Capital One Bank*, No. 3:08CV242, 2008 WL 2661990, at *2–3 (E.D. Va. July 3, 2008).
255. *Id.* at *2.
256. 512 F.3d 1213 (9th Cir. 2008).
257. *Id.* at 1219.
258. 161 P.3d 1000 (Wash. 2008).

rights.[259] Because the waiver was not severable, the entire arbitration agreement was unenforceable.[260] Recently, the U.S. District Court for the Western District of Washington emphasized that *Lowden* and *Scott* do not impose a per se ban on class action waivers, but rather require a case-by-case substantive unconscionability analysis of the specific terms of class action waivers.[261]

West Virginia

In *Schultz v. AT&T Wireless Services, Inc.*, the U.S. District Court for the Northern District of West Virginia rejected a challenge to an arbitration agreement containing a class action waiver.[262] The plaintiff relied heavily on a West Virginia case, *State ex rel. Dunlap v. Berger*,[263] that had invalidated a class action waiver as unconscionable, but the court held that the case was distinguishable because it applied only to "small dollar/high volume" claims, whereas the plaintiff's claim in the instant case sought a high damage award, including attorney fees and punitive damages.[264] Moreover, the court noted that even if the *Dunlap* holding were applicable, it would be preempted by Section 2 of the FAA, as the holding in *Dunlap* was impermissibly based on arbitration clauses uniquely, rather than contract law generally.[265]

Wisconsin

In *Hawkins v. Aid Association for Lutherans*,[266] the court rejected arguments that an arbitration provision was unconscionable because plaintiffs had "no opportunity to review, negotiate, or comment" on it and because it potentially limited certain remedies available to them.[267] The court limited itself to determining whether the parties "agreed to arbitrate or if the claims are within the scope of that agreement" and held that concerns with particular provisions of the arbitration clause, including a bar on pursuing a class action, were questions for the arbitrator, not a court.[268] More recently, the Wisconsin Supreme Court has indicated that Wisconsin may heavily scrutinize attempts to limit class treatment.[269] The court found an arbitration provision was unconscionable after an extensive examination of both

---

259. *Lowden*, 512 F.3d at 1218–19.
260. *Id.* at 1219.
261. *Coneff v. AT&T Corp.*, 620 F. Supp. 2d 1248, 1259 (W.D. Wash. 2009).
262. 376 F. Supp. 2d 685, 690–91 (N.D. W. Va. 2005).
263. 567 S.E.2d 265 (W. Va. 2002).
264. *Schultz*, 376 F. Supp. 2d at 690–91.
265. *See id.* at 669 (citation omitted).
266. 338 F.3d 801 (7th Cir. 2003).
267. *Id.* at 806.
268. *Id.* at 806–07.
269. *Wis. Auto Title Loans, Inc. v. Jones*, 714 N.W.2d 155 (Wis. 2006).

procedural and substantive aspects of the arbitration provision.[270] Although not addressing the effect of a class action waiver, the court approvingly cited California cases finding that class action waivers are unenforceable.[271]

Wyoming

There do not appear to be any cases applying Wyoming law to class action waivers.

---

270. *Id.* at 175.
271. *Id.* at 175 n.61.

RES JUDICATA AND COLLATERAL ESTOPPEL ISSUES IN CLASS LITIGATION

ANDREW S. TULUMELLO
MARK WHITBURN

I. Introduction

Res judicata (or claim preclusion) and collateral estoppel (or issue preclusion) bar future litigants from asserting claims or litigating issues that a court has already finally determined in connection with prior litigation. The need for such doctrines is clear. Without them, litigants could endlessly relitigate the same claims and issues with no hope of eventual finality. But implementation of these doctrines in the class action context—in both litigated and settled cases—raises complex issues. This chapter discusses the doctrines that govern claim and issue preclusion in the class action context.

II. Preclusive Effect of Judgments in Litigated Class Actions

In general, litigated judgments have the same preclusive effect in class actions as in any other action. As the U.S. Supreme Court stated in *Cooper v. Federal Reserve Bank of Richmond*, "[t]here is of course no dispute that under elementary principles of prior adjudication a judgment in a properly entertained class action is binding on class members in any subsequent litigation."[1] Traditional claim and issue preclusion principles apply. With respect to claim preclusion, the Supreme Court in *Cooper* explained that "[a] judgment in favor of the plaintiff class extinguishes their claim, which merges into the judgment granting relief[, while] [a] judgment

---

1. 467 U.S. 867, 874 (1984) (citing, *inter alia*, *Supreme Tribe of Ben-Hur v. Cauble*, 255 U.S. 356 (1921)).

in favor of the defendant extinguishes the claim, barring a subsequent action on that claim."[2] With respect to issue preclusion, the Court observed that "[a] judgment in favor of either side is conclusive in a subsequent action between them on any issue actually litigated and determined, if its determination was essential to that judgment."[3]

Federal courts must give judgments litigated either in the same court or in other federal courts full preclusive effect.[4] Pursuant to 28 U.S.C. § 1738, federal courts must afford state court judgments "the same preclusive effect as would be given that judgment under the law of the State in which the judgment was rendered."[5] As multiple federal and state class actions concerning the same or similar factual allegations frequently proceed in parallel, not only to one another but also to individual actions, courts and litigants must understand precisely who is bound by class action judgments and what preclusive effects those judgments will have. The following sections explore these topics.

A. PERSONS OR ENTITIES BOUND BY PRIOR JUDGMENT

Once a court has certified a class, any litigated judgment entered in the action will bind all members of that class.[6] In class actions brought under Rule 23(b)(3), absent class members have the opportunity to opt out of the class. If they do so, a litigated judgment entered in the action will not apply to them. Rules 23(b)(1) and 23(b)(2), on the other hand, do not expressly allow for opt-outs. Even so, where plaintiffs seek solely nonmonetary relief, judgments in actions brought under these provisions will bind absent class members. However, where plaintiffs seek monetary relief as well in such actions, some courts have held that a judgment cannot preclude later individual damages actions. Because class members had no opt-out opportunity, preclusion of later actions would violate these individuals' due process rights.[7] Other courts have refused to dilute preclusion principles in this manner

---

2. *Id.*

3. *Id.*

4. *Id.* at 872–74.

5. *Migra v. Warren City Sch. Dist. Bd. of Educ.*, 465 U.S. 75, 81 (1984); *see also Kremer v. Chem. Constr. Corp.*, 456 U.S. 461, 466 (1982) ("Section 1738 requires federal courts to give the same preclusive effect to state court judgments that those judgments would be given in the courts of the State from which the judgments emerged.").

6. *See, e.g., Hansberry v. Lee*, 311 U.S. 32, 40 (1940) ("[T]he judgment in a 'class' or 'representative' suit, to which some members of the class are parties, may bind members of the class or those represented who were not made parties to it.").

7. *See, e.g., Brown v. Ticor Title Ins. Co.*, 982 F.2d 386, 392 (9th Cir. 1992) ("Because Brown had no opportunity to opt out of the MDL 633 litigation [in which settlement was reached in a class certified under Rules 23(b)(1) and 23(b)(2)], we hold there would be a violation of minimal due process if Brown's damage claims were held barred by *res judicata*."); *Payton v. County of Kane*, No. 99-C-8514, 2005 WL 1500884, *3 (N.D. Ill. June 10, 2005). Where plaintiffs have brought 23(b)(1) or 23(b)(2) class actions seeking *only* declaratory or injunctive relief, courts have again differed in their approach with respect to

and have avoided the dilemma by refusing to certify 23(b)(1) or 23(b)(2) classes, where plaintiffs seek any monetary damages.[8] This issue seems destined for eventual Supreme Court resolution.[9]

The court entering a litigated judgment in a class action generally does not determine the preclusive effects of that judgment.[10] However, that court will describe the class bound by the judgment. Pursuant to Rule 23(c)(3), "the judgment in a class action must: (A) for any class certified under Rule 23(b)(1) or (b)(2), include and describe those whom the court finds to be class members; and (B) for any class certified under Rule 23(b)(3), include and specify or describe those to whom the Rule 23(c)(2) notice was directed, who have not requested exclusion, and whom the court finds to be class members."

B. CLAIM PRECLUSION

Claim preclusion bars "successive litigation of the very same claim, whether or not relitigation of the claim raises the same issues as the earlier suit."[11] In the class action context, a judgment for or against a certified class extinguishes the claims brought on behalf of that class, through merger into the judgment.[12]

---

later individual damages actions. Some have refused to preclude these later damages suits because preclusion would violate due process. *See, e.g., Frank v. United Airlines, Inc.*, 216 F.3d 845, 851–52 (9th Cir. 2000). However, other courts have refused to certify classes seeking only injunctive or declaratory relief because the class representative could not adequately represent members of the putative class whose individual damages claims the class action might preclude. *See, e.g., Colindres v. QuitFlex Mfg.*, 235 F.R.D. 347, 369–72, 374–76 (S.D. Tex. 2006); *but see Ammons v. La-Z-Boy*, No. 1:04-CV-67-TC, 2008 WL 5142186, *16 (D. Utah Dec. 5, 2008).

8. *See, e.g., Allison v. Citgo Petroleum Corp.*, 151 F.3d 402, 413 (5th Cir. 1998) ("[A]s claims for individually based money damages begin to predominate, the presumption of cohesiveness decreases while the need for enhanced procedural safeguards to protect the individual rights of class members increases, thereby making class certification under (b)(2) less appropriate." (citations omitted)); *Jefferson v. Ingersoll Int'l Inc.*, 195 F.3d 894, 897 (7th Cir. 1999) ("It is an open question in this circuit and in the Supreme Court whether Rule 23(b)(2) *ever* may be used to certify a no-notice, no-opt-out class when compensatory or punitive damages are in issue." (citation omitted; emphasis in original)).

9. The Supreme Court granted certiorari in *Ticor* but ultimately dismissed the writ as improvidently granted. 511 U.S. 117 (1994). The Court noted the issue again in *Adams v. Robertson*, 520 U.S. 83, 88–89 (1997), but refused to reach it in light of the Court's conclusion that it had not been properly presented in the lower courts.

10. *See, e.g., Midway Motor Lodge v. Innkeepers' Telemanagement & Equip. Corp.*, 54 F.3d 406, 409 (7th Cir. 1995) ("In the law of preclusion . . . the court rendering the first judgment does not get to determine that judgment's effect; the second court is entitled to make its own decision . . . ."); *Brown v. R.J. Reynolds Tobacco Co.*, 576 F. Supp. 2d 1328, 1339 (M.D. Fla. 2008) ("It is the duty of the second trial court—which knows both what the earlier finding was and how it relates to a later case—to independently determine what preclusive effect a prior judgment may be given.").

11. *New Hampshire v. Maine*, 532 U.S. 742, 748 (2001); *see also Taylor v. Sturgell*, 128 S. Ct. 2161, 2171 (2008) (same).

12. *Cooper*, 467 U.S. 867, 874.

In evaluating whether a class action judgment extinguishes claims brought in a later action, courts analyze whether the new claims arise from the same "operative nucleus of fact" at issue in the earlier litigation. As the Eleventh Circuit explained in *Adams v. Southern Farm Bureau Life Insurance Co.*, "[c]laim preclusion applies not only to the precise legal theory presented in the previous litigation, but to all legal theories and claims arising out of the same operative nucleus of fact."[13]

Determining whether claims arise out of the same operative nucleus of fact is not always straightforward. Despite the general rule articulated in cases like *Adams*, at least in the context of employment discrimination, the Supreme Court held in *Cooper* that a litigated judgment in favor of a defendant against a certified class asserting "pattern-or-practice" claims did not preclude individual class members from later asserting individual discrimination claims.[14] Although most have perceived *Cooper* as the key Supreme Court case on the operation of preclusion principles in class actions, at least one academic commentator has observed that *Cooper* clashes with the general rules of claim preclusion by not requiring plaintiffs to have asserted in the original proceeding all claims that arose from the same transaction or set of transactions.[15]

C. ISSUE PRECLUSION

Issue preclusion forecloses "successive litigation of an issue of fact or law actually litigated and resolved in a valid court determination essential to the prior judgment, whether or not the issue arises on the same or a different claim."[16] Only issues "actually litigated and necessary to the outcome of the first action" have

---

13. 493 F.3d 1276, 1289 (11th Cir. 2007) (citation and internal quotation marks omitted); *see also, e.g., Capitol Hill Group v. Pillsbury, Winthrop, Shaw, Pittman, LLC*, 569 F.3d 485, 490 (D.C. Cir. 2009); *Herman v. Meiselman*, 541 F.3d 59, 62 (1st Cir. 2008); *Channer v. DHS*, 527 F.3d 275, 280 (2d Cir. 2008); *Laurel Sand & Gravel, Inc. v. Wilson*, 519 F.3d 156, 162 (4th Cir. 2008); *United States v. Davenport*, 484 F.3d 321, 326 (5th Cir. 2007); *Okoro v. Bohman*, 164 F.3d 1059, 1062 (7th Cir. 1999); *Lane v. Peterson*, 899 F.2d 737, 742 (8th Cir. 1990); *Constantini v. Trans World Airlines*, 681 F.2d 1199, 1201–02 (9th Cir. 1982).

14. 467 U.S. 867.

15. Tobias Barrington Wolf, *Preclusion in Class Action Litigation*, 105 COLUM. L. REV. 717, 724–31 (2005):

> *Cooper* . . . is a Title VII opinion, not an opinion about the preclusive effects of class action judgments. The Court confronted a limited question [about Title VII] and it offered an answer informed primarily by Title VII policy, making no attempt to explain its result with reference to general preclusion principles . . . . [T]he opinion . . . provides little guidance for the array of preclusion problems that can arise . . . in . . . class action litigation.

16. *New Hampshire*, 532 U.S. at 748–49; *see also Taylor*, 128 S. Ct. at 2171 (same).

preclusive effect.[17] Under the doctrines of nonmutual collateral estoppel, issue preclusion can be invoked by or against non-parties to the initial proceeding.[18]

D. WHO MAY ASSERT ISSUE PRECLUSION?

Some courts have voiced concern about the doctrine of nonmutual collateral estoppel in the class action context, noting that opt-out opportunities in Rule 23(b)(3) cases might tempt some individuals to wait on the sidelines while others litigate a class action and then make offensive use of the preclusive effect of any ensuing judgment in later individual litigation.

In *Premier Electrical Construction Co. v. National Electrical Contractors Association*,[19] the Seventh Circuit held that opt-outs could not invoke the doctrine of offensive nonmutual collateral estoppel. The Seventh Circuit observed that

> [t]he more attractive it is to opt out—and giving the parties who opt out the benefit of preclusion makes it very attractive—the fewer settlements there will be, the less the settlements will produce for the class, and the more cases courts must adjudicate. This is not judicial economy at work![20]

The Seventh Circuit recited the difficulties with Rule 23's predecessor—difficulties that authors of the new Rule sought to avoid when they drafted it in 1966. Under the old rule, plaintiffs could style a case a "class action" without binding absent class members to any judgment.[21] If plaintiffs prevailed, absent class members would intervene and share in the rewards.[22] If not, then absent class members would wait for the next plaintiff to have a go.[23] As unfair as such a device may have been, the current rule would prove equally unfair, according to the Seventh Circuit, if it permitted opt-outs to use collateral estoppel. In that court's view, "[w]hether class members should get the benefit of a favorable judgment, despite

---

17. *In re Microsoft Corp. Antitrust Litig.*, 355 F.3d 322, 326 (4th Cir. 2004) ("To apply collateral estoppel or issue preclusion to an issue or fact, the proponent must demonstrate that (1) the issue or fact is identical to the one previously litigated; (2) the issue or fact was actually resolved in the prior proceeding; (3) the issue or fact was critical and necessary to the judgment in the prior proceeding; (4) the judgment in the prior proceeding is final and valid; and (5) the party to be foreclosed by the prior resolution of the issue or fact had a full and fair opportunity to litigate the issue or fact in the prior proceeding.").

18. *See, e.g.*, *Blonder-Tongue Labs., Inc. v. Univ. of Ill. Found.*, 402 U.S. 313, 329 (1971); *Parklane Hosiery Co. v. Shore*, 439 U.S. 322, 327–28 (1979).

19. 814 F.2d 358, 366–67 (7th Cir. 1987) (Easterbrook, J.).

20. *Id.* at 366. *See also* *Polk v. Montgomery County*, 782 F.2d 1196, 1202 (4th Cir. 1986) (holding that a class member who opts out may not take advantage of a judgment favoring the class).

21. *Premier Electrical*, 814 F.2d at 362.

22. *Id.*

23. *Id.*

not being bound by an unfavorable judgment, was considered and decided in 1966. That decision binds us still."[24]

However, not all courts have shied away from permitting opt-out plaintiffs to invoke the doctrine of offensive collateral estoppel. In *Saunders v. Naval Air Rework Facility*,[25] the Ninth Circuit held that a class member who opts out of the damages portion of a class action under Rule 23(b)(2), but remains in the class to seek injunctive relief, may invoke collateral estoppel in later individual damages litigation.[26] As the Ninth Circuit observed,

> [t]he opt-out practice as we understand it, limited as it is to (b)(3) actions, assumes the relief sought in the independent action to be separate and apart from that awarded to the class by injunction or declaratory judgment. It does not assume the relitigation of that which has been settled by class-wide injunctive or declaratory relief.[27]

E. ISSUES INVOLVING CLAIMS THAT HAVE NOT BEEN CERTIFIED

The general rule of claim preclusion bars the relitigation of claims that plaintiffs asserted, or could have asserted, in earlier litigation based on the common nucleus of operative facts.[28] Some courts, however, have held that claim preclusion should apply in the class action context only to claims actually certified in the prior class action.[29] These courts appear to endorse a type of "claim splitting" in which class members may assert particular claims (for example, claims for declaratory or injunctive relief, or even claims for noneconomic damages) in one class proceeding, and yet remain free to assert other claims, arising from the very same facts, in a later individual action.[30] Other courts have expressed doubts about this principle, several holding that a putative class representative fails the adequacy and typicality prongs of Rule 23(a) by failing to assert the full array of potential claims arising

---

24. *Id.* at 364.

25. 608 F.2d 1308, 1312 (9th Cir. 1979).

26. Courts continue to debate whether these types of class actions can be certified under (b)(2). *See supra* note 8 and accompanying text. *See also generally Dukes v. Wal-Mart*, 509 F.3d 1168 (9th Cir. 2007), *vacated and en banc rehearing ordered by* 556 F.3d 919 (9th Cir. 2009). As *Saunders* demonstrates, courts have applied principles of issue preclusion to parties to a 23(b)(1) or 23(b)(2) class action in a later damages action; *see also Ammons*, 2008 WL 5142186, at *16; *McGee v. E. Ohio Gas Co.*, 200 F.R.D. 382, 392 & n.14 (S.D. Ohio 2001).

27. *Saunders*, 608 F.2d at 1312.

28. *See supra* note 13 and accompanying text.

29. *See, e.g., Becherer v. Merrill Lynch, Pierce, Fenner, & Smith, Inc.*, 193 F.3d 415, 428–29 (6th Cir. 1999); *Scarver v. Litscher*, 371 F. Supp. 2d 986, 988 (W.D. Wisc. 2005); *Shuford v. Ala. State Bd. of Educ.*, 920 F. Supp. 1233, 1239 (M.D. Ala. 1996).

30. *Aspinall v. Philip Morris Cos., Inc.*, 813 N.E.2d 476, 488 n.19 (Mass. 2004) (holding that claim preclusion "would not operate to bar a member of a class certified to proceed . . . only on an economic theory of damages from future pursuit of claims for personal injury unsuitable for class treatment").

from a common nucleus of facts.[31] Several courts have applied this reasoning in holding the line against a recent trend of plaintiffs seeking to smooth their path to certification of 23(b)(3) classes by excluding personal injury claims.[32] Moreover, the reexamination clause of the 7th Amendment of the U.S. Constitution may complement traditional preclusion principles as an additional barrier to relitigation of any issues determined in an initial class action.[33]

Complicated preclusion also can arise if a court grants summary judgment to a defendant against the named plaintiff *before* making a class certification determination. Some courts insist that certification issues be decided before merits issues are considered at all.[34] However, other courts allow such summary judgment determinations prior to a certification decision.[35] Generally, if a court does allow for such merits determinations against the named plaintiffs prior to certifying a class, the judgment will not preclude future litigation by the absent class members.[36]

---

31. *See, e.g., In re Methyl Tertiary Butyl Ether Prods. Liab. Litig.*, 209 F.R.D. 323, 339 (S.D.N.Y. 2002) ("Plaintiffs fail to cite, and this Court cannot find, any authority for the proposition that absent class members with personal injury or property claims can be adequately represented by class representatives seeking only injunctive relief."); *see also Thompson v. Am. Tobacco Co.*, 189 F.R.D. 544, 550–51 (D. Minn. 1999); *In re Teflon Prods. Liab. Litig.*, 254 F.R.D. 354, 366–68 (S.D. Iowa 2008); *Feinstein v. Firestone Tire & Rubber Co.*, 535 F. Supp. 595, 606–07 (S.D.N.Y. 1982); *Pearl v. Allied Corp.*, 102 F.R.D. 921, 922–24 (E.D. Pa. 1984); *Krueger v. Wyeth, Inc.*, No. 03CV2496 JLS, 2008 WL 481956, *2–4 (S.D. Cal. Feb. 19, 2008); *Small v. Lorillard Tobacco Co., Inc.*, 252 A.D.2d 1, 11–12 (N.Y. App. Div. 1998).

32. *See, e.g., Stearns v. Select Comfort Retail Corp.*, 08-2746 JF, 2009 WL 4723366, *15–16 (N.D. Cal. Dec. 4, 2009); *In re Methyl Tertiary Butyl Ether Prods. Liab. Litig.*, 209 F.R.D. at 339 (citing cases); *but see Beaulieu v. EQ Indus. Servs., Inc.*, 5:06-CV-00400-BR, 2009 WL 2208131, *19 (E.D.N.C. July 22, 2009).

33. *See, e.g., Allison*, 151 F.3d at 422–25:

In sum, the existence of factual issues common between the plaintiffs' disparate impact and pattern or practice claims precludes trial of the disparate impact claim in a class action severed from the remaining nonequitable claims in the case. The claims for injunctive relief, declaratory relief, and any equitable or incidental monetary relief cannot be litigated in a class action bench trial (in the same case prior to certification of any aspects of the pattern or practice claim) without running afoul of the Seventh Amendment. Nor may they be advanced in a *subsequent* class action without being barred by res judicata and collateral estoppel, because all of the common factual issues will already have been decided, or could have been decided, in the prior litigation. (citations omitted; emphasis in original).

However, at least one commentator has taken issue with the Fifth Circuit's interpretation of and application of the reexamination clause in this context. *See* Wolf, *supra* note 15, at 776–82.

34. *See, e.g., Nance v. Union Carbide Corp.*, 540 F.2d 718, 723 n.9 (4th Cir. 1976) ("The language of Rule 23(c) makes it quite clear that the determination of class status is to be made before the decision on the merits." (internal quotation marks omitted)), *vacated in part on other grounds*, 431 U.S. 952 (1977); *see also* Chapter 1, "Precertification."

35. *See, e.g., Cowen v. Bank United of Texas, FSB*, 70 F.3d 937, 941–42 (7th Cir. 1995); *Wright v. Schock*, 742 F.2d 541, 543–44 (9th Cir. 1984).

36. *See, e.g., Muhammad v. Giant Food Inc.*, 108 F. App'x 757, 765 n.5 (4th Cir. 2004) ("While the rejection of the named employees' individual claims is binding as to those employees, it does not preclude later efforts to certify a class action against Giant or bar any individual claims that might be asserted in such an action."); *Cowen*, 70 F.3d at 941 (observing that, if summary judgment is granted against the named

F. ISSUES INVOLVING DENIALS OF CERTIFICATION OR DECERTIFICATION

Although individual plaintiffs can assert their own claims in individual actions after certification is denied, it is less clear whether plaintiffs may assert, in later state court proceedings, the same class claims that a federal court has previously declined to certify. The Supreme Court has not decided this issue, and a split exists among lower courts. The Third and Fifth circuits have allowed later state class actions to go forward, holding that the earlier federal decision not to certify class claims lacked finality (and, accordingly, preclusive effect) and necessarily involved discretion that a state court might choose to exercise differently.[37] On the other hand, the Seventh Circuit has held that its previous determination that manageability problems prevented certification of a nationwide class precluded both named plaintiffs and absent class members from seeking certification of nationwide class actions in various state courts on the same claims.[38] In so holding, the court stated that a contrary rule would enable plaintiffs to "roll the dice as many times as they please—when nationwide class certification sticks (because it subsumes all other suits) while a no-certification decision has no enduring effect."[39]

Moreover, some courts have held that actions in which a court ultimately *decertifies* the class may have some preclusive effects. For example, in *Engle v. Liggett Group, Inc.,*[40] the Florida Supreme Court considered a case in which a Florida trial court certified a class of individuals who had suffered from medical conditions allegedly caused by their addiction to cigarettes, a jury made numerous factual findings relevant to the defendants' conduct, and then a Florida court of appeals decertified the class based on predominance and superiority considerations. Although accepting the appellate court's decertification ruling, the Florida Supreme Court nevertheless determined that the "pragmatic solution" was to give certain of the jury's factual findings preclusive effect in the individual suits that would necessarily arise in the wake of that decertification, including, *inter alia,* (1) that cigarettes cause some of the diseases at issue; (2) that nicotine is addictive; (3) that the defendants placed cigarettes on the market that were defective and unreasonably dangerous; and (4) that the defendants made a false or misleading statement of

---

plaintiffs but no class is certified, "the defendant loses the preclusive effect on subsequent suits against him of class certification"); *Wright,* 742 F.2d at 544 (same).

37. *See J.R. Clearwater, Inc. v. Ashland Chem. Co.,* 93 F.3d 176, 179–80 (5th Cir. 1996); *In re Gen. Motors Corp. Pick-Up Truck Fuel Tank Prods. Liab. Litig.,* 134 F.3d 133, 146 & n. 7 (3d Cir. 1998).

38. *In re Bridgestone/Firestone, Inc., Tires Prods. Liab. Litig.,* 333 F.3d 763, 767 (7th Cir. 2003). The Seventh Circuit derived the preclusive force of its certification denial from *issue* preclusion rather than *claim* preclusion. *Id.* Only the latter requires a final judgment in place before it is triggered. *Id.*

39. *Id.*

40. 945 So. 2d 1246 (Fla. 2006).

material fact with the intention of misleading smokers.[41] Ultimately, "[c]lass members [could] choose to initiate individual damages actions and the . . . common core findings [approved as noted would] have res judicata effect in those trials."[42] The Supreme Court denied certiorari in an appeal of the Florida Supreme Court's decision in *Engle*.[43]

Engle's holding on preclusive effect of findings in a decertified class action has spawned significant litigation, and many individual plaintiffs from the now-decertified class have filed individual lawsuits to take advantage of the Florida Supreme Court's "pragmatic solution." One federal district court has refused to accord preclusive effect to the jury findings at issue,[44] holding that (1) claim preclusion did not apply because the findings had never been merged into any judgment as to liability; (2) issue preclusion did not apply because the findings were too broad for application in the context of an individual plaintiff's lawsuit; and (3) application of the findings to individual cases would violate due process because it was impossible to determine which findings applied to which individual defendants. This decision is currently on appeal to the Eleventh Circuit.[45]

Thus, both state and federal courts continue to debate the issue and may not resolve it in the near future.

III. Preclusive Effect of Class Settlements

As class action defendants enter into settlements expecting to buy global peace, they have a particular interest in maximizing the preclusive effect of those settlements. As a settlement is simply a contract, it has, for the most part, the operative effect supplied by its terms. The more the parties can make explicit in the language of the settlement itself, the more secure they are with respect to its future implications.

A. SCOPE OF RELEASE

Settling parties in class actions generally have latitude to set the scope of the settlement's release. For example, settling parties in state court class action litigation

---

41. *Id.* at 1269.

42. *Id.*

43. 552 U.S. 941 (2007).

44. *Brown*, 576 F. Supp. 2d 1328.

45. Some state courts have declined to accord preclusive effect to factual findings made in class litigation where the class is later decertified. *See, e.g., Spitzfaden v. Dow Corning Corp.*, 833 So. 2d 512, 524 (La. Ct. App. 2002); *Stern v. Carter*, 82 A.D.2d 321, 342 (N.Y. App. Div. 1981); *Mateza v. Polaroid Corp.*, 76-3379, 1981 WL 11479, *54 (Mass. Super. July 30, 1981).

can release claims that are exclusively federal[46] and vice versa.[47] Class action litigants may release claims through settlement even if the named plaintiffs never had standing to bring the released claims[48] or the claims were not ripe at the time of settlement.[49] Moreover, claims can be released even if they were not pursued by the named plaintiffs at all or are asserted against parties not named as defendants in the settled action.[50]

Before concluding the settlement, the settling parties also can amend the relevant pleadings to expand the class claims and allegations or to settle a broader set of claims than those at issue in the operative complaint.[51] However, if the parties have not shown that settlement as to these new claims is fair and adequate in light of the expanded release, the court might reject the settlement.[52] Moreover, the settlement must include appropriate notice and opt-out opportunities with respect to the new claims.[53] Despite these provisos, courts have approved extremely broad settlement releases.[54]

IV. Collateral Attacks on Class Judgment or Settlement

A collateral attack on a class judgment or settlement occurs when a putative class member challenges the validity of that judgment or settlement sometime *after* its entry. The collateral attack generally alleges that the earlier settlement or judg-

---

46. *See, e.g., Matsushita Elec. Indus. Co. v. Epstein*, 516 U.S. 367 (1996) (class settlement in state court can release exclusively federal claims); *see also Nottingham Partners v. Trans-Lux Corp.*, 925 F.2d 29 (1st Cir. 1991) (holding that a class settlement in a state court class action against a corporate defendant for securities violations could release federal securities claims, even though those claims were in the exclusive jurisdiction of the federal courts).

47. *See, e.g., Ass'n for Disabled Am., Inc. v. Amoco Oil Co.*, 211 F.R.D. 457, 471 (S.D. Fla. 2002) ("[F]ederal class action settlements containing a release of state law claims are both common and presumptively valid[.]").

48. *See, e.g., Monaco v. Mitsubishi Motors Credit of Am., Inc.*, 01-3700, 2002 U.S. App. LEXIS 6839 (3d Cir. Apr. 12, 2002) (claims can be released with respect to which named plaintiffs had no standing).

49. *See, e.g., Williams v. GE Capital Auto Lease*, 159 F.3d 266 (7th Cir. 1998) (claims can be released although not ripe at time of settlement).

50. *See, e.g., Reyn's Pasta Bella LLC v. Visa USA, Inc.*, 442 F.3d 741, 748 (9th Cir. 2006) ("A class settlement may . . . release factually related claims against parties not named as defendants . . . .").

51. *See, e.g., Malchman v. Davis*, 761 F.2d 893, 900 (2d Cir. 1985); *Weinberger v. Kendrick*, 698 F.2d 61, 76–77 (2d Cir. 1982).

52. *See, e.g., Weinberger*, 698 F.2d at 76–77.

53. *Id.*

54. *See, e.g., Wal-Mart Stores, Inc. v. Visa USA, Inc.*, 396 F.3d 96, 106 (2d Cir. 2005) ("Broad class action settlements are common, since defendants and their cohorts would otherwise face nearly limitless liability from related lawsuits in jurisdictions throughout the country. Practically speaking, class action settlements simply will not occur if the parties cannot set definitive limits on defendants' liability." (citations and internal quotation marks omitted)).

ment does not bind absent class members because the named plaintiffs did not adequately represent them or the parties did not give them adequate notice of the settlement. These cases derive from the Supreme Court's decision in *Hansberry v. Lee*,[55] which set forth the principle that "there has been a failure of due process . . . in those cases where it cannot be said that the procedure adopted[ ] fairly insures the protection of the interests of absent parties who are to be bound by it."[56] Absent class members may raise these challenges even if the parties contested these issues in the initial class proceeding and obtained a ruling from the court. The law in this area is unsettled in many respects.

A. STANDARD OF REVIEW

When a court considers a collateral attack to a class action settlement or judgment, it must first determine how much deference to assign to the manner in which the initial court resolved the relevant issue when it first approved the class settlement. Courts have disagreed over what standard of review to apply.

The Ninth Circuit has adopted an approach grounded in claim preclusion principles and procedural due process—if a collateral attack plaintiff had a "full and fair" *opportunity* to raise the alleged defect in the class settlement court, that plaintiff may not raise the defect now by way of collateral attack.[57] In *Epstein v. MCA, Inc.*,[58] it held that the only question a court considering a collateral attack should ask is whether the initial court followed the appropriate procedures—for example, whether it held a fairness hearing or whether it followed the notice and opt-out procedures outlined in Rule 23. If the initial court did follow those procedures, the reviewing court should not engage in "collateral second-guessing of those determinations and that review."[59]

Conversely, the Second Circuit has held that a court should analyze the issues raised in a collateral attack by using, in effect, issue preclusion principles—if the parties did not *actually* litigate the asserted defect before the rendering court and obtain a ruling from that court, the court presiding over the collateral attack

---

55. 311 U.S. 32.

56. *Id.* at 42; *see also id.* at 42–43:

It is familiar doctrine of the federal courts that members of a class not present as parties to the litigation may be bound by the judgment where they are in fact adequately represented by parties who are present, or where they actually participate in the conduct of the litigation in which members of the class are present as parties. (citations omitted).

57. *Epstein v. MCA, Inc.*, 179 F.3d 641, 648 (9th Cir. 1999) (applying claim preclusion principles and asking whether the collateral attack plaintiff had a "full and fair" opportunity to raise the alleged constitutional defect in the class settlement court).

58. *Id.*

59. *Id.*

should review the issue de novo.[60] In *Stephenson v. Dow Chemical Co.*,[61] the Second Circuit addressed a collateral challenge to a class settlement involving military personnel injured in Vietnam by Agent Orange and related chemicals. The settlement clearly stated that "[t]he Class specifically includes persons who have not yet manifested injury."[62] On direct appeal from the initial settlement, the Second Circuit had affirmed the class certification, the settlement approval, and the distribution plan outlined by the settlement, and had rejected both adequacy of representation and predominance objections.[63]

Yet almost 20 years later, in *Stephenson*, the Second Circuit ruled that individuals who had not manifested injuries at the time of the earlier settlement could still pursue claims against the chemical manufacturers because the named plaintiffs who had ostensibly settled their claims in the original class proceedings had not adequately represented them.[64] The court reasoned that its decision was consistent with the Ninth Circuit's decision in *Epstein* in that *Epstein* merely prohibited a collateral attack when the original certifying court had specifically found adequate representation of individuals situated similarly to those raising the collateral attack.[65] Accordingly, because the district court and appellate court handling the original Agent Orange settlement had not explicitly determined that the named plaintiffs adequately represented absent class members without manifested injuries, a court presiding over a collateral challenge by such absent class members need accord no deference to the earlier judicial settlement approvals.[66]

The Third Circuit has also weighed in on this area of the law, holding that "[n]o collateral review is available when class members have had a full and fair hearing and have generally had their procedural rights protected during the approval of the Settlement Agreement."[67] The Third Circuit has also stated that "[c]ollateral review is only available when class members are raising an issue that was not properly considered by the District Court at an earlier stage in the litigation."[68]

The Supreme Court has yet to weigh in definitively on this possible split in authority. The Supreme Court did affirm in part the ruling in *Stephenson*; however, it affirmed the ruling through a 4–4 per curiam decision, without Justice Stevens's participation, and thus set no binding precedent for the other appellate courts.[69]

---

60. *See Wolfert v. Transamerica HomeFirst, Inc.*, 439 F.3d 165 (2d Cir. 2006) (applying issue preclusion principles and asking whether the asserted defect was actually litigated and determined in the rendering court).

61. 273 F.3d 249 (2d Cir. 2001).

62. *Id.* at 252.

63. *Id.* at 253.

64. *Id.* at 251.

65. *Id.* at 258 n.6.

66. *Id.* at 258.

67. *See In re Diet Drugs Prods. Liab. Litig.*, 431 F.3d 141, 145–47 (3d Cir. 2005).

68. *Id.*

69. *Dow Chem. Co. v. Stephenson*, 539 U.S. 111 (2003).

Courts may thus look to the Second Circuit's limitation of *Epstein* in *Stephenson* as the only way to reconcile the divergent decisions of the circuits: when the original court followed the appropriate procedures, absent class members similarly situated to plaintiffs who raised objections in the prior action may not raise those same objections later by way of collateral attack. However, if the original court did *not* follow appropriate procedures or if the collateral attack plaintiffs are *not* raising issues put forward by similarly situated individuals during the earlier action, the collateral attack court will review the issue de novo.

B. TYPES OF COLLATERAL ATTACKS

A collateral attack on a class settlement or judgment generally takes one of two forms: a claim of inadequate representation in the earlier action or a claim of inadequate notice of the earlier settlement.

1. Inadequate Representation

Prior judgments do not bind absent class members if deeming them so bound would violate their due process rights. As a matter of due process, named plaintiffs in the prior action must have adequately represented absent class members.[70]

Amchem Products, Inc. v. Windsor is the Supreme Court's most authoritative examination of adequate representation issues in class actions.[71] In *Amchem*, the parties attempted to settle a sprawling asbestos class that encompassed "hundreds of thousands, perhaps millions, of individuals tied together by this commonality: Each was, or some day may be, adversely affected by past exposure to asbestos products manufactured by one or more of 20 companies."[72] Among other holdings, the Supreme Court held that the named plaintiffs—who had manifested asbestos-related injuries—could not adequately represent a class that also consisted of class members whose injuries had not yet manifested. An intraclass conflict arose because "for the currently injured, the critical goal is generous immediate payments . . . [and] [t]hat goal tugs against the interest of exposure-only plaintiffs in ensuring an ample, inflation-protected fund for the future."[73] Following *Amchem*, courts have held that injured plaintiffs cannot represent classes consisting of injured and uninjured consumers, and vice versa.[74]

---

70. *See, e.g., Hansberry*, 311 U.S. at 42–43.

71. 521 U.S. 591 (1997).

72. *Id.* at 597.

73. *Id.* at 626.

74. *See, e.g., Ortiz v. Fibreboard Corp.*, 527 U.S. 815, 856 (1999) ("[I]t is obvious after *Amchem* that a class divided between holders of present and future claims (some of the latter involving no physical injury and attributable to claimants not yet born) requires division into homogeneous subclasses under Rule 23(c)(4)(B), with separate representation to eliminate conflicting interests of counsel."); *Stephenson*, 273 F.3d at 260 (same); *cf. Wall v. Sunoco*, 211 F.R.D. 272, 279–80 (M.D. Pa. 2002) (denying certification on adequacy grounds because the named plaintiff "claims to have present injuries while she is attempting to represent a class of presently asymptomatic persons.").

Class representatives also can fail to adequately represent absent class members in other ways, including, for example, failing to assert or lacking standing to assert claims possessed by other members of the putative class,[75] attempting to represent a class containing subgroups with inherent rivalries or historical antagonisms,[76] differing from other putative class members in the degree to which claims are vulnerable to certain defenses,[77] or retaining inadequate counsel.[78]

2. Inadequate Notice

In a class action brought under Rule 23(b)(3), the named plaintiffs must provide class members with meaningful notice and an opportunity to exclude themselves from the class.[79] Generally, due process requires that "the means employed [to give notice] . . . be such as one desirous of actually informing the absentee might reasonably adopt to accomplish it."[80] Notice must be "reasonably calculated, under all the circumstances, to apprise interested parties of the pendency of the action and afford them an opportunity to present their objections."[81] It is "widely recognized that for the due process standard to be met it is not necessary that every class member receive actual notice, so long as class counsel acted reasonably in selecting means likely to inform persons affected."[82] Applying these standards, courts have held that notice was adequate even when challenged collaterally by class members who received notice after the opt-out date or never received notice at all.[83] But there

---

75. See supra note 31 and accompanying text; see also, e.g., In re FedEx Ground Package Sys., Inc., Employment Practices Litig., 662 F. Supp. 2d 1069, 1081–83 (N.D. Ind. 2009) (holding named representatives inadequate because they lacked standing to assert certain class claims); Lantz v. Am. Honda Motor Co., Inc., No. 06 C 5932, 2007 WL 2875239, *6 (N.D. Ill. Sept. 27, 2007) (same); Williams v. Boeing Co., No. C98-761P, 2005 WL 2921960, *6–9 (W.D. Wash. Nov. 4, 2005) (same).

76. See, e.g., Gen. Tel. Co. of the Nw., Inc. v. EEOC, 446 U.S. 318, 331 (1980) ("In employment discrimination litigation, conflicts might arise, for example, between employees and applicants who were denied employment and who will, if granted relief, compete with employees. . . . Under Rule 23, the same plaintiff could not represent these classes."); Kamean v. Local 363, Int'l Bhd. of Teamsters, 109 F.R.D. 391, 395 (S.D.N.Y. 1986); Pruitt v. Allied Chem. Corp., 85 F.R.D. 100, 106 (E.D. Va. 1980).

77. See, e.g., Langbecker v. Elec. Data Sys. Corp., 476 F.3d 299, 313 n.26 (5th Cir. 2007) (observing that adequacy of representation may be an issue where named plaintiffs did not sign releases of claims against the defendant, but many of the putative class members did); Spann v. AOL Time Warner, Inc., 219 F.R.D. 307, 320 (S.D.N.Y. 2003) (same).

78. See, e.g., Danner v. U.S. Civil Serv. Comm'n, 635 F.2d 427, 433 (5th Cir. 1981) (affirming lower court holding that a class representative was inadequate in virtue of the fact that plaintiffs' counsel did not appear at the class certification hearing).

79. See Eisen v. Carlisle & Jacquelin, 417 U.S. 156, 173 (1974).

80. Mullane v. Cent. Hanover Bank & Trust Co., 339 U.S. 306, 315 (1950).

81. Id. at 314.

82. In re Prudential Secs. Inc. Ltd. P'ships Litig., 164 F.R.D. 362, 368 (S.D.N.Y. 1996) (citing, inter alia, Weigner v. City of New York, 852 F.2d 646, 649 (2d Cir. 1988)).

83. See, e.g., Reppert v. Marvin Lumber & Cedar Co., Inc., 359 F.3d 53, 56–57 (1st Cir. 2004) (upholding dismissal of collateral challenge to settlement based on certain class members' failure to receive notice of settlement and noting that "[a]fter . . . appropriate notice is given, if the absent class members fail to opt

are limits, as some federal and state courts have refused to accord preclusive effect where they believed the notice plan in the original proceeding was inadequate.[84]

Among other things, the Supreme Court's decision in *Mullane v. Central Hanover Bank & Trust*[85] has been interpreted to require that the class members be provided notice of the types of claims that are being settled. For example, the Eleventh Circuit held in *Twigg v. Sears, Roebuck & Co.*[86] that the notice disseminated must inform recipients that the claims they possess are at issue. In *Twigg*, notice of a class settlement described the claims at issue as involving allegations that "Sears and other defendants violated federal and state law by allegedly making *unnecessary and/or improper* repairs to its customers' automobiles."[87] However, "[t]he notices do not alert a reader that the prior action included claims by Sears customers based upon being billed for services that Sears never performed."[88] As Twigg's claim was of the latter type, the Eleventh Circuit allowed his case to go forward and rejected Sears's contention that the earlier settlement should have preclusive effect.[89]

Far more notice plans have withstood collateral attacks than have succumbed to them, however. Some courts have simply found that the notice plans at issue were adequate.[90] Others have refused to consider the challenge because the original court

out of the class action, such members will be bound by the court's actions, including settlement and judgment, even though those individuals never actually receive notice.").

84. *See, e.g., State v. Homeside Lending, Inc.*, 826 A.2d 997, 1009–10 (Vt. 2003) (refusing to give preclusive effect to settlement of nationwide class action in Alabama because notice did not disclose to class members the true magnitude of the plaintiff's lawyers fee request, i.e., that many class members would pay more in attorney fees to class counsel than the economic benefit they received in the settlement); *Moody v. Sears, Roebuck & Co.*, No. 02 CVS 4892, 2007 WL 2582193, *6–10 (N.C. Super. May 7, 2007) (refusing to give preclusive effect to settlement of nationwide class in Illinois because, *inter alia*, notice was not properly distributed in North Carolina, notice was distributed right before the opt-out date, and the notice contained insufficient information about the relative amounts received by class members and class counsel), *rev'd by* 664 S.E.2d 569 (N.C. App. 2008) (*see infra* note 91); *see also In re Integra Realty Res., Inc.*, 262 F.3d 1089, 1106 (10th Cir. 2001) (citing cases); *Stephenson*, 273 F.3d at 261 n.8.

85. 153 F.3d 1222 (11th Cir. 1998).

86. 153 F.3d 1222 (11th Cir. 1998).

87. *Id.* at 1228 (emphasis in original).

88. *Id.*

89. *Id.* at 1229; *see also Fidel v. Farley*, 534 F.3d 508, 515 (6th Cir. 2008):

Finally, we note that individual class members who do not receive timely notice are not without recourse. If an individual [class member] later claims he did not receive adequate notice and therefore should not be bound by the settlement, he can litigate that issue on an individual basis when the settlement is raised as a bar to a lawsuit he has brought. (citation and internal quotation marks omitted).

90. *See, e.g., Learner v. Marvin Lumber & Cedar Co.*, No. 08-CV-177-JL, 2008 WL 5285028, *6 (D.N.H. Dec. 19, 2008) (recognizing that "the prevailing view holds that a party may collaterally attack a class action judgment on the grounds that it was entered with insufficient notice" but holding notice sufficient where it consisted of "notification by mail to all known members of the certified class, and the publication of this notice being placed in 33 newspapers of general circulation throughout the United States, including a toll-free number and the address of a web-site, established to provide potential class members

specifically considered and approved the notice plan as conforming to due process requirements.[91]

V. Conclusion

With all the complexities of preclusion issues in the class action context, the issue currently looming above all others as requiring prompt resolution is the extent to which classes certified under Rules 23(b)(1) or 23(b)(2) require notice and opt-out opportunities as a matter of due process, if they include claims not simply for declaratory or injunctive relief, but for monetary relief as well. The Supreme Court has noted this issue but has not yet decided it.[92] Both courts and litigants confront uncertainty about when a court may certify such classes. Similarly, it remains uncertain whether a court can or should accord full preclusive effect to a settlement under Rules 23(b)(1) or 23(b)(2) that embraces damages claims or related requests for relief. If absent class members are permitted to challenge it through collateral attack, the global peace for which the litigants bargained may be jeopardized.[93]

---

with information about the class action . . . ." (citation and internal quotation marks omitted)); *Patrowicz v. Transamerica HomeFirst, Inc.*, 359 F. Supp. 2d 140, 149–53 (D. Conn. 2005) (rejecting collateral attack on notice program where "the notice clearly stated that recipients must request exclusion in writing by sending certain basic information to the settlement administrator, whose address was clearly noted" and observing that "[a]ll that the Due Process Clause required is that absent Class members be informed of their right to opt out of the class and the procedures for doing so.").

91. *See, e.g., Brooks v. Wachovia Bank, N.A.*, No. Civ. A. 06-00955, 2007 WL 2702949, *5 (E.D. Pa. Sept. 14, 2007) ("Once issues of due process protections for class members have been decided by a court, they may not be relitigated. . . . A judge of the Philadelphia Court of Common Pleas approved the *Parsky* settlement, including its method of notice. . . . Therefore, Plaintiff may not collaterally attack the *Parsky* settlement agreement."); *Caruso v. Candie's, Inc.*, 201 F.R.D. 306, 314–15 (S.D.N.Y. 2001); *Moody*, 664 S.E.2d at 581–82.

92. *See supra* note 9 and accompanying text.

93. *See supra* notes 7 and 8 and accompanying text.

MULTISTATE CLASS ACTIONS AND CHOICE OF LAW

ANDREW S. TULUMELLO
GEOFFREY C. WEIEN

I. Introduction

Multistate class actions are those implicating the substantive law of multiple jurisdictions. In a typical multistate class action, the named plaintiff purports to bring state law claims on behalf of non-forum-state residents. For example, a plaintiff might sue an automobile manufacturer for breaches of express and implied warranties (governed by state law), purporting to represent a class of all vehicle owners in the United States.[1] As another example, an insurance policyholder, on behalf of a class of all similar policyholders nationwide, might sue an insurance company for violations of the federal securities laws and state common law.[2] The plaintiff may allege that one state's laws should apply to the entire class,[3] or may instead allege that any variations in state substantive law do not preclude class certification.[4] As courts of appeals have recognized, certification of a multistate or, especially, a nationwide class increases the stakes of litigation and can create significant settlement pressure for defendants.[5] Not surprisingly, certification decisions in multistate class actions are intensely litigated.

The U.S. Constitution, Rule 23 of the Federal Rules of Civil Procedure, and the Rules Enabling Act require a choice of law analysis to be conducted, at some stage, in every multistate class action, and each of these limits the power of federal

---

1. *See Cole v. Gen. Motors Corp.*, 484 F.3d 717, 720 (5th Cir. 2007).
2. *See In re Prudential Ins. Co. of Am. Sales Litig.*, 148 F.3d 283 (3d Cir. 1998).
3. *See, e.g., In re Bridgestone/Firestone, Inc.*, 288 F.3d 1012, 1015 (7th Cir. 2002).
4. *See, e.g., Zinser v. Accufix Research Inst., Inc.*, 253 F.3d 1180, 1188–90 (9th Cir. 2001).
5. *See, e.g., In re Rhone-Poulenc Rorer, Inc.*, 51 F.3d 1293, 1298 (7th Cir. 1995).

courts to certify class actions that would require the application of laws from multiples states.[6]

First, under the Constitution, *Erie Railroad Co. v. Tompkins*,[7] *Klaxon Co. v. Stentor Electric Manufacturing Co.*,[8] and *Phillips Petroleum Co. v. Shutts*[9] establish the following three principles, respectively: (1) federal courts sitting in diversity must apply the substantive law of the forum state in which they sit; (2) state choice of law rules are substantive law; and (3) states ordinarily may not apply their laws to conduct and transactions that occur outside their borders.

Second, the Rules Enabling Act provides that the Federal Rules "shall not abridge, enlarge or modify any substantive right."[10] The Rules Enabling Act confirms that a class action is a procedural device that should not deprive litigants (including absent class members) of the right to have the appropriate substantive law govern the disposition of their claims and defenses, even if there otherwise would be procedural efficiencies to adjudicating the claims on an aggregated basis.[11]

Third, several subsections of Rule 23—including section (a)(2)'s commonality requirement, section (b)(3)'s predominance requirement, section (b)(3)'s superiority requirement, and section (b)(3)(D)'s manageability factor—require courts to conduct a choice of law analysis, and to ascertain whether variations in state law make the action unsuitable for class treatment, at some point in the proceedings.

This chapter explains the doctrines governing choice of law analysis in multistate class actions.

II. Choice of Law Analysis Under the Constitution and the Rules Enabling Act

A. THE CONSTITUTION: *SHUTTS*

The starting point for analyzing constitutional limits on choice of law rules in class actions is the U.S. Supreme Court's decision in *Phillips Petroleum Co. v. Shutts*.[12] In

---

6. *See, e.g.*, Chapter 30, "Other Due Process Challenges to the Class Device."

7. 304 U.S. 64 (1938).

8. 313 U.S. 487 (1941).

9. 472 U.S. 797, 823 (1985).

10. 28 U.S.C. § 2072(b).

11. *See Amchem Prods., Inc. v. Windsor*, 521 U.S. 591, 613 (1997) ("Rule 23's requirements must be interpreted in keeping with Article III constraints, and with the Rules Enabling Act."); *id.* at 628–29 ("The argument is sensibly made that a nationwide administrative claims processing regime would provide the most secure, fair, and efficient means of compensating victims of asbestos exposure. Congress, however, has not adopted such a solution. And Rule 23, which must be interpreted with fidelity to the Rules Enabling Act and applied with the interests of absent class members in close view, cannot carry the large load [plaintiffs] and the District Court heaped upon it.").

12. 472 U.S. 797.

Shutts, the Court considered the claims of a nationwide class of plaintiffs who brought suit in Kansas state court against Phillips Petroleum, an out-of-state corporation. Plaintiffs had sued to recover interest on allegedly delayed royalty payments on oil and gas leases, the majority of which related to oil and gas deposits outside of Kansas. The state courts agreed with plaintiffs that Kansas law should govern the claims of the entire class, citing the plaintiffs' choice of Kansas as the forum and that state's preference for applying its own law in its own courts absent exceptional circumstances.

The Supreme Court reversed, holding that Kansas could not constitutionally apply its own law to the claims of the entire class in light of the commands of the due process clause and full faith and credit clause of the federal Constitution. Even though Kansas had personal jurisdiction over the defendant (through its conduct of business in that state) and the plaintiff class members, these contacts were insufficient to justify applying Kansas law to the dispute.[13] Moreover, because there was a material conflict between the substantive law of Kansas and that of Texas and Oklahoma (the other possible sources of law), the due process rights of the parties were violated by imposing Kansas law upon them.[14] According to the Court, the state whose law is applied "must have a significant contact or aggregation of contacts to the claims asserted *by each member of the plaintiff class*, contacts creating state interests, in order to ensure that the choice of that law is not arbitrary or unfair."[15]

In *Shutts*, the Supreme Court also held that choice of law analysis cannot be relaxed or excused simply to give effect to the class action as a favored forum of adjudication. The Constitution's restrictions on a state's power to apply its law beyond its borders are not "altered by the fact that it may be more difficult or more burdensome to comply . . . because of the large number of transactions which the States proposes to adjudicate in a single action."[16]

Shutts arose out of the Supreme Court of Kansas and therefore was not an interpretation of Federal Rule of Civil Procedure 23. Rather, *Shutts* establishes constitutional limitations on the power of a state to apply its law to conduct that occurs beyond its borders and shows that those limitations are not relaxed or suspended in a class action.

The Supreme Court has echoed many of the same concerns expressed in *Shutts* in a line of cases imposing due process limitations on punitive damage awards. The most recent and strongest articulation of the principle is in *State Farm Mutual Automobile Insurance Co. v. Campbell*.[17] There, the Court invalidated the Utah Supreme

---

13. *Id.* at 819–20.
14. *See id.* at 817–18.
15. *Id.* (emphasis added).
16. *Id.* at 821 (citing *Allstate Ins. Co. v. Hague*, 449 U.S. 302, 312–13 (1981)).
17. 538 U.S. 408, 421–22 (2003).

Court's imposition of a $145 million punitive damages judgment, in part because the record demonstrated that the jury had relied on the defendant's out-of-state conduct when awarding punitive damages. The Court observed that states "cannot punish . . . conduct that may have been lawful where it occurred," and cited *Shutts* for the proposition that "[a]ny proper adjudication of conduct that occurred outside Utah to other persons would require their inclusion [in the case], and, to those parties, the Utah courts, in the usual case, *would need to apply the laws of their relevant jurisdiction.*"[18] *State Farm* confirms the presumption, reflected in *Shutts*, that states cannot apply their law to conduct and transactions that occur outside their borders.

III. The Rules Enabling Act

Under the Rules Enabling Act, no Federal Rule of Civil Procedure, including Rule 23, may "abridge, enlarge or modify any substantive right."[19] In *Amchem Products, Inc. v. Windsor,*[20] the Supreme Court observed that the Act places important constraints on the interpretation and application of Rule 23. Even when a nationwide class action might be "the most secure, fair, and efficient means of compensating victims," class treatment is impermissible where "bold aggregation techniques" would violate the Act by abridging, enlarging, or modifying substantive rights.[21] The Rules Enabling Act precludes courts from using the class action device in ways that either negate or make it impossible for one or more of the parties to assert otherwise available claims and defenses or to do so under the state law that would apply outside the class action context.

IV. Choice of Law Analysis Under Rule 23

Separate and apart from constitutional and statutory requirements, Rule 23 requires courts to engage in a choice of law analysis. Rule 23(a) requires the claims of the named plaintiffs to be "typical" of and "common" with the members of the putative class; and, in damages class actions under Rule 23(b)(3), a putative class representative must show that individualized issues do not "predominate" over common issues in the proposed litigation, and that the proposed class action is both "manageable" and "superior" to other forms of adjudication.

The courts have construed each of these requirements—commonality, typicality, predominance, manageability, and superiority—as imposing a limit on their

---

18. *Id.* (emphasis added).
19. 28 U.S.C. § 2072(b).
20. 521 U.S. 591.
21. *Id.* at 628–29.

authority to certify classes that would involve the application of laws from many different states. Different courts have identified different elements of Rule 23 as the source of that constraint, as these representative statements from the federal appellate courts demonstrate:

> No class action is proper unless all litigants are governed by the same legal rules. Otherwise the class cannot satisfy the commonality and superiority requirements of Fed. R. Civ. P. 23(a), (b)(3). . . . Because these claims must be adjudicated under the law of so many jurisdictions, a single nationwide class is not manageable.[22]

> Given the multiplicity of individualized factual and legal issues, magnified by choice of law considerations, we can by no means conclude "that the questions of law or fact common to the members of the class predominate over any questions affecting only individual members."[23]

> [A] district court must consider how variations in state law affect predominance and superiority. . . . In a multi-state class action, variations in state law may swamp any common issues and defeat predominance.[24]

> [T]he law on predominance requires the district court to consider variations in state law when a class action involves multiple jurisdictions.[25]

Separately and in combination, these provisions of Rule 23 impose two types of constraints upon the certification of multistate class actions. One constraint is procedural: Rule 23 requires a choice of law analysis to be conducted at some stage in class proceedings. The second constraint is substantive: beyond a certain point, the need to apply the laws of different jurisdictions renders an action unsuitable for class treatment under the Rule.

V. Procedural Requirement: A Choice of Law Analysis Must Be Conducted

In most jurisdictions, a district court must analyze choice of law issues before certifying a class.[26] Several district courts have stated that failing to conduct a choice

---

22. *In re Bridgestone/Firestone*, 288 F.3d at 1015, 1018.

23. *Georgine v. Amchem Prods., Inc.*, 83 F.3d 610, 630 (3d Cir. 1996), *aff'd sub nom.*, *Amchem*, 521 U.S. 591.

24. *Castano v. Am. Tobacco Co.*, 84 F.3d 734, 741 (5th Cir. 1996).

25. *Lozano v. AT&T Wireless Servs., Inc.*, 504 F.3d 718, 728 (9th Cir. 2007).

26. *See In re LifeUSA Holding Inc.*, 242 F.3d 136, 147 (3d Cir. 2001); *Gariety v. Grant Thornton, LLP*, 368 F.3d 356, 370 (4th Cir. 2004); *Castano*, 84 F.3d at 740–41; *In re Am. Med. Sys.*, 75 F.3d 1069, 1085 (6th Cir. 1996); *Szabo v. Bridgeport Machs., Inc.*, 249 F.3d 672, 674 (7th Cir. 2001); *In re St. Jude Med., Inc.*, 425 F.3d 1116, 1121 (8th Cir. 2005); *Lozano*, 504 F.3d at 728; *Andrews v. Am. Tel. & Tel. Co.*, 95 F.3d 1014, 1024 (11th Cir. 1996); *Walsh v. Ford Motor Co.*, 807 F.2d 1000, 1016–17 (D.C. Cir. 1986).

of law analysis before certification violates due process.[27] As the Seventh Circuit has explained, "[n]o class action is proper unless all litigants are governed by the same legal rules"—and therefore the choice of law analysis must be conducted at the certification stage.[28] A failure to conduct this analysis (or postponing it) can be grounds for reversal of the certification order.[29]

The requirement to conduct the choice of law analysis before a class is certified flows from two sources. First, several courts have explained that the timing is based on the need to "find," rather than presume, that all of the Rule 23 standards have been met: "'In order to make the findings required to certify a class action under Rule 23(b)(3) . . . one must initially identify the substantive law issues which will control the outcome of the litigation.'"[30]

Second, the need to conduct a choice of law analysis at the certification stage may also derive from the need to provide meaningful notice to class members, which is mandatory upon certification under (b)(3) and discretionary under (b)(1) and (b)(2).[31] The class notice must "concisely and clearly state . . . the class claims, issues or defenses."[32] Unless the applicable substantive state law has been identified, class members may not have sufficient information to make an informed choice about whether to opt out of the class (or to intervene in a (b)(1) or (b)(2) proceeding).

In some jurisdictions, the courts have been less precise about whether a district court must conduct a choice of law analysis before class certification.[33] These

---

27. *See Yadlosky v. Grant Thornton, L.L.P.*, 197 F.R.D. 292, 300 (E.D. Mich. 2000) ("Due process requires individual consideration of the choice of law issues raised by each class member's case before certification."); *Chin v. Chrysler Corp.*, 182 F.R.D. 448, 457 (D.N.J. 1998) (same); *In re Ford Motor Co. Ignition Switch Prods. Liab. Litig.*, 174 F.R.D. 332, 348 (D.N.J. 1997) (same).

28. *In re Bridgestone/Firestone*, 288 F.3d at 1015.

29. *See, e.g., Castano*, 84 F.3d at 739, 741–43:

The [district] court noted that any determination of how state law variations affect predominance was premature, as the court had yet to make a choice of law determination. . . . A thorough review of the record demonstrates that, in this case, the district court did not properly consider how variations in state law affect predominance. The court acknowledged as much in its order granting class certification, for, in declining to make a choice of law determination, it noted that "[t]he parties have only briefly addressed the conflict of laws issue in this matter."

30. *Id.* at 741 (quoting *Alabama v. Blue Bird Body Co.*, 573 F.2d 309, 316 (5th Cir. 1978)); *see Gariety*, 368 F.3d at 365, 370.

31. *See* FED. R. CIV. P. 23(c)(2)(B).

32. *Id.*

33. *See Maywalt v. Parker & Parsley Petroleum Co.*, 147 F.R.D. 51, 58 (S.D.N.Y. 1993); *In re LILCO Sec. Litig.*, 111 F.R.D. 663, 670 (E.D.N.Y. 1986); *Bussie v. Allmerica Fin. Corp.*, 50 F. Supp. 2d 59, 71 (D. Mass. 1999); *In re United Telecomms., Inc. Sec. Litig.*, No. 90-2251, 1992 WL 309884, at *4 (D. Kan. Sept. 15, 1992).

courts generally reason that choice of law questions will be clarified as the litigation proceeds, and that any state law complexities can be addressed at a later juncture—even after certification. The certification decision in *In re LILCO Securities Litigation* is representative of this line of cases: "In the event that there are material variations in the law of the fifty states, the Court may employ subclasses or decertify those state law subclasses whose adjudication becomes unmanageable."[34]

VI. Procedural Requirement: The Plaintiff Bears the Burden of Proof

Most courts of appeals have held that plaintiffs bear the burden of proof in establishing that all of Rule 23's requirements are met before a class can be certified.[35] This point has been disputed in the past,[36] but the debate was largely put to an end by the Supreme Court's decision in *Amchem*, which stated that "[i]n addition to satisfying Rule 23(a)'s prerequisites, *parties seeking class certification must show* that the action is maintainable under Rule 23(b)(1), (2), or (3)."[37]

Because the plaintiff bears the burden of demonstrating that Rule 23's requirements are satisfied,[38] class action plaintiffs generally must provide the district court with a choice of law analysis.[39] In the words of the Fourth Circuit, "[t]he plaintiffs have the burden of showing that common questions of law predominate, and they cannot meet this burden when the various laws have not been identified and compared."[40]

Some courts have shifted the burden to class action defendants to prove that the forum state's law should *not* be applied on a classwide basis, on the ground that "the proponent of foreign law" bears the burden under the state's choice of law

---

34. 111 F.R.D. at 670.

35. *See, e.g., Cole,* 484 F.3d at 724; *In re Am. Med. Sys.,* 75 F.3d at 1086.

36. *See* 1 HERBERT B. NEWBERG, NEWBERG ON CLASS ACTIONS: A MANUAL FOR GROUP LITIGATION AT FEDERAL AND STATE LEVELS § 2076 (1st ed. 1977) ("Burden of proof concepts . . . are not appropriate in dealing with a determination respecting whether [an action brought under Rule 23] should be permitted to be maintained.").

37. *Amchem,* 521 U.S. at 614 (emphasis added); *see also In re Hydrogen Peroxide Antitrust Litig.,* 552 F.3d 305, 315–16 (3d Cir. 2008) ("[I]t is clear that the party seeking certification must convince the district court that the requirements of Rule 23 are met."); *In re Initial Pub. Offering Sec. Litig.,* 471 F.3d 24, 30 (2d Cir. 2006).

38. *See, e.g., Cole,* 484 F.3d at 724; *see Amchem,* 521 U.S. at 614 ("In addition to satisfying Rule 23(a)'s prerequisites, parties seeking class certification must show that the action is maintainable under Rule 23(b)(1), (2), or (3).").

39. *See, e.g., Cole,* 484 F.3d at 725.

40. *Gariety,* 368 F.3d at 370.

principles.[41] A few academic commentators advocate this burden shift.[42] When the plaintiff does not provide a choice of law analysis, district courts might conduct one sua sponte,[43] but there do not appear to be any cases in which a district court has certified a multistate class when the plaintiff failed to identify and compare the relevant states' laws.

VII. Procedural Requirement: What the Choice of Law Analysis Must Show

The first step in the choice of law analysis is to ascertain whether meaningful differences exist in the laws of the potentially relevant states.[44] The plaintiff's analysis on this point must be comprehensive, not cursory. As the Third Circuit has held, putative class members must conduct an "extensive analysis" of state law variations.[45]

The plaintiff must demonstrate that the potentially applicable state laws do not vary in meaningful ways.[46] Where there are no differences, the application of the laws from multiple states generally will not preclude class certification. In practice, this has prompted parties to file significant "state law appendices" to their class

---

41. *See Mazza v. Am. Honda Motor Co.*, 254 F.R.D. 610, 620 (C.D. Cal. 2008) (holding that "the foreign law proponent must identify the applicable rule of law in each potentially concerned state and must show it materially differs from the law in California"); *Payne v. Goodyear Tire & Rubber Co.*, 216 F.R.D. 21, 27–28 (D. Mass. 2003) (same); *but see S. States Police Benevolent Ass'n, Inc. v. First Choice Armor & Equip., Inc.*, 241 F.R.D. 85 (D. Mass. 2007) (disagreeing with *Payne* and holding that a defendant does not carry a burden at the choice of law stage). Following class certification in *Mazza*, the Ninth Circuit granted defendant's Rule 23(f) petition, and the appeal (9th Cir. Case No. 09-55376) is pending at the time of this writing.

42. *See* Stephen B. Burbank, *The Class Action Fairness Act of 2005 in Historical Context: A Preliminary View*, 156 U. Penn. L. Rev. 1439, 1507 n.264 (2008):

> Class counsel may also be aware of . . . [an] interesting argument that choice of law and class certification burdens are analytically discrete and that, by conflating them, some federal courts have erroneously placed both burdens on the party seeking class certification. *See* Patrick Wooley, Erie *and Choice of Law after the Class Action Fairness Act*, 80 Tul. L. Rev. 1723, 1739–43 (2006). On this view, state courts so inclined can blunt some of the force of *Shutts* and of recent federal and state case law emphasizing the plaintiff's burden of demonstrating compliance with Rule 23 (or its state equivalent). Thus, they can insist that the choice of law question be addressed first, invoke a presumption that forum law is applicable, and place on the party seeking to displace that law the burden of demonstrating that some other law is applicable.

43. *See, e.g., In re Panacryl Sutures Prods. Liab. Cases*, 263 F.R.D. 312, 318 (E.D.N.C. 2009) (explaining that the plaintiffs had not "identified and compared the laws of all interested states and ha[d] thus failed to carry [the Rule 23] burden," but then conducting a full choice of law analysis apparently sua sponte).

44. *Shutts*, 472 U.S. at 816 ("We must first determine whether Kansas law conflicts in any material way with any other law which could apply. There can be no injury in applying Kansas law if it is not in conflict with that of any other jurisdiction connected to this suit.").

45. *See In re Sch. Asbestos Litig.*, 789 F.2d 996, 1010 (3d Cir. 1986).

46. *See Walsh*, 807 F.2d at 1016.

certification briefing.[47] As a general matter, some legal claims or doctrines have been considered to be materially identical across the states, while others have been deemed to vary greatly. (Note that some doctrines appear in both of the following lists.) Legal claims that have been thought to be sufficiently similar across jurisdictions include breach of contract,[48] fraud,[49] breach of fiduciary duty,[50] limitations periods,[51] securities fraud,[52] and implied warranties.[53] Claims or doctrines that have been considered to vary materially from state to state include breach of contract,[54] limitations periods,[55] breach of fiduciary duty,[56] negligence,[57] fraud,[58] the duty of disclosure,[59] products liability law,[60] medical monitoring doctrines,[61] the assumption of the risk defense,[62] negligent infliction of emotional distress,[63] consumer protection laws,[64] warranty doctrines (including reliance, notice of breach, and privity requirements),[65] securities fraud, including the fraud-on-the-market presumption,[66] unjust enrichment,[67] implied covenants to market in oil and gas leases,[68] gaming laws,[69] and provisions of the Uniform Commercial Code.[70]

---

47. *See, e.g., Cole,* 484 F.3d at 725 ("[P]laintiffs have provided the district court with an extensive catalog of the statutory text of the warranty and redhibition laws of the fifty-one jurisdictions implicated in this suit . . . . [Defendant] provided the district court with extensive charts of authority concerning express and implied warranty actions from the fifty-one jurisdictions showing, *inter alia,* variations among the states in regard to reliance, notice of breach, vertical privity, and presumptions of merchantability.").

48. *See Klay v. Humana, Inc.,* 382 F.3d 1241, 1263 (11th Cir. 2004); *Steinberg v. Nationwide Mut. Ins. Co.,* 224 F.R.D. 67, 76–78 (E.D.N.Y. 2004).

49. *See Bresson v. Thomson McKinnon Sec. Inc.,* 118 F.R.D. 339, 343 (S.D.N.Y. 1988).

50. *Id.* at 343.

51. *See Waste Mgmt. Holdings, Inc. v. Mowbray,* 208 F.3d 288, 296 (1st Cir. 2000).

52. *See Amchem,* 521 U.S. at 625.

53. *See Walsh,* 807 F.2d at 1003.

54. *See Agostino v. Quest Diagnostics, Inc.,* 256 F.R.D. 437, 460 (D.N.J. 2009).

55. *See Doll v. Chicago Title Ins. Co.,* 246 F.R.D. 683, 688–89 (D. Kan. 2007).

56. *See id.* at 690–91.

57. *See In re Rhone-Poulenc,* 51 F.3d at 1300 ("The law of negligence, including subsidiary concepts such as duty of care, foreseeability, and proximate cause, may . . . differ among the states only in nuance[,] . . . [b]ut nuance can be important."); *Zinser,* 253 F.3d at 1188; *Bresson,* 118 F.R.D. at 344.

58. *See Castano,* 84 F.3d at 743 n.15.

59. *See id.*

60. *See id.; Zinser,* 253 F.3d at 1188.

61. *See Zinser,* 253 F.3d at 1188.

62. *See id.*

63. *See id.*

64. *See In re St. Jude,* 425 F.3d at 1120; *In re Bridgestone/Firestone,* 288 F.3d at 1018.

65. *See Cole,* 484 F.3d at 726–28.

66. *See Gariety,* 368 F.3d at 370.

67. *See Steinberg,* 224 F.R.D. at 67.

68. *See Stirman v. Exxon Corp.,* 280 F.3d 554, 564–65 (5th Cir. 2002).

69. *See Andrews,* 95 F.3d at 1024.

70. *See Walsh,* 807 F.2d at 1016.

If the laws of the potentially relevant jurisdictions differ, the district court must apply the forum state's choice of law rules to determine which state's substantive law will apply to each class member's claim.[71] In consolidated multidistrict litigation, the court applies the choice of law rules of the state in which each action was originally filed.[72]

VIII. Substantive Requirement: Classes Cannot Be Certified Where the Laws of Several States Must Be Applied and Those Laws Are Materially Different

Where the state laws applicable to the claims of class members differ, courts generally will decline to certify the class on the ground that variations in state law defeat the commonality requirement under section (a)(2), the predominance, superiority, and manageability standards of section (b)(3), or some combination. In *In re Bridgestone/Firestone*, for example, the Seventh Circuit, after conducting a choice of law analysis and determining that all 50 states' laws should be applied to the claims of a putative class, held that "a single nationwide class is not manageable."[73]

There is no clear quantitative limit of the number of distinct state laws beyond which a class cannot be certified. The Fifth Circuit has suggested that no variations are permissible: "In order for common issues to predominate, each of the states whose law is at issue must recognize an implied covenant to market, which is the heart of this class action. . . . The relevant state laws must be uniform in other necessary aspects as well."[74] In *In re American Medical Systems*, the Sixth Circuit characterized a permissible limit as "a few" variations: "If more than a few of the laws of the fifty states differ, the district judge would face an impossible task of instructing a jury on the relevant law."[75] In *Klay v. Humana, Inc.*, the Eleventh Circuit stated:

> It goes without saying that class certification is impossible where the fifty states truly establish a *large number* of different legal standards governing a particular claim.

---

71. States generally follow one of three general choice of law approaches: the "*lex loci*" test, the "most significant relationship" test, or the "government interest" test. *See generally Thompson v. Jiffy Lube Int'l, Inc.*, 250 F.R.D. 607, 627 (D. Kan. 2008) (explaining the *lex loci* approach); RESTATEMENT (SECOND) OF CONFLICT OF LAWS (1971) §§ 6, 145 (explaining the "most significant relationship" test); and *In re Mercedes-Benz Tele Aid Contract Litig.*, 257 F.R.D. 46, 55 (D.N.J. 2009) (explaining the "government interest" test).

72. *See Ferens v. John Deere Co.*, 494 U.S. 516, 532 (1990).

73. 288 F.3d at 1018; *see also Andrews*, 95 F.3d at 1024 (holding that variations in state laws rendered a proposed class action unmanageable).

74. *Stirman*, 280 F.3d at 564-55 & n.9.

75. 75 F.3d at 1085.

Similarly, if the applicable state laws can be sorted into a *small number* of groups, each containing materially identical legal standards, then certification of subclasses embracing each of the dominant legal standards can be appropriate.[76]

Even in courts that might tolerate some variation in the law applicable to the claims of class members, only a very small number of different state law doctrines appear to be permissible. In *In re School Asbestos Litigation*, the Third Circuit affirmed the district court's certification of a nationwide class when the plaintiffs had grouped relevant state law into four categories.[77] The court expressed some doubts about the manageability of four legal regimes, but based on the plaintiffs' "extensive analysis" that "satisfied the district court," the court affirmed the certification. In *In re Telectronics Pacing Systems, Inc.*, the district court certified two negligence subclasses and four strict liability subclasses.[78]

If varying state laws are applicable to the claims of class members, the plaintiff must submit a plan for managing the different laws through subclasses, separate trials, or special jury instructions.[79] In reversing a class certification order, for example, the Fifth Circuit held, "By not providing the district court with a sufficient basis for a proper choice of law analysis or a workable sub-class plan, the plaintiffs failed to meet their burden of demonstrating that common questions of law predominate."[80] Courts have found class certification inappropriate where plaintiffs have failed to submit detailed, workable plans that address the need to apply multiple states' substantive laws.[81]

IX. Special Issues

A. SUBCLASSES

Rule 23(c)(5) provides that "[w]here appropriate, a class may be divided into subclasses that are each treated as a class under this rule." Some courts have relied

---

76. 382 F.3d at 1261 (emphasis added).

77. *See* 789 F.2d at 1010.

78. 172 F.R.D. 271, 291 (S.D. Ohio 1997).

79. *See Zinser*, 253 F.3d at 1189.

80. *Spence v. Glock*, 227 F.3d 308, 316 (5th Cir. 2000).

81. *See, e.g., id.* at 313 ("Nor did the plaintiffs provide the court with a sub-class plan in case the court disagreed that Georgia law controlled."); *Agostino*, 256 F.R.D. at 466–67 ("In cases where numerous state laws are potentially applicable to a proposed class, the plaintiffs bear the burden to 'creditably demonstrate, through an extensive analysis of state law variances, that class certification does not present insuperable obstacles.' . . . Plaintiffs have not suggested how the many permutations in state consumer protection law can be managed by the Court. . . . The Court concludes that the Plaintiffs have not met their burden of proving that the legal variations among state consumer fraud statutes and the factual variations among the Class members can be managed in a practical manner in this litigation." (quoting *Walsh*, 807 F.2d at 1017)).

upon this provision to address the problems of multistate class actions by creating subclasses in which the laws of one state (or of all states with similar laws) would apply. As the Eleventh Circuit explained in *Klay*, "if the applicable state laws can be sorted into a small number of groups, each containing materially identical legal standards, then certification of subclasses embracing each of the dominant legal standards can be appropriate."[82]

But the mere availability of subclassing is, in and of itself, not sufficient to overcome the problems created by the need to apply the law of multiple states. In affirming a denial of class certification, the Ninth Circuit in *Zinser v. Accufix Research Institute* made clear that a plaintiff must conduct a rigorous analysis and show what the subclasses are and that each subclass meets Rule 23's requirements.[83] As one district court recently noted, "[w]hile numerous courts have talked-the-talk that grouping of multiple state laws is useful and possible, very few courts have walked the grouping walk" by appropriately analyzing whether variations within the proposed subclass are meaningful or not.[84]

Similarly, any effort to bypass subclassing by instructing the jury on a "compromise" set of legal standards would likely violate the *Erie* doctrine. As the Seventh Circuit held in *In re Rhone-Poulenc Rorer*, district courts may not make new substantive law in the service of facilitating aggregated litigation.[85] In that case, the district court certified a nationwide negligence class, intending to apply a single "Esperanto"-like jury instruction covering the laws of all 50 states, despite not being the "actual law of any jurisdiction." Using such a hybrid jury instruction, the Seventh Circuit held, was flatly prohibited: "The diversity jurisdiction of the federal courts is, after *Erie*, designed merely to provide an alternative forum for the litigation of state law claims, not an alternative system of substantive law for diversity cases."[86]

B. SETTLEMENT-ONLY CLASSES

Under Rule 23(e), class action settlements require court approval, and settlements also present choice of law dilemmas. In *Amchem*, the Supreme Court expressly held that "[s]ettlement is relevant to class certification" because "confronted with a request for settlement-only class certification, a district court need not inquire whether the case, if tried, would present intractable management problems, for the proposal is that there be no trial."[87] But the Court went on to state that "the *other* specifications of the Rule—those designed to protect absentees by blocking unwar-

---

82. 382 F.3d at 1262.
83. 253 F.3d at 1190.
84. *In re Pharm. Indus. Average Wholesale Price Litig.*, 252 F.R.D. 83, 94 (D. Mass. 2008).
85. 51 F.3d at 1300.
86. *Id.*
87. 521 U.S. at 619.

ranted or overbroad class definitions—demand undiluted, even heightened, attention in the settlement context."[88] Indeed, the Court ultimately affirmed an order decertifying a class because, among other reasons, "[d]ifferences in state law . . . compound[ed] the[ ] disparities" among class members' claims.[89]

Relatively few courts of appeals have addressed the extent to which choice of law problems should receive less weight in a settlement class than in a litigation class and whether settlement is relevant solely to the manageability prong of Rule 23(b)(3) or also to the "predominance" requirement. As a practical matter, most courts reviewing settlements provide broader latitude to settling parties on choice of law issues than they do when class proceedings are contested. For example, in *In re Warfarin Sodium Antitrust Litigation*, the Third Circuit held that divergent state laws did not preclude certification of a settlement class.[90] While the court stated that "there may be situations where variations in state laws are so significant so as to defeat commonality and predominance even in a settlement class certification," any variations in state consumer fraud and antitrust laws for the claims in *Warfarin* "were insufficient to defeat the requirements of Rule 23."[91] Similarly, in *In re Mexico Money Transfer Litigation*, the Seventh Circuit held that where federal and state law claims have been brought together, and where federal law is the principal theory of recovery, variations in state law theories were not sufficient to preclude the settlement.[92]

This is not to say that the general trend toward court approval of class settlements involving multistate claims can be cleanly reconciled with *Amchem*'s injunction that the requirements of Rule 23(a) and of Rule 23(b) *other than* manageability retain all of their force. In *Hanlon v. Chrysler Corp.*, for example, the Ninth Circuit approved a settlement class relating to an automobile defect that involved varying state laws of products liability, breaches of express and implied warranties, and "lemon laws."[93] The court believed the common factual questions, particularly the defendant's prior knowledge of the design defect, overrode any variations in state law. This decision could be in tension with the "extensive analysis" of state law variations that must take place in contested class proceedings.[94] It may well be that—for the practical purpose of promoting settlement—the predominance requirement of Rule 23(b)(3) is applied with less force at the settlement stage than

---

88. *Id.* at 620.
89. *Id.* at 624.
90. 391 F.3d 516, 529 (3d Cir. 2004).
91. *Id.* at 530.
92. 267 F.3d 743, 746–47 (7th Cir. 2001).
93. 150 F.3d 1011, 1022–23 (9th Cir. 1998).
94. *E.g., Cole*, 484 F.3d at 724.

when the propriety of class certification is disputed. At least one court of appeals has so stated.[95]

X. Trends and Open Issues

In recent years, the federal courts have become increasingly reluctant to certify multistate or nationwide class actions on the ground that variations in state law render the action unsuitable for class treatment.[96] To avoid this outcome, the proponents of class certification have contended, with increasing frequency, that under the forum state's choice of law analysis, the law of a single state—often the state of the defendant's headquarters or principal place of business—should govern all claims.[97] In *Bridgestone/Firestone*, the Seventh Circuit cast doubt on whether such a choice of law rule existed for products liability claims: "Neither Indiana nor any other state has applied a uniform place-of-the-defendant's-headquarters rule to products-liability cases."[98] Yet some district court decisions come close to approving such a "place of the defendant's headquarters" rule, and have concluded—under conflicts of law analysis—that the law of a single state is appropriately applied to the claims of all class members. In *Simon v. Philip Morris, Inc.*,[99] for example, the court held that it could apply New York law to a nationwide class of cigarette smokers because:

- The defendants' principal places of business and headquarters were in New York;
- Much of the alleged conduct, including the agreement initiating a conspiracy and the development of a public relations plan, took place in New York;
- Corporate entities in furtherance of the alleged conspiracy were incorporated in New York; and
- Defendants had business investors and lawyers based in New York.

---

95. *See Gunnells v. Healthplan Servs., Inc.*, 348 F.3d 417, 440 (4th Cir. 2003) (explaining that "settlement is relevant to class certification" under *Amchem* and that "Rule 23(e) affects a court's evaluation of predominance.").

96. *See, e.g., Powers v. Lycoming Engines*, 328 F. App'x 121 (3d Cir. 2009); *Cole*, 484 F.3d 717; *In re St. Jude*, 425 F.3d 1116; *Gariety*, 368 F.3d 356; *Zinser*, 253 F.3d 1180; *In re Bridgestone/Firestone*, 288 F.3d 1012; *Andrews*, 95 F.3d 1014; *In re Panacryl Sutures Prods. Liab. Cases*, 2009 WL 3874347, at *2 (E.D.N.C. Nov. 13, 2009); *Doll*, 246 F.R.D. 683.

97. *See, e.g., In re Mercedes-Benz*, 257 F.R.D. 46 (certifying nationwide class under New Jersey law based on New Jersey choice of law principles); *Mazza*, 254 F.R.D. at 620 (certifying nationwide class under California law); *Ysbrand v. DaimlerChrysler Corp.*, 81 P.3d 618 (Okla. 2003) (certifying nationwide class under Michigan law); *Daniel v. AON Corp.*, Nos. 1-06-0240 et al., 2008 Ill. App. LEXIS 1147 (Ill. App. Ct. Nov. 10, 2008) (unreported) (order denying rehearing regarding certification of nationwide class under Illinois law).

98. 288 F.3d at 1016.

99. 124 F. Supp. 2d 46, 53 (E.D.N.Y. 2000).

Similarly, in *In re Mercedes-Benz Tele Aid Contract Litigation*, the district court certified a nationwide class action under New Jersey's consumer protection statute on the ground that, under New Jersey choice of law rules, New Jersey law should govern because the defendant's principal place of business was in New Jersey, the major decisions involved in the litigation were made in New Jersey, and New Jersey had a strong interest in regulating the conduct of corporations headquartered within the state.[100]

In a reversal of the customary litigation positions, in a New Jersey state court case, *Meng v. Novartis Pharmaceuticals Corp.*, the defendants argued in favor of a "headquarters test" for the punitive damages portion of the claim.[101] (The parties had agreed that the law of each plaintiff's state of residence would govern compensatory damages claims.) In this case, the defendant sought the protection of New Jersey's statutory cap on punitive damages. The court agreed with the defendants: "Defendant should reasonably expect to be governed by the punitive damages law of the state in which it maintains its principal place of business and be punished by New Jersey's punitive damages law for any wrongdoing it may have committed at its corporate headquarters."[102]

These decisions have brought the multistate issues full circle. In *Shutts*, the Supreme Court made clear that choice of law issues must be examined carefully in class actions. Following *Shutts*, the federal courts of appeals became largely unreceptive to multistate class suits that would require the application of more than one state's law. In turn, the proponents of multistate class actions have turned to choice of law theories that resemble but can arguably be distinguished from the theories that the *Shutts* Court held insufficient to justify the application of Kansas law to a nationwide class. In *Shutts*, for example, the defendant was not headquartered and did not have its principal place of business in-state, and the Supreme Court concluded that it would not have been foreseeable to the defendant or to its contractual partners from other states that Kansas law would apply to their claims. The application of a so-called "headquarters test" or "principal place of business test" would appear to be in significant tension with *Shutts* and *State Farm*, and most federal appellate courts to have considered such a test have rejected it because

---

100. 257 F.R.D. at 48–60.

101. Nos. L-7670-07MT, L-6027-08MT, 278, 2009 WL 4623715 (N.J Super. Ct. Law Div. Nov. 23, 2009).

102. *Id.; cf. Aguirre Cruz v. Ford Motor Co.*, 435 F. Supp. 2d 701 (W.D. Tenn. 2006) (granting defendant's motion to dismiss non-class punitive damages claims because, even if Tennessee law governed compensatory claims, Michigan law would govern punitive damages claims under relevant choice of law principles, and Michigan law prohibited punitive damages).

of a failure to conduct a proper choice of law analysis.[103] But whether these new rationales will be sufficient to justify the application of a single state's law to the claims of a multistate or nationwide class will no doubt be a key front in the battleground of future class certification wars.

---

103. *See In re St. Jude*, 425 F.3d at 1120 (reversing the district court's certification of a nationwide class on a headquarters theory because the court had failed to "analyze the contacts between Minnesota and each plaintiff class member's claims," but stating "we suspect Minnesota lacks sufficient contacts with all the parties' claims, and the different states have material variances between their consumer protection laws and Minnesota's," citing *Shutts*); *Zinser*, 253 F.3d at 1188; *Agostino*, 256 F.R.D. at 460–65 (rejecting a "headquarters test" approach for a multistate class, under New Jersey choice of law principles, for consumer fraud and breach of contract claims); *see generally* Richard A. Nagareda, *Bootstrapping in Choice of Law after the Class Action Fairness Act*, 74 U. Mo. Kan. City L. Rev. 661 (2006).

PARENS PATRIAE ACTIONS AND THE LIMITS OF STATE SOVEREIGNTY

RICHARD L. FENTON[1]

KENDRA HARTMAN

I. Introduction

A close cousin of the class action, but utilized far less often, is the *parens patriae* action. *Parens patriae* literally translates to "parent of the country."[2] In a *parens patriae* action, the state in its sovereign capacity, typically acting through its attorney general, asserts a claim for injury to its sovereign or quasi-sovereign interests. The action has its origins in the "royal prerogative" exercised by the King of England in his capacity as "Father of the Country." The *parens patriae* power was traditionally used for the assertion of rights on behalf of persons who were under disability and incapable of acting on their own. "Blackstone refers to the sovereign or his representative as 'the general guardian of all infants, idiots, and lunatics,' and as the superintendent of 'all charitable uses in the kingdom.'"[3] This "royal prerogative" and its attendant *parens patriae* function were passed on to the states via the 10th Amendment.[4]

---

1. Mr. Fenton successfully argued both the *Road Home* and the *Caldwell* cases referenced in this chapter.

2. *Alfred L. Snapp & Son, Inc. v. Puerto Rico*, 458 U.S. 592, 600, n.8 (1982); *see also Mormon Church v. United States*, 136 U.S. 1, 57 (1890).

3. *Hawaii v. Standard Oil Co.*, 405 U.S. 251, 257 (1972) (quoting 3 WILLIAM BLACKSTONE, COMMENTARIES ON THE LAWS OF ENGLAND, 47).

4. *See* U.S. CONST. amend. X; *Hawaii*, 405 U.S. at 257–58.

II. Judicial Limits on Parens Patriae Actions for Damages

Except in a few rare circumstances, common law *parens patriae* actions have generally been confined to actions for injunctive or declaratory relief.[5] Courts have historically been hesitant to expand the doctrine of *parens patriae* to include damage recoveries on behalf of individual citizens where class action relief is available. In *Hawaii v. Standard Oil Co.*,[6] for example, the Supreme Court refused to allow the state of Hawaii (suing as *parens patriae*) to assert a claim for damages to its general economy as a result of alleged restraints of trade in the market for refined petroleum products.

The Supreme Court's ruling in *Hawaii* arguably could be explained on the narrow ground that damages to a state's general economy are not within the scope of recoverable damage to "business or property" under section 4 of the Clayton Antitrust Act.[7] However, less than one year later, the Ninth Circuit held in *California v. Frito-Lay, Inc.*[8] that the state of California was prohibited from suing as *parens patriae* for recovery on behalf of individual citizens of the state who had been injured as a result of alleged price-fixing. The court left no doubt that there was serious tension between the procedural class action safeguards under Rule 23 and the expansive view of *parens patriae* power being asserted by the state:

> The proposed *parens patriae* device would disregard all of Rule 23's safeguards without providing new guidelines as to when such wholesale determination of claims may be appropriate or even within the bounds of due process. Furthermore, since a *parens patriae* suit for the benefit of consumers would not necessarily preclude a class action on behalf of the same individuals, defendants could well be faced with two massive actions based on identical claims.[9]

Hawaii and *Frito-Lay* defined the limits of common-law *parens patriae* in damages cases and indicate that due process concerns can be met by a grant of legisla-

---

5. In the environmental arena, the state of Maine was permitted to recover damages on a *parens* theory where an oil spill damaged coastal waters. *See, e.g., Maine v. Tamano*, 357 F. Supp. 1097, 1102 (D. Me. 1973). However, in that case, the state's asserted interest in its coastal waters and the fish that occupied those waters was more akin to a proprietary interest than in the traditional type of quasi-sovereign interest typically asserted in *parens patriae* actions. Similarly, in *Texas v. Am. Tobacco Co.*, 14 F. Supp. 2d 956, 963 (E.D. Tex. 1997), *reconsidered on other grounds*, 1997 U.S. Dist. LEXIS 23289 (E.D. Tex. Dec. 9, 1997), the court found that the state had established a sufficient quasi-sovereign interest in the health of its citizens to pursue a suit against the major tobacco companies for recovery of Medicaid payments made by the state for tobacco-related medical care.

6. 405 U.S. at 263–64.

7. Clayton Act § 4, 15 U.S.C. § 15(a).

8. 474 F.2d 774, 778 (9th Cir. 1973), *cert. denied*, 412 U.S. 908 (1973).

9. *Id.* at 777 n.11.

tive authority coupled with the other necessary procedural devices, such as notice, opt-out rights, and court approval of settlements.[10]

III. Statutory Parens Patriae *Damage Actions Under Hart-Scott-Rodino and Its State Law Analogs*

In response to the "judicial invitation extended in *Frito-Lay*,"[11] Congress in 1976 created a statutory *parens patriae* damage remedy for federal antitrust damage suits as part of the Hart-Scott-Rodino Act (HSRA) amendments to the Clayton Antitrust Act.[12] HSRA authorizes the attorney general of any state to "bring a civil action in the name of such State as *parens patriae* on behalf of natural persons residing in such State . . . to secure monetary relief as provided in this section for injury sustained by such natural persons to their property by reason of any violation of" the Sherman Act.[13]

HSRA and analogous state laws include a number of class action type safeguards. For example, HSRA includes specialized provisions to prevent duplication of recovery, notice, and opt-out provisions, and judicial approval of settlements.[14] However, a significant difference between an HSRA *parens patriae* action and a class action is that a statutory *parens* action does not require court approval or certification before the action can proceed.

Several courts have confronted situations where plaintiffs in a private class action sought certification of a class whose interests were also represented by a state in an HSRA *parens patriae* action. In both cases, the courts denied class certification on the ground that a Rule 23 class action is not the superior method for adjudication where the state attorney general had previously filed a *parens patriae*

---

10. *See Hawaii*, 405 U.S. at 264, 265–66; *Frito-Lay*, 474 F.2d at 775, 777.

11. H.R. REP. No. 94-499(1) at 8, *reprinted in* 1976 U.S.C.C.A.N. 2572, 2578.

12. *See* Hart-Scott-Rodino Antitrust Improvements Act of 1976, Pub. L. No. 94-435, tit. III (codified as amended 15 U.S.C.A. §§ 15c–15h (Supp. 1977)).

13. 15 U.S.C. § 15c(a)(1). Although *Hawaii*, *Frito-Lay*, and HSRA all dealt with remedies available under federal antitrust law, most states have their own antitrust laws modeled on the Sherman and Clayton acts. In response to HSRA, 13 states have enacted similar procedural amendments authorizing the state attorney general to bring a *parens* action for recovery of antitrust damages. *See, e.g.*, ALASKA STAT. § 45.50.577 (Alaska); ARK. CODE ANN. § 4-7-315 (Arkansas); CAL. BUS. & PROF. CODE § 16760 (West) (California); COLO. REV. STAT. § 6-4-111 (Colorado); DEL. CODE ANN. tit. 6, § 2108 (b)–(c), (e)–(g) (Delaware); FLA. STAT. § 542.22 (Florida); IOWA CODE § 48.108 (Iowa); OKLA. STAT. ANN. tit. 79, § 205 (Oklahoma); OR. REV. STAT. § 646.775 (Oregon); R.I. GEN. LAWS § 6-36-12 (Rhode Island); S.D. CODIFIED LAWS §§ 37-1-23, 37-1-25 to -32 (South Dakota); W. VA. CODE § 47-18-17 (West Virginia); *see also* CONN. GEN. STAT. § 35-52 (Connecticut) (containing an explicit bar against duplicative damage recoveries and granting the court discretion to require the attorney general to bring a class action instead of a *parens patriae* action where the interests of justice so require).

14. *See* 15 U.S.C. § 15c(a)(1), (b), and (c).

action under HSRA. In *Commonwealth of Pennsylvania v. Budget Fuel Co.*,[15] the Pennsylvania attorney general brought a *parens patriae* action under section 4C of the Clayton Act as the statutory representative of persons allegedly injured by an alleged price-fixing conspiracy involving home heating oil. On that same day, a private putative class action was filed, also involving allegations that fuel dealers conspired to fix retail prices of home heating oil. The court struck the class allegations and refused to certify the private class, holding:

> A *parens patriae* action is superior to a class action as a means for adjudication of collective claims. The superiority of the *parens patriae* action over the class action is evidenced by the lack of any provision or requirement for court approval or certification of a *parens patriae* action. *Cf., e.g.*, 15 U.S.C. § 15c(b)(1) (directing that notice be sent to persons represented by the state attorney general "[i]n any action brought under subsection (a)(1) of this section . . .") with Federal Rule of Civil Procedure 23(c)(2) (directing notice to class members only after the action has been determined to be maintainable as a class action). In addition, Rule 23(b)(3) of the Federal Rules of Civil Procedure permits class certification only where "a class action is superior to other available methods for the fair and efficient adjudication of the controversy."[16]

The second case, *In re Montgomery County Real Estate Antitrust Litigation*,[17] was a class action brought by private plaintiffs on behalf of a class of purchasers of real estate services, alleging that defendants conspired to fix the price of real estate brokerage commissions in Montgomery County, Maryland. The court had certified a class of purchases from 1974 to 1976, and the court had previously approved a settlement of those claims. The Maryland attorney general, however, had brought a *parens* action under HSRA representing the interests of purchasers who closed their real estate transactions between 1976 and 1977.[18] The private class action plaintiffs then sought to expand the class to include the 1976–1977 purchasers and to approve a settlement of those claims to which the attorney general had not agreed. The court refused to expand the class, holding the that the attorney general's *parens patriae* action was the superior method of resolving the claims of the 1976–1977 purchasers, and that expanding the class would create duplicative and potentially conflicting representation of the class.[19] The court likewise refused to approve the settlement without the concurrence of the attorney general.[20]

---

15. 122 F.R.D. 184 (E.D. Pa. 1988).

16. *Id.* at 185–86.

17. No. B-77-513, 1988 WL 125789 (D. Md. July 17, 1988).

18. *Id.* at *1.

19. *Id.* at *2.

20. *Id.*

IV. The Impact of CAFA: Treating Parens Patriae Actions as Class Actions for Purposes of Federal Jurisdiction

Prior to the advent of the Class Action Fairness Act (CAFA),[21] *parens patriae* actions based on state law claims generally would not be heard in federal courts. States and their respective attorneys general are not regarded as "citizens" for purposes of ordinary diversity jurisdiction under 28 U.S.C. § 1332.[22] Accordingly, the presence of the state as a party would normally defeat the requirement of complete diversity for ordinary diversity jurisdiction under 28 U.S.C. § 1332. The same was true for class actions brought by a state attorney general as class representative, whether pursuant to express statutory authorization or pursuant to its general or inherent authority to represent the interests of the state and it citizens.

CAFA eliminated the complete diversity requirement in the class action context and permitted a class action to be either filed in or removed to federal court based on minimal diversity, provided that the action seeks more than $5 million in aggregate damages and involves claims of more than 100 plaintiffs.[23] CAFA also provides that mass actions shall be treated as class actions for purposes of federal jurisdiction, and defines a mass action as

> any civil action . . . in which monetary relief claims of 100 or more persons are proposed to be tried jointly on the ground that the plaintiffs' claims involve common questions of law or fact, except that jurisdiction shall exist only over those plaintiffs whose claims in a mass action satisfy the jurisdiction amount requirement under [28 U.S.C. § 1332(a)].[24]

So whereas federal jurisdiction over a class action under CAFA may be established based on minimal diversity and an aggregate amount in controversy exceeding $5 million, regardless of the amount in controversy for each class member, federal jurisdiction over a mass action meeting the same criteria will exist only as to those plaintiffs whose individual claims exceed the ordinary amount in controversy requirement of 28 U.S.C. § 1332(a), which is currently $75,000.[25] Under CAFA:

---

21. Pub. L. No. 109-2, 119 Stat. 4 (codified at 28 U.S.C. §§ 1332(d), 1453, and 1711–1715 (2005)).

22. *See Moor v. County of Alameda*, 411 U.S. 693, 717 (1973) ("There is no question that a State is not a 'citizen' for purposes of the diversity jurisdiction.").

23. 28 U.S.C. § 1332(d).

24. *Id.* at § 1332(d)(11)(B)(I).

25. CAFA contains numerous exceptions to the assertion of federal jurisdiction based on the presence of nondiverse defendants or the local nature of the controversy. *See, e.g.*, 28 U.S.C. § 1332(d). These exceptions are beyond the scope of this chapter and are covered in detail in Chapter 10, "The Class Action Fairness Act of 2005," and Chapter 11, "Mass Actions Under the Class Action Fairness Act."

[T]he definition of 'class action" is to be interpreted liberally. Its application should not be confined solely to lawsuits that are labeled "class actions" by the named plaintiff or the state rulemaking authority. Generally speaking, lawsuits that resemble a purported class action should be considered class action for the purpose of applying these provisions.[26]

The possible application of CAFA to attorney general actions was recognized during the Senate debates on CAFA. Congress specifically rejected a proposed amendment to CAFA that would have exempted state attorney general actions from the reach of CAFA jurisdiction. Senator Orrin Hatch (R-Utah) observed during the Senate debates on the amendment that

[a]t worst, [the amendment] will create a loophole that some enterprising plaintiffs' lawyers will surely manipulate in order to keep their lucrative class action lawsuits in State court. . . . If this legislation enables State attorneys general to keep all class actions in State court, it will not take long for plaintiffs' lawyers to figure out that all they need to do to avoid the impact of [CAFA] is to persuade a State attorney general to simply lend the name of his or her office to a private class action.[27]

Thus, CAFA's legislative history suggests Congress recognized the potential for state attorney general actions, whether denominated as class actions or as *parens patriae* suits, to fall within the jurisdictional ambit of CAFA and under certain circumstances be heard in federal court, even where the underlying claims were based solely on state law.

Two cases filed by the Louisiana attorney general in the aftermath of Hurricane Katrina explored the relationship between *parens patriae* actions, class actions, state sovereignty, and federal jurisdiction under CAFA. In *Louisiana v. AAA Insurance (Road Home)*,[28] the Louisiana attorney general filed a class action in Louisiana state court, asserting claims against several hundred insurance companies for alleged failure to fully pay covered insurance claims in the aftermath of Hurricane Katrina to claimants under the state's "Road Home" relief program. The attorney general asserted rights as a representative of a class of citizens who had allegedly been injured, and also asserted claims on behalf of the state itself in its capacity as assignee of insurance claims under assignments executed in favor of the state in exchange for Road Home grants.[29]

---

26. S. REP. NO. 109-14, at 35 (2005), *reprinted in* 2005 U.S.C.C.A.N. 34.

27. 151 CONG. REC. S1157, 1163–64 (2005 WL 309648).

28. 524 F.3d 700 (5th Cir. 2008). Because the case involved claims relating to the state's "Road Home" relief program, the case has been referred to in subsequent cases and will be referred to here as *Road Home*.

29. Although the Fifth Circuit's opinion in *Road Home* does not specifically address the state's argument that it had the ability to sue in state court as *parens patriae*, the issue was briefed by the parties, and the sovereign and quasi-sovereign nature of the state's claims clearly underlie the court's discussion of sovereign immunity.

Defendants removed the action to federal district court under CAFA.[30] The district court denied the state's motion to remand.[31] The state petitioned the Fifth Circuit for interlocutory review of the order denying remand pursuant to 28 U.S.C. § 1453(c)(1) and the Fifth Circuit allowed the appeal.

On appeal, the state argued that, as sovereign, it was entitled to enforce its own laws in its own courts and that CAFA did not apply because the state—which was the sole plaintiff, albeit in part in a representative capacity—has never been regarded as a "citizen" for diversity purposes.[32] The state also argued that the doctrine of sovereign immunity precluded the exercise of federal jurisdiction over claims brought by the state, whether in a representative capacity or in a sovereign or quasi-sovereign capacity.[33]

The Fifth Circuit affirmed.[34] With respect to the requirements of CAFA, the court rejected the state's contention that as plaintiff it was the sole party in interest. By asserting representative claims on behalf of individuals, the court held that the state was not the sole party in interest and that CAFA's minimal diversity requirement was met based on the claims of absent class members.[35] Therefore, federal jurisdiction would lie under CAFA unless considerations of state sovereignty required otherwise. Judge Higginbotham explained:

> We agree that a state is not a citizen under the diversity statutes, including CAFA. But that is not this case. Louisiana seeks relief for both the State and the citizens as "recipients" of insurance. While it is true that as partial assignees and assignors, both the State and the citizens are likely real parties in interest, we need not pause to examine its force. With citizens of Louisiana joined as plaintiffs there is minimal diversity. CAFA supplies federal jurisdiction and a path to removal unless state sovereignty turns away its exercise.[36]

The court then turned to the state's assertion that principles of sovereignty prohibited the exercise of federal jurisdiction over the state's efforts to enforce its own laws in the courts of Louisiana. The court first rejected defendants' argument that sovereign immunity is a doctrine that relates only to suits against the state and is inoperative where the state is a plaintiff.[37] The court proceeded to explore the constitutional underpinnings of the doctrine of immunity and raised serious questions as to whether federal jurisdiction could, as a threshold matter, ordinarily be invoked to force a state to litigate in a federal forum questions of state law against

---

30. *Road Home*, 524 F.3d at 702.
31. *Id.*
32. *Id.*
33. *Id.*
34. *Id.* at 712.
35. *Id.*
36. *Id.* at 706 (footnotes omitted).
37. *Id.* at 707.

defendants over whom it had regulatory authority.[38] However, the court ultimately concluded that the state waived any sovereign immunity protection by joining a class of individual citizens who were clearly not entitled to such immunity:

> In sum, we are persuaded that we ought to rest our decision on the most narrow of grounds—waiver and its predicate that any immunity the State may have cannot be conferred by the State upon the prosecution of suits by private citizens. We are persuaded that the State cannot pull these citizens under its claimed umbrella of protection in frustration of a congressional decision to give access to federal district courts to defendants exposed to these private claims, presumably for reasons not far removed from those that led the first Congress to confer diversity jurisdiction—known then and now to the trial bar as "home cooking."[39]

However, while holding that the state had waived sovereign immunity by joining a class of private citizens, the court did instruct the district court to explore on remand whether the claims of the state acting in its sovereign capacity could be separated from the claims pertaining to class members, and, if so, whether it would be appropriate to remand the state's own claims to state court while retaining jurisdiction over the class claims.[40]

Just three months later, the Fifth Circuit again addressed the interplay between CAFA and actions brought by the Louisiana attorney general in its sovereign or quasi-sovereign capacity in *State of Louisiana ex rel. Caldwell v. Allstate Insurance Company* (*Caldwell*).[41] In *Caldwell*, the Louisiana attorney general sued a number of insurance companies and certain third-party software companies in state court under the Louisiana Monopolies Act for alleged manipulation of the value of claims payouts and premiums in connection with the settlement of Hurricane Katrina losses.[42] Unlike the attorney general's action in *Road Home*, *Caldwell* was not filed as a class action, and the attorney general claimed to be suing solely in its capacity as *parens patriae*. Defendants removed the action to federal court under CAFA, asserting that the action, although denominated as a *parens patriae* suit, was either a class action or, alternatively, a mass action under CAFA because individual claimants were the real parties in interest.[43] As in *Road Home*, the Fifth Circuit granted discretionary interlocutory review following entry of an order by the district court denying remand.

After discussing the nature of *parens patriae* suits, the court ultimately concluded that the label was unimportant. For purposes of determining whether

---

38. *Id.*
39. *Id.* at 711 (footnotes omitted).
40. *Id.* at 712.
41. 536 F.3d 418 (5th Cir. 2008).
42. *Id.* at 423–24.
43. *Id.* at 423.

federal jurisdiction was appropriate under CAFA, the court would look to the substance of the claim and the nature of the interests at issue.[44] The court agreed with the district court's conclusion that the prayer for treble damages on behalf of the citizens of the state made the individual citizens, not the state, the real parties in interest.[45] As such, the claim was at a minimum a "mass action" under CAFA:

> The parties vigorously debate whether the Attorney General's *parens patriae* authority is extensive enough to allow the State to sue for treble damages in a representative capacity under state law. We need not address that issue. Even assuming *arguendo* that the Attorney General has standing to bring such a representative action, the narrow issue before this court is who are the real parties in interest: the individual policyholders or the State. We conclude that as far as the State's request for treble damages is concerned, the policyholders are the real parties in interest. The text of § 137 of the Monopolies Act, which authorizes the recovery of treble damages, plainly states that "any person who is injured in his business or property" under the Monopolies Act "shall recovery [treble] damages." The plain language of that provision makes clear that individuals have the right to enforce this provision. Accordingly, we agree with the district court and hold that under § 137 the policyholders, and not the State, are the real parties in interest.
>
> . . . .
>
> Having determined that the policyholders are real parties in interest, we agree that this action was properly removed pursuant to CAFA because the requirements of a "mass action" are easily met given the factual circumstances of this case: this is a civil action involving the monetary claims of 100 or more persons that is proposed to be tried jointly on the ground that the claims involve common questions of law or fact; the aggregate amount in controversy is at least $5 million, this action involves claims of more than 100 Louisiana citizens who are minimally diverse from Defendants, and it is being brought in a representative capacity on behalf of those who allegedly suffered harm. *See* 28 U.S.C. § 1332(d)(11)(B)(I). Since we have concluded that this case was properly removed under CAFA's "mass action" provision, we need not address whether this lawsuit could, following further proceedings on remand, properly proceed as a class action under CAFA.[46]

As in *Road Home*, the court rejected the state's contention that sovereign immunity prohibited removal under CAFA, but again raised the possibility that on remand the district court might explore ways in which the claims of the state in its sovereign capacity might be severed from the claims of individual citizens and be remanded to state court. Specifically, the court explained that the state's assertion of its sovereign interest was much greater with respect to its claims for injunctive

---

44. *Id.*
45. *Id.* at 428.
46. *Id.* at 429–30.

and declaratory relief—the traditional remedies sought in *parens patriae* actions—and that such claims might possibly be severed from the treble damage claims.[47]

Judge Southwick dissented on the ground that the attorney general had not brought the action pursuant to Louisiana's analog to Rule 23 and therefore did not meet CAFA's requirement that the action be filed "under rule 23 of the Federal Rules of Civil Procedure or similar State statute or rule of judicial procedure authorizing an action to be brought by 1 or more representative persons as a class action."[48] While Judge Southwick acknowledged that there was a question as to whether the attorney general indeed possessed the power to seek treble damage relief on behalf of private citizens, he noted that he would have remanded the action to state court for a determination of whether the Louisiana attorney general had standing under Louisiana law to seek treble damages in a *parens patriae* capacity, rather than force the attorney general to litigate the matter as a class or mass action in order to confer federal jurisdiction.[49]

The teaching of *Road Home* and *Caldwell* is that attorney general actions, even when purportedly filed in a state's sovereign capacity and not as a class action, may well be subject to federal jurisdiction and removal under CAFA. This is particularly true where the attorney general seeks monetary relief on behalf of citizens of the state, as opposed to injunctive or declaratory relief or damages suffered by the state itself in its proprietary capacity. While principles of sovereign immunity may preclude the state from being dragged into federal court even as a plaintiff in the latter situation, any such protection is waived when the state attempts to act as a representative of private interests for monetary recovery.

---

47. *Id.* at 430.
48. *Id.* at 434.
49. *Id.*

CLASS ACTIONS INVOLVING FOREIGN PARTIES

ROBERT TED PARKER

CHARLES F. RYSAVY[1]

I. Introduction

The judicial system in the United States has long been attractive to foreign plaintiffs, whether businesses or individuals, as a venue to seek redress for their grievances. Numerous advantages may be available to a foreign plaintiff in litigating his or her claim in the United States as opposed to in his or her native country. These include substantive legal theories, procedures, and categories of damages available in U.S. courts but not elsewhere—extensive pretrial discovery, strict liability, jury trials, and punitive damages.[2] Plaintiffs in most civil law countries face the potential for financial ruin from attorney fees being awarded to the prevailing party, in contrast to U.S. courts where fee shifting to parties who do not prevail is the rare exception.[3] Compensatory damages awarded by U.S. juries also typically dwarf recoveries for the same injuries in other countries.[4] Exchange rates and threats of foreign currency devaluation can also make compensation in U.S. dollars more

---

1. Mr. Parker served as trial and appellate counsel for the foreign prevailing party in a case cited in this chapter, *Alfadda v. Fenn*, 159 F.3d 41 (2d Cir. 1998). Mr. Rysavy served as lead counsel for one of the defendants in the international products liability litigation against manufacturers of military radar systems discussed in this chapter, *Blum v. Gen. Elec. Co.*, 547 F. Supp. 2d 717 (W.D. Tex. 2008).

2. *Piper Aircraft Co. v. Reyno*, 454 U.S. 235, 252 n.18 (1981); Andrew W. Davis, *Federalizing Foreign Relations: The Case for Expansive Federal Jurisdiction in Private International Litigation*, 89 MINN. L. REV. 1464 n.1 (2005).

3. Manuel A. Gomez, *Like Migratory Birds: Latin American Claimants in U.S. Courts and the Ford-Firestone Rollover Litigation*, 11 SW. J. L. & TRADE AM. 281, 297 (2005).

4. *Id.* at 295.

attractive.[5] Finally, most foreign countries have no contingent fee system, and many expressly prohibit the practice.[6]

The relative benefits to foreign plaintiffs of litigating their claims in the United States are particularly apparent when those claims have the potential to be aggregated into a class action. The American-style class action is unique among civil justice systems. Most countries have no procedural mechanism whatsoever for aggregating claims into a collective action,[7] and the relatively small number of countries that do allow collective actions have declined to adopt American-style class actions.[8] Foreign claimants, therefore, are attracted by many of the same strategic and financial benefits that attract U.S. plaintiffs to file claims seeking to redress their own grievances and those of "all others similarly situated."[9]

II. Class Actions Involving Foreign Plaintiffs

Most issues that arise in class actions involving foreign plaintiffs also arise in class actions involving domestic plaintiffs or in suits involving foreign plaintiffs suing individually. Some that may arise rarely in other contexts, however, arise consistently in putative class actions involving foreign plaintiffs. Most of these issues are likely to play a central role in the class certification process or in motions to dismiss or for summary judgment.

A. ENFORCEABILITY OF FOREIGN JUDGMENTS/RES JUDICATA

One issue that can impact a class action by foreign plaintiffs in numerous ways is whether the plaintiffs' home jurisdiction will recognize a judgment entered by the U.S. court.

Most U.S. courts will recognize and enforce a judgment entered by the court of a foreign country pursuant to the Uniform Foreign-Country Money Judgments Recognition Act (UFCMJRA).[10] The UFCMJRA provides that a judgment entered by a foreign court that is "final and conclusive and enforceable where rendered" is enforceable in the same manner as a judgment of a sister state that is entitled to full faith and credit.[11] There is no analog to the UFCMJRA, however, among international treaties or agreements, and the courts of many foreign countries will

---

5. *Id.* at 296.

6. *Id.*; Herbert M. Kritzer, *The Wages of Risk: The Returns of Contingency Fee Legal Practice*, 47 DePaul Rev. 267 (1998).

7. Davis, *supra* note 2, at 1464.

8. Stephen J. Choi & Linda J. Silberman, *Transnational Litigation and Global Securities Class-Action Lawsuits*, 2009 Wis. L. Rev. 465, 485–88 (2009) (discussing claim aggregation procedures utilized in Germany, England, Sweden, Canada, and Australia).

9. Gomez, *supra* note 3, at 294–97.

10. Unif. Foreign Country Money Judgments Recognition Act § 3, 13 U.L.A. 39 (2005).

11. *Id.*

refuse to recognize a judgment entered by a U.S. court.[12] In the 1990s, at the suggestion of the U.S. delegation, the Hague Conference on Private International Law agreed to begin work on a multilateral judgments convention, the Convention on Jurisdiction and the Recognition and Enforcement of Foreign Judgments in Civil and Commercial Matters.[13] The draft convention that circulated in 1999[14] was so unpopular, even with the U.S. delegation, that the vote was postponed.[15] To date, only one country, Mexico, has signed on to the convention.[16] The result is that a foreign court may ignore the judgment and findings of a U.S. court and decide de novo some or all of the issues litigated in a U.S. action.[17]

There are several reasons why a foreign jurisdiction may not recognize a particular U.S. court decision or judgment, including (1) the foreign court does not recognize the U.S. court's jurisdiction over the claim;[18] (2) the foreign court requires execution of a reciprocity treaty before recognizing a judgment from another country;[19] (3) the foreign court does not recognize punitive damages as a remedy;[20] (4) the foreign court does not consider an opt-out class binding on absent class

---

12. See, e.g., In re DaimlerChrysler AG Sec. Litig., 216 F.R.D. 291, 300–01 (D. Del. 2003) (discussing the possibility of foreign courts' nonrecognition of verdict); CL Alexanders, Laing & Cruickshank v. Goldfeld, 127 F.R.D. 454, 459–60 (S.D.N.Y. 1989) (same); In re Cable & Wireless, PLC, Sec. Litig., 321 F. Supp. 2d 749, 764–65 (E.D. Va. 2004) (same); see also Teena-Ann V. Sankoorikal, David A. Herman & Stephanie N. Grace, Current Legal Issues Relating to the Inclusion of Foreign Plaintiffs in Securities Class Actions, in MANAGING COMPLEX LITIGATION 2008: LEGAL STRATEGIES AND BEST PRACTICES IN "HIGH-STAKES" CASES 11, 28 (PLI 2008) (discussing foreign courts' refusal to recognize judgments from American courts).

13. Hague Convention on Private International Law, Final Act of the Eighteenth Session, in Proceedings of the Eighteenth Session 29, 47 (1996) (The Hague, 1999).

14. Hague Convention on Private International Law, Enforcement of Judgment, Preliminary Draft Convention on Jurisdiction and Foreign Judgments in Civil and Commercial Matters adopted by the Special Commission and Report by Peter Nygh and Fausto Pocar, Prelim. Doc. 11 (Aug. 2000), available at http://www.hcch.net/upload/wop/jdgmpd11.pdf.

15. See Ralf Michaels, Two Paradigms of Jurisdiction, 27 MICH. J. INT'L L. 1003, 1009–10 (2006) (discussing the failed Hague Convention).

16. Status Table of the Hague Convention, available at http://www.hcch.net/index_en.php?act=conventions.status&cid=98. The unpopularity of this convention is a stark contrast to the United Nations Convention on the Recognition and Enforcement of Arbitral Awards of 1958, to which 144 countries, including the United States, are signatories. 21 U.S.T. 2517, T.I.A.S. 6997, 330 U.N.T.S. 38 (effective in the United States on Dec. 29, 1970), codified at 9 U.S.C. §§ 201–08. See UNCITRAL, Status 1958—Convention on the Recognition and Enforcement of Foreign Arbitral Awards, available at http://www.uncitral.org/uncitral/en/uncitral_texts/arbitration/NYConvention_status.html. By this convention, member countries agree to enforce arbitration clauses and recognize and enforce arbitration awards made in other states.

17. See, e.g., In re DaimlerChrysler, 216 F.R.D. at 300–01 (discussing the possibility of foreign courts' nonrecognition of verdict because of jurisdictional concerns); CL Alexanders, 127 F.R.D. at 459–60 (same).

18. See, e.g., In re DaimlerChrysler, 216 F.R.D. at 300–01.

19. See, e.g., In re Vivendi Universal, S.A. Sec. Litig., 242 F.R.D. 76, 102 (S.D.N.Y. 2007) (discussing the necessity of a formal reciprocal agreement for Austria to recognize U.S. judgments).

20. See, e.g., Order of German Fed. Constitutional Court (Bundesverfassungsgericht) of 25 July 2003, 2 BVerfGE 1198/03 (refusing service of process upon defendant because the U.S. class action device and punitive damages were abusive and unconstitutional).

members;[21] or (5) the foreign court simply does not recognize U.S. class action suits as a legitimate method of resolving disputes.[22] Regardless of the reason, however, the danger of nonrecognition and nonenforcement by foreign courts may affect a court's willingness to hear a class action involving foreign parties.

Even the *reasonable possibility* that a foreign court will reject a judgment entered in a U.S. class action proceeding has great tactical, procedural, and substantive implications for the practitioner in this area. As discussed *infra*, this fact alone may be a sufficient basis upon which to dismiss the action in its entirety on forum non conveniens or indispensable party grounds, or to deny class certification.

B. FORUM NON CONVENIENS

A motion to dismiss on forum non conveniens grounds is frequently a defendant's first attack against a putative class action brought on behalf of foreign plaintiffs and is frequently the most significant barrier for a foreign putative class representative.[23] The essence of forum non conveniens is that a federal court may "decline to exercise its jurisdiction when it appears that the convenience of the parties and the court and the interests of justice indicate that the action should be tried in another forum."[24] The Supreme Court long ago declared that dismissal on forum non conveniens grounds is an exceptional remedy that should rarely be granted.[25] Even so, a number of courts have used this exceptional remedy to dismiss putative class actions brought by foreign plaintiffs.[26]

One reason why forum non conveniens motions are granted more frequently in actions brought by foreign plaintiffs is that the substantial deference ordinarily afforded a plaintiff's choice of forum is not afforded when a plaintiff chooses not to sue in his or her home forum,[27] especially when "it appears that the plaintiff's choice of a U.S. forum was motivated by forum-shopping reasons," including such

---

21. *See, e.g.*, *CL Alexanders*, 127 F.R.D. at 459–60 (denying plaintiff's motion for class certification noting that British court would not recognize a foreign judgment in an "opt-out" class action because the British subject had done nothing to invoke the assistance of the U.S. court).

22. *See, e.g.*, *Vivendi Universal*, 242 F.R.D. at 232–33 (noting that Germany does not recognize the class action).

23. Anne McGinness Kearse, Note, *Forfeiting the Home-Court Advantage: The Federal Doctrine of* Forum non conveniens, 49 S.C. L. Rᴇᴠ. 1303 (1998).

24. *Baumgart v. Fairchild Aircraft Corp.*, 981 F.2d 824, 828 (5th Cir. 1993).

25. *Gulf Oil Corp. v. Gilbert*, 330 U.S. 501, 509 (1947).

26. *See, e.g.*, *Gilstrap v. Radianz Ltd.*, 233 F. App'x 83 (2d Cir. 2007); *Carijano v. Occidental Petroleum Corp.*, 548 F. Supp. 2d 823 (C.D. Cal. 2008); *Aguinda v. Texaco, Inc.*, 303 F.3d 470 (2d Cir. 2002); *Warlop v. Lernout*, 473 F. Supp. 2d 260 (D. Mass. 2007); *In re Vioxx Prods. Liab. Litig.*, 448 F. Supp. 2d 741 (E.D. La. 2006); *Gilstrap v. Radianz Ltd.*, No. 05 Civ. 7947 (PKC), 2006 WL 2088187 (S.D.N.Y. July 26, 2006); *Minadeo v. Alcon Labs.*, 168 S.W.3d 699 (Mo. App. 2005).

27. *Piper Aircraft*, 454 U.S. at 255–56; *see also Koster v. Lumbermens Mut. Cas. Co.*, 330 U.S. 518, 524 (1947); *Windt v. Quest Commc'n Int'l Inc.*, 529 F.3d 183, 190 (3d Cir. 2008).

things as "the habitual generosity of juries in the United States or in the forum district . . . or the inconvenience and expense to the defendant resulting from litigation in that forum" when "convenience would be better served by litigating in another country's courts."[28]

In an effort to secure greater deference to a foreign plaintiff's choice of a U.S. court, foreign class actions filed in the United States frequently include a small handful of U.S. residents as named class representatives or class members.[29] This tactic has met with some success,[30] although courts still dismiss such actions in their entirety if the circumstances indicate that the U.S. citizens have been added to a fundamentally foreign controversy primarily to legitimize plaintiffs' choice of venue.[31] Moreover, plaintiffs may find that they have won the forum non conveniens battle, but lost the class certification war by agglomerating U.S. and foreign plaintiffs' claims. A single class composed of members from different countries substantially increases the chance that the court will conclude that the proposed class fails to satisfy the elements of commonality, superiority, and manageability.[32]

The defendant seeking dismissal on forum non conveniens grounds first must show that there is an "available" alternative forum.33 This is easily done if the defendant consents to jurisdiction in the foreign court, since an alternative forum is "available" as long as the entire case and all parties to it come within the jurisdiction of that forum.[34] When dismissing cases on the grounds of forum non conveniens, courts may enter "conditional dismissals" to protect the plaintiff from being penalized.[35] Often one such condition is upon the party's consent to jurisdiction

28. *Piper Aircraft*, 454 U.S. at 255–56.

29. *Koster*, 330 U.S. at 524; *see also Piper Aircraft*, 454 U.S. at 255–56 (citations omitted); *Forsythe v. Saudi Arabian Airlines Corp.*, 885 F.2d 285, 290–91 (5th Cir. 1989) (American plaintiff's choice of his home forum in an otherwise Saudi Arabian controversy cannot be given dispositive weight).

30. *Sarei v. Rio Tinto PLC*, 221 F. Supp. 2d 1116 (C.D. Cal. 2002) (applying the strong presumption in favor of plaintiff's choice of forum because "one of the named plaintiffs is a resident of the United States"), *reh'g granted*, 499 F.3d 923 (9th Cir. 2007). However, the inclusion of U.S. plaintiffs in a predominantly foreign class may have little effect on a court, as the court may dismiss only the foreign class while maintaining action for U.S. plaintiffs. *See, e.g., In re Vioxx*, 448 F. Supp. 2d 741 (dismissing French and Italian classes, but not entire action); *Blum*, 547 F. Supp. 2d 717 (severing part of foreign class and discussing lower level of deference paid to this class's forum selection). *Cf. In re Dow Corning Corp.*, 255 B.R. 445, 526–27 (E.D. Mich. 2000) (applying different degrees of deference to foreign and domestic claimants in bankruptcy action).

31. *See Iragorri v. United Techs. Corp.*, 274 F.3d 65, 72 (2d Cir. 2001) ("[T]he more it appears that the plaintiff's choice of a U.S. forum was motivated by forum-shopping reasons . . . the less deference the plaintiff's choice commands").

32. *See* section II.E, *infra*.

33. *See Gonzalez v. Chrysler Corp.*, 301 F.3d 377, 380 (5th Cir. 2002).

34. *Id.* (internal citations omitted); *see also* Kearse, *supra* note 23, at 1315.

35. *Blanco v. Banco Industrial de Venezuela, SA*, 997 F.2d 974, 984 (2d Cir. 1993) ("[F]orum non conveniens dismissals are often appropriately conditioned to protect the party opposing dismissal.").

in the foreign forum.[36] The failure of a guarantee of the valid jurisdiction of the alternative forum is grounds to reverse a dismissal.[37]

The defendant next must show that the alternative forum is "adequate."[38] Courts generally find that common law jurisdictions are adequate forums.[39] A foreign forum is "adequate" as long as "the parties will not be deprived of *all* remedies or treated unfairly, even though they may not enjoy the same benefits as they might receive in an American court."[40] It is not necessary that there be complete identity of procedures, causes of action, or remedies, and plaintiffs can be significantly disadvantaged in terms of the governing substantive and procedural laws in the foreign court relative to their chosen U.S. forum.[41] A foreign forum may still be considered "adequate" even though it does not allow class actions or contingent fee arrangements, there is no pretrial discovery, and the damages awarded in that forum are likely to be far less than amounts awarded in American courts.[42] Such differences do not merit "conclusive or even substantial weight" in the forum non conveniens analysis.[43] Plaintiffs, therefore, cannot defeat a motion to dismiss on forum non conveniens grounds merely by demonstrating that the substantive law of the alternative forum is less favorable than that of their chosen forum.[44]

Alternate forums have been found inadequate, however, when the legitimacy of the country's judicial system is in question, such as during a civil war.[45] An

---

36. *R. Maganlal & Co. v. M.G. Chem. Co.*, 942 F.2d 164, 167 (2d Cir. 1991); *Mercier v. Sheraton Int'l, Inc.*, 981 F.2d 1345, 1349 (1st Cir. 1993).

37. *See Jota v. Texaco, Inc.*, 157 F.3d 153, 159 (2d Cir. 1998) (reversing dismissal because of lack of stipulation as to jurisdiction of foreign forum).

38. *McLennan v. Am. Eurocopter Corp., Inc.*, 245 F.3d 403, 424 (5th Cir. 2001).

39. Peter J. Carney, Comment, *International* Forum non conveniens: *"Section 1404.5"—A Proposal in the Interest of Sovereignty, Comity, and Individual Justice*, 45 AM. U. L. REV. 415, 437 n.130 (1995).

40. *In re Air Crash Disaster*, 821 F.2d 1147, 1165 (5th Cir. 1987) (emphasis added (citing *Piper Aircraft*, 454 U.S. at 255 n.22)).

41. *Id.*

42. *See Piper Aircraft*, 454 U.S. at 247 (holding that a plaintiff cannot defeat a motion to dismiss on forum non conveniens grounds merely by showing that the substantive law of the alternative forum is less favorable than that of the chosen forum); *Aguinda*, 303 F.3d at 478 (absence of a class action procedure does not make a foreign forum "inadequate"); *Coakes v. Arabian Am. Oil Co.*, 831 F.2d 572, 576 (5th Cir. 1987) (absence of contingent fee arrangements); *Pain v. United Tech. Corp.*, 637 F.2d 775, 794–95 (D.C. Cir. 1980) (dismissal may be granted on forum non conveniens grounds even though the law in the applicable forum is less favorable to the plaintiff's recovery), *overruled in part by Piper Aircraft*, 454 U.S. at 247 (rejecting third part of *Pain* test); *Fitzgerald v. Texaco, Inc.*, 521 F.2d 448, 453 (2d Cir. 1975); *Anastasiadis v. S.S. Little John*, 346 F.2d 281, 283 (5th Cir. 1965); *Anglo-American Grain Co. v. The S/T Mina D'Amico*, 169 F. Supp. 908 (E.D. Va. 1959); *Pavlov v. Bank of N.Y. Co.*, 135 F. Supp. 2d 426, 434 (S.D.N.Y. 2001) (same); *Martin v. Vogler*, No. 93 C 3870, 1993 WL 462853, at *2 (N.D. Ill. Nov. 9, 1993) ("While the remedy is obviously deficient in the plaintiff's eyes, it is indisputable that [the alternative foreign forum] does recognize the cause of action at issue and that *some* remedy is available.").

43. *Id.*; *see also* Kearse, *supra* note 23, at 1315; *Baumgart*, 981 F.2d at 829.

44. *Piper Aircraft*, 454 U.S. at 247.

45. *Kadic*, 70 F.3d at 250.

alternative forum may also be inadequate for reasons peculiar to the plaintiffs' particular claims. If the alternative forum will apply different laws than the chosen forum, and those laws would deprive plaintiff of all available remedies (for example, because of a shorter statute of limitations), the alternative forum is not adequate.[46] If the court finds that no adequate alternative forum exists, a foreign plaintiffs' action will remain in the chosen forum.[47]

If the court determines that an adequate and available alternative forum exists, it must analyze "convenience factors" to decide if "the chosen forum serves justice and protects the litigants' rights to a fair trial."[48] In doing this, the court compares the convenience of the possible forums by examining both "private interest factors" that affect the convenience of the litigants and "public interest factors" that affect the convenience of the forum.[49] Through these private and public interest factors, the defendant must prove that the chosen forum is "unnecessarily burdensome or unreasonably inconvenient, and that the alternative forum is more convenient."[50]

The private interest factors center on "fairness and convenience at trial" and the "relative ability of litigants to gather and present evidence."[51] The relative ease of access to sources of physical, documentary, and testimonial proof is one of the most important of these factors.[52] It is questionable whether the ability to access documents and other materials remains a critical issue in modern litigation where such materials can be produced electronically and their actual physical location is largely irrelevant.[53]

---

46. *Mowrey v. Johnson & Johnson*, 524 F. Supp. 771 (W.D. Pa. 1981). *But see In re Union Carbide Corp. Gas Plant Disaster in Bhopal, India*, 809 F.2d 195, 203–04 (2d Cir. 1987) (conditioning dismissal upon agreement to waive any statute of limitations defense); *Ilusorio v. Ilusorio-Bildner*, 103 F. Supp. 2d 672, 675 n.4 (S.D.N.Y. 2000) (same).

47. Kearse, *supra* note 23, at 1304; *In re Air Crash Disaster*, 821 F.2d at 1164.

48. Kearse, *supra* note 23, at 1303; *Gulf Oil*, 330 U.S. at 508.

49. *Gulf Oil*, 330 U.S. at 508; *Piper Aircraft*, 454 U.S. at 259.

50. *Carlenstolpe v. Merck & Co.*, 638 F. Supp. 901, 904 (S.D.N.Y. 1986), *appeal dismissed*, 819 F.2d 33 (2d Cir. 1987); *Tramp Oil & Marine, Ltd. v. M/V Mermaid I*, 743 F.2d 48, 50 (1st Cir. 1984); *In re Air Crash Disaster*, 821 F.2d at 1159 n.15.

51. Kearse, *supra* note 23, at 1317; *Gulf Oil*, 330 U.S. at 508.

52. *Gilbert*, 330 U.S. at 508; *Piper Aircraft*, 454 U.S. at 238–39.

53. *See Overseas Nat'l Airways, Inc. v. Cargolux Airlines Int'l, S.A.*, 712 F.2d 11, 14 (2d Cir. 1983) (Oakes, J., concurring) (noting that modern advances make international travel and communication easier); *Itoba Ltd. v. LEP Group PLC*, 930 F. Supp. 36, 44 (D. Conn. 1996) ("[T]he entire doctrine of forum non conveniens should be reexamined in light of the transportation revolution . . . ."). The factors considered to determine whether to grant dismissal in a forum non conveniens analysis have been called anachronistic, imprecise, and incoherent. *See, e.g.*, Martin Davies, *Time to Change the Federal* Forum non conveniens *Analysis*, 77 TUL. L. REV. 309, 311 (2002). The ease of international postal services and electronic transfers has rendered the discovery procedure less inconvenient. *See, e.g.*, Gregoire Andrieux, *Declining Jurisdiction in a Future International Convention on Jurisdiction and Judgments—How Can We Benefit from Past Experiences in Conciliating the Two Doctrines of* Forum non conveniens *and Lis Pendens?*, 27 LOY. L.A. INT'L & COMP. L. REV. 323, 353–54 (2005); Alex Wilson Albright, *In Personam Jurisdiction: A Confused and Inappropriate Substitute for* Forum non conveniens, 71 TEX. L. REV. 351, 362 n.52 (1992) ("Even proponents of forum

The ability to access testimonial proof, however, and in particular the availability of compulsory process for attendance of unwilling witnesses, remains a pivotal issue.[54] This is especially true when a significant number of nonparty witnesses reside in foreign countries, where testimony at best can be secured by utilizing the expensive, time-consuming, and frequently difficult process of the Hague Convention—or at worst cannot be secured at all.[55] The often substantial travel and ancillary cost involved in deposing foreign witnesses is also a factor, even when such witnesses can be compelled to testify or are willing to do so voluntarily.[56] It is more difficult for a defendant to prevail on this point when a plaintiff has chosen a forum where the defendant's witnesses and evidence are located.[57] Courts also consider the need to translate documents from a foreign language into English as a factor, but its importance will depend on the total volume of such documents and the relative number in the control of each party.[58] The likelihood that a foreign court will not enforce a judgment entered by a U.S. court and the U.S. proceedings may be for naught weighs strongly in favor of dismissal.[59] Whether a defendant

---

non conveniens dismissals admit that private convenience is often of little importance in today's world of electronic communication and jet travel."). These technologies make a litigant less credible when arguing about geographic inconveniences because of long-distance telephones, facsimiles, cellular phones, teleconferences, and electronic mail. *See* Michael M. Karayanni, *The Myth and Reality of a Controversy: "Public Factors" and the* Forum non conveniens *Doctrine*, 21 Wis. Int'l L.J. 327, 380–81 (2003).

54. *Piper Aircraft*, 454 U.S. at 257–59.

55. The Hague Evidence Convention streamlined the process by which testimonial evidence is obtained from foreign nationals in a foreign country by obligating the courts of participating countries to comply with discovery requests. The Convention allows the requesting U.S. court to send a letter of request directly to the central authority in the foreign country. Davies, *supra* note 53, at 333. The receiving country then has only two very narrow grounds to reject the request: if execution of the request does not fall within the functions of the judiciary, or if the receiving country would be prejudiced by the granting of the request. *Id.* There are no reported cases of a country rejecting on either of these grounds. However, the Hague Convention does not cover all countries, and the process is still not simple. *Id.* So there are still countries in which depositions may be unattainable if witnesses are unwilling to voluntarily testify. Moreover, under the Convention, only depositions may be obtained, or in limited circumstances a witness may "appear" live at trial via live video feed. *See* Fed. R. Civ. P. 43(a) ("Permitting 'contemporaneous transmission' of evidence for 'good cause shown in compelling circumstances and upon appropriate safe guards'"); *see also Beltran-Tirado v. INS*, 231 F.3d 1179, 1185 (9th Cir. 2000) (permitting witness's testimony to occur via telephone in open court).

56. *See, e.g., Slight v. E.I Du Pont de Nemours & Co.*, 979 F. Supp. 433, 440 (S.D. W. Va. 1997) (noting the expenses of the "frequent shuttling of documents and attorneys").

57. *See Igragorri v. United Techs. Corp.*, 275 F.3d 65, 75 (2d Cir. 2001) (en banc).

58. *Borja v. Dole Food Co.*, No. Civ. A 397CV308L, 2002 WL 31757780, at *6 (N.D. Tex. Nov. 29, 2002); *Baumgart*, 981 F.2d at 836; *Sequihua v. Texaco, Inc.*, 847 F. Supp. 61, 64 (S.D. Tex. 1994); *Vasquez v. Bridgestone/Firestone*, 192 F. Supp. 2d 715, 725 (E.D. Tex. 2001). *But see Ingram Micro, Inc. v. Airoute Cargo Express, Inc.*, No. 99 Civ. 12480, 2001 U.S. Dist. LEXIS 2912, at *14 (S.D.N.Y. Mar. 21, 2001) (finding that the need for translation of documents alone is not a hardship of sufficient magnitude to justify dismissal).

59. *Baumgart*, 981 F.2d at 835–36; *Kearse*, *supra* note 23, at 1318 n.137; *Borja*, 2002 WL 31757780 at *6.

can meet its burden of proof on the private interest factors varies with the particular facts of each case.[60]

If the private interest factors weigh in favor of dismissal, a court need not consider the public interest factors.[61] If, however, the private interest factors weigh in favor of the court retaining jurisdiction or are in equipoise, the public interest factors can tip the balance in the forum non conveniens analysis because of the unfairness of burdening a local forum with controversies that have little or no relation to the citizens of that community.[62] When the practical and administrative inconveniences between the forums weigh equally, however, the case will likely remain in the chosen forum.[63] The public interest factors include the administrative difficulties flowing from court congestion; the local interest in having localized controversies resolved at home; the interest in having the trial of a case in the forum that is familiar with the law that must govern the action; avoiding unnecessary problems in conflicts of law or in application of foreign law; and the unfairness of burdening citizens in an unrelated forum with jury duty.[64] Under a forum non conveniens analysis, the need to apply foreign law generally favors dismissal because of the administrative and substantive difficulties in interpreting another country's laws.[65] While federal courts are "fully capable of applying foreign law,"[66] the application of foreign law is a factor that may be considered with the totality of the circumstances and weight in favor of dismissal.[67]

C. SUBJECT MATTER JURISDICTION

1. Some Basics

Subject matter jurisdiction is an issue of great importance when foreign class members seek application of U.S. statutes in litigation involving transactions that occurred abroad. Federal courts are courts of limited subject matter jurisdiction, authorized to decide only those cases that the U.S. Constitution and Congress authorize them to adjudicate: cases raising issues of federal law; cases to which the

---

60. *Piper Aircraft*, 454 U.S. at 249; *Koster*, 330 U.S. at 527; *Williams v. Green Bay & W. R. Co.*, 326 U.S. 549, 557 (1946); *Ernst v. Ernst*, 722 F. Supp. 61, 64 (S.D.N.Y. 1989) (citing *Piper Aircraft*, 454 U.S. at 249–50); *Syndicate 420 at Lloyd's London v. Early Am. Ins. Co.*, 796 F.2d 821 (5th Cir. 1986); *Watson v. Merrell Dow Pharm., Inc.*, 769 F.2d 354 (6th Cir. 1985); *In re Assicurazioni Generali S.P.A. Holocaust Ins. Litig.*, 228 F. Supp. 2d 348 (S.D.N.Y. 2002); *Doe v. Hyland Therapeutics Div.*, 807 F. Supp. 1117 (S.D.N.Y. 1992); *Derensis v. Coopers & Lybrand Chartered Accountants*, 930 F. Supp. 1003 (D.N.J. 1996).

61. *Baumgart*, 981 F.2d at 837; *Empresa Lineas Maritimas v. Schichau-Unterweser*, 955 F.2d 368, 376 (5th Cir. 1992).

62. *Gilbert*, 330 U.S. at 508–09.

63. *Kearse, supra* note 23, at 1313; *Lacey v. Cessna Aircraft Co.*, 932 F.2d 170, 180 (3d Cir. 1991).

64. *Baumgart*, 981 F.2d at 837 n.14; *Gulf Oil*, 330 U.S. at 508–09.

65. *Piper Aircraft*, 454 U.S. at 260 n.29.

66. *Rationis Enters. Inc. of Panama v. Hyundai Mipo Dockyard Co.*, 426 F.3d 580, 587 (2d Cir. 2005).

67. *See, e.g., Pollux Holding Ltd.*, 329 F.3d 64, 76 (2d Cir. 2002) (upholding dismissal where majority of the claims of the majority of plaintiffs must be considered under English law).

United States is a party; and cases in which parties have diversity of citizenship, which includes cases "between a State, or the Citizens thereof, and foreign States, Citizens or Subjects."[68] Where foreign class plaintiffs seek to have a U.S. federal statute applied to predominantly foreign transactions, the court must decide whether the facts are too remote or will reasonably permit its exercise of subject matter jurisdiction. The court considers "whether Congress would have wished the precious resources of the [U.S.] courts . . . to be devoted to them rather than [to] leave the problem to foreign countries."[69]

A federal court's subject matter jurisdiction remains an issue throughout the case. *Lack of* jurisdiction cannot be waived by any party or the court, and may be raised for the first time even on appeal.[70] Jurisdiction cannot be imposed where none exists by virtue of a party's failure to challenge jurisdiction,[71] but a party may be estopped from denying a jurisdictional fact, such as a prior claim of citizenship.[72] A federal court determines its own subject matter jurisdiction, and its findings, pro or con, are entitled to res judicata preclusion after appellate rights are exhausted.[73] Defects in subject matter jurisdiction usually cannot later be raised by collateral attack.[74] Federal and state courts have concurrent jurisdiction over most diversity or federal question cases,[75] but federal courts have exclusive jurisdiction over bankruptcy cases,[76] patent and copyright cases,[77] securities cases under SEC Rule 10b-5,[78] ERISA beneficiary claims for fiduciary breach,[79] cases under the Clay-

---

68. U.S. Const. art. III, § 1. *See, e.g., Kokkonen v. Guardian Life Ins. Co.*, 511 U.S. 375, 380 (1994).

69. *Bersch v. Drexel Firestone, Inc.*, 519 F.2d 974, 989 (2d Cir. 1975). *See also* Restatement (Third) of the Foreign Relations Law of the United States § 402 (1987) ("A state has jurisdiction to prescribe law with respect to . . . conduct outside its territory that has or is intended to have substantial effect within its territory."); *id.* At § 420(9)(c).

70. *Attorneys Trust v. Videotape Computer Prods., Inc.*, 93 F.3d 593, 594 (9th Cir. 1996).

71. *Hajek v. Burlington N. R.R. Co.*, 186 F.3d 1105, 1108 (9th Cir. 1999).

72. *Lydon v. Boston Sand & Gravel Co.*, 175 F.3d 6, 12 (1st Cir. 1999).

73. *United States v. United Mine Workers of Am.*, 330 U.S. 258, 291 (1947).

74. *Chicot County Drainage Dist. v. Baxter State Bank*, 308 U.S. 371, 376–77 (1940); *Ins. Corp. of Ireland, Ltd. v. Compagnie des Bauxites de Guinee*, 456 U.S. 694, 702 (1982). But collateral attack may be allowed where a "manifest abuse of authority" occurred, or the court lacked capability to adequately determine its own jurisdiction. *In re Bulldog Trucking, Inc.*, 147 F.3d 347, 353 (4th Cir. 1998); Restatement (Second) of Judgments § 12 (1982).

75. *Gulf Offshore Co. v. Mobil Oil Corp.*, 453 U.S. 473, 478 (1981).

76. 28 U.S.C. § 1334.

77. 28 U.S.C. § 1338(a). State courts have concurrent jurisdiction in trademark cases. *1st Nat'l Reserve v. Vaughan*, 931 F. Supp. 463, 465 (E.D. Tex. 1996). State courts also have jurisdiction over patent and copyright claims raised as a defense or counterclaim, as the case does not "arise under" federal law. *Lear, Inc. v. Adkins*, 395 U.S. 653 (1969).

78. 15 U.S.C. § 78aa; *Watson v. Roberts, Scott & Co.*, 466 F.2d 1348 (9th Cir. 1972). But state courts have concurrent jurisdiction over securities registration and disclosure claims arising under the Securities Act of 1933, 15 U.S.C. § 77v, which are not removable to federal court if commenced in state court. *Wilko v. Swan*, 346 U.S. 427 (1953).

79. 29 U.S.C. §§ 1104, 1109, 1132(e)(1).

ton Act[80] and other antitrust cases,[81] and in rem admiralty cases.[82] Class actions alleging claims under any of these provisions must be filed in federal court.

2. Subject Matter Jurisdiction with Foreign Elements

Despite exclusive federal jurisdiction over certain types of cases, a federal court will decline to assert subject matter jurisdiction if the case has an insufficient factual nexus with the United States. In a proposed class action without sufficient U.S. nexus, the court may exclude foreign claimants from the class and dismiss their claims. The decision depends on the degree of U.S. contacts, plus the area of substantive law invoked. In securities and antitrust class actions involving foreign parties and transactions, federal courts either assert or decline subject matter jurisdiction based on the principles discussed hereafter.

a. Securities Cases

Cases alleging securities law violations generally are said to be appropriate for class action treatment,[83] as they often meet the predominance and superiority requirements of Rule 23(b)(3).[84] When common issues of fact and law predominate in a securities fraud action, courts usually conclude that a class action would be manageable.[85]

i. The Conduct and Effects Tests

For securities law cases that involve predominantly foreign parties or transactions, the Second Circuit has developed "conduct" and "effects" tests to determine whether Congress would have intended courts to apply the antifraud provisions of the federal securities laws. The "conduct and effects" tests ask "(1) whether any wrongful conduct occurred in the United States and (2) whether that wrongful conduct had a substantial effect in the United States or upon United States citizens."[86] The two tests need not be applied separately, and in fact, "an admixture or combination of the two often gives a better picture if there is sufficient United States involvement to justify the exercise of jurisdiction."[87] But joint consideration of the two tests "is unlikely to provide any additional benefit to foreign plaintiffs

---

80. 15 U.S.C. § 15(a).

81. *Washington v. Am. League of Prof'l Baseball Clubs*, 460 F.2d 654, 658 (9th Cir. 1972) (finding subject matter jurisdiction "by necessary implication," even though not expressly made exclusive to federal courts by statute).

82. *Am. Dredging Co. v. Miller*, 510 U.S. 443, 446 (1994).

83. *See Mills v. Elec. Auto-Lite Co.*, 396 U.S. 375, 382 (1970).

84. *See, e.g., Amchem Prods., Inc. v. Windsor*, 521 U.S. 591, 625 (1997); *Eisenberg v. Gagnon*, 766 F.2d 770, 785 (3d Cir. 1985).

85. *In re Turkcell Iletisim Hizmetler, S.A. Sec. Litig.*, 209 F.R.D. 353, 363 (S.D.N.Y. 2002). *But see Newton v. Merrill Lynch, Pierce, Fenner & Smith, Inc.*, 259 F.3d 154, 162 (3d Cir. 2001).

86. *S.E.C. v. Berger*, 322 F.3d 187 (2d Cir. 2003).

87. *Itoba Ltd. v. LEP Group PLC*, 54 F.3d 118, 122 (2d Cir. 1995).

in a class action lawsuit who purchased a foreign company's stock on a foreign exchange."[88]

A leading case is *Bersch v. Drexel Firestone, Inc.*,[89] a class action in which the named plaintiff claimed to bring the action on behalf of all purchasers of stock, including numerous foreign residents. The appellate court held that there was subject matter jurisdiction as to the domestic plaintiffs' claims. But as to the foreign plaintiffs' claims, U.S. securities laws "do not apply to losses from sales of securities to foreigners outside the United States unless acts [or culpable failures to act] within the United States directly caused such losses."[90] The court found that defendants' conduct in the United States was neither substantial nor direct enough to confer jurisdiction over the foreign plaintiffs' claims. Any fraud occurred at the time when the allegedly false prospectus was placed in the foreign purchasers' hands, and the U.S. activities beforehand (meetings in the United States of underwriters and other professionals, and also some drafting) were "merely preparatory" and "small in comparison" to activity abroad.[91] The court also declined to exercise pendent jurisdiction over the foreign plaintiffs' claims, because of uncontradicted evidence that foreign courts would not give preclusive effect to a judgment in the defendants' favor.[92]

ii. The Conduct Test

Under the conduct test, subject matter jurisdiction exists where (1) substantial acts in furtherance of fraud were committed within the United States that are "more than merely preparatory" to a fraud committed elsewhere, and (2) the acts within the United States *directly caused* the losses.[93] Acts may be "merely preparatory" if they "take the form of culpable nonfeasance and are relatively small in comparison to those abroad,"[94] or are "far removed from the consummation of the fraud,"[95] or "where the bulk of the activity was performed in foreign countries."[96] Acts within the United States that are "merely incidental" to the fraud, such as filing reports with the SEC or disseminating shareholder materials in the United States, are usually insufficient to confer jurisdiction.[97]

Congress did not intend "to allow the United States to be used as a base for manufacturing fraudulent security devices for export, even when these are peddled

---

88. *In re SCOR Holding (Switz.) AG Litig.*, 537 F. Supp. 2d 556, 562 (S.D.N.Y. 2008) (citations omitted).
89. 519 F.2d 974.
90. *Id.* at 993.
91. *Id.* at 987.
92. *Id.* at 986–87.
93. *Id.* at 993.
94. *Id.* at 987.
95. *Psimenos v. E.F. Hutton & Co., Inc.*, 722 F.2d 1041, 1046 (2d Cir. 1983).
96. *Alfadda v. Fenn*, 935 F.2d 475, 478 (2d Cir. 1991).
97. *Psimenos*, 722 F.2d at 1045.

only to foreigners."[98] Conduct may be "more than merely preparatory" and serve as a basis for jurisdiction where: (1) "the fraudulent scheme was masterminded and implemented by [the defendant] in the United States;"[99] (2) "conduct material to the completion of the fraud occurred in the United States;"[100] (3) "substantial acts in furtherance of the fraud were committed in the United States;"[101] (4) the "culminating acts of the fraudulent scheme" occurred in the United States;[102] or (5) the U.S. conduct was "an essential link" in the fraud.[103] The Second Circuit has conceded that "the distinction [between the factors above] is a fine one,"[104] and "the presence or absence of any single factor which was considered significant in other cases dealing with . . . transnational securities cases is not necessarily dispositive in future cases."[105]

Apart from these general guidelines, however, courts since *Bersch* have differed as to the extent to which U.S.-based conduct must have caused the fraud and resultant harm in order to justify application of U.S. securities laws. Some courts have required a direct connection between plaintiffs' alleged losses and the alleged wrongdoing.[106] Other courts have adopted a somewhat less stringent standard, requiring that some degree of conduct within the United States contribute to and further the alleged fraud.[107] Thus, a slight lack of concurrence persists among federal appellate courts in the *degree* of causation required pursuant to Judge Friendly's observation that "[t]he antifraud provisions of the federal securities laws . . . do not apply to losses from sales of securities to foreigners outside the United States unless acts (not 'merely preparatory') within the United States directly caused such losses."[108]

iii. The Effects Test

The effects test "focuses principally on the impact of overseas activity on U.S. investors and securities traded on U.S. securities exchanges."[109] The effects test was

---

98. *Id.*

99. *Berger*, 322 F.3d at 194.

100. *Alfadda*, 935 F.2d at 478.

101. *Berger*, 322 F.3d at 193.

102. *Psimenos*, 722 F.2d at 1044.

103. *Leasco Data Processing Equip. Corp. v. Maxwell*, 468 F.2d 1326, 1335 (2d Cir. 1972).

104. *IIT v. Vencap, Ltd.*, 519 F.2d 1001, 1018 (2d Cir. 1975).

105. *IIT v. Cornfeld*, 619 F.2d 909, 918 (2d Cir. 1980). The discussion at note 115 follows the court's opinion in *In re SCOR Holding*, 537 F. Supp. 2d at 563 (Cote, J.).

106. *Robinson v. TCI/US W. Commc'ns, Inc.*, 117 F.3d 188, 192 (5th Cir. 1997); *Kauthar SDN BHD v. Sternberg*, 149 F.3d 659, 665 (7th Cir. 1998).

107. *Cont'l Grain (Austl.) Pty. Ltd. v., Pacific Oilseeds, Inc.*, 592 F.2d 409, 421 (8th Cir. 1979); *Grunenthal GmbH v. Hotz*, 712 F.2d 421, 424 (9th Cir. 1983).

108. *Bersch*, 519 F.2d at 993.

109. *Europe & Overseas Commodity Traders, S.A. v. Banque Paribas, London*, 147 F.3d 118, 128 (2d Cir. 1998).

first applied in *Schoenbaum v. Firstbrook*,[110] where a Canadian corporation listed on a U.S. securities exchange was sued under the Securities Exchange Act. The appellate court found subject matter jurisdiction, holding that Congress intended that Act "to protect domestic investors who purchase foreign securities on American exchanges, and to protect the domestic securities market from the effects of improper foreign transactions in American securities."[111] Subsequent cases have applied the effects test more broadly to justify subject matter jurisdiction where investors were U.S. residents, not necessarily U.S. nationals, and where the purchases were not necessarily made through a U.S. securities exchange.[112] Courts typically hold that "generalized effects," such as diminished investor confidence in U.S. markets or a decline in purchase by foreign investors, are insufficient to support jurisdiction.[113] Some cases have required "concrete harm to U.S. investors and markets."[114] In sum, foreign investors who seek relief from securities fraud through collective action are unlikely to satisfy the effects test unless the issuer is American or the purchase was made on a U.S. securities exchange.[115]

This presents a formidable obstacle for "foreign-cubed" claimants—i.e., foreign investors that purchased securities of a foreign company on a foreign securities exchange, thus placing all usual touchstones outside the United States. Foreign-cubed plaintiffs who purchased securities abroad may not establish jurisdiction by "bootstrapping their losses to independent American losses."[116] A foreign-cubed plaintiff cannot rely on incidental U.S. activity when the overall securities fraud scheme culminated abroad.[117] False statements in a foreign issuer's SEC filings are insufficient conduct on which to base subject matter jurisdiction,[118] and phone calls and facsimiles to and from the United States, when a transient foreign investor temporarily travels here, are also insufficient.[119]

iv. Lead Plaintiff

The presence of foreign plaintiffs can affect another early issue—the appointment of a lead plaintiff. The Private Securities Litigation Reform Act sets the procedure

---

110. 405 F.2d 200 (2d Cir. 1968).

111. *Id.* at 206.

112. *See Europe & Overseas Commodity Traders*, 147 F.3d at 128.

113. *Bersch*, 519 F.2d at 988.

114. *In re SCOR Holding*, 537 F. Supp. 2d at 562.

115. *Id.* at 563 (although claims of European investors who bought Swiss shares on the SWX Swiss Exchange were dismissed, the court certified a class of U.S. residents who also bought on the SWX Exchange, because 10 percent of the Swiss issuer's shares also traded on the New York Stock Exchange during the class period, and the 10 percent U.S. "float" would have a substantial effect on U.S. citizens).

116. *Tri-Star Farms Ltd. v. Marconi, PLC*, 225 F. Supp. 2d 567, 573 n.7 (W.D. Pa. 2002).

117. *Id.* at 578.

118. *In re Rhodia S.A. Sec. Litig.*, 531 F. Supp. 2d 527 (S.D.N.Y. 2007).

119. *Europe & Overseas Commodity Traders*, 147 F.3d at 129.

for appointment of a lead plaintiff: it should be the plaintiff "most capable of adequately representing the interests of class members" and ordinarily is the investor who has the largest financial interest in the relief sought.[120] This could be a foreign investor that either bought shares of a U.S. issuer or foreign issuer's ADRs on a U.S. exchange or has affected a U.S. securities exchange. But otherwise qualified foreign investors have not been allowed to act as lead plaintiff where (1) a credible showing is made to cast doubt on whether its home courts will grant preclusive effect to a U.S. class action judgment, or (2) serious questions exist about the court's subject matter jurisdiction. The "preclusive effect" concern recently disqualified a group of German investors as lead plaintiffs, despite their holding the largest financial share.[121] Another court allowed a foreign-cubed investor to act as lead plaintiff, however, because the statutory presumption that this foreign investor with the largest financial interest was the most adequate plaintiff was not overcome.[122] In that case, the plaintiff was a sophisticated institutional investor, and any subject matter jurisdiction challenge would not be unique to it, as most other class members would also be foreign investors.

b. Antitrust Cases with Foreign Elements

As with securities cases, numerous courts have found that class treatment is the superior method of adjudicating many antitrust suits. Class certification serves to promote private antitrust enforcement as a supplement to government suits, especially where individual claims are too small to justify individual action.[123] Because antitrust cases often involve small and widely dispersed claims, putative class members usually have little interest in individual control over the litigation.[124]

In the "predominance" context, most courts conclude that the need for individual antitrust damages determinations does not create insurmountable manageability problems.[125] On class certification, the "manageability" issue is whether the proof necessary to demonstrate antitrust impact as to each class member is particular to that class member or whether the necessary proof of impact is common and generalized to all class members.[126]

---

120. 15 U.S.C.A. § 78u-4(3)(B)(i).

121. *Borochoff v. GlaxoSmithKline, PLC*, 246 F.R.D. 201 (S.D.N.Y. 2007); *see also In re Royal Ahold N.V. Sec. & ERISA Litig.*, 219 F.R.D. 343 (D. Md. 2003) (denying lead plaintiff status to a foreign-cubed investor on both jurisdiction and enforceability grounds).

122. *Corwin v. Seizinger*, Nos. 07 CIV 6728 (DC), 07 CIV 7016 (DC), 07 CIV 7476 (DC), 2008 WL 123846 (S.D.N.Y. Jan. 8, 2008).

123. *See, e.g., DeLoach v. Philip Morris Cos., Inc.*, 206 F.R.D. 551, 567 (M.D.N.C. 2002); *Town of New Castle v. Yonkers Contracting Co., Inc.*, 131 F.R.D. 38, 41 (S.D.N.Y. 1990).

124. 1 JOSEPH M. MCLAUGHLIN, MCLAUGHLIN ON CLASS ACTIONS, § 5:71 (5th ed. 2009).

125. *Id.* n.9 (collecting cases).

126. *Id.* n.11.

i. Early Expansive Application

Extraterritorial application of U.S. antitrust laws has been a well-established fact of U.S. jurisprudence. The U.S. Supreme Court decided its first antitrust case involving foreign commerce in 1909 with *American Banana v. United Fruit Co.*[127] In 1917, the Supreme Court decided *Thomsen v. Cayser*,[128] concluding that a combination between U.S. entities and foreigners may violate the Sherman Act, even though no act was done in the United States and the acts were lawful where performed, if the agreement affects U.S. foreign commerce.

A notable peak came in 1945 with Judge Learned Hand's opinion in *United States v. Aluminum Co. of America (Alcoa)*,[129] extending the ambit of the Sherman Act to a completely foreign cartel of French, Swiss, and British ingot producers and a Canadian producer owned by Alcoa. There was no proof of any adverse effect on U.S. domestic commerce, but the court held the cartel agreements illegal because they were *intended* to affect U.S. imports, and thus defendants bore the obligation to rebut any actual restrictive effect on U.S. domestic commerce. This shift of burden of proof may have exceeded the scope of section 18 of the Restatement of Foreign Relations Law of the United States,[130] which would permit a state to prescribe rules for conduct outside its territory that causes an effect within, if it is shown (by claimant) that the effect within is substantial and occurs as a direct and foreseeable result of the conduct outside.[131]

ii. Recent Pullback—FTAIA

Congress thereafter enacted a new section 7 of the Sherman Act,[132] the Foreign Trade Antitrust Improvements Act of 1982 (FTAIA), intended to limit the exterritorial reach of that Act.[133] The FTAIA excludes from antitrust scrutiny any anticompetitive conduct that causes only foreign injury, then creates a limited exception if the foreign conduct has a direct, substantial, and foreseeable effect on U.S. domestic commerce that gives rise to a Sherman Act claim. "The FTAIA thus confers subject matter jurisdiction over the anticompetitive export conduct of U.S. firms only when that conduct would have a direct, substantial, and reasonably foresee-

---

127. 213 U.S. 347, 357 (1909).

128. 243 U.S. 66 (1917).

129. 148 F.2d 416, 444 (2d Cir 1945).

130. RESTATEMENT OF FOREIGN RELATION LAW OF THE UNITED STATES § 18 (1965).

131. *Id.* ("A state has jurisdiction to prescribe a rule of law attaching legal consequences to conduct outside its territory that causes an effect within its territory if: . . . (i) the conduct and its effect are constituent elements of activity to which the rule applies; (ii) the effect within the territory is substantial; (iii) it occurs as a direct and foreseeable result of the conduct outside the territory . . . .").

132. 15 U.S.C. § 6a (1982).

133. Pub. L. No. 97-290, tit. IV, §§ 402 & 403, 96 Stat. 1246 (Oct. 8, 1982), 15 U.S.C. § 6a; *Eurim-Pharm GmbH v. Pfizer, Inc.*, 593 F. Supp. 1102 (S.D.N.Y. 1984) first interpreted the amendment as limiting the extraterritorial reach of the Sherman Act.

able effect on trade or commerce within the United States or on import trade or commerce [of the United States]."[134]

The first case decided under the FTAIA signaled the pullback. In *Eurim-Pharm GmbH v. Pfizer, Inc.*,[135] a German plaintiff complained that Pfizer, a U.S. company, had licensed its antibiotic to companies in various countries with strict territorial confinement of the licensees' sales activities and prices fixed for their various levels of distribution, plus continuation of these limitations beyond the expiration of Pfizer's patent. The court dismissed the complaint, holding that the FTAIA was intended to exempt from U.S. antitrust law any conduct by U.S. companies operating abroad that causes no harmful domestic effect. The *Eurim-Pharm* complaint had alleged only artificially high prices and distribution restraints in foreign countries, but failed to allege any effect on U.S. trade or commerce.[136] Thus, the complaint was barred by the FTAIA general exemption of foreign trade, as it alleged no entitlement under the FTAIA exception for foreign anticompetitive activity creating a foreseeable effect within the United States.

The Supreme Court considered the FTAIA exception for foreseeable effects on domestic commerce in 2004 in the *Empagran I* case.[137] The complaint alleged a price-fixing conspiracy among vitamin producers around the world, leading to higher vitamin prices in the United States and also leading to higher prices in other countries. The Court confirmed that the FTAIA insulates export and other commercial activities abroad, unless they adversely affect domestic commerce.[138] But it held that the causal link between the domestic effect of the anticompetitive conduct and the foreign injury is not satisfied when the foreign injury is *independent of* the domestic effect.[139] The Court then remanded the case to the D.C. Circuit to determine whether the causal link is satisfied when the foreign injury is linked to, and not independent of, domestic effects.[140] On remand, the D.C. Circuit in *Empagran II* concluded that the statutory language "gives rise to" requires a direct or proximate causal relationship, rather than a lesser "but for" relationship.[141] The court then concluded that plaintiff's theory, that the domestic effect of conduct "gave rise to" their foreign injury because defendants could not have maintained

---

134. U.S. Dep't of Justice, Antitrust Guidelines for International Operations § 4.1 (1988), *reprinted in* 4 Trade Reg. Rep. (CCH) 13,109. Footnote 159 of the *Antitrust Guidelines* adds that "the Department is concerned only with adverse effects on competition that would harm U.S. consumers by reducing output or raising prices."

135. 593 F. Supp. 1102.

136. *See also United Phosphorus, Ltd. v. Angus Chem. Co.*, 322 F.3d 942 (7th Cir. 2003) (no evidence that plaintiffs would have made any U.S. sales).

137. *F. Hoffmann-La Roche, Ltd. v. Empagran, S.A.*, 542 U.S. 155 (*Empagran I*).

138. *Id.* at 161.

139. *Id.* at 164.

140. *Id.* at 175.

141. *Empagran, S.A. v. F. Hoffmann-LaRoche, Ltd.*, 417 F.3d 1267, 1271 (D.C. Cir. 2005) (*Empagran II*).

their global vitamin price-fixing without fixing prices in the United States, was only a "but for" cause of plaintiffs' injuries, not a direct or proximate cause, and thus the FTAIA exception could not apply.[142] The D.C. Circuit's *Empagran II* opinion requiring proximate, not "but for," causation has since been concurred in by the Eighth[143] and Ninth[144] circuits.

Thus, *Empagran I* and *II* and their progeny set the bar very high for foreign plaintiffs seeking to bring class action litigation in U.S. courts for anticompetitive injury suffered abroad. Not only will such foreign claimants have to allege and prove U.S. anticompetitive injury as well as foreign injury, but they must show that the U.S. injury was very substantial, and that the foreign injury was not caused by a factor other than the U.S. injury. U.S. appellate courts appear ready to apply the FTAIA amendment as allowing U.S. exporters to commit any anticompetitive activity in foreign markets so long as significant domestic injury does not result within the United States. To date, all alleged simultaneous injury in foreign and U.S. markets has been seen by courts as merely stating "but for" relationships that do not fulfill the FTAIA "proximate cause" or "direct injury" requirement. The FTAIA thus represents a definite step back for U.S. extraterritorial jurisdiction since the mid-20th century, when *Alcoa* applied the Sherman Act to exclusively foreign activity. As the Ninth Circuit described this new attitude: "[plaintiff] made its purchases entirely outside of the United States. It has recourse under its own country's antitrust laws."[145]

D. FEDERAL DIVERSITY JURISDICTION ISSUES—FOREIGN PARTIES

Diversity of citizenship is the sole federal court basis for jurisdiction in cases presenting no federal issue or party. For foreign parties planning class litigation, the basic diversity jurisdiction statute recognizes diversity of citizenship sufficient for federal jurisdiction in cases (1) between citizens of a state and citizens or subjects of a foreign state, or (2) between citizens of different states in which citizens or

---

142. *Id.* at 1270–71.

143. *In re Monosodium Glutamate Antitrust Litig.*, 477 F.3d 535, 540 (8th Cir. 2007) (no proximate cause because U.S. injury was "not significant enough to constitute the direct cause of the appellants' injuries, as they constituted merely one link in the causal chain . . . . at best only an indirect connection" between U.S. and foreign prices).

144. *In re Dynamic Random Access Memory (DRAM) Antitrust Litig.*, 546 F.3d 981, 989 (9th Cir. 2008) ("The defendants' conspiracy may have fixed prices in the United States and abroad, and maintaining higher U.S. prices might have been necessary to sustain the higher prices globally, but [plaintiff] has not shown that the higher U.S. prices proximately caused its foreign injury of having to pay higher prices abroad. Other actors or forces may have affected the foreign prices. . . . [Plaintiff] does not show that the effect in the United States, rather than the overall price-fixing conspiracy itself, proximately caused the effect abroad.").

145. *Id.* at 988.

subjects of a foreign state are additional parties.[146] To be a "citizen of a state," a person must be both a citizen of the United States and domiciled in one particular state. Thus, a U.S. citizen who lives abroad permanently is not a "citizen of a state" for diversity purposes and cannot sue or be sued in federal court on the basis of diversity jurisdiction.[147] Class action claimants, foreign or domestic, who seek to obtain federal jurisdiction based on diversity of citizenship enjoy some special dispensations from the normally strict rules otherwise applicable. First, a review of the usual rules is in order.

Diversity of citizenship must exist at the time the lawsuit is filed. It need not exist earlier, nor is it required to continue later.[148] A defendant's third-party complaint has supplemental jurisdiction as to nondiverse third parties on claims arising out of the same transaction or occurrence.[149]

Diversity jurisdiction can be based on alienage, which exists where there are one or more aliens on one side of the lawsuit and one or more citizens of a state on the other.[150] The phrase "citizens of a state" includes citizens of *different states*, so that a foreign party may bring a single action against defendants who are citizens of more than one state.[151] But an alien lawfully admitted for permanent residence under U.S. immigration laws is, for diversity purposes, "deemed a citizen of the State in which such alien is domiciled."[152]

There is no alienage jurisdiction in actions by one foreign subject against another.[153] As noted, aliens lawfully admitted to permanent U.S. residence are deemed "citizens" of their state of domicile, but courts split on whether this creates an exception to the rule that denies diversity in suits solely between aliens. At least one court allows a diversity suit by one alien against another if one is lawfully admitted to permanent residence in the United States,[154] while others refuse to create diversity jurisdiction between aliens, reading the diversity statute as limiting, not

---

146. 28 U.S.C. § 1332(a). Note that corporations are deemed to be citizens of both the state of incorporation and also the state of principal place of business. *Bank of Cal. v. Twin Harbors Lumber Co.*, 465 F.2d 489, 491 (9th Cir. 1972).

147. *Newman-Green, Inc. v. Alfonzo-Larrain*, 490 U.S. 826, 828 (1989).

148. *See Grupo Dataflux v. Atlas Global Group, LP*, 541 U.S. 567, 571 (2004).

149. 28 U.S.C. § 1367(b). Even if the original basis for diversity jurisdiction terminates (e.g., plaintiff's claim is settled or dismissed), the court may exercise discretion to retain defendant's supplemental claims against third parties. *See Hill v. Rolleri*, 615 F.2d 886, 889 (9th Cir. 1980).

150. 28 U.S.C. § 1332(a)(2)–(4); *Allendale Mut. Ins. Co. v. Bull Data Sys., Inc.*, 10 F.3d 425, 427 (7th Cir. 1993).

151. *Iraola & CIA, S.A. v. Kimberly-Clark Corp.*, 242 F.3d 854, 860 (5th Cir. 1998).

152. 28 U.S.C. § 1332(a). Conversely, foreign nationals *not* admitted by the INS as permanent residents are *not* "citizens" of their state of domicile, no matter how long they live there. *Karazanos v. Madison Two Assocs.*, 147 F.3d 624, 628 (7th Cir. 1998).

153. *Verlinden B.V. v. Cent. Bank of Nigeria*, 461 U.S. 480, 491 (1983).

154. *See, e.g., Singh v. Daimler-Benz, A.G.*, 9 F.3d 303, 309 (3d Cir. 1993).

expanding, the scope of jurisdiction.[155] Under this latter view, there is no diversity where a citizen of Mexico sues a citizen of Canada who is a U.S. permanent resident, as aliens are on both sides of the case.[156]

If an alien is a dual national, the court will consider only the American citizenship when determining the existence of diversity jurisdiction.[157] But if an *entity* party is a dual national and the entity has several citizenships (e.g., a partnership or corporation with both local and foreign citizenships), *each* of its citizenships is considered in determining jurisdiction.[158] This can be a major trap when asserting alienage jurisdiction, as jurisdiction is lacking where one party is an alien and the opposing party is a partnership or LLC with even just one member who is an alien. Without *complete* diversity, an independent basis for federal jurisdiction is required (e.g., a "federal question") in order to maintain a lawsuit against nondiverse parties in federal court.[159]

1. Complete Diversity in Separate Actions

The requirement of complete diversity undercuts the liberal joinder provisions of Rule 20(a) allowing joinder of all persons against whom the plaintiff asserts a right to relief. The plaintiff must limit selection to those persons who are citizens of other states or foreign subjects. A court will ordinarily order a plaintiff to join additional parties where joinder would destroy diversity, unless the court determines that such parties are truly "indispensable," in which case it must dismiss the action.[160]

In an action between citizens of different states, complete diversity is not affected by the presence of aliens as additional parties on either or both sides, if they are not U.S. permanent residents.[161] But there must be a real dispute between the U.S. citizens who are joined by aliens; it cannot be a gambit between aliens, as the court can make a determination of which are the principal adverse parties.[162] Aliens may be additional parties to lawsuits between citizens of different states,[163] but there is no alienage diversity jurisdiction when an alien *alone* sues both a U.S. citizen and an alien defendant, since there are aliens on each side and no diversity.[164]

---

155. *See, e.g., Saadeh v. Farouki*, 107 F.3d 52, 60 (D.C. Cir. 1997).

156. *China Nuclear Energy Indus. Corp. v. Anderson, LLP*, 11 F. Supp. 2d 1256, 1258 (D. Colo. 1998).

157. *Mutuelles Unies v. Kroll & Linstrom*, 957 F.2d 707, 711 (9th Cir. 1992).

158. *See Gen. Tech. Applications, Inc. v. Exro Ltda*, 388 F.3d 114, 121 (4th Cir. 2004) (citizenship of both U.S. and foreign members of limited liability company must be considered).

159. *See Romero v. Int'l Terminal Operating Co.*, 358 U.S. 354, 381 (1959).

160. *See* section II.D.1, *infra*.

161. 28 U.S.C. § 1332(a)(3); *Transure, Inc. v. Marsh & McLennan, Inc.*, 766 F.2d 1297, 1299 (9th Cir. 1985).

162. *Dresser Indus., Inc. v. Underwriters at Lloyd's*, 106 F.3d 494, 498 (3d Cir. 1997).

163. 28 U.S.C. § 1332(a)(3).

164. *Faysound, Ltd. v. United Coconut Chems., Inc.*, 878 F.2d 290, 294 (9th Cir. 1989).

There is also no alienage jurisdiction where there are foreign entities on both sides of an action without also the presence of citizens of a state on *both* sides.[165]

2. Class Actions and Diversity

In class actions, however, complete diversity need exist *only* between the named plaintiff(s) and the named defendant. The fact that the action is brought on behalf of other, nondiverse, class members does not affect diversity jurisdiction.[166] The same rule applies for a class action brought on behalf of an unincorporated association under Federal Rule 23.2.[167] Thus, the class representative may be chosen whose citizenship is diverse from that of the defendants. Each class member's claim in class actions must also satisfy the amount-in-controversy rule,[168] but if one plaintiff's claim satisfies the $75,000 threshold, the court may exercise supplemental jurisdiction "over all other claims that . . . form part of the same case or controversy under Article III."[169] This requires that all claims "arise from a common nucleus of operative facts" so that "considerations of judicial economy, convenience and fairness to litigants" support a single case.[170]

3. "Minimal Diversity"

Although the complete diversity requirement applies to class actions generally, even broader federal jurisdiction exists under the Class Action Fairness Act (CAFA), which allows "minimal diversity" for class actions brought on behalf of at least 100 members seeking relief in the amount of at least $5 million. Diversity of citizenship between any class member (not just the named plaintiff) and *any defendant* will suffice.[171] Similarly, for "minimal diversity," an unincorporated association is deemed a citizen *only* of the state where organized or where its principal place of business is located.[172]

A corporation created under the laws of a foreign state is deemed a citizen or subject of the foreign state for purposes of alienage diversity jurisdiction.[173] An alien corporation may also be deemed to have dual citizenship, as a citizen

---

165. *Gschwind v. Cessna Aircraft Co.*, 232 F.3d 1342, 1345 (10th Cir. 2000).

166. *Snyder v. Harris*, 394 U.S. 332, 356 (1969); *In re Prudential Ins. Co. of Am. Sales Litig.*, 148 F.3d 283, 303 (3d Cir. 1998).

167. *Aetna Cas. & Sur. Co. v. Iso-Tex, Inc.*, 75 F.3d 216, 218 (5th Cir. 1996).

168. Separate and distinct claims by class members cannot be aggregated for jurisdictional purposes. Each class member must individually satisfy the $75,000 amount-in-controversy requirement, despite that all claims arose out of the same transaction. *Snyder*, 394 U.S. at 338.

169. 28 U.S.C. § 1367(a); *see also Exxon Mobil Corp. v. Allapattah Servs., Inc.*, 545 U.S. 546, 549 (2005). The "supplemental jurisdiction" concept now incorporates both the former concepts of "ancillary jurisdiction" (claims and parties joined by defendant) and "pendent jurisdiction" (nonfederal claims in federal question cases).

170. *United Mine Workers of Am. v. Gibbs*, 383 U.S. 715, 726 (1966).

171. 28 U.S.C. § 1332(d)(2).

172. 28 U.S.C. § 1332(d)(10).

173. *JPMorgan Chase Bank v. Traffic Stream (BVI) Infrastructure Ltd.*, 536 U.S. 88, 91 (2002).

also of the state in which it maintains its principal place of business.[174] Even if alien corporations have dual citizenship under 28 U.S.C. § 1332(c), however, they are still subject to the limitations on alienage. Like domestic corporations, alien corporations may be examined under either the "nerve center" test for executive and administrative functions[175] or the "place of operations" test for location of its plants, personnel, sales, and physical operations.[176] The current trend, however, is for courts to examine the entity's "total activities," taking into account all aspects of the entity's business.[177] Where the alien corporation's activities are truly global, conducted in numerous countries, the court will place primary emphasis on the "nerve center" location of its executive offices.[178]

As noted, a corporation may have dual citizenship, but for purposes of "minimal diversity" under CAFA a corporation must be a citizen of a state different from "any member of a class of plaintiffs."[179] One court has held that, for CAFA purposes, a corporation cannot be a citizen of the same state as any plaintiff, so its dual citizenship in another state does not establish "minimal diversity" under CAFA.[180]

Certain securities and corporate governance claims cannot be maintained as "minimal diversity" class actions: (1) claims involving securities covered under the Securities Act or the 1934 Securities Exchange Act; (2) claims relating to rights and obligations created by any security; or (3) state law claims relating to a business entity's internal affairs or governance.[181] This provision of CAFA preserves the jurisdictional provisions of the Securities Litigation Uniform Standards Act of 1988 (SLUSA), which preclude state law class actions for securities fraud on purchase or sale of a "covered security" in either state or federal court, and provides for removal of state court actions to federal court.[182]

An exception (the "Delaware carve-out") preserves state court jurisdiction of class actions based on the law of defendant's state of incorporation, which actions

---

174. *See, e.g., Jerguson v. Blue Dot Inv. Corp.*, 659 F.2d 31, 35 (5th Cir. 1981). It is not clear whether dual citizenship exists where the alien corporation's principal place of business in the U.S. is not its principal place of business worldwide. *See Roby v. Gen. Tire & Rubber Co.*, 500 F. Supp. 480, 483 (D. Mo. 1980).

175. *See, e.g., Diaz-Rodriguez v. Pep Boys Corp.*, 410 F.3d 56, 60 (1st Cir. 2005).

176. *See, e.g., Kelly v. U.S. Steel Corp.*, 284 F.2d 850, 854 (3d Cir. 1960).

177. *See, e.g., MacGinnitie v. Hobbs Group, LLC*, 420 F.3d 1234, 1239 (11th Cir. 2005); *Teal Energy USA, Inc. v. GT, Inc.*, 369 F.3d 873, 876 (5th Cir. 2004).

178. *See, e.g., J.A. Olson Co. v. Winona*, 818 F.2d 401, 407 (5th Cir. 1987).

179. 28 U.S.C. § 1332(D)(2)(A).

180. *See Johnson v. Advance Am.*, 549 F.3d 932, 936 (4th Cir. 2008). *But see In re Hannaford Bros. Co. Customer Data Sec. Breach Litig.*, 592 F. Supp. 2d 146 (D. Me. 2008).

181. 28 U.S.C. § 1332(d)(9).

182. 15 U.S.C. §§ 77p(b–c), 78bb(f); *see also Falkowski v. Imation Corp.*, 309 F.3d 1123, 1128 (9th Cir. 2002) (state law "completely preempted"). A "covered security" is one traded nationally and listed on a regulated national exchange. *See* 15 U.S.C. §§ 77p(f)(3), 78bb(f)(5)(E).

involve transactions with the corporation regarding its shares, e.g., tender offers.[183] SLUSA authorizes removal and dismissal based solely on the allegations of the state court complaint. No evidentiary showing is required from either party, although the court may permit the defendant to support removal with supplemental evidence.[184] Plaintiff may seek leave to amend the complaint to avoid a SLUSA dismissal (i.e., by removing the securities allegations).[185]

A U.S. corporation whose principal place of business is abroad is not an alien corporation, but a citizen solely of the state in which incorporated.[186] Unless they are alter egos, a parent and subsidiary corporation will have their respective citizenship determined separately.[187] Thus, in a suit by or against a subsidiary, its parent's citizenship is not considered for diversity purposes,[188] and vice versa.[189] Separate divisions of a corporation, even if maintained entirely abroad, are not separate citizens for diversity purposes.[190]

E. CLASS CERTIFICATION

Attaining class certification of a class that includes foreign plaintiffs is generally more difficult than for a class of U.S.–only plaintiffs, even when the latter involves members from different states. The difficulties include more complex choice of law issues, the pernicious problem of a foreign court that may not recognize the U.S. court's judgment, and the knotty legal and factual issues that can be expected to arise when claims by citizens of different countries are litigated together.

1. Choice of Law

When ruling on a motion to certify a class, a court first must identify the substantive legal issues that will control the outcome of the litigation and then determine which country's laws will apply to each of those issues.[191] That is, the court must undertake a choice of law analysis as to *each issue in the litigation*, not just

---

183. 15 U.S.C. § 77p(d)(1).

184. *U.S. Mortgage, Inc. v. Saxton*, 494 F.3d 833, 842 (9th Cir. 2007).

185. *Id.* at 843.

186. *MAS Capital, Inc. v. Biodelivery Scis. Int'l, Inc.*, 524 F.3d 831, 832 (7th Cir. 2008) (Nevada corporation's principal business in Taiwan did not defeat diversity in action against Delaware corporation); *Torres v. S. Peru Copper Corp.*, 113 F.3d 540, 543 (5th Cir. 1997) (Delaware corporation's principal business in Peru did not defeat diversity against Peruvian defendants).

187. *See, e.g., Taber Partners, I v. Merit Builders, Inc.*, 987 F.2d 57, 61 (1st Cir. 1993).

188. *See, e.g., Topp v. CompAir, Inc.*, 814 F.2d 830, 835 (1st Cir. 1987).

189. *See, e.g., Danjaq, S.A. v. Pathe Commc'ns Corp.*, 979 F.2d 772, 775 (9th Cir. 1992). The *Danjaq* court, however, held that if either corporation is sued as the "alter ego" of the other, the court analyzes the *combined* business of the entities for diversity analysis. Other courts, however, hold that "alter ego" can only be used to *defeat* diversity, not to preserve it. *See, e.g., Pyramid Sec., Ltd. v. IB Resolution, Inc.*, 924 F.2d 1114, 1120 (D.C. Cir. 1991).

190. *See, e.g., Schwartz v. Elec. Data Sys., Inc.*, 913 F.2d 279, 284 (6th Cir. 1990).

191. *Castano v. Am. Tobacco Co.*, 84 F.3d 734, 741 (5th Cir. 1996) (quoting *Alabama v. Blue Bird Body Co.*, 573 F.2d 309, 316 (5th Cir. 1978)).

the proffered common issues,[192] and that analysis must be made for *each* class member and *each* claim,[193] including any affirmative defenses raised in the pleadings.[194] The result is that a court may be required to apply the laws of multiple foreign and domestic jurisdictions in a single putative class action brought by foreign plaintiffs.[195] Moreover, after determining which jurisdictions have an interest in an action, so as to require that their laws be applied to one or more of the claims asserted, the court must determine whether there are variations in the laws of those jurisdictions, whether those variations can be resolved, and how those variations would affect "how a trial on the merits would be conducted."[196]

When this analysis requires application of the laws of numerous jurisdictions, both domestic and foreign, satisfying the commonality, predominance, superiority, and manageability criteria under Rule 23(b)(3) can be very difficult. Commonality requires at least one common issue of fact or law such that, when the common question is answered for one class member, it is answered for all.[197] Both the Fifth and the Seventh circuits and district courts in Kansas and the Southern District of New York have held that there can be no common issues unless all litigants are governed by the same legal rules.[198] When determining whether plaintiffs have satisfied the predominance and superiority requirements, courts must consider the entire cause of action, including viable defenses, with a particular eye toward the manageability of legal and factual variations.[199] In doing so, the need to apply multiple jurisdictions' laws makes it considerably less likely that the court will conclude that a class action is the superior vehicle for resolving plaintiffs' claims and that resolution of the common issues would materially advance the case.[200] For

---

192. *Castano*, 84 F.3d at 742–43 n.15.

193. *Vasquez v. Bridgestone/Firestone, Inc.*, 325 F.3d 665, 675 (5th Cir. 2003); *Delgado v. Shell Oil Co.*, 231 F.3d 165, 181 (5th Cir. 2000).

194. *See In re Am. Med. Sys., Inc.*, 75 F.3d 1069, 1085 (6th Cir. 1996); *Thompson v. Am. Tobacco Co., Inc.*, 189 F.R.D. 544, 556 (D. Minn. 1999).

195. *Castano*, 84 F.3d at 740–42; *In re Rhone-Poulenc Rorer Inc.*, 51 F.3d 1293, 1301 (7th Cir. 1995); *Am. Med. Sys.*, 75 F.3d at 1085; *In re N. Dist. of Cal., Dalkon Shield Litig.*, 693 F.2d 847, 850 (9th Cir. 1982).

196. *Castano*, 84 F.3d at 743; *Spence v. Glock*, 227 F.3d 308, 311 n.6 (5th Cir. 2000).

197. *Barnes v. Am. Tobacco Co.*, 161 F.3d 127, 140 (3d Cir. 1998); *In re Am. Med. Sys., Inc.*, 75 F.3d at 1080–81. *See also Feinstein v. Firestone Tire & Rubber Co.*, 535 F. Supp. 595, 605–06 (S.D.N.Y. 1982) (finding that commonality was not satisfied when purported class members had breach of warranty claims whose elements varied across states).

198. *See In re Bridgestone/Firestone, Inc.*, 288 F.3d 1012, 1015 (7th Cir. 2002); *Simon v. Merrill Lynch, Pierce, Fenner & Smith, Inc.*, 482 F.2d 880, 882–83 (5th Cir. 1973); *Thompson v. Jiffy Lube Int'l, Inc.*, 250 F.R.D. 608, 625 (D. Kan. 2008) (applying *Bridgestone/Firestone*); *Lewis Tree Serv., Inc. v. Lucent Techs., Inc.*, 211 F.R.D. 228, 233 (S.D.N.Y. 2002) (same).

199. *Castano*, 84 F.3d at 745 n.21. *See In re Jackson Nat. Life Ins. Co. Premium Litig.*, 183 F.R.D. 217 (W.D. Mich. 1998); *Kemp v. Metabolife Int'l Inc.*, Civ. No. 00-3513 "C"(5), 2002 U.S. Dist. LEXIS 2435, at *13 (E.D. La. Jan. 25, 2002); *Arch v. Am. Tobacco Co.*, 175 F.R.D. 469, 496 (E.D. Penn. 1997).

200. *Castano*, 84 F.3d at 741 ("In a multi-state class action, variations in state law may swamp any common issues and defeat predominance."); *In re Rhone-Poulenc*, 51 F.3d at 1301 (variations in negligence

example, "[i]f more than a few of the laws of the [interested jurisdictions] differ, the district judge would face an impossible task of instructing a jury on the relevant law . . . ."[201]

2. Res Judicata

"Claim preclusion, or *res judicata*, is typically viewed as a fundamental aspect of the class action mechanism."[202] In *Phillips Petroleum Co. v. Shutts*,[203] the Supreme Court stated that the defendant "has a distinct and personal interest in seeing the entire plaintiff class bound by *res judicata* just as [defendant] is bound." Some courts take the view that the res judicata issue is part of Rule 23(b)(3) superiority requirement.[204] However, such treatment is not universal.[205]

The specter of a foreign court refusing to acknowledge a judgment or settlement entered in a U.S. class action, and some members of the plaintiff class thereby having a second bite at the apple in their home jurisdictions, weighs heavily against a finding that the U.S. class action would be a superior method for resolving the parties' dispute. Courts have taken somewhat divergent approaches on the tolerable level of certainty that a foreign court would not recognize a U.S. judgment.[206] Once the applicable threshold is met, however, courts are strongly inclined to deny class certification or carve foreign plaintiffs out of a U.S. class action because of lack of "superiority" and "commonality."[207] A named class representative is also less likely to be deemed an "adequate" class representative under Rule 23(a) if he hails from a jurisdiction that will not recognize a U.S. judgment.[208]

laws of 51 states preclude certification of class); *In re Am. Med. Sys., Inc.*, 75 F.3d at 1085; *Dalkon Shield Litig.*, 693 F.2d at 850.

201. *In re Am. Med. Sys., Inc.*, 75 F.3d at 1085; *Dalkon Shield Litig.*, 693 F.2d at 850; *Castano*, 84 F.3d at 743, n.15.

202. Sankoorikal et al., *supra* note 12, at 24–25.

203. 472 U.S. 797, 805 (1985).

204. *See In re Vivendi Universal*, 242 F.R.D. at 95 ("*Res judicata* concerns have been appropriately grafted onto the superiority inquiry.").

205. *See* Sankoorikal et al., *supra* note 12, at n.49, 52. For a more detailed discussion of this topic generally, see Chapter 23, "Res Judicata and Collateral Estoppel Issues in Class Litigation."

206. In *Bersch*, 519 F.2d 974, the Second Circuit held that foreign shareholders could not be included in a Rule 23(b)(3) opt-out class because it was a "near certainty" that a foreign court would not recognize an eventual judgment in the U.S. action. In *Cromer Fin. Ltd. v. Berger*, 205 F.R.D. 113 (S.D.N.Y. 2001), the district court stated that there is a difference between a mere "possibility" that a foreign court would not recognize a judgment and a "near certainty" that it would not recognize a judgment and held that a mere "possibility" was insufficient to exclude foreign shareholders from the proposed class. Other district courts in the Second Circuit seem to require less than a "near certainty," utilizing a sliding scale and stating that "[t]he closer the likelihood of non-recognition is to being a 'near certainty,' the more appropriate it is for the Court to deny certification of foreign claimants." *In re Vivendi Universal*, 242 F.R.D. at 95.

207. *See* Sankoorikal et al., *supra* note 12, at n.53 (citing *In re DaimlerChrysler*, 216 F.R.D. at 300–01; *CL Alexanders*, 127 F.R.D. at 459–60; *Ansari v. N.Y. Univ.*, 179 F.R.D. 112, 116–17 (S.D.N.Y. 1998).

208. *See, e.g., Borochoff*, 246 F.R.D. at 203–05 (refusing to appoint German institutional shareholder as lead plaintiff on the grounds that "any judgment in this action (whether favoring plaintiffs or defendants)

F. ACTIONS INVOLVING AN ARM OF A FOREIGN GOVERNMENT

It is not unusual for an arm of a foreign government to have a direct or indirect interest in litigation involving a class composed of its citizens or domestic business entities. For example, claims are frequently made by foreign military personnel for personal injuries from the use or exposure to toxic materials in ordnance or equipment manufactured in the United States.[209] If the defendant is held liable, the role of the foreign military in directing the actions that caused plaintiffs' alleged injuries must be resolved through a claim for contribution or indemnification by the defendant against the foreign government or its military.[210]

It likewise is common in many foreign countries for the government to own businesses either directly or indirectly, or otherwise exert substantial control over them. In these cases, the business entity itself may be an arm of the government or, at a minimum, the government will have a direct interest in the outcome of litigation involving the business entity.[211]

State-operated healthcare systems in foreign countries and the provision of free healthcare for military personnel are also common scenarios that create an interest for a foreign government in litigation. In those jurisdictions, claims for injuries against a third party may be assigned to the foreign government as the subrogated health insurer of the plaintiff.[212] If the defendant is found liable in any respect for the conditions for which plaintiffs claim they required medical care, the foreign government will have subrogation claims against the defendant.[213] A foreign government likewise may have an interest in the outcome of such lawsuits where plaintiffs seek injunctive relief in the form of medical monitoring that, if ordered, will take place within the foreign country.[214]

---

may be refused enforcement by a German court"); *In re Royal Ahold N.V. Sec. & ERISA Litig.*, 219 F.R.D. 343, 352 (D. Md. 2003) (holding that the presumption that the proposed lead plaintiff was the most adequate plaintiff was rebutted where it was a foreign purchaser of securities on a foreign exchange, and "[f]oreign courts might not recognize or enforce . . . a decision from an American court, which would allow foreign plaintiffs in the class to file suit against the defendant again in those foreign courts").

209. *See, e.g., Blum*, 547 F. Supp. 2d 717 (ruling on a products liability action against the manufacturer of a radar system that subjected class of American and German military personnel to radiation).

210. *Id.* at 731–32 (considering defendants' inability to implead German government as a factor weighing in favor of dismissal in a forum non conveniens analysis).

211. *See, e.g., Jota*, 157 F.3d 153 (upholding dismissal for failure to join an indispensable party only to part of complaint seeking to enjoin activities under oil company after the Republic of Ecuador became the sole owner).

212. *Krueger v. Cartwright*, 996 F.2d 928 (7th Cir. 1993).

213. *United States v. Aetna Cas. & Sur. Co.*, 338 U.S. 366, 382 (1949).

214. *See Sequihua*, 847 F. Supp. at 63; *Aquinda v. Texaco, Inc.*, 945 F. Supp. 625, 628 (S.D.N.Y. 1996), *vacated on other grounds and remanded by Jota*, 157 F.3d 153.

1. Foreign Government as an Indispensable Party

When a foreign government has a direct interest in the outcome of a lawsuit, defendants may be able to secure dismissal of the action for failure to join an "indispensable party."[215] Federal Rule of Civil Procedure 19, also known as the "compulsory joinder rule," sets out the process by which a court may determine whether the absence of a party that cannot be joined to a lawsuit is so critical that the lawsuit should be dismissed. The court first must determine whether a party is "necessary."[216] The factors listed in the Rule include:

> (1) in the person's absence complete relief cannot be accorded among those already parties or (2) the person claims an interest relating to the subject of the action and is so situated that the disposition of the action in the person's absence may . . . leave any of the persons already parties subject to a substantial risk of incurring double, multiple, or otherwise inconsistent obligations by reason of the claimed interest.[217]

This provision helps protect defendants from "needless multiple litigation" and from "incurring . . . inconsistent obligations."[218] The goal of Rule 19(a) is complete adjudication of a claim, elimination of relitigation, and prevention of inconsistent obligations.[219] In this way, judicial economy is aided by ensuring that courts do not enter "partial or hollow judgments"—judgments that do not effectively resolve the parties' entire controversy.[220] "[T]he court must always consider the possibility of shaping a decree . . . [and] in this vein the court must guard against the formulation of 'paper' decrees which neither adjudicate nor, in the end, protect rights."[221]

In the scenarios discussed above in which an arm of a foreign government has an interest in the litigation, the foreign government would be considered a "necessary" party. For example, where an absent party plays a significant role in the provision of some form of injunctive relief, courts are likely to conclude that complete relief cannot be accorded among the existing parties in the case.[222] Requests for injunctive relief in the form of medical monitoring and surveillance in a foreign country, but supervised by a U.S. court, are especially problematic.[223] "In the

---

215. FED. R. CIV. P. 19.

216. *Pulitzer-Polster v. Pulitzer*, 784 F.2d 1305, 1309 (5th Cir. 1986); *HS Resources, Inc. v. Wingate*, 327 F.3d 432, 439 (5th Cir. 2003).

217. FED. R. CIV. P. 19(a).

218. *Schutten v. Shell Oil Co.*, 421 F.2d 869, 871, 873 (5th Cir. 1970); FED. R. CIV. P. 19(a)(2)(ii).

219. 4 JAMES WM. MOORE ET AL., MOORE'S FEDERAL PRACTICE § 19.03[2][a] (3d ed. 1997).

220. *Id.*; *HS Resources*, 327 F.3d at 439; *Pulitzer-Polster*, 784 F.2d at 1309.

221. *Schutten*, 421 F.2d at 871, 873; *Bakia v. County of L.A.*, 687 F.2d 299, 301 (9th Cir. 1982). *See also Rose v. Simms*, No. 95-C1466, 1995 U.S. Dist. LEXIS 17686, at *9 (S.D.N.Y. Nov. 29, 1995).

222. *Rose*, 1995 U.S. Dist. LEXIS 17686, at *9.

223. *See Sequihua*, 847 F. Supp. at 63 (stating that "to step into the shoes of the Ecuadorian Health Ministry and supervise a medical monitoring scheme of unknown cost, scope or duration . . . fully and completely involve[s] the relationship between the United States through this Court and the Republic of Ecuador"); *Aquinda*, 945 F. Supp. at 628.

absence of [the foreign government], any order of [a court] granting any material part of the [foreign government]-directed equitable relief demanded by plaintiffs would be unenforceable on its face, prejudicial to both present and absent parties, and an open invitation to international political debacle."[224]

A foreign government with subrogation claims against a defendant is also a "necessary" party.[225] More importantly, a foreign court may resolve the foreign government's subrogation claim, or a defendant's contribution claim, de novo, and may not accept the judgment entered by the U.S. court.[226] Thus, a defendant in some foreign courts may be held responsible for the foreign government's subrogation claims, irrespective of the extent of liability assessed in the action venued in the United States, *and even if the defendant is found free of liability in the underlying case in the United States*. The defendant, therefore, would be "at a substantial risk of incurring double, multiple or otherwise inconsistent obligations,"[227] making the foreign government a necessary party to the U.S. action. Similarly, if the foreign court refuses to recognize the judgment of the U.S. court, the defendant may find itself unable to collect the foreign government's share of the judgment. This would leave the defendant saddled with a disproportionate share of the liability—literally without an avenue of redress in any court in the world.[228]

If the court determines that a foreign government is a necessary party, but that it cannot be joined, the court then must determine whether the action can go forward without the party, using the standards set forth in subpart (b) of Rule 19. If the action cannot go forward without the party, then the party is "indispensable," and the action should be dismissed.[229] The factors set out in Rule 19(b) that the court must consider include the extent to which judgment rendered in the person's absence will prejudice current parties; the extent to which prejudice can be lessened or avoided by protective provisions in the judgment, shaping the relief, or other measures; whether judgment rendered in the person's absence will

---

224. *Aquinda*, 945 F. Supp. at 628.

225. *United States v. Aetna*, 338 U.S. at 382; *Krueger*, 996 F.2d at 931–32; *Arkwright-Boston Mfrs. Mut. Ins. Co. v. City of N.Y.*, 762 F.2d 205, 209 (2d Cir. 1985); *Va. Elec. & Power Co. v. Westinghouse Elec. Corp.*, 485 F.2d 78, 85 (4th Cir. 1973); *Garcia v. Hall*, 624 F.2d 150, 152 (10th Cir. 1980).

226. *See, e.g., Crutcher v. Aetna Life Ins. Co.*, 746 F.2d 1076, 1080 (5th Cir. 1981). Germany, the Netherlands, Norway, Spain, and the United Kingdom, among others, will not necessarily recognize U.S. court judgments and can litigate subrogation claims de novo. *See* Russell J. Weintraub, *Symposium, How Substantial Is Our Need for a Judgments-Recognition Convention and What Should We Bargain Away to Get It?*, 24, BROOK. J. INT'L L. 167, 177–84 (discussing various countries' refusal to recognize U.S. judgments).

227. FED. R. CIV. P. 19(a)(1)(B)(ii).

228. Since, as noted *supra*, damages awarded in courts in other jurisdictions are likely to be smaller than those awarded in U.S. courts, the risk is substantial that the defendant will be saddled with a disproportionate share of liability in a de novo review of its cross-claims for contribution.

229. *Pulitzer-Polster*, 784 F.2d at 1308–09; *Shelton v. Exxon Corp.*, 843 F.2d 212, 216 (5th Cir. 1988), *rev'd on other grounds*, 921 F.2d 595 (5th Cir. 1991).

be adequate; and whether the plaintiff will have an adequate remedy if the action is dismissed for nonjoinder.[230]

When a foreign government is a "necessary" party to an action, it is also per se an "indispensable" party under Rule 19 because foreign states are immune from suit in federal or state courts in civil actions under the Foreign Sovereign Immunities Act.[231] The doctrine of sovereign immunity carries great weight in a Rule 19(b) analysis. Indeed, some courts have concluded that the weighing of other factors is hardly necessary, given the "paramount importance accorded the doctrine of sovereign immunity under Rule 19."[232] Even if the court considers the other guidelines for determining when a party is "indispensable," it is likely to conclude that the action must be dismissed. The sovereignty of a foreign government means that it may be impossible to fashion any relief that will protect the parties in the case. Regardless of what a U.S. court orders, it cannot bind the foreign government and cannot compel the foreign government to honor a U.S. judgment for purposes of a subrogation claim against the defendant or the defendant's right of contribution. When the relief requested is injunctive in the form of medical monitoring, it cannot be administered adequately, if it can be administered at all, without the approval and participation of a foreign government providing the healthcare. Furthermore, ordering such relief without the participation of the foreign government would violate the principles of international comity, which contain a "rule of 'local restraint' which guides courts reasonably to restrict the extraterritorial application of sovereign power."[233]

2. Act of State Doctrine

In class actions brought by foreign plaintiffs, where a foreign government potentially bears some liability for the injury suffered by the plaintiffs, a defendant may move under Federal Rule of Civil Procedure 12 to dismiss the complaint as

---

230. FED. R. CIV. P. 19(b); *see also Doty v. St. Mary Parish Land Co.*, 598 F.2d 885, 887 (5th Cir. 1979).

231. 28 U.S.C. §§ 1602–1611, 1604 (1988).

232. *Fluent v. Salamanca Indian Lease Auth.*, 928 F.2d 542, 548 (2d Cir. 1991); *see also Enterprise Mgmt. Consultants, Inc. v. United States ex rel. Hodel*, 883 F.2d 890, 894 (10th Cir. 1989) (when a necessary party under Rule 19(b) is immune from suit, there is very little room for balancing other factors set out in Rule 19(b) since immunity is itself a compelling interest); *Gore v. Grand Casinos of La., Inc.*, Civ. A. 98-1253A, 1998 U.S. Dist. LEXIS 23257 (W.D. La. Sept. 29, 1998) (joinder not feasible where immune sovereign could not be joined).

233. *Karaha Bodas Co. LLC v. Perusahaan Pertambangan Minyak Dan Gas Bumi Negara*, 335 F.3d 357, 371 (2003); *Crutcher*, 746 F.2d at 1080 n.8 ("[T]he receivers of [Camballin Farms] are indispensable parties. . . . [I]f we granted the relief requested by Crutcher, rescinding and canceling the receivership, Camballin Farms would be placed in the position of being declared free of the receivership by an American court and remaining subject to the receivership under Australian law, [which would present] an international conflict between the courts of Australia and the United States . . . .").

nonjusticiable under the "act of state" doctrine.[234] The act of state doctrine provides that, "in the absence of a treaty or other unambiguous agreement regarding controlling legal principles, courts in the United States will generally refrain from . . . sitting in judgment on . . . acts of a governmental character done by a foreign state within its own territory and applicable here."[235] This is not a jurisdictional issue, but an issue of comity once jurisdiction has been established. "The act of state doctrine . . . requires that, in the process of deciding, the acts of foreign sovereigns taken within their own jurisdictions shall be deemed valid."[236] It seeks to avoid conflict between the judicial and legislative/executive branches and unwarranted judicial interference with international affairs.[237]

Courts must undertake a flexible analysis that considers a number of factors that further the underlying goals of the act of state doctrine.[238] The court must weigh the degree of involvement of the foreign state in the factual circumstances of the case and the effect a judicial decision will have on U.S. foreign relations.[239] It also must consider whether a decision will involve the adjudication of the laws, conduct, or motivation of a foreign government.[240] The purpose of these factors is to determine whether there is a potential conflict between the judicial and executive/legislative branches and whether an adjudication of claims involving the foreign nation's actions will constitute unwarranted judicial interference into international affairs.[241]

The doctrine applies not only in cases brought against a sovereign nation, but also to the adjudication of claims asserted against privates entities, including cor-

---

234. *W.S. Kirkpatrick & Co. v. Environ. Tectonics Corp.*, 493 U.S. 400, 409 (1990); *De Sanchez v. Banco Central de Nicaragua*, 770 F.2d 1385, 1389 (5th Cir. 1985).

235. RESTATEMENT (THIRD) OF THE FOREIGN RELATIONS LAW OF THE UNITED STATES § 443 (1986).

236. *Kirkpatrick*, 493 U.S. at 409.

237. *See generally Rozenkier v. Schering (In re Nazi Era Cases Against German Defendants Litig.)*, 196 F. App'x 93, 99 (3d Cir. 2006) ("[J]udicial review of Rozenkier's claims would express a lack of respect for the Executive Branch's longstanding foreign policy interest in resolving Nazi-era claims through intergovernmental negotiation."); *Wei Ye v. Jiang Zemin*, 383 F.3d 620, 626 (7th Cir. 2004); *Harisiades v. Shaughnessy*, 342 U.S. 580, 588–89 (1952) ("It is pertinent to observe that any policy toward aliens is vitally and intricately interwoven with contemporaneous policies in regard to the conduct of foreign relations, the war power, and the maintenance of a republican form of government. Such matters are so exclusively entrusted to the political branches of government as to be largely immune from judicial inquiry or interference.").

238. *Banco Nacional de Cuba v. Sabbatino*, 376 U.S. 398, 428 (1964).

239. *Kirkpatrick*, 493 U.S. at 406; *Sabbatino*, 376 U.S. at 428; *Braka v. Bancomer, S.N.C.*, 762 F.2d 222, 224 (2d Cir. 1985); *Republic of the Philippines v. Marcos*, 806 F.2d 344, 359 (2d Cir. 1986).

240. *Airline Pilots Ass'n Int'l v. TACA Int'l Airlines, S.A.*, 748 F.2d 965, 970 (5th Cir. 1984); *Grupo Protexa, S.A. v. All Am. Marine Slip*, 20 F.3d 1224, 1237 (3d Cir. 1994).

241. RESTATEMENT (THIRD) OF THE FOREIGN RELATIONS LAW OF THE UNITED STATES § 443 cmt. a (1986); *Jota*, 157 F.3d 153 (some of the claims against the Ecuadoran government should have been dismissed because the relief sought required substantial participation by the government; however, not all claims should have been dismissed for failure to join the government: court considered whether the parties could get complete relief without joining the government).

porations, if the litigation calls into question the official acts of a foreign sovereign.[242] One potential limitation on the act of state doctrine is the "commercial exception," which would limit the application of the doctrine in situations where a foreign nation is acting in a purely commercial capacity. In those cases, the foreign nation would be subject to domestic law in the same way as a private entity.[243]

It is important to note the difference between the act of state doctrine and the sovereign immunity doctrine. Although both are based on respect for foreign governments, the act of state doctrine guards against judicial scrutiny of activities of foreign states in their own territories, as opposed to acts related to the U.S. court's territory, which sovereign immunity is designed to protect. In addition, while sovereign immunity is concerned with the initial question of jurisdiction, the act of state doctrine is concerned with the permissible scope of inquiry by courts into issues related to foreign governments after jurisdiction has been established.[244]

3. Political Question Doctrine

Closely related to the act of state doctrine is the "political question" doctrine, which recognizes that courts lack the constitutional jurisdiction or competence to decide political issues or questions because they do not present "cases" or "controversies" within the meaning of Article III.[245] The doctrine "prevents courts from adjudicating issues that are constitutionally committed to the 'political branches' of the federal government."[246] As the Supreme Court has explained, such decisions "frequently turn on standards that defy judicial applications or involve the exercise of a discretion demonstrably committed to the executive or legislature."[247] Before deciding issues involving an arm of a foreign state, a court must examine the particular area

242. *See, e.g., Callejo v. Bancomer, S.A.,* 764 F.2d 1101, 1113 (5th Cir. 1985).

243. *W.S. Kirkpatrick & Co. v. Envtl. Tectonics Corp.,* 847 F.2d 1052, 1059 (3d Cir. 1988), *aff'd,* 493 U.S. 400 (1990); *Callejo,* 764 F.2d at 1115; *Arango v. Guzman Travel Advisors Corp.,* 621 F.2d 1371, 1380-81 (5th Cir. 1980); *Dominican Republic v. AES Corp.,* 466 F. Supp. 2d 680, 695 (E.D. Va. 2006). Note that the exception has yet to be accepted by the majority of the Supreme Court and all circuits. *Alfred Dunhill of London v. Republic of Cuba,* 425 U.S. 682, 695-706 (1976); *Glen v. Mediterranee, S.A.,* 450 F.3d 1251, 1254 n.2 (11th Cir. 2006) (court does not recognize a commercial activity exception to the act of state doctrine).

244. RESTATEMENT (THIRD) OF THE FOREIGN RELATIONS LAW OF THE UNITED STATES § 443, reporters' note 11 (1986).

245. *Occidental of UMM al Qaywayn, Inc. v. A Certain Cargo of Petroleum,* 577 F.2d 1196, 1203 (5th Cir. 1978); *Eveland v. Dir. of CIA,* 843 F.2d 46, 49 (1st Cir. 1988); *State of New Jersey v. United States,* 91 F.3d 463, 469-70 (3d Cir. 1996); U.S. CONST. art. III, § 2.

246. Christopher R. Chase, *The Political Question Doctrine: Preventing the Challenge of U.S. Foreign Policy in 767 Third Avenue Associates v. Consulate General of Socialist Federal Republic of Yugoslavia,* 50 CATH. U. L. REV. 1045, 1045 (2000-2001); *Barclay's Bank v. Franchise Tax Bd. of Cal.,* 512 U.S 298, 328-29 (1994); *Japan Whaling Assoc. v. Am. Cetacean Soc'y,* 478 U.S. 221, 230 (1986); *Baker v. Carr,* 369 U.S. 186, 212 (1962).

247. *Baker,* 369 U.S. at 221; *Haig v. Agee,* 453 U.S. 280, 292 (1981); *First Nat'l City Bank v. Banco Nacional de Cuba,* 406 U.S. 759 (1972).

of international relations implicated and decide whether it should defer to another governmental branch and dismiss the claim as nonjusticiable.[248]

Although not reducible to a precise formula,[249] the Supreme Court in *Baker v. Carr*[250] established six "independent tests" for the existence of a political question.[251] A suit should be dismissed as a nonjusticiable political question when the claim involves (1) a textual commitment in the Constitution for another branch of government to decide the issue; (2) a lack of judicial standards for deciding the issue; (3) the impossibility of deciding the issue without the court making a nonjudicial policy determination; (4) the impossibility of a judicial resolution of the issue without encroaching upon another branch's constitutional prerogatives; (5) the obedient adherence to a previously made political decision; or (6) the potential chance of multifarious pronouncements by various departments within the three branches on the same question.[252] Because the first factor is derived from Article III of the U.S. Constitution, it is considered the weightiest consideration.[253] The second and third factors take a "functional approach" to deciding the issue by questioning whether the judiciary has the ability and resources to make a decision about the issue.[254] The last three factors focus on whether the judicial resolution of an issue would unduly interfere with a governmental policy interest established by the legislative or executive branches.[255] Any conflict within one or more of the six categories will make a claim inappropriate for judicial resolution.[256]

Generally, if a claim does not challenge a particular foreign policy but involves a substantive area of the law or implementing procedures for a policy or law, the claim will be justiciable.[257] For example, when federalism or the rights of individuals are implicated, the judiciary is more likely to retain a case involving foreign policy issues because they concern implementing policies or substantive areas of the law.[258] "A minimal invasion into the areas of foreign relations does not make a claim a nonjusticiable political question."[259]

---

248. *Baker*, 369 U.S. at 217.

249. *Saldano v. O'Connell*, 322 F.3d 365, 367 (5th Cir. 2003).

250. 369 U.S. at 186.

251. *Vieth v. Jubelirer*, 541 U.S. 267, 277–78 (2004).

252. *Baker*, 369 U.S. at 217.

253. *Id.*

254. *Id.*

255. *767 Third Ave. Assocs. v. Consulate General of Socialist Federal Republic of Yugoslavia*, 60 F. Supp. 2d 267, 272 (S.D.N.Y. 1999); *see also* CHARLES A. WRIGHT, LAW OF THE FEDERAL COURTS § 14 (4th ed. 1983).

256. *767 Third Ave. Assocs.*, 60 F. Supp. 2d at 272; WRIGHT, *supra* note 255, at § 14.

257. *Flynn v. Schultz*, 748 F.2d 1186, 1191 (7th Cir. 1984); *Can v. United States*, 14 F.3d 160, 162 (2d Cir. 1995).

258. *Ukrainian-Am. Bar Ass'n Inc. v. Baker*, 893 F.2d 1374, 1380 (D.C. Cir. 1990); *Richardson v. Simon*, 560 F.3d 501, 502 (2d Cir. 1977).

259. *Lamont v. Woods*, 948 F.2d 825, 832 (2d Cir. 1991); *Planned Parenthood Fed'n of Am., Inc. v. Agency for Int'l Dev.*, 838 F.2d 649, 650 (2d Cir. 1988).

As with the act of state doctrine, the political question doctrine is broad enough to include claims between private entities if they center on a foreign country's political or military decisions or actions.[260] Thus, the political question doctrine has been applied by numerous courts to dismiss claims against defense contractors for wrongful death and personal injuries caused by the manufacturing or deployment of ordnance.[261] Courts likewise have dismissed claims that center on other aspects of foreign policy or national security, on the basis that they are political matters not subject to judicial review.[262]

4. State Secrets Privilege

The final issue likely to arise when foreign plaintiffs are seeking to adjudicate their claims as a class action in a U.S. court is the state secrets privilege. The Supreme Court has long recognized an evidentiary privilege belonging to the government that protects against revealing military and state secrets.[263] The purpose of the state secrets privilege is to protect national security.[264] The privilege is especially relevant in class actions involving foreign claimants because of the danger that domestic state secrets will be revealed to foreign nationals, who may then share that information with their own governments. The privilege does not belong to exclusively to the U.S. government, and foreign governments have been permitted to assert the state secrets privilege in cases pending in U.S. courts.[265]

In determining if the privilege exists, a court must balance the public interest in maintaining the secrecy and security of military and diplomatic information with the "public and private interest[s] in maintaining fairness and efficiency in

---

260. *Aktepe v. United States*, 105 F.3d 1400, 1404 (11th Cir. 1997) (rebuffing plaintiff's efforts to categorize suit challenging adequacy of military training as "common negligence action," and affirming dismissal on political question grounds); *Gilligan v. Morgan*, 413 U.S. 1, 8 (1973) ("Trained professionals, subject to day-to-day control of the responsible civilian authorities, necessarily must make comparative judgments on the merits as to evolving methods of training, equipping, and controlling military forces with respect to their duties under the Constitution. It would be inappropriate for a district judge to undertake responsibility in the unlikely event that he possessed requisite technical competence to do so.").

261. *See, e.g., Nejad v. United States*, 724 F. Supp. 753 (C.D. Cal. 1989) (wrongful death action brought by families of Iranians killed in Airbus downed by U.S.S. *Vincennes* in Persian Gulf); *Benztlin v. Hughes Aircraft Co.*, 833 F. Supp. 1486 (C.D. Cal. 1993) (wrongful death action brought by families of military personnel killed in "friendly fire" accident during Operation Desert Storm); *Zuckerbraun v. Gen. Dynamics Corp.*, 755 F. Supp. 1134 (D. Conn. 1990) (wrongful death action on behalf of Navy sailors killed from Iraqi attack on U.S.S. *Stark*), *aff'd on other grounds*, 935 F.2d 544 (2d Cir. 1991).

262. *Haig*, 453 U.S. at 292; *Harisiades*, 342 U.S. at 589; *First Nat'l City Bank*, 406 U.S. at 759; *Ams. United for Separation of Church & State v. Reagan*, 786 F.2d 194, 201–02 (3d Cir. 1986).

263. *United States v. Reynolds*, 345 U.S. 1, 6 (1953).

264. James Zagel, *The State Secrets Privilege*, 50 MINN. L. REV. 875 (1966); *Reynolds*, 345 U.S. at 1.

265. *In re Extradition of Smyth*, 826 F. Supp. 316, 322 (N.D. Cal. 1993). In developing the privilege, the Supreme Court spoke of protecting national security, but did not specify that this was limited to the national security of the United States. *Reynolds*, 345 U.S. at 10; *Smyth*, 826 F. Supp. at 322.

litigation."[266] The Supreme Court has held that applying the privilege is appropriate when a court is satisfied "from all the circumstances of the case, that there is a reasonable danger that compulsion of the evidence will expose military matters which, in the interest of national security, should not be divulged."[267]

The state secrets privilege belongs exclusively to the government and cannot be claimed or waived by a private party.[268] As such, the government must intervene to assert the privilege if it is not already a party to the action.[269] Because of the serious risk that a plaintiff may lose his day in court if the privilege is successfully asserted, the formalities involved in asserting the privilege are very important and noncompliance will be enough to defeat any claim of privilege.[270] There must be a formal claim of privilege lodged by the head of the department that has control over the matter, or by a high-ranking official in the branch of the military that is in control of the sensitive information, after actual consideration by the department head or official.[271] Additionally, the claim should be supported by an unclassified declaration of the privilege as well as a classified one, which may be reviewed by the district court in camera.[272]

The information covered by the privilege must constitute a state or military secret.[273] The court must find that public release of information would cause a severe negative impact on national security or international relations.[274] This requirement is satisfied by proof of "a reasonable danger" that release of the information "will expose . . . matters which, in the interest of national security, should not be divulged."[275] This may include, for example, specifications on the manufacture of weapons and defense systems.[276] It also may include (1) the plans and capabilities of specific combat operations; (2) the official estimates of the military plans and capabilities of potential enemy nations; (3) the existence, design, and production of new weapons or equipment or the existence and results of research programs specifically directed toward producing new weapons and equipment; (4) the existence and nature of special ways and means of organizing combat oper-

---

266. Zagel, *supra* note 264, at 877.

267. *Reynolds*, 345 U.S. at 10; *Halkin v Helms*, 690 F.2d 977, 990 (D.C. Cir. 1982) (*Halkin II*); *Ellsberg v. Mitchell*, 709 F.2d 51 (D.C. Cir. 1983).

268. *Reynolds*, 345 U.S. at 7.

269. *Zuckerbraun*, 935 F.2d at 546; *Bareford v. Gen. Dynamics Corp.*, 973 F.2d 1138, 1140 (5th Cir. 1992); *Fitzgerald v. Penthouse Int'l Ltd.*, 776 F.2d 1236, 1237 (4th Cir. 1985).

270. *Doe v. Tenet*, No. 01-35419, 2003 WL 21231897, at *13 (9th Cir. May 29, 2003), *rev'd on other grounds*, 544 U.S. 1 (2005).

271. *Reynolds*, 345 U.S. at 8; *Zuckerbraun*, 935 F.2d at 546; *Kasza v. Browner*, 133 F.3d 1159, 1163 (9th Cir. 1998).

272. *Kasza*, 133 F.3d at 1163.

273. *Id.* at 1165–66; Zagel, *supra* note 264, at 884–85.

274. *Reynolds*, 345 U.S. at 10.

275. *Id.*; *Zuckerbraun*, 935 F.2d at 546.

276. *Zuckerbraun*, 935 F.2d at 546; *Bareford*, 973 F.2d at 1140.

ations; (5) the identity and location of vulnerable areas, such as production facilities, critical supply depots, or weapons installations; (6) the existence and nature of clandestine intelligence operations, special plans, or data; (7) the keys to communication codes; and (8) the existence and nature of international agreements relative to military plans and capabilities and the exchange of intelligence.[277] This list is not exhaustive, and the government may use the privilege to withhold a broad range of information.[278]

The privilege may be asserted as to specific facts or issues in the case, or as to the entire subject matter of the litigation. The subject matter of a suit is privileged if the issues cannot be resolved or even put into dispute because of the classified nature of the required information, and there is a threat of disclosure if the case is permitted to proceed.[279] If the sensitive information is separable from nonsensitive information, the privilege may be denied or may be upheld as to only some information. If the court finds that the information is separable, and thus that the very subject matter of the litigation is not itself a state secret, then the government is denied the privilege.[280] The "mosaic theory" of state secrets may argue for a different result, however.[281] "[I]f seemingly innocuous information is part of a classified mosaic, the state secrets privilege may be invoked to bar its disclosure and the court cannot order the government to disentangle this information from other classified information."[282] The danger sought to be avoided here is making too much information available to a "sophisticated intelligence analyst."[283]

In order for the privilege to be invoked successfully, the information must currently remain a secret.[284] It is not fatal to the privilege that the information was not always considered classified—it could have been classified at a date some time after it was created, or even declared classified for the first time for purposes of invoking the state secrets privilege in the present litigation.[285] Secrecy is not destroyed when certain civilian government employees and consultants have knowledge of the information.[286] "So long as the government agency . . . insists that its private

---

277. Zagel, *supra* note 264, at 884–85.

278. *Kasza*, 133 F.3d at 1166.

279. *Zuckerbraun*, 935 F.2d at 547; *Fitzgerald*, 776 F.2d at 1241; *Bareford*, 973 F.2d at 1140.

280. *In re United States*, 872 F.2d 472, 478 (D.C. Cir. 1989).

281. *Kasza*, 133 F.3d at 1166; *see also In re United States*, 872 F.2d at 475.

282. *Kasza*, 133 F.3d at 1166.

283. *In re United States*, 872 F.2d at 475 (quoting *Halkin v. Helms*, 598 F.2d 1, 10 (D.C. Cir. 1978)) (*Halkin I*); *Fitzgerald*, 776 F.2d at 1242–43.

284. *Miller v. United States Dep't of State*, 779 F.2d 1378, 1388 (8th Cir. 1986).

285. *Id.*

286. *Reynolds*, 345 U.S. at 3 (permitting the privilege where civilian observers were aboard the aircraft when it crashed).

contractors follow tight security procedures, the government can share secrets with these contractors without losing the protection of the privilege."[287]

The state secrets privilege is absolute.[288] If the court sustains the government's assertion of the privilege, the government withholds the privileged information from the parties,[289] and does not even need to confirm or deny that the subject matter of the privilege exists.[290] Any evidence involving the privileged information is simply unavailable to the parties.[291] It is as though a witness had died, and the case continues without the evidence.[292] Once the privilege is accepted, there is no special rule regarding the consequences of the privilege. The parties suffer "the usual impact of the burdens of production and persuasion when potentially valuable evidence is unavailable."[293] The greater consequence, dismissal, hinges on whether the underlying litigation may proceed without the privileged evidence and without causing harm to national security.[294] The privilege may result in a dismissal in three ways:[295]

- The plaintiff's case goes forward based on evidence not covered by the privilege. If, after further proceedings, the plaintiff cannot prove the prima facie elements of his claim with nonprivileged evidence, the court dismisses the claim as it would with any plaintiff who cannot prove his case.
- The privilege deprives the defendant of information that would otherwise give the defendant a valid defense to the claim, entitling the defendant to summary judgment in its favor.[296]
- Notwithstanding the plaintiff's ability to produce nonprivileged evidence, the very subject matter of the action is a state secret, requiring the court to dismiss the plaintiff's action based solely on the invocation of the state secrets privilege.[297]

---

287. EDWARD J. IMWINKELRIED, THE NEW WIGMORE: EVIDENTIARY PRIVILEGES § 8.3 at 155 (2002).

288. *In re United States*, 872 F.2d at 476.

289. *Id.*

290. *Black v. United States*, 900 F. Supp. 1129, 1134 (D. Minn. 1994).

291. *Farnsworth Cannon, Inc. v. Grimes*, 635 F.2d 268, 270–73 (4th Cir. 1980).

292. *In re United States*, 872 F.2d at 476.

293. *Farnsworth Cannon*, 635 F.2d at 271.

294. *Tenet*, 2003 WL 21231897, at *8, *rev'd on other grounds*, 544 U.S. 1 (2005).

295. *Kasza*, 133 F.3d 1159.

296. One way a defendant proves that the privileged information is essential to defend plaintiffs' claims is showing that the defendant is unable to effectively cross-examine the plaintiffs' witnesses without resorting to the classified information concerning the device at issue. *Bareford*, 973 F.2d at 1141–42. Dismissal of the plaintiff's case when the privileged information prevents a defense to the claim has been permitted in the Second, Fifth, Ninth, and D.C. circuits. *Kasza*, 133 F.3d at 1166; *Zuckerbraun*, 935 F.2d at 547; *In re United States*, 872 F.2d at 476; *see also Molerio v. F.B.I.*, 749 F.2d 815, 822 (D.C. Cir. 1984) (recognizing the theory but affirming dismissal on other grounds).

297. *Kasza*, 133 F.3d at 1166 (quoting *Reynolds*, 345 U.S. at 11 n.26 (internal quotation omitted)). *See also Farnsworth Cannon*, 635 F.2d at 274, 281. Dismissal may be appropriate even if the plaintiffs only

Before coming to the conclusion that the state secrets privilege requires dismissal of the case, all possibilities to continue the litigation must be considered and rejected.[298]

G. CLASS ACTIONS INVOLVING FOREIGN DEFENDANTS

The first issue likely to be faced by the practitioner defending a foreign defendant named in a putative class action in a U.S. court is likely to be whether personal jurisdiction exists over the client. Personal jurisdiction is a court's power to render a judgment that either commands the defendant's personal obedience or imposes obligations on the defendant that other courts will also enforce.[299] In personam jurisdiction is required whenever a judgment is sought that would, if granted, impose an obligation on the defendant personally, i.e., a judgment for money damages, or an injunction commanding an action or restraint from action. Unless waived, a judgment rendered by a court that lacks personal jurisdiction violates constitutional due process, and is voidable by direct or collateral attack.[300] This section is limited to some special considerations for obtaining jurisdiction in personam over foreign defendants in a class action suit.

If "minimum contacts" exist between defendant and the forum state, the court has a basis for personal jurisdiction, but cannot exercise jurisdiction until the defendant has been served properly under Federal Rule of Civil Procedure 4.[301] Ordinarily, federal courts have no broader power over persons outside the forum state than do the local state courts.[302] Service of summons in a federal case establishes personal jurisdiction over a defendant who is "subject to the jurisdiction of a court of general jurisdiction in the state where the district court is located."[303] So, the starting point is the forum state's "long-arm" statute, but if that statute does not enable plaintiff to serve the defendant, plaintiff will be unable to obtain personal jurisdiction in state court, and likely not in federal court either.[304]

---

produce nonprivileged information to support their case, if the use of nonprivileged materials in the case would "touch upon" privileged materials, or efforts to probe as close as possible to the privileged information would inevitably reveal aspects of the privileged information. *Reynolds*, 345 U.S. at 11; *Bareford*, 973 F.2d at 1143; *Fitzgerald*, 776 F.2d at 1243.

298. *Tenet*, 2003 WL 21231897, at *8, *rev'd on other grounds*, 544 U.S. 1 (2005).

299. *Burnham v. Superior Court*, 495 U.S. 604, 609 (1990).

300. *Id.* at 608–10.

301. *Murphy Bros., Inc. v. Michetti Pipe Stringing, Inc.*, 526 U.S. 344, 350 (1999).

302. *Omni Capital Int'l, Ltd. v. Rudolph Wolff & Co.*, 484 U.S. 97, 104 (1987).

303. Fed. R. Civ. P. 4(k)(1)(A).

304. *Omni Capital*, 484 U.S. at 104.

There are several types of cases in which Congress has authorized nationwide service of process. These include ERISA,[305] CERCLA,[306] RICO,[307] and certain receivership actions.[308] Of importance for foreign defendants, other federal statutes authorize *worldwide* service of process, including securities fraud actions to enforce liability under the Securities Exchange Act of 1934 and SEC Rule 10b-5,[309] and antitrust actions to enforce liability under section 12 of the Clayton Act.[310] Where these statutes apply, so long as a properly served defendant has "minimum contacts" with the United States as a whole, defendant *may* be subject to personal jurisdiction in any federal district.[311] In such cases, the scope of due process is defined by sovereignty—as the individual is within the territory of the "sovereign" (the United States) that is exercising jurisdiction.[312] To obtain personal jurisdiction under statutes authorizing nationwide or worldwide service of process, plaintiff must serve the defendant pursuant to the service provisions of the statute, not simply allege that the claim arises under such statute.[313]

Even in the absence of a federal statute authorizing nationwide or worldwide service, foreign defendants who are not otherwise subject to jurisdiction in any state but who have "national contacts," i.e., contacts with the nation *as a whole*, are subject to personal jurisdiction on claims *arising under federal law*.[314]

Federal Rule of Civil Procedure 4(k)(2) also allows federal courts to exercise personal jurisdiction in federal question cases even where no statute specifically authorizes worldwide service of process. Rule 4(k)(2) has been successfully invoked in an action for copyright and trademark infringement under federal law, where the defendant, who operated a website selling materials to U.S. residents in violation of U.S. copyright and trademark laws, was not subject to jurisdiction in any state—his website contacts with the United States as a whole satisfied due process

---

305. 29 U.S.C. § 1132(a)(3) (ERISA enforcement action allowing service "in any other district where a defendant resides or may be found.").

306. 42 U.S.C. § 9613(e).

307. 18 U.S.C. § 1965(d). Courts split, however, on whether RICO permits nationwide service on all defendants, or whether at least one defendant must be subject to in personam jurisdiction where the action is filed. *Compare Republic of Panama v. BCCI Holdings (Lux.) S.A.*, 119 F.3d 935, 942 (11th Cir. 1997), *with Butcher's Union Local No. 498 v. SDC Inv., Inc.*, 788 F.2d 535, 538 (9th Cir. 1986).

308. 28 U.S.C. § 1692; *see also S.E.C. v. Bilzerian*, 378 F.3d 1100, 1103 (D.C. Cir. 2004).

309. 15 U.S.C. §§ 77aa & 78aa; *see also Busch v. Buchman, Buchman & O'Brien Law Firm*, 11 F.3d 1255, 1258 (5th Cir. 1994); *Pinker v. Roche Holdings, Ltd.*, 292 F.3d 361, 369 (3d Cir. 2002).

310. 15 U.S.C. § 22.

311. *Bourassa v. Desrochers*, 938 F.2d 1056, 1058 (9th Cir. 1991).

312. *Med. Mut. of Ohio v. deSoto*, 245 F.3d 561, 567 (7th Cir. 2000).

313. *Gen. Cigar Holdings, Inc. v. Altadis, S.A.*, 205 F. Supp. 2d 1335, 1340 (S.D. Fla. 2002) (plaintiff sued foreign defendant under Clayton Act § 12, which authorizes worldwide service, but plaintiff served defendant under the Hague Convention, and could not invoke worldwide service).

314. FED. R. CIV. P. 4(k)(2); *see also Pebble Beach Co. v. Caddy*, 453 F.3d 1151, 1155 (9th Cir. 2006).

requirements.[315] Foreign defendants whose U.S. contacts are wholly through cyberspace may be increasingly subject to attempts at obtaining Rule 4(k)(2) jurisdiction on claims arising under the federal law.[316] This is an area of federal common law, as it involves personal jurisdiction in federal question cases where no statute authorizes service abroad.[317] In effect, the rule operates as a federal long-arm statute.

A plaintiff must prove three facts in order to establish personal jurisdiction under Rule 4(k)(2) based on a defendant's aggregated national contacts: (1) that defendant is not subject to the personal jurisdiction of any state court of general jurisdiction; (2) that the claim arises under federal law; and (3) that the court's exercise of personal jurisdiction comports with due process.[318] Practically speaking, the doctrine applies to defendants located or domiciled abroad, since anyone with U.S. domicile would have sufficient contacts with at least one state.[319]

Aside from personal jurisdiction, the most acute issue facing a U.S. practitioner when a foreign client is named as a defendant in a class action may be explaining the peculiarities of the U.S. class action mechanism and, thereafter, easing the *in terrorem* effect on the client of a single lawsuit that aggregates the claims of dozens, hundreds, or perhaps thousands of individuals and can bring financial ruin to the client with a single jury verdict.

---

315. *Graduate Mgmt. Admission Council v. Raju*, 241 F. Supp. 2d 589, 596 (E.D. Va. 2003).

316. FED. R. CIV. P. 4(k)(2); *see also Pebble Beach*, 453 F.3d at 1155; *Holland Am. Line, Inc. v. Wartsila N. Am., Inc.*, 485 F.3d 450, 461 (9th Cir. 2007).

317. *See Committee Notes to 1993 Amendments to FRCP 4*, 146 F.R.D. 401, 571 (1993).

318. FED. R. CIV. P. 4(k)(2); *see also Pebble Beach*, 453 F.3d at 1158; *Holland Am. Line*, 485 F.3d at 461.

319. *W. Africa Trading & Shipping Co. v. London Int'l Group*, 968 F. Supp. 996, 999 (D.N.J. 1997).

MANAGEMENT TECHNIQUES AND DEVICES FOR SEGMENTING AGGREGATE LITIGATION

EDWARD F. SHERMAN

I. Introduction

The paradigm for the American civil trial is a single event between two private parties in which witnesses and evidence are presented seriatim in a continuous proceeding. In a classic article in 1976, Professor Abram Chayes pointed to the emergence of a different model for "public law litigation," such as school desegregation, employment discrimination, antitrust, securities fraud, corporate reorganizations, union governance, consumer fraud, and environmental management.[1] Such cases, he said, involve multiple parties, a sprawling and amorphous structure, need for discovery of large amounts of information, lengthy pretrial preparation, and complex forms of relief.[2]

Many of the "public law" cases described by Professor Chayes were declaratory or injunctive suits tried to a judge, and thus the protracted and segmented nature of the litigation did not have to contend with juries. But the structural changes in public law litigation he described had their genesis in the "case management" movement that arose out of an avalanche of federal court antitrust damage suits against the electrical equipment industry in the 1960s.[3] A single-event trial simply

---

1. Abram Chayes, *The Role of the Judge in Public Law Litigation*, 89 HARV. L. REV. 1281, 1284 (1976).

2. *Id.*

3. This led to the passage of the Multidistrict Litigation Act, 28 U.S.C. § 1407, which provides that the Judicial Panel on Multidistrict Litigation may transfer similar cases in federal courts to a single judge for pretrial disposition. *Lexecon, Inc. v. Milberg Weiss Bershad Hynes & Lerach*, 523 U.S. 26, 40 (1998), held that once pretrial proceedings have been completed, the transferee judge must transfer the cases back to their

would not work for such complex aggregate litigation—that is, litigation in which the claims of many individuals are aggregated, whether by joinder,[4] consolidation,[5] or class certification.[6] The case management movement, as particularly reflected in the 1969 *Manual for Complex Litigation*,[7] prescribed a protracted litigation process divided into various segments en route to ultimate resolution, not so much by a single-event trial as through such means as motions, summary judgments, partial disposition of claims or parties, and settlement at various stages.[8]

A second movement in the last several decades that coincided with the case management movement has also had an effect of segmenting litigation and deviating from the single-event trial model. This is the alternative dispute resolution (ADR) movement that took root in the 1960s and ultimately came to be "court-annexed" in the 1980s and 1990s as an integral part of the litigation process.[9] The ADR movement experimented with nonbinding settlement processes, which, true to the label of "alternative," have been largely conducted by private mediators, arbitrators, and dispute resolution organizations and professionals. Although the ADR movement is more focused on settlement without trial than is case management (which ostensibly seeks to prepare cases for trial), both have a common objective of achieving resolution without trial. The result has been the segmentation of litigation through a variety of devices that focus on certain parts for early disposition, schedule separate disposition or trial of discrete issues, and look to trial runs or extrapolation from other cases to aid in settlement.

---

original jurisdictions for trial. For a more detailed discussion of multidistrict litigation, *see* Chapter 12, "Multidistrict Litigation."

4. *See* FED. R. CIV. P. 19 (mandatory joinder); FED. R. CIV. P. 20 (permissive joinder); FED. R. CIV. P. 22 (interpleader); FED. R. CIV. P. 24 (intervention).

5. FED. R. CIV. P. 42(a):

> When actions involving a common question of law or fact are pending before the court, it may order a joint hearing or trial of any or all the matters in issue in the actions; it may order all the actions consolidated; and it may make such orders concerning proceedings therein as may tend to avoid unnecessary costs or delays.

6. FED. R. CIV. P. 23.

7. *See* MANUAL FOR COMPLEX LITIGATION (THIRD), originally published in 1969, which sets out detailed procedures for the disposition of complex cases, at xiii (1995).

8. Judge William Schwarzer described the focus of case management in pretrial by comparing a complex case to a tree overgrown with tangled branches that represent the issues. Pretrial procedures seek to prune off the branches when there is no support in law or fact. Over the course of pretrial, the tree should be carefully shaped so that only the essential branches are left for summary disposition, settlement, or trial. WILLIAM W. SCHWARZER, MANAGING ANTITRUST AND OTHER COMPLEX LITIGATION: A HANDBOOK FOR LAWYERS AND JUDGES 18–19 (1982).

9. *See* ALAN SCOTT RAU, EDWARD F. SHERMAN & SCOTT R. PEPPET, PROCESSES OF DISPUTE RESOLUTION: THE ROLE OF LAWYERS 305–08 (4th ed. 2006) (noting that ADR processes once independent of the court system are now often an integral part of litigation despite the persistence of the "alternative" label).

The procedural devices that have developed out of these two movements have had a significant impact on the trial process in aggregated cases. Unlike the "public law litigation" model, these developments apply primarily to private suits for damages. Like the public law model, the model for aggregate litigation involves segmenting of the trial process, extensive case management, and complex remedies. But since aggregated cases generally anticipate a jury trial (although a high percentage never reach that point because of settlement), the model must also provide mechanisms for presenting manageable segments to juries and use intertwining case management and ADR procedures to facilitate settlement at various stages. Finally, the model for aggregate litigation must deal with issues that require individualized treatment, including the award of damages, while still preserving the cohesive nature of the overall controversy and the presentation of the case—or portions of the case—in unitary proceedings with introduction of evidence applicable to all. Defendants have raised challenges to this model, including such constitutional issues as a due process right to individualized treatment and a right to trial by the same jury of nonseparable issues. The extent to which courts can segment the litigation process, which inferentially bears on whether aggregation itself is permissible, is often at the center of disputes these days between plaintiffs and defendants in complex litigation.

II. Nonbinding Trial Runs

The ADR movement has involved a great deal of experimentation with processes that provide the parties an evaluation of their cases and "reality test" their confidence in the strength of their cases. It has thus added another phase or segment to litigation, which, under rules in many jurisdictions, must be exhausted as a prerequisite to being allowed to go to trial.[10] Mediation has been the favored process, an unstructured meeting of the parties and their lawyers presided over by an impartial mediator who facilitates discussion. The mediator encourages a dialogue, which includes gathering information, identifying problems, testing the parties' perceptions, generating opinions, and bargaining with the aim of achieving settlement.[11] More structured processes have also emerged that go beyond the objective of reality testing to provide a nonbinding[12] "trial run" of the case before a suitable

---

10. *See* Elizabeth Plapinger & Donna Stienstra, *ADR and Settlement in the Federal District Courts: A Sourcebook for Judges and Lawyers, in* ALTERNATIVE DISPUTE RESOLUTION: THE LITIGATOR'S HANDBOOK (Nancy F. Atlas, Stephen K. Huber & E. Wendy Trachte-Huber eds., 2000).

11. *See* RAU, SHERMAN & PEPPET, *supra* note 9, at 312–45.

12. Nonbinding trial runs can be combined with binding arbitration. A mediation-arbitration hybrid ("med-arb") begins as mediation, but if the parties cannot reach a settlement, the mediator is authorized to decide the case as an arbitrator. To agree to this, the parties must obviously be willing ultimately to roll the dice with the arbitrator, rather than preserving their right to a jury trial. Sometimes limitations are

neutral. The principal trial run processes are early neutral evaluation, nonbinding arbitration, mini-trial, and summary jury trial.

These four trial-run processes offer rather different approaches to "reality testing," involving presentations before different kinds of neutrals at different times in the litigation process.[13] Under *early neutral evaluation*, a neutral lawyer (often assisting the court by serving pro bono) meets with the parties and their lawyers not long after a suit is filed, hears a narrative presentation of their cases and positions, and gives them a frank, nonbinding evaluation of the issues. *Nonbinding arbitration—*often called *court-annexed arbitration—*takes place after there has been more discovery and preparation of each side's case. It typically involves a panel of three arbitrators (usually three neutral lawyers) listening to a summarized presentation of the case and rendering a nonbinding decision. Afterward, the parties have an opportunity to discuss the case informally with the arbitrators. At a *mini-trial* the parties present summaries of the evidence to the corporate officials or decision makers for each side who have settlement authority. This presentation is followed by discussions between the parties and a neutral advisor in an attempt to reach a settlement. The mini-trial has generally been used in complex commercial cases and takes place when the case is almost ready for trial. A *summary jury trial* takes place when the case is ready for trial and is held in a courtroom before a judge and jury who hear a summary of the evidence and some short testimony from key witnesses. The jury then renders a decision, which can be appealed by either side. The summary jury trial is the only trial-run process that is administered within the court.

There has been less use of trial-run processes in aggregate litigation than might be expected. This may be because trial runs seem better suited to settling individual rather than aggregated cases. Aggregated cases are often settled en masse, and a global settlement is often a key objective of pretrial administration.[14] As will be discussed in the next section, the actual trial of a small number of "bellwether" or "test" cases may be more useful for informing the parties and lawyers of the strength and value of the totality of the cases. However, mediation, with its informality and flexibility, has often been used to promote settlement in complex aggregate litigation. Federal judges to whom large numbers of cases have been

---

placed on the power of the arbitrator to award damages, as in "high-low" arbitration in which the parties agree in advance on a high and low damage figure, and the arbitrator's decision must be within those parameters. A further variation is "final offer arbitration" (sometimes called "baseball arbitration" because it has often been used in disputes over players' salaries) in which the arbitrator must accept the offer of one of the parties. *See* Harold I. Abramson, Mediation Representation: Advocating in a Problem-Solving Process 282–302 (2004).

13. For a more detailed description of these processes, *see* Rau, Sherman & Peppet, *supra* note 9, at 545.

14. A common trial may be contemplated for aggregate litigation (for example, in a class action the manageability and superiority of a classwide trial is a prerequisite for class certification), but individualized issues must sometimes be severed and resolved separately, and the time and expense of such additional proceedings can provide an incentive for a global settlement.

transferred under the Multidistrict Litigation (MDL) Act[15] routinely order mediation in an attempt to achieve partial or global settlements. These mediations tend to differ from mediations in other cases by being more structured and prolonged. There is thus considerable room for mediation/trial-run hybrids in which certain issues are presented to a neutral person or persons to gauge their reactions to the issues. We can expect experimentation to continue along these lines.

III. Bellwether Trials

Because a trial run can never exactly duplicate a real trial, a court management technique often used in complex aggregate litigation is to try a small number of selected cases to give the parties a sense of how the legal and factual issues play out in different cases to a jury.[16] Bellwether cases[17] (also called "test cases" or "representative plaintiff trials") are selected as lead cases for settling all the aggregated cases. The parties can agree to have a bellwether trial be binding on all cases,[18] but this is rare. Multiple bellwether case verdicts might not be given preclusive effect when their outcomes differ,[19] but even without preclusive effect, they offer an accurate picture of how different juries would view different cases across the spectrum of weak and strong cases that are aggregated. They have been especially used by federal courts to which cases have been transferred under the Multidistrict Litigation Act to provide information as to the dollar value of various kinds of injuries and damages in product liability, pharmaceutical, and environmental litigation.[20]

Bellwether trials, of course, still only provide a judgment for those cases that are tried, and thus how the cases are selected is of vital importance. There are various methods of selection, ranging from having each party select a certain number of cases (which obviously will usually be their strongest cases) to having the court make the selection. Bellwether cases have been used recently in Vioxx litigation where the prescription medication was alleged to have caused heart attacks and

---

15. 28 U.S.C.A. § 1407(a) (West 2006) ("When civil actions involving one or more common questions of fact are pending in different districts, such actions may be transferred to any district for coordinated or consolidated pretrial proceedings."). Some states, such as Texas, also provide for transfer to a state MDL court. TEX. GOV'T CODE ANN. § 74.161-63 (Vernon 2005).

16. MANUAL FOR COMPLEX LITIGATION (THIRD) § 33.28 (1995).

17. The term comes from a lead sheep in a flock that wears a bell.

18. *See In re Air Crash Disaster at Stapleton Int'l Airport*, 720 F. Supp. 1505 (D. Colo. 1989) (noting that the trial plan adopted by the MDL court to which cases arising out of the air crash in question were transferred provided that plaintiffs and defendants in all cases would be bound to the verdicts returned in an "exemplar" trial), *rev'd on other grounds*, 964 F.2d 1059 (10th Cir. 1992).

19. *See Hardy v. Johns-Manville Sales Corp.*, 681 F.2d 334, 345–46 (5th Cir. 1982) (stating that preclusive effect could not be accorded to previous judgment against defendant asbestos manufacturer because there were conflicting judgments in other trials, and it could not be said that the issues and circumstances were the same).

20. PAUL D. RHEINGOLD, MASS TORT LITIGATION §§ 16-26 to -29 (1996).

strokes in certain patients. More than 4,000 (ultimately increased to 20,000) suits were filed in federal courts against its manufacturer, Merck, which were trans-ferred by the Panel on Multi-District Litigation for pretrial disposition by Judge Eldon Fallon of the U.S. District Court for Eastern District of Louisiana. The par-ties submitted proposals for bellwether cases, and Judge Fallon selected six cases with differing characteristics, such as length of use of the drug, the age and medi-cal condition of the plaintiff at the time of use, and the injury claimed (death or lesser health complications).[21] The first case, involving a middle-aged man who died after taking Vioxx for only three weeks and who had preexisting medical con-ditions, resulted, perhaps not unpredictably, in a defense verdict.[22] Plaintiffs pre-vailed in other cases, and a number of state court cases resulted in both high plaintiff verdicts and defendant verdicts.[23]

At Judge Fallon's encouragement, negotiations with the defendant Merck took place over an extended period. Settlement was complicated because an even larger number of Vioxx cases were pending in state courts (some 30,000, mostly in New Jersey, California, and Texas), and the federal transferee court had no jurisdiction over them. However, there was close coordination between Judge Fallon and the state court judges as to bellwether trials and encouragement of settlement. Repre-sentative counsel from the state cases were included in the negotiations, and on November 9, 2007, a global settlement was announced between Merck and the Plaintiffs' Steering Committee in the federal MDL and representatives of plain-tiffs' counsel in the coordinated proceedings in the three state courts where most of the state cases were pending. Merck agreed to pay $4.85 billion pursuant to a complex administrative and claims procedure.[24] Judge Fallon, sitting with the coor-dinated proceedings judges from New Jersey and California, received the agreement in open court. The agreement settled the claims in all Vioxx cases then pending in federal and state courts if the plaintiffs opted in within a certain date.[25]

Judge Fallon has since created a Bellwether Trial Committee for third-party payor claims against Merck (that were not resolved by the *Vioxx* settlement).[26] He

---

21. *Vioxx Prods. Liab. Litig.*, MDL-1657, http://vioxx.laed.uscourts.gov.

22. *Plaintiffs Plan to Challenge Defense Verdict in Federal Lawsuit Alleging Vioxx Claims*, Prod. Liab. Daily (BNA) (Mar. 6, 2006); *Merck Loses Vioxx Suit in Texas: $32 Million Award to Short-Term User*, N.Y. TIMES, Apr. 22, 2006, at B1.

23. *See Vioxx Cases Near Trial on the West Coast*, NAT'L LAW J., Mar. 14, 2006 (stating that out of 1,800 Vioxx suits filed in California, a Los Angeles Superior Court judge narrowed the list of 36 cases to go to trial first by eliminating all but victims of myocardial infarction, an ailment similar to a heart attack). For a description of the process in *Vioxx*, see Eldon E. Fallon, Jeremy T. Grabill & Robert Pitard Wynne, *Bellwether Trials in Multidistrict Litigation*, 82 TUL. L. REV. 2323 (2008); Edward F. Sherman, *The MDL Model for Resolv-ing Complex Litigation if a Class Action Is Not Possible*, 82 TUL. L. REV. 2205 (2008).

24. *See Analysts See Merck Victory in Vioxx Deal*, N.Y. TIMES, Nov. 10, 2007, at 1.

25. *See* Settlement Agreement Between Merck & Co., Inc. and the Counsel Listed on the Signature Pages Hereto, at art. 8. The agreement can be found at http://www.officialvioxxsettlement.com/documents/.

26. Pretrial Order No. 41, *In re Vioxx Prods. Liab. Litig.*, May 19, 2009 (MDL No. 1657, E.D. La.).

also ordered bellwether trials to begin within six months after the MDL transfer to him of the Chinese Drywall Cases.[27] Bellwether trials have also been ordered in the FEMA Trailer Formaldehyde Products litigation after refusal to certify a class action.[28]

Bellwether trials can sometimes spell the end of litigation. For example, a bellwether trial in the U.S. District Court for the Southern District of Florida of four out of 400 plaintiffs seeking damages alleged to have been caused by negligently navigating the M/V *Norwegian Dawn* into a storm and freak wave resulted in a defense verdict, and thereafter the plaintiffs stipulated to dismissal with prejudice.[29]

Bellwether trials can be expensive; the parties in the *Vioxx* cases spent several million dollars in litigating only a handful of bellwether trials, an indication of the importance they placed on them for settlement purposes. Defense lawyers James Beck and Marc Herrmann have commented that "a bellwether trial in an MDL (or statewide coordinated) proceeding isn't very informative" since "trying one or two cases out of a collection of hundreds, or thousands, certainly doesn't give any statistical information about the value of the cases."[30] But they ask "what's the alternative?": "[d]iscovering up 5,000 cases simultaneously without trying any," or "setting them all for trial," or "cobbling together classwide trials in situations that don't merit them," all of which are undesirable.[31] Professor Alexandra Lahav, on the other hand, would give even more weight to bellwether trials particularly if social science methods, such as random sampling, were used:

> The bellwether trial procedure reintroduces the jury into an area of law where settlement rules. They can and should be conducted using reliable social science methods, including random sampling, so that they can provide a valid litigation alternative in settlement for mass tort cases.[32]

Bellwether cases can play an especially useful role in immature litigation—cases in which issues of causation based on expert medical and scientific testimony, as well as the legal issues, have not been tested in many individual trials. This contrasts with asbestos cases, which were tried in large numbers over the

---

27. *In re Chinese-Manufactured Drywall Prods. Liab. Litig.*, MDL 2047 (E.D. La. 2010), http://www.laed .uscourts.gov/Drywall/Orders/order3.pdf; *Federal Judge Puts Chinese Drywall Cases on "Rocket Docket,"* DAILY BUS. REV., Aug. 11, 2009.

28. *FEMA Trailer Formaldehyde Prods. Liab. Litig.*, 07-MDL-1873 (E.D. La. 2009) (Engelhardt, J.), http:// www.laed.uscourts.gov; Sean Wajert, FEMA Trailer MDL Selects First Bellwether Trial (Apr. 10, 2009), http://www.masstortdefense.com/2009/04/articles/fema-trailer-mdl-selects-first-bellwether-trial/.

29. Mase & Lara, *Attorneys at Law* Newsletter, Miami, Fla., June 2007.

30. James Beck & Marc Herrmann, Ruminations on Bellwether Trials (Jan. 19, 2007), http://drugand devicelaw.blogspot.com/2007/01/ruminations-on-bellwether-trials.html.

31. *Id.*

32. Alexandra Lahav, *Bellwether Trials*, GEO. WASH. L. REV. 576 (2008); *see also* Alexandra Lahav, *Recovering the Social Value of Jurisdictional Redundancy*, 82 TUL. L. REV. 2369 (2008).

past three decades with many of the same expert scientific witnesses testifying again and again, and therefore bellwether trials are of less utility. In rejecting class certification, the Fifth Circuit in *Castano v. American Tobacco Co.*,[33] a suit against the tobacco companies based on a new cause of action for "nicotine addiction," noted that the factual and legal issues had not previously been litigated. The use of bellwether or test cases before class certification, or upon transfer and consolidation under MDL, would permit the working through of novel issues in individual litigation before either an aggregate trial or, much more likely, a global settlement. The techniques for overseeing and administering bellwether or test case trials are still being refined.

IV. Sample Trials and Extrapolation

Bellwether cases resolve the particular cases tried, but unless they are deemed persuasive by the parties for reaching a settlement, the mass of similar aggregated cases remain unresolved. However, if the cases to be tried were selected randomly according to probability principles, they could have statistical validity for the entire field of cases. We accept statistical reliability based on sampling in many situations where it is burdensome or impossible to test every representative of a field. Examples are public opinion polls, sampling of products in customs or agricultural inspections, and testing of mass-produced products.[34] In recognition of this reality, Judge Robert Parker, who was faced with a docket of some 3,000 asbestos cases, proposed the use of sample trials from which damage awards would be extrapolated for all of the cases. In *Cimino v. Raymark Industries, Inc.*,[35] 169 asbestos cases were selected by random means and tried to a jury. The verdicts from the trials of cases within each of five disease categories were then averaged and applied to each plaintiff in that category. A statistics professor testified as to the "goodness-of-fit" between the sample cases tried and the rest of the claimants in each disease category.[36] The judge noted that statistical evidence has been used in a large number of litigation contexts, including civil rights cases to show unequal treatment of racial minorities, antitrust cases to project pre- and post-merger market share and concentration, and tort cases to show life expectancy or mortality for determining damages.[37]

---

33. 84 F.3d 734, 737 (5th Cir. 1996).

34. See cases cited in *Cimino v. Raymark Indus., Inc.*, 751 F. Supp. 649, 662 (E.D. Tex. 1990), including *United States v. 449 Cases Containing Tomato Paste*, 212 F.2d 567 (2d Cir. 1954) (approving inspector's testing of samples, rather than requiring the opening of all cases) and *United States v. 43 1/2 Gross Rubber Prophylactics*, 65 F. Supp. 534 (D. Minn. 1946) (determining shipment was misbranded based on evidence of a sample that indicated a potential of defective prophylactics), *aff'd*, 159 F.2d 881 (8th Cir. 1947); *see also* Chapter 18, "Statistical Sampling as a Basis for Extrapolating Liability and/or Damages."

35. 751 F. Supp. at 660.

36. *Id.* at 664.

37. *Id.* at 660–62.

The Fifth Circuit rejected Judge Parker's trial method.[38] It pointed out that the plaintiffs' statistical expert did not independently validate the variables he used to support his conclusion about "goodness-of-fit," but accepted information reported by plaintiffs' lawyers.[39] More fundamentally, it emphasized that the extrapolation provided no occasion for individual examination of claimants' circumstances to make a determination regarding causation, something that it viewed as required by Texas law and the 7th Amendment. It said:

> The only juries that spoke to actual damages received evidence only of the damages to the particular plaintiffs before them, were called on to determine only, and only determined, each of those some one hundred seventy particular plaintiffs' actual damages individually and severally, and were not called on to determine, and did not determine or purport to determine, the damages of any other plaintiffs or group of plaintiffs.[40]

At the heart of the difference in approach between Judge Parker and the Fifth Circuit panel is whether leeway may be given in aggregated cases to allowing determination of damages on a basis other than a strict individualized examination as to each plaintiff. Prior to taking the statistical approach in *Cimino*, Judge Parker had tried another aggregate approach for avoiding individualized trials on damages by extrapolating damages for some 3,000 class members from trials of 11 class representatives. The Fifth Circuit, in *In re Fibreboard Corp.*,[41] granted a writ of mandamus against that procedure, stating:

> We are also uncomfortable with the suggestion that a move from one-on-one "traditional" modes is little more than a move to modernity. Such traditional ways of proceeding reflect far more than habit. They reflect the very culture of the jury trial and the case and controversy requirement of Article III. It is suggested that the litigating unit is the class and, hence, we have the adversarial engagement or that all are present in a "consolidated" proceeding. But, this begs the very question of whether these 3,031 claimants are sufficiently situated for class treatment; it equally begs the question of whether they are actually before the court under Fed. R. Civ. Proc. Rules 23 and 42(b) in any more than a fictional sense. Ultimately, these concerns find expression in defendants' right to due process. . . . We are persuaded on reflection that the procedures here called for comprise something other than a trial within our authority. It is called a trial, but it is not.[42]

Cimino attracted a good deal of academic comment. Professors Michael Saks and Peter Blanck argued that statistical methods might actually produce more

---

38. *Cimino v. Raymark Indus., Inc.*, 151 F.3d 297 (5th Cir. 1998).

39. *Id.* at 321 n.48.

40. *Id.* at 320.

41. 893 F.2d 706 (5th Cir. 1990).

42. *Id.* at 711, 712.

accurate decisions.[43] "Every verdict is itself merely a sample from the large population of potential verdicts" that would result from trying the same case repeatedly.[44] Each case could have been tried in different contexts: "before the same jury; before different juries; or by different lawyers using exactly the same facts" or "using different permutations of the same facts or different facts and arguments that could have been assembled out of the same basic case."[45] Therefore a more accurate "true award" in any case would be "the average of the population of possible awards."[46] Professor Robert Bone, in reply, found that this analysis underestimated the additional risk of error resulting from statistical sampling and rejected sampling from both a process or rights-based and efficiency analysis.[47]

There have been few attempts since *Cimino* to resurrect sampling to avoid individualized trials for damages in complex aggregated cases.[48] Most settlements, however, do adopt schedules or grids based on prior damage awards and damage estimates that involve extrapolation and averaging.[49] Likewise, various bankruptcy agreements and legislative solutions to mass tort crises have allocated trust funds based on detailed grids derived from case verdicts and settlements to determine individual damage awards.[50] But the Fifth Circuit's refusal to make accommodations in aggregated cases that would avoid individualized determinations of causation and damages has thus far prevailed.

---

43. Michael Saks & Peter Blanck, *Justice Improved: The Unrecognized Benefits of Sampling and Aggregation in the Trial of Mass Torts*, 44 STAN. L. REV. 815, 833–35 (1992).

44. *Id.* at 833.

45. *Id.* at 833–34.

46. *Id.*

47. Robert G. Bone, *Statistical Adjudication: Rights, Justice and Utility in a World of Process Scarcity*, 46 VAND. L. REV. 561 (1993).

48. *But see Hilao v. Estate of Marcos*, 103 F.3d 767 (9th Cir. 1996) (using trials of 137 randomly selected class members to determine individual damage awards).

49. Both plaintiffs' and defendants' lawyers in specialized areas of litigation such as asbestos keep careful track of verdicts and settlements in other cases, and this information provides the basis for considerable agreement as to the settlement value of individual cases.

50. *See, e.g., In re Dow Corning Corp.*, 255 B.R. 445 (E.D. Mich. 2000) (using such methods for breast implant claimants), *aff'd in part*, 280 F.3d 648 (6th Cir. 2002); *In re A.H. Robins Co., Inc.*, 88 B.R. 742 (E.D. Va. 1988) (using such methods in bankruptcy court for the Dalkon Shield claimants), *aff'd*, 880 F.2d 694 (4th Cir. 1989); *In re Johns-Manville Corp.*, 36 B.R. 727 (Bankr. S.D.N.Y. 1984) (using such methods for asbestos claimants); *see also* discussion in RHEINGOLD, *supra* note 20, § 18.24. The Fairness in Asbestos Injury Resolution Act of 2004 (FAIR), S. 2290, 108th Cong. (2004), proposed abrogating the right of asbestos victims to sue in return for the right to make claims against a trust fund with an elaborate schedule of payments based on a variety of circumstances. *See* Mona Lisa Wallace & Edward F. Sherman, *Compensation Under a Trust Fund Solution to Asbestos Claims: Is It Really Fair?*, BRIEF, Winter 2005, at 48 (ABA Tort Trial & Ins. Prac. Sec.).

V. Bifurcation

A. GENERALLY

Federal Rule of Civil Procedure 42 provides that "[t]he Court, in furtherance of convenience or to avoid prejudice, or when separate trials will be conducive to expedition and economy, may order a separate trial of any claim."[51] Such separate trials would normally be before different juries. Called bifurcation (or trifurcation or polyfurcation if separate trials are ordered for more than two claims), this authority has been especially important in courts' dispositions of aggregate litigation.[52] The most common form of bifurcation that goes back many years is between liability and damages. A verdict could be rendered on liability, and individual damages would be determined later through such methods as individual or small-group trials[53] or some form of administrative or ministerial determination, including an ADR process.[54] The justification for this procedure in mass-tort class actions was stated in *Sterling v. Velsicol Chemical Corp.*:[55]

> In mass tort accidents, the factual and legal issues of a defendant's liability do not differ dramatically from one plaintiff to the next. No matter how individualized the issue of damages may be, these issues may be reserved for individual treatment with the question of liability tried as a class action.[56]

A number of courts have moved beyond liability/damages bifurcation to ordering separate trials on various damage or liability issues.[57] Rule 23(c)(4) provides

---

51. FED. R. CIV. P. 42(b).

52. *See Simon v. Philip Morris, Inc.*, 200 F.R.D. 21, 32 (E.D.N.Y. 2001) ("Bifurcation procedure has evolved to accommodate the modern emphasis on active judicial management of complex cases, particularly in the realm of mass tort disputes.").

53. *See* discussion at notes 85–87, *infra*.

54. If damages can be determined by resort to a noncontroverted standard (such as the price paid for a product), they might be apportioned and awarded to the individuals through a court surrogate or a claims process without the need for individual trials. See further discussion in text at notes 108–112, *infra*.

55. 855 F.2d 1188 (6th Cir. 1988).

56. *Id.* at 1196–97; *see also Simon*, 200 F.R.D. at 44:

The very nature of injuries arising from mass production and mass marketing efforts makes trial judges' discretion to sever issues for trial one of the most necessary and natural in their arsenal of tools required for the shaping of these types of cases for efficient adjudication. . . . Because modern marketing of most products is directed to anonymous consumers, the determination of the defendant's responsibility for its mass production and sales decisions should be aggregated to reflect that scheme.

57. *See, e.g., Sanford v. Johns-Manville Sales Corp.*, 923 F.2d 1142, 1145 (5th Cir. 1991) (trying liability and punitive damages before one jury and compensatory damages before another in asbestos litigation); *In re Bendectin Litig.*, 857 F.2d 290, 309 (6th Cir. 1988) (affirming district court's trifurcation into liability, causation, and damages in product liability suits brought against pharmaceutical company for

authority in class actions to certify classes "with respect to particular issues."[58] In cases where causation through exposure to a product, substance, or environmental condition is a centrally disputed issue, courts have approved bifurcating and trying first the issue of general or "generic" causation (that is, whether the injury could have been caused by the product, substance, or condition) and leaving for later determination the question of individual causation.[59] Some courts have adopted "reverse bifurcation" by which the issue of damages and remedy are tried first, with liability left for later.[60]

B. SEVENTH AMENDMENT REEXAMINATION CLAUSE CONCERNS

Courts have differed on their willingness to find that such methods comport with standards of efficiency and fairness. One of the most serious challenges is whether use of different juries for bifurcated trials violates the reexamination clause of the 7th Amendment.[61] Bifurcation has been said to be limited in "recognition of the fact that inherent in the Seventh Amendment guarantee of a trial by jury is the general right of a litigant to have only one jury pass on a common issue of fact."[62] The test, based on *Gasoline Products Co. v. Champlin Refining Co.*,[63] a 1931 case concerning a partial new trial on the question of damages (which it found "so interwoven with that of liability that the former cannot be submitted to the jury"[64]), is that an issue may only be separated if so distinct and separable from others that a trial of it alone may be had without injustice. Although there may be some overlapping of evidence in different segments of a bifurcated case, courts

---

manufacturing an antinausea medication for expectant mothers that allegedly caused birth defects); *In re Copley Pharm., Inc.*, 161 F.R.D. 456, 469 (D. Wyo. 1995) (ordering common issues of liability to be tried in classwide trial in products liability suit while ordering individual questions of causation, injury, and compensatory damages to be tried separately before separate juries).

58. *See also* Chapter 28, "Creative Application of Rule 23(c)(4): How Issue Certification Interacts with the Requirements of Rule 23(b)(3)."

59. *See Jenkins v. Raymark Indus., Inc.*, 782 F.2d 468, 473 (5th Cir. 1986) (ordering a first classwide trial to determine which asbestos products were capable of producing fibers sufficient to cause harm; which were defective and unreasonably dangerous; what date each defendant knew or should have known of the risk (i.e., "state of the art" defense); and what amount of punitive damages should be awarded).

60. Reverse bifurcation can be useful where the parties have excellent information about the likelihood of success on the issue of liability and the real sticking points are individual issues of causation and damages. *See, e.g., Angelo v. Armstrong World Indus., Inc.*, 11 F.3d 957, 964–65 (10th Cir. 1993) (approving reverse bifurcation in asbestos case where the procedure would save time and money and would not prevent plaintiffs from developing a history of their exposure to defendant's product); *Developments in the Law— Confronting the New Challenges of Scientific Evidence*, 108 HARV. L. REV. 1481, 1591–93 (1995) (discussing reverse bifurcation as a method of managing cases that present complex evidentiary issues).

61. The 7th Amendment provides that "no fact tried by a jury, shall be otherwise re-examined in any Court of the United States, than according to the rules of the common law." U.S. CONST. amend. VII.

62. *Alabama v. Blue Bird Body Co.*, 573 F.2d 309, 318 (5th Cir. 1978).

63. 283 U.S. 494, 500 (1931).

64. *Id.* at 500.

have generally found that such issues as liability, damages, causation, and affirmative defenses satisfy the "distinct and separable" test, and there is no violation of the 7th Amendment. "[The] Seventh Amendment prohibition is not against having two juries review the same evidence, but rather against having two juries decide the same essential issues."[65]

Cases in two circuits have found a 7th Amendment violation in the use of bifurcation. In *In re Rhone-Poulenc Rorer, Inc.*,[66] the trial court certified a class action and ordered an initial trial limited to the question of the negligence of the defendant manufacturers of blood solids for hemophiliacs that resulted in their being infected with AIDS. The order stated that if negligence were found in the initial trial, the class members could file individual suits, which would use special verdicts and the preclusion doctrine to avoid relitigation of the issue of negligence.[67] In finding that the court exceeded its authority, Judge Posner stated that issues of comparative negligence and proximate cause that would arise in the individual suits overlapped the issue of negligence and thus improperly allowed reexamination by different juries.[68] The Fifth Circuit adopted this analysis in *Castano*, rejecting a proposed classwide trial of "core liability" issues relating to defendant tobacco companies' conduct concerning "nicotine addiction," which was to be followed by trials of the individual issues of class members. The Fifth Circuit panel found a risk of reexamination,[69] since comparative fault was a central issue, given the longtime warnings on tobacco packages and general recognition of health risks in smoking.[70] It reasoned:

> There is a risk that in apportioning fault, the second jury could reevaluate the defendant's fault, determine that the defendant was not at fault, and apportion 100% of the fault to the plaintiff. In such a situation, the second jury would be impermissibly reconsidering the findings of a first jury.[71]

Undoubtedly issues that are not sufficiently freestanding to warrant a separate trial should not be the subject of bifurcation. But presumably a second jury would be instructed that it had to accept the first jury's findings. Judge Rovner, dissenting in *Rhone-Poulenc*, noted that the trial judge could modify severance orders, procedural decisions, and certification rulings to avoid any 7th Amendment problems.[72] Judge Weinstein commented in *Simon v. Philip Morris, Inc.*[73] that "there is some

---

65. *In re Paoli R.R. Yard PCB Litig.*, 113 F.3d 444, 452 n.5 (3d Cir. 1997) (quotation omitted).
66. 51 F.3d 1293 (7th Cir. 1995).
67. *Id.* at 1302.
68. *Id.* at 1303.
69. *Castano*, 84 F.3d at 750.
70. *Id.* at 751.
71. *Id.*
72. 51 F.3d at 1308.
73. 200 F.R.D. 21.

doubt about whether a second jury would be reexamining the first jury's findings of the defendant's negligence when it found the plaintiff also contributorily liable to some percentage (assuming that the first jury did not put an end to the case by finding no negligence)."[74] But he also found that reexamination could be avoided in bifurcation by appropriate judicial supervision.

Rhone-Poulenc and *Castano* have not been followed by most courts that have continued to order bifurcation in appropriate class action cases, expressing no 7th Amendment problem even as to issues such as comparative fault and proximate cause.[75] The American Law Institute's *Principles of the Law of Aggregate Litigation*[76] recognized "the practical difficulties that attend the aggregate treatment of liability issues when applicable substantive law does not separate cleanly issues of liability from dispute affirmative defenses."[77] However, it noted that *Gasoline Products* was a simple, nonaggregate case that "focused on relitigation of the liability issue—one as to which no error occurred in the original trial—not the reconsideration of evidence presented initially as to an issue different from those now for determination by the fact finder."[78] It urged that the relitigation question be given "a functional perspective based on the aims of aggregation":[79]

> Given the tendency of evidence in many instances to be relevant to multiple aspects of a claim, it is not realistically possible to insist that no reconsideration of evidence whatsoever may occur across the aggregate proceeding and subsequent proceedings. The question is one of degree and, as such, calls for the exercise of judicial discretion, in keeping with the discretionary nature of the determination whether to authorize aggregate treatment.[80]

C. PRACTICAL EFFECTS OF BIFURCATION ON OUTCOME

Bifurcation may have an effect on the outcome of the case. In routine personal injury cases, it has been reported that the defense wins almost twice as frequently when the liability issues are tried separately.[81] This experience with routine cases

---

74. *Id.* at 48.

75. *See* cases cited *id.* at 107–120.

76. American Law Institute, Principles of the Law of Aggregate Litigation, Proposed Final Draft (Apr. 1, 2009), § 2.03, cmt. b, at 109.

77. American Law Institute, Principles of the Law of Aggregate Litigation, Preliminary Draft No. 5 (Sept. 12, 2008), § 2.06, cmt. a.

78. American Law Institute, *supra* note 76.

79. American Law Institute, *supra* note 77.

80. American Law Institute, *supra* note 76, § 2.03, cmt. b, at 99.

81. *See* Warren F. Schwartz, *Severance—A Means of Minimizing the Role of Burden and Expense in Determining the Outcome of Litigation*, 20 VAND. L. REV. 1197 (1967); Jack B. Weinstein, *Routine Bifurcation of Jury Negligence Trials: An Example of the Questionable Use of Rule Making Power*, 14 VAND. L. REV. 831 (1961).

has also been found in research on mass torts.[82] An economic analysis concluded that

> a sequential trial lowers the expected cost of litigation compared to a unitary trial for both the plaintiff and defendant because it holds out the prospect of avoiding litigation on subsequent issues if the defendant wins the current issue or the parties settle the remaining issues after the current one is decided.[83]

It has also been found that "the bifurcation of general causation in the separated trial condition produces greater disbelief about causation, yielding fewer verdicts for the plaintiffs."[84] There are thus strategic considerations for courts and counsel in the use of bifurcation, but it has become a significant device for the segmenting and ultimate disposition of aggregate litigation.

VI. Hybrid Class Actions

The use of "hybrid class actions" is an application of bifurcation. This vehicle has had particular importance in employment discrimination cases in which class members seek both classwide injunctive or declaratory relief and an individual remedy in the form of back pay. Federal Rule of Civil Procedure 23(b)(2) allows a class action for injunctive or declaratory relief, while Rule 23(b)(3) provides for a class action for damages. Using the hybrid approach, a court would certify a (b)(2) class action for injunctive or declaratory relief, to be followed by a (b)(3) class action for individualized awards of back pay. Since there is an opt-out right only in a (b)(3) class action, notice of a right to opt out would only be given after the (b)(2) trial had been held.[85]

Hybrid class actions have also been resorted to in cases other than employment discrimination.[86] *Simon v. World Omni Leasing, Inc.*[87] was a class action against an auto leasing company on behalf of persons who had entered into long-term leases. It sought a declaration that the disclosure statement violated the Truth in Lending

---

82. Kenneth S. Bordens & Irwin A. Horowitz, *Mass Tort Civil Litigation: The Impact of Procedural Changes on Jury Decisions*, 73 JUDICATURE 22, 25–26 (1989) (empirical experiments using 66 juries showed that plaintiffs received favorable verdicts significantly more often in unitary trials than in bifurcated trials, although the damages awarded were significantly lower).

83. William M. Landes, *Sequential Versus Unitary Trials: An Economic Analysis*, 22 J. LEGAL STUD. 99, 100–01 (1993).

84. Bordens & Horowitz, *supra* note 82, at 27.

85. *See Cox v. Am. Cast Iron Pipe Co.*, 784 F.2d 1546 (11th Cir. 1986) (holding that an opt-out procedure was inappropriate before the monetary relief stage of a hybrid Rule 23(b)(2) class action).

86. As some courts have adopted restrictive applications of the predominance, superiority, and manageability requirements that only apply to (b)(3) classes, class lawyers have sometimes tried to structure their cases as (b)(2) classes, even when they seek substantial damages. *See, e.g.*, Chapter 14, "The Special Role of 23(b)(2) Classes."

87. 146 F.R.D. 197 (S.D. Ala. 1992).

Act, an injunction against the leases' enforcement, and also monetary refunds. The district court certified the class in two stages, the first to determine liability, as to which there would be no opt-out right, and the second for monetary relief, as to which class members could opt out and pursue their own private rights of action.

Hybrid class actions have been viewed by some courts as an improper way to avoid the requirements of both (b)(2) and (b)(3) class actions. The Fifth Circuit led the opposition, refusing in *Allison v. Citgo Petroleum Corp.*[88] to extend (b)(2) class actions to cases in which additional money damages do not flow directly from the equitable relief and would require individualized determinations.[89] It has also taken a strict view of the "predominance of common questions," superiority, and manageability requirements for a (b)(3) class action, rejecting class treatment of many cases.[90] Thus, employment discrimination cases in which money damages (as opposed to back pay) are sought would not be certifiable under either (b)(2) or (b)(3).[91] Under this view, certifying a hybrid class would not solve the problem because the damages portion of the case could not be certified under (b)(3) and furthermore would violate the 7th Amendment by reexamining the first jury's findings.[92]

---

88. 151 F.3d 402 (5th Cir. 1998).

89. The Advisory Committee notes to Rule 23(b)(2) provide that a (b)(2) class action "does not extend to cases in which the appropriate final relief relates exclusively or predominantly to money damages." FED. R. CIV. P. 23(b) advisory committee note (1966). This issue came to a head when the Civil Rights Act of 1991, 42 U.S.C.A. § 1981a(a)(1) (West 2000), accorded for the first time a right to compensatory and punitive damages in employment discrimination cases. Unlike back pay, which was considered equitable and therefore consistent with a (b)(2) class action, compensatory and punitive damages are clearly "money damages." *Allison* held that for monetary relief to be allowed in a (b)(2) class action, it must "flow directly from liability to the class *as a whole* on the claims forming the basis of the injunctive or declaratory relief" and must be "incidental," that is, "capable of computation by means of objective standards and not dependent in any significant way on the intangible, subjective differences of each class member's circumstances." 151 F.3d at 415 (emphasis added); *accord Murray v. Auslander*, 244 F.3d 807, 812 (11th Cir. 2001).

90. *See Castano*, 84 F.3d at 745 (finding class action for nicotine addiction not certifiable under (b)(3)); *Allison*, 151 F.3d at 419–20 (finding employment discrimination suit for injunction and damages not certifiable under (b)(3)). *Allison* also equated the predominance, superiority, and manageability requirements in (b)(3) with an inherent requirement of "cohesiveness" in (b)(2) classes, concluding that "the predomination requirement of Rule 23(b)(2) serves essentially the same functions as the procedural safeguards and efficiency and manageability standards mandated in (b)(3) class actions." *Id.* at 414–15.

91. *See* Melissa Hart, *Will Employment Discrimination Class Actions Survive?*, 37 AKRON L. REV. 813 (2004) (questioning whether employment discrimination class actions can continue to be certified under the *Allison* approach).

92. Cases certifying hybrid class actions

> stand for the proposition that it may be appropriate to use a bifurcated or hybrid trial process in Rule 23(b)(2) cases when class-wide injunctive relief is appropriate, followed by individualized awards of back pay. Significantly, these cases do not hold that such a process is appropriate (much less required, as plaintiffs would have it) when highly individualized awards of compensatory and punitive damages are at stake.

Cooper v. Southern Co., 390 F.3d 695, 721 (11th Cir. 2004).

Other circuit and district courts are more permissive as to allowing damages in a (b)(2) class action,[93] as well as to the predominance question in (b)(3) classes[94] and the reexamination clause of the 7th Amendment.[95] Thus, a hybrid approach is still possible in a number of circuits. Even the Fifth Circuit modified its strict *Allison* approach to (b)(2) class actions in a civil rights case in which it found that damages were incidental where they could be determined on a classwide basis, and therefore, a (b)(2) class was permissible.[96] That case, however, did not rely on a hybrid class action, but on a finding that the damages were allowable in a (b)(2) class action as only incidental. The split between the circuits goes not only to impediments to hybrid class actions and bifurcation, but also to fundamental disagreement as to predominance and cohesiveness in class actions, and would seem to require Supreme Court review at some point.

VII. *Subclassing*

Subclassing provides a mechanism for allowing a class action despite certain differences between class members who can nevertheless fit into subgroups.[97] "Subclassing is possible only if different class members coalesce into discrete, identifiable groups."[98] The only reference to subclasses in the federal rules is in Rule 23(c)(4) and states that "[w]hen appropriate (A) an action may be brought or maintained as a class action with respect to particular issues, or (B) a class may be divided into subclasses and each subclass treated as a class. . . ." Thus court cases and accepted practice have to be looked to in order to flesh out the dimensions of subclasses.[99]

Subclassing may serve as an adjunct to bifurcation. "Once the trial has been bifurcated, subclasses may also be necessary for handling various damage

---

93. The Second Circuit would allow even substantial money damages in a (b)(2) class action if, on an ad hoc basis, a reasonable plaintiff would have sought injunctive or declaratory relief even if money damages were not available. *Robinson v. Metro-North Commuter R.R.*, 267 F.3d 147 (2d Cir. 2001); *accord Molski v. Gleich*, 318 F.3d 937 (9th Cir. 2003). *See also Berger v. Xerox Ret. Income Guar. Plan*, 338 F.3d 755 (7th Cir. 2003) (holding that a suit for declaratory relief regarding determination of lump-sum distributions could be certified under (b)(2)).

94. *See, e.g., Chiang v. Veneman*, 385 F.3d 256 (3d Cir. 2004) (finding a "uniform course of conduct" sufficiently subject to common proof to sustain partial (b)(3) class certification; *Klay v. Humana*, 382 F.3d 1241 (11th Cir. 2004) (finding that reliance could be proven on a classwide basis to satisfy predominance).

95. *See* text accompanying notes 72–80, 110–123, *infra*.

96. *In re Monumental Life Ins. Co.*, 365 F.3d 408 (5th Cir. 2004).

97. *See Harris v. Pan Am. World Airways, Inc.*, 74 F.R.D. 24 (C.D. Cal. 1977) ("[T]he court may provide for the protection of separable interests by resort to Rule 23(c)(4) and direct that 'a class . . . be divided into subclasses and each subclass be treated as a class . . . .' *See Rodriguez v. East Texas Motor Freight*, 505 F.2d 40, 51 (5th Cir. 1974), *cert. granted*, 425 U.S. 990, 96 S. Ct. 2200, 48 L. Ed.2d 814 (1976).").

98. *Developments in the Law, supra* note 60, at 1479–82.

99. *See* Scott Dodson, *Subclassing*, 27 Cardozo L. Rev. 2351 (2006).

claims."[100] Subclassing may be structured around the type of remedy or damages sought by different groups. For example, in an action arising out of an environmental catastrophe, there may be subclasses based on the degree of exposure, the severity or type of physical injury, or the loss in the value of real property depending on the distance from the hazard.[101]

Subclasses may also be structured around differences of fact or law between class members who nevertheless rely on the same basic claim regarding the conduct of the defendant. Thus, subclasses are often approved for a class action by employees alleging employment discrimination, based on such features as their job or position, the time period of their employment, or the particular employer's conduct that they claim as discriminatory.[102] In consumer class actions, subclasses may be based on the time or circumstances in which misrepresentations were received or the nature and extent of the injury alleged.[103]

"Subclasses are often called for as well when it appears that the class representatives and class members have conflicting factual or legal positions."[104] However, if differences in their positions would put them into conflict as to objectives and litigation strategy, it may be necessary that the subclasses have different lawyers.[105] Subclassing can sometimes provide a solution to commonality and conflict problems caused by potential differences between class members. By subclassing, additional

---

100. THOMAS A. DICKERSON, CLASS ACTIONS: THE LAWS OF 50 STATES § 8.03[1], pp. 8–10 (2003).

101. *See Turner v. Murphy Oil USA, Inc.,* Civ. Act. No. 05-4206, 2006 U.S. Dist. LEXIS 4472 (E.D. La. Jan. 30, 2006) (subclassing based on geographical location regarding pollution caused by breach in tank); *Floyd v. Philadelphia* (No. 2), 8 Pa. D. & C. 2d 380 (Pa. Comm. Pleas 1970), discussed in DICKERSON, *supra* note 100, which subclassed as to adults, children, persons sick for the first time, and persons whose preexisting condition was aggravated by a chlorine leak.

102. *Gen. Tel. Co. of the Sw. v. Falcon,* 457 U.S. 147 (1982), held that a Mexican-American who claimed race discrimination in the denial of a promotion was not an adequate class representative for Mexican-Americans who claimed discrimination in not being hired. This defect might have been remedied by subclasses with different class representatives. *See Johnson v. Am. Credit Co.,* 581 F.2d 526, 533 n.13 (5th Cir. 1978):

When faced with a situation when no named plaintiff can represent a subclass, a trial court should consider whether it is in the interests of justice and judicial economy to postpone dismissal as to the subclass for a specified period in which members of the subclass could become plaintiffs by amendment of the Complaint or by intervention and thereby save the subclass action.

103. *See, e.g., Kashmiri v. Regents of the Univ. of Cal.,* 156 Cal. App. 4th 809, 67, Cal. Rptr. 3d 635 (2007), challenging a fee increase, which created subclasses for spring 2003 students, summer 2003 students, and professional students.

104. ROBERT H. KLONOFF, CLASS ACTIONS AND OTHER MULTI-PARTY LITIGATION 117 (1999).

105. *See Amchem Prods., Inc. v. Windsor,* 521 U.S. 591 (1997) (rejecting settlement, *inter alia,* because there was an irreconcilable conflict between the interests of class members who had manifested medical conditions from exposure to asbestos and class members who had not); *Ortiz v. Fibreboard Corp.,* 527 U.S. 815 (1999) (rejecting certification of a settlement class composed of present and future claimants and stating that courts should divide such classes into homogeneous subclasses under Rule 23(c)(4)(B) with separate counsel to eliminate conflicting interests).

named plaintiffs can be added to the suit that represent a subclass with a more discrete commonality of interests:

> By dividing a class, a judge may be able to redefine the responsibilities of class attorneys and named plaintiffs in terms of the interests of distinct and relatively unified portions of a class. The necessity for the ranking of class interests by the parties may therefore diminish, and the likelihood that diverse absentee interests will be presented to the court increase.[106]

Subclassing does not obviate a careful Rule 23 analysis. To the contrary, "the litigation as to each subclass is treated as a separate law suit. . . . Under the provisions of Rule 23(c)(4)(B), a class may be divided into subclasses and each subclass treated as a class with the provisions of the rule to be construed and applied accordingly to each class."[107] Thus there must be a proper class representative for each subclass, and all other requirements of Rule 23 must be satisfied.

VIII. Phased Trials

Phased trials are an extended application of bifurcation. Once bifurcation is permitted, a trial might be viewed as a continuous series of phases. Like bifurcation, authority for phased trials can be found in Federal Rule of Civil Procedure 42's authorization of "a separate trial of any claim."[108] In class actions there is also authority under Rule 23(c)(4) to certify classes "with respect to particular issues," often referred to as "issues classes." Thus, certain phases in a trial could involve certification of "issue" class actions, while other phases will not involve a classwide trial (as when individual issues such as causation, reliance, affirmative defenses, and damages are to be decided in individual or small-group trials or by resort to administrative processes).[109]

Phased trials have been particularly attractive to class action lawyers as a way to keep individual questions from predominating so as to satisfy the "predominance of common questions" requirement for a Rule 23(b)(3) class action.[110] Asbestos cases were among the first to rely on phased trials to meet class certification requirements. Over decades, class actions had been regularly denied in cases for personal injuries from exposure to asbestos. Although there were common

---

106. *Developments in the Law, supra* note 60, at 1479.

107. *Betts v. Reliable Collection Agency, Ltd.*, 659 F.2d 1000 (9th Cir. 1981).

108. FED. R. CIV. P. 42(b).

109. *See* RHEINGOLD, *supra* note 20, § 16.25 ("[Mini-trials may be used] to try damages and other individual or local issues in a mass tort litigation after general issues, usually liability and causation, have been resolved globally. Small ("mini") groups of cases are tried together, one group after another, as has been the practice in the asbestos cases.").

110. FED. R. CIV. P. 23(b)(3) (requiring a court to find that "the questions of law or fact common to the members of the class predominate over any questions affecting only individual members").

questions, such as the defectiveness of the product and knowledge of the risk by the manufacturers, individual questions such as the circumstances of exposure, likelihood of other causes, and injury were found to predominate.[111] In the early 1990s, Judge Parker, confronted with over 5,000 asbestos cases on his docket, certified a class action with common issues to be tried in a classwide first-phase trial.[112] Individual issues such as causation, affirmative defenses, and injury were left for a later phase, to be conducted as individual or mini-trials of a small number of similar cases.[113] The Fifth Circuit upheld this approach in *Jenkins v. Raymark Industries*,[114] commenting that "courts are now being forced to rethink the alternatives and priorities by the current volume of litigation and more frequent mass disasters." There was a settlement before the later individualized phases had to be conducted.

Phased trials have been adopted in a large number of class actions, as to such matters as injuries from an antinausea drug,[115] a supper club fire resulting in 164 deaths,[116] a tanker accident discharging 11 million gallons of oil into an Alaskan sound,[117] an explosion in an oil refinery,[118] property damage claims by homeowners for defective hardboard siding,[119] personal injury claims by opt-outs from a breast implant settlement,[120] claims of 10,000 persons who were tortured, exe-

---

111. A nationwide class of schools against three asbestos manufacturers for costs of removing asbestos from buildings was certified in *In re Asbestos School Litigation*, 789 F.2d 996, 998–99 (3d Cir. 1986). Predominance of common questions could be met since the circumstances of exposure were similar, and causation and injury were not individualized as in personal injury cases.

112. *See supra* note 56 for the special issues submitted to the jury relating to defendants', rather than plaintiffs', conduct and product in a first-phase of the class action. *Jenkins*, 782 F.2d at 471 n.3.

113. Such mini-trials have generally been limited to about ten cases in the belief that a jury can only adequately keep in mind the circumstances of that number of cases.

114. 782 F.2d at 473.

115. *In re Bendectin Prod. Liab. Litig.*, 749 F.2d 300 (7th Cir. 1984) (using a trifurcated procedure in which the first-phase trial as to "generic causation" resulted in a defense verdict, thus ending the immediate litigation).

116. *In re Beverly Hills Fire Litig.*, 695 F.2d 207, 210 (6th Cir. 1982) (using a three-phase trial in which the first phase addressed whether the wiring could have caused the fire).

117. *In re The Exxon Valdez*, Order No. 180 (Feb. 25, 1994) & Order No. 180 Supplement (Mar. 8, 1994) (four phases), No. A89-0595-CV (HRH) (D. Alaska); *see also generally* Elizabeth Cabraser, *Beyond Bifurcation: Multi-Phase Trial Structures in Mass Tort Class Actions, in* 7 CLASS ACTIONS & DERIVATIVE SUITS 2, 5–6 (1997).

118. *Watson v. Shell Oil Co.*, 979 F.2d 1014, 1018 (5th Cir. 1992) (ordering a phase-one trial of common issues regarding liability in suit growing out of refinery explosion, to be followed by three more phases).

119. *Ex Parte Masonite*, 681 So. 2d 681 (Ala. 1996); *see also* Cabraser, *supra* note 117, at 10–12. *But see In re Masonite Corp. Hardboard Siding Prods. Liab. Litig.*, 170 F.R.D. 417, 420–24 (E.D. La. 1997) (refusing to certify a nationwide class of purchasers of defective siding, finding the state laws on many issues varied substantially, and stating that "this Court cannot imagine managing a trial under the law of 51 jurisdictions on the defectiveness of Masonite siding").

120. *Spitzfaden v. Dow Corning Corp.*, 619 So. 2d 795 (La. App. 1993) (using four phases, with a first-phase trial as to defendant's conduct, knowledge, intent, negligence, and duty), *writ denied*, 624 So. 2d 1237 (La. 1993). For a more detailed account, see Dawn M. Barrios, *The Long and Winding Road for Spitzfaden, Louisiana's Breast Implant Class Action: Ad Astra Per Aspera*, 74 TUL. L. REV. 1941 (2000).

cuted, or "disappeared" against the former dictator of the Philippines,[121] and claims of employees for injuries resulting from a casino ship's defective ventilation system.[122] A class action was certified by a federal judge in Louisiana on behalf of several thousand people claiming property damage from the rupture of an oil storage tank during Hurricane Katrina. A three-phase trial plan was approved with phase one concerning common issues of liability, phase two common issues regarding punitive damages, and phase three compensatory damages for class members.[123]

Separate individualized phases may sometimes be unnecessary if it is possible to present individualized issues through classwide evidence. Take the issue of individual causation and damages in an aggregated asbestos case. If extensive evidence must be taken as to when and where each plaintiff was exposed to the asbestos products of various defendant manufacturers, there would have to be individual determinations after a unitary trial on the common issues. However, in an asbestos case involving claims of exposure at a single facility (such as an oil refinery), proof of class members' exposure to a defendant's asbestos might be presented by common evidence as to which asbestos products were present in which workplace locations during which time periods.[124] The jury would be asked to complete a grid reflecting the asbestos products present at various locations where class members worked during relevant time periods. Then each class member's exposure could be determined administratively or ministerially by a special master, court surrogate, or claims processor through an examination of the company employment records indicating when and where each class member worked.

Some courts have rejected such attempts to present classwide evidence in order to avoid the "predominance of common issues" requirement for (b)(3) class certification. In *McLaughlin v. American Tobacco Co.*,[125] the Second Circuit decertified a class of "light" cigarette smokers alleging fraud under the federal RICO Act. It found that individualized issues of reliance, loss causation, and damages and injury predominated. Plaintiffs' attempt to prove causation and injury with classwide evidence was also rejected. Rather than requiring individual proof as to which class members were harmed, the district court had proposed to allow the plaintiffs to demonstrate how much the entire class suffered in the aggregate. The circuit court held that this was a kind of "fluid recovery" that violates the defendants' due process rights.

---

121. *Hilao*, 103 F.3d at 772–82 (holding separate trials as to liability, exemplary damages, and compensatory damages in which a special master used claims of 137 randomly selected cases to determine individual damage awards).

122. *Mullen v. Treasure Chest Casino LLC*, 186 F.3d 620, 623 (5th Cir. 1999) (using a two-phase trial, with the first phase addressing the issues of negligence and unseaworthiness of the vessel).

123. *Turner*, 2006 U.S. Dist. LEXIS 4472.

124. This approach was taken in the phased trial plan in *Cimino*, 751 F. Supp. 649, *rev'd on other grounds*, 151 F.3d 297 (5th Cir. 1998).

125. 522 F.3d 215 (2d Cir. 2008).

Use of classwide evidence may be feasible as to certain issues in consumer suits. For example, plaintiffs may argue that purchase of a defective product by individual class members can be determined by a court, surrogate, or claims process through submission of proofs of purchase, and thus a determination of injury could be made administratively. Courts increasingly require counsel seeking class certification to submit a "trial plan" as to how the various issues will be determined: whether in phases, whether classwide evidence will be presented as to certain issues, and how individualized issues will be determined.[126]

Despite the widespread use of phased trials, concerns remain in some courts. The 7th Amendment issue discussed in relation to bifurcation is equally applicable to phased trials.[127] Those accepting the *Rhone-Poulenc* and *Castano* analysis that a jury in a later phase would have to reexamine the findings of the first jury would find 7th Amendment problems in many phased-trial cases.[128]

An additional issue is whether, in the class action context, Rule 23(c)(4)'s authorization to certify only an "issue" class will enable a partial class action to satisfy the predominance requirement. Plaintiffs argue that individual issues can be separated off for resolution in a later phase, and thus an earlier "issues" phase, looked at by itself, would easily satisfy predominance. This argument was rejected in *Castano*, where the court said that "a cause of action, as a whole, must satisfy the predominance requirement of (b)(3) and that (c)(4) is a housekeeping rule that allows courts to sever the common issues for a class trial."[129] Particularly in the Fifth Circuit, some panels have rejected phased trials as "an attempt to 'manufacture predominance through the nimble use of subdivision (c)(4).'"[130] This view is supported by Professor Laura Hines, who examined the drafting history of this provision and concluded that there is a "complete absence of evidence that the Committee ever conceived of (c)(4)(A) as anything other than a 'usable detail.'"[131]

---

126. The Fifth Circuit, in *Castano*, 84 F.3d at 744–45, criticized the lower court for believing that it could not go past the pleadings in deciding class certification, saying that the court must understand the claims, defenses, relevant facts, and applicable substantive law in order to make a meaningful determination. *See* Edward F. Sherman, *Class Action Practice in the Gulf South*, 74 TUL. L. REV. 1603, 1615 (2000):

> It is unclear just how detailed a blueprint of how the case will proceed is required, given that discovery may not be complete, and there are many unknowns while the case is still being prepared for trial. It appears, however, that troublesome issues, like those matters that require individualized evidence, will have to be addressed in the trial plan.

127. *See supra* notes 61–80, 110–123.

128. *See Allison*, 151 F.3d at 420–21 (upholding lower court's refusal to certify an initial-stage class action for injunctive relief as to employment discrimination because of 7th Amendment concerns).

129. 84 F.3d at 745 n.21.

130. *Allison*, 151 F.3d at 422 (quoting *Castano*, 84 F.3d at 745 n.21).

131. *Compare* Laura Hines, *Challenging the Issue Class Action End-Run*, 52 EMORY L.J. 709, 758 (2003) (arguing that expansive issue class actions are not authorized under the current rules) *with* Jon Rom-

Many courts, however, seem to take the view expressed by Judge Weinstein that "trial judges have the discretion to sever issues under the more particular Rule 23(c)(4)(A) in a fashion that facilitates class adjudication of common issues,"[132] and thus apply the predominance requirement only to the "issue" phase of a phased trial.[133] Again, there is a fundamental difference of approach as to segmentation of litigation. The advocates of phased trials view an "issues" class as a case management device that can properly sever off individual issues into a discrete segment for later determination, while opponents maintain that the litigation must be viewed as a whole for a predominance determination and that segmenting is inconsistent with the class action rules.

IX. Claims Procedures

Questions over the propriety of bifurcation, hybrid classes, and phased trials discussed above come full circle with claims procedures. In ordering phased trials, courts leave individual issues to later phases, often without clearly identifying how they will be administered. If there have to be later individual trials or small-group mini-trials, there is a question whether any efficiency has really been obtained by certifying a class action for common issues. When a later phase requires separate trials of such individualized issues as reliance, causation, and damages, some of the same evidence necessary for the common trial may have to be presented again.

On the other hand, issues that normally require individualized evidence can sometimes be made susceptible to common proof. For example, in an asbestos case involving claims of exposure at a single facility, proof of class members' exposure to a defendant's asbestos could be presented by common evidence that the asbestos was present in certain rooms and locations during certain periods of time.[134] Then each class member's exposure could be determined administratively without having to present individualized evidence at the trial. Likewise, the issue of damages in an aggregated case for monetary relief can sometimes be resolved ministerially on a classwide basis, for example, when damages can be determined mathematically by an appropriate formula or by resorting to undisputed financial or statistical records. In employment discrimination cases, courts have permitted evidence

---

berg, *Half a Loaf Is Predominant and Superior to None: Class Certification of Particular Issues Under Rule 23(c)(4)(A)*, 2002 UTAH L. REV. 249 (urging expanded use of issue classes).

132. *Simon*, 200 F.R.D. at 32; *see also Cent. Wesleyan Coll. v. W.R. Grace & Co.*, 6 F.3d 177, 189 (4th Cir. 1993) ("Rule 23(c)(4) makes[s] plain that district courts may separate and certify certain issues for class treatment.").

133. *See Cent. Wesleyan Coll.*, 6 F.3d at 185 (stating that district courts should "take full advantage" of Rule 23(c)(4) to "reduce the range of disputed issues in complex litigation" and to achieve judicial efficiencies).

134. This approach was taken in the phased trial plan in *Cimino*, 751 F. Supp. at 662, *rev'd on other grounds*, 151 F.3d 297 (5th Cir. 1998).

of what positions, promotions, and pay an average employee would have had over the relevant time period but for the discrimination in order to determine back pay on a classwide basis, rather than requiring individualized evidence as to the facts of each class member's employment.[135] In other cases, however, damages may have to be determined on an individual basis. Courts have generally held, however, that this will not prevent class certification and that the issues may be bifurcated.

Claims resolution facilities have been created, primarily by private entities working in conjunction with court personnel, to conduct claims procedures, and a body of standards and practices is being developed for claims processes.[136] Claims facilities are usually the product of a settlement of complex aggregated cases, and there is no problem in assigning to administrators both factual determinations (such as whether each individual claimant purchased the product or meets other eligibility criteria) and an assessment of individual damage awards. But if a case is not settled and goes to trial, can the final step in the litigation—determining damages—be assigned to an administrative claims process? Is the defendant entitled to a jury trial as to each plaintiff's damages?

Claims procedures have been analogized to the use of special masters to gather information and present findings to the court. This is particularly applicable to economic damages. If the damages are susceptible of determination by formula, or by reference to undisputed or stipulated records, or by extrapolation from factual determinations made by the jury (such as findings that all plaintiffs were subjected to a certain supracompetitive percentage increase in prices due to defendant's price fixing[137]), courts have often been willing to approve a claims process for the final stage in litigation. But if substantial gathering of information will be required, this is not usually feasible before the jury renders its verdict on liability or on liability phases, and a claims assessor would have to report such information to the court after the jury is discharged. The question then arises whether distinct factual or mixed law and fact issues are being improperly taken from the jury and decided by the court upon the recommendation of the claims processor. The disagreement over segmentation of cases and the reach of the 7th Amendment that we have discussed concerning bifurcation and phased trials comes to the fore here as well. We would have much the same kind of division between courts on the claims-process issue depending on their views of the other segmentation issues.

---

135. *Pettway v. Am. Cast Iron Pipe Co.*, 494 F.2d 211, 258–63 (5th Cir. 1974); *see also Pettway v. Am. Cast Iron Pipe Co.*, 576 F.2d 1157, 1222 (5th Cir. 1978) (reiterating approval of the classwide remedy approach).

136. *See* Francis E. McGovern, *The What and Why of Claims Resolution Facilities*, 57 Stan. L. Rev. 1361 (2005) (examining the characteristics, advantages, and disadvantages of claims resolution facilities).

137. *See In re S. Cent. States Bakery Prods. Antitrust Litig.*, 86 F.R.D. 407 (M.D. La. 1980) (allowing econometric models used to demonstrate the impact of price fixing); *In re Corrugated Container Antitrust Litig.*, 80 F.R.D. 244 (S.D. Tex. 1978) (allowing proof of nationwide impact of price fixing).

Since most cases settle, it is rare that a claims process will take place in a litigated case. However, the issue can come up on class certification, with defendants arguing that damages cannot be left for individual determination by claims processors and thus individual questions predominate because of the individualized nature of the damages. Most courts hold that the need for individualized evidence as to damages is not necessarily a bar to class certification.[138] Personal injury damages are the paradigm of individualized damages, and it is generally recognized that such damages will have to be determined by individual or mini-trials rather than a claims process. This is one reason that class lawyers have been attracted to claims for economic damages based on contract, warranty, or statutory penalties that are more susceptible to determination by formula and/or reference to undisputed facts.

Approval of administrative or ministerial determination of damages may depend on how susceptible to classwide proof or formulaic determination the damages will be. Again, how a court views the segmentation issues and the 7th Amendment impediment is likely to color its view of this issue. In plaintiffs' favor is that most courts have experience with claims procedures in settlement cases and view them as a reliable and cost-efficient way to assess damages. This may make them more inclined to aggregate cases or certify a class on the representation that this is a case in which claims processors may properly be assigned responsibility for determining damages without usurping jury functions. Both ADR and case management techniques have been adopted in defining the role of claims processes.[139]

---

138. *In re Visa Check/MasterMoney Antitrust Litig.*, 280 F.3d 138–40 (2d Cir. 2001) ("[C]ommon issues may predominate when liability can be determined on a class-wide basis, even when there are some individualized damage issues."); *Bertulli v. Indep. Ass'n of Cont'l Pilots*, 242 F.3d 290, 298 (5th Cir. 2001) (affirming district court's determination that common issues predominated because "[a]lthough calculating damages will require some individualized determinations, it appears that virtually every issue prior to damages is a common issue"); *Bogosian v. Gulf Oil Corp.*, 561 F.2d 434, 456 (3d Cir. 1977) (stating that although calculation of damages in an antitrust action would involve some individualized issues, "it has been commonly recognized that the necessity for calculation of damages on an individual basis should not preclude class determination when the common issues which determine liability predominate"); *Blackie v. Barrack*, 524 F.2d 891, 905 (9th Cir. 1975) ("The amount of damages is invariably an individual question and does not defeat class action treatment.").

139. The American Bar Association Task Force on Terrorism and the Law recommended a mediation option for the procedures adopted for the September 11 Victim Compensation Fund, but it was not adopted. Mary S. Elcano & Cynthia J. Hallberlin, *Sept. 11 and ADR: Meeting the Challenge, The Claims Process: Procedural Justice, or Just Procedure?*, 8 DISP. RESOL. MAG. 5 (2002). Mediation was considered for the claims procedures contained in the settlement of MDL cases concerning the drug Propulsid, but was not ultimately adopted. *See Propulsid Products Liab. Litig.*, MDL 1355 (E.D. La. 2001), Orders/Minute Entries, at http://propulsid .laed.uscourts.gov/ (last visited June 8, 2009). A proposal of the Tort Claimants Committee in the Dow Corning bankruptcy of six summary jury trials to aid the court in estimating the value of nondisease breast implant claims was not adopted. *In re Dow Corning Corp.*, 211 B.R. 545 (E.D. Mich. 1997).

X. Conclusion

The paradigmatic American single-event trial was dramatically changed by public law litigation more than three decades ago and by the more recent expansion of aggregate litigation. Devices arising out of two movements that spanned the public law and aggregate litigation phenomena—case management and ADR—have been instrumental in transforming the aggregate litigation process. That has involved protracting and segmenting litigation into manageable parts, which can be subjected to separate decision or settlement.

Eight devices have been examined in this chapter. *Nonbinding trial runs* are an ADR device that add a nonbinding proceeding in which shortened presentations of the evidence are made to different kinds of neutrals to obtain their evaluation of each side's case. *Bellwether cases* are actual trials of a small number of cases selected out of the aggregate litigation that normally do not have preclusive effect but offer a picture of how different juries view different cases across the spectrum of the aggregate litigation. *Sample trials* and extrapolation involve use of statistical analysis to derive individual damage verdicts from the trial of sample cases, or from determination by a jury of aggregate damages, but have generally been rejected by the courts. *Subclassing* provides a mechanism for allowing a class action despite certain differences between class members who can fit into subgroups and can sometimes provide a solution to commonality and conflict problems caused by potential differences between class members. *Bifurcation, hybrid class actions,* and *phased trials* are devices for segmenting issues in aggregated litigation, allowing a jury to determine certain issues whose resolution might lead to settlement without the need to litigate all issues and which might avoid predominance of individual issues that could prevent aggregate or class treatment. Defendants and some courts have raised constitutional and other impediments to such devices, and the courts are fundamentally divided on many of the principles and techniques used. *Claims procedures* are a device for allowing certain issues, particularly damages, to be determined ministerially by court surrogates or administrative processors to avoid the necessity of individual trials at the end of bifurcated litigation. The permissible scope of such proceedings is controversial, and the exact requirements and processes are in flux.

Since aggregate litigation generally involves private suits against corporate defendants as to which there is a right to trial by jury, the procedural devices must comply with the 7th Amendment, as well as due process. Defendants, who have generally opposed aggregation, have raised impediments to the segmented model based on denial of due process (because of lack of individualized treatment as to each element of each case), failure to provide a trial by the same jury of nonseparable issues, and violation of the standards and requirements of class actions and aggregate devices. These issues are still in dispute, and the form and scope of the segmented model and the devices used to accomplish it are very much in transition.

CREATIVE APPLICATION OF RULE 23(C)(4): HOW ISSUE CERTIFICATION INTERACTS WITH THE REQUIREMENTS OF RULE 23(B)(3)

CARI K. DAWSON

I. Introduction

Traditionally, Federal Rule 23 has been interpreted to permit certification of a 23(b)(1), (b)(2), or (b)(3) class. That is, a practitioner must prove that all the criteria of Rule 23(a) were satisfied, as well as the criteria of 23(b)(1), (2), and/or (3), in order to certify a class. Recently, however, courts have begun to question whether Rule 23(c)(4) provides them with an alternative class certification mechanism, referred to as "issue certification." Rule 23(c)(4)[1] provides, "When appropriate, an action may be brought or maintained as a class action with respect to particular issues."[2] Some courts have relied upon this language to conclude that Rule 23 authorizes courts in certain cases to isolate the common issues under Rule 23(c)(4) and proceed with class treatment of those particular issues—even if the common questions do not predominate over the individual questions in the litigation—so that class certification of the action as a whole is warranted. These courts maintain that "partial certification," "issue certification," or "issue classes" can be ordered and are authorized under Federal Rule of Civil Procedure 23.

The meaning and proper interpretation of Rule 23(c)(4) has become a hotly contested issue between the plaintiff and defense bar with the district and circuit courts issuing a number of divergent interpretations and opinions regarding the

---

1. Prior to December 2007, issue classes were dealt with in Rule 23(c)(4)(A). As of December 2007, Rule 23 was amended as part of the general stylistic restyling of the Federal Rules of Civil Procedure, and the provision on issue classes was given its own subsection—23(c)(4). For this reason, all but the most recent citations reference Rule 23(c)(4)(A), the precursor of Rule 23(c)(4).

2. FED. R. CIV. P. 23(c)(4).

propriety of issue classes/issue certification. The dichotomy in views is most starkly illustrated by the division between the Fifth and Seventh circuits and the Ninth and Second[3] circuits. The former have held that Rule 23(c)(4) certification as to specific issues is available *only if* common questions predominate in the claim as a whole, while the latter have held that Rule 23(c)(4) is available to certify as to particular issues, regardless of whether the claims as a whole satisfy Rule 23(b)(3)'s predominance requirement.[4] This chapter will explore the origins of issue certification and some of the recent decisions interpreting Rule 23(c)(4) to assist practitioners in navigating the waters in this controversial area of the law.

II. The Foundation of the Modern Class Action

The 1966 amendments to Rule 23 basically defined what we know of today as the modern class action.[5] The 1966 amendments established a two-pronged inquiry under parts 23(a) and 23(b) that must be satisfied before a class action can be certified by a district court. Rule 23(a) sets forth four distinct factors—numerosity, commonality, typicality, and adequacy of representation—all of which must be present to initiate a valid class action. Having satisfied the prerequisites under 23(a), it must then be determined whether a class of litigants properly falls within one of the categories of class actions permissible under 23(b). Section 23(b)(1) authorizes class actions with no right to opt out for situations in which individual interests could be harmed by inconsistent adjudications or individual adjudications that would essentially be dispositive of the claims asserted by other members of the proposed class. Section 23(b)(2) authorizes class actions with no right to opt out where injunctive or declaratory relief is sought by putative class members. Thus, both sections 23(b)(1) and 23(b)(2) permit the creation and maintenance of a mandatory class.

Section 23(b)(3) is different. Section 23(b)(3) empowers a court to certify an opt-out class, as opposed to a mandatory class, but only if the following additional conditions are met:

> (3) the court finds that the questions of law or fact common to class members predominate over any questions affecting only individual members, and that a class action is superior to other available methods for fairly and efficiently adjudicating the controversy. The matters pertinent to the findings include: (A) the class members' interests in individually controlling the prosecution or defense of sepa-

---

3. While there is precedent approving issue certification that remains good law within the Second Circuit, beginning in 2008 the Second Circuit has issued opinions that limit the scope of issue certification and restrict the circumstances in which it should be granted. *See* section VI, *infra*.

4. *See* section V, *infra*.

5. *See, e.g.,* FED. R. CIV. P. 23 advisory committee notes (1966 amendment).

rate actions; (B) the extent and nature of any litigation concerning the controversy already begun by or against class members; (C) the desirability or undesirability of concentrating the litigation of the claims in the particular forum; and (D) the likely difficulties in managing a class action.[6]

The heightened scrutiny under 23(b)(3) highlights the distinctive nature of subsection (b)(3), as compared to its mandatory class counterparts in (b)(1) and (b)(2). Rule 23(b)(3) includes the additional requirements of predominance and superiority, which serve a vital purpose.[7] They are there to make certain that the claims of the class members are more alike than different and that the named representatives are appropriate representatives for the entire class.[8] If those fundamental criteria are not satisfied, then the entire purpose of a class action is defeated. Accordingly, plaintiffs' contentions concerning predominance and superiority of a class action must not only be scrutinized rigorously, but also critically, to ensure that a class action is, in fact, superior to other available methods for the fair and efficient adjudication of the controversy.

III. What Is Issue Certification?

Admittedly, the language of Rule 23(c)(4) does leave some ambiguity as to its purpose and limitations. Defense practitioners argue that Rule 23(c)(4) is not a stand-alone provision and should be read in context with the entirety of the rule. In reviewing Rule 23 in its entirety, the location of part (c)(4) within the statute as a whole is of great significance. Part (a) of Rule 23, simply titled "Prerequisites," identifies the essential elements that must be satisfied to bring a class action: numerosity, commonality, typicality, and adequacy of representation.[9] Part (b) of Rule 23, entitled "Types of Class Actions," unambiguously states that not only must the prerequisites of 23(a) be satisfied, but, *in addition*, one of the subsections of part (b) must apply in order to maintain a class action.[10]

Part (c), by contrast, has a more cumbersome title and addresses a variety of different issues. It is a significant departure from parts (a) and (b), which identify the elements a plaintiff must satisfy in order to certify and maintain a class action. Part (c) provides direction to the court concerning when to reach the issue of class certification, the contents of any order certifying a class, the ability to amend a class certification order, notice to the class, the content of a class judgment,

---

6. FED. R. CIV. P. 23(b)(3).

7. *See Amchem Prods., Inc. v. Windsor*, 521 U.S. 591, 620 (1997) (discussing safeguards of Rule 23 class-qualifying criteria).

8. *Id.*

9. FED. R. CIV. P. 23(a).

10. *Id.* 23(b).

and options available to the court once it has determined that class treatment is appropriate.[11] Notably, the title of part (c), "Certification Order; Notice to Class Members; Judgment; Issues Classes; Subclasses," although unwieldy, can be more easily understood by matching each phrase to the appropriate subsection of part (c).[12] For instance, (c)(1)(A) deals with the "Time to Issue" the certification order, (c)(1)(B) concerns "Defining the Class; Appointing Class Counsel," (c)(1)(C) addresses "Altering or Amending the Order," (c)(2) addresses "Notice," (c)(3) explains the process for entering class "Judgment," (c)(4) involves "Particular Issues," and (c)(5) involves "Subclasses."[13]

Associating the appropriate title with each subsection facilitates an understanding of the section as a whole, as it becomes clear that each subsection addresses what many courts and commentators have referred to as a "housekeeping" function of the rule.[14] Indeed, none of the other subsections of Rule 23(c) authorizes the certification of another type of class action not sanctioned by part 23(b). In other words, as with the other "housekeeping" provisions of Rule 23(c), 23(c)(4) appears to simply provide the court with some guidance as to how it can manage a class action *after* the court has determined that the case meets the requirements set forth in 23(a) and 23(b).

Defense practitioners argue that a class action still must be brought and maintained under parts 23(a) and 23(b) prior to any issue certification and that subsection (c)(4) is merely a reaffirmation of a court's existing power under 23(b)(3) to either certify a class where some individual issues remain, certify certain causes of action within an action as opposed to the action as whole, or bifurcate a trial between a liability and damages phase.

Practitioners from the plaintiffs' bar disagree with this interpretation. Plaintiffs' counsel and some commentators contend that Rule 23(c)(4) can play a central role in class action litigation by sanctioning class treatment for suits that otherwise would not be able to meet the qualifications for certification under 23(a) and (23)(b).[15] Viewed in this light, 23(c)(4) can be characterized as a revival device—if your class definition does not pass muster under the traditional Rule 23 analysis, it could be revived by finely parsing the issues and claims under 23(c)(4). The foundation of this theory, its advocates contend, is in the vague and indefinite wording of

---

11. *Id.* 23(c).

12. *Id.*

13. *Id.*

14. *See, e.g.*, *Castano v. Am. Tobacco Co.*, 84 F.3d 734, 745 n.21 (5th Cir. 1996); Laura J. Hines, *Challenging the Issue Class Action End-Run*, 52 EMORY L.J. 709, 710–11 (2003); Laura J. Hines, *The Dangerous Allure of the Issue Class Action*, 79 IND. L.J. 567, 587–88 (2004).

15. *See, e.g.*, Jon Romberg, *Half a Loaf Is Predominant and Superior to None: Class Certification of Particular Issues Under Rule 23(c)(4)(A)*, 2002 UTAH L. REV. 249, 334 (2002) (concluding Rule 23(c)(4)(A) "provides courts with a finely calibrated tool . . . to slice apart 'downstream' cases . . . into their constituent issues").

23(c)(4), which lends itself to this expansive interpretation and arguably empowers courts to use their discretion in the application of the rule.[16]

The proper interpretation of the interaction of Rule 23(c)(4) and Rule 23(b)(3) cannot be resolved by a review of the plain language of Rule 23. It does not provide a simple, dispositive answer. Courts continue to grapple with these complex certification issues and struggle as well to reconcile the language within Rule 23 and the case law interpreting it.

IV. What's Old Is New Again

Significantly, issue certification under Rule 23(c)(4) is not a novel concept. In fact, it is actually a revival of a tactic used by plaintiff practitioners and embraced by certain courts in the 1970s and 1980s. During the era when mass tort cases were clogging the federal court system, plaintiffs' counsel and judges began to look to Rule 23 as a management tool. Early attempts at using Rule 23 to assist with mass torts began with single-event mass disasters, where, for instance, a fire injured many people at a single point in time.[17] Later, in the mid-1980s, the courts began to use Rule 23 to help them control their exploding asbestos dockets.[18]

The mass tort phenomenon encouraged the courts to respond with novel procedural solutions to control their dockets. As a result, some courts began looking to issue certification as a case management tool.[19] We are now seeing the reemergence of issue certification—only the trend this time around espouses an even broader, more expansive reading of 23(c)(4), to arguably bypass Rule 23(b)(3)'s predominance requirement.

V. Decoding the Mixed Signals from the Courts

Very few federal appellate courts have addressed the proper use and application of 23(c)(4) and its interaction with 23(b)(3), and the circuits are split on the issue.[20]

---

16. See id. at 262–65.

17. See, e.g., Am. Trading & Prod. Corp. v. Fischbach & Moore, Inc., 47 F.R.D. 155 (N.D. Ill. 1969) (using Rule 23 to manage mass tort litigation arising from a fire in an exhibition hall); Hernandez v. Motor Vessel Skyward, 61 F.R.D. 558 (S.D. Fla. 1973) (using Rule 23 to manage mass tort litigation arising from food poisoning on a cruise ship), aff'd, 507 F.2d 1278 (5th Cir. 1975).

18. See, e.g., John C. Coffee, Jr., Class Wars: The Dilemma of the Mass Tort Class Action, 95 COLUM. L. REV. 1343, 1356 (1995).

19. See, e.g., Sch. Dist. of Lancaster v. Lake Asbestos of Que., Ltd. (In re Sch. Asbestos Litig.), 789 F.2d 996, 1008 (3d Cir. 1986) (citing 23(c)(4)(A) when noting trend in favor of mass tort class actions); In re Tetracycline Cases, 107 F.R.D. 719, 725 (W.D. Mo. 1985) (observing that 23(c)(4)(A) permits class adjudication for one or more common issues).

20. It bears noting that the Eleventh Circuit has sidestepped the issue, declining to rule on the class certification argument under Rule 23(c)(4)(A) because of its determination that summary judgment

In *Valentino v. Carter-Wallace, Inc.*,[21] the U.S. Court of Appeals for the Ninth Circuit explained the intersection between 23(c)(4) and 23(b)(3)'s predominance requirement in a single sentence. The appellate court stated, "Even if the common questions do not predominate over the individual questions so that class certification of the entire action is warranted, Rule 23 authorizes the district court in appropriate cases to isolate the common issues under Rule 23(c)(4)(A) and proceed with class treatment of these particular issues."[22] Regrettably, for all sides, however, the court did not expand on this analysis any further; nor did it provide any guidance as to what would be an "appropriate" case for the kind of isolation of common issues advocated by the opinion. By its ruling, the Ninth Circuit became the first appellate court to date to arguably favor using 23(c)(4) to sidestep the predominance requirement of 23(b)(3) and authorize the isolation of common issues when individual issues predominate the action as a whole. The Ninth Circuit has yet to fully develop its analysis and rationale for issue certification, but its principle continues to be embraced.[23]

The Ninth Circuit's holding in *Valentino* was taken a step further by the Second Circuit in *Augustin v. Jablonsky (In re Nassau County Strip Search Cases)*.[24] *Nassau County* involved a series of cases contesting Nassau County Correctional Center's blanket strip search policy for newly admitted misdemeanor detainees. Plaintiffs appealed a series of orders entered in the district court denying their repeated motions for class certification on the ground that individual issues predominated over common issues. Plaintiffs sought to certify a Rule 23(b)(3) class solely on the issue of liability under Rule 23(c)(4). Recognizing the split in the circuit courts of appeals regarding the interpretation of Rule 23(c)(4), the Second Circuit began

---

was properly granted to the defendants. *See Rink v. Cheminova, Inc.*, 400 F.3d 1286, 1297 (11th Cir. 2005). In the recent decision of *Williams v. Mohawk Industries, Inc.*, 568 F.3d 1350, 1360 (11th Cir. 2009), the issue was sidestepped again, although the court instructed the district court on remand to consider the propriety of a "hybrid class action" to certify a claim under § 16-4-4(c) of the Official Code of Georgia Annotated under Rules 23(b)(2) and (c)(4). Additionally, the Fourth and Eighth circuits have acknowledged that there is a circuit split on the issue, but have left the correct interpretation of Rule 23(c)(4) an open question. *See Grovatt v. St. Jude Med., Inc. (In re St. Jude Med., Inc.)*, 522 F.3d 836, 841 (8th Cir. 2008) (noting that even if issue certification were allowed, the class should not be certified because treatment as an issue class would not advance the litigation); *Gunnells v. Healthplan Servs., Inc.*, 348 F.3d 417, 439, 444–45 (4th Cir. 2003) (refusing to "enter [the] fray" because the court found the "*cause of action* as a whole" satisfied the Rule 23 requirements); *Chiang v. Veneman*, 385 F.3d 256 (3d Cir. 2004) (recognizing that discretion is vested in courts to certify a class under Rule 23(c)(4), but not shedding light on the overall contours of that discretion).

21. 97 F.3d 1227 (9th Cir. 1996).

22. *Id.* at 1234.

23. *See, e.g., Sepulveda v. Wal-Mart Stores, Inc.*, 275 F. App'x 672 (9th Cir. Apr. 25, 2008) (holding that the district court abused its discretion in denying class certification and ordering on remand that the district court reconsider class certification under Rule 23(b)(2) and also reconsider using Rule 23(c)(4) to certify specific issues under the Rule 23(b)(2) standard).

24. 461 F.3d 219 (2d Cir. 2006).

its analysis by noting that whether a court may employ Rule 23(c)(4) to certify a class as to a specific issue where the entire claim does not satisfy Rule 23(b)(3)'s predominance requirement is a matter of first impression in the Second Circuit.[25]

On appeal, the circuit court concluded that, contrary to the district court's reservations, a court may employ Rule 23(c)(4) to certify a class on a particular issue even if the action as a whole does not satisfy Rule 23(b)(3)'s predominance requirement and cited to *Valentino* for support. The Second Circuit held that a court may employ subsection (c)(4) to certify a class as to liability regardless of whether the claim as a whole satisfies Rule 23(b)(3)'s predominance requirement. Of particular significance is the fact that the circuit court reached that conclusion without considering whether the district court should have certified a class as to the plaintiff's entire claim.[26] Accordingly, the court severed the issue of liability from damages and certified an issue class because it concluded that the primary issue—whether defendants had a blanket policy for strip searching and were liable for implementing such a policy—was ascertainable through generalized, common proof applicable to the class as a whole. *Nassau County* is a significant decision, as it represents a recent circuit court ruling on issue certification under Rule 23(c)(4) and its relationship to Rule 23(b)(3).

The holding in *Nassau County* was reaffirmed in *Cordes & Co. Financial Services, Inc. v. A.G. Edwards & Sons, Inc.*[27] The Second Circuit, citing to *Nassau County*, states explicitly that it had "adopted . . . the Ninth Circuit's view that Rule 23(c)(4)(A) is available to certify particular issues 'regardless of whether the claim as a whole satisfies Rule 23(b)(3)'s predominance requirement.'"[28] The circuit court reversed the district court's denial of class certification on appeal and ordered that, on remand, if the district court concludes that the action cannot be certified in its entirety because it does not meet the predominance requirement under Rule 23(b)(3), then plaintiff "may seek certification of a class to litigate the first element of their antitrust claim—the existence of a Sherman Act violation—pursuant to Rule 23(c)(4)(A) and *Nassau County*."[29]

The Seventh and Fifth circuits, on the other hand, view the function of Rule 23(c)(4) as more limited and have authorized its use only as a management tool after the predominance and superiority requirements of 23(b)(3) have been met. In *In re Rhone-Poulenc Rorer, Inc.*,[30] the Seventh Circuit, in the first appellate opinion to really touch on this issue, reversed a district court decision to partially certify a nationwide plaintiff class of hemophiliacs alleging they had contracted the AIDS

---

25. *Id.* at 226.
26. *Id.* at 225–26.
27. 502 F.3d 91 (2d Cir. 2007).
28. *Id.* at 109 (quoting *Nassau County*, 461 F.3d at 227).
29. *Id.*
30. 51 F.3d 1293 (7th Cir. 1995).

virus through defendants' blood products. Granting the extraordinary remedy of mandamus, the Seventh Circuit, in an opinion written by Judge Posner, ruled that the district court's partial certification of the plaintiff class "exceed[ed] the permissible bounds of discretion in the management of federal litigation" because it had bifurcated the case in a manner that created the potential for the same issues to be reexamined by different juries in violation of the 7th Amendment to the U.S. Constitution.[31] The district judge below had certified the partial class "'as a class action with respect to particular issues'" pursuant to Rule 23(c)(4) and determined that, while the negligence claim was susceptible to common proof, the issues of proximate causation and damages were not and would have to be tried before separate juries.[32] The Seventh Circuit held that such a bifurcation scheme was impermissible because the issues of proximate causation and damages were inextricably intertwined with the negligence claim to be decided by common proof and therefore would result in an overlap and reexamination of evidence.[33] As such, the predominance and superiority requirements of Rule 23(b)(3) could not be met.

Similarly, in *Castano v. American Tobacco Co.*,[34] the Fifth Circuit reversed a district court order certifying a plaintiff class alleging bodily injury from nicotine addiction and proposing a four-phase trial plan. The appellate court held that the district court had erred in considering the predominance and superiority requirements of Rule 23(b)(3) and abused its discretion by not including an analysis as to how a trial on the merits would be conducted or how variations in state law would play out when evaluating the predominance element. Specifically, with respect to the district court's use and application of Rule 23(c)(4), the Fifth Circuit observed:

> Severing the defendants' conduct from reliance under rule 23(c)(4) does not save the class action. A district court cannot manufacture predominance through the nimble use of subdivision (c)(4). The proper interpretation of the interaction between subdivisions (b)(3) and (c)(4) is that a cause of action, *as a whole*, must satisfy the predominance requirement of (b)(3) and that (c)(4) is a housekeeping rule that allows courts to sever the common issues for a class trial . . . Reading rule 23(c)(4) as allowing a court to sever issues until the remaining common issue predominates over the remaining individual issues would eviscerate the predominance requirement of rule 23(b)(3); the result would be automatic certification in every case where there is a common issue, a result that could not have been intended.[35]

---

31. *Id.* at 1297.
32. *Id.*
33. *Id.* at 1303.
34. 84 F.3d at 737–38.
35. *Id.* at 745 n.21 (citations omitted) (emphasis added).

Thus, the Fifth Circuit outright rejected the district court's suggestion that Rule 23(c)(4) could be used as a back door to evade the additional requirements of 23(b)(3).

As with the plain language analysis, assessing this sparse landscape of appellate decisions on the appropriate use of Rule 23(c)(4) does not provide courts or litigants with a definitive answer on this issue. There is, however, some value in taking a close look at these four appellate opinions. In particular, it bears noting that the Ninth Circuit's analysis in *Valentino* is indisputably the least developed. Moreover, and importantly, the Ninth Circuit actually vacated and remanded the district court's decision to certify the issues as classes under 23(c)(4) because, even after considering the option of issue certification, it found that the district court had failed to adequately explain how common issues predominated and how the trial of the common issues would be managed and promote greater efficiency.[36]

While the *Nassau County* decision includes more detailed analysis and cites to a number of leading legal scholars and commentators who have endorsed the liberal use of issue classes under Rule 23(c)(4), as explained in section VI of this chapter the scope of that decision has been limited by subsequent Second Circuit decisions. By contrast, the other two appellate opinions attempting to tackle this issue—*Rhone-Poulenc* and *Castano*—offer a much more detailed analysis of the reasoning behind their shared conclusion that the predominance and superiority requirements cannot be read out of Rule 23(b)(3) as an administrative convenience. As such, weighing the persuasive authority of the four appellate opinions addressing this issue, the scale tips in favor of a more strict constructionist approach to interpreting Rule 23(c)(4).

The most recent appellate decision to weigh in on these issues is *Hohider v. United Parcel Service, Inc.*[37] While the Third Circuit found that the district court abused its discretion in granting certification, it also noted that a court does have discretion to certify a class as to particular issues under Rule 23(c)(4). Of particular interest is that the Third Circuit noted that "a court's decision to exercise its discretion under Rule 23(c)(4), like any other certification decision under Rule 23, must be supported by rigorous analysis."[38] The Third Circuit further expressed its views on issue classes by identifying factors to be considered in weighing the propriety of (c)(4) certification:

> [W]e believe several considerations are relevant to determining "[w]hen [it is] appropriate" for a court to certify a class only "with respect to particular issues". . .: the type of claim(s) and issue(s) in question; the overall complexity of the case and the efficiencies to be gained by granting partial certification; the substantive law

---

36. *Valentino*, 97 F.3d at 1234.

37. 574 F.3d 169 (3d Cir. 2009).

38. *Id.* at 201.

underlying the claim(s), including any choice-of-law questions it may present; the impact partial certification will have on the constitutional and statutory rights of both the class members and the defendant(s); the potential preclusive effect that resolution of the proposed issues class will have; and so forth.[39]

Significantly, the Third Circuit acknowledged that it had not yet explicitly addressed the interaction between the requirements for class certification under Rule 23(a) and (b) and the authorization of issue classes under Rule 23(c)(4). It found that it did not need to resolve that question in *Hohider*, thus leaving the issue open in the Third Circuit.

Because the appellate courts have offered limited guidance as to whether Rule 23(c)(4) may appropriately be used as an alternative class certification mechanism or merely a housekeeping tool, it is not surprising that district court interpretations of Rule 23(c)(4) have run the gamut. One particularly interesting case study of a district court's attempt to follow appellate court guidance on the proper application of issue certification under Rule 23(c)(4) is the Northern District of Illinois' analysis in *In re Factor VIII or IX Concentrate Blood Products Litigation*.[40] The Northern District of Illinois was originally inclined to adopt the more expansive reading of Rule 23(c)(4), like that espoused by the Ninth Circuit, as evidenced by its ruling in *Wadleigh v. Rhone-Poulenc Rorer, Inc.*[41] As discussed above, however, the court was decisively reversed by the Seventh Circuit in its *Rhone-Poulenc* opinion. Indeed, the Seventh Circuit felt so strongly about this issue that, in granting the exceptional mandamus remedy, it determined that the court's order so far "exceed[ed] the proper bounds of judicial discretion as to be legitimately considered usurpative in character, or in violation of a clear and indisputable legal right, or, at the very least, patently erroneous."[42]

The *Blood Products* litigation was an outgrowth of the same litigation as *Rhone-Poulenc*. It consisted of the "second generation" of plaintiffs (mostly from foreign countries), but this second generation was similarly alleging the wrongful contraction of HIV and/or hepatitis C from the use of defendants' factor blood concentrate.[43] Consequently, the Northern District of Illinois was navigating a fine line when asked for a second time to determine whether it could certify one or more issue classes under Rule 23(c)(4).

When analyzing, in *Blood Products*, the question of issue certification in light of the lessons learned from *Rhone-Poulenc*, however, the Northern District of Illinois (perhaps in spite of itself considering its earlier *Wadleigh* opinion) unmistakably

---

39. *Id.*

40. No. 93 C 7452, 2005 WL 497782 (N.D. Ill. Mar. 1, 2005).

41. 157 F.R.D. 410 (N.D. Ill. 1994) (certifying a class with respect to particular issues only under Rule 23(c)(4)(A)).

42. *In re Rhone-Poulenc*, 51 F.3d at 1295.

43. *Blood Prods.*, 2005 WL 497782, at *1.

underscores the practical impossibilities that arise with issue certification.[44] The *Blood Products* court placed the ball back in plaintiffs' court with respect to issue certification, asking plaintiffs' counsel to draft ten questions that could potentially be certified as class issues without running afoul of the Seventh Circuit's rulings in *Rhone-Poulenc*.[45] Plaintiffs' counsel were unable to meet the challenge issued by the court. They could not draft a single question that did not implicate the very weighty and significant concerns addressed by *Rhone-Poulenc*.[46]

Many of the questions submitted by plaintiffs' counsel that could not pass muster under *Rhone-Poulenc* were basically mixed questions of both law and fact. Such questions were troubling to the Seventh Circuit and, consequently, to the *Blood Products* court, because the "legal overlay" meant that some legal standard would have to be applied in order for the jury to answer the question.[47] This was problematic in the *Blood Products* case because the proposed class was nationwide, and, as the Seventh Circuit concluded in *Rhone-Poulenc*, any legal standard to be applied would necessarily vary from state to state.[48]

In short, in declining to certify these issues with a "legal overlay" under Rule 23(c)(4), the *Blood Products* court essentially found that the predominance requirement could not be met. Because of the material variations in the legal standards, the issues to be potentially certified were more different than alike when considering the class as a whole. Thus, with respect to the issues framed by the plaintiffs, the class did not meet the traditional guarantees of representational litigation essential to a class action.

The interaction between Rules 23(b)(3) and 23(c)(4) is addressed by the district courts in a variety of ways. In *Blain v. SmithKline Beecham Corp.*,[49] the district court evaluated the two conflicting schools of thought regarding issue certification when the parent of a child who committed suicide while under the influence of the antidepressant Paxil and a patient who had attempted suicide while under the influence of Paxil as a minor filed a motion for nationwide class certification in a products liability action against the drug manufacturer. The plaintiffs urged the district court to certify an issue class, arguing that even if common questions did not predominate over individual questions, the court could isolate the common issues and perform the predominance evaluation solely with respect to their proposed common issues.[50] The district court rejected plaintiffs' argument and held that issue certification did not obviate the need to evaluate predominance. While

---

44. *See id.* at *2.
45. *Id.*
46. *See id.* at *3–9.
47. *Id.* at *3.
48. *Id.* at *5.
49. 240 F.R.D. 179 (E.D. Pa. 2007).
50. *Id.* at 190.

acknowledging the ruling by the Ninth Circuit in *Valentino*, the district court found the analysis of the Fifth Circuit in *Castano* persuasive and held that only after the court has found that the cause of action satisfies the predominance requirement of Rule 23(b)(3) may it certify common issues pursuant to Rule 23(c)(4).

Similarly, in *Taylor v. CSX Transportation, Inc.*,[51] plaintiffs sought certification of a class composed of engineers and conductors "diagnosed with asthma, COPD, or emphysema" who claimed they were harmed as a result of alleged exposure to diesel exhaust in the cabs of the defendants' locomotives. The district court noted it had discretion to "bifurcate portions of the trial" under Rule 23(c)(4), and that there was debate about whether the provision could apply when the predominance standard was not satisfied for the cause of action as a whole.[52] The district court agreed with the holding from the Fifth Circuit in *Castano* and other district courts in the Sixth Circuit that "Rule 23(c)(4) should not be interpreted to eviscerate the class certification requirements of Rule 23(b)(3)" and refused to certify the class.[53]

VI. *Efficiency Considerations and the 7th Amendment*

The additional requirements of Rule 23(b)(3) are there to ensure that the proposed class or proposed subclasses "are sufficiently cohesive to warrant adjudication by representation."[54] Although the predominance requirement does not insist that all issues be common to all plaintiffs, it does instruct that the "'*resolution* of the common questions affect all or a substantial number of the class members.'"[55] Thus, predominance not only requires that common questions predominate over individual ones with respect to class claims/causes of action, it also requires that there be common *answers* to those predominant questions. That is the only way that the core purpose of the predominance requirement—class cohesion sufficient to merit representational adjudication—is met.

To be sure, there are almost always common issues prevalent in any action brought as a putative class action. Indeed, that is why the 23(a) requirement of commonality is easily satisfied in nearly every case. The mere existence of a common nucleus of operative fact is generally sufficient to satisfy commonality. No real qualitative or quantitative analysis is performed at that stage.[56] In this sense, issue certification appears to be an outgrowth of the commonality requirement—where simply identifying common issues circumvents predominance.

---

51. No. 3:05CV7383, 2007 WL 2891085, at *1 (N.D. Ohio Sept. 28, 2007).

52. *Id.* at *14.

53. *Id.* at *15.

54. *Amchem*, 521 U.S. at 623.

55. *Watson v. Shell Oil Co.*, 979 F.2d 1014, 1022 (5th Cir. 1992) (emphasis added) (quoting *Jenkins v. Raymark Indus., Inc.*, 782 F.2d 468, 472 (5th Cir. 1986)).

56. *See Markham v. White*, 171 F.R.D. 217, 222 (N.D. Ill. 1997).

Resolution of a single common issue or a few common issues in the face of multiple individualized issues, facts, and circumstances does very little, if anything, to advance the ball toward the overall end goal of the case: trying the class claims by common proof. In fact, in the vast majority of cases, issue certification would likely unnecessarily postpone this goal. Instead of proceeding straight to a full trial on his claims, a class plaintiff affected by an issue certification order would be forced to wait until the jury renders a decision on a few "common" issues before the merits of a particular cause of action could be tried before yet another jury. Given this effect, issue certification can be viewed as an outgrowth of bifurcation, and, therefore, may potentially run afoul of the 7th Amendment.[57]

As plainly held by *Rhone-Poulenc*, the 7th Amendment prohibits a scenario where multiple juries are presented with the same testimonial and/or documentary evidence, as it guarantees litigants to have factual issues decided by a single jury to prevent against inconsistent jury verdicts.[58] In *Castano*, the Fifth Circuit elaborated:

> [T]his Court has cautioned that separation of issues is not the usual course that should be followed, and that the issue to be tried must be so distinct and separable from the others that a trial of it alone may be had without injustice. This limitation on the use of bifurcation is a recognition of the fact that inherent in the Seventh Amendment guarantee of a trial by jury is the general right of a litigant to have only one jury pass on a common issue of fact.[59]

In *In re Conagra Peanut Butter Products Liability Litigation*,[60] the district court followed the 7th Amendment analysis of the *Castano* court when it refused to certify an issue class of plaintiffs personally injured by salmonella-contaminated peanut butter, in part because of a concern that a "second jury would have to reconsider" liability issues determined by the common issues jury in violation of the 7th Amendment. Certainly, a class action cannot be the superior method of litigating plaintiffs' claims when evidence pertaining to certain claims must later be reintroduced and re-examined in a second trial.[61]

---

57. *See also* Chapter 27, "Management Techniques and Devices for Segmenting Aggregate Litigation."

58. 51 F.3d at 1303.

59. 84 F.3d at 750.

60. 251 F.R.D. 689, 691–92, 698–99 (N.D. Ga. 2008).

61. Based on the case law analyzing the 7th Amendment issue to date, it appears that the way plaintiffs' counsel or the district court proposes to structure the trial plan may have some bearing on whether it is ultimately determined to violate the 7th Amendment. *See Castano*, 84 F.3d at 750; *In re Gen. Motors Corp. Dex-Cool Prods. Liab. Litig.*, 241 F.R.D. 305, 323–24 (S.D. Ill. 2007); *In re Tri-State Crematory Litig.*, 215 F.R.D. 660, 699 (N.D. Ga. 2003); *see generally* 7AA CHARLES A. WRIGHT, ARTHUR R. MILLER & MARY K. KANE, FEDERAL PRACTICE AND PROCEDURE § 1790 (3d ed. 2005) (noting that 7th Amendment "concerns suggest caution in utilizing Rule 23(c)(4), not that it is never appropriate" and advocating using "careful structuring" including subclasses to avoid the 7th Amendment problem). Thus, although most district courts will likely view proposed issue certification trial plans with skepticism in light of *Rhone-Poulenc* and *Castano*,

As explained by the Fifth Circuit in *Castano*, in the course of conducting its predominance inquiry, a trial court must consider how a trial on the merits would be conducted as a practical matter.[62] This is likely why it was important to the conclusion reached in *Blood Products* that resolution of any potential issue that may legitimately qualify for certification under Rule 23(c)(4) would not materially advance the litigation.[63] Carving out issues that are not liability determinative does not advance the litigation. Rather, the misuse of Rule 23(c)(4) management tools would merely obfuscate the principal issue in determining the propriety of class treatment: Can liability and damages be established through common proof? After undertaking such an analysis, many courts have reached the same holding as ultimately reached in the *Blood Products* case—no.[64]

A majority of the courts advocating an expansive view of 23(c)(4) have ultimately concluded that, as a practical matter, issue certification still cannot save the putative class action under consideration.[65] Significantly, in *McLaughlin v. American Tobacco Co.*,[66] the Second Circuit itself—less than two years after its decision in *Nassau County*—refused to certify an issue class because certification of the issue class would not have advanced the litigation. Plaintiffs in *McLaughlin* brought an action under RICO alleging they overpaid for cigarettes as a result of "defendants' implicit representation" that "light" cigarettes were healthier for them.[67] The Second Circuit found that common issues did not predominate over individual issues (such as reliance, causation, and injury) in its 23(b)(3) analysis. While the circuit court acknowledged this did not preclude issue certification, the court found issue certification would not "'promote judicial economy.'"[68] "Certifying, for example, the issue of defendants' scheme to defraud, would not materially advance the liti-

---

conceivably there may be a trial plan proposed by plaintiffs' counsel that does not run afoul of the 7th Amendment.

62. *See Castano*, 84 F.3d at 740–41.

63. *Blood Prods.*, 2005 WL 497782, at *8.

64. *See, e.g., Farrar & Farrar Dairy, Inc. v. Miller-St. Nazianz, Inc.*, 254 F.R.D. 68, 77 (E.D.N.C. 2008) (finding that even if issue certification were allowed, "a district court should decline to certify issues where there are so many individual issues in the case that certifying the common issues would have a negligible effect on judicial efficiency"); *In re Genetically Modified Rice Litig.*, 251 F.R.D. 392, 400 (E.D. Mo. 2008) (same).

65. *See, e.g., Rattray v. Woodbury County, Iowa*, 253 F.R.D. 444, 464–65 (N.D. Iowa 2008) (denying plaintiffs' motion for class certification under 23(c)(4) because the court found "it [was] unlikely that the proposed class action . . . would achieve economies of time, effort, and expense"); *In re Baycol Prods. Litig.*, 218 F.R.D. 197, 209 (D. Minn. 2003) (denying plaintiffs' motion for class certification even under 23(c)(4) because individual issues were inextricably intertwined with common issues); *Emig v. Am. Tobacco Co.*, 184 F.R.D. 379, 395 (D. Kan. 1998) (same).

66. 522 F.3d 215, 234 (2d Cir. 2008).

67. *Id.* at 220.

68. *Id.* at 234 (quoting *Robinson v. Metro-North Commuter R.R.*, 267 F.3d 147, 168 (2d Cir. 2001)).

gation because it would not dispose of larger issues, such as reliance, injury, and damages."[69] *McLaughlin* was recently followed in *Dungan v. Academy at Ivy Ridge.*[70]

The Second Circuit's opinion highlights not only the difficulty of identifying an issue susceptible to classwide proof that will advance the litigation, but also that the inquiry into whether certification will advance the litigation necessarily requires consideration of issues outside of the specific issue being certified. Therefore, even those courts that have endorsed issue certification have acknowledged that the liability-determinative nature of the so-called common issues will still have to be considered in determining whether issue certification is appropriate.[71] As a district court in the Second Circuit recently noted, "[t]he Court is aware that . . . Plaintiffs are not seeking certification of the reliance and/or damages issue. The Court disagrees, however, that those issues are, therefore, rendered irrelevant to the overall Rule 23 analysis, including the issue certification under Rule 23(c)(4)(A)."[72]

Even in those jurisdictions where courts have approved issue certification, district court judges have declined to certify an issue class where individual trials will still be required to determine issues of causation, damages, and applicable defenses. In other words, where issue certification does not materially advance the litigation, but rather serves to unnecessarily complicate and delay the final resolution of the litigation, it has been rejected. As summarized by the district court for the Northern District of Georgia in *Conagra Peanut Butter Products*:

> [T]he Plaintiffs' case for class certification collapses when it confronts the fact that certification of a common issues class will not dispose of a single case or eliminate the need for a single trial. Any saving in judicial resources is speculative at best. Under the Plaintiffs' trial plan, at least 6,000 individual trials on exposure, injury, causation, damages and other individual issues will have to be prosecuted whether or not a class is certified . . . . This is not a case where class certification avoids clogging the federal courts with innumerable individual suits litigating the same issues repeatedly. If class certification is denied, these cases will go forward in essentially

---

69. *Id.*

70. No. 08-3870-CV, 2009 WL 2604356 (2d Cir. Aug. 20, 2009) (acknowledging that the Second Circuit had held that a court may employ Rule 23(c)(4) to certify a class as to liability regardless of whether the claim as a whole satisfied Rule 23(b)(3)'s predominance requirement, but ultimately concluding that the number of individual questions that would remain for individual adjudication made issue certification improper).

71. *See generally In re St. Jude Med.*, 522 F.3d at 841 ("Even courts that have approved 'issue certification' have declined to certify such classes where the predominance of individual issues is such that limited class certification would do little to increase the efficiency of the litigation."); Manual for Complex Litigation (Fourth) § 21.24 (2004) ("Certification of an issues class is appropriate only if it permits fair presentation of the claims and defenses and materially advances the disposition of the litigation as a whole.").

72. *Dungan v. Acad. at Ivy Ridge*, 249 F.R.D. 413, 414, 417 (N.D.N.Y. 2008) (denying certification of an issue class because it would not "meaningfully reduce the range of issues in dispute and promote judicial economy and [would] lead to potential confusion and redundancy in the presentation of proof").

the same manner they would if a class were certified, only without an expensive, unnecessary, meaningless, and largely uncontested "common" issues trial.[73]

As these cases demonstrate, where issue certification does little to increase the efficiency of the litigation and thereby conserve judicial resources, it continues to be rejected.

VII. Conclusion

Short of consideration by the U.S. Supreme Court or an amendment to Rule 23, it is unlikely that courts, litigants, and counsel will have final resolution on the proper use and application of Rule 23(c)(4) and its interaction with Rule 23(b)(3) in the near future. The weight of authority suggests that Rule 23(c)(4) simply allows courts to sever particular issues in certain factually specific contexts if the cause of action, as a whole, satisfies the predominance requirement. The efficiencies created through issue certification may be far outweighed by the delayed manageability problems that will arise as a result of individualized inquiries necessary to establish liability and/or damages. However, it is clear that discretion is vested in the district courts to utilize Rule 23(c)(4) to certify particular issues, and under certain circumstances, issue certification may withstand appellate scrutiny and be upheld by the circuit courts.

---

73. 251 F.R.D. at 701 (citations omitted).

MODIFICATION AND DECERTIFICATION OF CLASSES

J. BENJAMIN KING

I. Introduction

Although either party may bring a motion for class decertification, such motions are usually brought by defendants, and they tend to send a shiver of fear down the backs of class counsel. A motion for decertification of course occurs after plaintiffs have successfully obtained class certification and usually after surviving a Rule 23(f) appeal (or attempted appeal). They likely occur late in the case, after additional evidence not available prior to the original class certification decision has been developed, and after plaintiffs (and perhaps class counsel) have devoted substantial additional resources to the case. Plaintiffs may take comfort in the fact that the court has already granted class certification, but the battle over class certification is likely the most important in a class case. Losing a motion for decertification, after having certification in hand, would surely be a bitter pill for plaintiffs. For defendants, on the other hand, a motion for decertification is their opportunity to yank victory from the jaws of, if not defeat, then at least substantial exposure.

Rule 23(c)(1)(C) provides that a district court may alter or amend its class certification decision before final judgment. The U.S. Supreme Court has held that, "[e]ven after a certification order is entered, the judge remains free to modify it in the light of subsequent developments in the litigation."[1] A federal district court is "charged with the duty of monitoring its class decisions in light of the evidentiary development of the case."[2] Thus, a district court not only may modify or decertify a class at any time, but, in fact, has the affirmative obligation to ensure that class

---

1. *Gen. Tel. Co. of the Sw. v. Falcon*, 457 U.S. 147, 160, 102 S. Ct. 2364, 2372 (1982).
2. *Richardson v. Byrd*, 709 F.2d 1016, 1019 (5th Cir. 1983).

certification is appropriate as a case progresses after certification.[3] A decision of whether to modify or decertify a class is left to the district court's discretion.[4]

Decertification may be had at any point where the original basis for the class certification decision is no longer valid. Rather than complete decertification, a court may redefine the class, create subclasses, or partially decertify the class, as is warranted in a particular situation.[5] This is modification of a class.

The overarching issues in a motion for decertification or modification are the same as in the original class certification decision—whether the requirements of Rule 23 are met. However, there are several issues unique to a motion for decertification or modification, which this article addresses: (1) the deference shown the original certification decision and the burden of proof; (2) the relationship between a ruling on a motion for decertification or modification and Rule 23(f) appeals; and (3) the notice to class members required upon decertification or modification of a class.

II. The Deference Shown the Original Certification Decision and the Burden of Proof

One important issue upon which there is not agreement among the federal courts is the deference a district court should show to its prior certification decision.[6] The most widely cited case on this issue is *Sley v. Jamaica Water and Utilities, Inc.*[7] The court there held:

> Applying a "law of the case" rationale, a class once certified on the basis of the requirements of rule 23(a) and 23(b) should be decertified only where it is clear there exist changed circumstances making continued class action treatment improper.[8]

There are compelling arguments in favor of this deference to the prior certification decision. Absent this deferential standard, parties opposing class certification (usually defendants) will have strong incentives to move for decertification

---

3. *Wu v. Mamsi Life & Health Ins. Co.*, 256 F.R.D. 158, 162–63 (D. Md. 2008); *Chisolm v. TranSouth Fin. Corp.*, 194 F.R.D. 538, 544 (E.D. Va. 2000).

4. *Smilow v. Sw. Bell Mobile Sys., Inc.*, 323 F.3d 32, 37 (1st Cir. 2003); *Culpepper v. Irwin Mortgage Corp.*, 491 F.3d 1260, 1275 (11th Cir. 2007). The Ninth Circuit states the deference given district courts even more strongly: "A district court's decision to decertify a class is subject to 'very limited review' and will be reversed only upon a 'strong showing that the district court's decision was a clear abuse of discretion.'" *Westways World Travel, Inc. v. AMR Corp.*, 265 F. App'x 472, 475 (9th Cir. 2008) (citing *Dukes v. Wal-Mart, Inc.*, 509 F.3d 1168, 1175 (9th Cir. 2007)).

5. *Boucher v. Syracuse Univ.*, 164 F.3d 113, 118 (2d Cir. 1999); *Richardson*, 709 F.2d at 1019.

6. *See Muise v. GPU, Inc.*, 371 N.J. Super. 13, 32–34, 851 A.2d 799, 810–12 (N.J. Super. Ct. 2004) (discussing varying approaches of the federal courts).

7. 77 F.R.D. 391 (E.D. Pa. 1977).

8. *Id.* at 394.

repeatedly, even based on the same arguments and evidence previously rejected, because the most important event in a class action is almost invariably the certification decision. In addition, the parties will make important strategic decisions and expend substantial resources litigating the case in reliance on the class certification decision. Moreover, particularly after class notice has been issued, absentee class members may rely on the existence of a class to protect their interests. A variety of courts in different jurisdictions have cited to *Sley* as setting forth the appropriate standard.[9]

Courts may be particularly likely to defer to their original rulings when a motion to decertify comes late in the litigation. In *Langley v. Coughlin*, the court certified a class under Rule 23(b)(1)(A) and 23(b)(2) because, at that time, the primary relief sought by the class was injunctive and declaratory.[10] After the parties settled the injunctive and declaratory claims, defendants moved to decertify the class, claiming that certification under Rule 23(b)(3) was not appropriate.[11] In addressing the burden the parties bore on the motion to decertify, the court found that it was "doubtful" that plaintiffs carried "precisely the same burden as when they originally sought certification."[12] The court held that it "must take into consideration that an eve-of-trial decertification could adversely and unfairly prejudice class members, who may be unable to protect their own interests."[13] Echoing *Sley*, the court also held that the defendants had a steep burden to satisfy with respect to its prior finding regarding the Rule 23(a) requirements:

> Since the Rule 23(a) standards are preconditions for any form of class certification, this Court's 1985 certification order necessarily reflects the appropriate findings. Absent some significant intervening event, those findings may be deemed to be the law of the case, and they reflect that plaintiffs have satisfied the requirements of Rule 23(a).[14]

The court ultimately certified the class as a Rule 23(b)(3) class.[15] Other courts have agreed with *Langley*'s requirement that the party seeking decertification

---

9. *In re Nat'l Student Mktg. Litig.*, MDL Docket No. 105, 1981 WL 1617, at *8 (D.D.C. 1981) (quoting *Sley*, 77 F.R.D. at 394); *Robin v. Doctors Officenters Corp.*, 686 F. Supp. 199, 203 (N.D. Ill. 1988) ("Decertification should only occur where it is clear that changed circumstances make continuation of the class action improper." (citing *Sley*, 77 F.R.D. at 394); *In re Asbestos Sch. Litig.*, No. 83-0286, 1990 WL 2194, at *1 (E.D. Pa. Jan. 11, 1990) (quoting the *Sley* standard); *McLendon v. M. David Lowe Pers. Servs., Inc.*, 83 F.R.D. 204, 206 (S.D. Tex. 1979) (citing *Sley*, 77 F.R.D. 391).

10. 715 F. Supp. 522, 551 (S.D.N.Y. 1989).

11. *Id.*

12. *Id.* at 552.

13. *Id.*

14. *Id.* at 553.

15. *Id.* at 565; *see also Doe v. Karadzic*, 192 F.R.D. 133, 136–37 (S.D.N.Y. 2000) (recognizing that motions for decertification at the "early stages" of a litigation may fare better than those brought at a "late juncture").

demonstrate "some significant intervening event" justifying decertification[16] and have otherwise recognized that defendants bear a heavy burden in obtaining decertification.[17] Although many courts hold that the party seeking decertification bears the burden of establishing that decertification is appropriate, cases denying a motion to decertify simply because a party failed to come forward with evidence of changed circumstances are rare.[18]

Courts may be particularly disinclined to reverse their original certification decision after class notice has been issued. In *General Telephone Co. of the Southwest v. Falcon*, the Supreme Court stated that "particularly during the period before any notice is sent to members of the class," a class certification order "is inherently tentative."[19] Subsequent courts have cited this distinction for the proposition that after notice is sent, the class certification order becomes less tentative, and vice versa.[20]

As noted, the federal courts are not uniform on the deference owed the original class certification decision or whether the party challenging class certification bears the burden of proof on a motion for decertification or modification. Some

---

16. *In re Atl. Fin. Sec. Litig.*, Civ. A. No. 89-645, 1992 WL 50072, at *2 (E.D. Pa. Feb. 28, 1992) ("[W]hen seeking decertification of a class, the defendant bears a heavy burden to show that there exist clearly changed circumstances that make continued class action treatment improper."); *see also* 6A FED. PROC., L. ED. § 12:296 (updated Sept. 2008) ("An action once certified as a class action may be decertified where new facts have been developed to justify such a redetermination"); HERBERT B. NEWBERG & ALBA CONTE, NEWBERG ON CLASS ACTIONS: A MANUAL FOR GROUP LITIGATION AT FEDERAL AND STATE LEVELS § 7:47 (updated 2008) ("In the absence of materially changed or clarified circumstances, or the occurrence of a condition on which the initial class ruling was expressly contingent, courts should not condone a series of rearguments on the class issues by either the proponent or the opponent of class, in the guise of motions to reconsider the class ruling.").

17. *Gordon v. Hunt*, 117 F.R.D. 58, 61 (S.D.N.Y. 1987) ("At the outset, it is noted that defendants bear a heavy burden to prove the necessity of either the drastic step of decertification or the less draconian or still serious step of limiting the scope of the class."); *In re Vivendi Universal, S.A. Sec. Litig.*, No. 02 Civ. 5571 (RJH) (HBP), 2009 WL 855799, at *3 (S.D.N.Y. Mar. 31, 2009) ("[D]ecertifying or redefining the scope of a class should only be done where defendants have met their 'heavy burden' of proving the necessity of taking such a 'drastic' step." (citing *Gordon*, 117 F.R.D. at 61)); *Slaven v. BP Am., Inc.*, 190 F.R.D. 649, 651 (C.D. Cal. 2000) ("A party seeking class certification bears the burden of demonstrating that the proposed class satisfies the four elements of Rule 23(a), as well as the elements of at least one provision of Rule 23(b). . . . It follows, therefore, that a party seeking *decertification* of a class should bear the burden of demonstrating that the elements of Rule 23 have *not* been established."); *Gonzales v. Arrow Fin. Servs. LLC*, 489 F. Supp. 2d 1140, 1153 (S.D. Cal. 2007) ("The burden is on the party seeking decertification to demonstrate the elements of Rule 23 have not been established."); *Clarke v. Ford Motor Co.*, 228 F.R.D. 631, 633 (E.D. Wis. 2005) (quoting *Slaven*, 190 F.R.D. at 651).

18. *But see In re J.P. Morgan Chase Cash Balance Litig.*, 255 F.R.D. 130, 133–34 (S.D.N.Y. 2009).

19. *Falcon*, 457 U.S. at 160, 102 S. Ct. at 2372 (citation omitted). The *Falcon* decision was issued prior to the 2003 amendments to Rule 23, which altered the time for when a district judge should issue a class certification ruling from "as soon as practicable after the commencement of an action" to "at an early practicable time." The change was made in recognition of the discovery and detailed analysis needed prior to a class certification decision. FED. R. CIV. P. 23 advisory committee notes (2003).

20. *Karadzic*, 192 F.R.D. at 136; *Hickey v. Great W. Mortgage Corp.*, No. 94 C 3638, 1995 WL 121534, at *10 n.6 (N.D. Ill. Mar. 17, 1995).

courts have held that the burden of persuasion remains on the party supporting certification throughout the litigation,[21] and at least one court has indicated that its prior decision on class certification could be altered absent a finding of a significant intervening event.[22] There is some merit to this position, as well, because a judgment in a case with a certified class will resolve the claims of the absentee class members as well as the claims of the class representatives, even though the absentee class members will have no control over the litigation. Thus, the court must make sure that the class action treatment is appropriate for the sake of the rights of the absentee class members. Even where the certification decision was made by a different judge, a district court may reexamine the certification order with very little deference.[23]

The *Manual for Complex Litigation (Third)* recognizes that, while a district court may alter a class certification order "for good cause," as where "the discovery of new facts" necessitates reconsideration, the court should also consider any unfair prejudice to the class or the parties.[24] This formulation cuts both ways, as there may be unfair prejudice to either the proponent or objector to class certification, depending on the circumstances.

Research has not uncovered a case where the court considered the impact of a denial of a Rule 23(f) petition, or the affirmance of a class certification decision on an interlocutory appeal, on a motion to decertify or modify. Certainly in the latter situation, the party supporting the original class certification decision will argue from a strong position, absent a truly significant intervening event. In such a case, rehashing the same arguments is unlikely to be successful. But even where the Rule 23(f) petition is simply denied—and the circuit court never rules on the merits of the class certification decision—the proponent of the certification order may have

---

21. *See Smith v. Armstrong*, 968 F. Supp. 50, 53 (D. Conn. 1997) ("The burden of persuasion throughout the litigation remains with the party desiring to maintain certification."); *E. Maine Baptist Church v. Union Planters Bank, N.A.*, 244 F.R.D. 538, 541 n.3 (E.D. Mo. 2007) (holding, in a case where a class was certified by a state court prior to removal, that "the legal standard required for motions to certify the claims is identical to the legal standard required for motions to decertify the claims, and . . . the burden of proof is identical with respect to both"); *Ellis v. Elgin Riverboat Resort*, 217 F.R.D. 415, 419 (N.D. Ill. 2003) (holding that "on a motion to decertify the class," the party supporting class certification "bears the burden of producing a record demonstrating the continued propriety of maintaining the class action").

22. *Chisolm*, 194 F.R.D. at 548 n.5.

23. *Wu*, 256 F.R.D. at 163 n.2.

24. MANUAL FOR COMPLEX LITIGATION (THIRD) § 30.18, at 223 (1995) ("In deciding whether to modify its original decision, the court should consider not only the requirements of Rule 23(a) and (b) in light of the facts and issues of the case, but also whether the parties or the class would be unfairly prejudiced by a change in the proceedings at that point."); *see also In re Harcourt Brace Jovanovich Sec. Litig.*, 838 F. Supp. 109, 115 (S.D.N.Y. 1993) (considering prejudice to defendants in deciding whether to amend class certification order to allow class representatives to withdraw); *Cook v. Rockwell Int'l Corp.*, 181 F.R.D. 473, 477 (D. Colo. 1998) (quoting MANUAL FOR COMPLEX LITIGATION (THIRD) § 30.18, at 223 (1995)); *O'Connor v. Boeing N. Am., Inc.*, 197 F.R.D. 404, 409–10 (C.D. Cal. 2000).

an advantage, depending on the standards used in the circuit to assess the propriety of an interlocutory appeal and the reasons for the rejection of the petition.

III. The Effect of a Ruling on a Motion to Decertify or Modify and the Timing of a Rule 23(f) Petition

Although the denial of a motion to decertify or modify a class may be a significant event in a class action litigation, that denial does not provide a party with the opportunity to seek interlocutory appeal via Rule 23(f). A denial of a motion to decertify is not "an order granting or denying class-action certification."[25] Thus, the denial of a motion to decertify does not revive the ten-day period during which a party may seek a Rule 23(f) appeal.[26] If the rule were otherwise, "by styling a motion to reconsider as a motion to decertify the class, a litigant could defeat the function of the ten-day line drawn in Rule 23(f)."[27] However, a motion to reconsider filed within ten days of a ruling on a motion for class certification does toll the running of the Rule 23(f) clock until the court rules on the motion to reconsider.[28]

On the other hand, an order granting a motion to decertify triggers appellate rights under Rule 23(f). Although Rule 23(f) applies to "order[s] granting or denying class certification," an order decertifying a class has the same effect as an order denying class certification in the first place, and Rule 23(f) review is permitted:

> We recognize that Rule 23(c)(1)(C) permits the district court to alter or amend a certification decision. And parties may suggest such changes as the factual record and legal theories develop. All we are saying is that there can be no Rule 23(f) appeal from the denial of such a suggestion. An order that leaves class-action status unchanged from what was determined by a prior order is not an order "granting or denying class action certification." Of course, when the district court accepts a suggestion and the certification decision is changed, the new order, to the extent it modifies the prior order, is indeed such an order and an interlocutory appeal under Rule 23(f) is permitted.[29]

As is evident from the preceding quote from the Seventh Circuit, a decision modifying a class may provide grounds for a Rule 23(f) appeal. Such an order alters the status quo. However, at least one court has held that if an interlocutory appeal

---

25. Fed. R. Civ. P 23(f). *See also In re DC Water & Sewer Auth.*, 561 F.3d 494, 496 (D.C. Cir. 2009); *Gutierrez v. Johnson & Johnson*, 523 F.3d 187, 193 (3d Cir. 2008); *Jenkins v. BellSouth Corp.*, 491 F.3d 1288, 1291–92 (11th Cir. 2007); *Carpenter v. Boeing Co.*, 456 F.3d 1183, 1191–92 (10th Cir. 2006); *McNamara v. Felderhof*, 410 F.3d 277, 281 (5th Cir. 2005).

26. *See, e.g., DC Water & Sewer Auth.*, 561 F.3d at 496–97.

27. *Gary v. Sheahan*, 188 F.3d 891, 893 (7th Cir. 1999).

28. *Gutierrez*, 523 F.3d at 192–93; *Carpenter*, 456 F.3d at 1191–92.

29. *Carpenter*, 456 F.3d at 1191 (citing *Gary*, 188 F.3d at 893).

pursuant to Rule 23(f) could do no more than result in a modification of a class certification order, such a case is a poor candidate for Rule 23(f) review.[30]

IV. Notice to Class Members May Be Required upon Decertification or Modification of a Class

Rule 23(d)(1)(B) provides that a court may issue orders requiring that notice be given to the class members of "any step in the action." A court is likely to require notice to the former class members after the decertification of a class. Where absentee class members may have relied on the existence of a class action in failing to bring their own individual claims, they should be notified once the class is decertified so that they can act to protect their rights.[31] Where the absentee class members did not rely on the existence of a class action to protect their rights, or where the absentee class members will not suffer prejudice where notice is withheld, no notice of the decertification is necessary.[32] Of course, determining that the absentee class members did not rely on the existence of a class action to protect their rights is difficult. There would seem to always be some chance that the absentee class members relied. However, one court found that notice is not necessary where the class was never provided with notice of the original certification decision and where there was no publicity regarding the case.[33] On the other hand, the Seventh Circuit has held that a court must order notice to the absentee class members of a decertification decision unless the risk of prejudice "is nil."[34]

In addition, notice may be required after a court modifies a class order. Notice to the absentee class members of a modification would be particularly needed where modification altered the class composition so that persons previously within the class were now excluded. Such persons would have as much interest in receiving notice of such a modification as the members of a completely decertified class.

---

30. *Sumitomo Copper Litig. v. Credit Lyonnais Rouse, Ltd.*, 262 F.3d 134, 139–40 (2d Cir. 2001).

31. *See Puffer v. Allstate Ins. Co.*, 614 F. Supp. 2d 905, 912 (N.D. Ill. 2009).

32. *See Culver v. City of Milwaukee*, 277 F.3d 908, 915 (7th Cir. 2002).

33. *See Chesner v. Stewart Title Guar. Co.*, No. 1:06CV00476, 2009 WL 585821, at *8 (N.D. Ohio Feb. 24, 2009).

34. *Culver*, 277 F.3d at 915.

OTHER DUE PROCESS CHALLENGES TO THE CLASS DEVICE

CHRISTOPHER CHORBA
BLAINE H. EVANSON[1]

I. Introduction

By their very nature, group litigation and the class action procedure implicate the protections afforded by the due process clauses of the 5th and 14th Amendments to the U.S. Constitution. From the earliest days of the class device, courts have struggled with the inherent tension between the basic right of any litigant to due process of law and the efficiencies of adjudicating the rights of unnamed parties through a class action. Every class action involves the balancing of these competing interests. The keystone for this analysis is safeguarding the rights of absent class members while protecting the rights of defendants facing potentially annihilating liability.

While other chapters discuss these issues, this chapter will focus on the due process concerns that permeate any class action, as well as due process objections that defendants may raise in opposing class certification and class judgments. Many of the requirements the drafters of Rule 23 incorporated into the Rule are both based in and required by constitutional due process and therefore arise every time a court is faced with the question whether to certify a class under Rule 23. Courts typically focus on due process issues in certain contexts where the risks of abuse by class representatives and class counsel are particularly acute, such as in putative nationwide class actions, hybrid Rule 23(b)(2)/(b)(3) actions, defendant classes, and class settlements. In addition, some types of claims and remedies raise unique and complex due process problems when a plaintiff seeks to certify them

---

1. Gibson Dunn summer associates Stephanie Kantor, Alison M. Kelly, Kensie K. Kim, and Brandon J. Stoker contributed valuable research assistance in preparing this chapter.

as a class. For example, plaintiffs may not constitutionally subject a defendant to a nationwide class that involves claims from multiple jurisdictions with conflicting laws or that otherwise applies the law of a given state in an arbitrary or fundamentally unfair manner. And due process concerns arise in putative classes that seek to adjudicate claims and remedies in such a way that constricts the defenses a defendant is permitted to raise or otherwise alters the substantive law that would govern in an individual action. With respect to each of these issues, courts are guided by concerns with unduly binding absent class members to judgments in which they were not represented effectively, and with ensuring that defendants are able to defend themselves as fully as they could in individual actions.

II. Due Process and Rule 23

The familiar elements of Rule 23 of the Federal Rules of Civil Procedure—that a plaintiff must satisfy the preliminary requirements of Rule 23(a) (numerosity, commonality, typicality, and adequacy) and then one or more of the requirements of Rule 23(b)—have an essential due process component. Each requirement serves to ensure that classes are only certified when they involve homogenous and cohesive claims such that the class representative, in litigating his or her action, effectively litigates the claims of each absent class member as well, therefore making it appropriate to bind the absent class members based on the class representative's case. The requirements that the class representative be adequate, present common issues typical of the claims of the absent class members, and, in claims involving monetary damages, that common issues *predominate* over any individualized issues attempt to ensure the cohesiveness necessary to constitutionally bind the absent class members.

The historical development of Rule 23 reflects the symbiotic relationship between class actions and due process. As originally designed, Rule 23 suffered from potentially fatal ambiguities. The Rule allowed certification of classes under different categories, defined by the rights involved in the action, but it did not detail the requirements that plaintiffs seeking certification needed to satisfy and it afforded courts no mechanisms to ensure that the rights of absent class members were protected.[2] For example, the Advisory Committee determined that its original rule did not adequately confront "the measures that might be taken during the course of the action to assure procedural fairness, particularly giving notice to

---

2. *See* Benjamin Kaplan, *Continuing Work of the Civil Committee: 1966 Amendments of the Federal Rules of Civil Procedure (I)*, 81 HARV. L. REV. 356, 380–94 (1967) (detailing the problems with original Rule 23 and providing an account of the Advisory Committee's development of the new rule); FED. R. CIV. P. 23 advisory committee note (1966) (explaining the deficiencies of the original rule).

members of the class, which may in turn be related in some instances to the extension of the judgment to the class."[3]

Accordingly, in 1966, the Advisory Committee amended Rule 23 and produced the modern procedural vehicle for class action litigation. The most revolutionary change to Rule 23 was the Committee's proposed solution to the constitutional defects in the original rule—the requirements of notice and the right to opt out of a class action that seeks money as the predominant form of relief.[4] Several other amendments to Rule 23 had their roots in due process as well, and are set forth below.[5]

A. DUE PROCESS UNDERPINNINGS OF THE RULE 23(A) REQUIREMENTS

The Rule 23(a) requirements of adequate representation, commonality, and typicality[6] also are rooted in due process concerns.[7] Because class actions can bind class members to judgments in actions in which they did not participate, and about which they may not even have been aware, due process mandates that courts carefully scrutinize proposed class counsel and class representatives seeking to act on

---

3. FED. R. CIV. P. 23 advisory committee note (1966). *See also Eisen v. Carlisle & Jacquelin*, 391 F.2d 555, 568 (2d Cir. 1968) ("The Advisory Committee in its note has suggested that the mandatory notice pursuant to 23(c)(2) and the discretionary notice under 23(d)(2) were intended to fulfill the requirements of due process.").

Some courts have even held that class action defendants have a due process right to secure a determination of the issues related to certification prior to the determination of the merits of the case, *Rose v. City of Hayward*, 126 Cal. App. 3d 926, 937 (1981), and to have the case result in a final binding resolution of the dispute, *State ex rel. Union Planters Bank, N.A. v. Kendrick*, 142 S.W.3d 729, 740 (Mo. 2004). Rule 23 prohibits "one-way intervention," whereby putative class members could sit on the sidelines, watch how the case unfolded, and then decide whether to exercise their opt-out rights, FED. R. CIV. P. 23(c)(2), and some courts have held that due process prohibits this gamesmanship, because it places all of the risk of a class action on the defendant, without any offsetting benefit of a final judgment that binds the class. *See, e.g., Am. Pipe & Constr. Co. v. Utah*, 414 U.S. 538, 547–49 (1974); *Home Sav. & Loan Ass'n v. Superior Court*, 42 Cal. App. 3d 1006, 1010–11 (1974).

4. FED. R. CIV. P. 23 advisory committee note (1966); *see also* Stephen B. Burbank, *The Class Action Fairness Act of 2005 in Historical Context: A Preliminary View*, 156 U. PA. L. REV. 1439, 1488 (2008) ("The Advisory Committee settled on notice and opt-out rights to meet the expressed concern that (b)(3) classes might be used by class counsel, in league with the defendants, to force those with substantial individual claims into group litigation inimical to their interests.").

5. There have been other amendments to Rule 23 since 1966, and some of these were substantial. For example, in 1998 the Advisory Committee added subdivision (f), which provides for interlocutory review of a district court's certification decision, and in 2003 the Committee amended subdivision (c)(1)(C) to preclude "conditional certification," and mandated that "[a] court that is not satisfied that the requirements of Rule 23 have been met should refuse certification until they have been met." FED. R. CIV. P. 23 advisory committee note (2003). But these amendments did not effect the same revolutionary change on the due process rights of plaintiffs and defendants as the 1966 amendments.

6. *See* Chapter 3.B, "Numerosity, Commonality, and Typicality," and 3.C, "Adequacy Requirements."

7. *Newton v. Merrill Lynch, Pierce, Fenner & Smith, Inc.*, 259 F.3d 154, 182 n.27 (3d Cir. 2001) (explaining that these Rule 23(a) requirements "constitute a multipart attempt to safeguard the due process rights of absentees").

behalf of the absent class members.[8] Class representatives have a strict fiduciary duty to represent and protect the interests of absent class members.[9]

The Supreme Court established this rule in the landmark case of *Hansberry v. Lee*.[10] In that case, the defendant appealed a state court's decision rejecting a class certification order in a dispute over a racially restrictive land use covenant. The state court had held that the plaintiffs were members of a prior class and that the claim challenging the covenant was therefore barred by res judicata. The Supreme Court reversed and held that the appointment of class representatives implicates the due process rights of absent class members. The Court explained that "a selection of representatives . . . whose substantial interests are not necessarily or even probably the same as those whom they are deemed to represent, does not afford that protection to absent parties which due process requires."[11] The Advisory Committee cited *Hansberry* and recognized this due process limitation in its 1966 amendments to Rule 23(a).[12]

In determining whether a proposed class representative adequately represents the interests of absent class members and comports with due process, courts consider several factors, including (1) the gravity, quantity, and degree of conflicts between proposed class counsel and/or class representatives on the one hand and absent class members on the other; (2) the viability of alternatives to the class device; (3) the feasibly available procedures to limit the effect of conflicts (e.g., supervision by the court, the creation of subclasses, or the court's discretionary authority under Rule 23(d) and (e)); (4) whether there are other proposed representatives; and (5) any other facts bearing on the procedural fairness.[13] Further, a class representative also must convince the court that he or she will "vigorously prosecute the interests of the class through qualified counsel."[14] In assessing these

---

8. *See, e.g., Hansberry v. Lee*, 311 U.S. 32, 43 (1940); *Kincade v. Gen. Tire & Rubber Co.*, 635 F.2d 501, 506–08 (5th Cir. 1981); *Susman v. Lincoln Am. Corp.*, 561 F.2d 86, 90 (7th Cir. 1977); *Dosier v. Miami Valley Broad. Corp.*, 656 F.2d 1295, 1299 (9th Cir. 1981); *see also Daly v. Harris*, 209 F.R.D. 180, 189 (D. Haw. 2002) (explaining that Rule 23(a)(4)'s adequacy requirement is of paramount importance in all class actions because it "serves to protect the due process rights of absent class members who will be bound by the judgment").

9. *Hansberry*, 311 U.S. at 35.

10. *Id.* at 43.

11. *Id.* at 45.

12. FED. R. CIV. P. 23 advisory committee note (1966).

13. *Blackie v. Barrack*, 524 F.2d 891, 910 (9th Cir. 1975); *see also* FED. R. CIV. P. 23(g) ("[I]n appointing class counsel, the court . . . may consider any other matter pertinent to counsel's ability to fairly and adequately represent the interests of the class.").

14. *Piazza v. Ebsco Indus., Inc.*, 273 F.3d 1341, 1346 (11th Cir. 2001).

factors, courts often are skeptical of class counsel's motivations.[15] The court's obligation to assess these concerns continues throughout the litigation.[16]

Separately, the due process clause adds an additional layer of protection on the Rule 23(a) requirements.[17] Absent class members are not bound by a judgment where their claims were not "typical" or "common" to those of the class representative. These requirements serve a function similar to that of adequacy, in that they require a court to ensure that the claims prosecuted by the named plaintiff do not differ from the claims of the absent class members.[18] As the Third Circuit explained, "a court cannot infer that the rights of the *entire* class were vindicated without having assured that commonality and typicality were satisfied."[19]

B. DUE PROCESS ISSUES IN 23(B)(3) CLASSES

In addition to establishing the factors required by Rule 23(a), a class action plaintiff must satisfy the requirements of one or more of the subparagraphs of Rule 23(b).

1. Class Notice and the Right to Opt Out

If the plaintiff seeks certification of a class action under Rule 23(b)(3), that plaintiff must establish "that the questions of law or fact common to the members of the class predominate over any questions affecting only individual members, and that a class action is superior to other available methods for the fair and efficient adjudication of the controversy."[20] Rule 23(b)(3) requires that putative class members receive notice[21] and a right to opt out of the class.[22] The Advisory Committee included these requirements to address its concerns about fairness and due

---

15. *See, e.g., Weinberger v. Great N. Nekoosa Corp.*, 925 F.2d 518, 524 (1st Cir. 1991) (expressing "fear that class actions will prove less beneficial to class members than to their attorneys[, which] has been often voiced by concerned courts and periodically bolstered by empirical studies" (internal citations omitted)).

16. *McNeil v. Guthrie*, 945 F.2d 1163, 1167 (10th Cir. 1991) ("[T]he district court must constantly scrutinize class counsel to determine if counsel is adequately protecting the interests of the class."); *Kemp v. Birmingham News Co.*, 608 F.2d 1049, 1054 (5th Cir. 1979); *Wetzel v. Liberty Mut. Ins. Co.*, 508 F.2d 239, 248 (3d Cir. 1975); *Gonzales v. Cassidy*, 474 F.2d 67, 73 n.11 (5th Cir. 1973).

17. *See, e.g., Hansberry*, 311 U.S. at 44–45; *Newton*, 259 F.3d at 182; *Turner v. A.B. Carter, Inc.*, 85 F.R.D. 360, 369 (E.D. Va. 1980); *McKernan v. United Techs. Corp.*, 120 F.R.D. 452, 455 (D. Conn. 1988).

18. *In re Gen. Motors Pick-Up Truck Fuel Tank Prods. Liab. Litig.*, 55 F.3d 768, 796 (3d Cir. 1995).

19. *Id.* (emphasis in original).

20. FED. R. CIV. P. 23(b)(3).

21. FED. R. CIV. P. 23(c)(2)(B).

22. FED. R. CIV. P. 23(c)(2)(B)(v). For a more detailed discussion of the notice and opt-out requirements of Rule 23(c), *see* Chapter 3.E, "Predominance and Superiority," and Chapter 20, "Special Issues Relating to Class Notice."

process,[23] and several courts have held that due process requires these rights when money damages are involved.[24]

In mandatory and hybrid classes where plaintiffs do not seek predominantly monetary damages, the due process requirements are less clear.[25] The Supreme Court stated in *Phillips Petroleum Co. v. Shutts* that the due process right to notice and the opportunity to opt out were "limited to those class actions which seek to bind known plaintiffs concerning claims wholly or predominately for money judgments,"[26] and the lower courts have therefore not extended notice and opt-out rights to mandatory classes.[27] In hybrid classes involving both monetary and equi-

---

23. *See* FED. R. CIV. P. 23 advisory committee note (1966) ("[M]andatory notice pursuant to subdivision (c)(2), together with any discretionary notice which the court may find it advisable to give under subdivision (d)(2), is designed to fulfill requirements of due process to which the class action procedure is of course subject.").

24. The Supreme Court hinted at this requirement in *Mullane v. Cent. Hanover Bank & Trust Co.*, 339 U.S. 306, 313 (1950), and *Phillips Petroleum Co. v. Shutts*, 472 U.S. 797, 812 (1985), and a subsequent per curiam decision raised the issue as well, *Ticor Title Ins. Co. v. Brown*, 511 U.S. 117, 121 (1994), but it has never squarely held that due process requires that plaintiffs receive notice and be able to opt out of a class. Many lower courts have held that opt-out rights are required by due process. *Lindsay v. Gov't Employees Ins. Co.*, 448 F.3d 416, 420 (D.C. Cir. 2006) ("Because members of a class seeking substantial monetary damages may have divergent interests, due process requires that putative class members receive notice and an opportunity to opt out."); *In re Telectronics Pacing Sys., Inc.*, 221 F.3d 870, 881 (6th Cir. 2000) ("[C]onstitutional considerations of due process and the right to a jury trial all lead to the conclusion that in an action for money damages class members are entitled to personal notice and an opportunity to opt out."); *In re Prudential Ins. Co.*, 148 F.3d 283, 306 (3d Cir. 1998) ("The combination of reasonable notice, the opportunity to be heard and the opportunity to withdraw from the class satisfy the due process requirements of the Fifth Amendment.").

25. For a more detailed discussion of mandatory and hybrid classes, *see* Chapter 3.D, "Nonmonetary Relief," and Chapter 14, "The Special Role of 23(b)(2) Classes."

26. 472 U.S. at 811–12 n.3. *See also Ortiz v. Fibreboard Corp.*, 527 U.S. 815, 848 n.24 (1999) (noting that "an important caveat" to the notice and right to opt-out protections enunciated in *Shutts* is the limitation of these protections to "out-of-state class members whose claims were 'wholly or predominantly for money judgments'"); *Matsushita Elec. Indus. Co., Ltd. v. Epstein*, 516 U.S. 367, 395 (1996) (Ginsburg, J., concurring and dissenting in part) ("In [*Shutts*], this Court listed minimal procedural due process requirements a class action money judgment must meet if it is to bind absentees; those requirements include notice, a right to opt out, and adequate representation.").

27. *See, e.g., In re Veneman*, 309 F.3d 789, 792 (D.C. Cir. 2002) ("Because members of a class seeking substantial monetary damages may have divergent interests, due process requires that putative class members receive notice and an opportunity to opt out. By contrast, Rule 23(b)(2) imposes no similar requirements." (citations omitted)); *Molski v. Gleich*, 318 F.3d 937, 948 (9th Cir. 2003); *Reeb v. Ohio Dep't of Rehab. & Corr.*, 435 F.3d 639, 645 (6th Cir. 2006) ("Rule 23(b)(1) and Rule 23(b)(2) authorize 'mandatory' class actions under which potential class members do not have an automatic right to notice or a right to opt out of the class."); *McManus v. Fleetwood Enters., Inc.*, 320 F.3d 545, 553 (5th Cir. 2003) ("Unlike Rule 23(b)(3), class members are not permitted to opt-out of a Rule 23(b)(2) class to pursue their claims individually."); *Robinson v. Metro-North Commuter R.R. Co.*, 267 F.3d 147, 165 (2d Cir. 2001) ("Where class-wide injunctive or declaratory relief is sought in a (b)(2) class action for an alleged group harm, there is a presumption of cohesion and unity between absent class members and the class representatives such that adequate representation will generally safeguard absent class members' interests and thereby satisfy the strictures of due process."); *Lemon v. Int'l Union of Operating Eng'rs*, 216 F.3d 577, 580 (7th Cir. 2000).

table relief, courts differ on whether absent class members must also be able to opt out.[28] Several courts have held that due process requires opt-out rights in hybrid classes.[29]

The due process clause not only governs whether notice is required, but it also imposes several requirements on the form and content of the notice. The touchstone of the due process analysis is the Supreme Court's instruction in *Shutts* that the "best notice practicable under the circumstances be given."[30] At a minimum, the notice must provide putative class members with enough details about the case to allow them to evaluate whether to participate or opt out.[31] But in practice, this broad standard varies depending on the individual circumstances of each case. In some cases, this requires individual notice via first-class mail to those class members who can be identified through reasonable effort,[32] while other courts require further publication in newspapers, periodicals, or television commercials.[33] Courts

---

28. *See, e.g., Compaq Computer Corp. v. Lapray*, 135 S.W.3d 657, 667–68 (Tex. 2004) ("[T]rial courts considering certification under (b)(2) must consider, and due process may require, individual notice and opt-out rights to class members who seek monetary damages under any theory."); *see generally* Robert L. Serenka, Jr., Annotation, *Propriety of Allowing Class Member to Opt Out in Class Action Certified Under Subsections (b)(1) or (b)(2) of Rule 23 of Federal Rules of Civil Procedure*, 146 A.L.R. FED. 563 (2009).

29. *See, e.g., Ayers v. Thompson*, 358 F.3d 356, 375–76 (5th Cir. 2004) (a hybrid class action "begins to resemble a 23(b)(3) action, and there has been more concern with protecting the due process rights of the individual class members to ensure they are aware of the opportunity to receive the monetary relief to which they are entitled" (quoting *Penson v. Terminal Transp. Co.*, 634 F.2d 989, 994 (5th Cir. 1981))); *Johnson v. Gen. Motors Corp.*, 598 F.2d 432, 438 (5th Cir. 1979) ("Where, however, individual monetary claims are at stake, the balance swings in favor of the provision of some form of notice. It will not always be necessary for the notice in such cases to be equivalent to that required in (b)(3) actions."); *Williams v. Burlington N., Inc.*, 832 F.2d 100, 104 (7th Cir. 1987); *see also Ortiz*, 527 U.S. at 845–48; *Ticor*, 511 U.S. at 121–22 (raising, but not deciding, this issue).

Many courts that have granted opt-out rights in Rule 23(b)(2) classes have relied on the discretionary authority granted them under Rule 23(d)(2). *See, e.g., Penson*, 634 F.2d at 994; *Johnson*, 598 F.2d at 437; *Molski*, 318 F.3d at 947 (noting that "a district court may require notice and the right to opt-out under its discretionary authority provided in Rule 23(d)(2)"). But there is some disagreement on whether the use of 23(d)(2) to create a right to opt out is appropriate. *See generally* Serenka, *supra* note 28 (examining the different approaches that courts have taken with respect to opt-outs in (b)(1) and (b)(2) actions).

30. 472 U.S. at 812.

31. *Kyriazi v. W. Elec. Co.*, 647 F.2d 388, 395 (3d Cir. 1981).

32. *See, e.g., Shutts*, 427 U.S. at 811–12; *Greenfield v. Villager Indus., Inc.*, 483 F.2d 824, 832 (3d Cir. 1973); *Mountain States Tel. & Tel. Co. v. Dist. Court*, 778 P.2d 667, 672–73 (Colo. 1989); *Nat'l Lake Devs., Inc. v. Lake Tippecanoe Owners Ass'n, Inc.*, 417 So. 2d 655, 657 (Fla. 1982); *Client Follow-Up Co. v. Hynes*, 434 N.E.2d 485, 490 (1982).

33. *See, e.g., In re Orthopedic Bone Screw Prods. Liab. Litig.*, 246 F.3d 315, 318, 327 n.11 (3d Cir. 2001); *In re Diet Drugs Prods. Liab. Litig.*, Nos. 1203, 99-20593, 2000 WL 1222042, at *34–35 (E.D. Pa. Aug. 28, 2000); *see also* Chapter 20.A, "Quantifying Notice Results in Consumer, Mass Tort, and Product Liability Class Actions—the *Daubert/Kuhmo Tire* Mandate."

also differ on the degree of detail that the notice must contain.[34] The trial courts enjoy considerable discretion to formulate a notice plan.[35]

Courts continue to struggle with applying these requirements in the electronic age, as new and less expensive means of service become available and as privacy concerns present new challenges on the use of these methods.[36] For example, there is a split of authority on whether due process allows notice via e-mail. Some jurisdictions approve of e-mail notice, particularly where the class members' contact with the defendant is through an Internet website.[37] But even those courts that are willing to accept e-mail notice often require that the parties also provide notice by U.S. mail for class members whose e-mail addresses are unavailable and/or inactive.[38] Other courts have disapproved altogether of e-mail as a form of service.[39]

2. Manageability

Rule 23(b)(3) also requires that a class be "manageable" and that courts weigh this factor in determining whether a proposed class satisfies the superiority requirement.[40] Some courts have held that this factor has a constitutional component,

---

34. *Compare Gottlieb v. Wiles*, 11 F.3d 1004, 1013 (10th Cir. 1993) (no due process violation where formula for calculating potential damages awards for individual class members not included) *with Penn. Ass'n for Retarded Children v. Penn.*, 343 F. Supp. 279, 304 (E.D. Pa. 1972) ("The notice shall describe the proposed action in detail, including specification of the statute or regulation under which such action is proposed and a clear and full statement of the reasons therefor, including specification of any tests or reports upon which such action is proposed."); *see also, e.g., Ford Motor Co. v. Sheldon*, 22 S.W.3d 444, 453 (Tex. 2000); *Haitian Ctrs. Council, Inc. v. McNary*, 969 F.2d 1326, 1337–38 (2d Cir. 1992); *Noble Park, L.L.C. of Vancouver v. Shell Oil Co.*, 95 P.3d 1265, 1270 (Wash. 2004).

35. *Kyriazi*, 647 F.2d at 395; *In re "Agent Orange" Prod. Liab. Litig.*, 818 F.2d 145, 168 (2d Cir. 1987) ("Rule 23, of course, accords considerable discretion to a district court in fashioning [settlement] notice to a class."); *Grunin v. Int'l House of Pancakes*, 513 F.2d 114, 121 (8th Cir. 1975) ("[T]he mechanics of the notice process are left to the discretion of the court subject only to the broad 'reasonableness' standards imposed by due process."); *Crow v. Citicorp Acceptance Co.*, 354 S.E.2d 459, 466 (N.C. 1987).

36. *See* Chapter 20.C, "Reality Check: The State of New Media Options for Class Notice."

37. *See, e.g., Browning v. Yahoo! Inc.*, No. C04-01463 HRL, 2007 U.S. Dist. LEXIS 86266, at *13 (N.D. Cal. Nov. 16, 2007); *Lundell v. Dell, Inc.*, No. C05-3970 JW/RS, 2006 U.S. Dist. LEXIS 90990, at *2–3 (N.D. Cal. Dec. 5, 2006); *Larson v. Sprint Nextel Corp.*, No. 07-5325 (JLL), 2009 U.S. Dist. LEXIS 39298, at *7–8 (D.N.J. Apr. 30, 2009).

38. *See, e.g., Browning*, 2007 U.S. Dist. LEXIS 86266, at *13; *Lundell*, 2006 U.S. Dist. LEXIS 90990, at *2–3.

39. *See, e.g., Karvaly v. eBay, Inc.*, 245 F.R.D. 71, 93 (E.D.N.Y. 2007) (explaining that notice via e-mail "does not produce the same degree of reassurance that every member of the proposed class will receive individual notice of the settlement that a plan of notification by first class mail would"); *Reab v. Elec. Arts, Inc.*, 214 F.R.D. 623, 630 (D. Colo. 2002) (rejecting e-mail notice because e-mail could, among other things, "be copied and forwarded to other people via the internet with commentary that could distort the notice approved by the Court").

40. FED. R. CIV. P. 23(b)(3)(D). For a more detailed discussion of the manageability and superiority requirements in Rule 23(b)(3), *see* Chapter 3.E, "Predominance and Superiority" and Chapter 17, "Manageability and Predominance Concerns in Particular Class Actions."

in that an unmanageable class also violates due process.[41] In determining whether a class is manageable, courts must weigh "the whole range of practical problems that may render the class action format inappropriate for a particular suit."[42] Courts generally do not deny certification of a class solely based on manageability problems,[43] although concerns over manageability often also raise questions regarding whether common issues predominate over individual issues[44] and the sheer number of issues presented.[45]

III. Due Process Issues in Defendant Classes

Defendant classes raise unique and important due process concerns, and courts have exercised special cautions to ensure fairness and protect defendants' due process rights.[46] For example, the Tenth Circuit has cautioned that "defendant class actions create a special need to be attentive to the due process rights of absent parties."[47] Although the articulated adequacy standard for defendant classes is the same as the standard for plaintiff classes, courts are particularly cautious about the selection of class representatives in a defendant class, because of the risk that plaintiffs, for strategic reasons, may select weaker adversaries to represent the class.[48]

---

41. *See, e.g., Murry v. Griffin Wheel Co.,* 172 F.R.D. 459, 462 (N.D. Ala. 1997) ("'[D]ue process' . . . requires manageability as well as fairness.").

42. *Eisen v. Carlisle & Jacquelin,* 417 U.S. 156, 164 (1974).

43. *In re Visa Check/Mastermoney Antritrust Litig.,* 280 F.3d 124, 140 (2d Cir. 2001). *But see Andrews v. Am. Tel. & Tel. Co.,* 95 F.3d 1014, 1023 (11th Cir. 1996) ("[I]f the court finds 'that there are serious problems *now appearing,* it should not certify the class merely on the assurance . . . that some solution will be found.'" (citation omitted) (emphasis in original)).

44. *Klay v. Humana, Inc.,* 382 F.3d 1241, 1273 (11th Cir. 2004).

45. *Robinson v. Tex. Auto Dealers Ass'n,* 387 F.3d 416, 426 (5th Cir. 2004) ("[P]arties have an interest in ensuring that the jurors will have a reasonable chance of remembering which party presented which evidence. The sheer number of individual defendants and the incentive to offer individual defenses create the possibility of jurors' having to base their determinations on evidence offered throughout a long proceeding.").

46. *Marchwinski v. Oliver Tyrone Corp.,* 81 F.R.D. 487, 489 (W.D. Pa. 1979).

47. *In re Integra Realty Res., Inc.,* 262 F.3d 1089, 1105 (10th Cir. 2001).

48. *Ameritech Benefit Plan Comm. v. Commc'n Workers of Am.,* 220 F.3d 814, 820 (7th Cir. 2000) ("Defendant classes, initiated by those opposed to the interests of the class, are more likely than plaintiff classes to include members whose interests diverge from those of the named representatives, which means they are more in need of the due process protections afforded by (b)(3)'s safeguards."); *The Flying Tiger Line, Inc. v. Cent. States, Sw. & Se. Areas Pension Fund,* No. 86-304 CMW, 1986 WL 13366, at *4 (D. Del. Nov. 20, 1986) ("Defendant class actions, while appropriate, require special care before certification."); *Thillens, Inc. v. Cmty. Currency Exch. Ass'n of Ill., Inc.,* 97 F.R.D. 668, 674 (N.D. Ill. 1983) ("The crux of the distinction is: the unnamed plaintiff stands to gain while the unnamed defendant stands to lose.").

IV. Class Settlements

In evaluating class settlements, courts often view themselves as the guardians of the absent class members' due process rights against the risk of collusion between the named parties.[49] In particular, courts are suspicious of settlements that compensate the class representatives and their counsel and grant the defendant a broad release of all class claims, while providing very little meaningful relief for the class.[50]

Many proposed settlements that present indicia of potential collusion also feature other criteria that trouble courts, such as the lack of any proposed notice to class members or a right to opt out, large attorney fees awards that appear disproportionate to the amount of work expended on the action and/or the relief obtained for the class, an early settlement and compromise of damages claims before class counsel has had an opportunity to conduct an investigation and evaluate the merits of the claims, or other factors suggesting potential collusion.[51] Some courts therefore require a stricter review of class settlements reached *before* certification.[52]

As with certification of classes for litigation, courts require that the notice sent to putative class members be "reasonable,"[53] and the best practicable under the cir-

---

49. For a more detailed discussion of the ethical and tactical issues inherent in class settlements, *see* Chapter 7, "Settlements," and Chapter 32, "Ethical Issues in Class Actions."

50. *See Molski*, 318 F.3d at 954 ("In sum, the class members received nothing; the named plaintiff and class counsel received compensation for his injury and their time; and the defendant escaped paying any punitive or almost any compensatory damages."); *Crawford v. Equifax Payment Servs., Inc.*, 201 F.3d 877, 882 (7th Cir. 2000) (finding settlement was "substantively troubling" because the named plaintiff "and his attorney were paid handsomely to go away; the other class members received nothing (not even any value from the $5,500 'donation'), and lost the right to pursue class relief"); *Tornabene v. Gen. Dev. Corp.*, 88 F.R.D. 53, 60 (E.D.N.Y. 1980) ("'An attorney may be willing to settle a class action, without due regard for the best interests of class members in order to avoid the risk of defeat at trial.'" (quoting *Developments in the Law—Class Actions*, 89 HARV. L. REV. 1318, 1605 (1976))).

51. *Molksi*, 318 F.3d at 947–49; *Crawford*, 201 F.3d at 882.

52. *Hanlon v. Chrysler Corp.*, 150 F.3d 1011, 1026 (9th Cir. 1998); *In re Gen. Motors Prods. Liab. Litig.*, 55 F.3d at 805 ("We affirm the need for courts to be even more scrupulous than usual in approving settlements where no class has yet been formally certified."); *see also Mars Steel Corp. v. Cont'l Ill. Nat'l Bank & Trust*, 834 F.2d 677, 681 (7th Cir. 1987) ("*Simer* and *Weinberger* emphasize . . . that when class certification is deferred, a more careful scrutiny of the fairness of the settlement is required. We agree."); *Weinberger v. Kendrick*, 698 F.2d 61, 73 (2d Cir. 1982) ("[D]istrict judges who decide to employ such a procedure are bound to scrutinize the fairness of the settlement agreement with even more than the usual care."); MANUAL FOR COMPLEX LITIGATION (THIRD) § 30.45 (1995) ("Approval under Rule 23(e) of settlements involving settlement classes . . . requires closer judicial scrutiny than approval of settlements where class certification has been litigated.").

53. *Fowler v. Birmingham News Co.*, 608 F.2d 1055, 1059 (5th Cir. 1979); *Simer v. Rios*, 661 F.2d 655, 686 (7th Cir. 1981); *Grunin*, 513 F.2d at 121.

cumstances of a particular case.[54] Courts often consider whether the notice of the proposed settlement is sufficiently detailed in order to help absent class members be informed enough to decide whether to opt out of the settlement,[55] although the notice need not contain any and all information class members might want in making their decision, and courts rely on class members to undertake some investigation on their own.[56]

V. Due Process Defenses to Nationwide Classes

Nationwide class actions present unique due process problems because of the risk that a defendant may be subject to numerous and potentially conflicting state laws based on certification in a single forum or because plaintiffs without any connection to that state will have their claims adjudicated based on the laws of a foreign state.[57]

Once again, *Shutts* provides the framework for this analysis. In that case, the courts had applied Kansas law to a nationwide class even though 97 percent of the class members had no apparent connection to Kansas other than the litigation itself.[58] The Supreme Court ruled that the absence of contacts with Kansas, coupled with the substantive conflicts between Kansas law and the laws of the other affected jurisdictions, rendered the application of Kansas law "sufficiently *arbitrary* and *unfair* as to exceed constitutional limits."[59] The Court explained that "for a State's substantive law to be selected in a constitutionally permissible manner, that State must have a significant contact or significant aggregation of contacts, creating state interests, such that choice of its law is neither *arbitrary* nor *fundamentally unfair*."[60]

Equally impermissible is a court's attempt to meld the law of numerous states together in a class action. The landmark Seventh Circuit decision in *In re Rhone-Poulenc Rorer, Inc.*[61] reversed certification of a nationwide class because the district court had assumed that the negligence standards of the 50 states and the District of Columbia were essentially uniform and could be abstracted in a single jury

---

54. *In re Four Seasons Sec. Laws Litig.*, 502 F.2d 834, 840 (10th Cir. 1974); *Hill v. Art Rice Realty Co.*, 66 F.R.D. 449, 453 (N.D. Ala. 1974), *aff'd*, 511 F.2d 1400 (5th Cir. 1975); *Ballard v. Martin*, 79 S.W.3d 838, 852 (Ark. 2002); *see also Oppenlander v. Standard Oil Co.*, 64 F.R.D. 597, 602–03 (D. Colo. 1974).

55. *Barkema v. Williams Pipeline Co.*, 666 N.W.2d 612, 616 (Iowa 2003).

56. *Id.*; *Rubenstein v. Republic Nat'l Life Ins. Co.*, 74 F.R.D. 337, 348 (N.D. Tex. 1976).

57. For a more detailed discussion of issues related to nationwide classes, *see* Chapter 24, "Multistate Class Actions and Choice of Law."

58. 472 U.S. at 815.

59. *Id.* at 822 (emphases added).

60. *Id.* at 818 (emphases added) (citing *Allstate Ins. Co. v. Hague*, 449 U.S. 302, 312–13 (1981)).

61. 51 F.3d 1293 (7th Cir. 1995).

instruction.[62] Writing for the majority, Judge Posner explained that the different states all "sing negligence with a different pitch,"[63] and therefore the claims could not constitutionally be adjudicated in a single nationwide class action.[64]

Litigants sometimes urge federal courts to enjoin state or federal lawsuits that raise issues similar to those in the immediate class action before the court, but due process substantially limits the court's power to issue so-called anti-suit injunctions in the class action context.[65] Aside from principles of comity and statutory restrictions, due process limits the reach of a court's injunctive powers to those parties subject to the court's personal jurisdiction. While a court may thus enjoin subsequent suits by the plaintiff against the defendant arising from the same subject matter before the court,[66] the court may generally not enjoin other plaintiffs outside the jurisdiction.[67] Superior methods for handling related suits in different jurisdictions include stay of proceedings, transfer under 28 U.S.C. § 1404(a), and consolidation under 28 U.S.C. § 1407.[68]

Due process thus precludes nationwide classes brought solely under a single state's substantive law when the out-of-state plaintiffs would not be able to sue under that law and prohibits plaintiffs from combining the varying and conflicting laws of other states.

---

62. *Id.* at 1300.

63. *Id.* at 1301.

64. *Id.* at 1302. *See also Thorogood v. Sears, Roebuck & Co.*, 547 F.3d 742, 746 (7th Cir. 2008) ("The instructions to the jury on the law it is to apply will be an amalgam of the consumer protection laws of the twenty-nine jurisdictions and procedural rules by which particular jurisdictions expand or contract relief will be ignored."); *Zinser v. Accufix Research Inst., Inc.*, 253 F.3d 1180, 1190 (9th Cir. 2001) ("The complexity of the trial would be further exacerbated to the extent that the laws of forty-eight states must be consulted to answer such questions."); *Castano v. Am. Tobacco Co.*, 84 F.3d 734, 743 n.15 (5th Cir. 1996) ("[B]ecause we must apply an individualized choice of law analysis to each plaintiff's claims, the proliferation of disparate factual and legal issues is compounded exponentially." (citing *Georgine v. Amchem Prods.*, 83 F.3d 610, 627 (3d Cir. 1996))).

65. *See* 3 HERBERT B. NEWBERG & ALBA CONTE, NEWBERG ON CLASS ACTIONS: A MANUAL FOR GROUP LITIGATION AT FEDERAL AND STATE LEVELS § 9:25, at 360–65 (4th ed. 2002). *But see In re Bridgestone/Firestone, Inc. Tires Prods. Liab. Litig.*, 333 F.3d 763, 767, 768–69 (7th Cir. 2003) ("[U]nnamed class members have the status of parties for many purposes and are bound by the decision whether or not the court otherwise would have had personal jurisdiction over them. *Just as they receive the fruits of victory, so an adverse decision is conclusive against them.*" (emphasis added) (citations omitted)); *In re Diet Drugs Liab. Litig.*, 282 F.3d 220, 236 (3d Cir. 2002) (upholding injunction against competing state class action, reasoning that "[i]n complex cases where certification or settlement has received conditional approval, or perhaps even where settlement is pending, the challenges facing the overseeing court are such that it is likely that almost any parallel litigation in other fora presents the genuine threat to the jurisdiction of the federal court").

66. *See Kerotest Mfg. Co. v. C-O-Two Fire Equip. Co.*, 342 U.S. 180, 185–86 (1952).

67. *Alemite Mfg. Corp. v. Staff*, 42 F.2d 832, 832 (2d Cir. 1930) ("[N]o court can make a decree which will bind anyone but a party; a court . . . cannot lawfully enjoin the world at large, no matter how broadly it words its decree. If it assumes to do so, the decree is *pro tanto brutum fulmen* and the persons enjoined are free to ignore it.").

68. NEWBERG, *supra* note 65, § 9:25, at 362–63.

VI. Due Process Objections to Changes in Substantive Law

Due process also animates the common rule that class action procedure may not be used in a way that alters the underlying substantive law. The Rules Enabling Act, in giving authority to the Advisory Committee to establish procedural rules, limited that authority to *procedural* rather than *substantive* rulemaking.[69] Accordingly, any procedural rule, such as Rule 23, that changes the *substantive* law is in violation of this key limit in the Rules Enabling Act.[70]

Defendants also often argue that in addition to the Rules Enabling Act's prohibition on changing substantive law, the due process clause precludes the certification of a class that would prevent a defendant from raising defenses it otherwise would have been able to assert in an individual action.[71] The Supreme Court has held that "[t]he fundamental requisite of due process of law is the opportunity to be heard."[72] And a litigant's "right to litigate the issues raised" is "guaranteed . . . by the Due Process Clause,"[73] including the right "to present every available defense."[74] Most recently, the Supreme Court held in *Philip Morris USA v. Williams* that "the Due Process Clause prohibits a State from punishing an individual

---

69. 28 U.S.C. § 2072 (2009).

70. *Stonebridge Life Ins. Co. v. Pitts*, 236 S.W.3d 201, 205 (Tex. 2007); *Compaq Computer Corp. v. Albanese*, 153 S.W.3d 254, 261 n.6 (Tex. App. 2004); *City of San Jose v. Superior Court*, 525 P.2d 701, 711 (Cal. 1974).

71. Preserving this federal constitutional challenge is particularly important after the Supreme Court's decision in *Shady Grove Orthopedic Assocs. v. Allstate Ins. Co.*, No. 08-1008, 2010 U.S. LEXIS 2929 (U.S. 2010). The plurality opinion in *Shady Grove* held that the New York rule at issue in that case—which prohibited class actions seeking penalties—did not apply in a federal diversity action. *Shady Grove* held that because the New York procedural rule conflicts with Rule 23, which "creates a categorical rule entitling a plaintiff whose suit meets the specified criteria to pursue his claim as a class action," Rule 23 governs. *Id.* at *11. Whether the Court's fractured opinion will invalidate other state restrictions remains to be seen, but in the meantime the federal constitutional protections remain an important safeguard against using the class device to enlarge substantive rights.

72. *Goldberg v. Kelly*, 397 U.S. 254, 267 (1970).

73. *United States v. Armour & Co.*, 402 U.S. 673, 682 (1971).

74. *Lindsey v. Normet*, 405 U.S. 56, 66 (1972). *See also Amchem Prods., Inc. v. Windsor*, 521 U.S. 591, 615 (1997) (class certification should not "sacrifice[ ] procedural fairness"); *Nat'l Union Fire Ins. Co. of Pittsburgh v. City Sav., F.S.B.*, 28 F.3d 376, 394 (3d Cir. 1994) (an interpretation of a statute preventing "parties . . . from presenting defenses . . . to claims which ha[d] been filed against them" must be avoided); *W. Elec. Co. v. Stern*, 544 F.2d 1196, 1199 (3d Cir. 1976) (defendants have a federal due process "right to present a full defense," which includes the right to present "any relevant rebuttal evidence," such as that there was no violation "against one or more members of the class"); *Sanchez v. Wal-Mart Stores, Inc.*, No. Civ. 2:06-CV-02573-JAM-KJM, 2009 U.S. Dist. LEXIS 48428, at *12 (E.D. Cal. May 28, 2009) ("Beyond the Rule 23 requirements, certification of a class here would violate Defendants' constitutional rights to due process. 'Due process requires that there be an opportunity to present every available defense.'" (quoting *Lindsey*, 405 U.S. at 66)).

without first providing that individual with 'an opportunity to present *every* available defense.'"[75]

VII. Due Process Objections to Remedies

A. PUNITIVE DAMAGES AND OTHER STATUTORY PENALTIES

As discussed in Chapter 19,[76] the pursuit of aggregated civil penalties, statutory damages, and/or punitive damages in a class action presents complex due process issues. Courts have denied certification on the basis that the due process concerns with aggregating civil penalties or statutory damages render the class action a less superior method of adjudication than individual litigation.[77] Other courts have held that the individualized inquiries involved in the due process defenses to large aggregated damage awards outweigh any common issues and that classes seeking certification of penalties or punitive damages thus fail the predominance requirement under Rule 23(b)(3).[78]

Defendants also have asserted broader arguments that punitive damages are inappropriate in any class action. Recent Supreme Court precedent limits punitive damages to harm against actual parties that are present and participating in the litigation. For example, in *State Farm Mutual Life Insurance Co. v. Campbell*, the Supreme Court stated that the conduct giving rise to punitive damages "must have a nexus to the specific harm suffered by the plaintiff."[79] However, because class actions by their definition aggregate claims of a large group of plaintiffs, class actions necessarily have difficulty satisfying the constitutionally mandated "nexus" that the Supreme Court requires. *State Farm* also held that the precise punitive award in any case "must be based upon the facts and circumstances of the

---

75. 549 U.S. 346, 353 (2007) (emphasis added) (internal quotations and citation omitted). *See also Nelson v. Adams USA, Inc.*, 529 U.S. 460, 468 (2000); *Hovey v. Elliott*, 167 U.S. 409, 432 (1897); *Bell v. Farmers Ins. Exch.*, 9 Cal. Rptr. 3d 544, 480 (2004) (agreeing that "the trial management plan would raise due process issues if it served to restrict [defendant's] right to present evidence against [plaintiffs'] claims" (citation omitted)); Allan Erbsen, *From "Predominance" to "Resolvability": A New Approach to Regulating Class Actions*, 58 VAND. L. REV. 995, 1040–41 (2005) ("[T]here is a plausible reason to believe that using the class action device to deny a defendant its otherwise applicable right to raise defenses to individual claims, or to relieve class members of their obligation to prove otherwise required elements of their individual claims, would violate the defendant's rights to procedural due process."). *But see Hilao v. Estate of Marcos*, 103 F.3d 767, 786 (9th Cir. 1996).

76. *See* Chapter 19, "Aggregation or Stacking of Penalties or Punitive Measures."

77. *See, e.g., Kline v. Coldwell, Banker & Co.*, 508 F.2d 226, 233–35 (9th Cir. 1974); *Ratner v. Chem. Bank N.Y. Trust Co.*, 54 F.R.D. 412, 414 (S.D.N.Y. 1972).

78. *See, e.g., Cooper v. Southern Co.*, 390 F.3d 695, 721 (11th Cir. 2004) (punitive claims "require *detailed, case-by-case fact finding*, carefully calibrated for each individual employee" (emphasis added)); *Lemon*, 216 F.3d at 581 (punitive awards require "a fact-specific inquiry into [each] plaintiff's circumstances"); *Allison v. Citgo Petroleum Corp.*, 151 F.3d 402, 418–20 (5th Cir. 1998).

79. 538 U.S. 408, 422 (2003).

defendant's conduct and the harm to the plaintiff."[80] This highly individualized inquiry is inherently at odds with class actions. Based on this argument, a number of lower courts have relied on *State Farm* in rejecting certification of claims for punitive damages.[81]

Philip Morris also commands that punitive damages must be tethered to the defendant's conduct towards a particular plaintiff.[82] The logical extension of this argument suggests that classwide determinations of punitive damages are inherently suspect under, if not precluded altogether by, the due process clause. Although *Philip Morris* was not a class action, the Supreme Court's opinion strongly implies that punitive damages cannot constitutionally be awarded on a representative basis: "[T]he Constitution's Due Process Clause forbids a State to use a punitive damages award to punish a defendant for injury that it inflicts upon nonparties or those whom they directly represent, *i.e.*, injury that it inflicts upon those who are, essentially, strangers to the litigation."[83]

A final due process protection regarding punitive damages relates to the constitutionally permissible outer limit on the *amount* of punitive damages if they are allowed in a class action. In *State Farm*, the Supreme Court held that "[w]hen compensatory damages are substantial," a small ratio of 1:1 may be the highest allowed by the due process clause.[84] Courts have divided on what qualifies as a "substantial" amount of compensatory damages,[85] but the Supreme Court has observed that whether a damage award in a class action is "substantial" depends on the *aggregate* class recovery, and not the size of individual awards to class members.[86] Thus, even in class actions where compensatory awards to individual class members are small, if the aggregated amount of damages is "substantial," the punitive damages available to the class should be limited to the amount of compensatory damages.[87]

B. FLUID RECOVERY SCHEMES AND ALTERNATIVE DISPUTE RESOLUTION

Some courts have struck down so-called fluid recovery schemes whereby an aggregate damages award is determined at trial, but the actual amounts individual

---

80. *Id.* at 425.

81. *See, e.g., In re Simon II Litig.*, 407 F.3d 125, 139 (2d Cir. 2005); *Johnson v. Ford Motor Co.*, 113 P.3d 82, 94–95 (Cal. 2005); *Engle v. Liggett Group, Inc.*, 945 So. 2d 1246, 1265 (Fla. 2006).

82. 549 U.S. at 353.

83. *Id.*

84. *State Farm*, 538 U.S. at 425. *Accord Exxon Shipping Co. v. Baker*, 128 S. Ct. 2605, 2634 n.28 (2008).

85. *Compare Action Marine, Inc. v. Cont'l Carbon Inc.*, 481 F.3d 1302, 1321, 1322 n.24 (11th Cir. 2007) (upholding a $17.5 million punitive award despite compensatory damages and attorney fees that amounted to $3.2 million) *with Williams v. ConAgra Poultry Co.*, 378 F.3d 790, 799 (8th Cir. 2004) (holding that due process required remitting punitive damages to equal $600,000 compensatory damages).

86. *Exxon Shipping*, 128 S. Ct. at 2634 n.28.

87. *See id.; see also State Farm*, 538 U.S. at 425, 429 (holding that $1 million awarded in compensatory damages was "substantial," and "likely would justify a punitive damages award at or near the amount of compensatory damages").

plaintiffs are entitled to are adjudicated after the trial before special masters. Courts have based their holdings invalidating these distribution plans on both the defendant's right to a civil jury under the 7th Amendment and the due process clause.[88] For example, in *McLaughlin v. American Tobacco Co.*,[89] the district court approved a three-step plan, based on estimates and averaging, in which (1) collective damages would be proven on a classwide basis, (2) individual class members would make simplified claims, and (3) unclaimed damages would be distributed according to the principle of cy pres.[90] The Second Circuit held that the distribution scheme offended both the due process clause and the Rules Enabling Act.[91] The court explained that "[r]oughly estimating the gross damages to the class as a whole and only subsequently allowing for the processing of individual claims would inevitably alter defendants' substantive right to pay damages reflective of their actual liability," while the "mass aggregation of claims" caused the defendants to lose the right "to challenge the allegations of individual plaintiffs."[92]

In addition, the Seventh Circuit struck down such a scheme because even if there were a jury in the second phase, it would be a different jury and would therefore violate the 7th Amendment:

> [M]ost of the separate "cases" that compose this class action will be tried, after the initial trial in the Northern District of Illinois, in different courts, scattered throughout the country. The right to a jury trial in federal civil cases, conferred by the Seventh Amendment, is a right to have juriable issues determined by the first jury impaneled to hear them (provided there are no errors warranting a new trial), and not reexamined by another finder of fact.[93]

Some courts have rejected, as a violation of due process, distribution schemes that disburse any unclaimed balance of the class recovery to the "next best" class of persons, such as existing class members, charities, or the state.[94] Dividing the unclaimed balance among existing class members, for example, essentially ensures

---

88. *Compare In re Rhone-Poulenc*, 51 F.3d at 1303 (citing *Gasoline Prods. Co. v. Champlin Ref. Co.*, 283 U.S. 494, 500 (1931); *McDaniel v. Anheuser-Busch, Inc.*, 987 F.2d 298, 305 (5th Cir. 1993); *Alabama v. Blue Bird Body Co.*, 573 F.2d 309, 318 (5th Cir. 1978)), *with Eisen v. Carlisle & Jacquelin*, 479 F.2d 1005, 1018 (2d Cir. 1973), *vacated and remanded on other grounds*, 417 U.S. 156 (1974) ("[T]he courts . . . have to reject [fluid class recovery] as an unconstitutional violation of the requirement of due process of law.").

89. 522 F.3d 215 (2d Cir. 2008).

90. *Id.* at 231.

91. *Id.*

92. *Id.* at 231–32.

93. *In re Rhone-Poulenc*, 51 F.3d at 1303.

94. *Van Gemert v. Boeing Co.*, 553 F.2d 812, 815 (2d Cir. 1977); *Eisen*, 479 F.2d at 1018. Of course, courts frequently employ cy pres awards where class members cannot be identified. *See, e.g., In re Matzo Food Prods. Litig.*, 156 F.R.D. 600, 606 (D.N.J. 1994) ("Typically, the court employs *cy pres* where class members cannot be located or where individual recoveries would be so small as to make distribution economically impossible.").

that silent class members' compensation will be expropriated in windfall recoveries by class members who already collected their share of the damages.[95] This procedure may thus encourage "the bringing of class actions likely to result in large uncollected damage pools . . . [and] raises serious questions as to the adequacy of representation where the interests of the named plaintiffs lie in keeping the other class members uninformed."[96] Although courts are divided on this issue, some require that class recovery funds not distributed to class members as compensation for their claims be returned to the defendant.[97]

These principles apply similarly when parties engage in dispute resolution procedures, including arbitration, mediation, conciliation, negotiation, summary trials, and bifurcated trials, as well as use of ombudsmen, neutral experts, or settlement judges.[98] Class action litigants often use arbitration as an efficient means of resolving individual causation issues and determining damages suffered by individual class members.[99] Courts also routinely refer class action cases to mandatory, nonbinding arbitration or mediation prior to trial as an expeditious and economical alternative to traditional adjudication.[100] While due process does not require formal proceedings or fixed procedures, the alternative dispute resolution (ADR) methods must provide, at a minimum, an opportunity for a hearing and defense.[101] In some cases, informal ADR methods are not appropriate given the unique circumstances of the litigation.[102] Depending on the nature of the controversy, courts should balance the informality and nonadversarial nature of ADR methods with the protections inherent in more formal adjudicatory proceedings.[103]

---

95. *Van Gemert*, 553 F.2d at 815.

96. *Id.* at 816.

97. *See, e.g., Wilson v. Sw. Airlines, Inc.*, 880 F.2d 807, 816 (5th Cir. 1989); *Kennedy v. Nicastro*, 546 F. Supp. 267, 270 (N.D. Ill. 1982). *But see Powell v. Georgia-Pacific Corp.*, 119 F.3d 703, 706–07 (8th Cir. 1997) (approving cy pres distribution of remaining class recovery balance to a scholarship fund); *In re Motorsports Merch. Antitrust Litig.*, 160 F. Supp. 2d 1392, 1395 (N.D. Ga. 2001) (approving cy pres distribution of remaining class recovery balance to various charitable organizations).

98. NEWBERG, *supra* note 65, § 9:67, at 461–63.

99. *See, e.g.,* Chapter 21, "Arbitration and Class Actions."

100. *See, e.g., Rhea v. Massey-Ferguson, Inc.*, 767 F.2d 266, 268 (6th Cir. 1985); *Davison v. Sinai Hosp. of Balt., Inc.*, 462 F. Supp. 778, 779 (D. Md. 1978), *aff'd*, 617 F.2d 361 (4th Cir. 1980).

101. *Ballard v. Hunter*, 204 U.S. 241, 255 (1907).

102. *See, e.g., In re Yahoo! Litig.*, 251 F.R.D. 459, 467–69 (C.D. Cal. 2008) (declining to enforce an unconscionable class action waiver clause); *Discover Bank v. Superior Court*, 113 P.3d 1100, 1165–66 (2005); *Gentry v. Superior Court*, 165 P.3d 556, 573 (Cal. 2007).

103. *See* Richard A. Posner, *The Summary Jury Trial and Other Methods of Alternative Dispute Resolution: Some Cautionary Observations*, 53 U. CHI. L. REV. 366, 389–92 (1986); Judith Resnik, *Failing Faith: Adjudicatory Procedure in Decline*, 53 U. CHI. L. REV. 494, 536–38 (1986).

VIII. Conclusion

As discussed above and throughout this volume, due process concerns arise at various stages of class action certification and adjudication, and practitioners should assert (and anticipate) these objections at every stage. The adequacy of the class representative and the proffered counsel, the existence of issues common to the class, and the requirement that the named plaintiffs' claims be typical of the class claim are all concerns required not only by Rule 23(a), but also by due process. And these due process rights are especially scrutinized in class settlements and defendant classes. In claims for monetary damages under Rule 23(b)(3), the rights to notice of the class, to opt out, and for the class to be "manageable" are similarly required not only by Rule 23, but also by due process. These notice and opt-out rights do not apply with equal force in mandatory classes, but many courts have held that they apply in hybrid classes, certified for both injunctive and monetary relief.

Particular issues arise in putative nationwide classes, and there are due process limits both on the certification of claims from multiple and conflicting jurisdictions and on allowing plaintiffs without any connection to the forum state to obtain certification of a class within that state. And a class action that would have the effect of changing the substantive law applicable to plaintiffs' claims not only is impermissible by virtue of the Rules Enabling Act but is barred by the due process clause as well. Finally, due process concerns arise when plaintiffs seek to certify penalties and/or punitive damages, as these penalties may render the proposed class inferior to individual actions and/or require numerous individualized inquiries that predominate over any common issues.

Particularly in class actions brought under state law in state courts, where the standards required by Rule 23 may not be as rigorous or developed, the due process arguments discussed in this volume may be important to protect clients' interests, as well as to preserve arguments for further review after adjudication in state appellate courts. Practitioners should raise these arguments at every stage of the proceedings to ensure that the arguments are preserved for later appeal.

USE OF SPECIAL MASTERS IN CONNECTION WITH CLASS PROCEEDINGS

F. A. LITTLE, JR.[1]

I. Introduction

This chapter discusses the practical aspects of using a special master[2] in the context of a class action. In keeping with the other chapters in this volume, the following pages do not examine the use of a special master from an abstract or academic standpoint. Instead, this chapter focuses on the practical aspects—the "hows"—of using a special master.

II. What Benefits Does a Special Master Bring to the Litigation?

As most practitioners in the class action field know, or are presently finding out, a class action lawsuit can be an unwieldy beast. It can often resemble coordinated chaos with countless moving parts. Many of these parts are not found in the non-class action setting, and they are often administrative in nature. They are parts, though, that are crucial to achieving a speedy, efficient, and just resolution of the underlying dispute, and using a special master is often the fastest and most efficient way of keeping these parts moving forward toward that goal.

Herein lies the first benefit of the special master—speed and efficiency. Since the special master, as discussed below, is not a resource within the judiciary, but is engaged by the judiciary, he does not have a competing docket. He will give the

---

1. The author appreciates the professional heavy lifting done in preparation of this chapter by Zachary L. Wool, a New Orleans lawyer with the firm of Barrios, Kingsdorf & Casteix.

2. Although Rule 53 uses the term "master," the term "special master" is far more common in practice.

litigants the extra and prompt attention that the nature of a class action demands. The limited resources of the court can be freed to adjudicate other matters on the court's crowded docket. Further, the special master is a valuable resource when used by the court in areas of fact gathering that are highly specialized. In short, a special master will assist the court in its primary function—the resolution of the case.

III. What Desirable Qualities Should a Special Master Possess?

Three qualities form the backbone of any good special master—experience, knowledge, and time. Experience and knowledge are crucial to the role of a special master because he is appointed by the court to make factual or legal determinations that a court would ordinarily make. Further, a special master will need to have the free time to devote himself to working with the parties. Thus, the parties should seek a person with a deep knowledge of federal practice and class actions, such as a retired federal judge or experienced practitioner with time available to devote to the needs of the parties. In certain circumstances where expertise in a particular field of study is essential, courts have gone outside of the legal field and appointed physicians, accountants, and engineers as special masters.[3]

IV. Which Federal Rule of Civil Procedure Applies to the Appointment, Authority, and Conduct of the Special Master?

Federal Rule of Civil Procedure 53 (Rule 53) governs the use of special masters in all contexts, including class actions. Following a study completed by the Federal Judicial Center in 2000,[4] Rule 53 was amended and expanded in 2003 to conform with prevailing practices in the federal judiciary.

Two of the changes to the expanded Rule 53 warrant noting. First, a court may now appoint a special master for "pretrial and posttrial matters that cannot be effectively and timely addressed by an available district or magistrate judge."[5] Before the 2003 change in the rule, a court could only make such an appointment when there was an exceptional condition warranting the delegation of authority. That extra requirement has since been removed. Second, a court may now appoint a special master to any role "so long as the parties consent to such an

---

3. Timothy E. Willging, et al., Special Master's Incidence and Activity 40 (Federal Judicial Center 2000) [hereinafter Federal Judicial Center Report].

4. *Id.*

5. Fed. R. Civ. P. 53(a)(1)(C) (1938) (amended 2003).

appointment."[6] This added instance when a court can appoint a special master vastly increases the opportunities for parties to employ a special master. But the notes accompanying Rule 53 make it clear that the court retains the final word on appointing a special master, even when both parties consent. In addition, Rule 53 contains two provisions that require the special master to keep the court informed of his activities. Rule 53(d) requires that the special master file any order with the court and also serve it on the parties. Rule 53(e) pertains to reports of the special master, and it requires that he file any reports with the court and serve them on the parties, unless the court orders otherwise.

Rule 53(c) governs the special master's authority. Unless the appointing order directs otherwise, a special master may "regulate all proceedings,"[7] and "take all appropriate measures to perform the duties [assigned in the appointing order] fairly and efficiently."[8] To help the special master accomplish the latter goal, Rule 53 expressly authorizes the special master to impose sanctions pursuant to Rule 37 (for failure to make disclosures or to cooperate in discovery) or 45 (for failure to obey a subpoena) and further allows the special master to recommend contempt sanctions against a party and sanctions against a nonparty.[9] Further, Rule 53(c)(1) (C) permits the special master, when conducting an evidentiary hearing, to exercise the appointing court's powers to compel, take, and record evidence.

V. How Is a Special Master Appointed?

Rule 53 lays out the steps that the parties and court must follow to appoint a special master.

Any party may make a request to the court for the appointment of a special master. Moreover, the court may initiate the mechanism for special master appointment itself. In fact, the 2000 report by the Federal Judicial Center reveals that in 54 percent of the cases in which a special master was appointed, the court itself initiated the process.[10] Further, the report noted that only 15 percent of the motions to appoint a special master came jointly from the two sides, with most of the remainder being in the form of a motion from one party. However, courts are generally hesitant to appoint a special master without the consent of both parties because of the cost.[11] Indeed, Rule 53 requires the court to consider "the fairness of

---

6. FED. R. CIV. P. 53(a)(1)(A).

7. FED. R. CIV. P. 53(c)(1)(A).

8. FED. R. CIV. P. 53(c)(1)(B).

9. FED. R. CIV. P. 53(c)(2).

10. FEDERAL JUDICIAL CENTER REPORT, *supra* note 3, at 30.

11. *Compare id. with In re World Trade Ctr. Disaster Site Litig.*, No. 21 MC 100 (AKH), 2008 WL 793578, at *1–2 (S.D.N.Y. Mar. 24, 2008) (finding the usefulness of a special master to oversee vast amounts of data outweighs a party's objection to the cost).

imposing the likely expenses on the parties" and to "protect against unreasonable expense or delay."[12]

Prior to the appointment of a special master, Rule 53 requires that the court give notice and an opportunity for the parties to be heard on the matter. The Rule allows any party to suggest a candidate for appointment.

Rule 53 requires that the proposed special master file an affidavit stating whether there are actual or potential grounds for his disqualification as a special master.[13] The revised Rule 53 explicitly states that the special master must not have "a relationship to the parties, attorneys, action, or court that would require disqualification"[14] under the rules of disqualification applying to judges and magistrates.[15] Even if there are grounds for disqualification, Rule 53 allows for the person to serve as the special master, so long as the parties and the court are aware of the conflict and consent to it after the disclosure in the special master's affidavit.[16] For example, a judge would be prohibited from adjudicating a case if he or she owned one share of stock in the litigant corporation. A special master candidate, on the other hand, could be appointed if stock ownership is disclosed and the conflict is waived by the parties to the litigation.

Next, the court issues the order appointing the special master. While this act may seem perfunctory, Rule 53 places specific requirements on the contents of the order. Given that a court will often request that the litigants write a proposed order, it is helpful for practitioners to familiarize themselves with Rule 53(b)(2)'s requirements. The order must contain the following:

- A list of the special master's duties and any limitations on the special master's authority;
- The circumstances under which ex parte communication between the court or litigants and the special master may take place;
- The records that the special master must keep to help build a record of the special master's activities;
- The procedures for using the special master, along with the standards for reviewing any findings; and
- The method of compensation.

The court may amend its order of appointment of a special master. The amended order is preceded by notice to the parties, which will give all concerned an opportunity to comment upon the proposed amendment.[17]

---

12. FED. R. CIV. P. 53(a)(3).
13. FED. R. CIV. P. 53(b)(3)(A).
14. FED. R. CIV. P. 53(a)(2).
15. The rules regarding disqualification can be found at 28 U.S.C. § 455.
16. FED. R. CIV. P. 53(b)(3)(B).
17. FED. R. CIV. P. 53(b)(4)

VI. How Is a Special Master Different from a Magistrate, and Should One Be Preferred over the Other?

Special masters and magistrates can perform overlapping functions. Both serve, for instance, as overseers of pretrial discovery. Indeed, Rule 53 specifically contemplates that a magistrate can be appointed as a special master.[18] And while special masters are governed by Rule 53 and the order that appoints them, magistrates are governed by the Magistrates Act,[19] which lists more specifically the roles that a magistrate can fill. This list is more limiting than Rule 53, unless the magistrate is appointed specifically as a special master.

One benefit to using a special master over a magistrate stands head and shoulders above the rest. Simply put, a special master is not a limited court resource. District court judges and magistrates must apportion their time among all of the many cases on their dockets. Well-qualified special masters, however, do not have such constraints. The special master can make fast and efficient findings and decisions without competition from other cases.

VII. Can a Magistrate Appoint a Special Master?

A court will often employ the use of a magistrate to help oversee a large, complex class action. It is, therefore, becoming more common for a magistrate to appoint a special master to fulfill one of the nondispositive roles of the magistrate, such as overseeing a privilege dispute.[20] Although there is no statutory or jurisprudential authority that restricts a magistrate, and because the Magistrates Act does not expressly authorize it, it is advisable to have the district court judge's consent when the magistrate makes an appointment of a special master.

VIII. What Can a Special Master Do?

There is no single, detailed answer that anyone can give to this question. This section aims to illustrate various common functions that a special master can fulfill. It is by no means a complete or exhaustive list.

This section will be broken into two parts. The first part will discuss the language of Rule 53 and in what circumstances a court has the authority to appoint a special master. Because the language of Rule 53 is broad, the second part of this

---

18. FED. R. CIV. P. 53(h).

19. 28 U.S.C. § 631.

20. *See, e.g., Wachtel v. Guardian Life Ins. Co.,* 2:01-CV-04183-FSH-PS, slip op. at 1–2 (D.N.J. June 24, 2005).

section will delve into how parties and courts use and interpret the rule on a day-to-day basis.

A. THE LANGUAGE OF RULE 53

Rule 53 allows a court to appoint a special master in three instances. The Advisory Committee notes to Rule 53 describe the special masters that can be appointed in these three instances as "consent masters," "trial masters," and "pretrial and post-trial masters."

A consent master can "perform duties consented to by the parties."[21] Again, it should be noted that the court retains the authority to reject the use of a special master, even if both parties consent to the use. Second, a trial master is a master that can "hold trial proceedings and make or recommend findings of fact on issues to be decided without a jury if appointment is warranted by (i) some exceptional condition or (ii) the need to perform an accounting or resolve a difficult computation of damages."[22] Finally, a pretrial and post-trial master can "address pretrial and post-trial matters that cannot be effectively and timely addressed by an available district judge or magistrate judge of the district."[23]

B. THE USE OF RULE 53

A special master can work well in highly fact-intensive situations that would otherwise require a large amount of judicial time and resources. The following list illustrates different occasions in which Rule 53 has been used to appoint a special master.

1. Overseeing All Nondispositive Pretrial Discovery

In *Gipson v. Southwestern Bell Telephone Co.*,[24] a class action filed in the Middle District of Kansas, the court found itself with 115 pretrial motions and 462 docket entries less than a year after the class action had been filed. Faced with the overwhelming task of ruling on these motions, the court ordered the parties to meet and confer on a means of quickly and efficiently resolving these discovery disputes, most of which were administrative in nature. Absent an agreement of the parties to resolve the dispute in its entirety, the court ordered the parties to meet and confer "to agree on the selection of a person to be appointed as special master."[25] The special master would have the ability to "address pretrial discovery matters" and to enter orders relating thereto.[26] Such a flexible grant of authority would allow the

---

21. FED. R. CIV. P. 53(a)(1)(A).

22. FED. R. CIV. P. 53(a)(1)(B).

23. FED. R. CIV. P. 53(a)(1)(C).

24. No. 08-2-17-EFM-DW (D. Kan. Dec. 23, 2008).

25. *Id.*, slip op. at 2.

26. *Id.*

special master to oversee all of the administrative elements of discovery before the trial, relieving the court of the burden and saving the court's time to rule on the parties' substantive pretrial motions.[27]

2. Overseeing Production of Electronically Stored Information

In *In re Seroquel Products Liability Litigation*,[28] a multidistrict litigation from the Middle District of Florida, the court found itself with a defendant that was sluggish in its production of electronically stored information. Since the court did not have the resources to constantly monitor the production to make sure that the defendant was timely in its compliance with the court's orders, it decided to delegate the task to a special master. The duties of this special master, once chosen, were laid out in an order that directed him to "*assist* and, when necessary, *direct* the parties in completing required discovery of electronically stored information with reasonable dispatch and efficiency."[29]

3. Overseeing Compliance with Document Retention Orders

In *Hohider v. United Parcel Service, Inc.*,[30] the plaintiff class alleged that UPS had not retained documents in compliance with the court's order. Seeing the complexity of the task ahead of it, the court appointed a special master to oversee the inquiry into whether UPS had retained the necessary documents. It ordered the special master to familiarize himself with UPS's electronic systems and to make specific findings of fact as to whether UPS had failed to preserve the necessary documents.

4. Overseeing Attorney-Client Privilege and Work-Product Disputes

In *In re Vioxx Products Liability Litigation*,[31] a multidistrict litigation in the Eastern District of Louisiana, the trial court undertook the daunting task of reviewing 30,000 documents over a two-week period. As a result of the collapsed time frame in which the court reviewed the documents, the court "produced over 200 documents in which it reached inconsistent determinations, concluding that one copy of a document was privileged and that exact duplicates of the same document were not privileged."[32] Given the circumstances, the Fifth Circuit ordered the court to come up with a better procedure for reviewing the documents in dispute, all the while recognizing how large cases "sorely [tax] the processes attending our traditional binary structure in civil cases."[33]

In response to the Fifth Circuit, and in recognition of its limited resources, the trial court appointed a special master to review a 2,000-document representative

---

27. *Id.*
28. No. 6 MD 1769 (M.D. Fla. Oct. 5, 2007).
29. *Id.* at 1.
30. No. 04-363 (W.D. Pa. Dec. 19, 2003).
31. No. 06-30378-9, 2006 WL 1726675, at *2 (5th Cir. 2006).
32. *Id.*
33. *Id.* at *3.

sampling of the documents at issue.[34] The court realized that it did not have the resources or the time to do the job as thoroughly as was necessary without neglecting its other responsibilities, and it found that such a process—using a special master—would "afford plaintiffs the benefit of an *in camera* review, while giving Merck the opportunity to support its claim of privilege when it is necessary to do so."[35]

5. Overseeing Settlement Negotiations

In *In re Genetically Modified Rice Litigation*,[36] a multidistrict litigation in the Eastern District of Missouri, the court sought to assist the parties with settlement negotiations while maintaining its neutrality. The court proposed, sua sponte, and then the parties consented to, appointing a special master to aid in settlement talks. Specifically, the court ordered the special master to "supervise settlement discussions" and to "use his expertise to assist the parties in any way he deems appropriate to try to resolve [the] case." The order went so far as to give the special master the ability to order the parties into mediation should he deem it necessary.[37]

6. Overseeing Fee Disputes

In *Alvarado v. FedEx Corp.*,[38] the plaintiff class discharged one of its lawyers before the case settled for $55 million. Up to that point, the lawyer had worked for them for roughly three years. From those three years, she claimed that she was owed fees of approximately $700,000, a sum that was double her usual hourly charge. The discharged lawyer's former cocounsel, though, vigorously disputed the claim. Given the fact-intensive nature of such a fee dispute, the court appointed a special master to oversee and resolve the dispute. The special master also considered allegations that another lawyer for the class had engaged in bad faith in connection with three fee petitions seeking a total of $2.2 million, and the district court adopted the recommendation of the special master to sanction the lawyer, although it increased the sanctions at the request of the defendant.[39]

7. Overseeing Settlement Administration

Post-trial or post-settlement special master appointments, though, are not limited to fee disputes. In the aforementioned *Vioxx* litigation, the court appointed a special master and two deputy special masters to oversee any dispute involving the case's settlement administration.[40] That case reflects an instance where the

---

34. *In re Vioxx Prods. Liab. Litig.*, No. 2:05-md-01657-EEF-DEK (E.D. La. Apr. 26, 2007).

35. *Id.* at 3 (internal citations and quotations omitted).

36. 4:06-md-01811-CDP, slip op. at 2 (E.D. Mo. Nov. 24, 2008).

37. *Id.* at 4.

38. No. C 04-0098, 2009 WL 734683 (N.D. Cal. Mar. 19, 2009).

39. *Id.* at *16.

40. *In re Vioxx*, MDL 1657 (E.D. La. Jan. 14, 2008); *see also id.*, 2008 WL 3285912, at *3 n.7 (E.D. La. Aug. 7, 2008).

parties, of their own volition in the settlement agreement, specifically contemplated the use of a special master and two deputy special masters to oversee the administration of the settlement and payment of claims. Once the parties agreed as to the duties of the special master and his deputies, they petitioned the court to make the appointment. The court's order was pithy—it appointed the special master and two deputies to perform the duties detailed in the settlement agreement. One unique feature worthy of mention in the parties' settlement agreement is that they deemed the special master's decisions to be final and nonappealable.

IX. How Is the Special Master Compensated?

Typically, the order appointing the special master contains provisions governing compensation. Rule 53 lists three headlight issues of compensation that must be addressed. First, the court must decide how much the special master should be compensated.[41] Second, the court must determine the mechanics for payment of the special master.[42] Finally, the court must decide who should pay the special master (i.e., whether the parties should jointly shoulder the burden or whether one party should have sole payment responsibility).[43]

The first consideration of special master compensation is that of quantum, or how much the special master should be paid. In determining reasonable compensation for special masters, "a court should consider factors such as time necessarily spent, thoroughness of the services, importance of the matter, and the assistance provided to a final disposition of the issues referred."[44] To quantify the issue, courts have approved hourly rates from $400 to $600.[45] Once the court sets the amount of compensation, it may revisit the issue and adjust the rate after giving notice to the parties and an opportunity for them to be heard.[46]

Second, the court must decide the methodology for paying the special master. Rule 53 provides for two options. The obligor may pay the special master directly,[47] or the special master can be paid "from a fund or subject matter subject to the court's control."[48] For example, the parties may pay into a fund controlled by the court, and the special master may submit statements to the court to be paid from the fund.

---

41. FED. R. CIV. P. 53(g)(1).

42. FED. R. CIV. P. 53(g)(2).

43. FED. R. CIV. P. 53(g)(3).

44. *United States v. May*, 67 F.3d 706, 708 (8th Cir. 1995).

45. *See, e.g., Wachtel*, slip op. at 3–4 (approving $600 per hour); *Smart Parts, Inc. v. WDP Ltd.*, No. 02-1557, 2005 WL 35834, at *6 (D. Or. Jan. 7, 2005) (approving $500 per hour); *Triple Five of Minn. v. Simon*, No. Civ. 99-1894, 2003 WL 22859834, at *2 (D. Minn. Dec. 1, 2003) (approving $400 per hour).

46. FED. R. CIV. P. 53(g)(1).

47. FED. R. CIV. P. 53(g)(2)(A).

48. FED. R. CIV. P. 53(g)(2)(B).

The court has wide discretion to determine responsibility for the payment of costs. Rule 53 explicitly states that a court "must allocate payment among the parties after considering the nature and amount of the controversy, the parties' means, and the extent to which any party is more responsible than other parties for the reference to the master."[49] The court can also amend the order governing which among the parties is responsible for payment to reflect the decision on the merits.[50] Further, a division of responsibility for costs may await a decision on the merits of the case. A party that provokes unnecessarily the appointment of a special master may be tagged for the entire cost of the fees and expenses of the special master. As an example, in *Brock v. Ing*,[51] the court of appeals found that the district court had "abused its discretion" splitting the high costs of using a special master because the "wrongdoer" made the special master necessary.

X. What Procedures Are Available to Appeal a Ruling from a Special Master?

The amendments to Rule 53 changed the standards of review of a special master's actions. The standards vary depending upon the type of action or decision of a special master.[52] For findings of law and fact, the current Rule 53 requires that the district court review such findings de novo.[53] Interestingly, the parties may stipulate in advance that issues of fact be reviewed only for clear error or that the decision of the special master be final and unappealable.[54]

All procedural matters related to a special master's decisions, which are the bulk of what a special master does in the class action context, are reviewed only for an abuse of discretion unless otherwise decided by the court.[55]

If the special master makes findings or a report that is adopted by the district court, the decision is subject to appellate review like any district court decision.[56] If findings of the special master are not adopted by the trial court, the appeals court may directly review the special master's decision using the same standard the district court would use to review the decision.[57]

---

49. FED. R. CIV. P. 53(g)(3).

50. *Id.*

51. 827 F.2d 1426, 1428 (10th Cir. 1987).

52. FED. R. CIV. P. 53(g)(3).

53. *Turner v. Murphy Oil USA, Inc.*, 582 F. Supp. 2d 797 (E.D. La. 2008) (holding that a district court reviews the decision of a special master de novo).

54. FED. R. CIV. P. 53(f)(3)(B).

55. FED. R. CIV. P. 53(g)(5).

56. *In re Exxon Valdez*, 228 F. App'x 667, 668 (9th Cir. 2007).

57. *U.S. Energy Corp. v. Nukem, Inc.*, 400 F.3d 822, 830 (10th Cir. 2005) ("Where the district court rejects a factual finding by the master, [this court], like a majority of circuit courts, directly review[s] the

No matter what type of review it is, a party must file its objection to the special master's order, report, or recommendation "within 20 days after a copy is served, unless the court sets a different time."[58]

XI. Conclusion

A class action is a Serbonian Bog. Docket sheets often spiral out of control, and keeping track of all of the moving parts can be difficult both for the litigants and the court. Fortunately, Rule 53 provides everyone involved with a creative means of lightening the court's docket and efficiently resolving disputes. A well-chosen special master with a detailed list of responsibilities can resolve the action with celerity. True, there is some expense in the special master process. But the benefits far outweigh the costs. Hopefully, litigants will realize the advantages of Rule 53 and will work to use the office of the special master to its full potential.

---

findings of the special master, thereby effectively ignoring the district court's review of the master's findings." (citations omitted)).

58. FED. R. CIV. P. 53(f)(2).

ETHICAL ISSUES IN CLASS ACTIONS

ROBERT D. PHILLIPS, JR.[1]

I. Introduction

Complex class actions raise unique ethical considerations, particularly in the course of settlement negotiations.[2] Indeed, considering that the vast majority of class actions settle before trial, the class action settlement gives rise to many of the reported ethics concerns. Failure to consider and address the full range of issues applicable to a potential class action settlement may enable objectors to successfully attack the settlement and cause the court to reject it. This chapter will address issues relating to fee negotiations, the Class Action Fairness Act of 2005, restrictions on a lawyer's right to practice, confidentiality provisions, incentive payments to class representative plaintiffs, lawyers serving as class representative plaintiffs, and reverse auctions.

II. Fee Negotiations During the Settlement Process

During settlement discussions, a lawyer may not subordinate a client's interest in a favorable settlement to the lawyer's interest in fees. Class counsel must be careful not to create a conflict by negotiating an attorney fees deal that creates a benefit for counsel that is greater than the benefit conferred on the class as a whole.[3] This problem may arise in a variety of contexts.

Most courts and commentators agree that class counsel should negotiate settlement terms and the amount of the common fund separately from, and before

---

1. The author wishes to thank associates Eugenia Chern, Samuel Park, and Renee Feldman of Reed Smith LLP's San Francisco office for their work on this chapter.

2. *See, e.g.,* Chapter 7, "Settlements."

3. *See Ramirez v. Sturdevant,* 21 Cal. App. 4th 904, 916–17 (1994).

any discussion of, attorney fees.[4] In *Prandini v. National Tea Co.*,[5] the Third Circuit imposed a "bright line" rule and held that the settlement of the damages aspect of the class action must be concluded separately from and prior to the negotiation and award of attorney fees.[6] This "bright line," however, has its critics. The difficulty presented by a sequential approach is rooted in settlement negotiation dynamics—the parties generally want to know what the total cost of the settlement is before giving final agreement. This difficulty discourages settlements when a "bright line" rule is applied.

The U.S. Supreme Court recognized this difficulty in *Evans v. Jeff D.*[7] The Court commented that "a rule prohibiting the comprehensive negotiation of all outstanding issues in a pending case might well preclude the settlement of a substantial number of cases."[8] "[The] potential liability for attorney's fees may overshadow the cost of relief on the merits and darken prospects for settlement if fees cannot be negotiated."[9] Parties may refuse to settle if the issue of attorney fees remains open.[10] This would result in an unnecessary burden to the judicial system.[11] The Court concluded that simultaneous negotiations of a party's liability on the merits and liability on attorney fees should not be prohibited.[12] "[W]hen the parties find such negotiations conducive to settlement, the public interest, as well as that of the parties, is served by simultaneous negotiations."[13] However, subsequent decisions suggest that this holding may be limited to civil rights actions and thus inapplicable to class actions not involving civil rights.[14]

California also recognizes the difficulty associated with the sequential approach. In *Ramirez v. Sturdevant*,[15] the court "decline[d] to find that the inherent conflict in dual negotiations necessarily invalidate[d] any resulting settlements."[16] Although the court discouraged simultaneous negotiations, it concluded that the

---

4. *See, e.g., Turner v. Murphy Oil USA, Inc.*, 472 F. Supp. 2d 830, 844 (E.D. La. 2007); *see also* MANUAL FOR COMPLEX LITIGATION (FOURTH) § 21.7 (2004) ("[T]he simultaneous negotiation of class relief and attorney's fees creates a potential conflict. Separate negotiation of the class settlement before an agreement on fees is generally preferable.").

5. 557 F.2d 1015 (3d Cir. 1977).

6. *Id.* at 1021.

7. 475 U.S. 717 (1986).

8. *Id.* at 733 (citations omitted).

9. *Id.* at 735.

10. *Id.* at 736.

11. *Id.* at 736–37.

12. *Id.* at 738 n.30.

13. *Id.*

14. *See, e.g., Ayers v. Thompson*, 358 F.3d 356, 375 (5th Cir. 2004) (permitting simultaneous negotiation in school desegregation context); *Acosta v. Trans Union, LLC*, 243 F.R.D. 377, 397–99 (C.D. Cal. 2007) (refusing to approve settlement in consumer credit reporting context in part because of class counsel's willingness to simultaneously negotiate attorney fees with class relief).

15. 21 Cal. App. 4th 904.

16. *Id.* at 924.

better approach was to consider each settlement agreement on its own merits for any conflicts of interest.[17]

A modified approach to this problem is the "clear sailing agreement" in which essentially two things happen: (1) the parties negotiate both the basic settlement and attorney fees simultaneously, but they only agree to a ceiling on fees, and (2) the court reviews the settlement, as required under Federal Rule of Civil Procedure 23(e), and retains the authority to lower the attorney fees below the ceiling. This approach solves the practical problem of piecemeal settlement negotiations, but essentially retains the original problem of simultaneous negotiations with its potential for trade-off between maximum settlement for the class and maximum attorney fees for the lawyer.[18] Courts have applied "heightened scrutiny" when evaluating clear sailing agreements.[19] But judicial oversight has its limits.[20] One commentator has proposed a ban on clear sailing agreements, allowing the parties to negotiate the settlement and fees as a lump sum, followed by court determination of fees out of the lump sum at a hearing in which the class is represented by a guardian ad litem.[21]

Submitting conflicts to mediation may be a solution to resolving ethical issues regarding fee negotiation during settlement in some circumstances. Allowing a third party to effectively facilitate the negotiation can eliminate some of the ethical concerns or appearance of impropriety that often arise in such situations.[22] In particular, the use of retired judges who are experienced in class action litigation can facilitate working through the intertwined ethical and tactical challenges in such negotiations.

III. Fairness of Settlements and Fee Awards Under the Class Action Fairness Act

Prior to the enactment of the Class Action Fairness Act of 2005 (CAFA), class actions routinely resulted in settlements in which plaintiffs' lawyers collected large attorney fee awards but class members were left with only coupons or discounts

---

17. *Id.* at 924–25.

18. *See* William D. Henderson, *Clear Sailing Agreements: A Special Form of Collusion in Class Action Settlements*, 77 Tul. L. Rev. 813 (2003).

19. *See Weinberger v. Great N. Nekoosa Corp.*, 925 F.2d 518, 525 (1st Cir. 1991); *In re TJX Cos. Retail Sec. Breach Litig.*, 584 F. Supp. 2d 395, 399 (D. Mass. 2008); *Stokes v. Saga Int'l Holidays, Ltd.*, 376 F. Supp. 2d 86, 89–90 (D. Mass. 2005).

20. Henderson, *supra* note 18, at 824 n.50 ("In the class action context, an admonition for heightened judicial scrutiny is like dieting: a healthy and heartfelt aspiration that seldom produces results.").

21. *Id.* at 816–17, 830–38.

22. *See* Mark Richard Cummisford, *Resolving Fee Disputes and Legal Malpractice Claims Using ADR*, 85 Marq. L. Rev. 975, 985–87 (2002).

that had little or no value to them.[23] For example, when a class action against a video rental chain settled, class counsel collected $9 million in attorney fees, but class members received only two free rentals.[24] Likewise, in a class action against a retail company, plaintiffs' counsel received $1 million while class members were compensated with the opportunity to purchase select items on sale for one week.[25]

Congress designed provisions of CAFA to protect class members from these types of abusive coupon settlement practices.[26] CAFA seeks to ameliorate these abuses by limiting attorney fees in coupon settlements, as well as regulating the fairness of settlements that include coupons.[27]

Under CAFA, contingent attorney fees in coupon settlements are calculated based on the value of the coupons *actually redeemed*.[28] Previously, attorney fees were based on the value of the *total* coupons *issued*. By linking the class members' coupon redemption rate with attorney fees, class counsel has an incentive to make the coupons valuable to the class members and easy to use.[29] If the value of the coupons is not used to determine attorney fees, the fee award is based on the amount of time class counsel reasonably expended working on the litigation.[30]

Before approving a proposed coupon settlement, the court must hold a hearing and make a written determination that "the settlement is fair, reasonable, and adequate for class members."[31] Although the "fair, reasonable, and adequate" standard applicable in coupon settlements reads the same as the general standard for approving class actions in Rule 23(e)(2), courts have interpreted coupon settlements to require a greater level of scrutiny than other class action settlements.[32]

In *Figueroa v. Sharper Image Corp.*,[33] the court considered the fairness of a proposed settlement under CAFA's heightened scrutiny. The settlement included

---

23. *Synfuel Techs., Inc. v. DHL Express (USA), Inc.*, 463 F.3d 646, 654 (7th Cir. 2006) (citing Pub. L. No. 109-2, § 2(a)(3)(A), 119 Stat. 4, 4).

24. Gary L. Sasso, *Class Actions: De Minimis Curat Lex?*, 31 Litig. 15, 18 (Summer 2005).

25. *Id.*

26. *Figueroa v. Sharper Image Corp.*, 517 F. Supp. 2d 1292, 1320 (S.D. Fla. 2007).

27. *See* 28 U.S.C. § 1712.

28. *Id.* at § 1712(a).

29. J. Brendan Day, *My Lawyer Went to Court and All I Got Was This Lousy Coupon! The Class Action Fairness Act's Inadequate Provision for Judicial Scrutiny over Proposed Coupon Settlements*, 38 Seton Hall L. Rev. 1085, 1098 (2008); Steven M. Puiszis, *Developing Trends with the Class Action Fairness Act of 2005*, 40 J. Marshall L. Rev. 115, 175 (2006); James Tharin & Brian Blockovich, *Coupons and the Class Action Fairness Act*, 18 Geo. J. Legal Ethics 1443, 1449 (2005).

30. 28 U.S.C. § 1712(b).

31. *Id.* at § 1712(e).

32. *See Synfuel Techs.*, 463 F.3d at 654 ("[I]n [§ 1712], Congress required heightened judicial scrutiny of coupon-based settlements."); *Figueroa*, 517 F. Supp. 2d at 1321 ("[T]he undersigned interprets [§ 1712] to imply the application of a greater level of scrutiny to the existing criteria than existed pre-CAFA.").

33. 517 F. Supp. 2d 1292.

the distribution of $19 Sharper Image merchandise credits to all class members who purchased an allegedly defective and dangerous air purifier.[34] First, the court addressed the procedural fairness of the settlement.[35] The court concluded that the settlement was procedurally unfair because plaintiffs "negotiated from a position of weakness" because of defendant's threat to stay the case for jurisdictional reasons and because plaintiffs had limited information about the merits of the case when they negotiated the settlement.[36]

Next, the court addressed the substantive fairness of the settlement by applying the six-factor test articulated in *Bennett v. Behring Corp.*[37] Regarding the first factor, likelihood of success at trial, the court found that plaintiffs had a strong likelihood of success on the merits, thus favoring rejection of the settlement.[38] In discussing the second and third factors simultaneously, the range of possible recovery and the point on or below the range of recovery at which a settlement is fair, the court concluded that the $19 credit toward purchases at defendant's store was unfair because the settlement would result in increased sales for defendant rather than meaningful disgorgement of its wrongfully obtained profits.[39] Regarding the fourth factor, complexity and expense of litigation, the court found that this factor also favored rejection of the settlement because the parties already had completed most of the discovery necessary for trial and the risk of getting nothing at trial was worth taking in light of the small credit offered.[40] The court also found that the fifth factor, substance and amount of opposition to the settlement, supported rejection of the settlement because the attorneys general of 35 states had opposed the credit settlement at some point during the litigation.[41] Lastly, the court concluded that the sixth factor, stage of the proceedings in which settlement was achieved, also favored rejection of the settlement because the parties negotiated the settlement before class certification, when plaintiffs had insufficient information to evaluate the merits of their case.[42] Because all six substantive fairness factors supported rejection of the settlement, the settlement was not substantively fair. The lack of both procedural and substantive fairness led the court to deny approval of the settlement.[43]

---

34. *Id.* at 1294–95.
35. *Id.* at 1321–23.
36. *Id.* at 1322–23.
37. 737 F.2d 982 (11th Cir. 1984) (discussed in *Figueroa*, 517 F. Supp. 2d at 1323–28).
38. *Figueroa*, 517 F. Supp. 2d at 1326.
39. *Id.* at 1327.
40. *Id.* at 1327–28.
41. *Id.* at 1328.
42. *Id.*
43. *Id.* at 1329.

Some commentators believe that, in enacting CAFA, Congress intended to discourage or prohibit coupon settlements entirely.[44] Other commentators, however, believe that coupon settlements, if structured correctly, can be used effectively in settling class action lawsuits.[45]

IV. Restrictions on the Right to Practice

Where large numbers of similar cases or several major class actions are pending against a single defendant, that defendant may wish to prevent the best plaintiffs' lawyers from bringing additional related lawsuits. But Model Rule of Professional Conduct 5.6 (Rule 5.6) provides, "[a] lawyer shall not participate in offering or making . . . an agreement in which a restriction on the lawyer's right to practice is part of the settlement of a client controversy."[46] Many jurisdictions have the same or similar disciplinary rules. For example, in California, "[a] member shall not be a party to or participate in offering or making an agreement, whether in connection with the settlement of a lawsuit or otherwise, if the agreement restricts the right of a member to practice law."[47]

An agreement in which a plaintiffs' lawyer agrees, as part of the settlement, not to take on similar types of cases in the future or not to represent future plaintiffs in similar cases against the same defendant is therefore prohibited by Rule 5.6(b). Such a restrictive agreement creates a conflict of interest between the lawyer and the settling client, between the lawyer and any present non-settling clients, and between the lawyer's current client and any "future" clients.[48] The Rule also seeks to prevent awards to plaintiffs that do not flow from the merits of the case, but rather turn on the monetary value of having plaintiffs' lawyer "disappear" from future lawsuits of the same nature.[49] Provisions that *indirectly* restrict the right to practice are also ethically impermissible. For example, a lawyer may not enter into an agreement in which the defendant will retain plaintiff's lawyer in the future as

---

44. *See* Laurens Walker, *The Consumer Class Action Bill of Rights: A Policy and Political Mistake*, 58 HastINGS L.J. 849, 859 (2007); *see also* Nicole Ochi, *Complex Litigation in California and Beyond: Are Consumer Class and Mass Actions Dead? Complex Litigation Strategies after CAFA & MMTJA*, 41 Loyola L.A. L. Rev. 965, 973 (2008).

45. *See* Tharin & Blockovich, *supra* note 29, at 1445.

46. Model Rules of Prof'l Conduct R. 5.6(b) (2003).

47. Rules of Prof'l Conduct of the State Bar of Cal. R. 1-500 (2005); *see also* Cal. Bus. & Prof. Code § 16600 (2005) (providing that "every contract by which anyone is restrained from engaging in a lawful profession, trade, or business of any kind is to that extent void").

48. Yvette Golan, *Restrictive Settlement Agreements: A Critique of Model Rule 5.6(b)*, 33 Sw. U. L. Rev. 1, 14 (2003).

49. *Id.*

a consultant or lawyer in order to use the conflict of interest rules to prevent that lawyer from representing future clients against the defendant.[50]

The Rule acknowledges the reality that these agreements injure future plaintiffs by allowing defendants to "buy off" lawyers who might be the best candidates to represent these plaintiffs, leaving them without the services of the most experienced and knowledgeable counsel.[51]

Courts have disfavored practice restrictions in settlement agreements, regardless of how cleverly construed. In *In re Zaruba*, a former in-house lawyer at Warner-Lambert was suspended from the practice of law for one year for violating New Jersey Rules of Professional Conduct 5.6(b) (offering or making an agreement in which a restriction on the lawyer's right to practice is part of the settlement) and 8.4(a) (violating or attempting to violate the Rules of Professional Conduct and knowingly assisting or inducing another to do so).[52] The Office of Attorney Ethics accused Zaruba of paying off plaintiffs' lawyers to drop a mass breach of warranty suit over Warner-Lambert's Nix head-lice shampoo.[53] He was accused of agreeing with opposing counsel, Mark Hager of Washington, D.C. and John Traficonte of Massachusetts, on a deal in which the 90 plaintiffs got $10,000 and their lawyers got $225,000.[54] The agreement barred Traficonte and Hager from disclosing these terms to their clients and from helping anyone else bring a case regarding Nix.[55] In reviewing the *Zaruba* matter, the Disciplinary Review Board stated that attempts to "buy off plaintiffs' counsel by secret agreements . . . will be viewed as extremely serious, warranting substantial suspensions."[56]

---

50. *Ethical Guidelines for Settlement Negotiations*, 2002 ABA LITIG. SEC. 40–41, § 4.2.1.

51. *Golan, supra* note 48, at 21–22; *see also Ethical Guidelines, supra* note 50, at 40, § 4.2.1 (stating that a "provision that 'buys off' a party's lawyer unjustifiably deprives future litigants of the opportunity to employ that lawyer"); *see also* David A. Dana & Susan P. Koniak, *Secret Settlements and Practice Restrictions Aid Lawyer Cartels and Cause Other Harms*, 2003 U. ILL. L. REV. 1217, 1227, 1240 (2003) (finding that there is "no social value in allowing defendants to use the settlement process to limit the pool and scope of practice of the lawyers who are most familiar with the kind of claims that may arise from the defendant's conduct," making it harder for future plaintiffs with claims against the defendant "to learn about those claims and secure willing and effective counsel," which distorts the market for legal services); ABA Comm. on Ethics and Prof'l Responsibility, Formal Op. 93-371 (1993) [hereinafter ABA Formal Op. 93-371] ("While the Model Rules generally require that the client's interests be put first, forcing a lawyer to give up future representations may be asking too much, particularly in light of the strong countervailing policy favoring the public's unfettered choice of counsel."); Colo. Bar Ass'n Ethics Comm'n. Op. 92 (1993) ("A claimant's attorney should not agree to a settlement restriction giving the attorney significantly less discretion in the prosecution of a claim than an attorney independent of the agreement would have.").

52. 832 A.2d 317 (N.J. 2003).

53. *Suspended While Retired*, 174 N.J.L.J. 271 (2003).

54. *Id.*

55. *Id.*

56. Mary P. Gallagher, *Suspension for an In-House Lawyer Who Bribed Adversaries Not to Sue*, 173 N.J.L.J. 561 (2003).

The ethical concern resulting from the Nix deal was that Zaruba effectively "closed the door" on many future Nix lawsuits.[57] The provisions of the agreement insured that any future lawyer representing plaintiffs in a Nix lawsuit would have to start from scratch and would not get any help from Traficonte or Hager.[58] The deal provided that Traficonte and Hager had to preserve the secrecy of "facts, legal theories, or potential witnesses [from] anyone who might bring such a case."[59]

Plaintiffs also filed ethics charges against Hager with the D.C. Bar Counsel in *In re Hager*.[60] The court found Hager to be in violation of Rule 1.2(a), which states that a "lawyer shall abide by a client's decision whether to accept an offer of settlement of a matter," as well as Rule 5.6(b).[61] Noting the paucity of case law in the area,[62] the court found that it was unethical for Hager to accept an arrangement restricting his future practice.[63] The *Hager* court also cautioned that several ethics opinions have stated that a defense lawyer who proposed a restriction on practice as a settlement provision also engages in unethical conduct, even if plaintiffs' lawyer does not accept the offer.[64]

Several ethics opinions also address this type of restriction on the practice of law. In ABA Formal Opinion 93-371, the leading opinion on this issue, the American Bar Association's Standing Committee on Ethics and Professional Responsibility stated that a restriction on the right of plaintiffs' counsel to represent present and future claimants against a defendant in a mass tort class action as part of a global settlement of existing clients' claims is an impermissible restriction on the right to practice.[65] Any demand for, or acceptance of, such a restriction as part of a settlement violates Model Rule 5.6(b).[66] Such a settlement may be in the interests of some of the lawyer's present clients because the defendant may be willing to offer more consideration than it might have without the restrictive agreement.[67]

---

57. *Id.*

58. *Id.*

59. *Id.*

60. 812 A.2d 904, 911 (D.C. App. 2002).

61. *Id.* at 917.

62. *Id.* at 918.

63. *Id.* at 919 (citing D.C. Bar Op. 130 and D.C. Bar Op. 35).

64. *Id.* at 919 n.18; *see also* ABA Formal Op. 93-371 (stating that prohibitions on such restrictions apply to both the lawyer accepting the restriction and the defense lawyer offering or requiring the restriction).

65. ABA Formal Op. 93-371. Ethics opinions in various states unanimously affirm that the policies of the rules are best served by prohibiting negotiated practice restrictions on a lawyer's right to practice as a condition of a settlement agreement. *See* N.C. Ethics Op. RPC 179 (1994); Phila. Ethics Op. 95-13 (1995) ("buy off' disguised as a "reimbursement of fees and costs" did not eliminate the effect of the condition that limited lawyer's involvement on behalf of future clients); Or. Ethics Op. 1991-47 (1991); N.Y.C. Ethics Op. 1993-3 (1993) (prohibitions on restrictions on the right to practice apply to both the lawyer whose practice would be restricted and the lawyer who proposes such an agreement); Alaska Ethics Op. 2000-2 (2000).

66. ABA Formal Op. 93-371.

67. *Id.*

If such clients wished to accept such a settlement containing this restriction, normally under Rule 1.2 a lawyer would be required to abide by the client's instruction.[68] But Rule 1.2 must be read in conjunction with the limits of Rule 5.6, which expressly prohibits these restrictions.[69] Finally, although such restrictions often arise in a good faith attempt to settle complicated litigation, such intentions cannot overcome ethical requirements.[70]

California Ethics Opinion 1988-104[71] also addresses the practice restriction issue. In that opinion, the California State Bar Standing Committee on Professional Responsibility and Conduct (Cal. Committee) concluded that Rule 1-500 "clearly prohibits both plaintiff's and defendant's attorney from offering or accepting a provision as a condition of settlement which would preclude plaintiff's attorney from subsequently suing the settling defendant because such a provision restricts the plaintiff's attorney's right to practice law."[72] The Cal. Committee reasoned that such a provision gave the opposing party the ability to control the lawyer's representation of subsequent clients, thereby denying the subsequent clients' access to the most experienced lawyer.[73] Basically, a practice restriction provision of this nature "limits the autonomy of attorneys and the ability of clients to freely choose an attorney."[74] Furthermore, the Cal. Committee concluded that Rule 1-500 prohibited a defendant's lawyer from directly *or indirectly* proposing a practice restriction provision.[75]

Parties and their counsel have attempted from time to time to circumvent the prohibitions of Rule 5.6 through various ploys or indirect restrictions. For example, a defendant may hire a plaintiff's lawyer, after a suit is settled, as a "consultant" on the subject matter of the suit.[76] The resulting conflict of interest between the defendant and future clients of the lawyer prevents the lawyer from taking on subsequent suits dealing with the same issues against this defendant.[77] It has been argued that the availability of such "evasive techniques" undermines the arguments in support of Model Rule 5.6.[78] Opponents of Rule 5.6 stress the values of promoting settlements, zealous representation, and freedom of contract to support the

---

68. *Id.*

69. *Id.*

70. *Id.*

71. Cal. Ethics Op. 1988-104 (1988).

72. *Id.*

73. *Id.*

74. *Id.*

75. *Id.*

76. *See Golan, supra* note 48, at 44.

77. *Id.* Some states permit these arrangements if the parties make them after settlement, rather than making them a condition to the settlement agreement. *Id.* at 9–10; *see also, e.g., In re Conduct of Brandt*, 10 P.3d 906, 918 n.13 (Or. 2000); *Adams v. BellSouth Telecomms., Inc.*, No. 96-2473-CIV, 2001 WL 34032759, at *9 (S.D. Fla. Jan. 29, 2001). Both *Brandt* and *BellSouth* are discussed in this section.

78. *Golan, supra* note 48.

proposition that restrictive agreements should be allowed.[79] It is helpful to examine how attempts to use such alternatives have fared in the courts or before ethics committees.

In *In re Conduct of Brandt*,[80] the defendant offered to retain plaintiffs' counsel with the apparent motive to prevent them from subsequently representing "similarly situated" plaintiffs.[81] The plaintiffs' lawyers argued that the retainer agreement only indirectly restricted the right to practice and thus did not violate any ethical rules.[82] They further argued that "if a retainer agreement merely requires the lawyer to provide valuable legal services, with its concomitant disqualification from representing adverse parties, the agreement does not restrict the lawyer's right to practice law" and should instead be regulated merely by conflict of interest rules.[83] The *Brandt* court found that the ethical rules do not prohibit *all* agreements that restrict the practice of law, but only those made *in connection with* the settlement of a case.[84] Both direct and indirect methods of restricting practice undercut the purpose of the ethical rules and, if made in connection with the settlement of a case, are prohibited.[85]

In *Adams v. BellSouth Telecommunications, Inc.*,[86] BellSouth proposed to enter into a consulting arrangement with plaintiffs' counsel in order to prevent their future representation of parties against the company. BellSouth insisted that the money for the consulting fee be taken directly out of the global settlement, as a condition of the agreement.[87] The lawyers never informed plaintiffs of the consulting agreement.[88] Upon being charged with several ethical violations, the lawyers argued that this consulting agreement was a "limited" restriction on the lawyer's right to practice.[89] The court found that the restriction in this case was in no way designed in a limited manner, for example, to protect confidential information, which the court might have permitted.[90] The court stated that the purpose of the restriction was "a payoff to Plaintiffs' counsel to make them go away and never come back" and thus was a violation of ethical provisions prohibiting restric-

---

79. *Id.* at 45–47.
80. 10 P.3d at 917.
81. *Id.*
82. *Id.*
83. *Id.*
84. *Id.* at 918.
85. *Id.*
86. 2001 WL 34032759.
87. *Id.* at *1.
88. *Id.*
89. *Id.* at *3.
90. *Id.* at *6; *see also* discussion of confidentiality provisions in section V.

tions on the right to practice.[91] The public policy underlying Model Rule 5.6 is to "prohibit corporate 'buyouts' of plaintiffs' attorneys."[92] "[T]here is a strong public interest in having available plaintiffs' attorneys for future clients, an interest which outweighs allowing lawyers to restrict their future representation autonomy even where it would increase the overall size of a settlement (and thereby maximize a present client's recovery)."[93]

Furthermore, the *Adams* court found fault with the fact that the restriction in this case was put in place to protect the opposing party, not the plaintiffs' counsel.[94] Any permissible exception to the prohibition on such indirect restrictions arises only when necessary to safeguard the confidential disclosures the client made to his or her lawyer.[95] In this case, the lawyers did not even notify plaintiffs of these provisions.[96] Rather, these restrictions placed plaintiffs' counsel in direct conflict with their clients.[97] The court found that both lawyers committed ethical violations because the scope of Model Rule 5.6's prohibition of restriction on the right to practice applies to both the lawyer agreeing to the restriction and the lawyer offering or requiring the provision.[98]

Finally, the court found that by allowing counsel to directly take an amount of the settlement funds, they were in a financial conflict of interest with their clients, which is a clear ethical violation.[99] This is distinguishable from a situation in which a lawyer agrees to a restriction in exchange for a settlement in the client's best interests (i.e., increasing the client's recovery).[100] Here, the lawyers agreed to these restrictions merely to increase their own gain.[101] Because these types of consulting agreements were becoming more common, the court warned that "ethical rules should hold firm against allowing contemporaneous negotiations over settlement and consulting agreement terms. Further, settlement and consulting fees should never be co-mingled together into a singular pool . . . these steps are necessary to avoid any appearance of ethical wrongdoing in this area."[102]

91. *Id.*
92. *Id.* at *7.
93. *Id.*
94. *Id.* at *6.
95. *Id.*
96. *Id.*
97. *Id.*
98. *Id.* at *7.
99. *Id.* at *8.
100. *Id.*
101. *Id.*
102. *Id.* at *9.

V. Confidentiality Provisions in Settlement Agreements

Confidentiality provisions present special, heightened concerns in the class action context. Absent class members are rarely aware of such restrictions, and the general public may be adversely affected by such constraints.

If confidentiality provisions of a settlement agreement restrict a lawyer from using confidential information, they may be ethically prohibited as an indirect restriction on the lawyer's right to practice.[103] Such provisions indirectly prohibit a lawyer from taking on certain clients in the future whose representation would necessarily involve the use of such information.[104] Similarly, such an agreement may violate ethical guidelines if it restricts a lawyer from revealing information that is not otherwise subject to the lawyer's duty of confidentiality.[105]

A lawyer may participate in a settlement agreement that prohibits him from revealing confidential information relating to the representation of a client. However, a lawyer may not ethically participate in a settlement agreement that would prevent him from using information gained during the representation in later representations against the same opposing party, or a related party if the information is not subject to the lawyer's duty of confidentiality.[106] Such a provision in a settlement agreement may act as an indirect restriction on practice if, by prohibiting a lawyer's use of certain information, he would be precluded from effectively representing certain clients in the future in situations where the lawyer might have the need to use information that was not protected under the duty of confidentiality but that was covered by the settlement terms.[107] Such a provision may, as a practical matter, bar the lawyer from future representations because "the lawyer's inability to use certain information may materially limit his representation of the future client and, further, may adversely affect that representation":[108]

> A settlement proposal that calls on the lawyer to agree to keep confidential, for the opposing party's benefit, information that the lawyer ordinarily has no duty to protect, creates a conflict between the present client's interests and those of the lawyer

---

103. *See* CALIFORNIA PRACTICE GUIDE: CIVIL PROCEDURE BEFORE TRIAL ch. 12(II)-H § 12:1033 (Rutter Group 2005) ("To the extent such 'secrecy' clauses limit the attorney's disclosure to other clients or future clients of the attorney, they probably violate CPRC 1-500(A)."); *see generally* Jon Bauer, *Buying Witness Silence: Evidence-Suppressing Settlements and Lawyers' Ethics*, 87 OR. L. REV. 481 (2008) (arguing that secrecy provisions violate Model Rules 3.4(f) and 8.4(d)).

104. *See Ethical Guidelines, supra* note 50, at 48, § 4.2.6; *see also, e.g.*, ABA Comm. on Ethics and Prof'l Responsibility, Formal Op. 00-417 (2000).

105. *See Ethical Guidelines, supra* note 50, at 48, § 4.2.6; *see also, e.g.*, N.Y. Ethics Op. 730 (2000).

106. N.Y. Ethics Op. 730 (2000).

107. *Id.*

108. ABA Comm. on Ethics and Prof'l Responsibility, Formal Op. 00-417 (2000); *see also* N.Y. Ethics Op. 730 (2000).

and future clients—precisely the problem at which [New York Disciplinary Rule DR 2-108(B)] is aimed.[109]

Simply put, settlement agreements should not contain provisions that effectively prevent a lawyer from taking on future clients where the lawyer's need to use such information might arise.[110] Because confidentiality agreements can act as indirect restrictions that also harm potential future clients by restricting their access to lawyers with the most knowledge and experience pertinent to their case, such restrictions reduce the public's access to lawyers because the lawyers who "by virtue of their background and experience, might be the very best available talent to represent" future clients against the same opposing party might be precluded from taking on such clients.[111]

In addition, if the potential result of a confidentiality provision will be to indirectly restrict the lawyer's right to practice, client consent will not remedy the ethical violation.[112] A lawyer may not accept such a proposal even if such a provision would be favorable to his client.[113] Neither principles of client autonomy nor the duty of zealous representation can overcome these ethical constraints.[114] The general rule is that confidentiality provisions that have the indirect effect of restricting the right to practice by barring use of information that would be available to the lawyer but for the confidentiality provisions likely constitute an ethical violation.

Another concern of courts and commentators relating to confidentiality agreements is the effect that such agreements have on the rights of the public. For example, "secrecy agreements," which are often used in mass tort settlements, may affect third parties and the public in general, raising ethical concerns.[115] Internal company documents may reveal knowledge of a dangerous or defective product, and settlement agreements may contain provisions designed to ensure that such information remains secret.[116] This poses a conflict for a lawyer, because while a promise to maintain the confidentiality of such documents may be a valuable

109. N.Y. Ethics Op. 730 (2000) (interpreting New York Disciplinary Rule DR 2-108(B), New York's equivalent of Model Rule 5.6(b)). This New York Ethics Opinion also notes that an agreement restricting a lawyer's right to practice may be enforceable even if it violates a disciplinary rule. *See Feldman v. Minars*, 658 N.Y.S.2d 614 (N.Y. App. Div. 1997) (stating agreement may be enforceable even though it is deemed to be a restriction on the right to practice and thus violates ethical provisions).

110. Heather Waldbeser & Heather DeGrave, *A Plaintiff's Lawyer's Dilemma: The Ethics of Entering a Confidential Settlement*, 16 GEO. J. LEGAL ETHICS 815, 821–22 (2003); *see also Gen. Steel Domestic Sales, LLC v. Steel Wise, LLC*, No. 07-CV-01145-DME-KMT, 2009 U.S. Dist. LEXIS 4872, *21–28 (D. Colo. Jan. 23, 2009) (finding secrecy provision invalid that essentially muzzled potential claimants' future testimony).

111. ABA Comm. on Ethics and Prof'l Responsibility, Formal Op. 00-417 (2000).

112. *Id.*

113. *Id.*

114. *But see* Waldbeser & DeGrave, *supra* note 110, at 825–26.

115. *See* Marc Z. Edell & Philip J. Duffy, *Ethical Pitfalls Confronting the Mass Tort Lawyer*, 166 N.J. LAW. 32, 33 (1995).

116. *Id.*

settlement tool for a plaintiff, it may harm the public good by preventing access to information relating to public concerns such as health and safety.[117] Other potential claimants may not be able to discover information relevant to their alleged harm, and members of the public may not learn of the danger associated with such products. In many cases, the real or alleged danger is known to the public because the allegations of a complaint supply information to the public about possible dangers.[118] But where a particular danger is unknown, the impact of confidentiality agreements on the general public is less clear.

Such provisions are occasionally upheld, but are sometimes nullified or rejected when required to protect the public.[119] Opponents of such agreements argue that injuries can be prevented if such information pertaining to safety is allowed to come to light.[120] Others suggest that the interests protected by these private settlement provisions could be just as easily protected by other means, such as court orders.[121] By using the court system to accomplish the same objectives, an external mechanism would thus be put in place to monitor when such agreements were being used to protect legitimate privacy rights, such as trade secrets, and when they were being used to restrict public access to important information that would generate additional suits.[122] Proponents of this alternative believe that the judicial system would be a more appropriate forum for the resolution of such concerns.[123]

VI. Incentive Payments to Plaintiff Class Representatives

Ethical issues also arise in the context of "incentive awards" to plaintiff class representatives. The ethical concerns raised by such payments have been heightened by the recent publicity involving undisclosed payments to class representatives by prominent plaintiffs' firms, but even where such payments are fully disclosed, important ethical issues arise. Class representatives may receive incentive awards as settlement compensation for their extensive involvement in a class action law-

---

117. *Id.*

118. This problem may be akin to the duty of a lawyer to breach his duty of confidentiality to his client in order "to prevent the client or another person . . . (1) from committing a criminal, illegal or fraudulent act that the lawyer reasonably believes is likely to result in death or substantial bodily harm or substantial injury to the financial interest or property of another." N.J. RULES OF PROF'L CONDUCT R. 1.6(b) (2005).

119. Edell & Duffy, *supra* note 115, at 33; *see, e.g., In re Zyprexa Prods. Liab. Litig.*, 253 F.R.D. 69, 208–09 (E.D.N.Y. 2008) (finding public access desirable because litigation involved issues of "great public interest"); *In re "Agent Orange" Prod. Liab. Litig.*, 104 F.R.D. 559 (E.D.N.Y. 1985) (protective orders modified to permit disclosure of certain materials in the absence of good cause where the public's "right-to-know" outweighed the need for confidentiality), *aff'd*, 821 F.2d 139 (2d Cir. 1987).

120. Waldbeser & DeGrave, *supra* note 110, at 818–19.

121. *See* Dana & Koniak, *supra* note 51, at 1226.

122. *Id.*

123. *Id.* at 1226–27.

suit.[124] Incentive awards are allocations to class representatives over the amount of any judgment obtained by other class members.[125] Courts typically analyze incentive awards for fairness to the absent class members.[126] To assist in conducting this fairness analysis, courts generally consider five factors: (1) the risk to the plaintiff in commencing the suit, both financially and otherwise; (2) the notoriety and/or personal difficulties encountered by the representative plaintiff; (3) the extent of the plaintiff's personal involvement in the suit in terms of discovery responsibilities and/or testimony at depositions or trial; (4) the duration of the litigation; and (5) the plaintiff's personal benefit (or lack thereof) purely in his capacity as a member of the class.[127] Courts apply some or all of these factors to dispel potential ethical concerns associated with incentive awards. Ethical concerns include conflicts of interest between class representatives and other class members; collusion between class representatives, class counsel, and defendants; the possibility of bidding wars among lawyers to attract class representatives; and the potential for frivolous litigation. The manifestation of these ethical concerns can lead a court to invalidate an incentive award or, in the case of a frivolous claim, invalidate the lawsuit altogether.

The first issue with incentive awards lies in their ability to create a potential conflict of interest between the class representative receiving the award and the class members not receiving the award.[128] As a general rule, a class representative is a fiduciary to the entire class.[129] "If class representatives expect routinely to receive special awards in addition to their share of the recovery, they may be tempted to accept suboptimal settlements at the expense of the class members whose interests they are appointed to guard."[130] When class representatives "are provided with special 'incentives' in the settlement agreement, they may be more concerned with maximizing those incentives than with judging the adequacy of the settlement as it applies to class members at large."[131] Therefore, "applications for incentive awards are scrutinized carefully by courts who sensibly fear that incentive awards

---

124. *Hadix v. Johnson*, 322 F.3d 895, 897 (6th Cir. 2003); *see also Sauby v. City of Fargo*, No. 3:07-CV-10, 2009 U.S. Dist. LEXIS 70270, *4–5 (D.N.D. July 16, 2009).

125. Comm. on Prof'l Responsibility, Ass'n of the Bar of the City of N.Y., *Financial Arrangements in Class Actions, and the Code of Professional Responsibility*, 20 FORDHAM URB. L.J. 831, 833–34 (1993).

126. *See* FED. R. CIV. P. 23(e)(1)(C) (2005); *see also* Clinton A. Krislov, *Scrutiny of the Bounty: Incentive Awards for Plaintiffs in Class Litigation*, 78 ILL. B.J. 286, 289–90 (1990).

127. *See, e.g., Allapattah Servs. v. Exxon Corp.*, 454 F. Supp. 2d 1185, 1222 (S.D. Fla. 2006); *In re U.S. Bioscience Sec. Litig.*, 155 F.R.D. 116, 121 (E.D. Pa. 1994); *In re Janney Montgomery Scott LLC Fin. Consultant Litig.*, Master File No. 06-32-2, 2009 WL 2137224, at *12 (E.D. Pa. Jul. 16, 2009).

128. Comm. on Prof'l Responsibility, *supra* note 125, at 840.

129. *Wesley v. Spear, Leeds & Kellogg*, 711 F. Supp. 713, 720 (E.D.N.Y. 1989).

130. *Id.* (citations omitted); *see also Stevens v. Safeway, Inc.*, No. CV-05-01988, 2008 U.S. Dist. LEXIS 17119 (C.D. Cal. Feb. 25, 2008) (citing *Wesley*, 711 F. Supp. at 720).

131. *Staton v. Boeing Co.*, 327 F.3d 938, 977 (9th Cir. 2003); *see also Rodriguez v. West Publ'g Corp.*, 563 F. 3d 948, 960 (9th Cir. 2009) (extending reasoning behind *Staton* to incentive agreements).

may lead [class representatives] . . . to compromise the interest of the class for personal gain."[132]

In *Wesley v. Spear, Leeds & Kellogg*, plaintiffs' counsel asked the court to award the class representative a $5,000 incentive award.[133] Although the class representative took time away from work to respond to the defendant's document requests and attend depositions, the court found that he did not perform any extraordinary services for the class to warrant such an award.[134] In denying the request for the incentive award, the court noted the class representative's motivations for bringing the action.[135] The court remarked that "[i]n light of [the class representative's] reasons for commencing suit he will no doubt be well satisfied with the settlement and content to share in it equally with the Class."[136] Thus, the court in *Weseley* mitigated any potential conflicts between the class representative and the other class members by denying the request for the incentive award and awarding the class representative a share equal to that of the other class members.

In *Staton v. Boeing Co.*, the incentive award amount for the class representatives and other identified class members was more than 16 times greater than the amount received by other class members.[137] The court held that there was no justification for the "very large differential in the amount of damage awards," and therefore the settlement agreement was unfair.[138] The court reasoned that if the class representatives supported the settlement agreement, and the agreement treated other class members equally, then "the likelihood that the settlement is forwarding the class's interests to the maximum degree practically possible increases."[139] However, here, the agreement substantially failed to treat other class members equally.[140] The court's concern was that class representatives were more focused on their own interests than the interests of the class as a whole.[141]

Incentive awards may also facilitate collusion between class representatives, class counsel, and defendants, causing many courts to view them with heightened skepticism. Collusion may occur when the class representative and the defendants essentially make what amounts to a separate deal—the incentive award—against the interests of other class members.[142] Class representatives "with something

---

132. *Hadix*, 322 F.3d at 897 (citations omitted); *see also Sauby*, 2009 U.S. Dist. LEXIS 70270, at *4–5.

133. 711 F. Supp. 713, 720.

134. *Id.*

135. *Id.* at 721.

136. *Id.*

137. 327 F.3d 938, 946.

138. *Id.* at 978.

139. *Id.* at 977.

140. *Id.*

141. *Id.*

142. *Women's Comm. for Equal Employment Opportunity v. Nat'l Broad. Co.*, 76 F.R.D. 173, 180 (S.D.N.Y. 1977).

extra to gain are not motivated to hold out for higher awards for the rest of the class."[143] This raises "grave problems of collusion."[144] The class action mechanism should not be "used as a hammer at the head of the defendant for the purpose of extracting benefits for [class representatives] at the expense of members of the class."[145] Therefore, "[s]ettlements entailing disproportionately greater benefits to [class representatives] are proper only when the totality of circumstances combine to dispel the 'cloud of collusion which such a settlement suggests.'"[146]

In *Franks v. Kroger Co.*, one class representative received an incentive award of $10,000 and a promotion.[147] The other class representative received $500.[148] The remaining class members merely received an opportunity to present individual claims and the defendant's general agreement to treat its employees equally.[149] The court invalidated the incentive award because it was unfair, unreasonable, and completely against the best interests of the class members, and failed to treat class representatives and other class members equally.[150] In concurrence, Justice Merritt was concerned with possible collusion between the class representatives and the defendant because of the huge disparity between the class representatives' awards and the other class members' relief.[151]

In *Women's Committee for Equal Employment Opportunity v. National Broadcasting Co.*, one aspect of the settlement agreement provided for a separate payment to class representatives.[152] The court expressed reservations about this aspect of the agreement.[153] Nevertheless, the court approved the class representatives' incentive award.[154] In doing so, the court reasoned that many factors in the case combined "to dispel the cloud of collusion which such a settlement suggests."[155] First, the court examined the effect of the settlement to the entire class, finding that it afforded substantial relief to the entire class.[156] Second, the court considered the likelihood of collusion, finding that it was minimized by the participation of the

---

143. Comm. on Prof'l Responsibility, *supra* note 125, at 840.

144. *Women's Comm. for Equal Employment Opportunity*, 76 F.R.D. at 180.

145. *Franks v. Kroger Co.*, 649 F.2d 1216, 1227 (6th Cir. 1981) (Merritt, J., concurring), *rev'd on other grounds after reh'g*, *Franks v. Kroger*, 670 F.2d 71 (6th Cir. 1982); *see also* Comm. on Prof'l Responsibility, *supra* note 125, at 840 n.55.

146. *Holmes v. Cont'l Can Co.*, 706 F.2d 1144, 1148 (11th Cir. 1983) (citing *Women's Comm. for Equal Employment Opportunity*, 76 F.R.D. at 182).

147. 649 F.2d 1216, 1225.

148. *Id.*

149. *Id.*

150. *Id.*

151. *Id.* at 1227.

152. 76 F.R.D. at 180.

153. *Id.* at 175.

154. *Id.* at 182.

155. *Id.*

156. *Id.* at 181.

Equal Employment Opportunity Commission in the settlement negotiations.[157] Third, the court noted the lack of objections to the agreement at the settlement hearing.[158] Fourth, the court reasoned that the agreement did not foreclose other class members from bringing individual claims.[159] Fifth, the court examined the class representatives' involvement in the litigation and found that the representatives "undertook significant obligations, perhaps at some risk to job security and good will with coworkers, resulting in broad-ranging benefits to the class."[160] Finally, the court remarked on the general public policy in favor of amicable settlement of legal disputes, especially in cases involving Title VII, as in this litigation.[161] These six factors alleviated concerns of collusion between the class representatives, class counsel, and the defendants at the expense of other class members.

Another ethical concern associated with incentive awards is the possibility that they will lead to bidding wars among class counsel to attract class representatives.[162] As a result, plaintiffs will be persuaded to sign up with the highest-bidding lawyer.[163] "It is not difficult to envision a scenario . . . of prospective named plaintiffs becoming involved in a bidding war (with the ante spiraling upward for their 'services') with prospective class counsel."[164] In *In re Gould Securities Litigation*, several class representatives moved the court for an order allocating part of the settlement as an incentive award.[165] The class representatives argued that they deserved the award because they undertook the burden and responsibility of litigating the class action.[166] The court denied the request for an incentive award.[167] The court reasoned that "the real danger [of incentive awards] is a potentially undesirable precedent where every named plaintiff would expect a 'fee' or 'bounty' for the use of his or her name to create a class action."[168] The court's primary concern was that incentive awards would potentially lead to bidding wars among potential class counsel in future cases. On this basis, the court refused to approve the incentive award.[169]

However, the Committee on Professional Responsibility for the Bar Association of New York City (the Committee) does not accept the proposition that the risk of

---

157. *Id.*
158. *Id.*
159. *Id.* at 182.
160. *Id.*
161. *Id.*
162. Comm. on Prof'l Responsibility, *supra* note 125, at 839.
163. *Id.*
164. *In re Gould Sec. Litig.*, 727 F. Supp. 1201, 1209 (N.D. Ill. 1989).
165. *Id.* at 1208–09.
166. *Id.* at 1209.
167. *Id.*
168. *Id.*
169. *Id.*

bidding wars is sufficient to implement a complete ban on incentive awards.[170] The Committee believes that "[s]ince the incentive award is not granted until the class action has neared or reached completion, the trial court can at that point assess whether any improprieties have occurred in the retention of the attorney by the named plaintiff (or vice versa)."[171] Thus, the Committee relies heavily on the judicial system to ferret out and deter any bidding wars among class counsel to attract class representatives.

The ethical concerns associated with incentive awards to plaintiff class representatives are numerous and often complex. They present an ethical minefield and invite objections to the settlement. Any proposed payments to class representatives must be tailored with the guidelines outlined above in mind. More importantly, the parties must disclose fully to the court the details of the rationale and amount of such payments—whether paid by plaintiffs' counsel or the defendant—particularly in the "post–Milberg Weiss" world in which judges scrutinize such payments.

VII. Lawyers as Plaintiffs in Class Actions

Another ethical issue arises in class actions when a lawyer concurrently serves as class representative and class counsel. Similarly, ethical issues arise when a lawyer's firm serves as class counsel while a lawyer within the firm acts as class representative. Ethical problems also materialize when a person close to a class counsel, such as a relative or lawyer from another firm, serves as class representative.[172] In such situations, courts may either disqualify the class counsel or refuse to certify the class.[173] A class representative who is, or has a close relationship with, class counsel may not adequately protect the interests of the class because of the inherent conflict of interest resulting from the potential recovery of attorney fees.[174]

In California, a lawyer may not concurrently serve as both class representative and class counsel because of the inherent conflict of interest.[175] The class representative's primary duty is to advance the interests of the class, especially during

---

170. Comm. on Prof'l Responsibility, *supra* note 125, at 840.

171. *Id.*

172. *See Kesler v. Ikea, Inc.*, No. SACV 07-00568-JVS, 2008 U.S. Dist. LEXIS 97555, at *11–12 (C.D. Cal. Feb. 4, 2008).

173. *See Apple Computer, Inc. v. Superior Court*, 126 Cal. App. 4th 1253, 1267 (2005).

174. *See* Debra Lyn Bassett, *When Reform Is Not Enough: Assuring More than Merely "Adequate" Representation in Class Actions*, 38 GA. L. REV. 927, 950 (2004).

175. *Apple Computer*, 126 Cal. App. 4th at 1272. A majority of jurisdictions prohibit a lawyer from concurrently serving as both class representative and class counsel. *See, e.g., Shroder v. Suburban Coastal Corp.*, 729 F.2d 1371, 1375 (11th Cir. 1984); *Susman v. Lincoln Am. Corp.*, 561 F.2d 86, 90 (7th Cir. 1977); *Kramer v. Scientific Control Corp.*, 534 F.2d 1085, 1090 (3d Cir. 1976); *Turoff v. May Co.*, 531 F.2d 1357, 1360 (6th Cir. 1976); *King v. Frank*, 328 F. Supp. 2d 940, 950 (W.D. Wis. 2004); *Miller v. Mercedes-Benz USA, LLC*, No. CV 06-05382 ABC, 2009 U.S. Dist. LEXIS 45512, at *6–7 (C.D. Cal. May 15, 2009).

settlement negotiations.[176] When one lawyer serves dual roles of class counsel and class representative, there is an overwhelming temptation to sacrifice the interests of the class in favor of maximizing attorney fees.[177] The class counsel may recommend less favorable settlement terms to the class members because a large attorney fee may be part of the bargain.[178] The court's goal is to ensure that the class representative is concerned with the class members' interests throughout the litigation.[179] Therefore, "[i]f the interests of the class are to be fairly and adequately protected, if the courts and the public are to be free of manufactured litigation, and if proceedings are to be without cloud, the roles of class representative and of class attorney cannot be played by the same person."[180]

The same rationale applies when a lawyer's firm serves as class counsel and a lawyer or other employee in that firm acts as class representative.[181] As the class representative, the lawyer has an obligation to seek the maximum recovery for the class; however, the lawyer's firm may have an interest in maximizing their recovery of attorney fees.[182] The lawyer must choose between his duty as the class representative and his motivations as a firm employee. This results in an "insurmountable conflict of interest."[183]

In addition, those close to class counsel, such as a relative or lawyer from another firm with a close business connection to the class counsel, should not serve as the class representative—at least in California.[184] For relatives, the concern is that

> [i]n situations where there is a close familial bond between the class counsel and class representative . . . [,] there is a clear danger that the representative may have some interests in conflict with the best interests of the class as a whole when making decisions that could have an impact on attorney fees.[185]

Where a lawyer from another firm acts as class representative, the test in California for possible disqualification of counsel of record is whether there is a "close business connection" between the class counsel and the lawyer who is serving as class representative.[186] The class representative's close business connection to the

---

176. *Apple Computer*, 126 Cal. App. 4th at 1265.

177. *Id.*

178. *Id.* at 1278.

179. *Id.*

180. *Id.* (citations omitted).

181. *Id.* at 1261.

182. *Id.*

183. *Id.*

184. *Id.* at 1279. Other jurisdictions also follow this rule. *See, e.g., Zylstra v. Safeway Stores, Inc.*, 578 F.2d 102, 104 (5th Cir. 1978); *Susman*, 561 F.2d 86; *Hale v. Citibank, N.A.*, 198 F.R.D. 606 (S.D.N.Y. 2001); *Jaroslawicz v. Safety Kleen Corp.*, 151 F.R.D. 324 (N.D. Ill. 1993).

185. *Petrovic v. Amoco Oil Co.*, 200 F.3d 1140, 1155 (8th Cir. 1999).

186. *Apple Computer*, 126 Cal. App. 4th at 1274.

class counsel may result in "a significant financial interest in maintaining" the class counsel's goodwill.[187] The class representative may be tempted to choose her own financial interest over the class's interests. As a result, the class representative's financial interests and the class's interests are in conflict.[188]

In *Apple Computer, Inc. v. Superior Court*, a plaintiff's lawyer, Lawrence Cagney, filed a class action on behalf of himself and others similarly situated against Apple Computer.[189] The complaint alleged a violation of California's unfair competition law.[190] Cagney was the class representative in the lawsuit.[191] Cagney's own law firm, Westrup Klick, and another firm, Law Offices of Allan A. Sigel (Sigel), served as class counsel.[192] In the past, Sigel had served as cocounsel with Westrup Klick in a number of class actions.[193] Troubled by the representation, Apple Computer filed a motion to disqualify both Westrup Klick and Sigel; however, the trial court denied the motion.[194] On appeal, the court commanded the trial court to vacate its order denying Apple Computer's motion to disqualify Westrup Klick and Sigel.[195] The court ordered the trial court to grant Apple's disqualification motion, thereby precluding Westrup Klick and Sigel from representing Cagney and the class.[196]

As to Westrup Klick's disqualification, the court's concern was that Cagney, as the class representative, would choose to maximize his firm's attorney fees over the class members' recovery.[197] The court feared Cagney would permit less favorable settlement terms for the class in exchange for a more favorable attorney fee award for his firm.[198] Therefore, the court concluded that if Westrup Klick acted as class counsel, Cagney could not adequately protect the interests of the class.[199] Westrup Klick's disqualification as class counsel remedied this concern.

As to Sigel's disqualification, the court examined the close business connection between Cagney, Westrup Klick, and Sigel.[200] The court noted that "'a conflict of interest [may exist] based on the relationship between the class representative and class counsel even though the class representative will not share in attorney fees from that case.'"[201] Then the court focused on the fact that Sigel and

---

187. *Id.* at 1276.
188. *Id.*
189. *Id.* at 1262.
190. *Id.*
191. *Id.* at 1261.
192. *Id.* at 1262.
193. *Id.*
194. *Id.*
195. *Id.* at 1279–80.
196. *Id.* at 1279.
197. *Id.* at 1261.
198. *Id.* at 1264–65.
199. *Id.* at 1265.
200. *Id.* at 1274.
201. *Id.* at 1275 (citations omitted).

Westrup Klick were cocounsel on 13 other class actions.[202] More importantly, six of those actions were still pending.[203] The court reasoned that because Cagney, as an employee of Westrup Klick, could benefit from attorney fees in the other actions, he was not sufficiently independent to serve as the class representative in the current action.[204] "Here, in light of the financial relationship and interdependence between Cagney and [Sigel], Cagney may acquiesce in, rather than monitor, [Sigel]'s decisions, and [Sigel] may benefit from the situation by seeking to maximize its recovery of attorneys' fees."[205] The court feared that Cagney would protect the business relationship with Sigel over the interests of the class.[206] Sigel's disqualification remedied this concern.

In the wake of *Apple Computer*, it is clear that a lawyer may not concurrently serve as both class representative and class counsel in California. Moreover, those close to class counsel, such as a relative or lawyer from another firm with a close business connection to the class counsel, should not serve as the class representative because of the apparent, if not inherent, conflict of interest associated with such representation. Class counsel should be aware of these principles and concerns when selecting a class representative in any state. Counsel also should recognize the California courts' increasing concern with "manufactured" class actions and the need for truly independent class representatives.

VIII. Ethical Challenges Presented by Reverse Auctions

Closely related to concerns regarding class representation are the ethical challenges presented by reverse auctions. The term "reverse auction" generally refers to situations involving different teams of plaintiffs' lawyers in various actions involving the same underlying allegations where defense lawyers seek out the plaintiffs' lawyer willing to agree to the lowest settlement.[207] A reverse auction is often a result of structural collusion and allows the defense lawyers to shop for favorable settlement terms by contacting numerous plaintiffs' lawyers or inducing them to compete against one another until the lowest bidder among the plaintiffs' lawyers wins the right to settle with the defendant.[208] Many courts view reverse auctions as a

---

202. *Id.* at 1276.

203. *Id.*

204. *Id.*

205. *Id.* at 1276–77.

206. *Id.* at 1276.

207. *See* John C. Coffee, Jr., *Class Wars: The Dilemma of the Mass Tort Class Action*, 95 COLUM. L. REV. 1343, 1369–73 (1995) (coining the term "reverse auction"); *see also Reynolds v. Beneficial Nat'l Bank*, 288 F.3d 277, 282 (7th Cir. 2002) (referring to reverse auction as situation in which defendant chooses "the most ineffectual class lawyers to negotiate a settlement with in the hope that the district court will approve a weak settlement that will preclude other claims against the defendant").

208. Coffee, *supra* note 207, at 1354.

legitimate threat to class action plaintiffs.[209] Other courts, however, view reverse auction arguments with greater skepticism, requiring more concrete evidence of collusion among the parties.[210]

Scholars often place the blame for reverse auctions on greedy plaintiffs' lawyers who may be willing to unscrupulously collude with defense counsel to ensure the plaintiffs' counsel receives attorney fees.[211] This is because plaintiffs' lawyers fear that rejecting a defendant's low settlement offer will cause the defendant to look elsewhere for a lower settlement, in turn causing the lawyer to miss out on attorney fees altogether.[212] However, not all plaintiffs' lawyers who find themselves in potential reverse auction situations are entirely self-serving. In some instances, the plaintiffs' lawyer has incurred significant expenses in prosecuting the case, potentially even rejecting settlement offers they deem not to be in their clients' best interest, only to be undercut by another, less honorable, plaintiffs' lawyer.[213] Still other scholars place equal, if not greater, blame on defendants and defense counsel who they claim seek out the least effective plaintiffs' counsel and improperly leverage their bargaining power to effect a settlement that is not in the best interest of the class members.[214]

Regardless of which lawyer is to blame, current and potential class members often bear the brunt of the detrimental effects of reverse auctions. Because of the fact that a final judgment in any court in which the various plaintiffs' claims are pending will have res judicata effect, plaintiffs' counsel are faced with the prospect of an entirely different lawyer who knows nothing about their clients' best interests settling their clients' claims.[215] This is also true in federal courts, where res judicata effect must be given to valid state court judgments, even where a state

---

209. *See, e.g., In re Comty. Bank of N. Va.*, 418 F.3d 277, 308 (3d Cir. 2005); *Reynolds*, 288 F.3d at 282; *Figueroa*, 517 F. Supp. 2d at 1306.

210. *Negrete v. Allianz Life Ins. Co. of N. Am.*, 523 F.3d 1091, 1099–1100 (9th Cir. 2008); *Rutter & Wilbanks Corp. v. Shell Oil Co.*, 314 F.3d 1180, 1189 (10th Cir. 2002) (noting "reverse auction argument would lead to conclusion that no settlement could ever occur in the circumstances of parallel or multiple class actions—none of the competing cases could settle without being accused by another of participating in a collusive reverse auction."); *see also Int'l Union, United Auto., Aerospace & Agric. Implement Workers of Am. v. Gen. Motors Corp.*, 497 F.3d 615, 628 (6th Cir. 2007) (noting that "courts customarily demand evidence of improper incentives for the class representative or class counsel . . .").

211. Samuel Issacharoff & Richard Nagareda, *Class Settlements under Attack*, 156 U. PA. L. REV. 1649, 1667–68 (2008); Chris Brummer, *Sharpening the Sword: Class Certification, Appellate Review and the Role of the Fiduciary Judge in Class Action Lawsuits*, 104 COLUM. L. REV. 1042, 1048 n.50 (2004).

212. Brian W. Warwick, *Class Action Settlement Collusion: Let's Not Sue Class Counsel Quite Yet . . .*, 22 AM. J. TRIAL ADVOC. 605, 613 (1999).

213. *Id.*

214. *Id.* at 612; *see also* Issacharoff & Nagareda, *supra* note 211, at 1667–68; Allan Kanner & Tibor Nagy, *Exploding the Blackmail Myth: A New Perspective on Class Action Settlements*, 57 BAYLOR L. REV. 681, 699 (2005) (noting defendant has "options" and is not bound by settlement demands of single plaintiff).

215. *See Matsushita Elec. Indus. v. Epstein*, 516 U.S. 367, 369 (1996); Kanner & Nagy, *supra* note 214, at 699.

court judgment incorporates a class action settlement releasing claims exclusively within the federal courts' jurisdiction.[216]

While plaintiffs' claims are clearly impacted by res judicata, the collusive nature of reverse auctions may also lead to attempts by defense counsel to convince a court to enjoin other courts from hearing related cases even *before* a judgment or settlement is reached in the enjoining court. For example, in *Negrete v. Allianz Life Insurance Co. of North America*,[217] the district court considered class action allegations that had led to related lawsuits in other federal and state courts. The district court issued an order requiring (1) authorization of all settlement discussions in the other cases by the *Negrete* plaintiffs' counsel and (2) authorization by the *Negrete* court of any proposed settlement in one of those courts that resolved the claims before the *Negrete* court.[218]

Although the district court did not technically issue an injunction, the Ninth Circuit analyzed the order as such because it had the practical effect of an injunction and had potentially irreparable consequences for the plaintiffs in the other jurisdictions.[219] The court then considered the order under the All Writs Act,[220] which permits federal courts to issue all necessary and appropriate writs in aid of their jurisdiction, and the Anti-Injunction Act,[221] which precludes federal courts from granting injunctions to stay state proceedings in all but three specific situations.[222] The court noted first that the district court abused its discretion under the All Writs Act because it is improper for a district court to enjoin parties before other district courts from participating in or reaching a bona fide settlement.[223] This is especially so when, as in the case before the *Negrete* court, there is no settlement pending in the enjoining court.[224]

The court also found that the case before the district court did not fall within one of the three specifically defined exceptions to the Anti-Injunction Act, rendering the district court's attempts to enjoin settlement discussion in the pending state actions improper.[225] The court found that the district court abused its discre-

---

216. *Matsushita*, 516 U.S. at 373–74.

217. 523 F.3d at 1094–95.

218. *Id.* at 1095.

219. *Id.* at 1097.

220. 28 U.S.C. § 1651.

221. 28 U.S.C. § 2283.

222. *Id.* at 1090, 1100–01 (citing *Atl. Coast Line R.R. Co. v. Bhd. of Locomotive Eng'rs*, 398 U.S. 281, 286–87 (1970)); *see also* 28 U.S.C. §§ 1651, 2283.

223. *Negrete*, 523 F.3d at 1099 (citing *Grider v. Keystone Health Plan Cent., Inc.*, 500 F.3d 322, 326–27 (3d Cir. 2007)).

224. *Id.*

225. *Id.* at 1103.

tion by issuing the order, noting that the court "must live with the vicissitudes and consequences of our elegantly messy federal system."[226]

The *Negrete* court's protection of plaintiffs in suits pending in multiple jurisdictions appears to be an example of the judiciary acting in a fiduciary capacity with respect to class action plaintiffs.[227] Many courts subscribe to this theory, noting that the district judge in the settlement phase of a class action suit is a fiduciary of the class and is subject to a heightened duty of care.[228] As a result of their heightened duty of care, judges have an obligation to scrutinize closely proposed settlements reached in circumstances that appear susceptible to collusion.[229] This is especially true when parties reach a proposed settlement prior to class certification because the parties will have had little, if any, opportunity to conduct discovery on the merits.[230] When courts properly fulfill their duty, this heightened scrutiny provides further protection for class action plaintiffs from potential collusion between counsel.

Although the courts play a major role in protecting class members from collusion, various scholars have suggested additional approaches for combating reverse auctions. Among these are consolidation of cases, exit, and ex post bids. First, reverse auctions may be minimized if courts take steps to transfer all class actions filed on behalf of the same class to a single court and consolidate them into a single proceeding.[231] Consolidation would arguably alleviate pressure on plaintiffs' counsel to beat one another to a settlement while minimizing waste.[232]

A second approach would be to enhance the "exit" option by increasing the opt-out rights of class members.[233] If class members have greater opportunities to opt out of a given class action suit, they may be more likely to do so. Those who do choose to opt out would not be bound by any release of claims granted by plaintiffs' counsel in that action.[234]

Finally, at least one scholar has suggested the use of an ex post bid approach.[235] An ex post bid approach is one in which a member of the class who objects to a

---

226. *Id.*

227. *But see* John C. Coffee, Jr., *Class Action Accountability: Reconciling Exit, Voice, and Loyalty in Representative Litigation*, 100 COLUM. L. REV. 370, 392 n.54 (noting author's opinion that current interpretation of All Writs Act provides little protection for class members).

228. *See, e.g., In re Comty. Bank of N. Va.*, 418 F.3d at 318–19; *Culver City v. City of Milwaukee*, 277 F.3d 908, 915 (7th Cir. 2002); *Reynolds*, 288 F.3d at 279–80; *see also* Brummer, *supra* note 211, at 1052–53.

229. *Reynolds*, 288 F.3d at 284.

230. *See D'Amato v. Deutsche Bank*, 236 F.3d, 78, 85 (2d Cir. 2001); *County of Suffolk v. Long Island Lighting Co.*, 907 F.2d 1295, 1323 (2d Cir. 1990).

231. Rhonda Wasserman, *Dueling Class Actions*, 80 B.U. L. REV. 461, 508 (2000).

232. *Id.; see also* Chapter 12, "Multidistrict Litigation."

233. Coffee, *Class Action Accountability*, *supra* note 227, at 377.

234. *Id.* at 434.

235. *See* Geoffrey P. Miller, *Competing Bids in Class Action Settlements*, 31 HOFSTRA L. REV. 633, 639 (2003).

proposed settlement would guarantee (e.g., in the form of a bond for the amount of the recovery proposed in the settlement) that the class would not be less well off if the court transferred lead class counsel rights to another plaintiffs' lawyer.[236] An ex post bid might be beneficial in the reverse auction context where (1) counsel for overlapping class actions have a strong incentive to object to a collusive settlement in order to protect their own investment and clients; (2) the lawyer has a wealth of knowledge about the case; and (3) the lawyer knows with some certainty that the proposed settlement falls short of what the class could obtain absent collusion.[237] While each of these solutions involves various pros and cons, they demonstrate the legal community's recognition of the reverse auction problem, thereby highlighting the need for lawyers to understand and avoid the problem.

---

236. *Id.*
237. *Id.* at 649.

PART III

JURISDICTIONAL SURVEY OF LOCAL REQUIREMENTS GOVERNING CLASS ACTIONS

ALABAMA

KERMIT L. KENDRICK

I. Introduction

Since its enactment, Alabama Rule of Civil Procedure 23 has mirrored Federal Rule of Civil Procedure 23 (as amended in 1966),[1] and has generally been applied in an analogous fashion. This symmetry was interrupted beginning in 1998 with a series of amendments to the Federal Rule.[2] However, despite these amendments, the Alabama Supreme Court has recently stated that "Rule 23 of the Alabama Rules of Civil Procedure reads the same as Rule 23 of the Federal Rules, and we consider federal case law on class actions to be persuasive authority for the interpretation of our own Rule 23."[3]

II. Pre–Class Certification Procedure

Alabama Code Section 6-5-641,[4] enacted in 1999, outlines the procedure for class certification in Alabama and represents the most significant difference between Alabama and Federal Rule 23. Section 6-5-641(b) requires an Alabama state court judge, as soon as practicable, to "hold a conference among all named parties to the action for the purpose of establishing a schedule . . . for any discovery in which the parties may wish to engage which is allowed under the Alabama Rules of Civil Procedure 26-37, and are (2) germane to the issue of whether the requested class should be certified." At this conference, the court can set the date for a hearing on the issue of class certification, but not sooner than 90 days after the date on which

---

1. Rule 23 of the Alabama Rules of Civil Procedure does not apply in state small claims court.

2. *See* Appendix A for the text of each amendment and excerpts from the committee notes.

3. *See, e.g., Ryan v. Patterson*, 23 So. 2d 12, 17 (Ala. 2009) (citing *Adams v. Robertson*, 676 So. 2d 1265, 1268 (Ala. 1995)); *Reynolds Metals Co. v. Hill*, 825 So. 2d 100, 104 n.1 (Ala. 2002); Gregory C. Cook, *The Alabama Class Action: Does It Exist Any Longer? And Does It Matter?*, 66 ALA. LAWYER 289 (2005).

4. *See* Appendix B for the text of ALA. CODE § 6-5-641.

the court issues its scheduling order. Additionally, upon motion of either party, a state court judge must stay all discovery on the merits until the court makes its decision regarding certification.[5] Accordingly, Alabama has a mandatory bifurcated class certification process. There is no corresponding process under the Federal Rule.

III. Time to Appeal Class Certification Decisions

As mentioned above, in 1998 Congress began amending Rule 23 of the Federal Rules of Civil Procedure. In one such amendment, subpart (f) was added to make available interlocutory appeal from a class certification decision. The Alabama Rule did not provide for an interlocutory appeal process, thereby evidencing a gap between the Federal Rules and the Alabama Rules. The Alabama legislature reconciled this difference in 1999 by enacting Alabama Code Section 6-5-642,[6] which established a right of appeal from a class certification decision. The Alabama legislature went farther than Congress by making it mandatory for an Alabama appeals court to accept appeals from class certification decisions. Under the Federal Rule, the appeal is taken at the discretion of the appeals court. Additionally, the time to appeal in Alabama is different from the Federal Rule. Currently, Section 6-5-642 provides a 42-day window to appeal a class certification decision, and the Federal Rule only provides for a 14-day window.

IV. Appointment of Class Counsel

Unlike Federal Rule 23, the Alabama Rule contains no corresponding provision regarding the appointment of class counsel.

V. Attorney Fees

Subpart (h) of the Federal Rule provides guidance for the federal court in assessing attorney fees. It does not purport to provide a new mechanism for awarding such fees, but serves only to guide the court when fee awards are already available by statute. Again, these provisions reinforce the aim of active judicial supervision of the federal class action. Alabama has not yet adopted any provisions like subpart (h). Instead, Alabama courts will usually apply either the lodestar theory or the common benefit theory to award attorney fees in class actions.[7]

---

5. ALA. CODE § 6-5-641(c).

6. *See* Appendix B for the text of ALA. CODE § 6-5-642.

7. *Ala. Alcoholic Beverage Control Bd. v. City of Pelham*, 855 So. 2d 1070 (Ala. 2003); *City of Birmingham v. Horn*, 810 So. 2d 667 (Ala. 2001); *see also* Chapter 8, "Attorney Fee Awards and Incentive Payments."

APPENDIX A: FEDERAL RULE OF CIVIL PROCEDURE 23[8]

1998 AMENDMENT

(f) APPEALS. A court of appeals may in its discretion permit an appeal from an order of a district court granting or denying class action certification under this rule if application is made to it within ten days after entry of the order. An appeal does not stay proceedings in the district court unless the district judge or the court of appeals so orders.[9]

2003 AMENDMENT

(c) [Determination] Determining by Order Whether to Certify a Class Action [to Be Maintained]; Appointing Class Counsel; Notice and Membership in Class; Judgment: [Actions Conducted in Partially as Class Actions] Multiple Classes and Subclasses.

(1) [As soon as practicable after the commencement of an action brought] (A) When a person sues or is sued as a representative of a class, the court must—at an early practicable time—determine by order whether to certify the action as a class action [, the court shall determine by order whether it is to be so maintained].

(B) An order certifying a class action must define the class and the class claims, issues, or defenses, and must appoint class counsel under Rule 23(g).

(C) An order under [this subdivision may be conditional, and] Rule 23(c) (1) may be altered or amended before [the decision on the merits] final judgment.

(2) [In] (A) For any class certified under Rule 23 (b)(1) or (2), the court may direct appropriate notice to the class.

(B) For any class [action maintained] certified under [subdivision (b)(3)] Rule 23(b)(3), the court [shall] must direct to [the] class members [of the class] the best notice practicable under the circumstances, including individual notice to all members who can be identified through reasonable effort. The notice [shall advise each member that (A)] must concisely and clearly state in plain easily understood language:

- the nature of the action,
- the definition of the class certified,
- the class claims, issues, or defenses,

---

8. All underlined portions of an amendment are additions; all bracketed language has been removed.
9. 5 JAMES WM. MOORE ET AL., MOORE'S FEDERAL PRACTICE § 23App.06(1) (3d ed. 1999).

- that a class member may enter an appearance through counsel if the member so desires,
- that the court will exclude [the member] from the class [if the] any member [so] who requests [by a specified date; (B) the judgment, whether favorable or not, will include all members who do not request exclusion; and (C) any member who does not request exclusion may, if the member desires, enter an appearance through counsel] exclusion, starting when and how members may elect to be excluded, and
- the binding effect of a class judgment on class members under Rule 23(c)(3).

(3) The judgment in an action maintained as a class action under subdivision (b)(1) or (b)(2), whether or not favorable to the class, shall include and describe those whom the court finds to be members of the class. The judgment in an action maintained as a class action under subdivision (b)(3), whether or not favorable to the class, shall include and specify or describe those to whom the notice provided in subdivision (c)(2) was directed, and who have not requested exclusion, and whom the court finds to be members of the class.

(4) When appropriate (A) an action may be brought or maintained as a class action with respect to particular issues, or (B) a class may be divided into subclasses and each subclass treated as a class, and the provisions of this rule shall then be construed and applied accordingly.

(e) **Settlement, Voluntary Dismissal, or Compromise.** [A class action shall not be dismissed or compromised without the approval of the court, and notice of the proposed dismissal or compromise shall be given to all members of the class in such manner as the court directs.]

(1) (A) The court must approve any settlement, voluntary dismissal, or compromise of the claims, issues, or defenses of a certified class.

(B) The court must direct notice in a reasonable manner to all class members who would be bound by a proposed settlement, voluntary dismissal, or compromise.

(C) The court may approve a settlement, voluntary dismissal, or compromise that would bind class members only after a hearing an on finding that the settlement, voluntary dismissal, or compromise is fair, reasonable, and adequate.

(2) The parties seeking approval of a settlement, voluntary dismissal, or compromise under Rule 23(e)(1) must file a statement identifying and agreement made in connection with the proposed settlement, voluntary or dismissal, or compromise.

(3) In an action previously certified as a class action under Rule 23(b)(3), the court may refuse to approve a settlement unless it affords a new opportunity to request exclusion to individual class members who had an earlier opportunity to request exclusion but did not do so.

(4) (A) Any class member may object to a proposed settlement, voluntary dismissal, or compromise that requires court approval under Rule 23(e)(1)(A).

(B) An objection made under Rule 23(e)(4)(A) may be withdrawn only with the court's approval.

(g) **Class Counsel.**

(1) *Appointing Class Counsel.*

(A) Unless a statute provides otherwise, a court that certifies a class must appoint class counsel.

(B) An attorney appointed to serve as class counsel must fairly and adequately represent the interests of the class.

(C) In appointing class counsel, the court

(i) must consider:

- the work counsel has done in identifying or investigating potential claims in the action,
- counsel's experience in handling class actions, other complex litigation, and claims of the type asserted in the action,
- counsel's knowledge of the applicable law, and
- the resources counsel will commit to representing the class;

(ii) may consider any other matter pertinent to counsel's ability to fairly and adequately represent the interests of the class;

(iii) may direct potential class counsel to provide information on any subject pertinent to the appointment and to propose terms for attorney fees and nontaxable costs; and

(iv) may make further orders in connection with the appointment.

(2) *Appointment Procedure.*

(A) The court may designate interim counsel to act on behalf of the putative class before determining whether to certify the action as a class action.

(B) When there is one applicant for appointment as class counsel, the court may appoint that applicant only if the applicant is adequate under Rule 23(g)(1)(B) and (C). If more than one adequate applicant seeks appointment as class counsel, the court must appoint the applicant best able to represent the interests of the class.

(C) The order appointing class counsel may include provisions about the award of attorney fees or nontaxable costs under Rule 23(h).

(h) **Attorney Fees Award.** In an action certified as a class action, the court may award reasonable attorney fees and nontaxable costs authorized by law or by agreement of the parties as follows:

(1) *Motion for Award of Attorney Fees.* A claim for an award of attorney fees and nontaxable costs must be made by motion under Rule 54(d)(2), subject to

provisions of this subdivision, at a time set by the court. Notice of the motion must be served on all parties and, for motions by class counsel, directed to class members in a reasonable manner.

(2) *Objections to Motion.* A class member, or a party from whom payment is sought, may object to the motion.

(3) *Hearing and Findings.* The court may hold a hearing and must find the facts and state its conclusions of law on the motion under Rule 52(a).

(4) *Reference to Special Master or Magistrate Judge.* The court may refer issues related to the amount of the award to a special master or to a magistrate judge as provided in Rule 54(d)(2)(D).[10]

COMMENTARY

Subdivision (c). Subdivision (c) is amended in several respects. The requirement that the court determine whether to certify a class "as soon as practicable after commencement of an action" is replaced by requiring determination "at an early practicable time." The notice provisions are substantially revised.

Paragraph (1). Subdivision (c)(1)(A) is changed to require that the determination whether to certify a class be made "at an early practicable time." The "as soon as practicable" exaction neither reflects prevailing practice nor captures the many valid reasons that may justify deferring the initial certification decision. *See* Willging, Hooper & Niemic, *Empirical Study of Class Actions in Four Federal District Courts: Final Report to the Advisory Committee on Civil Rules 26-36* (Federal Judicial Center 1996).

Time may be needed to gather information necessary to make the certification decision. Although an evaluation of the probable outcome on the merits is not properly part of the certification decision, discovery in aid of the certification decision often includes information required to identify the nature of the issues that actually will be presented at trial. In this sense it is appropriate to conduct controlled discovery into the "merits," limited to those aspects relevant to making the certification decision on an informed basis. Active judicial supervision may be required to achieve the most effective balance that expedites an informed certification determination without forcing an artificial and ultimately wasteful division between "certification discovery" and "merits discovery." A critical need is to determine how the case will be tried. An increasing number of courts require a party requesting class certification to present a "trial plan" that describes the issues likely to be presented at trial and tests whether they are susceptible of class-wide proof. *See Manual for Complex Litigation (Third)* § 21.213, at 44; § 30.11, at 214; § 30.12, at 215 (1995).

---

10. *Id.* at § 23App.07(1).

Other considerations may affect the timing of the certification decision. The party opposing the class may prefer to win dismissal or summary judgment as to the individual plaintiffs without certification and without binding the class that might have been certified. Time may be needed to explore designation of class counsel under Rule 23(g), recognizing that in many cases the need to progress toward the certification determination may require designation of interim counsel under Rule 23(g)(2)(A).

Although many circumstances may justify deferring the certification decision, active management may be necessary to ensure that the certification decision is not unjustifiably delayed.

Subdivision (c)(1)(C) reflects two amendments. The provision that a class certification "may be conditional" is deleted. A court that is not satisfied that the requirements of Rule 23 have been met should refuse certification until they have been met. The provision that permits alteration or amendment of an order granting or denying class certification is amended to set the cut-off point at final judgment rather than "the decision on the merits." This change avoids the possible ambiguity in referring to "the decision on the merits." Following a determination of liability, for example, proceedings to define the remedy may demonstrate the need to amend the class definition or subdivide the class. In this setting the final judgment concept is pragmatic. It is not the same as the concept used for appeal purposes, but it should be flexible, particularly in protracted litigation.

The authority to amend an order under Rule 23(c)(1) before final judgment does not restore the practice of "one-way intervention" that was rejected by the 1966 revision of Rule 23. A determination of liability after certification, however, may show a need to amend the class definition. Decertification may be warranted after further proceedings.

If the definition of a class certified under Rule 23(b)(3) is altered to include members who have not been afforded notice and an opportunity to request exclusion, notice—including an opportunity to request exclusion—must be directed to the new class members under Rule 23(c)(2)(B).

Paragraph (2). The first change made in Rule 23(c)(2) is to call attention to the court's authority—already established in part by Rule 23(d)(2)—to direct notice of certification to a Rule 23(b)(1) or (b)(2) class. The present rule expressly requires notice only in actions certified under Rule 23(b)(3). Members of classes certified under Rules 23(b)(1) or (b)(2) have interests that may deserve protection by notice.

The authority to direct notice to class members in a (b)(1) or (b)(2) class action should be exercised with care. For several reasons, there may be less need for notice than in a (b)(3) class action. There is no right to request exclusion from a (b)(1) or (b)(2) class. The characteristics of the class may reduce the need for formal notice. The cost of providing notice, moreover, could easily cripple actions that do not seek damages. The court may decide not to direct notice after balancing the risk that notice costs may deter the pursuit of class relief against the benefits of notice.

When the court does direct certification notice in a (b)(1) or (b)(2) class action, the discretion and flexibility established by subdivision (c)(2)(A) extend to the method of giving notice. Notice facilitates the opportunity to participate. Notice calculated to reach a significant number of class members often will protect the interests of all. Informal methods may prove effective. A simple posting in a place visited by many class members, directing attention to a source of more detailed information, may suffice. The court should consider the costs of notice in relation to the probable reach of inexpensive methods.

If a Rule 23(b)(3) class is certified in conjunction with a (b)(2) class, the (c)(2)(B) notice requirements must be satisfied as to the (b)(3) class.

The direction that class-certification notice be couched in plain, easily understood language is a reminder of the need to work unremittingly at the difficult task of communicating with class members. It is difficult to provide information about most class actions that is both accurate and easily understood by class members who are not themselves lawyers. Factual uncertainty, legal complexity, and the complication of class-action procedure raise the barriers high. The Federal Judicial Center has created illustrative clear-notice forms that provide a helpful starting point for actions similar to those described in the forms.

Subdivision (e). Subdivision (e) is amended to strengthen the process of reviewing proposed class-action settlements. Settlement may be a desirable means of resolving a class action. But court review and approval are essential to assure adequate representation of class members who have not participated in shaping the settlement.

Paragraph (1). Subdivision (e)(1)(A) expressly recognizes the power of a class representative to settle class claims, issues, or defenses.

Rule 23(e)(1)(A) resolves the ambiguity in former Rule 23(e)'s reference to dismissal or compromise of "a class action." That language could be—and at times was—read to require court approval of settlements with putative class representatives that resolved only individual claims. *See Manual for Complex Litigation (Third)* § 30.41. The new rule requires approval only if the claims, issues, or defenses of a certified class are resolved by a settlement, voluntary dismissal, or compromise.

Subdivision (e)(1)(B) carries forward the notice requirement of present Rule 23(e) when the settlement binds the class through claim or issue preclusion; notice is not required when the settlement binds only the individual class representatives. Notice of a settlement binding on the class is required either when the settlement follows class certification or when the decisions on certification and settlement proceed simultaneously.

Reasonable settlement notice may require individual notice in the manner required by Rule 23(c)(2)(B) for certification notice to a Rule 23(b)(3) class. Individual notice is appropriate, for example, if class members are required to take action—such as filing claims—to participate in the judgment, or if the court orders a settlement opt-out opportunity under Rule 23(e)(3).

Subdivision (e)(1)(C) confirms and mandates the already common practice of holding hearings as part of the process of approving settlement, voluntary dismissal, or compromise that would bind members of a class.

Subdivision (e)(1)(C) states the standard for approving a proposed settlement that would bind class members. The settlement must be fair, reasonable, and adequate. A helpful review of many factors that may deserve consideration is provided by *In re Prudential Insurance Co. America Sales Practice Litigation Agent Actions*, 148 F.3d 283, 316–24 (3d Cir. 1998). Further guidance can be found in the *Manual for Complex Litigation*.

The court must make findings that support the conclusion that the settlement is fair, reasonable, and adequate. The findings must be set out in sufficient detail to explain to class members and the appellate court the factors that bear on applying the standard.

Settlement review also may provide an occasion to review the cogency of the initial class definition. The terms of the settlement themselves, or objections, may reveal divergent interests of class members and demonstrate the need to redefine the class or to designate subclasses. Redefinition of a class certified under Rule 23(b)(3) may require notice to new class members under Rule 23(c)(2)(B). See Rule 23(c)(1)(C).

Paragraph (2). Subdivision (e)(2) requires parties seeking approval of a settlement, voluntary dismissal, or compromise under Rule 23(e)(1) to file a statement identifying any agreement made in connection with the settlement. This provision does not change the basic requirement that the parties disclose all terms of the settlement or compromise that the court must approve under Rule 23(e)(1). It aims instead at related undertakings that, although seemingly separate, may have influenced the terms of the settlement by trading away possible advantages for the class in return for advantages for others. Doubts should be resolved in favor of identification.

Further inquiry into the agreements identified by the parties should not become the occasion for discovery by the parties or objectors. The court may direct the parties to provide to the court or other parties a summary or copy of the full terms of any agreement identified by the parties. The court also may direct the parties to provide a summary or copy of any agreement not identified by the parties that the court considers relevant to its review of a proposed settlement. In exercising discretion under this rule, the court may act in steps, calling first for a summary of any agreement that may have affected the settlement and then for a complete version if the summary does not provide an adequate basis for review. A direction to disclose a summary or copy of an agreement may raise concerns of confidentiality. Some agreements may include information that merits protection against general disclosure. And the court must provide an opportunity to claim work-product or other protections.

Paragraph (3). Subdivision (e)(3) authorizes the court to refuse to approve a settlement unless the settlement affords class members a new opportunity to request exclusion from a class certified under Rule 23(b)(3) after settlement terms are known. An agreement by the parties themselves to permit class members to elect exclusion at this point by the settlement agreement may be one factor supporting approval of the settlement. Often there is an opportunity to opt out at this point because the class is certified and settlement is reached in circumstances that lead to simultaneous notice of certification and notice of settlement. In these cases, the basic opportunity to elect exclusion applies without further complication. In some cases, particularly if settlement appears imminent at the time of certification, it may be possible to achieve equivalent protection by deferring notice and the opportunity to elect exclusion until actual settlement terms are known. This approach avoids the cost and potential confusion of providing two notices and makes the single notice more meaningful. But notice should not be delayed unduly after certification in the hope of settlement.

Rule 23(e)(3) authorizes the court to refuse to approve a settlement unless the settlement affords a new opportunity to elect exclusion in a case that settles after a certification decision if the earlier opportunity to elect exclusion provided with the certification notice has expired by the time of the settlement notice. A decision to remain in the class is likely to be more carefully considered and is better informed when settlement terms are known.

The opportunity to request exclusion from a proposed settlement is limited to members of a (b)(3) class. Exclusion may be requested only by individual class members; no class member may purport to opt out other class members by way of another class action.

The decision whether to approve a settlement that does not allow a new opportunity to elect exclusion is confided to the court's discretion. The court may make this decision before directing notice to the class under Rule 23(e)(1)(B) or after the Rule 23(e)(1)(C) hearing. Many factors may influence the court's decision. Among these are changes in the information available to class members since expiration of the first opportunity to request exclusion, and the nature of the individual class members' claims.

The terms set for permitting a new opportunity to elect exclusion from the proposed settlement of a Rule 23(b)(3) class action may address concerns of potential misuse. The court might direct, for example, that class members who elect exclusion are bound by rulings on the merits made before the settlement was proposed for approval. Still other terms or conditions may be appropriate.

Paragraph (4). Subdivision (e)(4) confirms the right of class members to object to a proposed settlement, voluntary dismissal, or compromise. The right is defined in relation to a disposition that, because it would bind the class, requires court approval under subdivision (e)(1)(C).

Subdivision (e)(4)(B) requires court approval for withdrawal of objections made under subdivision (e)(4)(A). Review follows automatically if the objections are withdrawn on terms that lead to modification of the settlement with the class. Review also is required if the objector formally withdraws the objections. If the objector simply abandons pursuit of the objection, the court may inquire into the circumstances.

Approval under paragraph (4)(B) may be given or denied with little need for further inquiry if the objection and the disposition go only to a protest that the individual treatment afforded the objector under the proposed settlement is unfair because of factors that distinguish the objector from other class members. Different considerations may apply if the objector has protested that the proposed settlement is not fair, reasonable, or adequate on grounds that apply generally to a class or subclass. Such objections, which purport to represent class-wide interests, may augment the opportunity for obstruction or delay. If such objections are surrendered on terms that do not affect the class settlement or the objector's participation in the class settlement, the court often can approve withdrawal of the objections without elaborate inquiry.

Once an objector appeals, control of the proceeding lies in the court of appeals. The court of appeals may undertake review and approval of a settlement with the objector, perhaps as part of appeal settlement procedures, or may remand to the district court to take advantage of the district court's familiarity with the action and settlement.

Subdivision (g). Subdivision (g) is new. It responds to the reality that the selection and activity of class counsel are often critically important to the successful handling of a class action. Until now, courts have scrutinized proposed class counsel as well as the class representative under Rule 23(a)(4). This experience has recognized the importance of judicial evaluation of the proposed lawyer for the class, and this new subdivision builds on that experience rather than introducing an entirely new element into the class certification process. Rule 23(a)(4) will continue to call for scrutiny of the proposed class representative, while this subdivision will guide the court in assessing proposed class counsel as part of the certification decision. This subdivision recognizes the importance of class counsel, states the obligation to represent the interests of the class, and provides a framework for selection of class counsel. The procedure and standards for appointment vary depending on whether there are multiple applicants to be class counsel. The new subdivision also provides a method by which the court may make directions from the outset about the potential fee award to class counsel in the event the action is successful.

Paragraph (1) sets out the basic requirement that class counsel be appointed if a class is certified and articulates the obligation of class counsel to represent the interests of the class, as opposed to the potentially conflicting interests of individual class members. It also sets out the factors the court should consider in assessing proposed class counsel.

Paragraph(1)(A) requires that the court appoint class counsel to represent the class. Class counsel must be appointed for all classes, including each subclass that the court certifies to represent divergent interests.

Paragraph (1)(A) does not apply if "a statute provides otherwise." This recognizes that provisions of the Private Securities Litigation Reform Act of 1995, Pub. L. No. 104-67, 109 Stat. 737 (1995) (codified in various sections of 15 U.S.C.), contain directives that bear on selection of a lead plaintiff and the retention of counsel. This subdivision does not purport to supersede or to affect the interpretation of those provisions, or any similar provisions of other legislation.

Paragraph (1)(B) recognizes that the primary responsibility of class counsel, resulting from appointment as class counsel, is to represent the best interests of the class. The rule thus establishes the obligation of class counsel, an obligation that may be different from the customary obligations of counsel to individual clients. Appointment as class counsel means that the primary obligation of counsel is to the class rather than to any individual members of it. The class representatives do not have an unfettered right to "fire" class counsel. In the same vein, the class representatives cannot command class counsel to accept or reject a settlement proposal. To the contrary, class counsel must determine whether seeking the court's approval of a settlement would be in the best interests of the class as a whole.

Paragraph (1)(C) articulates the basic responsibility of the court to appoint class counsel who will provide the adequate representation called for by paragraph (1)(B). It identifies criteria that must be considered and invites the court to consider any other pertinent matters. Although couched in terms of the court's duty, the listing also informs counsel seeking appointment about the topics that should be addressed in an application for appointment or in the motion for class certification.

The court may direct potential class counsel to provide additional information about the topics mentioned in paragraph (1)(C) or about any other relevant topic. For example, the court may direct applicants to inform the court concerning any agreements about a prospective award of attorney fees or nontaxable costs, as such agreements may sometimes be significant in the selection of class counsel. The court might also direct that potential class counsel indicate how parallel litigation might be coordinated or consolidated with the action before the court.

The court may also direct counsel to propose terms for a potential award of attorney fees and nontaxable costs. Attorney fee awards are an important feature of class action practice, and attention to this subject from the outset may often be a productive technique. Paragraph (2)(C) therefore authorizes the court to provide directions about attorney fees and costs when appointing class counsel. Because there will be numerous class actions in which this information is not likely to be useful, the court need not consider it in all class actions.

Some information relevant to class counsel appointment may involve matters that include adversary preparation in a way that should be shielded from disclosure to other parties. An appropriate protective order may be necessary to preserve confidentiality.

In evaluating prospective class counsel, the court should weigh all pertinent factors. No single factor should necessarily be determinative in a given case. For example, the resources counsel will commit to the case must be appropriate to its needs, but the court should be careful not to limit consideration to lawyers with the greatest resources.

If, after review of all applicants, the court concludes that none would be satisfactory class counsel, it may deny class certification, reject all applications, recommend that an application be modified, invite new applications, or make any other appropriate order regarding selection and appointment of class counsel.

Paragraph (2). This paragraph sets out the procedure that should be followed in appointing class counsel. Although it affords substantial flexibility, it provides the framework for appointment of class counsel in all class actions. For counsel who filed the action, the materials submitted in support of the motion for class certification may suffice to justify appointment so long as the information described in paragraph (g)(1)(C) is included. If there are other applicants, they ordinarily would file a formal application detailing their suitability for the position.

In a plaintiff class action the court usually would appoint as class counsel only an attorney or attorneys who have sought appointment. Different considerations may apply in defendant class actions.

The rule states that the court should appoint "class counsel." In many instances, the applicant will be an individual attorney. In other cases, however, an entire firm, or perhaps numerous attorneys who are not otherwise affiliated but are collaborating on the action will apply. No rule of thumb exists to determine when such arrangements are appropriate; the court should be alert to the need for adequate staffing of the case, but also to the risk of overstaffing or an ungainly counsel structure.

Paragraph (2)(A) authorizes the court to designate interim counsel during the pre-certification period if necessary to protect the interests of the putative class. Rule 23(c)(1)(B) directs that the order certifying the class include appointment of class counsel. Before class certification, however, it will usually be important for an attorney to take action to prepare for the certification decision. The amendment to Rule 23(c)(1) recognizes that some discovery is often necessary for that determination. It also may be important to make or respond to motions before certification. Settlement may be discussed before certification. Ordinarily, such work is handled by the lawyer who filed the action. In some cases, however, there may be rivalry or uncertainty that makes formal designation of interim counsel appropriate. Rule 23(g)(2)(A) authorizes the court to designate interim counsel to act on behalf of the putative class before the certification decision is made. Failure to make the formal designation does not prevent the attorney who filed the action from proceeding in it. Whether or not formally designated interim counsel, an attorney who acts on behalf of the class before certification must act in the best interests of the class as a whole. For example, an attorney who negotiates a pre-certification settlement must seek a settlement that is fair, reasonable, and adequate for the class.

Rule 23(c)(1) provides that the court should decide whether to certify the class "at an early practicable time," and directs that class counsel should be appointed in the order certifying the class. In some cases, it may be appropriate for the court to allow a reasonable period after commencement of the action for filing applications to serve as class counsel. The primary ground for deferring appointment would be that there is reason to anticipate competing applications to serve as class counsel. Examples might include instances in which more than one class action has been filed, or in which other attorneys have filed individual actions on behalf of putative class members. The purpose of facilitating competing applications in such a case is to afford the best possible representation for the class. Another possible reason for deferring appointment would be that the initial applicant was found inadequate, but it seems appropriate to permit additional applications rather than deny class certification.

Paragraph (2)(B) states the basic standard the court should use in deciding whether to certify the class and appoint class counsel in the single applicant situation—that the applicant be able to provide the representation called for by paragraph (1)(B) in light of the factors identified in paragraph (1)(C).

If there are multiple adequate applicants, paragraph (2)(B) directs the court to select the class counsel best able to represent the interests of the class. This decision should also be made using the factors outlined in paragraph (1)(C), but in the multiple applicant situation the court is to go beyond scrutinizing the adequacy of counsel and make a comparison of the strengths of the various applicants. As with the decision whether to appoint the sole applicant for the position, no single factor should be dispositive in selecting class counsel in cases in which there are multiple applicants. The fact that a given attorney filed the instant action, for example, might not weigh heavily in the decision if that lawyer had not done significant work identifying or investigating claims. Depending on the nature of the case, one important consideration might be the applicant's existing attorney-client relationship with the proposed class representative.

Paragraph (2)(C) builds on the appointment process by authorizing the court to include provisions regarding attorney fees in the order appointing class counsel. Courts may find it desirable to adopt guidelines for fees or nontaxable costs, or to direct class counsel to report to the court at regular intervals on the efforts undertaken in the action, to facilitate the court's later determination of a reasonable attorney fee.

Subdivision (h). Subdivision (h) is new. Fee awards are a powerful influence on the way attorneys initiate, develop, and conclude class actions. Class action attorney fee awards have heretofore been handled, along with all other attorney fee awards, under Rule 54(d)(2), but that rule is not addressed to the particular concerns of class actions. This subdivision is designed to work in tandem with new subdivision (g) on appointment of class counsel, which may afford an opportunity for the court to provide an early framework for an eventual fee award, or for monitoring the work of class counsel during the pendency of the action.

Subdivision (h) applies to "an action certified as a class action." This includes cases in which there is a simultaneous proposal for class certification and settlement even though technically the class may not be certified unless the court approves the settlement pursuant to review under Rule 23(e). When a settlement is proposed for Rule 23(e) approval, either after certification or with a request for certification, notice to class members about class counsel's fee motion would ordinarily accompany the notice to the class about the settlement proposal itself.

This subdivision does not undertake to create new grounds for an award of attorney fees or nontaxable costs. Instead, it applies when such awards are authorized by law or by agreement of the parties. Against that background, it provides a format for all awards of attorney fees and nontaxable costs in connection with a class action, not only the award to class counsel. In some situations, there may be a basis for making an award to other counsel whose work produced a beneficial result for the class, such as attorneys who acted for the class before certification but were not appointed class counsel, or attorneys who represented objectors to a proposed settlement under Rule 23(e) or to the fee motion of class counsel. Other situations in which fee awards are authorized by law or by agreement of the parties may exist.

This subdivision authorizes an award of "reasonable" attorney fees and nontaxable costs. This is the customary term for measurement of fee awards in cases in which counsel may obtain an award of fees under the "common fund" theory that applies in many class actions, and is used in many fee-shifting statutes. Depending on the circumstances, courts have approached the determination of what is reasonable in different ways. In particular, there is some variation among courts about whether in "common fund" cases the court should use the lodestar or a percentage method of determining what fee is reasonable. The rule does not attempt to resolve the question whether the lodestar or percentage approach should be viewed as preferable.

Active judicial involvement in measuring fee awards is singularly important to the proper operation of the class-action process. Continued reliance on caselaw development of fee-award measures does not diminish the court's responsibility. In a class action, the district court must ensure that the amount and mode of payment of attorney fees are fair and proper whether the fees come from a common fund or are otherwise paid. Even in the absence of objections, the court bears this responsibility.

Courts discharging this responsibility have looked to a variety of factors. One fundamental focus is the result actually achieved for class members, a basic consideration in any case in which fees are sought on the basis of a benefit achieved for class members. The Private Securities Litigation Reform Act of 1995 explicitly makes this factor a cap for a fee award in actions to which it applies. *See* 15 U.S.C. §§ 77z-1(a)(6) and 78u-4(a)(6) (fee award should not exceed a "reasonable percentage of the amount of any damages and prejudgment interest actually paid to the class"). For a percentage approach to fee measurement, results achieved is the basic starting point.

In many instances, the court may need to proceed with care in assessing the value conferred on class members. Settlement regimes that provide for future payments, for example, may not result in significant actual payments to class members. In this connection, the court may need to scrutinize the manner and operation of any applicable claims procedure. In some cases, it may be appropriate to defer some portion of the fee award until actual payouts to class members are known. Settlements involving nonmonetary provisions for class members also deserve careful scrutiny to ensure that these provisions have actual value to the class. On occasion the court's Rule 23(e) review will provide a solid basis for this sort of evaluation, but in any event it is also important to assessing the fee award for the class.

At the same time, it is important to recognize that in some class actions the monetary relief obtained is not the sole determinant of an appropriate attorney fees award. *Cf. Blanchard v. Bergeron*, 489 U.S. 87, 95 (1989) (cautioning in an individual case against an "undesirable emphasis" on "the importance of the recovery of damages in civil rights litigation" that might "shortchange efforts to seek effective injunctive or declaratory relief").

Any directions or orders made by the court in connection with appointing class counsel under Rule 23(g) should weigh heavily in making a fee award under this subdivision.

Courts have also given weight to agreements among the parties regarding the fee motion, and to agreements between class counsel and others about the fees claimed by the motion. Rule 54(d)(2)(B) provides: "If directed by the court, the motion shall also disclose the terms of any agreement with respect to fees to be paid for the services for which claim is made." The agreement by a settling party not to oppose a fee application up to a certain amount, for example, is worthy of consideration, but the court remains responsible to determine a reasonable fee.

"Side agreements" regarding fees provide at least perspective pertinent to an appropriate fee award.

In addition, courts may take account of the fees charged by class counsel or other attorneys for representing individual claimants or objectors in the case. In determining a fee for class counsel, the court's objective is to ensure an overall fee that is fair for counsel and equitable within the class. In some circumstances individual fee agreements between class counsel and class members might have provisions inconsistent with those goals, and the court might determine that adjustments in the class fee award were necessary as a result.

Finally, it is important to scrutinize separately the application for an award covering nontaxable costs. If costs were addressed in the order appointing class counsel, those directives should be a presumptive starting point in determining what is an appropriate award.

Paragraph (1). Any claim for an award of attorney fees must be sought by motion under Rule 54(d)(2), which invokes the provisions for timing of appeal in Rule 58 and Appellate Rule 4. Owing to the distinctive features of class action fee motions, however, the provisions of this subdivision control disposition of fee motions in class actions, while Rule 54(d)(2) applies to matters not addressed in this subdivision.

The court should direct when the fee motion must be filed. For motions by class counsel in cases subject to court review of a proposed settlement under Rule 23(e), it would be important to require the filing of at least the initial motion in time for inclusion of information about the motion in the notice to the class about the proposed settlement that is required by Rule 23(e). In cases litigated to judgment, the court might also order class counsel's motion to be filed promptly so that notice to the class under this subdivision (h) can be given.

Besides service of the motion on all parties, notice of class counsel's motion for attorney fees must be "directed to the class in a reasonable manner." Because members of the class have an interest in the arrangements for payment of class counsel whether that payment comes from the class fund or is made directly by another party, notice is required in all instances. In cases in which settlement approval is contemplated under Rule 23(e), notice of class counsel's fee motion should be combined with notice of the proposed settlement, and the provision regarding notice to the class is parallel to the requirements for notice under Rule 23(e). In adjudicated class actions, the court may calibrate the notice to avoid undue expense.

Paragraph (2). A class member and any party from whom payment is sought may object to the fee motion. Other parties—for example, nonsettling defendants— may not object because they lack a sufficient interest in the amount the court awards. The rule does not specify a time limit for making an objection. In setting the date objections are due, the court should provide sufficient time after the full fee motion is on file to enable potential objectors to examine the motion.

The court may allow an objector discovery relevant to the objections. In determining whether to allow discovery, the court should weigh the need for the information against the cost and delay that would attend discovery. See Rule 26(b)(2). One factor in determining whether to authorize discovery is the completeness of the material submitted in support of the fee motion, which depends in part on the fee measurement standard applicable to the case. If the motion provides thorough information, the burden should be on the objector to justify discovery to obtain further information.

Paragraph (3). Whether or not there are formal objections, the court must determine whether a fee award is justified and, if so, set a reasonable fee. The rule does not require a formal hearing in all cases. The form and extent of a hearing depend on the circumstances of the case. The rule does require findings and conclusions under Rule 52(a).

Paragraph (4). By incorporating Rule 54(d)(2), this provision gives the court broad authority to obtain assistance in determining the appropriate amount to award. In deciding whether to direct submission of such questions to a special master or magistrate judge, the court should give appropriate consideration to the cost and delay that such a process might entail.[11]

2007 AMENDMENT

Comment: The language of Rule 23 has been amended as part of the general restyling of the Civil Rules to make them more easily understood and to make style and terminology consistent throughout the rules. These changes are intended to be stylistic only.

Amended Rule 23(d)(2) carries forward the provisions of former Rule 23(d) that recognize two separate propositions. First, a Rule 23(d) order may be combined with a pretrial order under Rule 16. Second, the standard for amending the Rule 23(d) orders, not the more exacting standard for amending Rule 16 orders.

As part of the general restyling, intensifiers that provide emphasis but add no meaning are consistently deleted. Amended Rule 23(f) omits as redundant the explicit reference to court of appeals discretion in deciding whether to permit an interlocutory appeal. The omission does not in any way limit the unfettered discretion established by the original rule.

2009 AMENDMENT

Rule 23. Class Actions

(f) Appeals. A court of appeals may permit an appeal from an order granting or denying class-action certification under this rule if a petition for permission to appeal is filed with the circuit clerk within 14 days after the order is entered. An

---

11. *Id.* at § 23App.06(2).

appeal does not stay proceedings in the district court unless the district judge or the court of appeals so orders.

Comment: This amendment merely adjusts the time computation, apparently for internal consistency with the rules for appellate practice and bankruptcy.

APPENDIX B: ALABAMA CODE CLASS ACTION PROVISIONS

Section 6-5-640

Scope and effect on other laws or rules.

This article shall apply to and govern all civil class actions brought in the state courts of Alabama pursuant to Alabama Rule of Civil Procedure 23. The provisions of this article, where inconsistent with any Alabama Rule of Civil Procedure, including, but not limited to, Ala. R. Civ. P. 23, shall supersede such rules or parts of rules.

(Act 99-250, p. 329, §1.)

Section 6-5-641

Certification of classes.

(a) No class of civil litigants shall be certified or recognized by any court of the State of Alabama unless there shall have been compliance with the procedures for certification of the class set forth in this article.

(b) As soon as practicable after the commencement of an action in which claims or defenses are purported to be asserted on behalf of or against a class, or as soon as practicable after such assertions in an amended pleading, but in no event prior to the time allowed by law for each party (including, but not limited to, counterclaim, cross-claim, and third-party defendants) to file an answer or other pleading responsive to the complaint, counterclaim, cross-claim, or third-party claim, the court shall hold a conference among all named parties to the action for the purpose of establishing a schedule, in the same manner and to the same extent contemplated by Ala. R. Civ. P. 16, for any discovery in which the parties may wish to engage which is both (1) allowed by Ala. R. Civ. P. 26-37, and (2) germane to the issue of whether the requested class should or should not be certified. At this conference, the court may set a date for a hearing on the issue of class certification, but such hearing may not be set sooner than 90 days after the date on which the court issues its scheduling order pursuant to the conference unless a shorter time is agreed to by all parties.

(c) Upon motion of any party, the court shall, except for good cause shown and even then only if the interests of justice require that it not do so, stay all discovery directed solely to the merits of the claims or defenses in the action until the court shall have made its decision regarding certification of the class. In considering such a motion, the court shall consider whether any prejudice to the plaintiff exists because of the filing by the defendant of a Rule 56 motion for summary judgment prior to the court's decision regarding class certification.

(d) The court shall, on motion of any party, hold a full evidentiary hearing on class certification. The hearing shall be recorded, and all named parties to the action shall be given notice of the date, time, and place of the hearing by written notification given to the party's attorney (or if appearing pro se, to the party) no later than 60 days prior to the date set for the hearing. At the hearing, the parties shall be allowed to present, in the same manner as at trial, any admissible evidence in support of or in opposition to the certification of the class.

(e) When deciding whether a requested class is to be certified, the court shall determine, by employing a rigorous analysis, if the party or parties requesting class certification have proved its or their entitlement to class certification under Ala. R. Civ. P. 23. The burden of coming forward with such proof shall at all times be on the party or parties seeking certification, and if such proof shall not have been adduced, the court shall not order certification of the class. In making this determination, the court shall analyze all factors required by Ala. R. Civ. P. 23 for certification of a class and shall not order certification unless all such factors shall have been established. In announcing its determination, the court shall place in the record of the action a written order addressing all such factors and specifying the evidence, or lack of evidence, on which the court has based its decision with regard to whether each such factor has been established. In so doing, the court may treat a factor as having been established if all parties to the action have so stipulated on the record and if the court shall be satisfied that such factor could be proven to have been established.

(f) Nothing in this article shall affect, or be construed to affect, Ala. R. Civ. P. 12 or Ala. R. Civ. P. 56, including the provisions of Rule 56(f).
(Act 99-250, p. 329, §2.)

Section 6-5-642

Appeal of certification order.

A court's order certifying a class or refusing to certify a class action shall be appealable in the same manner as a final order to the appellate court which would otherwise have jurisdiction over the appeal from a final order in the action. Such appeal may only be filed within 42 days of the order certifying or refusing to certify the class. The filing of such appeal, the failure to file an appeal, or the affirmance of the certification or denial order shall in no way affect the right of any party, after the entry of final judgment, to appeal the earlier certification of, or refusal to certify, the class. If the appeal is not the first appeal taken by the party, the subsequent appeal shall be based upon the record at the time of final judgment and shall be considered by the court only to the extent that either the facts or controlling law relevant to certification have changed from that which existed or controlled at the time of the earlier certification or refusal to certify. During the pendency of any such appeal, the action in the trial court shall be stayed in all respects. Following adjudication on appeal (or, if the initial appeal is to an intermediate appellate court, adjudication of the action on any writ of certiorari granted by the Supreme Court of Alabama), if the class is not to be certified, the stay in the trial court shall automatically dissolve and the trial court may proceed to adjudicate any remaining individual claims or defenses. If, after such appeal or procedure on writ of certiorari, the class is to be certified, the stay shall likewise dissolve and the trial court shall proceed with adjudication on the merits, except that the trial court shall at all times prior to entry of a final order retain jurisdiction to revisit the certification issues upon motion of a party and to order decertification of the class if during the litigation of the case it shall become evident to the court that the action is no longer reasonably maintainable as a class action pursuant to the factors enumerated in Ala. R. Civ. P. 23(b).

(Act 99-250, p. 329, §3.)

ALASKA

ANDREW F. BEHREND

I. Introduction

Alaska Rule of Civil Procedure 23 closely parallels the pre-1998 version of Federal Rule 23. Federal authorities interpreting Rule 23 are "especially persuasive" in interpreting Alaska Rule 23.[1] Key differences between Alaska Rule 23 and the current Federal Rule 23[2] relate to (1) the right to appeal or otherwise obtain review of a decision granting or denying class certification; (2) the notice provided to the class regarding settlements and attorney fee award requests; and (3) methods for determining attorney fee awards.

II. Class Certification

The language of Alaska Rule 23 subsections (a) and (b) is functionally identical to the language of Federal Rule 23 subsections (a) and (b).[3] Just as with Federal Rule 23, to maintain a class action under Alaska Rule 23, a party must satisfy all of the requirements listed in Alaska Rule 23(a) and at least one of the requirements listed in Alaska Rule 23(b).[4] In applying these factors and deciding whether to certify or decertify a class, the trial court may not consider the merits of the alleged claims.[5]

---

1. *Bartek v. State*, 31 P.3d 100, 102 (Alaska 2001) (citing *Nolan v. Sea Airmotive, Inc.*, 627 P.2d 1035, 1041 (Alaska 1981)).

2. All future references to Federal Rule 23 will be to the current rule unless otherwise specifically indicated.

3. *Compare* ALASKA R. CIV. P. 23(a) & (b) *with* FED. R. CIV. P. 23(a) & (b).

4. *See Bartek*, 31 P.3d at 103–04; *Int'l Seafoods v. Bissonette*, 146 P.3d 561, 566–67 (Alaska 2006).

5. *Shook v. Alyeska Pipeline Serv. Co.*, 51 P.3d 935, 937–38 (Alaska 2002) (citing *Eisen v. Carlisle & Jacquelin*, 417 U.S. 156 (1974)). *But see State v. Alex*, 646 P.2d 203, 214 (Alaska 1982) (defendants waived objection to court deciding merits before class certification where defendants filed summary judgment motions while certification motion was pending).

A. STANDING TO SEEK CLASS CERTIFICATION

Alaska courts treat the determination of whether a plaintiff has standing to seek certification of a class as "an inherent prerequisite to the class certification inquiry."[6] Where named plaintiffs lack standing to represent a class, they must be given a fair opportunity to amend their complaint to add plaintiffs having such standing.[7]

B. TIMING OF THE CLASS CERTIFICATION DECISION

Alaska has not adopted the 2003 change to Federal Rule 23(c)(1) providing that the determination of whether to certify a class action be made "at an early practicable time after a person sues or is sued as a class representative."[8] Alaska Rule 23 instead retains the previous provision requiring that the certification decision be made as "[a]s soon as practicable after the commencement of an action brought as a class action."[9] As the official commentary to Federal Rule 23 notes, the change in the language of Federal Rule 23(c)(1) recognized that class certification often is not decided at the earliest practicable moment and that there may be valid reasons for deferring the certification decision.[10]

No reported Alaska cases have explored this difference between Federal Rule 23(c)(1) and Alaska Rule 23(c)(1). But the Alaska Supreme Court has observed that notwithstanding the "as soon as practicable" language in Alaska Rule 23(c)(1), considerations of judicial economy require that courts be allowed latitude in deciding what issues may be determined before addressing class certification.[11] This interpretation echoes the concerns expressed in the advisory notes regarding the 2003 amendment. Accordingly, it is unlikely that this difference between the federal and Alaska rules signals any practical difference as to when courts in those jurisdictions will consider the issue of class certification.

C. RULE 23(A) PREREQUISITES TO CLASS CERTIFICATION

Alaska courts apply the same class action prerequisites of numerosity, commonality, typicality, and adequacy of representation as the federal courts apply under federal Rule 23(a).[12] The numerosity requirement is satisfied if the class is so numerous

---

6. *Neese v. Lithia Chrysler Jeep*, 210 P.3d 1213, 1222 (Alaska 2009) (citing *Adams v. Pipeliners Union 798*, 699 P.2d 343, 346 (Alaska 1985)). In *Neese*, plaintiffs who had not purchased vehicles from two defendants lacked standing to represent a class with claims against those defendants. *Id.*

7. *Id.* at 1224–25.

8. *See* Fed. R. Civ. P. 23(c)(1)(A).

9. Alaska R. Civ. P. 23(c)(1).

10. *See* Fed. R. Civ. P. 23(c)(1) advisory committee note (2003).

11. *Gold Bondholders v. Atchison, Topeka*, 649 P.2d 947, 951 (Alaska 1982).

12. *Bissonette*, 146 P.3d at 566–67; *Bartek*, 31 P.3d at 103–04 (citing Alaska R. Civ. P. 23(a)(1)–(4)).

that joining the proposed class members as parties would be impracticable.[13] The Alaska Supreme Court has noted that while there is no "magic number" of putative class members that satisfies the numerosity requirement, a proposed class of more than forty members will be presumed to meet the numerosity requirement.[14] Broad geographic dispersion of putative class members supports a finding that their joinder would be impracticable.[15]

The requisite commonality exists if the named class representatives share at least one question of fact or law with the putative class.[16] The typicality requirement is satisfied when each putative class member's claim arises from the same course of events, and each class member makes similar legal arguments to prove the defendant's liability.[17]

For a putative class representative to be an adequate representative, the class representative's lawyer must be qualified to handle the matter, and there must be no conflict of interest between the class representative and the other members of the class.[18] The requirement that there be no conflict of interest is satisfied where the putative class representative and the other members of the class have the same interests and damages, and any putative class member who does not wish to participate in the class action has the opportunity to opt out of the class.[19] As a matter of law, a pro se plaintiff who is not an experienced class action lawyer cannot adequately represent a class under Alaska Rule 23.[20]

D. RULE 23(B) CLASS ACTION CATEGORIES

Alaska Rule 23(b) is virtually identical to Federal Rule 23(b), and the available categories of class actions under Alaska law mirror those under federal law.[21] Accordingly, once all of the prerequisites under Alaska Rule 23(a) have been satisfied,

---

13. *Bissonette*, 146 P.3d at 567; ALASKA R. CIV. P. 23(a)(1).

14. *Bissonette*, 146 P.3d at 567 (citing *Cox v. Am. Cast Iron Pipe Co.*, 784 F.2d 1546, 1553 (11th Cir. 1986)); *see also State v. Andrade*, 23 P.3d 58, 67 (Alaska 2001) (requisite numerosity existed where there were 20 named plaintiffs and hundreds of others allegedly either were similarly situated to the named plaintiffs or would be affected by the outcome of the case).

15. *See Bissonette*, 146 P.3d at 567 (joining 110 putative class members who lived variously in Alaska, Washington, Maryland, Colorado, Oregon, California, and other states would be impracticable).

16. *Id.* (citing *Baby Neal ex rel. Kanter v. Casey*, 43 F.3d 48, 56 (3rd Cir. 1994)); *see also Andrade*, 23 P.2d at 67 (commonality requirement met where the state's alleged systematic discrimination in favor of certain categories of legal aliens was asserted by a class consisting of legal aliens and children of legal aliens who claimed discrimination).

17. *Bissonette*, 146 P.3d at 567 (citing *Marisol A. ex rel. Forbes v. Giuliani*, 126 F.3d 372, 376 (2d Cir. 1997)).

18. *Id.* at 567 (citing *Marisol A.*, 126 F.3d at 378).

19. *Id.*

20. *Hertz v. Cleary*, 835 P.2d 438, 442 n.3 (Alaska 1992) (pro se plaintiff cannot properly represent a class because such a plaintiff lacks the required qualifications and expertise required by Rule 23(a)).

21. *Compare* FED. R. CIV. P. 23(b) *with* ALASKA R. CIV. P. 23(b).

a party seeking class certification must also establish at least one of the three requirements set forth in Alaska Rule 23(b)(1)–(3).[22]

The Alaska Supreme Court has affirmed certification of both a Rule 23(b)(1)(B) class and a mandatory (non-opt-out) Rule 23(b)(2) class seeking declaratory relief in a case involving the constitutionality of an Alaska statute and the associated conduct of the state of Alaska that was generally applicable to the class members.[23] Although the reported Alaska cases relating to Rule 23(b)(3) "opt-out" class actions have not analyzed the predominance requirement in detail, the Alaska Supreme Court has affirmed decisions certifying such classes after finding that questions of law and fact common to the class predominate over questions affecting individual class members.[24]

E. PRECERTIFICATION DISCOVERY AND EVIDENTIARY HEARINGS

Alaska Rule 23 does not require either an evidentiary hearing or discovery prior to a court's class certification decision, although discovery and/or a hearing may be appropriate under the particular circumstances of a case.[25] It is within the court's discretion to decide whether to hold an evidentiary hearing or to permit discovery before granting class certification.[26] In making that decision, the court should determine whether there are factual disputes that should be resolved at a precertification hearing after discovery.[27]

F. REVIEW OF CLASS CERTIFICATION DECISION

Unlike Federal Rule 23, Alaska Rule 23 does not provide for immediate appellate review of a decision to grant or deny class certification.[28] Consequently, a party seeking appellate review of a class certification decision prior to conclusion of litigation in the trial court must file a petition for interlocutory review under Alaska Rule of Appellate Procedure 402.[29] Review under Rule 402 is discretionary. It will be granted only where "the sound policy behind the rule requiring appeals to be taken only from final judgments is outweighed" by certain enumerated circumstances, such as where postponing review will result in injustice due to unnecessary delay or expense or where advancing the ultimate termination of the litigation

---

22. *Bissonette*, 146 P.3d at 567 (citing ALASKA R. CIV. P. 23(b)); *Bartek*, 31 P.3d at 104.

23. *Andrade*, 23 P.3d at 63–64, 67–68.

24. *See, e.g., Bissonette*, 146 P.3d at 567–68 (affirming certification under both Rule 23(b)(1)(A) and Rule 23(b)(3)).

25. *Bartek*, 31 P.3d at 103.

26. *Id.*

27. *Id.*

28. *Compare* ALASKA R. CIV. P. 23 (no certification review provision) *with* FED. R. CIV. P. 23(f) (providing for immediate discretionary appellate review).

29. *See* ALASKA R. APP. P. 402 (regarding petitions for review of nonappealable orders or decisions).

could result from immediate review.[30] Although some of the circumstances enumerated in Appellate Rule 402(b) may be found in the context of class actions, in practice, Rule 402 petitions for review of class certification decisions are not commonly granted.[31]

Where review of a class certification decision is available, whether by means of a Rule 402 petition for review or on appeal after final judgment, the class certification decision is subject to an abuse of discretion standard of review.[32] Accordingly, the trial court's class certification decision will only be overturned when the appellate court is "left with a definite and firm conviction, after reviewing the record as a whole, that the trial court erred in its ruling."[33] Factual findings made by the trial court in the context of a class certification decision will be reversed only if they are clearly erroneous.[34]

III. Postcertification Notice

Alaska has not adopted the significant changes to the class notice provisions made to Federal Rule 23(c) in 2003.[35] Alaska's class notice provision requires that the "best practicable" notice be given to members of a class certified under Alaska Rule 23(b)(3), along with the opportunity to opt out of the class.[36] This notice provision does not contain many of the specific requirements of Federal Rule 23(c)(2)(B)(i)–(vii). But in practice, the categories of information required by Federal Rule 23(c)(2)(B) typically are included in Rule 23(b)(3) class notices issued by Alaska courts.

Unlike Federal Rule 23, Alaska Rule 23 makes no provision for optional notice to members of classes certified under Alaska Rule 23(b)(1) or 23(b)(2).[37] The Alaska

---

30. ALASKA R. APP. P. 402(b).

31. *See, e.g.*, Bissonette, 146 P.3d at 566 n.14 (noting in an opinion affirming on appeal the trial court's class certification decision that a previous Rule 402 petition for review relating to the same decision had been denied). The Alaska Supreme Court has stated that petitions for interlocutory review should be granted only where injustice would result from delaying review of a nonfinal decision by the trial court and are not intended to be used as a substitute for an appeal. *Jefferson v. Moore*, 354 P.2d 373, 375 (Alaska 1960).

32. *Bissonette*, 146 P.3d at 566; *Andrade*, 23 P.3d at 65 (expressly adopting the abuse of discretion standard applied by the U.S. Supreme Court in *Gulf Oil Co. v. Bernard*, 452 U.S. 89, 100 (1981)).

33. *Bissonette*, 146 P.3d at 566 (citing, *inter alia*, *City of Kodiak v. Samaniego*, 83 P.3d 1077, 1082 (Alaska 2004)).

34. *Andrade*, 23 P.3d at 68; *see also Alex*, 646 P.2d at 214 (the determination of whether an individual is an adequate class representative is a finding of fact subject to reversal only upon a finding of clear error).

35. *Compare* FED. R. CIV. P. 23(c)(2) *with* ALASKA R. CIV. P. 23(c)(2).

36. ALASKA R. CIV. P. 23(c)(2).

37. *Compare* ALASKA R. CIV. P. 23(c)(2) (no reference to notice to members of Rule 23(b)(1) or 23(b)(2) classes) *with* FED. R. CIV. P. 23(c)(2)(A) (providing for discretionary "appropriate" notice to classes certified under Rule 23(b)(1) and 23(b)(2)).

Supreme Court has held that no such notice is required under Alaska Rule 23.[38] If potential conflicts of interest exist or arise between members of an Alaska Rule 23(b)(2) class, however, some form of class notice and potentially the opportunity to opt out of the class should be given.[39]

IV. Postcertification Discovery

Class representatives are subject to discovery.[40] Discovery generally is not available against absent class members except that discovery via interrogatories may be available when (1) the information requested is relevant to the decision of common questions; (2) the discovery requests are offered in good faith and are not overly burdensome; and (3) the information is not available from the class representatives.[41] Whether to allow such discovery is within the trial court's discretion.[42]

A court has broad discretion to choose whether to impose discovery sanctions in class actions, including sanctions against absent class members who fail to respond to appropriate discovery requests.[43] A sanction for such failure may be severe, intermediate, or mild at the discretion of the court after reviewing the circumstances.[44] The exercise of that discretion will be overturned only where the Alaska Supreme Court finds a manifest abuse of discretion.[45]

V. Class Action Settlements

Alaska courts use the same analysis to determine whether to approve a proposed class action settlement as the federal courts.[46] Accordingly, a proposed settlement will be reviewed to determine whether it is, on the whole, fair, adequate, and reasonable.[47] In making that determination, Alaska courts consider seven factors: (1) comparison between the likely result of litigation and the remedy in the settlement; (2) expense, complexity, and likely duration of further litigation; (3) reaction of the class to the settlement, number of objectors, and nature of objections; (4) experience and views of counsel; (5) defendant's ability to pay (feasibility of

---

38. *State v. Okuley*, 214 P.3d 247, 257–58 (Alaska 2009).

39. *Id.* at 257 (implying that such notice should include an opportunity to opt out of the class) (citing *Holmes v. Cont'l Can Co.*, 706 F.2d 1144, 1156 (11th Cir. 1983)).

40. *See Bissonette*, 146 P.3d at 568–69.

41. *Id.* at 568 (citing *Transamerican Ref. Corp. v. Dravo*, 139 F.R.D. 619, 621 (S.D. Tex. 1991)).

42. *Id.* at 568–69.

43. *Id.* at 569 (citing *Hikita v. Nichiro Gyogyo Kaisha, Ltd.*, 85 P.3d 458, 460 (Alaska 2004)).

44. *Id.* (affirming the "intermediate sanction" of excluding from evidence documents not identified or produced and oral statements not disclosed during discovery).

45. *Id.*

46. *See Weiss v. State*, 939 P.2d 380, 387 (Alaska 1997).

47. *See id.* at 387.

settlement); (6) extent of discovery completed; and (7) presence of collusion in settlement negotiations.[48] A trial court's approval of a class action settlement is subject to the same abuse of discretion standard of review applied under Federal Rule 23.[49]

VI. Lawyers and Attorney Fees

Subsections (g) ("Class Counsel") and (h) ("Attorney's Fees and Nontaxable Costs") of Federal Rule 23 are not included in Alaska Rule 23. As discussed above, however, a certified class must be represented by legal counsel.[50] The rules applicable to attorney fee awards in class actions under Alaska law differ in several respects from those applicable to attorney fee awards in cases subject to Federal Rule 23. These differences arise from several sources, including (1) Alaska's "partial English" rule for shifting attorney fees;[51] (2) the fee-shifting provisions of Alaska's offer of judgment rule;[52] and (3) the common fund doctrine. An award of attorney fees in a class action will be overturned only upon a showing of either abuse of discretion or that the award is manifestly unreasonable.[53]

A. ALASKA RULE OF CIVIL PROCEDURE 82

Unlike other states, Alaska has a rule of general application that functions to shift responsibility for part of a prevailing party's attorney fees to the losing party in civil cases under Alaska law unless a statute provides otherwise.[54] This rule, Alaska Rule of Civil Procedure 82, applies in class actions.[55]

The amount of a Rule 82 fee award is calculated by means of tables and formulas contained in the rule. If a money judgment has been obtained, then a Rule 82 fee award will be calculated using a table set forth in the rule that provides for fee awards calculated as percentages of certain components of the money judgment.[56] If no money judgment has been obtained, then Rule 82 provides for recovery of a certain percentage of the reasonable, actual attorney fees incurred by the prevailing

---

48. *Id.* at 386–87 (citing, *inter alia*, *Class Plaintiffs v. City of Seattle*, 955 F.2d 1268, 1291 (9th Cir. 1992)).

49. *Id.* at 386 (citing *Barber v. Barber*, 837 P.2d 714, 716 n.2 (Alaska 1992)).

50. *See Hertz*, 835 P.2d at 442 n.3 (a pro se plaintiff cannot properly represent a class).

51. Alaska R. Civ. P. 82.

52. Alaska R. Civ. P. 68.

53. *Bissonette*, 146 P.3d at 566.

54. *See Edwards v. Alaska Pulp Corp.*, 920 P.2d 751, 755 (Alaska 1996) (Alaska is the only state with a generally applicable "English rule" for fee-shifting).

55. *Okuley*, 214 P.3d at 250; *Bissonette*, 146 P.3d at 572–73; *Municipality of Anchorage v. Gentile*, 922 P.2d 248, 263 (Alaska 1996); *Edwards*, 920 P.2d at 755.

56. Alaska R. Civ. P. 82(b)(1).

party, typically 20 percent for cases decided without trial and 30 percent for cases decided at trial.[57]

Fee awards calculated without any variation under Rule 82(b)(1) and Rule 82(a)(2) are standard awards.[58] The trial court may, at its discretion, depart either upward or downward from a standard Rule 82 award based on its analysis of factors set forth in Rule 82(b)(3).[59] Factors relevant to a decision as to whether to vary a standard Rule 82 fee award include (1) the complexity of the litigation; (2) the length of any trial; (3) the reasonableness of the lawyer's hourly rates and the number of hours worked on the case; (4) the reasonableness of the number of lawyers used; (5) efforts to minimize fees; (6) the reasonableness of the claims and defenses pursued by the parties; (7) vexatious or bad faith conduct; (8) the relationship between the amount of work performed and the significance of the matters at stake; (9) the extent to which the award would risk chilling the use of the courts by similarly situated parties; (10) any evidence that the fees were incurred for reasons apart from the case at bar, such as to discourage claims by others against the prevailing party or its insurer; and (11) "other equitable factors" deemed relevant by the court.[60]

Because Rule 82 fees may be recovered by a prevailing party in a class action regardless of party status, both plaintiff classes and defendants potentially can recover Rule 82 fees if they succeed on their claims or defenses.[61] The Alaska Supreme Court has held, however, that attorney fees obtained under Rule 82 cannot be recovered from absent class members.[62] Consequently, among class members, only nonprevailing named class plaintiffs are subject to assessment of Rule 82 fees.[63] Rule 82 fee awards against named class plaintiffs, however, must be based solely on fees incurred litigating the merits of their individual claims and not on fees incurred litigating class certification or other class members' claims.[64]

In practice, significant fee awards against nonprevailing named class plaintiffs are rarely imposed. This is perhaps not surprising since a common feature of class actions is that an individual named plaintiff's claim is relatively small compared to the potential large attorney fees that may be incurred in opposing class certifi-

---

57. ALASKA R. CIV. P. 82(b)(2).

58. *See, e.g.*, McGlothlin v. Municipality of Anchorage, 991 P.2d 1273, 1277 (Alaska 1999) (fee awards made pursuant to the schedule in Rule 82(b)(1) are presumptively correct).

59. ALASKA R. CIV. P. 82(b)(3); *see also* Bissonette, 146 P.3d at 573 (affirming enhanced attorney fee award under Rule 82(b)(3) in class action).

60. ALASKA R. CIV. P. 82(b)(3)(A)–(K).

61. *See* Turner v. Alaska Comm'ns, 78 P.3d 264, 268–69 (Alaska 2003).

62. *Id.* at 266.

63. *Id.* at 269.

64. Monzingo v. Alaska Air Group, Inc., 112 P.3d 655, 668 (Alaska 2005).

cation and otherwise defending a class action. Under those circumstances, a large fee award might deter plaintiffs from using the courts to litigate similar claims.[65]

B. ALASKA RULE OF CIVIL PROCEDURE 68

The Alaska Rules of Civil Procedure also contain a powerful fee-shifting provision as part of its "offer of judgment" rule, Rule 68.[66] Rule 68 provides that any party asserting or defending a claim may serve an offer of judgment upon any other party, by which the offering party offers to allow judgment to be entered in complete satisfaction of the claim in exchange for money, property, or other consideration.[67] The offeree has ten days within which to accept a Rule 68 offer of judgment in writing.[68] If the offer of judgment is not accepted, it is considered withdrawn and the litigation continues.[69] Multiple offers of judgment may be made by a party.[70]

When judgment is entered in a case, it is compared to offers of judgment made during the case. If the actual judgment is sufficiently less favorable to the offeree than an unaccepted offer of judgment—as measured by criteria included in Rule 68—the offeror may recover from the other party the costs and partial attorney fees incurred from the date of the offer.[71] Under Rule 68, therefore, even a party that "loses" on its claims or defenses may recover costs and a fee award from a "winning" party when the actual relevant judgment is less favorable to the offeree than the offer of judgment.[72] For an offer of judgment to be valid to shift attorney fees under Rule 68, it must be reasonable in amount and timing and must constitute a good faith attempt to settle the litigation or to encourage negotiation.[73]

The percentage of attorney fees that may be recovered range from 30 to 75 percent of reasonable actual fees incurred between the date the offer of judgment was made and the conclusion of the case.[74] The actual percentage of fees that may be

---

65. *See* ALASKA R. CIV. P. 82(b)(3)(I); *Turner*, 78 P.3d at 269–70.

66. *See* ALASKA R. CIV. P. 68.

67. ALASKA R. CIV. P. 68(a).

68. *Id.*

69. *Id.*

70. *Id.*

71. *See* ALASKA R. CIV. P. 68(b).

72. *See Catalina Yachts v. Pierce*, 105 P.3d 125, 129 (Alaska 2005) (Rule 68 allows attorney fees to defendants who do not prevail at trial).

73. *Beal v. McGuire*, 216 P.3d 1154, 1178 (Alaska 2009) (citing *Beattie v. Thomas*, 668 P.2d 268, 274 (1983)). The Alaska Supreme Court in *Beal* indicated that courts evaluating the validity of offers of judgment should consider the following factors: (1) whether the plaintiff's claims were brought in good faith; (2) whether the offer of judgment was reasonable and in good faith in both its timing and amount; (3) whether the decision to reject the offer and proceed to trial was grossly unreasonable or in bad faith; and (4) whether the fees sought by the offeror are reasonable and justified in amount. *Id.*

74. ALASKA R. CIV. P. 68(b).

recovered depends on the timing of the offer of judgment, with earlier offers generating greater percentage awards.[75]

An offering party who is eligible to receive costs and a fee award under Rule 68(b) may recover either the appropriate Rule 68 fee award or a fee award under Rule 82, whichever is greater.[76] Rule 68 expressly provides that a party entitled to a fee award under Rule 68 is considered the prevailing party for purposes of a Rule 82 award.[77] This latter provision eliminates any confusion or conflict between Rule 68, where a party that "loses" its case nevertheless may be entitled to fee-shifting based on an offer of judgment, and Rule 82, where a "prevailing party" is typically the one who succeeds on its claims or defenses.

Alaska Rule 68 probably applies to class actions under Alaska Rule 23, although that issue is not addressed in either rule. Rule 68 does not refer to either class actions or Rule 23.[78] Nor does Rule 23 refer to either Rule 68 or offers of judgment.[79] One reported Alaska Supreme Court decision strongly implies that Rule 68 applies in class actions, analogizing the application of Rule 68 to the non-class consumer plaintiffs in that case to the application of Rule 82 to named class representatives expressly approved in the *Turner v. Alaska Communications* case.[80] Based on the general applicability of Rule 68 and the fact that Rule 82 applies in Rule 23 class actions, as discussed above, it is very likely that Rule 68 also applies in class actions. It also is likely that limitations on Rule 68 fee-shifting in favor of class action defendants track those applicable to Rule 82. Accordingly, such fee-shifting probably is available only against named class plaintiffs and then only with respect to fees incurred in litigating the merits of their individual claims.[81]

C. COMMON FUND FEE AWARDS

Alaska courts also may award attorney fees to class counsel under the common fund doctrine.[82] Under that doctrine, "a litigant or a lawyer who recovers a common fund for the benefit of persons other than himself or his client is entitled to a reasonable attorney's fee from the fund as a whole."[83] The purposes of the com-

---

75. ALASKA R. CIV. P. 68(b)(1)–(3).

76. ALASKA R. CIV. P. 68(c). Notably, fee-shifting under Rule 68 can apply even where a statute provides a separate mechanism for shifting fees. *See Catalina Yachts*, 105 P.3d at 128 (Rule 68 could operate to shift fees to a defendant who prevailed on claims including one under a federal statute that provided for fee-shifting only to prevailing plaintiffs). This differs from fee-shifting under Rule 82, which does not apply to claims arising under a statutory scheme that provides a separate fee-shifting mechanism. *Id.*

77. ALASKA R. CIV. P. 68(c).

78. *See* ALASKA R. CIV. P. 68.

79. ALASKA R. CIV. P. 23.

80. *See Catalina Yachts*, 105 P.3d at 131 (citing *Turner*, 78 P.3d at 268, 269).

81. *Cf. Monzingo*, 112 P.3d at 668 (imposing these limitations on Rule 82 fee awards in class actions).

82. *See Okuley*, 214 P.3d at 252; *Gentile*, 922 P.2d at 265; *Edwards*, 920 P.2d at 754–56.

83. *Edwards*, 920 P.2d at 754 (citing *Boeing Co. v. Van Gemert*, 444 U.S. 472, 478 (1980)).

mon fund doctrine include (1) to avoid unjust enrichment of persons who obtain the benefit of a lawsuit without contributing to its cost and (2) to ensure reasonable compensation to counsel who participate in obtaining the common fund or benefit.[84]

In calculating an appropriate common fund fee award, Alaska courts may apply either a percentage-of-the-fund method or a modified lodestar method.[85] Neither method is generally preferred over the other because the application of each could be unfair under certain circumstances; therefore, the choice of method is left to the discretion of the trial court.[86] If the percentage approach is taken, the court should begin with a baseline of 25 percent of the common fund and then modify that baseline based on factors such as the size of the common fund, whether class members have substantial objections to the fee request, nonmonetary benefits conferred by the result of the litigation, the economies of scale involved in the class action, and the so-called *Johnson-Kerr* factors used by federal courts.[87]

Under the modified lodestar approach, the trial court determines a lodestar amount of fees based on a reasonable hourly rate and the number of hours reasonably expended on the case.[88] The court may then award that lodestar amount or, at its discretion, determine an amount by which the lodestar should be multiplied to establish a final attorney fee award.[89] Factors to be considered in determining what, if any, multiplier to use include the *Johnson-Kerr* factors, the risk to class counsel in taking the case, achievement of extraordinary results, the quality of representation, and any substantial delay in payment.[90]

The Alaska Supreme Court held expressly in *Edwards v. Alaska Pulp Corp.* that the common fund doctrine does not conflict with Alaska Rule 82.[91] The two rules serve different purposes. While the common fund doctrine is a mechanism for spreading fees among class members in order to avoid unjust enrichment of some class members based on the efforts of a few and to ensure reasonable compensation

---

84. *Id.* at 754–55, 756.

85. *See Okuley*, 214 P.3d at 252 (citing *Edwards*, 920 P.2d at 758).

86. *Edwards*, 920 P.2d at 758 (citing *Wash. Pub. Power Supply Sys. Sec. Litig.*, 19 F.3d 1291, 1296 (9th Cir. 1994)). The percentage method may be inappropriate, for example, where (1) class counsel quickly negotiates an enormous settlement and would obtain an "inordinate windfall" if that method was used; (2) it is difficult to measure the common benefit obtained; or (3) the common fund is enormous. *Okuley*, 214 P.3d at 253 (citing, *inter alia*, *Edwards*, 920 P.2d at 758; *Gentile*, 922 P.2d at 266). The lodestar approach may be inappropriate where counsel recovers a small fund, most or all of which would be "devoured" by an award based on lodestar. *Id.*

87. *See id.* at 252–53; *see also Edwards*, 920 P.2d at 757 (setting out the 12 *Johnson-Kerr* factors) (citing *Johnson v. Ga. Highway Express, Inc.*, 488 F.2d 714, 717–19 (5th Cir. 1974); *Kerr v. Screen Extras Guild, Inc.*, 526 F.2d 67, 69–70 (9th Cir. 1975)).

88. *Okuley*, 214 P.3d at 253; *Edwards*, 920 P.2d at 757.

89. *Okuley*, 214 P.3d at 253; *Edwards*, 920 P.2d at 757.

90. *Edwards*, 920 P.2d at 757 (citing *Wash. Pub. Power Supply*, 19 F.3d at 1301–05).

91. *Id.* at 755–56.

to class counsel, Rule 82 is a fee-shifting mechanism that provides partial reimbursement of a prevailing party's attorney fees.[92] Because Rule 82 was not intended to cap recovery of attorney fees under other doctrines, it "does not preempt the applicability of the common fund doctrine, wholly or in part."[93] Accordingly, in an appropriate case, the common fund doctrine and Rule 82 may both be applied. For example, the common fund doctrine can be used to set an appropriate fee award from the common fund, and Rule 82 can then be applied to determine what portion of that common fund fee, if any, will be shifted to any nonprevailing party or parties.[94]

Where the trial court intends to award attorney fees from a common fund in a class action, it is desirable, but not required, that class members be provided with notice because the use of the common fund to pay attorney fees poses a risk of conflict of interest between class counsel and the class.[95] But such notice is not required by either Alaska Rule 23 or considerations of due process, at least where class counsel's request for fees from a common fund is formal, vigorously opposed by other parties, closely scrutinized by the trial court, and would result in only small deductions from each class member's individual recovery.[96]

VII. Punitive Damages

Alaska has statutory caps on punitive damages.[97] Neither the statute imposing the punitive damages cap nor any reported Alaska case addresses the application of such caps to class actions.

---

92. *Id.* at 755.

93. *Id.* at 755–56.

94. *See, e.g., Okuley,* 214 P.3d at 250 (class awarded fees from a common fund and a Rule 82 fee award from the defendant). In such cases, the Rule 82 fee award will be offset against the fee to be taken from the common fund, thereby increasing the amount of the fund available to benefit the class. *See Gentile,* 922 P.2d at 265.

95. *Okuley,* 214 P.3d at 257–58.

96. *Id.* at 258. The Alaska Supreme Court in *Okuley* noted that in light of these circumstances, the interests of class members were as well protected as if individual notice had been provided and at lower cost and with reduced delays. *Id.*

97. ALASKA STAT. § 09.17.020(f)–(h).

ARIZONA

ROBERT B. CAREY
AMY M. WILKINS

I. Introduction

While Arizona Rule of Civil Procedure 23 (Arizona Rule 23) used to be identical to Federal Rule 23, Arizona has not adopted the 1998 or 2003 amendments to Federal Rule 23. As a result, Arizona Rule 23 does not contain provisions concerning interlocutory appeals from class action determinations, the appointment of class counsel, procedures for settling or compromising class actions, the contents of class notices, and the award of attorney fees.

Although the two rules are no longer identical, federal cases are still persuasive authority in Arizona courts where the particular part of the rule is identical.[1] Where the rules differ, however, federal case law will be less persuasive.

II. Comparison with Federal Rule 23

A. INTERLOCUTORY APPEALS

Paragraph (f) to Federal Rule 23, added in 1998, permits interlocutory appeals of class certification decisions. "A court of appeals may permit an appeal from an order granting or denying class certification under this rule . . . ."[2] The rule provides a court of appeals with discretion to grant interlocutory review. The Advisory

---

1. *See, e.g., Fernandez v. Takata Seat Belts, Inc.*, 108 P.3d 917, 920 (Ariz. 2005) ("Given that our class action rule mirrors the federal rule, we find these [U.S.] Supreme Court cases persuasive in deciding the issue presented by this case."); *Lennon v. First Nat'l Bank*, 518 P.2d 1230, 1232 n.3 (Ariz. Ct. App. 1974) ("[F]ederal cases construing Fed. R. Civ. P. Rule 23, while not controlling, are authoritative.").

2. FED. R. CIV. P. 23(f); *see also* Chapter 5, "Interlocutory Appeals."

Committee notes advise that "[p]ermission is most likely to be granted when the certification decision turns on a novel or unsettled question of law, or when, as a practical matter, the decision on certification is likely dispositive of the litigation."[3]

Unlike its federal counterpart, Arizona Rule 23 does not provide for interlocutory appeals, nor is there a statutory right to do so as in some states. Instead, the proper procedure is to file a petition for special action in the court of appeals. In *Garza v. Swift Transportation Co.*,[4] the Arizona Supreme Court rejected the death-knell doctrine, reversing *Reader v. Magma-Superior Copper Co.*[5] The *Reader* court had held that a plaintiff could take an interlocutory appeal from a denial of class certification pursuant to section 2101(D) of the Arizona Revised Statutes, which provides that an appeal can be taken "from any order affecting a substantial right made in any action when the order in effect determines the action and prevents judgment from which an appeal might be taken."[6] The *Reader* court had determined that denial of class certification, which "as a practical reality . . . forecloses the appellants from pursuing their action further" due to the enormous costs of the litigation, fell within section 2101(D).[7] The *Garza* court held that an order denying class certification did not determine the action within the meaning of section 2101(D) because the individual plaintiffs could continue to seek a final judgment.[8] Although the *Garza* court advised that a party could seek relief from a class certification order by petitioning for a special action in the court of appeals, as a practical matter, this is a limited solution; the court of appeals does not accept jurisdiction of the majority of petitions for special actions.

B. APPOINTMENT OF CLASS COUNSEL

Federal Rule 23(g) provides that a court that certifies a class must appoint class counsel and provides a procedure for doing so. The specific procedure depends on whether there is more than one applicant for class counsel. The Federal Rule further provides that a court may appoint interim class counsel prior to certifying a class.[9]

Arizona does not have a comparable provision in Arizona Rule 23. Instead, the adequacy of class counsel is tied into Rule 23(a)(4), which provides that "the rep-

---

3. FED. R. CIV. P. 23(f) advisory committee note (1998).
4. 213 P.3d 1008, 1014 (Ariz. 2008).
5. 494 P.2d 708, 709 (Ariz. 1972).
6. ARIZ. REV. STAT. § 12-2101(D).
7. *Id.*
8. *Garza*, 213 P.3d at 1012–13.
9. FED. R. CIV. P. 23(g)(2)(A).

resentative parties will fairly and adequately protect the interests of the class."[10] As the Arizona Court of Appeals explained, "[t]o protect the interests of those whom the named plaintiffs claim to represent, the court inquires not only into the character and quality of the named representatives but it also considers the quality and experience of the attorneys representing the class."[11] Class counsel "must be 'qualified, experienced and generally able to conduct the proposed litigation.'"[12]

C. CLASS ACTION SETTLEMENTS

Federal Rule 23(e) was amended in 2003 to strengthen the process of reviewing proposed class action settlements and now provides for particular procedures that must be applied to a proposed settlement, voluntary dismissal, or compromise. Arizona Rule 23(e) has not been amended, and provides only that a class action shall not be dismissed or compromised without the approval of the court.

D. CLASS ACTION NOTICES

Federal Rule 23(c)(2) now provides specific items that must be included in notice to a class certified under Rule 23(b)(3). Arizona Rule 23(c)(2) has a less specific requirement and simply states that the notice must explain the exclusion rules in any class action certified under Arizona Rule 23(b)(3).

E. ATTORNEY FEES

Federal Rule 23(h) provides that a court may award attorney fees and provides procedures for their award. Arizona Rule 23 is silent as to attorney fees. Fees are regularly awarded in class actions, either under the common fund doctrine or pursuant to statute or contract. "Under the common fund doctrine a court may award attorneys' fees to counsel for the prevailing side whose efforts in litigation create or preserve a common fund from which others who have undertaken no risk or cost will nevertheless benefit."[13]

III. *Construction and Application of Arizona Rule 23*

Arizona Rule 23 is to be construed liberally, and doubts concerning whether to certify a class should be resolved in favor of certification.[14]

---

10. Ariz. R. Civ. P. 23(a)(4).

11. *London v. Green Acres Trust*, 765 P.2d 538, 543 (Ariz. Ct. App. 1988).

12. *Id.* (quoting *Eisen v. Carlisle & Jacquelin*, 391 F.2d 555, 562 (2d Cir. 1968)).

13. *Kerr v. Killian*, 3 P.3d 1133, 1137–38 (Ariz. Ct. App. 2000).

14. *See ESI Ergonomic Solutions, LLC v. United Artists Theatre Circuit, Inc.*, 50 P.3d 844, 848 (Ariz. Ct. App. 2002).

IV. Nuances of Arizona Rule 23(a)

A. NUMEROSITY

There is no bright line rule in Arizona for numerosity.[15] The test in Arizona, as in the federal rule, is whether it would be impracticable to join the affected class members as parties; numerosity—as used in the rule—encompasses more than just sheer numbers.

In *London v. Green Acres Trust*, the court noted that there must be evidence to defeat an allegation of numerosity. The defendants in that case alleged that the class was not numerous because there were only eight potential members. The court rejected that argument, because defendants had not submitted evidence (just argument of counsel) that there were only eight members.[16] Thus, in Arizona, courts will require evidence or a reasonable estimate of the number of class members.

B. COMMONALITY/TYPICALITY

While commonality and typicality are separate elements of Rule 23(a), there is some overlap in how they are treated in the case law.

Commonality, when reviewed separately from other elements, requires only a single common issue of law or fact.[17]

The view of typicality in Arizona is expansive. Arizona Rule 23(a)(3) provides that "the claims or defenses of the representative parties are typical of the claims or defenses of the class."[18] Arizona cases take several approaches to typicality. As the appellate court in *Lennon v. First National Bank*[19] summarized:

> Under Rule 23(a)(3) the claims of the representative party must be "typical" of the claims of the class. Some courts have held that the typicality requirement is satisfied when common questions of law or fact exist. Others have held a representative's claim typical if the interests of the representative are not antagonistic to those of absent class members. Still others require the representative to demonstrate that absent class members have suffered the same grievances of which he complains.[20]

The *Lennon* court did not choose a particular test, but found that all three tests were met in that case.

In *Godbey v. Roosevelt School District*,[21] the court noted that the three tests described in *Lennon* overlapped with other parts of Rule 23:

---

15. *See London*, 765 P.2d at 543.
16. *Id.* at 543.
17. *See Lennon*, 518 P.2d at 1233.
18. ARIZ. R. CIV. P. 23(a)(3).
19. 518 P.2d 1230 (Ariz. Ct. App. 1974).
20. *Id.* at 1233.
21. 638 P.2d 235 (Ariz. Ct. App. 1981).

[T]he second test is the most liberal and is clearly met in this case. The first and third tests overlap with the requirement of Rule 23(a)(2) that there exist questions of law and fact common to the class, and the possible additional requirement of Rule 23(b)(3) that such common questions predominate.[22]

In other words, the typicality test is somewhat amorphous in Arizona. To the extent that the test overlaps with commonality, it will likewise overlap with predominance because Arizona courts often combine the queries of whether common issues of law or fact exist with whether those issues predominate.[23]

C. ADEQUACY

As discussed above, Arizona courts examine the "character and quality" of both the named plaintiffs and their counsel.[24] If a plaintiff does not have standing, that plaintiff is not adequate to maintain a class action on behalf of others who would have standing.[25]

V. Nuances of Arizona Rule 23(b)

A. RULE 23(B)(1)

Arizona Rule 23(b)(1) authorizes a class action where the prosecution of separate actions creates the possibility that individual adjudications would, as a practical matter, dispose of the interests of other class members not party to the litigation or impede their ability to protect those interests. There is no case law in Arizona further developing this requirement. In *Godbey*, the parties obtained certification under Rule 23(b)(1) and (b)(2). On appeal, the parties briefed certification issues as if proceeding under Rule 23(b)(3), which shed little light on the proper application of Rules 23(b)(1) and (b)(2) in Arizona.[26]

B. RULE 23(B)(2)

Arizona Rule 23(b)(2) authorizes a class action where the party opposing the class has acted or refused to act on grounds generally applicable to the class. This type of class action is limited to instances where injunctive or declaratory relief is sought.

---

22. *Id.* at 239.

23. *See Reader v. Magma-Superior Copper Co.*, 515 P.2d 860, 862 (Ariz. 1973); *Lennon*, 518 P.2d at 1233.

24. *London*, 765 P.2d at 543.

25. *Karbal v. Ariz. Dept. of Revenue*, 158 P.3d 243, 245 (Ariz. Ct. App. 2007) ("A putative class representative who does not have standing cannot maintain a class action on behalf of others who could allege standing."); *Fernandez*, 108 P.2d at 920 (same).

26. *Godbey*, 638 P.2d at 239.

Arizona case law developing Rule 23(b)(2), like Rule 23(b)(1), is undeveloped, although classes have been certified under Rule 23(b)(2).[27]

C. RULE 23(B)(3)

Arizona Rule 23(b)(3) permits a class action where questions of law or fact common to class members predominate over individual questions and the class action is the superior vehicle for resolving the controversy.

1. Predominance

The predominance requirement means that common questions should predominate over questions affecting individual members. This requirement does not mean that all questions of law or fact must be common questions.[28] The common questions need not be dispositive of the entire action.[29]

2. Superiority

The court must find that a class action is superior to other available methods for the fair and efficient adjudication of the controversy. Like the Federal Rule, Arizona Rule 23(b)(3) lists four factors to be considered:

> (A) the interest of members of the class in individually controlling the prosecution or defense of separate actions; (B) the extent and nature of any litigation concerning the controversy already commenced by or against members of the class; (C) the desirability or undesirability of concentrating the litigation of the claims in the particular forum; (D) the difficulties likely to be encountered in the management of a class action.[30]

"The four factors are not exclusive, and the court, in its discretion, may consider other relevant factors."[31]

In *ESI Ergonomic Solutions, LLC v. United Artists Theatre Circuit, Inc.*, the court held that the lack of other lawsuits demonstrated the superiority of the class action as a method of adjudicating the controversy.[32] Moreover, the court considered and rejected the argument that the prospect of "annihilating damages" could be a factor in the superiority analysis. The court rejected the idea that "fairness of the consequences to the defendants should a plaintiff class prevail" should be considered

---

27. *See, e.g., Arnold v. Ariz. Dep't of Health Servs.*, 775 P.2d 521, 523 (Ariz. 1989) (special action to compel treatment for chronically mentally ill).

28. *See Home Fed. Sav. & Loan Ass'n v. Pleasants*, 534 P.2d 275, 278 (Ariz. Ct. App. 1975) ("Maintenance of a class action does not depend upon commonality of all questions of fact and law, but only that such questions predominate over questions affecting individual members of the class.").

29. *See id.*

30. Ariz. R. Civ. P. 23(b)(3).

31. *ESI Ergonomic Solutions*, 50 P.3d at 848.

32. *Id.* at 850.

rather than "the procedural fairness of adjudicating the matter through a class action versus some other method."[33]

For a class action not to be superior to other methods, there must be some viable alternative for adjudicating the dispute that is superior to the class action. For example, in *Lennon*, the court considered the alternative of individual suits, but found it "highly unlikely that any significant number of absent class members would individually file lawsuits against the [defendant] in light of the relatively small individual recoveries."[34] In *ESI*, defendant suggested the alternative of bankruptcy court, but the court rejected this proposal because the notice sent to class members had not satisfied Rule 23's requirement of giving the best notice practicable.[35]

Manageability is also part of the superiority analysis. Courts have held that class actions are manageable despite the existence of individual counterclaims. In *Lennon*, the defendant asserted that the existence of individualized defenses would render the action unmanageable. The court, however, concluded that because the amounts owed by each class member were liquidated and within the records of the defendant, these counterclaims did not render the class action unmanageable.[36] Moreover, because the claims asserted by plaintiffs in the case might negate the defenses if proven, the court found there would be little if any litigation on the defenses.[37]

VI. Other Features of Arizona Class Action Law

A. CLASS CERTIFICATION HEARING

There is no requirement in Arizona that the court conduct an evidentiary hearing prior to certification. As one court commented, "[w]hile there may be no absolute right to have an evidentiary hearing, there are situations when a hearing is appropriate."[38] The *London* court concluded that a hearing was not necessary in that case when the trial court had extensive pleadings and memoranda, which included discovery material supporting and opposing certification.[39]

---

33. *Id.*
34. *Lennon*, 518 P.2d at 1235.
35. *ESI Ergonomic Solutions*, 50 P.3d at 852.
36. *Lennon*, 518 P.2d at 1234–35.
37. *Id.* at 310–11; *see also Godbey*, 638 P.2d at 240 (following *Lennon*).
38. *London*, 765 P.2d at 140.
39. *Id.*

B. SECURITIES CASES

Arizona has enacted a state version of the federal Private Securities Litigation Reform Act.[40] The act imposes procedural requirements on class actions involving violations of Arizona's securities statutes. The statutory scheme requires plaintiffs to file a sworn certification with the court that, among other things, they reviewed and authorized the complaint, that they did not purchase the security at issue at the direction of counsel, and that they are willing to serve as class representatives. Moreover, within 20 days after filing the complaint, the plaintiffs must arrange for the publication of a notice to advise members of the putative class of the action and the claims, and the notice must advise potential class members that they may move to serve as lead plaintiff.

C. CLASS ACTIONS IN ADMINISTRATIVE SETTINGS

Arizona permits class actions in administrative settings. In *Arizona Department of Revenue v. Dougherty*,[41] the Arizona Supreme Court held that class actions were permitted in tax court. The court reasoned that nothing in Rule 23 precluded its application in tax proceedings. Moreover, the court reasoned that because the legislature had provided that proceedings in the tax court were governed by the Arizona Rules of Civil Procedure, the legislature had implicitly endorsed the use of Rule 23 in tax court.

D. ARBITRATION OF CLASS ACTIONS

The Arizona Court of Appeals has upheld an arbitration clause in a class action context. In *Harrington v. Pulte Home Corp.*,[42] a putative class of homeowners appealed the trial court's decision to enforce an arbitration clause. The homeowners did not argue that they could not have a class action in arbitration, but instead argued that the clause violated the reasonable expectations of the parties and was unconscionable. The court held, "[w]e do not find that the presence of a potential class renders this arbitration clause unenforceable."[43] The court rejected the argument that the clause violated the reasonable expectations of the parties even though it did not specifically reference a jury trial waiver or provide notice of the arbitration fees that would have to be paid by plaintiffs. The court further rejected the argument that the clause was substantively unconscionable simply because it required plaintiffs to pay fees, considering that the costs of arbitration were small "when

---

40. *See* Ariz. Rev. Stat. §§ 44-2081 to 44-2087.
41. 29 P.3d 862, 865 (Ariz. 2001).
42. 119 P.3d 1044 (Ariz. Ct. App. 2005).
43. *Id.* at 1049.

compared to the amount they seek to recover and compared to the amount they would likely have to pay in litigation expenses if arbitration were not available."[44]

E. THE DOCTRINE OF VIRTUAL REPRESENTATION

In *Bohn v. Waddell*,[45] the tax court adopted the doctrine of virtual representation:

> The doctrine of virtual representation provides that a judgment or decree may adjudicate the rights of a person not a party to the adjudication, if the absent party is so well represented by a party who is before the court, that the interests of the absent party receive actual and efficient representation. The doctrine rests on considerations of necessity, convenience, and efficiency in the administration of justice.[46]

Bohn involved a putative class of taxpayers who had paid state taxes on federal pensions and who sought refunds of the state tax paid from the state.

The tax court explained:

> The doctrine is most commonly found in litigation in which one of the parties is a government entity, and the other party or parties are persons subject to the authority of the government party. The issue which the Court is asked to determine is whether the government party has encroached upon a right or interest of the non-government party. In all cases, the non-government party shares with numerous non-parties the same relationship with the government party.[47]

On appeal, the Arizona Court of Appeals declined to consider the doctrine of virtual representation, resolving the appeal on other grounds.[48]

F. STANDING

As discussed above in section IV.C, a plaintiff does not have standing to bring a class claim if the plaintiff does not have an individual claim against the defendant.[49]

On appeal, if the final judgment is not favorable to an individual plaintiff, that plaintiff has standing to challenge an adverse certification ruling.[50] By contrast, "[g]enerally, when a court enters judgment in favor of a party, that party is not 'aggrieved' and thus has no standing to appeal."[51]

---

44. *Id.* at 1056.

45. 790 P.2d 772 (Ariz. Tax Ct. 1990).

46. *Id.* at 787.

47. *Id.*

48. *Bohn v. Waddell*, 848 P.2d 324 (Ariz. Ct. App. 1992).

49. *Fernandez*, 108 P.2d at 920 ("[T]he proper inquiry in a class action lawsuit must initially focus on whether the plaintiff has an individual claim against the defendant. If she does not, she cannot maintain a class action against that defendant.").

50. *See Markiewicz v. Salt River Valley Water Users' Ass'n*, 576 P.2d 517, 529 (Ariz. Ct. App. 1978).

51. *Douglas v. Governing Bd. of Window Rock Consol. Sch. Dist. No. 8*, 210 P.3d 1275, 1279 (Ariz. Ct. App. 2009).

In *Douglas v. Governing Board of Window Rock Consolidated School District No. 8*, the individual plaintiffs brought a class action and then accepted a Rule 68 offer of judgment on their claims. The court of appeals held that they did not have standing to appeal the denial of class certification since they had consented to judgment in their favor.[52] Although the plaintiffs asserted that they had not accepted judgment of the class claims, the court held that they had accepted the offer of judgment as to all claims. The plaintiffs then argued that they had standing to appeal the denial of class certification because they had filed a motion to substitute named plaintiffs after they accepted the Rule 68 offer of judgment, but before termination of the case. The court rejected the argument, finding that the plaintiffs could not file that motion after accepting an offer of judgment.[53] As a result, the court of appeals lacked jurisdiction over the appeal.[54] Thus, the best practice for plaintiffs is to arrange for substitute or additional class representatives, if necessary, before accepting an offer of judgment. Alternatively, it seems possible that potential new plaintiffs might be able to file a motion to intervene, but clearly such an approach would be risky and could be rejected.[55]

---

52. *Id.* at 1279–80.

53. *Id.* at 1282–83.

54. *Id.* at 1283.

55. *See id.* ("Thus, we do not have before us, and consequently do not decide, whether the Douglases' acceptance of the offer of judgment precluded putative class members from intervening under Rule 24(b) and appealing the denial of class certification.").

ARKANSAS

LYN P. PRUITT

I. Prerequisites to Class Certification in Arkansas

Rule 23 of the Arkansas Rules of Civil Procedure (Arkansas Rule) governs class actions and provides, in pertinent part:

> (a) *Prerequisites to Class Action.* One or more members of a class may sue or be sued as representative parties on behalf of all only if (1) the class is so numerous that joinder of all members is impracticable, (2) there are questions of law or fact common to the class, (3) the claims or defenses of the representative parties are typical of the claims or defenses of the class, and (4) the representative parties and their counsel will fairly and adequately protect the interests of the class.
>
> (b) *Class Actions Maintainable.* An action may be maintained as a class action if the prerequisites of subdivision (a) are satisfied, and the court finds that the questions of law or fact common to the members of the class predominate over any questions affecting only individual members, and that a class action is superior to other available methods for the fair and efficient adjudication of the controversy. At an early practicable time after the commencement of an action brought as a class action, the court shall determine by order whether it is to be so maintained. For purposes of this subdivision, "practicable" means reasonably capable of being accomplished. An order under this section may be altered or amended at any time before the court enters final judgment. An order certifying a class action must define the class and the class claims, issues, or defenses.[1]

---

1. ARK. R. CIV. P. 23(a)–(b) (2009).

II. Variance from Federal Rule 23

Arkansas Rule 23(a) is similar to Federal Rule of Civil Procedure 23(a). Arkansas Rule 23(b) tracks Federal Rule 23(b)(3), but the Arkansas Rule does not contain provisions for a class to be certified as set forth in Federal Rule 23(b)(1) or (2).

Arkansas Rule 23 is often compared to Federal Rule 23, but the interpretation of the predominance and superiority requirements of the Arkansas Rule is very different from the interpretation of predominance and superiority set forth by the vast majority of federal courts.

The Arkansas Rule tracks Federal Rule 23 provisions concerning notice, conducting the action, and dismissal or compromise, but is silent on issues of class counsel and attorney fees and nontaxable costs. Practically, as to the last two issues the Arkansas Rule has been applied consistent with Federal Rule 23.

III. Court Decisions

A. CLASS DEFINITION

Arkansas law requires that in order for a class to be certified, the following six elements must be present: (1) numerosity; (2) commonality; (3) typicality; (4) adequacy; (5) predominance; and (6) superiority. In addition, under Arkansas law, though not discussed in Arkansas Rule 23, certain requirements exist concerning the class definition.

With respect to class definition, it is axiomatic that for a class to be certified, a class must exist.[2] The definition of the class to be certified must first meet a standard that is not explicit in the text of Arkansas Rule 23, that the class be susceptible to precise definition. This is to ensure that the class is neither amorphous nor imprecise. Thus, before a class can be certified under Arkansas Rule 23, the class description must be sufficiently definite that it is administratively feasible for the court to determine whether a particular individual is a member of the proposed class. Furthermore, for a class to be sufficiently defined, the identity of the class members must be ascertainable by reference to objective criteria.[3]

B. PREDOMINANCE AND SUPERIORITY

The Arkansas Supreme Court has interpreted the requirements of predominance and superiority somewhat differently than federal courts in several respects. First, the Arkansas Supreme Court uses the following standard in reviewing an order granting class certification:

---

2. *Asbury Auto. Group, Inc. v. Palasack*, 366 Ark. 601, 237 S.W.2d 462 (2006).

3. *Id.*

We begin by noting that it is well settled that this court will not reverse a circuit court's ruling on a class certification absent an abuse of discretion. In reviewing a lower court's class certification order, "this court focuses on the evidence in the record to determine whether it supports the trial court's conclusion regarding certification." We have held that neither the trial court nor the appellate court may delve into the merits of the underlying claim in determining whether the elements of Rule 23 have been satisfied. Our court has said on this point that "*a trial court may not consider whether the plaintiffs will ultimately prevail, or even whether they have a cause of action.*" We, thus, view the propriety of a class action as a procedural question.[4]

The Arkansas Supreme Court has inferred and discussed the fact that a "rigorous analysis" of Rule 23's class certification factors is not required and in fact may be prohibited if it requires the trial court to delve into the merits of the underlying claim. In *General Motors Corp. v. Bryant*,[5] the court explained,

> we have previously rejected any requirement of a rigorous-analysis inquiry by our circuit courts. Instead, we have given the circuit courts of our state broad discretion in determining whether the requirements for class certification have been met, recognizing the caveat that a class can always be decertified at a later date if necessary. As our rule so clearly provides, "[a]n order under this section may be altered or amended at any time before the court enters final judgment."[6]

The Arkansas approach, under which a class certification determination is purely procedural, appears to affect all aspects of evaluating the predominance as well as the superiority factors and, in at least one Arkansas Supreme Court opinion, the choice-of-law analysis; unlike the federal courts, a circuit court in Arkansas need not engage in choice-of-law analysis before certifying a class.[7]

The Arkansas Supreme Court interprets the predominance factor of Arkansas Rule 23 by starting with an analysis of whether a common wrong has been alleged against the defendant.[8] If a case involves preliminary, common issues of liability and wrongdoing that affect all class members, the predominance requirement of Rule 23 is satisfied even if the circuit court must subsequently determine individual damage issues in bifurcated proceedings. The Arkansas Supreme Court has recognized that a bifurcated process of certifying a class to resolve preliminary, common issues and then decertifying the class to resolve individual issues, such as damages, is consistent with Rule 23. In addition, the court has said that

---

4. *Carquest of Hot Springs, Inc. v. Gen. Parts, Inc.*, 367 Ark. 218, 223, 238 S.W.3d 916, 919–20 (2006) (emphasis in original) (internal citations omitted) (quoting *Van Buren Sch. Dist. v. Jones*, 365 Ark. 610, 613, 232 S.W.3d 444, 447 (2006)).

5. 374 Ark. 38, 285 S.W.3d 634 (2008).

6. *Id.* at 46–47, 285 S.W.3d at 641 (internal citations omitted) (quoting ARK. R. CIV. P. 23(b)).

7. *Id.*

8. *ChartOne, Inc. v. Raglon*, 373 Ark. 275, 283 S.W.3d 576 (2008).

[t]he predominance element can be satisfied if the preliminary, common issues may be resolved before any individual issues. In making this determination, we do not merely compare the number of individual versus common claims. Instead, we must decide if the issues common to all plaintiffs "predominate over" the individual issues, which can be resolved during the decertified stage of bifurcated proceedings.[9]

The inquiry is whether there is a predominating question that can be answered before determining any individual issues.[10] In addition, the Arkansas Supreme Court has held that the mere fact individual issues and defenses may be raised by the defendant regarding the recovery of individual members cannot defeat class certification where there are common questions concerning the defendant's alleged wrongdoing that must be resolved for all class members.[11]

The Arkansas Supreme Court has stated that conducting a trial on the common issues in a representative fashion can achieve judicial efficiency. The court has expressed its approval for a bifurcated approach to the predominance element by allowing circuit courts to divide a case into two phases: (1) certification for resolution of the preliminary common issues and (2) decertification for the resolution of individual issues.[12] The bifurcated approach has been disallowed, however, where the preliminary issues to be resolved were individual issues rather than common ones.[13]

Up to this point, the court has declined to address constitutional concerns that might arise as a result of this "bifurcation approach,"[14] and this suggested bifurcation has never actually taken place at the trial court level. Decertification is also cited as a way to deal with any manageability issues that might arise after a class is certified. Again, due process and constitutional concerns surrounding this approach have not yet been addressed by the Arkansas Supreme Court, and in one instance the court has declined to do so.[15]

IV. Appeal

The trial court's decision to grant or deny class certification is immediately appealable to the Arkansas Supreme Court.[16] A notice of appeal must be filed within 30 days of entry of the order granting or denying class certification.

---

9. *Id.* at 286, 283 S.W.3d at 584 (quoting *Georgia-Pacific Corp. v. Carter*, 371 Ark. 295, 301, 265 S.W.3d 107, 111 (2007)).

10. *Gen. Motors Corp.*, 374 Ark. at 44, 285 S.W.3d at 639.

11. *FirstPlus Home Loan Owner 1997-1 v. Bryant*, 372 Ark. 466, 277 S.W.3d 576 (2008).

12. *Ark. Blue Cross & Blue Shield v. Hicks*, 349 Ark. 269, 78 S.W.3d 58 (2002).

13. *Id.*

14. *See Gen. Motors Corp.*, 374 Ark. at 50, 285 S.W.3d at 643.

15. *Id.* at 49–52, 285 S.W.3d at 643–45.

16. Ark. R. App. P. 2(a)(9) (2009).

V. Notice

If class certification is granted and affirmed, the procedure for notice and opting out tracks the federal procedure. There is one unique case in Arkansas that deals with intervenors and objectors.[17] This case states that if a putative class member has the opportunity to opt out of the class, he or she cannot later intervene for the purpose of objecting to the certification.

VI. Compromise

The requirements of Arkansas Rule 23 apply to a certification for settlement purposes just as to a certification for a trial on the merits. Like its federal counterpart, Arkansas Rule 23(e) requires court approval of any settlement or dismissal of claims or defenses with respect to a certified claim.[18] The notice and procedure necessary when a class has been certified track those set forth in Federal Rule 23.[19]

VII. Class Counsel and Attorney Fees

The sections in Federal Rule 23 entitled "Class Counsel" and "Attorney's Fees and Nontaxable Costs" are not included in the Arkansas Rule. Although case law does not exist concerning attorney fees awarded in a class action, the trial court's award of fees would likely be affirmed if deemed to be reasonable.

---

17. *DeJulius v. Sumner*, 373 Ark. 156, 282 S.W.3d 753 (2008).
18. Ark. R. Civ. P. 23(e).
19. *Id.*

CALIFORNIA

ROBERT D. PHILLIPS, JR.
LINDA B. OLIVER
MARK G. SCHROEDER

I. Introduction

The California rules governing class actions are set forth in the California Rules of Court adopted by the California Judicial Council, California Rules of Court 3.760–3.771. Before statewide rules were adopted, state courts looked to Rule 23 of the Federal Rules of Civil Procedure governing class action procedures.[1] State courts in California only follow Federal Rule 23 where there are gaps in the Rules of Court.[2] In contrast, California's Consumers Legal Remedies Act[3] closely follows Federal Rule 23.[4]

II. Statutory Authority for Class Actions in California

The statutory authority for class actions in California is found in California Code of Civil Procedure section 382, which authorizes class action suits "when the question is one of a common or general interest, of many persons, or when the parties are numerous, and it is impracticable to bring them all before the court . . . ." Section 382 does not provide any formal procedures for class certification, which are found in the California Rules of Court, Rule 3.760 *et seq.* and in case law.

---

1. *City of San Jose v. Superior Court*, 12 Cal. 3d 447, 453 (1974).

2. *Bell v. Am. Title Ins. Co.*, 226 Cal. App. 3d 1589, 1603 (1991).

3. CAL. CIV. CODE § 1750 *et seq.*

4. *Hypertouch, Inc. v. Superior Court*, 128 Cal. App. 4th 1527, 1544 (2005); *Ticconi v. Blue Shield of Cal. Life & Health Ins. Co.*, 160 Cal. App. 4th 528, 546 (2008).

III. Standards for Class Certification in California

The party seeking class certification must meet his or her burden of establishing the existence of (1) an ascertainable class and (2) a well-defined community of interest among the putative class members.[5]

A. THE CLASS MUST BE ASCERTAINABLE

A "class is ascertainable if it identifies a group of unnamed plaintiffs by describing a set of common characteristics sufficient to allow a member of that group to identify himself or herself as having a right to recover based on the description."[6] "Whether a class is ascertainable is determined by examining (1) the class definitions, (2) the size of the class, and (3) the means available for identifying class members."[7] In contrast to Federal Rule 23, which requires numerosity, California allows a far smaller number of members to form a class; it requires only the number to be large enough that bringing them all to court is "impracticable."[8]

B. COMMUNITY OF INTEREST REQUIREMENT—THREE FACTORS

"'The community of interest requirement embodies three factors: (1) predominant common questions of law or fact; (2) class representatives with claims or defenses typical of the class; and (3) class representatives who can adequately represent the class.'"[9] "[P]laintiffs' burden on moving for class certification . . . is not merely to show that some common issues exist, but, rather, to place substantial evidence in the record that common issues *predominate*."[10] Thus, in assessing whether common issues of law and fact predominate, "the trial court *must* examine the issues as framed by the pleadings and the causes of action as alleged."[11]

The "commonality" requirement is that common issues *predominate*. This is required because, at its heart, the commonality element is essentially a procedural one, asking "whether . . . the issues which may be jointly tried, when compared with those requiring separate adjudication, are so numerous or substantial that the maintenance of a class action would be advantageous to the judicial process and

---

5. *Lockheed Martin Corp. v. Superior Court*, 29 Cal. 4th 1096, 1103–04 (2003); *Sav-On Drug Stores, Inc. v. Superior Court*, 34 Cal. 4th 319, 326 (2004).

6. *Bartold v. Glendale Fed. Bank*, 81 Cal. App. 4th 816, 828 (2000).

7. *Reyes v. Bd. of Supervisors*, 196 Cal. App. 3d 1263, 1271 (1987).

8. CAL. CIV. P. CODE § 382.

9. *Lockheed Martin Corp.*, 29 Cal. 4th at 1104 (quoting *Richmond v. Dart Indus., Inc.*, 29 Cal. 3d 462, 470 (1981)).

10. *Id.* at 1108 (emphasis in original).

11. *Brinker Rest. Corp. v. Superior Court*, 165 Cal. App. 4th 25 (2008) (emphasis in original).

to the litigants."[12] Common issues do not predominate when each putative class member is

> required to individually litigate numerous and substantial questions to determine his [or her] right to recover following the class judgment; and the issues which may be jointly tried, when compared with those requiring separate adjudication, must be sufficiently numerous and substantial to make the class action advantageous to the judicial process and to the litigants.[13]

"[I]f a class action will splinter into individual trials, common questions do not predominate and litigation of the action in a class format is inappropriate."[14]

Class certification may be denied if there is a showing that there will be a need for individualized proof on damages or affirmative defenses.[15] However, "[a]s a general rule if the defendant's liability can be determined by facts common to all members, a class will be certified even if the members must individually prove their damages."[16]

When deciding whether common questions predominate, a court must identify common and individual issues, consider the manageability of those issues, and weigh the common issues against the individual issues to determine which predominate.[17]

Typicality requires that a class representative possess the same interest and suffer the same injury as the putative class members.[18] However, the class representative's claim does not have to be completely identical to the claims of other class members, but must be similarly situated to them so that he or she will have a motive to litigate on their behalf.[19] It is not necessary that all class representatives have personally incurred all of the damages suffered by all of the other class

---

12. *Sav-On Drug Stores*, 34 Cal. 4th at 326 (quoting *Collins v. Rocha*, 7 Cal. 3d 232, 238 (1972)); *Ticconi*, 160 Cal. App. 4th at 538) (quoting *Lockheed Martin Corp.*, 29 Cal. 4th at 1104–05).

13. *Bomersheim v. Los Angeles Gay and Lesbian Ctr.*, 184 Cal. App. 4th 1471 (2010) (quoting *City of San Jose*, 12 Cal. 3d at 460).

14. *Arenas v. El Torito Rest., Inc.*, 183 Cal. App. 4th 723, 732 (2010) (internal quotations and citation omitted); *see also Wash. Mut. Bank v. Superior Court*, 24 Cal. 4th 906, 913 (2001).

15. *Akkerman v. Mecta Corp.*, 152 Cal. App. 4th 1094, 1102–03 (2007) (class certification rejected where restitution calculation would vary for each case); *Kennedy v. Baxter Healthcare Corp.*, 43 Cal. App. 4th 799, 809–10 (1996) (proof of individual damages would defeat the purpose of a class action); *Walsh v. IKON Office Solutions, Inc.*, 148 Cal. App. 4th 1440, 1450 (2007) ("The question . . . is not whether [the defendant] proved its defense, but whether it presented evidence from which the trial court could reasonably conclude that the adjudication of the defense would turn more on individualized questions than on common questions."); *Keller v. Tuesday Morning, Inc.*, 179 Cal. App. 4th 1389, 1399 (2009) (motion for decertification granted based upon showing that work performed by the store manager plaintiffs varied significantly from store to store and week to week).

16. *Hicks v. Kaufman & Broad Home Corp.*, 89 Cal. App. 4th 908, 916 (2001).

17. *Dunbar v. Albertson's, Inc.*, 141 Cal. App. 4th 1422, 1432–33 (2006).

18. *Caro v. Procter & Gamble Co.*, 18 Cal. App. 4th 644, 663 (1993).

19. *Classen v. Weller*, 145 Cal. App. 3d 27, 45 (1983).

members.[20] The representative plaintiff has a *fiduciary duty* to protect absent putative class members and to fulfill this duty must "raise those claims 'reasonably
expected to be raised by the members of the class.'"[21]

A class cannot be certified unless it is superior to individual lawsuits and "other
alternative procedures for resolving the controversy."[22] As part of this superiority
analysis, courts evaluate the difficulties likely to be encountered in the management of a class action. Commonly referred to as "manageability," this consideration encompasses the whole range of practical problems that may render the class
action format inappropriate for a particular suit.[23]

IV. Statutory Representative Actions Under California's Unfair Competition Law

Under California's Unfair Competition Law (UCL),[24] a plaintiff may sue as a statutory (class) representative to enjoin ongoing wrongful business activities, including
"unlawful, unfair or fraudulent" business practices or "unfair, deceptive, untrue
or misleading advertising" that is likely to deceive, on behalf of the aggrieved persons.[25] The purpose of the UCL "is to protect both consumers and competitors by
promoting fair competition in commercial markets for goods and services."[26]

The scope of the UCL has been viewed by California courts as "quite broad."[27]
"Because the statute is framed in the disjunctive, a business practice need only
meet one of the three criteria—unlawful, unfair, or fraudulent—to be considered
unfair competition."[28] It can encompass violations of other laws, treating them as
unlawful practices that are independently actionable under the unfair competition
law, but a practice can be deemed unfair even if not specifically proscribed by some

---

20. *Wershba v. Apple Computer, Inc.*, 91 Cal. App. 4th 224, 228 (2001).

21. *City of San Jose*, 12 Cal. 3d at 464 (quoting *Technograph Printed Circuits, Ltd. v. Methode Elecs.*, 285
F. Supp. 714, 721 (N.D. Ill. 1968)).

22. *Capitol People First v. Dep't of Dev. Servs.*, 155 Cal. App. 4th 676, 689 (2007); *accord Linder v. Thrifty
Oil Co.*, 23 Cal. 4th 429, 435 (2000).

23. *Hamwi v. Citinational-Buckeye Inv. Co.*, 72 Cal. App. 3d 462, 473 (1977) (affirming denial of class
certification where interpretation of lease provision would involve a separate trial examining the extrinsic
evidence involved in each class member's lease transaction); *Kavruk v. Blue Cross of Cal.*, 108 Cal. App.
4th 773, 786–87 (2003) (affirming denial of class certification on fraud and unfair competition claims
because oral representations of insurance agents "would require proof on a subscriber by subscriber basis").

24. CAL. BUS. & PROF. CODE § 17200 *et seq.*

25. *Id.* at § 17200.

26. *Delano Farms Co. v. Cal. Table Grape Comm'n*, 623 F. Supp. 2d 1144 (E.D. Cal. 2009) (citing *Kasky v.
Nike, Inc.*, 27 Cal. 4th 939, 949 (2002)).

27. *McKell v. Wash. Mut., Inc.*, 142 Cal. App. 4th 1457, 1471 (2006).

28. *Id.*

other law.[29] Thus, in order to state a claim under the UCL, a plaintiff must "show that 'members of the public are likely to be deceived.'"[30]

Relief under the UCL is not mandatory even when an unfair business practice has been shown.[31] Thus, a mere regulatory violation that causes no harm to a plaintiff cannot furnish an equitable basis for restitution under the UCL, especially where the plaintiff received something of value from the defendant.[32]

The passage of Proposition 64 in November 2004 changed the statute considerably. Before the passage of Proposition 64, there was no standing requirement—any person could sue under the UCL as a representative of those affected by the business practice. The original statute was therefore a magnet for plaintiffs' lawyers, because anyone could sue as a private attorney general, even if the plaintiff had had no dealings with the defendants at all. Plaintiffs could also sue for classlike relief without meeting class certification requirements, which meant that a judgment had no res judicata effect. Proposition 64 changed the statute to limit standing to a plaintiff "who has *suffered injury in fact* and has *lost money or property* as a result of such unfair competition."[33] Proposition 64 also imposed new causation requirements, so that any injury and money/property loss must be "as a result of such" unfair competition or false advertising.[34] Proposition 64 also imported the traditional requirements for class certification to representative actions brought under the UCL.[35]

Proposition 64 has been the subject of much appellate controversy since it was enacted. At first, the application of class action principles to revised section 17200 seemed to require classwide proof of causation, and most courts of appeal agreed. The California Supreme Court granted review and consolidated multiple cases on this issue, leaving the issue unresolved for several years. In May 2009, the California Supreme Court issued its ruling in *In re Tobacco II Cases*.[36] At issue was the viability of UCL actions that seek to certify a class despite the fact that not all putative plaintiffs suffered injury as a result of a defendant's allegedly unfair practice. Also at issue was the causation requirement for purposes of establishing standing under the UCL, and in particular what the meaning is of the phrase "as a result of" in section 17204.

---

29. *Cel-Tech Commc'ns, Inc. v. Los Angeles*, 20 Cal. 4th 163, 180 (1999).

30. *Paduano v. Am. Honda Motor Co., Inc.*, 69 Cal. App. 4th 1453, 1469 (2009) (citing *Bank of the W. v. Superior Court*, 2 Cal. 4th 1254, 1267 (1992)).

31. *Cortez v. Purolator Air Filtration Prods.*, 23 Cal. 4th 163, 180 (2000).

32. *See Olson v. Cohen*, 106 Cal. App. 4th 1209, 1215 (2003) (failure of law corporation to register with state bar did not justify disgorgement of fees to client under UCL because the client still received the services of the lawyer and therefore disgorgement would be "disproportionate to the wrong").

33. CAL. BUS. & PROF. CODE §§ 17204, 17535 (emphasis added).

34. *Id.*

35. CAL. BUS. & PROF. CODE §§ 17203, 17535.

36. 46 Cal. 4th 298 (2009).

The gravamen of the plaintiffs' complaint in *Tobacco II* was that defendant tobacco manufacturers and researchers engaged in a decades-long conspiracy to conceal the health effects and addictiveness of cigarettes and, in so doing, made numerous false and misleading statements to consumers. The court of appeal had unanimously affirmed the trial court's holding that *every* class member must have suffered injury in order to maintain a class action under the UCL.

The California Supreme Court concluded that "standing requirements are applicable only to the class representatives, and not all absent class members."[37] The court also repeated the "likely to deceive" standard and concluded "the language of section 17203 with respect to those entitled to restitution—to restore to any person in interest any money or property, real or personal, which *may have been acquired*" by means of the unfair practice—is patently less stringent than the standing requirement for the class representative—"any person who has suffered injury in fact and has lost money or property *as a result of* the unfair competition."[38] The court found that Proposition 64 did not address the standing of nonrepresentative plaintiffs and recognized that it was specifically meant to address the harm of suits filed by uninjured plaintiffs to shake down businesses.

In *Tobacco II*, the California Supreme Court also found that "a class representative proceeding on a claim of misrepresentation as the basis of his or her UCL action must demonstrate actual reliance on the allegedly deceptive or misleading statements, in accordance with well-settled principles regarding the element of reliance in ordinary fraud actions."[39] Class representatives, however, need not plead or prove that they actually relied on a particular advertisement or statement when the unfair practice is a fraudulent advertising campaign.[40]

As to whether class representatives have standing, the California Supreme Court concluded that Proposition 64

> imposes an actual reliance requirement on plaintiffs prosecuting a private enforcement action under the UCL's fraud prong. This conclusion, however, is the beginning, not the end, of the analysis of what a plaintiff must plead and prove under the fraud prong of the UCL. . . . While a plaintiff must show that the misrepresentation was an immediate cause of the injury-producing conduct, the plaintiff need not demonstrate it was the only cause. "It is not . . . necessary that [the plaintiff's] reliance upon the truth of the fraudulent misrepresentation be the sole or even the predominant or decisive factor influencing his conduct. . . . It is enough that the representation has played a substantial part, and so had been a substantial factor, in influencing his decision."

---

37. *Id.* at 306.

38. CAL. BUS. & PROF. CODE § 17204 (emphasis added).

39. 46 Cal. 4th at 306.

40. *Id.*

Moreover, a presumption, or at least an inference, of reliance arises wherever there is a showing that a misrepresentation was material. . . . Nor does a plaintiff need to demonstrate individualized reliance on specific misrepresentations to satisfy the reliance requirement.[41]

A few recent cases have clarified the holdings in *Tobacco II*. In *Kaldenbach v. Mutual of Omaha*,[42] a life insurance vanishing premium case, the court of appeal stated that *Tobacco II* only holds that standing does not apply for absent class members "where class requirements have otherwise been found to exist."[43] The court found that the trial court had not abused its discretion in denying class certification where individualized issues predominated.[44]

In *Cohen v. DirecTV, Inc.*,[45] the court of appeal found that "standing" is not a substitute for "commonality." A satellite television subscriber brought a class action against a company and asserted a UCL violation based upon allegedly degraded high definition channels and claimed reliance on printed materials. However, other television subscribers confirmed in declarations that their decisions had nothing to do with the materials, and that they had not been exposed to the representations. Although the trial court decision was pre-*Tobacco II*, the court of appeal affirmed the denial of certification, on grounds of exposure, not of reliance.

Proposition 64's standing requirements have led the plaintiffs' bar to seek precertification discovery to identify potential class representatives in cases where the original plaintiff may lack standing. Whether or not discovery has been permitted has varied. In *Best Buy Stores, LP v. Superior Court*,[46] a lawyer sought class relief under the UCL for illegal fees for return of merchandise, but intervening law disqualified him to be counsel and class representative simultaneously. Precertification discovery was permitted to identify a substitute class representative, but this holding in part depended on counsel's former status as a class member who once had standing.

In *First American Title Insurance Co. v. Superior Court*,[47] a class representative without standing sought precertification discovery to find a substitute plaintiff. The court of appeal found that a plaintiff without standing could not seek discovery because to allow it would be an end run around Proposition 64. The proposed class representative had never been a class member, and his persistence in bringing his claim, despite knowing it to be without merit, was viewed as a "fishing expedition." Because plaintiff was never a member of the class, he had no cognizable

---

41. *Id.* at 326–27 (citation omitted).
42. 178 Cal. App. 4th 830 (2009).
43. *Id.* at 848.
44. *Id.* at 851.
45. 178 Cal. App. 4th 966 (2009).
46. 137 Cal. App. 4th 772 (2006).
47. 146 Cal. App. 4th 1564 (2007).

interest in seeing it proceed, so the potential abuses of the class procedures outweighed the minimal interest of plaintiff.

V. Class Actions Under the Consumers Legal Remedies Act

California's Consumers Legal Remedies Act (CLRA),[48] originally enacted in 1970, provides a more detailed statutory scheme for class actions, but is limited to actions brought by a consumer on behalf of others similarly situated alleging unfair or deceptive acts or practices in connection with "the sale or lease of goods or services to any consumer . . . ."[49] If a consumer suffers damage as a result of such an unlawful act, the consumer may bring an action under the CLRA for actual damages, injunctive relief, restitution, punitive damages, and other relief,[50] including an additional award in certain class actions by senior citizens or disabled persons,[51] and attorney fees and costs.[52] The CLRA is to be "liberally construed . . . to promote its underlying purposes . . . to protect consumers . . . ."[53] A consumer must allege actual damage for standing to sue under the CLRA; it is not enough to simply be exposed to the unlawful practice.[54]

Certain transactions, such as real estate leases, the sale of entire residences, or credit card transactions, are excluded from the reach of the CLRA unless the seller of the good or service is extending the credit.[55] The California Supreme Court also recently clarified that life insurance is not a "service" subject to the CLRA's provisions.[56]

Under the CLRA, the consumer must notify the potential defendant of the alleged wrongdoing in writing by certified or registered mail at least 30 days before filing a lawsuit and demand that the defendant "correct, repair, replace, or otherwise rectify the goods or services alleged to be in violation . . . ."[57] The potential defendant can avoid damages if the problem is corrected or agreed to be corrected

---

48. CAL. CIV. CODE § 1750 *et seq.*

49. CAL. CIV. CODE § 1770(a).

50. *See* CAL. CIV. CODE § 1780(a); *Wilens v. TD Waterhouse Group, Inc.*, 15 Cal. Rptr. 3d 271, 274 (Cal. App. 2003).

51. *See* CAL. CIV. CODE § 1780(b).

52. *See* CAL. CIV. CODE. § 1780(d).

53. CAL. CIV. CODE § 1760; *see also Quaccia v. DaimlerChrysler Corp.*, 19 Cal. Rptr. 3d 508, 517 (Cal. App. 2004).

54. *Meyer v. Sprint Spectrum L.P.*, 45 Cal. 4th 634, 640 (2009) ("[T]he statute provides that in order to bring a CLRA action, not only must a consumer be exposed to an unlawful practice, but some kind of damage must result.").

55. CAL. CIV. CODE § 1754; *see also Berry v. Am. Exp. Publ'g, Inc.*, 147 Cal. App. 4th 224, 230 (2007).

56. *Fairbanks v. Superior Court (Farmers New World Life Ins. Co.)*, 46 Cal. 4th 56 (2009).

57. CAL. CIV. CODE § 1782(a)(1)–(2).

within 30 days and the defendant can prove that the violation was the unintentional result of a bona fide error.[58]

Class action procedures under the CLRA are set forth in California Civil Code section 1781, which essentially "adopted the federal approach" under Federal Rule 23.[59] Unlike class actions under California Code of Civil Procedure, a plaintiff moving to certify a class under the CLRA is not required to show substantial benefit to litigants or the court, or a probability that each class member will come forward to prove his or her separate claim to a portion of the recovery.[60]

The standards for class certification under the CLRA closely follow the requirements of Federal Rule 23. A class will be certified if the following conditions are met:

1. It is impracticable to bring all members of the class before the court.
2. The questions of law or fact common to the class are substantially similar and predominate over the questions affecting the individual members.
3. The claims or defenses of the representative plaintiffs are typical of the claims or defenses of the class.
4. The representative plaintiffs will fairly and adequately protect the interests of the class.[61]

No other factors may be considered in a case brought under the CLRA, and courts lack discretion under the CLRA to deny certification for other considerations.[62] Often, however, a complaint alleging violations of the CLRA will include other causes of action, so courts will also consider factors under Code of Civil Procedure section 382 unless the case is strictly limited to the CLRA. The CLRA specifically provides that its provisions are not exclusive, and that if any practice also constitutes a cause of action under another statute or the common law, the consumer may also assert that cause of action under the procedures and remedies provided for under that law.[63]

If a CLRA class action is permitted, the trial court may direct notice to class members, and notice may be given by publication if personal notification is unreasonably expensive or it appears that all class members cannot be notified

---

58. CAL. CIV. CODE § 1782(b)–(d).

59. *See Hypertouch, Inc. v. Superior Court*, 27 Cal. Rptr. 3d 839, 849 (2005).

60. *See Mass. Mut. Life Ins. Co. v. Superior Court*, 119 Cal. Rptr. 2d 190, 193 n.1 (Cal. App. 2002); *Hogya v. Superior Court*, 142 Cal. Rptr. 325, 334 (Cal. App. 1997).

61. CAL. CIV. CODE § 1781(b)(1)–(4).

62. *See Dean Witter Reynolds, Inc. v. Superior Court*, 259 Cal. Rptr. 789, 793 (Cal. App. 1989); *Hogya*, 75 Cal. App. 3d at 138; *see also* CAL. CIV. CODE § 1752 (CLRA consumer class actions "shall be governed exclusively by" CLRA chapter 4).

63. CAL. CIV. CODE § 1752.

personally.[64] The trial court may direct either party to pay the cost of class notice.[65] Class notice must include, among other things, an opt-out provision.[66] Although summary judgment motions are not permitted in class actions commenced under the CLRA, a "no-merit determination" constitutes grounds for denying class certification and dismissal.[67]

VI. Rules for Class Notice in California

Rule 3.766 of the California Rules of Court governs the procedures for providing notice to class members. Once a class is certified, the court may require either party to notify the class of the action in the manner specified by the court.[68] The class representative must submit a statement regarding class notice and a proposed notice to class members to the court, which must include the following items: (1) whether notice is necessary; (2) whether class members may exclude themselves from the action; (3) the time and manner in which notice should be given; (4) a proposal for which parties should bear the costs of notice; and (5) if cost-shifting or sharing is proposed under subdivision (4), an estimate of the cost involved in giving notice.[69] While generally the court will order the plaintiff to provide notice and incur the cost of doing so, under appropriate circumstances a defendant may be required to bear or share costs.[70] Even if the plaintiff pays for the notice, it may be recoverable from defendant if the plaintiffs win the case.[71]

The Rule also provides that upon certification of a class, or as soon thereafter as practicable, the court must make an order determining the following: (1) whether notice to class members is necessary; (2) whether class members may exclude themselves from the action; (3) the time and manner of notice; (4) the content of the notice; and (5) the parties responsible for the cost of notice.[72]

The content of the class notice is subject to court approval. If class members are to be given the right to request exclusion from the class, the notice must include the following: (1) a brief explanation of the case, including the basic contentions or denials of the parties; (2) a statement that the court will exclude the member from the class if the member so requests by a specified date; (3) a procedure for

---

64. *See* CAL. CIV. CODE § 1781(d).

65. *See id.*

66. *See* CAL. CIV. CODE § 1781(e).

67. *See* CAL. CIV. CODE § 1781(c)(3); *Smith v. Wells Fargo Bank, N.A.*, 38 Cal. Rptr. 3d 653, 665 (Cal. App. 2005); *Dean Witter*, 259 Cal. Rptr. at 794.

68. CAL. RULES OF COURT, R. 3.766(a).

69. CAL. RULES OF COURT, R. 3.766(b).

70. *Hypertouch*, 128 Cal. App. 4th at 1551–55.

71. CAL. CODE CIV. PROC. § 1033.5(c)(2), (4).

72. CAL. RULES OF COURT, R. 3.766(c).

the member to follow in requesting exclusion from the class; (4) a statement that the judgment, whether favorable or not, will bind all members who do not request exclusion; and (5) a statement that any member who does not request exclusion may, if the member so desires, enter an appearance through counsel.[73]

In determining the manner of the notice, the court must consider (1) the interests of the class; (2) the type of relief requested; (3) the stake of the individual class members; (4) the cost of notifying class members; (5) the resources of the parties; (6) the possible prejudice to class members who do not receive notice; and (7) the potential res judicata effect on class members.[74]

If personal notification is unreasonably expensive, the stake of individual class members is insubstantial, or if it appears that all members of the class cannot be notified personally, the court may order a means of notice reasonably calculated to apprise the class members of the pendency of the action, such as publication in a newspaper or magazine; broadcasting on television, radio, or the Internet; or posting or distribution through a trade or professional association, union, or public interest group.[75]

VII. Discovery of Unnamed Class Members in California

Rule 3.768 of the California Rules of Court provides that certain types of discovery is permitted from unnamed class members, including an oral or written deposition or a deposition for the production of business records and things.[76] The number of depositions must be "reasonable."[77] Interrogatories require a court order.[78] The rule also provides that a party representative or the deponent may move for a protective order to preclude or limit the discovery.[79] In deciding whether to allow discovery, the court must consider the timing of the request, the subject matter to be covered, the materiality of the information sought, the likelihood that class members have such information, the possibility of reaching factual stipulations that eliminate the need for such discovery, whether class representatives are seeking discovery on the subject to be covered, and "whether discovery will result in annoyance, oppression, or undue burden or expense for the members of the class."[80]

---

73. CAL. RULES OF COURT, R. 3.766(d).

74. CAL. RULES OF COURT, R. 3.766(e).

75. CAL. RULES OF COURT, R. 3.766(f).

76. *S. Cal. Edison Co. v. Superior Court,* 7 Cal. 3d 832, 840 (1972).

77. *Nat'l Solar Equip. Owners' Ass'n, Inc. v. Grumman Corp.,* 235 Cal. App. 3d 1273, 1284 (1991).

78. CAL. RULES OF COURT, R. 3.768(c).

79. CAL. RULES OF COURT, R. 3.768(b).

80. CAL. RULES OF COURT, R. 3.768(d).

VIII. Settlement of Class Actions in California

Settlement of a class action in California, regardless of whether a class has been certified, requires court approval and a hearing.[81] After settlement, any party may file a motion for preliminary approval with a copy of the settlement agreement and a proposed notice to class members.[82] If the settlement includes an agreement to pay attorney fees, the attorney fee provision must be set forth in full.[83] The court may make an order approving or denying certification of a provisional settlement class after the preliminary settlement hearing.[84] If the preliminary approval is granted, the order must include the time, date, and place of the final approval hearing; the notice to be given to the class; and any other matters deemed necessary for the proper conduct of a settlement hearing.[85]

If the court has certified the action as a class action, notice of the final approval hearing must be given to the class members in the manner specified by the court.[86] The notice must contain an explanation of the proposed settlement and procedures for class members to follow in filing written objections to it and in arranging to appear at the settlement hearing and state any objections to the proposed settlement. The trial court has broad discretion in determining whether the settlement is fair.[87] The court will consider such factors as the strength of plaintiffs' case, the settlement amount, the amount of discovery, and the risk of further litigation. There is a presumption of fairness when the parties engage in arm's-length negotiation, there are few objectors, the parties have engaged in sufficient investigation, and the parties are represented by experienced counsel.[88]

If the court approves the settlement agreement after the final approval hearing, the court must make and enter judgment.[89] The judgment must include a provision for the retention of the court's jurisdiction over the parties to enforce the terms of the judgment.

---

81. CAL. RULES OF COURT, R. 3.769(a).
82. CAL. RULES OF COURT, R. 3.769(c).
83. CAL. RULES OF COURT, R. 3.769(b).
84. CAL. RULES OF COURT, R. 3.769(d).
85. CAL. RULES OF COURT, R. 3.769(e).
86. CAL. RULES OF COURT, R. 3.769(f).
87. *Dunk v. Ford Motor Co.*, 48 Cal. App. 4th 1794, 1801 (1996).
88. *In re Microsoft I-V Cases*, 135 Cal. App. 4th 706, 723 (2006).
89. CAL. RULES OF COURT, R. 3.769(h).

IX. Dismissal of Class Actions in California

Dismissal of a class action, or of any party or cause of action in a class action, requires court approval, whether or not a class has been certified.[90] Court approval prevents fraud, collusion, or unfairness to the class.[91] Requests for dismissal must be accompanied by a declaration setting forth the facts on which the party relies. The declaration must clearly state whether consideration, direct or indirect, is being given for the dismissal and must describe the consideration in detail.[92]

The court may grant the request without a hearing.[93] If the request is disapproved, notice of tentative disapproval must be sent to the lawyers of record. Any party may seek, within 15 calendar days of the service of the notice of tentative disapproval, a hearing on the request. If no hearing is sought within that period, the request for dismissal will be deemed denied.

If the court has certified the class, and notice of the pendency of the action has been provided to class members, notice of the dismissal must be given to the class in the manner specified by the court.[94] If the court has not ruled on class certification, or if notice of the pendency of the action has not been provided to class members in a case in which such notice was required, notice of the proposed dismissal may be given in the manner and to those class members specified by the court, or the action may be dismissed without notice to the class members if the court finds that the dismissal will not prejudice them.

---

90. CAL. RULES OF COURT, R. 3.770(a).
91. *Dunk*, 48 Cal. App. 4th at 1800.
92. CAL. RULES OF COURT, R. 3.770(a).
93. CAL. RULES OF COURT, R. 3.770(b).
94. CAL. RULES OF COURT, R. 3.770(c).

COLORADO

RUSSELL O. STEWART

I. Introduction

Colorado Rule of Civil Procedure 23 is "virtually identical" to Federal Rule of Civil Procedure 23.[1] Accordingly, Colorado courts give "considerable deference to federal interpretation" of Federal Rule 23 and look to federal decisions for guidance on issues not previously addressed by Colorado state courts.[2] Colorado Rule 23, however, has not been updated to reflect several 2003 amendments to its federal counterpart.[3] The federal amendments, along with Colorado statutes and case law, create subtle differences between Colorado and federal class action law.

II. Class Certification

Several differences between Colorado and federal class action law pertain to class certification, as explained below.

A. CERTIFICATION TIMING AND PROCEDURES

Colorado Rule 23(c)(1) requires state courts to grant or deny class certification "as soon as practicable," while Federal Rule 23(c)(1)(A) has been amended to permit federal courts to rule on certification "at an early practicable time." The Advisory Committee amended the federal rule to follow "prevailing practice" and to capture "the many valid reasons that may justify deferring the initial certification decision."[4] But Colorado Rule 23(c)(1) suggests at least that Colorado courts should determine class certification at an earlier stage of the case.

---

1. *Mountain States Tel. & Tel. Co. v. Dist. Court*, 778 P.2d 667, 671 (Colo. 1989); *see also State v. Buckley Powder Co.*, 945 P.2d 841, 844 (Colo. 1997); COLO. R. CIV. P. 23; FED. R. CIV. P. 23.

2. *Goebel v. Colo. Dep't of Insts.*, 764 P.2d 785, 794 n.12 (Colo. 1988); *Buckley Powder*, 945 P.2d at 844.

3. FED. R. CIV. P. 23 advisory committee note (2003); *cf.* COLO. R. CIV. P. 23.

4. FED. R. CIV. P. 23(c)(1)(A) advisory committee note (2003).

Despite the language of Colorado Rule 23(c)(1), however, Colorado courts frequently hold evidentiary hearings before ruling on certification[5] similar to the "prevailing practice" of federal courts.[6] Although an evidentiary hearing is not a "mandatory precondition" to class certification under the Colorado rule, certification requires "factual allegations" beyond "mere mimicry" of the rule's language.[7] Previously granted class certifications are not determinative of later certifications.[8] Accordingly, fact-finding is customary prior to certification rulings[9] and not specifically time-limited.[10] As such, Colorado's time line for certification resembles federal practice.

B. PLAINTIFF'S BURDEN OF PROOF FOR CERTIFICATION

In Colorado, a class action proponent must satisfy each of the Colorado Rule 23 requirements by a preponderance of the evidence,[11] and courts must apply the same "rigorous analysis" as federal courts.[12] Although Colorado courts should not resolve the merits of a dispute at the certification stage, courts should rigorously examine the nature of the class claims, the evidence the class plaintiffs will need to offer, and any viable defenses available to the defendants before ruling on class certification.[13] Thus, when there are conflicting expert opinions that may affect the appropriateness of class certification, the court should "compare the relative weight of [the] opinions in ruling on a motion for class certification."[14] Although Colorado courts should not "prejudge the merits of the case,"[15] the court can "weigh the conflicting [expert] testimony and make specific findings, under the preponderance of the evidence standard, concerning [the disputed factual issues] . . . but only to the extent necessary to deciding whether an identifiable class . . . has been established."[16]

---

5. *E.g., Levine v. Empire Sav. & Loan Ass'n*, 592 P.2d 410, 413 (Colo. 1979).

6. *Id.* at 412–13 (noting that courts are bound to ensure "the class nature of the suit" and have "a greater responsibility to ensure a just resolution of the maintainability of class actions," but holding that when over a year had passed and plaintiffs had neither conducted discovery nor brought any supporting evidence, the trial court did not abuse its discretion in dismissing the case based on pleadings alone).

7. *Id.* at 413.

8. *Toothman v. Freeborn & Peters*, 80 P.3d 804, 810 (Colo. App. 2002).

9. *Reyher v. State Farm Mut. Auto. Ins. Co.*, 171 P.3d 1263, 1267 (Colo. App. 2007) ("Whether the requirements of C.R.C.P. 23 are met is a 'fact-driven, pragmatic inquiry' . . . ." (quoting *Medina v. Conseco Annuity Assurance Co.*, 121 P.3d 345, 348 (Colo. App. 2005))).

10. *See Levine*, 592 P.2d at 413–14.

11. *Jackson v. Unocal Corp.*, No. 09CA0610, 2009 WL 2182603, at *4 (Colo. App. Jul. 23, 2009).

12. *Id.* at *1.

13. *Id.*

14. *Id.* at *8 (citing *In re Urethane Antitrust Litig.*, 251 F.R.D. 629, 637 (D. Kan. 2008)).

15. *Id.* at *9 (citing *Farmers Ins. Exch. v. Benzing*, 206 P.3d 812, 818 (Colo. 2009)).

16. *Id.* at *10.

C. CONDITIONAL CERTIFICATION

Colorado Rule 23(c)(1) continues to allow "conditional" certification orders, a provision the Advisory Committee removed from Federal Rule 23(c)(1) because "a court that is not satisfied that the requirements of [Federal] Rule 23 have been met should refuse certification until they are met."[17] Unlike federal courts, Colorado courts may certify classes that do not meet class requirements at the time of certification, but initial certifications by Colorado courts are deemed "inherently tentative."[18] Although both the Colorado and the Federal Rule allow courts to amend certification orders,[19] the increased malleability of certification orders in Colorado could weigh against discretionary interlocutory appellate review.[20]

D. CERTIFICATION AMENDMENTS

Colorado Rule 23(c)(1) allows courts to amend certification orders "before the decision on the merits" is made, while Federal Rule 23(c)(1)(C) allows amendment "before final judgment." The Advisory Committee revised the federal rule in part to allow courts to subdivide or amend classes when necessary to properly apply certain class remedies[21]—a tool potentially unavailable to Colorado courts. Because a decision on the merits is generally a final appealable judgment,[22] Colorado trial courts may conclude that they lack jurisdiction to amend certification orders following decisions on the merits.

E. CERTIFICATION NOTICE

Colorado Rule 23(c)(2) does not address whether courts may direct notice to members of classes certified under Colorado Rule 23(b)(1) or Colorado Rule 23(b)(2). In contrast, Federal Rule 23(c)(2)(A) now explicitly permits courts to direct notice to members of classes certified under Federal Rule 23(b)(1) or Federal Rule 23(b)(2). No Colorado court has addressed the effect of the different language, and Colorado courts may ultimately direct notice to members of (b)(1) and (b)(2) classes notwithstanding the silence of the rule. The issue is unlikely to arise because (b)(1) and (b)(2) class members have no right to exclude themselves from actions,

---

17. FED. R. CIV. P. 23(c)(1)(C) advisory committee note (2003).

18. *Levine*, 592 P.2d at 413–14 (quoting *Officers for Justice v. Civil Serv. Comm'n*, 688 F.2d 615, 633 (9th Cir. 1982)); *see also Benzing*, 206 P.3d at 818.

19. *See* COLO. R. CIV. P. 23(c)(1) (a certification order "may be altered or amended . . . .") *and* FED. R. CIV. P. 23(c)(1) (a certification order "may be altered or amended . . . .").

20. *See Clark v. Farmers Ins. Exch.*, 117 P.3d 26, 30 (Colo. App. 2004).

21. FED. R. CIV. P. 23(c)(1)(C) advisory committee note (2003) (reasoning that "[t]his change avoids the possible ambiguity in referring to 'the decision on the merits.' Following a determination of liability, for example, proceedings to define the remedy may demonstrate the need to amend the class definition or subdivide the class. In this setting, the final judgment concept is pragmatic.").

22. *Baldwin v. Bright Mortgage Co.*, 757 P.2d 1072, 1074 (Colo. 1988) (holding that a decision on the merits is a final judgment for the appeal purposes even where the issue of attorney fees is outstanding).

making notice unnecessary in most cases.[23] Notice costs may cripple purely injunctive or declaratory actions, making the direction of notice unpalatable for (b)(2) class actions.[24]

F. THRESHOLD ISSUES

As a threshold matter, class action plaintiffs face unique specific barriers to certification in Colorado.

1. The Necessity Doctrine in Colorado

The necessity doctrine holds that class certification is unnecessary and will be denied when relief will automatically extend to all putative plaintiffs.[25] Although federal courts are divided on whether to apply the necessity doctrine,[26] Colorado courts can consider necessity for classes under Colorado Rule 23(b)(3), but not for classes under Colorado Rule 23(b)(2).[27] The Colorado Supreme Court reasoned that "when addressing subsection (b)(2) . . . need must be rejected as a qualification because it would virtually eliminate [Colorado] Rule 23(b)(2) certification given that there would rarely be a need for a whole class to challenge the constitutionality of a statute."[28]

2. Causation

To satisfy the "predominance" prong of Colorado Rule 23, Colorado class action plaintiffs must advance a "theory of class-wide causation sufficient to maintain a class action."[29] In *Farmers Insurance Exchange v. Benzing*, the Colorado Supreme Court held that plaintiffs could not base class certification on a "fraud on the market" theory of causation if the class relied on omissions of fact by defendants in face-to-face transactions rather than on market prices or an inefficient market.[30] The court also held that a plaintiff may not base an appeal of an order denying class certification on a particular theory of causation not raised at trial.[31]

---

23. *See* FED. R. CIV. P. 23(c)(2) advisory committee note (2003) ("There is no right to request exclusion from a (b)(1) or (b)(2) class"); *see also Buckley Powder*, 945 P.2d at 845 n.3.

24. *See Jahn ex rel. Jahn v. ORCR, Inc.*, 92 P.3d 984, 989–91 (Colo. 2004).

25. Daniel Tenny, Note, *There Is Always a Need: The "Necessity Doctrine" and Class Certification Against Government Agencies*, 103 MICH. L. REV. 1018, 1019 (2005).

26. *Id.* at 1019–20.

27. *Buckley Powder*, 945 P.2d at 845–46 ("[W]hen addressing subsection (b)(2), we agree that need must be rejected as a qualification because it would virtually eliminate Rule 23(b)(2) certification given that there would rarely be a need for a whole class to challenge the constitutionality of a statute.").

28. *Id.*

29. *Benzing*, 206 P.3d at 815.

30. *Id.* at 820–23.

31. *Id.* at 823.

III. Tolling the Statute of Limitations

Colorado courts follow the class action tolling doctrine of *American Pipe & Construction Co. v. Utah*, so the filing of a class action complaint tolls the statute of limitations for the benefit of all putative class members.[32] In *State Farm Mutual Automobile Insurance Co. v. Boellstorff*, the Tenth Circuit, interpreting and applying Colorado law, extended *American Pipe* to putative class members who had filed their claims before class certification, but after the statute of limitations had expired.[33] Accordingly, a plaintiff who brings an individual action in Colorado "while the class action is pending can still claim the benefit of the *American Pipe* tolling doctrine."[34] The Tenth Circuit application of *American Pipe* differs from that of the First and Sixth circuits, which have not extended the *American Pipe* doctrine to individual plaintiffs who filed their claims before class certification.[35]

IV. Class Settlements

Colorado Rule 23(e) lacks the comprehensive procedural framework for judicial review of class settlements found in Federal Rule 23(e). The Advisory Committee added the comprehensive framework to the federal rule to codify the practices of federal courts in performing mandatory review of class settlements under Federal Rule 23(e).[36] Although Colorado courts have not adopted all the language of Federal Rule 23(e) pertaining to settlement certification,[37] they generally follow the federal framework.[38]

The Advisory Committee added Federal Rule 23(e)(1)(A) in 2003 to clarify that federal courts need not approve settlements of putative class actions that only resolve individual claims.[39] Colorado Rule 23, however, may still be read to approve review of individual settlements in putative class action cases.[40]

---

32. 414 U.S. 538 (1974); *State Farm Mut. Auto. Ins. Co. v. Boellstorff*, 540 F.3d 1223, 1229 (10th Cir. 2008).

33. 540 F.3d at 1230.

34. *Id.*

35. *Glater v. Eli Lilly & Co.*, 712 F.2d 735 (1st Cir. 1983); *Wyser-Pratte Mgmt. Co. v. Telxon Corp.*, 413 F.3d 553 (6th Cir. 2005).

36. FED. R. CIV. P. 23(e) advisory committee note (2003) ("Subdivision (e) is amended to strengthen the process of reviewing proposed class-action settlements. Settlement may be a desirable means of resolving a class action. But court review and approval are essential to assure adequate representation of class members who have not participated in shaping the settlement.").

37. For example, the Supreme Court urged "heightened attention" in *Amchem Prods., Inc. v. Windsor*, 521 U.S. 591, 620 (1997) and "rigorous adherence" to Fed. R. Civ. P. 23(e) in *Ortiz v. Fibreboard Corp.*, 527 U.S. 815, 849 (1999) (citation omitted).

38. *See, e.g., Medina*, 121 P.3d at 347–48.

39. FED. R. CIV. P. 23(e)(1)(A) advisory committee note (2003).

40. *See* COLO. R. CIV. P. 23(e).

V. Interlocutory Certification Appeals

Colorado Rule 23(f) lacks the provisions for interlocutory appeals found in Federal Rule 23(f) and instead incorporates by reference section 13-20-901 of the Colorado Revised Statutes.[41] Section 13-20-901 allows interlocutory appeals from orders denying class certification if made within ten days of the trial court's order.[42] Colorado courts have suggested that Section 13-20-901 is "substantially similar" in its effect to Federal Rule 23(f).[43]

VI. Class Counsel

The selection of class counsel and the provision of attorney fees in Colorado class actions differ from federal practice in a couple of important respects, as explained below.

A. APPOINTMENT OF CLASS COUNSEL

Colorado Rule 23 lacks the explicit guidance for appointing class counsel enumerated in Federal Rule 23(g). Because Colorado courts need not specifically scrutinize class counsel, class counsel selection effectively collapses into the class representative adequacy analysis under Colorado Rule 23(a)(4).[44]

B. ATTORNEY FEES

Colorado Rule 23 lacks the guidelines for awarding attorney fees enumerated in Federal Rule 23(h). Colorado courts recognize the federal "common fund" doctrine, awarding attorney fees at their discretion from damages awards and settlement funds.[45] Colorado courts are likely to follow similar principles to Federal Rule 23(h),[46] but section 13-17-203 of the Colorado Revised Statutes[47] limits plaintiffs' attorney fees to $250,000 if the defendant is a public entity.[48]

---

41. See COLO. REV. STAT. § 13-20-901 (2003).

42. Id.

43. E.g., Clark, 117 P.3d at 29; see also Andrew M. Low, Class Action Appeals, COLO. LAW., June 2006, at 85.

44. See Jahn, 92 P.3d at 988–90.

45. Kuhn v. State, 924 P.2d 1053, 1060 (Colo. 1996); Brody v. Hellman, 167 P.3d 192, 198 (Colo. App. 2007); see also Spensieri v. Farmers Alliance Mut. Ins. Co., 804 P.2d 268, 271 (Colo. App. 1990) (noting that a preexisting fee arrangement is not binding and is only one of many factors for a court to consider in determining whether to award attorney fees).

46. See Brody, 167 P.3d at 198 (noting the objection of a class member to an award of attorney fees and the requirement of the trial court to consider "findings sufficient to allow meaningful appellate review of an award").

47. COLO. REV. STAT. § 13-17-203 (2008).

48. See Buckley Powder Co. v. State, 70 P.3d 547, 560–63 (Colo. App. 2002) (holding the statute constitutional); COLO. REV. STAT. § 24-10-103(5) (2008) (defining public entities).

CONNECTICUT

DAVID M. BIZAR

I. Introduction

Class actions in Connecticut are governed by sections 9-7 through 9-10 of the Connecticut Practice Book (Practice Book).[1] The Practice Book rules, which are Connecticut's rules of civil procedure, are similar in most respects to Rule 23 of the Federal Rules of Civil Procedure, but there are notable differences.

As required under the Federal Rules, Connecticut courts must conduct a "rigorous analysis" to determine whether the plaintiffs have satisfied their burden of proving that the requirements for class certification have been met.[2] The trial court must take the substantive allegations of the complaint as true, but the court is not limited to the pleadings.[3] Indeed, the court's determination of whether to certify a class usually involves considerations that are "enmeshed in the factual and legal issues" comprising the cause of action.[4] The question is whether the plaintiffs have satisfied the prerequisites of certification, not whether the plaintiffs have stated a cause of action or will prevail on the merits.[5] The trial court has broad discretion to determine whether a suit should proceed as a class action, but the Connecticut Supreme Court has instructed that "[d]oubts regarding the propriety of class certification should be resolved in favor of certification."[6] Finally, as under the Federal

---

1. Connecticut Practice Book §§ 9-7 to 9-10.

2. *Artie's Auto Body, Inc. v. The Hartford Fire Ins. Co.*, 287 Conn. 208, 212–13 (2008) (citation omitted) (internal quotation marks omitted).

3. *Id.* at 213.

4. *Id.*

5. *Id.*

6. *Arduini v. Auto. Ins. Co. of Hartford*, 23 Conn. App. 585, 589 (1990); *Rivera v. Veteran's Mem'l Med. Ctr.*, 262 Conn. 730, 743 (2003) (citation omitted) (internal quotation marks omitted).

Rules, Connecticut courts may "revisit the issue of class certification" throughout the proceedings.[7]

II. Prerequisites to Class Actions

Practice Book section 9-7 has the same requirements as Federal Rule of Civil Procedure 23(a). Both require proof of numerosity of potential class members, commonality and typicality of issues of law and fact, and adequacy of representation. Connecticut courts look to federal case law for guidance because the requirements to certify a class are the same.[8]

A. NUMEROSITY

The numerosity requirement is satisfied when "the difficulty or inconvenience of joining all class members make the use of the class action device appropriate."[9] The courts do not use a "magic number" in determining whether the class is so numerous that joinder of the parties will be impractical.[10] Plaintiffs are not required to prove that the joinder of all parties is impossible.[11] The Connecticut Supreme Court has instructed that the determination of numerosity requires a flexible inquiry that considers the entirety of the action.[12]

B. COMMONALITY

The commonality requirement is "easily satisfied" because there must only be one question that is common to the class.[13] The resolution of the common question must advance the litigation, however.[14] The commonality requirement is satisfied, for example, when the members of a class allege that the defendant's policy has adversely affected them and the policy is the focus of the litigation.[15]

C. TYPICALITY

Plaintiffs satisfy the typicality requirement by showing that "each member's claim arises from the same course of events, and each class member makes similar legal

---

7. *Rivera*, 262 Conn. at 744.

8. *Collins v. Anthem Health Plans, Inc.*, 275 Conn. 309, 322–23 (2005) (*Collins II*); *Rivera*, 262 Conn. at 738.

9. *Town of New Hartford v. Conn. Res. Recovery Auth.*, 291 Conn. 433, 476 (2009) (internal quotation and citation omitted).

10. *Id.* at 475 (internal quotation and citations omitted).

11. *Id.* at 476 (citation omitted) (internal quotation marks omitted).

12. *Id.* at 475 (citation omitted) (internal quotation marks omitted).

13. *Collins II*, 275 Conn. at 323.

14. *Id.* (citation omitted) (internal quotation marks omitted).

15. *Id.* (citation omitted) (internal quotation marks omitted).

arguments to prove the defendant's liability."[16] The named representatives are not required to base their claims on identical facts as the class members, but the questions of law or fact in dispute must share characteristics that are central to their claims.[17] Class certification is inappropriate if the representatives are subject to "unique defenses" that have the potential of becoming the focus of the litigation.[18]

D. ADEQUACY

The adequacy requirement addresses concerns about conflicts of interest and the competency of class counsel.[19] Adequacy is met when the representatives "(1) have common interests with the unnamed class members; and (2) will vigorously prosecute the class action through qualified counsel."[20] The plaintiffs must prove that the representatives can protect the interests of the persons who would be included in the class and that the representatives' interests are not antagonistic to the interests of the class members.[21]

III. Class Actions Maintainable

Practice Book section 9-8 is similar to Rule 23(b) of the Federal Rules of Civil Procedure. It requires that the plaintiff establish that common issues of law or fact predominate over individual issues and that the maintenance of a class action is superior to other potential methods of adjudication. The Connecticut and Federal Rules are different in two respects, however. First, the Practice Book does not include the grounds specified in Rule 23(b)(1) and 23(b)(2) that allow certification to avoid the risk of inconsistent or varying adjudications or where the party opposing the class has acted or refused to act on grounds that apply generally to the class so that final injunctive relief or corresponding declaratory relief is appropriate respecting the class as a whole. Second, section 9-8 of the Practice Book does not contain the factors listed in Rule 23(b)(3) for a court to consider in determining whether the predominance and superiority requirements are met. Nevertheless, the Connecticut Supreme Court has utilized the factors of the Federal Rule to assess whether the predominance and superiority requirements are satisfied under the Connecticut rule.[22]

---

16. *Collins v. Anthem Health Plans, Inc.*, 266 Conn. 12, 34 (2005) (*Collins I*) (citation omitted) (internal quotation marks omitted).

17. *Id.*; *Robichaud v. Hewlett Packard Co.*, 82 Conn. App. 848, 854–55 (2004).

18. *Macomber v. Travelers Prop. & Cas. Corp.*, 277 Conn. 617, 630 (2006).

19. *Collins II*, 275 Conn. at 326 (citation omitted) (internal quotation marks omitted).

20. *Id.*

21. *Id.* at 327.

22. *Collins I*, 266 Conn. at 48–49.

A. PREDOMINANCE

Predominance is "far more demanding" than the commonality requirement.[23] The Connecticut Supreme Court has held that "[c]ommon issues of fact and law predominate if they have a direct impact on every class member's effort to establish liability and on every class member's entitlement to injunctive and monetary relief."[24] Additionally, "[o]nly when common questions of law or fact will be the object of most of the efforts of the litigants and the court will the predominance test be satisfied."[25]

The Connecticut Supreme Court has set forth a three-part inquiry with regard to the determination of predominance: (1) "the court should review the elements of the causes of action that the plaintiffs seek to assert on behalf of the putative class"; (2) "the court should determine whether generalized evidence could be offered to prove those elements on a class-wide basis or whether individualized proof will be needed to establish each class member's entitlement to monetary or injunctive relief"; and (3) "the court should weigh the common issues that are subject to generalized proof against the issues requiring individualized proof in order to determine which predominate."[26]

The presence of individualized damages does not prevent a finding that the predominance requirement has been satisfied, however.[27] If damages can be computed "according to some formula, statistical analysis, or other easy or essentially mechanical methods," individualized damages determinations do not preclude class certification.[28] In contrast, cases involving "significant individualized questions going to liability" that require individualized assessments of damages are inappropriate for certification.[29]

B. SUPERIORITY

The class action must be the best available method for the fair and efficient adjudication of the controversy.[30] In Connecticut, the superiority requirement is intertwined with predominance to the extent that "[i]f the predominance criterion is satisfied, courts generally will find that the class action is a superior mechanism

---

23. *Id.* at 48 (citing *Amchem Prods., Inc. v. Windsor*, 521 U.S. 591, 624 (1997)).

24. *Collins II*, 275 Conn. at 330 (citation omitted) (internal quotation marks omitted).

25. *Id.* at 332 (citation omitted) (internal quotation marks omitted).

26. *Id.* at 331–32 (citations omitted).

27. *Id.* at 330 (citation omitted) (internal quotation marks omitted).

28. *Id.* at 331 (citation omitted) (internal quotation marks omitted). *See also Artie's Auto Body*, 287 Conn. at 225.

29. *Collins II*, 275 Conn. at 33 (citation omitted) (internal quotation marks omitted).

30. *Collins I*, 266 Conn. at 56.

even if it presents management difficulties."[31] The more individualized issues predominate, "the less superior and more unmanageable a class action will be."[32]

IV. Dismissal or Compromise of Class Action

Connecticut has not adopted the changes made in the 2003 amendments to Rule 23(e) of the Federal Rules of Civil Procedure, which concern the procedure for the approval and notice of settlements, voluntary dismissals, or compromises. Both Practice Book section 9-9 and former Rule 23(e) require court approval to settle or voluntarily withdraw a certified class action. The 2003 amendments to the federal rule were a clarification that the court's approval was not required to approve the dismissal or compromise of an uncertified class.[33] It is unsettled in Connecticut whether the court's approval must be obtained to dismiss or compromise an individual settlement of a putative class suit. Additionally, section 9-9 of the Practice Book provides that the judicial authority can require that notice of the proposed dismissal or compromise be given.

V. Orders to Ensure Adequate Representation

Practice Book section 9-10 authorizes the judicial authority to impose terms that fairly and adequately protect the interests of the class at any stage of the action. Section 9-10 further provides that the judicial authority

> may order that notice be given, in such a manner as it may direct, of the pendency of the action, of a proposed settlement, of entry of judgment, or of any other proceedings in the action, including notice to the absent persons that they may come in and present claims and defenses if they so desire.[34]

This provision is more lenient than Rule 23(c)(2) of the Federal Rules. As a practical matter, however, it has been suggested that "trial courts follow all the provisions of Federal Rule 23(c), none of which are inconsistent with the state class action rules."[35]

Unlike Rule 23(c)(4), which specifically authorizes partial class actions, the Practice Book does not expressly provide for them. The Connecticut Supreme Court has held, however, that partial class actions may be brought in state court.[36]

---

31. *Collins II*, 275 Conn. at 347.
32. *Id.*
33. Fed. R. Civ. P. 23(e)(1) advisory committee note (2003).
34. Connecticut Practice Book §§ 9-10.
35. 1 W. Horton & K. Knox, Connecticut Practice: Practice Book Annotated §§ 9-10, Authors' Comments.
36. *Collins I*, 266 Conn. at 25-27.

Finally, pursuant to section 9-10, the class allegations can be removed from a class action complaint to allow judgment to be entered as to only the named representatives and those that the court determines to be adequately represented. Specifically, when class representation appears inadequate to fairly protect the interests of the absent parties, the judicial authority may order an amendment of the pleading that eliminates any reference to representation of the class.[37]

VI. Appeals

Connecticut has not adopted a provision similar to Rule 23(f) of the Federal Rules of Civil Procedure, which permits interlocutory appeals of class certification determinations. The Connecticut Senate Judiciary Committee has proposed legislation that would amend section 52-105 of the Connecticut General Statutes to make it similar to the federal rule in this regard.[38] Until such legislation is enacted or the relevant Practice Book sections are revised, however, Connecticut case law provides the only legal authority regarding the right to take an immediate appeal of the courts' decisions concerning class certification.

Connecticut precedent is clear that "[a]n otherwise interlocutory order is appealable in two circumstances: (1) where the order or action terminates a separate and distinct proceeding, or (2) where the order or action so concludes the rights of the parties that further proceedings cannot affect them."[39] If an order does not satisfy either of the above prongs, which are referred to as the *Curcio* test, the lack of a final judgment "is a jurisdictional defect" and the appeal must be dismissed.[40]

The Connecticut Supreme Court has applied the *Curcio* test to hold that an order denying class certification is not a final judgment that may be appealed.[41] Specifically, the court found that a denial of a class certification motion does not satisfy the first prong "because it is too intertwined with the named plaintiffs' lawsuit and is an order capable of review after a final judgment in the lawsuit."[42] A denial of class certification also cannot satisfy the second prong because there is no right to maintain a class action until the court exercises its discretion to certify the class and, upon denial of class certification, putative class members are free to file their own lawsuits or to seek to intervene in the ongoing litigation.[43]

---

37. HORTON & KNOX, *supra* note 35, at § 9-10.
38. S.B. 1143, Gen. Assem., Jan. Sess. (Conn. 2009).
39. *State v. Curcio*, 191 Conn. 27, 31 (1983).
40. *Rivera*, 262 Conn. at 734 (citation omitted) (internal quotation marks omitted).
41. *Palmer v. Friendly Ice Cream Corp.*, 285 Conn. 462, 482 (2008).
42. *Id.* at 472.
43. *Id.* at 470–72, 482.

In contrast, an order that decertifies a class action constitutes a final judgment.[44] The Connecticut Supreme Court has held that a decertification order satisfies the second prong of the *Curcio* test because when plaintiffs were certified as a class, they "secured the right to proceed in a class action against the defendant," which "provided to the plaintiffs an economically efficient means to proceed in an action that they otherwise might be unable to pursue."[45] When the trial court decertified the class, "the right to proceed as a class was irretrievably lost and the plaintiffs were irreparably harmed."[46] For these reasons, the order decertifying the class constituted an appealable final judgment.[47]

Additionally, the Connecticut Unfair Trade Practices Act (CUTPA)[48] contains a provision allowing for the immediate appeal of class certification decisions. Specifically, CUTPA provides as follows: "As soon as practicable after the commencement of an action brought as a class action, the court shall determine by order whether it is to be so maintained. . . . An order issued under this section shall be immediately appealable by either party."[49] The Connecticut Supreme Court has held that when non-CUTPA causes of action are "inextricably intertwined" with CUTPA claims, both are immediately reviewable.[50]

VII. *Appointment of Counsel and Attorney Fees*

Connecticut has not adopted provisions similar to Rule 23(g) of the Federal Rules of Civil Procedure regarding the appointment of class counsel or Rule 23(h) governing attorney fees and nontaxable costs.

---

44. *Rivera*, 262 Conn. at 731–32.
45. *Id.* at 734–35.
46. *Id.* at 735–36 (citation omitted) (internal quotation marks omitted).
47. *Id.* at 736.
48. CONN. GEN. STAT. § 42-110h.
49. *Id.*
50. *Collins I*, 266 Conn. at 29.

DISTRICT OF COLUMBIA

JOHN M. SIMPSON

I. Introduction

Understanding class action procedure in the District of Columbia requires an understanding of the judicial system in that jurisdiction. Although not a state, the District of Columbia has a local court system that, for individuals and entities residing in or doing business within the District, functions procedurally and substantively in much the same way as any state court system. The current configuration was established in 1970 when, pursuant to Article I of the Constitution,[1] Congress created the District of Columbia Court of Appeals as the highest appellate court and the Superior Court for the District of Columbia as the unitary trial court for the District.[2] This local court system is separate from the federal court system in the District—the U.S. Court of Appeals for the District of Columbia Circuit and the U.S. District Court for the District of Columbia—that Congress created under Article III of the Constitution.[3] Since this chapter is part of a state-law survey, its focus will be on class action procedure under the local law of the District.

Class actions in the District are governed by rules 23 and 23-I of the District of Columbia Superior Court Rules of Civil Procedure (D.C. Rules).[4] The current version of D.C. Rule 23, in effect since 1999, tracks the 1998 version of Federal Rule 23, except for certain parts of subsections (c)(1) and (c)(2) concerning shifting the costs of class notice to the defendant.[5] D.C. Rule 23-I, last amended in May 2002,

---

1. U.S. CONST. art. I.

2. Court Reorganization Act of 1970, Pub. L. No. 91-358, 84 Stat. 475 (1970); D.C. CODE ANN. § 11-102 (LexisNexis 2001).

3. U.S. CONST. art. III. *See Palmore v. U.S.*, 411 U.S. 389, 398 (1973).

4. D.C. SUPER. CT. R. CIV. P. 23 & 23-I (2009).

5. D.C. SUPER. CT. R. CIV. P. 23, cmt. *Compare* D.C. SUPER. CT. R. CIV. P. 23 *with* 5 JAMES WM. MOORE ET AL., MOORE'S FEDERAL PRACTICE §§ 23App.04(1) to 23App.06(2) (3d ed. 2010) [hereinafter MOORE'S] (FED. R. CIV. P. 23, as amended in 1966, 1987, & 1998). Pursuant to D.C. Rule 23(c)(2), the trial court, upon

prescribes procedures for handling class actions and was based upon Local Rule 23.1 of the U.S. District Court for the District of Columbia.[6] Because D.C. Rule 23 is derived from Federal Rule 23, it will be construed "'in light of the meaning of that federal rule.'"[7]

II. Prerequisites to Class Certification Under Rule 23(a)

D.C. Rule 23(a) tracks the comparable Federal Rule 23(a) requirements of numerosity, commonality, typicality, and adequacy of representation. The burden is on the party seeking class certification to show that these requirements are satisfied.[8] Whether that burden has been discharged is a matter that is committed to the trial court's discretion, whose decision in this regard will not be reversed unless that discretion has been abused.[9]

A vague and imprecise class definition can lead to a determination that the numerosity requirement has not been satisfied. Thus, in an action by a purported class of automobile owners against the city and certain towing companies, the court of appeals affirmed the trial court's denial of class certification on the ground, *inter alia*, that because of the "vagueness and speculative nature" of the class definition, the class could either be "'gargantuan' . . . [or] much smaller."[10]

The court of appeals has observed that the "core concept underlying the class action device is found in the requirement of Rule 23(a)(2) that there be questions of law or fact common to the class."[11] To satisfy this element, it is not necessary that every issue of fact or law be the same for each class member. "'[F]actual variations among the class members will not defeat the commonality requirement, so long as a single aspect of or feature of the claim is common to all proposed class members.'"[12]

In determining whether the typicality requirement has been satisfied, the courts in the District consider "the allegations in the complaint, the nucleus of facts underlying the allegations, and the evidence necessary to prove those facts."[13]

---

conducting a hearing under D.C. Rule 23-I(c)(3), may shift the costs of providing class notice to the defendant in a (b)(3) class action. D.C. SUPER. CT. R. CIV. P. 23(c)(2). The Rule was amended in response to the decision in *Eisen v. Carlisle & Jacqueline*, 417 U.S. 156 (1974), holding that the costs of notice normally cannot be shifted to the defendant. *See* D.C. SUPER. CT. R. CIV. P. 23, cmt.

6. *See* D.C. SUPER. CT. R. CIV. P. 23-I, cmt.

7. *Ford v. ChartOne, Inc.*, 908 A.2d 72, 85 n.13 (D.C. 2006) (quoting *Taylor v. Wash. Hosp. Ctr.*, 407 A.2d 585, 590 n.4 (D.C. 1979)).

8. *Snowder v. D.C.*, 949 A.2d 590, 597 (D.C. 2008); *Ford*, 908 A.2d at 84; *Cowan v. Youssef*, 687 A.2d 594, 602 (D.C. 1996); *Yarmolinsky v. Perpetual Am. Fed. Sav. & Loan Ass'n*, 451 A.2d 92, 94 (D.C. 1982).

9. *Snowder*, 949 A.2d at 597; *Ford*, 908 A.2d at 84; *Cowan*, 687 A.2d at 602; *Yarmolinsky*, 451 A.2d at 94.

10. *Snowder*, 949 A.2d at 597 (quoting trial court's order).

11. *Ford*, 908 A.2d at 85.

12. *Id.* (quoting *Bynum v. D.C.*, 214 F.R.D. 27, 33 (D.D.C. 2003)).

13. *Yarmolinsky*, 451 A.2d at 95.

The purpose of typicality is to ensure that the class representatives' claims are sufficiently similar to the absent class members' claims so that the former's acts are on behalf of and safeguard the interests of the latter.[14] If that purpose is achieved, then "as with commonality, '[f]actual variations between the claims of class representatives and the claims of other class members . . . do not negate typicality.'"[15]

As to adequacy of representation, D.C. courts apply two criteria: (1) whether the named representative has antagonistic or conflicting interests with the unnamed members of the class, and (2) whether the named representative can vigorously prosecute the interests of the class through qualified class counsel.[16]

Applying these principles, the court of appeals has held that the trial court properly denied certification of a class of real estate sellers in an action against a lender because the defendant's liability turned upon the terms of individual contracts: "By their very nature, breach of contract claims do not lend themselves to class action solution."[17] On the other hand, in an action claiming that the fees charged for copying medical records were unconscionably high, the court held that the individual cost variations cited by the trial court were immaterial and, therefore, that a class should have been certified since the relevant analysis was the defendant's average costs.[18] The court of appeals has also held, in an antitrust action claiming that defendant vitamin manufacturers had engaged in price fixing and market allocation, that the separately certified consumer and commercial classes of purchasers suffered similar enough injuries that any conflicts between them were not significant enough to preclude representation by common class counsel.[19]

---

14. *Ford*, 908 A.2d at 86.

15. *Id.* (quoting *Bynum*, 214 F.R.D. at 34).

16. *Id.* (citing *Twelve John Does v. D.C.*, 117 F.3d 571, 575 (D.C. Cir. 1997)).

17. *Yarmolinsky*, 451 A.2d at 96; *see also Snowder*, 949 A.2d at 598 (class action treatment properly denied in action by automobile owners against city and towing companies to recover towing fees where named representatives, who received tickets and notice of towing, had claims distinct from those members of the class whose automobiles had been stolen and towed to impoundment lot without notice); *Goss v. Med. Serv.*, 462 A.2d 442, 446 (D.C. 1983) (affirming denial of class certification motion in action brought on behalf of individuals insured under certain medical policies who may have been denied coverage on the ground that a certain condition is a dental rather than a medical condition; "A determination of the medical necessity of any treatment requires individualized review. The necessity of such individualized inquiries defeats the purpose of a class action, ..." (citations omitted)); *Kleibomer v. D.C.*, 458 A.2d 731, 733 (D.C. 1983) (since recovery of invalid tax requires filing of individual administrative refund request by taxpayer, named representatives and all class members must have filed administrative refund requests for action to proceed as class action); *Smith v. Murphy*, 294 A.2d 357, 360 (D.C. 1972) (where exhaustion of administrative remedies was requirement of any claim asserted on behalf of class, representatives who had not exhausted administrative remedies did not satisfy commonality requirement).

18. *Ford*, 908 A.2d at 90–91. Cf. *Hooker v. Edes Home*, 579 A.2d 608, 617 (D.C. 1990) (individuals who satisfied admission criteria for home for indigent, elderly widows had standing to bring action on behalf of all eligible potential residents of the home).

19. *Boyle v. Giral*, 820 A.2d 561, 565–66 (D.C. 2003). Cf. *Calvin-Humphrey v. D.C.*, 340 A.2d 795, 800 (D.C. 1975) (individual representing class of residential property owners should have been allowed to

III. Rule 23(b) Requirements

"Any action that satisfies the requirements of Rule 23(a) may be maintained as a class action provided that it also meets the requirements of one or more of the subdivisions of Rule 23(b)."[20] D.C. Rule 23(b) follows the requirements of Federal Rule 23(b).[21] The court of appeals does not appear to have directly addressed Rule 23(b)(1), but has indicated that Rule 23(b)(1) is the proper vehicle for an action by taxpayers to recover an invalid tax collected by the District, provided that other prerequisites for such a suit are satisfied.[22]

The court of appeals has viewed the (b)(2) class action as "'intended for cases where broad, class-wide injunctive or declaratory relief is necessary to redress a group-wide injury'" and not applicable to cases "'in which the appropriate final relief relates exclusively or predominantly to money damages.'"[23] The court follows the principle that "'insignificant or sham requests for injunctive relief should not provide cover for (b)(2) certification of claims that are brought essentially for monetary recovery.'"[24] Thus, the court affirmed a trial court's determination that an action by a class of medical records purchasers to challenge the defendant's allegedly unconscionable fee schedule was properly denied (b)(2) certification because it was an action predominantly for monetary rather than injunctive relief.[25]

The court of appeals has observed that "[c]lass actions seeking mainly monetary relief usually fall under Rule 23(b)(3), which not only implicates class member notification and opt-out rights but also mandates additional findings by the trial court."[26] While there is "'no magic formula'" for determining whether common questions predominate, predominance will arise for (b)(3) purposes when generalized evidence tends to prove or disprove an element on a classwide basis or where the defendant's activities present a common course of conduct.[27] Thus, "[c]onsumer actions alleging various types of systematic overcharging often have been certified as (b)(3) class actions under the foregoing principles."[28] However, an action by a putative class of tenants claiming breach of the implied warranty

---

intervene in action by class of commercial property owners seeking to enjoin assessment of property tax; neither the commercial owners nor the government adequately represented the interests of the residential owners).

20. *Ford*, 908 A.2d at 86.

21. *Compare* D.C. Super. Ct. R. Civ. P. 23(b) *with* Fed. R. Civ. P. 23(b).

22. *Kleibomer*, 458 A.2d at 732 (referring to trial court's grant of class certification pursuant to Rule 23(b)(1)(A)).

23. *Ford*, 908 A.2d at 87 (citations omitted).

24. *Id.* (quoting *Robinson v. Metro-North Commuter R.R. Co.*, 267 F.3d 147, 164 (2d Cir. 2001)).

25. *Id.* at 92–93.

26. *Id.* at 88.

27. *Id.* (citations omitted).

28. *Id.* (action to recover unconscionable medical records fees properly certified as (b)(3) class action) (citing *Dist. Cablevision Ltd. P'ship v. Bassin*, 828 A.2d 714, 719 (D.C. 2003)). While the *District Cablevision*

of habitability was properly denied (b)(3) certification because resolution of such a claim "'will turn largely on individual factual determinations concerning . . . each apartment.'"[29]

IV. Class Action Procedure in the Trial Court

With one notable exception (discussed below), paragraphs (c), (d), and (e) of D.C. Rule 23 are the same as the 1966 version of Federal Rule 23(c)–(e).[30] Therefore, D.C. Rule 23 does not contain the provisions in the current version of Federal Rule 23 addressing settlement, voluntary dismissal or compromise,[31] class counsel,[32] or attorney fees.[33]

The major difference between D.C. Rule 23(c) and its 1966 federal predecessor is the provision in paragraph (c)(2) regarding the cost of class notice. Pursuant to D.C. Rule 23(c)(2):

> The cost of notice shall be paid by the plaintiff unless the Court, upon conducting a hearing pursuant to Rule 23-I(c)(3), concludes (1) that the plaintiff class will more likely than not prevail on the merits and (2) that it is necessary to require the defendant to pay some or all of that cost in order to prevent manifest injustice.[34]

As explained by the Comment to D.C. Rule 23, this provision "was made necessary by [*Eisen v. Carlisle & Jacqueline*, 417 U.S. 156 (1974)] which held that under the language of [Federal Rule 23], the costs of notice could not be shifted to the defendant, except perhaps in cases involving a fiduciary, and, the Court could not make a preliminary determination of the merits of a case."[35]

D.C. Rule 23-I, which is patterned after a similar local rule of the U.S. District Court for the District of Columbia,[36] prescribes additional procedures to be followed in superior court class actions. Rule 23-I(a) specifies the pleading requirements for class action complaints, including references to the specific provisions of Rule 23 that the pleader intends to rely upon, the size of the class, the basis upon which the representatives are claimed to be adequate, and the questions of law and

---

case was certified as a (b)(3) class action, the court of appeals' decision in that case did not address class certification issues.

29. *Cowan*, 687 A.2d at 603 (quoting trial court's order).
30. *Compare* D.C. SUPER. CT. R. CIV. P. 23(c)–(e) *with* 5 MOORE'S, *supra* note 5, § 23App.04(1) (FED. R. CIV. P. 23(c)–(e), as amended in 1966).
31. FED. R. CIV. P. 23(e).
32. FED. R. CIV. P. 23(g).
33. FED. R. CIV. P. 23(h).
34. D.C. SUPER. CT. R. CIV. P. 23(c)(2).
35. D.C. SUPER. CT. R. CIV. P. 23(c)(2) cmt.
36. D.C. SUPER. CT. R. CIV. P. 23-I cmt.; *see also* D.D.C. LOCAL CIV. R. 23.1 (2009).

fact that are common and allegations supporting (b)(3) status when that provision is invoked.[37]

Rule 23-I(b)(1) requires that a plaintiff seeking to pursue a class action file a motion to certify the class within 90 days after the filing of the complaint and specifies the contents of the moving papers.[38] Rule 23-I(b)(2) provides the opposing party ten days in which to respond to the certification motion and specifies the contents of the opposition, noting that the court may assume that the facts stated by the plaintiff are admitted except those that the opponent asserts "in good faith [are] controverted in a statement filed in opposition to the motion."[39] Rule 23-I(b)(3) requires the court to act "promptly" upon the motion and grants the court discretion to conduct a hearing or to permit discovery in connection with the motion.[40] Rule 23-I(b)(3) specifically preserves the defendant's right to move at any time to strike the class action allegations or to dismiss the complaint.[41] The court of appeals has suggested, without directly deciding the point, that despite the 90-day requirement, a class certification motion can be postponed pending a ruling on the defendant's motion to dismiss.[42] Absent compliance with the certification procedures of Rules 23(b) and 23-I(b), a case will not be regarded as a class action, regardless of how it is pleaded or what relief the trial court ultimately may order.[43]

Rule 23-I(c)(1) and (2) prescribe procedures for the plaintiff to propose notice and for the defendant to oppose what plaintiff has proposed.[44] Rule 23-I(c)(3) addresses court action upon the proposed notice, including the conduct of a hearing on the proposed notice, the allowance of discovery in connection with the proposed notice, and a determination as to who shall bear the costs of notice.[45] Rule 23-I(d) provides that all of the foregoing procedures are applicable, "with appropri-

---

37. D.C. SUPER. CT. R. CIV. P. 23-I(a)(1) & (2)(i)-(iv).

38. D.C. SUPER. CT. R. CIV. P. 23-I(b)(1).

39. D.C. SUPER. CT. R. CIV. P. 23-I(b)(2).

40. D.C. SUPER. CT. R. CIV. P. 23-I(b)(3).

41. Id.

42. Chamberlain v. Am. Honda Fin. Corp., 931 A.2d 1018, 1019 n.1 (D.C. 2007).

43. Id. (absent a certification order, "this court will not consider any hypothetical claims of the unnamed class members in its review of the lower court's decision"); see also Washkoviak v. Student Loan Mktg Ass'n, 900 A.2d 168, 172 (D.C. 2006) (only claims of named plaintiffs considered in appeal of order dismissing complaint; "[a]lthough they characterized it as a class action complaint, [plaintiffs] concede that they never moved for certification as required by D.C. Super. Ct. Civ. R. 23-I(b)(1)"); In re Inquiry into Allegations of Misconduct Against Juveniles Detained & Committed at Cedar Knoll, 430 A.2d 1087, 1092 (D.C. 1981) (trial court had no authority to grant relief on behalf of all individuals detained at a certain facility without "even rudimentary trial level attempts to comply with Rule 23"); Apartment & Office Bldg. Ass'n v. Washington, 343 A.2d 323, 327 (D.C. 1975) (even though case had been pleaded as class action and trial court granted partial classwide relief on the merits, case not properly treated as a class action because trial court did not comply with Rule 23 or Rule 23-I).

44. D.C. SUPER. CT. R. CIV. P. 23-I(c)(1)-(2).

45. D.C. SUPER. CT. R. CIV. P. 23-I(c)(3).

ate adaptations," to "any counterclaim or cross-claim alleged to be brought for or against a class."[46]

The court of appeals has enforced a forum selection clause in a contract involving District residents and dismissed a putative class action even though the forum selected by the contract was "one of only two states that lacks a class action procedure similar to Super. Ct. Civ. R. 23 & 23-I."[47] As the court observed, "We fail to see . . . why the absence of one particular remedy in a foreign jurisdiction should be elevated beyond all other possible jurisprudential consequences of a forum selection clause."[48]

V. Appellate Procedure

D.C. Rule 23(f) is the same as the 1998 version of Federal Rule 26(f) and provides that the court of appeals may, in its discretion, "permit an appeal to be taken from an order of the Superior Court granting or denying class action certification under this Rule if application is made to it within ten days after entry of the order."[49] D.C. Rule 23(f) further provides that such an appeal will not stay the action in the trial court unless the trial court enters an order to that effect.[50]

Despite the plain language of D.C. Rule 26(f), and in contrast to the practice in federal court under Federal Rule 23(f) in which the appeal of a class certification order may proceed solely by leave of the appellate court, the D.C. Court of Appeals has held that D.C. Rule 26(f) "does not authorize [the court of appeals] to permit an interlocutory appeal from the grant or denial of class action certification without the written statement by the trial judge that D.C. Code § 11-721(d) requires."[51] Therefore, in addition to obtaining permission from the court of appeals to appeal, the appellant must also obtain a certification from the trial judge that the class certification order "involves a controlling question of law as to which there is a substantial ground for difference of opinion and that an immediate appeal . . . may materially advance the ultimate termination of the litigation or case."[52] The trial court's certification is a "jurisdictional condition imposed by D.C. Code § 11-721(d) that Rule 23(f) cannot abrogate."[53] The court of appeals reasoned that, while Federal Rule 23(f) "was intended to enlarge [federal] appellate

---

46. D.C. SUPER. CT. R. CIV. P. 23(d).

47. *Forrest v. Verizon Comm'ns, Inc.*, 805 A.2d 1007, 1011 (D.C. 2002).

48. *Id.*

49. D.C. SUPER. CT. R. CIV. P. 23(f). *Cf.* 5 MOORE'S, *supra* note 5, § 23App.06(1) (FED. R. CIV. P. 23(f), as amended in 1998).

50. D.C. SUPER. CT. R. CIV. P. 23(f).

51. *Ford v. ChartOne, Inc.*, 834 A.2d 875, 881 (D.C. 2003).

52. D.C. CODE ANN. § 11-721(d) (LexisNexis 2001). This provision of the D.C. Code parallels 28 U.S.C. § 1292(b).

53. *Ford*, 834 A.2d at 877.

jurisdiction beyond what the otherwise applicable jurisdictional statute allowed," the U.S. Supreme Court had the power to reach that result by rule under 28 U.S.C. § 1292(e).[54] However, "[t]here is no analogous provision in the District of Columbia Code (or in the United States Code, for that matter) expressly authorizing the Superior Court to promulgate a jurisdiction-enlarging rule such as Rule 23(f)."[55]

Because of the court of appeals' limiting interpretation of Rule 23(f), the only practical way to obtain interlocutory appellate review of an order on class certification is by leave of both the trial and appellate courts under the standard described above. Following U.S. Supreme Court precedent, the court of appeals has held that an order denying class certification is not appealable as of right because it sounds the "death knell" for the plaintiff's case.[56] Nor does it present "an issue likely to 'evade end-of-the-case review' and come[ ] within the collateral order doctrine."[57]

The current D.C. provision addressing dismissal or compromise of a class action—Rule 23(e)—parallels the 1966 version of Federal Rule 23(e).[58] The court of appeals has followed federal precedent in holding that appellate review of an order approving the settlement of a class action is limited and quite deferential to the trial court.[59]

---

54. *Id.* at 880.

55. *Id.*

56. *Id.* at 881 (citing *Coopers & Lybrand v. Livesay*, 437 U.S. 463 (1978)).

57. *Id.*

58. *Compare* D.C. SUPER. CT. R. CIV. P. 23(e) *with* 5 MOORE'S, *supra* note 5, at § 23App.04(1) (FED. R. CIV. P. 23(e), as amended in 1966).

59. *Shepherd Park Citizens Ass'n v. Gen. Cinema Beverages, Inc.*, 584 A.2d 20, 22 (D.C. 1990).

CHAPTER 33

DELAWARE

JUSTICE JOSEPH T. WALSH
DANIEL M. SILVER

I. Introduction

Like many states, Delaware has adopted a framework modeled on the Federal Rules of Civil Procedure (Federal Rules) to govern civil matters within its trial courts.[1] Delaware, however, unlike federal courts or the court systems of many states, maintains two separate and distinct courts where class actions may be brought: (1) the Court of Chancery, a court of equity with limited jurisdiction, and (2) the Superior Court, a court of law with general jurisdiction.

II. Requisites to Class Action

Both the Court of Chancery and Superior Court Civil Rule 23(a) are nearly identical to Federal Rule 23(a).[2] Both the Court of Chancery and the Superior Court look to the requirements of numerosity, commonality, typicality, and adequacy of representation.[3] However, the Court of Chancery Rule, in subsection (aa), adds an additional requirement, that each prospective class representative file an affidavit, under oath, stating that the representative

> has not received, been promised or offered and will not accept any form of compensation, directly or indirectly, for prosecuting or serving as a representative party in the class action in which the person or entity is a named party except for (i) such damages or other relief as the Court may award such person as a member of the class, (ii) such fees, costs or other payments as the Court expressly approves to be paid to or on behalf of such person, or (iii) reimbursement, paid by such person's

---

1. *See Plummer v. Sherman*, 861 A.2d 1238, 1242 (Del. 2004).
2. *Compare* DEL. CH. CT. R. 23(a) and DEL. SUPER. CT. R. CIV. P. 23(a) *with* FED. R. CIV. P. 23(a).
3. *See* DEL. CH. CT. R. 23(a); DEL. SUPER. CT. R. CIV. P. 23(a).

attorneys, of actual and reasonable out-of-pocket expenditures incurred directly in connection with the prosecution of the action.[4]

This affidavit must be filed within ten days of the commencement of a class action.[5] Superior Court Civil Rule 23 does not contain this additional requirement.[6]

Because of Delaware's preeminence as a top forum for stockholder litigation, there are numerous cases interpreting and applying Court of Chancery Rule 23. With regard to the numerosity requirement, the Court of Chancery has held that a class of 14 stockholders was insufficient to satisfy the requirements of Court of Chancery Rule 23,[7] though precedent exists for certifying a class of similar size when the defendant does not contest that numerosity is met.[8] Importantly, the focus on numerosity in the Delaware Court of Chancery is upon the *impracticality* of having all class members join as parties, and not *impossibility*.[9]

There are notably fewer cases applying Superior Court Civil Rule 23, but certain decisions illuminate the Superior Court's approach to class actions. In one case, the court approved a class of high-ranking employees, even though they were not identically situated, in an action to enforce their rights under an incentive compensation plan upon finding that it was the most efficient manner in which to proceed.[10] In another case, the Superior Court held that a plaintiff proceeding *in forma pauperis* could not adequately represent the class.[11]

III. Class Actions Maintainable

Both Court of Chancery and Superior Court Civil Rule 23 contain a provision that is nearly identical to Federal Rule 23(b) regarding the types of actions maintainable as class actions.[12] The Court of Chancery and the Superior Court have both held that fraud claims cannot be maintained as class actions because the individual issues presented predominate over common questions of law and fact.[13]

---

4. DEL. CH. CT. R. 23(aa).

5. *See id.*

6. *See generally* DEL. SUPER. CT. R. CIV. P. 23.

7. *See Erickson v. Centennial Beauregard Cellular LLC*, No. 19974, 2003 Del. Ch. LEXIS 38, at *7 (Apr. 11, 2003).

8. *See id.* at *12 n.18.

9. *See Leon N. Weiner & Assocs. v. Krapf*, 584 A.2d 1220, 1225 (Del. 1991).

10. *See generally Smith v. Hercules*, No. 01C-08-291 WCC, 2003 Del. Super. LEXIS 38 (Jan. 31, 2003).

11. *See Alston v. Minner*, No. 01C-07-039, 2001 Del. Super. LEXIS 472, at *3 (Oct. 19, 2001), *aff'd*, 796 A.2d 654 (Del. 2002).

12. *Compare* DEL. CH. CT. R. 23(b) and DEL. SUPER. CT. R. CIV. P. 23(b) *with* FED. R. CIV. P. 23(b).

13. *See Dieter v. Prime Computer, Inc.*, 681 A.2d 1068, 1076 (Del. Ch. 1996); *Benning v. Wit Capital Group, Inc.*, No. 99C-06-157 MMJ, 2004 Del. Super. LEXIS 411, at *14 (Nov. 30, 2004), *rev'd on other grounds*, No. 568, 2005 Del. LEXIS 536 (June 20, 2005).

IV. Determination by Order Whether Class Action to Be Maintained; Notice; Judgment; Actions Conducted Partially as Class Actions

Court of Chancery and Superior Court Civil Rule 23(c) are very similar to Federal Rule 23(c).[14] Both Delaware rules require the court to determine whether to certify a class as soon as practicable, as did Federal Rule 23 before 2003.[15] In keeping with the spirit of Federal Rule 23, both Court of Chancery and Superior Court Civil Rule 23 require "the best notice [to the class members] that is practicable under the circumstances" and require specific provisions in any notice being provided to a class certified pursuant to Rule 23(b).[16] The Court of Chancery has the discretion to provide class members with the right to opt out of the class, but where the relief sought is primarily equitable in nature, the court is not required to provide class members with the right to opt out.[17] The Delaware rules, like their federal counterpart, contain provisions for treating an action as a partial class action or dividing a class into subclasses.[18]

V. Orders in Conduct of Actions

Court of Chancery and Superior Court Civil Rule 23(d) are nearly identical to their federal counterpart.[19] Despite the similarity in rules, Delaware courts follow the *McWane* doctrine—which dictates that a Delaware court abstain from adjudicating an action where an earlier-filed action on similar issues is pending in another jurisdiction in the interests of comity and judicial economy—as well as the doctrine of forum non conveniens (in the case of a contemporaneously filed action in another jurisdiction), and apply those doctrines with equal force to class and derivative actions, staying or dismissing them as appropriate.[20]

VI. Dismissal or Compromise

Though the spirit of Federal Rule 23(e) is captured by its Delaware counterparts, the text of Court of Chancery and Superior Court Civil Rules 23(e) deviates from

---

14. *Compare* DEL. CH. CT. R. 23(c) and DEL. SUPER. CT. R. CIV. P. 23(c) *with* FED. R. CIV. P. 23(c).

15. *See* DEL. CH. CT. R. 23(c); DEL. SUPER. CT. R. CIV. P. 23(c).

16. DEL. CH. CT. R. 23(c); DEL. SUPER. CT. R. CIV. P. 23(c).

17. *See In re MCA, Inc.*, 598 A.2d 687, 692 (Del. Ch. 1991).

18. *See* DEL. CH. CT. R. 23(c)(4); DEL. SUPER. CT. R. CIV. P. 23(c)(4).

19. *Compare* DEL. CH. CT. R. 23(d) and DEL. SUPER. CT. R. CIV. P. 23(d) *with* FED. R. CIV. P. 23(d).

20. *See, e.g., In re Bear Stearns Cos., Inc. S'holders Litig.*, No. 3643-VCP, 2008 Del. Ch. LEXIS 46, at *15 (Apr. 9, 2008) (discussing *McWane Cast Iron Pipe Corp. v. McDowell-Wellman Engineering Co.*, 283 A.2d 281 (Del. 1970), and forum non conveniens doctrines).

Federal Rule 23(e).[21] Court of Chancery Rule 23(e) requires a class representative to file an additional affidavit akin to what is required by subsection (aa), in conjunction with a motion for approval of a settlement, affirming once again that the class representative has not received any extraordinary consideration in exchange for agreeing to the settlement.[22] Superior Court Civil Rule 23(e) does not contain a similar requirement.[23]

Delaware courts take very seriously the obligation of evaluating and approving class settlements. Particularly in the realm of stockholder suits, the Court of Chancery diligently examines whether a proposed settlement is fair, and has on more than one occasion rejected such settlements.[24] The Court of Chancery typically requires at least 30 days' notice to class members prior to the approval of a compromise.[25]

VII. The Delaware Rules Omit Provisions Comparable to Federal Rule 23(f), (g), and (h)

Court of Chancery and Superior Court Civil Rules 23 do not contain subsections (f), (g), and (h) found in Federal Rule 23.[26] Federal Rule 23(f) provides for a discretionary, interlocutory appeal from a presiding district court to the court of appeals upon the grant or denial of a class certification.[27] Under the governing procedural rules in Delaware, an aggrieved party is required to pursue an interlocutory appeal to the Delaware Supreme Court under Supreme Court Rule 42, which requires that the prospective appellant first seek certification from the trial court.[28] As with all requests for interlocutory appeals, a request for an interlocutory appeal to the Delaware Supreme Court on the issue of class certification may be denied if no novel legal issue is presented.[29]

While Court of Chancery and Superior Court Civil Rules 23 are silent on appointment of class counsel and awards of fees, the Delaware courts have the ability to appoint class counsel and award counsel fees. At least one court has interpreted the requirement of adequate representation contained in Rule 23(a)(4) to require an adequate class representative *and* adequate class counsel.[30] In the event of a contest for appointment of a class representative and class counsel, the

---

21. *Compare* DEL. CH. CT. R. 23(e) and DEL. SUPER. CT. R. CIV. P. 23(e) *with* FED. R. CIV. P. 23(e).

22. *See* DEL. CH. CT. R. 23(e).

23. *See* DEL. SUPER. CT. R. CIV. P. 23(e).

24. *See In re Prime Hospitality, Inc. S'holders Litig.*, No. 652-N, 2005 Del. Ch. LEXIS 61 (May 4, 2005).

25. *See In re Coleman Co. S'holder Litig.*, 750 A.2d 1202, 1210 (Del. Ch. 1999).

26. *Compare* DEL. CH. CT. R. 23 and DEL. SUPER. CT. R. CIV. P. 23 *with* FED. R. CIV. P. 23(f)-(h).

27. *See* FED. R. CIV. P. 23(f).

28. *See* DEL. SUP. CT. R. 42.

29. *See, e.g., Erickson*, 2003 Del. Ch. LEXIS 143, at *1; *Smith*, 2003 Del. Super. LEXIS 87, at *4-9.

30. *See Benning v. Wit Capital Group, Inc.*, 2001 Del. Super. LEXIS 7, at *21.

court will typically appoint the chosen representative's counsel as class counsel, assuming counsel is qualified to represent the class.[31]

With regard to counsel fees, Delaware courts have rejected a fixed, mathematical process for determining counsel fees.[32] Instead, courts have wide discretion in determining an award of counsel fees. In the Court of Chancery, equitable principles predominate.[33] For example, the Court of Chancery has approved an award that resulted in a fee award of over $2,600 per hour, finding that the size of the benefit conferred upon the class by the efforts of class counsel was more important than the per-hour fee award.[34] The Superior Court has approved a fee award representing one-third of the settlement fund obtained for the benefit of the class.[35] The Supreme Court of Delaware has recognized that the lawyers, in seeking a fee award, are no longer acting solely in a fiduciary capacity, and therefore the court must carefully scrutinize a fee application.[36]

VIII. Derivative Actions in the Court of Chancery

Court of Chancery Rules 23.1 and 23.2 are similar to Federal Rules 23.1 and 23.2 regarding derivative actions.[37] The Superior Court Rules do not contain an analogous provision because Delaware views derivative actions as being equitable in nature, and therefore, properly brought only in the Court of Chancery.[38] Derivative actions in the Court of Chancery are not required to meet the requirements contained in Court of Chancery Rule 23(a).

---

31. *See, e.g., Dutiel v. Tween Brands, Inc.*, Nos. 4743-CC & 4845-CC, 2009 Del. Ch. LEXIS 171, at *6–7 (Oct. 2, 2009).

32. *See Goodrich v. E.F. Hutton Group, Inc.*, 681 A.2d 1039, 1050 (Del. 1996).

33. *See id.* at 1049.

34. *See In re AXA Fin., Inc. S'holders Litig.*, No. 18268, 2002 Del. Ch. LEXIS 57, at *26 (May 16, 2002).

35. *See Crowhorn v. Nationwide Mut. Ins. Co.*, 836 A.2d 558, 566 (Del. Super. Ct. 2003).

36. *See Goodrich*, 681 A.2d at 1045.

37. *Compare* DEL. CH. CT. R. 23.1 and 23.2 *with* FED. R. CIV. P. 23.1 and 23.2.

38. *See generally Harf v. Kekorian*, 324 A.2d 215, 218 (Del. Ch. 1974), *modified*, 347 A.2d 133 (Del. 1975).

FLORIDA

G. CALVIN HAYES

I. Introduction

In Florida, class actions are governed by Florida Rule of Civil Procedure 1.220.[1] In 1980, the Florida Supreme Court completely revised the Rule to bring it into line with modern practice.[2] The current Rule 1.220 is based on Federal Rule of Civil Procedure 23,[3] and Florida courts may consider federal cases as persuasive authority when interpreting the Florida Rule.[4]

II. Pleading

In contrast to the Federal Rule 23, Florida's Rule 1.220 has specific pleading requirements.[5] As a general matter, next to the case caption, class-related pleadings must contain the designation "Class Representation."[6] Additionally, "[a]ny pleading, counterclaim, or cross-claim" including class allegations must contain a separate heading designated "Class Representation Allegations."[7]

Under the "Class Representation Allegations" heading, there must be a specific recitation of the "particular provision of subdivision (b)" of 1.220 under which the class is sought to be maintained.[8] In this section, the pleading must also specifically recite the "questions of law or fact that are common to the claim or defense"

---

1. Florida Rule of Civil Procedure 1.220 will also be referred to as the "Rule" and the "Florida Rule."
2. FLA. R. CIV. P. 1.220 committee notes (1980 Amend.).
3. *Id.* Federal Rule of Civil Procedure 23 will also be referred to as the "Federal Rule."
4. *Concerned Class Members v. Sailfish Point, Inc.,* 704 So. 2d 200, 201 (Fla. 4th DCA 1998).
5. FLA. R. CIV. P. 1.220(c).
6. *Id.*
7. FLA. R. CIV. P. 1.220(c)(1).
8. FLA. R. CIV. P. 1.220(c)(2)(A).

of the class representative and each member of the class.[9] Additionally, this section must contain the "particular facts and circumstances" that show the existence of the typicality prerequisite, the representative party's ability to adequately protect the interests of the class, and support for the conclusions required for the court to maintain the action as a class action.[10] Finally, the pleading must contain a specific recitation of the approximate number of class members and the class definition.[11]

III. Prerequisites to Class Certification

Like its federal counterpart, the Florida Rule allows courts to maintain class actions as either plaintiff or defendant classes.[12] The Rule also allows courts to maintain a class action by utilizing one or more representative parties.[13] As with the Federal Rule, Florida's Rule requires that before a class can be certified, the court must first conclude (1) the class is so numerous that separate joinder of the class members is impracticable; (2) the class representative's claims or defenses raise questions of law or fact common to the members of the class; (3) the class representative's claim or defense is typical of each of the class members; and (4) the class representative can fairly and adequately protect the interests of the class members.[14] Accordingly, cases interpreting the four 1.220(a) prerequisite requirements often look for guidance in the federal cases that interpret Rule 23. For example, Florida's Fourth District Court of Appeal has ruled that the actual number of putative class members is not the only determining factor when deciding whether the numerosity requirement is met.[15] In so ruling, the court reasoned, "'Whether a given number is sufficient is not susceptible to hard and fast standards since numerosity is tied to impracticability of joinder under specific circumstances.'"[16]

As with the Federal Rule, if the prerequisites of subdivision (a) are met the court must then determine whether the proposed class action fits one or more of the categories identified in subdivision (b). The Rule 1.220(b) requirements are patterned after Federal Rule 23(b) and in some instances are virtually identical to the federal rule's requirements.[17] Florida's First District Court of Appeal has held

---

9. FLA. R. CIV. P. 1.220(c)(2)(B).

10. FLA. R. CIV. P. 1.220(c)(2)(C)–(E).

11. FLA. R. CIV. P. 1.220(c)(2)(D)(i)–(ii).

12. FLA. R. CIV. P. 1.220(a) ("[b]efore any claim or defense may be maintained by one party or more suing or being sued as the representative of all the members of a class . . . .").

13. Id.

14. FLA. R. CIV. P. 1.220(a)(1)–(4).

15. Smith v. Glen Cove Apartments Condos. Master Ass'n, Inc., 847 So. 2d 1107, 1110 (Fla. 4th DCA 2002).

16. Id. (quoting Fifth Moorings Condo., Inc. v. Shere, 81 F.R.D. 712, 715–16 (S.D. Fla. 1979) (internal quotations omitted)).

17. Compare FED. R. CIV. P. 23(b) with FLA. R. CIV. P. 1.220(b).

that, like Federal Rule 23(b)(1)(A), Florida Rule 1.220(b)(1)(A) "is satisfied only if inconsistent judgments in separate suits would place the party opposing the class in the position of being unable to comply with one judgment without violating the terms of another judgment."[18] Florida courts have also followed the lead of the federal courts in holding that classes seeking compensatory damages cannot be certified under 1.220(b)(1)(A).[19] Further, Florida courts have followed federal precedent and recognized that 1.220(b)(1)(B) certifications include, for example, "limited funds cases," which involve numerous persons making claims against a fund insufficient to satisfy all of the claims.[20]

As with the federal counterpart, in order for a Florida court to certify a class under subsection (b)(2), the grounds for relief must be generally applicable to all class members.[21] Such general applicability requires a determination that the opposing party "'acted in a consistent manner towards members of the class so that his actions may be viewed as part of a pattern of activity.'"[22] Additionally, a class cannot be certified under (b)(2) when "'the appropriate final relief relates exclusively or predominantly to money damages.'"[23] For certification under subsection (b)(2), declaratory or injunctive relief must be the exclusive or predominant remedy requested for the putative class.[24]

In order for a Florida court to approve the certification of a (b)(3) class, the claim or defense should not be maintainable under either (b)(1) or (b)(2), the questions of law or fact common to the claim or defense of the representative party and the class members must "predominate" over any question of law or fact affecting only individual members of the class, and the class action device must be "superior" to other available methods for adjudicating the controversy.[25] Similarly to Rule 23, Florida Rule 1.220(b)(3) elaborates the considerations of superiority, stating that the court should derive these conclusions from all the relevant facts and circumstances, including (1) the interests of each member of the class in individually controlling the prosecution of separate claims or defenses; (2) the nature and extent of any pending litigation involving a member of the class concerning questions of law or fact to be adjudicated in the class action; (3) the desirability of

---

18. *Seven Hills, Inc. v. Bentley*, 848 So. 2d 345, 354 (Fla. 1st DCA 2003) (quoting 5 JAMES WM. MOORE ET AL., MOORE'S FEDERAL PRACTICE § 23.4l(2)(a) (3d ed. 1997)).

19. *Cheatwood v. Barry Univ., Inc.*, No. 01-0003986, 2001 WL 1769914, at *12 (Fla. Cir. Ct. Dec. 26, 2001).

20. *Id.* at *13.

21. FLA. R. CIV. P. 1.220(b)(2).

22. *Freedom Life Ins. Co. v. Wallant*, 891 So. 2d 1109, 1117 (Fla. 4th DCA 2004) (quoting *In re Managed Care Litig.*, 209 F.R.D. 678, 685–86 (S.D. Fla. 2002)).

23. *Id.* (quoting *Allison v. Citgo Petroleum Corp.*, 151 F.3d 402, 411 (5th Cir. 1998)).

24. *Id.* at 1117–18.

25. FLA. R. CIV. P. 1.220(b)(3).

concentrating the litigation in the forum where the class action is pending; and (4) the difficulties in the management of the class action.[26]

IV. Determination of Class Representation

Florida's Rule requires an earlier determination of whether the case will proceed as a class action than does Rule 23. Rule 1.220 requires that "[a]s soon as practicable after service of any pleading alleging the existence of a class," the court shall, after a hearing, determine whether the claim or defense is maintainable as a class action.[27] Florida's Rule specifically allows the court to make such a determination on its own initiative or on application of any party.[28] The Florida Rule also specifically requires the court to enter an order determining whether the action will proceed as a class action, with the order "separately stat[ing] the findings of fact and conclusions of law upon which the determination is based."[29] However, the court can defer this determination pending the completion of discovery as to the maintainability of the class.[30] As with Rule 23, Florida's Rule 1.220 makes special provisions for the court to alter or amend, at any time prior to final judgment, an order granting or denying class certification.[31] Only the Florida Rule specifically provides for conditional certifications.[32] Federal Rule 23's provisions allowing conditional certifications were deleted with the 2003 amendments.[33]

V. Notice Requirements and Judgment

Once certification of a class has occurred, and notice to class members becomes an issue, Rule 1.220 and Rule 23 diverge.[34] If a Florida court determines to maintain the class under subsection (b)(3), the court must provide the notice set out in subsection (d)(2).[35] If the court decides to maintain the class pursuant to subsections (b)(1) or (b)(2), it must instead provide the notice set out in subsection (d)(2),

---

26. *Id.*

27. *Compare* FLA. R. CIV. P. 1.220(d)(1) *with* FED. R. CIV. P. 23(c)(1)(A) (requiring court to make determination "[a]t an early practicable time").

28. FLA. R. CIV. P. 1.220(d)(1).

29. *Id.*

30. *Id.*

31. *Compare* FLA. R. CIV. P. 1.220(d)(1) *with* FED. R. CIV. P. 23(c)(1)(C).

32. FLA. R. CIV. P. 1.220(d).

33. FED. R. CIV. P. 23 advisory committee note (2003).

34. *Compare* FLA. R. CIV. P. 1.220(d)(1) *with* FED. R. CIV. P. 23(c)(2).

35. FLA. R. CIV. P. 1.220(d)(1).

"except when a showing is made that the notice is not required."[36] In this instance, "the court may provide for another kind of notice to the class as is appropriate."[37]

Subsection 1.220(d)(2) requires that notice be provided to all members of the class "[a]s soon as is practicable" after the court determines a class is maintainable.[38] The party asserting the existence of the class must give (d)(2) notice to "each member of the class who can be identified and located through reasonable effort[,]" and to other class members in a manner most practicable under the circumstances.[39] This notice must inform class members that they may be excluded from the class if they file a request to opt out, the judgment will include all members who do not opt out, and any member who does not opt out may make a separate appearance.[40] Unlike the silence of the federal rule, 1.220(d) specifically states the party asserting the existence of the class will initially pay for the cost of the notice.[41]

The contents of a judgment determining a claim or defense maintained on behalf of a class are determined by Florida Rule 1.220(d)(3) and Federal Rule 23(c)(3). Rule 1.220's requirements for the contents of this judgment closely approximate the requirements of Federal Rule 23, and like the federal rule, address those requirements depending on which (b) subdivision of the Rule the judgment encompasses.[42]

VI. Particular Issues and Subclasses

As with the Federal Rule, Rule 1.220 allows a claim or defense to be brought or maintained as a class regarding particular issues.[43] Similarly, both the Florida Rule and Federal Rule 23 allow the court to divide class representation into subclasses that may be each treated as a separate class.[44]

---

36. *Id.*

37. *Id.*

38. FLA. R. CIV. P. 1.220(d)(2).

39. *Id.*

40. FLA. R. CIV. P. 1.220(d)(2)(A)–(C).

41. FLA. R. CIV. P. 1.220(d)(2). *Accord Eisen v. Carlisle & Jacqueline*, 417 U.S. 156 (1974) (stating class representative petitioner in federal court must bear the cost of notice to all class members). *But cf. Oppenheimer Fund, Inc. v. Sanders*, 437 U.S. 340, 350, 355–56 (1978) (granting trial court discretion to allocate costs to the defendant for tasks that the court has appropriately ordered the defendant to perform).

42. *Compare* FLA. R. CIV. P. 1.220(d)(3) *with* FED. R. CIV. P. 23(c)(3).

43. FLA. R. CIV. P. 1.220(d)(4).

44. *Id.*

VII. Dismissal or Compromise

Once a court has certified a claim or defense for class treatment, both Rule 1.220 and the Federal Rule 23 require court approval before the claim or defense is voluntarily withdrawn, dismissed, or compromised.[45] While Rule 23 has additional limitations not found in the Florida Rule, both rules require notice to the class in certain circumstances.[46]

Unlike Rule 23(e)(5), the Florida Rule does not specifically provide class members the ability to object to the proposal of dismissal or compromise.[47]

VIII. Miscellaneous

Unlike its federal counterpart, Rule 1.220 does not expressly provide guidelines for the appointment of class counsel or awarding attorney fees and nontaxable costs.[48]

---

45. FLA. R. CIV. P. 1.220(e).
46. *Compare* FLA. R. CIV. P. 1.220(e) *with* FED. R. CIV. P. 23(e)(1).
47. *Compare* FLA. R. CIV. P. 1.220(e) *with* FED. R. CIV. P. 23(e)(5).
48. *Compare* FLA. R. CIV. P. 1.220 *with* FED. R. CIV. P. 23(g)–(h).

GEORGIA

LAURIE WEBB DANIEL
KIMBERLY R. WARD

I. Introduction

Georgia's class action statute, codified at O.C.G.A. section 9-11-23, generally mirrors federal practice. Indeed, the Georgia Court of Appeals has noted that "Georgia courts may rely on federal class action cases as persuasive authority."[1] The discussion below summarizes the routine issues encountered in class action litigation in Georgia and highlights the occasional peculiarities of Georgia class action law.

II. Precertification Considerations

A. MANAGEMENT ORDERS

O.C.G.A. section 9-11-23(d) grants the trial court authority to make appropriate orders determining the course of class action proceedings or prescribing measures to prevent undue repetition or complication in the presentation of evidence or argument.[2] For example, the court may impose conditions on the representative parties or on intervenors.[3] Additionally, the court may require that pleadings be amended to eliminate allegations as to representation of absent persons, and that the action proceed accordingly.[4] Orders issued pursuant to O.C.G.A. section 9-11-23(d) may be altered or amended by the court as may be desirable from time to time.[5]

---

1. *Liberty Lending Servs. v. Canada*, 293 Ga. App. 731, 738 n.9, 668 S.E.2d 3, 10 n.9 (2008).
2. O.C.G.A. § 9-11-23(d)(1).
3. O.C.G.A. § 9-11-23(d)(3).
4. O.C.G.A. § 9-11-23(d)(4).
5. O.C.G.A. § 9-11-23(d).

B. DISCOVERY

Georgia law requires bifurcated discovery in all class actions absent a court order to the contrary based on good cause.[6] Under O.C.G.A. section 23(f)(2), "[e]xcept for good cause shown, the court shall stay all discovery directed solely to the merits of the claims or defenses in the action until the court has issued its written decision regarding certification of the class."[7] Thus, class-related discovery is permissible prior to certification but merits-based discovered is precluded.[8]

III. Certification Requirements and Issues

As under federal law, the party seeking class certification in Georgia bears the burden of establishing the right to it.[9] A class action may be certified if all prerequisites of O.C.G.A. section 9-11-23(a) are satisfied, including numerosity, commonality, typicality, and adequacy, and at least one of the factors listed in O.C.G.A. section 9-11-23(b) is also satisfied.[10] A trial court may deny class certification where a plaintiff fails to establish any one of the required Rule 23 factors.[11]

A. THE O.C.G.A. SECTION 9-11-23(A) FACTORS

1. Numerosity

In Georgia, the class action device stems from the equitable doctrine that members of a numerous class may be represented by a few of the class.[12] Numerosity is the threshold factor in class action certification.[13] The numerosity requirement is met when the persons constituting the class are so numerous as to make it impracticable to bring them all before the court.[14] If the number of plaintiffs is so large that each cannot practically represent himself, either in the same or a separate lawsuit, then the court may allow a representative suit to bind each of them, if the other factors to be considered favor it.[15] As long as the plaintiff proves that the class is sufficiently numerous, the plaintiff need not specify the exact number of putative class members, and the trial court will not compel the defendant to go

---

6. O.C.G.A. § 9-11-23(f)(2).

7. O.C.G.A. § 9-11-23(f)(2).

8. *See McGarry v. Cingular Wireless, LLC*, 267 Ga. App. 23, 599 S.E.2d 34 (2004); *Ford Motor Credit Co. v. London*, 175 Ga. App. 33, 332 S.E.2d 345 (1985).

9. *UNUM Life Ins. Co. v. Crutchfield*, 256 Ga. App. 582, 568 S.E.2d 767 (2002).

10. *Earthlink v. Eaves*, 293 Ga. App. 75, 76, 666 S.E.2d 420, 423 (2008); O.C.G.A. § 9-11-23.

11. *Roland v. Ford Motor Co., Inc.*, 288 Ga. App. 625, 628, 655 S.E.2d 259, 263 (2007); *Hooters of Augusta, Inc. v. Nicholson*, 245 Ga. App. 363, 368, 537 S.E.2d 468, 472 (2000).

12. *Ford Motor Credit Co.*, 175 Ga. App. at 35–36, 332 S.E.2d at 347.

13. *Id.*

14. *Hammond v. Carnett's, Inc.*, 266 Ga. App. 242, 244, 596 S.E.2d 729, 732 (2004), *overruled on other grounds by Carnett's, Inc. v. Hammond*, 279 Ga. 125, 610 S.E.2d 529 (2005).

15. *Id.*

to great expense to assist the plaintiff in determining the exact number of class members.[16] There is no threshold number required to satisfy the numerosity prerequisite. Georgia courts have found a class consisting of as few as 25 persons sufficiently numerous,[17] a potential class numbering over 100 members sufficiently numerous,[18] and a class, which the parties agreed was "large," sufficiently numerous to satisfy numerosity.[19]

2. Commonality

While the class certification movant must meet each of the Rule 23 prerequisites, the primary contention in many cases is the issue of commonality. The commonality question is often discussed as incorporating the element of predominance. To properly certify a class, the movant must show that common questions of law and fact predominate.[20] And resolution of those common questions must also resolve the ultimate issues of the case.[21] Common issues of fact and law predominate if they have a direct impact on every class member's effort to establish liability and on every class member's entitlement to injunctive and monetary relief.[22] It is not sufficient that there exist *some* common questions of law and fact.[23] For instance, commonality does not exist when a common question is presented by the defendant's conduct and the answer, which is determinative of whether the member is properly part of the class, varies among class members.[24] Hence, when the plaintiffs must still introduce a great deal of individualized proof or argue a number of individualized legal points to establish most or all of the elements of their individual claims, the claims are not suitable for class certification.[25] Stated differently, class certification is precluded when proof of the claims requires a highly individualized, case-by-case determination as to each putative class member and the individual questions play a prominent role in the determination of liability.[26] Thus, if the determination whether a particular individual is a member of the putative class would require a separate mini-trial, class certification is improper.[27]

---

16. *Ford Motor Credit Co.*, 175 Ga. App. at 36, 332 S.E.2d at 347.

17. *Sta-Power Indus., Inc. v. Avant*, 134 Ga. App. 952, 216 S.E.2d 897 (1975).

18. *Stevens v. Thomas*, 257 Ga. 645, 361 S.E.2d 800 (1987).

19. *Ford Motor Credit Co.*, 175 Ga. App. at 35–36, 332 S.E.2d at 347–48.

20. See *Life Ins. Co. of Ga. v. Meeks*, 274 Ga. App. 212, 216–17, 617 S.E.2d 179, 184 (Ga. Ct. App. 2005).

21. *Id.*, 274 Ga. App. at 217, 617 S.E.2d at 184.

22. *Rollins, Inc. v. Warren*, 288 Ga. App. 184, 187, 653 S.E.2d 794, 797 (2007).

23. See *Meeks*, 274 Ga. App. at 216–17, 617 S.E.2d at 184.

24. *Roland*, 288 Ga. App. at 631, 655 S.E.2d at 264 (class action treatment inappropriate); *Carnett's*, 279 Ga. at 129, 610 S.E.2d at 532.

25. *Rollins*, 288 Ga. App. at 187, 653 S.E.2d at 797.

26. *Id.*, 288 Ga. App. at 188, 653 S.E.2d at 798; *Meeks*, 274 Ga. App. at 218, 617 S.E.2d at 185; *Duffy v. Landings Ass'n, Inc.*, 254 Ga. App. 506, 508, 563 S.E.2d 174, 176 (2002); *Winfrey v. Sw. Cmty. Hosp.*, 184 Ga. App. 383, 384, 361 S.E.2d 522, 523 (1987).

27. *Rollins*, 288 Ga. App at 188, 653 S.E.2d at 798.

"There need not be a total absence of individual questions of law or fact as long as the common questions predominate."[28] For instance, variation in the application of a defense against the class members' claims does not foreclose class certification as long as a "sufficient constellation of common issues binds the class members together."[29] Moreover, conflict of law issues requiring inquiries into each state's law do not preclude certification where common issues otherwise predominate over these individual issues.[30] And minor variations in the amount of damages do not destroy the class when the legal issues are common.[31]

3. Typicality

The typicality requirement under O.C.G.A. section 9-11-23(a) is satisfied upon a showing that the defendant committed the same unlawful acts in the same method against an entire class.[32] Hence, the named plaintiff must allege that he was the victim of the same conduct for which putative class members seek relief. A plaintiff cannot represent class members who have causes of action against other defendants against whom the plaintiff has no cause of action and from whose hands he suffered no injury.[33]

4. Adequacy of Representation

The privilege of representing absentee class members by the formation and certification of a class also carries with it the responsibility of providing adequate representation to all the members of the class.[34] To satisfy this obligation, the class representative must vigorously prosecute the interests of the class through quali-

---

28. *Trend Star Cont'l v. Branham*, 220 Ga. App. 781, 782, 469 S.E.2d 750, 752 (1996); *see also Fortis Ins. Co. v. Kahn*, 299 Ga. App. 319, 324, 683 S.E.2d 4, 9 (Ga. Ct. App. 2009) (commonality requirement met where class members received same standard, uniform written documents and same kind of policy); *Liberty Lending Servs.*, 293 Ga. App. 731, 668 S.E.2d 3 (commonality requirement met where class members received security deeds containing materially similar language); *JMIC Life Ins. Co. v. Toole*, 280 Ga. App. 372, 377, 634 S.E.2d 123, 128 (2006) (commonality requirement met where it was undisputed that class members executed materially similar form contracts).

29. *Fortis*, 299 Ga. App. at 324; 683 S.E.2d at 9 (concluding that differing defenses, including the statute of limitations, does not preclude class certification) (quoting *Augustin v. Jablonsky*, 461 F.3d 219, 225 (2d Cir. 2006)).

30. *Liberty Lending Servs.*, 293 Ga. App. at 740, 668 S.E.2d at 11.

31. *Fortis*, 299 Ga. App. at 325, 683 S.E.2d at 9–10; *Bd. of Regents of the Univ. Sys. of Ga. v. Rux*, 260 Ga. App. 760, 764, 580 S.E.2d 559, 563 (2003).

32. *Liberty Lending Servs.*, 293 Ga. App. at 738, 668 S.E.2d at 10 (typicality requirement satisfied where named plaintiffs alleged defendant committed same conduct with respect to the named plaintiff and proposed class members); *JMIC Life Ins.*, 280 Ga. App. 372, 634 S.E.2d 123 (proof that named plaintiff is entitled to the return of portion of his premium establishes a similar entitlement for all members of the class); *Duffy*, 254 Ga. App. 506, 563 S.E.2d 174 (concluding named plaintiffs would not share common issues with other putative class members).

33. *Hill v. Gen. Fin. Corp. of Ga.*, 144 Ga. App. 434, 437, 241 S.E.2d 282, 286 (1977).

34. *Graham v. Dev. Specialists, Inc.*, 180 Ga. App. 758, 762, 350 S.E.2d 294, 298 (1986).

fied counsel.[35] Indeed, one of the most significant aspects of adequacy of representation is whether the plaintiff's counsel is experienced and competent.[36] Counsel's failure to follow local rules or obey court orders indicates that counsel would not fairly and adequately protect the interests of absentee members of the class.[37] Moreover, the withdrawal of counts pleaded in a class action complaint without a showing of absence of harm raises doubt that the rights of some or all of the absentees would be protected adequately in a class action.[38] And a pro se plaintiff who lacks the requisite skill and financial means cannot adequately represent putative class members.[39]

The plaintiff must also show that his interests are not antagonistic to those of the class.[40] In essence, the named plaintiff must show that he is a member of the class he seeks to represent.[41] When the named plaintiff has no valid claim against the defendant, he is not eligible to represent the purported class. Accordingly, the named plaintiff cannot provide adequate representation when summary judgment has been entered against him.[42] However, an argument that the plaintiff is not an adequate representative because he or she will not ultimately prevail on the claim is not an appropriate basis for denying class certification.[43]

B. THE O.C.G.A. SECTION 9-11-23(B) FACTORS

O.C.G.A. section 9-11-23(b) allows for class certification if the four requirements of numerosity, commonality, typicality, and adequacy of representation set forth in O.C.G.A. section 9-11-23(a) are satisfied and (1) the prosecution of separate actions would create a risk of inconsistent adjudications or would impair other parties' ability to protect their interests; (2) the defendant has acted or refused to act on grounds generally applicable to the class, thereby making appropriate final injunctive relief or declaratory relief with respect to the whole class; or (3) questions of law or fact common to members of the class predominate over any questions affecting only individual members, and a class action is superior to other available methods for the fair and efficient adjudication of the controversy.[44]

---

35. Id.

36. *Taylor Auto Group v. Jessie*, 241 Ga. App. 602, 603–04, 527 S.E.2d 256 (1999).

37. Id.

38. Id.

39. *Otwell v. Floyd County Bd. of Comm'rs*, 200 Ga. App. 596, 408 S.E.2d 799 (1991) (denying class certification where named plaintiff was without counsel and neither trained in the law nor licensed to practice law and financially unable to represent class).

40. *Taylor Auto Group*, 241 Ga. App. at 603–04, 527 S.E.2d at 258.

41. *McGarry*, 267 Ga. App. at 25, 599 S.E.2d at 36.

42. *Meeks*, 274 Ga. App. at 218, 617 S.E.2d at 185.

43. *Taylor Auto Group*, 241 Ga. App. at 603, 527 S.E.2d at 258.

44. O.C.G.A. § 9-11-23(b).

It should be noted that certification under O.C.G.A. section 9-11-23(b)(2) is inappropriate if the predominant relief sought in the action is monetary damages.[45] "[M]onetary damages claims are not merely incidental" to injunctive or declaratory relief "when the damages claims of each individual class member 'would require detailed, case-by-case fact-finding' at mini-trials."[46] With respect to the superiority requirement of section 9-11-23(b)(3), the issue is not whether a class action will be difficult to manage.[47] Instead, the trial court is to consider the relative advantages of a class action suit over other forms of litigation that might be available.[48] There is no need to burden either the court system or the individual class members by requiring each member of the class to pursue his or her own action to recover a relatively small amount of damages.[49]

C. SUBCLASSES

Not all questions of fact and law must be common to all class members for a class to be certified. When appropriate, an action may be brought or maintained as a class action with respect to particular issues; or a class may be divided into subclasses and each subclass treated as a class.[50] A trial court may also certify an action as to common questions of law or fact and then order individual trials as to the remaining questions.[51] And, a trial court may bifurcate a class into a declaratory and injunctive relief class and a damages class where there are issues for trial common to the members of the class.[52] However, courts will not certify an action as to common questions and order individual trials as to the remaining questions where individual questions predominate over questions of law and fact common to the class members.[53]

---

45. *Rollins*, 288 Ga. App. at 192, 653 S.E.2d at 800.

46. *Id.*, 288 Ga. App. at 194, 653 S.E.2d at 802 (quoting *Cooper v. S. Co.*, 390 F.3d 695, 721(II)(C) (11th Cir. 2004)).

47. *Earthlink*, 293 Ga. App. at 77, 666 S.E.2d at 424.

48. *Id.*

49. *Id.*

50. O.C.G.A. § 9-11-23(c)(4).

51. *Trend Star*, 220 Ga. App. at 783, 469 S.E.2d at 752.

52. *Griffin Indus., Inc. v. Green*, 297 Ga. App. 354, 355, 677 S.E.2d 310, 311 (Ga. Ct. App. 2009) (bifurcation of damages issue does not mean that class certification is inappropriate); *Barnes v. City of Atlanta*, 275 Ga. App. 385, 389, 620 S.E.2d 846, 850 (2006) (trial court was authorized to bifurcate classes based on commonality or rights), *overruled on other grounds by Barnes v. City of Atlanta*, 281 Ga. 256, 637 S.E.2d 4 (2006); *State Farm Mut. Auto. Ins. Co. v. Mabry*, 274 Ga. 498, 499, 556 S.E.2d 114, 116–17 (2001) (trial court may bifurcate classes into declaratory and injunctive relief class and damages class based on commonality of rights and issues).

53. *Duffy*, 254 Ga. App. at 509, 563 S.E.2d at 176.

D. SPECIAL CONSIDERATIONS FOR FRAUD CASES

In Georgia—although claims based upon oral misrepresentations generally are not appropriate for class treatment "because the reliance element must be proved factually for each individual class-member"—the courts sometimes will certify a class action based on written representations.[54] For example, in *Fortis Insurance Co. v. Kahn*,[55] the court affirmed class certification of a fraud action based on representations in insurance policies. The court noted that the fact that reliance is an element of the cause of action is not a complete bar to class certification because "[i]n claims of fraud based upon written representations, the reliance element may sometimes be presumed."[56] It then reasoned that a jury could "infer that the class members' continued *renewal* of their policies after receiving the uniform, standard documents from appellants constitutes proof of reliance that is common to all class members."[57] In *Liberty Lending Services v. Canada*, the Georgia Court of Appeals also affirmed class certification of RICO claims against a lender based on similar reasoning: "'[T]he simple fact that reliance is an element in a cause of action is not an absolute bar to class certification.' . . . Given the fact that similar written representations were common to all the security agreements at issue, the circumstantial evidence that can be used to show reliance is also common to the whole class."[58]

IV. Certification Procedure

Rule 23(c)(1) directs that the trial court shall determine by order whether an action is to be maintained as a class action as soon as practicable after the commencement of the action.[59] The party seeking class action status must first file a motion to have the action certified as a class action.[60] The trial court must hold a hearing on the issue of class certification and enter a written order addressing whether the Rule 23 factors for class certification have been met and specifying the findings of fact and conclusions of law on which the court has based its decision with regard to whether each factor has been established.[61] The trial court must specifically address the issues of numerosity, commonality, typicality, adequacy of representation, and

---

54. *Fortis*, 299 Ga. App. at 322–23, 683 S.E.2d at 8.

55. *Id.*

56. *Id.*

57. *Id.* (emphasis in original).

58. 293 Ga. App. at 741, 668 S.E.2d at 12 (quoting *Klay v. Humana, Inc.*, 382 F.3d 1241, 1258(II)(C)(2) (11th Cir. 2004)).

59. O.C.G.A. § 9-11-23(c)(1).

60. *Seamans Estate v. True*, 247 Ga. 721, 279 S.E.2d 447 (1981).

61. O.C.G.A. §§ 9-11-23(f)(1), (f)(3); *McDonald Oil Co. v. Cianocchi*, 285 Ga. App. 829, 830, 648 S.E.2d 154, 155 (2007).

superiority in its order.[62] The court may treat a factor as having been established if all parties to the action have so stipulated on the record.[63] The order must be sufficiently detailed to provide a basis upon which appellate courts may evaluate whether the trial court properly exercised its discretion.[64] Appellate courts may vacate an order of certification when the trial court fails to enter a detailed order with findings of fact and conclusions of law.[65] However, an order that does not address each of the Rule 23 factors is not automatically vacated if the trial court's order references the factors it relied upon in denying class certification, giving a brief description of the facts and law it relied upon in arriving at its conclusions.[66] This is because a trial court may deny class certification where a plaintiff fails to establish even one of the required Rule 23 factors.[67]

Merits-based disputes are not ripe for adjudication at the class certification stage.[68] Therefore, the trial court must steer clear of questions regarding whether the plaintiffs have stated a cause of action or may ultimately prevail on the merits and limit its consideration to whether the requirements of O.C.G.A. section 9-11-23 have been met.[69] "Any assertion that the named plaintiff cannot prevail on her claims does not comprise an appropriate basis for denying class certification."[70]

A trial court may certify a class though the definition of the proposed class differs from the definition originally proposed in the motion for class certification, even when the proponent fails to amend the motion for class certification.[71] The class definition included in the consolidated pretrial order supersedes the pleadings and controls the subsequent scope and course of the action.[72] Even so, certification orders are inherently tentative and the trial court retains jurisdiction to modify or even vacate them, as may be warranted by subsequent events in the litigation.[73] Thus, despite the trial court's findings of fact when ruling on a motion to certify a class, the issue of whether or not a class exists, or whether any particular plaintiff

---

62. *McDonald Oil Co.*, 285 Ga. App. at 830, 648 S.E.2d at 155.

63. O.C.G.A. § 9-11-23(f)(3).

64. *Griffin Indus. v. Green*, 280 Ga. App. 858, 860, 635 S.E.2d 231 (2006).

65. *See, e.g., Gay v. B.H. Transfer Co.*, 287 Ga. App. 610, 652 S.E.2d 200 (2007) (vacating portion of class certification order for more detailed findings of fact and conclusions of law on superiority and adequacy of representation); *McDonald Oil Co.*, 285 Ga. App. 829, 648 S.E.2d 154 (vacating order certifying class where trial court did not hold hearing and certification order did not address any of the factors); *Griffin Indus.*, 280 Ga. App. 858, 635 S.E.2d 231 (vacating order certifying class and remanding case to trial court for a more detailed order with findings of fact and conclusions of law).

66. *Roland*, 288 Ga. App. at 628, 655 S.E.2d at 263.

67. *Id.*; *Hooters*, 245 Ga. App. at 368, 537 S.E.2d at 472.

68. *Village Auto Ins. Co., Inc. v. Rush*, 286 Ga. App. 688, 691–92, 649 S.E.2d 862, 866 (2007).

69. *Id.*

70. *Id.* (internal quotations and citation omitted).

71. *Meeks*, 274 Ga. App. at 216, 617 S.E.2d at 183–84.

72. *Id.*

73. *Fortis*, 299 Ga. App. at 326, 683 S.E.2d at 10; O.C.G.A. § 9-11-23(c)(1).

or subclass of plaintiffs is in fact damaged, are matters that may be raised at trial.[74] To proceed as a class action, however, the court must enter an order certifying the class.[75] If the trial court denies class action status, the suit proceeds upon the underlying action of the representative plaintiffs in the form of their individual actions.[76]

V. Notice to Class Members

The party seeking to represent the class must, at the direction of the court, mail an initial notice of the class action to each class member.[77] Such notice must be the best notice practicable under the circumstances and includes individual notice to all members who can be identified through reasonable effort.[78] The notice must advise each class member that (1) the court will exclude the member from the class if the member so requests by a specified date;[79] (2) the judgment, whether favorable or not, will include all members who do not request exclusion;[80] and (3) any member who does not request exclusion may, if the member desires, enter an appearance through counsel.[81] Rule 23(d)(2) also permits the court to make appropriate orders requiring that notice be given in such manner as the court may direct to some or all of the class members of (1) any step in the action, (2) of the proposed extent of the judgment, or (3) of the opportunity of members to signify whether they consider the representation fair and adequate, to intervene and present claims or defenses, or otherwise to come into the action.[82] Additionally, notice of a proposed dismissal or compromise must be provided to all class members in such manner as the court directs.[83] To satisfy procedural due process for absent class members and to bind them by judgment, there must be (1) notice and reasonable opportunity to be heard; (2) an opportunity to opt out of the proceeding; and (3) adequate class representation.[84] These conditions will likely be satisfied where the class member received actual notice of the class action by mail and is represented by a knowledgeable and competent lawyer.[85]

---

74. *Griffin Indus.*, 297 Ga. App. at 355, 677 S.E.2d at 311.

75. *Ford Motor Credit Co.*, 175 Ga. App. 33, 332 S.E. 2d 345.

76. *Perkins v. Dept. of Med. Assistance*, 252 Ga. App. 35, 37, 555 S.E.2d 500, 503 (2001).

77. *Hill*, 144 Ga. App. at 436, 241 S.E.2d at 285; O.C.G.A. § 9-11-23(c)(2).

78. O.C.G.A. § 9-11-23(c)(2).

79. O.C.G.A. § 9-11-23(c)(2)(A).

80. O.C.G.A. § 9-11-23(c)(2)(B).

81. O.C.G.A. § 9-11-23(c)(2)(C).

82. O.C.G.A. § 9-11-23(d)(2).

83. O.C.G.A. § 9-11-23(e).

84. *Smith v. AirTouch Cellular of Ga., Inc.*, 244 Ga. App. 71, 72–73, 534 S.E.2d 832, 835 (2000).

85. *Id.*

VI. *Evidentiary Issues: Statistical and Economic Evidence*

Where minor variations in damages exist among class members, statistical or economic evidence may be used to prove classwide damages.[86] In the class action setting, however, statistical and economic evidence may not always prove liability. If the issue of liability turns upon highly individualized facts, a plaintiff's generalized pattern and practice evidence cannot establish the defendant's liability as to any one particular class member.[87] For example, in *Rollins, Inc. v. Warren*, even though statistical evidence demonstrated that a pest control company engaged in a widespread practice of failing to perform reinspections, the court found that this evidence could not establish that the pest control company breached its duty to any given class member.[88]

VII. *Appeals*

Georgia law allows as a matter of right an expedited appeal of an order granting or denying class certification as long as the appeal is filed within 30 days of the order—and stays all proceedings in the trial court while the appeal is pending:

> A court's order certifying a class or refusing to certify a class shall be appealable in the same manner as a final order to the appellate court which would otherwise have jurisdiction over the appeal from a final order in the action. The appellate courts shall expedite resolution of any appeals taken under this Code section. Such appeal may only be filed within 30 days of the order certifying or refusing to certify the class. During the pendency of any such appeal, the action in the trial court shall be stayed in all respects.[89]

Further, Georgia allows cross-appeals in class actions where the parties comply with the procedures for obtaining interlocutory review under O.C.G.A. section 5-6-34(b).[90]

Most class certification rulings should be appealed to the Georgia Court of Appeals because that court has general appellate jurisdiction under the Georgia constitution.[91] The notice of appeal should specify that the appeal is to the Georgia Supreme Court, however, if the case involves an issue subject to that court's juris-

---

86. *Fortis*, 299 Ga. App. at 325, 683 S.E.2d at 9–10; *see also* Chapter 18, "Statistical Sampling as a Basis for Extrapolating Liability and/or Damages."

87. *Rollins*, 288 Ga. App. at 191–92, 653 S.E.2d at 800 (statistical evidence indicating that pest control company failed to complete between 66 and 98 percent of reinspection services in sample of 389 customers did not prove that any one particular class member failed to receive adequate reinspection services).

88. *Id.*

89. O.C.G.A. § 9-11-23(g).

90. *See Dryvit Systems, Inc. v. Stein*, 256 Ga. App. 327, 568 S.E.2d 569, 570 (Ga. Ct. App. 2002).

91. *See* GA. CONST. art. VI, § 5, ¶ III.

diction, such as a constitutional or equity question.[92] If the wrong court is designated, the clerk's office will simply transfer the appeal to the appropriate court.

Although the Georgia legislature has granted litigants an automatic right to appeal class certification rulings, review is pursuant to the abuse of discretion standard.[93] The Georgia courts apply the "clearly erroneous" standard of review to factual findings underlying class certification orders.[94] "'Under the "clearly erroneous" test, factual findings must be affirmed if supported by any evidence.'"[95]

Because trial courts have broad discretion in determining whether to certify a class action, class certification orders are rarely reversed in Georgia.[96]

In addition to granting a right of appeal for class certification orders, the Georgia Code authorizes an immediate appeal of an order granting summary judgment on any issue in a class action (as in other types of Georgia cases), even if the ruling does not dispose of the entire case.[97] Although the denial of summary judgment rulings is not appealable as a matter of right, a party can seek interlocutory review of the denial of summary judgment pursuant to O.C.G.A. section 5-6-34.[98] The Georgia courts historically have been more liberal in granting interlocutory review of the denial of summary judgment than the federal courts.

92. *See* GA. CONST. art VI, § 6, ¶ III; *State Farm*, 274 Ga. 498, 556 S.E.2d 114.

93. *See Hammond*, 266 Ga. 242, 596 S.E.2d 729; *UNUM*, 256 Ga. App. 582, 568 S.E.2d 767.

94. *Liberty Lending Servs.*, 293 Ga. App. at 735, 668 S.E.2d at 8.

95. *R.S.W. v. Emory Healthcare, Inc.*, 290 Ga. App. 284, 286, 659 S.E.2d 680, 683 (2008) (quoting *Village Auto Ins. Co.*, 286 Ga. App. 688, 649 S.E.2d 862).

96. *Roland*, 288 Ga. App. at 627, 655 S.E.2d at 262.

97. O.C.G.A. § 9-11-56(h).

98. *See also id.*

HAWAI`I

JASON H. KIM
PETER S. KNAPMAN
WITH PAUL ALSTON AND LOUISE K.Y. ING

I. Introduction

Hawai`i Rule of Civil Procedure Rule 23 (Hawai`i Rule) is largely identical to its federal counterpart circa 2000. There are a number of minor variations because the Hawai`i Rule does not reflect the most recent amendments to the corresponding Federal Rule. Hawai`i's version of Rule 23 was last amended effective January 1, 2000. Substantive differences are noted below.

II. Hawai`i Rule of Civil Procedure Rule 23

Like Federal Rules of Civil Procedure Rule 23, subpart (a) of the Hawai`i Rule requires (1) numerosity; (2) common questions of law or fact; (3) typicality; and (4) adequacy of representation. Subpart (b) of the Hawai`i Rule authorizes the same three types of class actions as are authorized by Federal Rules of Civil Procedure Rule 23(b) once the requirements of subpart (a) are satisfied. Subparts (c) and (d) of the Hawai`i Rule are also substantively identical to their federal counterparts.[1]

In a putative class action, the burden of proving entitlement to class certification falls on the party seeking to certify the class.[2] The trial court has broad discretion in

---

1. For class actions pending in the U.S. District Court for the District of Hawai`i, the district's local rules require that "[i]n any action sought to be maintained as a class action, the complaint, and any counterclaim or cross-claim, shall bear below the title of the pleading the legend 'Class Action.'" D. HAW. LOC. R. 10.2(h). There is no counterpart to that rule in Hawai`i state courts.

2. *Life of the Land v. Land Use Comm'n*, 63 Haw. 166, 180, 623 P.2d 431, 443 (1981).

deciding whether to certify a class.[3] The Hawai'i appellate courts have held that the burden of timely seeking certification falls on both parties.[4]

Subpart (e) of the Hawai'i Rule is not as detailed as its federal counterpart in that it does not specify the procedures the court is required to follow before approving the dismissal or settlement of a class action. Subpart (e) merely provides that "[a] class action shall not be dismissed or compromised without the approval of the court, and notice of the proposed dismissal or compromise shall be given to all members of the class in such manner as the court directs." Unlike the Federal Rule, subpart (e) of the Hawai'i Rule does not expressly require a fairness hearing.

The Hawai'i Rule contains no counterpart to subpart (f) of the federal rule, which allows for discretionary interlocutory appeal of an order certifying or denying class certification. An interlocutory appeal may be available, however, under section 641-1(b) of the Hawai'i Revised Statutes,[5] which provides that "an appeal in a civil matter may be allowed by a circuit court in its discretion from . . . any interlocutory judgment, order, or decree whenever the circuit court may think the same advisable for the speedy termination of litigation before it." The Hawai'i appellate courts have considered interlocutory appeals from class certification orders; however, state trial-level courts (circuit courts) tend to exercise their discretion under section 641-1(b) with restraint.[6] Federal cases that predate Federal Rule of Civil Procedure Rule 23(f) and decide whether an order granting or denying class certification qualified for discretionary appeal pursuant to 28 U.S.C. § 1292(b) may also be instructive for interpreting section 641-1(b) in this context.

The Hawai'i Rule also contains no counterpart to subparts (g) and (h) of the Federal Rule, which govern respectively (1) appointment of class counsel and (2) awards of attorney fees and costs. As explained below, however, Hawai'i courts have recognized that class counsel may be entitled to payment of their attorney fees pursuant to the common fund and common benefit doctrines.

Because the Hawai'i Rules of Civil Procedure are modeled after the Federal Rules of Civil Procedure, Hawai'i courts have repeatedly held that cases interpreting the federal rules are "highly persuasive" authority as to the interpretation of the analogous Hawai'i rules.[7]

---

3. *Garner v. State of Haw. Dep't of Educ.*, 122 Haw. 150, 164, 223 P.3d 215, 229 (2009) (citing *Life of the Land*, 623 P.2d at 443).

4. *Levi v. Univ. of Haw. Prof'l Assembly*, 67 Haw. 90, 679 P.2d 129 (1984) ("The burden of seeking certification rests on all parties to the case[.]" (citation omitted)).

5. HAW. REV. STAT. § 641-1(b).

6. *Life of the Land*, 623 P.2d at 443; *see also Levi*, 67 Haw. 90, 679 P.2d 129.

7. *See, e.g.*, *Ditto v. McCurdy*, 103 Haw. 153, 159, 80 P.3d 974, 980 (2003).

III. Application of Rule 23 by Hawai`i Courts

In researching Hawai`i authority, practitioners should note that Hawai`i Rule of Appellate Procedure Rule 35 essentially bars citation to unpublished opinions prior to July 1, 2008 in any court in Hawai`i.[8] Memorandum opinions or summary disposition orders after July 1, 2008 may be cited "for persuasive value."[9]

In considering the requirements of Rule 23(a), the few reported Hawai`i decisions focus on the (a)(3) and (a)(4) requirements of adequacy and typicality of the class representative. The Hawai`i Supreme Court held in *Life of the Land v. Land Use Commission*[10] that the numerosity requirement is satisfied when the class consists of only 150 members. The *Life of the Land* court nevertheless held that a proposed defendant class was improperly certified because the purported class representative was not demonstrably going to represent the various interests of the absent parties. The court noted that "[w]here colorable defenses may derive from particular circumstances, rather than from those common to the putative defendant class," a class certification is improper.[11]

The Hawai`i cases addressing the typicality requirement focus on an absence of conflict of interest between the class representative and other class members. More recently, in *Kemp v. State of Hawai`i Child Support Enforcement Agency*,[12] the Hawai`i Supreme Court added that the named plaintiff's claims must be "essentially similar" to the claims of the class. The *Kemp* court strictly scrutinized the claims of a purported class representative suing the State of Hawai`i Child Support Enforcement Agency on behalf of three related classes: (1) persons whose child support checks were not disbursed in a timely manner; (2) parents who received but did not cash support checks; and (3) parents whose checks were returned because of a bad address. The Hawai`i Supreme Court held that, as a parent who had received and cashed support checks, the plaintiff could not adequately represent the "uncashed check" and "bad address" parents and therefore reversed the circuit court's certification of those classes. Because she did not "possess the same interest and suffer the same injury," she was not a proper representative.[13]

In *Sheehan v. Grove Farm Co.*,[14] the court upheld the trial court's denial of class certification by a disgruntled shareholder seeking to bring an action challenging the vote to allow a merger between two corporations. Because the plaintiff

---

8. HAW. R. APP. P. 35.

9. *Id.*

10. 63 Haw. at 182, 623 P.2d at 444.

11. *Id.*, 63 Haw. at 184, 623 P.2d at 445 (citing *Kline v. Coldwell Banker & Co.*, 508 F.2d 226 (9th Cir. 1974)).

12. 111 Haw. 367, 385–86, 141 P.3d 1041, 1032–33 (2006).

13. *Id.*, 111 Haw. at 386, 141 P.3d at 1033.

14. 114 Haw. 376, 163 P.3d 179 (2005).

acknowledged that he was aware of alleged omissions in the challenged proxy statement prior to the vote, the court found that he was not an adequate representative, as he was subject to unique defenses. The court reasoned that the plaintiff's defenses would not be "coextensive" with the class and, therefore, absentees would be "unlikely to be afforded representation consistent with notions of fairness and justice."[15] Judgment against the plaintiff on his individual claim was affirmed.

In *Garner v. State of Hawai`i Department of Education*, the Hawai`i Intermediate Court of Appeals affirmed the circuit court's denial of class certification for a class of persons with separate but related claims.[16] A number of substitute teachers challenged the per diem pay paid by the State of Hawai`i Department of Education, and the circuit court certified a class. A separate proposed class of part-time employees sought to join the action as a separate subclass on the ground that there was a common issue relating to the underlying statutory pay scale since the part-time employees' hourly pay was, by rule, a fraction of the per diem rate. The circuit court rejected this attempt and the intermediate court of appeals affirmed, finding that the broad discretion afforded class certification decisions justified the ruling that the class representatives for the full-time substitute teachers would be unlikely to pursue the part-time employees' claims with the same vigor.

IV. Attorney Fees in Class Actions

Although Hawai`i Rule 23—unlike its federal counterpart—does not expressly allow for judicial supervision of attorney fee awards, the Hawai`i Supreme Court has recognized that class counsel is entitled to an award of attorney fees pursuant to the common fund/common benefit doctrine when class counsel "create, discover, increase, or preserve a fund to which others also have a claim" and that the trial court has considerable discretion as to how to calculate an appropriate fee award.[17] A true "common fund" is not necessary; an award may also be based on the value of a common benefit to the class.[18]

Under the common fund/common benefit doctrine, the attorney fees to be awarded to class counsel may be calculated in one of two ways at the discretion of the trial court. First, the trial court may calculate the attorney fees as a percentage of the fund created for the benefit of the class.[19] Alternatively, the trial court may calculate the attorney fees based on the lodestar method.[20] The trial court is

---

15. *Id.*, 114 Haw. at 388, 163 P.3d at 191 (internal quotations and citation omitted).

16. 2009 Haw. App. LEXIS 700.

17. *Chun v. Bd. of Trs. of the Employees' Retirement Sys.*, 92 Haw. 432, 439, 992 P.2d 127, 134 (2000) (quoting *Montalvo v. Chang*, 64 Haw. 345, 352, 641 P.2d 1321, 1327 (1982)).

18. *Id.* at 92 Haw. 439 n.7, 992 P.2d at 134 n.7.

19. *Id.* at 92 Haw. 444–45, 992 P.2d at 139–40.

20. *Id.*

to select the method that "most equitably compensates plaintiffs' counsel, while at the same time protecting the interests of the class members for whose benefit the common fund was created."[21]

Separate and apart from the common fund/common benefit doctrine, various Hawai`i laws create a substantive entitlement to attorney fees, regardless whether an action is brought on behalf of a class.[22] Practitioners should be aware that the Hawai`i courts have expressly ruled that recoverable costs do not include computer research, messenger fees, or any other costs broadly thought to be within a law firm's "overhead."[23]

21. *Id.* at 92 Haw. 445, 992 P.2d at 140.

22. *See, e.g.,* HAW. REV. STAT. § 617-14 (attorney fees available in actions in the nature of assumpsit); HAW. REV. STAT. § 480-13(a)(1)–(2) and (b)(1)–(2) (attorney fees available in actions for unfair methods of competition and unfair or deceptive trade practices in the conduct of trade or commerce); HAW. REV. STAT. § 607-14.5 (attorney fees available where opposing party has taken a position based on frivolous grounds, defined as not reasonably supported by law or fact or a good faith argument for the extension or modification of existing law).

23. *County of Haw. v. C&J Coupe Family Ltd. P'ship*, 120 Haw. 400, 415, 208 P.3d 713, 728 (2009).

IDAHO

JAMES C. DALE

I. Introduction

Rule 23 of the Idaho Rules of Civil Procedure governs class actions in Idaho. Although patterned after its federal counterpart, the current version of Idaho's rule does not contain many of the more recent amendments to Rule 23 of the Federal Rules of Civil Procedure. Because the Idaho rules on class actions are taken from the federal rules, the Idaho Supreme Court has noted that "federal authority is relevant."[1] The question remains whether Idaho courts will rely on federal precedent interpreting recent amendments that have not been specifically adopted in Idaho. It is unlikely such authority would be ignored.

II. Variance from Federal Rule

Because Idaho did not adopt the 2003 amendments to the federal rule, Idaho's class action rule retains language suggesting that a court should certify a class "as soon as practicable."[2] Likewise, Idaho's class action rule does not reflect the federal rule's concept of permissive notice for actions certified under Rule 23(b)(1) or (2).[3] Idaho has not adopted the change to Federal Rule 23(e) strengthening the process by which proposed class action settlements are reviewed.[4] The 2003 amendment to Federal Rule 23(f), providing for a permissive appeal following an order granting or denying certification, has also not been adopted in Idaho. Consequently, interlocutory appeal of an order granting or denying certification in Idaho would

---

1. *O'Boskey v. First Fed. Sav. & Loan Ass'n of Boise*, 112 Idaho 1002, 1005 n.2, 739 P.2d 301, 304 n.2 (Idaho 1987).
2. IDAHO R. CIV. P. 23(c)(1).
3. FED. R. CIV. P. 23(c)(2).
4. IDAHO R CIV.P. 23(e).

require permission of the Idaho Supreme Court pursuant to the Idaho Appellate Rules.[5] Finally, the Idaho rules have not incorporated the current language of Federal Rules 23(g), appointment of class counsel, and 23(h), addressing fee awards.

III. Court Decisions

Only a handful of cases have substantively addressed class actions in Idaho. Most of those opinions do little more than either acknowledge the existence of such a claim or identify the sort of claims that will not be available for class action treatment.[6] In this regard, Idaho courts have refused to recognize a "class action" appeal from a decision of a local zoning board despite the fact that the municipality's actions "would have a deleterious impact upon a large group of landowners whose property adjoined the parcel being rezoned."[7] The Idaho Supreme Court has also held that Idaho Rule 23 does not apply to proceedings before the Idaho Industrial Commission seeking workers' compensation benefits.[8]

As is the case with actions brought under federal law, class actions in Idaho must satisfy the requirements of Rule 23(a) and at least one of the enumerated subsections in Rule 23(b). Addressing the requirement of numerosity contained in Rule 23(a)(1), the Idaho Supreme Court rejected a class action where only 17 putative class members existed, finding that joinder was not impracticable.[9]

Practitioners in Idaho should take note that a class action defendant who elects to submit an issue on its merits prior to a ruling on certification "assumes the risk that an unfavorable judgment will benefit the class ultimately determined."[10] The advantages to a defendant of moving for summary judgment at an early stage may not outweigh the risks of an adverse ruling.

Idaho follows well-established federal authority that certification under Rule 23(b)(3) involves questions of law or fact common to class members and that such questions predominate over questions involving individual members. That a complaint raises alleged antitrust violations is only one facet of a claim for damages and is not, in and of itself, determinative of whether common, as opposed to individual, questions predominate.[11]

---

5. IDAHO APP. R. 21.

6. *Kerner v. Johnson*, 99 Idaho 433, 444–45, 583 P.2d 360, 371–72 (1978) (plaintiffs must establish satisfaction with prerequisites and conditions found in Rules 23(a), (b), and (f) to maintain class action).

7. *Burt v. City of Idaho Falls*, 105 Idaho 65, 70 n.1, 665 P.2d 1075 (Idaho 1983).

8. *Monroe v. Chapman*, 105 Idaho 269, 270, 668 P.2d 1000, 1001 (Idaho 1983).

9. *BHA Invs., Inc. v. City of Boise*, 141 Idaho 168, 172, 108 P.3d 315, 319 (Idaho 2005).

10. *O'Boskey*, 112 Idaho at 1006, 739 P.2d at 305.

11. *Pope v. Intermountain Gas Co.*, 103 Idaho 217, 238–39, 646 P.2d 988, 1009–10 (1982).

The standard of review for a grant or denial of class certification on appeal is under an abuse of discretion standard.[12] However, where the trial court fails to provide a basis for determining whether the requirements for certification were properly considered, an independent review of the record is permitted.[13]

---

12. *Id.*, 103 Idaho at 217, 237–38, 646 P.2d at 988, 1008–09.
13. *Id.*

ILLINOIS

JASON M. ROSENTHAL
KENNETH E. KRAUS

I. Introduction[1]

The Illinois Code of Civil Procedure[2] contains four prerequisites for a class action:

1. The class is so numerous that joinder of all members is impracticable;
2. There are questions of fact or law common to the class, which common questions predominate over any questions affecting only individual members;
3. The representative parties will fairly and adequately protect the interest of the class; and
4. The class action is an appropriate method for the fair and efficient adjudication of the controversy.

The proponent of the class action bears the burden of establishing these four prerequisites.[3]

"Section 2-801 is patterned after Rule 23 of the Federal Rules of Civil Procedure, and because of this close relationship between the state and federal provisions, 'federal decisions interpreting Rule 23 are persuasive authority with regard to questions of class certification in Illinois.'"[4] As discussed below, however, there are differences in the two rules. Thus, in certain instances, federal case law may be either inapplicable or distinguishable.

---

1. For a general reference on Illinois Class Actions, *see* CLASS ACTIONS 2007 EDITION, ILLINOIS INSTITUTE OF CONTINUING LEGAL EDUCATION SMARTBOOKS, https://www.iicle.com/SmartBooks (subscription required).

2. 735 ILL. COMP. STAT. 5/2-801.

3. *Avery v. State Farm Mut. Auto. Ins. Co.*, 835 N.E.2d 801, 819 (Ill. 2005); *Cruz v. Unilock Chicago, Inc.*, 892 N.E.2d 78, 89 (Ill. App. Ct. 2d. Dist. 2008).

4. *Cruz*, 892 N.E.2d at 89 (quoting *Avery*, 835 N.E.2d at 819).

II. Initial Illinois Law Distinctions

Even if a motion for class certification is unopposed, the trial court nonetheless has an independent obligation to ensure that a class action is appropriate and to protect absent class members. This includes a continuing obligation to adjust to changing factual circumstances that may require modification of class certification rulings.[5]

In determining whether a class action is appropriate, the trial court may conduct any factual inquiry necessary to resolve the issue of class certification. But the inquiry is limited to whether the plaintiff will satisfy the requirements of section 2-801, rather than a determination of the merits at that stage. On appeal regarding questions of class certification, however, the reviewing court is to assess the discretion exercised by the trial court and may not instead assess the facts and determine in its own view whether the case is well-suited for a class action.[6]

If certain individual questions exist, they may be handled within subclasses, as long as the common issues predominate.[7] This is true even where conflicting or differing state laws might apply. If at a later point a subclassification becomes unmanageable, the court may set aside the class certification or a portion thereof. Unlike Federal Rule 23(b), however, the Illinois statute does not distinguish between different types of class actions. While Federal Rule 23 allows class actions even where common issues do not predominate (pursuant to either Rule 23(b)(1) or (b)(2)), the Illinois statute requires common issues to predominate for all forms of class actions.[8]

Illinois law requires that a class action be an "appropriate" method for the just and efficient adjudication of the controversy. This is less stringent than Federal Rule 23's requirement that a class action be "superior" to other available methods. However, the Illinois Supreme Court has held that Illinois courts should consider federal rulings on superiority to decide appropriateness.[9]

Moreover, unlike Federal Rule 23's requirement that the class representative's claim be typical of those of the class, Illinois has adopted a more liberal approach. Illinois only requires that the class representative "fairly and adequately" protect the interests of the class. Thus, "a class representative may not be disqualified merely because his claim is not exactly the same as the claims of other potential

---

5. *Cohen v. Blockbuster Entm't, Inc.*, 878 N.E.2d 132, 138 (Ill. App. Ct. 1st Dist. 2007).

6. *Cruz*, 892 N.E.2d at 89.

7. *Purcell & Wardrope Chartered v. Hertz Corp.*, 530 N.E.2d 994, 998 (Ill. App. Ct. 1st Dist. 1988).

8. *Mele v. Howmedica, Inc.*, 808 N.E.2d 1026, 1044 (Ill. App. Ct. 1st Dist. 2004) ("Unlike the Illinois statute, the federal rule does not have a predominance requirement applicable to all class actions."), *overruled on other grounds by Calles v. Scripto-Tokai Corp.*, 864 N.E.2d 249 (2007).

9. *McCabe v. Burgess*, 389 N.E.2d 565, 570 (Ill. 1979).

class members."[10] Instead, Illinois courts have found that "[i]t is only necessary that the representative not seek relief antagonistic to the interest of other potential class members."[11]

III. Notice to Class Members

In terms of notice, the Illinois Code of Civil Procedure provides little guidance. It simply states that "the court in its discretion may order such notice that it deems necessary to protect the interests of the class and the parties."[12] Additionally, an order certifying the class may be conditioned upon "the giving of such notice as the court deems appropriate."[13] In damages class actions that include nonresident class members, due process requires notice to all readily identifiable nonresident members.[14] Notice may be required if class members have differing interests or opinions on the desirability of relief requested in the complaint.[15]

Under Federal Rule 23, classes certified under either 23(b)(1) or 23(b)(2) are mandatory classes, and individual class members cannot opt out of the judgment. "Unlike the federal statute, the Illinois statute does not provide for a mandatory class in which class members cannot seek exclusion."[16] As a result, persons may opt out of any form of class action such that a class action judgment would not affect their substantive rights.[17]

Under the Illinois statute, the trial court's power to amend a class certification order is more circumscribed than under the Federal Rule. The Illinois Code of Civil Procedure allows a trial court to amend a certification order until a "decision on the merits."[18] By contrast, Federal Rule 23 allows amendments or decertification until "final judgment."[19] Thus, a decision under the Illinois statute "does not have to be 'final' to have a limiting effect on the power of the trial court."[20]

---

10. *Carrao v. Health Care Serv. Corp.*, 454 N.E.2d 781, 790 (Ill. App. Ct. 1st Dist. 1983).

11. *Purcell*, 530 N.E.2d at 1000.

12. 735 ILL. COMP. STAT. 5/2-803.

13. *Id.*

14. *Miner v. Gillette*, 428 N.E.2d 478, 482 (Ill. 1981).

15. *Frank v. Teachers Ins. & Annuity Assoc.*, 376 N.E.2d 1377, 1381 (Ill. 1978).

16. *In re Chicago Flood Litig.*, 682 N.E.2d 421, 427 (Ill. App. Ct. 1st Dist. 1997); *see also* 735 ILL. COMP. STAT. 5/2-804(b) ("Any class member seeking to be excluded from a class action may request such exclusion and any judgment entered in the action shall not apply to persons who properly request to be excluded.").

17. *In re Chicago Flood*, 682 N.E.2d at 427.

18. 735 ILL. COMP. STAT. 5/2-803(a).

19. FED. R. CIV. P. 23(c)(1)(C).

20. *Rosolowski v. Clark Ref. & Mktg.*, 890 N.E.2d 1011, 1016 (Ill. App. Ct. 1st Dist. 2008).

IV. Statue of Limitations Tolling

Many jurisdictions provide that the statute of limitations is tolled for all purported class members upon the filing of a class action complaint. The U.S. Supreme Court rationalized that without such a rule, unnamed class members "would feel compelled to file motions to intervene in the action before the expiration of the limitations period in order to prevent loss of their claims in the event class status was ultimately denied after the limitation deadline."[21]

The Illinois Supreme Court, however, refused to adopt such a tolling rule. It reasoned that "[u]nless all states simultaneously adopt the rule of cross-jurisdictional class action tolling," tolling a state statute of limitations "may actually increase the burden on that state's court system, because plaintiffs from across the country may elect to file a subsequent suit in that state solely to take advantage of the generous tolling rule."[22] Accordingly, the court "refuse[d] to expose the Illinois court system to such forum shopping," and held that an Illinois statute of limitations was not tolled during the pendency of a class action in federal court.[23]

V. Appeals

Appeals of class certification rulings are permissive, as they are under federal law.[24]

VI. Attorney Fees

If no statutory right to attorney fees is available, attorney fees in Illinois class actions, as in some federal class actions, may be awarded under the common-fund doctrine.[25]

---

21. *Portwood v. Ford Motor Co.*, 701 N.E.2d 1102, 1104 (Ill. 1998) (citing *Am. Pipe & Constr. Co. v. Utah*, 414 U.S. 538 (1974)).

22. *Id.*

23. *Id.*

24. *Compare* Fed R. Civ. P. 23(f) *with* Ill. Sup. Ct. R. 308(a)(8).

25. *Scholtens v. Schneider*, 671 N.E.2d 657, 662–63 (Ill. 1996); *Brundidge v. Glendale Fed. Bank*, 659 N.E.2d 909, 911 (Ill. 1995).

INDIANA

JASON M. ROSENTHAL
KENNETH E. KRAUS

I. Introduction[1]

The Indiana Code of Civil Procedure[2] contains four primary prerequisites for a class action:

1. The class is so numerous that joinder of all members is impracticable;
2. There are questions of law or fact common to the class;
3. The claims or defenses of the representative parties are typical of the claims or defenses of the class; and
4. The representative parties will fairly and adequately protect the interests of the class.

In addition, a plaintiff must meet one of the requirements of Trial Rule 23(B), which largely tracks the language of Federal Rule 23(b).[3]

Indeed, Indiana law on class certification is almost identical to federal law. The Indiana rule was taken nearly verbatim from Federal Rule of Civil Procedure 23, and it thus is a "virtual carbon copy" of Federal Rule 23.[4] Accordingly, Indiana courts commonly look to federal law interpreting Federal Rule 23 to guide their interpretations of Indiana law.[5]

---

1. For a general reference on Indiana Class Actions, *see* STEPHEN E. ARTHUR, INDIANA PRACTICE § 18 (2007).

2. IND. R. TRIAL P. 23.

3. *Compare* IND. R. TRIAL P. 23(B) *with* FED. R. CIV. P. 23(b).

4. *Budden v. Bd. of Sch. Comm'rs*, 698 N.E.2d 1157, 1163 (Ind. 1998); *see also Associated Med. Networks, Ltd. v. Lewis*, 824 N.E.2d 679, 685 (Ind. 2005) ("The text of 23(B)(3) is identical in both rules.").

5. *Associated Med. Networks*, 824 N.E.2d at 685 (interpreting Trial Rule 23(B)(3)); *Reel v. Clarion Health Partners, Inc.*, 855 N.E.2d 343, 349–56 (Ind. App. Ct. 2006) (interpreting Trial Rule 23(C)(1)); *Wal-Mart Stores, Inc. v. Bailey*, 808 N.E.2d 1198, 1207 (Ind. App. Ct. 2004) (interpreting Trial Rule 23(B)(2)).

II. Indiana Law Distinctions

One significant difference between the two rules is that Indiana requires that a hearing take place on the class certification issue.[6] This requirement is triggered by the filing of the complaint, not the filing of a motion to certify the class.[7] As a result, Indiana permits a party to request special findings of fact and conclusions of law prior to the hearing, unlike federal law.[8] For nearly every other class certification issue, however, Indiana courts will look to federal law.[9]

With respect to attorney fees, both Indiana law and the Federal Rules of Civil Procedure provide for the recovery of reasonable fee awards.[10] Indiana courts look to federal cases for guidance on the reasonableness of a class action fee award.[11]

Although Indiana law lacks a precise analogue to Federal Rule 23(g) for appointment of class counsel, it does provide substantial discretion to trial courts to appoint class counsel and otherwise control the class action under Trial Rule 23(D)(1)–(5). When interpreting this rule, Indiana courts once again look to Federal Rule 23: "It is clear that an analysis of the trial court's duties under Federal Rule 23 is fully applicable under our Ind. R. Tr. P. 23 as our rule is based upon the federal rule."[12]

III. Appeals

The appellate court may, in its discretion, review the trial court's grant or denial of class certification.[13]

---

6. *Connorwood Healthcare, Inc. v. Estate of Herron*, 683 N.E.2d 1322, 1326 n.3 (Ind. App. Ct. 1997). Indiana law also contains an express provision for attorney fees, which the Federal Rules did not contain until the 2003 amendments. *See* FED. R. CIV. P. 23(h).

7. *Am. Cyanamid v. Stephen*, 623 N.E.2d 1065, 1070 (Ind. App. Ct. 1993).

8. *Id.* at 1071.

9. *Associated Med. Networks*, 824 N.E.2d at 685 ("Indiana's Trial Rule 23 is based upon Rule 23 of the Federal Rules of Civil Procedure, and it is thus appropriate to consider federal court interpretations when applying the Indiana rule.").

10. *Compare* IND. R. TR. P. 23(D) ("The court shall allow reasonable attorney's fees and reasonable expenses incurred from a fund recovered for the benefit of a class under this section and the court may apportion such recovery among different attorneys.") *with* FED. R. CIV. P. 23(h) ("In a certified class action, the court may award reasonable attorney's fees and nontaxable costs that are authorized by law or by the parties' agreement.").

11. *See Cmty. Care Ctrs., Inc. v. Ind. Family & Soc. Servs. Admin.*, 716 N.E.2d 519, 551–52 (Ind. Ct. App. 1999).

12. *State ex rel. Harris v. Scott Circuit Court*, 437 N.E.2d 952, 953 (Ind. 1982) (looking to federal cases for guidance on appointment of class counsel for absent members).

13. IND. R. APP. P. 14(C).

IOWA

ANN BROWN-GRAFF

I. Introduction

The Iowa rules governing class actions are set forth in the Iowa Rules of Civil Procedure 1.261–1.279. Iowa is one of only two states that have adopted the Uniform Class Action Rules promulgated by the National Conference of Commissioners on Uniform State Laws.[1] While Iowa's rules share many similarities with Federal Rule of Civil Procedure 23, particularly relating to the general prerequisites for class certification, there are also significant differences including specific and detailed requirements for providing notice to class members both of class certification and of settlement, counterclaims by and against the class, the discovery available, relief available to the class, and attorney fees and costs.[2]

II. Prerequisites to Certification

Iowa has not adopted the language of Federal Rule 23(a) and (b). However, Iowa's rules relating to class certification have been read to require the same prerequisites to certification as Rule 23, including numerosity, commonality, predominance, and adequacy of representation.[3] The Iowa Supreme Court has stated that Iowa's class action rules "should be construed liberally and the policy should favor maintenance of class actions."[4]

---

1. *Vignaroli v. Blue Cross*, 360 N.W.2d 741, 743 (Iowa 1985); *Martin v. Raytheon Co.*, 497 N.W.2d 818, 820 (Iowa 1993). North Dakota is the only other state to have adopted the Uniform Rules.

2. Iowa R. Civ. P. 1.261–1.264, 1.266, 1.269–1.271, 1.275 & 1.276; *see also Voss v. Farm Bureau Life Ins. Co.*, 667 N.W.2d 36, 44 (Iowa 2003) ("Iowa Rules of Civil Procedure 1.261 to 1.263, the rules regarding class actions, closely resemble Federal Rule of Civil Procedure 23.").

3. *Voss*, 667 N.W.2d at 44–46; *Comes v. Microsoft Corp.*, 696 N.W.2d 318, 325–26 (Iowa 2005).

4. *Ackerman v. Int'l Bus. Mach. Corp.*, 337 N.W.2d 486, 489 (Iowa 1983) (citing *Lucas v. Pioneer Inc.*, 256 N.W.2d 167, 175 (Iowa 1977)).

Rule 1.261 provides that a class action can be commenced if (1) the class is so numerous or so constituted that joinder of all members, whether or not otherwise required or permitted, is impracticable; and (2) there is a question of law or fact common to the class.[5] Rule 1.262 sets forth the requirements for class certification and provides that, in addition to the above requirements of Rule 1.261 (numerosity and commonality), the court may certify a class if (1) "a class action should be permitted for the fair and efficient adjudication of the controversy" and (2) "the representative parties fairly and adequately will protect the interests of the class."[6] The Iowa Rules differ from the Federal Rules because they do not expressly require typicality. However, the Iowa Supreme Court has essentially read the typicality requirement into the Iowa Rules.[7]

Iowa Rule 1.263 sets forth 13 criteria not found in Federal Rule 23 to be considered by the court in determining whether a class action should be allowed for the fair and efficient adjudication of the controversy.[8] The criteria in Rule 1.263 "have two broad considerations: achieving judicial economy by encouraging class litigation while preserving, as much as possible, the rights of litigants—both those presently in court and those who are potential litigants."[9] The court is not required to give any particular weight to any of the criteria listed.[10] Additionally, while the court is required to "state the reasons for the court's ruling and its findings of fact with regard to the criteria," the court is not required to "make written findings as to each factor under Rule 1.263(1)."[11]

A notable difference between the Iowa Rules and Federal Rule 23 is that the court is required to hold a hearing before issuing a certification order.[12] "Because Iowa is a notice-pleading state 'it may be necessary for the Court to probe behind the pleadings before coming to rest on the certification question.'"[13] However, unless the facts alleged in the pleadings are "merely speculative," the plaintiffs' "burden is light."[14] The class certification determination does not involve an inquiry into the merits of the case.[15] The district court's determination regard-

---

5. IOWA R. CIV. P. 1.261.

6. IOWA R. CIV. P. 1.262(2).

7. FED. R. CIV. P. 23(a)(3); *see Hammer v. Branstad*, 463 N.W.2d 86, 89–90 (Iowa 1990) (quoting 1 HERBERT B. NEWBERG & ALBA CONTE, NEWBERG ON CLASS ACTIONS § 2:05, at 48 (2d ed. 1985) ("[T]he claims of the plaintiff must be typical of the claims of the class, ...")).

8. IOWA R. CIV. P. 1.263.

9. *Vignaroli*, 36 N.W.2d at 744.

10. *Id.*

11. *Id.; see also Voss*, 667 N.W.2d at 45.

12. *Compare* IOWA R. CIV. P. 1.262(1) *with* FED. R. CIV. P. 23(c)(A).

13. *Comes*, 696 N.W.2d at 324 (quoting *Voss*, 667 N.W.2d at 48).

14. *Id.* (quoting *City of Dubuque v. Iowa Trust*, 519 N.W.2d 786, 791 (Iowa 1994)).

15. *Vignaroli*, 36 N.W.2d at 745.

ing class certification or decertification is appealable but only reviewed under the abuse of discretion standard.[16]

III. Notice of an Action

The requirements for notifying members of the class of a pending class action are set forth in Rule 1.266. The notice requirements vary slightly from the notice requirements set forth in Federal Rule 23(c)(2). Rule 1.266(2) provides that the notice must include (1) a description of the action; (2) the relief sought; (3) the names and addresses of representative parties; (4) a statement that any member of the class can opt out of the class and the manner and deadline for opting out; (5) a description of the potential financial consequences to the class; (6) a description of any counterclaim and the relief sought in such counterclaim; (7) a statement that the judgment will bind class members; (8) a statement that any member of the class may appear personally or through a lawyer; (9) an address to which inquiries may be directed; and (10) other information the court deems appropriate. Rule 1.266(4) provides that every member of a class whose potential recovery is estimated to exceed $100 shall be given personal or mailed notice if the class members' identity and whereabouts can be ascertained by the exercise of reasonable diligence.[17]

IV. Discovery Against Class Members

Iowa requires an order of the court before discovery can be directed against class members who are not representative parties and have not otherwise appeared.[18] Factors the court considers in determining what, if any, discovery to allow against nonrepresentative class members include (1) the timing of the request; (2) the subject matter to be covered; (3) whether the representative parties are seeking discovery on the subject matter; and (4) the annoyance, oppression, undue burden, or expense imposed on members of the class.[19]

V. Counterclaims

The Iowa Rules allow the defendant to assert counterclaims (1) against the entire plaintiff class if the counterclaim is certified; (2) against a plaintiff subclass if the

---

16. *Voss*, 667 N.W.2d at 44; *Comes*, 696 N.W.2d at 320.
17. Iowa R. Civ. P. 1.266(4).
18. Iowa R. Civ. P. 1.269(1).
19. *Id.*

counterclaim is certified; or (3) against an individual member of the class.[20] Counterclaims of a defendant against a plaintiff class must be asserted before notice of certification is sent to the class, pursuant to Rule 1.266.[21] A defendant class, defendant subclass, or individual member of a defendant class may also plead a counterclaim against the named plaintiff.[22] The court is required to order notice to the defendant class of the aforementioned counterclaims.[23] The defendant's failure to plead, or the court's refusal to allow, a counterclaim in a class action does not bar the defendant from asserting the claim in a subsequent action.[24]

VI. Notice of Settlement

The Iowa Rules also have specific requirements for the notice given to class members in the event of settlement. Rule 1.271(3) sets forth the notice requirements in the event of settlement or dismissal. This Rule requires that the notice include (1) the procedure available for modification of the settlement or dismissal; (2) full disclosure of the reasons for the dismissal or settlement; (3) any payments made in connection with the settlement; (4) the anticipated effect of the settlement on class members; (5) a description of any settlement agreement; (6) a description and evaluation of alternatives considered by the representative party; and (7) an explanation of any other circumstances giving rise to the proposed settlement.[25] All settlements must be approved by the court after a hearing.[26]

VII. Relief Afforded

Iowa Rule 1.274 sets forth the types of relief available to the class, the method for distributing proceeds from a judgment in favor of the class, and the criteria and methods for distributing any unclaimed funds to the state.[27] The court has broad powers to award "any form of relief consistent with the certification order," including "equitable, declaratory, monetary, or other relief."[28] The court can award relief to individual members of the class or the class as a whole.[29] In the event that a judgment is entered in favor of the class, the parties are responsible for identi-

---

20. IOWA R. CIV. P. 1.270(1).
21. IOWA R. CIV. P. 1.270(2).
22. IOWA R. CIV. P. 1.270(4).
23. Id.
24. IOWA R. CIV. P. 1.270(6).
25. IOWA R. CIV. P. 1.271(3).
26. IOWA R. CIV. P. 1.271.
27. IOWA R. CIV. P. 1.274.
28. Id.
29. IOWA R. CIV. P. 1.274(1).

fying class members, and the court oversees the identification process as well as the distribution process.[30] Unclaimed awards of individual class members can be distributed to any state where members of the class to whom distribution could not be made were last known to reside or to the defendant.[31] There are six factors for the court to consider in determining whether to distribute the money to a state or the defendant: (1) any unjust enrichment of the defendant; (2) the willfulness or lack of willfulness on the part of the defendant; (3) the impact on the defendant of the relief granted; (4) the pendency of other claims against the defendant; (5) any criminal sanction imposed on the defendant; and (6) the loss suffered by the plaintiff class.[32] The court also has the right to impose conditions respecting the use of any funds distributed to the defendant.[33]

VIII. Attorney Fees

Unlike Rule 23, the Iowa Rules do not require that the court appoint class counsel.[34] The Iowa Rules provide that attorney fees may be awarded to counsel for the representative party.[35] The Iowa Rules also set forth mandatory factors for the court to consider in determining the amount of attorney fees to be awarded. These factors are (1) the time and effort expended by the lawyer in the litigation, including the nature, extent, and quality of services rendered; (2) results achieved and benefits conferred upon the class; (3) the magnitude, complexity, and uniqueness of the litigation; and (4) appropriate criteria in the Iowa Rules of Professional Conduct.[36] Counsel for the representative party is required to file a copy of any written fee agreement or fee-sharing agreement or a summary of any oral fee agreement or fee-sharing agreement before certification or at other time as directed by the court.[37] The district court has broad discretion in awarding attorney fees, and decisions regarding fees are only reviewed for abuse of discretion.[38]

---

30. Iowa R. Civ. P. 1.274(3).
31. Iowa R. Civ. P. 1.274(3)(e)–(h).
32. Iowa R. Civ. P. 1.274(3)(f).
33. Iowa R. Civ. P. 1.274(3)(g).
34. *Compare* Fed. R. Civ. P. 23(g) *with* Iowa R. Civ. P. 1.275.
35. Iowa R. Civ. P. 1.275.
36. Iowa R. Civ. P. 1.275(5).
37. Iowa R. Civ. P. 1.276.
38. *King v. Armstrong*, 518 N.W.2d 336, 337 (Iowa 1994).

KANSAS

JAMES A. WALKER

I. Introduction

The class action procedure in Kansas is governed by Kansas Statutes Annotated 60-223 (Kansas Rule), which was last amended in 2010 by Kansas House Bill 2656, which became effective July 1, 2010. The current statute now resembles the 2009 version of Federal Rule of Civil Procedure 23.[1] Although the Kansas Rule was not identical to Rule 23 prior to the 2010 amendments, Kansas has usually followed the federal court's interpretations of Rule 23.[2]

II. Treatment of Threshold Elements Under the Kansas Scheme

The four threshold elements for class maintenance, well known by their abbreviated labels as numerosity, commonality, typicality, and adequacy, are all required in Kansas.[3] A trial court must conduct a rigorous analysis to confirm these elements.[4] The courts of Kansas have had occasion to interpret some of these elements in particular.

A. NUMEROSITY

In the context of an alleged multistate class action involving claims arising in six different states, the Kansas Supreme Court upheld the trial court's findings of numerosity and impracticality where the total class had 242 members and was divided into subclasses by state.[5] The trial court denied certification of subclasses

---

1. The previous version of the Kansas Rule was patterned after Federal Rule 23, though not identical.

2. *Steele v. Sec. Benefit Life Ins. Co.*, 602 P.2d 1305, 1309 (Kan. 1979).

3. *See* KAN. STAT. ANN. 60-223(a)(1)–(4).

4. *See Dragon v. Vanguard Indus., Inc.*, 89 P.3d 908 (Kan. 2004) (*Dragon I*); *Farrar v. Mobil Oil Corp.*, 2010 Kan. App. LEXIS 64 (Kan. Ct. App. June 11, 2010).

5. *Sternberger v. Marathon Oil Co.*, 257 Kan. 315, 894 P.2d 788 (Kan. 1995).

composed of members in two states for failure to satisfy numerosity, but certified subclasses composed of members of four of the six states.[6] The smallest approved subclass included 38 members. The court observed that the possibility of 38 separate lawyers would not be efficient judicial administration.[7] It concluded that there is no set number that must be shown to warrant class certification.[8]

In another case, the court upheld the trial court's refusal to certify a class composed of all 23 royalty owners under a mineral lease.[9]

B. ADEQUACY

Kansas decisions have considered the adequacy element from several different perspectives. The first involved whether a class representative could remain adequate upon abandoning certain causes of action and narrowing the scope of a class to facilitate certification. Litigation against Vanguard Industries, Inc. concerning polybutylene pipe was initially brought as a nationwide class action asserting a variety of causes of action. The trial court initially certified a nationwide class, but the Kansas Supreme Court reversed on several grounds, including because the record provided no basis to review matters concerning choice of law to determine issues of commonality.[10]

On remand, the plaintiffs filed an amended petition narrowing the scope of the class to include only consumers in four states and abandoning some of the various causes of action previously asserted. The trial court refused to certify another class, expressing concern that the narrowed class and claims reflected an attitude that the class representatives and counsel were willing to abandon claims in order to more easily secure certification.[11] On appeal from that ruling, the Kansas Supreme Court concluded that the deletion of claims did not automatically destroy adequacy for two reasons.[12] First, only claims actually litigated are precluded from being litigated elsewhere. Second, dropping claims may serve valid strategies of the class representative and need not necessarily threaten inadequacy. The court did appreciate the paradox that while dropping claims may serve certain aspects of certification, it may also highlight other problems with certification, such as superiority, if numerous individual suits appear likely to follow.[13]

Another vantage point from which the Kansas Supreme Court has considered adequacy is coextensiveness. In testing adequacy, the coextensiveness factor does

---

6. *Id.* at 257 Kan. at 341, 894 P.2d at 806. The subclasses for these two states had 21 and 18 members, respectively.

7. *Id.* at 257 Kan. at 343–44, 894 P.2d at 806–07.

8. *Id.* at 257 Kan. at 344, 894 P.2d at 807.

9. *Schupback v. Cont'l Oil Co.*, 394 P.2d 1 (Kan. 1964).

10. *Dragon I*, 89 P.3d at 917–18.

11. *Dragon v. Vanguard Indus., Inc.*, 144 P.3d 1279, 1283 (Kan. 2006) (*Dragon II*).

12. *Id.* at 1288.

13. *See id.* at 1288–89.

not require that the position of the class representative be identical to those of the rest or even the majority of the class. Even if the representative's interests go beyond those of the class, such as where the class representative is also a competitor of the defendant, it is not enough to defeat certification.[14]

C. RIGOROUS ANALYSIS

The most significant recent development in class action practice in Kansas is the court's express rejection in *Dragon I*[15] of the "face of the pleadings" approach to class certification. Prior to *Dragon I*, class representatives relied on *Eisen v. Carlisle & Jacqueline*[16] to argue that a preliminary factual inquiry of the certification requirements is unauthorized.

In *Dragon I*, the Kansas Supreme Court determined that trial courts must fully determine factual issues related to the prerequisites for commonality, typicality, predominance, and superiority and to rigorously analyze them. In so doing, the trial court should consider evidence when submitted.[17] An appellate court reviews a trial court's certification of a class action under the abuse of discretion test. A trial court abuses its discretion if it fails to conduct a rigorous analysis to determine whether the statutory elements have been met.[18]

The analysis required in Kansas for settlement classes may be less rigorous because of the absence of certain manageability issues, but the other considerations of class certification remain vitally important.[19]

Class certification decisions should be made as soon as practicable as statutorily directed, but only after the parties have had opportunity to develop and present facts relevant to class certification.[20]

D. CHOICE OF LAW, FINDINGS AND CONCLUSIONS, AND STATUTES OF LIMITATION

In multistate classes, Kansas trial courts have been cautioned to consider "any possible conflict of law problems" where liability is determined according to inconsistent state laws, thus bearing on one or more of the certification prerequisites and factors.[21] The fact that certification is modifiable and subject to creation of subclasses does not ease the plaintiff's burden of establishing the prerequisites.

---

14. *Connolly v. Frobenius*, 574 P.2d 971, 975–76 (Kan. 1978).
15. 89 P.3d 908.
16. 417 U.S. 156 (1974).
17. *Dragon I*, 89 P.3d 908; *Farrar*, 2010 Kan. App. LEXIS 64.
18. *Farrar*, 2010 Kan. App. LEXIS 64.
19. *Dragon I*, 89 P.3d at 919–20.
20. *Id.* at 914.
21. *Id.* at 915, 916.

The general rule that the party asserting a conflict between the applicable law and that of the forum has the burden to establish the existence of a conflict does not apply in a class certification context. Instead, the proponent of the class has the burden to show that there are no significant differences in the law or that the differences are manageable.[22]

Any party appealing a decision on class certification based on lack of rigorous analysis risks an adverse appellate decision where no additional or amended findings and conclusions were requested pursuant to Kansas Statutes Annotated 60-252(b).[23]

The appellate court is not required, however, to assume that the trial court made the necessary findings or conclusions and may remand for further findings to permit a meaningful review.[24]

When denying certification, it is not mandatory that the trial court make findings on all the requirements and factors for class treatment. But requesting findings on all factors is recommended, as it permits more meaningful review.[25]

A putative member of a proposed class has the right to file a separate action, and that right is preserved pending a determination of whether the matter may be maintained as a class action.[26] Subsequent actions by putative class members are preserved from statute of limitation defenses where the denial of class certification is based on lack of numerosity and assuming the separate filing is timely made and in compliance with tolling concepts or the savings statute.[27] It is an open question as to whether denial of class certification on some other basis, such as lack of typicality, would preserve the right to separately file if the statute would have otherwise run but for the class action filing.

E. DAMAGES

Generally, in order to maintain a suit as a class action, courts should consider whether the damage to individual class members can be proved by a common methodology. There is a Kansas class action case, however, where the court held that the named representative assumes the burden of proving the total classwide damages, rather than individual damages of each member.[28] It remains to be seen whether Kansas will permit class treatment in cases where the damages to individual class members cannot be proved by common methodology, but aggregate classwide damages can be proved.

---

22. *Id.* (quoting *Shutts Ex'r v. Phillips Petroleum Co.*, 567 P.2d 1292 (Kan. 1977)).
23. *Id.* at 918–19.
24. *Dragon II*, 144 P.3d at 1286.
25. *Id.*
26. *Id.* at 1287–88.
27. *Waltrip v. Sidwell Corp.*, 678 P.2d 128, 132 (Kan. 1984).
28. *Gilley v. Kan. Gas Serv. Co.*, 169 P.3d 1064, 1067 (Kan. 2007).

KENTUCKY

BARBARA B. EDELMAN[1]

I. Introduction

Kentucky Rule of Civil Procedure 23 (Kentucky Rule)[2] closely resembles Federal Rule of Civil Procedure 23 because it is derived from the 1966 version of the federal rule.[3] Accordingly, Kentucky courts often look to federal precedent for guidance in interpreting the Kentucky Rule.[4] The Kentucky Rule, however, varies from its federal counterpart in that it generally grants the trial court judge greater discretion in deciding matters related to class actions. A complete discussion of how the Kentucky Rule differs from Federal Rule 23 is provided below.

---

1. The author would like to thank Kelley R. Williams, an associate at Dinsmore & Shohl, LLP, for his assistance in the preparation of this chapter.

2. KY. R. CIV. P. 23.01–23.05.

3. 6 KY. PRAC. R. CIV. PROC. ANN. R. 23.01, cmt. 2 (6th ed. 2009). In 2008, the Kentucky Supreme Court commissioned the Mass Tort and Class Action Litigation Committee to consider possible revisions to the Kentucky Rule. The revisions to the Kentucky Rule, if any, are expected to be adopted in late 2010. The issues being considered by the committee derive in large part from a recent Kentucky class action involving the weight loss drug Fen-phen in which the handling of settlement funds by three Kentucky lawyers received national attention. *See* Adam Liptak, *Lawyers' Payday in Diet-Pill Case Is Called Fraud*, N.Y. TIMES, Mar. 24, 2007, at A1. Two of the lawyers, William J. Gallion and Shirley A. Cunningham, Jr., were found civilly liable for defrauding their clients by retaining more of the settlement funds than they were entitled to under their fee arrangements, *id.*, and were later convicted criminally. *See* Beth Musgrave, *Fen-phen Attorneys Sentenced to Decades in Prison*, LEXINGTON HERALD-LEADER, Aug. 18, 2009, *available at* http://www.kentucky.com/181/story/898627.html. The class action issues raised within the trials included, among other issues, the requirement of giving notice to class members and putative class members. *See* United States v. Gallion, 257 F.R.D. 141, 150–51 (E.D. Ky. 2009).

4. *See, e.g., Lamar v. Office of the Sheriff of Daviess County*, 669 S.W.2d 27, 31 (Ky. Ct. App. 1984); *Bellarmine Coll. v. Hornung*, 662 S.W.2d 847, 848 (Ky. Ct. App. 1983).

II. Class Certification

Kentucky courts must certify a class action based on the same four prerequisites and three types of class actions as federal courts.[5] Kentucky courts, however, have greater discretion in the granting of class certification. Whereas a federal court's certification order must set forth certain mandated details including the class, the class claims, issues, or defenses, and class counsel,[6] a Kentucky court is only required to "determine by order whether [the class action] is to be maintained."[7] This standard requires only that the trial court make findings of fact sufficient to prove that the requirements of Kentucky Rules 23.01 and 23.02 are satisfied.[8] Therefore, the additional details in the class certification order required by Federal Rule 23, such as the appointment of class counsel, are not required. Additionally, a Kentucky court's order certifying a class action may be conditional, a procedure that is no longer available in federal courts.[9]

Kentucky Rule 23.03 and Federal Rule 23(c) differ in their wording of the timing and notice requirements of a trial court's class certification order, but they are substantially the same in application.[10] In terms of timing, although Kentucky Rule 23.03(1)'s requirement of certifying the class action "as soon as practicable" seems to be earlier than Federal Rule 23(c)(1)(A)'s "at an early practicable time," these two time frames are not significantly different.[11] In terms of notice, Kentucky Rule 23.03, unlike Federal Rule 23(c)(2)(a), does not specifically state that a trial court may provide appropriate notice of class certification under Kentucky Rule 23.02(a) and 23.02(b) class actions (which are substantially the same as Federal Rules 23(b)(1) and 23(b)(2) class actions). A Kentucky court, however, has discretion to give such notice under Kentucky Rule 23.04(b). Additionally, the notice required in Kentucky Rule 23.03(c) class actions (which are substantially the same as Federal Rule 23(b)(3) class actions) is the same "best notice practicable" standard required under Federal Rule 23(c)(2)(B) even though the Kentucky and federal rules require slightly different details to be included in the notice.[12]

In terms of the order granting or denying class certification, the Kentucky Court of Appeals, although in an unpublished opinion, has held that a trial court

---

5. *Compare* FED. R. CIV. P. 23(a), (b) *with* KY. R. CIV. P. 23.01, 23.02.

6. FED. R. CIV. P. 23(c)(1)(B).

7. KY. R. CIV. P. 23.03(1).

8. *Rose v. Council for Better Educ., Inc.*, 790 S.W.2d 186, 202 (Ky. 1989); *Brockman v. Jones*, 610 S.W.2d 943, 945 (Ky. Ct. App. 1980).

9. KY. R. CIV. P. 23.03(1).

10. *Compare* FED. R. CIV. P. 23(c) *with* KY. R. CIV. P. 23.03.

11. *See* FED. R. CIV. P. 23 advisory committee note (2003) (explaining that the 2003 amendment of Federal Rule 23(c)(1)(A) from "as soon as practicable" to "at an early practicable time" was consistent with the prevailing practice of trial courts).

12. *Compare* FED. R. CIV. P. 23(c)(2)(B) *with* KY. R. CIV. P. 23.03(2).

may in its discretion order that notice be issued to the putative class members when class certification is denied.[13] In exercising this discretion, the trial court must consider the competing interests of (1) the prejudice to the putative class members by not giving notice of the denial of certification, and (2) the cost and judicial economy of giving notice.[14] Evidence that the putative class members had actual knowledge of the pending class action and that the putative class members were reasonably relying on the action to protect their interests are relevant to this determination.[15] In particular, the amount of publicity that the action has received is an important factor to be considered.[16] On appeal, the trial court's determination is reviewed under an abuse of discretion standard.[17]

III. Dismissal or Compromise

Once a class action is certified, Kentucky and federal courts generally have the same authority and discretion in conducting the class action.[18] In Kentucky courts, however, a trial judge has greater discretion in dismissing or allowing a compromise of a class action. Under Kentucky Rule 23.05, a class action can only be dismissed or compromised upon (1) the court's approval and (2) notice to the class members.[19] Additional requirements like the provisions contained in Federal Rule 23(e)(2)–(5) are not imposed on a Kentucky trial court judge.[20] Therefore, a Kentucky court can approve the dismissal or settlement of a class action without holding a fairness hearing or mandating a new opportunity for class members to request exclusion.

IV. Appeals

Under Kentucky law, an order granting or denying class certification is interlocutory and thus nonappealable.[21] Kentucky Rule 23, unlike Federal Rule 23, does not provide a special rule for appeal from such an order.[22] Therefore, the party that is adversely affected by an order granting or denying class certification must wait

---

13. *Hager v. Allstate Ins. Co.*, No. 2007-CA-002599-MR, 2009 WL 3320938, at *11 (Ky. Ct. App. Oct. 16, 2009). At the time of the writing of this chapter, Hager was in the process of seeking discretionary review from the Kentucky Supreme Court on the issue of notice to the putative class members.

14. *Id.*

15. *Id.*

16. *Id.* at *11–12.

17. *Id.* at *14.

18. *Compare* FED. R. CIV. P. 23(d) *with* KY. R. CIV. P. 23.04.

19. KY. R. CIV. P. 23.05.

20. *Compare* FED. R. CIV. P. 23(e) *with* KY. R. CIV. P. 23.05.

21. *Bellarmine Coll.*, 662 S.W.2d at 849.

22. *See* FED. R. CIV. P. 23(f) (allowing an immediate appeal at the discretion of the court of appeals if a petition is filed within 14 days).

until a trial has resulted in an adverse verdict to appeal the class certification ruling.[23] Furthermore, the order granting or denying class certification is not immediately appealable by a writ of mandamus.[24]

V. Appointment of Class Counsel

Federal Rule 23(g)'s list of mandatory and permissive considerations in appointing class counsel is not included in Kentucky Rule 23.[25] Instead, the appointment of class counsel in Kentucky courts is left to the trial judge's discretion, which is restrained only by the requirement that the representative parties must "fairly and adequately protect the interests of the class."[26]

VI. Attorney Fees

Unlike Federal Rule 23, Kentucky Rule 23 does not provide a special rule regarding class action attorney fees.[27] As such, the procedure for granting attorney fees in a class action is left to the trial judge, in whose discretion the attorney fees' reasonableness is determined.[28] The judge's ruling on attorney fees is reviewed under an abuse of discretion standard by the court of appeals.[29]

---

23. *Garrard County Bd. of Educ. v. Jackson*, 12 S.W.3d 686, 690–91 (Ky. 2000).

24. *Id.* at 691.

25. *Compare* FED. R. CIV. P. 23(g) *with* KY. R. CIV. P. 23.

26. KY. R. CIV. P. 23.01(d).

27. *Compare* FED. R. CIV. P. 23(h) *with* KY. R. CIV. P. 23.

28. *Dingus v. Fada Serv. Co.*, 856 S.W.2d 45, 50 (Ky. Ct. App. 1993).

29. *Id.*

LOUISIANA

S. AULT HOOTSELL III
J. ALAN HARRELL

I. Introduction

Class actions in Louisiana courts are governed by articles 591 through 597 of the Louisiana Code of Civil Procedure.[1] Prior to 1997, Louisiana followed somewhat loosely the pre-1966 version of Federal Rule of Civil Procedure 23, as adopted in 1937.[2] With the passage of Act No. 839 (1997), Louisiana's legal framework for class actions came to track closely the post-1966 provisions of Rule 23.[3]

II. The Louisiana Code Articles Generally

Louisiana Code of Civil Procedure Article 591 contains the substantive requirements under Louisiana law for certifying a class action,[4] and Article 592 governs the primary procedural issues for class actions.[5] The remaining Code articles,

---

1. LA. CODE CIV. PROC. ANN. arts. 591–597 (1997).

2. *Brooks v. Union Pac. R.R. Co.*, 2008-2035 (La. 5/22/09); 2009 WL 1425972, at *6; *see also* FED. R. CIV. P. 23.

3. *See* Act of July 10, 1997, No. 839, § 1. Further, a number of articles have been written since the 1997 legislative amendments that contain excellent discussions of Louisiana law (pre- and post-amendments) regarding Louisiana class actions. These articles include: Stephen H. Kupperman & David G. Radlauer, *Louisiana Class Actions*, 74 TUL. L. REV. 2047 (2000); Kent A. Lambert, *Class Action Settlements in Louisiana*, 61 LA. L. REV. 89 (2000); Donald C. Massey, Louis C. LaCour, Jr. & Valerie M. Sercovich, *Curtailing the Tidal Surge: Current Reforms in Louisiana Class Action Law*, 44 LOY. L. REV. 7 (1998); and Kent A. Lambert, *Certification of Class Actions in Louisiana*, 58 LA. L. REV. 1085, 1087–88 (1998).

4. The complete text of Article 591 is set forth in Appendix A.

5. The complete text of Article 592 is set forth in Appendix B.

articles 593 through 597, address venue,[6] dismissal or compromise,[7] award of expenses of litigation and security for costs,[8] prescription and suspension,[9] and effect of judgment.[10]

III. *Certification of a Litigation Class Under Louisiana Law*

When interpreting and applying articles 591 through 597, Louisiana courts look to federal and state jurisprudence interpreting Rule 23 as well as the provisions

---

6. Article 593 of the Louisiana Code of Civil Procedure provides:

>   A. An action brought on behalf of a class shall be brought in a parish of proper venue as to the defendant.
>   B. An action brought against a class shall be brought in a parish of proper venue as to any member of the class named as a defendant.

7. The complete text of Article 594 is set forth in Appendix C.
8. Article 595 of the Louisiana Code of Civil Procedure provides:

>   A. The court may allow the representative parties their reasonable expenses of litigation, including attorney's fees, when as a result of the class action a fund is made available, or a recovery or compromise is had which is beneficial, to the class.
>   B. The court, on contradictory motion at any stage of the proceeding in the trial court prior to judgment, may require the plaintiff in a class action to furnish security for the court costs which a defendant may be compelled to pay. This security for costs may be increased or decreased by the court, on contradictory motion of any interested party, on a showing that the security furnished has become inadequate or excessive.

9. Article 596 of the Louisiana Code of Civil Procedure provides:

>   Liberative prescription on the claims arising out of the transactions or occurrences described in a petition brought on behalf of a class is suspended on the filing of the petition as to all members of the class as defined or described therein. Prescription which has been suspended as provided herein, begins to run again:
>   (1) As to any person electing to be excluded from the class, from the submission of that person's election form;
>   (2) As to any person excluded from the class pursuant to Article 592, thirty days after mailing or other delivery or publication of a notice to such person that the class has been restricted or otherwise redefined so as to exclude him; or
>   (3) As to all members, thirty days after mailing or other delivery or publication of a notice to the class that the action has been dismissed, that the demand for class relief has been stricken pursuant to Article 592, or that the court has denied a motion to certify the class or has vacated a previous order certifying the class.

10. Article 597 of the Louisiana Code of Civil Procedure provides:

>   A definitive judgment on the merits rendered in a class action concludes all members of the class, whether joined in the action or not, if the members who were joined as parties fairly insured adequate representation of all members of the class.

of Rule 23 for guidance.[11] While modeled on the federal statute, Louisiana's code articles governing class actions are different in a number of ways from Rule 23. The primary differences are discussed below.

A. ARTICLE 591(A)(5)

Article 591(A)(5) adds a fifth requirement to Rule 23(a)'s four enumerated predicates to class certification—numerosity, commonality, typicality, and adequate representation. Specifically, Article 591(A)(5) provides that "[t]he class is or may be defined objectively in terms of ascertainable criteria, such that the court may determine the constituency of the class for purposes of the conclusiveness of any judgment that may be rendered in the case." This requirement is referred to in the Louisiana jurisprudence as "identifiability"[12] or the "objectively definable class" requirement.[13] It amounts simply to a requirement that the class be adequately defined. It should be noted that, while not expressly set forth in Rule 23(a), the requirement that the class be adequately defined is found elsewhere in Rule 23 and is addressed in federal jurisprudence.[14]

Despite the language of Article 591(A)(5), some Louisiana appellate courts have relied on the authority of the trial court to redefine the class after an initial ruling on certification[15] to permit class certification notwithstanding a finding that the class definition is inadequate.[16] Other Louisiana courts have refused to certify the proposed class when the class definition failed to "ensure that the class is not amorphous, indeterminate, or vague, so that any potential class members can readily determine if he/she is a member of the class."[17]

---

11. *Ford v. Murphy Oil U.S.A., Inc.*, 96-2913 (La. 9/9/97); 703 So. 2d 542, 546; *Stevens v. Bd. of Trs. of Police Pension Fund*, 309 So. 2d 144, 151 (La. 1975); *Howard v. Willis-Knighton Med. Ctr.*, 40,634, p. 8 (La. App. 2 Cir. 3/8/06); 924 So. 2d 1245, 1252; *Duhé v. Texaco, Inc.*, 1999-2002, p. 11 (La. App. 3 Cir. 2/7/01); 779 So. 2d 1070, 1078, *writ denied*, 2001-0637 (La. 4/27/01); 791 So. 2d 637; *see also Banks v. New York Life Ins. Co.*, 1998-0551, pp. 7–8 (La. 7/2/99); 737 So. 2d 1275, 1280.

12. *Howard*, 40,634, p. 27 (La. App. 2 Cir. 3/8/06); 924 So. 2d 1245, 1260, *writ denied*, 2006-850 (La. 6/14/06); 929 So. 2d 1268 and 2006-1064 (La. 6/14/06); 929 So. 2d 1271.

13. *Display S., Inc. v. Graphics House Sports Promotions, Inc.*, 2007-0925 (La. App. 1 Cir. 6/6/08); 992 So. 2d 510, 518.

14. *See* FED. R. CIV. P. 23(c)(1)(B) and (c)(3); 7A CHARLES A. WRIGHT, ARTHUR R. MILLER & MARY K. KANE, FEDERAL PRACTICE AND PROCEDURE § 1760 (3d ed. 1998); *see also* MANUAL FOR COMPLEX LITIGATION (FOURTH) § 21.222 (2004) (addressing the need for a "precise, objective, and presently ascertainable" class definition).

15. *See* LA. CODE CIV. PROC. art. 592(A)(3)(c).

16. *See, e.g., Chalona v. La. Citizens Prop. Ins. Corp.*, 2008-0257, pp. 10–12 (La. App. 4 Cir. 6/11/08); 3 So. 3d 494, 503 (citing *Duhé*, 1999-2002, pp. 14–15 (La. App. 3 Cir. 2/7/01); 779 So. 2d 1070, 1080, *writ denied*, 2001-0637 (La. 4/27/01); 791 So. 2d 637).

17. *Bourgeois v. A.P. Green Indus., Inc.*, 06-87, p. 11 (La. App. 5 Cir. 7/28/06); 939 So. 2d 478, 492, *writ denied*, 2006-2159 (La. 12/8/06); 943 So.2d 1095 (citing *Clement v. Occidental Chem. Corp.*, 97-246 (La. App. 5 Cir. 9/17/97); 699 So. 2d 1110, 1113). In *Bourgeois*, the trial court found improper the use of the term "significant exposure" in the class definition, observing that the term made it difficult to distinguish members of the class from the many former workers who may not have been exposed to asbestos, and that

B. ARTICLE 591(B)(3)

Article 591(B)(3) employs nearly identical language to its federal counterpart, Rule 23(b)(3). However, Louisiana's rule lists two additional factors not mentioned in the federal Rule:

> (e) the practical ability of individual class members to pursue their claims without class certification; [and]

> (f) the extent to which the relief plausibly demanded on behalf or against the class, including the vindication of such public policies or legal rights as may be implicated, justifies the costs and burdens of class action[.][18]

Despite the inclusion of these factors, the "predominance" and "superiority" analyses of Louisiana courts seem to differ little from those of the federal courts. Louisiana courts interpreting these "additional" factors have utilized federal jurisprudence in their analyses.[19] And, as the list of factors under Rule 23(b)(3) is "nonexhaustive" and federal courts may consider any factors relevant to the predominance and superiority determination,[20] federal courts have routinely considered in their analyses issues very similar to those raised by Louisiana's Article 591(B)(3)(e) and (f).[21]

C. ARTICLE 591(C)

Article 591(C)'s provision that "[c]ertification should not be for the purpose of adjudicating claims or defenses dependent for their resolution on proof individual to a member of the class" has no express analogue in Rule 23.

The proscription appears to address what has been described as a prior willingness of some Louisiana courts to "divvy up essential elements of a liability case for separate trials"[22] under old Article 593.1 (repealed in 1997). However, while Rule 23 does not contain similar language, it is doubtful that the language in Article

---

former workers had difficulty understanding whether they were members of the proposed class. The appellate court noted that "multiple classes more narrowly and specifically defined may overcome this issue." *Bourgeois*, 939 So. 2d at 492.

18. LA. CODE CIV. PROC. art. 591(B)(3)(e) & (f).

19. *See Martello v. City of Ferriday*, 2001-1240 (La. App. 3 Cir. 3/6/02); 813 So. 2d 467 (citing *Amchem Prods., Inc. v. Windsor*, 521 U.S. 591 (1997)); *see also Daniels v. Witco Corp.*, 03-1478 (La. App. 5 Cir. 6/1/04); 877 So. 2d 1011.

20. *See Amchem*, 521 U.S. at 615.

21. *See id.* (noting that the most dominant reason for a Rule 23(b)(3) class action is the vindication of the rights of groups of persons with negative value claims); *Bayridge Volvo Am., Inc. v. Volvo Cars of N. Am., Inc.*, No. 01-Civ.-1890-RMB(KNF), 2004 WL 1824379 (S.D.N.Y. 2004) (taking into consideration the practical ability of individual class members to pursue claims without certification); *In re Gen. Motors Corp. Engine Interchange Litig.*, 594 F.2d 1106 (7th Cir. 1979) (noting that the purpose of the class action device is to vindicate the interests of the victims of mass production wrongs and that, unless the anticipated recovery justifies the cost, the aggrieved person will not seek to vindicate his rights).

22. Kupperman & Radlauer, *supra* note 3, at 2073–78.

591(C) represents a meaningful departure from federal law. For example, in *Ford v. Murphy Oil U.S.A., Inc.*,[23] the Louisiana Supreme Court, after discussing with approval the U.S. Supreme Court's analysis in *Amchem Products, Inc. v. Windsor*[24] under federal law, held that under Louisiana law only mass torts arising from a "common cause or disaster" could be brought as a class action.[25] This analysis "was inherently based on the fact that causation is an essential part of the liability determination and if causation is not the same for each plaintiff, individual trials on causation could be required which would defeat the purpose of the class action device."[26]

D. ARTICLE 592(A)(1)

Article 592(A)(1) mandates that class proponents file a motion to certify the action as a class action within "ninety days after service on all adverse parties of the initial pleading demanding relief by or against a class." This article provides a more objective and arguably more restrictive time limit on proceeding with certification than found in Rule 23(c)(2), which requires that class certification be determined "[a]t an early practicable time after a person sues or is sued as a class representative."[27] Article 592(A)(1) provides expressly that the 90-day time period may be extended by stipulation of the parties or for good cause shown.

Importantly, Article 592(A)(2) provides that if the motion to certify is not filed timely under Article 591(A)(1), any adverse party may seek to have the class allegations stricken.[28] However, this article also allows stricken class allegations to be "reinstated upon a showing of good cause."[29] Louisiana appellate courts have repeatedly upheld lower court decisions striking class allegations because of the failure of class proponents to meet the deadlines set forth in Article 592(A)(1).[30]

E. ARTICLE 596

Article 596[31] provides that the statute of limitations—or liberative prescription, as it is known in Louisiana—is "suspended" during the pendency of a class action,

---

23. 96-2913 (La. 9/9/97); 703 So. 2d 542.

24. *See* 521 U.S. 591.

25. *Ford*, 703 So. 2d at 549–50.

26. *Brooks*, 2009 WL 1425972, at *7.

27. FED. R. CIV. P. 23(c)(2). Note the federal courts in Louisiana, by local rule, have incorporated into their procedures a provision virtually identical to Article 592(A)(1), although the 90-day period runs from filing rather than service. *See* D. LA. L.R. 23.1(B).

28. LA. CODE CIV. PROC. 592(A)(2).

29. *Id.*

30. *See, e.g., Sellers v. El Paso Indus. Energy, L.P.*, 08-403, pp. 6-11 (La. App. 5 Cir. 2/10/09); 8 So. 3d 723, 726–29 and the cases cited therein.

31. *See supra* note 9.

while Rule 23 is silent on the question of tolling, leaving the issue to be addressed jurisprudentially by the courts.

In *Katz v. Allstate Insurance Co.*,[32] the court found that because Article 596 does not reference limitations periods imposed by contract, the filing of a class action would not suspend a *contractual* prescriptive period.[33] A different panel of the same appellate court, however, subsequently reached a contrary conclusion in *Pitts v. Louisiana Citizens Property Insurance Corp.*[34] The *Pitts* court relied in part on the Louisiana Supreme Court's opinion in *State v. All Property & Casualty Insurance Carriers*,[35] which had found that the Louisiana legislature had constitutionally extended the prescriptive period on certain insurance claims arising from hurricanes Katrina and Rita.[36] The *Pitts* court described this conclusion as a determination "that contractual prescriptive periods can be subject to interruption."[37]

As used in Article 596, the term "suspended" is to be contrasted with "interrupted." In the case of suspension, the clock essentially stops. When the suspension ends, the prescriptive period picks up where it left off. In contrast, a prescriptive period that has been interrupted runs anew once the interruption ends. In other words, time that had accrued before the interruption is no longer counted toward the running of prescription on the claim(s).[38]

The suspension of prescription under Article 596 is effective on the filing of the petition and operates in favor of all class members. Once suspended, prescription begins to run again:

1. As to any person electing to be excluded from the class, from the submission of that person's election form;

2. As to any person excluded from the class pursuant to Article 592, 30 days after mailing or other delivery or publication of a notice to such person that the class has been restricted or otherwise redefined so as to exclude him; or

3. As to all members, 30 days after mailing or other delivery or publication of a notice to the class that the action has been dismissed, that the demand for class relief has been stricken pursuant to Article 592,[39] or that the court

---

32. 2004-1133 (La. App. 4 Cir. 2/2/05); 917 So. 2d 443.

33. Specifically in *Katz*, the contractual prescriptive period related to an insurance policy. The court was influenced by the plaintiff's filing of his own individual action after the prescriptive period lapsed, signaling he did not intend to participate in the class action.

34. 2008-1024 (La. App. 4 Cir. 1/7/09); 4 So. 3d 107, *writ denied*, 2009-0286 (La. 4/3/09); 6 So. 3d 772. Two of the judges who were on the *Katz* panel were also on the *Pitts* panel.

35. 06-2030 (La. 8/25/06); 937 So. 2d 313.

36. *Id.* at 327.

37. *Pitts*, 4 So. 3d at 110.

38. *See* LA. CIV. CODE arts. 3466 and 3472.

39. Article 596's references to Article 592 (discussed in section III.D.), particularly in Article 596(3), incorporate the concept of striking a demand for class relief if the proponents fail to timely move for

has denied a motion to certify the class or has vacated a previous order certifying the class.[40]

With the exception of a putative class member who elects to opt out of the class (where prescription begins to run again from the submission of the election form), in each of the other circumstances identified in Article 596, it is necessary to provide class members with notice in order to restart the prescriptive period. Once restarted, 30 days (after mailing or other delivery or publication) is added to the time period that had remained when prescription was suspended initially by the filing of the petition. Understanding this requirement at the outset of the suit may be important, as the cost for providing such notice could be significant.

In many instances where class allegations are dismissed prior to class certification, putative class members would likely not have received any notice of the class action and, thus, would not have actually relied upon the pendency of the class action and its tolling effect. Nevertheless, even if the putative class action was dismissed prior to certification and with no prior notice to class members, Article 596 read literally requires that notice of the dismissal be issued to putative class members to restart the running of prescription.[41]

While at the time of this writing there are no reported cases addressing the issue specifically, the language of Article 596 suggests that notice to class members under Article 596 to trigger the running of prescription delays is required even if the demand for class relief is stricken simply because of the proponent's failure to timely move for certification. Similarly, Article 596 does not expressly address the elimination of class allegations through voluntary amendment, an issue that also has not been addressed by current case law. Louisiana courts may conclude that the elimination of class allegations in this fashion should be treated no differently than the dismissal of the class action or the involuntary striking of class allegations under Article 596. If this proves to be the case, it would follow that these courts could also conclude that under these circumstances notice must be given to class members to end the tolling of prescription.[42]

---

certification. Article 592 also provides for continuation of an action between the named parties upon the court's denial of class certification, and for redefining the constituency of the class.

40. LA. CODE CIV. PROC. art. 596.

41. *See, e.g., Akins v. Parish of Jefferson*, 551 So. 2d 1331 (La. 1989) (decided under the prior law); *see also* LA. CODE CIV. PROC. art. 596.

42. At least before the 2003 amendments to Rule 23, federal courts would typically examine whether any prejudice to the class would result if voluntary dismissal without notice was allowed. *See* 4 HERBERT B. NEWBERG & ALBA CONTE, NEWBERG ON CLASS ACTIONS §§ 11:72, 11:74 (4th ed. 2008). For a case determining that no such notice is necessary under amended Rule 23(e) because it applies only to "a certified class," *see Buller v. Owner Operator Independent Driver Risk Retention Group, Inc.*, 461 F. Supp. 2d 757 (S.D. Ill. 2006).

In addition, Article 596 does not contain an express provision for extending the suspensive effect on prescription through the appeal of an order denying class certification, striking class allegations, or dismissing the class action. Presumably, if faced with the question, a Louisiana court interpreting current Article 596 would conclude that if notice of the district court's order has been provided to the class, an appeal of that order has no tolling effect. In fact, one Louisiana court applying pre–Article 596 law concluded that tolling did not continue during an appeal from an order denying certification.[43]

The requirements of Article 596 under Louisiana law would seem to contrast with the U.S. Supreme Court's pronouncement of federal law on the question of when the statute of limitations, once interrupted or suspended, begins to run again. In *Crown, Cork & Seal Co.*,[44] the Court held that under federal law the statute of limitations (prescription) on a federal cause of action is suspended upon commencement of the action, and "it remains tolled for all members of the putative class until class certification is denied."[45]

Although some federal courts have ordered that putative class members be notified of the denial of class certification in part to alleviate potential prejudice from prescription beginning to run again without their knowledge, the actual trigger for restarting the statute of limitations (prescription) remains the order denying certification.[46] In contrast, under Article 596, the trigger is notice.

Finally, the notice requirements under Louisiana law found in Article 594(A)(2) and Article 596(3) should not be confused. Article 594(A)(2) requires notice of "the *proposed* dismissal of an action *previously certified* as a class action."[47] This requirement allows class members an opportunity to object to the proposed settlement or dismissal. By contrast, Article 596(3) includes provisions to restart prescription by "notice to the class that the action *has been dismissed*," and by its terms is not limited to previously certified class actions.[48]

---

43. *See Bordelon v. City of Alexandria*, 2002-48 (La. App. 3 Cir. 7/10/02); 822 So. 2d 223, *writ denied*, 2002-2390 (La. 11/22/02); 829 So. 2d 1044 (following *Armstrong v. Martin Marietta Corp.*, 138 F.3d 1374 (11th Cir. 1998)). *But see Taylor v. United Parcel Serv., Inc.*, 554 F.3d 510 (5th Cir. 2008) (finding that although an appeal of the denial of class certification does not extend the tolling effect on the statute of limitations, an appeal of the merits dismissal of a certified class does).

44. 462 U.S. 345 (1983); *see also Am. Pipe & Constr. Co. v. Utah*, 414 U.S. 538 (1974).

45. *Crown*, 462 U.S. 354.

46. *See, e.g., Puffer v. Allstate Ins. Co.*, 614 F. Supp. 2d 905 (N.D. Ill. 2009).

47. *See* Appendix C, *infra* (emphasis added).

48. La. Code Civ. Proc. art. 596(3) (emphasis added).

IV. Class Action Settlements Under Louisiana Law—Article 591(B)(4)

Louisiana law offers a more relaxed inquiry than found under federal decisional law for certification of settlement classes. Specifically, Article 591(B)(4) allows for certification of a settlement class if the factors set forth in Article 591(A) are satisfied and "[t]he parties to a settlement request certification under Subparagraph B(3) [Louisiana's analogue to Rule 23(b)(3)] for purposes of settlement, even though the requirements of Subparagraph B(3) might not otherwise be met."[49]

The Federal Rules Advisory Committee had proposed an amendment to Rule 23(b) very similar to Article 591(B)(4), upon which Louisiana's article was modeled.[50] However, this proposed amendment was never adopted by the federal courts. As a result, Article 591(B)(4) currently stands in contrast with federal decisional law, which requires heightened scrutiny in consideration of the Rule 23(b) factors even in a class settlement context.[51]

V. Additional Provisions That Differ Between Louisiana and Federal Law

The following nuances of Louisiana's class action articles are worth mention:

- Louisiana law does not contain a provision similar to Rule 23(e)(3) that requires the party seeking settlement approval to identify any other agreements made in connection with the proposal.
- Louisiana law does not have a counterpart to Rule 23(e)(4)'s provision that in an action previously certified under Rule 23(b)(3), the court may refuse to approve a settlement that does not afford a new opportunity for class members to request exclusion. Still, it is doubtful that a Louisiana court would feel that it was without authority to impose such a requirement if it believed it to be necessary.[52]
- Article 592(A)(3)(d) provides that no class action order "shall be rendered after a judgment or partial judgment on the merits of common issues has

---

49. LA. CODE CIV. PROC. art. 591(B)(4). Prior to the 1997 amendments, at least one Louisiana appellate court had followed the guidance of the Supreme Court in *Amchem* requiring full if not heightened scrutiny of settlement classes. *White v. Gen. Motors Corp.*, 1997-1028 (La. App. 1 Cir. 6/29/98); 718 So. 2d 480.

50. The proposed (but ultimately not adopted) amendment to Rule 23 would have, like the provision Louisiana adopted, allowed for certification of a settlement class even though the requirements of Rule 23(b)(3) might not have been met for trial purposes. *Amchem*, 521 U.S. at 617–19.

51. *See, e.g., Amchem*, 521 U.S. 591, 619–21. The *Amchem* Court excepted only Rule 23(b)(3)(D) regarding manageability of the class action. *Id.* at 620.

52. *See, e.g.,* LA. CODE CIV. PROC. art. 592(E) (granting Louisiana courts broad authority over class action procedure).

been rendered against the party opposing the class and over such party's objection."[53]

- Article 592(B)(3) provides that unless the parties agree otherwise, the class proponents shall bear the expense of class notice under Article 592(B). The court may tax such expenses as costs.[54]

- Article 592(B)(2) provides more detail regarding the content of class notice than its counterpart in Rule 23(c)(2)(B); however, this additional information is what is typically expected in a federal class action notice.[55]

- Article 594(E) governing dismissal and compromise includes a provision that, in connection with a class settlement, the court having jurisdiction over the class action can approve the settlement and order the distribution of funds without the necessity of prior qualification for representatives of minors, interdicts, successions, or other incompetents or absentees, provided the court makes appropriate provisions to insure that all funds adjudicated for the benefit of such represented persons are placed in appropriate safekeeping pending the completion of appropriate qualification procedures.[56]

---

53. *Duhé*, 1999-2002 (La. App. 3 Cir. 2/7/01); 779 So.2d 1070, *writ denied*, 2001-0637 (La. 4/27/01), 791 So.2d 637. In *Duhé*, the court determined that the granting of partial summary judgment on the plaintiffs' "single business enterprise" claim did not lessen the plaintiffs' burden of proof and did not concern the merits. Therefore, the court reasoned that the ruling was not a judgment or partial judgment on the merits of a common issue for purposes of Article 592(A)(3)(d).

54. LA. CODE CIV. PROC. art. 592(B)(3).

55. *Id.* art. 592(B)(2).

56. *Id.* art. 594(E).

APPENDIX A

Article 591 provides:

A. One or more members of a class may sue or be sued as representative parties on behalf of all, only if:

(1) The class is so numerous that joinder of all members is impracticable.

(2) There are questions of law or fact common to the class.

(3) The claims or defenses of the representative parties are typical of the claims or defenses of the class.

(4) The representative parties will fairly and adequately protect the interests of the class.

(5) The class is or may be defined objectively in terms of ascertainable criteria, such that the court may determine the constituency of the class for purposes of the conclusiveness of any judgment that may be rendered in the case.

B. An action may be maintained as a class action only if all of the prerequisites of Paragraph A of this Article are satisfied, and in addition:

(1) The prosecution of separate actions by or against individual members of the class would create a risk of:

(a) Inconsistent or varying adjudications with respect to individual members of the class which would establish incompatible standards of conduct for the party opposing the class, or

(b) Adjudications with respect to individual members of the class which would as a practical matter be dispositive of the interests of the other members not parties to the adjudications or substantially impair or impede their ability to protect their interests; or

(2) The party opposing the class has acted or refused to act on grounds generally applicable to the class, thereby making appropriate final injunctive relief or corresponding declaratory relief with respect to the class as a whole; or

(3) The court finds that the questions of law or fact common to the members of the class predominate over any questions affecting only individual members, and that a class action is superior to other available methods for the fair and efficient adjudication of the controversy. The matters pertinent to these findings include:

(a) The interest of the members of the class in individually controlling the prosecution or defense of separate actions;

(b) The extent and nature of any litigation concerning the controversy already commenced by or against members of the class;

(c) The desirability or undesirability of concentrating the litigation in the particular forum;

(d) The difficulties likely to be encountered in the management of a class action;

(e) The practical ability of individual class members to pursue their claims without class certification;

(f) The extent to which the relief plausibly demanded on behalf of or against the class, including the vindication of such public policies or legal rights as may be implicated, justifies the costs and burdens of class litigation; or

(4) The parties to a settlement request certification under Subparagraph B(3) for purposes of settlement, even though the requirements of Subparagraph B(3) might not otherwise be met.

C. Certification shall not be for the purpose of adjudicating claims or defenses dependent for their resolution on proof individual to a member of the class. However, following certification, the court shall retain jurisdiction over claims or defenses dependent for their resolution on proof individual to a member of the class.[57]

---

57. *Id.* art. 591.

APPENDIX B

Article 592 provides:

A. (1) Within ninety days after service on all adverse parties of the initial pleading demanding relief on behalf of or against a class, the proponent of the class shall file a motion to certify the action as a class action. The delay for filing the motion may be extended by stipulation of the parties or on motion for good cause shown.

(2) If the proponent fails to file a motion for certification within the delay allowed by Subparagraph A(1), any adverse party may file a notice of the failure to move for certification. On the filing of such a notice and after hearing thereon, the demand for class relief may be stricken. If the demand for class relief is stricken, the action may continue between the named parties alone. A demand for class relief stricken under this Subparagraph may be reinstated upon a showing of good cause by the proponent.

(3) (a) No motion to certify an action as a class action shall be granted prior to a hearing on the motion. Such hearing shall be held as soon as practicable, but in no event before:

(i) All named adverse parties have been served with the pleading containing the demand for class relief or have made an appearance or, with respect to unserved defendants who have not appeared, the proponent of the class has made due and diligent effort to perfect service of such pleading; and

(ii) The parties have had a reasonable opportunity to obtain discovery on class certification issues, on such terms and conditions as the court deems necessary.

(b) If the court finds that the action should be maintained as a class action, it shall certify the action accordingly. If the court finds that the action should not be maintained as a class action, the action may continue between the named parties. In either event, the court shall give in writing its findings of fact and reasons for judgment provided a request is made not later than ten days after notice of the order or judgment. A suspensive or devolutive appeal, as provided in Article 2081 et seq. of the Code of Civil Procedure, may be taken as a matter of right from an order or judgment provided for herein.

(c) In the process of class certification, or at any time thereafter before a decision on the merits of the common issues, the court may alter, amend, or recall its initial ruling on certification and may enlarge, restrict, or otherwise redefine the constituency of the class or the issues to be maintained in the class action.

(d) No order contemplated in this Subparagraph shall be rendered after a judgment or partial judgment on the merits of common issues has been rendered against the party opposing the class and over such party's objection.

B. (1) In any class action maintained under Article 591(B)(3), the court shall direct to the members of the class the best notice practicable under the circumstances, including individual notice to all members who can be identified through reasonable effort. This notice, however given, shall be given as soon as practicable after certification, but in any event early enough that a delay provided for the class members to exercise an option to be excluded from the class will have expired before commencement of the trial on the merits of the common issues.

(2) The notice required by Subparagraph B(1) shall include:

(a) A general description of the action, including the relief sought, and the names and addresses of the representative parties or, where appropriate, the identity and location of the source from which the names and addresses of the representative parties can be obtained.

(b) A statement of the right of the person to be excluded from the action by submitting an election form, including the manner and time for exercising the election.

(c) A statement that the judgment, whether favorable or not, will include all members who do not request exclusion.

(d) A statement that any member who does not request exclusion may, if the member desires, enter an appearance through counsel at that member's expense.

(e) A statement advising the class member that the member may be required to take further action as the court deems necessary, such as submitting a proof of claim in order to participate in any recovery had by the class.

(f) A general description of any counterclaim brought against the class.

(g) The address of counsel to whom inquiries may be directed.

(h) Any other information that the court deems appropriate.

(3) Unless the parties agree otherwise, the proponents of the class shall bear the expense of the notification required by this Paragraph. The court may require the party opposing the class to cooperate in securing the names and addresses of the persons within the class defined by the court for the purpose of providing individual notice, but any additional costs reasonably incurred by the party opposing the class in complying with this order shall be paid by the proponent of the class. The court may tax all or part of the expenses incurred for notification as costs.

C. The judgment in an action maintained as a class action under Article 591(B) (1) or (B)(2), whether or not favorable to the class, shall include and describe those whom the court finds to be members of the class. The judgment in an action maintained as a class action under Article 591(B)(3), whether or not favorable to the class, shall include and specify or describe those to whom the notice provided in

Paragraph B was directed, and who have not requested exclusion, and whom the court finds to be members of the class.

D. When appropriate an action may be brought or maintained as a class action with respect to particular issues, or a class may be divided into subclasses and each subclass treated as a class, and the provisions of Article 591 and this Article shall then be construed and applied accordingly.

E. In the conduct of actions to which Article 591 and this Article apply, the court may make any of the following appropriate orders:

(1) Determining the course of proceedings or prescribing measures to prevent undue repetition or complication in the presentation of evidence or argument.

(2) Requiring, for the protection of the members of the class or otherwise for the fair conduct of the action, that notice be given in such manner as the court may direct to members of the class of any step in the action, or of the proposed extent of the judgment, or of the opportunity of members to signify whether they consider the representation fair and adequate, to intervene and present claims or defenses, or otherwise to come into the action.

(3) Imposing conditions on the representative parties or on intervenors.

(4) Requiring that the pleadings be amended to eliminate therefrom allegations as to representation of absent persons, and that the action proceed accordingly.

(5) Dealing with similar procedural matters, including but not limited to case management orders providing for consolidation, duties of counsel, the extent and the scheduling of and the delays for pre-certification and post-certification discovery, and other matters which affect the general order of proceedings; however, the court may not order the class-wide trial of issues dependent for their resolution on proof individual to a member of the class, including but not limited to the causation of the member's injuries, the amount of the member's special or general damages, the individual knowledge or reliance of the member, or the applicability to the member of individual claims or defenses.

(6) Any of the orders provided in this Paragraph may be combined with an order pursuant to Article 1551,[58] and may be altered or amended as may be desirable from time to time.[59]

---

58. Article 1551 of the Louisiana Code of Civil Procedure allows for pretrial scheduling conferences and orders.

59. LA. CODE CIV. PROC. art. 592.

APPENDIX C

Article 594 of the Louisiana Code of Civil Procedure provides:

A. (1) An action previously certified as a class action shall not be dismissed or compromised without the approval of the court exercising jurisdiction over the action.

(2) Notice of the proposed dismissal of an action previously certified as a class action shall be provided to all members of the class, together with the terms of any proposed compromise that the named parties have entered into. Notice shall be given in such manner as the court directs.

B. After notice of the proposed compromise has been provided to the members of the class, the court shall order a hearing to determine whether the proposed compromise is fair, reasonable, and adequate for the class. At such hearing, all parties to the action, including members of the class, shall be permitted an opportunity to be heard.

C. The court shall retain the authority to review and approve any amount paid as attorney fees pursuant to the compromise of a class action, notwithstanding any agreement to the contrary.

D. Any agreement entered by the parties to a class action that provides for the payment of attorney fees is subject to judicial approval.

E. If the terms of the proposed compromise provide for the adjudged creation of a settlement fund to be disbursed to and among members of the class in accordance with the terms thereof, the court having jurisdiction over the class action is empowered to approve the compromise settlement of the class action as a whole and issue a final judgment accordingly, following a finding that the compromise is fair, reasonable, and adequate for the class, and to order the distribution of the settlement fund accordingly, without the necessity of prior qualification of representatives of minors, interdicts, successions, or other incompetents or absentees, or prior approval of the terms of the settlement or the distribution thereof by another court; provided, that in such cases the court having jurisdiction over the class action shall include in the orders of settlement and distribution of the settlement fund appropriate provisions to ensure that all funds adjudicated to or for the benefit of such incompetents, successions, or absentees are placed in appropriate safekeeping pending the completion of appointment, qualification, and administrative procedures otherwise applicable in this Code to the interests and property of incompetents, successions, and absentees.[60]

---

60. *Id.* art. 594.

MAINE

DAVID W. BERTONI
STACY O. STITHAM

I. Introduction

Class actions in Maine are governed by Rule 23 of the Maine Rules of Civil Procedure (Maine Rule), which is based on its federal counterpart, Rule 23 of the Federal Rules of Civil Procedure. While the rules are substantially similar, there are important distinctions of which the practitioner should be aware. Moreover, Maine courts do not have substantial experience in class action lawsuits, obligating practitioners on both sides of each case to be especially mindful of procedural nuances. Often, the only guidance that can be obtained is in unreported decisions of the Superior Court.[1]

In addition to the differences set forth below, the Maine Rule contains *no* provisions for appeals, class counsel, or attorney fees and nontaxable costs. Faced with no guidance in the Rule regarding appeals, the Maine Supreme Judicial Court held that class certification orders are generally not appealable on an interlocutory basis under any of the recognized exceptions to the final judgment rule.[2] This is in

---

1. *See, e.g., Karofsky v. Abbott Labs.*, No. CV-95-1009, 1997 WL 34504652 (Me. Super. 2007) (noting that Maine's highest court "has not had an opportunity to opine in detail regarding the prerequisites to class certification"). Twelve years after *Karofsky*, there remain no reported Maine decisions on that issue. *Karofsky*, written by the judge who is now the Chief Judge of the Maine Supreme Judicial Court, represents the best available guidance for Maine practitioners on the nuances of certification, including issues of numerosity, typicality, adequacy of representation, predominance, and manageability. *See Millett v. Atl. Richfield Co.*, No. Civ. A CV-98-555, 2000 WL 359979 (Me. Super. 2000) (applying *Karofsky* and justifying reliance on federal case law because of the similarity of the rules and "the almost complete lack of Maine case law on class actions"); *see also Pease v. Jaspar Wyman & Son*, No. Civ. A CV-00-015, 2002 WL 1974081 (Me. 2000).

2. *Millett v. Atl. Richfield Co.*, 2000 Me. 178, 760 A.2d 250 (2000) (recognizing the split in state authority on the question). The *Millett* court did open the door to possible appeals where it could be shown that the named plaintiffs' claims are "so small or because their resources are too minimal to allow them to proceed in the absence of the prospect of class recovery." *Id.* at ¶ 13.

contrast with Federal Rule 23(f), which empowers the federal circuit courts of appeal to grant permission to a party to appeal within 14 days from a class certification decision.

II. Prerequisites to Class Certification

This provision is identical to its federal counterpart. Although there are no reported decisions in Maine on the requirements of Maine Rule 23(a) or (b), the trial courts have required that plaintiffs "show under a strict burden of proof that they have satisfied the requirements of Rule 23" in consumer products class action cases.[3]

III. Class Actions Maintainable

This provision is identical to its federal counterpart.

IV. Determination by Order Whether Class Action to Be Maintained, Notice, Judgment, and Actions Conducted Partially as Class Actions

Under Maine Rule 23(c)(1), a certification order may be altered or amended *before the decision on the merits*—in contrast to federal law which, under Federal Rule 23(c)(1)(c), permits the order to be altered or amended at any time before *final judgment*. In addition, the Maine Rule does not contain *any* express requirements for the content of the class certification order as found in Federal Rule 23(c)(1)(B). The content of the order is left to the discretion of the trial court, and it is essential that, to the extent the court deems it appropriate, proposed orders reflect the fundamental matters set out in the Federal Rule, including the definition of the class, the issues at stake, defenses, and the appointment of class counsel.

Under Maine Rule 23(c)(2), requirements as to the issuance and content of class notice are far less precise than those of Federal Rule 23(c)(2)(B). Again, practitioners are advised to review the Federal Rule to determine any other categories of information that would be prudent to include in the notice, including, but not limited to, the nature of the action and the definition of the certified class. Moreover, the Maine Rule on notice is limited to actions arising under Maine Rule 23(b)(3) and fails to address the appropriate content of notices to classes arising

---

3. *See, e.g., Melnick v. Microsoft Corp.*, Nos. CV-99-709; CV-99-752, 2001 WL 1012261 (Me. Super. 2001). In *Melnick*, the trial judge reasoned that this strict burden of proof was necessary because "certification [of] mass tort actions dramatically affects stakes for defendants, strengthens the numbers of unmeritorious claims, results in significantly higher damage awards, and creates 'insurmountable pressure on defendants to settle.'" *Id.* at *16 (citing *Millett*, 2000 WL 359979, at *18–19).

under subsections 23(b)(1) and (b)(2), giving the courts even broader discretion as to what constitutes appropriate notice in such cases.

V. Orders in Conduct of Action

This provision is identical to its federal counterpart.

VI. Dismissal or Settlement

Unlike its federal counterpart, Maine Rule 23(e) contains no guidance at all governing the approval of any notice of dismissal or settlement except by noting that any such action must be approved by the court and notice given "in such manner as the court directs." In contrast, Federal Rule 23(e) requires binding orders to be approved after a hearing and based on a finding that the resolution was fair and adequate, and it also provides a mechanism for class member objections, among other things.

MARYLAND

SCOTT H. MARDER[1]

I. Introduction

This chapter examines and compares the federal and Maryland class action rules, focusing on the distinctions and nuances between the two bodies of law. The chart at the end of the chapter is a summary of Maryland's class action law with useful citations to authority.

II. Maryland Rule 2-231

In 1984, Maryland performed a wholesale revision of the Maryland Rules, including former class action rule 209, which became Maryland Rule 2-231 (Rule 2-231). Rule 2-231 was derived from the 1966 version of Federal Rule of Civil Procedure 23. Since its adoption, Maryland appellate courts have had limited opportunity to interpret the class action rule. Nonetheless, Maryland appellate courts have looked to federal and other state courts' analyses of the specific requirements for class certification under similar or identical class action rules.[2] The Court of Appeals of Maryland has stated that analysis of Maryland's rule "shall be informed by cases interpreting Federal Rule 23 and other analogous state rules outlining class certification requirements."[3] Although Maryland authority directly addressing Rule 2-231 is sparse, substantial guidance can be found in two leading Maryland Court

---

1. The author would like to thank Laurie Goon for her hard work and assistance on this chapter. Laurie is a third-year law student at the University of Maryland, and is expected to receive her J.D. in 2010.

2. *See Creveling v. Gov't Employees Ins. Co.*, 828 A.2d 229, 239 n.4 (Md. 2003) (noting that decisions as to the construction of Rule 2-231 "shall be informed by cases interpreting Federal Rule 23 and other analogous state rules outlining class certification requirements").

3. *See id.*

of Appeals cases, *Creveling v. Government Employees Insurance Co.*[4] and *Philip Morris, Inc., v. Angeletti.*[5]

III. Statutory Construction

Every subsection of Rule 2-231, other than subsection (g) dealing with discovery, was derived in whole or in part from the 1966 version of Federal Rule 23.[6] Although based on the 1966 Federal Rule, the Maryland rule differs, both structurally and substantively, in various respects discussed herein. Rule 2-231 is specifically derived as follows:

- Section (a) is derived from the 1966 version of Federal Rule 23(a) and former Rule 209(a).
- Section (b) is derived from the 1966 version of Federal Rule 23(b)(1), (2), and (3).
- Section (c) is derived from the 1966 version of Federal Rule 23(c)(1).
- Section (d) is derived from the 1966 version of Federal Rule 23(c)(4).
- Section (e) is derived from the 1966 version of Federal Rule 23(c)(2).
- Section (f) is derived from the 1966 version of Federal Rule 23(d).
- Section (g) is new.
- Section (h) is derived from the 1966 version of Federal Rule 23(e) and former Rule 209(d).
- Section (i) is derived from the 1966 version of Federal Rule 23(c)(3).

Among the federal courts, the general trend has been to liberally construe Rule 23.[7] Although the Court of Appeals of Maryland has held that Rule 2-231 is to be "informed" by federal precedent, the Court of Special Appeals of Maryland has stated that Maryland has rejected liberal constructions of the class action rule applied by certain federal and state courts.[8] Instead, Maryland follows a more exacting and conservative analysis of the class certification requirements under its interpretation of Rule 2-231.[9] Maryland courts have not yet resolved this seeming incongruity, although their decisions continue to look to federal case law with approval when interpreting Rule 2-231.

---

4. *Id.*

5. 752 A.2d 200 (Md. 2000).

6. *See* MD. R. 2-231.

7. *Kidwell v. Transp. Commc'ns Int'l Union*, 946 F.2d 283, 305 (4th Cir. 1991); *Cutler v. Wal-Mart*, 927 A.2d 1, 14 (Md. Ct. Spec. App. 2007).

8. *Cutler*, 927 A.2d at 14.

9. *Id.*

IV. Discovery

In adopting its version of the 1966 Federal Rule 23, Maryland added subsection (g) to Rule 2-231 governing discovery. For purposes of discovery, Rule 2-231(g) presumptively treats only the class representatives as parties to the suit.[10] The putative class members are not required to respond to discovery requests, other than as nonparties.[11] Any party opposing the class may seek an order to obtain discovery from putative class members.[12] Maryland's appellate courts have not yet addressed under what circumstances such a motion should be granted or denied by the trial court. However, Maryland courts will likely look to federal precedent to determine whether to permit discovery of class members.[13]

Rule 23 contains no explicit discovery provision, and there is some disagreement in the federal courts on the extent of discovery permitted of absent class members.[14] In *Brennan v. Midwestern United Life Insurance Co.*,[15] the court permitted discovery of members of a class and held that discovery should be allowed from absent class members when such discovery is necessary or helpful to the proper presentation and correct adjudication of the principal suit, and adequate precautionary measures are taken to ensure that the absent members are not misled or confused. On the other hand, other federal courts have refused to treat class members as parties for purposes of discovery.[16] In *Wainwright v. Kraftco Corp.*, the court noted that the usefulness of Rule 23 would end if class members were subjected to party discovery and were forced to spend time, and perhaps retain counsel, to answer detailed interrogatories.[17] The *Wainwright* court expressed additional concern that dismissing with prejudice nonparty class members who had not responded to interrogatories would present "serious constitutional problems."[18]

---

10. MD. R. 2-231(g); JOHN A. LYNCH, JR. & RICHARD W. BOURNE, MODERN MARYLAND CIVIL PROCEDURE 4-98 (2d ed. LexisNexis Matthew Bender 2004).

11. MD. R. 2-231(g).

12. *Id.*

13. LYNCH & BOURNE, *supra* note 10.

14. HERBERT B. NEWBERG & ALBA CONTE, NEWBERG ON CLASS ACTIONS § 16:3 (4th ed. 2002) [hereinafter NEWBERG]; LYNCH & BOURNE, *supra* note 10 (citing 7B CHARLES A. WRIGHT & ARTHUR K. MILLER, FEDERAL PRACTICE AND PROCEDURE § 1796.1 (2d ed. 1986)).

15. 450 F.2d 999 (7th Cir. 1971).

16. *See Wainwright v. Kraftco Corp.*, 54 F.R.D. 532 (N.D. Ga. 1972); *Fischer v. Wolfinbarger*, 55 F.R.D. 129 (W.D. Ky. 1971).

17. 54 F.R.D. at 534.

18. *Id.*

V. Class Certification

Rule 2-231 contains a number of substantive differences from Rule 23 in its procedure for class certification. Although Rule 2-231(b) is derived from Rule 23(b), Maryland accords trial courts extra discretionary power in determining class certification. Specifically, Rule 2-231(b) provides that an action may be maintained as a class action if the prerequisites are met, "unless justice requires otherwise." The federal rule contains no such additional language. While this language appears to provide an additional basis for denying class certification, Maryland's appellate courts have not yet interpreted this provision.

Another difference involves the timing of class certification. In 2003, Rule 23(c)(1)(A) was amended to provide that the court should determine whether the suit will be maintained as a class action, "at an early practicable time." The 2003 amendment effectively relaxed the time frame for class certification in federal court.[19] According to the Advisory Committee, time may be needed to gather information necessary to make the certification decision, to explore designation of class counsel, or to allow the party opposing the class sufficient time to win dismissal or summary judgment.[20] The Advisory Committee notes recognized that active case management may be necessary to ensure that the certification decision is not unjustifiably delayed.

Maryland has made no such amendment to its corollary provision.[21] Continuing to adhere to the 1966 version of Rule 23, Rule 2-231(c) states that the court shall determine "as soon as practicable" whether the suit should be maintained as a class action. Ordinarily in Maryland, when a motion for class certification is pending, the maintainability of a lawsuit as a class action should be determined before any substantive issue in the case is decided.[22] Following the amendment to Rule 23, Maryland has not addressed whether the new federal rule creates a distinguishable difference in the timing of the ruling on class certification.

Maryland and federal class action law also provide potentially different procedures for class certification hearings. Pursuant to Rule 2-231(c), Maryland courts are required to hold a hearing on the issue of class certification at the request of either party. Rule 23(c)(1) contains no such requirement. In addition, Rule 2-231(c) specifically permits the court to determine on its own motion whether a suit should be certified as a class action. Although federal law provides that the party seeking certification must demonstrate that a suit warrants class action certification,[23]

---

19. FED. R. CIV. P. 23 advisory committee note (2003).
20. *Id.*
21. MD. R. 2-231(c).
22. *See Kirkpatrick v. Gilchrist*, 467 A.2d 562, 566 (Md. Ct. Spec. App. 1983).
23. *See, e.g., Carracter v. Morgan*, 491 F.2d 458, 459 (4th Cir. 1973).

there is a split in the federal circuits as to whether the court may also certify a class on its own motion.[24]

VI. Interlocutory Appeals

Another significant difference between federal and Maryland class action law is in the area of interlocutory appeals from class certification orders. The 1998 amendment to Rule 23 permits the federal courts of appeal to hear interlocutory appeals of district court orders granting or denying class certification.[25] Maryland, in contrast, ordinarily does not permit interlocutory appeals from class certification orders.[26] In the decade since the amendment of Rule 23, the Court of Appeals of Maryland has not amended Maryland's class certification rule to authorize interlocutory appeals.[27]

The Court of Special Appeals of Maryland, however, has explicitly recognized that Rule 23 was amended to authorize federal courts of appeal to permit interlocutory appeals from class certification orders.[28] In *Royal Financial Services v. Eason*,[29] the plaintiff filed a class action complaint seeking damages from Royal Financial Services, Inc., for allegedly violating Maryland's mortgage laws. The trial court certified the case as a class action, and Royal Financial Services appealed the class certification order. The court of special appeals dismissed the appeal based on lack of jurisdiction, noting that the court of appeals "has shown no inclination to change [Maryland's] existing law" on interlocutory appeals.[30] In a subsequent case, the court of special appeals carved out an exception, holding that an order determining the sufficiency of class notice constitutes a final, appealable order for purposes of the final judgment rule.[31]

In an unusual case, expressly limited to its facts, the Court of Appeals of Maryland issued a writ of mandamus, directing a trial court to vacate its class certification order in a mass tobacco litigation case.[32] In *Angeletti*, the court took this unusual step based on the "unique factual circumstances and procedural nature"[33] of the case, where the court had significant concerns over predominance, manageability, and the extreme burden the case would place on the busiest circuit court in Maryland.

---

24. NEWBERG § 7:6, p. 18–19.
25. FED. R. CIV. P. 23(f).
26. *Royal Fin. Servs. v. Eason*, 961 A.2d 1161, 1164 (Md. Ct. Spec. App. 2008).
27. *Id.* at 1164 n.2.
28. *Id.*
29. *Id.* at 1162.
30. *Id.* at 1164 n.2.
31. *Anne Arundel County, Md. v. Cambridge Commons*, 892 A.2d 593, 598 (Md. Ct. Spec. App. 2005).
32. *Angeletti*, 752 A.2d at 254.
33. *Id.* at 218.

VII. Notice

Rule 23(c)(2) outlines the federal requirements for notice to class members. The federal rule is more specific and detailed than the corollary Maryland provision, Rule 2-231(e). Rule 23(c)(2) provides that the court direct "the best notice practicable under the circumstances," including individual notice attempts to all members who can be "identified through reasonable effort." In contrast, the Maryland Rule simply provides that notice be accomplished "in the manner the court directs."[34] Under federal practice, Rule 23(c)(2) has been controversial because individual notice to a large class may be quite expensive.[35] The difference between the Maryland and federal rules in this respect appears to represent an attempt by the Maryland Standing Committee on the Rules of Practice and Procedure to avoid the "political" issue of notice that has arisen in federal practice.[36]

Although Rule 2-231(e) is not as specific as the federal notice rule, in *Anne Arundel County, Maryland v. Cambridge Commons*[37] the Court of Special Appeals of Maryland looked to federal precedent in interpreting Maryland's notice requirements. As with federal practice, the court of special appeals acknowledged the general rule that the cost and resulting task of effecting class notification rests on the plaintiff. However, the court noted that this burden is not absolute. In some instances, the defendant may be able to perform a necessary task with less difficulty or expense than could the representative plaintiff.[38] In such cases, the trial court may properly exercise its discretion to order the defendant to perform the task in question.[39]

VIII. Federal Provisions Absent from Rule 2-231

A. CLASS COUNSEL

In 2003, Rule 23 was amended to include subsection (g), which provides additional requirements for the appointment and conduct of class counsel, in addition to those found in Rule 23(a)(4). Maryland continues to scrutinize class counsel solely under Rule 2-231(a)(4),[40] which requires that "the representative parties will fairly and adequately protect the interests of the class." In assessing the adequacy of class

---

34. MD. R. 2-231(e).

35. LYNCH & BOURNE, *supra* note 10, at 4-96 n.569.

36. *Id.*

37. 892 A.2d at 601–04.

38. *Id.*

39. *Id.* at 603.

40. *Angeletti*, 752 A.2d at 228 (stating that the adequacy of representation prerequisite ensures that both the class representatives and class counsel are adequate to represent the interests of all class members).

counsel, Maryland courts look to counsel's vigor, experience, and diligence.[41] No Maryland case has yet addressed the additional language in Rule 23(g).

B. ATTORNEY FEES AND NONTAXABLE COSTS

The 2003 amendments to Rule 23 also added subsection (h), which governs fee awards that were previously addressed under Rule 54(d)(2).[42] The new federal subsection, however, did not create new grounds for an award of attorney fees or nontaxable costs. Maryland has made no similar amendment, and Maryland's appellate courts have not addressed the additional language in the federal rule.

IX. Miscellaneous Issues

A. TOLLING OF STATUTE OF LIMITATIONS

American Pipe & Construction Co. v. Utah[43] is currently the leading federal case on the class action tolling doctrine. The majority of states with class action rules similar to Rule 23 have followed *American Pipe* and endorsed a class action tolling rule.[44] The Court of Appeals of Maryland has recognized that "[s]tate court opinions endorsing *American Pipe* class action tolling and lower federal court opinions applying it, however, vary in terms of their depth of treatment, and, most significantly, in terms of the emphasis they place on ensuring that *American Pipe* is applied consistently with the purposes of statutes of limitations."[45]

In *Philip Morris USA, Inc. v. Christensen*,[46] the Court of Appeals of Maryland addressed whether to permit tolling of statutes of limitation, in accordance with the practice of the federal courts following *American Pipe*. The court of appeals adopted the federal tolling doctrine, holding that the pendency of a putative class action tolls the statute of limitations on the causes of action asserted in the class action complaint for the putative plaintiff class members, but only when the class action complaint gives the defendants in the class action complaint fair notice of the claims of the putative class members who claim the benefits of tolling. Thus, the court of appeals agreed with the U.S. Supreme Court's holding in *American Pipe* that "the commencement of a class action suspends the applicable statute of limitations as to all asserted members of the class who would have been parties had the suit been permitted to continue as a class action."[47]

---

41. *Id.*
42. Fed. R. Civ. P. 23 advisory committee note (2003).
43. 414 U.S. 538 (1974).
44. *Philip Morris USA, Inc. v. Christensen*, 905 A.2d 340, 354 (Md. 2006).
45. *Id.*
46. *Id.*
47. *Id.* at 352 (citing *Am. Pipe*, 414 U.S. at 554).

The court of appeals also held that the class action tolling doctrine must be applied in a manner consistent with the purposes of statutes of limitations,[48] meaning that the original class action complaint must provide the defendants with notice of the "number and generic identity of the potential plaintiffs."[49] The court of appeals rejected the defendants' argument that "mass torts" should be excluded from the class action tolling doctrine because there was no reason to assume that individual plaintiffs would be unable to meet the notice requirement in such cases.[50]

B. MASS TORT ACTIONS

The federal Advisory Committee warned federal courts that mass accidents resulting in injuries to numerous persons are ordinarily not appropriate for class action treatment.[51] Some federal and state courts have adhered to this commentary and refused to certify mass tort class actions.[52] Many other federal courts, although showing a conceptual reluctance toward certifying mass tort litigation, have, when deemed appropriate, certified classes in mass tort litigation.[53]

In *Angeletti*, the Court of Appeals of Maryland determined that there was no per se prohibition against mass-tort class action suits in Maryland, holding that Maryland would "abide by the view that courts should decide whether to certify a class action in mass tort litigation on a case-by-case basis."[54] Notwithstanding, the court of appeals issued a writ of mandamus directing the trial court to decertify the class, holding that issues of predominance, manageability, and superiority precluded certification. In this mass tobacco litigation case, the potential class consisted of tens of thousands of members, each of whom would have had to establish individual reliance to prevail. The trial court would also have had to conduct an individual choice of law analysis for each class member. Additionally, the court of appeals was concerned that a class action was not the proper vehicle for adjudicating an "immature tort" of medical monitoring, which was not yet recognized in Maryland.[55] Finally, the court of appeals expressed concern with the great burden this size class action would place on Maryland's busiest circuit court, in Baltimore City.

---

48. *Id.*

49. *Id.* at 357 (quoting *Am. Pipe*, 414 U.S. at 555).

50. *Id.* at 360.

51. FED. R. CIV. P. 23 advisory committee note (1966).

52. *Angeletti*, 752 A.2d at 221.

53. *Id.* at 222 (citing *Castano v. Am. Tobacco Co.*, 84 F.3d 734, 746–48 n.23 (5th Cir. 1996)).

54. *Id.*

55. *Id.* at 243–44.

C. ARBITRATION

Both federal and Maryland law favor arbitration agreements.[56] The majority of federal courts enforce arbitration clauses that bar class actions.[57] A minority of federal courts, however, refuse to enforce such provisions.[58] Maryland courts follow the majority view and will enforce contractual arbitration clauses that bar class action lawsuits.[59] The court of appeals has held that such arbitration clauses are not unconscionable and that Maryland's courts cannot ignore the strong public policy favoring the enforcement of arbitration agreements.[60]

D. AGGREGATION OF CLAIMS

Maryland appellate courts have opined on a number of issues that, although not directly distinct from federal law, help to clarify class action law in Maryland. As with federal practice, aggregation of individual claims to satisfy the amount-in-controversy requirement is permitted in Maryland where plaintiffs seek to enforce a joint, common, and single title or right in which they have common and undivided interest.[61]

E. SPECIAL MASTERS

Maryland has also recognized the use of special masters in class action proceedings.[62] Maryland has permitted the appointment of special masters to handle a number of matters, including making recommendations on attorney fees and expenses; issuing subpoenas to compel the attendance of witnesses and the production of documents; administering oaths; ruling on the admissibility of evidence; examining witnesses; convening and adjourning hearings; recommending contempt proceedings; and making recommended findings of fact and conclusions of law.[63]

F. PUNITIVE DAMAGES

With respect to determining punitive damages in a mass tort action, the Court of Appeals of Maryland has held that a class action jury may not award punitive damages based on a multiplier of individual, putative class members' compensatory

---

56. *Walther v. Sovereign Bank*, 872 A.2d 735, 750–51 (Md. 2005).

57. *See Snowden v. Checkpoint Check Cashing*, 290 F.3d 631, 638 (4th Cir. 2002).

58. *See Ting v. AT&T*, 319 F.3d 1126, 1150 (9th Cir. 2003) (applying California unconscionability law); *Walther*, 872 A.2d at 750–51.

59. *Walther*, 872 A.2d at 751.

60. *Id.*

61. MD. CODE ANN., CTS. & JUD. P. § 4-402(d)(1) (LexisNexis 2008 Supp.).

62. *See, e.g., Boyd v. Bell Atl.-Md., Inc.*, 887 A.2d 637, 648 (Md. 2005).

63. *Id.*

damages, which are not determined until later by second juries in individual trials for class members.[64] The court held that

> [a]llowing a single jury to set irrevocably the amount of punitive damages to be imposed relative to and on behalf of several, let alone thousands of individuals, whose actual damages are themselves determined separately from each other, does not enable the jury to properly assess the amount of punitive damages that are appropriate in specific relation to differing amounts of—and reasons for—actual damages.[65]

X. Conclusion

Maryland's class action law closely follows federal law in most respects. However, the practitioner must take care to identify those areas where Maryland and federal class action law diverge. Keeping this in mind, an experienced practitioner should be able to successfully handle class action matters in Maryland state courts.

---

64. *Angeletti*, 752 A.2d at 246.

65. *Id.* at 249.

SUMMARY OF MARYLAND CLASS ACTION LAW

Issue	Maryland Law[63]
RELATION TO FEDERAL LAW	The Maryland class action rule, enacted in 1984, is derived from the 1966 version of Federal Rule 23.[64] There is limited authority in Maryland analyzing the specific requirements of Rule 2-231. Maryland courts look to federal practice and state court decisions based on analogous rules for guidance in interpreting Rule 2-231.[65]
STATUTORY CONSTRUCTION	Unlike some federal circuits, Maryland does not liberally construe the class certification requirements.[66] Rather, Maryland requires a more exacting analysis. In Maryland, there is no statutory or constitutional right to pursue a class action. Rule 2-231 is simply "a procedural device, created by the judiciary's adoption of a court rule to facilitate management of multiple similar claims."[67]
CHOICE OF LAW	Trial courts must engage in an individualized choice of law assessment for each class member.[68] Maryland is in the minority of states that follow the *lex loci delecti* rule for analyzing choice of law issues for torts.[69]
AMOUNT-IN-CONTROVERSY STANDARD	Maryland law permits the aggregation of separate claims of proposed members of a class to meet the minimum amount in controversy in the circuit courts.[70]
PRECERTIFICATION DISCOVERY	See "Discovery from Class Members" below.

63. Italicized text below contains the actual language of Maryland Rule 2-231.
64. *Cambridge Commons*, 892 A.2d at 596.
65. *Angeletti*, 752 A.2d at 219.
66. *Cutler*, 927 A.2d at 14.
67. *Id.* at 7.
68. *Angeletti*, 752 A.2d at 232.
69. *Id.* at 230.
70. Md. Code Ann., Cts. & Jud. P. § 4-402(d)(ii) (LexisNexis 2008 Supp.).

Issue

Maryland Law

PRECERTIFICATION GENERALLY

Rule 2-231 sets forth several prerequisites that must be satisfied before a trial court may certify a class, all of which track the requirements found in Rule 23. Rule 2-231(a) presents the four threshold requirements of numerosity, commonality, typicality, and adequacy of representation. The requirements are necessary but not alone sufficient; a putative class must also fall into one of the three subcategories of Rule 2-231(b).[71] Rule 2-231(b) provides that "[u]nless justice requires otherwise, an action may be maintained as a class action if the prerequisites of section[s] (a) [and (b)] are satisfied." Rule 23 does not include the words "unless justice requires otherwise," suggesting that the Maryland Rule provides an additional ground to deny class certification, even where the specific requirements of 2-231(a) and (b) are satisfied. There is no case law interpreting this additional language.

NUMEROSITY

Rule 2-231(a)(1): the class is so numerous that joinder of all members is impracticable.

The first requirement of Rule 2-231 is that the class be so numerous that joinder of all members is impracticable. This requirement helps promote the objectives of judicial economy and access to the legal system, particularly for persons with small, individual claims. Whether numerosity is met depends on a court's practical judgment, given the facts of a particular case. Plaintiffs need not state a number with specificity; a good faith estimate is ordinarily sufficient. A class consisting of hundreds or thousands of members is likely to satisfy this requirement.[72]

COMMONALITY

Rule 2-231(a)(2): there are questions of law or fact common to the class.

The commonality requirement promotes convenience, uniformity of decision, and judicial economy. The threshold of commonality is not a high one and is easily met in most cases. The requirement does not require that all, or even most, issues be common, nor that common issues predominate, but only that common issues exist. An issue of law or fact should be deemed common only to the extent its resolution will advance the litigation of the entire case. This less demanding prerequisite of commonality is necessarily subsumed in the more exacting requirement of predominance of common issues over individual issues found in Rule 2-231(b)(3). A lack of commonality exists where previous litigation settled the alleged common issue.[73]

TYPICALITY

Rule 2-231(a)(3): the claims or defenses of the representative parties are typical of the claims or defenses of the class.

Representative claims need not be identical to those of the rest of the class; instead, there must be similar legal and remedial theories underlying the representative claims and the claims of the class. Factual distinctions in the named plaintiffs' cases are not fatal to a finding of typicality.[74]

ADEQUACY OF REPRESENTATION

Rule 2-231(a)(4): the representative parties will fairly and adequately protect the interests of the class.

Consistent with federal practice, both the class representatives and class counsel must be adequate to represent the interests of all class members. The named plaintiffs must have no conflict of interest with the class members and must prosecute the action vigorously on behalf of the class. In analyzing the adequacy of class counsel, Maryland courts look to the "vigor, experience, and diligence of counsel," as well as to whether any conflicts of interest exist.[75]

PARTIAL CLASS ACTIONS/ SUBCLASSES

Rule 2-231(d): Partial class actions; subclasses. When appropriate, an action many be brought or maintained as a class action with respect to particular issues, or a class may be divided into subclasses and each subclass treated as a class.

---

71. *Creveling*, 828 A.2d at 238.
72. *Angeletti*, 752 A.2d at 223–24.
73. *Creveling*, 828 A.2d at 241.
74. *Angeletti*, 752 A.2d at 227–28.
75. *Id.*

Issue	Maryland Law
CLASS DEFINITION	*Rule 2-231(b): Class actions maintainable. Unless justice requires otherwise, an action may be maintained as a class action if the prerequisites of section (a) are satisfied, and in addition:* *(1) the prosecution of separate actions by or against individual members of the class would create a risk of (A) inconsistent or varying adjudications with respect to individual members of the class that would establish incompatible standards of conduct for the party opposing the class, or (B) adjudications with respect to individual members of the class that would as a practical matter be dispositive of the interests of the other members not parties to the adjudications or substantially impair or impede their ability to protect their interests; or* *(2) the party opposing the class has acted or refused to act on grounds generally applicable to the class, thereby making appropriate final injunctive relief or corresponding declaratory relief with respect to the class as a whole; or* *(3) the court finds that the questions of law or fact common to the members of the class predominate over any questions affecting only individual members and that a class action is superior to other available methods for the fair and efficient adjudication of the controversy. The matters pertinent to the findings include: (A) the interest of members of the class in individually controlling the prosecution or defense of separate actions, (B) the extent and nature of any litigation concerning the controversy already commenced by or against members of the class, (C) the desirability or undesirability of concentrating the litigation of the claims in the particular forum, (D) the difficulties likely to be encountered in the management of a class action.*

Under Rule 2-231(b)(3), a court must find predominance (questions of law or fact common to the members of the class predominate over any questions affecting only individual members) and superiority (a class action is superior to other available methods for the fair and efficient adjudication of the controversy).[76] The predominance test does not require that common issues be dispositive of the action or determinative of the liability issues, but, rather, the court should inquire into whether the proposed classes are sufficiently cohesive to warrant adjudication by representation, and common issues must constitute a significant part of the individual cases.[77] The Court of Appeals of Maryland has held that an issue of law or fact is common only to the extent its resolution will advance the litigation of the entire case.[78] Superiority is met if it is the most efficient means of adjudicating the matter.[79] The greater the individual's stakes in the litigation, the greater their interest in controlling their own actions in individual litigation. The extent and nature of litigation concerning the controversy that has already been commenced is a factor in determining whether there is so much preexisting litigation that a class would be unproductive. The court must also look at whether a class action will prevent the duplication of effort and the possibility of inconsistent results and whether the forum chosen for the class action represents an appropriate place to settle the controversy, given the location of the interested parties and the manageability of the lawsuit as a class action.[80]

Rule 2-231(b)(2): the party opposing the class has acted or refused to act on grounds generally applicable to the class, thereby making appropriate final injunctive relief or corresponding declaratory relief with respect to the class as a whole.

Rule 2-231(b)(2) class members are bound by any resulting judgment, given that they are not afforded any opt-out mechanism. Consequently, a class action seeking equitable relief under Rule 2-231(b)(2) must exhibit cohesiveness as a condition precedent to class certification. Cohesiveness is more demanding and difficult to satisfy than the similar prerequisite of predominance.[81]

THE SPECIAL ROLE OF RULE 23(B)(2)

76. *Id.* at 221.
77. *Id.* at 230.
78. *Cutler*, 927 A.2d at 13.
79. *Angeletti*, 752 A.2d at 240.
80. *Id.* at 240–42.
81. *Id.* at 253.

Issue

Maryland Law

CERTIFICATION HEARINGS AND DECISIONS

Rule 2-231(c): On motion of any party or on the court's own initiative, the court shall determine by order as soon as practicable after commencement of the action whether it is to be maintained as a class action. A hearing shall be granted if requested by any party. The order shall include the court's findings and reasons for certifying or refusing to certify the action as a class action. The order may be conditional and may be altered or amended before the decision on the merits.

The party moving for class certification bears the burden of proving that the requirements for certification have been met. A court should accept the putative class representative plaintiffs' allegations as true in making its decision on class certification. The court may not rest its determination upon the merits of the underlying cause(s) of action.[82] Nevertheless, "the court can go beyond the pleadings to the extent necessary to understand the claims, defenses, relevant facts, and applicable substantive law in order to make a meaningful determination of the certification issues."[83] Ordinarily, questions about the maintainability of a lawsuit as a class action should be determined "as soon as practicable," before any substantive issue, especially when a motion for class certification is pending before the court.[84]

INTERLOCUTORY APPEALS

Unlike in federal practice, under Maryland law, interlocutory appeals from class certification orders are ordinarily not permitted.[85] However, in a mass tobacco class action, expressly limited to its facts, the court of appeals issued a writ of mandamus directing the trial court to decertify a class, based on concerns over predominance, manageability, and superiority.[86]

STANDARD OF REVIEW

Following federal case law, Maryland's appellate courts review trial court orders certifying class actions under an abuse of discretion standard and review de novo whether the lower court applied the correct legal standard to grant certification. The standard of review does not depend on whether the trial court granted or denied the class certification.[87]

CLASS NOTICE

Rule 2-231(e): Notice. In any class action, the court may require notice pursuant to subsection (f)(2). In a class action maintained under subsection (b)(3), notice shall be given to members of the class in the manner the court directs. The notice shall advise that (1) the court will exclude from the class any member who so requests by a specified date, (2) the judgment, whether favorable or not, will include all members who do not request exclusion, and (3) any member who does not request exclusion and who desires to enter an appearance through counsel may do so.

Notice is required for a class that is certified pursuant to Rule 2-231(b)(3). This rule was designed to ensure that members of the class would be identified before a trial on the merits and would be bound by all subsequent orders and judgments. Because individuals are included in the class and must then opt out, class members must be notified early enough to allow voluntary exclusion prior to a judgment in the suit and early enough to allow for effective appearance of counsel.[88]

Maryland follows the general rule that the cost and resulting task of effecting class notification rest on the plaintiff. That principle is not absolute, however, and in some instances the defendant may be able to perform a necessary task with less difficulty or expense than could the representative plaintiff. In such cases, the trial court may properly exercise its discretion to order the defendant to perform the task in question. If the defendant was required by law to have made and maintained appropriate records, the burden placed on the defendant should not be too onerous. If the defendant has failed to keep such records, the difficulty and expense of reproducing them should be borne by the defendant, rather than class representatives or members of the class.[89] Appeal from sufficiency of notice is permitted as an appeal of a final order for purposes of the final judgment rule, because it falls within the common law collateral order exception to the rule.[90]

DISCOVERY FROM CLASS MEMBERS

Rule 2-231(g): For purposes of discovery, only representative parties shall be treated as parties. On motion, the court may allow discovery by or against any other member of the class.

82. *Id.* at 220.
83. *Id.* (quoting *Emig v. Am. Tobacco Co., Inc.*, 184 F.R.D. 379, 384 (D. Kan. 1998)).
84. *Kirkpatrick*, 467 A.2d at 566.
85. *Royal Fin. Servs.*, 961 A.2d at 1164.
86. *Angeletti*, 752 A.2d at 200.
87. *Creveling*, 828 A.2d at 239–40.
88. *Cambridge Commons*, 892 A.2d at 596.
89. *Id.* at 601–03.
90. *Id.* at 598.

Issue	Maryland Law
TRIALS/COURT MANAGEMENT	*Rule 2-231(f): Orders in Conduct of Actions. In the conduct of actions to which this Rule applies, the court may enter appropriate orders: (1) determining the course of proceedings or prescribing measures to prevent undue repetition or complication in the presentation of evidence or argument, (2) requiring, for the protection of the members of the class or otherwise for the fair conduct of the action that notice be given in the manner the court directs to some or all of the members of any step in the action, or of the proposed extent of the judgment, or of the opportunity of members to signify whether they consider the representation fair and adequate, to intervene and present claims or defenses, or otherwise to come into the action, (3) imposing conditions on the representative parties or intervenors, (4) requiring that the pleadings be amended to eliminate allegations as to representation of absent persons, and that the action proceed accordingly, (5) dealing with similar procedural matters. The orders may be combined with an order under Rule 2-504, and may be altered or amended as may be desirable from time to time.*
CLASS SETTLEMENT	
NOTICE	Notice to class members of settlement that does not contain sufficient information regarding counsel fees may be found deficient.[91]
SETTLEMENTS	*Rule 2-231(h): A class action shall not be dismissed or compromised without the approval of the court. Notice of a proposed dismissal or compromise shall be given to all members of the class in the manner the court directs.*

FINAL FAIRNESS HEARING

Rule 2-231(h) requires court approval of any class action settlement but does not articulate any standards for determining either the fairness or the adequacy of the settlement.[92] There are also no appellate decisions in Maryland establishing such standards; however, Maryland trial courts have looked to Maryland federal class action decisions for guidance.[93] Maryland federal courts separately consider the fairness and adequacy of the settlement. Factors tending to reveal the fairness of the settlement are those that indicate the presence or absence of collusion among the parties. The settlement must be the result of good faith, arm's-length bargaining by the parties. Factors to consider in evaluating the good faith of the parties include the following: (1) the posture of the case at the time settlement is proposed; (2) the extent of discovery that has been conducted; (3) the circumstances surrounding the negotiations; and (4) the experience of counsel.

In evaluating the adequacy of the proposed settlement, the trial court must weigh the likelihood of the plaintiffs' recovery on the merits against the amount offered in settlement. In assessing the adequacy of the proposed settlement, courts should weigh the amount tendered against the following factors: (1) the relative strength of the plaintiff's case on the merits; (2) the existence of any difficulties of proof or strong defenses the plaintiffs will encounter if the case goes to trial; (3) the anticipated duration and expense of additional litigation; (4) the solvency of the defendants and the likelihood of recovery on a litigated judgment; and (5) the degree of opposition to the settlement.[94]

ATTORNEY FEES

Awards of attorney fees are reviewed under an abuse of discretion standard.[95] The trial court has wide discretion to award attorney fees under the lodestar method, the percentage of funds method, or a blend of both.[96] Attorney fees must be consistent with Maryland Rule of Professional Conduct 1.5, which governs the amount attorneys may charge.[97] The fee awarded must be appropriate to the value actually received by the class.[98]

91. See, e.g., Boyd, 887 A.2d 637.

92. Id. at 643.

93. See, e.g., Dotson v. Bell Atl.-Md., Inc., CAL 99-21004, CAL 00-09962, 2003 WL 23508428, at *4 (Md. Cir. Ct. Nov. 13, 2003).

94. Id. at *5 (quoting In re Montgomery County Real Estate Antitrust Litig., 83 F.R.D. 305 (D. Md. 1979)); see also In re Mid-Atl. Toyota Antitrust Litig., 564 F. Supp. 1379 (D. Md. 1983).

95. Head v. Head, 505 A.2d 868, 875 (Md. Ct. Spec. App. 1986); Dotson, 2003 WL 23508428, at *8.

96. Dotson, 2003 WL 23508428, at *8.

97. United Cable Television Ltd. P'ship v. Burch, 732 A.2d 887, 903 (Md. 1999), overruled by statute on other grounds, Plein v. Dep't of Labor, 800 A.2d 757 (Md. 2002).

98. Dotson, 2003 WL 23508428, at *10.

Issue	Maryland Law
MASS ACTIONS	There is no per se prohibition against mass-tort class action suits in Maryland. Certification decisions are to be performed on a case-by-case basis.[99] Nonetheless, the court of appeals has taken the extraordinary step of issuing a writ of mandamus directing a trial court to vacate its order certifying a mass tobacco class action.[100]
MEDICAL MONITORING CLASSES	Maryland has not yet determined whether it will recognize causes of action for, or relief in the form of, medical monitoring. The court of appeals has only once considered whether a demonstrated need for medical monitoring created a valid cause of action in Maryland. However, the court declined to reach the question.[101] The court did note in dicta, however, that a complaint asserting a cause of action for, or seeking relief in the form of, medical monitoring must seek injunctive relief and not exclusively or predominately monetary damages.[102] The court further noted that a medical monitoring claim may more accurately be deemed a remedy, rather than a distinct cause of action.[103] Insofar as medical monitoring constitutes only a form of relief, the class would still be required to assert and prove a valid cause of action.[104]
MANAGEABILITY AND PREDOMINANCE CONCERNS IN PARTICULAR CLASS ACTIONS	The legal nature of common law claims of fraud, deceit, and negligent representation (reliance-based torts) face predominance and manageability problems because, in many cases, plaintiffs must prove reliance and/or specific causation on an individual basis.[105] Issues of reliance will often vary from plaintiff to plaintiff.[106]
STATISTICAL SAMPLING AS A BASIS FOR EXTRAPOLATING LIABILITY AND/OR DAMAGES	No court in Maryland has decided whether statistical sampling can be used as a basis for extrapolating liability, damages, or both. In the only case touching on the issue, the court held that under the facts of the particular case, even if the expert's statistical reports were accepted as valid evidence, the reports alone were insufficient to establish the plaintiffs' claims. The court went on to reject the Ninth Circuit's reliance on statistical data, surveys, and anecdotal evidence to meet the burden of proving commonality of issues.[107]

PUNITIVE DAMAGES

A class action jury may not award punitive damages based on a multiplier of individual, putative class members' compensatory damages, which are later determined by second juries in individual trials for class members.[108] A jury must find compensatory damages as a foundation before it may award punitive damages.[109] Where the evidence warrants punitive damages, it is within the sound discretion of the trier of fact to award or deny such damages.[110]

ARBITRATION

Maryland courts will enforce arbitration clauses that bar class actions.[111]

RES JUDICATA/ COLLATERAL ESTOPPEL EFFECTS

Rule 2-231(i): The judgment in an action maintained as a class action under subsections (b)(1) and (2), whether or not favorable to the class, shall include and describe those whom the court finds to be members of the class. The judgment in an action maintained as a class action under subsection (b)(3), whether or not favorable to the class, shall include and specify or describe those to whom the notice provided in subsection (e)(1) was directed, and who have not requested exclusion, and whom the court finds to be members of the class.

SPECIAL MASTERS

Maryland has recognized the use of special masters in class action proceedings. Maryland has permitted the appointment of special masters to handle a number of matters, including making recommendations on attorney fees and expenses; issuing subpoenas to compel the attendance of witnesses and the production of documents; administering oaths; ruling on the admissibility of evidence; examining witnesses; convening and adjourning hearings; recommending contempt proceedings; and making recommended findings of fact and conclusions of law.[112]

99. *Angeletti*, 752 A.2d at 222.
100. *Id.* at 254.
101. *Id.* at 251.
102. *Id.*
103. *Id.* at 253.
104. *Id.*
105. *Id.* at 234.
106. *Id.* at 235.
107. *Cutler*, 927 A.2d at 13–14.
108. *Angeletti*, 752 A.2d at 248–49.
109. *Id.* at 246.
110. *Id.*
111. *Walther*, 872 A.2d at 750–51.
112. *See, e.g., Boyd*, 887 A.2d at 648.

Issue

Maryland Law

TOLLING OF STATUTE OF LIMITATIONS

Maryland has adopted the federal tolling doctrine from *American Pipe*. The pendency of a putative class action tolls the statute of limitations on the causes of action asserted in the class action complaint for the putative class members if the class action complaint gives the defendants in the class action complaint fair notice of the claims of the putative class members who claim the benefits of tolling.[113] The class action complaint must provide the defendants with notice of the "number and generic identity of the potential plaintiffs."[114]

---

113. *Christensen*, 905 A.2d at 342.
114. *Id.* at 352 (quoting *Am. Pipe*, 414 U.S. at 555).

MASSACHUSETTS

DONALD R. FREDERICO

I. Introduction

Rule 23 of the Massachusetts Rules of Civil Procedure (Massachusetts Rule) was enacted in 1973 and has been amended only once. Although the rule was modeled after Federal Rule 23, none of the recent amendments to the federal rule have been adopted. Thus, unlike the current federal rule, the Massachusetts Rule makes no express provision for the appointment of class counsel, for certifying classes with respect to limited issues, for certifying subclasses, or for attorney fee awards. Some of these procedural gaps have been filled by case law. For example, the Massachusetts Supreme Judicial Court has held that, because the rule contains no express authorization for courts to certify classes with respect to limited issues, courts may not do so.[1] The court more recently has suggested that liability classes may be certified despite the need for individualized inquiries regarding damages and that courts can avail themselves of "innovative management techniques" to deal with such difficulties, including conditional class certification, limited issue certification, bifurcated trials, use of special masters and magistrates, and cy pres distributions of residual funds.[2] Some Massachusetts judges have appointed lead counsel to represent certified classes despite the absence of any express provision authorizing them to do so, and some recognize the court's authority to certify subclasses despite the absence of any reference to subclass certification in the Rule. The Rule also includes no provision for appeals from orders granting or denying class certification, and any such appeals must be sought through the general rules governing interlocutory appeals.[3]

---

1. *Fletcher v. Cape Cod Gas Co.*, 394 Mass. 595, 602 (1985).

2. *Salvas v. Wal-Mart Stores, Inc.*, 452 Mass. 337, 368 (2008) (citing HERBERT B. NEWBERG & ALBA CONTE, NEWBERG ON CLASS ACTIONS: A MANUAL FOR GROUP LITIGATION AT FEDERAL AND STATE LEVELS § 4:32, at 287–88 (4th ed. 2002)).

3. *See* MASS. GEN. LAWS ch. 231, §§ 111, 118.

II. Rules 23(a) and (b)

Massachusetts Rule 23(a), like its federal counterpart, requires a party seeking class certification to establish the requirements of numerosity, commonality, typicality, and adequacy. Massachusetts Rule 23(b), however, differs from its federal counterpart by omitting any reference to the grounds for certification set forth in Federal Rule 23(b)(1) and (b)(2). Massachusetts Rule 23(b) is patterned after Federal Rule 23(b)(3) and requires that, for any case to be maintained as a class action, the court must find both predominance and superiority. Unlike the Federal Rule, however, the Massachusetts Rule does not specify any matters pertinent to the findings that bear on these requirements. The Massachusetts Supreme Judicial Court has held that the plaintiffs' burden of establishing predominance is satisfied by providing "information sufficient to enable the motion judge to form a reasonable judgment that the class meets the requirements of rule 23; they do not bear the burden of producing evidence sufficient to prove that the requirements [of rule 23] have been met."[4]

III. No Opt-Outs

Despite the similarities between Massachusetts Rule 23(b) and Federal Rule 23(b)(3), classes certified under the Massachusetts Rule differ dramatically from Federal Rule 23(b)(3) class actions because there is no right to opt out of a Massachusetts state class action.[5] The inability of class members to opt out of a Massachusetts state court class action has several practical consequences.

First, when a litigation class is certified, there is no need to send notice to class members, because there generally is nothing they can do if notified. Courts have discretion under Massachusetts Rule 23(d) to order class notice at the time of certification, but because such notice is generally pointless, they typically do not order the parties to incur the effort or expense of doing so.

Second, because class members are bound by a judgment in a class action without any individual procedural rights, there are constitutional limitations on the jurisdictional reach of class action lawsuits. In *Phillips v. Shutts*,[6] the U.S. Supreme Court held that, as a matter of constitutional due process, absent class members who have not had sufficient minimum contacts with a state to be subjected to personal jurisdiction within the state can be bound by the state's courts' judgments in class actions for money damages only if they receive notice and an opportunity to remove themselves from the case. Applying *Shutts* to the situation of an out-of-state class member who has no right to opt out of a damages class action, the

---

4. *Weld v. Glaxo Wellcome Inc.*, 434 Mass. 81, 87 (2001).
5. *Fletcher*, 394 Mass. at 602.
6. 472 U.S. 797 (1985).

Massachusetts Supreme Judicial Court has held that Massachusetts courts may not certify classes that include members who are beyond the reach of the Massachusetts long-arm statute.[7]

As a practical matter, the absence of an opt-out provision, combined with the *Shutts* due process holding, means that most Massachusetts state court class actions will be limited to classes that include only persons who are, or who were at relevant time periods, Massachusetts residents. Lawyers wishing to bring class actions for monetary relief in Massachusetts on behalf of classes that include non-resident members ordinarily will have to file in federal court or in the courts of other states. Parties wishing to enter into nationwide or multistate class settlements also will generally have to look to other jurisdictions for the resolution of their disputes. This jurisdictional limitation on Massachusetts state court class actions, the reluctance of many class action defendants to remain in state court, and the relative ease with which most multistate class actions can be removed under the federal Class Action Fairness Act (CAFA)[8] lead one to expect that, as a general rule, most class actions that will be litigated in the Massachusetts state court system will be limited to statewide classes and cases of relatively small value. To the extent this has not been the case to date, it may only be because a pipeline of pre-CAFA filings has continued to work its way through the state court system.

IV. Settlement

Massachusetts Rule 23(c) governs class action settlements. Like earlier versions of Federal Rule 23(c), it simply provides that "[a] class action shall not be dismissed or compromised without the approval of the court" and that "[t]he court may require notice of such proposed dismissal or compromise to be given in such manner as the court directs." The Rule provides no specifics concerning the standards for approving a class settlement and omits the relatively new federal provisions granting courts discretion to give class members an opportunity to opt out after a settlement has been reached. Despite the lack of specificity in the Rule, Massachusetts courts have adopted the federal standard that a settlement will be approved if the court is satisfied that it is fair, reasonable, and adequate.[9] Additionally, Massachusetts judges follow the same bifurcated procedure as federal judges. A proposed settlement will first be submitted for preliminary approval and conditional

---

7. *Moelis v. Berkshire Life Ins. Co.*, 451 Mass. 483 (2008).

8. Pub. L. No. 109-2, 119 Stat. 4 (codified at 28 U.S.C. §§ 1332(d), 1453, and 1711–15 (2005); *see also* Chapter 10, "The Class Action Fairness Act of 2005." Defendants seeking to remove Massachusetts class actions to federal court bear the burden of demonstrating a "reasonable probability" that the aggregate amount in controversy at the time of removal exceeds $5 million. *Amoche v. Guarantee Trust Life Ins. Co.*, 556 F.3d 41 (1st Cir. 2009).

9. *Sniffin v. Prudential Ins. Co.*, 395 Mass. 415, 420–22 (1985).

certification of the settlement class. Although there is "no controlling Massachusetts authority setting the appropriate standard for preliminary approval of a settlement," the courts apply a more lenient standard than the standard governing final approval.[10] Once preliminary approval is granted, the court will schedule a final approval hearing and direct that notice issue to the class. The only meaningful difference in the final approval process between Massachusetts and federal practice is that Massachusetts judges have no discretion to permit class members to opt out of a settlement they do not like, and therefore may apply heightened scrutiny when considering whether the settlement will be fair to class members who will be forced to accept it if approved. Moreover, although the standard for preliminary approval is lenient, it is not "an empty ritual," and a judge who intends to deny final approval of a proposed settlement may also deny preliminary approval.[11]

V. Rule 23(d): Ensuring Adequate Representation

Massachusetts Rule 23(d) grants the trial courts broad discretion to enter orders to ensure adequate representation during the course of a class action. The Rule specifically authorizes courts to order at any time that notice be given to class members concerning such matters as a proposed settlement, entry of judgment, or any other proceedings, "including notice to the absent persons that they may come in and present claims and defenses if they so desire."[12] This section of the Rule also permits a court to decertify class actions "[w]henever the representation appears to the court inadequate fairly to protect the interests of absent parties who may be bound by the judgment."[13]

VI. Rule 23(e): Residual Funds

Massachusetts Rule 23(e) was added by amendment in 2008 and addresses the use of funds remaining from a class action judgment or settlement after payment of class members' claims, expenses, litigation costs, attorney fees, and other approved disbursements, often referred to as cy pres distributions.[14] The purpose of the amendment was to help ensure that any residual funds from class action

---

10. *In re Mass. Smokeless Tobacco Litig.*, No. 03-5038-BLS1, 2008 WL 1923063, at *3 (Mass. Super. Ct. Apr. 9, 2008) (emphasis omitted).

11. *See id.* (denying preliminary approval of coupon settlement). The judge who denied preliminary approval of the smokeless tobacco coupon settlement has since been elevated to the Massachusetts Supreme Judicial Court.

12. MASS. R. CIV. P. 23(d).

13. *Id.*

14. Jayne B. Tyrell & Lisa C. Wood, *Residual Class Action Funds: Supreme Judicial Court Identifies IOLTA as Appropriate Beneficiary*, BOSTON B.J., Fall 2009, at 17.

settlements are directed to where the money is most needed, particularly to provide funding for legal services for the poor. Massachusetts Rule 23(e)(2) requires that where an order, judgment, or approved settlement results in residual funds remaining after all claims have been paid,

> [such] residual funds shall be disbursed to one or more nonprofit organizations or foundations (which may include nonprofit organizations that provide legal services to low income persons) which support projects that will benefit the class or similarly situated persons consistent with the objectives and purposes of the underlying causes of action on which relief was based, or to the Massachusetts IOLTA Committee to support activities and programs that promote access to the civil justice system for low income residents of the Commonwealth of Massachusetts.[15]

Despite the charitable purpose of this provision, Massachusetts Rule 23(e)(1) specifically permits parties to enter into, and courts to approve, settlements that do not create such residual funds. This flexibility helps to alleviate any concerns, as recognized by a recent Second Circuit decision,[16] that forcing a defendant to pay more than will be claimed by class members, and distributing the excess through cy pres distribution, violates due process. Whether the Massachusetts courts will force defendants to do so over due process objections remains an open issue.

VII. Consumer Class Actions

The Massachusetts Consumer Protection Act[17] contains its own class action provision and has spawned its own jurisprudence. Section 9(2) of chapter 93A provides:

> Any persons entitled to bring such action may, if the use or employment of the unfair or deceptive act or practice has caused similar injury to numerous other persons similarly situated and if the court finds in a preliminary hearing that he adequately and fairly represents such other persons, bring the action on behalf of himself and such other similarly injured and situated persons; the court shall require that notice of such action be given to unnamed petitioners in the most effective practicable manner. Such action shall not be dismissed, settled or compromised without the approval of the court, and notice of any proposed dismissal, settlement or compromise shall be given to all members of the class of petitioners in such manner as the court directs.[18]

The Massachusetts Supreme Judicial Court has issued subtly conflicting comparisons of this statutory standard with the standards of Massachusetts Rule 23.

---

15. MASS. R. CIV. P. 23(e)(2).

16. *McLaughlin v. Am. Tobacco Co.*, 522 F.3d 215, 231–32 (2d Cir. 2008).

17. MASS. GEN. LAWS ch. 93A.

18. *Id.*

A majority of the court in a landmark 2004 decision pointed out that the statutory "similarly situated" standard differs from Massachusetts Rule 23(a), and that, while Rule 23(a) provides a "useful framework for an analysis," judges deciding certification under chapter 93A

> must bear in mind "'a pressing need for an effective private remedy' for consumers, and that 'traditional technicalities are not to be read into the statute in such a way as to impede the accomplishment of substantial justice.'"[19]

More recently, the court reaffirmed its earlier holdings that "Section 9(2) requires satisfaction of the same elements of numerosity, commonality, typicality, and adequacy of representation as are required by Mass. R. Civ. P. 23(a)."[20] The court further held that, although the statute does not require a showing of predominance or superiority in consumer class actions, courts nevertheless have "discretion to consider issues of predominance and superiority" in deciding whether to certify a class action under chapter 93A.[21]

The courts have held that the certification provisions of section 9(2), like Rule 23, do not permit class members to opt out.[22] Also, the Massachusetts Supreme Judicial Court has held that there is a strong public policy in favor of consumer class actions and that this public policy renders void class action waivers contained in the arbitration provisions of consumer contracts.[23]

VIII. Wage and Hour Class Actions

Recently, plaintiffs seeking class certification of wage and hour cases have argued that the Massachusetts Wage Act[24] provides an independent basis for class certification because, like chapter 93A, it permits plaintiffs to maintain actions on behalf of themselves and others similarly situated. Unlike chapter 93A, however, the Wage Act provides no guidelines for class action procedure, and to date the only Massachusetts courts to have ruled on this issue have held that plaintiffs may seek certification of wage cases only through the provisions of Rule 23.[25]

---

19. *Aspinall v. Philip Morris Co.*, 442 Mass. 381, 391–92 (2004) (quoting *Fletcher*, 394 Mass. at 605, and *Baldassari v. Pub. Fin. Trust*, 369 Mass. 33, 40–41 (1975)).

20. *Moelis*, 451 Mass. at 489.

21. *Id.* at 490 (citing *Fletcher*, 394 Mass. at 605–06).

22. *Fletcher*, 394 Mass. at 602.

23. *Feeney v. Dell Inc.*, 454 Mass. 192 (2009); *see also* Donald R. Frederico, *Feeney v. Dell Inc.: Consumer Class Actions and Public Policy*, BOSTON B.J., Winter 2010, at 6; Chapter 22, "Class Action Waivers in Arbitration Provisions."

24. MASS. GEN. LAWS ch. 149, § 150.

25. *Shea v. Weston Golf Club*, No. 0201826, 2007 WL 1537665 (Mass. Super. May 18, 2007); *Calgano v. High Country Investor, Inc.*, No. 03-0707, 2005 WL 5417992 (Mass. Super. Dec. 20, 2005); *Williamson v. DTMgmt., Inc.*, No. 021827D, 2004 WL 1050582 (Mass. Super. Mar. 10, 2004).

MICHIGAN

JOANNE GEHA SWANSON[1]

I. Introduction

Michigan Court Rule 3.501 (Michigan Rule) governs class actions in Michigan.[2] The Michigan Rule "very closely mirror[s] the federal prerequisites for class certification"[3] and "similar purposes, goals, and cautions are applicable to both."[4] Case law interpreting Federal Rule 23 is instructive to Michigan courts. However, the Rules differ in significant respects.

II. Commencement of a Class Action

A. JURISDICTION

Generally, class actions may only be filed in Michigan's circuit courts, without regard to the amount in controversy.[5] However, one court has held that the Michigan Tax Tribunal has jurisdiction to entertain class actions as long as the allegations fall within the tribunal's exclusive jurisdiction.[6] Further, Michigan has permitted

---

1. Fred K. Herrmann, also a member of the commercial dispute and complex action groups at Kerr, Russell, and Davidde A. Stella, an associate with the firm's litigation group, have contributed invaluable assistance to this chapter.

2. For a detailed history of the evolution of Michigan's class action law before Michigan Rule 3.501, *see* J. Douglas Peters & David R. Parker, *The History, Law, and Future of State Class Actions in Michigan*, 44 WAYNE L. REV. 135 (1998).

3. *Henry v. Dow Chem. Co.*, 772 N.W.2d 301, 308 (Mich. 2009).

4. *Id.* at 309.

5. *Dix v. Am. Bankers Life Assurance Co.*, 415 N.W.2d 206, 210–11 (Mich. 1987). Circuit courts in Michigan are of general jurisdiction and have exclusive jurisdiction over civil controversies exceeding $25,000. MICH. COMP. LAWS §§ 600.601, 600.605.

6. *Wikman v. Novi*, 322 N.W.2d 103, 115 (Mich. 1982); *Sessa v. State Tax Comm'n*, 351 N.W.2d 863, 865 (Mich. Ct. App. 1984).

its court of claims to hear cases that involve class allegations.[7] At least one Michigan court has held that the Michigan's Workmen's Compensation Bureau did not have the authority to entertain a class action absent governing administrative rules or an explicit statutory grant of power.[8]

B. STANDING

Michigan requires that the proposed class representative be a member of the class. "A plaintiff who cannot maintain the cause of action as an individual is not qualified to represent the proposed class."[9] Similarly, each member of the class "must have suffered an actual injury to have standing to sue."[10] The fact that a named plaintiff receives a favorable judgment before class certification does not preclude that party from representing the class "if that is otherwise appropriate."[11]

C. DEFENDANT CLASSES

"An action that seeks to recover money from individual members of a defendant class may not be maintained as a class action."[12] Further, a representative of a defendant class other than a public body or officer may decline to defend the action in a representative capacity, absent the court's determination "that the convenient administration of justice otherwise requires."[13]

D. COUNTERCLAIMS

Counterclaims may be filed in a class action by or against a class or individual class member.[14] If the counterclaim is not being asserted against a representative party, a defendant has 56 days to file and serve the counterclaim from the time the class member intervenes or from the time the class member submits a claim for distri-

---

7. *Grunow v. Sanders*, 269 N.W.2d 683, 685 (Mich. Ct. App. 1978) (stating that the Michigan Court of Claims had jurisdiction to entertain class allegations regarding the adoption of Michigan's No-Fault Act). Since no published Michigan Court of Appeals decision post-1990 has adopted the *Grunow* holding, this decision is not binding on subsequent appellate courts. *See* MICH. CT. R. 7.215(J)(1).

8. *Stein v. Dir., Bureau of Workmen's Comp.*, 258 N.W.2d 179, 182 (Mich. Ct. App. 1977) ("That is, while we need not and do not decide whether the bureau, under properly promulgated administrative rules, could entertain claims brought in the nature of a class action, it certainly does not have the authority to do so absent either an explicit statutory grant of powers or such administrative rules.").

9. *Zine v. Chrysler Corp.*, 600 N.W.2d 384, 399–400 (Mich. Ct. App. 1999) (holding that where the class representative could not maintain his action under the Michigan Consumer Protection Act, class certification was properly denied); *Dishaw v. Somerville Assocs.*, No. 242048, 2003 Mich. App. LEXIS 1328, at *19 (June 3, 2003) (finding that where the plaintiff lacked standing to bring her claim as a taxpayer, she could similarly not represent the putative class).

10. *Zine*, 600 N.W.2d at 400.

11. MICH. CT. R. 3.501(D)(3); *Tinman v. Blue Cross and Blue Shield of Michigan*, No. 268448, 2008 Mich. App. LEXIS 339, at *2–3 (Feb. 14, 2008).

12. MICH. CT. R. 3.501(I)(1).

13. MICH. CT. R. 3.501(I)(2).

14. MICH. CT. R. 3.501(H)(1).

bution of the award recovered in the action (whichever is earlier), or within the time allowed by the court.[15] If notice of class certification has not been effected, the defendant may file a "notice of intent to file counterclaims" against absent class members.[16]

If class notice did not advise class members of the counterclaim, each class member against whom the counterclaim is asserted can elect to be excluded from the action, upon receiving notice of the counterclaim.[17] The court must prevent the counterclaims from making the class action unmanageable,[18] and it can sever the counterclaims or defer consideration of the counterclaims until after the defendant's liability is determined.[19]

Michigan courts do not interpret Rule 3.501(H) and (I) as preventing defendants in a class action from asserting class action counterclaims against the plaintiffs for money damages.[20] In that instance, Michigan courts apply Rule 3.501(H) (governing counterclaims in class actions) and not Rule 3.501(I).[21]

E. PENALTY ACTIONS

An action that seeks to recover a statutory penalty or minimum amount without regard to actual damages may not be maintained as a class action unless the statute specifically permits recovery by class action.[22]

F. STATUTORY ACTIONS

Certain Michigan statutes specifically authorize class actions to redress violations.[23] For example, the Michigan Consumer Protection Act expressly permits the Michigan attorney general[24] or individuals[25] to bring class actions. Other statutes expressly prohibit class actions.[26]

---

15. MICH. CT. R. 3.501(H)(3).
16. MICH. CT. R. 3.501(H)(2).
17. MICH. CT. R. 3.501(H)(4).
18. MICH. CT. R. 3.501(H)(5).
19. *Id.*
20. *Adair v. City of Detroit*, 498 N.W.2d 924, 925–26 (Mich. Ct. App. 1993).
21. *Id.*
22. MICH. CT. R. 3.501(A)(5).
23. These statutes primarily focus upon consumer protection issues. *See, e.g.*, MICH. COMP. LAWS § 14.310 *et seq.* (Public Safety Solicitation Act); MICH. COMP. LAWS § 257.1241 *et seq.* (Vehicle Protection Product Act); MICH. COMP. LAWS § 445.51 *et seq.* (Cooperative Identity Protection Act); MICH. COMP. LAWS § 445.351 *et seq.* (Pricing and Advertising of Consumer Items); MICH. COMP. LAWS § 445.811 *et seq.* (Advertisements); MICH. COMP. LAWS § 445.851 *et seq.* (Retail Installment Sales Act); MICH. COMP. LAWS § 445.901 *et seq.* (Michigan Consumer Protection Act); MICH. COMP. LAWS § 445.951 *et seq.* (Rental-Purchase Agreement Act); MICH. COMP. LAWS 445.1651 *et seq.* (Mortgage Brokers, Lenders, and Servicers Licensing Act); MICH. COMP. LAWS 445.1851 *et seq.* (Credit Reform Act); MICH. COMP. LAWS § 493.101 (Credit Card Arrangements).
24. MICH. COMP. LAWS § 445.910(1).
25. MICH. COMP. LAWS § 445.911(3).
26. MICH. COMP. LAWS §§ 445.1601–.1614 (Mortgage Lending Practices).

G. COORDINATION OR CONSOLIDATION OF MULTIPLE OVERLAPPING ACTIONS

Although not addressed in Michigan's class action rule, by petition to the Michigan Supreme Court for a writ of superintending control, it may be possible to obtain the transfer of overlapping class actions to a single court for coordinated pretrial and trial proceedings.[27]

H. STATUTE OF LIMITATIONS

Michigan Court Rule 3.501(F) "was modeled after" the U.S. Supreme Court's decision in *American Pipe & Construction Co. v. Utah*.[28] The filing of a complaint asserting a class action tolls the statute of limitations as to all persons within the class described in the complaint,[29] even if the action does not meet the requirements for class certification or is filed by a person who is not qualified to serve as the class representative.[30] The running of the statute of limitations resumes against class members other than representative parties and intervenors upon (1) the filing of a notice of failure to timely move for class certification; (2) the expiration of 28 days after the entry, amendment, or revocation of an order of certification eliminating the person from the class; (3) the entry of an order denying class certification; (4) the submission of a class member's election to be excluded; or (5) the final disposition of the action.[31] If, however, the circumstance that triggered resumption of the statute of limitations is superseded by court order, appellate reversal or otherwise, the statute of limitations shall be deemed to have been continuously tolled from the commencement of the action.[32]

Michigan courts also hold that the filing of a class action complaint tolls the period of limitations on a putative class member's claim that was not pled in the initial complaint if the claim arises out of the same factual and legal nexus and the defendant "has notice of the class member's claim and the number and generic identities of the potential plaintiffs."[33]

---

27. *See, e.g.*, Administrative Order 2000-5, *In re Microsoft Antitrust Litig.*

28. *Cowles v. Bank West*, 719 N.W.2d 94, 103 (Mich. 2006) (citing *Am. Pipe & Constr. Co. v. Utah*, 414 U.S. 538 (1974)).

29. MICH. CT. R. 3.501(F)(1).

30. *Cowles*, 719 N.W.2d at 108.

31. MICH. CT. R. 3.501(F)(2).

32. MICH. CT. R. 3.501(F)(3).

33. *Cowles*, 719 N.W.2d at 105. *Cowles* involved a complex situation where the original class representative alleged a Truth in Lending Act claim in a second amended complaint outside of the one-year statute of limitations, but within the one-year limitation for the intervening class representative's claim. *Id.* at 101–02. The Michigan Supreme Court recognized that Rule 3.501(F) incorporates the "class-action tolling doctrine" explained by the U.S. Supreme Court in *American Pipe & Construction Co. v. Utah*. *Id.* at 103. The Michigan Supreme Court agreed with cases from the Second and Ninth Circuits that recognized that "subsequent individual claims filed after class certification is denied need not be identical to the claims in

III. Class Certification Procedure

A. TIMING OF CLASS CERTIFICATION MOTION

Unlike the leeway granted under the federal Rule, in Michigan a motion for class certification must be filed within 91 days after filing a complaint "that contains class action allegations."[34] However, upon stipulation of the parties or on motion for good cause shown, the court may extend the time for filing.[35] Once the plaintiff moves for class certification in a timely fashion, subsequent motions for class certification do not implicate Rule 3.501(B)(1).[36]

If the plaintiff fails to file a timely motion, the defendant may file a notice of the failure.[37] The class allegations are "deemed stricken" upon the filing of the notice, and the action continues by or against the named parties only.[38] The class allegations can only be reinstated if excusable neglect is shown.[39] If class certification is denied or revoked, then the matter proceeds as to the named parties.[40]

Frequently the parties will stipulate to, or courts will grant motions seeking, a schedule that provides for fact and expert discovery, motion and briefing deadlines, and a hearing (which may include the presentation of evidence) on the class certification issues while holding merits discovery in abeyance. In Michigan, "[r]epresentative parties and intervenors are subject to discovery in the same manner as parties in other civil actions."[41] Other class members are subject to discovery in the same manner as nonparties, although they may be required to submit to discovery procedures applicable to parties if so ordered by the court.[42]

B. PROPOSALS FOR NOTICE

A motion for class certification must include a proposal regarding notice, which addresses "how, when, by whom, and to whom the notice shall be given; the content

---

the original class action for tolling to apply" as long as the "individual claims . . . share a common factual and legal nexus to the extent that the defendant would likely rely on the same evidence or witnesses in mounting a defense." *Id.* at 105 (citing *Tosti v. City of L.A.*, 754 F.2d 1485, 1489 (9th Cir. 1985) and *Cullen v. Margiotta*, 811 F.2d 698, 719 (2d Cir. 1987); *see also Crown, Cork & Seal Co. v. Parker*, 462 U.S. 345, 355 (1983) (Powell, J., concurring).

34. MICH. CT. R. 3.501(B)(1)(a).

35. MICH. CT. R. 3.501(B)(1)(b).

36. *Hill v. City of Warren*, 740 N.W.2d 706, 713 (Mich. Ct. App. 2007) (rejecting the defendant's argument that the plaintiff's renewed motion for class certification was untimely when the original certification motion was filed within the 91 days).

37. MICH. CT. R. 3.501(B)(2).

38. *Id.*

39. *Id.*

40. MICH. CT. R. 3.501(B)(3)(e).

41. MICH. CT. R. 3.501(G).

42. *Id.*

of the notice; and to whom the response to the notice is to be sent."[43] The plaintiff may elect to delay the notice proposal, but must state both the reasons why the determination cannot then be made and when it should be made.[44] A notice proposal must also accompany a motion for decertification or for an amended certification.[45]

C. TIMING OF COURT'S CONSIDERATION

Absent good cause, a court cannot consider a class certification motion until service has been accomplished on all named defendants or any unserved summons has expired.[46] Further, a court may postpone its ruling on a class certification motion pending discovery or other preliminary procedures.[47]

D. PREREQUISITES TO CLASS CERTIFICATION

Unlike Rule 23, Rule 3.501 does not have the procedural equivalents of the (b)(1), (b)(2), and (b)(3) classes. The Michigan Rule applies the requirements of numerosity, predominance of common issues, typicality, adequacy, and superiority to *all* class actions.[48]

E. NUMEROSITY

The Michigan Rule is the same as the federal Rule with respect to numerosity. One or more members may sue as representative parties only if "the class is so numerous that joinder of all members is impracticable."[49] Michigan does not require any "minimum number of members," and does not mandate that "the exact number of members . . . be known as long as general knowledge and common sense indicate that the class is large."[50] However, Michigan does require an "approximate number" and the plaintiff must present "some evidence" or a "reasonable estimate" of the number of class members.[51] In certain circumstances, Michigan courts have denied class certification because a reasonable estimate of the number of members who suffered an actual injury was not provided.[52] But Michigan courts have

---

43. MICH. CT. R. 3.501(C)(2)–(3).

44. MICH. CT. R. 3.501(C)(2).

45. *Id.*

46. MICH. CT. R. 3.501(B)(3)(a).

47. MICH. CT. R. 3.501(B)(3)(b).

48. *Henry,* 772 N.W.2d at 308.

49. MICH. CT. R. 3.501(A)(1)(a); FED. R. CIV. P. 23(a)(1).

50. *Zine,* 600 N.W.2d at 400; *see also Kennedy Masonry, Inc. v. Associated Builders & Contractors Workers Comp. Fund,* No. 247016, 2004 Mich. App. LEXIS 2943, at *15–16 (Nov. 2, 2004) (holding that a subclass of eight parties did not satisfy the numerosity requirement).

51. *Zine,* 600 N.W.2d at 400.

52. *Id.* (holding that the class representative's identification of 522,658 purchasers of automobiles, without showing approximately how many suffered an actual injury, did not suffice to establish the numerosity requirement); *Jackson v. Scott,* No. 258498, 2005 Mich. App. LEXIS 2975, at *7–12 (Nov. 29, 2005) (holding

rejected the argument that the "fluidity" of the class—where during the pendency of the lawsuit certain class members may fall in or fall out of the class by changes in circumstance—defeats numerosity.[53]

F. PREDOMINANCE OF COMMON ISSUES

1. Generally

A class action in Michigan must present "questions of law or fact common to the members of the class that *predominate* over questions affecting only individual members."[54] In this respect, class certification in Michigan differs from the federal Rule, which only requires the "predominance" of common issues in a Rule 23(b)(3) class.[55]

Michigan "does not require *all* issues in the litigation to be common; it merely requires the common issue or issues to predominate over those that require individualized proof."[56] In other words, the Rule requires that "the issues in the class action that are subject to generalized proof, and thus applicable to the class as a whole, must predominate over those issues that are subject only to individualized proof."[57]

Michigan courts generally emphasize that as long as there are common questions of liability that can be established by common classwide proof,[58] individual determinations of appropriate damages will not defeat predominance.[59] On the

that the plaintiffs' failure to offer any evidence as to the approximate size of the class of employees who were forced to work off the clock or sacrifice meal and rest breaks prevented the establishment of numerosity); *Royal Oak School Dist. v. MASB-SEG Prop. & Cas. PPL, Inc.*, No. 235260, 2003 Mich. App. LEXIS 2352, at *22 (Sept. 16, 2003) (holding that the plaintiff's proffered estimated evidence regarding certain school districts' expenditures on Y2K programs did not demonstrate that the districts were damaged or intended to assert a claim). *But see A&M Supply Co. v. Microsoft Corp.*, 654 N.W.2d 572, 582 (Mich. Ct. App. 2002) (finding that the estimation of "hundreds of thousands" of potential class members who purchased software was sufficient to satisfy the numerosity requirement).

53. *Hill*, 740 N.W.2d at 716.

54. MICH. CT. R. 3.501(A)(1)(b) (emphasis added).

55. FED. R. CIV. P. 23(b)(3).

56. *Hill*, 740 N.W.2d at 716 (emphasis in original).

57. *A&M Supply Co.*, 654 N.W.2d at 582 (internal citations and quotations omitted).

58. *See, e.g., VandenBroeck v. CommonPoint Mortgage Co.*, No. 236642, 2004 Mich. App. LEXIS 2098, at *13–15 (Aug. 10, 2004) (stating that in the case of a form contract, the plaintiffs' breach of contract allegations as to whether a company had a practice of charging loan discount fees without actually providing a loan discount satisfied the commonality requirement).

59. *See Hill*, 740 N.W.2d at 716–17 (holding that where the class established that a municipality's policy of planting trees caused damages to the homeowners' properties, the fact that each class member would have to prove individual damages did not defeat the commonality requirement); *Coponen v. Wolverine Pipe Line Co.*, Nos. 235692, 235693, 235694, 235695, 2004 Mich. App. LEXIS 2557, at *3–5 (Sept. 30, 2004) (finding in a gasoline pipeline breakage case that although the class members may have had individualized damages issues, the liability question was common to the class); *VandenBroeck*, 2004 Mich. App. LEXIS 2098, at *19–20 (holding that individualized damages consideration does not defeat commonality); *Briney v. Kelsey-Hayes*, No. 218621, 2001 Mich. App. LEXIS 1192, at *15–18 (Aug. 21, 2001) (holding that

other hand, Michigan courts typically reject class certification where the class members would have to prove liability with individualized evidence. Examples of this latter category include:

- Claims that an insurer would deny emergency room services based upon the patient's final diagnosis, since the determination of the insurer's liability would "vary from claimant to claimant" and involve "highly individualized inquiries";[60]
- Deceptive statements about lemon laws in booklets provided with automobiles;[61]
- Pregnancy discrimination;[62]
- "Disparate treatment" discrimination claims;[63]
- Insurance reimbursement claims for telephone and television use;[64]
- Breach of lease agreements;[65]
- Improper deductions from tenants' security deposits;[66]
- Employment claims based on an employer's policy of making employees not report all time worked and skip rest and meal breaks;[67]
- Contaminated catered food at three different events;[68] and
- False imprisonment of patrons of a gambling establishment.[69]

2. Particular Actions

a. Antitrust

Antitrust actions may present nuanced considerations of the predominance issue, particularly in indirect purchaser antitrust actions, which are allowed in Michigan under the Michigan Antitrust Reform Act (MARA).[70] MARA permits recovery of "actual damages sustained by reason of a violation of [the] act."[71] Class plaintiffs must therefore prove "actual damage" as to each class member to establish the "fact of injury" requisite to recovery. If they fail to set forth a viable method for

---

the plaintiffs established that the employer's elimination of certain accrued vacation time was a common question and individual determinations of compensation did not defeat class certification).

60. *Tinman v. Blue Cross and Blue Shield of Michigan*, 692 N.W.2d 58, 67–68 (2004).

61. *Zine*, 600 N.W.2d at 401.

62. *Lee v. Bd. of Educ. of Grand Rapids Public Schs.*, 459 N.W.2d 1, 2–4 (Mich. Ct. App. 1989).

63. *Commc'ns Workers Local 4100 v. Ameritech Servs., Inc.*, No. 232886, 2003 Mich. App. LEXIS 1494, at *9–16 (June 24, 2003).

64. *Hamilton v. AAA Mich.*, 639 N.W.2d 837, 845–46 (Mich. Ct. App. 2001).

65. *Williams v. Terra Energy, Ltd.*, No. 260725, 2006 Mich. App. LEXIS 2309, at *4–16 (July 25, 2006).

66. *Maier v. Cmty. Res. Mgmt. Co.*, No. 257958, 2006 Mich. App. LEXIS 708, at *4–5 (Mar. 16, 2006).

67. *Jackson*, 2005 Mich. App. LEXIS 2975, at *13–20.

68. *Peet v. The Sweet Onion, Inc.*, No. 251736, 2005 Mich. App. LEXIS 737, at *2–3 (Mar. 17, 2005).

69. *Stiglmaier v. Detroit Entm't, LLC*, Nos. 246465 & 246466, 2004 Mich. App. LEXIS 2292, at *8–11 (Aug. 31, 2004).

70. MICH. COMP. LAWS §§ 445.771–.788.

71. MICH. COMP. LAWS § 445.778.

proving actual damages or fact of injury on a classwide basis, class certification will be denied[72] because a plaintiff must demonstrate that "all members of the class had a common injury that could be demonstrated with generalized proof, rather than evidence unique to each class member."[73]

b. Consumer Protection

The Michigan Supreme Court has observed that the class action remedy contained in Michigan's Consumer Protection Act (MCPA) "should be construed liberally to broaden the consumers' remedy, especially in situations involving consumer frauds affecting a large number of persons."[74] The court consequently held that it is not necessary to prove every class member's individual reliance on an alleged misrepresentation. "It is sufficient if the class can establish that a reasonable person would have relied on the representations."[75] However, MCPA class actions are limited to claims for actual damages.[76] The $250 statutory remedy is not available in class actions.[77]

c. Fraud

Unlike MCPA claims, Michigan courts have held that fraud claims are not appropriate for determination in a class action because such claims typically require individual proof of reliance.[78]

G. TYPICALITY

Typicality requires that "the claims and defenses of the representative parties [must be] typical of the claims or defenses of the class."[79] This provision tracks the federal Rule.[80] Typicality looks to whether the class shares a legal theory and a "core of allegation."[81] Typicality may not exist if the defendant has genuine defenses to the claims of the representative parties that are inapplicable to unnamed class members.

---

72. *See, e.g., A&M Supply Co.*, 654 N.W.2d at 603.

73. *Id.* at 600.

74. *Dix*, 415 N.W.2d at 209.

75. *Id.*

76. MICH. COMP. LAWS § 445.911(3); *see Woods v. Wayland Ford*, No. 275177, 2008 Mich. App. LEXIS 796, at *2 (Apr. 17, 2008).

77. MICH. COMP. LAWS §§ 445.911(2) and (3).

78. *Freeman v. State-Wide Carpet Distribs., Inc.*, 112 N.W.2d 439, 443–44 (Mich. 1961); *see Williams*, 2006 Mich. App. LEXIS 2309, at *21–22.

79. MICH. CT. R. 3.501(A)(1)(c).

80. FED. R. CIV. P. 23(a)(3).

81. *Hill*, 740 N.W.2d at 717.

H. ADEQUACY

Adequacy mandates that "the representative parties will fairly and adequately assert and protect the interests of the class."[82] This is also the same as the federal Rule.[83] However, unlike the federal Rule,[84] the Michigan Rule lacks any detailed procedure for the evaluation of the adequacy of class counsel. Michigan courts ask first whether the named plaintiffs' counsel "is qualified to sufficiently pursue the putative class action" and second whether the members of the class "have antagonistic or conflicting interests."[85] Potential intraclass conflicts weigh heavily against a finding of adequacy.[86]

I. SUPERIORITY

The federal Rule considers whether "a class action is superior to other available methods for fairly and efficiently adjudicating the controversy" only when evaluating the certification of a "(b)(3)" class.[87] But, as noted above, similar to the predominance requirement, Michigan requires satisfaction of the superiority prong regardless of the type of certification sought.[88]

Superiority examines whether "maintenance of the action as a class action will be superior to other available methods of adjudication in promoting the convenient administration of justice."[89] The factors that must be considered in making this determination are similar to the requirements for Rule 23(b)(1), (2), and (3) classes. For example, Rule 3.501(A)(2)(a) parallels the requirements of a Rule 23(b)(1) class; Rule 3.501(A)(2)(b) recites one of the requirements for a Rule 23(b)(2) class; and Rule 3.501(A)(2)(c), (d), and (f) are similar to factors considered for establishing a Rule 23(b)(3) class. The superiority analysis under Rule 3.501(A)(2) requires that a court consider

    (a) whether the prosecution of separate actions by or against individual members of the class would create a risk of

---

82. MICH. CT. R. 3.501(A)(1)(d).

83. FED. R. CIV. P. 23(a)(4).

84. FED. R. CIV. P. 23(g).

85. *Neal v. James*, 651 N.W.2d 181, 186–87 (Mich. Ct. App. 2002), *overruled on other grounds, Henry*, 772 N.W.2d at 313 n.39.

86. *Jackson*, 2005 Mich. App. LEXIS 2975, at *23–24 (holding that where the class contained employees and their managers, class conflict was possible because the managers could have been the cause of the employees' complaints); *Kelley v. Thompson-McCully Co.*, No. 236229, 2004 Mich. App. LEXIS 2016, at *13–18 (July 24, 2004) (holding that where possibilities for intraclass conflict existed, and where the plaintiff could therefore not adequately represent the interests of the class, class certification was not possible).

87. FED. R. CIV. P. 23(b)(3).

88. MICH. CT. R. 3.501(A)(1)(e).

89. *Id.*

(i) inconsistent or varying adjudications with respect to individual members of the class that would confront the party opposing the class with incompatible standards of conduct; or

(ii) adjudications with respect to individual members of the class that would as a practical matter be dispositive of the interests of other members not parties to the adjudications or substantially impair or impede their ability to protect their interests;

(b) whether final equitable or declaratory relief might be appropriate with respect to the class;

(c) whether the action will be manageable as a class action;

(d) whether in view of the complexity of the issues or the expense of litigation the separate claims of individual class members are insufficient in amount to support separate actions;

(e) whether it is probable that the amount which may be recovered by individual class members will be large enough in relation to the expense and effort of administering the action to justify a class action; and

(f) whether members of the class have a significant interest in controlling the prosecution or defense of separate actions.[90]

Overall, the inquiry asks "whether a class action, rather than individual suits, will be the most convenient way to decide the legal questions presented, making a class action a superior form of action."[91]

The Michigan Supreme Court has recognized that this inquiry is essentially the same as the "convenient administration of justice" and is essentially a "practicality test."[92] Michigan often considers the superiority issue to be "intertwined" with the predominance requirement.[93] At least one Michigan court has held that the potential application of many other states' laws weighed against the convenient administration of justice.[94]

J. CERTIFICATION STANDARD

In *Henry v. Dow Chemical Co.*,[95] the Michigan Supreme Court recently addressed "the proper analysis a court must conduct when determining whether the prerequisites for class certification have been met." In considering that issue, the court observed that "a certifying court may not simply 'rubber stamp' a party's allegations that the class certification prerequisites are met."[96] The court also noted

---

90. Mich. Ct. R. 3.501(A)(2).

91. *A&M Supply Co.*, 654 N.W.2d at 601.

92. *Hill*, 740 N.W.2d at 717.

93. *A&M Supply Co.*, 654 N.W.2d at 603.

94. *Edgcumbe v. Cessna Aircraft Co.*, 430 N.W.2d 788, 790 (Mich. Ct. App. 1988).

95. 772 N.W.2d 301.

96. *Id.* at 311.

that the federal "rigorous analysis" standard applied by the U.S. Supreme Court in *General Telephone Co. of the Southwest v. Falcon*[97] "does not necessarily bind state courts."[98] The court concluded that "the plain language of Rule 3.501(A) provides sufficient guidance for class certification decisions in Michigan,"[99] and that the certifying court must be provided "*information* sufficient to establish that each prerequisite for class certification in Rule 3.501(A)(1) is in fact satisfied."[100] "Mere repetition" of the language of the rule is not enough; rather, "there must be an adequate statement of basic facts to indicate that each prerequisite is fulfilled."[101]

A class certification decision may be based "on the pleadings alone *only if* the pleadings set forth sufficient information to satisfy the court that each prerequisite is in fact met,"[102] such as where the facts necessary to support the finding are uncontested or admitted by the opposing party.[103] In other words, the court "may not simply accept as true a party's bare statement that a prerequisite is met unless the court independently determines that the plaintiff has at least alleged a statement of basic facts and law that are adequate to support that prerequisite."[104]

Similar to federal law, Michigan courts have "broad discretion to determine whether a class will be certified,"[105] but may not assess the merits of the asserted facts, law, claims, or defenses when making that determination.[106]

K. CLASS CERTIFICATION ORDERS

The class certification order must "set forth a description of the class."[107] Unlike the federal Rule, Michigan does not *require* that the class certification order define the class claims, issues, or defenses, or appoint class counsel.[108] However, as provided in the federal Rule, when appropriate the court may order that the class action be limited to particular issues or forms of relief, or that the proposed class be divided into separate classes.[109]

---

97. 457 U.S. 147 (1982).
98. *Henry*, 772 N.W.2d at 311.
99. *Id.*
100. *Id.* at 312 (emphasis added).
101. *Id.*
102. *Id.* at 311.
103. *Id.*
104. *Id.* at 312.
105. *Id.*
106. *Id.*
107. MICH. CT. R. 3.501(B)(3)(c).
108. *Id.*
109. MICH. CT. R. 3.501(B)(3)(d).

L. CLASS DECERTIFICATION

A party resisting class certification may bring a decertification motion at any time.[110] No time limit for decertification motions is specified in the Rule.[111] Moving for class decertification renews the plaintiff's burden to establish the Rule 3.501 requirements.[112]

IV. Notice to Class Members

Class members must receive notice in all Michigan class actions, unlike the federal Rule, which only requires that notice be given to a (b)(3) class.[113] Notice must be given to persons who become class members upon certification or amendment of a prior certification, or to persons who are excluded from a class by amendment or revocation.[114] Michigan's notice requirements do not distinguish among situations where a plaintiff is seeking money damages or injunctive or declaratory relief. "As soon as practicable," the trial court must determine the manner of notice, or may postpone the notice determination to allow the parties to conduct discovery, which may be limited to matters relevant to the notice determination.[115]

The court has discretion in determining the manner of notice.[116] The court may require that individual written notice be given to class members who can be identified with reasonable effort and/or in addition may formulate "another method reasonably calculated to reach the members of the class," including publication in a newspaper or magazine, radio or television broadcasting, posting, or distribution through a trade or professional publication.[117] When determining the manner of notice, the court is instructed to take into consideration the following factors, among others: (1) the extent and nature of the class; (2) the relief requested; (3) the cost of notifying members; (4) the plaintiff's resources; and (5) the possible prejudice to members of the class or others if notice is not received.[118]

---

110. *Tinman*, 692 N.W.2d at 66.

111. *Id.* at 65–66.

112. *Id.* at 66.

113. *Compare* MICH. CT. R. 3.501(C) *with* FED. R. CIV. P. 23(c)(2).

114. MICH. CT. R. 3.501(C)(1).

115. MICH. CT. R. 3.501(C)(3).

116. MICH. CT. R. 3.501(C)(4)(a); *see also Rennie v. Marblehead Lime Co.*, Nos. 269529 & 272637, 2007 Mich. App. LEXIS 2355, at *13–17 (Oct. 16, 2007) (holding that publication of notice of a settlement in a newspaper satisfied Rule 3.501(C)(5) even though the notice failed to contain the case caption number, the terms of the settlement agreement, or notice of a right to intervene and allowed only 16 days of notice before the settlement hearing).

117. MICH. CT. R. 3.501(C)(4)(b).

118. MICH. CT. R. 3.501(C)(4)(c).

The content of notice is prescribed in the Rule, although the court may order the inclusion of "other information the court deems appropriate."[119] The plaintiff is typically responsible for bearing the expense of notice and must reimburse the defendant for any additional costs it incurs in cooperating.[120] The prevailing party may be able to recover taxable costs and expenses of notification.[121] However, these cost provisions shall not apply if a statute provides for a different allocation of costs.[122] During the proceedings, the trial court may order that additional notice be given to some or all class members.[123]

V. Opting Out of the Class and Intervention

Class members have "the right to be excluded from the action in the manner provided in th[e] rule, subject to the authority of the court to order them made parties to the action pursuant to other applicable court rules."[124] Class members may also intervene in the action, subject to the court's authority "to regulate the orderly course of the action."[125]

VI. Judgment

The judgment "shall describe the parties bound."[126] If a judgment is entered before class certification, it is only binding on the named parties.[127] As explained above, a judgment entered in favor of a named plaintiff does not preclude that plaintiff from representing the class.[128] However, if not previously alleged, class allegations cannot be added to a complaint after judgment or partial judgment has been entered.[129] The judgment will bind all class members who did not opt out unless the court directs otherwise.[130]

VII. Attorney Fees

The Michigan class action rule does not have an attorney fee provision.

---

119. MICH. CT. R. 3.501(C)(5)(h).
120. MICH. CT. R. 3.501(C)(6)(a).
121. MICH. CT. R. 3.501(C)(6)(b).
122. MICH. CT. R. 3.501(C)(6)(c).
123. MICH. CT. R. 3.501(C)(7).
124. MICH. CT. R. 3.501(A)(3).
125. MICH. CT. R. 3.501(A)(4).
126. MICH. CT. R. 3.501(D)(1).
127. MICH. CT. R. 3.501(D)(2).
128. MICH. CT. R. 3.501(D)(3).
129. MICH. CT. R. 3.501(D)(4).
130. MICH. CT. R. 3.501(D)(5).

VIII. Dismissal or Compromise

If an action has been certified as a class action, it "may not be dismissed or compromised without the approval of the court, and notice of the proposed dismissal or compromise shall be given to the class in such manner as the court directs."[131] The Michigan Rule itself does not adopt the requirement of Rule 23(e)(2) that the trial court may only approve a settlement after a hearing and upon "finding that it is fair, reasonable and adequate." Nor does it require that class members be given an additional opportunity to opt out of the class, or provide for a class members' objections.[132] However, Michigan courts have followed the jurisprudence developed under the federal Rule[133] and recognize that "[t]here is an overriding public interest in favor of settlements in class-action lawsuits."[134] In deciding whether to approve a settlement, Michigan courts consider the following factors: (1) "whether the settlement's terms are fair and reasonable"; (2) "whether the settlement is a product of fraud, overreaching, or collusion"; (3) "the relative strengths and weaknesses of the plaintiffs' claims"; and (4) "the stage of the proceedings."[135]

A court's acceptance of a class action settlement will only be reversed for an abuse of discretion.[136] A trial court does not necessarily abuse its discretion if it accepts a class action settlement over the objections of the named representatives. However, an abuse of discretion may be found if the settlement is accepted over the objections of the named plaintiffs, the class's negotiating team, and the majority of class members.[137]

IX. Appellate Review of Class Certification Decisions

Unlike the federal Rule,[138] Michigan rules have no special provision governing an appeal of a class certification decision. A party must instead submit an application for leave to appeal and satisfy the general requirements for interlocutory review.[139]

The Michigan Supreme Court has recently clarified that because the class certification analysis often requires that a trial court make "findings of fact" and "discretionary determinations," a reviewing court will apply a "clear error" standard to

---

131. MICH. CT. R. 3.501(E).

132. FED. R. CIV. P. 23(e).

133. *Brenner v. Marathon Oil Co.*, 565 N.W.2d 1, 4 (Mich. Ct. App. 1997).

134. *Id.* at 3 (citing *Kincade v. Gen. Tire & Rubber Co.*, 635 F.2d 501, 507 (5th Cir. 1981)).

135. *Brenner*, 565 N.W.2d at 3 (citing *Priddy v. Edelman*, 883 F.2d 438, 447 (6th Cir. 1989) and *In re A.H. Robins Co.*, 880 F.2d 709, 748 (4th Cir. 1989)).

136. *Id.* (citing *Laskey v. Int'l Union (UAW)*, 638 F.2d 954, 956 (6th Cir. 1981)).

137. *Id.* at 3–4.

138. FED. R. CIV. P. 23(f).

139. MICH. CT. R. 7.203 & 7.205.

fact findings and an "abuse of discretion" standard to discretionary decisions.[140] In Michigan, "clear error" means "there is no evidentiary support for [factual findings] or where there is supporting evidence but the reviewing court is nevertheless left with a definite and firm conviction that the trial court made a mistake."[141] An "abuse of discretion" occurs when the trial court's decision falls outside the range of reasonable and principled outcomes.[142]

---

140. *Henry*, 772 N.W.2d at 307. Previously, Michigan courts applied a broad "clear error" standard to trial court decisions on class certification. *See, e.g., Hill*, 740 N.W.2d at 715.

141. *Hill*, 740 N.W.2d at 714.

142. *Maldonado v. Ford Motor Co.*, 719 N.W.2d 809, 817 (Mich. 2006).

MINNESOTA

JAMES A. O'NEAL
AMY BERGQUIST

I. Introduction

Minnesota Rule of Civil Procedure 23 "is modeled after" Federal Rule of Civil Procedure 23.[1] In 2006, Minnesota adopted amendments that "extensively revamped" Rule 23, and those changes "primarily adopt[ed] the amendments made to Federal Rule 23 in 2003."[2] The federal Advisory Committee notes accompanying the 2003 Federal Rule amendments "provide useful information . . . and may be consulted for interpretation of the [Minnesota] rules."[3] Minnesota's rule has not yet been "restyled" to correspond with the most recent federal Rule. Nonetheless, "[b]ecause of the substantial similarity between Minnesota's rule 23 and Federal Rule 23, federal precedent is instructive in interpreting [the Minnesota] Rule."[4] Minnesota first revised its Rule 23 to follow the federal Rule in 1968, and therefore "decisions under [the federal rule] may be of greater persuasive value than the Minnesota Supreme Court's pre-1968 rulings."[5] There is a "dearth of Minnesota Supreme Court decisions on many important class action issues," making federal cases particularly relevant in construing Minnesota's Rule 23.[6] Although federal cases interpreting Federal Rule 23 are "instructive," they are "not necessarily

---

1. *Lewy 1990 Trust ex rel. Lewy v. Inv. Advisors, Inc.*, 650 N.W.2d 445, 452 (Minn. Ct. App. 2002).

2. MINN. R. CIV. P. 23 advisory committee comment (2006).

3. *Id.*

4. *Whitaker v. 3M Co.*, 764 N.W.2d 631, 635 (Minn. Ct. App. 2009), *petition for further rev. denied* (Minn. July 22, 2009) (internal quotation marks omitted).

5. *Kochlin v. Norwest Mortgage, Inc.*, No. C3-01-136, 2001 Minn. App. LEXIS 848, at *3 n.1 (July 31, 2001) (quoting DAVID F. HERR & ROGER S. HAYDOCK, MINNESOTA PRACTICE § 23.2 (3d ed. 1998)) (alteration in *Kochlin*).

6. 1 DAVID F. HERR & ROGER S. HAYDOCK, MINNESOTA PRACTICE SERIES: CIVIL RULES ANNOTATED § 23:1 at 599 (5th ed. 2009).

controlling."[7] When citing federal cases, Minnesota courts may be more likely to cite decisions from the Eighth Circuit and the District Court of Minnesota than other lower courts.[8]

This chapter highlights several subtle differences between Minnesota and federal class action law.

II. Timing

Rule 23.03(a)(1) requires the district court to "determine by order whether to certify the action as a class action . . . at an early practicable time."[9] Minnesota's 2006 Advisory Committee comment observes that the "as soon as practicable" phrasing of the pre-2006 Rule "occasionally prompted courts to feel they did not have the leeway to defer ruling on certification until a later, more logical time. In many cases, certification cannot be decided without consideration of the practicalities of trying the case, making an early certification decision impractical."[10]

Practitioners should raise all possible grounds for class certification simultaneously. Minnesota courts have declined to consider a second certification motion under a different subsection of Rule 23.02 where that "request could have been made with [the] first request."[11] For example, a district court did not abuse its discretion in concluding that a plaintiff's purely strategic decision to defer a request for certification under Rule 23.02(c) until after the court rejected its motion for certification of a Rule 23.02(a)(1) class violated the "as soon as practicable" requirement under the old Rule.[12] The Minnesota Supreme Court has employed similar reasoning to conclude that a defendant waived objections to the class by failing to raise those objections in its first petition for review.[13] Therefore, the district court's obligation under Rule 23.03(a)(1) to determine whether to certify the class at an early stage in the proceedings imposes a similar obligation on the parties to raise all arguments related to class certification in a similarly timely manner. Consistent with this approach, a motion for alteration of a certification decision must be justified by changed circumstances or new information.[14] It cannot be used as an end run around Rule 23.03(a)(1).

---

7. *Lewy*, 650 N.W.2d at 452 (quoting *Johnson v. Soo Line R.R.*, 463 N.W.2d 894, 899 n.7 (Minn. 1990)).

8. *See, e.g., id.* at 452–57.

9. *Cf.* FED. R. CIV. P. 23(c)(1)(A) ("At an early practicable time after a person sues or is sued as a class representative, the court must determine by order whether to certify the action as a class action.").

10. MINN. R. CIV. P. 23 advisory committee comment (2006).

11. *Kochlin*, 2001 Minn. App. LEXIS 848, at *3–4.

12. *Id.*

13. *Peterson v. BASF Corp.* (*Peterson II*), 675 N.W.2d 57, 67–68 (Minn. 2004).

14. *Kochlin*, 2001 Minn. App. LEXIS 848, at *5.

Manageability concerns can also shape a court's determination of whether a motion for class certification is timely. In one case, the court of appeals affirmed a district court's determination that a motion for class certification filed ten months after the complaint was filed and two months prior to trial was untimely and "exacerbate[d] the management problems that this court would have if this class proceeded pursuant to Rule 23.02(c)."[15] Courts have been willing to entertain motions for class certification even after liability has been established, however, "where the merits of the litigation are fully determinable as a matter of law, based exclusively on judicial construction of controlling state statutes."[16] In an older case, the Minnesota Supreme Court was unwilling to penalize plaintiffs for making "no attempt . . . to comply with the requirements of Rule 23" before the district court granted summary judgment in their favor.[17] The court concluded that the district court erred in certifying a class on the basis of the pleadings alone and without issuing any order or giving notice to absent class members, but stated that the plaintiffs should "have the option on remand to pursue" a class action because "it appears that they may be able to establish a right to maintain it under the rules."[18]

III. Considerations for Certification

Minnesota Rule 23.01 contains the same prerequisites as Federal Rule 23(a), and Rule 23.02 lists the same types of class actions as Federal Rule 23(b). Hence, the same general considerations for class certification apply in Minnesota state courts. This section highlights some of the nuances of the Minnesota Rule.

A. CLASS DEFINITION

1. Ascertainability
Minnesota's appellate courts have not recognized a separate ascertainability requirement. Ascertainability challenges may succeed as stand-alone arguments,[19]

---

15. *Novack v. Nw. Airlines, Inc.*, 525 N.W.2d 592, 600 (Minn. Ct. App. 1995).
16. *Streich v. Am. Family Mut. Ins. Co.*, 399 N.W.2d 210, 214–15 (Minn. Ct. App. 1987).
17. *Beckman v. St. Louis County Bd. of Comm'rs*, 241 N.W.2d 302, 305 (Minn. 1976).
18. *Id.*
19. *Peridot, Inc. v. Kimberly-Clark Corp.*, No. MC98-012686, 2000 WL 673933, at *5–6 (Minn. Dist. Ct. Feb. 7, 2000) (citing *Esler v. Northrop Corp.*, 86 F.R.D. 20, 33 (W.D. Mo. 1979); 2 Herbert B. Newberg & Alba Conte, Newberg on Class Actions § 6:14 (4th ed. 2002)).

but may be better incorporated into challenges to numerosity,[20] typicality,[21] or manageability,[22] where relevant.

2. Issue Classes

There may be circumstances under which Minnesota courts would endorse the practice of segregating a single issue for class action determination, particularly to achieve the predominance required under Rule 23.02(c).[23] Typically, the single issue determines liability for the entire class, and the only remaining issues for individual determination relate to damages.[24] If, however, the individual damages proceedings would require the court to revisit "much of the same proof" that was presented at the liability stage, an issue class would not satisfy the superiority requirement.[25]

B. RULE 23.01 PREREQUISITES

1. Numerosity: Rule 23.01(a)

If a putative class is sufficiently small, a court may reject the class as lacking numerosity if additional potential class members are not readily ascertainable. For example, in one case there were fewer than 40 Minnesota residents who were members of the putative class of job applicants who did not meet an airline's height requirements. "The [district] court refused to consider an additional number of unknown nonresident applicants who may have had sufficient contacts with Minnesota," and the court of appeals affirmed the district court's conclusion that the class did not satisfy the numerosity requirement.[26] In another case, the court concluded that joinder did not appear to be impracticable because plaintiffs had formed an organization of city residents specifically for the purpose of obtaining the injunction sought in the suit.[27]

---

20. *Novack*, 525 N.W.2d at 600 ("The court refused to consider an additional number of unknown nonresident applicants who may have had sufficient contacts with Minnesota and found that the class, as modified, contained less than 40 Minnesota residents.").

21. *State ex rel. Neighbors Organized in Support of the Env't v. Dotty*, 396 N.W.2d 55, 58 (Minn. Ct. App. 1986).

22. *Forcier v. State Farm Mut. Auto. Ins. Co.*, 310 N.W.2d 124, 131 (Minn. 1981) (directing that in evaluating manageability on remand, the district court should "evaluate State Farm's claim with respect to ascertaining the names of potential class members, [and] how, if once ascertained, these claimants can be reimbursed").

23. *Rathbun v. W.T. Grant Co.*, 219 N.W.2d 641, 652 (Minn. 1974) ("[T]he trial court correctly segregated the issue of usury as the single item for class-action determination."); *Streich*, 399 N.W.2d at 218.

24. *Rathbun*, 219 N.W.2d at 652 ("Although this ruling recognizes the need for multiple proceedings to determine the individual damages of the class members, the predominance of a common issue of liability over individual questions of damage has been frequently recognized."); *Streich*, 399 N.W.2d at 218 ("In this case, liability has been established and all that remains is to determine individual damages. If this case does not go forward as a class suit, the injuries suffered by many members of the class will go unredressed.").

25. *Ario v. Metro. Airports Comm'n*, 367 N.W.2d 509, 515 (Minn. 1985).

26. *Novack*, 525 N.W.2d at 600.

27. *Dotty*, 396 N.W.2d at 58.

2. Commonality: Rule 23.01(b)

Several Minnesota decisions note in passing that "[t]he threshold for commonality is not high and requires only that the resolution of the common questions affect all or a substantial number of class members."[28] "For commonality to exist," however, "behavior causing a common effect must be subject to some dispute."[29] Even if the litigation has already resolved that dispute and only individual issues of damages remain, the common behavior "continues to provide the common link necessary to satisfy the commonality requirement."[30] But if the party opposing certification has admitted the common fact, it is a nonissue and cannot be used to establish commonality.[31]

3. Typicality: Rule 23.01(c)

The Minnesota Supreme Court has stated that "typicality refers to the potential for rivalry and conflict which may jeopardize the interests of the class."[32] If the class is defined so broadly that it includes individuals who have not been harmed, the class may not satisfy the typicality requirement.[33] The fact that some members of the putative class may prefer an alternate resolution of the conflict giving rise to the suit does not defeat typicality.[34] But, as described in the following section, if the requested relief could actually harm some members of the putative class, the party opposing class certification can argue that the representativeness requirement is not satisfied.[35]

4. "Representativeness": Rule 23.01(d)

Courts may question adequacy of class representation if the requested relief is arguably not in the best interests of all members of the putative class. In a case challenging the constitutionality of a statute authorizing orders for confining

---

28. *Streich*, 399 N.W.2d at 214; *see also Peterson v. BASF Corp.* (*Peterson I*), 618 N.W.2d 821, 825 (Minn. Ct. App. 2000). *But see In re Objections & Defs. to Real Prop. Taxes*, 335 N.W.2d 717, 719 (Minn. 1983).

29. *In re Objections*, 335 N.W.2d at 719; *Streich*, 399 N.W.2d at 214.

30. *Streich*, 399 N.W.2d at 215. *But see Nolan v. State Farm Mut. Auto. Ins. Co.*, 355 N.W.2d 492, 493 (Minn. Ct. App. 1984):

Nolan has failed to meet the commonality prerequisite. After *Prax*, there is no remaining question of law which is common to all members of the class. The only remaining questions are those between individual policyholders and State Farm, and relate to whether an individual is due some additional benefit and its amount. These issues are inherently individual in nature. It is not enough for Nolan to assert that all the claims are "related" through State Farm's erroneous interpretation of the law.

31. *In re Objections*, 335 N.W.2d at 719.

32. *Ario*, 367 N.W.2d at 513.

33. *Dotty*, 396 N.W.2d at 58 ("Clearly [a class consisting of] all persons owning real estate in Breezy Point who merely 'object' to the Club is too broadly defined to ensure that the members will have the necessary typicality under Rule 23.01.").

34. *Ario*, 367 N.W.2d at 513.

35. *State ex rel. Doe v. Madonna*, 295 N.W.2d 356, 360 (Minn. 1980).

individuals pending a determination of whether they should be committed to a mental institution, the plaintiffs sought to represent all persons who had been confined subject to the statute.[36] The Minnesota Supreme Court affirmed the district court's decision to deny class certification because the class did "not meet the requirement of representativeness."[37] The court concluded that "not all members of the class would be in favor of this action and thus would not want the commitment procedure to be struck down," and therefore "a potential conflict could exist between those individuals who would be subjected to an additional traumatic court action and the representatives of the class who foster such procedures."[38]

Rule 23.01(d) may be an effective mechanism to challenge a putative class where the class representative is not a member of the class or lacks standing. In rejecting certification of a class of defendants, the Minnesota Court of Appeals concluded that "representivity was lacking because a plaintiff who has no cause of action against the defendant can not fairly and adequately protect the interests of those who do have such causes of action."[39]

C. TYPES OF CLASS ACTIONS: RULE 23.02

1. Rule 23.02(b): Nonmonetary Relief

Minnesota courts follow federal law in concluding that Rule 23.02(b) is not appropriate if the claim is essentially for monetary relief, even if plaintiffs also request an injunction.[40] Certification under this subsection "is used where civil rights violations are alleged or where a statute is being challenged as unconstitutional, cases which make injunctive or declaratory relief appropriate."[41] But courts seem to be divided as to whether seeking an order directing the defendants to compute and pay retroactive benefits defeats certification under Rule 23.02(b). In one case, the Minnesota Court of Appeals held that such a claim was "essentially [a request] for monetary relief" and therefore Rule 23.02(b) certification was improper.[42] A somewhat more recent opinion of the same court reversed a district court's refusal to award retroactive benefits to members of a Rule 23.02(b) class, concluding that reimbursements of monies withheld pursuant to an unconstitutional statute amounted to equitable relief, rather than monetary damages.[43]

---

36. *Id.* at 359.
37. *Id.* at 360.
38. *Id.*
39. *Streich*, 399 N.W.2d at 215 (internal quotation marks omitted).
40. *Id.* at 216.
41. *Id.*
42. *Id.*
43. *Mitchell v. Steffen*, 487 N.W. 896, 906–07 (Minn. Ct. App. 1992).

2. Rule 23.02(c)

The Minnesota Supreme Court has recognized that a district court's authority to determine predominance and superiority under Rule 23.02(c) "approaches a grant of discretionary power to allow class actions whenever the court sees fit."[44] Moreover, "once convinced there is substantial merit to plaintiffs' claims, the court ordinarily does not let procedural difficulties stand in its way."[45] Although the four factors in Federal Rule 23(b)(3) also appear in Rule 23.02(c), Minnesota courts rarely make specific reference to them. Instead, the courts have developed their own considerations for evaluating predominance and superiority.

a. Predominance

Minnesota's "predominance inquiry is directed toward the issue of liability."[46] Courts examine the elements of liability for the particular cause of action, and if "the generalized evidence will prove or disprove an element on a simultaneous, class-wide basis," and the common issues "constitute a significant part of the individual cases," then the predominance requirement is satisfied.[47] One common element may be sufficient, provided that the elements remaining for individualized determination do not present manageability difficulties.[48]

Minnesota courts are open to bifurcating damages from liability in order to achieve predominance, but before doing so courts must consider whether "the damages . . . lend themselves to mechanical calculation" or whether they would require "a large number of mini-trials" on the issue of damages.[49] "[I]f a different damages calculation would be required for each [plaintiff], the necessity of separate calculations weighs against satisfaction of the predominance requirement."[50] Minnesota courts have been particularly reluctant to certify antitrust class actions if "any determination of fact or amount of individual damage will require thousands of factual examinations done on a retailer by retailer basis, and a transaction by transaction basis," degenerating quickly "into thousands and thousands of individual trials."[51]

---

44. *Ario*, 367 N.W.2d at 514 (quoting 2 Douglas McFarland & William J. Keppel, Minnesota Civil Practice § 1472 at 443 (1st ed. 1979)).

45. *Forcier*, 310 N.W.2d at 131.

46. *Lewy*, 650 N.W.2d at 455.

47. *Id.* at 455–56; *Streich*, 399 N.W.2d at 217.

48. *See, e.g., Cavanaugh v. Hometown Am. LLC*, No. A05-595, 2006 Minn. App. Unpub. LEXIS 265, at *6 (Mar. 21, 2006) ("[B]ecause one of the elements here is common to the class and predominates, certification is appropriate."); *Schaff v. Chateau Cmtys., Inc.*, No. A04-1246, 2005 Minn. App. Unpub. LEXIS 86, at *6 (July 26, 2005) (same).

49. *Lewy*, 650 N.W.2d at 456.

50. *Id.*

51. *Keating v. Philip Morris, Inc.*, 417 N.W.2d 132, 137 (Minn. Ct. App. 1987); *see also Peridot*, 2000 WL 673933, at *5 (rejecting plaintiffs' expert's "proposed mechanical calculations" of antitrust damages as "so insubstantial as to amount to no method at all").

"But the necessity of calculating separate damages does not destroy the appropriateness of the class-action method."[52]

b. Superiority

Minnesota courts consider "manageability, fairness, efficiency, and available alternatives" when evaluating superiority.[53]

Manageability concerns may include identification and notification of class members, choice of law issues,[54] "difficulties and inconsistencies that may result from a number of actions brought in the various counties of the state involving the same issue,"[55] and the need for individualized proof of damages. Although Minnesota courts look favorably on bifurcating class action proceedings so that individual damages determinations may take place after a classwide adjudication of liability, "[w]here proof of damage must be established on an individual basis for thousands of class members, the suit is unmanageable and class action treatment is inappropriate."[56] The Minnesota Supreme Court has also stated that if there is a "key fact issue" that must be decided at the liability stage and that "would again be presented in each individual [damages] action," "[w]e cannot see where it profits either the litigants or the administration of justice to have a repeat performance on" that key issue.[57] Under such circumstances, where "the proof needed in the individual [damages] action . . . will to a large extent duplicate the proof in any class action [on liability], we do not find the class action to be a superior method of handling this litigation."[58] However, "[w]hen collective adjudication promises substantial efficiency benefits . . . a class action is superior to other available methods for the fair adjudication of the controversy."[59]

Public policy concerns can influence a court's analysis of available alternatives. In determining superiority, Minnesota courts have considered that "[t]he purpose of the class action has been to take care of the smaller guy"[60] and have stated that the class action is particularly "needed in consumer suits where individual claims are small."[61] Courts have found class actions particularly appropriate in promoting the public purposes of usury statutes and "consumer fraud statutes to protect those who cannot protect themselves."[62]

---

52. *Lewy*, 650 N.W.2d at 457.
53. *Streich*, 399 N.W.2d at 218.
54. *Lewy*, 650 N.W.2d at 457.
55. *Klicker v. State*, 197 N.W.2d 434, 437 (Minn. 1972).
56. *Keating*, 417 N.W.2d at 137.
57. *Ario*, 367 N.W.2d at 515.
58. *Id.* at 516.
59. *Lewy*, 650 N.W.2d at 457.
60. *Streich*, 399 N.W.2d at 218; *see also Rathbun*, 219 N.W.2d at 653.
61. *Peterson I*, 618 N.W.2d at 826.
62. *Id.*

Prior to enactment of the federal Class Action Fairness Act (CAFA) in 2005, the Minnesota Supreme Court emphasized that the difficulty of aggregating small claims to qualify for federal class jurisdiction created an "even greater" need "for state class action statutes to provide a forum for such cases."[63] CAFA's more generous access to federal courts may therefore diminish the importance of these policy considerations favoring class certification under Minnesota law.

IV. Examining the Merits to Determine Certification

Minnesota district courts must "resolve factual disputes relevant to Rule 23 certification requirements, including relevant expert disputes."[64] In establishing this requirement, the Minnesota Court of Appeals recently recognized that "[t]he federal courts of appeal have addressed expert testimony related to class certification primarily in two contexts: securities litigation and antitrust litigation."[65] The court then applied the requirement of resolving relevant expert disputes in the context of an age discrimination class action.[66] The court rejected the argument that the federal antitrust and securities cases could be distinguished "as cases involving legal issues rather than factual disputes."[67] The court held that "parties moving for class certification under Minn. R. Civ. P. 23 must prove, by a preponderance of the evidence, that the certification requirements of the rule are met" and "district courts must address and resolve factual disputes relevant to class-certification requirements, including disputes among expert witnesses."[68] The court added that "the factual findings at the class-certification stage are not binding on the ultimate trier of fact."[69]

V. Interlocutory Appeals

As under federal law, there is no interlocutory appeal as of right from an order granting or denying a motion for class certification.[70] In determining what standards should guide a decision to exercise discretionary review under Rule 23.06, the Minnesota Supreme Court declined to "adopt[ ] any of the federal circuits' approaches wholesale," but instead established its own "nonexclusive list of

---

63. *Forcier*, 310 N.W.2d at 130; *see also* Chapter 10, "The Class Action Fairness Act of 2005."
64. *Whitaker*, 764 N.W.2d at 638.
65. *Id.*
66. *Id.*
67. *Id.* at 639.
68. *Id.* at 640.
69. *Id.* at 638.
70. *In re Objections*, 335 N.W.2d at 731.

factors . . . to consider . . . when making a determination whether to exercise discretionary review of a class certification decision."[71] The court held:

> The three primary factors that indicate when discretionary review should be granted are as follows:
>
> (1) when a questionable denial of class certification is the "death knell" of plaintiffs' case because their individual claims are too small to pursue individually;
>
> (2) when a questionable grant of class certification places inordinate pressure on the defendant to settle; and
>
> (3) whether the appeal will permit resolution of an important legal issue that is also important to the particular litigation.[72]

The court added that "special, compelling circumstances may exist that require a different result than a pure application of the factors identified herein," and cautioned that "exercise of the discretionary power of review is the exception rather than the norm" because the policy of Minnesota courts "is to avoid 'piecemeal appeals' that interrupt and delay litigation."[73]

A party objecting to a class certification decision has more time to file a petition for interlocutory review under Minnesota law. The federal Rule allows only ten days from the date the order is entered,[74] while the Minnesota Rules allow 30 days from the date the order is filed.[75]

VI. Settlements

Minnesota courts apply the same standards as federal courts in approving class action settlements.[76] In conducting that analysis, "[t]he court must compare the settlement's terms with the results the plaintiffs would have likely received after a full trial."[77] In evaluating the reasonableness of the settlement, the court "is not required to make . . . a comparison with different settlements in other districts" arising out of similar facts.[78] Minnesota recognizes the common-fund doctrine,

---

71. *Gordon v. Microsoft Corp.*, 645 N.W.2d 393, 401 (Minn. 2002).

72. *Id.* at 401–02 (paragraphing added).

73. *Id.* at 402–03.

74. Fed. R. Civ. P. 23(f).

75. Minn. R. Civ. App. P. 105.01 ("The petition shall be served on the adverse party and filed within 30 days of the filing of the order."); Minn. R. Civ. P. 23.06 ("An application to appeal must be sought within the time provided in Rule 105 of the Minnesota Rules of Civil Appellate Procedure, and shall be subject to the other provisions of that rule.").

76. *Heller v. Schwan's Sales Enters., Inc.*, 548 N.W.2d 287, 289 (Minn. Ct. App. 1996); *SST, Inc. v. City of Minneapolis*, 288 N.W.2d 225, 231 (Minn. 1979).

77. *Heller*, 548 N.W.2d at 289.

78. *Id.* at 291.

and under that doctrine Minnesota courts have approved a settlement in which class counsel receive a proportion of the amounts paid to class members.[79]

The class action settlement standards in Rule 23 also apply to settlements approved by an administrative law judge for claims brought by the Commissioner of Human Rights under Minnesota's Human Rights Act.[80]

VII. Attorney Fee Awards

The Minnesota Supreme Court has cautioned that

> [t]he common fund doctrine says only that class members must pay their attorney out of the fund recovered for the class. The doctrine has nothing to do with whether the defendant sued by the class must, in addition to the damages recovered against him, pay attorney fees. The general rule in this country, subject to well-defined exceptions, is that parties pay their own attorney fees.[81]

A plaintiff seeking to recover attorney fees must therefore establish that one of those exceptions applies. Courts will not award attorney fees simply because the class representative is successful in creating a fund for the class.[82] Some statutory provisions limit the award of attorney fees in certain class actions.[83]

Under the Minnesota Rules, a class action court has the authority "to assume exclusive jurisdiction over claims related to the class-action attorney-fee award," but is not required to do so.[84] If the class action court has entered final judgment or has not expressly retained exclusive jurisdiction prior to the entry of judgment, other district courts have subject matter jurisdiction over claims seeking a share of the attorney fee award.[85] Even though subject matter jurisdiction is not at issue, judicial comity and other prudential concerns may cause the second court to refer the case to the original class action court.[86]

79. *Id.*

80. *State ex rel. Wilson v. St. Joseph's Hosp.*, 366 N.W.2d 403, 406–07 (Minn. Ct. App. 1985).

81. *Gilchrist v. Perl*, 387 N.W.2d 412, 418 (Minn. 1986).

82. *Id.*

83. *See, e.g.*, MINN. STAT. § 17.9441 subdiv. 3 ("In a class action or series of class actions that arise from the use by a contractor of an agricultural contract found to violate section 17.943, the amount of attorney's fees and costs of investigation assessed against that contractor and in favor of the class or classes may not exceed $10,000."); MINN. STAT. § 325G.34 subdiv. 3 ("In any class action or series of class actions which arise from the use by a person of a particular consumer contract found to violate section 325G.31, the amount of attorney's fees and costs of investigation assessed against that person and in favor of the consumer class or classes may not exceed $10,000.").

84. *Boynton v. Nill*, Nos. A08-0244 & A08-0554, 2009 Minn. App. Unpub. LEXIS 262, at *15–16 (Mar. 17, 2009), *petition for further rev. denied* (Minn. May 27, 2009).

85. *Id.* at *8, 15–16.

86. *Id.* at *17–18.

VIII. Multistate Class Actions

The circumstances under which the Minnesota appellate courts may certify multistate class actions have not been clearly established. The Minnesota Court of Appeals has adopted the federal standards for multistate class actions, holding that "[a] state district court may exercise jurisdiction over a multistate class. The state court must provide minimal procedural due process protection, including a choice of law that is not arbitrary or fundamentally unfair."[87] Minnesota courts have approved multistate class action settlements.[88] With respect to litigated class actions, what little Minnesota appellate authority exists on the subject of multistate class actions may be of questionable precedential value.

The ambiguous status of multistate class actions under Minnesota law emerges from *Peterson v. BASF Corp.*,[89] a case with what the Minnesota Supreme Court acknowledged is a "unique procedural history." The district court in *Peterson* certified a nationwide class of plaintiffs under the New Jersey Consumer Fraud Act, concluding that "it was neither arbitrary nor fundamentally unfair to certify" the nationwide class.[90] Several months later, the district court denied defendant BASF's motion to decertify the class, but granted its motion for summary judgment.[91] The plaintiffs appealed the grant of summary judgment, and BASF on appeal challenged the district court's order certifying the class and its denial of the motion to decertify.[92] BASF argued on appeal, among other things, that "class certification was inappropriate because a detailed choice of law analysis was in order . . . and because different states' consumer protection laws" applied to the claims of class members, depending on where they purchased and used the product.[93]

The court of appeals reversed the district court's grant of summary judgment and also held that the decision to certify the class was not an abuse of discretion.[94] The court's cursory examination of the class certification issues did not mention choice of law or whether it was appropriate to apply the New Jersey Consumer Fraud Act to the claims of all class members.[95] In a subsequent lengthy procedural history, the Minnesota Supreme Court twice avoided addressing the class certification and conflict of law issues on procedural grounds.[96]

---

87. *Heller*, 548 N.W.2d at 289–90 (citation and internal quotation marks omitted).

88. *See, e.g., id.* at 290–92.

89. *Peterson II*, 675 N.W.2d at 68.

90. *Id.* at 63.

91. *Id.*

92. *Id.*

93. *Id.* at 67.

94. *Id.* at 64.

95. *See Peterson I*, 618 N.W.2d at 826.

96. *Peterson II*, 675 N.W.2d at 66–68; *Peterson I*, 618 N.W.2d at 825–26.

Both before and after *Peterson*, Minnesota district courts have engaged in rigorous choice of law analysis when deciding whether it is appropriate to certify a nationwide class.[97] In sum, Minnesota law on the certification of multistate classes, especially litigated as opposed to settlement classes, remains less than fully developed.

IX. *Minnesota Human Rights Act Class Actions*

Minnesota Rule 5000.1100 establishes a separate set of procedures by which the Minnesota Commissioner of Human Rights may sue on behalf of a class for violations of Minnesota's Human Rights Act. The Rule's prerequisites are "substantially like" Rule 23.01, but there is no numerosity prerequisite.[98] An administrative law judge determines whether the administrative equivalents of the Rule 23.01 prerequisites and Rule 23.02 requirements are satisfied and then oversees notice to the potential members of the class and conducts a hearing on the charge.[99] The administrative law judge's decision is a final agency decision subject to judicial review.[100] The Minnesota Supreme Court has held that "Rule 5000.1100 provides the [administrative law judge] no room for exercising discretion."[101] The administrative law judge may refuse to certify a class based on a factor in Rule 5000.1100, but may not do so based on a determination that certain claims cannot be proven.[102]

---

97. *See, e.g., Rupp v. Thompson*, No. C5-03-347, 2004 WL 3563775, at *3–4 (Minn. Dist. Ct. Mar. 17, 2004); *Graham v. Knutson Mortgage Corp.*, No. CT 94-11043, 1996 WL 407491, at *5–7 (Minn. Dist. Ct. June 18, 1996); *see also Lewy*, 650 N.W.2d at 457 ("Both IAI and the trustees agree that Delaware law applies, so the court will not be confronted with complex choice-of-law issues.").

98. *State ex rel. McClure v. Sports & Health Club, Inc.*, 370 N.W.2d 844, 854 (Minn. 1985). *Compare* Minn. R. 5000.1100 subpart 1 *with* Minn. R. Civ. P. 23.01(a).

99. Minn. R. 5000.1100 subpart 2, 3; Minn. Stat. § 363A.29.

100. Minn. R. 5000.1100 subpart 6; Minn. Stat. § 363A.30; Minn. Stat. § 14.001 *et seq.*; *Dep't of Human Rights v. Hibbing Taconite Co.*, 482 N.W.2d 504, 506 (Minn. Ct. App. 1992) ("This court may reverse or modify an ALJ's decision if it is in violation of constitutional provisions, in excess of an agency's statutory authority or jurisdiction, unsupported by substantial evidence, arbitrary or capricious, or affected by an error of law.").

101. *State ex rel. McClure*, 370 N.W.2d at 854.

102. *Id.*

MISSISSIPPI

LUTHER T. MUNFORD
ROBERT GREGG MAYER

I. Introduction

Mississippi does not permit class actions of any kind. When Mississippi adopted civil rules modeled on the Federal Rules of Civil Procedure, it expressly omitted Rule 23.[1] The Mississippi Supreme Court has even abolished the equitable class action that its chancery courts once recognized.[2] As a result, the state's joinder practices have played a significant and, with recent changes to the Rules, an increasingly restrictive role in multiplaintiff litigation.

II. Mississippi's Abolition of Class Actions

In adopting the Mississippi Rules of Civil Procedure in 1982, the state supreme court purposefully decided to exclude class action litigation.[3] The Mississippi Supreme Court explained that the state's court system was unable to manage class actions, though the court noted the Rules might be open to change.[4]

Historically, the absence of a class action rule had not precluded class actions in Mississippi chancery courts under general equity jurisdiction.[5] For example, equitable class actions would have been permitted in the "rare circumstance[ ]"[6]

---

1. In full, the Rule reads: "Rule 23. Class Actions. [Omitted]."
2. *See USF&G Ins. Co. of Mississippi v. Walls*, 911 So. 2d 463, 464 (Miss. 2005).
3. *See Am. Bankers Ins. Co. of Fla. v. Booth*, 830 So. 2d 1205, 1214 (Miss. 2002).
4. *Id.* at 1214.
5. *See Marx v. Broom*, 632 So. 2d 1315, 1322 (Miss. 1994) ("Prior to the enactment of the Rules of Civil Procedure, this Court recognized the possibility of class action suits as a matter of general equity jurisdiction in chancery court under limited circumstances.").
6. Guthrie T. Abbott & Pope Mallette, *Complex/Mass Tort Litigation in State Courts in Mississippi*, 63 MISS. L.J. 363, 393 (1994).

of plaintiffs seeking to enjoin governmental entities. There was even a statute that provided for class actions in equity.[7]

But in 2005, in *USF&G Insurance Co. of Mississippi v. Walls*,[8] the Mississippi Supreme Court ruled that class actions do not exist in any form in the state's courts: "[C]lass actions . . . are not a part of Mississippi practice—chancery, circuit, or otherwise."[9] Indeed, the Mississippi Supreme Court determined that the preexisting statutory authority for class actions in equity was "inconsistent" with the Mississippi Rules of Civil Procedure, and so the Rules trumped the statute.[10]

The absence of any formal class action rule, however, did not slow down the rush to file mass tort lawsuits in Mississippi in the 1990s and into the early 2000s. To the contrary, liberal joinder rules fueled a mass tort bonanza.

III. The 2004 Move to Restrict Liberal Joinder Rules

At one time, Mississippi was the "hotbed" of mass tort litigation.[11] The engine behind the Mississippi mass actions was the judiciary's liberal interpretation of Mississippi Rules of Civil Procedure 20 and 42, the rules governing the permissive joinder of parties and the consolidation of trials involving a common question of law or fact. At the mass tort peak, one case involved 6,000 plaintiffs with various asbestos-related injuries. To accommodate the sheer volume of participants, one circuit court held a jury trial at the county fairgrounds.[12]

But in February 2004, things changed. The Mississippi Supreme Court deleted a portion of the Comment to Rule 20 that provided that the "general philosophy of the joinder provisions of these rules is to allow *virtually unlimited joinder* at the pleading stage."[13] More dramatically, the court tightened the definition of a same "transaction or occurrence" within the Rules to require there be a "distinct litigable event linking the parties."[14]

In the same month as the amendments to Rule 20 were announced, the Mississippi Supreme Court handed down *Janssen Pharmaceutica, Inc. v. Armond*.[15] In

---

7. MISS. CODE ANN. § 11-53-37.

8. 911 So. 2d 463.

9. *Id.* at 468.

10. *Id.* at 467.

11. Howard M. Erichson, *Mississippi Class Actions and the Inevitability of Mass Aggregate Litigation*, 24 MISS. C.L. REV. 285 (2005).

12. Richard T. Phillips, *Class Action and Joinder in Mississippi*, 71 MISS. L.J. 447, 456 (2001).

13. MISS. R. CIV. P. 20 cmt. (pre-2004) (emphasis added); *see also MS Life Ins. Co. v. Baker*, 905 So. 2d 1179, 1183 (Miss. 2005).

14. *See* MISS. R. CIV. P. 20 cmt.

15. 866 So. 2d 1092 (Miss. 2004). In fact, *Armond* was handed down one day before the new Rule 20(a) took effect, eliminating the "virtually unlimited" joinder language; however, the court still found joinder improper under the old Rule. *See Baker*, 905 So. 2d at 1184.

Armond, 56 plaintiffs filed suit against their doctors, hospitals, and the Propulsid drug manufacturer. Although the claims all sought damages for the ingestion of Propulsid, the Mississippi Supreme Court held joinder was improper. It reversed a trial court's denial of a motion to sever because each plaintiff had "different medical histories; alleg[ed] different injuries at different times; ingested different amounts [of the drug]; [and] received different advice from different doctors who, in turn, received different information about the risks associated with the medication[,]" among other distinguishing events.[16] In short, there was no "distinct litigable event" linking the plaintiffs. Later in 2004, the Mississippi Supreme Court reversed a $48 million damages award against a Propulsid manufacturer in *Janssen Pharmaceutica, Inc. v. Bailey*.[17] It said the joinder of the ten different consumers in that lawsuit was improper under Mississippi's tightened joinder requirements.[18] With *Armond* and *Bailey*, the heyday of Mississippi's liberal joinder practice came to an end.

IV. Conclusion

In light of *Armond*, the tightening of the liberal joinder rules, and the complete absence of class actions in Mississippi state courts, some critics contend that it is time to swing the pendulum back the other way to allow for class actions in state courts.[19] Such a movement, however, has not seen much traction so far.

---

16. *Armond*, 866 So. 2d at 1096.
17. 878 So. 2d 31 (Miss. 2004). This award came in the first Propulsid case in the country to go through a trial and jury verdict.
18. *Id.* at 45–48.
19. *See* Erichson, *supra* note 11.

MISSOURI

ADAM E. MILLER[1]

I. Introduction

In Missouri, Supreme Court Rule 52.08 (Missouri Rule) governs the procedure for the certification of class actions. The Rule sets forth the necessary requirements and the types of class actions maintainable, as well as rules regarding class certification, notice to class members, judgments, partial class actions, court orders, dismissal, and appeals. Since the Missouri Rule is nearly identical to Federal Rule 23, Missouri courts find federal class action decisions highly persuasive.[2]

The purpose of Missouri's class action procedure is "to facilitate litigation when the number of persons having interest in a lawsuit is so great that it is impractical to join them as parties. In many cases this allows the accumulation of many relatively small but meritorious claims that would not otherwise be pursued."[3] Membership in the putative class must be readily ascertainable based on "definite and objective criteria" included in the class definition.[4] Ascertainment of class membership must not remain contingent on the outcome of some later merits determination. "[I]ndividualized hearings or 'mini-hearings' to determine who is a member of the class [are] 'incongruous with the efficiencies expected in a class action' and effectively 'render[ ] any class action inappropriate for addressing the claims at issue.'"[5]

---

1. The author gratefully acknowledges the assistance of Timothy Hodits in reviewing this chapter.

2. *Craft v. Philip Morris Co., Inc.*, 190 S.W.3d 368, 376 (Mo. Ct. App. 2005).

3. *Dale v. DaimlerChrysler Corp.*, 204 S.W.3d 151, 164 (Mo. Ct. App. 2006).

4. *Id.* at 166.

5. *Id.* (quoting *Senneman v. Chrysler Corp.*, 191 F.R.D. 441, 446 (E.D. Pa. 2000)).

II. Threshold Requirements for Certification

Under Rule 52.08, the party seeking certification bears the burden of proving the following four prerequisites:

> (1) the class is so numerous that joinder of all members is impracticable, (2) there are questions of law or fact common to the class, (3) the claims or defenses of the representative parties are typical of the claims or defenses of the class, and (4) the representative parties will fairly and adequately protect the interests of the class.[6]

The requirements "are not merely technical or directory, but are mandatory."[7]

A. NUMEROSITY

Rule 52.08 requires that the class demonstrate that "the class is so numerous that joinder of all members is impracticable."[8] Putative class size is "an important consideration in satisfying the numerosity requirement, but is not a dispositive one."[9] Whether the class is sufficiently numerous depends on the "circumstances in a given case."[10] "In making [the determination of numerosity], the courts have not developed arbitrary or rigid rules to define the required size of a class."[11] Rather, the primary consideration in determining whether the numerosity requirement has been satisfied is the practicability of joining the class members as parties.[12] The party seeking certification is not required to identify with great precision the number of putative class members, but must provide some evidence or a reasonable, good faith estimate of the number of putative class members.[13]

B. COMMONALITY

The putative class must also demonstrate the existence of "questions of law or fact common to the class."[14] This requirement is generally regarded as less demanding than the requirement that common questions predominate over individual questions under class actions authorized by 52.08(b)(3).

C. TYPICALITY

The "claims or defenses of the representative parties [must be] typical of the claims or defenses of the class."[15] Typicality ensures that the "class members share the

---

6. Mo. Sup. Ct. R. 52.08(a).

7. Id.

8. Id.

9. Doyle v. Fluor Corp., 199 S.W.3d 784, 792 (Mo. Ct. App. 2006).

10. Campbell v. Webb, 258 S.W.2d 595, 599 (Mo. 1953).

11. Dale, 204 S.W.3d at 167.

12. See Sheets v. Thomann, 336 S.W.2d 701, 710 (Mo. Ct. App. 1960); Dale, 204 S.W.3d at 164.

13. Dale, 204 S.W.3d at 164 (citing Linquist v. Bowen, 633 F. Supp. 846, 858 (W.D. Mo. 1986)).

14. Mo. Sup. Ct. R. 52.08(a)(2).

15. Mo. Sup. Ct. R. 52.08(c).

same interest and suffer the same injury" and "is fairly easily met so long as other class members have claims similar to the named plaintiff."[16] The typicality requirement "is designed to preclude class certification of actions involving legal or factual positions of the representative class which are markedly different from those of other class members."[17] "If the claim arises from the same event or course of conduct as the class claims, and gives rise to the same legal or remedial theory, factual variations in the individual claims will not normally preclude class certification."[18]

Affirmative defenses and differing damages unique to each class member may not be sufficient in and of themselves to defeat typicality.[19] "Defenses may affect the individual's ultimate right to recover, but they do not affect the presentation of the case as to liability for the named class representative's case."[20]

D. ADEQUACY OF REPRESENTATION

Finally, Rule 52.08(a)(4) requires that "the representative parties fairly and adequately protect the interests of the class."[21] "This requirement is particularly important because the due process rights of absentee class members may be implicated if they are bound by a final judgment in a suit where they were inadequately represented by the named plaintiff."[22]

The requirement applies to both class counsel and the named representative.[23] A class representative whose interests conflict with the interests of the putative class may not satisfy this requirement. In determining whether a conflict of interest exists, "the trial court not only considers whether there is an actual conflict of interest, but whether there is a likelihood that such a conflict may exist."[24]

Representativeness is an issue of fact and determined on a case-by-case basis.[25] Specifically, "[a] plaintiff must allege and prove facts showing that the [representative] has been fairly chosen and adequately represents the class."[26] The class representative must be a member of the class and "possess the same interest and suffer the same injury as the class members."[27] Missouri courts have rejected a per se

---

16. *Id.*

17. *Hale v. Wal-Mart Stores, Inc.*, 231 S.W.3d 215, 223 (Mo. Ct. App. 2007) (internal quotations omitted).

18. *Id.*

19. *Dale*, 204 S.W.3d at 171.

20. *Id.*

21. Shareholder derivative class actions brought under Missouri Supreme Court Rule 52.09 and class actions brought by or against unincorporated associations under Rule 52.10 also require the named plaintiff to fairly and adequately represent the interests of the class.

22. *State ex rel. Union Planters Bank, N.A. v. Kendrick*, 142 S.W.3d 729, 735–36 (Mo. 2004) (quoting *Key v. Gillette Co.*, 782 F.2d 5, 7 (1st Cir. 1986)).

23. *Vandyne v. Allied Mortgage Capital Corp.*, 242 S.W.3d 695, 698 (Mo. 2008).

24. *Dale*, 204 S.W.3d at 173.

25. *Id.*

26. *Craft*, 190 S.W.3d at 379.

27. *Koger v. Hartford Life Ins. Co.*, 28 S.W.3d 405, 410 (Mo. Ct. App. 2000) (internal quotations omitted).

rule excluding a relative of an employee of class counsel as class representative.[28] Instead, "Missouri courts utilize a case-by-case approach that vests the circuit court with discretion to determine whether, under the facts of individual cases," the class counsel will adequately represent the class.[29] "Under this approach, the circuit court is required to constantly monitor the case to ensure that the interests of the absent parties are being protected."[30]

III. Maintainable Class Actions

If the four prerequisites in Rule 52.08(a) are satisfied, the court must next determine whether the class action is maintainable under subsection (b) of the Missouri Rule. Rule 52.08(b) authorizes three types of class actions: (1) where independent actions could unfairly affect the class or the opposing party; (2) where classwide equitable relief is sought; and (3) where questions of law or fact common to the class predominate over individual questions and a class action is superior to other available methods for the adjudication of the controversy. "Although the class certification decision is independent of the ultimate merits of the lawsuit, the applicable substantive law is relevant to a meaningful determination of the certification issues."[31]

A. RISK OF SEPARATE SUITS

The first type of class action authorized under Rule 52.08(b) is appropriate when

> the prosecution of separate actions by or against individual members of the class would create a risk of (A) inconsistent or varying adjudications with respect to individual members of the class which would establish incompatible standards of conduct for the party opposing the class, or (B) adjudications with respect to individual members of the class which would as a practical matter be dispositive of the interests of the other members not parties to the adjudications or substantially impair or impede their ability to protect their interests.

This category of class actions is "concerned with the risk of inconsistent or varying determinations."[32] A class that seeks only money damages, as opposed to injunctive relief, presents "little risk that separate suits could establish incompatible standards for the party opposing the class."[33] An action for damages under Rule 52.08(b)(1) is maintainable when "only a common or limited fund is available to pay members of the class."[34]

---

28. *Dale*, 204 S.W.3d at 174.
29. *Vandyne*, 242 S.W.3d at 698.
30. *Id.*
31. *Green v. Fred Weber, Inc.*, 254 S.W.3d 874, 880 (Mo. 2008).
32. *Id.* at 884.
33. *Id.*
34. *Id.* at 885 n.12.

B. EQUITABLE RELIEF

Rule 52.08(b)(2) provides that a class action is maintainable if "the party opposing the class has acted or refused to act on grounds generally applicable to the class, thereby making appropriate final injunctive relief or corresponding declaratory relief with respect to the class as a whole." There are no Missouri cases discussing Rule 52.08(b)(2) actions.

C. COMMON QUESTIONS

The third type of class action maintainable under the Missouri Rule is available if "the court finds that the questions of law or fact common to the members of the class predominate over any questions affecting only individual members, and that a class action is superior to other available methods for the fair and efficient adjudication of the controversy."[35] "The object of Rule 52.08(b)(3) is to get at the cases where a class action promises important advantages of economy of effort and uniformity of result without undue dilution of procedural safeguards for members of the class or for the opposing party."[36]

Proving that the common questions predominate over the individual issues is a separate, and more demanding, requirement than "finding the existence of common questions under 52.08(a)(2)."[37] To meet the predominance requirement, every issue in the matter does not have to be common to the entire class, but substantial common issues must exist and predominate over the individual issues.[38] Moreover, "the common issues do not need to dispose of the entire action"; rather, "'one or more of the central issues in the action'" must predominate, even if other separate issues must be tried separately.[39] The touchstone of Rule 52.08(b)(3)'s "predominance" requirement rests in the valuation of the evidence to be presented on the class claims. "'If, to make a prima facie showing *on a given question*, the members of a proposed class will need to present evidence that varies from member to member, then it is an individual question.'"[40]

"The fact that an affirmative defense may be available against certain individual class members and affect them differently does not, by itself, show that individual issues predominate."[41]

---

35. Mo. Sup. Ct. R. 52.08(b)(3).

36. *State ex rel. Am. Family Mut. Ins. Co. v. Clark*, 106 S.W.3d 483, 489 (Mo. 2003).

37. *Craft*, 190 S.W.3d at 381.

38. *Am. Family Mut. Ins. Co.*, 106 S.W.3d at 488.

39. *Craft*, 190 S.W.3d at 382 (quoting 7A Charles A. Wright, Arthur R. Miller & Mary K. Kane, Federal Practice and Procedure: Civil 2d § 1778, at 529 (2d ed. 1986)).

40. *Id.* (quoting *Blades v. Monsanto Co.*, 400 F.3d 562, 566 (8th Cir. 2005) (emphasis added)).

41. *Id.* at 383.

Regardless of which type of class action is sought to be certified, the court must analyze whether a class action is "superior to other available methods."[42] When making this determination, the court should consider

> (A) the interest of members of the class in individually controlling the prosecution or defense of separate actions; (B) the extent and nature of any litigation concerning the controversy already commenced by or against members of the class; (C) the desirability or undesirability of concentrating the litigation of the claims in the particular forum; and (D) the difficulties likely to be encountered in the management of a class action.[43]

This list of factors is not exclusive, however, and "the trial court [should] balance, in terms of fairness and efficiency, the merits of a class action in resolving a controversy against those of alternative available methods of adjudication."[44]

IV. Class Member Notice

"In a class action, notice is a function of adequate representation."[45] Notice is required in Rule 52.08(b)(3) class actions; notice is merely discretionary in actions maintained under Rule 52.08(b)(1) and (b)(2).[46] Class actions proceeding under Rule 52.08(b)(3) require that members of the class receive "the best notice practicable under the circumstances, including individual notice to all members who can be identified through reasonable effort."[47] The notice must state that "(A) the court will exclude the member from the class if requested by a specified date; (B) the judgment, whether favorable or not, will include all members who do not request exclusion; and (C) any member who does not request exclusion may, if desired, enter an appearance through counsel."[48]

V. Settlement and Dismissal

Rule 52.08(e) provides that "[a] class action shall not be dismissed or compromised without the approval of the court, and notice of the proposed dismissal or com-

---

42. Mo. Sup. Ct. R. 52.08(b)(3).

43. Mo. Sup. Ct. R. 52.08. "Failure to certify an action on the sole ground that it would be unmanageable is disfavored by federal courts." *Craft*, 190 S.W.3d at 386. Notably, "[t]he existence of administrative complications in managing the distribution of different damage awards to a class does not suggest that a trial court abuses its discretion in finding a class manageable." *Id.*

44. *Dale*, 204 S.W.3d at 181.

45. *City of Excelsior Springs v. Elms Redevelopment Corp.*, 18 S.W.3d 53, 59 (Mo. Ct. App. 2000).

46. *State ex inf. Ashcroft v. Kansas City Firefighters Local No. 42*, 672 S.W.2d 99, 120 (Mo. Ct. App. 1984).

47. Mo. Sup. Ct. R. 52.08(c)(2).

48. *Id.*

promise shall be given to all members of the class."[49] This Rule imposes a lower standard than the provision governing notice of class certification; however, the notice of settlement must still satisfy due process.[50] To meet the requirements of due process, notice of settlement must "fairly apprise prospective members of the class of the terms of the settlement and of the options that are open to them in connection with [the] proceedings."[51] The information contained in a notice of settlement "need only be general in nature, and can refer the putative class members to the court or counsel for detailed information."[52]

In furtherance of its continuing duty to protect the interests of absent class members, the court need not accept a settlement proposed by the class representatives. In determining whether a settlement is satisfactory, courts will scrutinize the total dollar amount of the settlement, the attorney fees, the presence or absence of opposition to the settlement, and the likelihood of a successful result in litigation.[53]

In evaluating fairness and reasonableness,

> the court must consider: (1) the existence of fraud or collusion behind the settlement; (2) the complexity, expense, and likely duration of the litigation; (3) the stage of the proceedings and the amount of discovery completed; (4) the probability of the plaintiff's success on the merits; (5) the range of possible recovery; and (6) the opinions of class counsel, class representatives and absent class members.[54]

The most important of these considerations "is the strength of the plaintiff's case on the merits balanced against the offered settlement."[55]

In determining attorney fees for class counsel in the proposed settlement of a class action, "[t]he court should consider the percentage of recovery requested, the size of the total recovery on behalf of the class and the time and effort of the attorneys," among other factors.[56] "The court may also check the fairness of the proposed award by comparing it to the amount to which counsel would be entitled if their fee were figured on an hourly basis."[57] In addition, the trial court must "make certain that the amount of settlement is fixed and will remain the same even if

---

49. Mo. Sup. Ct. R. 52.08(e). Actions brought under Rule 52.10 against unincorporated associations must be dismissed or settled according to the procedures in 52.10. Shareholder derivative class actions under Rule 52.09 are distinguishable, however, because notice is not required, but rather given in the manner directed by the court. Mo. Sup. Ct. R. 52.09.

50. *State ex rel. Byrd v. Chadwick*, 956 S.W.2d 369, 385 (Mo. Ct. App. 1997).

51. *Id.* (quoting *Maywalt v. Parker & Parsley Petroleum Co.*, 67 F.3d 1072 (2d Cir. 1995)).

52. *Id.*

53. *Grantham v. J.L. Mason Group*, 811 F. Supp. 1386, 1390 (E.D. Mo. 1993).

54. *Ring v. Metro. St. Louis Sewer Dist.*, 41 S.W.3d 487, 492 (Mo. Ct. App. 2000).

55. *Id.*

56. *Byrd*, 956 S.W.2d at 388.

57. *Id.*

class counsel's fee is reduced in amount, and that the attorneys are not benefiting at expense of class."[58]

VI. Effect of Judgment

While the procedural utility of class actions is well recognized, it is also well recognized that by their very nature, class actions are a procedural exception to the "cardinal principle of jurisprudence that one is not bound by a judgment in personam entered in litigation to which he was not designated as a party or made a party by service of process or entry of appearance."[59] Members of a class who did not initiate the lawsuit have little or no control over the case, but are still bound by its result.[60] "[A]s long as the representation is adequate and faithful, there is no unfairness in giving res judicata effect to a judgment against all members of class even if they have not received notice."[61]

VII. Appeals and Review

Under Missouri Supreme Court Rule 52.08(f), "[a]n appellate court may permit an appeal from an order of a circuit court granting or denying class action certification . . . if a petition is timely filed as provided in Rule 84.035." Rule 52.08(f) does not permit an appeal of certification orders as a matter of right.[62] "The filing of a petition shall not stay the proceedings in the trial court unless the trial judge or the appellate court so orders."[63]

The appeal of an order granting class certification is reviewed solely for abuse of discretion.[64] The court of appeals "will err on the side of upholding certification in cases where it is a close question" because the class certification rule "provides for de-certification of a class before a decision on the merits."[65]

---

58. *Id.* The U.S. Supreme Court also established in *Evans v. Jeff D.*, 475 U.S. 717 (1986), that a court could not require that a settlement include attorney fees where they would have been required in a judgment in the plaintiff class's favor, if the settlement offer is still reasonable and fair to the class represented. *Id.* at 728.

59. *Beatty v. Metro. St. Louis Sewer Dist.*, 914 S.W.2d 791, 794 (Mo. 1995) (en banc) (internal citation omitted).

60. *Id.*

61. *Ashcroft*, 672 S.W.2d at 121 n.11 (internal citations omitted).

62. *State ex rel. Coca-Cola Co. v. Nixon*, 249 S.W.3d 855, 859 (Mo. 2008).

63. Mo. Sup. Ct. R. 52.08(f).

64. *Hale*, 231 S.W.3d at 221.

65. *Dale*, 204 S.W.3d at 164.

MONTANA

ALLAN MCGARVEY

I. Introduction

Rule 23 of Montana's Rules of Civil Procedure derives from and is practically identical to the pre-2003 version of Federal Rule 23, and the Montana courts are instructed by federal authority.[1] Montana, however, allows a direct, immediate appeal (as of right) from any order granting or denying class certification.[2]

II. Rule 23(a) Prerequisites to Class Certification

Montana courts apply the same requirements of numerosity, commonality, typicality, and adequacy of representation. The trial court exercises broad discretion in determining the need for discovery and/or evidentiary hearings in advance of the certification ruling.[3] The class certification decision is reviewed under an abuse of discretion standard.[4] The Montana Supreme Court has specifically held the common question may be one of either law or fact[5] and that the commonality standard is permissively applied:

> Rule 23(a)(2) does not require that every question of law or fact be common to every member of the class. The commonality requirement is satisfied "where the question of law linking the class members is substantially related to the resolution of the litigation even though the individuals are not identically situated."[6]

---

1. *McDonald v. Washington*, 261 Mont. 392, 400, 862 P.2d 1150, 1154 (1993).

2. MONT. R. APP. P. 6(3)(d).

3. *Mattson v. Mont. Power Co.*, 215 P.3d 675, 694–95 (Mont. 2009).

4. *Sieglock v. Burlington N. Santa Fe Ry. Co.*, 2003 MT 355, ¶ 18, 319 Mont. 8, ¶ 5, 81 P.3d 495, ¶ 18.

5. *Ferguson v. Safeco Ins. Co. of Am.*, 342 Mont. 380, 180 P.3d 1164, 2008 MT 109.

6. *McDonald*, 261 Mont. at 401, 862 P.2d at 1155 (quoting *Jordan v. County of L.A.*, 669 F.2d 1311, 1320 (9th Cir. 1982)).

Typicality is evaluated under the traditional tests to assure the appropriate "nexus" or "alignment" between the representative and the class such that a vigorous pursuit of the representative's claim will necessarily advance the interests of the class. These tests require a demonstration that the representative's claim "stems from the same event, practice, or course of conduct that forms the basis of the claims and is based on the same legal or remedial theory."[7] Montana has recognized that a class of individuals affected by the common practice of multiple defendants may be represented by a class member whose claim is against some, but not all, of the defendants so long as sufficient "juridical link" is established. For example, a juridical link may exist where "the various defendants are related instrumentalities of a single state" or where they have "industry-wide collective bargaining agreements, or any other type of industry-wide agreement, or through involvement in any type of holding entity or claims management association, or the like.[8]

Montana has a peculiar representation rule, 23(f) of the Montana Rules of Civil Procedure, which permits the defendant in a class action to demand the class representative to provide an undertaking for costs. The Rule is of little practical significance because the required undertaking may not exceed $1,000.

III. Rule 23(b) Categories

The Montana Supreme Court has expressly approved mandatory class actions under Rule 23(b)(2) to address, through declaratory or injunctive relief, conduct of the defendant generally applicable to the class.[9] In an "opt-out" class under Rule 23(b)(3), Montana allows the additional element of "predominance" to be established by the centrality of the liability question to the litigation, notwithstanding the need for calculation of widely varying damages on an individual basis.[10]

IV. Lawyers and Attorney Fees

Section (g), pertaining to class counsel, and section (h), addressing attorney fees and nontaxable costs, of Federal Rule 23 are not included in the Montana class action rule. Nevertheless, Montana follows the same underlying principles. Competency of class counsel is addressed as an element of the "adequacy of representation" element under Rule 23(a).

---

7. *Id.*

8. *Murer v. State Comp. Mut. Ins. Fund*, 257 Mont. 434, 439, 849 P.2d 1036, 1038 (1993) (*Murer I*).

9. *Ferguson*, 342 Mont. at 389–90, 180 P.3d at 1170.

10. *McDonald*, 261 Mont. at 403, 862 P.2d at 1157.

Montana allows assessment of attorney fees against the common fund or common benefit created for the class. In common-fund cases, the Montana Court has held that such recovery is "contingent upon success, and upon the existence of a fund from which the fees can be paid,"[11] and has adopted the standard of "fair, reasonable, and in the best interests of all affected."[12] The Montana Court has addressed recovery of common-fund fees in some depth in two cases that are not class actions.[13] The court embraced a broad meaning for "common fund" and held that the mechanism is "especially appropriate . . . where the individual damage from an institutional wrong may not be sufficient from an economic viewpoint to justify the legal expense necessary to challenge that wrong."[14]

V. Punitive Damages

Montana expressly recognizes class actions as an exception to the statutory cap on punitive damages.[15]

VI. Appeals

Orders granting or denying class certification are immediately appealable as a matter of right so long as the trial court has reached its "final decision" on the certification question.[16]

---

11. *Assoc. of Unit Owners of Deer Lodge Condo., Inc. v. Big Sky of Mont., Inc.*, 790 P.2d 967, 969, 242 Mont. 358, 362 (1990).

12. *Id.*

13. *Means v. Mont. Power Co.*, 191 Mont. 395, 625 P.2d 32 (1981); *Murer v. State Comp. Mut. Ins. Fund*, 283 Mont. 210, 942 P.2d 69 (1997) (*Murer II*).

14. *Murer II*, 283 Mont. at 222–23, 942 P.2d at 76.

15. Mont. Code Ann. § 27-1-220(3).

16. Mont. R. App. P. 6(3)(d).

NEBRASKA

MEGAN M. BELCHER

I. Introduction

Nebraska Statute Section 25-319 governs class actions in Nebraska.[1] That statute simply states, "When the question is one of a common or general interest of many persons, or when the parties are very numerous, and it may be impracticable to bring them all before the court, one or more may sue or defend for the benefit of all."[2] However, Nebraska's courts have interpreted that single sentence to parse out the various requirements for parties in Nebraska.

II. Requirements for Certification

The statute, in general, imposes two requirements. First, for a representative to bring an action on behalf of a class, the representative must bring suit for the benefit of the class (the commonality requirement).[3] The test to determine a "common interest" is whether all members of the class desire the same outcome as their representative.[4] If the class members have potentially conflicting interests, then that is incompatible with the recognition of a true class action.[5] In addition, an action may not be maintained as a class action by a plaintiff on behalf of himself and others unless he has the power as member of the class to satisfy judgment on behalf of the class.[6]

Second, a class action may only be brought when the question underlying the suit is one of common interest or where the parties are too numerous and

---

1. NEB. REV. STAT. § 25-319.
2. See id.
3. See Evans v. Metro. Utils. Dist. of Omaha, 176 N.W.2d 679 (Neb. 1970).
4. NEB. REV. ST. § 25-319; see also Hoiengs v. County of Adams, 516 N.W.2d 223 (Neb. 1994).
5. See Riha Farms, Inc. v. Sarpy County, 322 N.W.2d 797 (Neb. 1982).
6. See State ex rel. Sampson v. Kenny, 175 N.W.2d 5 (Neb. 1970).

it may be impracticable to bring all the actions before the court (the numerosity requirement).[7] Although the statute joins the two requirements with the word "or," the Nebraska Supreme Court has indicated that the conjunctive in fact should read as an "and," and therefore requires both showings.[8] Consequently, the filing representative must meet both requirements for the action to be proper under the statute.

As with federal law, implied in the commonality requirement is the requirement that there be the existence of an identifiable class. Both of these requirements assume the existence of an identifiable class. The existence of an identifiable class is therefore an implicit requirement for a class action.[9] Additionally, as one would anticipate with the selected language of "one or more may sue or defend for the benefit of all," the named parties must be able to demonstrate that they have appropriate standing as part of the class.[10] Should the named plaintiff's circumstances change such that he or she is no longer a member of the class, another class member may be substituted for the previously named class member.[11]

In Nebraska, the courts are empowered with broad discretion in determining whether the claiming party has properly brought an action as a class action.[12]

III. Notice and Pleading

The information contained in the pleading of the action will generally determine whether or not the suit may proceed as a class action.[13] With regard to providing notice under the Nebraska statute, generally notice to all class members is not required in class actions.[14] However, any member of a putative class not receiving notice would not be bound by a judgment entered into in the action.[15]

---

7. *See Archer v. Musick*, 23 N.W.2d 323 (Neb. 1946).

8. *See Hoiengs*, 516 N.W.2d at 240; *see also Lynch v. State Farm Mut. Auto. Ins. Co.*, 745 N.W.2d 291, 298 (Neb. 2008).

9. *See Kosowski v. City Betterment Corp.*, 1249 N.W.2d 481 (Neb. 1977) (class action improper because the class members could not be satisfactorily identified). The same is true at the federal level. *See* Chapter 3.A, "Class Definition."

10. Neb. Rev. Stat. § 25-319.

11. *See Hoiengs*, 516 N.W.2d at 230 (in class action involving county retirement contributions, a new named plaintiff was substituted after the original named plaintiff left his job and withdrew the funds giving him standing to file suit).

12. *See Riha Farms*, 322 N.W.2d 797; *Gant v. City of Lincoln*, 225 N.W.2d 549 (Neb. 1975); *Benesch v. City of Schuyler*, 555 N.W.2d 63 (Neb. App. 1996).

13. *See, e.g., Hoiengs*, 516 N.W.2d at 240–41.

14. *See Gant*, 225 N.W.2d 549.

15. *See Hoiengs*, 516 N.W.2d at 243.

IV. Certification

Nebraska sets forth no procedure by statute whereby the named plaintiff may seek a determination of whether or not the class is proper.[16] However, Nebraska's courts have borrowed the class certification theory from the Federal Rules.[17]

The Nebraska Supreme Court has implied that rather than certification, demurrer or summary judgment could be tools for challenging class action status.[18] However, such a process would be a somewhat tortured procedure for challenging class status, and the Nebraska Supreme Court has noted as much where the facts are disputed. However, it has noted that summary judgment may be an appropriate tool for determining class status when the facts are undisputed.[19]

With regard to the appealability of an order granting or denying class certification in Nebraska, that order is not final and therefore cannot be appealed.[20] If, upon the court's determination, the case may not proceed as a class action, the plaintiffs' causes of action on the merits do not necessarily end at that time. The actions may continue as individual actions.[21]

V. Due Process and Judicial Discretion

Nebraska courts have held that the procedure followed in class actions must comply with notions of due process to ensure the protection of absent parties who may be bound by any outcome.[22] It has also been noted that there may be a due process requirement of notice to absent class members even if there is no express statutory requirement that the parties do so.[23]

---

16. NEB. REV. STAT. § 25-319.

17. *See Johnsen v. State*, 697 N.W.2d 237, 240 (Neb. 2005); *Keef v. State, Dept. of Motor Vehicles*, 634 N.W.2d 751, 755 (Neb. 2001); *Mach v. County of Douglas*, 612 N.W.2d 237, 240 (Neb. 2000).

18. *See Twin Loups Reclamation Dist. v. Blessing*, 276 N.W.2d 185, 191 (Neb. 1979) (in holding that class action status could be challenged by demurrer or summary judgment, the court noted that unlike the Federal Rules, the Nebraska statutes do not contain a certification procedure).

19. *See Blankenship v. Omaha Pub. Power Dist.*, 237 N.W.2d 86, 90 (Neb. 1976).

20. *See Keef*, 634 N.W.2d at 759; *Lake v. Piper, Jaffray and Hopwood, Inc.*, 324 N.W.2d 660, 662 (Neb. 1982).

21. *See Roadrunner Dev., Inc. v. Sims*, 330 N.W.2d 915, 917 (Neb. 1983); *Blankenship*, 237 N.W.2d at 92; *Benesch*, 555 N.W.2d at 69.

22. *See Hoiengs*, 516 N.W.2d 223.

23. *See id.*

NEVADA

GEORLEN SPANGLER

Rule 23 of the Nevada Rules of Civil Procedure (Nevada Rule 23)[1] governs class actions in Nevada. This Rule was patterned on Federal Rule of Civil Procedure 23 before the 2003 amendments to the Federal Rule. Accordingly, Nevada courts find federal cases to be authoritative on class action issues.[2]

Although Nevada Rule 23 is modeled after Federal Rule 23, it no longer mirrors the Federal Rule.[3] Since its creation in 1971, Nevada Rule 23 has only been amended once. This occurred in 2005, and these amendments were purely technical. Neither the court nor the Advisory Committee considered the 2003 amendments to the Federal Rule. Therefore, Nevada Rule 23 does not reflect the Federal Rule's amendment that became effective December 1, 2003, that revised subdivisions (c) and (e) and added new subdivisions (g) and (h). Still, it appears that Nevada courts will continue using federal cases as authoritative on Nevada class action issues.[4]

---

1. The complete text of Nevada Rule 23 is set forth in Appendix A.

2. *Shuette v. Beazer Homes Holdings Corp.*, 121 Nev. 837, 124 P.3d 530 (2005) (citing federal cases).

3. *See, e.g., Jane Roe Dancer I-VII v. Golden Coin, Ltd.*, 124 Nev. 28, 176 P.3d 271 (2008); *Meyer v. Eighth Judicial Dist. Court*, 110 Nev. 1357, 885 P.2d 622 (1994).

4. *See, e.g., Marcuse v. Del Webb Communities, Inc.*, 123 Nev. 278, 163 P.3d 462 (2007); *Jane Roe Dancer I-VII*, 124 Nev. 28, 176 P.3d 271; *Shuette*, 121 Nev. 837, 124 P.3d 530.

APPENDIX A

Nevada Rule of Civil Procedure 23 provides:

(a) Prerequisites to a Class Action. One or more members of a class may sue or be sued as representative parties on behalf of all only if (1) the class is so numerous that joinder of all members is impracticable, (2) there are questions of law or fact common to the class, (3) the claims or defenses of the representative parties are typical of the claims or defenses of the class, and (4) the representative parties will fairly and adequately protect the interests of the class.

(b) Class Actions Maintainable. An action may be maintained as a class action if the prerequisites of subdivision (a) are satisfied, and in addition:

(1) the prosecution of separate actions by or against individual members of the class would create a risk of

(A) inconsistent or varying adjudications with respect to individual members of the class which would establish incompatible standards of conduct for the party opposing the class, or

(B) adjudications with respect to individual members of the class which would as a practical matter be dispositive of the interests of the other members not parties to the adjudications or substantially impair or impede their ability to protect their interests; or

(2) the party opposing the class has acted or refused to act on grounds generally applicable to the class, thereby making appropriate final injunctive relief or corresponding declaratory relief with respect to the class as a whole; or

(3) the court finds that the questions of law or fact common to the members of the class predominate over any questions affecting only individual members, and that a class action is superior to other available methods for the fair and efficient adjudication of the controversy. The matters pertinent to the findings include: (A) the interest of members of the class in individually controlling the prosecution or defense of separate actions; (B) the extent and nature of any litigation concerning the controversy already commenced by or against members of the class; (C) the desirability or undesirability of concentrating the litigation of the claims in the particular forum; (D) the difficulties likely to be encountered in the management of a class action.

(c) Determination by Order Whether Class Action to Be Maintained; Notice; Judgment; Actions Conducted Partially as Class Actions.

(1) As soon as practicable after the commencement of an action brought as a class action, the court shall determine by order whether it is to be so maintained. An order under this subdivision may be conditional, and may be altered or amended before the decision on the merits.

(2) In any class action maintained under subdivision (b)(3), the court shall direct to the members of the class the best notice practicable under the circumstances, including individual notice to all members who can be identified through reasonable effort. The notice shall advise each member that (A) the court will exclude the member from the class if the member so requests by a specified date; (B) the judgment, whether favorable or not, will include all members who do not request exclusion; and (C) any member who does not request exclusion may, if the member desires, enter an appearance through the member's counsel.

(3) The judgment in an action maintained as a class action under subdivision (b)(1) or (b)(2), whether or not favorable to the class, shall include and describe those whom the court finds to be members of the class. The judgment in an action maintained as a class action under subdivision (b)(3), whether or not favorable to the class, shall include and specify or describe those to whom the notice provided in subdivision (c)(2) was directed, and who have not requested exclusion, and whom the court finds to be members of the class.

(4) When appropriate (A) an action may be brought or maintained as a class action with respect to particular issues, or (B) a class may be divided into subclasses and each subclass treated as a class, and the provisions of this rule shall then be construed and applied accordingly.

(d) Orders in Conduct of Actions. In the conduct of actions to which this rule applies, the court may make appropriate orders: (1) determining the course of proceedings or prescribing measures to prevent undue repetition or complication in the presentation of evidence or argument; (2) requiring, for the protection of the members of the class or otherwise for the fair conduct of the action, that notice be given in such manner as the court may direct to some or all of the members of any step in the action, or of the proposed extent of the judgment, or of the opportunity of members to signify whether they consider the representation fair and adequate, to intervene and present claims or defenses, or otherwise to come into the action; (3) imposing conditions on the representative parties or on interveners; (4) requiring that the pleadings be amended to eliminate therefrom allegations as to representation of absent persons, and that the action proceed accordingly; (5) dealing with similar procedural matters. The orders may be combined with an order under Rule 16, and may be altered or amended as may be desirable from time to time.

(e) Dismissal or Compromise. A class action shall not be dismissed or compromised without the approval of the court, and notice of the proposed dismissal or compromise shall be given to all members of the class in such manner as the court directs.

NEW HAMPSHIRE

BRUCE W. FELMLY[1]

I. Introduction

New Hampshire Superior Court Rule 27-A (New Hampshire Rule or Rule 27-A) was enacted in 1983 and provides the standards and rules for class action practice in the state's courts. It replaced, or arguably codified, prior common law set forth in New Hampshire Supreme Court decisions that permitted class action proceedings since at least 1898.[2] Currently and historically, New Hampshire class action practice closely follows Federal Rule 23 and the cases construing it. In a recent New Hampshire Supreme Court case, *Cantwell v. J&R Properties Unlimited, Inc.*,[3] the court held that in interpreting Rule 27-A it would ". . . rely upon cases interpreting the Federal Rule as an analytic aid."

While Rule 27-A follows the federal model on important issues, the actual language, organization, and inclusiveness of the New Hampshire Rule reflects a number of differences. In many cases identical or closely related language from Federal Rule 23 is reordered or positioned differently in the New Hampshire Rule. Additionally, much of the procedural detail of the Federal Rule either is not incorporated or is simplified in its presentation in Rule 27-A. These changes and omissions will be noted below, but likely do not signal a significant substantive difference from the federal practice. In light of the pre-rule case law on class actions and the expressed intention of New Hampshire to track or draw on the federal body of class action law, the differences are more form than substance.

---

1. The author received very helpful advice regarding class action procedure and rulings from Edward K. O'Brien of the O'Brien Law Firm, P.C., located in Manchester, New Hampshire.

2. *Smith v. Bank of New England*, 69 N.H. 254, 45 A. 1082 (1898); *Textile Works Union v. Textron*, 99 N.H. 385, 111 A.2d 823 (1955); *State Employees Ass'n of N.H. v. Belknap County*, 122 N.H. 614, 448 A.2d 969 (1982).

3. 155 N.H. 508, 511, 924 A.2d 355, 358 (2007).

II. Prerequisites to a Class Action: Comparison to Federal Rule 23(a) and (b)

Rule 27-A(a) combines into one section the class action requirements of (1) numerosity, (2) commonality, (3) typicality, (4) predominance of class action questions over individual claims, (5) fair and adequate representation of class members, and (6) the superiority of the class action over other available methods of adjudication. This subdivision also sets forth the requirement that the lawyer for the representative parties must adequately represent the interests of the class.

Rule 27-A therefore departs from the federal format by bringing some elements contained in Rule 23(b) (types of class actions) into the provisions of subdivision (a). Rule 27-A does not set out expressly the provisions of Rule 23(b) contained at sections (1) and (2). The provisions of Rule 23(b)(3), dealing with predominance and superiority, are folded into Rule 27-A at subdivision (a), but do not contain the specific listing of matters "pertinent to these findings," which are detailed at Rule 23(b)(3)(A)–(D). The New Hampshire Supreme Court has not spoken on whether any substantive difference results from the assembly of these provisions in this manner, but it seems unlikely that the omission of some of the detailed provisions contained in Rule 23 operates to limit their consideration in a proper case. The factors set out illustrating issues of predominance or superiority do not operate as mandatory considerations in New Hampshire, but courts can no doubt consider them as deemed appropriate. This seems more an effort to simplify the Rule's language and maintain judicial discretionthan a substantive rejection of the provisions that are set out in more detail in Rule 23.

III. Standard of Review and Cases Interpreting Class Action Prerequisites

In 2007, the New Hampshire Supreme Court interpreted the provisions of Rule 27-A for the first time in two separate opinions. These cases remain the best judicial indication of the scope and nature of class action law in New Hampshire. In *Cantwell*,[4] the court ruled that the trial court's dismissal of a consumer-based class action was in error and held that the plaintiff should have been entitled to conduct a certain amount of discovery in order to develop proof on issues of commonality and typicality. The court remanded the case to permit the plaintiff discovery with respect to class claims. Importantly, in addition to stating it would rely upon cases interpreting Rule 23 as it construed Rule 27-A, the court also expressly adopted

---

4. *Id*; *Smilow v. Sw. Bell Mobile Sys., Inc.*, 323 F.3d 32, 38 (1st Cir. 2003); *Gen. Tel. Co. of Sw. v. Falcon*, 457 U.S. 147, 161, 102 S. Ct. 2364 (1982).

the federal standard of "rigorous analysis" in examining the prerequisites for class certification under Rule 27-A.

This level of scrutiny by the New Hampshire Supreme Court and its approach to class action prerequisites was further exemplified in *Petition of Bayview Crematory, LLC*.[5] In this case, the court accepted an appeal based on its original jurisdiction to review a certification order of the lower court after the lower court had denied the moving party's request to take an interlocutory appeal of the order. The case arose out of funeral operations, the plaintiffs claiming that the bodies of decedents were handled improperly, remains of multiple decedents were commingled, authorizations for cremations were forged, and alleging other unlawful conduct involving the management of remains. The family member plaintiffs based their legal theories for recovery on various claims of negligent infliction of emotional distress. The trial court ruled that the negligence claims were appropriate for class treatment, but contemplated the individual damage cases of the families would be handled in separate actions.

In reversing the trial court and rejecting class action certification, the supreme court adopted the federal "abuse of discretion" standard set forth in a series of First Circuit Court of Appeals cases interpreting Rule 23.[6] The actual New Hampshire lexicon to be applied was noted by the court as "an unsustainable exercise of discretion."[7] Applying that standard to issues of commonality and predominance, the court disagreed with the trial court findings, stating that under New Hampshire substantive law, claims of negligent infliction of emotional distress require evidence of physical manifestation of injury as part of the liability case. It rejected the notion that such a finding only bears on the plaintiffs' damage claims and could be dealt with in subsequent individual damage proceedings. Although stating that the commonality requirement is a low threshold, the court based its decision on the "far more demanding" requirement of predominance.[8] Because the nature of the various family claims and the evidence of emotional injury to be offered by the plaintiffs would be so different or individual, the court determined that the individual claims would predominate over common class claims.[9]

Taken together, the *Cantwell* and *Bayview Crematory* cases make it plain that the court will apply a rigorous standard in terms of examining the prerequisites of class certification and that the existing body of federal cases interpreting Rule 23 will be looked to for guidance.

---

5. 155 N.H. 781, 930 A.2d 1190 (2007).

6. *McKenna v. First Horizon Home Loan Corp.*, 475 F.3d 418, 422 (1st Cir. 2007); *In re Polymedica Corp. Sec. Litig.*, 432 F.3d 1, 4 (1st Cir. 2005); *Tardiff v. Knox County*, 365 F.3d 1, 4 (1st Cir. 2004).

7. *State v. Lambert*, 147 N.H. 295, 787 A.2d 175 (2001).

8. *Bayview Crematory*, 155 N.H. at 785, 930 A.2d at 1194.

9. *Id*. at 155 N.H. at 786-87, 930 A.2d at 1195.

IV. Certification Order, Jurisdictional Damage Aggregation, Description of the Claims, and Notice

Rule 27-A(b) sets out the requirement that the court make a determination on class action certification, permits the court's order to be conditional and subject to amendment, and indicates that the prerequisites for class certification set forth in subdivision (a) of the Rule are the touchstone of that decision. Actions for money damages in the New Hampshire Superior Court have modest jurisdictional amount limits, and subdivision (c) of the Rule permits aggregation of the class members' claims in order to satisfy those requirements. It is hard to imagine a class claim that would not be maintainable in the superior court as a result of jurisdictional amount.

Subdivision (d) requires the court's order to describe the class and specifies that the court may limit the class to those members who do not timely request exclusion after notice. Notice of the class action is governed by subdivision (e) and largely tracks the notice and informational requirements of Rule 23(c)(2). Although there is no express requirement that the notice set forth the nature of the class claims, presumably that information would be drawn out of the court's order set forth and described at subdivision (d).

V. Exclusion of Class Members, Judgment, Methods of Payment of Damages, and Partial Class Actions

Subdivision (f) of Rule 27-A specifically addresses exclusion of class members, limiting such election to plaintiff class members. A member of a defendant class cannot elect exclusion. Judgment is governed by subdivision (g) and substantially follows the provisions of Rule 23(c)(3). Rule 27-A(h) deals with payments of judgments and permits, when the court so orders, that payments may be made into court and a claim and filing process may occur to satisfy class member claims. Subdivision (i) permits class actions to be brought as to specific issues, and authorizes subclasses as appropriate in the manner of Rule 23(c)(4)(5).

VI. Conducting the Class Action

Rule 27-A(j) deals with court orders conducting or adjudicating class action cases and follows the practical provisions of Rule 23(d) seeking to avoid repetition or complication, as well as providing for notice to class members, giving them the opportunity to signify whether they deem representation of their interest fair and adequate.

VII. Dismissal and Discontinuance or Settlement

The provisions of subdivision (k) of Rule 27-A simply set forth the requirement of court approval regarding any dismissal, discontinuance, or settlement with appropriate notice to class members. Rule 23(e) provides more procedural detail with respect to such matters, including the requirement of a hearing, and has more specificity as to agreements of parties or withdrawal of objections. The absence of detail in Rule 27-A suggests these issues may be dealt with within the court's discretion as appropriate or necessary, but they are not mandated.

VIII. Class Counsel and Attorney Fees and Costs

Rule 23(g) contains detailed provisions on the appointment of class counsel, laying out specific criteria that the court must consider, establishing provisions to appoint interim counsel, and stating that it is the duty of class counsel to fairly and adequately represent the interest of the class. Rule 27-A incorporates the fair and adequate representation standard in subdivision (a) of the Rule, but does not otherwise set out or define the scope of the court's inquiry or determination as to class counsel's competence or abilities. Despite the absence of detailed provisions, it seems probable that in New Hampshire the court's evaluation of counsel will consider or draw on the federal provisions. There is no express provision addressing attorney fees for class counsel in Rule 27-A, as contrasted to the specific provisions and process that are set forth in Rule 23(h). The broad authority of subdivision (j) of Rule 27-A would seem to permit such awards of attorney fees, and New Hampshire's stated preference for looking to the federal Rule for guidance would obviously support such a procedure.

NEW JERSEY

ERIC L. PROBST
JEFFREY M. PYPCZNSKI

I. Introduction

The New Jersey Court Rule[1] on class action certification mirrors Federal Rule 23.[2] Thus, New Jersey courts rely heavily on their federal counterparts' interpretation of Rule 23 in determining whether certification of a class is appropriate.[3] Therefore, this chapter will not supply a general overview of New Jersey class action law, but instead will focus on several representative class action cases involving consumer fraud, products liability, medical monitoring, and arbitration, with an emphasis on those decisions where New Jersey courts have denied certification because of defects in the class's underlying claims.

II. Consumer Fraud

The New Jersey legislature enacted the Consumer Fraud Act (CFA)[4] to be one of the strongest consumer fraud statutes in the country.[5] The CFA prohibits the use of unconscionable business practices ("bad faith conduct"), affirmative misrepresentations, knowing omissions, and certain regulatory violations in connection with the sale or advertising of merchandise and real estate.[6] New Jersey is a favorite forum for plaintiffs because the statute permits them to recover attorney fees, costs of suit, and treble damages.[7] The New Jersey legislature implemented these

---

1. N. J. CT. R. 4:32-1-3 (2010).
2. *In re Cadillac V8-6-4 Class Action*, 461 A.2d 736, 742 (N.J. 1983).
3. *Delgozzo v. Kenny*, 628 A.2d 1080, 1090 (N.J. Super. Ct. App. Div. 1993).
4. N.J. STAT. ANN. 56:8-1.
5. Governor's Press Release for Assembly Bill No. 2402, at 1 (June 29, 1971).
6. N.J. STAT. ANN. 56:8-2; *Cox v. Sears Roebuck & Co.*, 647 A.2d 454, 462 (N.J. 1994).
7. N.J. STAT. ANN. 56:8-19.

severe remedies to encourage plaintiffs' lawyers to file lawsuits on behalf of private claimants in cases where the prospect of recovery is small.[8] Not surprisingly, similar to the federal courts, New Jersey courts hesitate to deny certification to a proposed New Jersey CFA class because a class action allows a group of consumers to seek monetary relief that the group members might not seek individually because the value of the individual claim is too small to justify the expense of maintaining the suit.[9] Nevertheless, assertion of a New Jersey CFA class does not automatically result in certification. The putative class representative must have standing to proceed with the claim, which requires demonstrating that it has suffered a quantifiable loss as a result of the CFA violation in order to survive a summary judgment motion.

A. STANDING: PROOF OF ASCERTAINABLE LOSS REQUIRED

In *Weinberg v. Sprint Corp.*,[10] the class alleged that defendant Sprint fraudulently failed to disclose its practice of rounding up customers' telephone call charges to the nearest minute. Besides monetary relief, the plaintiff sought an injunction to prevent defendant from continuing its rounding-up practice. At summary judgment, defendant successfully argued that the filed-rate doctrine[11] deprived plaintiff of standing because a customer is presumed to know the publicly filed rate (here, the rounding-up practice) and cannot seek monetary damages under a state fraud statute. The filed-rate doctrine, however, did not bar injunctive relief. As a result of being unable to plead an ascertainable loss in the form of monetary damages, the class advocated abandoning the CFA distinction between a public and private action to give it standing to seek injunctive relief, attorney fees, and costs. Thus, the New Jersey Supreme Court had to consider whether the class could obtain injunctive relief under Rule 4:32-1(b)(2) through the CFA without demonstrating an ascertainable loss.[12]

The New Jersey Supreme Court refused to waive the ascertainable loss standing requirement because the waiver would strip from the CFA its legislative intent that private claimants suffer an ascertainable loss to have standing to maintain a claim.[13] Thus, it held that a private plaintiff seeking injunctive relief under Rule 4:32-1(b)(2) must establish an ascertainable loss to have standing.[14] In dicta, the court noted that if a class can survive a summary judgment motion by proving

---

8. *In re Cadillac*, 461 A.2d at 747–48.

9. *Riley v. New Rapids Carpet Ctr.*, 294 A.2d 7, 12 (N.J. 1972).

10. 801 A.2d 281, 283 (N.J. 2002).

11. The filed-rate doctrine requires a telecommunications carrier to charge its customers the rate contained in the tariff filed with the Federal Communications Commission. *Id.* at 285–87.

12. *Id.* at 286–87, 293.

13. *Id.* at 293.

14. *Id.* at 292–93.

an ascertainable loss with reasonable certainty and get to the fact finder, it can seek injunctive relief, attorney fees, and costs even if the jury ultimately rejects its ascertainable loss claim.[15]

New Jersey courts have also rejected certification attempts that rely on a price inflation theory based on a failure of the ascertainable loss requirement. A year after *Weinberg*, a trial court denied class certification to a proposed nationwide class of Ricoh digital camera purchasers who allegedly overpaid for the camera because Ricoh's deceptive advertising increased the price and demand for the camera ("price inflation theory").[16] In the absence of proof of how the advertising increased the purchase price, the court held that the price inflation theory was too speculative to constitute an ascertainable loss.[17] Similarly, a potential class cannot rely on the "fraud on the market" theory to confer standing.[18] In *International Union of Operating Engineers Local No. 68 Welfare Fund v. Merck & Co., Inc.*,[19] a third-party payor of prescription medications and health benefits relied on a fraud on the market theory to demonstrate that Merck's marketing campaign inflated the price paid for the drug across all third-party prescription payment plans. The court granted Merck summary judgment because the fraud on the market theory is limited to federal securities litigation and the price effect could not satisfy the ascertainable loss and proximate cause elements of the CFA.[20]

B. MULTISTATE CLASS ACTIONS: CONFLICT OF LAW ANALYSIS

Under Rule 4:32-1(b)(3), New Jersey courts undertake a rigorous conflict of law analysis in multistate class action matters to determine whether state law variations overshadow common fact issues to defeat predominance. Indeed, the application of one state's law in a nationwide class action is rare and more problematic in consumer fraud actions.[21] In *Fink v. Ricoh Corp.*,[22] the court found significant differences between the states' consumer protection laws to justify denying a multistate class action. Notably, several states barred private action consumer fraud class actions and jury trials (New Jersey does not); did not provide for treble damages (New Jersey does); left the award to the discretion of the trial judge (New Jersey does not); imposed damage caps; required proof of reliance; applied different proximate cause standards; and required proof of intent to deceive when the defendant made an affirmative misrepresentation (unlike New Jersey). Applying New

---

15. *Id.*

16. *Fink v. Ricoh Corp.*, 839 A.2d 942 (N.J. Super. Ct. Law Div. 2003).

17. *Id.* at 964–65.

18. *Int'l Union of Operating Eng'rs Local No. 68 Welfare Fund v. Merck & Co., Inc.*, 929 A.2d 1076 (N.J. 2007).

19. *Id.* at 1088.

20. *Id.*

21. *Beegal v. Park W. Gallery*, 925 A.2d 684, 694 (N.J. Super. App. Div. 2007).

22. 839 A.2d at 974–82.

Jersey's governmental interest test and the *Restatement (Second) Conflict of Laws* section 148 factors, the court concluded that plaintiffs could not demonstrate that common fact and legal questions predominated.[23]

Further, the application of 50 states' consumer fraud statutes presented complex litigation management issues.[24] When confronted with a multistate consumer fraud class action, class counsel and trial courts have been instructed to consider the use of alternate litigation procedures, such as test cases or injunctive relief, when the class's "geographical diversity" complicates case management.[25]

III. Products Liability

A. THE PRODUCTS LIABILITY ACT: EXCLUSIVE REMEDY

The New Jersey Product Liability Act (PLA) is a plaintiff's exclusive cause of action for harm caused by a product. In 1987, the New Jersey legislature enacted the PLA[26] as remedial legislation to limit the expansion of common law products liability law.[27] A product liability action is broadly defined as "any claim or action brought by a claimant for *harm* caused by a product, irrespective of the theory underlying the claim, except actions for harm caused by breach of an express warranty."[28] "Harm" is defined as

> (a) physical damage to property, other than to the product itself; (b) *personal physical illness, injury or death*; (c) pain and suffering, mental anguish or emotional harm; and (d) any loss of consortium or services *or other loss deriving from any type of harm* described in subparagraphs (a) through (c) of this paragraph.[29]

This definition has commanded center stage in a recent products liability class action decision involving the pharmaceutical drug Vioxx.

In *Sinclair v. Merck & Co., Inc.*,[30] plaintiffs sought to certify a national medical monitoring class of individuals who ingested Vioxx but who had yet to suffer a physical injury. Plaintiffs claimed that they had an increased risk of "serious undiagnosed and unrecognized myocardial infarctions ('silent heart attacks') that required medical monitoring and a Merck-funded screening program."[31] Plaintiffs also alleged negligence, consumer fraud, breach of implied and express warran-

---

23. *Id.* at 986–92.
24. *Id.* at 992.
25. *Carroll v. Cellco P'ship*, 713 A.2d 509, 519–20 (N.J. Super. Ct. App. Div. 1998).
26. N.J. STAT. ANN. §§ 2A:58C-1a.
27. *Shackil v. Lederle Labs.*, 561 A.2d 511, 527 (N.J. 1989).
28. N.J. STAT. ANN. § 2A:58C-1(b)(3) (emphasis added).
29. N.J. STAT. ANN. § 2A:58C-1(b)(2) (emphasis added).
30. 948 A.2d 587 (N.J. 2008).
31. *Id.* at 589–91.

ties, and strict liability under the PLA.[32] The central issue before the court was whether plaintiffs could maintain a products liability medical monitoring class action under the PLA in the absence of proof of a physical injury.[33]

The court interpreted the terms "harm" and "manifest injury" in the definition section to require proof of a personal physical injury caused by a defective product.[34] Because no class members had suffered a heart attack, the court concluded that they had not been harmed and could not maintain a medical monitoring claim under the PLA.[35] Thus, in New Jersey, plaintiffs cannot seek medical monitoring in the absence of a physical injury.

B. CFA CLAIMS AND THE PLA

Significantly, the court in *Sinclair* also ruled that the PLA subsumed the class's CFA claims. Though it recognized the CFA's "broad reach," especially in the class action context, the court ruled that the PLA precludes a CFA claim in cases where the plaintiff claims that the product caused physical harm.[36] Similarly, a mere two weeks before the New Jersey Supreme Court decided *Sinclair*, an appellate division panel ruled that the PLA subsumed CFA claims asserted in a Vioxx personal injury matter.[37] The court initially recognized that plaintiffs' claimed CFA violation—Merck's fraudulent marketing of Vioxx—was a traditional products liability failure to warn claim encompassed within the PLA's statutory framework.[38] It subsequently refused to permit plaintiffs to recover treble damages and attorney fees in product defect matters because the recovery of these damages lacked legislative authorization.[39]

C. MEDICAL MONITORING

Sinclair should not be read to preclude any class claim for medical monitoring in New Jersey. A medical monitoring claim (also known as "medical surveillance") seeks damages in the form of costs necessary to establish a court-supervised program of regularly scheduled medical examinations and/or diagnostic testing to

---

32. *Id.* at 589.
33. *Id.* at 593.
34. *Id.* at 595.
35. *Id.*
36. *Id.* at 595–96.
37. *McDarby v. Merck & Co.*, 949 A.2d 223 (N.J. App. Div. 2008), *cert. granted in part, denied in part*, 960 A.2d 393 (N.J. 2008), *appeal dismissed as improvidently granted*, 129 S. Ct. 1187 (2009) (the matter was on the New Jersey Supreme Court's docket for the 2009–2010 term solely on the issue of whether the Federal Food, Drug, and Cosmetic Act preempts state law inadequacy of warning claims under the PLA. However, after the U.S. Supreme Court decision in *Wyeth v. Levine*, 129 S. Ct. 1187 (2009), the appeal was dismissed as improvidently granted).
38. *Id.* at 277–78.
39. *Id.* at 278.

monitor for known diseases or harmful health conditions due to exposure to a toxic substance or product.[40] The claim is built on a traditional, underlying liability claim, such as negligence, product liability, or nuisance. While *Sinclair* requires proof of a physical injury to proceed with a claim under the PLA, not all medical monitoring claims require proof of injury.[41]

Under New Jersey law, in order to recover the costs of medical monitoring, a plaintiff must demonstrate

> through reliable expert testimony predicated upon the significance and extent of exposure to chemicals, the toxicity of the chemicals, the seriousness of the diseases for which individuals are at risk, the relative increase in the chance of onset of disease in those exposed, and the value of early diagnosis, that such surveillance to monitor the effect of exposure to toxic chemicals is reasonable and necessary.[42]

The New Jersey Supreme Court has further modified the standard to allow medical monitoring damages "only if a plaintiff reasonably shows that medical surveillance is required because the exposure caused a distinctive increased risk of future injury *and* would require a course of medical monitoring *independent of any other that the plaintiff would otherwise have to undergo.*"[43] Indeed, the New Jersey Supreme Court has described medical surveillance damages as "a special compensatory remedy."[44]

Accordingly, in order to establish a medical monitoring class under Rule 4:32-1, the class plaintiff must demonstrate to the court (1) that all proposed class members experienced significant exposure to a chemical substance; (2) that the chemical at issue is toxic; (3) that the alleged exposure can cause serious disease; (4) that class members have a distinctive increased risk of some future disease; (5) the value of an early diagnosis; (6) that medical monitoring is reasonable and necessary; and (7) that the proposed course of monitoring is different from and independent of any other monitoring that a class member may need.[45]

Further, once the four prerequisites of Rule 4:32-1(a) are met, the class representative must demonstrate that the class has satisfied Rule 4:32-1(b)(2) or (b)(3). Certification under (b)(2) is warranted when the party opposing class certification has acted or refused to act on grounds typical to the class, making injunctive or declaratory relief appropriate.[46] Rule 4:32-1(b)(3) requires the court to find predominance and superiority of questions of law and fact. To satisfy either (b)(2) or

---

40. *See also* Chapter 15, "Medical Monitoring Classes."
41. *See Ayers v. Jackson*, 525 A.2d 287 (1987).
42. *Id.* at 312–13.
43. *Theer v. Philip Carey Co.*, 628 A.2d 724, 733 (N.J. 1993) (emphasis added).
44. *Id.*
45. *See id.*
46. N.J. Ct. R. 4:32-1(b)(2).

(b)(3), the class must demonstrate that the proposed class is "cohesive" by showing that each element of the medical monitoring claim can be proven through common evidence.[47] Before the court can even consider whether the plaintiffs have proven cohesiveness, the plaintiffs must prove that the relief sought is primarily injunctive or equitable. The class cannot seek medical monitoring under (b)(2) when they seek to have the defendants pay for their medical treatment directly or for a certain portion of their medical expenses.[48] However, a court-supervised medical monitoring program is a proper exercise of the court's equitable powers and will be viewed as injunctive relief under (b)(2).[49]

The cohesiveness requirement is the "vital core" of a (b)(2) class and requires the class to show that its claims have a certain degree of "homogeneity."[50] In *Goasdone v. American Cyanamid*,[51] the court noted why the existence of individual issues often precludes certification of a (b)(2) class. First, in contrast to (b)(3) actions, class members cannot opt out of a (b)(2) class; they are bound by the litigation.[52] "Thus, the court must ensure that significant individual issues do not pervade the entire action because it would be unjust to bind absent class members to a negative decision where the class representative's claims present different individual issues than the claims of the absent members present."[53] Second, the class action would become unmanageable if individual issues frequently arose during the litigation.[54]

Thus, the cohesiveness requirement creates a significant obstacle to establishing a medical monitoring class action claim in New Jersey. At least three of the elements (significant exposure, distinctive increased risk of disease, and the need for monitoring that is different and independent from any monitoring the class member may otherwise require) will almost always require an individual assessment of each class member, including but not limited to their personal medical history and current health condition; their predisposition to certain medical conditions; the type, manner, and length of alleged exposure; and exposure to other substances or environmental conditions that could produce the same or similar injury. For these reasons, the New Jersey Supreme Court has yet to endorse certification of a class action seeking medical monitoring.[55]

---

47. *Goasdone v. Am. Cyanamid*, 808 A.2d 159, 166–67 (N.J. Super. Ct. Law Div. 2002).

48. *Id.* at 167.

49. *Id.* at 167–68.

50. *Id.* at 167.

51. *Id.* at 167–68.

52. *Id.* at 168.

53. *Id.*

54. *Id.*

55. More recently, a New Jersey federal district court denied certification of a proposed medical monitoring class alleging exposure to a chemical known as PFOA. *See Rowe v. E.I. DuPont de Nemours & Co.*, Nos. 06-1810 & 06-3080, 2008 U.S. Dist. LEXIS 103528 (D.N.J. Dec. 23, 2008). The *Rowe* court also concluded that certification had to be denied because the presence of so many individualized issues precluded

VI. Forum Non Conveniens

Recently, a number of defendants have successfully defeated class certification by raising the forum non conveniens defense.[56] In *In re Vioxx Litigation*, a group of 98 United Kingdom citizens filed a PLA, CFA, and breach of warranty class action against Merck and its U.K. subsidiary claiming personal injuries suffered as a result of Vioxx ingestion. In its forum non conveniens motion, Merck contended that the U.K. provided the plaintiffs with an adequate forum to resolve the dispute. Plaintiffs objected, pointing out that the U.K. employed a "loser pays" system, prohibited contingency fee agreements, and did not provide for the recovery of punitive and loss of consortium damages.[57] The New Jersey Appellate Division upheld the dismissal of the complaint on forum non conveniens grounds because the "loser pays" system and absence of punitive damages did not deprive the plaintiffs of a fair trial. Further, plaintiffs' expert conceded that the U.K. consumer protection law was closely analogous to the New Jersey PLA.[58] The court also held that New Jersey trials would be "inconvenient" because a U.K. jury would have a greater interest deciding the U.K. plaintiffs' claims based on U.K. pharmaceutical product liability and regulatory law. Further, the U.K. court system was better equipped to handle the lawsuit than New Jersey's, as the plaintiffs, their experts, treating physicians, and medical records were located in the U.K.[59]

V. Arbitration

Class action waiver provisions in arbitration agreements are enforceable in New Jersey, but subject to the defense of unconscionability. In *Gras v. Associates First Capital Corp.*,[60] the appellate division considered, as a general rule, whether arbitration clauses precluding class actions resulting from an alleged CFA violation were per se unenforceable. The court held that such clauses were enforceable because the CFA does not create a private class action right, and plaintiffs can pursue their CFA claims (including seeking treble damages) in arbitration.[61] The court further

---

a finding of cohesiveness and rendered certification under Federal Rule 23(b)(2) and (b)(3) inappropriate. *Id.* at *59–66.

56. *In re Vioxx Litig.*, 928 A.2d 935 (N.J. Super. Ct. App. Div. 2007), *certif. denied*, 936 A.2d 968 (N.J. 2007).

57. *Id.* at 938–39.

58. *Id.* at 938–44.

59. *Id.* at 944–48.

60. 786 A.2d 886 (N.J. Super. Ct. App. Div. 2001), *certif. denied*, 171 N.J. 445 (2002).

61. *Id.* at 892.

found that there was no legislative mandate or overriding public policy to favor class actions for alleged CFA violations.[62]

The New Jersey Supreme Court, in a more factually narrow case, approved the *Gras* holding, but held the class action waiver clauses in an arbitration agreement unconscionable and unenforceable.[63] The court ruled that the waiver provision essentially shielded the defendant from suit because the potential recovery was so small (less than $600 even with the CFA's treble damages) that it essentially precluded an individual plaintiff from filing the suit in the absence of a class.[64] The court concluded that the public interest factor in providing an adequate forum for the plaintiff to pursue her statutory rights outweighed the defendant's interest in enforcing the arbitration agreement.[65]

---

62. *Id.* at 892–93.
63. *Muhammad v. County Bank*, 912 A.2d 88 (N.J. 2006), *cert. denied*, 549 U.S. 1338 (2007).
64. *Id.* at 99–100.
65. *Id.* at 100–01.

NEW MEXICO

TIMOTHY C. HOLM

I. Introduction

New Mexico's class action rule, Rule 1-023 (New Mexico Rule or Rule 1-023),[1] is patterned after Federal Rule 23. Accordingly, New Mexico courts look to federal law regarding Rule 23 for guidance in ruling on class action issues.[2] This is particularly true given that there is not an abundance of reported New Mexico decisions on class actions, with the great weight of the appellate cases being decided after 2003. Significantly, however, the New Mexico Rule does not (yet) incorporate the 2003 amendments/additions to Rule 23. Thus, New Mexico's current Rule 1-023 is virtually identical to the 2002 version of Rule 23. The annotations to the Federal Rules describing the 2003 amendments are therefore helpful in determining and understanding the differences in the provisions of the New Mexico Rule and the current Rule 23.

II. The New Mexico Class Action Rule: Virtually Identical to the 2002 Federal Rule

Most of the substantive differences between the language of the New Mexico Rule and Rule 23 appear in subsection (C) of the New Mexico Rule regarding the class certification order and subsection (E) of the New Mexico Rule regarding settlement. Also, the New Mexico Rule does not contain subpart (g) of Rule 23 regarding appointment of class counsel. Subsection (C) of the New Mexico Rule still provides for class determination "as soon as practicable," whereas Rule 23 now provides for class determination "at an early practicable time." Subsection (C) of the New

---

1. N.M. R. Civ. P. 1-023.

2. *Ferrell v. Allstate Ins. Co.*, 144 N.M. 405, 411, 188 P.3d 1156, 1162 (2008); *Armijo v. Wal-Mart Stores, Inc.*, 142 N.M. 557, 564, 168 P.3d 129, 136 (Ct. App. 2007); *Romero v. Philip Morris, Inc.*, 137 N.M. 229, 238, 109 P.3d 768, 777 (Ct. App. 2005).

Mexico Rule also still contains the pre-2003 Rule 23 language that "an order under this subparagraph may be conditional, and may be altered or amended before the decision on the merits." Subpart (e) of the Federal Rules explicitly sets forth the procedures for the court to apply to a proposed settlement (and/or dismissal) of a class action, whereas subsection (E) of the New Mexico Rule simply states that the settlement (and/or dismissal) must be approved by the court, with notice given to all class members. Subpart (g) of Rule 23 sets forth detailed provisions regarding appointment of class counsel and the award of attorney fees. The New Mexico Rule contains no comparable provision to subpart (g) of Rule 23.

Considering its traditional adherence to Rule 23, it is likely that New Mexico will ultimately modify its rule—or at least its class action practice—to conform with the 2003 amendments to Rule 23. Although it may in part depend on the particular judge assigned to the case, in practice the New Mexico district courts seem to follow the general nature and spirit of the 2003 amendments to the Federal Rules, even though the New Mexico Rule has not yet incorporated those changes. For example, under subsection (C), New Mexico district courts do not tend to make time "of the essence" in determining class certification despite the fact that the current language of subsection (C) (to the effect that class certification must be determined "as soon as practicable") suggests such a standard.

Generally speaking, the local rules of the 13 districts in New Mexico do not address class actions. However, since the local rules are amended from time to time, the practitioner should always check the local rules of the district in which the case is filed.

III. New Mexico Class Action Case Law

Although there is not an abundance of reported decisions in New Mexico regarding class actions, over the past six years there have been numerous significant decisions that provide guidance on particular issues.

A. CLASS DEFINITION

New Mexico follows the "Rule of Definiteness" as "an implicit requirement" of Rule 1-023.[3] The New Mexico Court of Appeals has explained that rule as follows:

> [P]laintiffs bear the burden to demonstrate the existence of an identifiable class that is capable of ascertainment under some objective standard. . . .

> This is not to say that the definition must be so precise that every potential member can be immediately identified or the precise number ascertained at the outset. . . . Nevertheless, given the notice requirement, it is especially incumbent on Rule

---

3. *Brooks v. Norwest Corp.*, 136 N.M. 599, 606, 103 P.3d 39, 46 (Ct. App. 2004).

1-023(B)(3) plaintiffs to identify a legally definable class that can be ascertained through reasonable effort. . . . The class definition must be sufficiently definite so that it is administratively feasible for the court to determine whether a particular individual is a member. . . .

Whether a class definition is legally sufficient depends on the facts of each case and must be determined on a case-by-case basis. As a general rule, definitions must bear some relation to defendant's activities. At minimum, a definition should include a common transactional fact or status predicated on the cause of action, the appropriate time span, and geographical boundaries, if applicable, or other pertinent facts or characteristics that would make the class readily identifiable and capable of accurate verification. When defining a class, Plaintiffs must avoid subjective criteria or circular definitions that depend on the outcome of the litigation. Imprecise, vague, or broad definitions that include persons with little connection to the claims will fail to meet the definiteness requirement.[4]

B. CLASS CERTIFICATION HEARING

Although district courts in New Mexico typically conduct an evidentiary hearing prior to making a certification decision, the New Mexico Court of Appeals has held, in some situations, that an evidentiary hearing may not be necessary.[5] For example, an evidentiary hearing was not deemed necessary where the district court reviewed a mass of documentary evidence and heard argument of counsel and where appellants did not specifically show any prejudice from the failure to hold such a hearing.[6]

C. STANDARD FOR CLASS CERTIFICATION

The district court must engage in a rigorous analysis to determine whether the requirements of Rule 1-023 are met.[7] Specifically, the standard is as follows:

While the party seeking class certification has the burden of demonstrating that each requirement of Rule 1-023 is met, the moving party is not required to prove its case at the certification stage. As such, a district court should avoid examining the merits of the moving party's case at the time class certification is sought.

Although it is not appropriate to examine the merits of Plaintiffs' claims at the certification stage, the district court should not simply presume that requirements of Rule 1-023 are met. At this stage, it is essential for the court to understand the substantive law, proof elements of, and defenses to the asserted cause of action to properly assess whether the certification criteria are met. If it is possible to make

---

4. *Id.* at 136 N.M. at 606–07, 103 P.3d 39, 46–47 (internal citations omitted); *see also Armijo*, 142 N.M. at 574, 168 P.3d at 146.

5. *Murken v. Solv-Ex Corp.*, 139 N.M. 625, 631, 136 P.3d 1035, 1041 (Ct. App. 2006).

6. *Id.*

7. *Armijo*, 142 N.M. at 565, 168 P.3d at 137.

such a determination simply on Plaintiffs' pleadings, then the court may do so. If necessary, however, the court may probe behind the pleadings and forecast what kind of evidence may be required or allowed at trial.[8]

Within the confines of Rule 1-023, the district court has broad discretion whether or not to certify a class. To the extent that the district court has applied the correct legal standard to the facts, its decision to certify a class will be affirmed when supported by substantial evidence.[9] While there is still a tendency for courts in New Mexico to follow a "when in doubt, certify" approach, this principle has been tempered in recent years by the rigorous analysis requirement.[10]

D. OTHER PROCEDURAL ISSUES NOT EXPLICITLY ADDRESSED IN THE NEW MEXICO RULE

1. Findings of Fact and Conclusions of Law

Although Rule 1-023 does not explicitly require the submission and entry of findings of fact and conclusions of law, the New Mexico Court of Appeals has indicated that specific findings of fact and conclusions of law should generally be entered by the district court.[11] Therefore, a party should generally submit requested findings of fact and conclusions of law to the district court.

2. Standard for Appeals of Certification Order

With respect to class certification appeals under Rule 1-023(F), which allows a party to appeal a class certification order within ten days after entry of the order, the court of appeals will ordinarily grant review of the class certification decision under the following circumstances:

> (i) when there is a death-knell situation for either the plaintiff or defendant that is independent of the merits of the underlying claims, coupled with a class certification decision by the district court that is questionable, taking into account the district court's discretion over class certification; (ii) when the certification decision presents an unsettled and fundamental issue of law relating to class actions, important both to the specific litigation and generally, that is likely to evade end-of-the-case review; and (iii) when the district court's class certification decision is manifestly erroneous.[12]

---

8. *Id.* (internal citations omitted); *see also Ferrell*, 144 N.M. at 411, 188 P.3d at 1162.

9. *Armijo*, 142 N.M. at 564, 168 P.3d at 136.

10. *See, e.g., Berry v. Fed. Kemper Life Assurance Co.*, 136 N.M. 454, 466, 99 P.3d 1166, 1178 (Ct. App. 2004); *Armijo*, 142 N.M. at 570, 168 P.3d at 142.

11. *See Armijo*, 142 N.M. at 567, 168 P.3d at 139.

12. *Salcido v. Farmers Ins. Exch.*, 134 N.M. 797, 800, 82 P.3d 968, 971 (Ct. App. 2004).

E. ATTORNEY FEES

In determining the appropriate award of attorney fees, New Mexico courts consider the following factors:

> (1) the time and labor required, the novelty and difficulty of the questions involved, and the skill requisite to perform the legal service properly; (2) the likelihood . . . that the acceptance of the particular employment will preclude other employment by the lawyer; (3) the fee customarily charged in the locality for similar legal services; (4) the amount involved and the results obtained; (5) the time limitations imposed by the client or by the circumstances; (6) the nature and length of the professional relationship with the client; (7) the experience, reputation and ability of the lawyer performing the services; and (8) whether the fee is fixed or contingent.[13]

F. OTHER NOTABLE NEW MEXICO CLASS ACTION DECISIONS

1. Fiser v. Dell Computer Corp.: *Contractual Prohibition on Class Action Unenforceable Against Consumer*

In *Fiser v. Dell Computer Corp.*,[14] the New Mexico Supreme Court held that a corporation's contractual requirement of arbitration and contractual prohibition on class action relief was unenforceable against a consumer. The plaintiff in *Fiser* purchased a computer from Dell Computer Corporation via the company's website. He subsequently filed a putative class action lawsuit contending that the defendant systematically misrepresented the memory size of its computers. The defendant argued that, pursuant to the terms and conditions on its website at the time of the purchase, plaintiff was required to individually arbitrate his claims and was precluded from proceeding on a classwide basis either in litigation or arbitration. The New Mexico Supreme Court rejected defendant's argument, explaining that "contractual prohibition of class relief, as applied to claims that would be economically inefficient to bring on an individual basis, is contrary to the fundamental public policy of New Mexico to provide a forum for the resolution of all consumer claims and is therefore unenforceable in this state."[15]

2. Ferrell v. Allstate: *Forum Selection and Conflicts of Laws Issues*

There are a number of New Mexico appellate decisions resulting from a series of putative nationwide/multistate class action lawsuits filed against insurance companies regarding premiums and installment fees.[16]

---

13. N.M. Rules of Prof. Conduct 16-105; *see also In re N.M. Indirect Purchasers Microsoft Corp. Antitrust Litig.*, 140 N.M. 879, 908, 149 P.3d 976, 1005 (Ct. App. 2006).

14. 144 N.M. 464, 188 P.3d 1215 (2008).

15. *Id.* at 144 N.M. at 471, 188 P.3d at 1222.

16. *See, e.g., Ferrell*, 144 N.M. 405, 188 P.3d 1156; *Berry*, 136 N.M. 454, 99 P.3d 1166; *Rivera-Platte v. First Colony Life Ins. Co.*, 143 N.M. 158, 173 P.3d 765 (Ct. App. 2007) (opinion withdrawn by New Mexico Supreme Court in *Platte v. First Colony Life Ins. Co.*, 194 P.3d 108 (2008)); *Azar v. Prudential Ins. Co. of Am.*, 133 N.M. 669, 68 P.3d 909 (Ct. App. 2003); *Enfield v. Old Line Life Ins. Co. of Am.*, 136 N.M. 398, 98 P.3d

In *Ferrell v. Allstate Insurance Co.*,[17] the New Mexico Supreme Court addressed several issues regarding choice of law, conflict of law, and certification in putative multistate class action cases. First, the court ruled that, in New Mexico, forum selection clauses contained in contracts are treated as venue defenses, which must be raised in the first responsive pleading or the defense will be waived. Secondly, the court held that the possibility of a potential conflict between the laws of various states in a putative multistate class action will not defeat the application of forum law. Rather, only proof of an actual conflict will preclude a district court from making a determination that it could apply forum law. The party opposing certification must establish that the laws of the relevant states actually conflict through clearly established, plainly contradictory law.[18]

1048 (Ct. App. 2004); *Smoot v. Physician's Life Ins. Co.*, 135 N.M. 265, 87 P.3d 545 (Ct. App. 2004); *Wilson v. Mass. Mut. Life Ins. Co.*, 135 N.M. 506, 90 P.3d 525 (Ct. App. 2004).

17. 144 N.M. 405, 188 P.3d 1156.

18. *Id.* at 144 N.M. at 418, 188 P.3d at 1169.

NEW YORK

PETER A. ANTONUCCI[1]

I. Introduction

Class action litigation in New York state courts is governed by Article 9 of the New York Rules of Civil Procedure (Article 9). Article 9 is modeled after Rule 23 of the Federal Rules of Civil Procedure (Rule 23), but contains some notable distinctions. This chapter will (1) summarize various provisions of Article 9, highlighting where Article 9 diverges from Rule 23, and (2) discuss the continued viability of securities class actions in New York state courts after the federal Class Action Fairness Act of 2005 (CAFA).[2]

II. Overview of Class Actions Under Article 9

A. LEGISLATIVE HISTORY

Article 9 was enacted in 1975 to broaden the availability of class action relief to aggrieved plaintiffs. Prior to 1975, New York courts applied a set of arcane and restrictive rules making the state inhospitable to class action litigation.[3] Article 9 "was the culmination of the efforts of the Judicial Conference beginning in 1972 to repeal the prior restrictive class action provision and enact a new bill more in keeping with the modern approach to class actions."[4] The legislature intended

---

1. Lauren B. Grassotti, an associate in the litigation group in Greenberg Traurig's New York office, assisted in the preparation of this chapter.

2. Pub. L. No. 109-2, 119 Stat. 4 (codified at 28 U.S.C. §§ 1332(d), 1453, and 1711–15 (2005)).

3. *See* Vincent C. Alexander, *Practice Commentaries*, N.Y. C.P.L.R. § 901, at C901:1 (2006) [hereinafter Alexander] (discussing the prior New York class action statute and the legislative history of Article 9); *see also* N.Y. Civ. Prac. CPLR, *Article 9 Class Actions*, ¶ 901.3 (describing the influx of "progressive" state class action statutes in the 1970s and 1980s in response to various Supreme Court rulings encouraging state class actions and circumscribing federal class action jurisdiction).

4. Alexander, *supra* note 3.

for Article 9 to "(1) set up a flexible, functional scheme whereby class actions could qualify without the present undesirable and socially detrimental restrictions; and (2) to prescribe basic guidelines for judicial management of class actions."[5] While Article 9 is modeled after Rule 23, it is generally more flexible and gives judges greater discretion in applying its requirements and managing class action litigations.[6]

B. REQUIREMENTS FOR MAINTAINING A CLASS ACTION

Article 9 of the New York Civil Practice Law and Rules (CPLR) defines the requirements for maintaining a class action in New York state courts. It is substantially similar to Rule 23 of the Federal Rules of Civil Procedure. In addition to requiring the establishment of numerosity, commonality, typicality, and adequacy as required under Rule 23(a), CPLR 901(a) also mandates the superiority requirement of Rule 23(b)(3) as a prerequisite to a class action.[7]

Moreover, as is the case with Rule 23, the plaintiff bears the burden of establishing all five elements before a class can be certified.[8]

Section 901(a) of the CPLR defines the requirements for maintaining a class action in New York State Court. "One or more members of a class may sue or be sued as representative parties on behalf of all" if:

> (1) the class is so numerous that joinder of all members, whether otherwise required or permitted, is impracticable; (2) there are questions of law or fact common to the class which predominate over any questions affecting only individual members; (3) the claims or defenses of the representative parties are typical of the claims or defenses of the class; (4) the representative parties will fairly and adequately protect the interest of the class; and (5) a class action is superior to other available methods for the fair and efficient adjudication of the controversy.[9]

---

5. *Id.*

6. *Id.* ("The article mirrors the general scheme of Rule 23 of the Federal Rules of Civil Procedure, but is simpler in structure and seeks to overcome the limitations imposed upon the rule, particularly with regard to notice"); *see also Friar v. Vanguard Holding Corp.*, 78 A.D.2d 83, 90, 434 N.Y.S.2d 698, 703 (2d Dep't 1980) (noting the "much-heralded flexibility and the functional terms contained" in Article 9).

7. *Sperry v. Crompton Corp.*, 9 N.Y.3d 204, 211 (2007); *Rabouin v. Metro. Life Ins. Co.*, 25 A.D.3d 349, 806 N.Y.S.2d 585 (1st Dep't 2006); *Colt Indus. S'holder Litig. v. Colt Indus. Inc.*, 77 N.Y.2d 185, 195 (1991); *Makastchian v. Oxford Health Plans, Inc.*, N.Y.L.J., Aug. 3, 1998, at *28, col. 1 (Sup. Ct. N.Y. County), *aff'd*, 704 N.Y.S.2d 44 (1st Dep't 2000).

8. *Kings Choice Neckwear, Inc. v. DHL Airways, Inc.*, 41 A.D.3d 117, 836 N.Y.S.2d 605, 606 (1st Dep't 2007); *Flemming v. Barnwell Nursing Home & Health Facilities*, 309 A.D.2d 1132, 1133, 766 N.Y.S.2d 241, 243–44 (3d Dep't 2003); *Bettan v. Geico Ins. Co.*, 296 A.D.2d 469, 470–71, 745 N.Y.S.2d 545, 547 (2d Dep't 2002).

9. N.Y. C.P.L.R. § 901(a).

Article 9 contemplates the possibility of a class of defendants, though such classes are rare in practice.[10] New York courts also permit counterclaims to proceed as class actions if the requirements of section 901(a) are met.[11] If an action has satisfied all of the prerequisites of CPLR section 901, the court must then consider the factors listed in CPLR section 902.[12] Though the section 902 factors are almost identical to those contained in Rule 23(b), the court must consider the factors in all cases, unlike under the Federal Rule.

Unlike Rule 23, Article 9 does not specify the types of substantive claims that may be brought as class actions. A class action may be established so long as a plaintiff can establish the existence of the above factors. "The representative for the proposed class has the burden of demonstrating that all five prerequisites have been met. . . . The showing must be made with competent evidence, not mere conclusory allegations."[13] However, Article 9 does specifically exclude one particular type of claim. Under section 901(b) a suit "to recover a penalty, or minimum measure of recovery created or imposed by statute may not be maintained as a class action" unless that statute "specifically authorizes the recovery thereof in a class action."[14] The Second Circuit has interpreted section 901(b)'s prohibition against class recovery of statutory damages as a substantive requirement, thereby foreclosing these types of actions in federal court as well.[15]

---

10. *See City of Rochester v. Chiarella*, 86 A.D.2d 110, 112, 449 N.Y.S.2d 112, 113 (4th Dep't 1982) (plaintiff city sued the named defendants "as representatives of all payers of real property taxes to the City for the fiscal years 1974–1979").

11. *See Compact Electra Corp. v. Paul*, 93 Misc. 2d 807, 808–09, 403 N.Y.S.2d 611, 611–12 (Sup. Ct. App. 2d Dep't 1977) (remanding for determination of whether defendant's statutory counterclaims satisfied the prerequisites of Article 9).

12. The factors listed in N.Y. C.P.L.R. § 902 are:

(1) [t]he interest of members of the class in individually controlling the prosecution or defense of separate actions; (2) [t]he impracticability or inefficiency of prosecuting or defending separate actions; (3) [t]he extent and nature of any litigation concerning the controversy already commenced by or against members of the class; (4) [t]he desirability or undesirability of concentrating the litigation of the claim in the particular forum; (5) [t]he difficulties likely to be encountered in the management of a class action.

13. Alexander, *supra* note 3, at C901:3 (citing *Katz v. NVF Co.*, 100 A.D.2d 470, 473, 475, 473 N.Y.S.2d 786, 789 (1st Dep't 1984)).

14. N.Y. C.P.L.R. § 901(b).

15. *See Shady Grove Orthopedic Assocs. v. Allstate Ins. Co.*, 549 F.3d 137, 143 (2d Cir. 2008) (holding "Rule 23 leaves room for the operation of CPLR 901(b), which is a substantive rule that eliminates statutory penalties under New York law as a remedy for class action plaintiffs"), *cert. granted*, 129 S. Ct. 2160 (2009).

1. Numerosity

CPLR section 901(a)(1) mandates that "the class is so numerous that joinder of all members, whether otherwise required or permitted, is impracticable."[16]

There is no set number of plaintiffs that will automatically fulfill the numerosity requirement; the court will exercise its discretion to determine whether a particular amount is numerous enough for class status based on the facts and circumstances of the particular case.[17] In accordance with federal jurisprudence, classes with at least 100 members are almost always sufficiently numerous; however, classes with fewer than 50 plaintiffs have been both certified and denied certification.[18]

2. Commonality

CPLR section 901(a)(2) requires that questions of law and fact that are common to the class predominate.[19] Article 9's commonality requirement is essentially an amalgam of Rule 23(a)(1) and (b)(3). There is no litmus test to be employed by a court in determining whether there exists a predominance of common questions of fact or law. Rather, courts look to "whether a class action achieves economies of time, effort, and expense and promotes uniformity of decision as to persons similarly situated."[20]

One of the earliest New York appellate courts to consider the predominance of the common issues requirement instructed that "the decision as to whether there are common predominating questions of fact or law so as to support a class action should not be determined by any mechanical test, but rather, 'whether the use of a class action would achieve economies of time, effort, and expense, and promote uniformity of decision as to persons similarly situated.'"[21] Subsequent courts generally follow this instruction and engage in a practical analysis as to predominance, looking at the facts and circumstances of the particular case, while not letting the presence of individual issues necessarily stand in the way of class certification.

New York judges are sometimes willing to grant class certification even when significant individual issues are present, so long as common issues generally predominate. This willingness is in part due to CPLR section 906, which affords the

---

16. *Rabouin*, 25 A.D.3d at 350, 806 N.Y.S.2d at 584, 585; *see also Klein v. Robert's Am. Gourmet Food, Inc.*, 28 A.D.3d 63, 69, 808 N.Y.S.2d 766, 772 (2d Dep't 2006).

17. *Friar*, 78 A.D.2d at 96, 434 N.Y.S.2d at 706 ("There is no 'mechanical test' to determine whether the first requirement numerosity has been met, nor is there a set rule for the number of prospective class members which must exist before a class is certified.").

18. *See* Alexander, *supra* note 3, at C901:4 (comparing cases).

19. *See Cherry v. Resource Am. Inc.*, 15 A.D.3d 1013, 1013, 788 N.Y.S.2d 911 (4th Dep't 2005) (citing *Friar*, 76 A.D.2d at 98, 434 N.Y.S.2d at 708).

20. *Michels v. Phoenix Home Life Mut. Ins. Co.*, No. 95/5318, 1997 WL 1161145, at *11 (Sup. Ct. Albany County Jan. 3, 1997).

21. *Friar*, 78 A.D.2d at 97, 434 N.Y.S.2d at 707 (quoting *LaMar v. H & B Novelty & Loan Co.*, 55 F.R.D. 22, 25 (D. Or. 1972)).

court the option to divide the class into subclasses and treat each subclass as a class, or to grant class status to try only a particular issue rather than all issues. This flexibility permits classes to be certified even where individual issues are present or class member interests are divergent.[22] As discussed above, the court may alter, amend, or decertify a class on its own motion or the parties' motion if it later appears that individual issues predominate, making class relief untenable. In the alternative, the court may allow the action to proceed as a class action with respect to particular issues only. In light of all of the flexibility afforded to judges in the management of state class action litigation, class decertification is not lightly granted.[23]

New York courts routinely grant class certification where damages must be determined on an individual basis, so long as common issues regarding liability predominate.[24] On the other hand, New York courts are reluctant to grant class certification where there are individual issues surrounding a reliance requirement. For example, in *Strauss v. Long Island Sports, Inc.*,[25] the Second Department held that individual reliance determinations precluded class relief. There, plaintiffs were purchasers of New York Nets season tickets seeking to recover damages based on the trade of a star player prior to the start of the season where plaintiffs allegedly relied on various newspaper articles touting that player in their decision to purchase season tickets.[26] The proposed class of plaintiffs had purchased their tickets over a several-month period, defendants had placed several different advertisements over a several-week period, and only some of the purchases actually occurred during a time when an advertisement was running.[27] In its analysis, the *Strauss* court contrasted the case with *Guadagno v. Diamond Tours & Travel*.[28] Class certification was granted in *Guadagno* where plaintiffs' allegations arose from alleged misrepresentations contained in defendant's marketing materials in connection with a travel

---

22. *See, e.g., City of Rochester v. Chiarella*, 86 A.D.2d 110, 116–17, 449 N.Y.S.2d 112, 116–17 (4th Dep't 1982) (ordering creation of a new subclass "to overcome any potential conflict within members of the class").

23. *See, e.g., Stellema v. Vantage Press, Inc.*, 121 Misc. 2d 1058, 1065, 470 N.Y.S.2d 507, 512 (Sup. Ct. N.Y. County 1983).

24. *See, e.g., Godwin Realty Assocs. v. CATV Enters., Inc.*, 275 A.D.2d 269, 712 N.Y.S.2d 39 (1st Dep't 2000) ("To the extent that there may be differences among the class members as to the degree in which they were damaged, the court may try the class aspects first and have the individual damage claims heard by a special master or create subclasses."); *Makastchian v. Oxford Health Plans, Inc.*, 270 A.D.2d 25, 26, 704 N.Y.S.2d 44, 45 (1st Dep't 2000); *Simon v. Cunard Line Ltd.*, 75 A.D.2d 283, 289, 428 N.Y.S.2d 952, 955 (2d Dep't 1980) ("Although the damages sustained may raise individual issues inappropriate for class action treatment, such individual issues need not preclude class action treatment at least as to liability.").

25. 60 A.D.2d at 501, 504, 401 N.Y.S.2d 233, 234 (2d Dep't 1978).

26. *Id.*

27. *Id.* at 60 A.D.2d at 507, 401 N.Y.S.2d at 235–36.

28. *Id.* at 60 A.D.2d at 507, 401 N.Y.S.2d at 236 (citing *Guadagno v. Diamond Tours & Travel, Inc.*, 89 Misc.2d 697, 392 N.Y.S.2d 783 (Sup. Ct. N.Y. County 1976)).

tour, because all of the plaintiffs had taken the same tour within a three-week period and received the same marketing materials.[29] Thus, reliance was a common issue allowing for class certification. It should be noted that some New York courts allow for a presumption of reliance in fraud class actions where the misrepresentation is material and actionable.[30] Mass tort and products liability plaintiffs are generally not successful in seeking class certification. Consistent with federal interpretations of Rule 23, New York judges generally hold that individual issues predominate in these cases and deny class certification.[31] In one of the few court of appeals cases addressing class certification, the court affirmed decertification of a class of over 5 million plaintiffs who "became or continued to be nicotine dependent as a result of buying and smoking cigarettes in New York that were manufactured by defendants."[32] It relied on the appellate division's findings that there could be no classwide presumption of reliance and that the individualized damages determination with respect to 5 million plaintiffs would render the class "unmanageable" and evidence that the named plaintiffs would not adequately represent the class.[33]

3. Typicality

CPLR section 901(a)(3) is identical to Rule 23(a)(3). The claims of the representative party must be typical of the claims of the class. Claims are typical when they arise from the same set of facts and legal theories that give rise to the claims of the class.[34]

4. Adequacy

Article 9's adequacy requirement, CPLR section 901(a)(4), is identical to its federal counterpart in Rule 23(a)(4). The determination as to whether a plaintiff can fairly and adequately represent the class members implicates a balancing of factors, including "whether any conflict of interest exists between the representative and the class members, the representative's familiarity with the lawsuit and his or her financial resources, and the competence and experience of class

---

29. *Id.*

30. *See Weinberg v. Hertz Corp.*, 116 A.D.2d 1, 7, 499 N.Y.S.2d 693, 696 (1st Dep't 1986).

31. *See, e.g., Geiger v. Am. Tobacco Co.*, 277 A.D.2d 420, 420–421, 716 N.Y.S.2d 108, 109–110 (2d Dep't 2000) (causation and the extent of each plaintiff's injury were individual issues precluding class certification); *Rosenfeld v. A.H. Robins Co., Inc.*, 63 A.D.2d 11, 19, 407 N.Y.S.2d 196, 201 (2d Dep't 1978) (denying class certification in products liability action based on the Dalkon Shield because predominance of common issues was lacking).

32. *Small v. Lorillard Tobacco Co., Inc.*, 94 N.Y.2d 43, 51, 720 N.E.2d 892, 894, 698 N.Y.S.2d 615, 617 (1999).

33. *Id.* at 94 N.Y.2d at 53–54, 720 N.E.2d at 896–97, 698 N.Y.S.2d at 619–20.

34. *Klein*, 28 A.D.3d at 69, 808, N.Y.S.2d at 772; *Pruitt v. Rockefeller Ctr. Props.*, 167 A.D.2d 14, 22, 574 N.Y.S.2d 672, 676 (1st Dep't 1991); *Dragnoli v. Spring Valley Mobile Vills.*, 165 A.D.2d 859, 859–60, 560 N.Y.S.2d 323, 324 (2d Dep't 1990).

counsel."[35] Moreover, one court has articulated three distinct factors that must be addressed in determining the adequacy of whether a plaintiff may represent the class. Those factors are "the qualifications of counsel, the ability of the class representatives to assist their counsel, and the relationship between the interests of the class representatives and the interests of other class members."[36]

5. Superiority

CPLR section 901(a)(5) requires a fifth element that is similar to Rule 23(b)(3). This requirement is the relatively obvious notion that the plaintiff prove that a class action is superior to other available methods for adjudication of the controversy.[37]

C. PROCEDURE AND TIMING OF CLASS CERTIFICATION

Procedurally, a class action is commenced, just as any other suit in New York, by filing a summons and complaint.[38] The named plaintiff's name appears in the caption along with an indication that the suit is being brought on behalf of others similarly situated. CPLR section 902 mandates that a plaintiff move to certify a class within 60 days after the defendant's time to serve a responsive pleading has expired[39] and New York courts strictly construe the 60-day period.[40] The court should hold what is called a "mini-hearing" on issues related to class certification and develop an evidentiary record on which it can base its class certification decision. It is reversible error to decide a class motion without such a hearing.[41] The merits of plaintiff's claims are generally not considered at the mini-hearing.[42] To

---

35. *Ackerman v. Price Waterhouse*, 252 A.D.2d 179, 202, 683 N.Y.S.2d 179, 194–95 (1st Dep't 1998); *see also Wilder v. May Dep't Stores Co.*, 23 A.D.3d 646, 648–49, 804 N.Y.S.2d 423, 425 (2d Dep't 2005).

36. *Michels*, 1997 WL 1161145, at *11.

37. *Small*, 94 N.Y.2d at 53, 720 N.E.2d at 896, 698 N.Y.S.2d at 619; *Cannon v. Equitable Life Assurance Soc'y*, 87 A.D.2d 403, 411, 451 N.Y.S.2d 817, 822 (2d Dep't 1982).

38. *See* N.Y. C.P.L.R. § 304 (acknowledging that an action may be also be commenced by filing a summons with notice).

39. N.Y. C.P.L.R. § 902; *see Colbert v. Rank Am., Inc.*, 295 A.D.2d 302, 742 N.Y.S.2d 905 (2d Dep't 2002); *see generally* C.P.L.R. art. 3 (containing permissible methods of service along with defendants' corresponding time to answer or appear).

40. *See Shah v. Wilco Sys., Inc.*, 27 A.D.3d 169, 173–74, 806 N.Y.S.2d 553, 556–57 (1st Dep't 2005) (denying plaintiff's motion for class certification as untimely where made four days past 60-day mark); *Am. Express Travel Related Servs., Inc. v. Caplan*, 266 A.D.2d 325, 697 N.Y.S.2d 519, 520 (2d Dep't 1999) (denying defendant's motion to extend the 60-day time period within which to move for certification of a counterclaim).

41. *See Chimenti v. Am. Express Co.*, 97 A.D.2d 351, 352, 467 N.Y.S.2d 357, 358 (1st Dep't 1983) (reversing class certification based on lower court's failure to "develop an evidentiary basis for class certification" and admonishing that the lower court "should have held [a] 'mini-hearing' . . . preceded by limited discovery, to determine whether the prerequisites to class certification listed in CPLR 901 are present, and to assess the feasibility considerations listed in CPLR 902 in relation to the particular facts.").

42. *See Simon*, 75 A.D.2d at 288, 428 N.Y.S.2d at 955 ("To the extent that inquiry into the merits of a claim is appropriate before certification of a class, the inquiry is to determine whether on the surface there appears to be a cause of action for relief which is neither spurious nor sham.").

aid in the development of the evidentiary record, plaintiffs are entitled to "limited discovery in order to adduce evidence to meet [their] burden of showing that the statutory prerequisites to certification of a class are met."[43] The court has several options after conducting the mini-hearing. Pursuant to section 902, the court may grant or deny class certification, grant conditional class certification, and can decertify, alter, or amend the class at any time before a decision on the merits, on a motion by the parties or sua sponte.[44]

D. MANAGING THE CLASS ACTION

CPLR section 907 governs the management of class actions generally. This provision allows the court to make "appropriate" orders:

(1) [d]etermining the course of proceedings or prescribing measures to prevent undue repetition or complication in presentation of evidence or argument; (2) [r]equiring, for the protection of the members of the class, or otherwise for the fair conduct of the action, that notice be given in such manner as the court may direct to some or all of the members of any step in the action, or of the proposed extent of the judgment, or of the opportunity of members to signify whether they consider the representation fair and adequate, or to appear and present claims and defenses, or otherwise to come into the action; (3) [i]mposing conditions on representative parties or intervenors; (4) [r]equiring that pleadings be amended to eliminate therefrom allegations as to representation of absent persons; and that the action proceed accordingly; (5) [d]irecting that a money judgment favorable to the class be paid either in one sum . . . or in such installments as the court may specify; (6) dealing with similar procedural matters.[45]

1. Opt-Out and Notice

The remaining provisions of Article 9 afford judges substantial flexibility in managing class action litigations. For instance, unlike Rule 23, which requires the right to opt out in actions for money damages, CPLR section 903 makes the right to opt out discretionary in all actions.[46]

As contemplated by the Judicial Conference, the opting out procedure would be used:

(i) when representation of the entire class is not needed for a just disposition of the controversy; (ii) when the class members have a significant practical interest in

---

43. *Chimenti*, 97 A.D.2d at 352, 467 N.Y.S.2d at 359.

44. N.Y. C.P.L.R. § 902.

45. N.Y. C.P.L.R. § 907.

46. N.Y. C.P.L.R. § 903 ("When appropriate the court may limit the class to those members who do not request exclusion from the class within a specified time after notice."); Alexander, *supra* note 3, § 903 ("According to the language of CPLR 903, the court's conferral of an opt-out right is wholly discretionary.").

individually controlling the litigation; and (iii) when individual notice is feasible without imposing a prohibitive economic or administrative burden on the parties.[47]

Despite CPLR section 903's discretionary opt-out procedure, due process requires that nonresident class members with minimal contacts with New York have the right to opt out in actions seeking money damages only.[48] This due process right does not attach in actions seeking "predominantly equitable relief."[49]

The provision regarding notice to class members grants the court similar discretion. Notice is not required in actions brought primarily for injunctive or declaratory relief, and "in all other class actions, reasonable notice of the commencement of a class action shall be given to the class in such manner as the court directs."[50] Section 904(c) lists several factors for the court's consideration in determining method of notice, including cost, the resources of parties, and the stake of each class member and likelihood that a significant number of members will want to opt out of the class.[51] The plaintiff generally bears the cost of notice, but the court can order the defendant to pay all or part of the cost, if justice requires, and can conduct a preliminary hearing on the issue of apportionment of notice costs.[52] The court must approve the contents of the notice, which should "present a balanced statement of the potential class member's rights and liabilities."[53] In one case, the court itself redrafted the notice and opt-out request provided by class counsel.[54]

Rule 23 does not contain a similar provision to CPLR section 907 allowing for installment payments of a money judgment or for the appearance of parties without formal joinder.[55] It should come as no surprise that pursuant to CPLR section 908, the court must approve dismissal or settlement of class actions and has discretion to order the particular method of notification to class members.[56]

2. Attorney Fees

Article 9 also contains a provision that grants the court discretion to "award attorneys' fees to the representatives of the class based on the reasonable value of legal services rendered and if justice requires, allow recovery of the amount awarded

---

47. Alexander, *supra* note 3, § 903.

48. *Colt Indus. S'holder Litig. v. Colt Indus. Inc.*, 77 N.Y.2d 185, 198, 566 N.E.2d 1160, 1167–68, 565 N.Y.S.2d 755, 762–63 (1991) (citing *Phillips Petroleum Co. v. Shutts*, 472 U.S. 797 (1985)).

49. *Id.*, 77 N.Y.2d at 195, 566 N.E.2d at 1165, 565 N.Y.S.2d at 760.

50. N.Y. C.P.L.R. § 904.

51. *Id.* § 904(c).

52. *Id.* § 904(d); *see Geelan v. Pan Am. World Airways, Inc.*, 83 A.D.2d 538, 539, 441 N.Y.S.2d 474, 474–75 (1st Dep't 1981) (holding that cost of notice should be paid either by plaintiff or a single defendant and not divided among both defendants).

53. *Vickers v. Home Fed. Sav. & Loan Assoc. of E. Rochester*, 56 A.D.2d 62, 65–66, 390 N.Y.S.2d 747, 749 (4th Dep't 1977).

54. *Id.*

55. *See* Alexander, *supra* note 3, § 907 (2005).

56. N.Y. C.P.L.R. § 908.

from the opponent of the class" if a judgment is rendered for the class.[57] "Although the statute speaks of a 'judgment' in favor of the class, CPLR § 909 applies with equal force to favorable settlements."[58] An award of attorney fees pursuant to section 909 is normally paid for out of any fund created for plaintiffs' recovery, but "attorneys' fees have been charged as costs against a defendant . . . where the defendant has been guilty of fraudulent, groundless, oppressive or vexatious conduct."[59] Where defendants are charged with class counsel's fees, liability must be apportioned among the defendants pro rata in accordance with each defendant's "share of the total value of the claims."[60] New York courts have applied the same two general approaches to awarding attorney fees that are employed by most federal courts—the lodestar/multiplier and the percentage of benefit methods. Under the lodestar/multiplier method, the court will consider certain factors, including (1) whether plaintiff's counsel had the benefit of a prior judgment or decree in a case brought by the government; (2) the standing of counsel at the bar—both counsel receiving the award and opposing counsel; (3) time and labor spent; (4) the magnitude and complexity of the litigation; (5) the responsibility undertaken; (6) the amount recovered; (7) the knowledge the court has of conferences, arguments that were presented, and work shown by the record to have been done by lawyers for the plaintiff prior to trial; (8) what it would be reasonable for counsel to charge a victorious plaintiff; (9) the contingent nature of the fee arrangement; and (10) the novelty of the issues presented.[61] Recent cases might portend a change to the percentage of the benefit approach. In at least one case, a court applied the percentage of the benefit method first and then checked its reasonableness by employing a lodestar analysis.[62] New York courts do not permit incentive awards for named plaintiffs.[63]

III. Securities Fraud Class Actions in New York State Courts

Class action plaintiffs asserting securities fraud claims in state court in New York have to contend with the broad removal provisions contained in both CAFA[64] and

---

57. N.Y. C.P.L.R. § 909.

58. Alexander, *supra* note 3, § 909 (2005) (citing *Becker v. Empire of Am. Fed. Sav. Bank*, 177 A.D.2d 958, 577 N.Y.S.2d 1001 (4th Dep't 1991)).

59. *Sternberg v. Citicorp Credit Servs.*, 110 Misc.2d 804, 809, 442 N.Y.S.2d 1017, 1020 (Sup. Ct. Nassau County 1981).

60. *Becker*, 177 A.D.2d at 959, 577 N.Y.S.2d at 1003.

61. *See Sternberg*, 110 Misc. 2d at 810, 442 N.Y.S.2d at 1021.

62. *Michels*, 1997 WL 1161145, at * 31–32.

63. *Flemming v. Barnwell Nursing Home & Health Facilities, Inc.*, 56 A.D.3d 162, 166, 865 N.Y.S.2d 706, 709 (3d Dep't 2008).

64. 28 U.S.C. § 1453; *see also* Chapter 10, "The Class Action Fairness Act of 2005."

the Securities Litigation Uniform Standards Act of 1998 (SLUSA).[65] SLUSA pre-empts state law securities fraud claims and provides for their removal to federal district court.[66] Despite the fact that the language of SLUSA refers only to state law securities claims, the Southern and Eastern districts of New York have permitted removal of claims arising solely under the Securities Act of 1933 (the '33 Act) pursuant to SLUSA.[67] Thus, class action plaintiffs asserting claims under the '33 Act in New York state courts should be prepared for a contentious battle over the forum in which their claims will be litigated and for the strong possibility, at least in the First and Second departments, that defendants will successfully remove the class action pursuant to SLUSA.

The future of securities fraud class actions in New York state courts after CAFA is also uncertain. In particular, the question of whether CAFA's removal provisions trump the prohibition against removal contained in the '33 Act remains unsettled. The Southern District has answered this question in the affirmative and permitted defendants to remove "a large, non-local securities class action dealing with a matter of national importance, the mortgage-backed securities crisis that is currently wreaking havoc with the national and international economy."[68] The court felt "constrained" by the Second Circuit's broad interpretation of CAFA, and this decision indicates a willingness by courts in the Second Circuit to stretch the literal meaning of CAFA so as to further its legislative intent.

Second Circuit courts also broadly construe CAFA's exceptions for certain types of securities claims. For example, in *Estate of Pew v. Cardarelli*,[69] the Second Circuit narrowly construed the exception for claims relating to the "rights, duties (including fiduciary duties), and obligations relating to or created by or pursuant to any

---

65. 15 U.S.C. § 77p(c); *see also* Chapter 17.G, "Securities."

66. 15 U.S.C. §§ 78bb(f). SLUSA provides that

> (1) [n]o covered class action based upon the statutory or common law of any State or subdivision thereof may be maintained in any State or Federal court by any private party alleging—
> (A) a misrepresentation or omission of a material fact in connection with the purchase or sale of a covered security; or
> (B) that the defendant used or employed any manipulative or deceptive device or contrivance in connection with the purchase or sale of a covered security.
> (2) . . . Any covered class action brought in any State court involving a covered security, as set forth in paragraph (1), shall be removable to the Federal district court for the district in which the action is pending, and shall be subject to paragraph (1).

15 U.S.C. §§ 78bb(f)(1)–(2).

67. *See Knox v. Agria Corp.*, 613 F. Supp. 2d 419, 425 (S.D.N.Y. 2009); *Rubin v. Pixelplus*, 06 CV 2964, 2007 U.S. Dist. LEXIS 17671, at *18–19 (E.D.N.Y. Mar. 13, 2007). *But see Bernd Bildstein IRRA v. Lazard Ltd.*, 05 CV 3388, 2006 U.S. Dist. LEXIS 61395, at *15 (E.D.N.Y. Aug. 14, 2006) (granting plaintiffs' motion to remand based on a narrow interpretation of SLUSA).

68. *N.J. Carpenters Vacation Fund v. Harborview Mortgage Loan Trust*, 581 F. Supp. 2d 581, 587–88 (S.D.N.Y. 2008).

69. 527 F.3d 25, 31–32 (2d Cir. 2008).

security . . . ."[70] and permitted removal of a class action relating to securities fraud but arising solely under New York's consumer fraud statute.[71] As one commentator noted, this decision "suggests that CAFA is a potentially powerful tool for removing securities cases that do not qualify for removal under SLUSA."[72] The Southern District has held that plaintiffs bear the burden of establishing the applicability of an exception to the removal provisions of CAFA.[73] This holding may have a devastating effect on securities class actions in New York state courts; one commentator has noted that "[w]hen there was such a shift in the burden of proof, the party desiring to litigate in federal court prevailed on the forum contest in 80% of the cases reviewed."[74] Thus, the future of securities fraud class actions in New York state courts is uncertain at best, and plaintiffs are sure to face stiff resistance to their choice of forum in light of the Second Circuit's overall policy of favoring removal of these types of actions.

---

70. 28 U.S.C. § 1453.

71. *Estate of Pew*, 527 F.3d at 31–32.

72. Andrew B. Kratenstein, *Controlling Opt Outs and Coordinated Cases: SLUSA, The All Writs Act, and CAFA*, in MANAGING COMPLEX LITIGATION 2008: LEGAL STRATEGIES AND BEST PRACTICES IN "HIGH STAKES" CASES, at 155 (PLI Litig., Course Handbook Series No. 786, 2008).

73. *Harborview Mortgage Loan Trust*, 581 F. Supp. 2d at 588.

74. Matthew O'Brien, *Choice of Forum in Securities Class Actions: Confronting "Reform" of the Securities Act of 1933*, 28 REV. LITIG. 845, 894 (2009).

NORTH CAROLINA

MATTHEW P. MCGUIRE
ANITRA GOODMAN ROYSTER

I. Introduction

Rule 23 of the North Carolina Rules of Civil Procedure (North Carolina Rule)[1] differs significantly from Rule 23 of the Federal Rules of Civil Procedure. Whereas Federal Rule 23 has been expanded and made significantly more detailed over the years, the North Carolina Rule is skeletal in nature and consists of only four subsections, two of which deal with discrete aspects of secondary actions by shareholders (Rule 23(b)) and tax class actions (Rule 23(d)).

Section (a) of North Carolina Rule 23 is derived from Federal Rule 23 as it existed prior to 1966. Whereas Federal Rule 23 has evolved to the point where it expressly covers most aspects of class certification and postcertification procedure, North Carolina's class certification jurisprudence has developed through a limited number of appellate decisions, the vast majority of which have been decided in the past 25 years.

II. Overview and Class Certification Prerequisites

Rule 23(a) of the North Carolina Rule provides, "If persons constituting a class are so numerous as to make it impracticable to bring them all before the court, such of them, one or more, as will fairly insure the adequate representation of all may, on behalf of all, sue or be sued." Rule 23 is to be liberally construed and "should not be loaded down with arbitrary and technical restrictions."[2] The party seeking certification of a class action has the burden of demonstrating that the prerequisites for

---

1. N.C. R. Civ. P. 23 (1967).
2. *English v. Holden Beach Realty Corp.*, 41 N.C. App. 1, 9, 254 S.E.2d 223, 230, *disc. rev. denied*, 297 N.C. 609, 257 S.E.2d 217 (1979).

certification are present.[3] While federal class action decisions are not binding on North Carolina courts, North Carolina courts have found the reasoning in such cases instructive, even though the rules are quite different.[4]

To certify a class in North Carolina, the party seeking certification must demonstrate that the following prerequisites are satisfied: (1) a class exists, in that "the named and unnamed members each have an interest in either the same issue of law or of fact, and which issue predominates over issues affecting only individual class members;" (2) there is numerosity, in that the class is so numerous as to make it impracticable to bring each member of the class before the court; (3) the party representing the class fairly and adequately ensures the representation of all class members, including those outside the jurisdiction of the court; and (4) adequate notice is given to the class members.[5] Even where all of the class certification prerequisites are satisfied, it is still within the trial court's broad discretion to determine whether a class action is superior to other available methods for the adjudication of the controversy.[6] Findings of fact are required by the trial court when rendering a judgment granting or denying class certification.[7]

A. EXISTENCE OF A CLASS: COMMONALITY AND PREDOMINANCE

A class exists when both the named and unnamed members have an interest in the same issues of either law or of fact, and those issues predominate over issues affecting only individual class members.[8] To determine whether common issues predominate over issues affecting only individual class members, the court will not simply compare the number of common issues against those that require individual consideration. Rather, the test is whether the individual issues are such that they will predominate over common ones as the focus of the court's and litigants' efforts.[9]

---

3. *Crow v. Citicorp Acceptance Co.*, 319 N.C. 274, 282, 354 S.E.2d 459, 465 (1987).

4. *Frost v. Mazda Motor of Am., Inc.*, 353 N.C. 188, 192–93, 540 S.E.2d 324, 327 (2000) (North Carolina courts are "attentive to the interpretation of Rule 23 by the federal courts" and are "guided by such interpretation when appropriate"); *see also In re Senergy*, 2000 N.C.B.C. 7, at ¶ 34 (N.C. Super. Ct. May 17, 2000) (Tennille, J.) (noting that the General Assembly drafted North Carolina's Rule 23 "with an eye toward" the federal equivalent and that the North Carolina Supreme Court therefore "considered federal authority in determining the requirements of a class under North Carolina Rule 23").

5. *Crow*, 319 N.C. at 280–84, 354 S.E.2d at 464–67.

6. *Id.* at 319 N.C. at 284, 354 S.E.2d at 467; *see also Harrison v. Wal-Mart Stores, Inc.*, 170 N.C. App. 545, 613 S.E.2d 322 (2005).

7. *Nobles v. First Carolina Commc'ns*, 108 N.C. App. 127, 133, 423 S.E.2d 312, 316 (1992).

8. *Faulkenbury v. Teachers' & State Employees' Ret. Sys. of N.C.*, 345 N.C. 683, 697, 483 S.E.2d. 422, 431 (1997) (quoting *Crow*, 319 N.C. at 280, 354 S.E.2d at 464).

9. *See Harrison*, 170 N.C. App. at 550–53, 613 S.E.2d at 327–28.

B. NUMEROSITY

To certify a class, the court must determine that class members are so numerous that it is impracticable to bring them all before the court. There is no hard and fast formula for determining whether the numerosity threshold is satisfied. Instead, a party seeking class certification must sufficiently demonstrate "substantial difficulty or inconvenience in joining all members of the class."[10] It is not required that the moving party demonstrate the impossibility of joining class members. Whether numerosity exists depends upon the factual circumstances of each case and is not subject to an arbitrary numerical threshold.[11]

C. ADEQUACY OF REPRESENTATION

The named class representatives must demonstrate that they will fairly and adequately represent the interests of all class members. It is within the court's discretion to determine what constitutes adequate representation in a potential class action.[12] The named representatives must show that there is no conflict of interest between them and the members of the class who are not named parties, so that the interests of the unnamed class members will be fairly protected.[13] The named representatives must also show that they have a personal, and not just a technical or an official, interest in the action.[14] Class representatives must also demonstrate that they will adequately represent those class members located outside of North Carolina.[15]

D. NOTICE

Due process and notions of fundamental fairness dictate that adequate notice be given to members of a certified class through the best means practicable under the circumstances.[16] Such notice should include individual notice to all members who can be identified through reasonable efforts and should be provided as soon as possible to allow the class members an opportunity to participate in the action.[17] The trial court may, in its discretion, apportion the responsibility for paying for the cost of providing notice to the class members.[18]

---

10. *Crow*, 319 N.C. at 283, 354 S.E.2d at 466.
11. *English*, 41 N.C. App. at 6, 254 S.E.2d at 229.
12. *Perry v. Union Camp Corp.*, 100 N.C. App. 168, 394 S.E.2d 681 (1990).
13. *Crow*, 319 N.C. at 282–83, 354 S.E.2d at 465.
14. *English*, 41 N.C. App. at 7, 254 S.E.2d at 230.
15. *Id.* at 41 N.C. App. at 6, 254 S.E.2d at 229.
16. *Crow*, 319 N.C. at 283–84, 354 S.E.2d at 466.
17. *Id.* at 319 N.C. at 284, 354 S.E.2d at 466.
18. *Frost*, 353 N.C. at 198, 540 S.E.2d at 331.

E. SUPERIORITY

Even if all of the prerequisites for class certification are satisfied, it is left to the trial court's discretion to determine whether a class action is superior to other available methods for the adjudication of a controversy.[19] This element typically is the battleground on which class certification determinations are fought in North Carolina. The North Carolina Supreme Court has noted that "class actions should be permitted where they are likely to serve useful purposes such as preventing a multiplicity of suits or inconsistent results."[20] The usefulness of the class action device must be balanced, however, against inefficiency or other drawbacks.[21]

When making this determination, the trial court is not limited to consideration of the class certification prerequisites.[22] Some proper considerations include, but are not limited to, the amount of recovery compared to the cost of administration of the lawsuit,[23] the interest of members of the class in individually controlling the prosecution or defense of separate actions, "'the extent and nature of any litigation concerning the controversy already commenced by or against members of the class,' 'the desirability or undesirability of concentrating the litigation of the claims in the particular forum,' and 'the difficulties likely to be encountered in the management of a class action.'"[24]

III. Practical Considerations Related to Class Certification

A. INQUIRIES INTO THE MERITS

While North Carolina courts have recognized that it may not be proper for a judge to make a determination on the merits at the class certification stage,[25] courts must undertake a "rigorous analysis before certifying a class."[26] When determining whether to certify a class, the court may conduct a preliminary inquiry into the legal measure of damages available to the plaintiff, and if this number is

---

19. *Crow*, 319 N.C. at 285, 354 S.E.2d at 466.

20. *Id.* at 319 N.C. at 284, 354 S.E.2d at 466.

21. *Pitts v. Am. Sec. Ins. Co.*, 144 N.C. App. 1, 11, 550 S.E.2d 179, 188 (2001) (quoting *Crow*, 319 N.C. at 284, 354 S.E.2d at 466), *disc. rev. allowed*, 355 N.C. 214, 560 S.E.2d 133 (2002), *aff'd without precedential value*, 356 N.C. 292, 569 S.E.2d 647 (2002).

22. *Nobles*, 108 N.C. App. at 132, 423 S.E.2d at 315.

23. *Maffei v. Alert Cable TV*, 316 N.C. 615, 621–22, 342 S.E.2d 867, 872 (1986).

24. *Pitts*, 144 N.C. App. at 11, 550 S.E.2d at 188.

25. *Maffei*, 316 N.C. at 618, 342 S.E.d 2d at 870.

26. *Pitts v. Am. Sec. Ins. Co.*, No. 96-CVS-658, 2000 WL 33915843, at *3 (N.C. Super. Ct. Feb. 2, 2000), *rev'd in part, vacated in part by* 144 N.C. App. 1, 550 S.E.2d 179 (2001).

found be inconsequential, the court may deny certification on the basis of judicial efficiency.[27]

B. APPEAL OF ORDER DENYING CERTIFICATION

Section 7A-27(d)(10) of the North Carolina General Statutes permits the review of interlocutory orders affecting a substantial right. An order denying class certification, although interlocutory in nature, has been held to affect a substantial right and is, therefore, immediately appealable.[28] In its review, an appellate court is bound by the trial court's findings of fact if they are supported by competent evidence.[29] Granting a class certification motion, on the other hand, usually has been found *not* to affect a substantial right, and thus such orders usually are not immediately appealable.[30]

C. MOTIONS TO DECERTIFY A CLASS ACTION OR MODIFY A CLASS DEFINITION

Another major difference between North Carolina Rule practice and its federal counterpart concerns the court's ability to revisit its class certification decision and decertify or modify the class definition. In North Carolina, civil litigation matters are not assigned to a specific judge. Because judges rotate through counties and judicial districts, it is the procedural norm for different judges to handle a case at various stages. In other words, the judge who rules on a Rule 23 motion for class certification likely will be a different judge than the one who ruled on a Rule 12 motion to dismiss at the outset of the case. And the judge who hears a Rule 56 motion for summary judgment likely will not be the same judge who heard the Rule 23 motion. This is procedurally significant because in North Carolina, one superior court judge cannot overrule a prior ruling of another superior court judge.[31]

Thus, if a class is certified, only the judge that enters the class certification order can revisit that decision upon a motion to decertify or modify the class definition. This fact alone makes it prudent to seek the designation of a putative class action as an exceptional civil case or a complex business case under Rule 2.1 of the General Rules of Practice for the Superior and District Courts, as such a designation ensures that the case will be assigned to a single judge for the duration of the matter.

---

27. *Maffei v. Alert Cable TV of N.C.*, 75 N.C. App. 473, 331 S.E.2d 188 (1985), *rev'd on other grounds*, 316 N.C. 615, 342 S.E.2d 867 (1986).

28. *Frost*, 353 N.C. at 192–93, 540 S.E.2d at 327.

29. *Nobles*, 108 N.C. App. at 132, 423 S.E.2d at 325.

30. *Frost*, 353 N.C. at 193, 540 S.E.2d at 328.

31. *Adams Creek Assocs. v. Davis*, 186 N.C. App. 512, 652 S.E.2d 677 (2007), *disc. rev. denied*, 362 N.C. 354, 662 S.E.2d 900 (2008).

It is true that "in an appropriate context a superior court judge has the power to modify an interlocutory order entered by another superior court judge."[32] For example, interlocutory orders are modifiable based on circumstances that changed the legal foundation of the prior order.[33] However, the addition of new defendants and new claim theories has been held not to constitute sufficient grounds to over-rule or modify a class certification order entered by a different judge.[34]

IV. Settlement of Class Actions in North Carolina

A. SETTLEMENT OF CERTIFIED CLASS ACTION

North Carolina Rule 23(c) states that a "class action shall not be dismissed or compromised without the approval of the judge." There is scant North Carolina case law regarding the standard a court should apply when evaluating a proposed settlement of a certified class, but approval is conditioned upon the court's finding that a settlement is "fair, adequate and reasonable."[35] As noted above, federal law is highly instructive on this issue in light of the void of North Carolina precedent. Rule 23(c) also provides that "notice of a proposed dismissal or compromise shall be given to all members of the class in such manner as the judge directs."

B. SETTLEMENT OF A PUTATIVE CLASS ACTION PRIOR TO A RULE 23 DETERMINATION

For many years, matters that were filed as putative class actions in North Carolina could be settled and/or dismissed prior to a Rule 23 determination without any court supervision. In recent years, the potential for abuse of this situation began to draw the attention of the North Carolina Business Court. In *Moody v. Sears Roebuck & Co.*,[36] the North Carolina Court of Appeals took up the issue of whether the requirements of North Carolina Rule 23(c) applied to precertification settle-ments or dismissals. The *Moody* court followed the reasoning of the Fourth Circuit in *Shelton v. Pargo*,[37] and held that North Carolina Rule 23(c) does not apply to precertification class action complaints.[38]

However, the court's inquiry did not end there, and it fashioned a new rule for court supervision of precertification dismissals of putative class action complaints:

---

32. *Dublin v. UCR, Inc.*, 115 N.C. App. 209, 219, 444 S.E.2d 455, 461 (1994).

33. *State v. Duvall*, 304 N.C. 557, 284 S.E.2d 495 (1981); *Carr v. Carbon Corp.*, 49 N.C. App. 631, 272 S.E.2d 374 (1980), *rev. denied*, 302 N.C. 217, 276 S.E.2d 914 (1981).

34. *Dublin*, 115 N.C. App. at 220, 444 S.E.2d at 461–62.

35. *Ruff v. Parex, Inc.*, No. 96 CVS 0059, slip op. at 3 (N.C. Super. Ct. Mar. 16, 2000).

36. 664 S.E.2d 569 (2008).

37. 582 F.2d 1298 (4th Cir. 1978).

38. *Moody*, 664 S.E.2d at 577.

Without some level of pre-certification court supervision, there is an unacceptable risk that parties may abuse the class-action mechanism in myriad ways. For example,

> defendants faced with a class action may be encouraged to try to avoid class resolution of claims by buying off individual named plaintiffs. These defendants could settle with strong class plaintiffs, and proceed with a class action when faced with weak or ineffectual named plaintiffs. In some situations, the defendants may be able to forum shop settling claims brought in undesirable forums. The other side of the coin is that plaintiffs with small claims may try to use class allegations to coerce unusually generous individual settlements from defendants.

5 MOORE'S FEDERAL PRACTICE § 23.64[2][a] (3d. ed 2008). Parties with such motives will be less likely to abuse the class-action mechanism if they know that a voluntary dismissal will be subject to the trial court's review. Further, when a plaintiff files a class-action complaint, the plaintiff has set out to the world a willingness to assume the role of a representative in a class-action lawsuit. Although the class is not yet certified, putative class members may rely on the named plaintiff's stated intentions to represent the class. Under such circumstances, trial courts have a duty to assure that putative class members will not be prejudiced, procedurally or otherwise, by voluntary dismissal of the class-action complaint.[39]

The North Carolina Court of Appeals thus held that "when a plaintiff seeks voluntary dismissal of a pre-certification class-action complaint, the trial court should engage in a limited inquiry to determine (a) whether the parties have abused the class-action mechanism for personal gain, and (b) whether dismissal will prejudice absent putative class members."[40] If the trial court is satisfied that proposed dismissal does not raise either of these concerns, the dismissal may be filed. If, on the other hand, the trial court has reason to believe that the dismissal may represent an abuse of the class action mechanism or prejudice absent putative class members, it may retain jurisdiction and take steps to address those concerns.[41]

---

39. *Id.* at 578–79.
40. *Id.* at 579.
41. *Id.*

NORTH DAKOTA

MARK G. SCHROEDER

I. Introduction

Class action procedure in North Dakota state courts is governed by Rule 23 of the North Dakota Rules of Civil Procedure (North Dakota Rule).[1] The North Dakota Rule is patterned after the Model Class Action Rule and is distinguishable from Rule 23 of the Federal Rules of Civil Procedure. The North Dakota Supreme Court takes a liberal approach in favor of class actions.

II. Comparison with Federal Rule of Civil Procedure 23

As noted, the North Dakota Rule, enacted in 1977, is patterned after the Model Class Action Rule.[2] Prior to 1977, the North Dakota Rule was the same as Rule 23 of the Federal Rules of Civil Procedure.[3] The North Dakota Rule now differs in significant ways from Federal Rule 23.[4] For example, the "superiority" standard appears in Federal Rule 23, but not North Dakota Rule 23.[5] The North Dakota Rule also lacks the "typicality" prerequisite found in the federal rule. In addition, the uniform rule adopted in North Dakota has a single broad category of class actions,

---

1. N.D. R. Civ. P. 23 (2010).

2. *See id.* (explanatory note); *see also Holloway v. Blue Cross of N.D.*, 294 N.W.2d 902, 906–07 (N.D. 1980). *See generally* 12 U.L.A. Uniform Law Commissioners' Model Class Action Rule (2008). Iowa is the only state besides North Dakota that has adopted Model Class Action Rule 23. *Id.* at 93.

3. *See* N.D. R. Civ. P. 23 (explanatory note); *Rogelstad v. Farmers Union Grain Terminal Ass'n, Inc.*, 226 N.W.2d 370, 374 (N.D. 1975).

4. *See Werlinger v. Champion Healthcare Corp.*, 598 N.W.2d 820, 829 (N.D. 1999) (North Dakota Rule 23 "is distinguishable from the federal rule"); *Peterson v. Dougherty Dawkins, Inc.*, 583 N.W.2d 626, 629 n.4 (N.D. 1998) ("Model Class Actions Rule . . . is similar but not identical to the federal rule").

5. *See Peterson*, 583 N.W.2d at 631 (comparing Fed. R. Civ. P. 23(b)(3) with N.D. R. Civ. P. 23(c)(1)(F) & (G)).

rather than the three types of class actions set forth in Federal Rule 23(b).[6] Other differences between North Dakota and federal class action practice are discussed below.

III. Requirements for Class Certification Under North Dakota Rule 23

Four essential requirements must be satisfied to certify a class action under the North Dakota Rule:[7]

> 1. "the class is so numerous or so constituted that joinder of all members, whether or not otherwise required or permitted, is impracticable;"[8]
> 2. "there is a question of law or fact common to the class;"[9]
> 3. "a class action should be permitted for the fair and efficient adjudication of the controversy;"[10] and
> 4. "the representative parties fairly and adequately will protect the interests of the class."[11]

A. NUMEROSITY

The numerosity determination under North Dakota Rule 23(a)(1) must be made in light of circumstances of the case, and the trial court may rely on common sense assumptions to support its findings.[12] North Dakota courts have found numerosity with a class as few as 48 members.[13]

B. COMMONALITY

The commonality requirement under North Dakota Rule 23(a)(2) is easily satisfied.[14] Commonality can be established through standardized conduct by defen-

---

6. *See Werlinger*, 598 N.W.2d at 829.

7. *See Rose v. United Equitable Ins. Co.*, 651 N.W.2d 683, 687 (N.D. 2002); *Klagues v. Maint. Eng'g*, 643 N.W.2d 45, 50 (N.D. 2002); *Ritter, Laber & Assocs., Inc. v. Koch Oil, Inc.* (*Ritter II*), 623 N.W.2d 424, 426 (N.D. 2001); *Ritter, Laber & Assocs., Inc. v. Koch Oil, Inc.* (*Ritter I*), 605 N.W.2d 153, 156 (N.D. 2000).

8. N.D. R. Civ. P. 23(a)(1).

9. N.D. R. Civ. P. 23(a)(2).

10. N.D. R. Civ. P. 23(b)(2)(B).

11. N.D. R. Civ. P. 23(b)(2)(C).

12. *See Werlinger*, 598 N.W.2d at 826.

13. *See Horst v. Guy*, 211 N.W.2d 723, 726 (N.D. 1973) (former North Dakota Rule 23); *see also Werlinger*, 598 N.W.2d at 826 (112 class members satisfied numerosity).

14. *See N.D. Human Rights Coal. v. Bertsch*, 697 N.W.2d 1, 4 (N.D. 2005).

dants toward members of the proposed class,[15] such as a company-wide policy.[16] Individual differences concerning damages do not defeat commonality.[17]

C. FAIR AND EFFICIENT ADJUDICATION OF THE CONTROVERSY

In determining whether a class action should be permitted for the fair and efficient adjudication of the controversy under North Dakota Rule 23(b)(2)(B), the trial court should consider and give appropriate weight to 13 criteria:

(A) whether a joint or common interest exists among members of the class;

(B) whether the prosecution of separate actions by or against individual members of the class would create a risk of inconsistent or varying adjudications with respect to individual members of the class that would establish incompatible standards of conduct for a party opposing the class;

(C) whether adjudications with respect to individual members of the class as a practical matter would be dispositive of the interests of other members not parties to the adjudication or substantially impair or impede their ability to protect their interests;

(D) whether a party opposing the class has acted or refused to act on grounds generally applicable to the class, thereby making final injunctive relief or corresponding declaratory relief appropriate with respect to the class as a whole;

(E) whether common questions of law or fact predominate over any questions affecting only individual members;

(F) whether other means of adjudicating the claims and defenses are impracticable or inefficient;

(G) whether a class action offers the most appropriate means of adjudicating the claims and defenses;

(H) whether members not representative parties have a substantial interest in individually controlling the prosecution or defense of separate actions;

(I) whether the class action involves a claim that is or has been the subject of a class action, a government action, or other proceeding;

(J) whether it is desirable to bring the class action in another forum;

(K) whether management of the class action poses unusual difficulties;

(L) whether any conflict of laws issues involved pose unusual difficulties; and

(M) whether the claims of individual class members are insufficient in the amounts or interests involved, in view of the complexities of the issues and the expenses of the litigation, to afford significant relief to the members of the class.[18]

The trial court is not required to specifically address each of these 13 factors when deciding whether a class action will provide a fair and efficient adjudication of the

---

15. *See Bice v. Petro-Hunt, L.L.C.*, 681 N.W.2d 74, 77–78 (N.D. 2004).

16. *See Werlinger*, 598 N.W.2d at 826–27.

17. *See Bice*, 681 N.W.2d at 78; *Ritter I*, 605 N.W.2d at 156.

18. N.D. R. Civ. P. 23(c)(1).

controversy.[19] Rather, the trial court must weigh these competing factors, and no single factor predominates over the other.[20]

If a trial court incorrectly analyzes some of the factors under North Dakota Rule 23(c)(1), rather than deny certification as a matter of law, the appropriate remedy would be to remand the case to the trial court for proper reconsideration of certification under all 13 factors.[21]

1. Joint/Common Interest[22]

A common interest exists if one plaintiff's failure to collect would increase the recovery of the remaining plaintiffs, or if the defendant's total liability does not depend on how the recovery of a claim is distributed among the class members.[23] A common question is not the same as a common interest that would give rise to a mandatory class action.[24]

2. Incompatible Standards[25]

Incompatible standards occur when a party opposing the class would be unable to comply with one judgment without violating the terms of another judgment.[26] Different results in actions for money damages, such as the risk of being found liable to some plaintiffs and not to others, does not qualify as an incompatible standard.[27] This factor is only applied to actions where the defendant is sued for different and incompatible affirmative relief, as opposed to actions seeking money damages.[28]

3. Adjudication of Individual Interest, Which As a Practical Matter Would Dispose of Nonparty Interests[29]

In analyzing this factor, North Dakota courts look to the similar provision under Federal Rule 23(b)(1)(B).[30] Unlike federal practice, this factor is not restricted in North Dakota to cases where there is a limited or insufficient fund.[31] Precedent plus some other practical matter could be sufficient for a class to qualify under this factor.[32]

---

19. *See Howe v. Microsoft Corp.*, 656 N.W.2d 285, 288 (N.D. 2003) (citing multiple cases).
20. *See id.*
21. *See id.* at 290; *Klagues*, 643 N.W.2d at 54.
22. *See* N.D. R. Civ. P. 23(c)(1)(A).
23. *See Klagues*, 643 N.W.2d at 51–52; *Ritter II*, 623 N.W.2d at 430; *Ritter I*, 605 N.W.2d at 157.
24. *See Werlinger*, 598 N.W.2d at 833.
25. *See* N.D. R. Civ. P. 23(c)(1)(B).
26. *See Ritter I*, 605 N.W.2d at 157 (citing *Werlinger*, 598 N.W.2d at 834).
27. *See id.* at 157–58 (citing *Werlinger*, 598 N.W.2d at 834).
28. *See id.* at 158.
29. *See* N.D. R. Civ. P. 23(c)(1)(C).
30. *See Ritter I*, 605 N.W.2d at 158.
31. *See Klagues*, 643 N.W.2d at 52.
32. *See Bice*, 681 N.W.2d at 79.

4. Predominance[33]

In analyzing the predominance factor, the North Dakota Supreme Court provides this guidance:

> There is no precise test governing the determination of whether common questions predominate over individual claims. Rather, a pragmatic assessment of the entire action and all of the issues is involved in making the determination. For common questions to predominate, it is not necessary the individual claims be carbon copies of each other. "Predominate" should not be automatically associated with "determinative" or "significant," and consequently when one or more central issues to the action are common and can be said to predominate, the class action will be proper. Class certification is not to be refused merely because individual issues will remain even after disposition of common issues. The common issues need not dispose of the case, and the presence of individual issues is of no obstacle to proceeding as a class action.[34]

The North Dakota courts have never suggested that a class plaintiff must show common proof on each element of a claim.[35] The presence of individual questions, such as significant individual questions of proximate cause and damages, does not preclude class certification.[36]

D. ADEQUACY OF REPRESENTATION

To determine adequate representation under North Dakota Rule 23(b)(2)(C), the court must find

> (A) the attorney for the representative parties will adequately represent the interests of the class;
> (B) the representative parties do not have a conflict of interest in the maintenance of the class action; and
> (C) the representative parties have or can acquire adequate financial resources, considering subdivision (q), to assure that the interests of the class will not be harmed.[37]

In North Dakota, it is not necessary that all class representatives meet the adequacy requirement.[38] Adequacy has been satisfied in North Dakota even where

---

33. *See* N.D. R. Civ. P. 23(c)(1)(E).

34. *Rose*, 651 N.W.2d at 688–89 (quoting *Werlinger*, 598 N.W.2d at 830 (citations omitted)).

35. *See Howe*, 656 N.W.2d at 289.

36. *See id.*; *Rose*, 651 N.W.2d at 688–89.

37. *See* N.D. R. Civ. P. 23(c)(2); *Werlinger*, 598 N.W.2d at 827.

38. *See Werlinger*, 598 N.W.2d at 828 (familial relationship between two class representatives and class lawyer was insufficient in itself to support charge of collusion to defeat the adequacy of representation requirement).

class counsel was also a class member.[39] If one representative satisfies the requirement, adequacy of representation is met.[40]

IV. Burden of Proof/Evidence

The party moving for class certification has the burden of demonstrating compliance with the prerequisites of the North Dakota Rule.[41]

The trial court must determine class certification without delving into or
resolving the merits of the case.[42] Thus, in deciding a class certification motion, it
is inappropriate to resolve battles between the parties' respective experts.[43] Instead,
the North Dakota Supreme Court advocates the use of a "lower *Daubert* standard"
at the class certification stage.[44]

V. Miscellaneous Issues

A. PURPOSE AND PHILOSOPHY

The "remedial" objectives of the North Dakota Rule include the efficient resolution of claims of many individuals in a single action, the elimination of repetitious
litigation, and an effective procedure for claims that would be uneconomical to
litigate individually.[45] The North Dakota Rule is traditionally construed to provide
an open and receptive attitude toward class actions.[46] As such, the North Dakota
courts are guided by a broad and liberal public policy in favor of class actions.[47]

B. CONTENTS OF CLASS ORDER

An order on certification must describe the class, state the relief sought, and specify reasons for the court's rulings.[48]

---

39. *See Bice*, 681 N.W.2d at 82–83.

40. *See Werlinger*, 598 N.W.2d at 828.

41. *See Vignaroli v. Blue Cross of Iowa*, 360 N.W.2d 741, 744 (Iowa 1985) (discussing burden under
Iowa's Uniform Class Action Rule).

42. *See Howe*, 656 N.W.2d at 291.

43. *See id.* at 293.

44. *See id.* at 295 (citing *Daubert v. Merrell Dow Pharms., Inc.*, 509 U.S. 579 (1993)).

45. *See Peterson*, 583 N.W.2d at 628–29 & n.4 (citing *Rogelstad*, 226 N.W.2d at 376 (noting the "judicial
philosophy expressed in *Rogelstad* remains unchanged")); *Old Broadway Corp. v. Hjelle*, 411 N.W.2d 81, 83
(N.D. 1987) (citing same).

46. *See Rose*, 651 N.W.2d at 686.

47. *See id.*

48. *See* N.D. R. Civ. P. 23(d)(1), (2); *Bertsch*, 697 N.W.2d at 4; *Holloway*, 294 N.W.2d at 906–07.

C. AMENDMENT OF CLASS ORDER/SUBCLASSES

Under the North Dakota Rule, certification orders may be amended before judgment, and may include subclasses,[49] especially to address substantive differences in state law.[50]

D. CLASS NOTICE

The required contents of class notice and the manner of notification are specified in the North Dakota Rule.[51] Each class member whose potential damages exceed $100 must be given personal or mailed notice if the person's identity or whereabouts can be ascertained with reasonable due diligence.[52] A plaintiff must advance the expense of notice to class members.[53] Due process requires an opportunity to opt out.[54]

E. NON–CLASS MEMBER PARTICIPATION

The North Dakota Rule permits mandatory class members to participate in the class action.[55] A nonrepresentative class member also has the right to appear and to be represented by separate counsel.[56] As such, the North Dakota Rule provides more due process protections than Federal Rule 23.[57]

F. DISCOVERY AGAINST CLASS MEMBERS

Discovery against class members who are not representative parties may be used only on court order based on relevant factors outlined in the North Dakota Rule.[58]

G. DISMISSAL/COMPROMISE

Unless certification has been refused, a class action shall not be dismissed or settled without court approval.[59] This includes motions for voluntary dismissal.[60]

---

49. *See* N.D. R. Civ. P. 23(e)(1); *Bice*, 681 N.W.2d at 80–81.
50. *See Peterson*, 583 N.W.2d at 630.
51. *See* N.D. R. Civ. P. 23(g).
52. *See* N.D. R. Civ. P. 23(g)(4).
53. *See* N.D. R. Civ. P. 23(g)(6); *Holloway*, 294 N.W.2d at 907.
54. *See Ritter I*, 605 N.W.2d at 160.
55. *See* N.D. R. Civ. P. 23(i)(1)(B)(iii).
56. *See* N.D. R. Civ. P. 23(i)(2).
57. *See Ritter II*, 623 N.W.2d at 431.
58. *See* N.D. R. Civ. P. 23(j).
59. *See* N.D. R. Civ. P. 23(l).
60. *See Glasow v. E.I. Dupont de Nemours and Co.*, 696 N.W.2d 531, 533 (N.D. 2005).

H. COSTS

The expenses of class notice under North Dakota Rule 23(g) are taxable as costs in favor of the prevailing party.[61]

I. FLUID RECOVERY

The North Dakota Rule specifically allows for a fluid recovery of damages to benefit the class as a whole where individual distribution of the class recovery is impracticable or a residual remains after the distribution.[62]

J. ATTORNEY FEES

The North Dakota Rule authorizes the trial court to award attorney fees in class action litigation.[63] The trial court must consider specified factors in awarding class action attorney fees.[64] When considering a request for attorney fees in a class action lawsuit, the court takes on a fiduciary role on behalf of the class members.[65]

K. FEE AGREEMENT AND EXPENSES

Any fee agreement between the class representative and class counsel must be produced prior to any class certification hearing.[66] If litigation expenses cannot be reasonably defrayed by the class representative, the court may authorize and control solicitation and expenditure of voluntary contributions for expenses from class members or advances by lawyers or others.[67]

L. TOLLING

Statutes of limitations are tolled for class members.[68]

M. ARBITRATION

The North Dakota Supreme Court has concluded that arbitration clauses waiving class actions are not substantively unconscionable, but such clauses may be procedurally unconscionable.[69]

---

61. *See* N.D. R. Civ. P. 23(n)(3).

62. *See* N.D. R. Civ. P. 23(o); *Ritter II*, 623 N.W.2d at 429.

63. *See* N.D. R. Civ. P. 23(p).

64. *See* N.D. R. Civ. P. 23(p)(5).

65. *See Ritter, Laber & Assocs., Inc. v. Koch Oil, Inc. (Ritter IV)*, 740 N.W.2d 67, 80 (N.D. 2007).

66. *See* N.D. R. Civ. P. 23(q)(1).

67. *See* N.D. R. Civ. P. 23(q)(2).

68. *See* N.D. R. Civ. P. 23(r) (explanatory note) (codifying *Am. Pipe & Constr. Co. v. Utah*, 414 U.S. 538 (1974)).

69. *See Strand v. U.S. Bank Nat'l Ass'n*, 693 N.W.2d 918 (N.D. 2005).

VI. Appeal

Unlike federal courts, in North Dakota state court practice an order certifying or refusing to certify a class action is appealable as of right.[70] An order amending the class certification order is also appealable.[71] Even orders that generally are nonappealable may be appealable when issued in a class action.[72]

The North Dakota Supreme Court reviews class certification orders under an abuse of discretion standard.[73] In the class certification context, the North Dakota Supreme Court employs a "highly deferential" standard of review.[74]

---

70. *See* N.D. R. Civ. P. 23(d)(3); *Peterson*, 583 N.W.2d at 628.
71. *See* N.D. R. Civ. P. 23(e)(4).
72. *See, e.g., Glasow*, 696 N.W.2d at 532–33 (order to dismiss without prejudice).
73. *See Peterson*, 583 N.W.2d at 628.
74. *See Rose*, 651 N.W.2d at 689.

OHIO

DAVID J. MICHALSKI
JEFFREY A. BRAUER

I. Introduction

Ohio's class action local practice is, in most respects, a mirror image of federal class action litigation, notwithstanding the fact that Ohio does not reflect the 2003 revisions to Federal Rule 23. Indeed, courts routinely observe that "the bulk of Ohio's class action rule, Civ.R. 23(A) through (E), is identical to the bulk of the federal class action rule, Fed.R.Civ.P. 23(a) through (e)."[1] Accordingly, federal practice often serves as a guide to class action litigation in Ohio. This chapter is intended to identify the few substantive differences between Ohio procedures and federal practice.

II. Ohio Rule 23

Rule 23 of the Ohio Rules of Civil Procedure (Ohio Rule 23), which became effective in 1970, was drafted to mirror the 1966 version of Rule 23 of the Federal Rules of Civil Procedure (Federal Rule 23).[2] From 1970 to 2003, Ohio Rule 23 was nearly identical to the Federal Rule, and Ohio courts routinely stated that federal case law was persuasive in interpreting Ohio Rule 23.[3] Not surprisingly, the case

---

1. *Vaccariello v. Smith & Nephew Richards, Inc.*, 763 N.E.2d 160, 162 (Ohio 2002).

2. The Staff Notes to Ohio Rule 23 make clear that it was intended to adopt "the unchanged language of [the 1966 version of] Federal Rule 23" with the exception of a unique Ohio provision, Ohio Rule 23(F), discussed in section IV, *infra*.

3. The 1987 amendments to Federal Rule 23 were purely technical; no substantive change was intended. *See* Advisory Committee notes to 1987 Amendment. The 1998 amendment to Federal Rule 23 added Rule 23(f), which authorized courts of appeal to permit an interlocutory appeal of an order granting or denying class certification. This provision, which differs from Ohio Rule 23, is discussed in detail in section III.

law reflected these similarities. In 2003, Federal Rule 23 was substantially revised, adding subdivision (g) and (h) and making changes to the provisions regarding class notice and settlement as well. While Ohio Rule 23 has not been amended to incorporate the changes to Federal Rule 23, the changes to the Federal Rules reflected past practice which was, in most cases, already in effect in Ohio. Accordingly, the two rules remain very similar in nearly every respect and virtually identical in terms of the prerequisites for certification and the types of class actions maintainable.[4]

III. Timing of Appeals

A significant practice difference between Federal Rule 23 and Ohio Rule 23 concerns the appeal of orders granting or denying class certification. Under Federal Rule 23(f), which was added in 1998, a party may seek an interlocutory appeal from an order granting or denying class certification. In federal court, an interlocutory appeal is permissive "in the sole discretion of the court of appeals."[5] While Ohio Rule 23 itself does not address interlocutory appeals, Ohio's final appealable order statute was amended in 1998 to provide that "[a]n order that determines that an action may or may not be maintained as a class action" is a final and appealable order.[6] "Accordingly, the aggrieved party must appeal, if at all, within 30 days of the judgment entry, or else waive that appeal and accept the decision."[7] Thus, unlike federal practice, the party losing the certification battle must seek an interlocutory appeal of the decision under Ohio law and cannot delay an appeal until the entire case is resolved.

IV. Aggregation of Claims

Ohio Rule 23 has a unique provision, Ohio Rule 23(F), permitting class members to aggregate their claims to reach the $500 minimum jurisdiction of the courts of common pleas, the courts of general jurisdiction in Ohio. In Ohio, county courts and municipal courts have "exclusive original jurisdiction" over civil actions for the recovery of sums below $500.[8] Ohio Rule 23(F) permits aggregation of claims in the class action context so that even very small class claims may be heard in the courts of common pleas.[9] Absent this provision, Ohio claimants with claims for very small amounts would not be able to reach Ohio's primary trial courts.

---

4. *Compare* Ohio R. Civ. P. 23(A) and (B) *with* Fed. R. Civ. P. 23(a) and (b).

5. *See* Fed. R. Civ. P. 23 advisory committee notes (1998).

6. Ohio Rev. Code § 2505.02(B)(5).

7. *Rehoreg v. Stoneco, Inc.*, No. 04CA008481, 2005 Ohio App. LEXIS 6, at *5 (9th Dist. Jan. 5, 2005).

8. *See* Ohio Rev. Code §§ 1907.03(A), 1901.18(A)(1).

9. *See* Ohio R. Civ. P. 23, staff notes.

V. Distinctions Arising from the 2003 Amendments

The remaining differences between Ohio Rule 23 and Federal Rule 23 all derive from the 2003 amendments to Federal Rule 23.[10] The 2003 amendments resulted in four significant differences between the rules. First, Ohio Rule 23(C)(1) provides that a court's certification decision should come "as soon as practicable after the commencement of an action brought as a class action," while Federal Rule 23(c)(1) now provides that the certification decision shall come at "an early practicable time."[11] The Advisory Committee notes to the 2003 amendments to Federal Rule 23 make clear that this change in language was meant to reflect the prevailing federal practice of deferring the certification decision to permit class discovery and briefing.[12] Regardless of the fact that Ohio retains the legacy "as soon as practicable" language, the timing of the certification decision is rarely, if ever, "as soon as practicable" in practice.[13] As in federal practice, Ohio litigants routinely engage in discovery and briefing in advance of any class certification. Thus, Ohio Rule 23 and Federal Rule 23 remain similar in practice, although not in text, with respect to the timing of the certification motion and decision.

Second, the 2003 amendments to Federal Rule 23 also authorize, but do not require, district courts to provide for class notice to members of classes certified under Federal Rule 23(b)(1) or 23(b)(2).[14] Such notice is not mandated, and courts are admonished that the discretion to provide such notice "should be exercised with care."[15] This provision has not been incorporated into Ohio Rule 23.[16] In contrast, classes under both Federal Rule 23(b)(3) and Ohio Rule 23(B)(3) do require notice. Arguably, Ohio's lack of the new Federal Rule 23(c)(2)(A) language would suggest that Ohio courts do not have authority to provide notice to potential class members under Ohio Rule 23(B)(1) and (2). Despite there being no explicit authorization, however, courts do direct notice to Ohio Rule 23(B)(1) and (2) class members on occasion. This may arise out the fact that Ohio courts are granted broad notice authority under Ohio Rule 23(D)(2) in administering class action litigation. It may also be based on the fact that Ohio's practice so strongly mirrors the federal practice.

---

10. This chapter does not attempt to point out every textual difference between Ohio Rule 23 and Federal Rule 23. Instead, it highlights the most important differences.

11. *Compare* OHIO R. CIV. P. 23(C)(1) *with* FED. R. CIV. P. 23(c)(1).

12. FED. R. CIV. P. 23(c)(1) advisory committee note (2003).

13. *See, e.g., Hansen v. Landaker*, Nos. 99AP-1125 & 99AP-1126, 2000 Ohio App. LEXIS 5676 (10th Dist. Dec. 7, 2000) (plaintiff's nine-month delay in seeking class certification was not a violation of Ohio Rule 23(C)(1)).

14. *See* FED. R. CIV. P. 23(c)(2)(A).

15. *See* FED. R. CIV. P. 23(c)(2)(A) advisory committee note (2003).

16. *Compare* FED. R. CIV. P. 23(c)(2) *with* Ohio R. CIV. P. 23(C)(2).

Third, the 2003 amendments to Federal Rule 23(e) were intended to "strengthen" the district court's authority to review class action settlements in federal court.[17] Federal Rule 23(e)(3) now requires the parties seeking approval of a class settlement to file a statement identifying "any agreement made in connection with the [settlement] proposal"—not just the settlement agreement itself—so the district court is fully informed of potential "side deals" that might impact the reasonableness of the terms. Furthermore, Federal Rule 23(e)(2) now expressly requires the district court to hold a settlement hearing as to any proposal that would bind absent class members and to approve the settlement only upon a finding that it is "fair, reasonable, and adequate." Any class member has the right to object to the settlement, and any objection can only be withdrawn with court approval under Federal Rule 23(e)(5). While these settlement procedures are not explicitly contained in Ohio Rule 23, Ohio courts applying Ohio Rule 23(e) have held hearings as to whether a proposed settlement is fair, reasonable, and adequate before approving class settlements, so the rules may not be that different in practice.[18]

Fourth, the 2003 amendments to Federal Rule 23 added new subsections 23(g) and (h), addressing the appointment of class counsel and the award of attorney fees and costs. These subsections are not found in Ohio Rule 23. This being said, Federal Rule 23(g) was not a true departure from prior federal practice as most, if not all, of the criteria for appointment had previously been used as part of the Federal Rule 23(a)(4) inquiry into the adequacy of counsel.[19] Ohio courts consider many of the same criteria set forth explicitly in Federal Rule 23(g) as part of the Ohio Rule 23(A)(4) inquiry into the adequacy of class counsel.[20] While the case law is not definitive, Ohio state courts appear to presume adequacy in the absence of a showing to the contrary.[21]

With respect to the award of attorney fees and costs, Ohio Rule 23 does not contain a provision governing the procedures for an award (as in Federal Rule

---

17. See FED. R. CIV. P. 23(e) advisory committee notes (2003). The amended Federal Rule 23(e) makes clear that these procedures only apply to settlement, voluntary dismissal, or compromise of "certified" class actions. See Aikens v. Deluxe Fin. Servs., Inc., No. 01-2427-CM, 2005 U.S. Dist. LEXIS 8079 (D. Kan. Mar. 2, 2005) (no need for notice to class or court approval with respect to precertification settlements by named plaintiffs). By contrast, Ohio Rule 23(E) requires notice and court approval whenever a "class action" is dismissed or compromised. Since the word "certified" is absent from the Ohio Rule, it might arguably be read to reach precertification settlement of individual claims.

18. See, e.g., Beder v. Cleveland Browns, Inc., 758 N.E.2d 307 (Ohio C.P. 2001) (approving class settlement after fairness hearing).

19. See FED. R. CIV. P. 23(a)(4) advisory committee note (2003).

20. See Lasson v. Coleman, No. 21524, 2007 Ohio. App. LEXIS 3151, at *16–19 (2d Dist. June 29, 2007) (discussing the adequacy of counsel inquiry).

21. Id. at *18 ("[W]e think the better rule is that in the absence of evidence that counsel is unable to handle complex litigation, there is no need for the trial court to require significant evidence of counsel's ability.").

23(h)), but Ohio courts do award reasonable attorney fees and costs as part of a class action judgment or settlement.[22]

VI. Conclusion

Federal Rule 23 and Ohio Rule 23 are nearly the same even though the rules are no longer worded identically. Practitioners are advised to be aware of the difference in the appealability of an order granting or denying certification. Otherwise, general practice applicable to federal class actions will ordinarily be applicable in Ohio state actions. Even when the Ohio rules are silent, Ohio courts are generally willing to consider federal best practices in interpreting Ohio procedures.

---

22. *See State ex rel. Montrie Nursing Home, Inc. v. Creasy*, 449 N.E.2d 763, 766–67 (Ohio 1983) (court has discretion to award reasonable attorney fees and costs from common fund created by class action).

OKLAHOMA

CLYDE A. MUCHMORE
MARK D. CHRISTIANSEN

I. Introduction

Oklahoma's class action rules are found at title 12, section 2023 of the Oklahoma Statutes. As of November 2009, Oklahoma amended these rules as part of a larger comprehensive lawsuit reform bill,[1] so practitioners should exercise caution when relying on earlier precedents. In places, this amendment has brought Oklahoma more in line with federal practice, while in other instances it has created more divergence. Where Oklahoma's rules are similar to the federal rules, Oklahoma courts will consider federal case law.[2] This chapter will primarily focus on those places in which Oklahoma class action practice differs from the federal norm, both in the newly amended rules and the still-applicable precedent.

II. Prerequisites and Types of Class Actions

Oklahoma's provisions regarding the prerequisites to a class action and the three primary types of class actions are substantially identical to their federal counterparts.[3] Following federal precedent, class certification under section 2023(B)(2) is only allowed if, among other requirements, injunctive or declaratory relief is the primary remedy requested for class members, and the defendant's behavior is generally applicable to the class as a whole. Monetary damages may be awarded, but

---

1. Comprehensive Lawsuit Reform Act of 2009, H.B. 1603, 2009 Okla. Sess. Law Serv. ch. 228 (West).

2. Oklahoma "case law recognizes the insight which can be garnered through consideration of federal court decisions addressing federally-evolved concepts reflected in Oklahoma's procedural regime." *Dewey v. Okla. ex rel. Okla. Firefighters Pension & Ret. Sys.*, 2001 OK 40, ¶ 18, 28 P.3d 539, 547.

3. *Compare* OKLA. STAT. tit. 12, § 2023(A)–(B) *with* FED. R. CIV. P. 23(a)–(b).

only if they are secondary or incidental to the primary injunctive or declaratory relief sought.[4]

The Oklahoma courts have reached varying decisions regarding whether fraud claims may be certified in some cases under section 2023(B)(3).[5] The Oklahoma Supreme Court has indicated that individualized issues may defeat a predominance finding for claims of unjust enrichment.[6]

III. Order Certifying Class

Oklahoma law is similar to the federal rules as to the timing of the decision to grant or deny class certification. However, in Oklahoma, an order determining the issue of class certification is immediately appealable and is now, by statute, subject to de novo appellate review.[7] While class certification is being appealed, the trial court explicitly retains jurisdiction to consider any settlements and discovery is stayed.[8]

The Oklahoma Statutes no longer allow for a limitation of individual notice to 500 class members. Instead, individual notice shall be provided to all members who can be identified through reasonable effort. However, Oklahoma has retained the statutory provision allowing those who do not receive individual notice to opt out of the class at any time prior to the determination of liability.[9]

---

4. *Harvell v. Goodyear Tire & Rubber Co.*, 2006 OK 24, ¶¶ 26–27, 164 P.3d 1028, 1037–38.

5. *See, e.g., Black Hawk Oil Co. v. Exxon Corp.*, 1998 OK 70, ¶¶ 29–30, 969 P.2d 337, 345 ("'The need to show individual reliance has not precluded class treatment in cases where standardized written misrepresentations have been made to class members.'" (quoting HERBERT B. NEWBERG & ALBA CONTE, NEWBERG ON CLASS ACTIONS: A MANUAL FOR GROUP LITIGATION AT FEDERAL AND STATE LEVELS § 22:49 (3rd ed. 1992)); *see also Masquat v. DaimlerChrysler Corp.*, 2008 OK 67, ¶ 23, 195 P.3d 48, 56 ("Where plaintiffs in a class action allege similar representations, the reliance issues may be presumed similar as well." (internal quotations and citation omitted)). The court may, however, delve into the process required to prove the fraud claims to assess whether, for example, common issues predominate. *KMC Leasing, Inc. v. Rockwell-Standard Corp.*, 2000 OK 51, ¶ 26, 9 P.3d 683, 691 ("Proof regarding liability and damages will require the trial court to analyze fraud issues under differing laws of numerous jurisdictions. Thus, individuality of issues will predominate . . . as to the very elements necessary to establish fraud."); *see also Masquat*, 2008 OK 67, ¶ 10, 195 P.3d at 52–53 ("The Oklahoma Supreme Court subscribes to the modern view that a court may consider the merits [but only] insofar as they inform what individual issues might be part of the adjudicatory process." (internal quotations and citation omitted)).

6. *Harvell*, 2006 OK 24, ¶ 21 & n.39, 164 P.3d at 1036 & n.39.

7. OKLA. STAT. tit. 12, § 2023(C)(2). Previously, reversal of an order denying or granting certification required an abuse of discretion. *KMC Leasing*, 2000 OK 51, ¶ 8, 9 P.3d at 687 (denying); *Masquat*, 2008 OK 67, ¶ 8, 195 P.3d at 52 (granting). If the new version of section 2023(C)(2) is interpreted to refer only to the second sentence of section 2023(C)(1), which would be the case if the modified standard of review applies only to orders entered on or after November 1, 2009, then it would appear that the de novo standard of review only applies to orders "granting" class certification, and that the previous abuse of discretion standard may still apply to orders "refusing to certify" a class.

8. OKLA. STAT. tit. 12, § 2023(C)(2).

9. OKLA. STAT. tit. 12, § 2023(C)(4).

IV. Class Membership

For class actions filed after November 1, 2009, class membership is limited—absent agreement of the defendant—to individuals or entities who are either (1) residents of Oklahoma or (2) nonresidents of Oklahoma who own an interest in property within Oklahoma that is relevant to the class action or who have a significant portion of their cause of action arising from conduct occurring within Oklahoma.[10]

Prior to this amendment, Oklahoma courts had, in some cases, allowed nationwide class actions,[11] although the courts also denied nationwide classes where, for example, the court found predominance lacking (such as where the substantive law of multiple jurisdictions applied).[12]

The court also has the power, but only after a class has been certified, to require parties to provide the names and addresses of potential class members "as they possess, subject to an appropriate protective order," for the sole purpose of providing notice to the class.[13]

V. Settlement/Voluntary Dismissal

Oklahoma's provisions on settlement of class actions are now identical to the federal rules, with one exception. Where the federal rules require court approval for the withdrawal of a class member's objection to settlement, the Oklahoma Statutes omit this provision.[14]

Oklahoma courts have also ruled that a defendant's agreement to the certification of a particular type of class for purposes of a class settlement does not mean that the defendant has agreed that such a class could be properly certified for litigation purposes in a later class action. The court noted that different issues are involved in class certification for settlement purposes as compared to certification of a class for litigation.[15]

---

10. OKLA. STAT. tit. 12, § 2023(D)(3).

11. *Masquat*, 2008 OK 67, ¶¶ 1, 6, 195 P.3d at 50–51.

12. *Harvell*, 2006 OK 24, ¶¶ 13, 16, 164 P.3d at 1033, 1034–35. In this context, one division of the Oklahoma Court of Civil Appeals had previously held that the burden was on the opponent of class certification to prove the existence of conflicting state laws. *Lobo Exploration Co. v. Amoco Prod. Co.*, 1999 OK Civ. App. 112, ¶ 11, 991 P.2d 1048, 1052–53. However, in 2000, the same appellate division found that the plaintiff bore the burden of proving that "other states' laws are in conformity with Oklahoma law." *Sias v. Edge Commc'ns, Inc.*, 2000 OK Civ. App. 72, ¶ 16, 8 P.3d 182, 187.

13. OKLA. STAT. tit. 12, § 2023(D)(4).

14. *Compare* FED. R. CIV. P. 23(e)(5) *with* OKLA. STAT. tit. 12, § 2023(E)(5).

15. *Gipson v. Sprint Commc'ns Co.*, 2003 OK Civ. App. 89, ¶¶ 31–33, 81 P.3d 65, 73–74.

VI. Attorney Fees

Oklahoma has added several provisions related to the award of attorney fees to class counsel that appear intended to make such awards more difficult to obtain and to lower the amounts awarded. Evidentiary hearings are now required for all fee motions to determine what is "fair and reasonable," taking into consideration 13 enumerated factors, and the court must "act in a fiduciary capacity on behalf of the class" when making this determination.[16] The court further has the option of appointing a lawyer to represent the class on the issue of fees, and any such lawyer or referee must be independent of the lawyers seeking the fees. Finally, if any portion of the benefits recovered for a section 2023(B)(3) class includes coupons, discounts, or other noncash common benefits, the attorney fee award must be cash and noncash in the same proportion as the class benefits.[17]

---

16. OKLA. STAT. tit. 12, § 2023(G)(4)(a), (b), (e).
17. OKLA. STAT. tit. 12, § 2023(G)(4).

OREGON

LOIS O. ROSENBAUM
DANIEL C. OCCHIPINTI

I. Introduction

Class actions in Oregon state courts are governed by Oregon Rule of Civil Procedure (Oregon Rule) 32. Several sections of Oregon Rule 32 are modeled after Federal Rule 23, and Oregon courts consider federal cases applying those sections "persuasive" when interpreting the Oregon counterparts.[1] However, there are several significant characteristics of class actions unique to Oregon practice. This chapter focuses on the distinctions between Oregon Rule 32 and the Federal Rule.

II. Prelitigation Requirements and Limitations on Class Actions

A. PRELITIGATION NOTICE

1. Requirement of Notice Generally

Oregon imposes a minimum 30-day notice requirement for class actions seeking damages.[2] At least 30 days prior to the commencement of such an action, the potential class representative must (1) notify the potential defendant of the particular alleged cause of action and (2) demand that such person "correct or rectify the alleged wrong."[3]

---

1. *Froeber v. Liberty Mut. Ins. Co.*, 193 P.3d 999, 1006 n.9 (Or. Ct. App. 2008). *But see Shea v. Chicago Pneumatic Tool Co.*, 990 P.2d 912, 915 (Or. Ct. App. 1999) (refusing to follow federal interpretation of class action rule where decision was published after adoption of Oregon Rule and analysis was "at odds" with language of Oregon Rule).

2. Or. R. Civ. P. 32H1, A5.

3. Or. R. Civ. P. 32H1a–b.

2. Form and Content of Notice

The prelitigation notice must be in writing and must be sent by certified or registered mail to one of the following: (1) the place where the transaction occurred; (2) the defendant's principal place of business within Oregon; or (3) for corporations or limited partnerships not authorized to transact business in Oregon, to the principal office or place of business of the corporation or limited partnership, and to any address that the class representative knows, or on the basis of reasonable inquiry has reason to believe, is most likely to result in actual notice.[4]

A plaintiff may file an action for equitable relief without providing the 30-day prelitigation notice and can later amend the action to include a request for damages without leave of court as long as (1) the request is made at least 30 days after commencement of the action, and (2) the plaintiff provides the proper notice to the defendant.[5] However, the defendant will then have an opportunity to correct the alleged harm and thereby preclude class certification.[6]

B. DEFENDANT'S OPPORTUNITY TO AVOID LITIGATION

Oregon allows a prospective class action defendant to avoid unnecessary litigation after receipt of the notice.[7] The rule applies only to actions for damages, but includes actions for equitable relief that are later amended to include a request for damages.[8] As set forth in Oregon Rule 32I, the defendant should be able to defeat class certification and/or obtain dismissal of the case if the defendant can show that:

1. All potential class members similarly situated have been identified, or a reasonable effort to identify others has been made;
2. All potential class members so identified have been notified that upon their request the defendant will make the appropriate compensation, correction, or remedy of the alleged wrong;
3. Such compensation, correction, or remedy has been, or in a reasonable time will be, given; and
4. The prospective defendant has ceased engaging in the methods, acts, or practices alleged to be violative of the rights of the potential class members. If immediate cessation is "impossible or unreasonably expensive under the circumstances," the defendant may satisfy this part of the rule upon showing that the allegedly violative conduct will cease within a "reasonable time." What constitutes "impossible or unreasonable under the circumstances" has not been adjudicated in Oregon.

---

4. OR. R. CIV. P. 32H2.
5. *See* OR. R. CIV. P. 32J.
6. *Id.; see also* section II.B, *infra.*
7. OR. R. CIV. P. 32I.
8. *Id.;* OR. R. CIV. P. 32J.

C. PROHIBITION ON CLASS ACTIONS FOR STATUTORY MINIMUM PENALTIES

Oregon specifically prohibits class actions that seek recovery of statutory minimum penalties for any class member.[9] Such statutory minimums include those set forth in Oregon's Unlawful Trade Practices Act,[10] the Federal Consumer Credit Protection Act,[11] or any other "similar statute."[12] However, the Oregon Court of Appeals has held that this prohibition applies only to class actions seeking statutory penalties under laws that "protect the consumer of goods or services."[13]

III. Commencement of Class Actions

A. PRELIMINARY REQUIREMENTS

Oregon Rule 32A sets forth the same four class action prerequisites that are found in the federal rule: (1) numerosity, (2) commonality, (3) typicality, and (4) adequacy of representation.[14] In addition, a class action for damages must comply with the prelitigation notice provisions of Oregon Rule 32H.[15] Because the Oregon rule mirrors Federal Rule 23, federal cases interpreting those sections are persuasive in Oregon courts.[16] "[A]s a matter concerning judicial administration, the trial court's assessment of the utility of a class action is entitled to wide latitude."[17] The plaintiff has the burden of demonstrating that the preliminary requirements of Oregon Rule 32A have been satisfied.[18]

1. Numerosity
The numerosity inquiry focuses on efficient judicial administration and whether it would be impractical, absent class certification, to have the multiple parties before the court.[19] Although several factors determine practicability, the number of parties is the most persuasive factor.[20]

---

9. OR. R. CIV. P. 32K.

10. OR. REV. STAT. § 646.638.

11. 15 U.S.C. § 1640(a).

12. OR. R. CIV. P. 32K.

13. *See Wilson v. Smurfit Newsprint Corp.*, 107 P.3d 61, 74 (Or. Ct. App. 2005) (upholding class certification involving statutes that "protect the *providers* of services").

14. OR. R. CIV. P. 32A1–4.

15. *See* section II.A, *supra*.

16. *See, e.g., Froeber*, 193 P.3d at 1006 n.9.

17. *Safeway, Inc. v. Or. Pub. Employees Union*, 954 P.2d 196, 201 (Or. Ct. App. 1998) (internal quotation marks and citation omitted).

18. *Id.*

19. *Newman v. Tualatin Dev. Co.*, 597 P.2d, 800, 801–02 (Or. 1979).

20. *Id.* (finding numerosity where 125 town home owners were affected and citing authority that class numbers "in the 25 to 30 range should have a reasonable chance of success on the basis of number alone").

2. Commonality

As under the Federal Rule, Oregon requires that the plaintiff demonstrate the existence of questions of law or fact common to the class. As a general rule, common questions must predominate in order for the class to be certified, and courts are hesitant to certify classes where there are substantial issues unique to each class member.[21] However, at least one Oregon court has certified an "issue class" even where common questions do not predominate the action as a whole.[22]

3. Typicality

The Oregon Supreme Court has adopted a test for typicality in which "a plaintiff's claim is typical if it arises from the same event or practice or course of conduct that gives rise to the claims of members and his or her claims are based on the same legal theory."[23] When certifying an issue class, the typicality test may be applied to the issues to be certified, rather than to the claims and defenses of the class as a whole.[24]

4. Adequacy

Oregon courts have found that the interests of the class are adequately protected if "(1) there are no disabling conflicts of interest between the class representatives and the class; and (2) the class is represented by counsel competent to handle such matters."[25]

5. Notice

For a discussion of the prelitigation notice that must be given prior to maintaining a class action under Oregon Rule 32A, *see* section II.A.

---

21. *See, e.g., Brown v. Lobdell*, 585 P.2d 4, 12 (Or. Ct. App. 1978) (upholding trial court's denial of certification motion on grounds that there were questions of fact not common to all members of the proposed class); *Pearson v. Philip Morris, Inc.*, No. 0211-11819, 2006 WL 663004 (Or. Cir. Feb. 23, 2006) (denying class certification where individual members would have to prove reliance and causation and noting that "when plaintiffs seek class certification and assert that something can be proved on a class-wide basis, they have the burden in the certification proceeding to present evidence in support of that proposition"). *But see Alsea Veneer, Inc. v. State*, 843 P.2d 492, 497 (Or. Ct. App. 1992) ("[T]he fact that damages may be different with respect to the individual policyholders, or even that some policyholders may not be entitled to damages, does not negate the existence of the common legal and factual issues concerning the consequences of [the defendant's alleged misconduct]."), *aff'd in part and rev'd in part on other grounds*, 862 P.2d 95 (Or. 1993).

22. *See Shea*, 990 P.2d at 917.

23. *Newman*, 597 P.2d at 802.

24. *Shea*, 990 P.2d at 916.

25. *Alsea Veneer*, 862 P.2d at 498 (citing *Penk v. Or. State Bd. of Higher Educ.*, 93 F.R.D. 45, 50 (D. Or. 1981)).

B. STATUTE OF LIMITATIONS TOLLING

Upon commencement of a class action, the statute of limitations is automatically tolled for all class members.[26] However, the statute of limitations resumes running against a prospective member of the class if

1. The class member files an election of exclusion;
2. The court enters an order of certification, or amends an order, that eliminates the class member from the class;
3. The court enters an order refusing to certify the class as a class action; or
4. The action is dismissed without an adjudication on the merits.[27]

C. "COMPLEX CASE" DESIGNATION

Oregon Uniform Trial Court Rule 7.030 provides that any party in a case may apply to the presiding judge to have the matter designated as a "complex case."[28] Complex cases in Oregon are assigned to a single judge who will thereafter have full or partial responsibility for the entire case.[29] Additionally, while civil cases must usually be tried within one year from the date of filing, complex cases may be set as far out as two years from the date of filing, or longer if good cause is shown.[30]

Lawyers desiring to have a case designated as "complex" should prepare a motion relying on as many of the following factors as possible: (1) the number of parties involved; (2) the complexity of the legal issues; (3) the expected extent and difficulty of discovery; (4) the anticipated length of trial; and (5) any other circumstances that make the case especially unusual, difficult, or time-consuming.[31] As a general rule, a party should attempt to obtain the consensus of all counsel before filing a motion seeking complex case designation. Cases not designated complex will not usually be assigned to a single judge, which may lead to motions being heard by different judges during the course of the case.

IV. Class Certification

A. TIMING

After commencement of a class action, Oregon courts are required to determine "as soon as practicable" whether, and with respect to what claims or issues, the action shall be maintained, and to "find facts specially and state separately [the

---

26. OR. R. CIV. P. 320.

27. *See id.; see also Loewen v. Galligan,* 882 P.2d 104, 114 (Or. Ct. App. 1994) (accounting for tolling effect of prior class action between commencement of action and date certification was denied).

28. OR. UNIF. TR. CT. R. 7.030(1).

29. OR. UNIF. TR. CT. R. 7.030(3).

30. *Id.*

31. *See* OR. UNIF. TR. CT. R. 7.030(2).

court's] conclusions thereon."[32] Although Oregon courts have not strictly defined the timing of the motion, the Oregon Rule mirrors the former language of Rule 23(c)(1)(a), and therefore federal cases interpreting that provision are persuasive.[33]

However, Oregon courts may postpone the certification determination where (1) a party has relied upon a statute or law that another party seeks to have declared invalid or (2) a party has in good faith relied upon any legislative, judicial, or administrative interpretation or regulation that would necessarily have to be voided or held inapplicable in order for a party to prevail in the class action.[34] In such situations, the court may wait until after it has made a determination as to the validity of the applicable statute, law, interpretation, or regulation before proceeding to determine class certification.[35]

B. FINDING SUPERIORITY OF CLASS ACTION MECHANISM

An action will not be certified for class action treatment in Oregon unless the court finds that (1) the five preliminary requirements of Oregon Rule 32A are satisfied,[36] and (2) "a class action is superior to other available methods for the fair and efficient adjudication of the controversy."[37] The plaintiff bears the burden of demonstrating superiority.[38] This section of the Oregon Rule varies from Rule 23(b). The Oregon Rule sets forth eight "matters" that are "pertinent" to the determination of whether or not a class action vehicle is superior.[39]

Included in those eight matters are the same seven considerations found in the Federal Rule: (1) risk of inconsistent adjudications or impeding the ability of non-parties to protect their interests; (2) applicability of injunctive or declaratory relief to the class; (3) predominance; (4) the interest of individual members in controlling separate actions; (5) the extent and nature of related litigation already commenced; (6) the desirability of concentrating the litigation in a particular forum; and (7) the likely difficulties in managing the class action, to which the Oregon rule adds the following: "that will be eliminated or significantly reduced if the controversy is adjudicated by other available means."[40] Of these criteria, courts tend to give predominance especially great weight, in part because this factor bears heavily on judicial resources and manageability.[41]

---

32. Or. R. Civ. P. 32C1.
33. See *Froeber*, 193 P.3d at 1006 n.9.
34. Or. R. Civ. P. 32C2.
35. *Id.*
36. See section III.A, *supra.*
37. Or. R. Civ. P. 32B.
38. See *Safeway*, 954 P.2d at 201.
39. Compare Or. R. Civ. P. 32B1–8 with Fed. R. Civ. P. 23(b)(1)–(3).
40. Or. R. Civ. P. 32B1–7.
41. See, e.g., *Pearson*, 2006 WL 663004, at *10.

Unique to Oregon, Rule 32 also provides that the court may consider an eighth factor—whether the claims of individual class members "are insufficient in amounts or interests involved, in view of the complexities of the issues and the expenses of the litigation, to afford significant relief to the members of the class."[42] At least one court applying this provision noted that it was "one of the most persuasive reasons for certification" where otherwise "the claims of the individual class members are not likely to be adequate to cover the costs of litigation."[43] The trial court need not consider each and every one of the listed factors in determining whether to certify a class.[44]

C. DISCRETION OF THE TRIAL COURT

Oregon trial courts are given "wide latitude" to determine whether a case should proceed as a class action[45] and "broad authority" to "make [certification] ruling[s] in class actions that can be tailored to the practical needs of individual cases and to a variety of circumstances."[46] Like federal courts, Oregon courts may issue "conditional" certification orders that may be altered or amended at any time before the decision on the merits.[47] Courts may also order that an action be maintained as a class action with respect only to particular claims or issues or by or against multiple classes or subclasses.[48] In such situations, each subclass must satisfy all the prerequisites of Oregon Rule 32A, except for the numerosity requirement.[49]

V. Interlocutory Appeals

A. DISCRETIONARY INTERLOCUTORY APPEALS IN CLASS ACTIONS

Oregon's discretionary interlocutory appeals rule is set forth in Oregon Revised Statute section 19.225 and is modeled after the general federal interlocutory appeal statute, 28 U.S.C. § 1292(b).[50] The statute applies to orders that are not otherwise appealable, including class certification orders.[51] The Oregon Court of Appeals has substantial discretion to allow or deny an interlocutory appeal, but the court

---

42. Or. R. Civ. P. 32B8.

43. *See Alsea Veneer*, 843 P.2d at 499.

44. *Belknap v. U.S. Bank Nat'l Ass'n*, No. AI38636, 2010 Or. App. LEXIS 652, at *14 (June 16, 2010).

45. *See id.* at *13.

46. *Greene v. Salomon Smith Barney, Inc.*, 209 P.3d 333, 336 (Or. Ct. App. 2009).

47. Or. R. Civ. P. 32C1.

48. Or. R. Civ. P. 32G.

49. *Id.; see* section III.A, *supra*.

50. *See also Pearson v. Philip Morris, Inc.*, 145 P.3d 298, 299 (Or. Ct. App. 2006) (when interpreting Or. Rev. Stat. § 19.225, Oregon courts assume that the legislature intended to incorporate interpretations of the federal counterpart existing at the time that the Oregon statute was enacted).

51. Or. Rev. Stat. § 19.225.

has held that such discretion should be reserved only for "exceptional" cases and should not be regularly employed.[52] The general policy in Oregon is to "disfavor piecemeal appeals."[53]

B. PRELIMINARY REQUIREMENTS

Three preliminary requirements must be satisfied in order for the court of appeals to permit an interlocutory appeal:

1. The trial court must state in its order that the decision involves a "controlling question of law."[54] "Controlling" does not mean that the issue need be dispositive, but rather that it will have a "significant effect on the outcome of the litigation."[55]

   Parties who wish to file an interlocutory appeal should request that this language be added to the proposed order. Parties are afforded this opportunity by Oregon Uniform Trial Court Rule 5.100, which requires that proposed orders be served on opposing counsel three days prior to submission to the court or be presented in open court. This gives the opposing party the opportunity to negotiate the language of the order or file objections to the proposed language.

2. A "substantial ground for difference of opinion" regarding the issues underlying the challenged order must exist.[56] This does *not* require a showing that the trial court erred, but rather that the order presents issues "about which reasonable appellate jurists could disagree."[57]

3. Finally, the immediate appeal must "materially advance the ultimate termination of the litigation."[58] This requirement is "inextricably intertwined" with the court's ultimate exercise of discretion regarding whether to allow the appeal.[59] As one court described it, the moving party should demonstrate that the appeal involves an "exceptional case" in which immediate resolution of the legal issues will necessarily result in "less expense for the parties, speedier resolution of the litigation, or more efficient use of judicial resources."[60]

---

52. *Id.*; *see also Pearson*, 145 P.3d at 304 (denying interlocutory review of circuit court order refusing to certify class).

53. *Pearson*, 145 P.3d at 304.

54. OR. REV. STAT. § 19.225.

55. *Pearson*, 145 P.3d at 304.

56. OR. REV. STAT. § 19.225.

57. *Pearson*, 145 P.3d at 304.

58. OR. REV. STAT. § 19.225.

59. *Pearson*, 145 P.3d at 304.

60. *Id.*

C. CONTENT AND TIMING

The specific practices and procedures governing applications for interlocutory appeals under Oregon Revised Statute section 19.225 are set forth in Oregon Rule of Appellate Procedure 10.05. The application must be submitted to the court of appeals within ten days of entry of the contested order.[61]

VI. Notice Requirements

A. NOTICE TO CLASS MEMBERS

Oregon courts have broad discretion in fashioning the notice to be served. Unlike the Federal Rule, which requires that notice in a class action for damages be given to *all* members who can be identified through reasonable effort, the Oregon Rule simply provides that the court shall direct that notice be given to "some or all members" of the class under subsection E2.[62] The discretion of the trial court is also provided in Oregon Rule 32E2, which allows the court to require, "for the protection of class members or otherwise for the fair conduct of the action, that notice be given in such manner as the court may direct to some or all class members."

Although every class member need not be identifiable, the class must be sufficiently ascertainable in order to permit the determination of the potential group to which notice must be sent.[63] For example, the Oregon Supreme Court has noted the difficulty of sustaining a proposed class defined in part on the members' states of mind (whether or not they had knowledge of an event) because it would be impossible to determine each individual's state of mind at the outset of the case.[64]

B. FORM, CONTENT, AND EXCLUSION FROM THE CLASS

Again, Oregon trial courts have broad authority to "determine when and how this notice should be given" and to decide "whether, when, how, and under what conditions putative members may elect to be excluded from the class."[65] Oregon law provides six factors that are "ordinarily" pertinent to the court's determination of the form and content of class notice:

1. The nature of the controversy;
2. The extent and nature of any member's injury or liability;
3. The interest of the party opposing the class in securing a final resolution of the matters in controversy;

---

61. OR. REV. STAT. § 19.225.
62. *Compare* FED. R. CIV. P. 23(c)(2) *with* OR. R. CIV. P. 32F1.
63. *See Bernard v. First Nat'l Bank*, 550 P.2d 1203, 1211 (Or. 1976).
64. *See id.*
65. OR. R. CIV. P. 32F1.

4. The inefficiency or impracticality of separately maintained actions to resolve the controversy;

5. The cost of notifying class members; and

6. The possible prejudice to members to whom notice is not directed.

With regard to notice of potential exclusion from the class, Oregon courts may condition exclusion on either (1) a prohibition against instituting or maintaining a separate action on some or all of the matters in controversy or (2) a prohibition against using any judgment rendered in favor of the class in a separately maintained action.[66]

C. COST OF NOTICE

As a default rule, Oregon class action plaintiffs are to bear the costs of any notice ordered prior to a determination of liability.[67] However, the court may require a defendant to bear all or part of the costs of any notice included with a regular mailing by the defendant to its current customers (persons who have purchased goods or services) or employees.[68] If a defendant provides such notice in a regular mailing to current customers or employees, no duty of compliance with due process notice requirements is imposed on defendant.[69]

VII. *Coordination of Pending Class Actions*

Oregon Rule 32 provides a unique mechanism for statewide coordination of pending class actions that share common questions of law or fact.[70] When such actions are pending in different Oregon courts, there is a three-step process by which the actions may be heard by the same judge. First, the trial court judge, on motion by any party or on its own initiative, may request the Oregon Supreme Court to assign a circuit court, court of appeals, or supreme court judge to determine whether coordination of the actions is appropriate.[71]

Second, the judge so assigned then evaluates whether coordination of the actions would "promote the ends of justice," considering such factors as whether common questions predominate, convenience to persons involved, the relative stages of the litigation, judicial calendars, potential problems with inconsistent outcomes, and

---

66. *Id.*

67. OR. R. CIV. P. 32F5.

68. *Id.; see also* OR. R. CIV. P. 32F7.

69. OR. R. CIV. P. 32F6.

70. OR. R. CIV. P. 32L; *see also* OR. R. APP. P. 12.15 (appellate procedural rules for coordination).

71. OR. R. CIV. P. 32L1a; OR. R. CIV. P. 12.151.

the likelihood of settlement.[72] During this process, the pending class actions, or any other action that is affected thereby, may be temporarily stayed.[73]

Finally, if the court determines that coordination is appropriate, then the chief justice of the Oregon Supreme Court must assign a single judge to hear and determine the pending class actions.[74]

VIII. Claims Forms in Class Actions for Damages

A. CLAIMS FORMS BY CLASS MEMBERS

1. Requirement Generally

Oregon requires class members seeking monetary damages to essentially "opt in" to the class action by submitting a claims form that requests affirmative relief from the defendant.[75] The claims forms are only required if class members may be entitled to individual monetary recovery. There is no similar requirement in class actions seeking equitable or declaratory relief.[76]

2. Timing

The court may require that class members submit a claims form at any time prior to the entry of judgment in the action.[77] Generally, the claims forms should be submitted after a general determination of liability. However, the legislative history suggests that the claims forms could go out earlier if the court so determines.[78] The court cannot order any payment of damages prior to the filing of claim statements and prior to the entry of judgment.[79]

3. Content of Claims Form

In addition to requesting affirmative relief, the claims form will usually require more specific information, such as the nature of the person's loss, the type of injury, details related to the claim, the existence of a transactional relationship with the defendant, and other information about damages.[80] In determining what type of information should be required, the court should consider "at least" the following five factors:

---

72. Or. R. Civ. P. 32L1b; Or. R. Civ. P. 12.15(3).

73. Or. R. Civ. P. 32L4.

74. Or. R. Civ. P. 32L2; Or. R. Civ. P. 12.15(5).

75. Or. R. Civ. P. 32F2i; *see also Benjamin Franklin Fed. Sav. & Loan Ass'n v. Dooley*, 601 P.2d 1248, 1251 (Or. 1979) (discussing "opt-in" policy); *accord Bernard*, 550 P.2d at 1217.

76. Or. R. Civ. P. 32F2i.

77. *Id.*

78. *See Bernard*, 550 P.2d at 1218 (Oregon Supreme Court discussing claim statements and legislative history).

79. *Benjamin Franklin*, 601 P.2d at 1251.

80. Or. R. Civ. P. 32F2i.

1. The nature of the acts of the defendant;

2. The amount of knowledge a class member would have about the extent of damages;

3. The degree of sophistication of the class members, special needs created by the class members' disabilities, and other considerations about the "nature of the class";

4. Whether the claims form should be in special format, such as large type, Braille, or a foreign language; and

5. The availability of relevant information from sources other than the individual class members.[81]

4. Effect of Claims Form

After the court receives the claims forms, both parties are entitled to contest the validity and/or timeliness of claims, and the court must ultimately determine the actual damages for each class member.[82] The total amount of damages assessed against the defendant may not exceed the total amount of damages determined to be allowable by the court for all individual class members who filed a claims form (plus assessable court costs and attorney fees, if any).[83]

If a class member fails to file the claims form within the time specified by the court, that person's claim for monetary recovery will be dismissed without prejudice to the right to maintain an individual, but not a class, action for such claim.[84]

B. ALTERNATIVE TO CLAIMS FORMS

1. Alternative Damages Notice

The court has discretion to not require claims forms from class members in cases where (1) the names and addresses of the class members can reasonably be determined from the defendant's business records and (2) the individual monetary recoveries are capable of calculation without the need for individualized adjudications.[85]

In such cases, instead of requiring a claims form, the court may direct the defendant to send each class member a notice that states (1) the amount of the monetary recovery that has been calculated for that person and (2) that person's right to request exclusion from the class.[86]

---

81. *See* OR. R. CIV. P. 32F2ii.
82. *Benjamin Franklin*, 601 P.2d at 1251.
83. OR. R. CIV. P. 32F2iv.
84. OR. R. CIV. P. 32F3.
85. OR. R. CIV. P. 32F2iii.
86. *Id.*

2. Effect of Alternative Damages Notice

All class members who are sent the alternative damages notice and who do not request exclusion from the class within the time specified by the court shall be deemed to have requested affirmative relief in the calculated amount.[87] The total amount of damages assessed against the defendant may not exceed the total amount of damages determined to be allowable by the court for all individual class members who are deemed to have requested affirmative relief (plus assessable court costs and attorney fees, if any).[88]

If a class member requests exclusion within the time specified by the court, that person's claim for monetary recovery shall be dismissed without prejudice to the right to maintain an individual action for such claim.[89]

C. COST OF NOTICE

The plaintiff generally bears the cost of providing notices, including notices regarding claims forms, prior to a determination of liability. However, the court has discretion to impose part or all of the cost on the defendant in certain circumstances.[90]

D. WAIVER

In any particular case, the requirement of a claims form or alternative damages notice may be waived if (1) the parties agree and (2) the court approves the waiver.[91]

IX. Settlement and Dismissal

Like its federal counterpart, Oregon Rule 32 generally requires judicial approval of any voluntary dismissal or settlement of a class action.[92] However, there are several subtle distinctions between Rule 23(e) and Oregon Rule 32D that should be noted for Oregon practice.

A. JUDICIAL APPROVAL FOR DISMISSAL PRIOR TO CERTIFICATION

Whereas the 2003 revisions to Rule 23(e) require judicial approval of settlement in cases that have been certified, the Oregon Rule requires judicial approval of the

---

87. *Id.*

88. Or. R. Civ. P. 32F2iv.

89. Or. R. Civ. P. 32F3.

90. For a more detailed discussion of notice requirements, *see* section VI, *supra*.

91. Or. R. Civ. P. 32F2v.

92. *Compare* Or. R. Civ. P. 32D *with* Fed. R. Civ. P. 23(e); *see also Froeber*, 193 P.3d at 1005 (relying on federal precedent to interpret Oregon Rule 32D and noting that the "universally applied standard is whether the settlement is fundamentally fair, adequate and reasonable" (internal quotation marks and citation omitted)).

settlement of "any action filed as a class action"—even if the court has not yet determined class certification.[93]

B. NOTICE NOT REQUIRED FOR ALL CLASS MEMBERS

Oregon courts must direct notice to "some or all members of the class," rather than to all class members who would be bound by the proposal.[94] As a practical matter, courts are often guided by general considerations for providing notice of settlement as set forth in other sections of Oregon Rule 32.[95]

C. TRIAL COURT DISCRETION

The Oregon Rule does not impose the federal requirements for a hearing to determine adequacy, statements indicating any agreements made in connection with the proposal, or new opportunities for class members to request exclusions.[96] Rather, Oregon Rule 32D gives great discretion to the trial court to direct notice of the proposal in any manner it chooses. However, the Rule explicitly notes that the court may require appropriate notice where the statute of limitations has run or may run against the claim of any class member.[97]

D. EXCEPTION TO NOTICE REQUIREMENT

Oregon Rule 32D provides an exception to the notice requirement. No notice is required for settlement or dismissal of class actions where all of the following conditions are met:

1. The dismissal is without prejudice, or with prejudice against a class representative only;
2. There is a showing that no compensation in any form has passed directly or indirectly from the party opposing the class to the class representative or to the class representative's lawyer; and
3. No promise for such compensation has been made.

X. Form of Judgment

Both Oregon Rule 32 and the Federal Rule require a judgment in a class action to describe those found to be members of the class or who, as a condition of exclusion, have agreed to be bound by the judgment.[98] However, when the judgment

---

93. *See also* section IV, *supra.*
94. *Compare* OR. R. CIV. P. 32D *with* FED. R. CIV. P. 23(e)(1).
95. For a more detailed discussion of notice, *see* section VI, *supra.*
96. *Compare* OR. R. CIV. P. 32D *with* FED. R. CIV. P. 23(e)(2)–(4).
97. OR. R. CIV. P. 32D.
98. OR. R. CIV. P. 32M; FED. R. CIV. P. 23(c)(3).

includes a monetary award, Oregon courts are also required to identify in the judgment, by name, each member of the class and the amount to be recovered by each member, when such identification is possible.[99]

XI. Class Counsel

Unlike Rule 23(g), Oregon does not require the court that certifies a class to also designate class counsel. Rather, a lawyer who brings the initial class action may serve as class counsel, although the court may review the competency of that lawyer in determining the adequacy of representation under Oregon Rule 32A4.[100]

XII. Attorney Fees

Detailed provisions regarding the award of attorney fees in class actions are set forth in Oregon Rule 32N. As a general matter, attorney fees for representing a class are subject to the control and discretion of the court.[101] However, a fee agreement between the representative parties and their lawyer must be considered.[102] The court may order the adverse party to pay to the prevailing class its reasonable attorney fees and litigation expenses if permitted by law in similar cases not involving a class.[103] Oregon courts may also properly award attorney fees for actions in other jurisdictions that were directed at obtaining the relief sought in the case before the Oregon court.[104]

A. ADVANCED DISCLOSURE TO COURT OF FEE ARRANGEMENT

Oregon statute requires that the representative parties and their lawyer(s) disclose fee arrangements to the court.[105] The disclosure is to be made prior to the certification hearing,[106] or at any other time the court directs.[107] The disclosure can be filed jointly or separately by the representative parties and their lawyer, and must provide the following:

---

99. Or. R. Civ. P. 32M.

100. *See Alsea Veneer*, 862 P.2d at 498 (court may evaluate whether "the class is represented by counsel competent to handle such matters").

101. Or. R. Civ. P. 32N1a.

102. Or. R. Civ. P. 32N2; *Kalman v. Curry*, 745 P.2d 1232, 1236 (Or. Ct. App. 1987).

103. Or. R. Civ. P. 32N1d.

104. *Kalman*, 745 P.2d at 1238.

105. Or. R. Civ. P. 32N.

106. *See* section IV, *supra*.

107. Or. R. Civ. P. 32N2.

1. A statement showing any amount paid or promised by any person for the services rendered or to be rendered in connection with the action, or for the costs and expenses of the litigation, and the source of all the amounts;

2. A copy of any written financial agreement or a "summary" of any oral financial agreement between the representative parties and their lawyer; and

3. A copy of any written agreement or a summary of any oral agreement in which the representative parties or their lawyer agreed to share the amounts described above with any person other than a member, regular associate, or regular of-counsel lawyer in the representative lawyer's law firm.[108] If such financial arrangements are made after the filing of the disclosure statement, the statement must be promptly supplemented.[109]

B. FACTORS FOR AWARDING FEES

The court must consider a wide range of factors when determining the amount of fees, if any, to award the lawyers for the prevailing class, including

1. The time and effort expended by the lawyer in the litigation, including the nature, extent, and quality of services rendered;
2. The results achieved and benefits conferred upon the class;
3. The magnitude, complexity, and uniqueness of the litigation;
4. The "contingent nature" of success;
5. The preclusion of other work for the lawyer who handled the case;
6. The fee customarily charged in the locality for similar services;
7. The time limitations imposed by the client or by the circumstances;
8. The nature and length of the professional relationship with the client; and
9. The experience, reputation, and ability of the lawyer performing the services.[110]

These factors are "particularly relevant" in evaluating the reasonableness of a contingent fee payable out of a settlement fund.[111]

C. DISTRIBUTION OF FEES

1. Fees Paid from Award

"If the prevailing class recovers a judgment that can be divided for the purpose," Oregon courts may order reasonable attorney fees and litigation expenses of the class to be paid from the recovery.[112]

---

108. OR. R. CIV. P. 32N2a–c.
109. OR. R. CIV. P. 32N2c.
110. OR. R. CIV. P. 32N1e; *see also* OR. R. PROF'L CONDUCT 1.5.
111. *Kalman*, 745 P.2d at 1236.
112. OR. R. CIV. P. 32N1c.

2. Fees Paid to Plaintiff Class

If a plaintiff is entitled to attorney fees, costs, or disbursements from a defendant class, the court may apportion the fees, costs, or disbursements among the members of the class.[113]

3. Fees Paid to Defendant Class

If a defendant or a defendant class is entitled to attorney fees, costs, or disbursements from a plaintiff class, only representative parties and those members of the class who have appeared individually are liable for those amounts.[114]

XIII. Appeal from Final Judgment

Oregon class actions are subject to the same appellate rules as other actions in the state. A notice of appeal must be served and filed within 30 days after a judgment is entered in the register.[115] Oregon law expressly permits the aggregation of the claims of all potential class members in order to satisfy the $250 minimum threshold in controversy required for an appeal.[116]

---

113. Or. R. Civ. P. 32N1b.
114. *Id.*
115. Or. Rev. Stat. § 19.255.
116. Or. Rev. Stat. §§ 19.205(4), 19.215.

PENNSYLVANIA

LARRY R. ("BUZZ") WOOD, JR.
ALLAN A. THOEN

I. Introduction

Class actions in Pennsylvania are governed by Rules 1701 to 1716 of the Pennsylvania Rules of Civil Procedure. These rules were promulgated in 1977 and based largely on Federal Rule of Civil Procedure 23.[1] Many of the provisions in the Pennsylvania class action rules are either identical to provisions of Rule 23 or derived from federal case law interpreting Rule 23. Consequently, federal case law is instructive in construing the Pennsylvania class action rules and is commonly cited as persuasive authority.[2] As explained in this chapter, however, some of the provisions of the Pennsylvania class action rules, as well as Pennsylvania class action practice, diverge from Rule 23 and federal class action practice. Where the language of the Pennsylvania rules differs from that of Rule 23, the difference is intentional.[3] The following sections discuss these differences and the unique quirks of the Pennsylvania class action rules and practice.

II. Commencement of a Class Action

A class action in Pennsylvania can be commenced only by the filing of a class action complaint, not by filing a writ as is otherwise permitted by the Pennsylvania rules of civil procedure for the commencement of an action.[4] The caption

---

1. PA. R. CIV. P. 1701–1716 explanatory cmt. (1977).

2. *Janicik v. Prudential Ins. Co.*, 451 A.2d 455, 454 n.3 (Pa. Super. 1982) (endorsing citation of federal case law); *Klusman v. Bucks County Court of Common Pleas*, 564 A.2d 526 (Pa. Commw. 1989) (same), *aff'd*, 574 A.2d 604 (Pa. 1990).

3. PA. R. CIV. P. 1701–1716 explanatory cmt. (1977).

4. PA. R. CIV. P. 1703(a).

of the complaint must include the designation "Class Action," and the complaint must include, under the heading "Class Action Allegations," averments of fact in support of all of the prerequisites for class certification.[5] Pennsylvania does not follow the federal notice pleading standard, but instead requires the pleading of specific facts essential to support the claim.[6] The requirement to plead class action factual allegations separately and specifically "is fundamental" and "impels the plaintiff to plead in detail all the facts which will support his right to this special remedy."[7] A class action cannot be commenced by an amendment to an individual complaint.[8]

III. Prerequisites for Certification

Pennsylvania Rule of Civil Procedure 1702 establishes the following prerequisites for class certification:

- *Numerosity*: joinder of all class members is impractical;
- *Commonality*: there are common questions of law or fact;
- *Typicality*: the claims or defenses of the representative parties are typical of the claims or defenses of the class;
- *Adequacy of representation*: the representative parties will fairly and adequately protect the interests of the class; and
- *Fair and efficient method*: a class action is a fair and efficient method to adjudicate the controversy.

These prerequisites are largely the same as those under Rule 23, with a few notable exceptions, as described in the following sections.

A. NUMEROSITY

The language of Pennsylvania Rule 1702(1) requiring that a proposed class be sufficiently numerous is identical to that of Rule 23(a)(1), although there is case law suggesting that Pennsylvania's numerosity requirement may be "less stringent . . . than its federal counterpart."[9] The party seeking class certification is not required to plead or prove the precise number of class members, but must be able to define

---

5. PA. R. CIV. P. 1704.

6. *See* PA. R. CIV. P. 1019(a); *see also, e.g., Lerner v. Lerner*, 954 A.2d 1227, 1235 (Pa. Super. 2008).

7. PA. R. CIV. P. 1704 cmt. (1977).

8. *Debbs v. Chrysler Corp.*, 810 A.2d 137, 149-51 (Pa. Super. 2002). *But see Foust v. SEPTA*, 756 A.2d 112, 115 (Pa. Commw. 2000) (class action commenced by addition of class allegations to previously filed individual complaint).

9. *See* PA. R. CIV. P. 1702(1); *Keppley v. School Dist.*, 866 A.2d 1165, 1173 (Pa. Commw. 2005). *But see Janicik*, 451 A.2d at 456 (citing federal case law).

the class with specificity and provide "sufficient indicia that more members exist than it would be practicable to join."[10]

B. COMMONALITY

The language of Pennsylvania Rule 1702(2) requiring that "there are questions of law or fact common to the class" is identical to that of Rule 23(a)(2). As set forth in greater detail below in section III.E, Rule 1702(a)(2), in conjunction with Rule 1708(a), requires the court to determine whether common questions of law or fact "predominate" over individual questions. Pennsylvania courts have held that "it is essential that there be a *predominance* of common issues."[11] In *Weinberg v. Sun Co.*,[12] the Pennsylvania Supreme Court held that common questions of law or fact did not predominate where the plaintiffs' cause of action required proof of individual reliance, barring class certification.[13] But, the Pennsylvania Supreme Court recently affirmed class certification explaining that breach of contract claims met the commonality requirement.[14] Pennsylvania appellate courts have also cited federal decisions applying and interpreting Rule 23 in determining whether individual questions, such as reliance, causation, and choice of law, preclude class certification.[15]

C. TYPICALITY

Pennsylvania Rule 1702(3) requires that "the claims or defenses of the representative parties are typical of the claims or defenses of the class." This language is

---

10. *Keppley*, 866 A.2d at 1171; *see also, e.g., Baldassari v. Suburban Cable TV Co., Inc.*, 808 A.2d 184, 190–91 (Pa. Super. 2002); *Foust*, 756 A.2d at 118 (Pa. Commw. 2000) (numerosity established where "the number of class members could conceivably number in the thousands"); *Weismer v. Beech-Nut Corp.*, 615 A.2d 428, 430 (Pa. Super. 1992) (numerosity requirement not satisfied where "the class definition is so poorly established that the court cannot even discern who the potential class members are"); *Kruth v. Liberty Mut. Ins. Co.*, 499 A.2d 354, 356 (Pa. Super. 1985) (numerosity not established by plaintiff's "request that the trial court take judicial notice of the number of vehicles insured in our Commonwealth").

11. *Eisen v. Independence Blue Cross*, 839 A.2d 369, 374 (Pa. Super. 2003) (quoting *Weismer*, 615 A.2d 428); *see also, e.g., Baldassari*, 808 A.2d at 191 (same); *Dunn v. Allegheny County Prop. Assessment Appeals & Review*, 794 A.2d 416, 424 (Pa. Commw. 2002) (same); *Foust*, 756 A.2d at 118 (same).

12. *777 A.2d 442 (Pa. 2001).*

13. *See also, e.g., Keppley*, 866 A.2d at 1173–74 (finding that although there were "some common questions . . . there is a lack of *predominance* of common questions"); *Eisen*, 839 A.2d at 373–75 (commonality absent where plaintiffs' claims required a "determination of medical necessity based on the particular needs of a given patient"); *Green v. Saturn Corp.*, No. 685, 2001 WL 1807390, at *5–7 (Pa. C.P. 2001) (denying certification of false advertising, misrepresentation and warranty claims); *Savage Hyundai, Inc. v. N. Am. Warranty Servs., Inc.*, No. 01-952, 2002 Pa. Dist. & Cnty. Dec. LEXIS 173 (C.P., Sept. 24, 2002) (same).

14. *Liss & Marion, P.C. v. Recordex Acquisition Corp.*, 983 A.2d 652 (Pa. 2009).

15. *See, e.g., Debbs*, 810 A.2d at 157-59; *Keppley*, 866 A.2d at 1173–74 (citing Fed. R. Civ. P. 23(a)(2)); *Foust*, 756 A.2d at 119–20 (citing federal toxic tort medical monitoring case).

identical to that of Rule 23(a)(3), and Pennsylvania courts have applied this standard in a way that does not materially differ from federal practice.[16]

D. ADEQUACY OF REPRESENTATION

Unlike Rule 23, which contains no specific criteria for determining whether the named parties will adequately represent the interests of the class, Pennsylvania Rule 1709 provides a nonexclusive list of criteria that the court must consider in determining adequacy of representation:

1. whether the lawyer for the representative parties will adequately represent the interests of the class;
2. whether the representative parties have a conflict of interest in the maintenance of the class action; and
3. whether the representative parties have or can acquire adequate financial resources to assure that the interests of the class will not be harmed.[17]

Despite this difference in the rule, in practice, Pennsylvania procedure closely tracks federal procedure on this point, as the criteria specified in Pennsylvania Rule 1709 are largely derived from federal case law.[18]

E. FAIR AND EFFICIENT METHOD FOR ADJUDICATION

Pennsylvania's requirement that a class action must be "a fair and efficient method for adjudication of the controversy" is set forth in Pennsylvania Rule 1702(a)(5). This requirement does not have a direct counterpart in the federal Rules, although the three subparts of Rule 23(b) are substantively similar and essentially provide the same analytical framework. As noted below, however, Pennsylvania courts do not consider whether the class action is "superior" to other available methods for fairly and efficiently adjudicating the controversy.

Pennsylvania Rule 1708 sets out a nonexclusive list of factors that the court must consider in determining whether a class action would be "fair and efficient." A trial court's consideration and application of the factors depends on whether the representative plaintiffs are seeking only monetary or only equitable relief, or both. Where both forms of relief are sought, all of the factors set forth in Rule 1708

---

16. *See, e.g., Keppley,* 866 A.2d at 1174–75 (citing federal case law and Fed. R. Civ. P. 23(a)(3)); *Eisen,* 839 A.2d at 375 (typicality absent where "it was unclear that the named representatives were continually, or even almost always, denied reimbursement for medically necessary chiropractic services as a result of [defendant health insurers'] allegedly improper practices"); *Baldassari,* 808 A.2d at 193 (citing federal case law on typicality); *Debbs,* 810 A.2d at 159–63 (finding lack of typicality); *Dunn,* 794 A.2d at 424–25.

17. PA. R. CIV. P. 1709. For cases applying these criteria, see, e.g., *Karn v. Quick & Reilly, Inc.,* 912 A.2d 329, 337 (Pa. Super. 2006) (citing federal authority); *Keppley,* 866 A.2d at 1175 (citing federal authority); *Buynack v. Dep't of Transp.,* 833 A.2d 1159, 1166–67 (Pa. Commw. 2003) (addressing adequacy of counsel); *Janicik,* 451 A.2d at 458–61.

18. PA. R. CIV. P. 1709, explanatory cmt. (1977).

must be considered and analyzed by the court. The relative weight of each factor in the court's analysis necessarily varies according to the circumstances of each case and is left to the court's discretion.[19]

In cases that involve only claims for monetary recovery, Pennsylvania Rule 1708(a) directs the court to consider the following factors in determining whether a class action would be fair and efficient:

1. whether common questions of law or fact predominate over any question affecting only individual members;[20]
2. the size of the class and the difficulties likely to be encountered in the management of the action as a class action;[21]
3. whether the prosecution of separate actions by or against individual members of the class would create a risk of
    i. inconsistent or varying adjudications with respect to individual members of the class that would confront the party opposing the class with incompatible standards of conduct;[22]
    ii. adjudications with respect to individual members of the class that would as a practical matter be dispositive of the interests of other members not parties to the adjudications or substantially impair or impede their ability to protect their interests;
4. the extent and nature of any litigation already commenced by or against members of the class involving any of the same issues;
5. whether the particular forum is appropriate for the litigation of the claims of the entire class;[23]
6. whether in view of the complexities of the issues or the expenses of litigation the separate claims of individual class members are insufficient in amount to support separate actions; and
7. whether it is likely that the amount that may be recovered by individual class members will be so small in relation to the expense and effort of administering the action as not to justify a class action.

---

19. *See Janicik*, 451 A.2d at 461; *Dickler v. Shearson Lehman Hutton, Inc.*, 596 A.2d 860, 866 (Pa. Super. 1991) ("Rule 1708 implies a great deal of discretion for the trial court by not according any specific weight to the listed criteria and by not insisting on the exclusivity of the list.").

20. For cases applying this factor, see section III.B, *supra* and notes 11–14.

21. For cases applying this factor, *see, e.g.*, *Debbs*, 810 A.2d at 159 (holding that trial court erred by applying Pennsylvania law to entire class, rather than addressing manageability issues raised by differences in state law); *Klusman*, 564 A.2d at 534 (difficulty of verifying claims by class members "would present an administrative nightmare"); *Janicik*, 451 A.2d at 462 (citing federal case law); *Parsky v. First Union Corp.*, No. 771, 2001 Pa. Dist. & Cnty. Dec. LEXIS 304, at *34–39 (C.P. 2001) (same).

22. For cases applying this factor, *see, e.g.*, *Baldassari*, 808 A.2d at 195; *Cambanis v. Nationwide Ins. Co.*, 501 A.2d 635, 641–42 (Pa. Super. 1985); *Janicik*, 451 A.2d at 462–63.

23. For cases applying this factor, *see, e.g.*, *Baldassari*, 808 A.2d at 195; *Cambanis*, 501 A.2d at 641.

The Explanatory Comments to Rule 1708 note that the first five of these factors "are taken almost verbatim from Federal Rule 23(b)(1), (2) and (3), except that the requirement of 'superiority' in class actions based on common questions of law or fact is specifically omitted."[24] Largely because the term "superior" could be ambiguous, the drafters of the Pennsylvania class action rules "deliberately decline[d] to adopt that part of Federal Rule 23 which requires that, in actions based on common questions of fact and law, a class action be 'superior to other available methods for the fair and efficient adjudication of the controversy.'"[25]

Another difference from Rule 23 in the Pennsylvania list of factors that courts must consider is the sixth factor, namely, whether the class members' claims are too small to litigate individually. Although that factor does not appear in Rule 23, it does find support in federal case law interpreting Rule 23.[26] Because this factor is explicitly contained in Pennsylvania Rule 1708, it has been addressed by numerous Pennsylvania courts.[27]

The seventh factor in Pennsylvania Rule 1708—whether the amount recovered by individual class members would be too small to justify the lawsuit—presents another difference from Rule 23. This recovery/cost analysis factor, which is drawn from the Uniform Class Action Act,[28] was addressed by the Pennsylvania Supreme Court in *Kelly v. County of Allegheny*.[29] In *Kelly*, the court held that although the average recovery of individual class members would be as low as $13.61, the aggregate class recovery would be sufficiently large that the cost of the litigation "would not consume the recovery."[30] Pennsylvania courts applying this analytic framework articulated in *Kelly* have tended to look at whether the aggregate class recovery would be sufficiently large to justify the expense of the action, rather than at the amount that individual class members might recover.[31]

---

24. PA. R. CIV. P. 1708, explanatory cmt. (1977); *see also Janicik*, 451 A.2d at 461.

25. PA. R. CIV. P. 1702, explanatory cmt. (1977) ("'Superior' is a comparative term . . . The court may weigh the need for class action relief objectively, without the need to search for other possible 'superior' judicial remedies").

26. *See* PA. R. CIV. P. 1708, explanatory cmt. (1977) ("This follows the Federal case law.").

27. *See, e.g., Janicik*, 451 A.2d at 463; *Dunn*, 794 A.2d at 427; *Savage Hyundai*, 2002 Pa. Dist. & Cnty. Dec. LEXIS 173, at *51 (claims were large enough to support individual actions); *Milkman v. Am. Travelers Life Ins. Co.*, No. 3775, 2001 WL 1807376, at *8 (Pa. C.P. 2001) (individual recoveries would be "low enough to preclude separate actions . . . yet large enough to justify the expense and effort of maintaining this suit as a class action").

28. PA. R. CIV. P. 1708, explanatory cmt. (1977).

29. 546 A.2d 608 (Pa. 1988).

30. *Id.* at 611–12 (holding that trial court abused its discretion by denying class certification on the ground that an average individual recovery of $13.61 per class member was insignificant where it was "clearly demonstrated that the potential costs would not consume the recovery" of the class as a whole).

31. *See, e.g., Baldassari*, 808 A.2d at 195 ("Assuming that class membership could exceed 600,000 in this case, and recovery by individual class members could be as low as $2.00, the aggregate potential claim would be $1.2 million. Thus, class certification is more than warranted under the instant facts."); *Milk-*

In cases where "equitable or declaratory relief" is sought, rather than monetary relief, Rule 1708(b) requires the court to consider factors (1) to (5) above, as well as "whether the party opposing the class has acted or refused to act on grounds generally applicable to the class, thereby making final equitable or declaratory relief appropriate with respect to the class."[32]

IV. Certification Procedure

Under Pennsylvania Rule 1707, a class action plaintiff must move for certification within 30 days after the pleadings are closed or the last required pleading was due.[33] Failure to follow this time limit, however, will not be a bar to certification. Under the express language of the Rule, if the plaintiff fails to make a timely motion for class certification, "the court if so notified shall promptly set a date for a certification hearing."[34] As such, another party may notify the court and request the class action hearing. In *Rauch v. United Instruments, Inc.*,[35] the court permitted the plaintiff to move for certification four years after the deadline had passed, where none of the parties had previously notified the trial court of the plaintiff's failure to make a timely motion.[36]

The court may defer a hearing on class certification pending the resolution of other motions or to permit discovery with respect to the class certification issues.[37] The hearing on class certification is limited to the "Class Action Allegations" in the complaint without consideration of the merits of the plaintiffs' claims.[38] The Pennsylvania Rule on this point may now be slightly different than the federal trend toward considering the merits of a claim where delving into the merits is necessary to perform the "rigorous analysis" required under Rule 23.[39]

---

man, 2001 WL 1807376, at *8 (individual recoveries would be "low enough to preclude separate actions . . . yet large enough to justify the expense and effort of maintaining this suit as a class action.").

32. *See Janicik*, 451 A.2d at 456 ("[Defendant] concedes that it applies a similar interpretation to all eight insurance riders in question, thus satisfying this criterion.").

33. PA. R. CIV. P. 1707(a); *see also, e.g., Cavenaugh v. Allegheny Ludlum Steel Corp.*, 528 A.2d 236, 239 (Pa. Super. 1987) ("[A] court may not make the initial class action determination until after the close of pleadings to ensure that the class proponent is presenting a non-frivolous claim capable of surviving preliminary objections.").

34. PA. R. CIV. P. 1707(a).

35. 533 A.2d 1382 (Pa. Super. 1987).

36. *See id.* at 1385 ("[W]e will not penalize [plaintiffs] for their untimeliness by dismissing the [certification] order on that basis.").

37. PA. R. CIV. P. 1707(b).

38. PA. R. CIV. P. 1707(c) & explanatory cmt. (1977); *see also, e.g., Baldassari*, 808 A.2d at 189; *Cavenaugh*, 528 A.2d at 240 ("Instead of focusing on the Plaintiff's obligation to establish the factors relevant to class certification, the lower court improperly examined the merits of the litigation itself.").

39. *See, e.g., In re Hydrogen Peroxide Antitrust Litig.*, 552 F.3d 305, 316–22 (3d Cir. 2008); *Oscar Private Equity Invs. v. Allegiance Telecom, Inc.*, 487 F.3d 261, 268 (5th Cir. 2007).

The burden of proof in the class certification proceeding is on the party seeking class certification.[40] In Pennsylvania practice, the burden is "not a heavy" one and is satisfied if the proponent presents "evidence sufficient to make out a prima facie case 'from which the court can conclude that the five class certification requirements are met.'"[41] It remains to be seen whether Pennsylvania will follow the federal trend toward more rigorous and critical weighing of the evidence presented for and against class certification.[42]

Pennsylvania Rule 1710 establishes requirements for the court's order certifying or refusing to certify a class action. As under the federal Rules, a court may certify the class only as to particular issues and may divide the class into subclasses. Pennsylvania Rule 1710(d) tracks the pre-2003 version of Rule 23(c)(1)(C).

As was the case under the pre-2003 Federal Rule, an order certifying a Pennsylvania class may be conditional and may be revoked or amended at any time before a decision on the merits.[43] By contrast, since 2003, Rule 23(c)(1)(C) no longer permits conditional certification and sets the cutoff point for revoking or amending a class certification decision at "final judgment" rather than at "a decision on the merits."[44] The phrase "before a decision on the merits" was interpreted recently by the Pennsylvania Supreme Court in *Basile v. H&R Block, Inc.*,[45] where the court explained that if a trial court's decision on the merits is reversed on appeal, the trial court may again be permitted to decertify the class on remand.

V. Interlocutory Appellate Review of Certification Decision

Unlike Rule 23 and federal practice, in Pennsylvania practice an order denying class certification is immediately appealable as of right, but an order granting certification is immediately appealable only if permission is obtained from the court. More specifically, under Pennsylvania Rule of Appellate Procedure 313, an order denying

---

40. *See, e.g., Kelly*, 546 A.2d at 612; *Debbs*, 810 A.2d at 153–54; *Cambanis*, 501 A.2d at 637.

41. *Baldassari*, 808 A.2d at 189; *Debbs*, 810 A.2d at 153–54.

42. *See, e.g., In re Hydrogen Peroxide*, 552 F.3d at 321 (holding that "proper analysis under Rule 23 requires rigorous consideration of all the evidence and arguments offered by the parties" and rejecting the view that "the burden on the party seeking certification is a lenient one (such as a prima facie showing or a burden of production) or that the party seeking certification receives deference or a presumption in its favor"); *Szabo v. Bridgeport Machs., Inc.*, 249 F.3d 672, 675 (7th Cir. 2001) ("The proposition that a district judge must accept all of the complaint's allegations when deciding whether to certify a class cannot be found in Rule 23 and has nothing to recommend it.").

43. PA. R. CIV. P. 1710(d).

44. FED. R. CIV. P. 23 advisory committee notes (2003).

45. 973 A.2d 417, 422–23 (Pa. 2009) ("[U]nder Rule 1710(d), the trial court was authorized to consider Block's motion for decertification after summary judgment was reversed"; waiver did not exist); *see also id.* at 422 n.9 (noting divergence between language of Pennsylvania Rule 1710(d) and Rule 23(c)(1)(C)).

class certification or decertifying a class is immediately appealable as a "collateral order." However, an order certifying a class is an interlocutory order that is immediately appealable only by permission under Pennsylvania Rule of Appellate Procedure 312.[46] The trial court's certification decision is a mixed question of law and fact and is reviewed for abuse of discretion.[47]

VI. Postcertification Procedure

A. OPT-IN/OPT-OUT RULES

Whereas federal practice provides an opt-out procedure only for classes certified under Rule 23(b)(3), under Pennsylvania Rule 1711, the default position is that all class actions are certified as opt-out classes.[48] In appropriate situations, however, the court retains authority to certify a mandatory class, such as in the circumstances that would justify a mandatory class under Rule 23(b)(1) or (b)(2).[49] Additionally, if the court finds that class members would have the resources and ability to pursue their claims individually or that other special circumstances exist, the court may certify an opt-in class under Pennsylvania Rule 1711(b).[50] This differs from federal practice under Rule 23, which contains no provision for an opt-in procedure before a person may be considered a member of the class.[51]

B. NOTICE TO CLASS MEMBERS

Notice to class members is governed by Pennsylvania Rule 1712, which differs from Rule 23 in two notable respects. Pennsylvania Rule 1712 requires notice in all class actions, while Rule 23 only requires notice in 23(b)(3) opt-out classes. However, Pennsylvania Rule 1712 dispenses with the federal requirement of individual notice to all class members and only requires that notice "be given through

---

46. *See Dunn*, 794 A.2d at 422; *Foust*, 756 A.2d at 116 n.3. In *Basile*, the Pennsylvania Supreme Court held that the defendant did not waive its right to challenge the trial court's class certification order by failing to cross-appeal the certification issue when the plaintiff appealed the trial court's grant of summary judgment in favor of the defendant.

47. *Kelly*, 546 A.2d at 610; *Weismer*, 615 A.2d at 430.

48. PA. R. CIV. P. 1711(a).

49. PA. R. CIV. P. 1711 & explanatory cmt. (1977).

50. For examples and additional discussion of opt-in classes under Pennsylvania Rule 1711(b), *see, e.g.*, *Milkman*, 2001 WL 1807376 (rejecting attorney general's request that class be certified as opt-in as to out-of-state class members); *Parsky v. First Union Corp.*, No. 771, 2001 WL 987764 (Pa. Com. Pl. 2001) (rejecting defendant's request that class be certified as opt-in rather than opt-out); *Katlin v. Tremoglie*, No. 9706-2703, 1999 WL 1577980 (Pa. C.P. 1999) (certifying opt-in class).

51. Opt-in procedures under federal law generally relate to collective actions brought under section 216 of the Fair Labor Standards Act, 29 U.S.C. § 216(b), including those brought under the Age Discrimination in Employment Act.

methods reasonably calculated to inform the members of the class of the pendency of the action," which may include "using a newspaper, television or radio or posting or distributing through a trade, union or public interest group."[52] Recently, in the context of deciding a collateral attack by a Pennsylvania resident on a New York class action judgment, the Pennsylvania Supreme Court reiterated that the due process standard for determining whether notice is adequate to bind class members is "flexible and non-technical" and that notice is constitutionally "adequate when it is reasonably calculated to inform a party of the pending action and provides the party an opportunity to present objections to the action."[53]

In Pennsylvania practice, the plaintiff must bear the expense of the notice, although the court "may require a defendant to cooperate in giving notice by taking steps which will minimize the plaintiff's expense," such as by including the notice in a regular mailing from the defendant to the class members.[54]

C. CONTACTS WITH CLASS MEMBERS

Like Rule 23(d), Pennsylvania Rule 1713 gives the court broad discretion to make "appropriate orders" governing the conduct of a class action. In *Pennsylvania Orthopaedic Society v. Independence Blue Cross*,[55] the Pennsylvania Superior Court cited federal case law under Rule 23(d) as support for upholding the trial court's order under Pennsylvania Rule 1713 restricting contacts by the defendant with members of the plaintiff class. There is also Pennsylvania case law holding that, under the Rules of Professional Conduct, the defendant may not engage in ex parte communications with members of a putative class.[56]

VII. Settlement and Attorney Fees

Pennsylvania Rule 1714 governs settlement of class actions. It differs from its federal counterpart, Rule 23(e), in that it applies not only to certified classes but also to class action complaints that have not yet been certified.[57] In *Dauphin Deposit Bank and Trust Co. v. Hess*,[58] the Pennsylvania Supreme Court set forth seven factors for trial courts to consider in determining whether to approve a proposed settlement:

---

52. PA. R. CIV. P. 1712.

53. *Wilkes ex rel. Mason v. Phoenix Home Life Mut. Ins. Co.*, 902 A.2d 366, 383 (Pa. 2006).

54. PA. R. CIV. P. 1712(c).

55. 885 A.2d 542, 548 (Pa. Super. 2002).

56. *Braun v. Wal-Mart Stores, Inc.*, 60 Pa. D. & C. 4th 13 (C.P. 2003).

57. *See* PA. R. CIV. P. 1714, cmt. (1977).

58. 727 A.2d 1076, 1079–80 (Pa. 1999); *see also, e.g., Brophy v. Phila. Gas Works*, 921 A.2d 80 (Pa. Commw. 2007); *Gregg v. Independence Blue Cross*, No. 03482, 2004 WL 869063 (Pa. C.P. 2004); *Milkman v. Am. Travelers Life Ins. Co.*, No. 3775, 2002 WL 778272 (Pa. C.P. 2002); *Milkman*, 2001 WL 1807376.

1. the risks of establishing liability and damages;
2. the range of reasonableness of the settlement in light of the best possible recovery;
3. the range of reasonableness of the settlement in light of all the attendant risks of litigation;
4. the complexity, expense, and likely duration of the litigation;
5. the state of the proceedings and the amount of discovery completed;
6. the recommendations of competent counsel; and
7. the reaction of the class to the settlement.

The standard of review of the trial court's acceptance or rejection of a proposed settlement is abuse of discretion.[59] The circumstances under which a trial court's order accepting or rejecting a proposed settlement may be immediately appealable are addressed in *Brophy v. Philadelphia Gas Works.*[60]

Furthermore, while Rule 23 does not specifically address attorney fees, Pennsylvania Rule 1716 specifies criteria the court should consider in awarding attorney fees, when attorney fees are "authorized under applicable law."[61] Pennsylvania Rule 1716 does not determine when attorney fees may be awarded, which is treated as a matter of substantive law, but "does empower the court, if fees are allowable, to regulate the amount of fees and expenses."[62] When awarding attorney fees under Pennsylvania Rule 1716, the court is not bound by the amount or percentage set forth in any fee agreement between the named plaintiff and counsel.[63]

VIII. Other Issues

A. TOLLING OF STATUTES OF LIMITATION

Several Pennsylvania cases have followed the class action tolling doctrine articulated in *American Pipe & Construction Co. v. Utah.*[64] Pennsylvania does not, however, recognize cross-jurisdictional tolling based on class actions filed in other states or in federal court.[65]

---

59. *Dauphin,* 727 A.2d at 1080.

60. 921 A.2d 80.

61. PA. R. CIV. P. 1716(1).

62. PA. R. CIV. P. 1716, explanatory cmt. (1977).

63. *Id.*

64. 414 U.S. 538 (1974); *see also, e.g., Cunningham v. Ins. Co., Inc.,* 530 A.2d 407, 408–09 (Pa. 1987); *Verrichia v. Commonwealth, Dep't of Revenue,* 639 A.2d 957, 964 n.13 (Pa. Commw. 1994); *Kruth,* 499 A.2d at 357.

65. *See Ravitch v. Pricewaterhouse,* 793 A.2d 939, 943–45 (Pa. Super. 2002); *Johnson v. Am. Home Prods. Corp.,* 62 Pa. D. & C.4th 20 (C.P. 2003), *aff'd,* 847 A.2d 765 (Pa. Super. 2004).

B. ARBITRATION AGREEMENTS

The Pennsylvania Superior Court addressed the enforceability of arbitration agreements between the defendant and plaintiff class members in *Thibodeau v. Comcast Corp.*[66] and *Dickler v. Shearson Lehman Hutton, Inc.*[67] In *Dickler*, the arbitration contracts between the defendant and class members did not specifically prohibit aggregate or classwide arbitration, and the court held that enforcement of the arbitration agreements could be accomplished through classwide arbitration:

> Given the three paths down which this litigation can be directed—compelled individual arbitration, class action in a court of law, or compelled classwide arbitration—the last choice best serves the dual interest of respecting and advancing contractually agreed upon arbitration agreements while allowing individuals who believe they have been wronged to have an economically feasible route to get injunctive relief from large institutions employing adhesion contracts.[68]

In *Thibodeau*, the arbitration agreement between the defendant and its customers required individual arbitration and specifically prohibited any aggregate or class arbitration.[69] The court refused to enforce the contract, holding that "preclusion of class wide litigation or class wide arbitration of consumer claims, imposed in a contract of adhesion, is unconscionable and unenforceable."[70]

---

66. 912 A.2d 874 (Pa. Super. 2006).
67. 596 A.2d 860; *see also Lytle v. CitiFinancial Servs., Inc.*, 810 A.2d 643 (Pa. Super. 2002).
68. 596 A.2d at 867.
69. 912 A.2d at 877.
70. *Id.* at 886.

RHODE ISLAND

PATRICIA K. ROCHA

NICOLE J. DULUDE

I. Introduction

Although not identical to its federal counterpart, Rhode Island Rule of Civil Procedure 23 (Rhode Island Rule) is substantially in accord with Federal Rule of Civil Procedure 23.[1] It differs primarily because Rhode Island has not adopted the 2003 amendments to Federal Rule 23.[2] In addition to this distinction, Rhode Island court decisions interpreting the rules governing class actions have shed light on several other nuances that have become apparent because of the courts' interpretation of Rhode Island Rule 23 and its interplay with other state statutes and rules.

II. Jurisdiction

As with any civil action, class actions must be commenced in a proper jurisdiction. Ordinarily class actions in Rhode Island are commenced in the superior court, which has original jurisdiction in all civil matters where the amount in controversy exceeds $10,000 and concurrent jurisdiction with the district court in civil matters where the amount in controversy is between $5,000 and $10,000.[3] However, the Rhode Island Supreme Court has suggested that the district court, which has original jurisdiction in civil actions where the amount in controversy is less than $5,000 and certain other matters specified by statute,[4] may entertain a class action notwithstanding the absence of any rule of procedure providing for such

---

1. *Zarella v. Minn. Mut. Life Ins. Co.*, 824 A.2d 1249, 1263 n.16 (R.I. 2003) ("Rhode Island Rule 23 is a carbon copy of Rule 23 of the Federal Rules of Civil Procedure.").

2. ROBERT B. KENT, ET AL., RHODE ISLAND CIVIL AND APPELLATE PROCEDURE § 23:4 (2006).

3. R.I. GEN. LAWS § 8-2-14.

4. R.I. GEN. LAWS § 8-8-3.

an action.[5] In *Seibert v. Clark*,[6] the Rhode Island Supreme Court noted that "[t]he absence of a specific rule permitting class actions in District Court does not prohibit them in all cases."[7] The court reasoned that class actions were available in the superior court long before the adoption of Rhode Island Rule of Civil Procedure 23 in 1966, therefore the fact that the district court has not adopted a similar version of Rule 23 does not foreclose the possibility of commencing a class action there.[8]

III. Class Certification

Having not adopted the 2003 amendments, the Rhode Island Superior Court is required to make class certification decisions "as soon as practicable."[9] Relying on federal case law construing the pre-2003 Federal Rule, however, the Rhode Island Supreme Court has noted that "although the words 'as soon as practicable' are not without effect, 'there is no set deadline by which the court must act.'"[10] Nevertheless, the court has held, given the facts and circumstances of one case, that an eight-and-a-half-year delay in seeking Rhode Island Rule 23 certification was untimely.[11] Conversely, however, the court has also affirmed a trial justice's conclusion that a plaintiff's motion, which sought class certification almost two years after the suit was initiated, was timely because the delay was caused by procedural issues that were resolved shortly before the plaintiff sought class certification.[12]

The hearing on a party's motion for class certification must be on the record and may not be substituted by an unrecorded chambers conference.[13] At this hearing, a party seeking class certification bears the burden of proof, but this burden is light.[14] Identical to the federal Rule, in Rhode Island a party seeking class certification must show "(1) there are a sufficient number of class members to make joinder impracticable; (2) there are common legal or factual issues which can be efficiently adjudicated by the court on a classwide basis; (3) the claims of the chosen representative are typical of those of the members of the class; and (4) the chosen representative and attorney will vigorously and adequately represent the interest of all

---

5. *Seibert v. Clark*, 619 A.2d 1108 (R.I. 1993).

6. *Id.*

7. *Id.* at 1112.

8. *Id.*

9. R.I. R. Civ. P. 23(c)(1).

10. *Zarrella*, 824 A.2d at 1263 n.16 (quoting *Ayuda, Inc. v. Reno*, 7 F.3d 246, 253 (D.C. Cir. 1993)).

11. *Cabana v. Littler*, 612 A.2d 678, 686 (R.I. 1992).

12. *Zarrella*, 824 A.2d at 1263 n.16.

13. *Cabana*, 612 A.2d at 684.

14. *Id.*

class members."[15] The court must make a finding that the class action will fairly ensure adequate representation of the parties, and the "parties may not usurp this power from the court nor can the court abdicate this responsibility."[16] Accordingly, "parties may not stipulate to the existence of a class in lieu of an independent judicial determination made after an on-the-record hearing."[17] In addition to these stated prerequisites, as is the case with federal class actions, class actions in Rhode Island must satisfy one of the subsections in Rhode Island Rule 23(b).[18] Taking guidance from the federal courts, the Rhode Island Supreme Court has expressed preference for certifying class actions under Rule 23(b)(1) or (2) over certifying an action under Rule 23(b)(3).[19]

IV. Lawyers and Attorney Fees

In view of the fact that Rhode Island has not adopted the 2003 amendments to Federal Rule 23, section (g) ("Class Counsel") and section (h) ("Attorney's Fees and Nontaxable Costs") of Federal Rule 23 are absent from Rhode Island Rule 23. In practice, however, these omissions likely have little substantive impact on a case. For example, although Federal Rule 23(h) includes a provision for attorney fees, as a practical matter, it does not create any new grounds for an award of attorney fees. Therefore, as in federal class actions, an award of attorney fees in Rhode Island is dependent on whether such fees are otherwise authorized for the particular action.[20]

V. Appeals

The Rhode Island Supreme Court affords great deference to a trial justice's decision to certify a class pursuant to Rule 23.[21] Therefore, a trial justice's decision "will not

---

15. *Id.* at 685.

16. *Id.*

17. *Id.* (concluding that the trial justice erred in accepting a stipulation from the parties of class certification).

18. *DeCesare v. Lincoln Benefit Life Co.*, 852 A.2d 474, 490 (R.I. 2004); *accord Cazabat v. Metro. Prop. & Cas. Ins. Co.*, C.A. No. KC99-544, 2001 R.I. Super. LEXIS 27, at *6 (Feb. 23, 2001).

19. *DeCesare*, 852 A.2d at 490 (recognizing that members of a class certified under Rule 23(b)(1) or (2) cannot opt out of the action, while members of a class certified under Rule 23(b)(3) are entitled to opt out).

20. *Compare Int'l Ass'n of Machinists & Aerospace Workers v. Affleck*, 504 A.2d 468, 471–72 (R.I. 1986) (upholding trial justice's award of attorney fees in class action suit where such fees were authorized by statute) *with W. Sur. Co. v. Lums of Cranston, Inc.*, 618 F.2d 854, 855 (1st Cir. 1980) (upholding district court's denial of attorney fees to a losing defendant class because Rhode Island law did not authorize such an award of fees).

21. *DeCesare*, 852 A.2d at 487 (likening the standard of review to that employed when reviewing findings of a trial justice sitting without a jury).

be disturbed unless the trial court misconceived material evidence, substantially abused its discretion, or was otherwise clearly wrong."[22]

VI. Statutory Authorization for Certain Class Actions

By statute, the Rhode Island General Assembly has authorized the maintenance of numerous class actions. As one example, subject to certain exceptions, Rhode Island General Laws section 6-47-1 authorizes the state's attorney general to maintain a class action on behalf of recipients of unsolicited advertisements received by facsimile.[23] Similarly, Rhode Island General Laws section 11-52.2-6 authorizes victims of software fraud and the state's attorney general to maintain class action suits for various forms of software fraud made unlawful under that chapter.[24] Despite the general assembly's statutory authorization of numerous forms of class actions, maintenance of such class actions remains subject to and governed by Rhode Island Rule 23.[25]

---

22. *Id.*

23. R.I. Gen. Laws § 6-47-1.

24. R.I. Gen. Laws §§ 11-52.2-6; 6-13.1-5.2.

25. R.I. Gen. Laws § 8-6-2(a) (specifying that Rhode Island's Rules of Civil Procedure prevail over conflicting state statutes); *see also Johnston Businessmen's Ass'n v. Aarussillo,* 108 R.I. 257, 261, 274 A.2d 433, 436 (1971).

SOUTH CAROLINA

JAMES D. MYRICK
JOHN C. HAWK IV

I. Introduction

South Carolina Rule of Civil Procedure 23 (South Carolina Rule) derives from Federal Rule of Civil Procedure 23.[1] There are, however, significant differences between the two rules, as discussed below, most notably the South Carolina Rule's omission of the requirements of Federal Rule 23(b). Because case law interpreting the state rule is sparse, South Carolina courts look to federal precedent for guidance.[2]

II. South Carolina Rule 23(a): Prerequisites to Class Certification

A trial judge may not consider the merits when deciding whether to certify a class; he must instead look to the prerequisites of South Carolina Rule 23(a).[3] South Carolina's Rule is identical to the federal Rule with regard to the requirements of numerosity, commonality, typicality, and adequacy of representation, but it adds a fifth requirement—an amount in controversy of $100 per class member.[4]

Courts must apply a rigorous analysis to determine that all the prerequisites have been satisfied, and a failure to satisfy any one requirement is fatal to class

---

1. S.C. R. CIV. P. 23 advisory committee notes.

2. *Gardner v. Newsome Chevrolet-Buick, Inc.*, 404 S.E.2d 200, 201 (S.C. 1991) ("Since our Rules of Procedure are based on the Federal Rules, where there is no South Carolina law, we look to the construction placed on the Federal Rules of Civil Procedure.").

3. *Tilley v. Pacesetter Corp.* (*Tilley I*), 508 S.E.2d 16, 21 (S.C. 1998), *subsequent appeal*, 585 S.E.2d 292 (S.C. 2003) (*Tilley II*).

4. *Compare* S.C. R. CIV. P. 23(a) *with* FED. R. CIV. P. 23(a).

certification.[5] The class certification decision is reviewed under the abuse of discretion standard.[6] Federal precedent is instructive for the first four prerequisites.[7]

The amount in controversy requirement is intended to limit the abuse of representative suits by making sure that the parties have a sufficient stake in the matter to litigate realistic issues and prevent cases that merely benefit the lawyers.[8] It is similar to the U.S. Supreme Court's former rule for class actions requiring that, when jurisdiction was based on diversity, each member of the class had to meet the jurisdictional amount.[9]

As long as a claim is apparently made in good faith, the amount in controversy is controlled by the plaintiff's claim.[10] Courts should consider the value of the object to be gained by the suit, and should not dismiss an action unless a plaintiff's failure to meet the minimum dollar amount is a legal certainty.[11] Punitive damages and attorney fees are not considered for the purposes of determining the amount in controversy.[12] Monetary damages of less than $100 per class member are permitted when the primary relief sought is equitable.[13]

III. Omission of the Requirements of Federal Rule of Civil Procedure 23(b)

Perhaps the most significant difference between South Carolina's Rule and the Federal Rule is the omission of the requirements of Federal Rule 23(b), "Types of Class Action." The drafters of the South Carolina Rule preferred to allow the prerequisites of South Carolina Rule 23(a) shape class actions without the additional Federal Rule 23(b) requirements. The South Carolina Rule thus expands the reach of class actions.[14] Arguably, a class action in South Carolina need not be superior to alternative methods of adjudication, as required by the federal Rule.[15]

---

5. *Waller v. Seabrook Island Prop. Owners Ass'n*, 388 S.E.2d 799, 801 (S.C. 1990).

6. *See id.*

7. *See Gardner v. S.C. Dep't of Revenue*, 577 S.E.2d 190, 200 (S.C. 2003) (citing *Boggs v. Divested Atomic Corp.*, 141 F.R.D. 58, 64 (S.D. Ohio 1991) for a definition of "commonality").

8. James F. Flanagan, South Carolina Civil Procedure 181 (S.C. Bar, CLE Division, 2d ed. 1996).

9. *See Zahn v. Int'l Paper Co.*, 414 U.S. 291 (1973). In 1990, Congress enacted 28 U.S.C. § 1367, which operated to overrule *Zahn's* ban on aggregation of claims in class actions to determine the amount in controversy. *See Exxon Mobil Corp. v. Allapattah Servs., Inc.*, 545 U.S. 546, 566 (2005) ("We hold that § 1367 by its plain text overruled *Clark* and *Zahn* and authorized supplemental jurisdiction over all claims by diverse parties arising out of the same Article III case or controversy.").

10. *Gardner*, 404 S.E.2d at 201 (citing *St. Paul Mercury Indem. Co. v. Red Cab Co.*, 303 U.S. 283, 289 (1938)).

11. *Id.* at 202 (citing *Swan Island Club v. Ansell*, 51 F.2d 337 (4th Cir. 1931)).

12. *Id.*

13. S.C. R. Civ. P. 23(a)(5).

14. *Littlefield v. S.C. Forestry Comm'n*, 523 S.E.2d 781, 784 (S.C. 1999).

15. *Compare* S.C. R. Civ. P. 23 *with* Fed. R. Civ. P. 23(b).

IV. Derivative Actions and Unincorporated Associations

South Carolina Rule 23(b)(1), "Derivative Actions by Shareholders," and Rule 23(b)(2), "Actions Relating to Unincorporated Associations," were written to mirror Federal Rules 23.1 and 23.2, respectively.[16] These sections apply state class action procedures to derivative actions and actions relating to unincorporated associations. In keeping with the federal practice of separating these two types of actions from regular class actions, proposed class actions arising under these sections are not required to meet the prerequisites of South Carolina Rule 23(a).[17]

V. Dismissal or Compromise

The South Carolina Rule on dismissal and compromise, South Carolina Rule 23(c), is similar to Federal Rule 23(e), only less detailed.[18] A class action may not be dismissed or compromised without the approval of the court and notice to the class. The South Carolina Rule, however, does not include provisions 2 through 5 of the federal Rule (requiring a hearing in certain circumstances, requirements for parties, and specifics on court approval). Instead, the trial court is given discretion on these matters.[19]

VI. South Carolina Rule 23(d): Broad Discretion to Conduct Actions

South Carolina Rule 23(d), "Orders in the Conduct of Actions," borrows from Federal Rule 23(c) and (d). Compared to the federal Rule, the South Carolina Rule leaves many decisions to the courts. By not providing courts with detailed instructions on issues such as notice to class members, the South Carolina Rule permits broad discretion in procedural matters. This discretion is intended to prevent abuse of the justice system in class actions.[20] South Carolina Rule 23(d) breaks down into three subsections.

South Carolina Rule 23(d)(1) calls for a determination of class certification "as soon as practicable." This provision is similar to the federal requirement that certification be determined "at an early practicable time."[21] Like the federal Rule,

---

16. *Compare* S.C. R. Civ. P. 23(b)(1) & (2) *with* Fed. R. Civ. P. 23.1 & 23.2.

17. Flanagan, *supra* note 8, at 185.

18. *Compare* S.C. R. Civ. P. 23(c) *with* Fed. R. Civ. P. 23(e).

19. *See Eldridge v. City of Greenwood*, 417 S.E.2d 532, 534 (S.C. 1992).

20. *Id.*

21. *Compare* S.C. R. Civ. P. 23(d)(1) *with* Fed. R. Civ. P. 23(c)(1)(A).

the South Carolina Rule allows the certification order to be conditional. It may be altered or amended at any time before the decision on the merits.[22]

South Carolina Rule 23(d)(2) corresponds loosely with the notice requirements of Federal Rule 23(c)(2). It states broadly, "[t]he court may at any time impose such terms as shall fairly and adequately protect the interest of the persons on whose behalf the action is brought or defended." It goes on to provide that, as part of this protection, the court "may" require notice. The Federal Rule, on the other hand, includes more detailed and mandatory notice provisions.[23] These stark differences led the South Carolina Supreme Court to note that the South Carolina Rule "provides a trial court with broader discretion to make decisions regarding class notification procedures than the federal rule."[24] According to the notes to the South Carolina Rule, however, those seeking to maintain an action on behalf of a class *must* notify potential members, and courts have generally required such notice.[25] Undoubtedly, though, courts are given more leeway under the South Carolina Rule.

Finally, South Carolina Rule 23(d)(3) addresses protection of absent class members, and is similar to Federal Rule 23(d). With typically broad language, it permits the trial court, "[w]henever the representation appears . . . inadequate," to impose additional conditions or amend the pleadings to protect parties that are not adequately represented. The court shall only enter a judgment that affects those parties who were adequately represented.[26]

The requirements of Federal Rule 23(c) regarding judgment, particular issues, and subclasses are not included in the South Carolina Rule. Again, South Carolina gives the trial court discretion to deal with these matters.

VII. Appeals

In South Carolina, orders granting or denying class certification are generally considered interlocutory and are not immediately appealable.[27] The federal procedure of filing a petition for permission to appeal is not available in the state context.[28]

---

22. *Compare* S.C. R. Civ. P. 23(d)(1) *with* Fed. R. Civ. P. 23(c)(1)(C).

23. *Compare* S.C. R. Civ. P. 23(d)(2) *with* Fed. R. Civ. P. 23(c)(2).

24. *Salmonsen v. CGD, Inc.,* 661 S.E.2d 81, 89 (S.C. 2008).

25. *See* S.C. R. Civ. P. 23 advisory committee notes; *Tilley II,* 585 S.E.2d at 302.

26. S.C. R. Civ. P. 23(d)(3).

27. *Ferguson v. Charleston Lincoln Mercury, Inc.,* 564 S.E.2d 94, 98 (S.C. 2002); *see also Eldridge,* 417 S.E.2d at 534 ("Orders under Rule 23, SCRCP are interlocutory and thus, immediately appealable only in certain circumstances.").

28. *Compare* S.C. R. Civ. P. 23 *with* Fed. R. Civ. P. 23(f).

VIII. Lawyers and Attorney Fees

Sections (g) ("Class Counsel") and (h) ("Attorney's Fees and Nontaxable Costs")
of Federal Rule 23 are not included in the South Carolina Rule. The broad language
of South Carolina Rule 23(d)(2) appears to grant courts the discretion to address
both of these matters. A trial court's award of fees will be affirmed unless not supported by "any competent evidence."[29]

IX. Multistate Class Actions

South Carolina's "door closing statute" determines which parties may bring actions
in state circuit court against foreign corporations.[30] Nonresident plaintiffs may
only bring an action if the cause of action arose within the state.[31] Because of
this statute, those plaintiffs who would not be allowed access to South Carolina
courts in individual lawsuits may likewise not participate in a class action in state
court against a foreign corporation.[32] South Carolina plaintiffs are thus precluded
from representing nationwide or multistate classes in state court.[33] Furthermore,
nationwide class action settlements and judgments are entitled to full faith and
credit in the state, and they preclude separate state actions.[34]

---

29. *Condon v. State*, 583 S.E.2d 430, 435 (S.C. 2003).

30. S.C. CODE ANN. § 15-5-150(2) (2008).

31. *Farmer v. Monsanto Corp.*, 579 S.E.2d 325 (S.C. 2003).

32. *Id.* at 328.

33. *Id.*

34. *See Hospitality Mgmt. Assocs., Inc. v. Shell Oil Co.*, 591 S.E.2d 611 (S.C. 2004); *Cowden Enters., Inc. v. E. Coast Millwork Distribs.*, 611 S.E.2d 259 (S.C. Ct. App. 2005).

SOUTH DAKOTA

MARK G. SCHROEDER

I. Introduction

Class action procedure in South Dakota state courts is governed by South Dakota Codified Laws section 15-6-23, which is virtually identical to a prior version of Rule 23 of the Federal Rules of Civil Procedure. South Dakota case law on class actions is limited. The South Dakota Supreme Court has for the most part construed section 15-6-23 consistent with Rule 23, but has tended to apply those principles in favor of class certification in questionable cases.

II. Comparison to Federal Rule 23

Section 15-6-23, last amended in 1985, is virtually identical to the then-existing Federal Rule 23,[1] with one principal exception.[2] Therefore, later revisions to Rule 23(a)–(e) are absent from its South Dakota counterpart. Likewise, no provisions in section 15-6-23 correspond with Rule 23(f), (g), or (h).

In interpreting section 15-6-23, federal case law is followed.[3]

III. Prerequisites

Besides numerosity, commonality, typicality, and adequacy of representation,[4] South Dakota adds a fifth class action prerequisite that is absent from Rule 23(a). Specifically, members of a class may sue as representative parties if "[t]he suit is

---

1. *See Trapp v. Madera Pac., Inc.*, 390 N.W.2d 558, 560 (S.D. 1986).
2. *See* S.D. CODIFIED LAWS § 15-6-23(a)(5), discussed *infra* section III.
3. *See In re S.D. Microsoft Antitrust Litig. (S.D. Microsoft Litig. I)*, 657 N.W.2d 668, 672 n.4 (S.D. 2003).
4. *See* S.D. CODIFIED LAWS § 15-6-23(a)(1), (2), (3) & (4).

not against this state for the recovery of a tax imposed by [specified South Dakota statutes]."[5]

To establish numerosity in South Dakota, "there [must] be at least some evidence of the number of class members," and courts have denied class certification with the lack of even a minimal showing of any class members other than the named plaintiff.[6] Numerosity has been met with as few as 100 plaintiffs.[7]

To establish typicality in South Dakota, the class representative must demonstrate the existence of other class members with similar grievances. Like the stance of South Dakota courts on numerosity, courts have denied class certification without a minimal showing to this effect.[8]

Legal construction of the commonality and the adequacy of representation prerequisites by the South Dakota courts is consistent with federal practice.[9]

IV. Superiority

In South Dakota, a class action must be superior to, and not just as good as, other methods for handling a controversy.[10] South Dakota courts analyze superiority by considering the same factors as in Rule 23(b)(3).[11] On the superiority issue, the South Dakota Supreme Court has remanded a case with a limited record to determine whether class members were risking more than nominal damages, whether class members could be effectively notified, and whether judicial efficiency was better served by the use of a class action as opposed to an administrative proceeding.[12]

V. Alteration of Certification Order

Like Rule 23(c)(1),[13] South Dakota case law permits modification of a class action order should new developments require.[14] The time in which to determine whether to maintain a class action is within the discretion of the trial court.[15]

---

5. *See* S.D. CODIFIED LAWS § 15-6-23(a)(5); *see also Lick v. Dahl*, 285 N.W.2d 594 (S.D. 1979) (taxpayer could not maintain class action lawsuit to recover allegedly illegal property tax payments).

6. *See Shangreaux v. Westby*, 281 N.W.2d 590, 593 (S.D. 1979).

7. *See Trapp*, 390 N.W.2d at 561.

8. *See Shangreaux*, 281 N.W.2d at 593.

9. *See, e.g., Trapp*, 390 N.W.2d at 561–62.

10. *See Beck v. City of Rapid City*, 650 N.W.2d 520, 523 (S.D. 2002).

11. *See* S.D. CODIFIED LAWS § 15-6-23(b)(3); *Beck*, 650 N.W.2d at 523.

12. *See Beck*, 650 N.W.2d at 525–26 & n.5.

13. *See* S.D. CODIFIED LAWS § 15-6-23(c)(1).

14. *See Beck*, 650 N.W.2d at 526.

15. *See Shangreaux*, 281 N.W.2d at 593.

VI. Burden of Proof/Evidence

In South Dakota, the party seeking class certification has the burden of proving that the statutory requirements of a class action have been met.[16] In making its determination, the trial court must conduct a "rigorous analysis" to determine whether the proponent has shown "actual, not presumed," conformance with class certification requirements.[17] Nevertheless, in questionable cases, any doubt as to whether to certify a class should be resolved in favor of certification.[18]

In South Dakota courts, plaintiffs are not required to prove their case on the merits at the class certification stage.[19] Where the parties present disputed expert testimony, any "battle of experts" should be resolved at trial, rather than on a motion for class certification.[20] The South Dakota Supreme Court has suggested use of a "lower *Daubert* standard" in analyzing the class certification issue.[21] Although the mere production of a self-professed expert is not enough to meet South Dakota class certification requirements, the South Dakota Supreme Court has refused to extend the gatekeeping function to usurp the factual-determination role of the ultimate trier of fact.[22]

VII. Tolling

South Dakota has adopted the doctrine of class action tolling.[23]

VIII. Attorney Fees

South Dakota has analyzed attorney fees awards in class action litigation under the common fund doctrine, the substantial benefit rule, and the lodestar method.[24] In applying the lodestar method, the South Dakota Supreme Court has limited

---

16. *See Beck*, 650 N.W.2d at 523.

17. *See S.D. Microsoft Litig. I*, 657 N.W.2d at 672, 674–75 (citing *Gen. Tel. Co. of Sw. v. Falcon*, 457 U.S. 147, 160–61 (1982)).

18. *See id.* at 672; *Beck*, 650 N.W.2d at 525.

19. *See S.D. Microsoft Litig. I*, 657 N.W.2d at 673.

20. *See id.* at 677.

21. *See id.* at 675 (citing *Daubert v. Merrell Dow Pharms., Inc.*, 509 U.S. 579 (1993)).

22. *See id.* at 679.

23. *See One Star v. Sisters of St. Francis*, 752 N.W.2d 668, 680–81 (S.D. 2008) (citing *Am. Pipe & Constr. Co. v. Utah*, 414 U.S. 538 (1974)).

24. *See In re S.D. Microsoft Antitrust Litig. (S.D. Microsoft Litig. II)*, 707 N.W.2d 85 (S.D. 2005) (lodestar method); *Van Emmerik v. Mont. Dakota Utils. Co.*, 332 N.W.2d 279 (S.D. 1983) (common-fund doctrine and substantial benefit rule). *See also* Chapter 8, "Attorney Fee Awards and Incentive Payments."

attorney fee awards where hourly rates were excessive and out-of-state counsel's rates exceeded prevailing local rates.[25]

IX. Appeals

In South Dakota, a class certification order is interlocutory in nature and not appealable as of right.[26] The South Dakota Supreme Court reviews class certification orders under an "abuse of discretion" standard.[27]

In the context of reviewing class certification orders, the abuse of discretion standard tends to be liberally applied. For example, the South Dakota Supreme Court has affirmed a trial court decision certifying a class, notwithstanding substantial questions as to numerosity and commonality.[28]

---

25. *See S.D. Microsoft Litig. II*, 707 N.W.2d at 102–06 (fee award remanded on various grounds, including use of improper multiplier).

26. *See Smith v. Tobin*, 311 N.W.2d 209, 210–11 (S.D. 1981), *overruling Rollinger v. J.C. Penney Co.*, 192 N.W.2d 699 (S.D. 1971); *see also S.D. Microsoft Litig. I*, 657 N.W.2d at 670 (granting discretionary appeal of class certification order).

27. *See S.D. Microsoft Litig. I*, 657 N.W.2d at 671 (citing *Trapp*, 390 N.W.2d at 560–61).

28. *See Trapp*, 390 N.W.2d at 561–62.

TENNESSEE

DANIEL W. OLIVAS

I. Introduction

This chapter offers a general overview of the fundamentals of maintaining a class action in Tennessee. With the exception of the notice requirement, the fundamentals under Tennessee Rule of Civil Procedure 23 (Tennessee Rule)[1] are substantially the same as those in the Federal Rule 23; consequently, federal authority is persuasive in this area.[2] Moreover, federal authority might be a necessary resource because, while Tennessee Rule 23 has most of the same moving parts contained in the Federal Rule, it has fewer interpretive or explanatory cases.

II. Synopsis of Tennessee Rule 23 Certification Requirements

A. RULE 23.01 PREREQUISITES, THE LESSER INCLUDED STANDARDS[3]

The first prerequisite, numerosity, requires that the size of the class be such that joinder of all members is impracticable.[4] The "size" language suggests that a particular number decides the question, but Tennessee places no numeric threshold on potential class actions.[5] There is no need to prove the precise number of class members, but there must be more than speculation as to size.[6]

---

1. TENN. R. CIV. P. 23 (2009).

2. *Compare* FED. R. CIV. P. 23 *with* TENN. R. CIV. P. 23; *Bayberry Assocs. v. Jones*, 783 S.W.2d 553, 557 (Tenn. 1990).

3. Martha S.L. Black, *Class Actions Pursuant to Tennessee Rule of Civil Procedure 23*, 46 TENN. L. REV. 556, 566 (1979).

4. TENN. R. CIV. P. 23.01(1).

5. Black, *supra* note 3, at 560–61.

6. *Id.* at 561.

In addition, there must be a "positive showing that [joinder] would be impracticable."[7] The determination of practicability depends "upon all the circumstances surrounding the case,"[8] including "the nature of the claim, the size of the individual claims, location of the [class members], and whether it would be impossible to obtain personal service over some [class members]."[9]

The second prerequisite, commonality, requires that questions of law or fact be common to the class.[10] However, commonality is only a threshold and a single common question might be enough.[11] Often, commonality is satisfied once the requirements of Rules 23.02(1), (2), or (3) have been met.[12]

The third prerequisite, typicality, requires the plaintiff's claims to be typical of the claims of all other class members.[13] They do not need to be identical to those of the class, "as long as they share the essential characteristics."[14] Therefore, claims are typical if they "'arise[ ] from the same event or practice or course of conduct that gives rise to the claims of other class members, and if [they] are based on the same legal theory.'"[15]

The fourth prerequisite, adequacy, ensures that "the representative parties will fairly and adequately protect the interests of the class."[16] Under this rule, the plaintiff stands in the role of fiduciary to the class members, and the focus is "on the ability of the class representative and its counsel to conduct litigation on behalf of the class."[17]

Adequacy tests whether the plaintiff will pursue the claims with vigor and whether the plaintiff's interests conflict with those of the class.[18] The search for conflicts of interest can call into question the plaintiff's credibility, although credibility questions must be substantial and demonstrate real conflict.[19]

---

7. *Albriton v. Hartsville Gas Co.*, 655 S.W.2d 153, 155 (Tenn. Ct. App. 1983) (quoting *DeMarco v. Edens*, 390 F.2d 836, 845 (2nd Cir. 1969)).

8. *Id.*

9. *Id.* (citing 7 Charles A. Wright & Arthur R. Miller, Federal Practice and Procedure § 1762, at 600 (1972)).

10. Tenn. R. Civ. P. 23.01(2).

11. Black, *supra* note 3, at 561.

12. *Id.*

13. Tenn. R. Civ. P. 23.01(3).

14. *Bayberry Assocs. v. Jones*, No. 87-261-II, 1988 Tenn. App. LEXIS 718, at *26 (Tenn. Ct. App. Oct. 28, 1988) (citations omitted).

15. *Freeman v. Blue Ridge Paper Prods., Inc.*, 229 S.W.3d 694, 703 (Tenn. Ct. App. 2007) (quoting *In re Am. Med. Sys., Inc.*, 75 F.3d 1069, 1082 (6th Cir. 1996)).

16. Tenn. R. Civ. P. 23.01(4).

17. *Bayberry Assocs.*, 1988 Tenn. App. LEXIS, at *31.

18. *Id.* at *32 (citations omitted).

19. *Id.* at *37–38.

Finally, adequacy examines the experience and qualifications of class counsel.[20] The Tennessee Rule, however, has no stand-alone class counsel provision like 23(g) of the Federal Rule.[21]

B. RULE 23.02 CLASSES

Despite stylistic differences, Tennessee Rule 23.02 is identical to its federal counterpart.[22] Consequently, certification depends upon the satisfaction of all of the prerequisites under Rule 23.01 and whether the claims fall into one of the three subsections in Rule 23.02.[23]

Subsection 23.02(1) creates a class out of the desire to prevent certain undesirable effects that might result from individual judgments.[24] In service of that principle, certification is permitted to avoid either of two circumstances: (1) where individual actions might result in inconsistent individual judgments[25] or (2) where individual judgments would decide the interests of nonparties or would substantially hobble their ability to protect their interests.[26]

To fit within the first circumstance, the effect of the individual judgment also must threaten to force the defendant "simultaneously to occupy inconsistent positions."[27] Claims that are appropriate under this subsection are those involving constitutional questions, the illegality of conduct of the class, or the need to establish "a common standard of conduct."[28] Notably, classes certified under this subsection have no opt-out rights.[29]

Class status under Rule 23.02(2) is based on the type of relief sought.[30] Certification is permitted where the principal relief prayed for is injunctive or declaratory.[31] That is not to say, however, that the Rule prohibits actions seeking damages, only that injunctive relief must be primary.[32]

---

20. *Id.* at *32.

21. *Compare* FED. R. CIV. P. 23 *with* TENN. R. CIV. P. 23.

22. *Compare* FED. R. CIV. P. 23 *with* TENN. R. CIV. P. 23.

23. TENN. R. CIV. P. 23.02.

24. *Gov't Employees Ins. Co. v. Bloodworth*, No. M2003-02986-COA-R10-CV, 2007 Tenn. App. LEXIS 404, at *9 (June 29, 2007).

25. TENN. R. CIV. P. 23.02(1)(a).

26. TENN. R. CIV. P. 23.02(1)(b).

27. Black, *supra* note 3, at 567.

28. *Id.* at 567–68.

29. *Freeman*, 229 S.W.3d at 702 n.1.

30. TENN. R. CIV. P. 23.02(2).

31. *Id.*

32. Black, *supra* note 3, at 570.

Rule 23.02(3) is the most general of the provisions and deserves considerable attention.[33] Like the Federal Rule, Tennessee's version has two elements that must be satisfied before certification is allowed.

First, there must be a question of fact or law common to the class[34] that predominates over any other questions affecting the individual members.[35] A question is common "to the extent its resolution will advance the litigation of the case."[36] Accordingly, the court must consider the elements of the cause of action and the facts needed to prove them.[37]

Predominance "depends on whether the class members will require individualized hearings to prove the elements of each cause of action."[38] Where the elements of a claim require substantial individual determinations, there is no predominance.[39] Predominance exists only where there is "generalized evidence which proves or disproves an element on a simultaneous, class-wide basis."[40]

Rule 23.02(3) also requires that the class device be the superior means of disposing of the claims.[41] That is, a class action must be better than, not simply as good as, other methods of resolving the claims.[42] To that end, the provision contains the same four factors relevant to superiority found in the Federal Rule.[43]

In addition, for classes certified under Rule 23.02(3), notice of the opt-out rights in Rule 23.03 must be given to all class members.[44] As will be discussed in section III, Tennessee's notice provision represents a significant departure from its federal counterpart.

III. *Procedure for Maintaining Class Action Suits in Tennessee*

Tennessee Rule 23.03 sets out the procedure for maintaining a class action suit. With the exception of notice, Tennessee's procedural requirements track those in the Federal Rule.

---

33. *Meighan v. U.S. Sprint Commc'n Co.*, 924 S.W.2d 632, 636 (Tenn. 1996).

34. TENN. R. CIV. P. 23.02(3).

35. *Id.*

36. *Bloodworth*, 2007 Tenn. App. LEXIS 404, at *44 (quoting *Philip Morris, Inc. v. Angeletti*, 752 A.2d 200, 226 (Md. Ct. App. 2000)).

37. *Id.*

38. *Freeman*, 229 S.W.3d at 704–05 (quoting *Couch v. Bridge Terminal Transp., Inc.*, No. M2001-00789-COA-R3-CV, 2002 WL 772998, at *4 (Tenn. Ct. App. Apr. 30, 2002)).

39. *Bloodworth*, 2007 Tenn. App. LEXIS 404, at *45–46.

40. *Id.* at *46 (quoting *Lockwood Motors, Inc. v. Gen. Motors Corp.*, 162 F.R.D. 569, 580 (D. Minn. 1995) (internal quotation marks omitted)).

41. TENN. R. CIV. P. 23.02(3).

42. *Bloodworth*, 2007 Tenn. App. LEXIS 404, at *54.

43. *Compare* FED. R. CIV. P. 23(b)(3)(A)–(D) *with* TENN. R. CIV. P. 23.02(3)(a)–(d).

44. TENN. R. CIV. P. 23.03.

First, Rule 23.03(1) directs the court to make a determination as to class certification "as soon as practicable after commencement of an action."[45] Of course, the meaning of "practicable" varies with the facts of each case, and neither the Rule nor the courts have established a set period of time for the determination.[46]

Nevertheless, practitioners should consult the local rules for any provisions affecting the timing of certification. For example, the local rules for the Circuit Court of Davidson County, home to Nashville, the state capital, provide that "within sixty (60) days after filing a complaint in a class action . . . the plaintiff shall move for a determination [of certification] . . . ."[47]

Next, Rule 23.03(2) provides that the "best notice practicable . . . including publication when appropriate or individual notice" must be given to all class members advising of the opt-out rights.[48] By permitting notice by publication, and making individual notice optional, the Tennessee formulation departs from the Federal Rule. Of course, a thorough discussion of the due process issues raised by publication, even where authorized by statute, is beyond the scope of this chapter.[49] To address those issues, the practitioner should turn to Tennessee case law.[50]

Further, Rule 23.03(2) does not specifically require that the notice contain a statement of the nature of the action, the class definition, or the claims or defenses involved in the action, unlike the Federal Rule.[51] But Tennessee courts, like federal courts, must determine the "best notice practicable under the circumstances," no matter how notice ultimately is given.[52]

Finally, Rule 23.03(4) is largely identical to Federal Rule 23(4) and (5). It appears that this Tennessee provision is rarely litigated, so federal authority should be consulted for disputes arising out of this rule.[53]

---

45. Tenn. R. Civ. P. 23.03(1).

46. Black, *supra* note 3, at 577.

47. Davidson County Local R. 26.14. *But see Tigg v. Pirelli Tire Corp.*, 232 S.W.3d 28, 35 (Tenn. 2007) (reserving "judgment as to whether Rule 26.14 of the Davidson County Circuit Court is consistent with statutory law and the procedural rules adopted by [the Tennessee Supreme Court]").

48. Tenn. R. Civ. P. 23.03(2).

49. *See* Chapter 30, "Other Due Process Challenges to the Class Device."

50. *See, e.g., Baggett v. Baggett*, 541 S.W.2d 407 (Tenn. 1976) (holding in the context of a divorce action that service of process by publication is a denial of due process where address of out-of-state adversary is known or easily ascertainable).

51. *Compare* Fed. R. Civ. P. 23(c)(2)(i)–(vii) *with* Tenn. R. Civ. P. 23.03(2)(a)–(c).

52. Tenn. R. Civ. P. 23.03(2).

53. *Meighan*, 924 S.W.2d at 637 n.2.

IV. Tennessee Trial Courts Conduct a Rigorous Analysis of the Rule 23 Requirements Before Deciding to Certify a Class

The decision to certify a class is within the trial court's discretion but that discretion is bound by Tennessee Rule 23's legal standards that the trial court must fully apply before certifying a class.[54] In 2007, the Tennessee intermediate appellate courts adopted the rigorous analysis requirement for trial court class certification decisions.[55]

Under the rigorous analysis requirement, the trial court is to "conduct a rigorous, thorough, and careful analysis of the issues related to the standards in [Rule 23] before certifying a class action."[56] A court's decision to certify a class will be overturned if the court fails to perform this analysis.[57]

The rigorous analysis standard is particularly important to those seeking certification under Rule 23.02(3), the common question class.[58] The language of that subsection limits certification to those circumstances where the "court finds that the question of law or fact common to the members of the class predominate" over individual questions and that the class action is the superior device to resolve the claims.[59] Thus, "rigorous analysis" means that the trial court must make these specific findings before allowing certification.[60]

V. Tolling Applicable Statute of Limitations

The federal courts recognize the doctrine of cross-jurisdictional tolling.[61] Under this doctrine, the "commencement of a class action suspends the applicable statute of limitation as to all asserted members of the class who would have been parties had the suit been permitted to continue as a class action."[62] The doctrine bears heavily on cases where the plaintiff untimely files suit in state court after failing to receive certification in federal court, where the action was first filed.[63]

Tennessee, however, does not recognize cross-jurisdictional tolling.[64] Furthermore, it recognizes neither intrajurisdictional tolling, which "tolls statutes of limi-

---

54. *Bloodworth*, 2007 Tenn. App. LEXIS 404, at *18–19.

55. *Id.* at *20, 22.

56. *Id.*

57. *Id.* at *24–25.

58. *Id.* at *27–28.

59. Tenn. R. Civ. P. 23.02(3).

60. *Bloodworth*, 2007 Tenn. App. LEXIS 404, at *28.

61. *Maestas v. Sofamor Danek Group, Inc.*, 33 S.W.3d 805, 807 (Tenn. 2000) (quoting *Crown, Cork & Seal Co. v. Parker*, 462 U.S. 345, 353–54 (1983) (internal quotation marks omitted)).

62. *Id.*

63. *Id.*

64. *Id.* at 808.

tations within the same court system during the pendency of a class action for potential members of the class," nor the doctrine of equitable tolling.[65]

VI. Final Considerations

The practical distinctions between Tennessee Rule 23 and the Federal Rule are few but important. Beyond that, there are several final considerations respecting class action practice in Tennessee that merit discussion.

As in the federal system, the residence of the named class representative governs venue for class actions brought in Tennessee.[66] Accordingly, the residence of unnamed class members cannot defeat certification.[67]

Appropriate venue notwithstanding, Tennessee forbids class actions in at least one circumstance and frowns upon it in another. Class actions are unavailable under the Tennessee Consumer Protection Act,[68] and Tennessee follows the federal approach in finding that fraud actions frequently are not well suited for certification because the predominance requirement is destroyed by the often varying degrees of representations made by the defendant to the class members.[69]

Regarding damage awards, Tennessee courts may award damages on a class-wide basis.[70] The court is under no duty to conduct individual damages inquiries. Rather, the court "may determine an aggregate damage amount for the class as a whole . . . [and it] may simply choose to divide the award among the members or [it] may allow each plaintiff to recover by proving his or her claims against the entire judgment."[71]

Finally, Tennessee trial courts are not required to consider the potential recovery of damages at trial before approving a settlement of a certified class action.[72] In this state, the "'dollar amount of the settlement by itself is not decisive . . . . Dollar amounts are judged . . . in light of the strengths and weaknesses of plaintiffs' case.'"[73] Instead, the "most important consideration [in determining whether a

---

65. *Tigg*, 232 S.W.3d at 33 (emphasis omitted).

66. *Meighan*, 924 S.W.2d at 639.

67. *Id.*

68. TENN. CODE ANN. §§ 47-18-101-125; *see also Walker v. Sunrise Pontiac-GMC Truck, Inc.*, 249 S.W.3d 301, 308–10 (Tenn. 2008).

69. *Walker*, 249 S.W.3d at 312.

70. *Freeman*, 229 S.W.3d at 707.

71. *Id.* (citation and quotations omitted).

72. *Denver Area Meat Cutters & Employers Pension Plan v. Clayton*, 209 S.W.3d 584, 591 (Tenn. Ct. App. 2006).

73. *Id.* (quoting *In re "Agent Orange" Prod. Liab. Litig.*, 597 F. Supp. 740, 762 (E.D.N.Y. 1984)).

settlement is fair] is the strength of plaintiffs' case on the merits weighed against the amount offered in settlement."[74]

Nor is the difference between attorney fees awarded and the per share recovery determinative of the fairness of a settlement.[75] Rather, the "appropriate point of inquiry is not the degree of disparity between these amounts, but rather whether each particular amount was unreasonable under the circumstances."[76]

---

74. *Id.* (quotation marks omitted).
75. *Id.* at 593.
76. *Id.*

TEXAS

MICHAEL S. TRUESDALE

I. Introduction

Texas rules and statutes authorize the use of class action lawsuits. The general procedures governing class actions are set forth in Rule 42 of the Texas Rules of Civil Procedure, while other statutes, including provisions of the Texas Civil Practice and Remedies Code, address various matters relevant to class action practice.[1]

When adopted in 1941, Rule 42 was patterned after Federal Rule of Civil Procedure 23.[2] Rule 42 was revised in 1977 to conform with the 1966 amendments to the federal Rule.[3] In light of that relationship between the Texas and federal class action rules, Texas courts treat authorities interpreting Rule 23 as persuasive.[4] Currently, Rule 42 closely mirrors its federal counterpart—with the exceptions discussed in this chapter.

Texas courts recognize that there is no right to litigate a claim as a class action.[5] Instead, a class may be certified only if the party satisfies the requirements of Rule 42.[6] Specifically, a party seeking certification must satisfy the four requirements of Rule 42(a) by demonstrating (1) the class is so numerous that joinder of all members is impracticable; (2) there are questions of law or fact common to the class; (3) the claims or defenses of the representative parties are typical of the claims or

---

1. *See generally* Tex. R. Civ. P. 42; Tex. Civ. Prac. & Rem. Code §§ 26.001–003, 26:051, 51.014; *see also* Tex. Bus. & Com. Code Ann. § 17.501; Tex. Ins. Code § 541.251 (authorizing certain insurance class actions to be brought by individuals or by the Texas Attorney General). *But see* Tex. Bus. & Com. Code Ann. § 321.109 (prohibiting the certification of certain statutory claims for e-mail abuses as class actions); Tex. Bus. & Com. Code Ann. § 502.002(f) (prohibiting certification of certain statutory claims for misuse of credit card information as class actions).

2. *See Ford Motor Co. v. Sheldon*, 22 S.W.3d 444, 452 (Tex. 2000).

3. *See Citizens Ins. Co. of Am. v. Daccach*, 217 S.W.3d 430, 449 (Tex. 2007).

4. *Id.* at 449; *Intratex Gas Co. v. Beeson*, 22 S.W.3d 398, 403 (Tex. 2000).

5. *Sheldon*, 22 S.W.3d at 452–53.

6. *Id.*

defenses of the class; and (4) the representative parties will fairly and adequately protect the interests of the class.[7] Additionally, the party must also satisfy one of the provisions of Rule 42(b), which track Federal Rule 23(b): (1) risks caused by prosecution of separate actions of inconsistent or varying adjudications or of adjudications that, as a practical matter, would be dispositive of the interests of others; (2) injunctive or declaratory relief based on the nonmovant's acts or refusal to act on grounds generally applicable to the class; or (3) the predominance/superiority of litigating questions of law or fact common to the class.[8]

II. Significant Differences Between Texas Rule 42 and Federal Rule 23

A. RULE 42(C)(1)(D): AMPLIFYING "RIGOROUS ANALYSIS"

In 2000, the Supreme Court of Texas issued several significant opinions that have had a lasting impact on class action practice in Texas.[9] In *Southwest Refining, Inc. v. Bernal*, the court explicitly rejected what it described as a "certify now and worry later" approach to class certification.[10] In doing so, it set in motion a shift in the process by which Texas trial courts are to decide certification issues.

These Texas Supreme Court precedents reaffirmed that the class action proponent has the burden to plead and prove the right to maintain a class action.[11] Texas trial courts may not presume that the requirements of Rule 42 are satisfied, but instead must meaningfully determine the class certification issues by inquiring beyond the pleadings to understand the claims, defenses, relevant facts, and applicable substantive law.[12] Thus, trial courts "must perform a 'rigorous analysis' to determine whether all prerequisites to certification have been met."[13]

Rule 42(c)(1)(B) tracks the requirement under Rule 23(c)(1)(B) that "[a]n order certifying a class must define the class and the class claims, issues or defenses and must appoint class counsel . . . ."[14] However, Texas requires additional information pursuant to Rule 42(c)(1)(D), which supplements the common law "rigorous analysis" requirement. By rule, Texas trial courts considering certification of a

---

7. TEX. R. CIV. P. 42(a).

8. TEX. R. CIV. P. 42(b)(1)–(3).

9. *See Sw. Refining, Inc. v. Bernal*, 22 S.W.3d 425 (Tex. 2000); *Sheldon*, 22 S.W.3d 444; *Beeson*, 22 S.W.3d 398.

10. *Bernal*, 22 S.W.2d at 433.

11. *Sheldon*, 22 S.W.3d at 453.

12. *Bernal*, 22 S.W.3d at 435; *see also Union Pac. Res. Group, Inc. v. Hankins*, 111 S.W.3d 69, 72 (Tex. 2003).

13. *Bernal*, 22 S.W.3d at 435.

14. *See* TEX. R. CIV. P. 42(c)(1)(B); FED. R. CIV. P. 23(c)(1)(B).

class under Rule 42(b)(3) must address eight specific subjects in its order granting *or* denying certification:

- The elements of each claim or defense asserted in the pleadings;
- Any issues of law or fact common to the class members;
- Any issues of law or fact affecting only individual class members;
- The issues that will be the object of most of the efforts of the litigants and the court;
- Other available methods of adjudication that exist for the controversy;
- Why the issues common to the members of the class do or do not predominate over individual issues;
- Why a class action is or is not superior to other available methods for the fair and efficient adjudication of the controversy; and
- If a class is certified, how the class claims and any issues affecting only individual members, raised by the claims or defenses asserted in the pleadings, will be tried in a manageable, time efficient manner.[15]

In conducting its "rigorous analysis" of a proposed class, the trial court must also "consider the risk that a judgment in the class action may preclude subsequent litigation of claims not alleged, abandoned, or split from the class action."[16] In fact, the trial court abuses its discretion "if it fails to consider the preclusive effect of a judgment on abandoned claims, as *res judicata* could undermine the adequacy of representation requirement."[17]

While the rule-based trial plan required by Rule 42(c)(1)(D) applies to "common question" classes under Rule 42(b)(3), a trial court considering certification of a declaratory or injunctive class pursuant to Rule 42(b)(2) must also engage in a "rigorous analysis" of the requirements for certification. That review focuses on all the four elements of Rule 42(a), as well as on the "cohesiveness" of the proposed class seeking declaratory/injunctive relief as required pursuant to Rule 42(b)(2).[18]

Even when certification is sought for settlement purposes only, a trial court still must engage in a "rigorous analysis" of the Rule 42 factors.[19] Such an analysis must precede the final approval, or fairness, hearing.[20]

When a court of appeals reverses a trial court's determination—made prior to its formulation of a trial plan—that Rule 42 factors do not warrant certification, the appellate court must remand to the trial court with instructions to "reconsider the class action requirements in light of the court of appeals' opinion and,

---

15. Tex. R. Civ. P. 42(c)(1)(D)(i)–(viii); *see also Texas Parks & Wildlife v. Dearing*, 240 S.W.3d 330, 340 (Tex. 2007) (noting that Rule 42(c)(1(D) codifies the trial plan requirement).

16. *Daccach*, 217 S.W.3d at 458.

17. *Id.*

18. *See Compaq Computer Corp. v. Lapray*, 135 S.W.3d 657, 670–71 (Tex. 2004).

19. *McAllen Med. Ctr., Inc. v. Cortez*, 66 S.W.3d 227, 231 (Tex. 2001).

20. *Id.*

consistent with that court's rulings, conduct such further proceedings as may be necessary to determine whether and how class claims can be tried in light of that opinion."[21] In the absence of a trial plan, the appellate court may not direct the trial court to certify a class, and the supreme court will not examine for itself whether certification was appropriate.[22]

B. DISCOVERY

Rule 42(f) provides that unnamed class members are not considered parties for purposes of discovery. This Rule has no express analog in Rule 23.

For purposes of precertification discovery from the class, discovery typically is limited to the particular issues governing certification in each case, mindful of the importance, benefit, burden, expense, and time needed to produce the proposed discovery.[23]

C. APPEALS

Rule 23(f) allows a court of appeals to permit an appeal from an order granting or denying class action for certification. An appeal from a federal class action certification ruling is subject to the discretion of the federal appellate court.[24]

Rule 42 contains no analog to Rule 23(f). However, by statute, an interlocutory appeal may be taken as a matter of right from an order that "certifies or refuses to certify a class in a suit brought under Rule 42 of the Texas Rules of Civil Procedure."[25]

Texas courts have strictly construed the types of class-related orders that may be raised in an interlocutory appeal. By statute, "a person may appeal from an interlocutory order of a district court, county court at law, or county court that . . . (3) certifies or refuses to certify a class in a suit brought under Rule 42 of the Texas Rules of Civil Procedure."[26] Jurisdiction is not conferred to authorize appeals from orders denying motions to decertify classes.[27] Nor does Rule 42 confer jurisdiction over orders striking corporate shareholder derivative claims.[28] When a trial court order materially alters an earlier certification order so as to fundamentally alter

---

21. *N. Am. Mortgage Co. v. O'Hara*, 153 S.W.3d 43 (Tex. 2004).

22. *Id.* Federal Rule 23(d) provides for conducting the class action, empowering the district court to issue and amend orders governing the course of proceedings, assuring adequate notice, and imposing certain conditions on representative parties and intervenors. Rule 42 does not contain a specific analog, but, as discussed above, has many particularized requirements for certain aspects of the process.

23. *In re Alford Chevrolet-Geo*, 997 S.W.2d 173, 180–82 (Tex. 1999).

24. FED. R. CIV. P. 23(f).

25. TEX. CIV. PRAC. & REM. CODE ANN. § 51.014(a)(3).

26. *Id.*

27. *See Bally Total Fitness Corp. v. Jackson*, 53 S.W.3d 352, 353 (Tex. 2001).

28. *Stary v. DeBord*, 967 S.W.2d 352, 352 (Tex. 1998).

the nature of the class, such an order may be immediately appealable.[29] An order preliminarily certifying a class for settlement purposes is ripe for appellate review, even when a court may later reconsider the certification issue during a fairness hearing.[30] However, during such appeal, the only issue subject to review is the certification; complaints about the adequacy of the proposed settlement may not be addressed except insofar as they may relate to review of the certification order.[31] When a class has been certified pursuant to both Rule 42 and the virtually identical provisions of the Texas Insurance Code, the exercise of jurisdiction applies to the entire case, allowing for review of certification under either provision.[32]

A trial court's decision whether to certify a class is reviewed for abuse of discretion on appeal.[33] However, that discretion cannot be supported exclusively by presumptions favoring the court's ruling.[34] Instead, "actual, not presumed, compliance with [Rule 42] remains indispensable," and must be demonstrated, not assumed.[35]

On appellate review of a certification order, a court may consider the standing of the class representative to assert classwide claims. If the named class representative has not suffered any actual or threatened injury, that party lacks standing to assert claims and to serve as a class representative, calling for the dismissal of the case.[36] If a trial court determines that the putative class representatives lack standing, the trial court does not abuse its discretion in denying a third party's request to intervene because no viable common claim exists as between the intervenor and the party seeking to represent the class.[37]

Historically, the Supreme Court of Texas lacked jurisdiction over most interlocutory class certification rulings. Thus, jurisdiction over interlocutory rulings terminated in the intermediate courts of appeals except under limited circumstances. In 2003, statutory amendments expanded the supreme court's jurisdiction to interlocutory orders that certified or refused to certify classes under Rule 42.[38] The exercise of that jurisdiction remains within the supreme court's discretion.

---

29. See De Los Santos v. Occidental Chem. Corp., 933 S.W.2d 493, 495 (Tex. 1996).

30. Cortez, 66 S.W.3d at 234.

31. Id.

32. See Farmers Group, Inc. v. Lubin, 222 S.W.3d 417, 421 (Tex. 2007). In Lubin, the supreme court assumed without deciding that section 51.014 of the Texas Civil Practice & Remedies Code only applied to certification orders under Rule 42. Id.

33. Bernal, 22 S.W.3d at 439; see also Gen. Motors Corp. v. Bloyed, 916 S.W.2d 949, 955 (Tex. 1996) ("Approval of a class action settlement is within the sound discretion of the trial court and should not be reversed absent an abuse of discretion.").

34. See Henry Schein, Inc. v. Stromboe, 102 S.W.3d 675, 691 (Tex. 2003).

35. Id. (quoting Bernal, 22 S.W.3d at 435).

36. See M.D. Anderson Cancer Ctr. v. Novak, 52 S.W.3d 704, 711 (Tex. 2001); DaimlerChrysler Corp. v. Inman, 252 S.W.3d 299 (Tex. 2008).

37. Texas Commerce Bank v. Grizzle, 96 S.W.3d 240 (Tex. 2003).

38. Tex. Gov't Code § 22.225(d).

Factors governing the exercise of that discretion include, among other things, the importance of the issue raised to the jurisprudence of the state, the existence of any conflict between the appellate court's ruling and the ruling of another coordinate or superior court (including the U.S. Supreme Court), and the existence of any disagreement among members of the appellate court panel from whose ruling review is sought.[39] Other statutes confer supreme court jurisdiction over particular types of class actions.[40]

D. SETTLEMENTS

Rule 42(e) generally tracks Rule 23(e) with the following exception: Rule 42(e)(4)(A) provides that a court "may not approve a settlement" unless the settlement affords a new opportunity for class members to request exclusion from the class.[41] By contrast, Rule 23(e)(4) states that a court "may refuse" to approve a settlement unless the settlement affords a new opportunity to request exclusion.[42]

The trial court acts as a guardian of the interests of the class, and that role takes on an enhanced importance when parties to a class action propose a classwide settlement.[43] In the context of a proposed settlement, the court must, as a threshold, "independently determine that the requirements of Rule 42 have been scrupulously met, in their entirety, before approving any class action settlement."[44]

As in federal court, upon preliminary approval of a settlement class, a Texas court must ultimately determine that the proposed settlement is fair, adequate, and reasonable. Such a determination is made at a fairness hearing conducted after adequate notice is provided to the class. Notice of a proposed settlement must advise the class members of the maximum amount of attorney fees sought by the class counsel and specify the proposed method of calculating the award.[45] Absent such notice, "class members cannot make informed decisions about their right to challenge the fee award at the hearing, including the allocation of the settlement proceeds between the class and its attorneys."[46]

---

39. *See* TEX. GOV'T CODE § 22.001(a)(1), (2), (6); *see also* TEX. R. APP. P. 56.1(a). Texas Government Code section 22.001(a) also confers jurisdiction over matters involving the construction of state statutes or constitutional provisions, matters involving state revenue, and matters involving the Texas Railroad Commission. TEX. GOV'T CODE § 22.001(a)(3)–(5).

40. *See, e.g.*, TEX. OCCUP. CODE § 2301.756 (conferring jurisdiction over interlocutory orders certifying a class brought against a motor vehicle licensee).

41. TEX. R. CIV. P. 42(e)(4)(A).

42. FED. R. CIV. P. 23(e)(4).

43. *Bloyed*, 916 S.W.2d at 954 (citations omitted).

44. *Id.* (citing *In re Gen. Motors Corp. Pick-Up Truck Fuel Tank Prods. Liab. Litig.*, 55 F.3d 768, 795–96 (3d Cir. 1995)).

45. *Id.* at 957–58.

46. *Id.*

At the final approval hearing, the trial court must examine "both the substantive and procedural aspects of the settlement: (1) whether the terms of the settlement are fair, adequate and reasonable; and (2) whether the settlement was the product of honest negotiations or of collusion."[47] This analysis is guided by six factors: "(1) whether the settlement was negotiated at arms' length or was a product of fraud or collusion; (2) the complexity, expense, and likely duration of the litigation; (3) the stage of the proceedings, including the status of discovery; (4) the factual and legal obstacles that could prevent the plaintiffs from prevailing on the merits; (5) the possible range of recovery and the certainty of damages; and (6) the respective opinions of the participants, including class counsel, class representatives, and the absent class members."[48]

Given the trial court's heightened responsibility in approving settlements, the general rule is that a fairness hearing should proceed by way of a plenary hearing with the opportunity for questioning by the court and cross-examination by counsel for objecting parties.[49] Such a hearing should confirm the two inquiries described above—that the certification requirements of Rule 42 are satisfied and that the settlement is fair, adequate, and reasonable, as well as determining the amount of attorney fees to be awarded.[50] These inquiries are separate, and findings supporting the settlement cannot be substituted for findings of compliance with Rule 42's requirements.

An unnamed class member is not required to intervene in order to appeal its objections to a class settlement or to the denial of a request to opt out of the class; instead, such objectors are deemed parties for those purposes under the doctrine of virtual representation.[51] A nonsettling defendant also has standing to appeal the certification of a settlement class if that defendant can show it is adversely affected by the settlement.[52]

E. ATTORNEY FEES: LODESTAR CAP

In 2003, as a part of wide-sweeping tort reform efforts, the Texas legislature directed the Texas Supreme Court to enact rules "to provide for the fair and efficient resolution of class actions."[53] Specifically, it directed the supreme court to

---

47. *Id.* at 955 (citing *Pettway v. Am. Cast Iron Pipe Co.*, 576 F.2d 1157, 1169 (5th Cir. 1978), *cert. denied*, 439 U.S. 1115 (1977)).

48. *Id.* (citing *Ball v. Farm & Home Sav. Ass'n*, 747 S.W.2d 420, 423 (Tex. App.—Fort Worth 1988, writ denied) (citing *Parker v. Anderson*, 667 F.2d 1204, 1209 (5th Cir. 1982))).

49. *Id.*

50. *Id.* at 958–59.

51. *City of San Benito v. Rio Grande Valley Gas Co.*, 109 S.W.3d 750, 755–56 (Tex. 2003).

52. *Cortez*, 66 S.W.3d at 235.

53. *See* Tex. Civ. Prac. & Rem. Code Ann. § 26.001.

adopt rules giving effect to mandatory guidelines governing the procedures to be used in awarding attorney fees in class actions.[54]

The mandatory guidelines contain two components. First, the legislature required the adoption of rules requiring trial courts to use the lodestar method[55] to calculate the amount of attorney fees to be awarded class counsel—with the discretion to increase or decrease the lodestar amount by no more than a factor of four based on specific factors.[56] Second, the legislature required the adoption of rules governing the calculation of attorney fees in cases in which any portion of the benefits recovered for the class are in the form of coupons or other noncash common benefits. In such cases, the attorney fees awarded must be in cash and noncash amounts in the same proportion as the recovery by the class.[57]

In response to these legislative directives, the Texas Supreme Court adopted Rule 42(i). Section (1) of that rule addresses the lodestar component:

> In awarding attorney's fees, the court must first determine a lodestar figure by multiplying the number of hours reasonably worked times a reasonable hourly rate. The attorney fees award must be in the range of 25% to 400% of the lodestar figure. In making these determinations, the court must consider the factors specified in Rule 1.04(b), Texas Disciplinary Rules, Professional Conduct.[58]

The factors to be considered in determining the lodestar rate, as well as any upward or downward adjustment to the overall award, are those set forth in Rule 1.04(b) of the Texas Disciplinary Rules of Professional Conduct:

(1) the time and labor required, the novelty and difficulty of the questions involved, and the skill requisite to perform the legal service properly;

(2) the likelihood, if apparent to the client, that the acceptance of the particular employment will preclude other employment by the lawyer;

(3) the fee customarily charged in the locality for similar legal services;

(4) the amount involved and the results obtained;

(5) the time limitations imposed by the client or by the circumstances;

(6) the nature and length of the professional relationship with the client;

(7) the experience, reputation, and ability of the lawyer or lawyers performing the services; and

---

54. *See id.* at § 26.002 ("Rules adopted under Section 26.001 must comply with the mandatory guidelines established by this chapter."); *id.* at § 26.003 (setting forth guidelines for calculating attorney fees).

55. The lodestar calculation determines a "reasonable" number of hours worked on a case multiplied by a "reasonable" hourly rate. *See* TEX. CIV. PRAC. & REM. CODE ANN. § 26.003(a). As noted, this amount can be enhanced by a multiplier under certain circumstances. *Id.*; *see also* Chapter 8, "Attorney Fee Awards and Incentive Payments."

56. TEX. CIV. PRAC. & REM. CODE ANN. § 26.003(a).

57. *Id.* at § 26.003(b).

58. TEX. R. CIV. P. 23(i)(1).

(8) whether the fee is fixed or contingent on results obtained or uncertainty of collection before the legal services have been rendered.[59]

No reported opinion has yet determined whether the factors analyzed in calculating the lodestar rate can also justify an adjustment to the final award; however, in other contexts, the same factors cannot be used both to set the lodestar rate and to justify a departure from the rate.

In addition to the statutory lodestar cap, Rule 42(i) also gives effect to the legislative directive concerning the calculation of fees in class actions awarding noncash benefits. Rule 42(i)(2) provides, "If any portion of the benefits recovered for the class are in the form of coupons or other noncash common benefits, the attorneys fees awarded in the action must be in cash and noncash amounts in the same proportion as the recovery for the class."[60]

Though the contours of Rule 42(i)(2) are still in the early stages of appellate scrutiny, certain issues are looming. Rule 42(i)(2) appears to strip any mechanism for recovering attorney fees in class actions seeking nonmonetary relief, such as injunctive or declaratory relief, other than through a fee agreement with class representatives. The Rule does not explain how proportions will be determined in cases seeking both cash recoveries and injunctive/declaratory relief. Finally, the Rule may in fact directly conflict with other statutes that authorize the award of both declaratory relief and attorney fees.[61]

---

59. TEX. DISCIPLINARY R. PROF'L CONDUCT 1.04(b)(1)–(8), *reprinted in* TEX. GOV'T CODE ANN. tit. 2, subtit. G App. A (Vernon Supp. 1997); *see also Arthur Andersen & Co. v. Perry Equip. Corp.*, 945 S.W.2d 812, 818 (Tex. 1997) (citing factors).

60. TEX. R. CIV. P. 42(i)(2); *see also* TEX. CIV. PRAC. & REM. CODE § 26.003(b).

61. *See, e.g.*, TEX. CIV. PRAC. & REM. CODE § 37.009 (authorizing the award of reasonable and necessary attorney fees in a declaratory judgment proceeding).

UTAH

LANCE SORENSON

I. Introduction

Utah Rule of Civil Procedure 23 subparts (a)–(e) are substantially similar to those of Federal Rule 23. Utah Rule 23 does not contain provisions corresponding to Federal Rule 23 subparts (f)–(h). Most significant of the subparts omitted by the Utah Rule is Federal Rule 23(f), permitting an interlocutory appeal of the grant or denial of class certification. Utah courts are instructed by federal authority when interpreting state rules that are nearly identical to federal rules.[1]

II. Rule 23(a) Prerequisites to Class Certification

Utah generally follows the same requirements of numerosity, commonality, typicality, and adequacy of representation as those of the federal Rule.[2]

III. Rule 23(b) Categories

Utah Rule 23(b) is nearly identical to its federal counterpart, and Utah generally follows principles expounded in federal case law. The Utah Supreme Court has stated that "although not bound to follow federal precedent . . . , those courts have developed useful principles . . . ."[3]

---

1. *See Olson v. Salt Lake Sch. Dist.*, 724 P.2d 960, 965 n.5 (Utah 1986); *see also Workman v. Nagle Constr., Inc.*, 802 P.2d 749, 751 (Utah Ct. App. 1990).
2. *See Nunnelly v. First Fed. Bldg. & Loan Ass'n of Ogden*, 154 P.2d 620 (Utah 1944).
3. *Utah Rest. Ass'n v. Davis County Bd. of Health*, 709 P.2d 1159, 1162–63 (Utah 1985).

IV. Rule 23(e)

Utah Rule 23(e) differs slightly from the federal Rule regarding the settlement of claims. The Utah Rule does not contain the requirement that a hearing be held before approval of the settlement, as required by Federal Rule 23(e)(2).

V. Rule 23(f)

As noted, the Utah Rule does not contain a provision corresponding to Federal Rule 23(f), expressly permitting an interlocutory appeal in the discretion of the appellate court. However, the Utah Supreme Court has allowed the interlocutory appeal of an order decertifying a class.[4] It has also allowed an interlocutory appeal so that a defendant could challenge the certifying of a class it contended was overly broad.[5] The standard of review of a certification decision is abuse of discretion.[6]

VI. Rule 23(g)–(h)

Sections (g), pertaining to class counsel, and (h), addressing attorney fees and nontaxable costs, of Federal Rule 23 are not included in the Utah class action rule. Utah allows for attorney fees to be collected from funds recovered by settlement or award so long as the fees are fair and reasonable.[7] The trial judge is charged with determining whether the fee award is fair and reasonable and may not abdicate his or her responsibility to do so.[8]

---

4. *See Houghton v. Dep't of Health*, 206 P.3d 287 (Utah 2008).

5. *See Brumley v. Utah State Tax Comm'n*, 868 P.2d 796 (Utah 1993); *see also Richardson v. Ariz. Fuels Corp.*, 614 P.2d 636 (Utah 1980).

6. *See Call v. City of W. Jordan*, 727 P.2d 180, 183 (Utah 1986).

7. *See Plumb v. State*, 809 P.2d 734 (Utah 1990).

8. *Id.*

VERMONT

JACOB B. PERKINSON

I. Introduction

The Vermont Supreme Court has taken a measured approach in its evaluation of its class action rule, Vermont Rule of Civil Procedure 23 (Vermont Rule).[1] The Vermont Rule derives from the pre-2003 version of Federal Rule 23,[2] and the Vermont courts are guided by the interpretation of the federal Rule.[3] While Vermont has not adopted a provision to parallel Federal Rule 23(g) or (h), Vermont Rule 23(f) was added in 2002 and follows its 1998 federal counterpart in providing an appeals process from orders granting or denying class certification.[4] Appeals are to the Vermont Supreme Court, as Vermont does not have intermediate appellate courts.

As under the federal Rule, Vermont requires that a determination of the question of class certification must be wholly divorced from a consideration of the merits of the action.[5] However, the Vermont Supreme Court has recently cautioned that an understanding of the merits of an action may be necessary to evaluate the

---

1. VT. R. CIV. P. 23; *see also George v. Town of Calais*, 135 Vt. 244, 245, 373 A.2d 553, 554 (1977) ("Class actions are intended to be of limited and special application, not to be casually resorted to or authorized"); *Salatino v. Chase*, 2007 Vt. 81, ¶ 11, 939 A.2d 482, 487 (2007) (noting "this is particularly true of the mandatory class actions authorized by Rules 23(b)(1)(B)"). *Compare State of Vt. v. Homeside Lending, Inc. & Bankboston Corp.*, 2003 Vt. 17, ¶ 67, 826 A.2d 997, 1020 (2003) ("We are not unmindful of the benefits that national class actions can bring to our citizens, without an accompanying burden on our judicial system.") *with Merrilees v. Treasurer of State of Vt.*, 159 Vt. 623, 625, 618 A.2d 1316 (1992) (noting the "obvious utility of aggregating small claims in a class action").

2. *See* VT. R. CIV. P. 23 reporter's notes.

3. *See* VT. R. CIV. P. 23 reporter's notes; *Chase*, 2007 Vt. 81, ¶ 7, n.4, 939 A.2d at 486; *Wright v. Honeywell Int'l, Inc.*, 2009 Vt. 123, ¶ 10. *But cf. Chase*, 2007 Vt. 81, ¶ 6, n.2, 939 A.2d at 485 (declining to follow Second Circuit trend of applying less deference to denial than to approval of class certification decisions).

4. VT. R. CIV. P. 23(f).

5. *Alger v. Dept. of Labor and Indus.*, 2006 Vt. 116, ¶ 41, 917 A.2d 508, 523 (2007).

elements of predominance and superiority in the context of considering certification of a class action brought under Vermont Rule 23(b)(3).[6]

In general, Vermont courts are encouraged to take a pragmatic approach to class certification to serve the ends of justice:

> Although trial courts must assure that questions common to the putative class predominate and that a class action would be superior to independent actions, they must not rigidly apply Rule 23 so as to prematurely determine the merits of the case and deny a class of indirect consumers, who as a practical matter cannot obtain relief for alleged antitrust violations in separate proceedings, the opportunity to present their case to a jury. Otherwise, legitimate plaintiffs may be left without a remedy, and defendants may secure unlawful gains without the risk of being sued or prosecuted.[7]

II. Vermont Rule 23(a) Prerequisites to Class Certification

Vermont courts apply the same requirements of numerosity, commonality, typicality, and adequacy of representation set forth in Federal Rule 23, and the trial court exercises broad discretion in determining the issues.[8]

Typicality, commonality, and numerosity have not been directly addressed by the Vermont Supreme Court except in summary citations to the language of the Vermont Rule.[9] Without specifically citing Vermont Rule 23(a)'s requirements, the Vermont Supreme Court has declared a standard apropos to each of these elements by holding that a class may not be "'defined so broadly that it encompasses individuals who have little connection with the claim being litigated' nor can the class definition be too 'amorphous.'"[10]

The adequacy prong has been directly addressed in Vermont and follows the two-part formulation generally set out in Federal Rule 23, requiring the named representative to act as a fiduciary on behalf of absent class members and that counsel be competent to prosecute the suit. Thus, a representative must "fairly and adequately protect the interests of the class."[11] This charge includes protecting the absent class members' interests "against the possibly competing interests of

---

6. *Wright*, 2009 Vt. 123, ¶¶ 12–13; *see also* section III.B, *infra*.

7. *Wright*, 2009 Vt. 123, ¶ 31.

8. *Chase*, 2007 Vt. 81, ¶ 6, 939 A.2d at 485.

9. *See, e.g., Am. Trucking Assocs., Inc. v. Conway*, 152 Vt. 383, 390 n.2, 566 A.2d 1335, 1339 (1989) (noting that commonality is a prerequisite to any class action under Rule 23(a)); *Wright*, 2009 Vt. 123, ¶ 8.

10. *Alger*, 2006 Vt. 116, ¶ 36, 917 A.2d at 522 (quoting 7A Charles A. Wright, Arthur R. Miller & Mary K. Kane, Federal Practice and Procedure § 1760, at 142–47 (3d ed. 2005)).

11. *Homeside*, 2003 Vt. 17, ¶ 38, 826 A.2d at 1012.

the attorneys" and requires that the class representative monitor counsel for any potential conflicts.[12]

To meet the adequacy requirement of Vermont Rule 23(a), counsel for the class "must be loyal to each member of it and not act based on interests antagonistic to it."[13] Of course, the need to compensate class counsel, while presenting an unavoidable conflict, does not render counsel inadequate. Notably, the Vermont Supreme Court specifically found representation to be inadequate in *State of Vermont v. Homeside Lending, Inc. & Bankboston Corp. (Homeside)*[14] and held that jurisdiction over Vermonters in that case could not exist because of the violation of due process occasioned by the economic conflict of the named representatives and class counsel with the members of the class.

III. Vermont Rule 23(b) Categories

A. RULE 23(B)(1)

The Vermont Supreme Court directly addressed mandatory class actions under Rule 23(b)(1) in *Salatino v. Chase*.[15] In *Chase*, the court addressed a proposed limited fund class action under subsection (B) of the rule. In *Chase*, the court adopted the limited fund factors promulgated in *Ortiz v. Fibreboard Corp.*,[16] distilling the *Ortiz* case to three primary factors: (1) that funds available to the defendant be demonstrably insufficient to pay all claims; (2) that the whole of the fund is to be dedicated to the claims of the class; and (3) that the class members "identified by a common theory of recovery be treated equitably among themselves."[17] The burden of demonstrating these factors is, of course, on the moving party.[18] In *Chase*, the court denied certification of a limited fund class based on the lack of liquidated damages by holding that the trial court's ruling that the mandatory attorney fees available under the Vermont Consumer Fraud Act were not the equivalent of "liquidated damages" for purposes of Vermont Rule 23(b)(1)(B).[19]

B. RULE 23(B)(3)

In a ruling issued December 10, 2009, the Vermont Supreme Court directly addressed the commonality and superiority elements of Vermont Rule 23(b)(3).[20]

---

12. *Id.*
13. *Id.* at 2003 Vt. 17, ¶ 40, 826 A.2d at 1013.
14. *Id.* at 2003 Vt. 17, ¶ 52, 826 A.2d at 1016.
15. 2007 Vt. 81, 939 A.2d 482.
16. 527 U.S. 815, 119 S. Ct. 2295, 144 L. Ed. 2d 715 (1999).
17. *Chase*, 2007 Vt. 81, ¶¶ 9–10, 939 A.2d at 487.
18. *Id.* at 2007 Vt. 81, ¶ 12, 939 A.2d at 487.
19. *Id.* at 2007 Vt. 81, ¶ 15, 939 A.2d at 488.
20. *Wright*, 2009 Vt. 123.

In doing so, the Vermont court waded into the debate over the merits-versus-certification debate that has grown over the last decade. In *Wright v. Honeywell International, Inc.*, the court concluded that the level of proof necessary at the certification stage is not equivalent to what is required to prevail at trial, holding that plaintiff need only present "common, generalized, logically probative methodologies to prove antitrust injury to class members, methodologies that are at the very least superficially acceptable to meet the predominance threshold."[21] In addition, in *Wright*, the court held that issues of individualized damages did not preclude a finding that common issues predominate under Vermont Rule 23(b)(3).[22]

The court also directly addressed Vermont Rule 23(b)(3)'s superiority requirement in *Wright*, holding:

> As a general rule, "if common questions are found to predominate in an antitrust action, then courts generally have ruled that the superiority prerequisite of Rule 23(b)(3) is satisfied." Further, most courts agree, "as a general proposition, that from a manageability perspective, a class action is a superior procedure to handle thousands of class members' small claims when common issues of fact and law predominate and common methods of proving those claims exist."[23]

IV. Notice

The Vermont Supreme Court has addressed the issue of notice to the class in three cases: *Homeside*, *Chase*, and *American Trucking Associates, Inc. v. Conway*.[24]

In *Homeside*, the court addressed notice under Vermont Rule 23(e) in an action brought by the state of Vermont challenging the jurisdiction of an Alabama trial court to bind Vermonters in a "negative value," opt-out class action filed in Alabama. The court in *Homeside* emphasized that adequate notice is essential to comply with due process of law and rejected claims of the Alabama court's personal jurisdiction in light of the lack of adequate notice to Vermonters in connection with the opt-out notice provided.[25] Under *Homeside*, the smaller the benefit, the greater the clarity and fairness of the notice must be.[26] In order to comply with due process, notice to the class must not use "impenetrable" language[27] and must

---

21. *Id.* at 2009 Vt. 123, ¶ 26.

22. *Id.* at 2009 Vt. 123, ¶¶ 26–28.

23. *Id.* at 2009 Vt. 123, ¶ 30 (quoting 7AA CHARLES A. WRIGHT, ARTHUR R. MILLER & MARY K. KANE, FEDERAL PRACTICE AND PROCEDURE § 1781, at 254–55 (3d ed. 2005)).

24. 152 Vt. 383, 566 A.2d 1335.

25. *Homeside*, 2003 Vt. 17, ¶ 28, 826 A.2d at 1009.

26. *Id.* at 2003 Vt. 17, ¶ 30, 826 A.2d at 1009.

27. *Id.*

clearly describe the benefits and costs attendant to participating in the action to allow an informed decision by a rational person.[28]

In *Homeside*, the Vermont Supreme Court cited with approval the notice parameters prescribed by the National Association of Consumer Advocates' Standards and Guidelines for Litigating and Settling Class Actions, which include describing the total amount of relief available to the class; the individual relief available to each member; and the total maximum fees (in dollars) sought by class counsel.[29] In rejecting the efficacy of the notice under consideration in *Homeside*, the court emphasized the failure to reveal the potential that class members could be forced to pay more in fees than they recovered under the terms of the settlement, which, in the estimation of the Vermont Supreme Court, converted the plaintiff class into a de facto defendant class for purposes of any due process analysis.[30]

In *Chase*, the court addressed the issue of whether a trial court is empowered to provide putative class members with notice of the denial of a motion for class certification, and while the supreme court held that such notice is authorized under Vermont Rule 23(d)(2) in the exercise of the trial court's discretion, that discretion was found to be exceeded in the particular circumstances of the *Chase* case.[31] After noting the distinction between the mandatory nature of notice under Vermont Rule 23(e) and the discretionary nature of Vermont Rule 23(d)(2),[32] the *Chase* court determined that the trial court had abused its discretion under Vermont Rule 23(d) because there was "no legal or factual basis for holding that there was any risk of prejudice to putative class members in this case."[33] Thus, in Vermont, absent a showing of risk of prejudice to absent class members, court-ordered notice of denial of class certification is not available.[34]

Conway addressed the issue of notice to a certified class under Vermont Rules 23(b)(1) and (2) and held that the stricter requirements of Vermont Rule 23(c)(2) notice do not apply to these cases and that the notice provisions of Vermont Rule 23(d)(2) provide much broader discretion to the court in formulating what notice is provided to the class and how.[35]

---

28. *Id.* at 2003 Vt. 17, ¶ 33, 826 A.2d at 1010–11.
29. *Id.* at 2003 Vt. 17, ¶ 32, 826 A.2d at 1010.
30. *Id.* at 2003 Vt. 17, ¶ 35, 826 A.2d at 1011.
31. *Chase*, 2007 Vt. 81, ¶ 18, 939 A.2d at 489.
32. *Id.* at 2007 Vt. 81, ¶ 19, 939 A.2d at 489–90.
33. *Id.* at 2007 Vt. 81, ¶ 22, 939 A.2d at 491.
34. *Id.*
35. *Conway*, 152 Vt. 383, 390–91, 566 A.2d at 1339.

V. Lawyers and Attorney Fees

Sections (g) ("Class Counsel") and (h) ("Attorney's Fees and Nontaxable Costs") of Federal Rule 23 are not included in the Vermont class action rule. Nevertheless, Vermont follows the same underlying principles. Competency of class counsel is addressed as an element of the "adequacy of representation" element under Vermont Rule 23(a).[36]

Vermont allows assessment of attorney fees against the common fund or common benefit created for the class. However, such fees will be closely scrutinized for "reasonableness," and the Vermont Supreme Court has noted reservations with "clear sailing" scenarios where defendants affirmatively commit not to comment or oppose plaintiffs' counsel's requests for an award of attorney fees in the class action context.[37]

VI. Punitive Damages

Vermont has no statutory cap on punitive damages.

VII. Appeals

Orders granting or denying class certification are appealable at the discretion of the trial court if such motion is made within ten days of the order on class certification.[38] Trial court rulings on class certification are reviewed under an abuse of discretion standard.[39]

Notably, the Vermont Supreme Court has recognized that a trial court has discretion to change its decision not to certify a class even after the appellate court has affirmed such denial should developments in the case on remand warrant such a decision.[40] Conversely, the court has also recognized that a class may be decertified even after certification is upheld by the appellate court if evidence develops that makes certification no longer appropriate.[41]

---

36. *See Homeside*, 2003 Vt. 17, ¶ 40, 826 A.2d at 1013.
37. *Id.* at 2003 Vt. 17, ¶ 50, 826 A.2d at 1015–16.
38. VT. R. CIV. P. 23(f).
39. *See, e.g., Alger*, 2006 Vt. 116, ¶ 36, 917 A.2d at 522.
40. *See, e.g., id.* at 2006 Vt. 116, ¶ 40, 917 A.2d at 523.
41. *Wright*, 2009 Vt. 123, ¶ 29:

> [O]ur decision today does not prevent the superior court from decertifying the class at a later time—for example, following the completion of discovery, if the court concludes that no reasonable jury could possibly determine that monopolistic overcharges passed through to end users. Nor does our decision preclude the court from certifying sub-classes to account for the various distribution channels.

VIII. Incentive Payments

In Vermont, incentive payments are recognized as common and proper compensation for class representatives.[42] However, such payments must be evaluated to ensure that they are not used merely as leverage to induce the named representatives to agree to a deal that is not otherwise in the best interests of the absent class members.[43]

IX. Tolling

The Vermont Supreme Court has expressly recognized and adopted the rationales of *Crown, Cork & Seal Co. v. Parker*[44] and *American Pipe & Construction Co. v. Utah*[45] in tolling limitations for putative class members' claims.[46] Thus, in Vermont, the filing of a class action tolls the statute of limitations for all putative class members, and the denial of certification commences the running of the same.[47]

---

42. *Homeside*, 2003 Vt. 17, ¶ 39, 826 A.2d at 1013 (noting awards ranging from $1,000 to $55,000).
43. *Id.*
44. 462 U.S. 345, 354, 102 S. Ct. 2392, 76 L. Ed. 2d 628 (1983).
45. 414 U.S. 538, 94 S. Ct. 756, 38 L. Ed. 2d 713 (1974).
46. *Chase*, 2007 Vt. 81, ¶ 18, 939 A.2d at 491–92.
47. *Id.*

VIRGINIA

DEBORAH M. RUSSELL
ROBERT L. HODGES
LISA M. SHARP

I. Introduction

Virginia has no provision for class actions in its state court procedures. Virginia is still a code pleading state that has maintained the traditional division between law and chancery, except that it has recently modified procedural rules that provide for a single form of civil action. Consequently, the default rule of joinder as to parties is that no party can be bound by the judgment or decree unless he or she is properly named and joined as a party in the case and served with process. The exceptions and limitations to this rule are discussed below.

Virginia has by statute and rule also liberalized the rules of joinder of causes of action and generally permits claims to be joined in a single action as long as the claims arise out of the same transaction or occurrence. Special provisions applicable to joinder of causes of action are also set forth below.

II. Joinder of Parties in Virginia

Although a Virginia court is empowered to adjudicate a cause in the absence of proper parties, it is powerless to proceed with a suit unless all necessary parties are properly before it. Virginia recognizes limited exceptions to this rule. Virginia permits a party's representative to have standing where authorized by statute, or under the limited doctrine of virtual representation.[1]

---

1. *See* VA. CODE § 8.01-316(A)(2) (permitting service by order of publication when the pleading states that there are or may be persons, whose names are unknown, interested in the subject matter and describes the interest); VA. CODE § 8.01-316(A)(3) (permitting service by order of publication when the number of persons actually served with process exceeds ten and those persons represent like interests with the

Misjoinder of parties occurs when plaintiffs or defendants are improperly joined. Misjoinder may be challenged by a motion to drop.[2]

III. Joinder of Causes of Action in Virginia

A. PRIOR LAW

Formerly, Virginia civil procedure prohibited plaintiffs from jointly suing multiple defendants unless the defendants' acts "concur[ed] in producing a single individual injury or damage."[3] However, in 1954, the Virginia legislature enacted Virginia Code section 8.01-272, allowing parties to join claims in tort and contract, and "as many matters, whether of law or fact, as he shall think necessary," provided that "all claims so joined arise out of the same transaction or occurrence."[4] Additionally, in 1974, a related code section was enacted to permit parties to "plead alternative facts and theories of recovery against alternative parties," again so long as "such claims . . . so joined arise out of the same transaction or occurrence."[5]

Accordingly, Virginia's current Supreme Court Rule 1:4(k) regarding joinder provides, in pertinent part:

> A party asserting . . . a claim . . . may plead alternative facts and theories of recovery against alternative parties, provided that such claims . . . arise out of the same transaction or occurrence. When two or more statements are made in the alternative and one of them if made independently would be sufficient, the pleading is not made insufficient by the insufficiency of one or more of the alternative statements. A party may also state as many separate claims . . . as he has regardless of consistency and whether based on legal or equitable grounds.[6]

Where joinder would not "attain the ends of justice," a Virginia trial court has the discretionary power to order a separate trial of any claim.[7]

---

remaining defendants not personally served); *White v. Nat'l Bank & Trust Co.*, 212 Va. 568, 570, 186 S.E.2d 21, 22–23 (1972) (invoking doctrine of virtual representation).

2. VA. CODE § 8.01-5.

3. *Norfolk Bus Term. v. Sheldon*, 188 Va. 288, 49 S.E.2d 338 (1948); *see also* W. HAMILTON BRYSON, BRYSON ON VIRGINIA CIVIL PROCEDURE § 6.02[4][b] 6–21 (4th ed. 2005) (stating that traditional common law practice was to join claims only "of the same nature and character" against a single defendant).

4. VA. CODE § 8.01-272; the statute was enacted, according to one commentator, "to avoid a conflict with the then-existing Rules of Court . . . so that a counterclaim need not arise out of the same transaction as the original claim." KENT SINCLAIR, GUIDE TO VIRGINIA LAW/EQUITY REFORM AND OTHER LANDMARK CHANGES at 75 (2006).

5. VA. CODE § 8.01-281.

6. VA. SUP. CT. R. 1:4(k).

7. VA. CODE § 8.01-272; *Deane v. Mady*, No. 05-57, 2006 WL 3456352 (Va. Cir. Ct. Dec. 1, 2006).

The Supreme Court of Virginia recognized the liberalization of the rules regarding joinder in *Fox v. Deese*.[8] Some claims were pursued against some defendants jointly, as well as against some defendants severally, and some claims related to separate, independent acts of different defendants.[9] The court, acknowledging that the import of Rule 1:4(k) and Virginia Code sections 8.01-272 and 8.01-281 "represent[s] a radical departure from . . . common-law pleading rule[s]," concluded that, under those authorities, Fox fairly pleaded "alternative theories of recovery against the same group of defendants and that the claims arise out of the same transaction or occurrence."[10]

B. MISJOINDER OF ACTIONS

Formerly, the equitable doctrine of multifariousness provided for the dismissal of insufficiently related claims impermissibly joined in a single suit. Today, improperly joined claims may be severed at law or in equity on the grounds that the claims do not arise out of the same transaction or occurrence, such as in *Powers v. Cherin*.[11]

In *Powers*, plaintiff joined a claim of malpractice against a doctor who treated her for injuries she sustained in a car accident with her claim of negligence against the driver of the vehicle involved in the accident. The Supreme Court of Virginia held that these claims were impermissibly joined because Virginia Code sections 8.01-272 and 8.01-281 require joined claims to arise out of the same transaction or occurrence, and the occurrence of negligent driving is distinct from the occurrence of malpractice in subsequent medical treatment.[12]

IV. Multiple Claimant Litigation Act (1995): Consolidation Criteria

In the early 1990s, the Supreme Court of Virginia requested that the Boyd-Graves Conference of the Virginia Bar Association examine how Virginia courts should handle mass tort cases. The resulting legislation was enacted in 1995 as the Multiple Claimant Litigation Act (MCLA or Act).[13] The MCLA requires all plaintiffs to be named parties and does not permit representational standing akin to class action procedure.

Under the MCLA, either a circuit court or a panel of circuit court judges designated by the supreme court may enter an order "joining, coordinating, consolidating or transferring several actions" upon finding that:

---

8. 234 Va. 412, 415, 362 S.E.2d 699, 701 (1987).

9. *Id.* at 234 Va. 422, 362 S.E.2d at 705.

10. *Id.* at 234 Va. 423, 362 S.E.2d at 705.

11. 249 Va. 33, 452 S.E 2d 666 (1995).

12. *Id.* at 249 Va. 37, 452 S.E 2d at 672.

13. VA. CODE §§ 8.01-267.1–8.01-267.9.

1. Separate civil actions brought by six or more plaintiffs involve common questions of law or fact and arise out of the same transaction, occurrence or series of transactions or occurrences;

2. The common questions of law or fact predominate and are significant to the actions; and

3. The order (1) will promote the ends of justice and the just and efficient conduct and disposition of the actions, and (2) is consistent with each party's right to due process of law, and (3) does not prejudice each individual party's right to a fair and impartial resolution of each action.[14]

The Act provides a nonexhaustive list of factors for courts to consider, including:

- the nature of the common questions of law or fact;
- the convenience of the parties, witnesses, and counsel;
- the relative stages of the actions and the work of counsel;
- the efficient utilization of judicial facilities and personnel;
- the court's calendar;
- the likelihood and disadvantages of duplicative and inconsistent rulings;
- the likelihood of prompt settlement without the entry of the order; and
- as to joint trials by jury, the likelihood of prejudice or confusion.[15]

The language in the Act—requiring claims to "arise out of the same transaction or occurrence or series of transactions or occurrences"—is identical to language used in federal and state joinder rules.[16] However, under the MCLA, common issues of law or fact must *predominate* and must be *significant* to the actions before consolidation is proper.[17] Additionally, the court must find that consolidation of the plaintiffs' claims would "promote the ends of justice and the just and efficient conduct and disposition of the actions, [be] consistent with each party's right to due process of law, and not prejudice each individual party's right to a fair and impartial resolution of each action."[18]

The case-management provisions of the MCLA, like provisions familiar to practitioners in federal multidistrict litigation, allow defendants to request that plaintiffs be grouped in like categories, or that certain plaintiffs be severed from other plaintiffs who have consolidated, common claims. The Act provides:

> The court may organize and manage the combined litigation . . . consistent with the right of each party to a fair trial . . . , including but not limited to orders which

---

14. VA. CODE § 8.01-267.5. For the procedure regarding joinder, coordination, transfer, or consolidation of actions filed in different circuit courts under the MCLA, *see* VA. CODE § 8.01-267.4.

15. VA. CODE § 8.01-267.1.

16. *See, e.g.*, FED. R. CIV. P. 20(a).

17. VA. CODE § 8.01-267.1.

18. *Id.*

organize the parties into groups with like interests; appoint counsel to have lead responsibility for certain matters; allocate costs and fees to separate issues in the common questions that require treatment on a consolidated basis and individual cases that do not; and to stay discovery on the issues that are not consolidated.[19]

Accordingly, some courts have consolidated actions for pretrial purposes only.[20] Some have considered additional factors, such as whether the issues will require different witnesses and evidence.[21] At least one Virginia court also required consolidated-case plaintiffs to be organized in a "Litigation Steering Committee."[22]

A. SEVERANCE

The Act states that "[o]n motion of a defendant, the actions so joined shall be severed unless the court finds that the claims of the plaintiffs were ones which, if they had been filed separately, would have met the standards of § 8.01-267.1 and would have been consolidated under § 8.01-267.3."[23] At least one circuit court has interpreted this language to require that "the court must either make the [required] findings and invoke the Act or grant Defendants' motions to sever."[24] Additionally, sua sponte consolidation appears to be prohibited.[25]

There are only a handful of reported cases in Virginia discussing the MCLA. A fair reading of the cases indicates that courts tend to favor consolidation, particularly when claims have overlapping facts. Nevertheless, there are circumstances where courts have found severance appropriate. In *Bay Point Condominium Association, Inc. v. RML Corp.*,[26] condominium owners sued a builder for defects in construction. The builder then sued every supplier or subcontractor involved in the

---

19. VA. CODE § 8.01-267.1(v); *see also Wright v. Eli Lilly & Co.*, 66 Va. Cir. 195, 217 (Portsmouth Cir. Ct. 2004) (dividing plaintiffs into subclasses under the MCLA).

20. *See Chesapeake v. Cunningham*, 268 Va. 624, 627 n.1, 604 S.E.2d 420, 422 n.1 (2004); *McClure v. Norfolk & W. Ry. Co.*, 54 Va. Cir. 322, 322 (City of Roanoke 2000) (stating that "[f]requently, cases are consolidated only for matters of discovery and pretrial economy but are tried separately"); *see also Doe v. Bruton Parish Church*, 42 Va. Cir. 467, 470–71 (Williamsburg Cir. Ct. 1997) (consolidating cases for discovery purposes but reserving right to sever for trial).

21. *Wright*, 66 Va. Cir. at 223. *But see Branch v. Purdue Pharma L.P.*, 64 Va. Cir. 159, 160 (Richmond Cir. Ct. 2004) (stating that the Act does not parallel Fed. R. Civ. P. 20).

22. *In re Zoning Ordinance Amendments*, 67 Va. Cir. 462 (Loudoun County 2004) (noting that Litigation Steering Committee was established in Decree of Consolidation, and further charging Committee to file a Master Supplemental Bill of Complaint containing the common issues to which the defendant might then respond).

23. VA. CODE § 8.01-267.5.

24. *Bruton Parish Church*, 42 Va. Cir. at 470.

25. *See Livingston v. County of Fairfax*, No. CL-2008-8875, 2009 Va. Cir. LEXIS 32, at *2 (Fairfax County Apr. 28, 2009) (concluding that severance sua sponte prohibited, but allowable "upon motion of the defendant"); *see also* Boyd Graves Conference, Report of the Committee on Mass Claims Litigation 7 (Oct. 11, 1993) (stating that "[i]f none of the parties want consolidation, for example, it should not be forced on the litigants by the courts").

26. 52 Va. Cir. 432 (City of Norfolk 2000).

project. The suppliers filed motions for severance, to which the builder objected on the grounds that, if the plaintiffs prevailed, it would suffer the burden of separately suing 16 suppliers and subcontractors.[27] In granting severance, the court found that a consolidated trial would result in jury confusion. The court also found that the presentation of evidence regarding each supplier-defendant would be "extremely burdensome on the third-party defendants with limited participation in the project or a more remote connection to the claimed damages."[28]

B. PHARMACEUTICAL CASES

Virginia trial courts have taken different approaches to interpreting "the same transaction or occurrence" in cases where plaintiffs seek to join both pharmaceutical defendants and prescribing or treating physicians for injuries.[29] On one hand, in *Branch v. Purdue Pharma, L.P.*,[30] defendants moved to sever the suits of various plaintiffs who claimed that the defendant makers of a prescription medicine, as well as their individual physicians, caused them harm. The court granted the motion, finding that "[e]ach Plaintiff's case is based upon an intervening act by their individual physician. This intervening act makes for a multitude of varying questions of fact for each Plaintiff."[31] On the other hand, in *Wright v. Eli Lilly & Co.*,[32] the court denied a motion to sever where the plaintiffs charged the pharmaceutical defendants with negligence and other claims related to the design of certain drugs, and in the same action sued their health care providers for negligence in providing treatment related to the drugs' prescription. The court denied severance on grounds that it was "conceivable that the pharmaceutical manufacturers could be held liable for the health-care providers' actions in prescribing and monitoring the drugs at issue if the pharmaceutical manufacturers' failure to properly warn and other breaches/actions combined with negligence by the health-care providers to produce the death."[33]

C. APPELLATE ISSUES

The MCLA permits a discretionary, interlocutory appeal from an order of a circuit court pursuant to the Act under certain circumstances. A party may appeal if the circuit court orders "a consolidated trial of claims joined or consolidated pursuant

---

27. *Id.* at 458.

28. *Id.*

29. VA. CODE § 8.01-267.1.

30. 64 Va. Cir. 159.

31. *Id.* at 160; *see also Lee v. Mann*, 51 Va. Cir. 465 (2000) (finding misjoinder and no common transaction or occurrence where plaintiff sued doctor for medical malpractice in prescribing a diet drug and drug manufacturer for products liability).

32. 66 Va. Cir. 195.

33. *Id.* at 214.

to [the MCLA]."[34] Where the order falls short of consolidating claims for trial, the order is appealable only if it states that it involves a controlling question of law, that there is substantial ground for difference of opinion, and that an immediate appeal from the order may materially advance the ultimate termination of the litigation.[35] If an appeal is taken, proceedings in the circuit court are not stayed unless the circuit court so orders.[36]

V. Conclusion

While Virginia has not adopted Federal Rule of Civil Procedure 23, it permits claims to be joined if they arise out of the same transaction or occurrence. Additionally, while not permitting representational standing, the MCLA allows for the initial joinder of six or more plaintiffs in a single action, or the consolidation of cases filed by at least that number of plaintiffs in different jurisdictions, where the claims arise out of the same transaction or occurrence.

---

34. VA. CODE § 8.01-267.8(A).
35. VA. CODE § 8.01-267.8(B).
36. VA. CODE § 8.01-267.8(C).

CHAPTER 33

WASHINGTON

JILL D. BOWMAN

I. Introduction

Class actions in Washington are governed by Civil Rule 23 (CR 23). Because the state Rule mirrors the former Federal Rule 23,[1] Washington courts interpreting CR 23 frequently look to federal cases for guidance.[2]

CR 23 "avoids multiplicity of litigation, 'saves members of the class the cost and trouble of filing individual suits[,] and . . . also frees the defendant from the harassment of identical future litigation.'"[3] Washington courts therefore favor a liberal approach to the rule.[4] At the same time, they recognize that class actions are specialized types of suits that must be brought and maintained in strict conformity with the rule's requirements[5] and that a "rigorous analysis" is necessary to determine whether those requirements are met.[6]

---

1. CR 23 is identical to the version of Federal Rule 23 that was in effect before the 1998, 2003, and 2007 amendments, with one exception. In late 2005, the state added a provision regarding the disposition of residual settlement funds. *See* discussion at section V, *infra*.

2. *See, e.g., Pickett v. Holland Am. Line-Westours, Inc.*, 145 Wash. 2d 178, 188, 35 P.3d 351 (2001); *Schnall v. AT&T Wireless Servs., Inc.*, No. 80572-5, 2010 Wash. LEXIS 61, at *11 (Jan. 21, 2010); *cf. Darling v. Champion Home Builders Co.*, 96 Wash. 2d 701, 706, 638 P.2d 1249 (1982) (considering federal decisions instructive, but not binding).

3. *Smith v. Behr Process Corp.*, 113 Wash. App. 306, 318, 54 P.3d 665 (2002) (quoting *Brown v. Brown*, 6 Wash. App. 249, 256–57, 492 P.2d 581 (1971)); *see also Scott v. Cingular Wireless*, 160 Wash. 2d 843, 851, 161 P.3d 1000 (2007) ("Washington's CR 23 . . . demonstrates a state policy favoring aggregation of small claims for purposes of efficiency, deterrence, and access to justice.").

4. *See Nelson v. Appleway Chevrolet, Inc.*, 160 Wash. 2d 173, 188–89, 157 P.3d 847 (2007); *Miller v. Farmer Bros. Co.*, 115 Wash. App. 815, 820, 64 P.3d 49 (2003); *Brown*, 6 Wash. App. at 256–57, 492 P.2d 581.

5. *DeFunis v. Odegaard*, 84 Wash. 2d 617, 622, 529 P.2d 438 (1974).

6. *See Oda v. State*, 111 Wash. App. 79, 92, 44 P.3d 8 (2002) (citing *Gen. Tel. Co. of the Sw. v. Falcon*, 457 U.S. 147, 160–61 (1982)); *accord Weston v. Emerald City Pizza LLC*, 137 Wash. App. 164, 168, 151 P.3d 1090 (2007).

II. Certification

When deciding a motion for class certification, the trial court assumes that the factual allegations in the complaint are true, but may look beyond the pleadings and examine the evidence in order to understand the claims, defenses, relevant facts, and applicable substantive law.[7] At this stage, the court is not permitted to conduct an inquiry into the merits and therefore may not weigh conflicting expert testimony, but may determine the admissibility of such evidence.[8]

A. THRESHOLD ISSUES: STANDING AND CLASS DEFINITION

Before reaching the specific requirements of CR 23, a Washington court may consider the threshold issue of standing. A putative class representative cannot litigate a claim that he or she could not pursue individually.[9] In other words, the class action device does not confer standing that a party does not otherwise possess.[10] If the case involves multiple defendants, the representative plaintiff has no standing to bring the action against all of the defendants unless he or she has a claim against each defendant or has a claim against one of them and is able to show the existence of a juridical link among all of them.[11]

Another threshold issue is the definition of the proposed class. "Class definition is critical because it identifies the persons (1) entitled to relief, (2) bound by a final judgment, and (3) entitled to notice in a Rule 23(b)(3) action."[12] A class must be defined objectively (i.e., not depend on subjective criteria), and the definition must not depend on the merits of the case or require extensive factual inquiry to determine whether a person falls within the class.[13]

B. CR 23 REQUIREMENTS

As with Federal Rule 23, certification is appropriate in Washington only if all of the CR 23(a) prerequisites are satisfied, together with at least one of the grounds

---

7. *Oda*, 111 Wash. App. at 94, 44 P.3d 8.

8. *Schwendeman v. USAA Cas. Ins. Co.*, 116 Wash. App. 9, 21 n.34, 26–27 & n.44, 65 P.3d 1 (2003).

9. *Wash. Educ. Ass'n v. Shelton Sch. Dist. No. 309*, 93 Wash. 2d 783, 790, 613 P.2d 769 (1980).

10. *Doe v. Spokane & Inland Empire Blood Bank*, 55 Wash. App. 106, 115, 780 P.2d 853 (1989).

11. *Id.* at 55 Wash. App. 114–18 & n.6, 780 P.2d 853; *cf. id.* at 55 Wash. App. 118–19 (also indicating that the "typicality" requirement of CR 23(a)(3) may not be met if the case involves multiple defendants and the putative class representative does not have a claim against every defendant).

12. *Barnett v. Wal-Mart Stores, Inc.*, No. 55491-3-I, 2006 WL 1846531, at *1 (Wash. Ct. App. July 3, 2006) (internal quotations and citations omitted) (unpublished opinion). [NB: General Rule 14.1(a) prohibits a party from citing as an authority an unpublished opinion of the court of appeals. Parties risk sanctions from the Washington courts if they violate this prohibition.]

13. *Id.*

set forth in CR 23(b).[14] The party moving for class certification bears the burden of proving the requirements are met.[15]

1. CR 23(a) Prerequisites

a. Numerosity

A class action may be certified only if "the class is so numerous that joinder of all members is impracticable."[16] The putative class representative need not show that it would be impossible to join all of the members of the proposed class, but must show that it would be "extremely difficult or inconvenient" to do so.[17] There is no "magic number" that satisfies the impracticability requirement, and Washington courts will look not only at the number of potential class members, but also at such factors as whether class members are geographically dispersed, the size of individual claims, the financial resources of class members, whether membership in the class changes over time, and whether it is possible to identify all of the class members.[18]

b. Commonality

A class action may be certified only if "there are questions of law or fact common to the class."[19] This requirement has "a low threshold" and may be satisfied with a showing of a single issue common to all members of the class.[20] Commonality exists "if the 'course of conduct' that gives rise to the cause of action affects all the class members and all class members share at least one of the elements of the cause of action."[21]

c. Typicality

A class action may be certified only if "the claims or defenses of the representative parties are typical of the claims or defenses of the class."[22] Putative class representatives "satisfy the typicality requirement if their claims arise from the same conduct that gives rise to the claims of other class members and are based on the same legal theory."[23] As long as the same unlawful conduct is alleged to have affected

---

14. CR 23(a) & (b); *Brown*, 6 Wash. App. at 251–52, 492 P.2d 581.

15. *Weston*, 137 Wash. App. at 168, 173, 151 P.3d 1090.

16. CR 23(a)(1).

17. *Miller*, 115 Wash. App. at 821, 64 P.3d 49.

18. *Id.* at 115 Wash. App. 822 n.1; *Johnson v. Moore*, 80 Wash. 2d 531, 532–33, 496 P.2d 334 (1972); *Zimmer v. City of Seattle*, 19 Wash. App. 864, 868, 578 P.2d 548 (1978).

19. CR 23(a)(2).

20. *Behr*, 113 Wash. App. at 320, 54 P.3d 665.

21. *Schnall v. AT&T Wireless Servs., Inc.*, 139 Wash. App. 280, 295–96, 161 P.3d 395 (2007), *rev'd on other grounds*, 2010 Wash. LEXIS 61.

22. CR 23(a)(3).

23. *Schnall*, 139 Wash. App. at 295–96, 161 P.3d 395, *rev'd on other grounds*, 2010 Wash. LEXIS 61.

both the representative parties and the class members, typicality is not defeated by the existence of varying fact patterns in the individual claims.[24]

d. Adequacy

A class action may be certified only if "the representative parties will fairly and adequately protect the interests of the class."[25] This prerequisite has two components: the absence of adversity within the proposed class and the adequacy of class counsel.[26]

2. CR 23(b) Requirements

a. CR 23(b)(1) and (b)(2)

A class action may be certified under CR 23(b)(1) when separate adjudications of the claims of individual class members could result in incompatible standards of conduct for the party opposing the class or could impede the ability of absent class members to protect their interests. More simply, "[c]lasses certified under CR 23(b)(1) are designed to avoid prejudice to the defendant or absent class members."[27] Class certification under CR 23(b)(2) may be granted when the party opposing the class has acted or refused to act on grounds generally applicable to the class, and injunctive or declaratory relief is sought with respect to the class as a whole.[28] "Classes certified under subsections (b)(1) and (b)(2) are 'mandatory' classes; that is, the results are binding on all class members, who may not choose to opt out of the class."[29] Notice to (b)(1) and (b)(2) class members is at the trial court's discretion.

When putative class representatives seek monetary damages, certification under (b)(1) or (b)(2) violates due process unless the monetary damages sought are merely incidental to the primary claim for injunctive or declaratory relief.[30] "Incidental damages are those that flow directly from liability to the class as a whole on the claims forming the basis of the injunctive or interlocutory relief."[31] The dam-

---

24. *Id.; see also King v. Riveland*, 125 Wash. 2d 500, 519, 886 P.2d 160 (1994) (observing that complete unanimity of position and purpose is not required).

25. CR 23(a)(4).

26. *See DeFunis*, 84 Wash. 2d at 622, 529 P.2d 438 (acknowledging that conflicting or antagonistic interests among class members may render a class action an improper vehicle for resolving the dispute); *Marquardt v. Fein*, 25 Wash. App. 651, 656, 612 P.2d 378 (1980) (declaring that an "essential concomitant of adequate representation" is that class counsel be "qualified, experienced, and generally able to conduct the litigation").

27. *Sitton v. State Farm Mut. Auto. Ins. Co.*, 116 Wash. App. 245, 251, 63 P.3d 198 (2003).

28. *See, e.g., King*, 125 Wash. 2d at 503–04, 518–20, 886 P.2d 160 (upholding certification of a (b)(2) class of former correctional center inmates who sought declaratory and injunctive relief prohibiting the release of information from sex offender treatment program files).

29. *Sitton*, 116 Wash. App. at 252, 63 P.3d 198.

30. *Nelson*, 160 Wash. 2d at 189, 157 P.3d 847.

31. *Sitton*, 116 Wash. App. at 252, 63 P.3d 198 (internal quotation marks omitted).

ages "must be cognizable by objective standards and not significantly dependent on each class member's subjective circumstances."[32]

b. CR 23(b)(3)

To obtain certification under CR 23(b)(3), a putative class representative must demonstrate that common questions of law or fact predominate over questions affecting only individual members and that a class action is superior to other methods of adjudication.[33] The "predominance" requirement of CR 23(b)(3) is more stringent than the commonality requirement of CR 23(a)(2).[34]

"The relevant inquiry for the predominance requirement is whether the proposed class is sufficiently cohesive to warrant adjudication by class representation."[35] When making this inquiry, a Washington court engages "in a pragmatic inquiry into whether there is a common nucleus of operative facts as to each class member's claim."[36] This inquiry is "not a rigid test," but rather a review of many factors, "the central question being whether 'adjudication of the common issues in the particular suit has important and desirable advantages of judicial economy compared to all other issues, or when viewed by themselves.'"[37] The common issue need not be dispositive or determinative, nor is it a matter of comparing the court time needed to adjudicate common issues versus individual issues.[38] Instead, the critical question is whether the common issue or issues are the overriding issue or issues in the litigation, even if the suit also entails numerous remaining individual questions.[39]

The superiority element of CR 23(b)(3) requires a comparison of available alternative methods of adjudication, such as joinder, intervention, or consolidation.[40] This discretionary determination involves "consideration of all the pros and cons of a class action as opposed to" individual lawsuits or other forms of adjudication.[41] Manageability is one consideration. Others may include "conserving time,

---

32. *Nelson*, 160 Wash. 2d at 189, 157 P.3d 847 (citing *Sitton*, 116 Wash. App. at 252, 63 P.3d 198).

33. *Weston*, 137 Wash. App. at 168, 170, 151 P.3d 1090; *Sitton*, 116 Wash. App. at 253, 63 P.3d 198.

34. *See Schnall*, 2010 Wash. LEXIS 61, at *10–18 (upholding trial court's determination that proposed nationwide consumer class action did not meet predominance requirements).

35. *Schwendeman*, 116 Wash. App. at 20, 65 P.3d 1 (citing *Amchem Prods., Inc. v. Windsor*, 521 U.S. 591, 623 (1997)).

36. *Id.* (quoting *Behr*, 113 Wash. App. at 323, 54 P.3d 665).

37. *Sitton*, 116 Wash. App. at 254, 63 P.3d 198 (quoting 1 HERBERT B. NEWBERG & ALBA CONTE, NEWBERG ON CLASS ACTIONS § 4:25, at 4-86 (3rd ed. 1992)).

38. *See id.*

39. *See id.; see also Behr*, 113 Wash. App. at 323, 54 P.3d 665 ("That class members may eventually have to make an individual showing of damages does not preclude class certification" under CR 23(b)(3)).

40. *See Schnall*, 2010 Wash. LEXIS 61, at *18–19; *Sitton*, 116 Wash. App. at 256, 63 P.3d 198.

41. *Miller*, 115 Wash. App. at 828, 64 P.3d 49.

effort and expense; providing a forum for small claimants; and deterring illegal activities."[42]

III. *Review of Class Certification Rulings*

Although Washington has not adopted the counterpart to Federal Rule 23(f), its appellate rules provide a mechanism for interlocutory review. Under Washington Rule of Appellate Procedure 2.3, a party may seek discretionary appellate review of nonfinal trial court rulings. The considerations governing acceptance of discretionary review are set forth in Appellate Rule 2.3(b). Interlocutory review of pretrial rulings is not generally favored, but class certification rulings have been accepted for review.[43]

Whether a challenge to a trial court's class certification ruling is raised on discretionary review or on appeal, the decision is reviewed for an abuse of discretion.[44] A trial court abuses its discretion if its decision is based on untenable grounds or is manifestly unreasonable or arbitrary.[45] Although the appellate courts "generally review decisions certifying a class liberally,"[46] certification is not automatically affirmed.[47] Failure to give appropriate consideration to the criteria of CR 23 and to articulate the court's application of the criteria to the facts will result in reversal and remand.[48] Remand may also be ordered if no abuse of discretion is apparent, but the definition of the class is unclear.[49]

---

42. *Sitton,* 116 Wash. App. at 257, 63 P.3d 198; *see also Schnall,* 139 Wash. App. at 297–99, 161 P.3d 395 (reversing determination that existence of individual issues rendered proposed national consumer class action unmanageable); *Schwendeman,* 116 Wash. App. at 29, 65 P.3d 1 (upholding determination that proposed class action would be difficult and unruly to manage, where evidence showed that liability determination would require resolution of many individual inquiries); *Miller,* 115 Wash. App. at 828, 64 P.3d 49 (acknowledging that "the advantages of the class action vehicle would all but disappear" if evidence showed that plaintiffs' job duties "varied too much to be established by representative testimony").

43. *See Sitton,* 116 Wash. App. 245, 63 P.3d 198; *Miller,* 115 Wash. App. 815, 64 P.3d 49; *Oda,* 111 Wash. App. 79, 44 P.3d 8.

44. *Nelson,* 160 Wash. 2d at 188, 157 P.3d 847; *Eriks v. Denver,* 118 Wash. 2d 451, 466, 824 P.2d 1207 (1992); *Sitton,* 116 Wash. App. at 250, 63 P.3d 198.

45. *Mader v. Health Care Auth.,* 149 Wash. 2d 458, 468, 70 P.3d 931 (2003); *Oda,* 111 Wash. App. at 91, 44 P.3d 8.

46. *Miller,* 115 Wash. App. at 820, 64 P.3d 49.

47. *See, e.g., Weston,* 137 Wash. App. at 174, 151 P.3d 1090 (reversing certification of a class of employees alleging violation of state minimum wage and overtime laws); *Oda,* 111 Wash. App. at 105, 44 P.3d 8 (reversing certification of a class of employees alleging gender discrimination and violation of state equal pay requirements).

48. *See Miller,* 115 Wash. App. at 821, 64 P.3d 49 (citing *Wash. Educ. Ass'n,* 93 Wash. 2d at 793, 613 P.2d 769).

49. *See Mader,* 149 Wash. 2d at 468–69, 70 P.3d 931.

IV. Settlement

CR 23(e) prohibits the dismissal or compromise of a class action without court approval. A proposed class settlement may be approved by the trial court if it is determined to be "fair, adequate and reasonable."[50] To determine if these criteria are met, the trial court generally will consider the likelihood of success by plaintiffs; the amount of discovery or evidence; the settlement terms and conditions; the recommendation and experience of counsel; future expense and likely duration of litigation; the recommendation of neutral parties, if any; the reaction of the class, as indicated by the number of objectors and the bases of objections; and the presence of good faith and the absence of collusion.[51] This list of factors is not exhaustive, and not every factor will be relevant in every case. Further, the weight to be given each factor depends on the nature of the claims at issue, the types of relief sought, and the specific facts and circumstances of the case. When making this determination, the trial court should not reach any ultimate conclusions on the contested issues of fact and law underlying the merits of the dispute.[52]

While the purpose of the inquiry conducted by the trial court is to protect those class members whose rights may not have been given due regard by the negotiating parties, it is not the trial court's duty to make sure that every party is content with the settlement.[53] Rather, the court's responsibility is to perform a sufficient inquiry to support a reasoned judgment that the settlement "is not the product of fraud or overreaching by, or collusion between, the negotiating parties, and the settlement, taken as a whole, is fair, reasonable and adequate to all concerned."[54]

To provide class members the opportunity to object to a proposed settlement, CR 23(e) mandates that notice of the proposed settlement "be given to all members of the class in such manner as the court directs." Although not required, CR 23(b)(3) class members may be given the opportunity to opt out of the settlement.[55]

Should an objector appeal the approval of a class action settlement, the trial court's finding that the class settlement was fair, adequate, and reasonable will be reviewed for an abuse of discretion.[56] The same standard applies when the trial court's administration of a class action settlement is challenged.[57]

---

50. *Pickett*, 145 Wash. 2d at 188, 35 P.3d 351.
51. *Id.* at 145 Wash. 2d at 188–89, 35 P.3d 351.
52. *Id.* at 145 Wash. 2d at 190–91, 35 P.3d 351.
53. *Id.* at 145 Wash. 2d at 189, 35 P.3d 351.
54. *Id.* (quoting *Officers for Justice v. Civil Serv. Comm'n*, 688 F.2d 615, 625 (9th Cir. 1982)).
55. *See id.* at 145 Wash. 2d at 188, 35 P.3d 351.
56. *Id.* at 145 Wash. 2d at 191–92, 35 P.3d 351.
57. *See In re Firestorm 1991*, 106 Wash. App. 217, 223, 22 P.3d 849 (2001).

V. Disposition of Residual Funds

Section (f) is the one part of CR 23 that does not track the former version of Federal Rule 23. This section of the Rule controls disbursement of "residual funds" (i.e., those "funds that remain after the payment of all approved class member claims, expenses, litigation costs, attorneys' fees, and other court-approved disbursements to implement the relief granted").[58] The Rule itself indicates that it is not intended to keep the parties from suggesting, or a trial court from approving, a settlement that does not create residual funds. But in a case where a class action judgment or an order approving settlement establishes a process for identifying and compensating members of the class, the judgment or order must specifically provide for the disbursement of any residual funds. At least 25 percent of the residual funds must be disbursed to the Legal Foundation of Washington to support activities and programs that promote access to the civil justice system for low-income residents of the state.[59] A court may order the balance to be distributed to the Legal Foundation of Washington "or to any other entity for purposes that have a direct or indirect relationship to the objectives of the underlying litigation or otherwise promote the substantive or procedural interests of members of the certified class."[60]

VI. Practical Considerations and Miscellaneous Tips

A. TIMING AND PROCEDURES FOR CLASS CERTIFICATION

CR 23 does not specify the procedures or timetables for class certification determinations.[61] A defendant therefore may find itself facing a class certification hearing sooner than it expects, with little time to prepare its opposition. In King County, for example, nondispositive motions (including motions for class certification) can be brought before the court for hearing without oral argument on six court days' notice.[62] The common practice, however, is for the parties to confer and agree upon a briefing schedule that reasonably accommodates both sides and for one party to

---

58. CR 23(f)(1).

59. CR 23(f)(2).

60. Id.

61. CR 23(c)(1) merely directs the trial court to make the class action determination "[a]s soon as practicable after the commencement" of the lawsuit. Local rules should be checked to determine whether there is a specific deadline.

62. See King County Local Rule 7(b). Opposition papers are due by noon two court days before the date the motion is set to be considered. KCLR 7(b)(4)(D).

contact the court to request a date and time for oral argument.[63] Class certification motions are usually decided on affidavits instead of evidentiary hearings.

B. TRIAL PLANS

A trial plan is a useful tool in the class certification process. For example, by identifying the elements of the claims at issue and then explaining how those elements can be proved with representative or expert testimony, a putative class representative of a (b)(3) class can show how the predominance and superiority requirements are met.[64]

C. SETTLEMENT OF INDIVIDUAL AND CLASS CLAIMS

A putative class representative will be allowed to appeal the denial of class certification after his or her individual claim has become moot, as long as that claim for relief was valid when class certification was sought.[65] Accordingly, a defendant who settles with an individual plaintiff after class certification is denied will want to ensure that the settlement agreement/release is appropriately worded to extinguish both the plaintiff's individual claim and his or her interest in having a class certified.[66]

D. CLASS ACTIONS IN ARBITRATION

Class actions are arbitrable in Washington.[67] In cases brought under the state's Consumer Protection Act, the Washington Supreme Court has invalidated class action waivers in arbitration agreements, holding the waivers unconscionable.[68]

---

63. It should be noted that oral argument rules and practices vary by county. In King County, for example, the courts do not hear oral argument on nondispositive motions without leave of the hearing judge. In some counties, the courts hear oral argument on all contested motions. Whether a special setting needs to be arranged will depend on the court.

64. *See Sitton,* 116 Wash. App. at 257–60, 63 P.3d 198 (vacating proposed trial plan, but suggesting a different plan might pass muster); *cf. Oda,* 111 Wash. App. at 95–96, 44 P.3d 8 (describing plaintiffs' two-stage trial plan).

65. *Schwendeman,* 116 Wash. App. at 16–17, 65 P.3d 1.

66. *Id.*

67. *See McKee v. AT&T Corp.,* 164 Wash. 2d 372, 395, 191 P.3d 845 (2008) (acknowledging class actions "are often arbitrated"); *McGinnity v. AutoNation, Inc.,* 149 Wash. App. 277, 280, 202 P.3d 1009 (2009) (affirming superior court's refusal to vacate arbitrator's attorney fee award to certified class).

68. *See McKee,* 164 Wash. 2d at 396–98, 191 P.3d 845; *Scott,* 160 Wash. 2d at 852–57, 161 P.3d 1000.

WEST VIRGINIA

NANCY L. PELL
JENNIFER CADENA

I. Introduction

West Virginia's Rule of Civil Procedure 23 (West Virginia Rule) mirrors Federal Rule 23 up to a point. Among the differences, West Virginia has not adopted the provisions added to Federal Rule 23 in 2003 that address the appointment of class counsel and attorney fees.[1] Even when the rules are the same, however, the West Virginia Supreme Court of Appeals has cautioned against relying too heavily on case law interpreting the Federal Rules lest the construction of West Virginia's rules "amount to nothing more than Pavlovian responses to federal decisional law."[2]

II. Prerequisites to a Class Action

While the language of the West Virginia Rule regarding class action prerequisites is nearly identical to the corresponding Federal Rule,[3] the West Virginia courts have provided additional guidance. First, as with the Federal Rule, the class must be so numerous that joinder of all members is impracticable.[4] There is no explicit reference regarding the minimum number of individuals required to satisfy the numerosity requirement,[5] but the West Virginia Supreme Court has indicated that 13

---

1. *See* FED. R. CIV. P. 23(g)–(h) (2004).
2. *Brooks v. Isinghood*, 584 S.E.2d 531, 537–38 (W. Va. 2003).
3. *Compare* W. VA. R. CIV. P. 23(a) *with* FED. R. CIV. P. 23(a).
4. W. VA. R. CIV. P. 23(a)(1).
5. *In re W. Va. Rezulin Litig.*, 585 S.E.2d 52, 65 (W. Va. 2003).

defendants is not numerous enough for joinder to be impracticable.[6] Impracticability does not mean that it is impossible to join all members, merely that it is difficult or inconvenient to join all members.[7] Moreover, it is not a proper objection to certification that the class as defined may include some members who do not have claims.[8]

Second, the party requesting class certification must meet the commonality test, meaning that there are questions of law or fact common to the class.[9] Similar to the Federal Rules, a common nucleus of operative facts or question of law is usually enough to satisfy the commonality requirement.[10] Although this low threshold requires only that the resolution of common questions affect all, or at least a substantial number, of the class members, the facts resulting in liability must be sufficiently similar. For example, commonality was lacking in a breach of contract suit where employees' claims were based on individual promises not common to all employees.[11]

Third, to satisfy the typicality requirement, the claim or defense must arise from the same event or practice or course of conduct that gives rise to the claims of other class members.[12] In addition, when potential class members are in other states, West Virginia requires that the same or "reasonably coextensive" cause of action be available in each state.[13] For example, in *West Virginia ex rel. Chemtall, Inc.*,[14] the representative plaintiffs, coal preparation plant workers or their children in West Virginia, alleged exposure of residual acrylamide by manufacturers, distributors, and representatives in West Virginia. The proposed class, however, consisted of coal preparation plant workers and their children who were exposed in coal preparation facilities in Illinois, Indiana, Ohio, Pennsylvania, Tennessee,

---

6. *Robertson v. Hatcher*, 135 S.E.2d 675, 679 (W. Va. 1964) (construed under the former rule, which also contained a numerosity requirement, specifically, that a class action could be brought "[i]f persons constituting a class are so numerous as to make it impracticable to bring them all before the court . . . "); *see also In re Rezulin Litig.*, 585 S.E.2d at 65–66 (referencing case law in other jurisdictions of a certified class action that contained 17 to 20 members (*Ark. Educ. Ass'n v. Bd. of Educ.*, 446 F.2d 763 (8th Cir. 1971)); 35 to 70 members (*Fidelis Corp. v. Litton Indus., Inc.*, 293 F. Supp. 164 (S.D.N.Y. 1968)); 70 members (*Korn v. Franchard Corp.*, 456 F.2d 1206 (2d. Cir. 1972)); 123 members (*Temple Univ. of Commonwealth Sys. of Higher Educ. v. Pa. Dep't of Pub. Welfare*, 374 A.2d 991 (Pa. Commw. 1977)); and 204 members (*Ablin v. Bell Tel. Co.*, 435 A.2d 208 (Pa. Super. 1981))).

7. *Mitchem v. Melton*, 277 S.E.2d 895, 902 (W. Va. 1981) (construing the former rule, which contained a similar impracticability requirement pertaining to numerosity).

8. *State ex rel. Metro. Life Ins. Co. v. Starcher*, 474 S.E.2d 186, 193 (W. Va. 1996).

9. W. Va. R. Civ. P. 23(a)(2).

10. *In re Rezulin Litig.*, 585 S.E.2d at 67.

11. *Ways v. Imation Enters. Corp.*, 589 S.E.2d 36 (W. Va. 2003).

12. W. Va. R. Civ. P. 23(a)(3).

13. *See W. Va. ex rel. Chemtall, Inc.*, 607 S.E.2d 772, 783–84 (W. Va. 2004).

14. *Id.* at 778.

and Virginia.[15] Of these states, Indiana, Tennessee, and Virginia did not recognize a medical monitoring cause of action.[16] The West Virginia Supreme Court, after issuing a writ of prohibition for the certification of the class action, held that exposure to acrylamide in the various states was insufficient for certification, reasoning that the other states must also recognize a medical monitoring cause of action that is reasonably coextensive with the medical monitoring cause of action available in West Virginia.[17]

Fourth, West Virginia Rule 23(a)(4) requires that the representative parties fairly and adequately protect the interests of the class. Although each class member does not need to be explicitly identified, the class itself must be objectively defined.[18] The class description must be "sufficiently definite" to allow the court to determine whether a particular person is a member.[19]

In West Virginia the "adequacy of representation" requirement serves two purposes. First, it assures that the lawyers representing the class are qualified to represent the class.[20] Specifically, class counsel should be competent, be experienced, and have enough resources to investigate the class claims and contact other class members.[21] Second, potential conflicts of interest between the named parties and the prospective class should be explored and resolved in order to certify a class.[22]

III. Procedural Considerations for Certification Decision

West Virginia Rule 23(c) differs from the corresponding Federal Rule, specifically regarding the information required in notice to class members. Both rules place a duty on the court to determine whether to certify the proceeding as a class action as soon as practicable.[23] However, although both rules allow for the order

---

15. *Id.*

16. *Id.* at 783.

17. *Id.* It is important to note that the court's decision to issue a writ in this case does not preclude the circuit judge in the future from certifying a class or subclasses involving out-of-state plaintiffs; one simply needs the judge to carefully analyze and explain why a plaintiff—who lived, worked, and was injured exclusively in a foreign jurisdiction—should be allowed or required to have his or her case heard by a West Virginia jury.

18. *Metro. Life Ins. Co.*, 474 S.E.2d at 193.

19. *Id.*

20. *In re Rezulin Litig.*, 585 S.E.2d at 63 (citing *In re Prudential Ins. Co. of Am. Sales Practice Litig.*, 148 F.3d 283, 312 (3d Cir. 1998) (internal citations omitted) and *Black v. Rhone-Poulenc, Inc.*, 173 F.R.D. 156, 162 (S.D.W.V. 1996) ("When assessing the class representatives' ability to adequately represent the interest of the class, the Court must consider the abilities of both the attorneys who represent the class representatives, and the class representatives themselves.")).

21. *Id.*

22. *Id.* at 69.

23. *Compare* W. Va. R. Civ. P. 23(c)(1) *with* Fed. R. Civ. P. 23(c)(1)(A).

certifying a class action to be altered or amended, West Virginia requires that the alteration or amendment be completed before the decision on the merits, whereas the Federal Rule requires that any amendment occur prior to the final judgment.[24] Additionally, the West Virginia Rule allows the class action order to be conditional, an option not explicitly provided for in the Federal Rules.[25]

A trial court has sound discretion in certifying a class action,[26] but certification cannot be based on whether the plaintiff stated a cause of action or will prevail on the merits. Rather, the dispositive question is whether all the requirements outlined in West Virginia Rule 23 have been satisfied.[27] The burden to make that showing is on the party seeking to establish class certification. If the party seeking certification lacks sufficient information to determine if class certification is possible, the court may allow discovery before ruling on class certification, especially if the pleadings and record are also insufficient.[28] Although the West Virginia Rules do not specify what must be included in a class certification order, the courts have clarified that class certification orders must be detailed and specific.[29] Additionally, the order must explain the rule basis for certification and the relevant facts that support the court's legal conclusions.[30]

An action may be brought or maintained as a class action with respect to particular issues.[31] Alternatively, a class may be divided into subclasses and each subclass treated as a class.[32] However, there is no requirement for the use of subclasses.[33]

The order denying or granting certification of a class is reviewable by the West Virginia Supreme Court of Appeals under an abuse of discretion standard. If certification is granted, it may be challenged by a writ of prohibition. Interpretation of the West Virginia Rules of Civil Procedure is a question of law subject to de novo review.[34]

---

24. *Compare* W. VA. R. CIV. P. 23(c)(1) *with* FED. R. CIV. P. 23(c)(1)(C).

25. *Compare* W. VA. R. CIV. P. 23(c)(1) *with* FED. R. CIV. P. 23.

26. *Evans v. Huntington Publ'g Co.*, 283 S.E.2d 854, 855 (W. Va. 1981) (construing pre-1988 rule).

27. *Id.* (citing *Miller v. Mackey Int'l, Inc.*, 452 F.2d 424, 427 (5th Cir. 1971)).

28. *See Love v. Georgia-Pacific Corp.*, 590 S.E.2d 677, 681 (W. Va. 2003); *Burks v. Wymer*, 307 S.E.2d 647, 654 (W. Va. 1983) (discussing the pre-1988 version of the class action rule but holding that "[a]n exploration beyond the pleadings is essential to make an informed judgment on the propriety of a proposed spurious class action").

29. *Chemtall*, 607 S.E.2d at 783.

30. *Id.*

31. W. VA. R. CIV. P. 23(c)(4)(A).

32. W. VA. R. CIV. P. 23(c)(4)(B).

33. *See Chemtall*, 607 S.E.2d at 783–84.

34. *See Keesecker v. Bird*, 490 S.E.2d 754, 763 (W. Va. 1997).

IV. Notice and Judgment in Certified Class Actions

Federal Rule 23 is explicit in allowing discretionary notice in (b)(1) and (b)(2) actions, while making notice in (b)(3) actions mandatory.[35] The West Virginia Rule makes no mention of notice in (b)(1) and (b)(2) cases, so like the Federal Rule, notice is discretionary as well.[36]

For West Virginia Rule 23(b)(3) actions, notice is mandatory.[37] West Virginia requires that the notice to each possible class member contain advice that (1) the member will be excluded if he or she requests exclusion by the court-set deadline; (2) the judgment, whether favorable or not, binds members who do not request exclusion; and (3) any member not requesting exclusion may make an appearance through counsel.[38] Unlike the instructions in the Federal Rule, however, West Virginia Rule 23 does not explicitly require that the notice needs to be clear and concise, and stated in plain, easily understood language.[39] Additionally, there is no provision in the West Virginia Rule requiring that notice state the nature of the action; the definition of the class certified; the class claims, issues, or defenses; the method by which the member must request exclusion; or the binding effect of the class judgment on the nonexcluded parties.[40] Although, as noted in section III, the order must be detailed and specific as to the grounds for certification.

The West Virginia judgment requirements for class actions under subdivision (b)(1), (b)(2), and (b)(3) are almost identical to the Federal Rule.[41] For a class certified under West Virginia Rule 23(b)(1) or (b)(2), the judgment must include and describe those whom the court finds to be class members.[42] For Rule 23(b)(3) cases, the judgment must include those individuals to whom notice was directed, those who have not requested exclusion, and those whom the court finds to be class members.[43]

---

35. *See* FED. R. CIV. P. 23(c)(2).
36. *See* W. VA. R. CIV. P. 23(c)(2).
37. *See* W. VA. R. CIV. P. 23(c)(3).
38. *See* W. VA. R. CIV. P. 23(c)(2).
39. *Compare* W. VA. R. CIV. P. 23(c) *with* FED. R. CIV. P. 23(c)(2).
40. *Compare* W. VA. R. CIV. P. 23(c) *with* FED. R. CIV. P. 23(c)(2).
41. *Compare* W. VA. R. CIV. P. 23(c) *with* FED. R. CIV. P. 23(b)(3).
42. W. VA. R. CIV. P. 23(c)(3).
43. *Id.*

V. Dismissal or Compromise

West Virginia Rule 23(e) differs from Federal Rule 23(e).[44] Both rules require that the court approve the dismissal or compromise of a class action.[45] The West Virginia Rule, however, only applies to the dismissal or compromise of class actions, not the dismissal or compromise of claims, issues, or defenses.[46] Another difference is that West Virginia does not specify any procedure that must be followed for a proposed settlement, voluntary dismissal, or compromise.[47]

---

44. *Compare* W. VA. R. CIV. P. 23(e) *with* FED. R. CIV. P. 23(e).
45. *Compare* W. VA. R. CIV. P. 23(e) *with* FED. R. CIV. P. 23(e).
46. *Compare* W. VA. R. CIV. P. 23(e) *with* FED. R. CIV. P. 23(e).
47. *See* W. VA. R. CIV. P. 23(e).

WISCONSIN

MARK G. SCHROEDER

I. Introduction

Class action lawsuits in Wisconsin state courts are authorized by Wisconsin Statutes section 803.08. Wisconsin's one-sentence class action rule, however, provides no guidance on the procedural aspects and requirements of state class actions. Although the Wisconsin courts have set forth class certification criteria and addressed other procedural issues, Wisconsin class action practice diverges somewhat from federal class action practice. In contrast, class action procedure under the Wisconsin Consumer Act is substantially similar to Federal Rule 23.

II. Text of Wisconsin's Class Action Rule

Section 803.08 provides, "When the question before the court is one of a common or general interest of many persons or when the parties are very numerous and it may be impracticable to bring them all before the court, one or more may sue or defend for the benefit of the whole."[1]

III. Comparison to Rule 23

Wisconsin's class action rule is patterned after the Field Code.[2] Section 803.08 is essentially the same as its predecessor statute.[3] When section 803.08 was adopted

---

1. WIS. STAT. § 803.08.

2. *See Schlosser v. Allis-Chalmers Corp.*, 222 N.W.2d 156, 164 (Wis. 1974) (*Schlosser I*) (discussing predecessor class action statute). The Field Code, enacted in New York during the nineteenth century to codify rules of civil practice, included the first state statute on class actions. *See* 12 U.L.A. Uniform Law Commissioners' Model Class Actions Act, at 93–94 (2008) (prefatory note).

3. *See Schlosser v. Allis-Chalmers Corp.*, 271 N.W.2d 879, 883 (Wis. 1978) (*Schlosser II*) (new Wisconsin class action rule under section 803.08 "essentially the same as the class action provision" in former Wis. Stat. § 260.12).

in 1978, the Wisconsin Judicial Council Committee considered, but declined to adopt, a class action rule patterned after Rule 23.[4]

Section 803.08 authorizes class actions, but specifies no procedure for class certification.[5] Wisconsin case law on state procedural requirements for class actions is limited.[6] While Wisconsin courts view federal decisions construing procedural counterparts to the Wisconsin Rules of Civil Procedure as persuasive,[7] interpretations of federal class action rules are not necessarily controlling with respect to Wisconsin state law class actions.[8]

IV. Criteria for Class Certification

Despite some debate as to whether the Wisconsin class action rule should be read "conjunctively or disjunctively," the Wisconsin Supreme Court has construed section 803.08 as presenting one set of three criteria:

> (1) the named parties must have a right or interest in common with the persons represented; (2) the named parties must fairly represent the interest or right involved so that the issue may be fairly and honestly tried; and (3) it must be impracticable to bring all interested persons before the court.[9]

More recent Wisconsin appellate decisions add "manageability" as a fourth "prerequisite" to class certification.[10]

V. Commonality or Community of Interest

The first prerequisite for class certification in Wisconsin state courts is commonality or community of interest. To establish this prerequisite, "[a]ll members of the class need not share all interests, but all must share a common interest."[11] The

---

4. *See* Charles D. Clausen & David P. Lowe, *The New Wisconsin Rules of Civil Procedure: Chapters 801-803*, 59 MARQ. L. REV. 1, 107 (1976).

5. *See Mercury Records Prod., Inc. v. Econ. Consultants, Inc.*, 283 N.W.2d 613, 617 (Wis. Ct. App. 1979).

6. *See id.*

7. *See Wilson v. Cont'l Ins. Co.*, 274 N.W.2d 679, 682 (Wis. 1979).

8. *See Mercury Records*, 283 N.W.2d at 617 (citing *Browne v. Milwaukee Bd. of Sch. Dir.*, 230 N.W.2d 704, 711 (Wis. 1975)).

9. *Schlosser I*, 222 N.W.2d at 165 (analyzing former Wis. Stat. § 260.12) (quotations omitted); *see also Mercury Records*, 283 N.W.2d at 617 (three prerequisites under section 803.08—common interest, adequate representation, and numerosity (citing *Schlosser I*, 222 N.W.2d at 164–65)).

10. *See In re Wal-Mart Employee Litig.*, 711 N.W.2d 694, 696 (Wis. Ct. App. 2006) ("[T]he proposed class must be manageable."); *Cruz v. All Saints Healthcare Sys., Inc.*, 625 N.W.2d 344, 350 (Wis. Ct. App. 2001) ("[W]e need to assess the manageability of the proposed class.").

11. *Mercury Records*, 283 N.W.2d at 617 (citing *State ex rel. Harris v. Larson*, 219 N.W.2d 335, 338 (Wis. 1974)).

common interest test "is whether all members of the purported class desire the same outcome of the suit that the alleged representatives of the class desire."[12] Where a case presents a common legal question and each class member's claim involves common issues of proof, commonality is demonstrated.[13]

VI. Adequate Representation

The second prerequisite for class certification in Wisconsin state courts is adequacy of representation. The determination of adequacy of representation in Wisconsin state courts is similar to Rule 23(a)(4). "[T]he primary criteria are: (1) whether the plaintiffs or counsel have interests antagonistic to those of absent class members; and (2) whether class counsel are qualified, experienced and generally able to conduct the proposed litigation."[14] An individual can serve as a class representative as long as the individual has a general understanding of the nature of the alleged class claims.[15]

VII. Numerousness

The third prerequisite for class certification in Wisconsin state courts is "numerousness." Like federal practice, there is no "numerical test" to determine this issue.[16] A class in excess of 150 employees has satisfied Wisconsin's numerousness prerequisite.[17]

VIII. Manageability

Early Wisconsin state court decisions discussed the concept of manageability, but not by name. According to the Wisconsin Supreme Court, the trial court must weigh "the benefits to be gained from disposing of the entire controversy in one proceeding against the difficulties inherent in a single action."[18] Stated another way, the trial court must determine whether "common issues far outweigh the

---

12. *Id.* (citing *Browne*, 230 N.W.2d at 710–11; *Pipkorn v. Vill. of Brown Deer*, 101 N.W.2d 623 (Wis. 1960)); *see also Hogan v. Musolf*, 459 N.W.2d 865, 872 (Wis. Ct. App. 1990) (quoting *Mercury Records*, 283 N.W.2d at 617), *rev'd on other grounds*, 471 N.W.2d 216 (Wis. 1991).

13. *See Cruz*, 625 N.W.2d at 351.

14. *Id.*

15. *See id.*

16. *See Pipkorn*, 101 N.W.2d at 626.

17. *See Browne*, 230 N.W.2d at 711.

18. *Schlosser II*, 271 N.W.2d at 883.

separate issues."[19] Ultimately, based on these prior state supreme court pronouncements, the Wisconsin Court of Appeals concluded that the trial court must "assess the manageability of the proposed class."[20]

Wisconsin courts have concluded that putative class actions were unmanageable where there were multiple and/or complicated affirmative defenses and application of different state laws,[21] where each and every member of a proposed class would need to be examined to test statistical conclusions and underlying data,[22] and where causation and damages issues were individualized.[23] In contrast, a Wisconsin court found that a class action was manageable where there were no individual issues on subclasses, defenses, or different state laws, and a single legal issue was common to all class members.[24]

IX. Class Notice

Section 803.08 is silent with respect to class notice. Wisconsin courts have embraced federal due process concepts in connection with class actions, such that absent class members cannot be bound by a class action judgment unless they receive adequate notice, an opportunity to decide whether to submit themselves to the court's jurisdiction, and proper representation.[25] The Wisconsin Supreme Court has approved opt-out notice procedures.[26]

X. Attorney Fees

The Wisconsin courts have awarded class action attorney fees under the common-fund doctrine.[27] In calculating attorney fees, the trial court has the discretion to

---

19. *Schlosser I*, 222 N.W.2d at 166; *see also Goebel v. First Fed. Sav. & Loan Ass'n*, 266 N.W.2d 352, 360 (Wis. 1978) ("[A] court must determine whether the issues common to the named plaintiffs and the class members are outweighed by the issues particular to the individual class members.").

20. *Cruz*, 625 N.W.2d at 350; *see also Sisters of St. Mary v. AAER Sprayed Insulation*, 445 N.W.2d 723, 725 (Wis. Ct. App. 1989) (concerns noted in *Schlosser I* "focus on the basic question: is the proposed class action manageable?").

21. *See Sisters of St. Mary*, 445 N.W.2d at 725–29.

22. *See In re Wal-Mart*, 711 N.W.2d at 696–98.

23. *See Markweise v. Peck Foods Corp.*, 556 N.W.2d 326, 333–34 (Wis. Ct. App. 1996); *see also Nolte v. Michels Pipeline Constr., Inc.*, 265 N.W.2d 482, 485–87 (Wis. 1978) (class action inappropriate where causation and damages issues were substantial and particular to each putative class member).

24. *See Cruz*, 625 N.W.2d at 352–53.

25. *See Schlosser II*, 271 N.W.2d at 886–87; *Mercury Records*, 283 N.W.2d at 617–19.

26. *See Schlosser II*, 271 N.W.2d at 887; *see also Bilda v. Milwaukee County*, 722 N.W.2d 116, 135 (Wis. Ct. App. 2006) ("due process requires . . . notice and an opportunity to opt out" when the class action lawsuit is predominantly for damages).

27. *See Wis. Retired Teachers Ass'n, Inc. v. Employee Trust Funds Bd.*, 558 N.W.2d 83, 97–99 (Wis. 1997).

base its award on either the percentage of the fund recovered or on the lodestar method.[28]

XI. Miscellaneous Issues

A. PURPOSE/PHILOSOPHY

In Wisconsin, the purpose of class actions is to simplify lawsuits and to avoid a multiplicity of litigation.[29] The Wisconsin Supreme Court advocates a "flexible" approach to class action litigation, and recently the courts have tended to take a "very permissive attitude."[30] Indeed, the public interest as declared by the legislature is served by permitting class actions when the Wisconsin state rule prerequisites are met.[31]

B. TYPES OF CLASS ACTIONS

Although Wisconsin has no counterpart to Rule 23(b)(2) or (b)(3), the Wisconsin courts allow class actions seeking either injunctive relief or damages.[32] Certain types of claims, such as a personal tort based on fraud, do not lend themselves to a class action.[33]

C. TIME TO DETERMINE CLASS

Wisconsin does not have a counterpart to Rule 23(c) in its class action rule. Although "an early determination of the class is essential," the Wisconsin courts have declined to specify time periods under which class certification and notification must be made.[34]

D. DAMAGES

The Wisconsin courts may permit individual issues on damages to be litigated subsequent to resolution of common issues where the damage questions would not be

---

28. *Id.* at 99.

29. *See Mercury Records*, 283 N.W.2d at 617 (citing *Hicks v. Milwaukee County*, 238 N.W.2d 509, 513 (Wis. 1976)).

30. *See Schlosser I*, 222 N.W.2d at 165 & n.35.

31. *See Mercury Records*, 283 N.W.2d at 617 (citing *Mussallem v. Diners' Club, Inc.*, 230 N.W.2d 717, 721 (Wis. 1975)).

32. *See Schlosser I*, 222 N.W.2d at 167.

33. *See Kaski v. First Fed. Sav. & Loan Ass'n*, 240 N.W.2d 367, 369 (Wis. 1976).

34. *See Mercury Records*, 283 N.W.2d at 619.

overly complicated.[35] But where damage issues are more complex and not subject to common proof, class certification may be inappropriate.[36]

E. MERITS

As in federal practice, the trial court's view of the merits is an improper basis on which to deny class certification.[37]

F. TYPICALITY, PREDOMINANCE, AND SUPERIORITY

Wisconsin case law does not explicitly discuss or analyze typicality,[38] predominance,[39] or superiority (except for the manageability prerequisite).[40]

XII. Class Actions Under the Wisconsin Consumer Act

The Wisconsin Consumer Act—Administration[41] permits consumer class actions under certain conditions for various violations of state and federal consumer credit law.[42] In contrast to section 803.08, the state class action procedures under the Wisconsin Consumer Act are substantially similar to Rule 23.[43]

XIII. Appeals

In Wisconsin, a class certification order is interlocutory, and thus an appeal may only be brought with leave of court.[44] The Wisconsin appellate courts review class certification orders under an abuse of discretion standard.[45]

---

35. *See Sisters of St. Mary*, 445 N.W.2d at 728 (discussing *Schlosser I*, 222 N.W.2d at 166; *Schlosser II*, 271 N.W.2d at 887).

36. *See, e.g., Markweise*, 556 N.W.2d at 333–34 (jury trial of individual causation and damages issues for each class member could take years); *Sisters of St. Mary*, 445 N.W.2d at 728 (damages issues not subject to mechanical calculation but require separate mini-trials) (citation omitted).

37. *See Tietsworth v. Harley Davidson, Inc.*, 661 N.W.2d 450, 456 (Wis. Ct. App. 2003), *rev'd on other grounds*, 677 N.W.2d 233 (Wis. 2004).

38. *But see Cruz*, 625 N.W.2d at 351 (representative parties' claims are "typical" of the class).

39. *But see Sisters of St. Mary*, 445 N.W.2d at 728 (damages may "predominate") (quotation omitted).

40. *See generally* section VIII, *supra*.

41. WIS. STAT. §§ 426.101–.301.

42. WIS. STAT. § 426.110(1)–(4).

43. WIS. STAT. § 426.110 (5)–(13).

44. *See In re Wal-Mart*, 711 N.W.2d at 695.

45. *See Schlosser II*, 271 N.W.2d at 887; *In re Wal-Mart*, 711 N.W.2d at 696.

WYOMING

MARK G. SCHROEDER

I. Introduction

Class action procedure in Wyoming state courts is governed by Wyoming Rule of Civil Procedure 23 (Wyoming Rule), which is patterned after a prior version of Rule 23 of the Federal Rules of Civil Procedure. Wyoming case law interpreting Wyoming Rule 23 is sparse. The availability of class actions in Wyoming state courts to assert claims for relatively small amounts of individual damages may be limited, depending on jurisdiction and statutory authorization.

II. Comparison to Federal Rule 23

Wyoming Rule 23, last amended in 1971, is patterned after then existing Federal Rule 23.[1] Therefore, later revisions to Federal Rule 23(a)–(e) are absent from its Wyoming counterpart. Likewise, no provisions in Wyoming Rule 23 correspond with Federal Rule 23(f), (g), or (h).

In interpreting Wyoming Rule 23, federal case law is considered "highly persuasive."[2]

---

1. *See* Wyo. R. Civ. P. 23, Wyo. Court Rules Ann. (Lexis 2009) ("This rule is similar to Rule 23 of the Federal Rules of Civil Procedure."); *Blount v. City of Laramie*, 510 P.2d 294, 297 (Wyo. 1973) (observing that Wyoming had adopted 1966 federal revisions to Rule 23).

2. *See Mut. of Omaha Ins. Co. v. Blury-Losolla*, 952 P.2d 1117, 1121 (Wyo. 1998) (finding federal class action precedent "persuasive"); *see also Kimbley v. City of Green River*, 642 P.2d 443, 445 n.3 (Wyo. 1982) (federal authority relative to Wyoming civil rules virtually identical to their federal counterparts are considered "highly persuasive").

III. Interpretive Case Law

In Wyoming, the purpose of a class action "is to prevent a multiplicity of law-suits . . . ."[3] Since 1971, no Wyoming Supreme Court decisions have interpreted or analyzed the procedural requirements of Wyoming Rule 23. Although a small handful of state supreme court cases discuss the prior version of Wyoming Rule 23, the court's analysis is limited, but consistent with federal authority.[4]

IV. Subject Matter Jurisdiction

The Wyoming circuit courts have exclusive jurisdiction in civil actions for money damages in an amount not exceeding $7,000.[5] This limitation represents a legislative mandate that such smaller cases may not be heard in the district courts.[6] Based on federal case law, the Wyoming Supreme Court has held that individual class members' claims cannot be aggregated to create jurisdiction in the district courts.[7] Wyoming Rule 23, however, is not applicable in the circuit courts for most matters.[8] As a result, class actions in Wyoming usually must be filed in the district courts, and if damages are sought, each individual class member's damage claim usually must exceed $7,000. With limited exceptions,[9] class actions asserting individual damage claims of $7,000 or less may not be maintained in Wyoming state courts.

---

3. *Beadle v. Daniels*, 362 P.2d 128, 132 (Wyo. 1961); *see also Hansen v. Smith*, 395 P.2d 944, 946 (Wyo. 1964) (purpose of class action is "to determine finally the rights of a numerous class of individuals by one common final judgment").

4. *See, e.g., Beadle*, 362 P.2d at 133 (conclusiveness of adjudication); *State v. Laramie Rivers Co.*, 136 P.2d 487 (Wyo. 1943) (standing, common interests, antagonistic representative).

5. *See* Wyo. Stat. Ann. § 5-9-128(a)(i) (Matthew Bender 2009).

6. *See Mut. of Omaha*, 952 P.2d at 1121 (discussing exclusive jurisdiction of predecessor county courts).

7. *See id.* (Wyoming class action procedures do not contemplate a modification of the district court's subject matter jurisdiction via aggregation of claims) (citing *Zahn v. Int'l Paper Co.*, 414 U.S. 291 (1973)).

8. *See* Wyo. R. Civ. P. Cir. Ct. 1.06 (Wyoming Rule 23 not applicable in circuit courts "unless and until circuit courts have statutory subject matter jurisdiction of cases in which such relief is requested"); *see also Mut. of Omaha*, 952 P.2d at 1120 n.2 (suggesting Wyoming Rule 23 did not apply in predecessor county courts or justice courts).

9. *See, e.g.,* Wyo. Stat. Ann. § 30-5-303 (Matthew Bender 2009) (granting jurisdiction to district courts for all proceedings brought under the Wyoming Royalty Payment Act); *see also* Wyoming consumer protection statutes, discussed in section V, *infra*.

V. Class Actions Under Wyoming Consumer Protection Statutes

Under the Wyoming Consumer Protection Act (CPA),[10] a person seeking "damages for an unlawful deceptive trade practice may bring a class action against such person on behalf of any class of persons of which he is a member and which has been damaged by such unlawful deceptive trade practice, subject to and pursuant to the Wyoming Rules of Civil Procedure governing class actions . . . ."[11] Private remedies available in a class action under the CPA include actual damages and reasonable attorney fees.[12]

The Wyoming Consumer Rental-Purchase Agreement Act (CRPAA)[13] also permits consumer class actions. Under the CRPAA, class action damages may be awarded in "the amount the court determines to be appropriate with no minimum recovery as to each member" (subject to a statutorily defined total recovery limit for class actions), together with costs and reasonable attorney fees.[14] Because the CRPAA specifically permits actions to be brought "in any court of competent jurisdiction,"[15] CRPAA class actions arguably could be commenced in either the circuit courts or the district courts.

---

10. *See* WYO. STAT. ANN. §§ 40-12-101 *et seq.* (Matthew Bender 2009).

11. WYO. STAT. ANN. § 40-12-108(b) (Matthew Bender 2009).

12. *Id.*

13. *See* WYO. STAT. ANN. §§ 40-19-101 *et seq.* (Matthew Bender 2009).

14. *See* WYO. STAT. ANN. § 40-19-119(a)(iii) (Matthew Bender 2009).

15. WYO. STAT. ANN. § 40-19-119(f) (Matthew Bender 2009).

Table of Cases

Index